THE DICTIONARY OF HISTORICAL THEOLOGY

THE DICTIONARY
of
HISTORICAL THEOLOGY

General Editor

Trevor A. Hart

Consulting Editors

Richard Bauckham
Jan Milič Lochman
Paul D. Molnar
Alan P. F. Sell

paternoster
press

William B. Eerdmans Publishing Company
Grand Rapids, Michigan

This edition first published jointly 2000
in the U.K. by
Paternoster Press
Paternoster Press is an imprint of Paternoster Publishing,
P.O. Box 300, Carlisle, Cumbria, CA3 0QS, UK /
P.O. Box 1047, Waynesboro, GA 30830-2047, USA
Website: paternoster-publishing.com

and in the United States of America by
Wm. B. Eerdmans Publishing Company
255 Jefferson Ave. S.E., Grand Rapids, Michigan 49503 /
P.O. Box 163, Cambridge CB3 9PU U.K.
www.eerdmans.com

Printed and bound in the United States of America

05 04 03 02 01 00   5 4 3 2 1

British Library Cataloguing in Publication Data

A catalogue record for this book is available from the British Library

Paternoster Press ISBN 1-84227-002-8

Library of Congress Cataloging-in-Publication Data

The dictionary of historical theology / general editor, Trevor A. Hart;
consulting editors, Richard Bauckham . . . [et al.].
p.   cm.
Includes bibliographical references and index.
Eerdmans ISBN 0-8028-3907-X (alk. paper)
1. Theology, Doctrinal — History — Encyclopedias.
I. Hart, Trevor A. II. Bauckham, Richard.

BT21.2.D53 2000
230'.09 — dc21
00-045323

Typeset by WestKey Ltd, Falmouth, Cornwall

Contents

Contributors

WILLEM J. VAN ASSELT is Lecturer in Church History at Utrecht University, The Netherlands.

PAUL AVIS is General Secretary of the Council for Christian Unity of the Church of England and Sub-Dean of Exeter Cathedral, Research Fellow in the Department of Theology at the University of Exeter and Director of the Centre for the Study of the Christian Church.

GARY D. BADCOCK is Professor of Systematic Theology at Huron College, University of Western Ontario, London, Canada.

DAVID V.N. BAGCHI is a Lecturer in Historical Theology at the University of Hull.

MARIE L. BAIRD is Assistant Professor of Theology at Duquesne University, Pittsburgh, Pennsylvania, USA.

RICHARD BAUCKHAM is Professor of New Testament Studies at St Mary's College, University of St Andrews.

GERALD BONNER is Reader Emeritus in Theology, University of Durham.

THOMAS J. BOONE, III is Lecturer for the Theology Department at Loyola University in Chicago, USA.

LOUISE BOURDUA is Associate Lecturer on the History of Art at the University of Aberdeen.

GERALD BRAY is Anglican Professor of Divinity at Beeson Divinity School, Samford University, Birmingham, Alabama, USA.

GIJSBERT VAN DEN BRINK is Lecturer in Philosophical Theology at Utrecht University, The Netherlands.

PETER NEWMAN BROOKS is Fellow Emeritus, Robinson College, Cambridge and Professor of Reformation Studies, Cranmer Theological House, Shreveport, Louisiana, USA.

DAVID BROWN lectures in the Department of Theology at the University of Durham.

JAMES BRUCE is Rector, St James Penicuik and St Mungo's West Linton, Scotland.

ROMANUS CESSARIO, OP is Professor of Systematic Theology at St John's Seminary, Brighton, Massachusetts, USA.

MARK D. CHAPMAN is Lecturer in Systematic Theology at Ripon College, Cuddesdon, Oxford.

JOHN CHRYSSAVGIS is Professor of Theology at Holy Cross School of Theology in Boston, Massachusetts, USA.

JOHN P.H. CLARK is Vicar of Chevington, Northumberland.

RICHARD CLUTTERBUCK is Principal, West of England Ministerial Training Course, Gloucester.

JOHN E. COLWELL is Tutor in Christian Doctrine and Ethics and Academic Dean, Spurgeon's College, London.

JON K. COOLEY is a postgraduate student at St John's College, Cambridge.

ANTHONY R. CROSS is a Research Fellow at the Centre for Advanced Theological Research, University of Surrey Roehampton, London.

RICHARD CROSS is Tutorial Fellow in Theology at Oriel College, Oxford

IVOR DAVIDSON is Lecturer in Systematic Theology at the University of Otago, New Zealand.

OLIVER DAVIES is Reader in Systematic Theology at the University of Wales, Lampeter.

EEF DEKKER is Lecturer in Philosophical Theology at Utrecht University, The Netherlands.

LORETTA DEVOY, OP is Associate Professor in the Department of Theology and Religious Studies at St John's College, St John's University, Jamaica, New York, USA.

J.A. DINOIA, OP is on the Adjunct Faculty in Systematic Theology and Philosophy at the Dominican House of Studies, Washington, DC, USA.

DENNIS M. DOYLE is Associate Professor of Religious Studies at the University of Dayton, Ohio, USA.

JOHN W. DRANE is Head of Practical Theology in the Department of Divinity, University of Aberdeen, Scotland and Adjunct Professor of Ministry at Fuller Seminary, Pasadena, California, USA.

AVERY DULLES, SJ is Laurence J. McGinley Professor of Religion and Society, Fordham University, Bronx, New York, USA.

HARVEY D. EGAN, SJ is Professor of Systematic and Mystical Theology, University of Boston College, Massachusetts, USA.

MARK W. ELLIOTT is Lecturer in Christian Studies at Liverpool Hope University College.

NOEL LEO ERSKINE is Associate Professor of Theology and Ethics at Candler School of Theology, Emory University, Atlanta, Georgia, USA.

DONALD FAIRBAIRN is Assistant Professor of Church History and Missions at Erskine Theological Seminary, South Carolina, USA and Visiting Lecturer in Theology at Donetsk Christian University, Ukraine.

DOUGLAS B. FARROW is Assistant Professor of Christian Theology at McGill University, Montreal, Quebec, Canada.

DAVID FERGUSSON is Professor of Divinity at New College, Edinburgh.

GERALD F. FINNEGAN, SJ is Assistant Professor of Theology at St Joseph's University, Philadelphia, Pennsylvania, USA.

CHRIS L. FIRESTONE is Assistant Professor of Philosophy at Trinity International University, Deerfield, Illinois, USA.

R.N. FROST is on the seminary faculty at Multnomah Biblical Seminary, Portland, Oregon, USA.

R. DOUGLAS GEIVETT is Professor of Philosophy and Department Chair at Talbot Department of Philosophy, Biola University, La Mirada, California, USA.

SHERIDAN GILLEY lectures in the Department of Theology at the University of Durham.

JAMES GINTHER is Lecturer in Medieval Theology, Religion and Society at the University of Leeds.

TIMOTHY GORRINGE is St Luke's Professor of Theological Studies at the University of Exeter.

GARRETT GREEN is Professor and Chair of the Department of Religious Studies at Connecticut College, New London, Connecticut, USA.

NIELS HENRIK GREGERSEN is Research Professor in Science and Theology at the University of Aarhus, Denmark.

DOUGLAS GROOTHUIS is Associate Professor of Philosophy at Denver Seminary, Colorado, USA.

JOHN W. DE GRUCHY is the Robert Selby Taylor Professor of Christian Studies at the University of Cape Town.

COLIN E. GUNTON is Professor of Systematic Theology at King's College, University of London.

STUART G. HALL is Emeritus Professor of Church History, King's College, London and Honorary Professor of Church History, University of St Andrews.

HARRIET A. HARRIS is Lecturer in Theology at the University of Exeter.

JOHN W. HART is Co-Pastor of the Presbyterian Church of Upper Montclair, New Jersey, USA.

TREVOR A. HART is Professor of Divinity and Dean of the Faculty of Divinity, St Mary's College, University of St Andrews.

NICHOLAS M. HEALY lectures in the Department of Theology and Religious Studies at St John's University, Staten Island, New York, USA.

BRIAN HEBBLETHWAITE is a Life Fellow of Queens' College, Cambridge and Canon Theologian of Leicester Cathedral.

DAVID S. HOGG is a postgraduate student at the University of St Andrews.

RICHARD HOSKINS is Senior Lecturer in Study of Religions at Bath Spa University College.

IOAN I. ICA, JR is Professor at the Orthodox Theological Faculty of the Babes-Bolyai State University, Cluj-Napoca, Romania and Director of the Deisis Publishing House, Sibiu, Romania.

MICHAEL JINKINS is Associate Professor of Pastoral Theology, Austin Presbyterian Theological Seminary, Austin, Texas, USA.

CHRISTOPHER M. JONES is a member of the Theology Faculty at St Peters College, Oxford.

ELAINE KAYE is a Non-Stipendiary Lecturer in Mansfield College, Oxford.

FERGUS KERR is Regent, Blackfriars Hall, University of Oxford and Honorary Senior Lecturer in the Faculty of Divinity, University of Edinburgh.

J. ANDREW KIRK lectures in the School of Mission and World Christianity at Selly Oak Colleges.

MARTIN I. KLAUBER is Visiting Professor of Church History at Trinity Evangelical Divinity School and Lecturer in Religious Studies at Barat College, Illinois, USA.

CHARLES M. KOVICH is Professor of English at Rockhurst University, Kansas City, Missouri, USA.

ANTHONY N.S. LANE is Director of Research and Senior Lecturer in Christian Doctrine, London Bible College.

EMMANUEL Y. LARTEY is Senior Lecturer in Pastoral Studies at the University of Birmingham.

DAVID R. LAW is Lecturer in Christian Thought at the University of Manchester.

JOSEPH T. LIENHARD, SJ is Professor of Theology at Fordham University, Bronx, New York, USA.

PAUL C.-H. LIM is a postgraduate student in the Faculty of Divinity, University of Cambridge.

ANN LOADES lectures in the Department of Theology at the University of Durham.

JAN MILIČ LOCHMAN is Emeritus Professor of Theology at the University of Basle, Switzerland.

ARTHUR J. LONG is Former Principal, Unitarian College Manchester and Honorary Lecturer in the Department of Religions and Theology, University of Manchester.

GERARD LOUGHLIN is Head of the Department of Religious Studies at the University of Newcastle.

ANDREW LOUTH is Professor and Chairman of the Department of Theology at the University of Durham.

NEIL B. MACDONALD is Meldrum Lecturer in Dogmatic Theology at New College, University of Edinburgh.

JOHN MACQUARRIE is Emeritus Lady Margaret Professor of Divinity in the University of Oxford.

JOSEPH L. MANGINA is Assistant Professor of Systematic Theology at Wycliffe College, Toronto, Ontario, Canada.

IAN MARKHAM holds the Liverpool Chair of Theology and Public Life at Liverpool Hope University College.

CLIVE MARSH is Senior Lecturer in Theology, College of Ripon and York, England.

I. HOWARD MARSHALL is Emeritus Professor of New Testament Exegesis and Honorary Research Professor, University of Aberdeen.

PETER MATHESON is Principal at the Theological Hall, Ormond College, Parkville, Victoria, Australia.

ANTHONY M. MATTEO is Professor of Philosophy at Elizabethtown College, Elizabethtown, Pennsylvania, USA.

MICKEY L. MATTOX is Assistant Professor of Historical Theology at Concordia University.

DOUGLAS MCCREADY is Adjunct Assistant Professor of Theology and Ethics at Alvernia College, Reading, Pennsylvania, and visiting Fellow at the Fletcher School of Law and Diplomacy, Tufts University, Medford, Massachusetts, USA.

LESLIE MCCURDY is Senior Pastor of Bayers Road Baptist Church, Halifax, Nova Scotia, Canada and Adjunct Professor at Atlantic Baptist University.

TIMOTHY S. MCDERMOTT is former Resident Scholar at the Center of Theological Inquiry, Princeton, New Jersey, USA.

JOHN M. MCDERMOTT, SJ is Laghi Chair Research Professor at the Pontifical College Josephinum, Columbus, Ohio, USA.

GRAHAM MCFARLANE is Lecturer in Systematic Theology at London Bible College.

ANDREW T.B. MCGOWAN is Principal of Highland Theological College, Dingwall, Scotland.

J.A. MCGUCKIN is Professor of Early Church History, Union Theological Seminary, New York, USA.

JOSEPH C. MCLELLAND is Professor Emeritus of McGill University and the Presbyterian College, Montreal, Canada.

JOHN L. MCPAKE is Convener, Panel on Doctrine, Church of Scotland and a Parish Minister.

JOANNE MCWILLIAM is Professor Emerita, University of Toronto, Canada.

PAUL D. MOLNAR is Professor of Systematic Theology, St John's University, Jamaica, New York, USA.

ROBERT C. MORGAN is University Lecturer in Theology (NT Studies) at Linacre College, Oxford.

RICHARD A. MÜLLER is P.J. Zondervan Professor of Historical Theology at Calvin Theological Seminary, Grand Rapids, Michigan, USA.

STUART MURRAY is Oasis Director of Church Planting and Evangelism and Tutor on the MTh in Baptist and Anabaptist Studies at Spurgeon's College.

EDWARD L. NANNO holds the PhD from the University of St Andrews.

BRADLEY NASSIF is Professor of Historical and Systematic Theology, Antiochian House of Studies (USA) in the Balamand University (Lebanon) and Adjunct Professor of Theology at Fuller Seminary, USA.

ROGER NEWELL lectures in the Department of Religion at George Fox University, Newberg, Oregon, USA.

GEORGE NEWLANDS is Professor of Divinity at the University of Glasgow.

DERON S. NEWMAN holds the PhD in Philosophical Theology from the University of Edinburgh.

BÉATRICE NICOLLIER is at l'Université de Genève, Institut d'Histoire de la Réformation.

FREDERICK W. NORRIS is Dean E. Walker Professor of Church History and Professor of Mission/ Evangelism at Emmanuel School of Religion, Johnson City, Tennessee, USA.

CHRISTOPHER OCKER is Associate Professor of Church History at the San Francisco Theological Seminary and the Graduate Theological Union at Berkeley, USA.

MICHAEL O'CONNOR is Warden, Royal School of Church Music, Surrey.

THOMAS O'LOUGHLIN is Lecturer in Theology at the University of Wales Lampeter.

ALAN G. PADGETT is Professor of Theology and Philosophy of Science at Azusa Pacific University, California, USA.

JAMES CARLETON PAGET is University Lecturer in New Testament Studies at the University of Cambridge and Fellow of Peterhouse.

KEN PARRY is Honorary Senior Research Fellow in the Department of Ancient History, Macquarie University, Sydney, Australia.

CHRISTOPHER PARTRIDGE is Senior Lecturer in Theology and Contemporary Religion in the Department of Theology and Religious Studies at Chester College.

ALVYN PETTERSEN is an Anglican priest, currently the vicar of Frensham, Surrey.

LYNNE PRICE is a freelance theologian engaged in a wide variety of work and is currently writing a theological biography of Walter Hollenweger.

A.T. STEPHEN PRICKETT is Professor in the Department of English Literature at the University of Glasgow.

ANNE PRIMAVESI is former Research Fellow in Environmental Theology at the University of Bristol.

BEN QUASH is Dean of Peterhouse, Cambridge.

HENRY D. RACK is the former Bishop Fraser Senior Lecturer in Ecclesiastical History at the University of Manchester.

EPHRAIM RADNER is Canon Missioner of the Sangre de Cristo Region in the Dicoese of Colorado, Rector of Ascension Episcopal Church and Adjunct Professor of Theology, Iliff School of Theology, Denver, Colorado, USA.

ESTHER REED is Lecturer in Theology and Ethics at the University of St Andrews.

MARJORIE REEVES is Honorary Fellow, St Anne's and St Hugh's Colleges, Oxford.

R.R. RENO is Associate Professor of Theology at Creighton University, Omaha, Nebraska, USA.

ARIE DE REUVER is Professor of Reformed Theology at the University of Utrecht, The Netherlands.

DAVID E. ROBERTS is a postgraduate student at the University of Edinburgh.

†T.A. ROBERTS was Professor of Philosophy at the University of Wales, Aberystwyth.

GREGORY ROCCA, OP is Associate Professor of Philosophy and Theology and President, Dominican School of Philosophy and Theology, Berkeley, California, USA.

HAROLD H. ROWDON is former Lecturer in Church History, London Bible College.

GEOFFREY ROWELL is Suffragan Bishop of Basingstoke.

DAVID T. RUNIA is Professor of Ancient and Medieval Philosophy at Leiden University and C.J. de Vogel Professor of Patristic Philosophy at Utrecht University, both in The Netherlands.

STANLEY H. RUSSELL is Honorary Research Fellow in the Department of Religions and Theology at the University of Manchester.

MARCEL SAROT is Lecturer in Philosophical Theology at Utrecht University, The Netherlands.

CHARLES J. SCALISE is Associate Professor of Church History at Fuller Seminary, Pasadena, California, USA.

GLEN G. SCORGIE is Professor of Theology at Bethel Theological Seminary West in San Diego, California, USA.

HENRY R. SEFTON is Teaching Fellow in Church History at the University of Aberdeen.

ALAN P.F. SELL is Professor of Christian Doctrine and Philosophy of Religion and Director of the Centre for the Study of British Christian Thought at the United Theological College, Aberystwyth.

D.W.D. SHAW is Emeritus Professor of Divinity, University of St Andrews.

DANIEL P. SHERIDAN is Vice President for Academic Affairs and Dean of the College and Professor of Theology at Saint Joseph's College of Maine, USA.

PETER SLATER is Professor Emeritus of Trinity College in the Toronto School of Theology, Canada.

DAVID SMITH is Associate Director of the Whitefield Institute in Oxford.

JAMES V. SMITH is Lecturer in Theology at Loyola University in Chicago, USA.

ALAN SPENCE has a PhD in Systematic Theology from King's College, London.

MAX L. STACKHOUSE is Stephen Colwell Professor of Christian Ethics at Princeton Theological Seminary, New Jersey, USA.

ALAN M. SUGGATE is Lecturer in the Department of Theology at the University of Durham.

R.S. SUGIRTHARAJAH is Senior Lecturer in Biblical Hermeneutics at the University of Birmingham.

GEORGE R. SUMNER, JR is Principal of Wycliffe College, Toronto, Canada.

WALTER SUNDBERG is Professor of Church History at Luther Seminary, Saint Paul, Minnesota, USA.

HANS SVEBAKKEN is a postgraduate student at Loyola University, Chicago, USA.

BRENDAN SWEETMAN is Associate Professor of Philosophy at Rockhurst University, Kansas City, Missouri, USA.

DAVID G.K. TAYLOR is Lecturer and Postgraduate Admissions Tutor at the University of Birmingham.

ANTHONY C. THISELTON is Professor of Christian Theology and Head of Department, University of Nottingham and Canon Theologian of Leicester Cathedral.

DAVID M. THOMPSON is University Lecturer, Modern Church History and Director, Centre for Advanced Religious and Theological Studies at Fitzwilliam College, Cambridge.

WILLIAM M. THOMPSON is Professor of Systematic Theology at Duquesne University, Pittsburgh, Pennsylvania, USA.

LARS THUNBERG is former Associate Professor of Systematic Theology at the universities of Uppsala/Lund, Sweden and Aarhus, Denmark.

DAVID TOMBS is Senior Lecturer in Theology and Religious Studies, University of Surrey Roehampton, Southlands College, London.

IAIN R. TORRANCE is Professor in Patristics and Christian Ethics at the University of Aberdeen.

CARL R. TRUEMAN is Lecturer in Church History at the University of Aberdeen.

JOHN MUNSEY TURNER is part-time lecturer in Methodism at Hartley Victoria College, Manchester.

KEVIN J. VANHOOZER is Research Professor of Systematic Theology at Trinity Evangelical Divinity School, Deerfield, Illinois, USA.

DERK VISSER is Professor of History, Emeritus, Ursinus College, Collegeville, Pennsylvania, USA.

JAMES B. WALKER is Chaplain and Assistant Hebdomadar (Welfare) at the University of St Andrews.

JOHN WEBSTER is Lady Margaret Professor of Divinity at the University of Oxford and Canon of Christ Church

TIMOTHY J. WENGERT is Professor of the History of Christianity at the Lutheran Theological Seminary in Philadelphia, Pennsylvania, USA.

STEVE WILKENS is Professor of Philosophy and Ethics at Azusa Pacific University, Azusa, California, USA.

LOREN WILKINSON is Professor of Interdisciplinary Studies and Philosophy at Regent College, Vancouver, BC, Canada.

GARRY WILLIAMS is Tutor in Church History and Doctrine at Oak Hill Theological College, London.

STEPHEN WILLIAMS is Professor of Systematic Theology at Union Theological College, Belfast, Northern Ireland.

R. MCL. WILSON is Emeritus Professor of Biblical Criticism at the University of St Andrews.

MATTHIAS WOLFES is Research Fellow at the Schleiermacher Research Institute in the University of Kiel, Berlin, Germany.

DAVID F. WRIGHT is Professor of Patristic and Reformed Christianity at New College, Edinburgh.

ROBERT W. YARBROUGH is Associate Professor of New Testament and Chairman of the Department of New Testament at Trinity Evangelical Divinity School, Deerfield, Illinois, USA.

DAVID S. YEAGO is Michael C. Peeler Professor of Systematic Theology at Lutheran Theological Southern Seminary, Columbia, South Carolina, USA.

DOUGLAS VINCENT YOUNG is Lecturer in Philosophy and the Philosophy of Religion in the Northern Congregational College, Manchester and Senior Extra-Mural Lecturer in Philosophy in the University of London.

JAMES V. ZEITZ is Associate Professor of Religious Studies at Our Lady of the Lake University, San Antonio, Texas, USA.

Abbreviations

Abbreviations for commonly cited works
CD	Karl Barth, *Church Dogmatics*
CH	Eusebius of Caesarea, *Ecclesiastical History*
Eph.	Ignatius, *Letter to the Ephesians*
Heresies	Irenaeus, *Against the Heresies*
Magn.	Ignatius, *Letter to the Magnesians*
Marcion	Tertullian, *Against Marcion*
Rom.	Ignatius, *Letter to the Romans*
Smyrn.	Ignatius, *Letter to the Smyrnaeans*
Trall.	Ignatius, *Letter to the Trallians*

Abbreviations for secondary sources: Journals, periodicals, major reference works and series
AAR	American Academy of Religion
ABD	*Anchor Bible Dictionary*
ACW	Ancient Christian Writers
Am Cath Ph Q	*American Catholic Philosophical Quarterly*
Am J Th	*American Journal of Theology*
Am Th L Assoc Proc	*American Theological Library Association Proceedings*
ANF	*Ante-Nicene Fathers*
Angl Th R	*Anglican Theological Review*
ANRW	*Aufstieg und Niedergang der römischen Welt: Geschichte und Kultur Roms im Spiegel der neuren Forschung*
Arch Fr Hist	*Archivum Franciscanum Historicum*
Arch Phil	*Archives de Philosophie*
Arch Ref	*Archiv für Reformationsgeschichte*
Aug Stud	*Augustinian Studies*
Bapt Q	*The Baptist Quarterly: Journal of the Baptist Historical Society*
BETL	Bibliotheca ephemeridum theologicarum lovaniensium
BHT	Beiträge zur historischen Theologie
Bib Arch Rev	*Biblical Archaeology Review*
BSR	Biblioteca di scienze religiose
BU	Biblische Untersuchungen
Bul Soc H Prot Fran	*Bulletin de la Société de l'Histoire du Protestantisme Français*
BUSE	Bibliothèque de l'Université Saint-Esprit
Cal Th J	*Calvin Theological Journal*
Cam J	*Cambridge Journal*
Cath Hist Rev	*Catholic Historical Review*
Cath Th S Pr	*Catholic Theological Society Proceedings*
CCCM	Corpus Christianorum: Continuatio mediaevalis
CCSG	Corpus Christianorum: Series graeca
CCSL	Corpus Christianorum: Series latina
Ch H	*Church History*

Ch Q R	*Church Quarterly Review*
CJR	*Christian Jewish Relations*
CMCS	*Cambridge Medieval Celtic Studies*
Cong Q	*Congregational Quarterly*
CPL	*Clavis patrum latinorum*
CS	*Cistercian Studies*
CSCO	Corpus scriptorum christianorum orientalium
CSEL	Corpus scriptorum ecclesiasticorum latinorum
CW	Die Christliche Welt: Evangelische Gemeindeblatt für Gebildete aller Stände
CWS	Classics of Western Spirituality
DNB	*Dictionary of National Biography*
DOP	*Dumbarton Oaks Papers*
Down Rev	*Downside Review: A Quarterly of Catholic Thought*
DTC	*Dictionnaire de théologie catholique*
Epworth R	*Epworth Review*
Ev Q	*Evangelical Quarterly*
Ev Th	*Evangelische Theologie*
Expos T	*Expository Times*
Faith Phil	*Faith and Philosophy*
FC	Fathers of the Church
Fr St	*Franciscan Studies*
GCS	Die griechische christliche Schriftsteller der ersten [drei] Jahrhunderte
Gr Or Th Rev	*Greek Orthodox Theological Review*
Gr	*Gregorianum*
Harv Th R	*Harvard Theological Review*
Hey J	*Heythrop Journal*
I C S	*Illinois Classical Studies*
Ir Th Q	*Irish Theological Quarterly*
J A A R	*Journal of the American Academy of Religion*
J E Chr St	*Journal of Early Christian Studies*
J Eccl H	*Journal of Ecclesiastical History*
J Ev Th S	*Journal of the Evangelical Theological Society*
J Hisp Ph	*Journal of Hispanic Philology*
J Hist Phil	*Journal of the History of Philosophy*
J Rel Ethics	*Journal of Religious Ethics*
J Rel	*Journal of Religion*
J Rom St	*Journal of Roman Studies*
J Th St	*Journal of Theological Studies*
LCC	Library of Christian Classics
LCL	Loeb Classical Library
Med St	*Mediaeval Studies*
Menn Q R	*Mennonite Quarterly Review*
Meth Rec	*Methodist Recorder*
Mod Ch	*Modern Churchman*
Mod Th	*Modern Theology*
Mystics Q	*Mystics Quarterly*
N T T	*Nederlands theologisch tijdschrift*
N Z Sys Th	*Neue Zeitschrift für Systematische Theologie und Religionsphilosophie*
Ned A Ker	*Nederlands archief voor kerkgeschiedenis*
NHS	Nag Hammadi Studies
NPNF¹	*Nicene and Post-Nicene Fathers*, Series 1
NPNF²	*Nicene and Post-Nicene Fathers*, Series 2
OECT	Oxford Early Christian Texts
P B Rev	*Patristic and Byzantine Review*

PG	Patrologia graeca
Ph-hist Kl	*Philosophisch-philologisch und historische Klasse*
PL	Patrologia latina
R Bén	*Revue bénédictine*
R E Aug	*Revue des études augustiniennes*
R Hist Ph Rel	*Revue d'histoire et de philosophie religieuses*
R Hist Sp	*Revue d'histoire de la spiritualité*
R S Ph Th	*Revue des sciences philosophiques et théologiques*
Recher Sci Rel	*Recherches de science religieuse*
Recher Th Anc Med	*Recherches de théologie ancienne et médiévale*
Ref R	*Reformed Review*
Rel G G	*Religion in Geschichte und Gegenwart*
Rel Life	*Religion in Life*
Rel St	*Religious Studies*
Rel T	*Religion Today*
Rev Phil	*Revue de philosophie*
RNSP	*Revue néo-scholastique de philosophie*
S Bapt J Th	*Southern Baptist Journal of Theology*
Sap	*Sapienza*
SC	Sources chrétiennes
Scot Bul Ev Th	*Scottish Bulletin of Evangelical Theology*
Scot J Th	*Scottish Journal of Theology*
SHCT	Studies in the History of Christian Thought
Sitz B Ak Wiss	*Sitzungsberichte der bayerischen Akademie der Wissenschaften*
Sixteen Cent J	*Sixteenth Century Journal*
SP	Studia Patristica
St Ans	Studia Anselmiana
St Mys	*Studia Mystica*
TDNT	*Theological Dictionary of the New Testament*
Th H	Théologie historique
Th Real	*Theologische Realenzyklopädie*
Th St	*Theological Studies*
Th Today	*Theology Today*
Th	*Theology*
Trinity J	*Trinity Journal*
TS	Texts and Studies
TU	Texte und Untersuchungen
Tyndale Bul	*Tyndale Bulletin*
VCSup	Vigiliae christianae Supplements
Vig Chr	*Vigiliae christianae*
WA	*Weimarer Ausgabe. D. Martin Luthers Werke: Kritische Gesamtausgabe*
West Th J	*Westminster Theological Journal*
WUNT	Wissenschaftliche Untersuchungen zum Neuen Testament
Z Kg	*Zeitschrift für Kirchengeschichte*
Z Rel Gg	*Zeitschrift für Religions- und Geistesgeschichte*
Z Th K	*Zeitschrift für Theologie und Kirche*

General abbreviations:

art.	article
bk.	book
ch/s.	chapter(s)
diss.	dissertation
ed./eds.	editor/editors
edn	edition

ET	English translation
fl.	*floruit* (Lat., 'flourished')
GE	German edition
LXX	Septuagint
n.d.	no date
NF	Neue Folge
NS	New Series
pt.	part
repr.	reprint
Revd	Reverend
revd	revised
s.v.	*sub voce*
SJ	Society of Jesus
Sp.	Spanish
trans.	translator

NB: An asterisk (*) preceding a word or phrase indicates a relevant article in the *Dictionary* under this (or a similar) heading.

Preface

This new dictionary is offered as a resource to all those with a serious interest in the history and development of Christian theology. While there is an abundance of material published in the field of historical theology, until now there has been no concise and reasonably comprehensive manual available to readers in the English language. It is hoped that *The Dictionary of Historical Theology* will fill this gap, serving as a ready reference to scholars, students, ministers of religion and informed lay people alike, and drawing together the best of contemporary scholarship on the key figures, movements and texts in the story of Christian theology from the early church to the present day.

While theology can never be separated from other aspects of the church's life, entries in this volume (which vary in length from 500 to 15,000 words) concentrate deliberately on figures, schools of thought and significant texts in the development of Christian theology. Contributors have been urged to include biographical and wider historical material only in so far as this is germane to the task of locating subjects within their theological contexts, and exploring their particular relationship and contributions to those contexts. Having located its subject within such a context, each entry proceeds to consider any significant developments and changes identifiable in the characteristic modes of thought and expression of its subject. Attention is also paid to intellectual antecedents and descendants, and to the subject's role in shaping the wider development of the Christian theological tradition.

Contributors to the dictionary have without exception been invited to participate on the basis of their proven expertise on particular topics. We have sought to provide access to scholarship of the highest order, and expect that the dictionary will be of use to other scholars seeking some brief but authoritative treatment of a particular subject. The essence of a dictionary, though, is to provide informative coverage for as wide a readership as possible, and we intend this volume to be of use to students writing essays and dissertations, ministers and priests writing sermons, and the informed layperson interested simply in furthering his or her general knowledge of the Christian tradition and its development. For those seeking a more substantial engagement with a topic, each entry concludes with a succinct bibliography of primary and secondary texts for further study.

By limiting the number of entries (to some 314 in all) scope has been provided for more extended and thorough treatment than might ordinarily be expected in a dictionary. This has meant that we have been unable to incorporate entries on all deserving candidates. This consideration is offset, however, by the provision of a carefully compiled index which enables the reader to track down references to many more subjects than those actually included in the list of entries. We hope that our overall coverage is reasonably comprehensive. We have also taken the opportunity to include entries on some subjects that the reader might not ordinarily expect to find treated at length in a volume of this size.

The dictionary is deliberately international and interdenominational in its choice of entries and its list of contributors. Its aim is to tell something of the story of Christian theology, a story which is wider and more complicated than any of the many individual strands of development to which Christians today may belong. The story looks different and is told differently by those belonging to different traditions within the Christian community. The hope of the editors is that this volume will allow many such perspectives to find a voice, to the illumination and benefit of all its readers.

Finally, as General Editor, I must offer thanks to all those who have been involved in the production of this volume during the last five years: to the Consulting Editors (Richard Bauckham, Jan Milič Lochman, Paul Molnar and Alan Sell) who offered invaluable advice on the list of entries, and who helped to produce a list of appropriate contributors to match; to all those who agreed to write entries, and produced them in a timely fashion and to a high standard; to my research assistant Steve Guthrie who helped to bear much of the administrative load at crucial stages of the project; to my wife Rachel, who provided a second pair of eyes in proof-reading; to Tara Smith for her patience and care in copy-editing the volume; to Jeremy Mudditt for his enduring interest in the project, and his patient nudging of it towards publishing deadlines; and to the Paternoster Press and Wm. B. Eerdmans for their willingness to publish it.

Trevor A. Hart
St Mary's College
St Andrews

Abelard, Peter (1079–1142)

Born in Le Pallet and trained in the cathedral schools of his day, Abelard studied under some of the foremost teachers in France. He began his studies under Roscelin, who advocated a *Nominalist view (universals, or abstract concepts, are not distinct from individuals, i.e. a being does not have separate parts) of the Trinity. In other words, Roscelin argued that either the three persons of the Trinity were three different beings or the Father and the Holy Spirit were also incarnate with the Son. On this view Roscelin was accused of Tritheism at the Council of Soissons in 1092, but managed to defend himself against the charges. It was not until several years later that Abelard finally rejected Roscelin's teaching and took up studies under William of Champeaux. Abelard could hardly have chosen more disparate teachers, for William, in contrast to Roscelin, taught Realism (that universals do in fact have an existence apart from individuals). Eventually, however, Abelard challenged William on the ground that he had conflated individuals and universals to such a degree that distinguishing the substance of the Godhead was impossible.

In his attempt to address the mysteries of the Trinity in a way that avoided the pitfalls of his previous masters, Abelard wrote the *Theologia Summi Boni*. In it he sought to preserve the individuality of the three persons of the Trinity, but not at the expense of eliminating the substance of the Godhead. The difficulty some (such as *Bernard of Clairvaux and Otto of Freising) had with Abelard's approach, was that he reduced the persons of the Trinity to abstract characteristics. He had identified the Father, Son and Holy Spirit as power, wisdom and goodness. This clearly contradicted the *Athanasian Creed which declared the Father, Son and Holy Spirit equally as almighty. Abelard appeared to have overstepped the bounds of acceptable theological discourse. He seemed to be arguing that certain qualities could be predicated of particular persons of the Trinity in a way which precluded every quality of the Godhead being predicated of all three equally.

Although Abelard protested the orthodoxy of his work vehemently, and his students seemed to have little difficulty in accepting it, the Council of Soissons condemned the work in 1121 and Abelard was made to recite the Athanasian Creed. Not surprisingly though, condemning and burning Abelard's book did not stop him from continuing his defence. Shortly after the council, Abelard wrote *Theologia Christiana*, which was a defence of his own Trinitarian position. This work was again revised in the 1130s under the title *Theologia Scholarium*. Although the final version reveals efforts to modify his expression so as to comport with the orthodoxy of the day, Bernard of Clairvaux again accused Abelard of heresy at the Council of Sens in 1140. This time Abelard decided to appeal to the pope directly, but on his way to Rome he became ill and, while taking refuge at Cluny with his friend and admirer Peter the Venerable, Abelard died.

In spite of such difficulties concerning his Trinitarian theology, Abelard was considered an able and competent commentator on the Bible. He is perhaps most famously remembered for his commentary on the book of Ezekiel, not only because he composed his lectures in a remarkably short time, but also because he did so in order to compete against his teacher, Anselm of Laon. Unfortunately, this work has been lost; we do, however, have Abelard's commentary on Romans. While much could be said about the nature of Abelard's exegesis, his commentary on Romans is best known for the brief appendix he adds to 3:19–26. In that short section Abelard asks how it is possible that Christ's death and resurrection effects salvation for those who believe. He answers that God, through the work of Christ, has bound Christians to himself by love, and that those who believe are motivated to love in the way that Christ did. What Abelard did was to equate love with righteousness. Those whose love imitates and is motivated by Christ's love win for themselves freedom from sin and redemption in Jesus.

As with much in Abelard's writings, this perspective on the atonement was not readily received. Even today scholars label Abelard's view as subjective and inadequate. The perceived problem is that Abelard has rested the efficacy of Christ's saving work on the activity of the believer rather than on Christ himself. Such a view stands in contrast to the objective view of the atonement which *St Anselm of Canterbury developed. The reader should, however, accept this interpretation of Abelard with some caution. We have already noted that Abelard's view on the atonement is found in a very short appendix of a work which was not intended to engage the matter in detail. Surely, all that

Abelard thought about the work of Christ is not contained in those few pages alone. Consequently, we may derive more profit from this aspect of his work if we confine ourselves to considering its merits within the context of his wider theological stance.

Other works of note that Abelard wrote include *Sic et Non, Dialogue of a Philosopher with a Jew and a Christian,* and *Historia Calamitatum. Sic et Non* reveals Abelard's theological method: doubt leads to inquiry, which leads to truth. This method reflects Abelard's dictum that 'nothing is believed unless it is first understood', which is a reversal of St Anselm of Canterbury's famous dictum, 'I do not understand in order that I might believe, but I believe in order that I might understand'. *Dialogue of a Philosopher with a Jew and a Christian* shows this method of inquiry at work in the course of a debate. *Historia Calamitatum* is of particular interest because it is an autobiography.

There are also a number of hymns and letters that remain available to us. One of the most interesting of Abelard's works is his *Ethics,* otherwise known as *Scito te ipsum* ('know yourself'), because it so closely reflects his concerns for Heloise. Heloise was Abelard's clandestine lover during his time at Notre Dame. After their affair was discovered Abelard was maliciously castrated and Heloise vested as a nun. During this tumultuous period Heloise wrote to Abelard that she felt both guilty and innocent – for while the church condemned her actions, her intentions (love for Abelard) were pure. Although Abelard never admits to writing his *Ethics* in response to Heloise's concerns, he argues there that actions are counted as good or evil based on the intention behind them. This does not mean that the moral value of one's intention is arbitrarily determined by the individual, for intentions must be measured against God's law, but what it does mean is that sin is defined as consent to an evil will.

The difficulties of this position are easily seen, but once again we must listen to Abelard carefully. It may be said that one of Abelard's greatest problems was his penchant to overemphasize certain perspectives. The consequence of this shortcoming was that his adversaries continually tormented Abelard; but it is also true that because of Abelard certain aspects of theology received greater attention than they had before.

DAVID S. HOGG

FURTHER READING: M.T. Clancy's work *Abelard: A Medieval Life* (Oxford, 1997) is an excellent study. Among D.E. Luscombe's works on Abelard *The School of Peter Abelard: The Influence of Abelard's Thought in the Early Scholastic Period* (London, 1969) is informative. Richard Weingart's book *The Logic of Divine Love: A Critical Analysis of the Soteriology of Peter Abelard* (London, 1970) is also very good.

African Theology

The term 'African theology' has been applied in several different ways. It is possible to understand it *historically,* as referring to the ways in which 'God-talk' has been engaged in at different points in the history in Africa. In that case it is necessary for African theology to be understood as an articulation of the concepts of God in traditional African religions. This point has been argued by J.K. Agbeti of Ghana and Jesse N.K. Mugambi of Kenya (*African Christian Theology,* 1989), John Mbiti in *Concepts of God in Africa* (1970) and Bolaji Idowu in *Olodumare: God in Yoruba Belief* (1962). In addition to a historical understanding, 'African theology' has been used to describe the differing *types* of 'God-talk' which have gone on in Africa – Christian, Muslim as well as traditional African. It has also been used to refer to the *nature* of the theology of Africans and peoples of African descent. By far the most widespread usage of the term has been with reference to African *Christian* discourse.

In the first centuries of Christianity, northern Africa provided some of the most thoughtful apologists and brilliant intellects for the Christian faith. Legend traces the founding of the Christian church in Africa to the preaching of St Mark the evangelist in Alexandria in the first century. Alexandria was the centre of Roman Africa. The Christian presence there from the end of the second century is well documented by theologians, writers and bishops such as the Egyptian *Origen (185–254), *Clement of Alexandria (c. 150–215) and *Athanasius, the 'Black dwarf' (c. 296–373). Carthage, to the west (in present-day Tunisia) produced such Christian thinkers as *Tertullian (c. 160–225), the first Christian to write in Latin whose terminology, such as that God is 'one substance consisting in three persons' set the course for Christian theology; *Cyprian (d. 258); and one of the greatest theologians in the history of the Christian church – *Augustine (354–430), Bishop of Hippo.

The Alexandrian church was largely responsible for taking the Christian faith south to Axum, north-eastern Ethiopia, in the fourth century. The Ethiopian Orthodox church of today originates from Axumite Christianity. Coptic Christians found it impossible to accept the definition agreed by the Council of *Chalcedon in 451, according to which Christ has two distinct and indivisible natures – human and divine. They preferred not to 'divide' Christ in this way and thus diminish his glorious divinity. Three African churches – the Coptic church in Egypt and the Nubian and Ethiopian churches – together with the Armenian and Jacobite church of Syria, became known as *Monophysite churches. To this day, the Coptic church in Egypt and the Ethiopian Orthodox church reflect the Monophysite Christology of their forebears and represent one of the oldest forms of Christianity.

Alexandrian and Axumite Christianity influenced the Christianizing of Nubia to the south. These churches resisted the Arab conquest launched in the seventh century and, with the exception of Nubia which was overcome by Muslims in the fourteenth century, remain a Christian minority in the midst of an almost completely Islamic North Africa.

Another significant contribution of Africa to world Christianity lies in the invention of monasticism. The beginnings of western monasticism have been traced to Coptic writings and disciplines. The rule of the Egyptian Pakhom (290–346) survives in Latin translation and influenced *John Cassian, Basil the Great and Benedict. Pakhom was one of the first desert fathers to emphasize the value of a life of moderate austerity lived in community.

Sub-Saharan African theology has its roots in the re-emergence of Christianity in Africa linked to the activities of European explorers and expansionists. Portuguese Roman Catholics arrived on the shores of southern and western Africa in the fifteenth century. The nature of African theology arising from different parts of the continent since that time is clearly connected with the interactions of Africans with Europeans.

Any account of African theology must consider the work of many great pioneers – Africans who struggled with and made use of whatever means and circumstances were at their disposal to articulate their heritage, faith, hopes, struggles and desires. Often they did this in the face of exploitation, inhumanity, slavery and brutality against their kind. A few such people can be mentioned. Ottobah Cugoano, a Fanti from the 'Gold Coast' and enslaved while a child, gained his freedom in England and published an influential book containing penetrating theological arguments entitled *Thoughts and Sentiments on the Evil and Wicked Traffic of Slavery and Commerce of the Human Species* (1787). Olaudah Equiano, baptized Gustavus Vassa, and similarly enslaved, later managed to purchase his freedom with money saved from his wages as a seaman. Equiano also published a narrative autobiography in 1789. Ignatius Sancho, born on a slave ship bound for the Caribbean, later settled in London and wrote extensively. Anton Wilhelm Amo was also from the 'Gold Coast'. Never a slave, he went to Europe under missionary auspices, mastered six languages (including Hebrew and Greek), and lectured for a number of years in philosophy at several German universities. Jacobus E.J. Capitein (1717–47), a Fanti former-slave from Elmina on the 'Gold Coast', presented a doctoral dissertation to the University of Leiden in 1742, in which he argued that slavery was not incompatible with Christian freedom. He thus became a forerunner, in a rather peculiar way, of those African theologians who have sought to promote all forms of western Christianity in Africa. Philip Quarcoo (1741–1816), the son of a 'Gold Coast' merchant, was taken to England when he was fourteen years old by the Anglican missionary Thomas Thompson. After his baptism in 1759 he went on to study theology and was later ordained and, like Capitein, was sent back to Africa as a missionary and served in his native Fantiland for 50 years.

A native of St Thomas, West Indies, Edward Wilmot Blyden (1832–1912), lived most of his life in Liberia. He was an accomplished writer, linguist, statesman, diplomat, clergyman and educator, who strongly defended the unique character of Africa and its people. Blyden challenged white racial theorists, arguing that Africans are 'distinct', not inferior. He analyzed African culture within the context of African social experience. Blyden perceived very acutely the reality of an African identity problem as a result of the European impact on Africa and was the first to propose the adoption of 'African personality' and the self-conscious cultivation of African indigenous values and attitudes.

Samuel Ajayi Crowther (c. 1814–91) has been

described as probably the best-known African Christian of the nineteenth century. Crowther, a Yoruba, was captured, enslaved, sold and freed as a child. He was sent to Fourah Bay, Sierra Leone where under the tutelage of Church Missionary Society missionaries Crowther's intellectual flair flourished. Ordained a priest in England in 1845, he went to Abeokuta in his native Nigeria as a missionary. In 1864 he was consecrated bishop of the territories of West Africa. Crowther recognized the value of African traditional religion and argued that for Christian mission to be effective it should involve the translation of Christian values into African traditional idiom. James 'Holy' Johnson (c. 1837–1917), Crowther's successor as leader of Nigeria's Christian community, was also a Yoruba who lived and studied in Freetown and then returned as a missionary to his home country. Johnson worked tirelessly for an African Christianity in which Africa and Europe were reconciled.

These pioneers wrestled with what has remained a central question of African theology to this day. Given the history of Christianity in Africa, *is it possible to be an African and a Christian at one and the same time?*

In the early 1950s the struggles for African nationalism were in the ascendancy. In the forefront of the struggle for independence were African intellectuals such as Kwame Nkrumah (Ghana) and Léopold Senghor (Senegal), mostly trained in western academic institutions. There were also grass-roots movements of workers and peasants which sought to end colonial rule. Out of the ferment of that period emerged concepts such as 'négritude', associated with the writings of Léopold Senghor in Senegal and the West Indian, Aimé Césaire. The term was used to cover the totality of black experience in terms of cognition, culture, values and especially spirituality in its distinctiveness from western analytical rationality. Similarly, 'African personality' is a concept arising from anglophone Africa that refers particularly to the perceived preference of African peoples for communal rather than individualistic social arrangements. It is possible to trace the significance of these influential ideas within the formal writings of African theologians since that period, although with differing degrees of acceptance of these concepts or their theological implications. It is also important to observe the phenomenal growth of 'independent' churches in Africa at this time, although

most of the well-established ones were in existence from before the 1930s. These churches, often grass-roots movements, made use of the vernacular into which the Bible and Christian teaching had been translated to embark on far-reaching innovations in church, ritual and theology. C.G. Baëta's *Prophetism in Ghana* (1962) was an early theological appraisal of some of these churches.

In 1956 a seminal work, perhaps meriting the recognition it has gained as the 'starting point of the modern African theology movement', was published. Entitled *Des Prêtres Noires s'Interrogent*, this collection of essays by African Roman Catholic priests contains the reflections of Africans on the relation of African culture and history to Christianity. Vincent Mulago's *Un Visage Africain du Christianisme* (1962) represents an attempt to take African culture, négritude and Pan-Africanism seriously in Christian faith in Africa. On the anglophone side, Bolaji Idowu's *Towards an Indigenous Church* (1965) clearly favours the 'Africanization' of Christianity.

African theologians such as John Mbiti, Bolaji Idowu, Harry Sawyerr, Vincent Mulago, Charles Nyamiti, John Pobee and Kwesi Dickson have been concerned with Africanization. Their analyses can be termed 'religio-cultural' because they encourage a Christian dialogue with African traditional religion and culture. Their quest is essentially for authentic African Christianity. Two terms have been used in this exploration – 'inculturation' and 'acculturation'. Inculturation has to do with the changes that come into African life and culture as a result of Christian faith. Acculturation refers to the efforts to use things African in the practice of Christianity. For these African theologians, *both* are necessary. A major criticism which has been levelled against these 'older' theologians has been that they have, by and large, been unable to free themselves from Eurocentric analyses and have tended to view African realities through European lenses. The influence of Edward Geoffrey Parrinder is clear in Mbiti's work, E.E. Evans-Pritchard in Idowu's and Placide Tempels in Mulago's. It is clear in their work that in any dialogue between African religion and western Christianity, the latter is the superior partner. A further charge is that their analyses fail to address seriously the current situation of grinding and increasing poverty, economic and political instability, oppression, sexism and repression in present-day Africa.

A more recent trend in African theology seeks to address these perceived shortcomings through social or contextual analyses. These analyses examine the socio-economic situations of countries as they exist at present and seek to critically engage with these situations in the light of the Christian gospel. The emergence of this new trend was discernible in the formation of the Ecumenical Association of Third World Theologians (EATWOT) in Dar es Salaam, Tanzania, in 1976. The call for African theology to be 'liberation' theology was issued most clearly in 1977 at the Pan-African Conference of Third World Theologians, as documented in Kofi Appiah-Kubi and Sergio Torres (eds.), *African Theology en Route* (1979). Leading African theologians of the liberationist persuasion include Jean-Marc Éla (*African Cry*, 1986), Engelbert Mveng and Eboussi Boulaga (all Cameroonians). In South Africa, African theology has taken the form of *black theology, akin to the African-American struggles against discrimination manifest in the Civil Rights and Black Power movements and clearly articulated in the work of *James Cone. Leading South African Black theologians in this regard include the veteran Archbishop Desmond Tutu, Itumeleng Mosala, Bonganjalo Goba, Takatso Mofokeng, Allan Boesak, Frank Chikane and Manas Buthelezi.

Several African theologians have sought to demonstrate the complementarity of religio-cultural and socio-liberative analysis in African theology. Among them would be the African women Mercy Amba Oduyoye and Musimbi Kanyoro, Barthélemy Adoukonou of Benin, Bénézet Bujo from Zaire, and Ghanaian Emmanuel Martey.

Among the issues that African theologians continue to wrestle with are questions of the nature of God – as the supreme, ultimate One; Christ – as brother, proto-ancestor or uncle; the Spirit – as enabler, community-builder or power-giver; human identity and dignity in the face of exploitation, poverty and dehumanization; the nature of the community of faith – extended family, clan or fellowship; and eschatology – the ultimate significance of all things. The touchstone in all of these issues, though, is the manner in which ritual, belief and practice relate to the well being of the African community within its social context.

EMMANUEL Y. LARTEY

FURTHER READING: E.W. Fasholé-Luke, R. Gray, A. Hastings and G. Tasie (eds.), *Christianity in Independent Africa* (London, 1978); Josiah U. Young III, *African Theology: A Critical Analysis and Annotated Bibliography* (Westport, CT, 1993); Kwesi A. Dickson, *Theology in Africa* (London / Maryknoll, NY, 1984); Kwame Bediako, *Theology and Identity* (Oxford, 1992); J.N.K. Mugambi, *African Christian Theology* (Nairobi, 1989); K. Appiah-Kubi and Sergio Torres (eds.), *African Theology en Route* (Maryknoll, NY, 1979); Bénézet Bujo, *African Theology in its Social Context* (Maryknoll, NY, 1992); Jean-Marc Éla, *African Cry* (Maryknoll, NY, 1986); John Parratt, *Reinventing Christianity: African Theology Today* (Grand Rapids / Trenton, NJ, 1995); Elizabeth Isichei, *A History of Christianity in Africa* (London, 1995).

Alacoque, Margaret Mary (1647–90)

Margaret Mary, daughter of Claude Alacoque and Philiberte Lamyn, was born on 22 July 1647 at Hautecour, in the province of Burgundy, France. Her father was a royal notary and judge in the baronial courts of Terrau, Corcheval and Pressy.

Margaret Mary's earliest years were spent in the home of her parents. At the age of four she went to live in Corcheval with her godmother, Madame de Fautrières. Her earliest education in catechism was entrusted to two ladies in the employ of her godmother. At the age of eight, shortly after the deaths of both her godmother and of her father, Margaret Mary was sent to a convent of Urbanist nuns, also called the Poor Clares, at Charolles. A pious and devout child, she was allowed to make her first communion at age nine, several years before the prevailing age. Because of illness, Margaret Mary returned home after only two years with the Urbanist nuns to a household filled with tension between her mother and her uncle who had taken over the care of Claude's estate after his death. Her uncle was a shrewd and successful manager, but his rigidity and that of his wife caused constant distress within the family. When Margaret Mary was seventeen her brother became of age, took over the management of the property, and the family settled into a life of comfort common to their class in seventeenth-century French society.

Having vowed virginity as a young child, Margaret Mary had intended to live an ascetic life with particular devotion to Christ in the Blessed Sacrament. This devotion had achieved a particular status during the Catholic reform which followed *Martin Luther's protest in the sixteenth century. An important part of Luther's protest was whether Christ's presence in the host extended beyond the action of the Lord's Supper. As part of the Roman Catholic response following the Council of Trent (1545–62), Roman Catholicism had encouraged devotion to Christ's real presence in the Blessed Sacrament before, during and after the action of the liturgy. The priests of the Society of Jesus, the *Jesuits, preached this devotion tirelessly.

Following the restoration of the family property, Margaret Mary's mother made it clear to her children that she expected them all to marry. Margaret Mary then began to enjoy social gatherings and amusements. Following the deaths of two of her brothers, Margaret Mary had a vision of Christ. Once again, she turned to the ascetic life.

On 20 June 1671, Margaret Mary entered the convent of the Visitation nuns at Paray-le-Monial as a postulant; two months later she was admitted as a novice. Originally founded by a Jesuit priest to be an active community of women religious, the Visitation nuns, sometimes called Holy Maries, had been cloistered by Rome and had as their special devotion reverencing Christ really present in the reserved host. During her time in the novitiate, Margaret Mary was a source of controversy among the nuns. Her extreme asceticism and continual prayer before the Blessed Sacrament was different from the usual life of the community at Paray-le-Monial. In a group where humility was expected and singularity rejected, the nuns doubted her ability to live as a Visitation nun. Finally, after the intercession of Father de la Colombière, SJ, Margaret Mary was admitted to vows. Although the controversy over her apparent singularity of life endured, without exception her biographers note that she bore the criticism of the nuns with great patience and unfailing charity.

During her life in the convent at Paray-le-Monial Margaret Mary experienced visions of Christ centred on his Sacred Heart. During many of her prayer hours before the Blessed Sacrament Margaret Mary experienced visions of Jesus in which he pointed to his heart laid bare, surrounded by a crown of thorns with a cross on top. Following his wishes, Margaret Mary spread the devotion to the Sacred Heart to all within her community and, as far as possible, beyond. Several healing miracles are attributed to Christ under this devotion through the work of Margaret Mary. She was tireless in making the Sacred Heart known and is credited as an influence in the Roman Catholic Church's inclusion of this feast in its liturgical calendar on the Friday after the octave of Corpus Christi. The now well-recognized picture of the Sacred Heart was popularized through her efforts. In addition, the devotional practice of dedicating the first Friday of every month to prayers to the Sacred Heart of Jesus is a result of Margaret Mary Alacoque's visions. Devotion to the Sacred Heart was officially approved by Pope Clement XIII in 1765.

Theologically, devotion to the Sacred Heart is rooted in St Paul's statement that Christians fill up in themselves what is wanting in the sufferings of Christ. That is, Christians carry on Christ's suffering, redemptive work in this world, all the while clinging in deep affection to Christ. His heart is the symbol of his unconditional and illimitable love for all. Thus, the devotion to the Sacred Heart interprets a biblical statement and the element of Christian belief that in Christ's heart all were included in his sacrifice on the cross.

With the help of the Jesuit priests, devotion to the Sacred Heart of Jesus spread quickly, especially throughout seventeenth-century southern France. Margaret Mary Alacoque has been known as the 'Apostle of the Sacred Heart of Jesus'. She was admired for her devotion to the sick, especially to those whose illnesses were severe. She was appointed Novice Director within her convent in 1685.

Margaret Mary Alacoque became ill and died on 17 October 1690. Her *Memoir*, or autobiography, is available in several languages. In 1920 Pope Benedict XV declared her a saint of the Roman Catholic Church.

LORETTA DEVOY, OP

FURTHER READING: Albert Barry, CSSR, *Life of Blessed Margaret Mary Alacoque* (London, 1889); Henri H. Gheon, *The Secret of St Margaret Mary* (New York, 1937); H.J. Heagney, *'Behold This Heart': The Story of St Margaret Mary Alacoque* (New York, 1947); Clarence A. Herbst, SJ, *Letters of Margaret Mary Alacoque* (Florida, 1976); Jesus Solano, SJ, *The Historical Development of Reparation in Devotion to the Heart of Jesus: From the First Century to St Margaret Mary Alacoque* (Rome, 1980).

Alexander of Hales (c. 1186–1245)

Little is known of Alexander's early years, except that he was born into a rural wealthy family in Halesowen, Shropshire. By 1210, he had completed his study in the arts faculty at Paris and had incepted as a teaching master. He soon entered the faculty of theology and by 1222 he was a master of the sacred page. He enjoyed a long and successful career, maintaining his teaching role until his death. The only years in which he did not teach were during the university strike (1229–31). The cessation of studies had been called in response to the harsh treatment of a student by the civil authorities, an act which appeared to threaten the autonomy of the university. Alexander left Paris for Angers, but he did not remain there for long; instead, he travelled to Rome and participated in negotiations with the papal court to find a solution to the strike. He may have aided in writing the papal bull 'Parens scientarum' (1231), which affirmed the university's independence from any other civil or ecclesiastical authority. Alexander did not return to Paris directly, but rather spent a short time in England. By 1232, he was once again teaching theology in Paris.

Around 1236, Alexander's life took a dramatic turn when he entered the *Franciscan order. We have no record as to what impelled him to make this decision, but it was of clear benefit to the minor brothers. For the first time they had an institutional link with the university, and they quickly turned Alexander's school in the faculty of theology into a centre for educating Franciscan brothers. Among the many students Alexander taught, John of La Rochelle, William of Melitona, Odo Rigaldus and *Bonaventura were the most notable. In 1245, Alexander travelled to Lyons to participate in the church council called by Innocent IV. He became ill on the return journey and died at Paris, possibly on 23 August.

Modern scholars have yet to establish a complete picture of Alexander as a theologian. Up until this century, it was thought that the Summa fratris Alexandri contained a full statement of his theology. The text was certainly begun by Alexander, with the intention of providing the Franciscan order with a comprehensive survey of scholastic theology. However, it remained incomplete at his death, and it was left to his students to finish writing the Summa. Hence, the work reflects the general interests of the Franciscan school, rather than any one individual. For Alexander's own theology one must turn instead to his collection of disputed questions, in which he touched upon almost the whole gamut of scholastic theology. This collection is one of the reasons he became known as the Doctor irrefragibilis. Equally important is his commentary on the Sentences of *Peter Lombard. Although he was not the first to complete a commentary on what would become the standard textbook of theology in the medieval university, he nonetheless introduced a new system of referencing the text (known as 'distinctions'), which made it easier to cite the Sentences and, most of all, easier to cross-reference while commenting.

Although Alexander is considered to be the first Franciscan theologian, his theological outlook was established well before he entered the order. Like most theologians of the period, he was fundamentally a follower of *Augustine, but he did not hesitate in appropriating new sources for his teaching. He employed the *Aristotelian corpus in his writings, although Roger Bacon would later accuse him of being a poor reader of the Stagirite. Of equal importance was the fact that Alexander was one of the first theologians to see the sacramental and pastoral implications of the teachings of Pseudo-Dionysius, particularly in his theology of holy orders. A careful reading of canon law also distinguished his sacramental theology.

The Christocentric character of Franciscan theology can be traced back to Alexander, who argued that the person of Christ represents an intermediary relation between creature and Creator. The incarnation is the greatest act of God, which allowed humanity to encounter God's grace and to come to understand the reality of creation. At the same time, Alexander is careful to delineate the ontological independence of God with respect to his creative acts. Creation was not a necessary act of God's being, but rather a volitional manifestation ad extra of his goodness. This also meant that while one could accept certain personal attributes within the Trinity (such as the power of the Father, the wisdom of the Son, and the goodness of the Holy Spirit), it remained an inviolable truth that every act of God reflected the Trinitarian reality as a whole. Here again one can see vestiges of Augustine, but reshaped by Alexander's reading of *Boethius and especially of *Richard of St Victor.

In addition to his theological influence, Alexander helped to direct the order in other ways. After the scandalous period under the leadership of Elias of Cortana (1231–39), the order became more vigilant in how it governed and administered itself. In 1241, the general chapter held at Montpellier requested that an authoritative commentary on the Rule be produced. Alexander joined two of his students, John of La Rochelle and Odo Rigaldus, along with a fourth theologian, Robert of Bascia, and together they produced the first commentary. While careful not to betray the intention of the Rule, the four masters wished to provide a more accurate picture of the implementation of the Rule, particularly in light of papal mandates that had been issued since Francis's death. This commentary laid the groundwork for the greater reconstruction of the order which took place under the leadership of Bonaventura.

JAMES GINTHER

FURTHER READING: *Texts:* The College of St Bonaventure in Quarrachi, Florence, have been responsible for producing the two critical editions of Alexander's work: *Glossa in quatuor libros Sententiarum Petri Lombardi* (4 vols.; 1951–57); *Quaestiones disputatae 'antequam esset frater'* (3 vols.; 1960). The disputed questions from his fraternal period survive in manuscript form, but as they were a key source for the *Summa fratris Alexandri*, the editors provide a large amount of detail about them in the edition's *Prolegomena* (1948). His biblical commentaries remain almost entirely unexamined, but see A.A. Young, '"*Accessum ad Alexandrium*": The *Praefatio* to the *Postilla in Iohannis Evangelium* of Alexander of Hales (1186–1245)', *Med St* 52 (1990), pp. 1–23. Alexander's *Exoticon*, a list of 'exotic' words found in Latin theological works, remains unedited. Alexander also produced some sermons, for which see J.B. Schneyer, 'Eine Sermonsreihe des Mgr. Alexander von Hales in der Hs. Pavias Univ. Aldinin 479, f. 128ra–180vb', *Arch Fr Hist* 58 (1965), pp. 537–51. *Studies:* There is no comprehensive study of Alexander's theology, but see K.B. Osborne, 'Alexander of Hales', in *The History of Franciscan Theology* (St Bonaventure, NY, 1994), pp. 1–38; V. Marcolino, *Das Alte Testament in der Heilsgeschichte* (Münster, 1970); Walter H. Principe, *Alexander of Hales' Theology of the Hypostatic Union* (Toronto, 1967); I. Brady, 'The Distinctions of Lombard's *Book of Sentences* and Alexander of Hales', *Fr St* 25 (1965), pp. 90–116.

Althaus, Paul (1888–1966)

German Protestant churchman and theologian whose work included *Luther studies,

systematic theology and New Testament research. His father, Paul Althaus Sr, was also a theologian and served as professor at Göttingen and Leipzig. The younger Althaus was trained at Tübingen, where he studied with *Adolf Schlatter, and at Göttingen, where he heard Carl Stange's lectures on Martin Luther. In 1913, Althaus published his first academic work under the title *Die Prinzipien der reformierten Dogmatik im Zeitalter der aristotelischen Scholastik*, thereby qualifying to teach in the German university system. His career was put on hold, however, by the outbreak of the First World War, during which he served as a hospital chaplain in Poland. From 1919–25 he served as professor in Rostock. In 1925 he accepted a position in Erlangen, where he served, in spite of offers from Halle and Tübingen, and a brief post-war hiatus, until his retirement in 1956. In 1926, he was chosen to succeed Karl Holl as president of the *Luthergesellschaft* ('Luther Society'), a position which he held until 1964.

From the very beginnings of his career, Althaus's theological work was set deeply in the context of his troubled times. For the most part, he chose positions that stood somewhere near the midpoint between the poles of competing ideas (so Ericksen). His work could be classified as conservative, in the sense that he identified with the traditions of Lutheran Protestantism and attempted to defend and develop them in response to the challenges of the day. His attempt to apply and develop that tradition marks him, however, as something other than a reactionary, and his theology certainly should not be understood as a simplistic effort to repristinate the theology of some supposedly classic period in Protestant thought. In one of Althaus's early essays, 'Gottes Gottheit als Sinn der Rechtfertigungslehre Luthers', he attempted to show that Luther's doctrine of justification, far from being man-centred, as Schlatter had asserted, was in fact a highly existential manner of asserting the 'Godness' of God. Likewise, in his study of Luther's interpretation of Romans 7, he concluded – again, contra Schlatter – that Luther's use of Paul to support his conclusion that the Christian is simultaneously a saint and a sinner was a justifiable extension of Paul's argument, even if it went somewhat beyond Paul's own intentions.

When the National Socialists came to power in 1933, Althaus enthusiastically supported them, probably because, like so many others, he was disappointed with the outcome and after-math of the First World War. 'Our Protestant churches', he claimed, 'have greeted the turning point of 1933 as a gift and miracle of God' (Erickson, p. 85). During the struggles of that year, he and his colleague Werner Elert went so far as to write an apology of sorts for the 'Aryan paragraph', a repressive Nazi law which excluded persons of Jewish descent from public service, including service as Lutheran pastors. In 1934, he also signed the *Ansbacher Ratschlag* (written by Elert) which, much to the delight of the so-called 'German Christian' party, opposed the *Barmen Declaration which had been pub-lished by the Confessing Church in opposition to the German Christians. His opposition to Barmen stemmed largely from his discomfort with *Karl Barth's notion of revelation, and his sense that the 'two kingdoms' theology of the Lutheran tradition entailed support for the state as a good gift of God, even when the state inter-fered in the church's internal affairs. After 1937, however, Althaus seems to have become disillu-sioned with the course of National Socialism, and he wrote nothing further in support of the state. In the years following the war, he could even speak of the 'evil spirit' that had ruled in Germany during the period of the Third Reich.

During 1947, Althaus found himself sus-pended from his university position on charges associated with his role in supporting the poli-cies and ideology of National Socialism. Cleared late in that same year, he spent the rest of his life teaching (until his retirement), writing and preaching in Erlangen. During this period, Althaus was strikingly productive, completing, among other things, the two works for which he is probably best known in the English-speaking world – *The Theology of Martin Luther* and *The Ethics of Martin Luther*. Each is a work of sound and judicious scholarship informed by many years of fruitful research, writing and vigorous participation in the controversies of his time. The *Theology of Martin Luther* is arranged more or less sequentially according to the categories used by later Christian dogmaticians. Placing Luther's rather unruly thought into such a dog-matic structure obviously entails the risk of obscuring rather than accenting his theological genius, tempting the reader to eschew careful historical study of Luther's writings in their own context in favour of a quick glance through Althaus. But the surefooted Althaus negotiates

the territory skilfully, with the result that the volume can still serve as a handy introduction to Luther's thought.

MICKEY L. MATTOX

FURTHER READING: *Texts: Grundriss der Dogmatik* (2 vols.; Erlangen, 1929–32); 'Gottes Gottheit als Sinn der Rechtfertigungslehre Luthers', in *Jahrbuch der Luthergesellschaft* 13 (1931), pp. 1–28; *Die deut-sche Stunde der Kirche* (Göttingen, 3rd edn, 1934); *Kirche und Staat nach lutherische Lehre* (Leipzig, 1935); *Obrigkeit und Führertum* (Gütersloh, 1936); *Paulus und Luther Über den Menschen* (Gütersloh, 1938); *Die Christliche Warheit* (2 vols.; Gütersloh, 1947–48); *Die Theologie Martin Luthers* (Gütersloh, 1962; ET *The Theology of Martin Luther* [trans. Robert C. Schultz; Philadelphia, 1966]); *Die Ethik Martin Luthers* (Gütersloh, 1965; ET *The Ethics of Martin Luther* [trans. Robert C. Schultz; Philadel-phia, 1972]), the preface to the ET includes a brief biography; *The Divine Command: A New Perspective on Law and Gospel* (trans. Franklin Sherman; Social Ethics Series 9; Philadelphia, 1966). *Studies*: Robert P. Ericksen, *Theologians Under Hitler: Gerhard Kittel, Paul Althaus and Emanuel Hirsch* (New Haven / London, 1985); Paul Knitter, *Towards a Protestant Theology of Religions: A Case Study of Paul Althaus and Contemporary Attitudes* (Marburg, 1974).

Ambrose (c. 339–97)

Ambrose was born at Trier, son of one of the chief officials of the Roman Empire, and received a Christian upbringing and classical education at Rome. He pursued a career in the imperial administrative service, and in c. 372/3 was appointed governor of the important prov-ince of Aemilia-Liguria, with a base in Milan. The see of Milan had been occupied since 355 by the Arian Auxentius. On Auxentius's death in the autumn of 374, the city was thrown into turmoil, as the pro-Nicene dissidents demanded a say in the appointment of his successor. Ambrose intervened, implicitly upholding the rights of the Nicenes, and found that he was claimed as the ideal candidate himself, though he had not even been baptized. Initially reluc-tant to accept the acclamation, Ambrose gave in once he had secured the sanction of the emperor, Valentinian I. After receiving baptism at the hands of a Catholic priest, Ambrose was ceremonially passed through the various clerical grades from doorkeeper to presbyter in the course of one week, and consecrated on 7 December 374. He was to hold office for more than twenty-two years and to exercise a considerable, if often misconstrued, influence on the subsequent course of western Christianity.

Ambrose's episcopacy was characterized by one grand strategy: the quest to create a role for the church on the stage of a Christian empire. The strategy was implemented in three areas: first, in opposition to *Arianism; second, in defining the relationship between political authority and the prerogatives of the ecclesiastical hierarchy; and third, in fostering an image of a civilized and cohesive church community as a model for society. The establishment of Ambrose's hegemony was in reality a far more difficult process than hagiographical accounts, ancient or modern, suggest. He struggled against significant opposition, and his achievement was won only through frequent improvisation and brinkmanship. The skills of the political operator and the theatricality of the demagogue were essential to his success.

Ambrose's polemic scarcely differentiates between the many forms of Arianism which existed in the late fourth century, but his principal target was the Homoean theology of a Christ who was 'like' God the Father but not consubstantial with him. An assiduous student of Greek authorities, Ambrose repackaged the theology of the eastern Nicenes in forceful Latin. His early efforts were as much an attempt to defend his own orthodox credibility as an engagement in constructive theological reflection, and the results are often unimpressive as intellectual arguments for any other than the converted. But they remain seminal in historical terms: by drawing on Basil and Didymus (d. 398), for example, Ambrose succeeded in producing the first western treatise on the Holy Spirit. Ambrose was not just dealing in rhetorical platitudes, either: for him, the Homoeans were a serious rival force in Milan. He could carry the day at the Council of Aquileia in 381, but he faced renewed opposition in the mid-380s, when the Milanese Arians, ably abetted by Justina, the mother of the boy-emperor Valentinian II, demanded a basilica in which to worship. At the high point of the crisis, at Easter 386, Ambrose and his supporters were besieged in church by imperial troops, and confronted real physical peril. The emperor backed down in the face of stage-managed resistance from a bishop who protested his inability to surrender God's own property. To yield space to the unsound was to

give tacit credence to the plausibility of their alternative theological manifesto. To promote solidarity among his people at this time, Ambrose introduced the Greek practice of congregational hymn singing. He composed simple yet evocative hymns celebrating a fully consubstantial Christ and a truly divine Spirit. The faithful community broadcast its orthodoxy with one voice, while the enemies of truth bared their teeth at the doors. The 'Ambrosian' hymn was to revolutionize the Latin liturgy.

Implicit in the confrontation of 386 was Ambrose's perspective on church-state relations. The presence of the western court in Milan from 381 brought him a privileged access to the machinery of government, and he exploited it to the full. His relations with a series of emperors, not only in the west but also in the east, were delicate and complex. He laboured to sustain an impression of awesome ecclesiastical authority, according to which the secular powers had no right to interfere in the affairs of the church and the emperor himself was subject to episcopal discipline. Ambrose could see to it that a pagan statue was not restored to the Roman senate house (384); or that legal penalties imposed upon a bishop who had orchestrated the burning of a synagogue at Callinicum were lifted (388); or that the emperor Theodosius I himself did public penance for having ordered an indiscriminate massacre at Thessalonica (390). Such coups were contrived, but it was the spectacle that mattered. Spiritual authority was in the end supreme; yet that very authority was tied to imperial stability and the political expansion of Catholic orthodoxy.

A similar obsession with appearance pervades Ambrose's pastoral ministry. One of the greatest orators of the patristic period, his sermons display an 'erudite suavity' which greatly impressed *Augustine. The allegorical exegesis of *Philo and *Origen is synthesized in a strongly neo-Platonist spirituality; the framework is biblical, yet allusions to classical literature and thought abound. Ambrose's most famous work, *On Duties*, transforms Cicero's textbook for aspiring politicians into a moral guide for the clergy, combining scriptural paradigms with Stoic ethics. Ecclesiastics are to be paragons of 'seemliness', so that the church will make an impression upon polite society. Ambrose did much to promote asceticism and to develop the cult of the martyrs. He engaged in an extensive church-building programme in Milan and dominated clerical affairs across northern Italy.

Ambrose's originality thus lay in the potency of the image he presented of a strong, holy, orthodox, other-worldly church, devoted to the service of Christ, the true emperor. His theological ideas were generally derivative, though he anticipated or influenced Augustinian thought in a number of areas, not least on the biological transmission of original sin (a theme also expounded by his brilliant contemporary, the otherwise unknown Roman commentator on Paul whom *Erasmus called Ambrosiaster). Ambrose also speaks, significantly, of a super-natural change taking place in the Eucharistic elements when the priest recites the dominical words. Western veneration of Mary was given some impetus by his focus on her as an example in his preaching on female asceticism. In the end, though, it is in his role as pioneer of Greek ideas in a Latin context, as pragmatic church-man and impresario rather than speculative theologian, that the genius of Ambrose must be measured.

IVOR DAVIDSON

FURTHER READING: Overview of texts in A. di Berardino (ed.), *Patrology* 4 (Westminster, MD, 1994), pp. 144–80. *Basic studies:* F. Homes Dudden, *The Life and Times of St Ambrose* (2 vols.; Oxford, 1935); N.B. McLynn, *Ambrose of Milan: Church and Court in a Christian Capital* (Berkeley, 1994); J.-R. Palanque, *Saint Ambroise et l'Empire Romain* (Paris, 1933); A. Paredi, *Saint Ambrose: His Life and Times* (Notre Dame, 1964); D.H. Williams, *Ambrose of Milan and the End of the Nicene-Arian Conflicts* (Oxford, 1995). *More specialized studies:* E. Dassmann, *Die Frömmigkeit des Kirchenvaters Ambrosius von Mailand* (Münster, 1965); Y.-M. Duval (ed.), *Ambroise de Milan* (Paris, 1974); R. Gryson, *Le Prêtre selon Saint Ambroise* (Louvain, 1968); G. Lazzati (ed.), *Ambrosius Episcopus* (2 vols.; Milan, 1976); G. Madec, *Saint Ambroise et la Philosophie* (Paris, 1974); B. Ramsey, *Ambrose* (London, 1997); H. Savon, *Ambroise de Milan* (Paris, 1997).

Ames, William (1576–1633)

William Ames was born in Suffolk, England of a family with *Puritan sympathies. He studied in Christ's College, Cambridge University, where he was a pupil of William Perkins, perhaps the most significant Puritan theologian of his day. Ames graduated in 1607 and became a fellow of Christ's College. He was recognized both as a fine academic and a godly churchman, and a life spent either in the university or the church seemed ahead of him. Both of these possible avenues of service were closed to him, however, due to the persecution of the Puritan cause by James VI and I after the failure of the Hampton Court Conference of 1604. Like many others Ames travelled to Holland where, in 1610, he settled first in Rotterdam and then in The Hague.

During these early years in Holland Ames ministered to English exiles, merchant seamen and soldiers. Even in The Hague, however, he was not safe from the influence of those in England who regarded him as an enemy of the state, and his ministry in The Hague was brought to an end in 1618. Finally, he became a professor of theology in the University of Franeker, taking up his appointment in 1622.

The years between losing his appointment in The Hague and taking up his professorship were not spent idly. Even at this early stage in his career, Ames was increasingly being recognized as one of the most able of the Puritan theologians. During the winter of 1618–19 he attended the Synod of Dort, contributed to its debates and clearly approved of the final doctrinal statements issued by the Synod, particularly the famous 'five points' of *Calvinism. He was not a delegate to the Synod but a paid consultant to the president.

This early period in Holland brought him into contact with some of those who would later become the 'New England Puritans'. His discussions with them, especially with their leader John Robinson, with whom he often seriously disagreed, led to Ames being one of the main influences on the development of Calvinist theology and church life in the New World. In particular, his views on covenant theology and his congregational church polity made a significant contribution to the thinking of these early settlers. He continued in correspondence with them until the end of his days and, by this means, influenced the development of reformed theology not only in Europe but also in America. Indeed, Sydney Ahlstrom has called him the 'chief theological mentor' of the New England Puritans.

It was Ames's ultimate objective, at the strong and repeated insistence of the New England Puritans, to go and minister among them – but it was not to be. Having left the University of

Franeker in 1632 to become associate minister of an independent congregation in Rotterdam, he died the following year, before his departure for the New World could be arranged.

It is, however, for his contributions to *Reformed theology that Ames is principally remembered. Like many of the Reformed theologians of his day, Ames's principal theological opponents were Roman Catholics and *Arminians (or Remonstrants). Against Roman Catholicism, particularly targeted against one of its leading scholars, he wrote a treatise entitled *Bellarmine Disarmed*. His volume *The Marrow of Theology*, first published in Latin in 1623 in Amsterdam, ranks alongside the finest volumes of Reformed theology to be published in the seventeenth century and was held in very high regard by the Reformed scholars of the day. In addition, he wrote *Conscience with the power and cases thereof* (1630, ET 1639) and numerous shorter works.

It was not only by his publishing, however, that Ames influenced the development of covenant theology. He was also tremendously influential on the next generation of covenant theologians. For example, *Johannes Cocceius (1603–69) was one of Ames's pupils who, in his own writings on covenant theology, carried forward the work of his master.

Ames was not only a fine theologian but also a godly man. Although a staunch opponent of the Church of England and its 'ceremonies', his was a moderate Calvinism which, while holding firm to the tenets of Dort, was conscious of the concerns of his theological opponents and the strengths of their arguments. For example, he regarded the Arminians not as heretics but as brothers who had fallen into serious error.

As to theological method he was, following Perkins, a Ramist (declaring deduction to be the final scientific method). The use of Ramist logic, in contrast to the prevailing *Aristotelianism, gave the Puritans a philosophical basis for their theology which, at the same time, helped to give structure and shape to the theology itself.

Like most of the Puritans, Ames had a great concern for Christian life and character. This emphasis on 'practical divinity' shines through all of his writings and is also evident in the ecclesiastical controversies in which he took part.

ANDREW T.B. MCGOWAN

FURTHER READING: *Text: The Marrow of Theology* (trans. and ed. J.D. Eusden; Boston, 1968). *Studies:* K.L. Sprunger, *The Learned Doctor William Ames* (Urbana, IL, 1972); Matthew Nethenus, Hugo Visscher and Karl Reuter, *William Ames* (trans. Douglas Horton; Cambridge, MA, 1965); D.K. McKim, *Ramism in William Perkins' Theology* (New York, 1987).

Amyraldianism

Amyraldianism is a system of Christian doctrine which seeks to understand Christ's atonement as being universal in its extent and intention, while at the same time holding to a particularist view of its effect. It is associated with the name of Moise Amyraut (1596–1664) and so-called because of the Latin form of his name (Amyraldus).

In fact, the system can be traced to John Cameron (1579–1625), Amyraut's teacher in the French Protestant Academy of Saumur. Cameron was a Scotsman who taught at Saumur from 1618–21. He had considerable influence on the theological development of Saumur, not least by his impact on several young scholars, of whom Amyraut is the most significant. Amyraut himself taught at Saumur from 1633 until his death in 1664.

The key to understanding Amyraldianism is its notion of a hypothetical universal covenant, which is why Amyraldianism is sometimes called 'hypothetical universalism'. The idea is that the covenant of grace is really two covenants. By this understanding, God made a covenant with all human beings wherein they would be saved on condition of repentance and faith. This was possible at a natural level (the human will was capable of making such a response) but impossible at a moral level (through the inability of human beings to respond because of their sin). This being the case, God made another covenant, this time an unconditional covenant, which guarantees the salvation of the elect.

Amyraldianism thus implies a twofold will of God, whereby he wills the salvation of all humankind on condition of faith but wills the salvation of the elect specifically and unconditionally. The theological difficulty of God's will having been frustrated by the fact that not all are saved is met by the argument that God only willed their salvation on the condition of faith. Where an individual has no faith, then God has not willed the salvation of that person.

This theological perspective also implies a twofold intention in the atonement whereby Christ dies in a (hypothetical) universalist sense for all humanity but in a particularist sense for the elect only. It is in this debate on the extent of the atonement that Amyraldianism (or a variant thereof) has maintained its influence to the present day. The debate as to whether or not *Calvin taught limited atonement or, if he did not, whether it is a natural and logical outworking of his other doctrines, rumbles on.

Amyraut's intention in developing this theological perspective was a noble one. He wanted to reconcile those of a *Reformed persuasion with their *Lutheran contemporaries, solve the impasse between those who believed in a universal atonement and those who believed in a limited atonement, and thus unite the Protestant cause. Amyraut had no intention of rejecting the Reformed heritage stemming from Calvin. He believed that the Scriptures do have a universalist as well as a particularist view of the atonement and that both of these had to be expressed in any theology of the atonement. The problem was that Amyraut's solution suited neither the universalists nor the particularists.

Amyraut's views were dealt with at the National Synod of Alencon (1637). Interestingly, although his views were rejected and he was admonished by the Synod, he was not condemned as a heretic.

Saumur became noted for several theological perspectives which differed from the prevailing orthodoxy as represented by the Synod of Dort (1615). As well as Amyraut's views on the nature and extent of the atonement, one of his contemporaries denied verbal inspiration and another taught a view of mediate imputation of Adam's sin to his posterity. All three of these positions were dealt with in the Formula Consensus Helvetica (1675), although particular attention was paid to Amyraldianism, which was rejected as being unorthodox.

The famous Amyraldian dictum that Christ died sufficiently for all but efficiently only for the elect was, in fact, a scholastic expression to which even Calvin was prepared to give assent. The Amyraldians, however, used it to mean something which Calvin and the later Reformed theologians rejected, namely, the notion of a universal atonement which was then applied particularistically. This Amyraldian version of the dictum has experienced something of a revival of late through the writings of R.T. Kendall and

Alan Clifford. Both have argued that Calvin held to a universal atonement while at the same time affirming a predestination of the elect alone to salvation.

ANDREW T.B. MCGOWAN

FURTHER READING: B. Armstrong, *Calvinism and the Amyraut Heresy* (Madison, WI, 1969); R. Nicole, *Moyse Amyraut: A Bibliography* (New York, 1981); B.B. Warfield, *Plan of Salvation* (Philadelphia, 1915); R.T. Kendall, *Calvin and English Calvinism to 1649* (Oxford, 1979); G. Michael Thomas, *The Extent of the Atonement: A Dilemma for Reformed Theology from Calvin to the Consensus* (Carlisle, 1997). For a list of Amyraut's writings see P. Schaff, *The Creeds of Christendom*, I (Grand Rapids, 1983), p. 481, footnote 1.

Anabaptists

Anabaptism was a radical renewal movement, contemporaneous with the sixteenth-century *Reformation, in territories which now comprise Switzerland, Austria, the Czech Republic, Germany, Alsace and the Netherlands. Its distinguishing characteristics included Christocentrism, emphasis on new birth and discipleship in the power of the Spirit, establishment of believers' churches free from state control, commitment to economic sharing, and a vision of restoring New Testament Christianity.

Anabaptism drew adherents primarily from poorer sections of the community, although early leaders included university graduates, monks and priests. Assessing its numerical strength is difficult, because it was driven underground by persecution; it certainly influenced many more people than those baptized as members. Historians identify four main Anabaptist branches – Swiss Brethren, South German/Austrian Anabaptists, Dutch Mennonites and the communitarian Hutterites – but each of these branches comprised numerous groups which gathered around charismatic leaders and developed distinctive practices and emphases.

Recent research has challenged earlier interpretations of Anabaptism as simply a radicalizing of the Reformers' convictions. Scholars now acknowledge the influence of *Thomas Müntzer (c. 1490–1525), the Zwickau prophets, radical Reformers like Andreas von Karlstadt (c. 1480–1541) and Spiritualists like Caspar Schwenckfeld (1489–1561) on the movement. Other possible influences on Anabaptism include monasticism, the *Franciscan Tertiaries, Humanism,

*Erasmus (c. 1469–1536), German mysticism, the '*devotio moderna*' and pre-Reformation radicals. Such influences have been challenged on the grounds that there is inadequate documentary evidence, that similarity of belief and practice need not imply derivation, and that the Anabaptists' restitutionist approach meant they looked to the New Testament for inspiration. However, all of the above were components in the context within which Anabaptism developed.

Dispute revolves around the terms 'monogenesis' and 'polygenesis' in relation to Anabaptist origins. Recent scholarship has challenged earlier historians who claimed Anabaptism originated among the disciples of *Ulrich Zwingli (1484–1531) in Zurich in 1525 and spread through central and northern Europe. The development of Anabaptism was complex, with various groups emerging independently, discovering one another and recognizing kindred spirits. The significance of peasant unrest, millenarian hopes and anticlericalism has become increasingly clear. Even where links cannot be established with earlier movements, the effects of these factors on lay piety, particularly among the poor, should not be underestimated. Anabaptists found considerable receptivity among communities which had quietly kept alive radical ideas that the official church thought had been smothered.

Some Mennonite historians have tended to identify the Swiss Brethren and Dutch Mennonites as normative – evangelical Anabaptists in contradistinction to others regarded as spiritualistic or revolutionary. These historians have been criticized for homogenizing these groups and for reading back later Mennonite convictions into early Anabaptism. As well as distinguishing Swiss, South German/Austrian, Dutch and Hutterite branches, it is necessary to consider different camps into which Anabaptists divided, especially in relation to principles of biblical interpretation. The main camps, which do not coincide precisely with geographical divisions, were 'literalists', 'spiritualists' and 'apocalypticists', although these were not mutually exclusive. The morphology of the movement is complicated further by the fact that some influential figures passed through it before renouncing Anabaptist beliefs.

Although other factors (such as social discontent) contributed to its emergence, Anabaptism must be understood in the context of the Reformation, to which the movement owed much, as its leaders freely acknowledged. There are several things which distinguished Anabaptists from the Reformers.

Radicalism. Anabaptists criticized *Luther (1483–1546) and Zwingli for their unwillingness to follow through with their biblical convictions. The Anabaptists were convinced that Scripture was authoritative for ethics and ecclesiology as well as for doctrine, which the Reformers seemed unwilling to admit. Much to their discomfort, Anabaptists reminded the Reformers of their own more radical early ecclesiological views, which they had jettisoned. Anabaptists championed immediate action rather than the Reformers' gradualist approach.

Restitution. Anabaptists believed the church was 'fallen' beyond mere reform. Thorough restoration of New Testament Christianity was necessary, which required freedom from both state control and ecclesiastical traditions. Anabaptists urged separation of church and society and rejected the Christendom system that had dominated European culture since the fourth century. They asserted that for centuries the church had been in error not only in certain doctrines, but also on the question of its identity and relationship with society.

An alternative tradition. Anabaptists have been described as 'step-children of the Reformers', but there was also resonance with earlier movements such as the *Unitas Fratrum*, Waldensians and Lollards. Anabaptists were neither Catholic nor Protestant, but heirs of an alternative tradition that had persisted throughout the centuries since Constantine. Often regarded as heretics and persecuted, these 'old evangelical brotherhoods' kept alive beliefs and practices which the official church ignored or marginalized.

A church of the poor. As these earlier groups mentioned above, Anabaptists were mostly poor and powerless with few wealthy, academic or influential members. They were regarded as subversives, although few were primarily politically or economically motivated. It is legitimate, however, to regard some Anabaptists as heirs of the failed Peasants' Revolt (1524–26), still pursuing their concerns through the alternative strategy of establishing communities where just practices were fostered. Anabaptism, a grass-roots revival with disturbing implications for the church/state amalgam at the heart of the European social order, was vehemently opposed by those whose vested interests were threatened. Some Anabaptist views owe much to their powerless position: for example, they were prepared to obey the Bible regardless of social consequences.

'Anabaptists'. Anabaptists called themselves Christians or 'brothers and sisters'; their opponents designated them 'enthusiasts', revolutionaries or 'Anabaptists'. This label, meaning 're-baptizers', had negative connotations. Anabaptists themselves objected to this name: they did not regard believers' baptism as rebaptism because they denied the validity of infant baptism. Also, baptism was not the main issue – although it symbolized their rejection of Christendom.

Anabaptism was a diverse, fluid but coherent movement. Various stimuli enabled it to develop in different places, resulting in regional variations and some sharp internal disagreements. It developed towards greater uniformity of belief and practice by mid-century. Most Anabaptists shared the following convictions:

The Bible. Anabaptists agreed with the Reformers about the Bible's authority but disagreed strongly about its interpretation and application. Anabaptists prioritized the New Testament, and particularly the life and teachings of Jesus. 'Christocentrism' was an Anabaptist hallmark and radically affected their hermeneutics. Balthasar Hubmaier (1481–1528), the leading Anabaptist theologian, explained: 'all the Scriptures point us to the spirit, gospel, example, ordinance and usage of Christ'. Anabaptists started from Jesus and interpreted everything in the light of him – unlike the Reformers, whom Anabaptists suspected of starting from doctrinal passages and trying to fit Jesus into these. Anabaptists refused to treat the Bible as a 'flat' book, regarding it as an unfolding of God's purposes, with the New Testament providing normative guidelines for ethics and ecclesiology. They challenged the Reformers' use of Old Testament models and disagreed with them about such issues as baptism, war, tithing, church government and swearing oaths. In debates, Anabaptists complained that the Reformers used Old Testament passages

illegitimately to set aside clear New Testament teaching.

Salvation. While the Reformers emphasized justification by faith and forgiveness of past sins, the Anabaptists emphasized new birth and the power to live as disciples. The Reformers feared Anabaptists were reverting to salvation by works; Anabaptists accused the Reformers of failing to address moral issues and tolerating unchristian behaviour in their churches. 'Shame on you for the easy-going gospel', chided Menno Simons (c. 1496–1561). Anabaptists emphasized the Spirit's work in believers and taught that Jesus was to be followed and obeyed as well as trusted. He was not only saviour but captain, leader and Lord. Dirk Philips (1504–68) wrote: 'Jesus with his doctrine, life and example is our teacher, leader and guide. Him we must hear and follow.' Michael Sattler (c. 1490–1527), author of the Schleitheim Confession (1527), complained that, whereas Catholics appeared to advocate works without faith, the Reformers taught faith without works, but he wanted faith that expressed itself in works. Hans Denck (1495–1527) insisted that faith and discipleship were interconnected: 'no one can truly know Christ unless he follows him in life, and no one may follow him unless he has first known him'.

The church. Anabaptists formed churches of committed disciples, denying that all citizens should be regarded as church members. They insisted on differentiating believers from unbelievers, so that church membership was voluntary and meaningful. They acknowledged the role of the state in government but resisted state control of their churches. They rejected infant baptism as unbiblical, forcibly imposed on children and a hindrance to developing believers' churches. They challenged clericalism, lack of church discipline and coercion in matters of faith. Although greater formalism gradually developed, early gatherings were sometimes charismatic and unstructured, concentrating on Bible study; some churches encouraged women to participate. A Congregational Order (1527) conveys their serious informality: 'when the brothers and sisters are together, they shall take up something to read together. The one to whom God has given the best understanding shall explain it ... when a brother sees his brother erring, he shall warn him according to the command of Christ, and shall admonish him in a Christian and brotherly way.'

Evangelism. The Reformers did not generally practise evangelism. Where they had state support, they relied on sanctions to coerce attendance (though there are examples of evangelism and church planting by Calvinists in Catholic France where Protestants could not coerce). The Reformers assumed within Protestant territories that church and society were indistinct, so their policy was to pastor people through the parish system, rather than evangelizing them as unbelievers. Anabaptists rejected this interpretation of church and society and refused to use coercion. They embarked on a spontaneous missionary venture to evangelize Europe. They travelled widely, preached in homes and fields, interrupted state church services, baptized converts and planted churches. Such evangelism by untrained men and women, ignoring national and parish boundaries, was regarded as outrageous.

Ethics. Anabaptists were socially deviant, challenging contemporary norms and living in anticipation of the kingdom of God. They questioned the validity of private property. Some groups practised community of goods. Most retained personal ownership, but all taught that their possessions were not their own but were available to those in need. The 1527 Congregational Order urged: 'Of all the brothers and sisters of this congregation, none shall have anything of his own, but rather, as the Christians in the time of the apostles held all in common, and especially stored up a common fund, from which aid can be given to the poor, according as each will have need, and as in the apostles' time permit no brother to be in need.' When they shared communion they confirmed this mutual commitment.

They rejected the use of violence, refusing to defend themselves by force. Conrad Grebel (1498–1526) described his congregation: 'Neither do they use worldly sword or war, since all killing has ceased with them.' They urged love for enemies and respect for human life. Anabaptists accepted that governments would use force but regarded this as inappropriate for Christians. Felix Mantz (c. 1498–1527) concluded: 'no Christian could be a magistrate, nor could he use the sword to punish or kill anyone'. Anabaptists aimed to build an alternative community, changing society from the bottom up. Many refused to swear oaths. Oaths were important in sixteenth-century Europe, encouraging truth-telling in court and loyalty to the state. Anabaptists rejected these oaths, citing Jesus' teaching in Matthew 5 and arguing that they should always be truthful, not just under oath. Nor would they swear loyalty to any secular authority.

Suffering. Anabaptists were not surprised by persecution. They knew they would be seen as revolutionaries, despite their commitment to non-violence; as heretics, despite their commitment to the Bible; and as disturbers of the *status quo*. They regarded suffering for obedience to Christ as unavoidable and biblical: suffering was a mark of the true church, as Jesus had taught in the Sermon on the Mount. That the Reformers persecuted the Anabaptists showed that the former were not building a biblical church.

Anabaptism was drowned in blood in many parts of Europe, but its legacy remains influential as progenitor of the free churches. Though many still accuse Anabaptism of sectarianism, legalism and irresponsibility, careful research has rehabilitated this radical renewal movement, made its writings and stories accessible, and indicated its significance for post-Christendom societies.

STUART MURRAY

FURTHER READING: Hans-Jurgen Goertz, *The Anabaptists* (London, 1996); Leland Harder, *The Sources of Swiss Anabaptism* (Scottdale, PA, 1985); Guy F. Hershberger (ed.), *The Recovery of the Anabaptist Vision* (Scottdale, PA, 1957); Walter Klaassen, *Anabaptism in Outline* (Scottdale, PA, 1981); H. Wayne Pipkin, *Essays in Anabaptist Theology* (Elkhart, IL, 1994); C. Arnold Snyder, *Anabaptist History and Theology* (Kitchener, Ontario, 1995); James Stayer, *The German Peasants' War and Anabaptist Community of Goods* (Montreal, 1991); James M. Stayer, Werner O. Packull and Klaus Deppermann, 'From Monogenesis to Polygenesis: The Historical Discussion of Anabaptist Origins', *Menn Q R* 69 (1995), p. 83; J. Denny Weaver, *Becoming Anabaptist* (Scottdale, PA, 1987); George H. Williams, *The Radical Reformation* (Kirksville, MO, 3rd edn, 1992).

Anselm of Canterbury (1033–1109)

Born in Aosta, North Italy, trained at Bec, Normandy and appointed Archbishop of Canterbury, England, Anselm was anything but provincial. Raised by a Christian mother and a pagan father, converted only later in life, taking a monastic vow and later joining the ranks of the secular clergy, Anselm was not unlike his mentor and, arguably, his greatest teacher, *Augustine. And yet, despite the evidence in Anselm's personal correspondence which suggests that his works enjoyed a certain degree of popularity in the monastic and wider ecclesial circles, it appears that what popularity and renown he had gained died with or shortly after him. Fortunately, this hiatus was evanescent.

The works of Anselm that remain tend to have an occasional quality about them. That is, they were written to address the questions and concerns of his contemporaries. The *De Grammatico*, for example, was intended as a kind of textbook for students on grammar and logic. It continues to be useful, however, since it sheds light on the methods theologians used. Indeed, other works such as *De Veritate, De Libertate Arbitrii, De Conceptu Virginali et de Peccato Originali* and *De Processione Sancti Spiritus*, to name only a few, were also written for the instruction of his students or at the request of his colleagues. But in each case the reader learns not only what ideas and questions engaged the minds of medieval theologians, but also gains a different perspective on issues that have since been subsumed into modern theological discussions.

Among the rest of Anselm's treatises two have enjoyed particular attention: the *Proslogion* and the *Cur Deus Homo*. The former continues to be a source of never-ending intrigue for philosophers and theologians alike as it addresses the question of the existence and nature of God. The latter also enjoys a great deal of attention, though mainly from theologians, since in it Anselm seeks to discover why God became a man. Unfortunately, many of the other preparatory and supplementary works that Anselm wrote are rarely considered in conjunction with these two.

When approaching the *Proslogion* many commentators and critics agree, in spite of other differences, that its greatest fault is the presupposition that God exists. Indeed, how can one seriously presume to provide irrefutable proof for the existence of God if that argument begins by assuming God's existence? It is for this reason that we must first question whether or not Anselm actually intended to prove God's existence in a way concordant with modern

western thought. Certainly, Anselm does say at the beginning of the *Proslogion* that his intention was to discover one single argument to demonstrate that God truly exists; but we should recognize that Anselm also wished to prove that this God does not depend on anyone else for his existence. Instead, Anselm argues, everything depends on him for both existence and well-being; and, as if this were not enough, Anselm further wished to prove the whole gamut of derivative beliefs about the divine nature – all by one single argument. Clearly, the scope of Anselm's lucubrations is broader than is often conceived.

We must remember that Anselm lived in eleventh-century Europe. He lived at a time and within a community that espoused two fundamental convictions. First, the Bible was the revelation of God and was sufficient for defining the boundaries of any and all questions for life and salvation. This is why Anselm insists here and elsewhere that he does not seek to understand in order to believe, but that he believes in order to understand, and that unless he believes he cannot understand. Second, and particularly pertinent to the *Proslogion*, the nature and being of God were not separable qualities. In other words, proving that God existed meant that one could simultaneously establish the nature of God (what God is like). Consequently, Anselm feels entirely justified in devoting the first chapter to petitioning God to reveal himself so that his existence can be demonstrated. Furthermore, Anselm has no compunction in deriving his definition of God from revelation. The medieval mind could not conceive of trying to prove God's existence apart from the revelation of God because his transcendence requires it. In truth, this is the point of greatest contention in the *Proslogion*, because in order to admit the need for divine revelation one must first admit the need to submit to that divinity.

It was not until later in his life, and while in exile, that Anselm completed the *Cur Deus Homo*. This work is divided into two sections. The first deals with humanity's need and the second addresses God's provision. It is interesting that Anselm states at the outset that he will accomplish this as if he knew nothing of Jesus Christ (*remoto Christo*). This strikes the reader as an odd claim to say the least, but by the end of the work it is clear that what Anselm has done is to mobilize the other doctrines of the faith in such a way as to show that only his doctrine of the atonement answers the questions they raise. Hamartiology, anthropology, soteriology and eschatology, to name just a few, are shown to cohere in the central doctrines of Christology, and, in particular, the doctrine of the atonement.

Essentially, Anselm argues that the effect of Adamic sin, which is endemic to all humans, has not only distorted the hearts and minds of all people, but has also offended God. Sin has offended God because, as Anselm defines it, it is not giving to God what is due to him. Initially, one might think that reconciliation might be restored through recompense of some kind, but Anselm explains that the extent of an offence is proportionate to the stature of the one offended. In this case the extent is infinite because God is infinite. Thus the debt is greater than the sum of all that is human. Obviously, this poses a problem for humanity. Where can a race of inherently sinful and finite creatures find a means of reconciliation that is sufficient to cover this offence? Anselm also informs his interlocutor that the individual chosen for this task must be God for two reasons. First, whoever frees humanity from this predicament commands their obedience. Second, in order for an individual to offer an acceptable satisfaction he must be 'all that is not God'. The answer to this difficulty, according to Anselm, is found in the God-Man Jesus Christ. For in Jesus humanity is represented, infinite satisfaction is rendered; obedience is still owed to God alone.

Although space does not permit an investigation into all of Anselm's writings, a word must be said about his *Prayers and Meditations*. In this collection of works Anselm covers a wide range of topics, but most remarkable is that the works exquisitely exemplify the unity between theology and piety, life and faith. Theology provides knowledge about God, and that knowledge ought to move us to worship. Humanity, according to Anselm, was created to enjoy immortality, but not for its own sake. The possibility of immortality through the redemption offered by Jesus Christ was designed as an opportunity to share in the glory and worship of God. This is the end to which Anselm wrote his *Prayers and Meditations* and the reason he struggled so hard to elucidate the doctrines of the faith for his students.

DAVID S. HOGG

FURTHER READING: The critical edition of Anselm's works is edited by F.S. Schmitt, *Sancti Anselmi Opera Omnia* (6 vols.; Edinburgh, 1938–68). A translation of these works is found in Jasper Hopkins and Herbert Richardson, *Anselm of Canterbury* (4 vols.; Toronto, 1975–76). For a general overview of Anselm's life, R.W. Southern's *Saint Anselm: A Portrait in a Landscape* (Cambridge, 1990) is informative. G.R. Evans' *Anselm and a New Generation* (Oxford, 1908) is also helpful. Eadmer's *The Life of St Anselm* (ed. and trans. R.W. Southern; London, 1962) should not be neglected as a source of contemporary insight. On Anselm's theological method and its application to the *Proslogion* Karl Barth's *Fides Quaerens Intellectum* (Pittsburgh, 1985) is perceptive. The standard work on the *Cur Deus Homo* is still John McIntyre's *St Anselm and His Critics: A Re-Interpretation of the Cur Deus Homo* (Edinburgh, 1954).

Apollinaris (c. 310 – c. 390)

Although Apollinaris was eventually condemned by Nicene leaders because of his Christology, both he and his father were supporters of *Athanasius, who had visited their home, early on in the *Arian controversies. Apollinaris was probably bishop of Laodicea by 360 and had a hand in consecrating his student Vitalis as yet another sitting Nicene bishop of Antioch. When Apollinaris and his father were faced with the emperor Julian's shrewd insistence that only those who believed in the Greek myths could teach Hellenic literature, they began to rework at least parts of the Old Testament into poetry and parts of the Gospels into dialogues. In that way Christian worshippers, whether children or adults, could claim the Hellenic heritage which Apollinaris and his father thought was rightfully theirs. Apollinaris wrote rather extensive attacks on both Julian and the Neoplatonist philosopher Porphyry which have not survived. These attacks would also have contributed to his being so well regarded by fellow Christians early in his career.

Apollinaris evidently wrote extensive comments on the Bible. Fragments of works on the first eight books of the Old Testament, Psalms, Matthew, John and Romans have been found in *cataenae* (anthologies of comments on biblical books). As a biblical exegete he works well within philological categories, but also as a theologian he insists that the intent or content of a text is the more important aspect. Sadly, almost all of the scriptural exegetical foundations for his Christological teaching have perished.

Although Basil of Caesarea was hesitant to say so, Apollinaris apparently had a profound influence on his thought. As a trusted ally of Athanasius, Apollinaris evidently led Basil toward the acceptance of three *hypostaseis*, 'persons', and one *ousia*, 'nature', within the Trinity. The correspondence between Basil and Apollinaris, which is probably genuine, indicates that he saw Apollinaris as a friend during the debates with the Eunomians. Apollinaris evidently insisted that the Father and the Son were of the same nature. He did not see the Son as a created figure of a secondary yet divine status as *Eunomius did. Gregory Nazianzen, however, warned in 382 that Apollinaris's doctrine of the Holy Spirit was insufficient. It is unlikely, then, that Apollinaris was the author of fully developed *Cappadocian Trinitarian thought. Yet Apollinaris's poetic works, evidently of some import among his followers, spurred Nazianzen toward writing his own poetry during retirement.

Apollinaris's solution to the Christological conundrums of his day was both creative and forceful, but it is difficult to reconstruct fully because of the fragmentary character of his suppressed writings. At the least he avoided the sense of Jesus Christ as only an inspired man comparable to the prophets. He has been read as offering a solution to *Plato and *Aristotle's problem of how humans could obtain saving knowledge of God. He conceived of the incarnation as the mind of God (the divine Son of God) becoming enfleshed. Human intellect and will were original gifts of God lost in Adam's sin; thus they could not be taken up when the mind of God became incarnate because they were not there to be assumed. If that reading is correct, the unsatisfactory character of Apollinaris's Christology is that it operates almost exclusively on the level of knowledge – although on that level it is quite strong.

Classically, Apollinaris has been seen as following the lead of Athanasius in rejecting Diodore of Tarsus's conception of two sons, one divine and one human. Apollinaris, however, intensified the sense of one subject, the mind of God incarnate, by not hesitating about what to do with the human soul of Jesus as a subject (as Athanasius did). Apollinaris slashed through the difficulties by insisting that the incarnate Son of God did not assume a human soul – whether that soul included a human intellect in a threefold anthropology or was by itself in a twofold anthropology. His construction has the merit of making certain that true divinity is involved in incarnation and that there is no possibility of intellectual, wilful rebellion in the person of Christ.

Diodore of Tarsus seemed to have understood Apollinaris's weaknesses well before others did. Diodore's teaching about the full humanity of Jesus Christ made him especially sensitive to the lack of full human presence in Apollinaris's Christology. Basil mumbled a bit, but serious refutation might have made him admit that Apollinaris was one of his teachers. Gregory of Nyssa wrote two tracts directly against Apollinaris. Although he also felt it necessary to renounce talk of two sons, for him Apollinaris's solution was unbalanced in that its sense of human nature was askew. Gregory Nazianzen attacked Apollinarianism in three theological letters (101, 102, 202). He asserted that two full natures could be united in one person and insisted that in the incarnation human intellect and will must be present. In the first point Nazianzen offered a model of union in which a greater and a lesser could interpenetrate each other. In the second he resurrected *Origen's principle, now known from the *Dialogue with Heracleides*: the unassumed is unhealed, what is taken up is saved. Human soul, including mind and will, must be assumed in the Son, not only because they are the best of humankind, but also because they are as much sources of evil as is the flesh. Although some synods moved against Apollinaris before Athanasius's death, the Alexandrian bishop may never have grasped clearly what the issues were and thus may not have rejected Apollinaris's Christology effectively.

Most of Apollinaris's work was suppressed, but Apollinarian forgeries (sometimes in Athanasius's name) circulated well beyond his death. *Cyril of Alexandria thought the Apollinarian phrase 'incarnate in one nature' was Athanasian. It slowed Cyril's recognition of what was at stake with *Nestorius and was not emphasized in his reconciliation with John of Antioch.

FREDERICK W. NORRIS

FURTHER READING: Henri de Riedmatten, 'La Correspondance entre Basile de Césarée et Apollinaire de Laodicée', *J Th St* NS 7 (1956), pp. 199–210; NS 8 (1957), pp. 53–70; Reinhard Hübner, 'Soteriologie, Trinität, Christologie: Von Markel von Ankyra zu Apollinaris von Laodicea', in *Gespräch mit dem dreieinen Gott: Elemente einer trinitarischen Theologie*, (Festschrift Wilhelm Breuning; eds. Michael Bohnke and Hanspeter Heinz; Düsseldorf, 1985), pp. 175–96; 'Gotteserkenntnis durch die Inkarnation Gottes', *Kleronomia (Thessalonika)* 4 (1972), pp. 131–61; Hans Lietzmann (ed.), *Apollinarius von Laodicea und seine Schule: Texte und Untersuchungen* (Tübingen, 1904); Ekkehard Mühlenberg, *Apollinaris von Laodicea*, Forschungen zur Kirchen und Dogmengeschichte 23 (Göttingen, 1969); Richard Norris, *Manhood and Christ: A Study in the Christology of Theodore of Mopsuestia* (Oxford, 1963), pp. 81–122; G.L. Prestige, *St. Basil the Great and Apollinaris of Laodicea* (ed. Henry Chadwick; London, 1956).

Apologists

The term 'apologists' is used of some early Christian writers who produced 'apologies', that is, books in defence of their faith. 'Apologetic(s)' has gone on throughout church history. Important apologies were written by *Clement of Alexandria, *Tertullian, *Origen, *Eusebius and *Athanasius. Those usually considered include the earliest, Quadratus, known only from a fragment, and Aristides, writing about 140, whose work is reconstructed from later writings. Aristides addresses his work to the emperor, as do *Justin Martyr in the 150s, and Melito, *Athenagoras and Tatian between 170 and 180. Justin also composed *The Dialogue with Trypho the Jew* to argue against Judaism. The books of *Theophilus of Antioch *To Autolycus* are also from about 180, and the anonymous *To Diognetus* is of uncertain date. The last of the early Greek apologists, Hermias, wrote in the early third century, as did the Latin Minucius Felix.

The apologists defended Christianity first by refuting charges against it. The persecutions under Marcus Aurelius provoked the writings of 170–80, which deal with the impieties alleged by the populace and government against Christians. These charges are chiefly atheism, cannibalism and incest. Atheism is godlessness, and Christians were known to reject the gods on whose favour the welfare of the state and its peoples rested (called the 'peace of the gods' by the Romans). It was true enough: the first duty of a Christian was to renounce and abstain from the gods of the cities and nations and from all the sport, theatre, government and military ceremonial that went with them. The other charges arise from the private nature of the church, which excluded the unbaptized from all their ritual meals and kept Christians from intermarriage with unbelievers: ideas of babyeating, blood-drinking and immoral orgies freely circulated. The apologists, therefore, tried to prove that they believed in God, and that they did so more perfectly than their critics. They also give long accounts of Christian behaviour, its high principles of faithfulness, sexual purity and honesty. Theophilus wrote a long account based on the Ten Commandments, and the writer *To Diognetus* pictures Christians as 'the soul of the world'. Athenagoras and others denounce cannibalism and incest as features of pagan myths which Christians do not believe or read. Justin, in his *First Apology*, has some frank and detailed descriptions of baptismal and Eucharistic rites which are very valuable to modern scholars; these were aimed to dispel rumours of dark deeds.

Secondly, the apologists aimed to present Christian thought in a favourable light, and to argue its truth while at the same time demonstrating how absurd and contradictory the alternatives are, whether the sacrificial religions of pagans and Jews (notably *To Diognetus*), or the theological ideas of poets and philosophers (Tatian and Hermias). They also argue from a legal standpoint against the injustice of persecution: Justin illustrates the absurdity of execution merely for bearing the name of Christian, rather than investigating their conduct, and Athenagoras, Melito and Minucius Felix appeal to imperial justice.

To demonstrate the truth of the gospel, the apologists invoked ideas already familiar to their critics. They claimed that Greek culture, no less than Hebrew, prepared the way for Christ. Theophilus writes at length to reconcile the chronology of Homer with that of Scripture. Athenagoras labours to prove the Greek poets are at heart monotheists. Many of the apologists' arguments against pagan religion are lifted from Greek philosophers, following Socrates and *Plato. Justin particularly praises the Athenian philosopher Socrates, the hero of Plato in the late fifth century BC. Socrates questioned the conventional poetic stories about the gods and was executed for it – a kind of pre-Christian martyr. Plato himself advocated a transcendent sort of theism, and *Aristotle and Zeno the Stoic refined and developed his philosophy in a theological direction. For Justin, God is invisible, unchangeable, indescribable and unnameable, in conventional Platonic fashion. But for Justin God has made himself known in creation and revelation: he has spoken his Word, his *logos*. In Greek that means not just spoken sound but articulate thought, which can either be inside us or uttered aloud – immanent or expressed. Building on contemporary Platonic ideas, Justin makes the *logos* mediate between the ineffable, unchanging God and the changing, mobile, perishable world. The Word remained inside God, till he uttered it and said, 'Let there be light.' After that, creation began, and God could hold converse with his Word as with another being. All that happens in the universe is done by the Word, but especially the revelation of God in the Old Testament: the Word appeared to Moses in the bush. The philosophers of the past, like the prophets, have genuine but incomplete revelations of this Word, who becomes fully embodied in Jesus Christ.

The apologists generally are occupied with fundamental theology. Theophilus expounds at length the six days of creation from Genesis, and he explains Christian behaviour in terms of the Ten Commandments and the Sermon on the Mount. He uses the word 'Trinity', *trias*, and argues that God's immanent *logos* was uttered or expressed in creation. But nowhere does he refer to Jesus Christ. The same is true of Athenagoras. This absence is partly due to the apologetic purpose – to demonstrate the rational basis before revealing the mysteries; it reflects also the order of baptismal preparation. Justin does not share these restraints, but openly discusses Christ both in his *Apologies* and in his arguments with Trypho, which are much concerned with the fulfilment of prophecy in the life, death and resurrection of Jesus. The apologists generally say little about the Holy Spirit, though the third Person of the Trinity plainly figured in the baptismal confession from which they worked. The Spirit also belonged chiefly to the inner secrets of the church, not to its argument with its unbelieving neighbours.

STUART G. HALL

FURTHER READING: *Critical texts: Clavis patrum graecorum I* (ed. Mauritius Geerard; Turnhout, 1983); Henry Chadwick, *Early Christianity and the Classical Tradition* (Oxford, 1966); *Early Christian Fathers* (ed. C.C. Richardson; London, 1953 [includes *To Diognetus*, Justin's *First Apology*, Athenagoras]); *Encyclopedia of the Early Church* (ed. Angelo di Berardino; trans. Adrian Walford; Cambridge, 1992); R.M. Grant, *Greek Apologists of the Second Century* (London, 1988); Stuart G. Hall, *Doctrine and Practice in the Early Church* (London, 1991); James Stevenson, *A New Eusebius: Documents Illustrating the History of the Church to* AD 337 (rev. W.H.C. Frend; London, 1987).

Apostles' Creed

The Apostles' Creed is a western baptismal creed, first attested in its present form in the early eighth century in southern Gaul and now used widely in western churches.

A creed is a concise statement of Christian faith and belief. The word 'creed' derives from the Latin word *credo*, 'I believe', which is the first word of many Latin creeds. In Greek, a creed was called a *symbolon* (borrowed by Latin as *symbolum*). Most true creeds have three articles: God, the Father; Jesus Christ, the Lord; and the Holy Spirit (with other doctrines often added to the third article). Creeds originated in the administration of baptism. Eastern creeds have two parts in the second article: one on the Son's pre-incarnate existence, the other on the history of the incarnate Christ from his conception to his second coming and eternal reign. Western creeds consistently lack the first part on the Son's pre-incarnate existence. The oldest form of creeds was probably interrogatory: the one administering baptism asked for a triple confession of faith (see below). Later, especially in the west, the custom of 'handing over' the creed to catechumens and having them 'hand it back' (that is, memorize and recite it), called *traditio* and *redditio*, fostered the development of declaratory creeds. The Apostles' Creed is one of the many variant forms of the Roman baptismal creed, often called the Old Roman Creed (which was probably first formulated in Greek). The name 'Apostles' Creed' derives from the legend, reported by Rufinus of Aquileia, that the twelve apostles composed the creed before they set out on their missions of evangelization. (Later forms of the legend have each apostle contributing one article.) The Apostles' Creed reads:

I believe in God, the Father almighty, creator of heaven and earth;
And in Jesus Christ, His only Son, our Lord, who was conceived by the Holy Spirit, born of

the Virgin Mary, suffered under Pontius Pilate, was crucified, died, and was buried; he descended into hell; on the third day he rose again from the dead, ascended into heaven, sits at the right hand of God the Father almighty; thence he will come to judge the living and the dead;

I believe in the Holy Spirit, the holy catholic Church, the communion of saints, the forgiveness of sins, the resurrection of the flesh, and eternal life. Amen.

The oldest witness to a western, Roman creed is *Hippolytus's *Apostolic Tradition* 21 (c. 220), which has a three-part interrogatory creed to be used at baptism. It reads:

Do you believe in God the Father almighty?

Do you believe in Jesus Christ, the Son of God, who was born by the Holy Spirit of the Virgin Mary, was crucified under Pontius Pilate, died, was raised up alive on the third day from among the dead, went up to heaven, and is seated at the Father's right hand?

Do you believe in the Holy Spirit in the holy Church?

By the early fourth century, the declaratory Old Roman Creed had emerged, attested in Greek in a letter addressed by Marcellus of Ancyra to Pope Julius c. 340, and attested more exactly in Latin by Rufinus of Aquileia, c. 404. As reconstructed from Rufinus's commentary, it reads:

I believe in God the Father almighty;

and in Jesus Christ, His only Son, our Lord, who was born from the Holy Spirit and the Virgin Mary; who was crucified under Pontius Pilate and buried; on the third day he rose again from the dead, ascended into heaven, sits at the right hand of the Father, whence he will come to judge the living and the dead;

and in the Holy Spirit, the holy Church, the forgiveness of sins, the resurrection of the flesh.

Many western churches used variants of the Old Roman Creed. *Augustine of Hippo, for example, quotes three creeds in his writings: the creeds of Milan and Carthage, and a variant of the Roman creed.

The Apostles' Creed differs from the Old Roman Creed mostly by its length: phrases are added to the former, but virtually none are removed. The two most noteworthy additions are 'he descended into hell' and 'the communion of saints'.

The eighth-century text reads *descendit ad inferna*, 'he descended into hell'; more recent usage prefers *descendit ad inferos*, 'he descended to those below', as being less problematic. Rufinus already knew a creed with a similar clause. The phrase may be eastern in origin. In ancient interpretations, the phrase was taken to mean that, between his death and his resurrection, Christ either preached the saving gospel to the righteous dead of the Old Testament or that he liberated those imprisoned in the underworld.

The most-discussed phrase in the Apostles' Creed is 'the communion of saints' (*sanctorum communio*). The words are first attested in the creed that Nicetas of Remesiana commented on (in the late fourth century). The phrase may simply paraphrase 'the holy catholic Church', if *sanctorum* is masculine in gender. But if *sanctorum* is neuter, it could mean 'sharing in the Eucharistic elements' and thus be a rare reference to the Eucharist in creeds. While this latter interpretation may be attractive, the former is more probable.

JOSEPH T. LIENHARD, SJ

FURTHER READING: *Texts:* August Hahn and G. Ludwig Hahn, *Bibliothek der Symbole und Glaubensregeln der Alten Kirche* (Breslau, 1897); J.N.D. Kelly, *Early Christian Creeds* (Harlow, 3rd edn, 1972). *Early commentaries:* Nicetas of Remesiana, *Explanation of the Creed* (trans. G.G. Walsh; FC 7; Washington, DC, 1949); Ambrose, *The Explanatio Symboli ad initiandos* (trans. R.H. Connolly; TS 10; Cambridge, 1952); Rufinus, *Commentary on the Apostles' Creed* (trans. J.N.D. Kelly; ACW 20; Westminster, MD, 1955); Augustine, *On the Creed to Catechumens* (trans. M. Liguori) and *On Faith and the Creed* (trans. Robert P. Russell; in FC 27; Washington, DC, 1955). *Studies:* C.H. Turner, *The History of the Use of Creeds and Anathemas* (London, 2nd edn, 1910); F.J. Badcock, *The History of the Creeds* (London, 2nd edn, 1938); G. Hedley, *The Symbol of the Faith: A Study of the Apostles' Creed* (New York, 1948).

Apostolic Fathers

The term 'Apostolic Fathers' designates those Christian authors who wrote between the end of New Testament times and c. 150. The term originated with J.B. Cotelier, who in 1672 designated five writers as '*Patres aevi apostolici*', or 'Fathers of the apostolic age'. In modern usage, the term designates seven or eight documents or groups of documents: *1 Clement*, a letter, and *2 Clement*, a homily; seven letters by Ignatius of Antioch; a letter by Polycarp of Smyrna, and a letter called the *Martyrdom of Polycarp*; an apocalypse, the *Shepherd*, by Hermas; the *Didache*, a church order; the *Epistle to Diognetus*, an apology; and sometimes the fragments of Papias's work on the Lord's sayings, and a fragment of the apology of Quadratus. J.A. Fischer, in his edition of the Apostolic Fathers published in 1956, tried to narrow the term to designate only authors who claimed to be disciples of apostles (*1 Clement*, the letters of Ignatius and Polycarp, and the fragment of Quadratus), but his thesis has not been accepted. Among the literary genres employed by the Apostolic Fathers, the letter or epistle predominates. This form continues the letter-writing common in New Testament times and illustrates the eagerness of early Christian communities to communicate with one another.

The occasion of *1 Clement*, a letter addressed by the church at Rome to the church at Corinth c. 96, was unrest in Corinth. Some younger members of the community had removed the presbyters, or elders, from office and replaced them with younger leaders. The church at Rome wrote collectively to Corinth and urged the Christians there to restore the elders to office. About a quarter of *1 Clement* comprises quotations from the Old Testament, which the author uses as a source book for models of virtue and order. *1 Clement* presupposes a church governed by 'bishops and deacons' (or 'overseers and servers'), who can also be called 'presbyters' or 'elders' (42, 4–5; 44, 5). They receive their office in orderly succession, beginning from the apostles. *1 Clement* also attests to the martyrdom of Peter and Paul in Rome. Authorship of *1 Clement* was traditionally attributed to a bishop of Rome by that name (see Dionysius of Corinth in Eusebius, *CH*, 4.23.11). *Irenaeus lists Clement as Peter's third successor as bishop of Rome (*Heresies* 3.3.3).

2 Clement is a homily delivered c. 150, probably in Corinth. The work is an exhortation to repentance. Eusebius (*CH* 3.38.4) wrote of a second letter by Clement; but *2 Clement* could not be that letter.

Ignatius of Antioch wrote seven letters. As bishop of Antioch, he was arrested there and condemned to death c. 110. Ten soldiers transported him across Asia Minor, to be thrown to the beasts in the arena at Rome. In western Asia Minor delegates from churches visited him, and he composed letters to several churches. From Smyrna he wrote to Ephesus, Magnesia and Tralles, as well as to the church at Rome, asking the Roman Christians not to prevent his martyrdom. From Troas he wrote to the churches at Philadelphia and Smyrna, as well as to Polycarp, the young bishop of Smyrna. In the fourth century, Ignatius's letters were expanded, and further letters added to the corpus; the original seven letters were restored only in the seventeenth century. Ignatius's letters are among the most personal, and most beloved, of the writings of the Apostolic Fathers.

One letter survives from Polycarp of Smyrna, who recalled hearing the teaching of the apostle John. Later Irenaeus recalled hearing Polycarp – a kind of apostolic succession. Irenaeus also recalls that Polycarp met *Marcion and called him the 'firstborn of Satan' (*Heresies* 3.3.4). We also know that Polycarp dealt with Anicetus of Rome on the date of Easter, c. 155. In his letter to the church at Philippi, Polycarp addressed himself to 'bishops and deacons and others at Philippi' and used *1 Clement* as one of his sources. P.N. Harrison (*Polycarp's Two Epistles to the Philippians* [1936]) suggested that the present letter was originally two. According to his interpretation chapter 13 is a note, written c. 110, that accompanied the copies of Ignatius's letters for which the Philippians had asked Polycarp; chapters 1–12 were written c. 135, when the community at Philippi was unsettled by Marcion's teaching; chapter 14 would fit either letter.

The *Martyrdom of Polycarp* is a letter from the church at Smyrna to the church at Philomelium in Phrygia. It was written by Marcion (not the heretic), to give an account of Polycarp's arrest, trial and death by burning at the stake when Polycarp was eighty-six years of age, probably on 22 February 156. This work is the oldest extant account of a Christian martyrdom, noteworthy for its simplicity and its portrayal of Polycarp's fidelity and courage.

The *Epistle of Barnabas* is perhaps the strangest writing among the collection of the Apostolic Fathers. The apostle Barnabas was probably not the author of the *Epistle*; despite many guesses, the author remains unknown. The work was written, probably in Alexandria, between 130 and 140, although some recent writers suggest a date c. 70. The author considers himself a teacher and holds that the Old Testament must be interpreted spiritually, and only spiritually. The Jews, he writes, were misled at Sinai by an evil angel into taking their Scriptures literally.

The *Epistle* thus represents the position diametrically opposite to Marcion's: Marcion took the Old Testament literally and threw it out of the church; Barnabas took the Old Testament spiritually and took it away from the synagogue. The last four chapters (18–21) of the *Epistle* describe the 'Two Ways', as the *Didache* does, calling them the ways of light and darkness.

The *Shepherd* of Hermas is the longest single work among the Apostolic Fathers. The author, Hermas, is a simple man, perhaps the brother of Pius (142–155), the bishop of Rome. The date of composition is c. 140–150. The work was usually divided into five visions, twelve mandates and ten similitudes, although recent editions adopt a simpler scheme of numbered paragraphs. Despite its apocalyptic elements, the main concern of the *Shepherd* is repentance. Several ancient authors (Irenaeus, *Tertullian, *Clement of Alexandria, and *Origen) considered the *Shepherd* part of the canonical New Testament.

The *Didache* is the oldest extant church order, written c. 150, perhaps in Syria; the text was only recovered in 1873. Chapters 1–6 comprise a moral instruction called the Two Ways, which probably has Jewish roots. The rest of the work describes Christian rites and prayers: a full account of the administration of baptism; prayers connected with the celebration of the Eucharist (citing Mal. 1:11 and calling the Eucharist a sacrifice); rules for receiving wandering apostles and prophets, among whom many charlatans were found; and finally an exhortation to communities to elect bishops and deacons, stable local officials. The *Didache* demonstrates the transition from charismatic to hierarchical leadership in the church.

The *Epistle to Diognetus*, which was never mentioned in antiquity, was discovered only in the modern era. This anonymous epistle, written in elegant Greek and addressed to an otherwise unknown pagan named Diognetus, was written in the latter part of the second century. The work is an explanation of, and apology for, Christianity. The end of the work is part of another writing, perhaps a homily.

Papias of Hierapolis wrote, c. 130, a work in five books entitled *Explanations of the Lord's Sayings*. It is a collection of accounts of the Lord's words and deeds gathered from the oral tradition. Only a few pages of fragments survive, including accounts of the origin of the Gospels according to Matthew and Mark, some account

of John, and a passage on Judas's death. Because of his chiliastic beliefs, Papias was later the object of disdain.

Quadratus, a disciple of the apostles, addressed an apology to the emperor Hadrian c. 120–130. Eusebius (*CH*, 4.3.1–2) quotes one paragraph from it.

The Apostolic Fathers do not represent high theological accomplishment (as Paul and John did), nor are they concerned with explaining the Christian faith to unbelievers (as the apologists would be). They provide glimpses into the turmoil and struggles of the first half of the second century as Christianity was establishing and organizing itself. Their works are plain writings that deal with matters within churches. Among their major concerns are ministry and church order; opposition to *Gnostics, Marcion and Judaizers; second penance; and understanding the Old Testament.

The Apostolic Fathers also attest to the state of Christian doctrine or teaching in their time. They had no New Testament canon. Their authorities for the truth are traditions about the Lord, the teachings of the apostles, the Old Testament (interpreted Christologically) and their own bishops and teachers.

The Apostolic Fathers are wholly convinced monotheists, but they also accept the divinity of Christ and show early forms of a Trinitarian confession. *1 Clement* assumes Christ's preincarnate existence (16.2). *2 Clement* urges its readers 'to think of Jesus Christ as of God'. Ignatius's letters contain a classic formulation of Christological doctrine: 'There is one physician, who is both fleshly and spiritual, begotten and unbegotten, God in man, true life in death, both from Mary and from God, first passible and then impassible, Jesus Christ our Lord' (*Eph.* 7.2). In its structure, this sentence anticipates the definition of Chalcedon. Barnabas writes that the Son of God came in the flesh (5.11; 12.10). For Hermas, Christ is flesh indwelt by the Holy Spirit (59.5).

1 Clement co-ordinates the names God, the Lord Jesus Christ and the Holy Spirit (58.2). Ignatius, too, uses triadic formulas (e.g., *Magn.* 13.1) and describes the intriguing image of God the Father building the faithful (who are compared to stones) into a temple, using Christ's cross as a crane and the Holy Spirit as the rope (*Eph.* 9.1). Hermas combines binitarianism and adoptionism, so that God the Father and the Holy Spirit exist before

Christ, and the Holy Spirit is incarnated as the Son of God (59.5).

The Apostolic Fathers reveal a sense of the church as universal. Hermas sees the church as an old woman, who has existed from the beginning (8.1). The *Epistle to Diognetus* calls the Christians a 'new race', distinguished from pagans and Jews. For Ignatius, the church is centred in the one bishop (*Eph.* 4.1, and often). He presupposes governance of a church by a monarchical bishop, a college of presbyters and deacons to serve the bishop. He is also the first Christian writer to use the phrase 'catholic church' (*Smyrn.* 8.2). The church at Rome, he writes, is distinguished by the role that Peter and Paul played there (*Rom.* 4.3).

A key passage in the *Shepherd* treats second penance, or the forgiveness of serious, public sin after baptism (31.1–7). The practice described by Hermas became the standard of the church for six or seven centuries. Only one reconciliation was possible, and that after an extended period of penance.

The *Didache* contains an extensive description of the rite of baptism (7). Ignatius places great emphasis on the real presence of Christ in the Eucharist and on the Eucharist as the sign of unity; he calls it the 'flesh of our Saviour' (*Smyrn.* 7.1), the 'medicine of immortality', and the 'antidote for death' (*Eph.* 20.2).

JOSEPH T. LIENHARD, SJ

FURTHER READING: *Editions and translations: The Apostolic Fathers with an English Translation* (ed. Kirsopp Lake; 2 vols.; London, 1912, 1913); *Die Apostolischen Väter* (ed. Joseph A. Fischer; Munich, 1956); *Early Christian Fathers* (trans. Cyril C. Richardson; London, 1964); *Early Christian Writings: The Apostolic Fathers* (trans. Maxwell Staniforth; Harmondsworth, 1968); *Die Apostolischen Väter* (ed. A. Lindemann and H. Paulsen; Tübingen, 1992). *Studies:* R.M. Grant (ed.), *The Apostolic Fathers: A New Translation and Commentary* (New York, 1964); L.W. Barnard, *Studies in the Apostolic Fathers and Their Background* (Oxford, 1966); William R. Schoedel, *A Commentary on the Letters of Ignatius of Antioch* (Philadelphia, 1985); Simon Tugwell, *The Apostolic Fathers* (London, 1990); Clayton N. Jefford, et al., *Reading the Apostolic Fathers: An Introduction* (Peabody, MA, 1996).

Aquinas, Thomas (1224/5–74)

St Thomas Aquinas, by common consent the greatest of the medieval theologians, was born near Naples in 1224/5, the youngest son of minor Italian nobility. He spent his childhood as a *Benedictine oblate at Cassino, but in 1239 he went to the University of Naples to study the arts. There he met, first, the *Aristotelian learning about nature, newly entering Europe through Islam, and, second, the Dominican order of preaching friars to which he attached himself in 1242/3 and which sent him to study philosophy and theology in Cologne under the Aristotelian scholar, Albert the Great. In 1251 Aquinas started his own teaching career as a bachelor at Paris, commenting Scripture and *Peter Lombard's *Book of Sentences*. In 1256 he incepted as master of theology, teaching in the Dominican *schola* and later in the theology faculty of the university. In 1259/60 he was recalled to Italy where he taught for the next eight years. From 1269 he spent a further turbulent three years as a master in Paris, embroiled in controversy with both *Franciscan theologians who thought him too Aristotelian, and so-called Latin Averroists in the arts faculty who thought him not Aristotelian enough. In 1272/3 he was transferred back to Naples where, on 6 December 1273, he was suddenly rendered unable to work further, and he died on 7 March 1274.

A large part of the nearly nine million words he wrote during his lifetime are the edited by-product of this uninterrupted life of lecturing and public disputation. His works include the *Scriptum super libros Sententiarum* (1252–56); his commentaries on Isaiah, Jeremiah and Lamentations, and on Paul (date doubtful), Matthew (1256–69), Job (1261–64), John (1269–72) and the Psalms (1272–73, unfinished); and the academic disputations *De Veritate* (1256–59), *De Potentia Dei* (1265–66), *De Malo* (1266–67), *De Spiritualibus Creaturis* (1267–68), *De Anima* (1269), *De Virtutibus* (1269–72), *De Unione Verbi Incarnati* (1272), and the *Quodlibets* (1256–59 and 1269–72). A further large part of his writing is work undertaken on commission (e.g., the *Catena Aurea* [1263–7], a gloss from Greek and Latin Fathers on the four Gospels, papally commissioned) or provoked by public controversies. But it was his own decision to comment Aristotelian texts as they appeared in new Latin translations (e.g., the *Physics*, *De Anima*, *De Sensu* and *De Memoria* [1269–70], the *De Interpretatione* and the *Ethics* [1270–71], the *Posterior Analytics*, *Metaphysics*, and *Politics* [1271–72], and the *De Caelo et Mundo*, the *Meteora* and the *De Generatione et Corruptione* [1272–3]); and to present his whole theology twice over in two masterly compendia: the *Summa contra Gentiles* (1259–64; 350,000 words) and the unfinished *Summa Theologiae* (1266–73; 1,500,000 words).

After his death his work was at first hotly disputed, and the bishop of Paris's condemnation of 219 Aristotelian and Averroist propositions in 1277 includes condemnation of certain of Aquinas's positions (though he is not mentioned by name). But gradually Aquinas's work became accepted as *the* orthodox articulation of theology – first in his own Dominican order, and later in the Roman Catholic Church at large. A great literature of *Thomist commentary grew up, from which the original Aquinas has only begun to be disentangled during the last one hundred years. Today, partly because of his own method of approach (discussed below) and partly because it is freer of official church oversight, his philosophy is studied more often than his theology, but this is slowly being redressed.

At the time Aquinas wrote, theology had only just begun to differentiate itself from scriptural exegesis, abstracting *quaestiones* (with the immediate text that provoked them) from their scriptural context and grouping them in *summae* in a systematic pattern of like questions. Aquinas boldly identified this process as the elaboration of a *science* in the strict Aristotelian sense, sharing in – by borrowing premises from – God's vision of himself by way of revelation and faith, in the way geometrical optics shares in and borrows premises from geometry. Aristotle's works on physical and natural science did not, like modern science, dig into the 'insides' of things (the inner works that explain in mathematical ways how the outsides work). Rather, they studied those 'outsides': the world as it immediately presents itself to us, and the sense things make at that level, by whatever mechanisms they have achieved their present stability. Aristotle does not know the mechanisms of 'natural selection', but he does know that things exist by environmental favour. He thought of such favour as fixed in its 'intentions', so that nature comprised harmoniously co-operating agencies fixed in species. Aquinas understood Aristotle's ventures 'beyond natural philosophy' (*meta-physics*) as a philosophical theology extrapolating the notion of environmental favour beyond the abstract immaterial-

ity of physics (its generalizations about material existents) to that really immaterial existent who gave nature ultimate favour. This extrapolation (at work in Aquinas's famous five ways of proving that there is god) founds a human philosophical learning in which the god appears as *auctor naturae*, the author nature reveals to us. But the divine teaching of Christian scriptural theology introduces us to God as he sees himself and as he reveals himself to us through faith. Theology is not a study *of* revelation, but a study of everything, starting with God, *in the light of* revelation. Indeed more is true: theology is the sacred teaching itself still active, not now in the mode of revelation planting the seeds of faith, but in the mode of explicating and developing those seeds in the soil of human reason, *fides quaerens intellectum*.

The relation of philosophical and scriptural theology then is not a relation of two subject matters, but of two lights in which any subject matter can be seen. Each light calls for the other, though in different ways. The light of revelation calls for the light of reason as *praeambulum fidei*, presupposed by faith, a handmaiden called on to fulfil its autonomous role. The light of reason calls for the light of revelation by a *desiderium naturale*, a natural craving to see what that is that favours nature into existence. This mutual call of light to light explains the structure of Aquinas's theology as he presents it in his two great *Summae*. In the *Summa contra Gentiles* (against non-believers) he explicitly contrasts the philosophical and scriptural approaches to God, correcting 'errors' of the former by philosophical argument when possible (in the first three books: God known through nature, the nature of human being and the providence of God for human being), but otherwise by exegesis of Scripture (in the final book: the Trinity, the incarnation and eschatology). The *Summa Theologiae* maintains this structure with minimal changes: the Trinity is moved forward to join God known through nature, and the providence of God for human being is expanded to include a survey of the whole Christian moral tradition, set in the framework of an Aristotelian ethic of virtue but allowed occasionally to refer forward to a Christ who will be studied in himself only later. This is a theology not now directed 'against non-believers', but done in the presence of those non-believers deprived of revelation (Aristotle, at the very least) who, Aquinas says, 'were saved by *implicit* faith in God's go-between, believing God's providence would have chosen some way to deliver men, and revealed it by his Spirit to seekers after truth somewhere' (*2a2ae 2,7.3m*).

In the *Summa Theologiae*, then, we meet a mature theology which, in order to take up its duty of sacred teaching, confronts Scripture and the world, revelation and reason. 'The fundamental aim of God's teaching', Aquinas writes, 'is to make God known not only in himself but as the beginning and end of all things, and of reasoning creatures especially. So we devote part one of this book to God, part two to the journey to God of reasoning creatures, part three to Christ who, as man, is our road to God.' Part one (*1a pars*) begins by letting reason show that a god exists as *auctor naturae* and that we can by analogy which is literal and not metaphorical talk truth about him, even if we cannot conceive what he is like in himself. Aquinas thinks we can prove God to exist with certainty though we cannot see what that means for him, in contrast with most philosophers who seem certain of what God means but doubtful whether he exists. Aquinas then makes clear what this means for the world: that within its own causal structures and even within those events that partly escape those causal structures (chance happenings and freely willed action), God's activity is present, not restricted to a *mediate* presence through the activity of created causes but also *immediately* present in his eternal subsistent existence to that intimately individual temporal existence of each thing which is God's doing. Even if, contrary to Scripture, the world were everlasting (as is reasonably possible and as Aristotle believed), nevertheless reason would have to acknowledge the world's absolute dependence at each temporal moment on the eternal presence of God. The being of the world is the doing of God. Or, adopting the distinction of interior act of will within external human agency which Aquinas will make later, we might call God the interior act of the universe, immediately immanent and eminently transcendent of the universe which is his external action.

The first part of part two of *Summa Theologiae* (*1a2ae*) begins to explore the return of this world to its creator, especially by the mediation of human being, a creature master of its own doing and setting its own ends, and thus imaging the God who is master and doer of all. Human being is a prudence that reflects God's providence, by nature a source of that law unto itself (the *natural law*) which reflects the eternal law unto himself that God is. It is at this point that reason craves revelation: humans are not content with the happiness (*felicitas* = *eudaimonia*) that Aristotle can offer, but crave the bliss (*beatitudo*) that God himself is. Of their nature they wish to see God in himself and by the grace of revelation are enabled to set themselves that end. So the morality of human actions and passions, determined by the end they ultimately tend to, must now be judged not only by conformity to reason and natural law and the balance of Aristotelian virtue. They must also be judged by the deiform virtues of faith, hope and charity (God's friendship) by which God's grace is accepted into human life, and by the restructuring of moral virtue towards that friendship and the earning of eternal life (studied in detail in the second part of part two, *2a2ae*). Grace is God's favour immediately present to our freedom in a new mode, not simply as *auctor naturae* but as *obiectum beatitudinis*, authoring in us a new 'second nature' that disposes us to be 'consorts of God's nature'.

All this, as comparison with the *Summa contra Gentiles* makes clear, is deliberately expressed in ways which a saved non-believer could recognize by implicit faith. It becomes explicit only when we name the bringer of God's grace, Jesus Christ, the climax of the *Summa*. In the later stages of the *1a2ae* the naming is prepared. The preparation begins in the analysis of the primary presupposition of Christianity: that human being, though not depraved in nature, has in history exchanged a state of rightness, in which he would not have suffered from natural impediments, for one of wrongness in which he does justly so suffer. The preparation continues in an examination of the status granted to human history (though not under that name): for we are invited to see in human laws reason's own adaptation of natural law to particular human societies and cultures and religions, and then to identity the old law as God's own adaptation of natural law to the society and culture and religion that was Israel. Finally, we are to see God using Israel's law to foretell symbolically a new law, identified with the 'second nature' that grace introduces into our hearts to make them responsive to God's Spirit. This is a liberation into a new and universal human being that springs from God's investment of himself in Jesus Christ and in 'the things done and suffered in his human nature by God's Son made flesh'. What has so far been discussed in general terms – an encounter of the two natures of God and human being, the interior act of the universe and the interior act of history – is now seen to spring from an actual historical uniting of these two natures in one person. Aquinas understands this incarnation with the help of an image drawn from the Greek Fathers: that of Christ's human nature as a 'joined tool' of the divine person existing in that nature, as hands are joined tools of human beings. The further this-worldly means which Christ uses in carrying out his divine mission are the 'separated tools' wielded by his human nature (e.g. the sacraments, and the church regarded as the mystical or sacramental body of Christ, its head). So Aquinas can say that 'Christ's passion considered as God's action *effects* our salvation, as willed by Christ's soul *earns* it, and as suffered in his flesh can be compared by theologians to a *making amends* (waiving punishment) or *ransom* (freeing from slavery) or *sacrifice* (reconciling to God)' (*3a 48,6*). The sacraments are the social celebratory ritual signs of this in the church, wielded by Christ's institution and ongoing presence, so that their signifying causes grace as separated tools of God's love and its joined tool, Christ's meriting. But about the glorious apotheosis of the world to which these sacraments point and of which they are the seed already present Aquinas is silent, because at this point in writing the *Summa* God called him into that apotheosis.

Aquinas's theology then stood at a crossroads in the history of the Christian tradition. It gave an autonomy to philosophy which profoundly shook that tradition, provoking reactions of fideism on the one hand and on the other that post-Tridentine failure of nerve which tries to dictate philosophical positions from theological standpoints. By emphasizing literal rather than allegorical interpretations of Scripture Aquinas precipitated a break between patristic and later theology which has not yet been fully healed. Nevertheless, what this theology gives us in principle is far more than it accidentally took away, and it remains a supreme model to be imitated in its approach to human sciences and cultures, and bettered in our approach to the interpretation of Scripture.

TIMOTHY S. MCDERMOTT

FURTHER READING: The Leonine Commission's critical edition of the Latin text of Aquinas's complete works is still incomplete (100 years after its start). CD-Roms of Latin works and English translations are available, and some texts are available on the Internet. Large libraries sometimes have R. Busa's *Index Thomisticus*, an immense concordance to Aquinas. The most accessible guide in English to Aquinas's life and works is J.A. Weisheipl, *Friar Thomas d'Aquino: His Life, Thought, and Works* (Washington, DC, 1983). The *Summa Theologiae* is available in English in 60 vols. (ed. T. Gilby; London, 1963), but T. McDermott's *Summa Theologiae: A Concise Translation* (London, 1989) is a good introduction. *Other classic studies:* M.D. Chenu, *Toward Understanding St Thomas* (trans. A.M. Landry and D. Hughes; Chicago, 1964); E. Gilson, *The Christian Philosophy of St Thomas Aquinas* (London, 1971); V.J. Bourke, *Studies of Thomas: 1920–1940*, in *Modern Schoolman* (1941); T.L. Miethe and V.J. Bourke, *Thomistic Bibliography, 1940–1978* (Westport, CT, 1980).

Arianism

Fourth-century Christological heresy. Arianism cannot be understood unless it is seen, in intention at least and in particular at its onset, as being biblically orientated. Arius (c. 250 – c. 336) claimed to be a conservative Christian, seeking not only to preserve the monotheism of God by denying the deity of the Son, but desiring at the same time to honour the Son. Following Scripture, the Arians worshipped the Son and used the threefold name of Father, Son and Spirit in baptism. Admittedly some of their phrases might seem derogatory of the Son, such as he is 'created' or 'founded', but they are qualified by other phrases, such as 'a creature but not as one of the creatures'. Arius thus emphatically asserted the difference in being between Father and Son. He chose the term 'creature' as the basic description of their relationship, but he was also intent to pay the highest honour to the Son.

This regard for the Son forms part of the reason why Arianism had such an impact in the years prior to and following the Council of Nicaea in 325. Clearly other aspects contributed to its ascendancy, such as the Arian insistence on monotheism and on the utter transcendence of God. What terrified *Athanasius, and at the same time attracted many others, was the Arian combination of monotheism with an overt Christocentrism. This distinguished it radically from a revived Judaism and gave it, in appearance at least, a biblical base. To many Christians, particularly those of an *Origenist bent, the Arian position presented, at least in its broad outline, a possible way forward in understanding the relation of Father and Son.

It is a mistake to think of Arianism as a coherent body of thought, with its adherents slavishly defending the thought of its founder. The Arians, who counted among their number several bishops, including Eusebius of Nicomedia and (initially) *Eusebius of Caesarea, believed themselves to be within the mainstream of Christian thought. Arius, originally a presbyter in a parish in Alexandria, eventually found more congenial episcopal company in Palestine once he had fallen foul of Alexander of Alexandria, his own bishop.

Some uncertainty exists over when precisely Arianism first emerged (though it seems unlikely to have been more than five or six years prior to the convening of the Council of Nicaea), and in what order its various documents (of which only a few are extant) were produced. No documents offering a sympathetic overview of Arian thought actually exist, and knowledge of the phenomenon relies heavily, therefore, on selections appearing in the writings of its opponents (not necessarily the best witnesses). This fact counsels a degree of caution in any attempt to describe it.

The Arians on the one hand distinguished the being of the Son from the being of creatures. They accorded to the Son the highest place next to God and held that he could not be grasped or probed by the mind of any other creature. On the other hand, they sought to distinguish the being of the created Son from the being of the ingenerate God, and although the Son's mode of beginning was acknowledged as inexpressible, the being of God is even more inexpressible. God is 'only one God, alone ingenerate, alone everlasting, alone unbegun' (Athanasius, *De Synodis*, 16) – with these being understood in an apophatic way. God was not always Father.

Origen had used 'creature' of the Son but had allied it with his eternal nature. The distinctiveness of the Arians lay in their connecting 'creature' with the phrases 'there was when he was not' and 'from nothing'. The Arians, when pressed, excluded a temporal element from the Son's beginning, insisting on its being 'before all ages' and 'apart from time'. Nevertheless, once 'from nothing' was introduced and contrasted with God's eternity, it was very hard to avoid a

suggestion of temporality, no matter what qualifications were adduced.

Arians adhered to some fundamental epistemological principles: (1) the difference in being between God and creatures is understood as a difference in kind, not of degree; (2) that which acts on something is superior to it. No matter, therefore, that God is triad – God and the Son are utterly 'different in kind'. The distance of God from creation is underlined when the Son is spoken of as being created 'for the works' (Prov. 8:22) and as the 'medium' between God and creation, brought into being for the creation's existence and life. Though created, the Son is the only begotten, the first created, with his own intrinsic grandeur, preferment and high office.

Up to the time of the Arian controversy, most theology occurred in a cosmological context. When the Arians separated the being of God from the being of creatures, the result was that they denied any inherent kinship or likeness between God and creatures. This had the effect of enabling the understanding of God to be slowly freed from a cosmological context, and of distinguishing between the being and the will of God. God exists in and by himself, with the creation existing not as a necessary consequence of his being but of his will and purpose.

The preferred title, in describing the second person of the Trinity, was 'Son' rather than 'Word'. God could not be (nor could he ever have been) without his 'Word'. But a Son could be different – he could be subordinate. Only with a subordinate Son did the Arians believe that the unity of God could be safeguarded. Further, a Son can be rewarded.

The Arians introduced the novel notion of the Son as 'changeable and alterable', although in practice the Son can be and is unchangeable. They took seriously the dynamic obedience or 'growth' of the Son (Luke 2:52), meaning that the Son, an ethical being, advanced or made progress towards God. This advance was not from a condition of sin to one of sinlessness, but it referred to the Son's continuing obedience in every new moral and religious situation that he faced. It is likely that, in Arian thinking, the Son replaced the soul in the human Jesus – so intent were they to argue, for the sake of salvation, that the Son truly faced all the difficulties and temptations which beset humanity.

As 'a creature but not as other creatures' the Son is liable to partake of the instability and frailty of all creatures. He is like other creatures in essence, but unlike them in terms of function, merit and mode of beginning. His different mode of beginning lay in his being directly created by God; his different function lay in the fact that he was himself to be the creator of all else. But both ultimately depended on his merit. In that God foreknew and foresaw his uprightness and obedience, he was chosen to be created first. His pre-eminence was real – accidental, perhaps – but real nevertheless, unsurpassed and unsurpassable.

Similarly, 'a creature but not as one of the creatures' meant that the Son is the vehicle for revelation, truly united to God's teaching. Trustworthiness in revelation lay not in similarity of being between Father and Son, but in the Son's being unchangeable in practice. The revelatory principle that only God can reveal God was still maintained, for God must initiate any revelatory action.

It is along similar lines that an Arian understanding of salvation could have developed. On the grounds of his foreseen obedience, God chose him to become and to be the Son, though it was equally open to all others to become and to be sons also. While it is theoretically possible for the Arians to develop a soteriology, nevertheless actual references to the cross, the conception and eschatology are conspicuously absent from their extant writings. This is not to say that they did not expound these subjects, and it is hard to understand how Arianism could have had any impact in the churches, or on the mission field, without these. It is difficult to imagine the Arians challenging Athanasius with texts such as 'Therefore God has highly exalted him', for example, without expounding in some measure the reason for the death of Christ.

Nevertheless, and here one must be careful with arguments from silence, right through the course of the controversy the questions that held the centre of attention were not the incarnation and soteriology but the nature of the pre-existent Son. No reference to, or hint of, the incarnation or soteriology occurred in the 'Confession of Faith' submitted to Alexander, nor was Alexander in his letters ever required to refute an Arian understanding of the incarnation and soteriology. In subsequent years the Arians carefully confronted Athanasius with the whole range of texts relating to the life of Christ, many of which have clear soteriological connotations. The prime intent of presenting these passages, if one can judge from the nature of Athanasius's answers on page after page, was to demonstrate the creatureliness of the Son. Athanasius, like Alexander before him, never appears to have been faced with an established Arian doctrine of soteriology.

Three reasons for this omission could be that the Arians: (1) never imagined that their soteriology would come under attack; (2) never realized the importance of presenting a soteriology in defending their position; and (3) put all their energies into defending the doctrine of the creaturely Son. Though wishing to give the highest praise, after God, to the Son, they inevitably had to appeal to texts that supported, or purported to support, their position. The strength of Alexander's and Athanasius's positions, in insisting that the controversial texts referred to the incarnate Son, meant that a soteriology must and could develop. The weakness of the Arian position, once these texts were applied to the Son in himself, was that a soteriology would be left on the sidelines in their replies to the debate.

How exactly the Arians might have developed their soteriology is speculation, and yet immense difficulties present themselves. Can God really be said and be known to be a God of love if he speaks of his love only through a subordinate, no matter how noble that creature is? What guarantee is there of God's forgiveness if the Son, though within the Trinity, differs from God even 'unto immensity'? How does one creature who is not as other creatures relate to humanity in the incarnation? Can a creature, however exalted, really become and act for another creature? What is the link between the obedient Jesus and the Son who was advanced as Son by adoption on the grounds of his obedience in the flesh? Can a creature, however honoured, be worshipped?

From this point on in Christian theology the church had to think through what it meant for God to be God in his inner being, and what it meant for a creature to be a creature in its own being. It had to take seriously the doctrines of revelation and soteriology, Trinity and Spirit, as well as the humanity and divinity of Jesus.

Following the Council of Nicaea in 325 Arianism waxed and waned a few times over a number of years. In the 350s a more radical group, known as Anomoeans or Eunomians, surfaced, holding that the Father and Son are unlike (*anomoios*) in being. Whereas earlier Arian thinkers had tended to emphasize the apophatic nature of knowledge of God, Aetius and his successor, *Eunomius, insisting on God as ingenerate, seemed to argue that God's essence was comprehensible by the human mind.

By the time of the Council of Constantinople of 381 Arianism was on the wane, with Nicene orthodoxy triumphant. The creed produced by this council (which emphatically endorsed the theology of Nicaea) included a phrase on the Spirit, who had figured little in Arian documents. In the 360s, however, a group known as Macedonians (but called 'Pneumatomachi' [Spirit-fighters] by its opponents) emerged. While accepting the Son as 'of one substance' with the Father, they denied this to the Spirit, on the grounds that nowhere in Scripture is the Spirit called God or is the Spirit worshipped. Athanasius perceived in this another form of Arianism, and he once again launched an attack. The upshot was a clear statement in the so-called *Niceno-Constantinopolitan Creed on the divinity of the Spirit.

JAMES B. WALKER

FURTHER READING: R.C. Gregg and D.E. Groh, *Early Arianism: A View of Salvation* (London, 1981); R.P.C. Hanson, *The Search for the Christian Doctrine of God* (Edinburgh, 1988); J.N.D. Kelly, *Early Christian Creeds* (London, 1972); *Early Christian Doctrines* (London, 1977); T.A. Kopecek, *A History of Neo-Arianism* (2 vols.; Cambridge, MA, 1979); R.D. Williams, *Arius: Heresy and Tradition* (London, 1987).

Aristotelianism

Aristotelianism represents a movement in western philosophy that followed the teachings of the great Greek philosopher Aristotle. This article does not expound Aristotelianism as a system of ideas but rather looks at its history of effects, and especially at Aristotle's influence on Christian thought. This influence grew from modest beginnings to dominate the relationship between theology and philosophy among Jews, Muslims and Christians in the Middle Ages. Aristotelian natural philosophy provided the background for the debate between theologians and early modern science in the seventeenth century. Having abandoned his natural philosophy, the modern age continues to be influenced by Aristotle's metaphysics, logic and ethics.

After Aristotle's death (322 BC), his school, the Lyceum, was headed by Theophrastus of Eresos (c. 371–288 BC). The tradition of Peripatetic philosophy was carried on (in its main literary remains) through a series of commentators and systemizers. It was taken up into Neoplatonism (see *Platonism) through the work of Plotinus and Porphyry. Some Neoplatonic works, in fact, were wrongly identified as Aristotle's own, including the so-called 'theology' of Aristotle (which in fact is a selection from Proclus, *Elements of Theology*).

While early Christian theologians were aware of the work of Aristotle, they did not esteem it. Plato, not Aristotle, was the philosopher of preference. For example, while *Lactantius in his *Divine Institutes* is aware of Aristotle's view of God, his rhetoric clearly favours Plato (I.5; *ANF* 7:14). Theologians in the west, at best, were in favour of Aristotle's logical works. *Boethius, in particular, translated the logical works of Aristotle into Latin. In the Greek-speaking east, Aristotle was also known but not widely used, apart from a few Christian thinkers such as Gregory Nazianzen and John Philoponus (sixth century). However, Syrian Christian philosophers introduced the works of Aristotle to Semitic culture, beginning in the fifth century. This began a significant Aristotelian movement among Muslim and Jewish philosophers in the Middle Ages. Because of the interest and use of Aristotle among thinkers in his culture, therefore, *John of Damascus (c. 665–749) used Aristotle more than any prior Greek father. This unity of Aristotelianism and Christian theology was to herald the work of the Latin west, especially *Thomas Aquinas, in the Middle Ages.

The works of Muslim and Jewish philosophers were soon translated into Latin. Averroes (Ibn Rushd, 1126–98), in particular, developed an Aristotelian philosophy that was a challenge to Christian theology. The breadth of Aristotelian thought cannot be summarized here, but a few elements which caused trouble in the thirteenth century, especially at the University of Paris, can be mentioned. Aristotelian metaphysics rejected the Platonic Forms and the immortality of the soul. It was seen by its opponents as too close to materialism. Aristotle also taught the eternity of the world, contrary to the doctrine of *creatio ex nihilo*. Aristotelian epistemology focused on scientific knowledge gained through experience and memory and built up through evidence and careful, logical argument. This seemed to conflict with knowledge gained by direct revelation, or holy Scriptures. In ethics, Aristotle provided a reasoned, humanistic foundation for moral truths, based upon virtue and character. This seemed in conflict with an ethics based upon divine commands founded upon the Bible.

The unification of the 'new' Aristotelian philosophy from Semitic sources, with Christian theology and tradition, was the great achievement of Thomas Aquinas and his teacher, Albert the Great, at the University of Paris. Although highly controversial in Aquinas's own time, this unification was soon broadly accepted. By the time of the canonization of Aquinas (1323), Aristotle was becoming the leading intellectual light in the universities of Europe. His logical and metaphysical tradition was key to the growth of scholastic thought. In the fourteenth to sixteenth centuries, Aristotelian psychology, logic, natural philosophy and metaphysics were triumphant. However, the close association of Aristotle with Christian theology soon led to a significant *faux pas*.

A Christian school of Humanism developed in the Renaissance, based for the most part outside universities. This humanist tradition prized the classical beauty of Greek and Latin literature, over against the logical 'sterility' of *Scholasticism. The humanists prized Aristotle for his *Rhetoric* and *Poetics*, rather than for his logical works. Eventually, Aristotelian-scholastic philosophy and theology were driven out of the universities of Europe. It was not the humanists alone, however, who accomplished this: scientists were involved as well. During the Renaissance, natural philosophy was to take a turn against the authority of Scholasticism. Early modern science was indebted to Aristotle, but it moved away from his conclusions and methods. In particular, the work of Galileo brought the new science into conflict with the older Aristotelian natural philosophy, which was then dominant in academia and in the church. By silencing Galileo the church won a battle, but lost a war. Aristotelianism was on the wane in the eighteenth century, and it has never recovered its dominant influence.

In theology, Aristotle continued to be influential through Aquinas and those who followed Catholic thought. *Erasmus followed Aristotle and Aquinas against *Luther on the freedom of the will. *Francisco de Suárez (1548–1617), a Spanish philosopher and *Jesuit priest,

developed Aristotelian philosophy in the area of metaphysics. The Anglican divine Richard Hooker (d. 1600) is an example of how Protestant thought could also be influenced by Aristotle, through Aquinas.

The major developments in Aristotelian thought in the nineteenth century were historical-critical. French, German and English scholars laboured to provide critical editions of Aristotle and his early commentators, along with modern translations of his work. Significant commentaries on the works of Aristotle were likewise produced. These included an important Oxford school of translators, commentators and scholars of Aristotle, such as W.D. Ross (1877–1971). Ross edited the complete works of Aristotle in English (Oxford, 1928).

In the twentieth century, the revival of neo-Thomism (see *Thomism) has kept alive the influence of Aristotle upon Christian theology. Already in 1879, Pope Leo XIII encouraged the revival of Thomas Aquinas in his encyclical 'Aeterni Patris', and he indirectly sparked greater interest in Aristotle. Among the most important figures in this movement were *Étienne Gilson (1884–1978) and *Jacques Maritain (1882–1973) in France; *Karl Rahner (1904–84) in Germany; and, among Anglo-American scholars, *E.L. Mascall (1905–93), *Bernard Lonergan (1908–84) and Alasdair MacIntyre (b. 1929). For example, in the area of religious epistemology, Maritain's *Degrees of Knowledge* and Lonergan's *Insight* both demonstrate the continuing power of Aristotle's influence. In contemporary moral philosophy, MacIntyre has revived the tradition of Aristotelian-Thomistic ethics for a postmodern culture. It appears that Aristotle's profound influence on western thought in general, and Christian theology in particular, is still with us some 2,300 years after his death.

ALAN G. PADGETT

FURTHER READING: A.H. Armstrong (ed.), *The Cambridge History of Later Greek and Early Modern Philosophy* (Cambridge, 1970); Victor L. Dowdell, *Aristotle and Anglican Religious Thought* (Ithaca, NY, 1942); Étienne Gilson, *A History of Christian Philosophy in the Middle Ages* (New York, 1955); Bernard Lonergan, *Insight* (New York, 1957); Alasdair MacIntyre, *Three Rival Versions of Moral Enquiry: Encyclopaedia, Genealogy, and Tradition* (Notre Dame, 1990); Jacques Maritain, *Degrees of Knowledge* (New York, 1959); R.P. McKeon, 'Aristotelianism in Western Christianity', in *Environmental Factors in Christian History* (ed. J.T. McNeill, et al.;

Chicago, 1939); F.E. Peters, *Aristotle and the Arabs* (New York, 1968); Richard Sorabji (ed.), *Aristotle Transformed* (London, 1990); 'The Ancient Commentators on Aristotle' (ed. J. Barnes and M. Schofield; London, 1978–); Ferdnan van Steenberghen, *Aristotle in the West* (1955; New York, repr. 1970); *Thomas Aquinas and Radical Aristotelianism* (Washington, DC, 1980).

Arminius and Arminianism

Jacob, or as he has been frequently identified, James Arminius (1559–1609), was born at Oudewater, near Rotterdam, probably in 1559 – although some sources indicate 1560. On his father's death, he left home for Marburg, where he lived and studied with Rudolf Snellius, who was then a fairly well-known philosopher and logician. In 1576, Arminius returned to the Netherlands and began his studies at the University of Leiden. After six years, the burgomasters of Amsterdam presented him with a stipend to enable him to attend the universities of Geneva and Basle. Apart from a brief academic stay in Padua to hear the famous Aristotelian logician, Jacopo Zabarella, Arminius's theological education was under Reformed tutelage.

Nonetheless, Arminius's theological training in Leiden and Geneva was not, as is often stated, so rigidly supralapsarian as to produce a massive reaction against Reformed orthodoxy in the young Arminius. In Leiden he sat under Guilhelmus Feuguereus and Lambert Daneau. The former was a biblical scholar and the editor of Augustin Marlorat's *Scripture Thesaurus* (1574) and the latter, though a scholastic in method, was influenced deeply by his studies of the Fathers and was distinctly infralapsarian in both his placement and his exposition of predestination. Arminius's studies in Geneva (1582–87) present a similar picture: despite the supralapsarian tendencies of *Beza, the *Harmony of Reformed Confessions* produced in that era and the student theses in the academy – we have a set in print from 1585 – were infralapsarian in their teaching. There is no evidence that a supralapsarian 'Bezan' orthodoxy was pressed on students in Geneva in the late sixteenth century. On the contrary, Arminius would have imbibed there, as in Leiden, a Reformed theology which respected *Bullinger as well as *Calvin, *Ursinus and Zanchi as well as Beza. In addition, as Arminius's later declarations make clear, his protest against Reformed predestinarianism was directed against all its forms, whether supra- or infralapsarian.

In 1588, Arminius left his studies behind for a pastoral appointment in Amsterdam. Although it is highly improbable that his views were altered because of an encounter with the synergistic teachings of Dirck Coornhert, Arminius was certainly well aware of the debates over predestination that troubled the Dutch church in his time. In any case, he wrote no response to Coornhert's work. Rather, he immersed himself in the study of Paul's epistle to the Romans. He first directed his attention to Romans 7 and the problem of the will. He moved away from the traditional *Augustinian pattern of the Reformers and argued that the inward struggle of Paul was a pre-conversion, not a post-conversion, struggle. Here already are hints of a synergism in which the human will takes the first step toward grace. He then addressed the problem of predestination in Romans 9 and engaged in a detailed and exceedingly cordial epistolary debate on that doctrine with Franciscus Junius. Here Arminius argued that Isaac and Ishmael, Jacob and Esau are not individuals but types, and that Romans 9 did not refer to individual predestination. Arminius then encountered William Perkins's *De praedestinatione modo et ordine* (1598) and reacted strongly against its doctrine – not only against the supralapsarianism of Perkins, but also against the general implications of the Reformed doctrine of predestination. Since these documents were not immediately published, the Reformed community did not become aware of the changes in his position. In 1602, Arminius, still a virtually unknown quantity, succeeded Junius as professor of theology at Leiden.

With this theological preparation in hand, Arminius began to manifest the change of mind that had taken place in his theology over the past decade. His pronouncements on predestination – and a Christological controversy in which he engaged – soon brought down on him the ire of the theological faculty, particularly of Francis Gomar (1563–1641) and Lucas Trelcatius, the younger (1573–1607). The debate occupied the remainder of Arminius's life: he argued his orthodoxy to the end, presenting in 1608 his *Declaration of Sentiments* before the highly Calvinistic Estates General of Holland.

The most important document left by Arminius concerning his doctrine of predestination is this *Declaration* he offered before the

Estates of Holland at The Hague in 1608. Here, Arminius finally published his views on the doctrines of predestination, providence, free choice, grace, assurance of salvation, the divinity of the second Person of the Trinity, justification and the revision of the *Belgic Confession* and the *Heidelberg Catechism*. Of all the topics treated in the *Declaration*, predestination receives the lengthiest exposition – and it is here also that Arminius most clearly states his divergence from the Reformed theology of his contemporaries. The document presents three Reformed views of predestination – the supralapsarian, a modified supralapsarian position, and the infralapsarian – and rejects them all in favour of a fourth position, Arminius's own.

On this point in particular, Arminius stepped consciously outside of the bounds of the Reformed faith and its confessions – giving substance to his proposal that the Belgic Confession and the Heidelberg Catechism be emended. On purely historical grounds, therefore, we must reject the argument that Arminius was a 'Reformed theologian' and that his theology represented a type of Reformed thought somewhat out of style in the late sixteenth century. The view of predestination that Arminius presented in his *Declaration* opposed Reformed teaching, whether of Calvin or Bullinger, Beza or Zanchi, Gomar or Junius, and it opposed the unaltered Reformed confessions.

Rather than describe a single eternal decree and its objects, Arminius's doctrine of the decree and its execution outlines four decrees and an order of priorities in the mind of God. The first of these is a general decree to appoint Christ as mediator of salvation, made without reference to individual people and expressing an antecedent gracious will of God to save and to save generally. The second decree expresses the divine will to save specifically those who will repent and believe, thus resting salvation entirely on divine foreknowledge of human choice. The third divine decree determines the means of salvation. Here Arminius speaks of the establishment of preaching, sacraments and the instrumental order of grace as a whole, as sufficient and efficacious for salvation. This sufficiency and efficacy is, however, qualified by human choice, drawing on Molina's doctrine of a divine 'middle knowledge' (*scientia media*). That is: God provides the conditions for the future contingent acts of individual human beings and acts on the basis of his foreknowledge of the

result. Only in the fourth and final decree does the decision of God relate to individual human beings: God decrees to save those whom he has foreknown will respond to and persevere in his offer of grace and to damn those whom he knows will not. Arminius does speak of prevenient and co-operating grace – but the former can be rejected and the latter only serves to reinforce.

On the issue of prevenient grace and its character, Arminius makes a fairly clear declaration in his *Apology against Thirty-one Defamatory Articles*. It was alleged against him that he claimed, in semi-Pelagian fashion, that a man might do good apart from grace and that he accepted a late medieval, semi-Pelagian maxim, 'To those who do what is in them, God will not deny grace.' Arminius countered that even Adam needed the assistance of grace to do good – what he meant was that the person 'who does what he can by the primary grace already conferred upon him' will receive from God further grace. This is in fact precisely the interpretation placed on the maxim by Gabriel Biel, the late-medieval semi-Pelagian whose theology *Luther so vociferously rejected at the outset of the Reformation. And, in Arminius's theology, this idea is linked, as in Biel's, to the belief that the prevenient grace of God is offered to all and is not irresistible.

When Arminius died in 1609, controversy was prolonged on the Arminian side by Simon Episcopius (1583–1644), Arminius's successor in the University of Leiden, and by Janus Uitenbogaert (1557–1644), an eminent preacher at The Hague. In 1610, Uitenbogaert and Episcopius presented the Arminian position in a five-point *Remonstrance* to the Estates of Holland. Article one of the *Remonstrance* contains a distillate of the doctrine of predestination found in Arminius's *Declaration*: it defines predestination as the eternal purpose of God in Christ to save those who believe and to damn those who reject the gospel and the grace of God in Christ. Here already the implication is synergistic and the will of God is viewed as contingent upon human choice. Next, in article two, the *Remonstrance* speaks of the universality of Christ's death: Christ died for all and the limitation of the efficacy of his death arises out of the choice of some not to believe. The third article argues the necessity of grace if fallen man is to choose the good and come to belief. In the fourth article, this insistence upon prevenient grace is drawn into relation with the synergism of the first two articles. Prevenient and subsequent assisting grace may be resisted and rejected: ultimately the work of salvation, in its efficacy and application, rests on human choice. The fifth and final article of the *Remonstrance* argues continuing gracious support of believers by God but refuses to decide on the issue of perseverance. When Reformed opponents answered with a Contra-Remonstrance, a conference was arranged for the following year at The Hague. This conference, together with a colloquy at Delft in 1613 and an edict from the Estates of Holland (1614) demanding cessation of theological dispute, only succeeded in deepening the controversy and leading to the National Synod at Dort, 1618–19.

The Synod of Dort, far from being a 'Dutch' Synod represented what has been called 'international Calvinism' or, more accurately, an international Reformed theology. It drew delegates from Britain, including the bishops of Chichester and Salisbury. The latter, John Davenant, was a learned theologian, and the bishop of Chichester was Samuel Ward, professor of divinity from Cambridge. Theodore Tronchin came from Geneva, a duo of eminent German Reformed theologians (Alting and Scultetus) came from Heidelberg, and a trio of renowned thinkers (Martinius, Isselburg and Crocius) came from Bremen. Basle, Berne and Zurich also sent representatives – as did all the Dutch provinces and universities. The combination of learning with diversity of views within a churchly consensus produced at Dort a document which was far from extreme and quite representative of the Reformed theology of its day. The decision reached by the Synod after six months of discussion and 154 formal sessions was, at least in a negative sense, a foregone conclusion: the Arminian articles were condemned; the Belgic Confession, against which the Arminians had protested, and the Heidelberg Catechism, which they sought to reinterpret, were affirmed as the standards of the Dutch church, together with the five Canons of Dort, in which the Arminian position was refuted.

The Arminian doctrines were clearly beyond the bounds of Reformed confessional orthodoxy. The Synod, we note, decided against the Arminians but not in favour of Arminius's bitter opponent, the supralapsarian Gomar. The Canons of Dort ought to be viewed as a magisterial interpretation of the extant Reformed confessional synthesis: they condemn predestination grounded on prior human choice; they deny a grace that is both resistible and acceptable by man; they affirm the depth of original sin, argue a limited efficiency of Christ's work of satisfaction and stress the perseverance of the elect by grace. None of these views modifies the earlier Reformed position – indeed, virtually all of these points can be elicited from Ursinus's exposition of the Heidelberg Catechism.

The *Confession of the Remonstrant Pastors* or *Confessio sive declaratio sententiae pastorum, qui in foederato Belgico Remonstrantes vocantur, super praecipuis articulis Religionis Christianae* was written by Arminius's theological successor in the University of Leiden, Simon Episcopius, and published in 1622. Episcopius had studied both philosophy and theology at Leiden under both Arminius and Gomar. His attachment to the theology of Arminius eventually led to conflict with Gomar and, within a year of Arminius's death, to Episcopius's departure from Leiden. He served as pastor in Bleyswick, near Rotterdam, during the year 1610. On Gomar's retirement from the university in 1611, Episcopius was called to succeed Gomar as professor of theology. Episcopius soon became the chief theological spokesman of the Arminian or Remonstrant party and was eventually condemned with twelve other Arminian pastors and theologians at the Synod of Dort in 1618. He lived for eight years in Brussels, banished from the Netherlands. When he was permitted to return to the Netherlands in 1626, he served first as preacher in the Remonstrant church in Amsterdam and, after 1634, as professor of theology in the Remonstrant college in Amsterdam. The *Confession of the Remonstrant Pastors*, together with Episcopius's *Apology for the Confession*, stand as the major Arminian confessional documents of the seventeenth century.

RICHARD A. MÜLLER

FURTHER READING: Jacobus Arminius, *Opera theologica* (Leiden, 1629); *The Works of James Arminius* (trans. James Nichols and William Nichols; 3 vols.; Grand Rapids, 1986); Carl Bangs, *Arminius: A Study in the Dutch Reformation* (Nashville, TN, 1971); 'Arminius as a Reformed Theologian', in *The Heritage of John Calvin* (ed. John H. Bratt; Grand Rapids, 1973), pp. 209–22; 'Recent Studies in Arminianism', *Rel Life* 32.3 (1963), pp. 421–28; Caspar Brandt, *Historia vita Jacobi Arminii*

(Brunswick, 1725); *The Life of James Arminius, D.D.* (trans. John Guthrie; intro. by T.O. Summers; Nashville, TN, 1857); Geeraert Brandt, *The History of the Reformation and Other Ecclesiastical Transactions in and about the Low Countries: From the Beginning of the Eighth Century, down to the Famous Synod of Dort* ... (4 vols.; London, 1720–23); Peter Y. DeJong (ed.), *Crisis in the Reformed Churches: Essays in Commemoration of the Great Synod of Dort, 1618–1619* (Grand Rapids, 1968); Eef Dekker, 'Jacobus Arminius and his Logic: Analysis of a Letter', *J Th St* NS 44 (1993), pp. 118–42; *Rijker dan Midas: Vrijheid, gebade en predestinatie in de theologie van Jacobus Arminius (1559–1609)* (Zoetermeer, 1993); 'Was Arminius a Molinist?', *Sixteen Cent J* 27 (1996), pp. 337–52; A.W. Harrison, *Arminianism* (London, 1937); *The Beginnings of Arminianism to the Synod of Dort* (London, 1926); G.J. Hoenderdaal, 'The Debate About Arminius Outside the Netherlands', in *Leiden University in the Seventeenth Century* (ed. Th. H. Lunsingh Scheurleer, et al.; Leiden, 1975), pp. 137–59; Gerald O. McCulloh (ed.), *Man's Faith and Freedom: The Theological Influence of Jacobus Arminius* (Nashville, TN, 1962); Richard A. Muller, 'God, Predestination, and the Integrity of the Created Order: A Note on Patterns in Arminius' Theology', in *Later Calvinism: International Perspectives* (ed. W. Fred Graham; Sixteenth-Century Essays & Studies; Kirksville, MO, 1994), pp. 431–46; *God, Creation and Providence in the Thought of Jacob Arminius: Sources and Directions of Scholastic Protestantism in the Era of Early Orthodoxy* (Grand Rapids, 1991); 'Grace, Election, and Contingent Choice: Arminius' Gambit and the Reformed Response', in *The Grace of God and the Bondage of the Will*, II (ed. Thomas Schreiner and Bruce Ware; 2 vols.; Grand Rapids, 1995), pp. 251–78; 'The Priority of the Intellect in the Soteriology of Jacob Arminius', *West Th J* 55 (1993), pp. 55–72; A.S. Wood, 'The Declaration of Sentiments: The Theological Testament of Arminius', *Ev Q* 65 (April 1993), pp. 111–29.

Asian Theologies

Asia is a theological and cultural mosaic, where major beliefs and moral traditions such as Hinduism, Buddhism, Confucianism, Islam, Sikhism and a countless range of popular and indigenous beliefs blend with one another, as well as with Christianity, secular ideologies and global humanism. Amidst this variety of religious and cultural practices, Christianity remains a minority faith, except in the Philippines. Although there have been pockets of Christians in various Asian countries from the earliest centuries of the Christian era in the form of the oriental churches, it was only after the advent of western colonialism that Christianity's presence was felt very widely. Unlike in the west, where Christian theology as we know it today arose as a response to denominational needs, *rationalism, problems of industrialization and secularization, in Asia it emerged as a way of responding to colonialism, and later to the process of nation building and often, more pertinently, in response to the presence of various religious and philosophical traditions. There is the risk of generalization in speaking of an Asian theology. However, surveying the literature emanating from Asia's diverse regions, one can identify the following theological emphases, at the same time noting that these are not mutually exclusive but often interpenetrative categories.

Heritagist. This is the attempt to find conceptual analogies in the high culture and textual traditions and philosophies of Asia. The task here is to trace Christian ideas in the Hindu, Buddhist, Confucian, Taoist and Shintoist thought worlds as a way of explaining the Christian gospel, thus bypassing, and at times going beyond, the familiar Semitic and Hellenistic images. The Bengali Christian Brahmabandhab Upadhyaya explored the Hindu *Vedanta*; the Sri Lankan Lynn de Silva made use of the Buddhist analysis of the human condition, *tilakkhana* (characteristic of existence); the Japanese Mashisa Uchimura appropriated *bushido* (the way of the warrior), the Samurai concept; and the Sirhak Christians of Korea, and later Korean Methodist theologians such as Yu Dong Shil, Yung Sung Bum and Byun Sun Whan, employed Confucian concepts as a way of working out an appropriate theology for their context. Missionaries also, such as Swami Abhishiktananda (Henri Le Saux) in India, Matteo Ricci in China and Alexandre de Rhodes in Vietnam, to name a few, played a critical role in utilizing profitably the high cultural and textual traditions of Asia. Delving into their heritage not only helped Asians to cope with colonialism and the missionary onslaught on their religious traditions, but it also helped them to create an identity, which enabled them to be part of the national life, and to avoid being seen in their own countries as de-nationalized and uprooted aliens.

Liberationist. The emphasis here is to rectify the one-sided attempts of heritagism to make the gospel relevant to Asia's religious traditions by shifting the emphasis to Asia's socio-economic realities. Long before Latin American theologians put the poo at the centre of theological discourse, Asians had been engaged with issues faced by the economically disadvantaged. For instance, Toyohiko Kagawa from Japan, and those who were inspired by him, like Shigeru Nakajima, had been involved with the problems of labour and had been reflecting theologically on them. What makes the current Asian theology of liberation different from that of the Latin Americans is the realization that no liberation can be simply confined to the Christian church. For liberation to be meaningful to 90 per cent of Asia's poor who are not Christian it must be interreligious, and it must take into account the prophetic and protest voices embedded in both the oral and the written traditions of Asia's religious and cultural heritage. The Korean minjung (common people) theology, while clearly informed by the liberation concept, derives much of its hermeneutical resources from the historical experience of the Korean people associated with the *han* (accumulated anger). Other examples of Asian liberation theologies are the Filipino 'theology of struggle', and the Taiwanese 'homeland theologies' which emerge from political oppression, martial law and conditions that deny a people rights and freedoms. The employment of Hindu *bhakti* (devotion) and the Korean shamanistic ritual of *gut* (offering to gods) in Asian Christian theologies demonstrates that there are resources within Asia's vast religious traditions which can be profitably utilized not only for theological illumination but also for political and social transformation.

Subalternist. This is the voice of those who have been excluded from the mainstream theological discourse by its failure to address the concerns of those who were outside the high culture and patriarchy. In India, the *dalits* (the name chosen by the outcastes of Indian society themselves) are trying to bring to the fore the glaring social reality of the caste system, and they are endeavouring to work out a theology based on the principle of equality. In Japan, the *burakumin*, the people who have been discriminated against on the basis of ceremonial pollution, have recovered the crown of thorns as a symbol which points both to the pain of marginalization and also to a future liberation.

Asian women have been trying to bring together two disparate but interconnected realities – Asianness and womanness. The tribal peoples of Asia draw upon two fundamental concepts, anti-pride and anti-greed, to work out a theology in opposition to caste pride and consumer greediness. These theologies, like theologies of emancipation, arise out of being wounded and hurt. Once sidelined, now the subalterns have emerged to tell their own stories on their own terms, and in the process they have discovered a new self-identity and self-worth and self-validation. Tero Kuryiabashi (*Burakumins*), Aravind Nirmal (*Dalits*), Nirmal Minz (tribals) and Asian women such as Aruna Gnanadason, Kwok Pui-Lan, Virginia Fabella and Chung Hyun Kyung were all pioneers not only in removing the distortion and mystification perpetuated by the reigning theologies of Asia, but also in using them to reinstate their legitimate position and affirm their wish to take their place in reinvigorating Asian theologies.

Postcolonialist. This is a recent approach undertaken by Asian scholars such as Wong Wai Ching, Archie Lee and R.S. Sugirtharajah, who find that the earlier Asian attempts were either deeply committed to the orientalist paradigm which saw Asia as spiritual and ascetic, or locked into the modernist idea of a salvation history model which was not always sympathetic to those outside the Christian fold. Those who hold to a postcolonial approach want to go beyond the contrastive east/west, orient/occident, evangelizer/evangelized categories in order to forge an identity which will be mutually transformative. In this view, gospel and church are no longer seen as in charge, and society and culture no longer belong to them. The gospel is seen as one among many divine manifestations. In the light of the postcolonial view, Christian theology and the church are in need of a huge reappraisal. This means seeking to reinvent from a position of humility and vulnerability.

Though the above categories seem to progress in a linear way, the emergence of one does not exhaust the other. These modes are still available and sit side by side and often interact. There is, however, another very vibrant theology available in Asia – namely evangelical theology. Evangelically inclined Asian Christians have worked out a theology drawing heavily on biblical insights to face Asian realities. For them, the Asian context is not necessarily a definitive factor for doing theology, and any such attempts are seen as relativizing the gospel. If these theologies make use of the terminology of indigenous tradition, it is always firmly subordinate to their particular understanding of biblical revelation. Asian evangelical theologies are closely tied to biblical revelation, and they are of the view that the gospel message is eternal and no culture escapes its judgement.

Over the years, Asian theologies have gone through different methodological processes which can be categorized as follows.

Accommodation. In this method, the missioner/evangelizer, with a view to presenting the gospel effectively, adopts the customs, manners and habits of the culture to which he or she is trying to bring the Christian message. Three outstanding examples of missioners who adopted this method are Robert de Nobili in India, Mateo Ricci in China and Alexandre de Rhodes in Vietnam. De Nobili, an Italian aristocrat, assumed that because high caste Brahmins were held in high esteem by the people, the best way to put the gospel across was to be identified with them. So he gave himself an Indian name, lived like a *sanyasin* (ascetic) with a topknot, wore sandals, learnt Tamil and Sanskrit and employed high caste servants. Ricci, in the same way, adopted the lifestyle of Confucian scholars – their language, teaching methods and vocabulary. Similarly, the French Jesuit de Rhodes dressed himself in Vietnamese robes, wore the heelless shoes which were common among the middle class and took to the local cuisine. In this model of interpretation, the message remains the same but it is the messenger who gets a new identity and form. The Christian Ashram movements in India fall within this accommodative category.

Indigenization. In some ecclesiastical circles this is called acculturation. This is seen as a process whereby the gospel is translated into a particular culture. It is the concept of incarnation, in which God is perceived as taking human form in a particular Palestinian culture, that provides the theological undergirding for this enterprise. Asian Christians have critically employed concepts and doctrines from other religious traditions as a way of interpreting the Christian message. The Hindu concept of *Ardhanareesvara* (expression of male and female

deity) was used to interpret the *imago dei*, and *avatara* was used to interpret the doctrine of incarnation. The Buddhist notion of *nirvana* was appropriated to explain the kingdom of God; the Japanese concept of tragedy, *tsura*, was taken as an analogy for God's suffering for humans; the fundamental concept of Confucianism, *Jen* (life), was compared with the Holy Spirit. The indigenous culture, however imperfect and impure, is seen as a convenient vehicle for transmitting the unchanging gospel truth. Although positive aspects of other faiths are acknowledged, the superiority of Christianity is assumed, affirmed and celebrated.

Contextualization. This method came to the fore in the 1970s when Asian theologians were compelled to address the questions posed by the rapid industrialization and urbanization that took place in various Asian countries, and the social and economic divide they brought in their wake. Unlike indigenization, which focused on religious and cultural elements, the aim here was to discern the gospel in all aspects of human life, including the economic, and to address questions of power and powerlessness. Though one of the pioneers of this method, the Taiwanese theologian Shoki Coe, advocated a double wrestle between the gospel and context, ultimately it was the gospel, and applying its critique to socio-economic realities, which was seen as primary.

All these methodological approaches are evangelistic and apologetic in content and tone. They are all concerned with translating or interpreting a given text and a given gospel for a culture. The Bible and the gospel are taken for granted. These modes of doing theology are all expressions of a one-way movement by a form of Christianity largely based on biblical presuppositions shaped by and infused with indigenous resources, in order to occupy and dislodge the local religions and cultures. The underlying presupposition is that the other cultures and religions have to be cleansed and transformed.

Hybridization. This is a recent method advocated by those who employ postcolonial categories. Unlike the aforementioned methods, hybridization calls for a critical integration, which is seen as a two-way process where both text and context, gospel and culture, are seen as interactive so that something new is created. The theological task here is seen as a way of re-forming and re-conceptualizing both Christian identity and the gospel. The postcolonial notion of hybridity is not about the dissolution of differences but about renegotiating the structures of power built on differences. It is not like those forms of assimilation which the missionaries and later Christian theologians advocated, but is a form of subversion which creates new theological openings and interpretations.

Some sources for doing theology include the following.

Extratextual. Besides the Christian Scriptures and church tradition, Asian theologians have often profitably delved into other, indigenous resources. Asian theologians have made use of the sacred texts of Asian religions – the *Veda*, the *Bhagavadgita*, the *Dhammapada*, *I Ching* and the *Holy Granth* etc., some of which provided spiritual nourishment to Asians even before Christian faith came into existence. These texts are not only mined for theological truths but also are put to use profitably in worship and liturgical arrangements.

Transtextual. Asian theologians have made creative use of stories and visual and performative art forms which are common to Asian cultures. Stories, dance and art have been pressed into service by various Asian theologians: mask dance by Korean minjung; storytelling by C.S. Song and later by Peter Lee; painting by various Asians, chief among them being Jyoti Sahi and Masao Takenaka; the Japanese Noh drama by Yuko Yusa; and shadow puppets by the Javanese Judo Poerwowidagdo. These are all indications that Asians not only attempt to grasp the mystery which is not always accessible through literal and written tradition, but that they also seek to communicate the message in visual, oral and aural forms as well.

Asian theologians are aware that these texts, stories and art forms have been used to legitimize, serve and preserve the interests of the dominant class, and therefore they realize that it is of vital importance to use these resources critically, unmasking their ideological biases and at the same time retrieving the liberative potential embedded in them. Notwithstanding their hegemonic tendencies, these stories and art forms have been used effectively, in preference to *Marxian materials, to disclose structures of oppression and signs of inequality.

There are two major theological issues which are crucial to Asian theologies – Christology and ecclesiology. Ever since the gospel reached Asia, an ongoing theological task has been to redefine Jesus in a context which brims with founders of religious truth and wisdom. Under colonial pressure and overtly negative missionary preaching, Jesus was seen as the fulfilment of Asia's religious expectations. It was K.M. Banerjee who first mooted the idea of Jesus as the fulfiller rather than the destroyer of Asia's religious heritage, an idea often credited to the missionary theologian J.N. Farquhar. Among others, the Japanese Matsumura Kaiseki and Kawai Shinsui also advocated such an idea. Then, during the days of nation building, as a way of repairing the earlier apologetic arrogance, Jesus was seen as exerting his presence from within Asia's religious and cultural traditions. Now, the subalterns who were left out of the discourse see him as a life-force who empowers them to claim their humanity and dignity.

The other major issue has to do with the existence of the Christian community amidst other religious communities. More than the questions about the existence of God, or methods of doing theology, the definition of Christian communal identity is crucial for Asian Christians. What it amounts to is how to work out a practical ecclesiology. The early converts faced with this issue struggled to configure their Christian identity by eliminating and leaving behind their cultural and religious heritage. In a changed context, it is no longer possible to characterize Christianity as historical and life-affirming, over against Asia's religions as spiritual and life-denying. Now that Asian religions contribute to justice causes, affirm the dignity of people and care for the earth, the current generation is trying to be Christian and at the same time willing to be transformed and cleansed by Asia's religious wisdom. The recognition of Christianity in Asia, and for that matter its survival, depends on the ability of Asian Christians to reconfigure their identity, which is so often viewed with suspicion and tainted with the recent colonial past. Ultimately, the question concerns one's willingness to be vulnerable in order to be both truly Asian and truly Christian.

R.S. SUGIRTHARAJAH

FURTHER READING: M. Amaladoss, *Life in Freedom: Liberation Theologies from Asia* (Maryknoll, NY, 1997); Hyun Kyung Chung, *Struggle to be the Sun*

Again: Introducing Asian Women Theology (Maryknoll, NY, 1990); D. Carr, *God, Christ and God's People in Asia* (Hong Kong, 1995); Yeow Choo Lak and John England (eds.), *Doing Theology with People's Symbols and Images* (Singapore, 1989); Virginia Fabella (ed.), *Asia's Struggle for Full Humanity* (Maryknoll, NY, 1980); Virginia Fabella and Sun Ai Lee Park (eds.), *We Dare to Dream: Doing Theology as Asian Women* (Maryknoll, NY, 1989); Aloysius Pieris, *An Asian Theology of Liberation* (London, 1988); R.S. Sugirtharajah, *Asian Biblical Hermeneutics and Postcolonialism* (Sheffield, 1999); R.S. Sugirtharajah (ed.), *Frontiers in Asian Christian Theology* (Maryknoll, NY, 1994); Masao Takenaka, *Christian Art in Asia* (Tokyo, 1975).

Athanasian Creed

A statement of faith in the Trinity and in the person and work of Christ, composed in Latin in the west, probably in the late-fifth or early-sixth century. The Athanasian Creed is sometimes called the *Quicunque vult*, from its opening words ('Whoever wishes to be saved ...'). The name 'Athanasian Creed' is late; until AD 1000 it was called 'The [Catholic] Faith of St Athanasius', or similar names. The Creed is certainly not by Athanasius and has little direct relationship to his theology. Nor is it technically a creed, since it lacks the words 'I believe' or 'We believe'.

J.N.D. Kelly divided the Athanasian Creed into 42 verses. Following that division, its structure is this:

- vv. 1–2: Introduction – the catholic faith is necessary for salvation
- vv. 3–27: The doctrine of the Trinity
- v. 28: Transition: this faith in the Trinity is necessary for salvation
- vv. 29–37: The doctrine of the person of Christ
- vv. 38–41: Articles on Christ's saving work, similar to articles in a creed
- v. 42: Closing statement – this faith is necessary for salvation

In its structure, the Athanasian Creed is unlike classical baptismal or conciliar creeds (see *Apostles' Creed), but similar to a series of confessional statements promulgated by the Councils of Toledo between 400 and 700, and to other western formulations.

The authorship of St Athanasius was accepted in the west until the middle of the sixteenth century. Gerhard Jan Voss (1577–1649) proved definitively that Athanasius could not be the author. The Creed has since been attributed to eight or ten western Fathers including *Ambrose, *Vincent of Lérins and Caesarius of Arles, but its author remains unknown.

The date of the creed can be determined better. In 1940, José Madoz published the rediscovered *Excerpta* of Vincent of Lérins (who died before 450), and showed that part of the Christological section of the Creed is taken almost verbatim from the *Excerpta*. Madoz concluded that Vincent must be considered its most immediate precursor. In 1931, Germain Morin rediscovered a manuscript at Stuttgart that contained a selection of Caesarius of Arles's sermons. One of the sermons (*sermo* 3 [CCSL 103, 20–21]) was in fact the Athanasian Creed, lightly retouched to make it look like a homily. Caesarius was bishop from 502 to 542; hence the Creed was composed between c. 450 and 540. The place of origin is most likely southern Gaul, probably the island-monastery of Lérins.

In its Trinitarian section, the Athanasian Creed teaches that there are in God three Persons, which are not to be confused, and one substance, which is not to be divided. Each of the three Persons is uncreated, infinite, eternal, omnipotent, God and Lord; yet there are not three uncreateds, etc., but only one. The Father is neither made nor created nor begotten. The Son is from the Father, neither made nor created but begotten. The Holy Spirit is from the Father and the Son, neither made nor created nor begotten but proceeding.

While it avoids most technical theological terms, the Athanasian Creed teaches the unity of the Godhead and the reality and equality of the three Persons. The Persons differ by relations of origin. The opponents that the Creed envisages are Sabellians, who denied the real distinction of Persons, and *Arians, who divided the substance of the Godhead by making the Son a creature. The Trinitarian theology of the Creed is clearly *Augustine's; J.N.D. Kelly calls it 'traditional, almost scholasticized Augustinianism'. Specifically, the Athanasian Creed teaches the *filioque ('and from the Son'), the distinctly western doctrine of the procession of the Holy Spirit from the Father and the Son. The doctrine of the *filioque* has its roots in Augustine's theology. Between the ninth and eleventh centuries the word *filioque* was added to the *Niceno-Constantinopolitan Creed in the west, and the doctrine has been a point of division between eastern and western churches ever since.

In the Christological section of the

Athanasian Creed, Christ is confessed as equally God and man, God from the Father's substance, man from his mother's substance, perfect God and perfect man. One clause clearly opposes *Apollinaris of Laodicea's doctrine, namely: 'composed of a rational soul and human flesh'. The Athanasian Creed is probably also meant to oppose *Nestorianism, although it lacks the precise terms of the *Chalcedonian definition ('one person and one *hypostasis* existing in two natures'), as well as the key word *theotokos*, 'God-bearer', applied to Mary. A problematic clause reads: 'For just as a rational soul, and flesh, are one man, so God and man are one Christ'. This expression was popular with *Monophysites; but orthodox theologians, eastern and western, also used it.

References to the Athanasian Creed are infrequent before AD 800. From the Carolingian era onward, the Athanasian Creed is frequently attested, and its popularity continued unabated through the nineteenth century. It was translated into Greek in the fourteenth century, but the attitude of the eastern church to the Athanasian Creed has been ambiguous, especially because of the presence of the *filioque*.

The Creed has been used in the liturgy of the Anglican, Lutheran and Roman Catholic communions. In the Roman Breviary promulgated after the Council of Trent, it was used each Sunday at Prime. Use of the Creed was later reduced to certain Sundays only, then to Trinity Sunday only. Since the reform of 1970, it is no longer used. In other communions its use is also diminishing, perhaps because of the clauses of condemnation it contains.

JOSEPH T. LIENHARD, SJ

FURTHER READING: *Editions and studies:* A.E. Burn, *The Athanasian Creed and Its Early Commentaries* (Cambridge, 1896); C.H. Turner, 'A Critical Text of the Quicunque Vult', *J Th St* 11 (1910), pp. 401–11; A.E. Burn, *The Athanasian Creed* (London / New York, 1912); G. Morin, 'L'Origine du symbole d'Athanase: Témoignage inédit de s. Césaire d'Arles' *R Bén* 44 (1932), pp. 207–19; V. Laurent, 'Le symbole "Quicunque" et l'église byzantine', *Échos d'Orient* 35 (1936), pp. 385–404; José Madoz, *Excerpta Vincentii Lirenensis* (Madrid, 1940); J.N.D. Kelly, *The Athanasian Creed* (London, 1964); J.M. Pero-Sanz, *El símbolo atanasiano* (Madrid, 2nd edn, 1998).

Athanasius (c. 296–373)

Bishop of Alexandria, in Egypt (from 328). His episcopacy was set in a period when the imperial court's support was crucial for a theological party's supremacy, when early *Arian thinking was being formulated, and when incipient eastern monasticism, both solitary and communal, was gaining influence.

Athanasius's theology led to at least three main developments upon those of earlier Christian thinkers. Firstly, his soteriology demanded that the Son was very God, and so he looked for elaboration upon the Son's relation to the Father within the context of a monotheistic faith. Secondly, with Arius (c. 250–336), Athanasius was a leader in articulating clearly a doctrine of 'creation from nothing'. Previous thinkers had placed the fundamental ontological distinction between the spiritual, to which realm God and the human soul belonged, and the material, of which the human body was part. Athanasius's doctrine placed the fundamental ontological distinction between God the Creator and all creation, to which latter both the human soul and body now naturally belonged. Thirdly, Athanasius's asserting matter's goodness, though not unprecedented (cf. *Irenaeus, c. 130 – c. 200), was particularly significant at a time when emerging monasticism was increasingly questioning the religious propriety of involvement in the world.

Developments also occurred within Athanasius's thinking. Firstly, the term *homoousios* was used at Nicaea (325) to describe the Son's 'consubstantiality' with the Father. Yet, though Athanasius assumed such a consubstantiality in his debates with the Arians, early on he largely avoided the term. Only after 360 did he use it more fully, and then as much to preclude the introduction of other less suitable terminology as to stress his theology's identity with Nicaea's (see Athanasius's *Tome*). Secondly, for most of his life Athanasius was content to affirm, along with Nicaea, unqualified belief 'in the Holy Spirit'. Only in *ad Serapionem 1–4* did he explore that belief, affirming the Spirit's 'consubstantiality' with the Godhead. Thirdly, Arius certainly denied the Son's assumption of a human soul. It is not clear that Athanasius countered this denial in his earlier works. In the later *Tome* and *ad Epictetum* Athanasius may have asserted that the divine Logos did not assume a 'body without a soul'. Yet, even if he did, it is much debated as to whether he made theological use of that assertion, despite his being aware of the principle that 'that which is not assumed is not healed' (cf. Gregory Nazianzen, *Ep. 101 ad Cledonium*).

Athanasius strongly maintained that the Son was very God. This revealed truth he saw 'evidenced' in, for example: Christ's fulfilling the Old Testament Scriptures (see *Contra Gentes*); Christ's miracles, which highlighted Christ's being Lord of those material things which some worshipped (see *De Incarnatione*); and Christ's being Saviour – which no creature could be, for no creature, however sublime, is able to redeem humanity, fellow creatures. Later, with respect to the Spirit, Athanasius argued similarly: no creature, however holy, could be the source of sanctification; thus the Spirit must be God.

Having asserted both the Father and Son's divinity, Athanasius had to address the issue of God's oneness. Wishing to maintain the uniqueness of both Father and Son within the one Godhead, Athanasius replaced a traditional image used to describe the Father and Son's oneness, that of 'one light' shared by two torches, with that of 'light and radiance', the one not possible without the other. He extended the new image's implied mutuality, asserting that the 'Father' eternally suggested the 'Son', and the 'Son' the 'Father'. Athanasius made a further contribution here by distinguishing the Greek verbs 'to beget' and 'to become', allowing him to maintain that the Son is 'eternally begotten' of the Father, and only 'becomes', or 'comes into being' when he 'becomes' flesh on entering the material, temporal world of 'becoming' (see his treatment of Prov. 8:22; John 1:14, etc.).

Athanasius's God is therefore not the solitary one, but the one good being who 'envies none existence'. God's infinitely good, generous nature lies behind several themes. It lies behind Athanasius's understanding of the Genesis account of all being brought not just into existence but into a blessed, joyous existence. It further lies behind Athanasius's conviction that God did not allow fallen creation to slip vainly back to the non-existence whence it was created. Indeed, this generous God did not just forgive humanity its sin, which would have treated the sin but not its consequences, mortality and corruptibility. But God became human, that in his assumed humanity God might renew humanity in God's own image, might die the death owed by all and resurrect humanity to new and eternal life. So, having become

'humanity that humanity might be made divine' (*De Incarnatione* 54), God returned humanity not to the prelapsarian state from which it might fall again, but to a secure salvation in Christ. Lastly, God's illimitable goodness also lies behind God's self-revelation through the human soul, made 'in God's image'; creation's harmony; the Old Testament prophets' words; and most particularly, the Christ (see *De Incarnatione*). When humanity failed to recognize and know God through a more sublime creaturely instrument, God revealed himself in a more accessible manner, and always for humanity's sake.

ALVYN PETTERSEN

FURTHER READING: *Texts: Contra Gentes* and *De Incarnatione* (ed. R.W. Thomson; Oxford, 1971); A. Robinson, 'St Athanasius: Select Works and Letters', *NPNF²* (Grand Rapids, 1971); *The Letters of Saint Athanasius Concerning the Holy Spirit* (ed. C.R.B. Shapland; London, 1951). *Studies:* A. Pettersen, *Athanasius* (London, 1995); P. Widdicombe, *The Fatherhood of God from Origen to Athanasius* (Oxford, 1994); E.P. Meijering, *Orthodoxy and Platonism in Athanasius: Synthesis or Antithesis?* (Leiden, 1968); J. Roldanus, *Le Christ et l'Homme dans la Théologie d'Athanase d'Alexandrie* (SHCT 4; Leiden, 1968); R.P.C. Hanson, *The Search for the Christian Doctrine of God: The Arian Controversy 318–381* (Edinburgh, 1988).

Athenagoras of Athens (c. 177–80)

Little is known about Athenagoras of Athens, apart from the fact that he was well educated according to the standards of classical rhetoric. The only way that we can date his works is by internal evidence. The first of his two extant treatises is called *An Embassy on Behalf of the Christians*. It was addressed to the Emperors Marcus Aurelius (161–80) and his son Commodus (176–92), so that it has to be placed at some point during the four-year period when they were co-emperors. In this work, Athenagoras presents a calm and elegant refutation of the standard charges made against Christians – that they were atheists, cannibals and incestuous. Like other Christian writers of his time, Athenagoras asks the pagan rulers to judge Christians on their merits and not according to the rumours which circulated about them. He was sure that, if they did so, the Christians would be exonerated and allowed to practise their religion freely.

Athenagoras's second treatise, written shortly

after the first, is *On the Resurrection of the Dead*. It is philosophical in tone and approach and argues the case for resurrection on the basis of reason. The first ten chapters seek to demonstrate that the idea of resurrection is in line with the nature of God, and the last fifteen chapters discuss the subject in relation to human nature. Athenagoras argues that the human race was created for eternal life, and that the resurrection represents the necessary reunion of body and soul, which is broken by death. He goes on to say that the body must rise again in order to share in both the punishments and the rewards due to people on account of their earthly deeds, because it would be unjust to let the soul alone take either the praise or the blame for them. He argues in conclusion that happiness is the goal of human striving, but that as it cannot be attained in this life we must expect to achieve it after death. That can only happen, of course, if there is a resurrection in which to enjoy this happiness.

Like most of his Christian contemporaries, Athenagoras felt the need to defend the Christian doctrine of God against charges of both atheism and polytheism, and he was remarkably sophisticated in his theological statements. He tried to demonstrate the necessity of monotheism, using the idea of creation as his main argument (*Embassy*, 8), and he had no hesitation in claiming full divinity for the Logos, as Son of God (*Embassy*, 10). He avoided subordinationism by claiming that the Logos is the indwelling thought process of the divine mind (*Nous*) and is therefore co-eternal with, and inseparable from, the Father. In the same passage he also describes the Holy Spirit as a ray of divine light, similar to a ray of the sun, bringing the glory of God down to earth and then returning to heaven again. Athenagoras also believed in the divine inspiration of the Bible, which he describes as similar to a musician playing musical instruments, the latter of which he identifies with the apostles and prophets of old.

Athenagoras's views of matrimony are also of interest. He preferred the celibate life in principle, but was prepared to accept marriage, which he believed was intended almost exclusively for the procreation of children. That he was not against this shows that he was relatively uninfluenced by the ascetic and millenarian tendencies which were gaining ground during his lifetime.

GERALD BRAY

FURTHER READING: *Texts:* Migne, *PG* VI, pp. 889–1024; W.R. Schoedel, *Athenagoras:* Legatio *and* De resurrectione (Oxford, 1972); B. Pouderon, *Athénagore* (SC 379; Paris, 1992). English translation by B.P. Pratten in ANF II (1885), pp. 129–62. *Studies:* J.H. Crehan, *Athenagoras* (ACW 23; Westminster, MD, 1956); L.W. Barnard, *Athenagoras* (Paris, 1972); T.D. Barnes, 'The Embassy of Athenagoras', *J Th St* NS 26 (1975), pp. 111–14; R.M. Grant, *Greek Apologists of the Second Century* (London, 1988), pp. 100–11; L.A. Ruprecht, 'Athenagoras the Christian, Pausanius the Travel Guide and a Mysterious Corinthian Girl', *Harv Th R* 85 (1992), pp. 35–49; T.F. Torrance, '*Phusikos kai theologikos Logos*, St Paul and Athenagoras at Athens', *Scot J Th* 41 (1988), pp. 11–26.

Augustine of Hippo (354–430)

Augustine, bishop of Hippo, left a lasting theological legacy to the western churches, both Catholic and Protestant. Of mixed Roman and Berber descent, he was born in 354 in Thagaste, a small town in North Africa. The son of a devoutly Christian mother (Monica), he was brought up as a Christian but not baptized. He tells us that as a young man he considered Christianity intellectually unacceptable and, while pursuing studies in rhetoric in Carthage, he became a Manichean because Manicheism promised a faith consonant with reason. He maintained the status of 'auditor' for almost a decade, although he became gradually disillusioned with Manichean doctrines. After teaching rhetoric in Carthage and Rome, he was appointed to the imperial court in Milan. There *Ambrose, the bishop, and other Christians in that city brought him to a more sympathetic understanding of Christianity. After a study/retreat of several months at Cassiciacum he was baptized on Easter eve 387. A year or so later he returned to North Africa where his outstanding talent was soon recognized. He was ordained to the priesthood in 391 and was encouraged to preach while still a priest (a practice virtually unknown at that time). He became bishop of Hippo in 395, a position he retained until his death in 430.

Augustine's extant writings form the largest single corpus from the patristic age. His works have been widely translated and the secondary Augustinian literature is immense. His fame and stature sparked as well a considerable body of pseudepigraphy. About three hundred letters (some discovered only recently) and five hundred sermons survive. His more formal writings are almost all occasional, elicited by controversy or personal attacks. His most famous works, *The City of God* and *The Confessions*, were inspired, respectively, by controversy and personal attacks. One important exception (although not entirely free of polemic) is *On the Trinity*. His chief theological contributions came in his writings 1) against the Donatists, 2) against the Manicheans, 3) against the *Pelagians, 4) the *City of God* and 5) *On the Trinity*.

The Donatist controversy. Augustine grew up in and returned to a North Africa where the Donatist church surpassed the Catholic in both numbers and influence. The premise of Donatist ecclesiology was that the integrity of the sacraments, notably baptism and ordination, depended on the worth of the minister, 'worth' meaning not only moral probity, but a genealogy of ordination free from any taint of apostasy. On this latter count the Donatists saw the Catholic church to have been remiss since early in the fourth century, and they did not recognize its sacraments. Both churches claimed the authority of *Cyprian, and considerable bad feeling, even violence, had erupted between the two. On his return to North Africa, Augustine took up his pen for the Catholics. His arguments, repeated in all his anti-Donatist writings (most notably *On Baptism*), were basically simple. Taking his cue from Cyprian's treatise *On the Unity of the Catholic Church*, Augustine argued that Cyprian abhorred schism more than anything and would therefore not have sided with the Donatists. Second, and more importantly, Augustine insisted that the sacraments belong to Christ, and that it is he who baptizes. While the holiness of the minister is highly to be desired, his unworthiness can in no way invalidate Christ's sacraments. Consistent with this point, Augustine recognized the validity of the Donatists' sacraments, although he considered them not spiritually efficacious (because the Holy Spirit would not be present to a schismatic church). Donatists converting to Catholicism, were, therefore, not rebaptized (Augustine insisted that there was no such thing as *re*baptism), but the Holy Spirit was invoked upon them. It is because of Augustine's eventual success in this controversy that the major churches of the west hold the sacramental doctrine *ex opere operato*.

The Manichean controversy. Augustine's writings against the Manicheans were intended both to show the falsity of their teachings and, positively, to demonstrate that he no longer held those teachings, as some alleged. His defence of the goodness of creation and of the Old Testament patriarchs was important, but it was his explanation of the origin and universality of human sin which cast the longest shadow. Against the Manichean teaching that sin is involuntary and due to human embodiment, Augustine's earliest writings defend the traditional Christian teaching on the freedom of the human will (*On Free Will*, books 1 and 2). From 396 on, however, his understanding of human freedom, of God's salvific will, and of God's dealing with humankind changed. (The occasion for the change may have been a challenge from the Manicheans to explain why God had chosen Jacob, but not Esau.) Beginning with the second part of his reply *To Simplicianum*, Augustine taught that, while God gives grace to all, the human will is so vitiated by Adam's sin that humankind is incapable, without divine compulsion, of accepting that grace and turning to God. It is only those God wishes to save who are given that compelling or irresistible grace, *gratia congruens*. Those not predestined to be saved will inevitably refuse the less forceful grace given them. Augustine's conviction that the human will is totally vitiated was based on his belief that humankind inherits not only the *results* of Adam's sin (as traditionally taught) but Adam's *guilt* as well. The exegetical basis of this conviction was a misreading of the *eph hō pantes hēmarton* of Romans 5:12 as 'in whom all sinned' rather than 'in that all sinned' (RSV). It is probable that other factors as well contributed to his increasingly pessimistic outlook. Even western churches which have not accepted Augustine's teaching of double predestination (it was rejected as early as 529 at the Second Council of Orange) have not totally escaped his bleak understanding of Christian anthropology.

The Pelagian controversy. This controversy, which lasted from 411 to the end of Augustine's life, had its roots in the shift in his thinking of the mid-390s. It started when Pelagius and his more vociferous follower, Coelestius, passed through North Africa on their way to Palestine from Rome, and were cited as saying that infant baptism was not necessary to remove the guilt of original sin. Pelagius was not denying the worth of infant baptism, but he was viewing it (in a way many twentieth-century Christians do) as the sacrament of initiation. Infants, in his eyes, do not need the forgiveness of sin because sin requires free will, which they do not have. From here the controversy grew. Augustine distinguished between 'freedom of choice' and 'freedom of will'. The former humankind does not have because, operating from its fallen nature, it can choose only evil. Only the will which has received irresistible grace is truly free and capable of willing the good. Augustine charged Pelagius with not appreciating the seriousness of sin; Pelagius replied that Augustine was playing down the salvific consequences of Christ's death. Pelagius's theology approached what would today be called 'creationism'. He did not at all deny grace (as Augustine charged), but saw it in the sacraments, in the teachings of Christ, in many of the external as well as the interior gifts of God. For Augustine, grace was completely hidden and mysterious, totally interior. The controversy lasted until the end of Augustine's life, and beyond into 'semi-Pelagianism'.

The City of God *(413–26)*. Pelagius was only one of thousands who fled Rome when it fell to the Goths in 411, and many came to North Africa. Reaction to the Eusebian euphoria over a Christian emperor of the previous century was strong: did the highly symbolic fall of the city (the empire dragged on until 476) entail the fall of the church? Augustine's reply was the working out of the theme of the two cities – that of God and that of humankind – and the contention that in all things spiritual the church is independent of, even indifferent to, the human city. The two cities, identified by the objects of their loves, would continue their parallel courses throughout history. It is a misinterpretation to think that Augustine identified the city of God with the church; he clearly did not. The true citizens of the city of God would be identified only at the eschaton. *The City of God* was a milestone in the church's relations with secular powers and was much read in the Middle Ages.

Trinitarian theology. Augustine's deepest and most consistent theological thought is found in his treatise *On the Trinity* (399 – early 420s). The Arian crisis had been officially resolved in 381, but *Arianism was far from dead, especially in the west, and no satisfactory answer,

particularly with reference to the Holy Spirit, had been offered to the question of the distinction of the Trinitarian 'persons' (Augustine was clear that the word 'person' is a label which tells us nothing of the nature of the Three). It was evident that neither divine attributes nor activities could be the answer if monotheism was to be maintained. Augustine built on the writings of the fourth century, particularly those of Gregory Nazianzen, to propose the divine relationships as the distinguishing force. True to his Plotinian background (see the *Soliloquies*, the earliest of his extant writings), Augustine turns inward to find the divine. '[I]f man is made in God's image ... perhaps we can attain the inwardness of God indirectly, through entry into the inwardness of man' (Hill, p. 52). In this vein Augustine presents three mental trinities – 1) mind, knowledge of self, love of self; (2) memory of self, thinking of self, willing self; (3) memory of God, understanding of God, willing God – as analogies revelatory of the divine Trinity. Yet, he writes in the epilogue: 'This same [divine] light has shown you [my soul] those three things in yourself, in which you can recognize yourself as the image of that supreme Trinity on which you are not yet capable of fixing your eyes in contemplation' (XV. 50; trans. Hill).

JOANNE McWILLIAM

FURTHER READING *(English only)*: W. Babcock, 'Augustine's Interpretation of Romans (A.D. 394–396)', *Aug Stud* 10 (1979), pp. 55–74; G. Bonner, 'Augustine as Biblical Scholar', in *Cambridge History of the Bible* (ed. P.R. Ackroyd and C.F. Evans; Cambridge, 1970), pp. 541–63; Peter Brown, *Saint Augustine of Hippo* (London, 1967); J. Patout Burns, *The Development of Augustine's Doctrine of Operative Grace* (Paris, 1980); J. Kevin Coyle, 'Augustine and Apocalyptic: Thoughts on the Fall of Rome, the Book of Revelation, and the End of the World', *Florilegium* 19 (1987), pp. 1–34; M. Djuth, 'Stoicism and Augustine's Doctrine of Human Freedom after 396', in J.C. Schnaubelt and F. Van Fleteren, *Collectanea Augustiniana* (New York, 1990), pp. 387–402; Edmund Hill, OP, *Saint Augustine: The Trinity* (Brooklyn, NY, 1991); C. Kirwan, *Augustine against the Skeptics: The Skeptical Tradition* (Berkeley, 1983); J. McWilliam, 'Augustine's Developing Understanding of the Cross', *Aug Stud* 17 (1986), pp. 15–33; R.A. Markus, *Conversion and Disenchantment in Augustine's Spiritual Career* (Saint Augustine Lecture, 1984; Villanova, 1989); M. Miles, *Augustine on the Body* (Missoula, MT, 1979); Robert J. O'Connell, *Augustine's Confessions: The Odyssey of Soul* (Cambridge, MA, 1969); *Saint Augustine's Platonism* (Villanova, 1984); J.J. O'Meara, 'The

Historicity of the Early Dialogues of Saint Augustine', *Vig Chr* 5 (1951), pp. 150–78; *The Young Augustine: An Introduction to the Confessions* (London, 1965); J. van Oort, *Jerusalem and Babylon: A Study into Augustine's 'City of God' and the Sources of his Doctrine of the Two Cities* (Leiden, 1991); B. Stock, *Augustine: The Reader* (Cambridge, MA, 1996).

Baillie, Donald Macpherson (1887–1954)

Donald Baillie was the son of a minister of the Free Church of Scotland who died when Donald was only three years old. His elder brother was the theologian *John Baillie. Donald was brought up by his mother in an atmosphere of Calvinistic piety and attended school in Inverness. He studied philosophy at the University of Edinburgh and theology at New College, Edinburgh. He also studied in Marburg, under *W. Herrmann (1846–1922) and A. Jülicher (1857–1938), and in Heidelberg under *E. Troeltsch (1865–1923) and J. Weiss (1863–1914). Baillie was licensed as a minister of the United Free Church of Scotland (later the Church of Scotland) and for 15 years was a parish minister. A life-long martyr to asthma, ill health forced him to abandon service with the YMCA in France during World War I. In 1934 he became professor of systematic theology at St Mary's College in the University of St Andrews, where he remained until his death in 1954.

Baillie belonged to the liberal evangelical tradition of his church. He shared the commitment of many scholars of his day to both literary and historical criticism, and also their respect for natural science and the fashionable disciplines of psychology and anthropology. In his thinking, teaching and, not least, preaching, he strove to expound Christian doctrine in a way which while respecting traditional formulations took account of the requirements of modern thought. Subject to bouts of severe depression himself, his sympathy for the doubts and religious difficulties of others gave a sensitive and attractive tone to his teaching. He was also a leading figure in Britain in the ecumenical movement.

In *Faith in God and its Christian Consummation* (1927) Baillie attempted to provide an apologetic for faith in the existence of God based on human moral commitment. Although this particular attempt is now generally thought to have been declared a failure by both philosophy and theology, Baillie's presentation does contain much that was original both on the dangers of the then prevailing Christocentrism and what he saw as docetic tendencies which obscured, or even denied, the humanity of Christ.

It is, however, his second book on which Baillie's reputation rests. *God Was in Christ: An Essay on Incarnation and Atonement* (1948) was much praised. According to *Rudolf Bultmann

it was 'the most significant book of our time in the theme of Christology'. What Bultmann appreciated was the manner in which Baillie engaged with traditions other than his own as well as with modern thought.

In his Christology, Baillie was entirely orthodox in insisting on the full humanity and deity of Christ. In expounding the humanity of Christ, he took issue with extreme historical scepticism and lack of interest in the Jesus of history exhibited by much contemporary theology. In particular, he took issue with *Karl Barth, suggesting that because of its total repudiation of all claims to know something of Jesus as a particular historical figure, the school of Karl Barth 'does not take the Incarnation quite seriously'.

As regards the deity of Christ, Baillie was at pains to assert this, although he criticized certain features of Christology then prominent. In particular, Baillie resisted attempts to expound the meaning of the incarnation on the basis of *anhypostasia* (i.e. the old conception that in Christ there was no distinct human personality but rather divine personality assuming human nature), and theories of *kenosis* (i.e. the divine Logos laid aside – 'emptied himself of' – his distinctively divine attributes and lived for a period on earth within the limitations of humanity).

Baillie found the clue to the understanding of incarnation in the concept of paradox – 'a self-contradictory statement' – unavoidable since God cannot be comprehended in any human words or categories of finite thought. Finding paradoxical elements in the doctrines of creation and providence, Baillie approached the central paradox (God incarnate in a particular human life) by way of Christian experience – the paradox of grace.

This is the experience enunciated by St Paul and loudly echoed in the history of Christian thought: 'By the grace of God I am what I am: and his grace which was bestowed upon me was not found in vain; but I laboured more abundantly than they all: yet not I but the grace of God which was with me' (1 Cor. 15:10). The Christian's actions are personal and responsible actions, yet the Christian experience is that God lives and acts in them: whatever good there is in life is 'all of God'.

It is this paradox of grace in its fragmentary form in Christian life which is a reflection of the union of God and man in the incarnation: the life of Jesus, which, being the perfection of humanity, is also the very life of God himself. Further, it is not only the clue to understanding the incarnation, but it can also be elaborated to throw light on the doctrine of the Trinity and on the meaning and necessity of atonement (using the 'faint analogy' of the generous yet painful forgiveness of a true friend for a grave wrong suffered).

Despite criticism – for example that the nature of the concept of paradox is not sufficiently explored, or that attempting to proceed from human experience to God is a dangerously false method (Barth) – Baillie's achievement can best be measured by the fact that there are very few subsequent works of Christology in the twentieth century which do not refer to his contribution.

D.W.D. SHAW

FURTHER READING: *Texts: Faith in God and its Christian Consummation* (Edinburgh, 1927); *God Was in Christ: An Essay on Incarnation and Atonement* (New York, 1948); *To Whom Shall We Go?* (New York, 1955); *The Theology of the Sacraments* (New York, 1957); *Out of Nazareth* (Edinburgh, 1958). *Studies:* D.W.D. Shaw (ed.), *In Divers Manners* (St Andrews, 1990); David Fergusson (ed.), *Christ, Church and Society: Essays on John and Donald Baillie* (Edinburgh, 1993).

Baillie, John (1886–1960)

John and *Donald Baillie were among the most significant Scottish theologians of the twentieth century, and indeed since *John McLeod Campbell. In the Baillies, the Scots theological tradition reached a peak and a maturity which it urgently needs to recover.

John Baillie was born in the Free Church of Scotland manse of Gairloch in 1886. Though John later recalled 'a rigorously Calvinistic upbringing' (mainly by their mother who was very soon widowed), there were also astonishingly liberal strands in nineteenth-century Free Church culture and a huge respect for learning, which drove the two brothers through brilliant academic careers in school at Inverness and university at Edinburgh. Both graduated with Firsts in philosophy, distinction in divinity and won every possible prize, medal and fellowship. They both became assistants in the philosophy department and spent some time in the YMCA in France during the First World War. Both wrote copious poetry and delighted in literary

circles of the sort that were fairly standard in the pre-war period.

There their paths diverged. John married in 1919 and immediately went off to Auburn Theological Seminary in New York state, being ordained in the Presbyterian church there in 1920. There followed six years of intensive teaching and research in theology, culminating in *The Roots of Religion in the Human Soul* and a large-scale work on *The Interpretation of Religion*, completed in 1925 but not published till 1929.

These books reflect an extraordinarily wide cultural and theological experience: the Calvinist manse; the strikingly liberal tradition of arts and divinity in Edinburgh before the war; the impact of four years with the YMCA in France; immersion in American culture – its poetry and politics; the polarization of church politics in the fundamentalism debate; and participation in conferences on the social gospel in New York in the early 1920s, long before such issues came to centre stage in church circles elsewhere.

John moved to Toronto in 1927, partly perhaps to be near the support of old friends from Scotland (his wife was in sanatoria with tuberculosis from 1923–30, and looking after their only son was not an easy task), partly because of the challenge of a new ecumenical college in the new United Church of Canada. Gospel and culture, social issues and ecumenical concern were to be the focal points of much of his later work. His return to America from Canada in 1930, to the Roosevelt Chair at Union Theological Seminary in New York, then arguably 'the world's greatest theological seminary', provided a forum for theology from which, along with Henry Sloane Coffin, Reinhold Niebuhr and Pitney Van Dusen, he was to have a major impact on western theology for the next two decades. In fact John moved to Edinburgh in 1934. But the transatlantic links remained very strong, and through visits and letters the group exerted huge influence on the new World Council of Churches, along with their friend bishop Henry Sherrill and others.

Baillie, Coffin, Niebuhr and Van Dusen differed in emphasis in several ways. But they agreed on a *via media* between extreme liberalism on the one hand, which they regarded as a dilution of the gospel, and a narrow *Barthianism on the other, which they regarded as an overreaction to an overreaction.

The overarching theme of the presence of God to faith was central to John Baillie's next three books, *And the Life Everlasting* (1933), *Our Knowledge of God* (1939) and *Invitation to Pilgrimage* (1942). The emphasis on spirituality and a combination of honest self-examination with concentration on God's reconciling grace was manifested in *A Diary of Private Prayer*, which sold (and still sells) tens of thousands of copies.

The next step, centred in John's year as Moderator of the General Assembly of the Church of Scotland in 1943, was the report of the Baillie Commission on *God's Will in Our Time*, which combined critique of the Nazis with a programme for social reconstruction after the war – a programme echoed in the Beveridge Reports. The subject matter of the report echoed visits to Germany in the 1930s and conversations with both sides in the German Church struggle, numerous Church of England and ecumenical gatherings, not to mention the Moot, an influential forum which met in Oxford in the late 1930s and early 1940s.

There is room here for only brief illustration from John Baillie's writings. In his last book, the Gifford Lectures published as *The Sense of the Presence of God*, we find a characteristic combination of appeal to experience together with an exploration of rational grounds for belief in God.

Chapter 1, 'Knowledge and Certitude', deals with some of the most basic problems in the philosophy of religion. Knowledge seems to imply certitude but often does not go beyond probabilities. The concept of faith always contains both the idea of knowing and the idea of not knowing fully. 'No Christian, then, can say that he knows nothing' (p. 5). But equally, 'all human thinking is defectible' (p. 6). There are indeed certainties – in the natural sciences, in moral and especially in our religious convictions. A distinction is drawn between knowledge of truth and knowledge of reality. Our knowledge of the realities is primary, and our knowledge of truths concerning them secondary. 'Gratitude is not only the dominant note of Christian piety but equally the dominant motive of Christian action in the world' (p. 236). This is *imitatio Christi*. We should also recognize vestigial forms of gratitude in those who are not explicitly Christian. The last chapter, 'Retrospect', reconsiders the argument. Analysis and clarity in linguistic analysis is not sufficient. But neither is Barthian exclusivism. Faith is trust. Propositions are necessary but not sufficient. We have to do with 'a God whose living and active presence among us can be perceived by faith in a large variety of human contexts and situations'. Baillie ends characteristically with Vaughan's prayer, 'Abide with us, O most blessed and merciful saviour, for it is towards evening and the day is far spent ...'

What, if anything, may be learned from John Baillie for the future? Both John and Donald were concerned to do theology in context, and to look to the future. Their work would appear to point to a theology and a church that remain both resolutely liberal and resolutely evangelical. This would mean resistance to an easy assimilation with the prevailing culture, in the name of the vulnerable Christ who is the judge of that exploitation and domination so common both in state and in church. It would also mean resistance to a complacent retreat to the calm of paradise the blessed, in a church and theological framework in which all answers are known in advance, and all nonconformists excluded.

GEORGE NEWLANDS

FURTHER READING: *Texts: The Roots of Religion in the Human Soul* (London, 1926); *The Interpretation of Religion* (Edinburgh, 1929); *And the Life Everlasting* (London, 1933); *Our Knowledge of God* (London, 1939); *Invitation to Pilgrimage* (London, 1942); *A Diary of Private Prayer* (London, 1936); *The Sense of the Presence of God* (London, 1962). *Study:* David Fergusson (ed.), *Christ, Church and Society: Essays on John Baillie and Donald Baillie* (Edinburgh, 1993).

Balthasar, Hans Urs von (1905–88)

Swiss Roman Catholic theologian. Balthasar was born into an upper-middle-class family in Lucerne. An extraordinary knowledge of European literature, philosophy and music pervades his theology and stems from university studies in German literature and philosophy at Vienna, Berlin and Zurich. His doctorate (1929) was an ambitious study of the eschatological idea in nineteenth- and early twentieth-century German thought, eventually published as *Die Apokalypse der deutschen Seele* (1937–39). In 1929 Balthasar entered the South German Province of the *Jesuits and continued his studies at Pullach (near Munich) and Fourvière (near Lyons). During this time two of his major intellectual relationships had their beginnings – with *Erich Przywara (1899–1972) and *Henri de Lubac (1896–1991). De Lubac awoke Balthasar to the rich exegetical and theological imagination of the patristic church, and this sustained him in the face of the 'dry' neo-scholastic pedagogy of much of his training. Balthasar actually went on to write monographs on *Origen (published as *Parole et mystère chez Origène* [1957; 2nd edn, 1998]), *Maximus the Confessor (*Kosmische Liturgie* [1941; 2nd edn, 1961]), and Gregory of Nyssa (*Présence et Pensée* [1942]) and to translate the Fathers into German. Przywara's work on *analogia entis* – and his development of the Fourth Lateran Council's definition of analogy (1215) – was crucial to the way that Balthasar began to envisage the internal structure of Catholic thought and its comprehensive interest in the activity of the human spirit (always oriented towards transcendence).

After his ordination in 1936 Balthasar was assigned to the staff of *Stimmen der Zeit*, the Jesuit monthly in Munich, before returning to his native Switzerland in 1940 as university chaplain at Basle. Here he formed two more key relationships. One was with the medical doctor Adrienne von Speyr, who converted to Roman Catholicism under Balthasar's direction and who was the recipient of a series of mystical graces which greatly influenced his theology. Balthasar devoted much of his life thereafter to editing her work (written and dictated) and promoting her vision. The other friendship was with *Karl Barth (1886–1968), an authoritative study of whose work he published in 1951 (ET 1992), and with whom he shared an overwhelming sense of the free and dramatic character of God's self-revelation (though Balthasar placed greater emphasis than Barth on the relative autonomy of the creature in relation to God). Under von Speyr's inspiration, Balthasar set up a secular institute (the Community of St John) whose members took vows but lived and worked 'in the world'. His commitment to this joint mission with von Speyr led to his departure from the Jesuits in 1950. At about this time Balthasar set up his own publishing house, initially to publish von Speyr's work. He was not invited to *Vatican II.

In the wake of Vatican II Balthasar moved from a firm alignment with the so-called progressive theologians of the *nouvelle théologie*, and an advocacy of the *aggiornamento* ('bringing up to date') in Catholic theology, towards a distrust of certain theological trends justified in Vatican II's name. He founded a rival periodical – *Communio* – to the post-conciliar liberal journal *Concilium*. Balthasar was nominated a cardinal in May 1988, just before his death.

Balthasar's corpus of works is vast, and ranges from short devotional pieces and essays (including *Skizzen zur Theologie*, I–IV [1960–74; ET *Explorations in Theology*, 1993]), to his great theological trilogy in multiple volumes (*Herrlichkeit: Eine theologische ästhetik* [1961–69; ET *The Glory of the Lord*, 1982–91], *Theodramatik* [1973–83; ET *Theo-Drama*, 1988–] and *Theologik* [1985]). In addition, Balthasar translated and wrote about the works of contemporary theologians (such as de Lubac [1976]) and playwrights, novelists and poets in the Catholic tradition (notably P.L.C. Claudel, Reinhold Schneider [1953] and Georges Bernanos [1954]). Balthasar also wrote biography (*Thérèse von Lisieux* [1950; ET 1953] and *Elisabeth of Dijon* [1952; ET 1956]), a meditation on the Paschal *triduum* (in *Mysterium Salutis* [ed. J. Feiner and M. Lëhrer; III/2; 1969; ET *Mysterium Paschale*, 1990]) and an important book on prayer (*Das betrachtendes Gebet* [1955; ET 1961]).

In his great theological trilogy, Balthasar interprets all of Christian theology's traditional themes through a sustained re-appropriation of the 'transcendentals': beauty, goodness and truth. Balthasar was frustrated by the abstraction of much modern philosophical thought, by its inattention to the revelatory power of the particular in its concern to find clear and precise ideas with a universal application. He believed that the proper way for a seeker of truth to dispose himself towards the object in which truth is sought – and find its real and God-given 'form' – was contemplatively and prayerfully, in an active receptivity. (As a consequence, Balthasar did not regard the historical-critical approach to biblical exegesis as an unalloyed good.) We do not command or compel reality, thereby 'gaining' our knowledge; rather, it 'gives itself' to us and enables our involvement with it. The discovery of truth is consequent upon such reception and participation. The three parts of the trilogy are ordered as they are precisely because Balthasar sees the true exercise of reason as consequent upon both an encounter with beauty (supremely, the glory of God in the concrete and yet universal form of Christ) and upon consent to receive a part in God's work (a 'mission', in the course of which one discovers one's identity and is drawn more deeply into the Marian heart of the church).

Balthasar believed that all creaturely freedom, culture and creativity were capable of being brought into the service of the divine revelation

– although all had first to be challenged, broken and recast by their relation to the form of Christ. God is 'always greater' than the shapes of our understanding. Przywara's work on analogy helped him to formulate this conviction.

While criticizing a 'narrowness' in the way Barth developed the implications of his Christology, Balthasar agreed with Barth on the central importance of the person of Christ for theology, in the context of a thoroughgoing Trinitarianism. The mutual self-giving of the Trinitarian Persons (graphically illustrated by Balthasar in his meditations on Christ's descent into hell) is what informs his characteristic understanding of true freedom as kenotic and 'self-emptying' (the main principle of his metaphysics). Christ in corpse-like obedience takes on the deadness and god-forsakenness of humanity. But, unlike *Moltmann, Balthasar places the accent less on Christ's human suffering and more on the unified Trinitarian working out of God's plan of love.

Balthasar is a strong advocate not only of the 'subjective' holiness of the church, but of the 'objective' holiness of her structures and offices. He maintains an *Ignatian emphasis on the importance of obedience in the Christian life – often backed up (controversially) by an analogy with the properly 'feminine' submissiveness of the creature over against God.

BEN QUASH

FURTHER READING: A comprehensive bibliography of Balthasar's works is *Hans Urs von Balthasar: Bibliographie 1925–1990* (ed. C. Capol; Freiburg, 1990). Good secondary works include J. Riches (ed.), *The Analogy of Beauty* (Edinburgh, 1986); G. O'Hanlon, *The Immutability of God in the Theology of Hans Urs von Balthasar* (Cambridge, 1990); J. O'Donnell, *Hans Urs von Balthasar* (London, 1992). See also A. Nichols' companion to Balthasar's trilogy, *The Word Has Been Abroad* (Washington, DC, 1998); and *New Blackfriars* 79.923 (1998), which is devoted to Balthasar's work.

Barlaam of Calabria (c. 1290–1348)

Greek scholar and philosopher who was educated in Italy and who settled in Constantinople in 1330 where he established himself as an authority on the writings of Pseudo-Dionysius. In 1339 the Byzantines entrusted him with a mission to Pope Benedict XII at Avignon to promote ecclesiastical union. He published works rejecting *Thomist Scholasticism and the *filioque, but although his anti-Latin stance endeared him to many Greeks, his wholesale embrace of apophatic theology was denounced by *Gregory Palamas. Palamas attacked him for his apophatic agnosticism, a kind of 'because we cannot know, we cannot say' position, which left no room for revelation and the incarnation. Barlaam went on to ridicule the hesychast monks for their apparent simplistic understanding of their experience of the uncreated light. In view of the prayer posture adopted by the hesychasts of putting their heads between their knees, he referred to them by the derogatory title of *omphalopsychoi* (those-with-their-souls-in-their-navels), equivalent to the modern expression 'navel-gazing'.

Barlaam and Palamas met on several occasions in Thessaloniki where they engaged in debate over the nature of the divine light and the status of pagan philosophy. The second of Palamas's famous *Triads in Defence of the Holy Hesychasts* is a refutation of a series of three works by Barlaam entitled *On the Acquisition of Wisdom*, *On Prayer* and *On the Light of Knowledge*. The third of Palamas's *Triads* is a refutation of another work by Barlaam entitled *Against the Messalians*. Barlaam's criticism of the hesychasts and his accusation of heresy earned him a rebuke by two synods meeting in Constantinople in 1341 which endorsed Palamite theology. He returned to Avignon shortly afterwards believing that he represented the true tradition of Byzantine thought. In France he converted to Catholicism and at one point he gave Greek lessons to the poet Petrarch.

If for nothing else Barlaam deserves to be remembered for the opportunity he gave Gregory Palamas to define and refine Byzantine mystical theology. It was as a result of the Palamite victory that hesychast spirituality spread to the rest of the Orthodox world, notably in Bulgaria where it was promoted by Theodosius of Turnovo and in Russia by Sergius of Radonezh.

KEN PARRY

FURTHER READING: J. Meyendorff (ed.), *Gregory Palamas: The Triads* (New York, 1983); J. Meyendorff, *Byzantine Hesychasm: Historical, Theological and Social Problems* (London, 1974); *St Gregory Palamas and Orthodox Spirituality* (New York, 1974); *A Study of Gregory Palamas* (London, 1964); G. Podskalsky, *Theologie und Philosophie in Byzanz* (Munich, 1977).

Barmen Declaration (1934)

Adolf Hitler came to power in Germany in January 1933. The principle he used in the political sphere, the *Führerprinzip* (leadership principle) maintained that one person have unified control over the State's political apparatus. Some of the leaders of the German Evangelical Church attempted to establish this *Führerprinzip* in the church. A large number of these leaders belonged to the so-called German Christians who attempted to fuse Nazi ideology with Protestant theology. There were two main goals for this program. Firstly, as the German church was organized independently in each German state, it had to be organized into one single *Reichskirche* (Reich church). Secondly, one person had to assume the leadership of the church – a *Reichsbischof* (Reich bishop). All of the clergy in the German Evangelical Church would be responsible to this bishop who would, in turn, be responsible to the German chancellor – Adolf Hitler. Thus the church would be closely bound together with the Third Reich.

Shortly after Hitler came to power, this Reich church was founded. The constitution of the German Evangelical Church was ratified on 11 July 1933. It maintained a separation of church and state, which required that the relationship between them be determined at a later date by treaty. In September 1933, Ludwig Müller was elected Reich bishop. By all accounts he was remarkably incompetent and was manipulated by those working in the background. The German Christians attempted to force all of the regional churches into the Reich church under the Reich bishop.

In response to these events, leaders of the Confessing Church (including churches from the *Lutheran, *Reformed and Unified traditions) called for a synod meeting from 29–31 May 1934 in Barmen, part of Wuppertal, a city in the German state of North-Rhein Westphalia. In preparation for this event a theological committee, consisting of *Karl Barth, Hans Asmussen and Thomas Breit, agreed to meet on 15 and 16 May in Frankfurt-on-Main to draft a theological declaration for the synod. This draft (which was to a large extent written by Barth) went through several revisions before the synod met. The meeting in Barmen was chaired by Kurt Koch and attended by 139 voting delegates (86 theologians and 53 laypersons – among whom there was only one woman delegate). Hans Asmussen led the discussion of the

declaration. There were two major concerns about the declaration: one was that it not be viewed as a step towards unifying the Lutheran and Reformed churches, and the other was that it failed to address certain issues raised by the German Christians, such as the aspirations of the *Volk*. Nonetheless, after two days the 'Theological Declaration of Barmen' was unanimously accepted.

The 'Declaration' consists of an introduction, six theses and a conclusion. It is important to note that, unlike other confessions, such as Luther's Small Catechism or the Heidelberg Catechism, Barmen does not attempt to summarize the whole of the Christian faith. It rather deals with issues raised by the particular situation in the German church following Hitler's rise to power. Each of the theses begins with New Testament references, followed by a positive statement of the text's meaning and, finally, a *damnatio* repudiating false teachings. The theses tend to be referred in literature by Roman numerals (e.g. Barmen I or Barmen III).

The introduction to the declaration begins by basing the synod's meeting in Barmen on the constitution of the German Evangelical Church dated 11 July 1933; especially Article I which states that the church is founded on the gospel of Jesus Christ as revealed in Holy Scripture and which came again to light in the creeds of the Reformation, and Article II which states that the German Evangelical Church consists of territorial churches. These two points were held to have been violated by the actions and teachings of the German Christians. Therefore, the leaders from the various confessions at Barmen felt they had to speak.

The first thesis states the epistemology, which informs the whole declaration and must be the basis of any church – Jesus Christ as attested in Holy Scripture is the one Word of God. There can therefore be no other source for the church's preaching and teaching. This thesis provides the foundation for the declaration as a whole, the remaining theses being concerned to expound its meaning in the current crisis. Thus, Barmen II states that Jesus Christ is Lord of the whole of our lives, with no area excluded. Barmen III and IV deal with ecclesiological issues, unfolding the claim that the church's external form is based on its confession and cannot be separated from it. Barmen III states that the church is the fellowship of those who accept Jesus as Lord, that all that this fellowship does is based on Jesus' lordship, and that therefore her task and witness cannot change due to any political or ideological change. Barmen IV carries this further, explicitly rejecting the *Führerprinzip* as in any way appropriate to the sort of authority recognized or practised within the church. Barmen V argues that, while the State is divinely ordered, its authority does not extend over all areas of human existence, but nor should the church attempt to usurp the State's role. Barmen VI argues that the church's primary purpose is to extend the message about God's free grace to all people, and this purpose can not be made subservient to any human goal.

For the most part, the German Christians ignored Barmen. The most significant opposition to the declaration came from the Lutherans who opposed the German Christian takeover but were not part of the Confessing Church. Werner Elert argued this position most notably in the *Ansbacher Ratschlag* (Ansbach Advice). He maintained that Barmen rejected the essential Lutheran teaching of the two kingdoms: one kingdom, the church, governed by God's grace; the other, the State, governed by God's law. Therefore, he concluded, Barmen is heretical. *Paul Althaus, another prominent Lutheran theologian, also signed the *Ansbacher Ratschlag*.

Since the war, the 'Theological Declaration of Barmen' has been incorporated into various churches to varying degrees. The Evangelical Church in Germany, which is made up of Lutheran, Reformed and Unified (Lutheran and Reformed) congregations, was established in 1945 to replace the German Evangelical Church and had its first synod meeting in 1949. Although they have not adopted the Barmen Declaration in the preamble of their constitution, which would give it confessional status, it is included in the first article. The United Presbyterian Church in the United States of America (now the Presbyterian Church in the USA) adopted the Barmen Declaration into its book of confessions in May 1967. The declaration has also been important to many churches dealing with an unjust government.

DAVID E. ROBERTS

FURTHER READING: Eberhard Jüngel, *Christ, Justice and Peace: Toward a Theology of the State* (Edinburgh, 1992). This book offers a critical theological analysis of the 'Barmen Theological Declaration', and contains a translation of the text of the declaration by Douglas S. Bax.

Barth, Karl (1886–1968)

Swiss Reformed theologian. Barth was born on 10 May 1886 in Basle. His parents were Johann Friedrich ('Fritz') Barth, a pastor and professor, and Ana Katharina, née Sartorius. Both of Barth's grandfathers were pastors in Basle. On the eve of his confirmation in 1902, Barth resolved to become a theologian so that he could gain 'a proper understanding of the creed in place of the rather hazy ideas that I had at that time' (Busch, *Karl Barth*, p. 31). The first book that really interested him was *Kant's Critique of Practical Reason* and later the *Critique of Pure Reason*. At Berlin, Barth studied with *Adolf von Harnack, was influenced by *Schleiermacher and became a committed pupil and follower of *Wilhelm Herrmann (1846–1922). Upon reading Herrmann's *Ethics*, Barth's 'own personal interest in theology began' (Busch, *Karl Barth*, p. 41). After studying at Tübingen, Barth went to Marburg in 1908 to study with Herrmann. Ordained in 1908, Barth became pastor of a German-speaking congregation in Geneva in 1909, where his sixteen-page sermons illustrated his markedly liberal theology. Barth took his Christocentric impulse from Herrmann. Accordingly, legitimate apologetics and a true understanding of humanity cannot:

> … start from the believing man but from Jesus Christ as the object and foundation of faith … as the one and only man ready for God, Jesus Christ has not only lived, died and risen for us once in time, so that the abounding grace of God might be an event and at the same time revelation among us, but that as this same One He stands before His Father now in eternity for us, and lives for us in God himself as the Son of God He was and is and will be … Jesus Christ Himself sees to it that in Him and by Him we are not outside but inside. (*CD* II, 1, p. 156)

Anthropology is thus irreversibly grounded in Christology. This is the hallmark of Barth's theology.

The main events of Barth's life which influenced his theology were his years as pastor at Safenwil (1911–21); the First World War; his involvement in politics; and his years as professor of theology at Göttingen, Münster, Bonn until 1935, when the Nazis forced him out, and finally at Basle until he retired in 1962. That year he made a seven-week trip to the United States and spoke in Princeton, Chicago and New York. On a first visit to Britain in 1930 Barth was initially astonished by the *Pelagian thinking he encountered; but by 1938 he had become so fond of the British that he said: 'If I were not Swiss, I would like best to be British' (Busch, *Karl Barth*, p. 287).

In Safenwil Barth became involved in politics, and in the struggle to preach to his congregation he concluded that the old liberal theology was not working. His views changed radically in 1914, when 93 German intellectuals issued a manifesto supporting the war policy of Kaiser Wilhelm II and the Chancellor. Almost all his German teachers were among the signatories. Their ethical lapse indicated to Barth a basic failure in exegesis. He soon developed a general attack on nineteenth-century theology, Schleiermacher included. Although Barth criticized the Social Democrat Party for its failures, he joined the party and became known as 'comrade pastor'.

For Barth, 'instead of doing all possible kinds of things, "we should begin at the beginning and recognize that God is God" ' (Busch, *Karl Barth*, p. 90). Part of his search for a new approach led to his first commentary on Romans (1919) and a thoroughly revised second edition (1921), which showed signs of *Kierkegaard's influence. Barth insisted on the infinite qualitative difference between God and humanity; he likened God's inconceivability and wholly otherness to a tangent which touches a circle without touching it, thus touching it as a *new* world. He viewed the church as a 'crater formed by an explosion', and he overemphasized eschatology: 'If Christianity be not altogether thoroughgoing eschatology, there remains in it no relationship whatever with Christ' (Barth, *The Epistle to the Romans* [trans. Edwyn C. Hoskyns; New York, 1975], p. 314). Years later, Barth claimed that there was nothing absolutely false in his eschatological view, but admitted its one-sidedness and its inability to speak clearly and positively about God as the hope of the future instead of just 'a general idea of limit or crisis' (*CD* II, 1, pp. 634–5). Barth wanted to overcome the idea that: 'God was always thought to be good enough to put the crowning touch to what men began of their own accord' (Busch, *Karl Barth*, p. 99). This key element of his theology led him to stress a genuine *need* for God so that no thinking, however practical or significant, could have the first and final word: that place is already occupied by God's intervention on our behalf in Jesus Christ and the Holy Spirit.

Barth's theology came to be called *dialectical theology, because conflicting ideas were juxtaposed in order to make a positive point: 'As ministers we ought to speak of God. We are human, however, and so cannot speak of God. We ought therefore to recognize both *our obligation and our inability* and by that very recognition give God the glory' (Barth, *The Word of God and the Word of Man* [trans. Douglas Horton; Gloucester, MA, 1978], p. 186; cf. also Busch, *Karl Barth*, p. 140). The point is that God alone can say 'Yes' to us, and he has done so in Christ, but he has done so in and through the veil of creation, which included its sinfulness and its difference from God. So what is impossible, humanly speaking, becomes possible for humans in and through the triumph of God's grace. Barth was very clear that dialectic cannot reveal God, since only God could do that: 'We count upon God's *grace*. But it is not our own! *Everything* depends upon that grace! But we do not bring it into being by any magic turn of our dialectic. He *is* and he *remains free*: else he were not God' (Barth, *The Word of God*, p. 178; cf. also pp. 186ff., 198–217). Election included God's 'Yes' and 'No', with emphasis upon the 'Yes'. Revelation involved God's veiling and unveiling himself. Sin, seen as the 'impossible possibility', results when the creature wants to be the Creator, a goal that can never be achieved, but one which creatures still attempt, since redemption is not yet complete and we are *simul justus et peccator*.

Barth's working relationships with Gogarten, *Brunner and *Bultmann (who were all seen as 'dialectical theologians') soured over the years as it became clear to him that each in his own way sought to ground theology in existential philosophy – thus compromising the very nature of theology as *fides quaerens intellectum*. One instance of this involved a journal, *Zwischen den Zeiten*, founded by Barth, Thurneysen (his long-time friend) and Gogarten in 1922, which ended in 1933 when Gogarten equated God's law with the law of the German people.

In a public lecture in 1917, Barth argued that there is a new world within the Bible which is unexpected and is not identical with history, morality, religion or our quests for human understanding.

> The Bible tells us not how we should talk with God but what he says to us; not how we find the way to him, but how he has sought and found

the way to us; not the right relation in which we must place ourselves to him, but the covenant which he has made with all who are Abraham's spiritual children ... The word of God is within the Bible. (Barth, *The Word of God*, p. 43)

Prior to beginning his *Church Dogmatics* (1930), Barth studied *Anselm and consequently wished to put aside any philosophical or anthropological justifications of doctrine. He adopted both Anselm's stress on the need for prayer as well as his contention that theology means *fides quaerens intellectum* and *credo ut intelligam*. But there was no shift *from* dialectic *to* analogy in Barth's theology at this time, or any new prioritizing of ontic over noetic necessity, as some have contended. In fact, both factors characterized Barth's theology from early on and throughout his career (cf. McCormack). Barth's own 'retractions' in *CD* I, 1, which stress his intention to erase the last vestiges of existential philosophy as a ground for theology in the *Church Dogmatics* in order to correct his *Christian Dogmatics* of 1927, clearly indicate that he had never tried to ground theology in this way – what he now wished to eliminate was any appearance of doing so (cf. McCormack, p. 440, who believes Barth distanced himself from the first edition for political reasons).

Several emphases set Barth's theology apart:

Reaction against natural theology. In the preface to *CD* I, 1, Barth wrote: 'I regard the *analogia entis* as the invention of Antichrist, and I believe that because of it it is impossible ever to become a Roman Catholic, all other reasons for not doing so being to my mind short-sighted and trivial' (*CD* I, 1, p. xiii). Barth's reaction to natural theology partially resulted from his reaction to the German church's capitulation to Nazism. An accord with Hitler could be struck only on the basis of some natural theology, but certainly not on the basis of the grace of God revealed in Christ. Barth composed the famous *'Barmen Declaration' of 1934 which rejected all authorities other than Jesus Christ and clearly illustrated his attitude in this matter. Natural theology suggests that there is some other court of appeal by which God can be known other than his grace. It cancels our human *need* for God and suggests, first, that we can rely on ourselves to know God either existentially or idealistically. Second, natural theology implies that revelation is a possibility we can choose,

and that we can in that sense domesticate and control God's free grace which always comes as a miracle – that is, it reaches us in our deepest need exactly in such a way that it, as God's act, supplies what we cannot, under any circumstances, supply ourselves. The epitome of natural theology for Barth is the idea that we can understand the possibility of revelation apart from God's actual revelation in Christ and by the Spirit. This amounts to some form of self-justification and just misses the meaning of the gospel, which is that our self-justification has been overcome in the history of Jesus Christ once and for all. The true meaning of human freedom is that we have been freed from having to be our own helper, saviour and friend in face of the riddles of existence.

The word of God. In the doctrine of the word of God, natural theology suggests that we can produce an apologetic for the gospel apart from acknowledging and living by faith from the gospel. Instead of *credo ut intelligam*, theology becomes grounded partially in experience and partially in God. This thinking leads exactly to the reversibility of the creature/Creator relation, and it is just this practical and theoretical reversal that twentieth-century theology inherited from the eighteenth and nineteenth centuries: the tendency to collapse theology into anthropology. Barth vigorously attacked Schleiermacher and *Feuerbach, rejecting Schleiermacher's attempt to bring the Christian religion 'under the common denominator of the concept of the "feeling of absolute dependence" ' since this thinking is 'an outrage to the essence of man ... for it opens the door to the establishment of every possible kind of caprice and tyranny and therefore to the profoundest disobedience to God' (*CD* II, 2, pp. 552–55; cf. also Paul D. Molnar, *Karl Barth and the Theology of the Lord's Supper: A Systematic Investigation* [New York, 1996], pp. 87f.). Barth insisted that dogmatics is ethics just because our holiness is 'hidden in Christ with God' (Col. 3:3). Thus the question about right conduct is an existential problem solved only by the ruling grace of God in Christ (cf. *CD* I, 2, pp. 22, 3).

Doctrine of God. In the doctrine of God, natural theology means that we may ask *whether* God is known instead of understanding God from the fact that he *is* known by grace, faith and revelation within the church. Our knowledge of

God is our inclusion within God's Trinitarian self-knowledge on the basis of grace. God is objective to himself in his triune life (primary objectivity) and objective to us in the veil of objects different from himself (secondary objectivity); they cannot be identified or separated, but God must be seen as the one who speaks in and through the medium (work/veil) (CD II, 1, pp. 16, 52). Since 'God is known only through God' (CD II, 1, p. 179), Barth spoke of the *analogia fidei* rather than the *analogia entis* in order to emphasize that knowledge of God takes place as grace on the basis of an act of God. Ultimately, Barth's attack on natural theology was an argument in favour of a proper understanding of the relationship of nature and grace. So Barth spoke of God as 'One who loves in freedom'. Instead of speaking of the divine attributes, he referred to the divine perfections in order to obviate any residue of *Nominalism, or the idea that God could exist as a hidden entity behind the revelation of God in Christ. Christ is present within the structures of alienated humanity as the one who is judged in our place. Indeed, Jesus Christ himself is the only one who actually experienced hell; he did so on our behalf so that hell could not triumph over anyone else (CD II, 2, p. 496).

Doctrine of election. This, of course, is the heart of Barth's doctrine of election – our predestination is not a *decretum absolutum* which remains hidden and unknown, but it is made known in the one who was elected Son of God and Son of Man from eternity. His doctrine of election, properly seen by *Hans Urs von Balthasar as the 'sum of the Gospel' (von Balthasar, p. 174), represents a major departure from the tradition because, in place of a *decretum absolutum* which would suggest bad news, arbitrariness or ultimate agnosticism, Barth insisted that Jesus Christ is both electing God and elected man. Election, therefore, is not a fixed inscrutable decree because it is identical with God's ever-active involvement with us in the history of Jesus Christ. Because he is 'God for us', humanity finds a place in the doctrine of God (cf. CD II, 2, pp. 509ff.). Barth's doctrine of election embodies his view of the relation between Israel and the church, his bold opposition to anti-Semitism, an extensive treatment of evil in relation to Judas, and an important ethical section. When accused of 'universalism', Barth responded: 'I do not teach it and I do not not

teach it.' Election is no static concept for Barth; such a view could make God a prisoner of his own freedom. God continually elects and chooses in favour of humanity, but the form and content of that election is actually known and visible only to faith in Jesus Christ himself. For Barth, God is both fully revealed and fully hidden in Christ. Thus, he advocated an *analogia fidei* which stressed that, while remaining hidden, God has made himself knowable and comparable in Christ. God is both veiled and unveiled in his revelation, and revelation never ceases to be an act of God.

Doctrine of creation. Barth insisted that creation was the external basis of the covenant, and that the covenant was the internal basis of creation. Hence, without understanding creation in faith and as an act of God that took place in and through Christ and the Holy Spirit, creation would not be seen as a benefit. Apart from this view, creation could be separated from the covenant, as *Marcion did, or viewed negatively, as did Schopenhauer. Without understanding the inner meaning of creation one could fall into pantheism or dualism. Barth's doctrine of creation is marked by the fact that creation took place in and through the Son with a view toward our reconciliation and redemption. Creation is essentially an act of the *triune* God who is simultaneously one and three *in se* and *ad extra*. CD III, 4 clearly illustrates that on specific ethical issues Barth is objective without being legalistic or casuistic. His considerations show that human freedom grounded in reconciliation and redemption leads to obedience and not to licence. That freedom is permission rather than an imposition, and it allows for exceptional circumstances grounded in God himself. In his doctrine of reconciliation Barth did not cease to reject natural theology in the sense that he continued to understand our human relations with God exclusively from Christ as the Lord in the form of a servant, and as the servant who was Lord. In Christ, God humbled himself in order to exalt humanity.

Doctrine of reconciliation. Barth's doctrine of reconciliation is a powerful expression of just how God includes us by judging us and setting us on the road to redemption. Barth argued that the Father's suffering was not part of his nature, but was rather his free ability to suffer in the abasement and sending of Jesus for our sakes

(*CD* IV, 2, p. 357). When speaking of the continuing effect of sin, even after the event of reconciliation in the cross of Jesus, Barth insisted that theology had to treat the existence of the devil with reserve. This reserve is necessary precisely because human resistance to our justification and sanctification can only exist negatively. It cannot alter the reality of our reconciliation. Our liberation is wholly and utterly the work of God. Thus we can be free only in obedience. This we resist. We would rather have a 'God or fate or Supreme Being which does not stoop to the being of man but is self-sufficient; and it [the resistance] wants this God as a supreme symbol for the self-resting and self-moved sovereignty, autarchy and self-sufficiency of human being' (*CD* IV, 3, p. 252).

Barth has been criticized for an insufficient doctrine of the Holy Spirit – though his writings demonstrate much relevant material on the Holy Spirit. He has also been criticized for a tendency toward *Docetism and for being a faith subjectivist and a modalist. His sacramental theology has been roundly criticized as the weakest part of the *Church Dogmatics*: it separates divine and human being and action too sharply; rejects infant baptism; sees Christ as the only sacrament; and subtly redefines the sacraments in terms of our ethical *response* rather than stressing our human inclusion in the life of the Trinity through Christ's high priestly mediation. Barth tried to avoid sacramentalism (ascribing sacramental validity to the visible action of the church rather than to the Holy Spirit) and moralism (ascribing sacramental validity to an individual's ethical disposition or behaviour rather than to the Holy Spirit's inclusion of that disposition and behaviour in the Trinitarian action *ad extra*). One can easily see that Barth's attempt to avoid both sacramentalism and moralism incorporated the basic insights of his *analogia fidei*, which stressed the positive fact that the church was the historical visible form of Christ's continued presence on earth. In the *Church Dogmatics* there is a distinct emphasis on Christ's humanity as the humanity of fallen creatures, on Jesus' particularity which is decidedly objectivist and anti-docetic and a stress on God's three-in-oneness. Barth was neither a subjectivist nor a modalist, and he frequently stressed that while God himself was directly present in his word and Spirit within history, he could not be known directly because knowing his presence took place by way of recollection and expectation of God's activity within history.

A genuine excitement emanates from the more than nine thousand pages of the *Church Dogmatics* which, in spite of its incomplete nature, was nine times as long as *Calvin's *Institutes* and nearly twice as long as *Aquinas's *Summa* and included 14 part-volumes. Barth's theology at once stressed God's positive freedom as the only self-moved being, his freedom from conditioning in his relations with creation, his ability not to be hindered by the sin or opposition of creatures, and the fact that God's freedom for us in Christ and through the Holy Spirit was a definite 'Yes' which was the basis for joy, thanksgiving and certitude. Barth's entire theology was marked in this way. Like few before him Barth had a sense of the fact that God is a *living* God. His theology consistently illustrated the fact that God was and is the one who initiates, sustains and completes the fellowship between us and him without in any way diminishing our human self-determination – but rather establishing it. From beginning to end, Barth was clear that it was the triune God who gives meaning to our faith and hope, and that the experiences of faith and hope could never become the themes of theology without ending with a '*mixophilosophicotheologia*', or a mixture of philosophy and theology (Barth, *Evangelical Theology: An Introduction* [trans. Grover Foley; Grand Rapids, 1963], p. xiii). Barth always demonstrated that knowledge of God, which took place as an event 'in the bosom of the divine Trinity', led to new and different insights that could not be gleaned apart from faith.

The esteem in which Barth was held by his peers is indicated in the fact that, although he never completed a doctorate, he received 11 honorary doctoral degrees during his career. Almost every twentieth-century theologian has been influenced by Barth's theology and has sensed a need to respond to him in some fashion: his commentary on the *Epistle to the Romans* (1921) 'fell like a bomb on the playground of the theologians' (Torrance, *Introduction*, p. 17). Barth's name is often associated with *Augustine, *Athanasius, Aquinas, *Luther and Schleiermacher because of his originality and his enormous contribution to theology. Barth's interest in Catholic theology led to important relationships with *Erich Przywara, Hans Urs von Balthasar and *Hans Küng; he took an active interest in the events of *Vatican II and met *Karl Rahner, *Josef Ratzinger and Pope Paul VI (who admired his work). He even suggested that he would have preferred the Roman Catholic approach to what he called the Neo-Protestant or Protestant modernist method. Nonetheless, Barth objected to the Roman Catholic strategy of co-ordinating nature and super-nature, creature and Creator, reason and revelation and philosophy and theology, thus obscuring the nature of grace, the divine command and the meaning of sin. But he also objected to modernist dogmatics, which was unaware that something which was unknown needed to be said to us by God and could not be spoken by us to ourselves: 'Modernist dogmatics hears man answer when no one has called him' (*CD* I, 1, pp. 61–2).

PAUL D. MOLNAR

FURTHER READING: *Text: Church Dogmatics* (ed. G.W. Bromiley and T.F. Torrance; trans. G.W. Bromiley; 4 vols. in 13 pts.; Edinburgh, 1975). *Studies:* Hans Urs von Balthasar, *The Theology of Karl Barth: Exposition and Interpretation* (trans. Edward T. Oakes, SJ; San Francisco, 1992); Geoffrey W. Bromiley, *Introduction to the Theology of Karl Barth* (Edinburgh, 1979); Eberhard Busch, *Karl Barth: His Life from Letters and Autobiographical Texts* (trans. John Bowden; Philadelphia, 1976); George Hunsinger, *How To Read Karl Barth: The Shape of His Theology* (New York, 1991); Eberhard Jüngel, *Karl Barth: A Theological Legacy* (trans. Garrett E. Paul; Philadelphia, 1986); Bruce L. McCormack, *Karl Barth's Critically Realistic Dialectical Theology: Its Genesis and Development 1909–1936* (New York, 1995); John Thompson, *Christ in Perspective: Christological Perspectives in the Theology of Karl Barth* (Grand Rapids, 1978); Thomas F. Torrance, *Karl Barth: Biblical and Evangelical Theologian* (Edinburgh, 1990); *Karl Barth: An Introduction to his Early Theology, 1910–1931* (London, 1962); John Webster, *Barth's Ethics of Reconciliation* (Cambridge, 1995).

Baur, F.C. (1792–1860)

Ferdinand Christian Baur, professor of New Testament, church history and history of dogma (including symbolics) in Tübingen from 1826 to his death, was the most important pioneer of critical historical methods in theology and may justly be called the 'father of historical theology'. His pupils were denied theological chairs and many of his conclusions were superseded, but his 'Tübingen school' of radical criticism left a powerful imprint on 150 years of New Testament scholarship.

Initially trained in the older Tübingen school which combined *Kant with supernaturalism, Baur was persuaded by *Schleiermacher's *Glaubenslehre* (1821–22) that modern theology should instead be based on human self-consciousness. As classics teacher at the Blaubeuren seminary (1817–26), Baur learned about source criticism from B.G. Niebuhr's *Römische Geschichte* (1811–12) and about ancient myth from G.F. Creuzer (1771–1858). Convinced that 'without philosophy history remains eternally dead and dumb', Baur's first book, *Symbolik und Mythologie* (3 vols.; 1824–25), also drew on Schelling's philosophy to help interpret the history of ancient religion.

In Tübingen Baur massively advanced the modern study of church history, especially the history of dogma, and produced the studies of Christian origins which proved both controversial and seminal. Around 1832 he found in *Hegel's philosophy of religion (published that same year) a key to interpreting the historical development of Christianity theologically. This discovery gave further religious motivation to his critical and speculative investigations of the dialectical unfolding of God's self-revelation as Spirit in history. In 1831, before any reference to Hegel, Baur's 'Die Christuspartei in der korinthischen Gemeinde, der Gegensatz des petrinischen und paulinischen Christenthums in der ältesten Kirche, der Apostel Petrus in Rom' (ed. E. Käsemann; repr. 1963) noticed the tensions in Corinth (1 Cor. 1:12) and interpreted them as a conflict between Jewish and Gentile (Pauline) Christianity. In 1835 Baur published a historically reasoned denial of the authenticity of the post-Pauline pastoral epistles and unleashed the conservative polemics which would accompany his career and memory. These lengthy essays, and one on the purpose and occasion of Romans (1836), inaugurated the modern historical (rather than doctrinal) study of Paul's epistles and point towards Baur's 1845 masterpiece, *Paulus der Apostel Jesu Christi* (ET 1875). Part I of this work is a brilliant analysis of Acts, denying its historicity, and part II questions the authenticity of all except the four major epistles. Part III draws on Hegelian conceptuality to interpret the apostle's thought, but when this philosophy faded around 1850 Baur greatly reduced his debt to it in his later articles on Paul and his posthumously published lectures on New Testament theology (1864).

It was Baur's critical judgements on the epistles and Gospels, rather than his theological interpretations, which were thought to undermine the authority of Scripture. In 1835, his former pupil *D.F. Strauss's *Leben Jesu* (ET 1846) stimulated Baur to pursue his own researches on the Gospels. He engaged in 'tendency criticism' (*Tendenzkritik*), observing the theological 'tendency' of each writing and hoping to locate it accordingly in its place in the development of early Christianity. His model of this was bi-linear, tracing the development of Jewish and Gentile Christianity to their eventual reconciliation in late second-century Catholicism. The model was defective. Baur denied the authenticity and early date of the seven Ignatian epistles, adhered to the traditional view of Matthean priority, and overvalued the Clementine literature. He dated the Gospels too late, but his gospel criticism of John (1844) and Luke (1846), summed up and extended in *Kritische Untersuchungen über die kanonischen Evangelien* (1847), and his monograph on Mark (1851) demonstrated that John should not be read as history but as the climax of New Testament theology.

The Church History of the First Three Centuries (1853; 2nd edn 1860; ET 2 vols.; 1878–79) fills in the picture of a historical development and insists on the importance of 'the founder' who contained within himself the germ of both his disciples' Messianism and St Paul's universalism. Baur finds the original Christian principle in the Sermon on the Mount. The beatitudes show what constitutes the inmost self-consciousness of the Christian, and the absolute moral command of the antitheses (Mt. 5:21–48) is directed to inner disposition and purity of heart. A shift to Kant's ethical idealism is apparent here.

Baur's five-volume church history, preceded by *Die Epochen der kirchlichen Geschichtsschreibung* (1852; ET 1968), occupied his final decade. Volume two appeared in 1859, the remaining three posthumously. The last volume, on the nineteenth century, was reprinted in 1970. Baur's other works have been less influential than his earlier pioneering work in the history of dogma, especially the great monographs on the history of the doctrine of the atonement (1838) and of the Trinity and incarnation (3 vols.; 1841–43), strongly influenced by Hegel. In 1968 his *Lehrbuch der christlichen Dogmengeschichte* (1847) was reprinted, and a few of his introductory lectures were translated by P.C. Hodgson. Baur's response (1833) to the *Symbolik* of his Roman Catholic colleague *J.A. Möhler (1796–1838) recalls a less ecumenical age. But in *Die christliche Gnosis* (1835), his comparison of second-century heresies with the modern *Religionsphilosophie* of Boehme, Schelling, Schleiermacher and Hegel is the first modern sympathetic interpretation of *Gnosticism. This also best reveals his own theological commitments.

Baur's prodigious output exceeds 20,000 pages, mostly of pioneering research. It gave a body to Schleiermacher's dictum which prefaces the nineteenth-century German achievement, that 'historical theology is the actual corpus of theological study' (*Brief Outline*, 28).

ROBERT C. MORGAN

FURTHER READING: Text: *Ausgewählte Werke in Einzelausgaben* (ed. Klaus Scholder; Stuttgart, 1963–75). In addition to *Paul* and *Church History* in English, see P.C. Hodgson (trans. and ed.), *Ferdinand Christian Baur on the Writing on Church History* (Oxford, 1968). *Studies:* J. Fitzer, *Moehler and Baur in Controversy, 1832–38* (Florida, 1974); W. Geiger, *Spekulation und Kritik* (Munich, 1964); H. Harris, *The Tübingen School* (Oxford, 1975); R. Harrisville and A.C. Sundberg, *The Bible in Modern Culture* (Grand Rapids, 1995); P.C. Hodgson, *The Formation of Historical Theology* (New York, 1966); E.P. Meijering, *F.C. Baur als Patristiker* (Amsterdam, 1986).

Baxter, Richard (1615–91)

A leading pastoral theologian of the *Puritan tradition, Baxter was known for his evangelistic fervour, pastoral sensitivity, commitment to ecclesiastical unity and a literary output which made him arguably the most prolific English theologian. Ordained in 1638 as a conforming Anglican, Baxter's first position as a preaching schoolmaster in Dudley lasted one year. After another year as a pastoral assistant in a larger town, Bridgnorth, Baxter was invited to be the lecturer at St Mary's, Kidderminster, Worcestershire in 1641. With an interlude from 1642 to 1647 as chaplain in the Parliamentarian Army, an experience which profoundly affected his view of religious radicalism, Baxter carried on an exemplary Puritan ministry in Kidderminster during the turbulent Civil War and interregnum years of 1641–60. His dedication to fulfilling the ideal of the English Reformation – not from the top down led by magistrates, but from the bottom up led by ministers – was to set a demanding benchmark for future generations of ministers.

In addition to fulfilling his pastoral duty, Baxter penned 47 books during this period. Furthermore, he had a leading role in creating a ministerial association for Worcestershire, designed to help the administration of pastoral discipline, enhance collegiality among pastors and create a solid basis for Christian unity. This association encompassed Presbyterian, Episcopal and Independent clergy. After the Restoration of monarchy in 1660 Baxter was made a royal chaplain ordinary, but he declined the offer of bishopric in 1662 to stand along with the soon-to-be marginalized group of Nonconformist ministers. His appeal for an episcopacy – patterned after Archbishop James Ussher's 'reduced episcopacy' – was comprehensive enough to embrace the ministers who were not episcopally ordained but who wanted to function within the restored Church of England. However, the 'Presbyterian' position, articulated by Baxter in the Savoy Conference of 1661, failed to convince the restored Anglican party. The breach between these two parties subsequently led to the expulsion of over fifteen hundred ministers on 24 August 1662.

During the period after the Act of Uniformity of 1662, Baxter emerged as the leader for the conservative faction among the Nonconformists. His constant self-designation as a 'mere Catholic' clearly demonstrated Baxter's distaste for denominational labelling and his desire for ecclesiastical mutuality and unity. Baxter suffered two imprisonments, failed in his endeavours to bring various Nonconformist parties back into the Church of England, and was subject to much misunderstanding regarding his occasional conformity. During these years Baxter published another 87 books, ranging from a defence of Nonconformity to pleas for church unity, from a highly complex systematic theology to guidebooks for the poor and their household instruction. Two years after the Act of Toleration of 1689, Baxter entered his 'saints everlasting rest' and was buried in London.

Even though Baxter was principally valued in the Nonconformist tradition for his practical writings, he engaged throughout his career in numerous theological controversies. Anti-antinomianism was a leading feature of Baxter's theology. Haunted by the spectre of his Civil War chaplaincy experience, where he witnessed the proliferation of antinomian teaching which tended to de-emphasize human responsibility and repentance, Baxter wrote his first book, *Aphorisms of Justification* (1649). Applying the teaching of the parable of the sheep and the goats (Mt. 25) into both phases of justification – initial and final – Baxter taught that the legal righteousness of Christ, although imputed to us, must be complemented by the evangelical righteousness of each believer. This modified *Reformed position caused a furore among his more *Calvinist colleagues, but Baxter was to retain it throughout his life. In 1690, Baxter published *The Scripture Gospel Defended* to refute the resurgent antinomianism, claiming that to neglect the significance of human righteousness was tantamount to derogating the sufficiency of Christ's atonement.

Anti-separatism was another major theme of Baxter's theological structure. Seeing himself standing in the line of Elizabethan and Jacobean Nonconformists, many of whom did not take the path of separatism but chose to conform and reform the ecclesiastical structure from inside, Baxter tirelessly spoke against the evil of separatism and warned of the danger of the centrifugal tendency of the Independents and other separatists. *Augustinian twofold ecclesiology, dividing the church into the visible and the invisible, was the conceptual framework for Baxter's tireless anti-separatism. Moreover, closely related to his anti-separatism was his endeavour for church unity, both locally and nationally. He encapsulated his ecclesiological convictions in *Christian Concord* (1653); *Catholick Unity* (1669); *Universal Concord* (1660); *The Cure of Church Divisions* (1670); *The True and Only Way of Concord* (1680); and *Church Concord* (1691). Baxter's extensive surviving correspondence with individuals such as John Dury, *John Owen, Thomas Manton and John Eliot attest his passionate commitment for ecclesiastical reunion. He even provided epistemological grounds for such unity in *Richard Baxter's Catholick Theology* (1675), in which his endeavour for reconciling *Lutherans, Reformed, *Arminians and Roman Catholics prompted him to argue that most doctrinal differences were not real but verbal.

In addition to Baxter's anti-antinomianism and anti-separatism, there is a sober pastoral realism about his theology. It was this dimension which made many of his writings so popular. *The Saints Everlasting Rest* (1650) was written to prepare his parishioners for the imminent eschatological rest. *A Call to the Unconverted* (1658) was a phenomenal success as it issued a clarion call to those who were nurtured in the church to seriously consider and endeavour for conversion. His best-known work, however, is *The Reformed Pastor* (1656) in which we see Baxter's theological perspectives brought together in a coherent whole. In it, Baxter urged his colleagues to realize the stupendous nature of their office and stressed that individual pastoral care, couched in the form of catechizing, must be carried out with vigour and faithfulness. Furthermore, he provided a comprehensive compendium for the clergy as well as for the laity in *A Christian Directory* (1674), which covers the entire gamut of the Christian existence; this would be the culmination of his pastoral experience and theological erudition.

With the exception of his eclectic 'reformed' soteriology, Baxter's importance as a leading voice of the moderate Puritan tradition of the seventeenth century can hardly be overestimated. Baxter was a transitional figure in Puritanism as he witnessed and contributed to the ecclesiastical structure of England which moved from a relatively cohesive national church to an amalgam of a weakened 'national' church and other permanently marginalized dissenting churches.

PAUL C.-H. LIM

FURTHER READING: *Texts: The Reformed Pastor* (ed. William Brown; Edinburgh, 1989); *A Holy Commonwealth* (ed. William Lamont; Cambridge, 1994). *Studies:* Han Boersma, *A Hot Pepper Corn: Richard Baxter's Doctrine of Justification in Its Seventeenth-century Context of Controversy* (Zoetermeer, 1993); N.H. Keeble, *Richard Baxter, Puritan Man of Letters* (Oxford, 1982); N.H. Keeble and Geoffrey F. Nuttall (eds.), *Calendar of the Correspondence of Richard Baxter* (2 vols.; Oxford, 1991); William Lamont, *Richard Baxter and the Millennium* (London, 1979); G.F. Nuttall, *Richard Baxter* (London, 1965); J.I. Packer, 'The Redemption and Restoration of Man in the Thought of Richard Baxter' (DPhil diss.; Oxford, 1954); F.J. Powicke, *A Life of the Reverend Richard Baxter 1615–1691* (London, 1924); *The Reverend Richard Baxter Under the Cross* (London, 1927).

Bede (c. 673–735)

Known as 'the venerable', Bede was born in the north of England and given by his parents to the monastery of Wearmouth, under Benedict Biscop (d. 690), when aged seven. Soon after that he was transferred to a daughter house,

Jarrow, which was not far distant along the river Tyne and lived under abbot Coelfrid (d. 716). For the remainder of his life he remained there, apart from a couple of short trips to gather information. Ordained a priest (c. 703), the life of his community and his work in Jarrow (teaching and writing) seem to have been his only concerns.

Towards the end of his life Bede drew up a list of his works. It is incomplete, but the 30 works mentioned can be divided thus: 21 pieces of exegesis, four pieces of hagiography (into this category he would have placed his historical writings), one work on science (and we could add others on chronology), two works on grammar, a book of letters, and a book of liturgical material (and we could add many homilies). The range is expressive of the concerns of theology at his time, and of the monastic curriculum in particular.

It is in his commentaries that we see Bede at his best. They are largely derivative from the great Latin Fathers: *Augustine, *Ambrose, *Jerome, and Gregory; but while Bede was anxious to display his dependence (he developed the use of marginal codes to identify sources) he did not simply excerpt material. His aim was to smooth over differences and omissions to provide a seamless exegesis that seems to show all four Fathers (and others) speaking 'with one voice'. It was this ability that made his work so popular. Bede is therefore the ideal of the pre-Carolingian schoolmaster.

Today Bede is less known as a theologian than as a historian, especially for his *Historia ecclesiastica gentis anglorum* ('churchly history of the English race'). His aim, however, was theological: to show that his own race was an elect one, a people that figure in God's providence. To this end he had to show that their pagan ancestors could be brought within the sphere of God's saving plans. While Bede in most matters followed Augustine closely, in this he developed Augustine's notion of the 'Egyptian Gold' beyond recognition to produce a theory of God's working outside the church as well as a theory of inculturation whereby missionaries could build upon pagan customs and practices by redirecting them towards their true end. This theory was an important element in the armoury of Anglo-Saxon missionaries.

Bede's larger legacy is complex: he fixed the message of the Fathers for much of the Middle

Ages, popularized the AD dating in historical writing, and, at a local level, canonized a particular picture of early Christianity in the British Isles.

THOMAS O'LOUGHLIN

FURTHER READING: *Catalogue: CPL* 1343–84; 1565–7; 2032; 2273; 2318–2323b; and 2333. *Studies:* G. Bonner (ed.), *Famulus Christi: Essays in Commemoration of the Thirteenth Centenary of the Birth of the Venerable Bede* (London, 1976); C.W. Jones, 'Some Introductory Remarks on Bede's Commentary on Genesis', *Sacris Erudiri* 19 (1969), pp. 115–98; B. Ward, *The Venerable Bede* (London, 1991).

Bellarmine, Robert (1542–1621)

Major Roman Catholic theologian of the post-Tridentine period, most famous for his writings against the Protestants. Born Roberto Bellarmino in Montepulciano in 1542, he entered the novitiate of the *Jesuit order in Rome in 1560, and was trained in philosophy and theology at, among other places, Rome, Padua and Louvain. In 1570 he was appointed professor at the Jesuit seminary in Louvain. In many of his lectures there, he was engaged with the refutation of *Luther, *Calvin and other important Protestant writers. He also became involved in the controversy around his Louvain colleague, Michael Baius (1513–89).

In 1576 Bellarmine was called to teach at the Roman College, in the recently founded 'chair of controversies'. He proved equal to the task, for his lectures resulted in his main work, the monumental *Disputationes de Controversiis Christianae Fidei, adversus hujus temporis Haereticos* ('disputations concerning the controversies of the Christian faith, against the heretics of these days'), published in three volumes between 1596 and 1593, and reprinted many times (from 1596 onward in four volumes). It is a comprehensive and extensive discussion of all areas in which controversy had been raised, in which he adduced arguments from biblical, patristic and medieval sources along with rational arguments. The *Disputationes* evoked many reactions among the Protestants (listed in Sommervogel, pp. 1165–80). In 1600, David Paraeus (1548–1622) founded a *Collegium Antibellarminianum* in Heidelberg. Bellarmine held, for example, that the signs of the true church were: confession of the true faith, sacraments and the acknowledgement of the

authority and superiority of the pope. The last point, of course, could not pass unchallenged by the Protestant theologians. During his years as a professor, Bellarmine published, among other works, a Hebrew grammar as well as a compendium of patristic and medieval theology, entitled *De scriptoribus ecclesiasticis*.

In 1592, he functioned as a rector of the Roman College, and from 1594 to 1597, he became provincial of the Jesuit province of Naples. Bellarmine published two catechisms which became immensely popular, the *Dottrina christiana breve* (meant for children, 1597), and the *Dichiarazione più copiosa della dottrina christiana* (for teachers, 1598). In 1599 Bellarmine was appointed cardinal, and became an adviser of the congregation *De auxiliis*, which was installed to settle the controversy between *Molinists and *'Thomists' concerning the nature of grace and its concord with human freedom.

In 1602, Bellarmine was appointed archbishop of Capua, and took residence there, according to the Tridentine rule. He held that position until 1605, when he was called in conclave for two subsequent popes (Leo XI and Paul V). The new pope wanted him in Rome again, and so he resigned the bishop's see. Again he became a member of the congregation (one of his many administrative duties during these years) which had to decide upon the aforementioned controversy. Bellarmine's suggestion was followed by the pope, who in 1607 decreed that the parties should not condemn their adversaries and that the doctrinal question remained to be settled (something which, up to now, has not happened).

Bellarmine also left his mark on the Vulgate edition, known as the Sixto-Clementine Vulgate. Pope Sixtus V put him to the task of revising the official text, but Sixtus himself had made rather arbitrary revisions in the text. Bellarmine convinced Clement VIII that these revisions had better be undone, and replaced by his own revisions.

Around 1611, Bellarmine became involved in the controversy surrounding his fellow Jesuit and follower of Baius, Leonhard Lessius (1554–1623). This controversy once again centred on the topic of grace and freedom, in which he sided with the Order General, Aquaviva, against Lessius (Bellarmine's views on this matter, known as 'Congruism', were posthumously published in Le Bachelet, *Auctarium Bellarminianum*).

Also very important was Bellarmine's membership of the Holy Office (Inquisition), in which capacity he delivered the command that Galileo was forbidden to teach a heliocentric universe (1616), since there was insufficient proof of it. We know from his private correspondence that Bellarmine was prepared to revise his interpretation of Scripture, in case Galileo would come with convincing evidence – but this did not happen.

Towards the end of his life, Bellarmine wrote, besides a commentary on the Psalms (1611), mainly devotional treatises, which once again became very popular. Two of them were recently translated into modern English as: *Mind's Ascent to God*, and *The Art of Dying Well*. Bellarmine died in 1621, was canonized in 1930 and made a Doctor of the Church in 1931. A renewed interest in Bellarmine's doctrine of the natural and its relation to the supernatural was raised by *Henri de Lubac's seminal work *Surnaturel* (Paris, 1946). De Lubac claimed that Bellarmine's doctrine was an example of the 'modern' view that a human being could attain a natural, inner-worldly fulfilment, over against the medieval, *Augustinian doctrine which held that a human being is naturally directed toward the supernatural, which it cannot naturally attain.

EEF DEKKER

FURTHER READING: *Texts: Opera Omnia* (12 vols.; Paris, 1870–74); see also Carlos Sommervogel, *Bibliothèque de la Compagnie de Jésus* (Brussels / Paris, 1890), Tome 1 s.v.; Galeota, ed. (below); *Spiritual Writings* (ed. and trans. John Patrick Donnelly and Roland J. Teske; New York, 1989). *Studies*: Manfred Biersack, 'Bellarmin und die "Causa Baii"', in *L'Augustinisme à l'ancienne faculté de théologie de Louvain* (ed. M. Lamberigts; BETL 111; Louvain, 1994), pp. 167–78. Richard J. Blackwell, *Galileo, Bellarmine and the Bible* (Notre Dame, IN / London, 1991); James Brodrick, *Robert Bellarmine: Saint and Scholar* (London, 1961), still the latest comprehensive biography in English – rewritten and updated version of a 2-vol. biography, published in 1928; L. Ceyssens, 'Bellarmin et Louvain (1569–1576)', in *L'Augustinisme à l'ancienne faculté de théologie de Louvain*, (ed. M. Lamberigts; BETL 111; Louvain, 1994), pp. 179–205; Gustavo Galeota, 'Bellarmini', *Th Real* 5, pp. 525–31; Gustavo Galeota (ed.), *Roberto Bellarmino: Arcivescovo di Capua teologo e pastore della riforma cattolica* (Atti del convegno internazionale di studi Capua 28 settembre–1 ottobre 1988; Capua, 1990), 2 vols. with an extensive bibliography of posthumously edited works (pp. 828–31) and of twentieth-century secondary literature (pp. 809–26, 832–72); Romeo de Maio, et al. (eds.), *Bellarmino e la Controriforma*. (Atti del simposio internazionale di studi Sora 15–18 ottobre 1986; Sora, 1990); Michael A. Mullett, *The Catholic Reformation* (London / New York, 1999), introductory book on the theology of the post-Tridentine theologians.

Benedictines

St Benedict of Nursia (480–c. 550). Little is known of the life of the 'father of western monasticism', and, contrary to popular opinion, he founded no order. The only information on his life comes from St Gregory's later hagiographical work entitled 'The Dialogues'. Despite its emphasis on the miraculous, a broad historical outline may be discerned.

Benedict was born in the village of Nursia in the Apennines. He was later sent to Rome for a classical education but became so disillusioned with the city's depravity that c. 500 he took refuge in a cave, east of Rome, in Subiaco. After spending several years as a hermit, a monastic community began to grow under his leadership.

In c. 525, he left Subiaco with a small band of monks and established a community at Monte Cassino. While he does not appear to have been ordained, he oversaw this community until his death by fever in 547.

The Rule of Benedict. It is clear that Benedict made use of earlier 'rules' such as those of *Augustine and Basil as well as the anonymous 'Rule of the Master' in the composition of his own Rule. In addition, Benedict was greatly influenced by *John Cassian's *De institutis coenobiorum* ('Institutes') and *Conlationes* ('Conferences'), which were written between 425 and 428. Cassian's works, which were largely informed by his monastic experiences in Egypt, were penned at the command of Castor, bishop of Apt, who turned to Cassian for advice for the fledgling monastic enterprise in Gaul.

Cassian created no formal 'Rule' because he feared that it might become inflexible. It is clear that Benedict was sensitive to Cassian's concerns when he formulated his own Rule. The Rule of St Benedict consists of 73 chapters which combine doctrinal teaching with practical observation. As Cassian had encouraged, Benedict adopted a coenobitic (community) form of monasticism in which the differences and needs of the individual were readily acknowledged. This common life was not simply understood to be a beginning stage towards what was understood by some as the solitary ideal. The monastic community under the direction of a wise and discerning abbot was to be a sufficient school of perfection and obedience to Christ in and of itself.

Cassian had little tolerance for those who professed to be monks but did not live under the authority of an elder, whom he called 'sarabites' (Conf. 18). Likewise, Benedict despised such monks, whom he labelled 'the worst' (ch. 1). While both Cassian and Benedict disapproved of Sarabitism, it would have certain advocates in the East such as John Climacus, whose *Ladder of Divine Ascent* continues to be read by Orthodox monks and the faithful, particularly during Lent.

The abbot who oversaw each monastery was to be elected by the monks. Obedience to the abbot's command was equated to obedience to the commands of God (ch. 5), and the desires of the individual were to have no place in the monastery (ch. 3). However, the abbot was admonished by the Rule not only to act as a stern master but also as an affectionate father (ch. 2). Thus stability in coenobitic monasticism and obedience in response to the authority of the abbot became hallmarks of Benedict's Rule.

The chief work of monks following Benedict's Rule was the *opus Dei* ('work of God'), or the daily office. The daily office consisted of eight periods of prayer interspersed throughout the day and night. The Benedictine day began with the office of Matins/Lauds, which occurred around 2 a.m. This was followed by Prime, then Tierce, Sext, None, Vespers and Compline. In addition to the daily office, monks performed a variety of manual labour tasks in keeping with their particular skills and at the discretion of the abbot (chs. 48, 57).

Monastic life followed two separate patterns in the Benedictine monastery: the summer order and the winter order. The summer order began with Easter. From Easter until Pentecost no fasting was allowed by the Rule. During this period of time, monks enjoyed two meals per day instead of the customary one meal per day. Fasting was resumed after Pentecost. The winter order included the Lenten penitential and fasting season. During this time, modifications were made in regard to the daily meal observance and devotional reading as well as manual labour.

The early medieval period. It would seem strange that there is no proof that the Rule of St Benedict was widely in use in Italy prior to the tenth century. Nevertheless, the Rule does appear to have been used in seventh-century England and Gaul. In both England and Gaul, the Rule of St Benedict seems to have been used in conjunction with the more austere Rule of St Columbanus. The Rule of St Benedict gradually superseded other rules in the west and, by the time of Carolingian Empire, it was being observed throughout western Europe.

During the ecclesiastical reforms of the eighth century, the Rule of St Benedict was frequently employed as a tool to reform both the secular clergy as well as the clergy who lived in the largely autonomous monasteries. In his desire to encourage and standardize education in this realm, Charlemagne made the Rule of St Benedict the *de facto* rule for the monasteries of his empire. By the demise and fall of the Carolingian Empire in the ninth century, the Rule of St Benedict had become *the* monastic rule of the west.

Cluny. A variety of attempts at collective reform were attempted in the years following the early medieval period. While the Benedictines often preferred to enact reform through the founding of new locally governed congregations, the centralizing tendencies of the Cluniac houses were to become exceptionally influential.

The monastery of Cluny was founded in 909, and it adopted a return to the strict observance of the Rule of St Benedict. All subsequent monasteries established by monks of Cluny were under the direct control of the abbot of Cluny, which insured a general uniformity not experienced in the autonomous local Benedictine houses. By the eleventh and twelfth centuries, Cluny enjoyed its height of influence and power in the Roman church with over one thousand houses. Its abbey church was the largest in Christendom until the construction of St Peter's basilica in Rome. However, by the late medieval period, the Cluniac system fell into serious decline. In 1790, the abbey was closed in the wake of the French Revolution.

The Cistercians. Another example of the reforming tendencies of the high medieval period was the establishment of the Cistercians. Robert of Molesme and several companions founded the monastery of Cîteaux in 1098, attempting to return to a strict observance of the Benedictine ideal. The prominence of the mother house of Cîteaux was secured by *St Bernard. Bernard was from Clairvaux, the fourth established monastery in the Cistercian system.

Cistercian monasteries were noted for their particularly secluded locations as well as their austerity. The Rule of St Benedict was to exercise an important place in the day-to-day life of Cistercian monks in matters such as food, clothing and the observance of silence. Unlike the Cluniac system, which exercised central authority from the mother house, each Cistercian monastery governed its own affairs – but in conformity to the decisions of the annual chapter meetings held at Cîteaux.

Internal attempts at reform continued even within the Cistercian order. In 1662, Armand Jean Le Bouthillier de Rance, the abbot of the Cistercian community at Notre Dame de la Trappe, introduced new reforms into his community. His reforms became so popular that the subsequent adherents of this 'strict observance' became known as Trappists. Adherence to the traditional Rule of St Benedict in matters of manual labour, the daily office and devotional reading were strictly followed. In addition, absolute silence was observed in these matters as well. In 1892, 230 years after de Rance's reforms, the Trappists were declared a separate order from those Cistercians who adhered to the 'common observance'.

Certainly the most notable Trappist of the twentieth century has been Thomas Merton. Merton resided in the largest Trappist abbey in the United States: Our Lady of Gethsemane, from 1941 to 1968. His works cover a wide range of issues from civil rights to peace, spiritual direction, liturgical renewal and ecumenism.

The Carthusians. In 1084, St Bruno settled with six fellow monks in the Chartreuse valley near Grenoble. This contemplative order originally possessed no formal Rule, however by the mid-twelfth century the *statuta antiqua* had been formulated. In subsequent years, several additions and elaborations were made to the Carthusian Rule. The Carthusians combined a traditional Benedictine coenobitic approach with the solitary ideal as originally expressed in the deserts of fourth- and fifth-century Egypt. Among their many distinguished mystics are included Richard Rolle, *Walter Hilton and the anonymous author of the *Cloud of Unknowing.

The author of the *Cloud of Unknowing* demonstrated the predilection among Carthusians for apophaticism and mental prayer.

The general of the order is also the prior of the mother house, La Grande Chartreuse. He is elected by the monks of that house, just as the abbot is elected in a Benedictine monastery. Each year a general chapter meeting is held with the priors of each of the Carthusian monasteries in attendance. The decisions of such annual meetings become binding legislation for the order in general. The Carthusians remain the most austere of all Roman Catholic religious orders.

JAMES V. SMITH

FURTHER READING: *Texts: The Rule of the Master* (trans. Luke Eberle; CS 6; Kalamazoo, MI, 1977); *The Rule of St Benedict in Latin and English with Notes* (ed. Timothy Fry; Collegeville, MN, 1981); *The Rule of St Benedict* (trans. Anthony C. Meisel and M.L. del Mastro; New York, 1975); *John Cassian: The Conferences* (trans. Boniface Ramsey; ACW 57; New York, 1997). *Studies:* Constance B. Bouchard, 'Merovingian, Carolingian and Cluniac Monasticism: Reform and Renewal in Burgundy', *J Eccl H* 41 (1990), pp. 365–88; Caroline W. Bynum, 'The Cistercian Conception of Community', *Harv Th R* 68 (1975), pp. 273–86; Karl S. Frank, *With Greater Liberty: A Short History of Christian Monasticism and Religious Orders* (CS 144; Kalamazoo, MI, 1993); Adrian Hastings, 'The Contribution of St Benedict to European Civilization' *Down R* 114 (1996), pp. 56–69; Robin B. Lockhart, *Halfway to Heaven: The Hidden Life of the Sublime Carthusians* (Spencer, MA, 1999); Jean Baptiste van Damme, *The Three Founders of Cîteaux* (CS 176; Spencer, MA, 1998).

Berdyaev, Nicholas (1874–1948)

Russian Orthodox philosopher and prolific author who wrote on religion, philosophy and politics. He was arrested as a young man for his involvement in socialism and for his criticism of existing institutions. In 1909 he was a contributor and editor with *Sergius Bulgakov (1871–1944) of the symposium *Vekhi* ('landmarks'), which opposed the materialism and positivism of the Russian intelligentsia. He was made a professor of philosophy at Moscow University in 1920, but he was forced to step down by the Bolsheviks in 1922. He spent the next 25 years of his life in exile, mainly in France. At least twenty of his books were translated into English between 1932 and 1954. During this period his writings exercised considerable influence in western intellectual circles and he gained something of a cult following.

Although Berdyaev was happy to be called an *existentialist, his primary interest was not in ontology, as found in other existentialist philosophers such as Heidegger and Sartre, but in the notion of freedom, both ideological and individual. His focus on freedom was derived partly from the Christian orientation of his thought, and partly in reaction to dialectical materialism and the development of *Marxism in the Soviet Union. For Berdyaev, freedom was embedded in the very fabric of the universe, being present before the creation of the world. It originated in the undifferentiated 'nothing' or *Ungrund*, a concept which he found in the writings of the seventeenth-century German theosophist Jakob Boehme, and which he developed in his essay *Freedom and Ungrund* (1935). He came under the influence of Vladimir Solovyov (1853–1900) as a young man and, like Sergius Bulgakov, developed an interest in sophiology, but Divine Wisdom (Sophia) never became a central theme of his writings as it did for Bulgakov.

Berdyaev developed a theory of person and personality based on spiritual freedom and responsibility. His personalism was also in some respects a reaction against the collective consciousness of Soviet Communism, but at the same time he was equally critical of capitalist exploitation. The way to transform human society was not through political or religious institutions, but through the human capacity for spiritual renewal and creativity. It was personal freedom that allowed human beings to transform themselves and, ultimately, to transform the societies in which they lived. If the end of history was the kingdom of God, then the realization of that end was a work of co-operation between God and humanity. For Berdyaev, the defence of human freedom was at the same time a defence of God's freedom to act through humanity. Any suppression of that freedom was a suppression of the spiritual dimension to human life and a violation of that inner space reserved for the encounter with the divine. As theology was largely a social construct, the only possible way to approach the divine was through personal experience and revelation.

Because he came from a Russian Orthodox background, Berdyaev was able to provide a fresh perspective on religious philosophy and the development of European thought. His Eastern Orthodox perspective on history, for example, particularly Russian history, gave westerners an alternative way of looking at the development of European civilization. This perspective is apparent in his critique of Communism in such works as *The Russian Revolution* (1935) and *The Origin of Russian Communism* (1937). It is as a Christian philosopher rather than as an Orthodox theologian that Berdyaev gives priority to human freedom and to the concept of the person as a spiritual category. Although an inspirational writer, his somewhat diffuse style tends at times to detract from his underlying message. His visionary approach to philosophical and religious problems made him a prophetic figure in the eyes of many of his admirers.

KEN PARRY

FURTHER READING: J.D. Kornblatt and R.F. Gustafson (eds.), *Russian Religious Thought* (Madison, WI, 1996); M.S. Shatz and J.E. Zimmerman (trans.), *Vekhi: Landmarks* (New York, 1994); F.C. Copleston, *Philosophy in Russia: From Herzen to Lenin and Berdyaev* (Notre Dame, IN, 1986); D.I. Lowrie, *Rebellious Prophet* (New York, 1960).

Berkeley, George (1685–1753)

George Berkeley was born near Kilkenny in Ireland in 1685. He entered Trinity College, Dublin, at the age of fifteen, and took his BA in 1704. He became a fellow of the college in 1707. In that year and the year following he filled two notebooks with reflections suggested to him by his reading of *Locke, Newton, Malebranche and others. These notebooks, now called the *Philosophical Commentaries* contain, in a nutshell, almost all of his philosophy. Some of the ideas contained in them are worked out in the *Essay towards a New Theory of Vision*, which appeared in 1709, and in Berkeley's best-known work, *A Treatise Concerning the Principles of Human Knowledge*, published in 1710. The *Three Dialogues between Hylas and Philonous* (1713) restate and expand some of the main arguments and theses of the *Principles*. These three works are Berkeley's most important. In 1724 Berkeley resigned his fellowship to become Dean of Derry. In 1734 he was appointed Bishop of Cloyne. In 1752 he settled in Oxford, where he died in 1753.

The central feature of Berkeley's philosophy is the thesis that to exist is the same as to perceive or to be perceived: *esse est percipi*. He discovered the principle as a young man of about twenty-two, and the discovery is recorded in his notebooks. The context of this principle is the work of Newton and Locke. Berkeley did not doubt the importance of Newton's scientific work and the discovery of universal physical laws. But he thought the validity of these discoveries independent of the existence of matter. His reaction to Locke's understanding of the concept of material substance was that it was without meaning, and moreover, that it was unnecessary as a hypothesis to explain the fact that we have ideas at all.

According to Berkeley, to see that existence is the same thing as perceiving or being perceived we are required only to consider what we might mean by the term 'exists'. He thought that if we did this we would be freed from a whole set of otherwise intractable problems – in physics and mathematics and in theology, for example. He argued that it was because of the misunderstanding of existence that many of the ancient philosophers had felt compelled to deny the existence of motion and other phenomena they detected through the normal mode of sense experience. The failure to ask what existence *was* was only a particular case of a more general philosophical deficiency. The universal cause of philosophical error was that human beings did not reflect properly on their own concepts. The source of the mistake did not lie in the concepts themselves – thing, substance, etc.; rather, it resided in improper reflection or lack of real reflection on them. Berkeley retained the terms but asked us to consider their necessary meaning in the light of his logical and conceptual analysis. With respect to the question of existence, the failure to examine the idea of existence is crucial. Pseudo-problems arise, Berkeley thought, as a result of the presupposition that there exist objects that neither perceive nor are perceived. The chief merit of Berkeley's principle is that it eliminates such problems and the accompanying perplexities at the point of origin.

Implicit in Berkeley's thesis is a particular world-picture, which he sometimes called *immaterialism*. In this world-view there exist two, and only two, sorts of objects – ideas and spirits. Spirits perceive ideas, or, perhaps better, have ideas. The existence of an idea consists in its being perceived or had by some spirit. The existence of a spirit consists in its having ideas and in its exercising acts of will. Only spirits perceive; only ideas are perceived; there cannot be any other kind of thing besides these two.

Because they exercise will, spirits are causal agents. They and they alone initiate changes in the world. Ideas are passive and owe their existence to spirits. There are two kinds of spirits. Human beings constitute finite spirits. The existence of God implies that there is at least one infinite spirit. For any given finite spirit, some of his or her ideas are caused by him or herself and some by God. The ideas caused by God have a tendency to come in collections or bundles. These we call tables, chairs, doors, et cetera, in accordance with the kind of ideas that constitute them. When finite spirits look at a table, they are perceiving or having ideas caused by God. When they think of or remember the same table, they are having ideas of which they themselves are the cause.

Berkeley believed that his immaterialist world-view would rid us once and for all of all metaphysical problems. Indeed, he thought that he had proved the conclusion that it was the only world-picture that did not result in metaphysical difficulties. Most surprisingly, he thought that it was the normal way of looking at the world, and that all of us, possibly without realizing it, are immaterialists before we are tempted into confusion by false science and improper philosophy. Paradoxically, Berkeley was persuaded that the logic of his immaterialist position would lead us back to normality.

The fate of Berkeley's thesis has not been a propitious one. In the eighteenth century there were no real attempts to come to grips with him. *Hume (1711–76, whose work appears not to be known to Berkeley) discerned the value of the work, but there were few others who did. Though *Kant had not read him, he claimed to repudiate him in a 'Refutation of Idealism'. The nineteenth-century attitude was much the same (Ueberweg's *History of Philosophy* at the end of the century confines Berkeley to a few words in a chapter on Locke). In the twentieth century, Berkeley's reputation suffered even more. In the context of G.E. Moore's common-sense philosophy, *Wittgenstein's later philosophy and Oxford 'ordinary language' philosophy, Berkeley was judged to be a philosopher who had generated philosophical nonsense through a gross misunderstanding of the logic of everyday language. It is the nature of paradox that Berkeley thought that those who rejected his view were in the grip of an equally captivating, though fundamentally illusory, picture of reality.

NEIL B. MacDONALD

FURTHER READING: *Texts: The Principles of Human Knowledge* (ed. Roger Woolhouse; London, 1993); *Three Dialogues Between Hylas and Philonous* (ed. and intro. by Robert Merrihew Adams; Indianapolis, IN, 1979); *Philosophical Works: Including the Works on Vision* (intro. and notes by M.R. Ayers; London, 1980); *Notebooks of George Berkeley* (with a postscript by Desiree Park; Oxford, 1984). *Studies:* Jonathan Dancy, *Berkeley: An Introduction* (Oxford, 1987); George Pitcher, *Berkeley* (London, 1977); J.O. Urmson, *Berkeley* (Oxford, 1982); G.J. Warnock, *Berkeley* (Oxford, 1982); Kenneth P. Winkler, *Berkeley: An Interpretation* (Oxford, 1994).

Bernard of Clairvaux (1090/1–1153)

A medieval monk and mystic, Bernard became a monk at the age of twenty-one, joining the recently-founded abbey of Cîteaux. Three years later he was appointed abbot of a new monastery at Clairvaux. Bernard went to Cîteaux to flee the world, but he became embroiled in most of the leading events of his time. He helped to secure the victory of Pope Innocent II over a rival pope; he opposed the teaching of *Peter Abelard and brought about its condemnation; he preached around Europe, raising support for the disastrous Second Crusade. In his era he was one of the most influential and widely-travelled leaders of the church.

In Bernard's time the new scholastic approach to theology, pioneered by *Anselm, was becoming established. Bernard, by contrast, was the last great representative of the earlier medieval tradition of monastic theology. The contrast between the two approaches is seen most starkly in Bernard's opposition to Abelard. Anselm, an important pioneer of *Scholasticism, had maintained the traditional Augustinian programme of 'faith seeking understanding' and had even used this as a title for his *Proslogion*. Abelard, by contrast, stated in the preface to his *Sic et Non* that 'by doubting we come to enquire and by enquiring we reach truth'. The approach of Bernard the mystical writer was very different – faith seeking experience.

The contrast between Bernard and Scholasticism should not, however, be overplayed. One of his earliest writings, on *Grace and Free Choice*, has some of the characteristics of scholastic theology. This work was influential upon early Scholasticism and also upon the later *Franciscan school. Bernard wrote warmly commending *Peter Lombard (*Ep.* 410) and

other scholastic theologians. He did not hesitate to make use of dialectical and other rational arguments in his theological works. Sommerfeldt goes too far in claiming that Bernard 'was, in short, a scholastic', but it is true that his opposition to Scholasticism should not be exaggerated.

Bernard preached regularly and many of his sermons survive. Some are unpolished, probably much as originally preached. Others are in a highly polished literary form designed for reading. These sermons are mostly based on various Sundays and saints' days throughout the church year. Bernard corresponded widely and more than five hundred of his letters survive, ranging from the personal and devotional to the official and political. Some are virtually treatises: on baptism, on the office of bishop and against the errors of Abelard.

Bernard wrote a number of treatises. Three of these are on monasticism: his *Apology* for the Cistercians against the Cluniacs, *Precept and Dispensation* on the correct interpretation of the *Rule of St Benedict* and a treatise *In Praise of the New Knighthood* on the new order of Templars. He also wrote a biography of Archbishop Malachy of Armagh (1094–1148), who helped to bring the Irish church into line with Roman practices.

In his early years Bernard wrote his masterly treatise on *Grace and Free Choice* in which he relates the work of grace and of the human will, along Augustinian lines. He argues that our good works are at the same time entirely the work of God's grace (thus leaving no room for boasting) and entirely the work of our free choice in that it is *we* who perform them (thus providing a basis for merit and reward). Grace so moves the will that it freely and willingly chooses the good.

Towards the end of his life Bernard wrote on *Consideration* for his former disciple, now Pope Eugenius III. Bernard urged him to find time for reflection or meditation in his busy life. He should consider himself (his person and his office), those placed under him, those around him at Rome and those above him (in the heavenly world). Bernard had a high view of the papacy, the pope being 'the unique vicar of Christ who presides not over a single people but over all' and has fullness of power. But Bernard is equally emphatic in his opposition to papal tyranny.

Bernard is best known as a spiritual writer. His book on *Loving God* has been called 'one of the most outstanding of all medieval books on mysticism'. In this work he describes the four degrees of love: loving oneself for one's own sake; loving God for one's own benefit; loving God for God's sake; and, finally, loving oneself for the sake of God (8:23–10:29). His *Steps of Humility and Pride* is based on the 12 steps of humility described in the *Rule of St Benedict*. But his best-known spiritual work is his *Sermons on the Song of Songs*, 86 sermons allegedly commenting on Song of Solomon 1:1 – 3:1, but in reality a treatise in sermonic form on the spiritual life of the monk and the steps towards mystical union with God.

Bernard has been called 'the last of the Fathers'. He was a brilliant writer, earning himself the title 'mellifluous' (sweet as honey). It is because of his literary skills and his considerable spiritual insight that Bernard has proved to be a 'man for all seasons', remaining popular in almost every generation.

ANTHONY N.S. LANE

FURTHER READING: *Texts: Sancti Bernardi Opera* (eds. Jean Leclercq, et al.; 8 vols.; Rome, 1957–77 [standard critical edition]); *The Works of Bernard of Clairvaux* (Kalamazoo, MI, 1970– [multi-volume modern translation]). *Studies:* Adriaan H. Bredero, *Bernard of Clairvaux between Cult and History* (Edinburgh, 1996); Michael Casey, *A Thirst for God: Spiritual Desire in Bernard of Clairvaux's Sermons on the Song of Songs* (Kalamazoo, MI, 1988); G.R. Evans, *The Mind of St Bernard of Clairvaux* (Oxford, 1983); Étienne Gilson, *The Mystical Theology of Saint Bernard* (London, 1940); Jean Leclercq, *Recueil d'études sur Saint Bernard et ses Écrits* (5 vols.; Rome, 1962–92); *Bernard of Clairvaux and the Cistercian Spirit* (Kalamazoo, MI, 1976); *A Second Look at Saint Bernard* (Kalamazoo, MI, 1990); J.R. Sommerfeldt, *The Spiritual Teachings of Bernard of Clairvaux* (Kalamazoo, MI, 1991); J.R. Sommerfeldt (ed.), *Bernardus Magister* (Kalamazoo, MI, 1992).

Bérulle, Pierre de (1575–1629)

Pierre de Bérulle was cardinal and founder of the French Oratory (in 1611) and a principal theologian and spiritual master in the renewal movement of the French Catholic 'Reformation'. Bérulle associated with many of the prominent spiritual leaders of his time and formed a constellation with the following people: Madeleine of Saint Joseph (1578–1637), the first French prioress of Paris's Great Carmel; Charles de Condren (1588–1641), Bérulle's successor as superior of the Oratory; Jean-Jacques Olier (1608–57), pastor of St Sulpice in Paris and founder of the 'Sulpicians', who were dedicated to establishing seminaries; Baron Gaston de Renty (1611–49), who disseminated the teachings of what has come to be called 'the French School' among influential laity, particularly through the reforming Company of the Blessed Sacrament; and Saint John Eudes (1601–80), a disciple of Olier's who founded male and female congregations. Contemporaneously influential constellations include those formed by the alliances between Francis de Sales and Jeanne de Chantal; Vincent de Paul and Louise de Marillac; *Pascal, *Descartes, and Malebranche; Richelieu and the Court. Some have suggested that all of this might be aptly characterized as constituting a French Catholic 'Golden Age', paralleling the earlier Spanish one.

Challenges from the Huguenots stimulated Bérulle to study the *patres*, the conciliar teachings, and the liturgical *lex orandi* carefully. These writings, together with the Scriptures, especially Paul and John, profoundly shaped his thought. In response, he wrote apologetic treatises on the ministry and the Eucharist. Bérulle was also able to draw on the patristic renaissance of the time. Mystical literature had just come in to France and was popular in the reformist circles of the 'devout' which the Cardinal frequented at Madame Acarie's salon. This tradition (the Rheno-Flemish northern current and the southern current of Spanish mysticism, especially Teresian and Ignatian) profoundly influenced his writing as well.

Bérulle's earlier thought is commonly said to reflect a more 'abstract mysticism', which regarded Jesus' humanity as an aid for beginners in the Christian life. But this 'abstract mysticism' is progressively transcended in his later thought by a kind of apophatic (non-conceptual) experience considered typical of the northern mystical current. There is now some question, however, concerning the adequacy of this characterization – both for Bérulle and for the northern mystical tradition as a whole. His *Bref Discours de l'abnégation intérieure* (1597), an adaptation of a treatise by Isabelle Bellinzaga which is usually regarded as Bérulle's apophatic writing par excellence, contains only a few references to Jesus as an example of our call to spiritual detachment. But how should one interpret this? Does 'example' simply mean that we are not always 'bound' to the Saviour, even in the highest stages of detachment? Or should we give the notion of 'example' a more 'exemplarist', Neoplatonic interpretation, in which it becomes the ontological foundation of our Christian existence?

From about 1602, when he completed *Ignatius's *Spiritual Exercises,* Bérulle became unambiguously Christocentric. Because he was co-superior of the discalced Carmelite nuns he helped establish in France he was able to deepen his contact with the spirituality of the Carmelite reformer *Teresa of Avila, who had experienced a Christocentric 'conversion' (see her *Life*, ch. 22). From 1615–23, Bérulle was involved in a controversy over the appropriateness of 'vows of servitude', which he advocated taking, to Mary and Jesus. Pope Urban VIII (who is credited with naming Bérulle 'the apostle of the incarnate Word', and who named him a cardinal in 1627) finally resolved this dispute in his favour. The debate forced Bérulle to ground his devotional practices in the soil of the Trinity and Christology, and the result was the apologetic *Grandeurs of Jesus* (1623).

These vows of servitude, first to Mary and then, in imitation of and participation in her grace, to Jesus, the incarnate Word, were an expression of the Bérullian Christocentric Trinitarianism. Servitude expresses the eternal Son's obedient relationship to the Father, manifested in the historical economy through the kenotic servitude of Jesus. The temporal origins of the incarnation emerged through Mary first sharing in this servitude in a singularly unique and intimate way. Sharing in the journey from Mary's servitude to that of Jesus was a sort of novitiate in spirituality for Bérulle. Taking these vows, finally explained as renewals of the baptismal promises, was a way of experientially personalizing doctrine. In this way he exemplified the unity between doctrine and spirituality sought by the French School of mysticism. Bérulle incorporates some restorationist and classical tendencies with a Renaissance and Baroque sensitivity to the human in, for example, his stress upon Jesus' incarnate humanity and our call to participate in this in both a common manner and in a way suited to our unique personal talents. 'Jesus … wishes that we have a unique share in [his] various states, according to the diversity of his will for us and our piety toward him' (*Oeuvres de Piété*, 17, col. 940, ed. Migne). Bérulle's thought is 'exemplarist' in the Neoplatonic sense – the Divine Life is the exemplary archetype in which all creation participates.

But Bérulle's thought is also biblical and Trinitarian, for Jesus is the incarnate *and* divine Word, who is the central link in a great 'chain of love' comprised of the Trinity, the incarnation and the Eucharist, according to his *Discourse on the State* and *Grandeurs of Jesus*, 6, 4, 130 (ed. W.M. Thompson). The incarnate Word is the centre or 'sun' – the 'Copernican Revolution' is the movement of the universe around the Son ('Sun'), he wrote (*Discourse*, disc. 2). This movement reflects on and enables us to participate in the Trinity on the one hand, and simultaneously through his Spirit gives the Christian life a Eucharistic shape and existence in the church on the other. Bérulle's 'science of the saints', as he called it, is an alternative to the rationalistic style of late *Scholasticism. But it also shares something in common with attempts to wed scholastic thought with affective sensitivity such as we find it in Louis Bail's *Théologie Affective, ou Saint Thomas en Méditations* (1638–50) or Guillaume de Contenson's *Theologia mentis et Cordis* (1668–87).

Bérulle's thinking is organic, seeking to unite what has been severely severed – whether that be authority, holiness and doctrine (in the priesthood, as he put it in a famous letter); theology and spirituality, or analogously faith and reason; church as institution and church as Eucharistic communion; or church and society. In stressing unity he also describes the image of the 'chain of love' as a 'chain of unity'. Thus, one needs to read him as a deeply textured thinker, one dimension penetrated by and opening out onto another. The image of a chain indicates differentiated, overlapping unity – not monochrome uniformity.

Contemporary scholarship emphasizes Bérulle's Christocentrism, in reaction to Henri Bremond, who stressed his accent on God's transcendence and our corresponding posture of worship and adoration. *Karl Rahner singled out the writings of Bérulle as among the rare theologically articulate reflections upon how the Christian actually shares in the living Christ. The temporal performance of the states and mysteries of Jesus is over, but their power and love are alive, present and eternally fruitful (*Oeuvres*, 77). The term 'states' would seem to stress the permanency of Jesus' mysteries, while 'mystery' brings out the sacramental dimension of Jesus' deeds as efficacious signs of God at work in history. (See *Catechism of the Catholic*

Church, nos. 512ff., which rehabilitates the appropriateness of this tradition, and centrally refers to John Eudes [no. 521].) Bérulle and his School contemplate the entire range of the mysteries, from the 'eternal birth' as the Father's Word to the temporal birth (incarnation), and then – after a fascinating contemplation of the full range of the earthly mysteries from infancy to death – the third birth into resurrection life (*Grandeurs*, dis. 8–12).

In the image of the chain the incarnation links creation with the Trinity on the one side, and with the Eucharist on the other. 'All the works of God lead us to a knowledge of a Trinity' (*Oeuvres*, 15E). Through participation in Jesus – a key notion in the French School – our lives are increasingly configured through the Spirit to the kenotic servitude and worship of the Son toward his Father. As we are deified, our sinful selves are healed by being brought into communion with all the works of the Trinity. The Eucharist, the third part of the chain, can represent the economy of the church, or those who make up the 'whole Christ' – the Virgin Mary pre-eminently, and after her the other saints. No artificial separation of Jesus from his ecclesial community exists. Bérulle's *Elevation on Mary Magdalene* is particularly exemplary in this regard, celebrating her as an apostle to the apostles and, next to the Virgin Mary, uniquely blessed in the mystery of love. The depth of participation in Jesus is the central focus of this celebration of Mary. Hence, we can see why the French School is so Marian, for it holds that no other saint shared more intimately in the life of the Saviour. The literary genres of the French School emerge from and foster this 'participation', which brings knowledge. As the gift of the Spirit's indwelling, this participation takes the form of prayer (both personal and liturgical), which lifts us up ('elevates') to the Triune God.

Bérulle's focus upon adoration, worship, and human sin is a reaction to *Pelagianism and extreme Humanism. The accent upon Jesus' humanity and our participation through it represents an integration of the human dimension with the divine, of the kataphatic with the apophatic, which remains provocatively challenging. Jesus himself remains unique. His 'lack' of a human hypostasis (in the conciliar sense) is interpreted as an ontological *kenosis,* a peerless servitude of the humanity of Jesus to the divine Word. This God-Man is the adored adorer, both in the triune life (the Son worshipfully obeying the Father), and in the economy in imitation of that triune life, as the humanity of Jesus is in kenotic servitude to the Word.

WILLIAM M. THOMPSON

FURTHER READING: *Texts:* Cerf (Paris) is currently publishing Bérulle's *Oeuvres complètes* (ed. M. Dupuy; 13 vols.); earlier and incomplete editions were published by Maison de l'Oratoire, Montsoult (2 vols.; 1960); and in 1 vol. by Migne in 1856. See also M. Dupuy (ed.),'Des nouveaux inédits de Bérulle', *R Hist Sp* 48 (1972), pp. 435–52; 52 (1976), pp. 345–86; 53 (1977), pp. 275–316; *R E Aug 26* (1980), pp. 266–85. *Interpretive anthologies:* W.M. Thompson (ed.), *Bérulle and the French School: Selected Writings* (trans. L.M. Glendon; CWS; New York, 1989); R. Deville, *The French School of Spirituality: An Introduction and Reader* (trans. A. Cunningham; Pittsburgh, 1994); M. Dupuy, *Pierre de Bérulle: Introduction et Choix de Textes* (Témoins de la Foi; Paris, 1964); H.U. von Balthasar (ed. and trans.), *Kardinal Pierre de Bérulle: Gründer des französischen Oratoriums* (Leben im Mysterium Jesu; Einsiedeln, 1984). *Studies:* H. Bremond, *The Triumph of Mysticism*, III: *A Literary History of Religious Thought in France* (trans. K. Montgomery; London, 1936); F. Guillén Preckler, *Bérulle Aujourd'hui 1575–1975: Pour une Spiritualité de l'Humanité du Christ* (Le Point Théologique; Paris, 1978); W.M. Thompson, *Christology and Spirituality* (New York, 1991). *Helpful:* L. Cognet, 'Ecclesiastical Life in France', in H. Jedin and J. Dolan (eds.), *History of the Church*, VI: *The Church in the Age of Absolutism and Enlightenment* (trans. G. Holst; New York, 1981), pp. 3–106; K. Rahner, 'Brief Observations on Systematic Christology Today', in *Theological Investigations*, XXI (trans. H. Riley; New York, 1988), pp. 228–38.

Beza, Theodore (1519–1605)

Theodore Beza was born to a noble family in Vézelay in Burgundy in 1519. He had an excellent humanist education. At the age of ten he was sent to learn Greek and Latin under the humanist teacher Melchior Wolmar, one of the best Greek scholars of his day. Beza remained for seven years with Wolmar, who had adopted the ideas of the *Reformation and who influenced him greatly. When in 1535 Wolmar decided that it would be safer to take refuge in Germany, the Beza family sent young Theodore to Orléans to read law. He finished his studies in 1539 and then returned to Paris (1539–48). He was above all a man of letters, interested in languages and literature. His personal income meant he could lead the life of a young nobleman and immerse himself in Virgil, Ovid, Catullus and Martialis, as well as the classical Greek authors. Such poetic activity enabled him to produce the famous *Poemata* (1548). They contain some light passages in the style of Ovid for which he was severely criticized when he became a 'Reformer'. Beza, however, remained attached to these poems, of which the 1548, 1569 and 1597 editions are extant, as are the final hand-written corrections which the author noted in his own personal copy. Though convinced by Wolmar's ideas, Beza lived as a 'Nicodemite' while in Paris: he was intellectually and spiritually estranged from the church and married (to Claudine Denosse). It was a secret wedding, because he did not want to lose his ecclesiastical income. But when he caught the plague and became seriously ill, the presence of death and the imminence of God's judgement led to his conversion. As a result of this psychological shock, he decided to leave Paris in 1548. His possessions were then confiscated and he was even condemned to be burnt in effigy at the stake. Beza settled in Lausanne, where Pierre Viret had invited him to teach Greek in the newly established university. He was its rector from 1552 to 1554 and remained in Lausanne for nine years. His abilities as a theologian, an exegete and a polemicist soon became manifest and led to him becoming *Calvin's closest disciple. He joined Calvin in Geneva in 1558, refusing to remain in the state church which the Bernese authorities had established in Lausanne. During this period he published his *Confession of the Christian Faith* (1559), which he wrote to prove to his father that he was neither an unbeliever nor a heretic. That this work was published more than thirty-five times in the sixteenth century – in French, Latin, English, German and Dutch – shows the extent to which his thought influenced Reformed circles.

From then on Beza stayed in Geneva, first of all alongside Calvin and then alone, leading and maintaining the work that the latter had begun. He arrived in Geneva just three years after Calvin had managed to impose on the city his conception of Christian living, and that victory was still fragile. This was also the time when Protestantism was making rapid progress in France; around 1560 it even seemed that the Reformation would prevail in Beza's native land. At the same time there was violent controversy with the German *Lutherans, and the Calvinist Reformation badly needed a gifted writer to face the challenge. So Beza set

to work on several fronts. He consolidated the institutions founded by Calvin: the Company of Pastors, the Consistory and the Academy. His skill and authority enabled him to keep them going for almost half a century, though he was obliged to negotiate constantly with the civil power. He made Geneva a model of a new society and a new religion, and impregnated it with that austere way of life that would later be called *Puritanism. He poured his energy into the Academy and became its first rector from its founding in 1559. He attracted to it first-class teachers (Hotman, Beroald, Daneau), but most of the time he alone taught theology. In 1586 the city no longer had the means to fund the university and decided it should close. But Beza, aged sixty-seven, continued to teach in private. That continuity made it easier to reopen the following year. Beza preached and taught regularly and ensured that refugees were made welcome. He remained a central figure in Genevan life until the beginning of the seventeenth century. He made a solid contribution to the stability of the Genevan model by maintaining excellent relationships with his Swiss counterparts in Zurich (*Bullinger, then Gwalther) and in Basle (Grynaeus) and by leading and co-ordinating the defence of Reformed orthodoxy.

Beza also played an important part in the events taking place in France. In 1560 he encouraged the future Henry IV's mother, Jeanne d'Albret, in her Protestant faith. She became one of the Reformation's firmest supporters. He was the spokesman for the Huguenots at the Poissy conference (1561), where he gave a famous *Harangue* in which he declared his faith and provoked a genuine scandal. After the failure of this conference, he remained in France for several months. As he was on good terms with some of the highest-ranking Protestant nobles, he became an adviser to their leaders, a role that he held throughout the wars of religion. He also worked at preserving the unity of the French Huguenots, fighting against the congregationalist ideas held by the followers of Pierre Ramus. He presided over several synods of the French churches, including the La Rochelle synod, which published the La Rochelle Confession of Faith, a basic reference for the French churches. The events surrounding the St Bartholomew's Day massacre made him lose all confidence in the French monarchy, whether it was responsible for the killing or forced into it. He then published anonymously his famous *De jure magistratum* (1574), which gave lower magistrates the right to oppose tyrants by force of arms if necessary. He also wrote *The Ecclesiastical History of the Reformed Churches in the Kingdom of France* (1580), a first-hand testimony to the struggles and suffering of the French Huguenots, intended for future generations.

All through his life, Beza also took an interest in relations between the Calvinist Reformation and Germany. He was sent three times to Germany between 1557 and 1558 to attempt a *rapprochement* with the Lutherans, but he was forced to admit that agreement was impossible. He tried in vain to stop the 'Formula of Concord' (1580) using the condemnation of the Reformed churches to bolster Lutheran unity. He steadfastly defended the Swiss position before German princes such as the Palatine of the Rhine and the Landgrave of Hesse, whom he thought might be disposed to support it, and he was involved in almost constant controversy with the more intransigent Lutherans such as Brenz, Selneccer and Jakob Andreae. Beza also maintained close contact with the numerous Reformed churches in Eastern Europe, in Hungary, Poland and Bohemia, as well as with those in England and Scotland. He trained many students who came to Geneva from these regions. But these diplomatic tasks did not prevent him from continuing his activities as a scholar, a theologian and an exegete. He developed and defended Calvin's doctrine of predestination, both at the outset of his career (*Tabula praedestinationis*, 1555) and much later (*De praedestinationis doctrina*, 1582). His main work is certainly the New Testament (*Novum Testamentum ... cum annotationibus*), the successive editions of which he revised as long as he lived. Beza began work on the New Testament in 1551. His annotations were not only philological notes but also a genuine commentary that Beza continually improved on despite the little time his other responsibilities allowed him. Beza's New Testament was published in his lifetime in 1558, 1565, 1582 and 1598; it created a truly Reformed tradition of the gospel text and was republished more than one hundred and fifty times right up to 1965. As regards literature, which Beza never neglected, we have his masterful translation of the Psalms, which was highly successful. In a lighter vein, he also published *Icônes* (1580), a kind of illustrated

dictionary of the great men of the Reformation, which was a very unusual undertaking.

BÉATRICE NICOLLIER

FURTHER READING: *Texts: Tractatus pius et moderatus de vera excommunicatione ...* (Geneva, 1590); *A Little Book of Christian Questions and Responses in which the Principal Headings of the Christian Religion are Briefly Set Forth* (trans. Kirk M. Summers; Allison Park, PA, 1986); *A Discourse Wrytten by M. Theodore de Beza, Conteyning in Briefe the Historie of the Life and Death of Maister John Calvin* (trans. I.S. London; Amsterdam / New York, 1972); *Correspondance* (ed. Aubert, Dufour, Nicollier, Bodenmann, et al.; 20 vols.; Geneva, 1960–98). *Studies:* Alexander Cunningham, *An Essay Concerning Church Government* (Edinburgh, 1703); Frédéric Louis Gardy, *Bibliographie des Oeuvres Théologiques, Littéraires, Historiques et Juridiques de Théodore de Bèze* (Geneva, 1960); P.F. Geisendorf, *Théodore de Bèze* (Geneva, 1949); F. Gardy, *Bibliographie des oeuvres ... de Théodore de Bèze* (Geneva, 1960); Philip C. Holtrop, *The Bolsec Controversy on Predestination, from 1551 to 1555: The Statements of Jerome Bolsec, and the Responses of John Calvin, Theodore Beza, and other Reformed Theologians* (Lewiston, NY, 1993); Tadataka Maruyama, *The Ecclesiology of Theodore Beza: The Reform of the True Church* (Geneva, 1978); Jill Raitt, *The Eucharistic Theology of Theodore Beza: Development of the Reformed Doctrine* (AAR Studies in Religion 4; Chambersburg, 1972).

Black Theology

The roots of black theology may be traced to the black church in North America. The role of the black church in the development of black theology reached a high point in two significant movements that emerged in the 1950s and 1960s in North America: the civil rights movement led by Baptist preacher Martin Luther King, Jr, and the black power movement led by Stokely Carmichael and Malcolm X (the son of a Baptist preacher). The black power movement is related to the black church not only because the term 'black power' was coined by a Baptist preacher from Harlem, Adam Clayton Powell, Jr, at a rally in Chicago in May 1965, but also because its philosophy of black dignity and black determination had its roots in the teaching of black church leaders such as Nat Turner, Denmark Vesey, Bishop Henry McNeil Turner and Marcus Garvey. The civil rights movement and the black power movement went in different directions. The civil rights movement aimed at a reformation of American life, and the black power movement demanded change in the structure of oppression. Each movement had immense influence upon the development and articulation of black theology. In the midst of the black power struggle, which came to a head with the issuance of James Foreman's 'Black Manifesto' to the white religious establishment, *James Cone, a little-known theologian, published his first book, *Black Theology and Black Power*. In this book, Cone contends that black power is the power of Jesus Christ: 'The existence of the church is grounded exclusively in Christ. And in twentieth century America, *Christ means Black Power*' (p. 112). In a chapter entitled 'Black Church and Black Power', Cone argues that his understanding of black power is not strange to the black church but rather emerged from its life and teaching. While grounding his work in the black power movement, and at the same time calling into question the love ethic of the civil rights movement, Cone writes:

> Some black preachers, like the Rev. Highland Garnet, even urged outright rebellion against the evils of white power. He knew that appeals to 'love' or 'goodwill' would have little effect on minds warped by their own high estimation of themselves. Therefore, he taught that the spirit of liberty is a gift from God, and God thus endows the slave with the zeal to break the chains of slavery. (p. 96)

Another significant voice in the development of black theology was Major Jones. His perspective on black power differs from that of Cone in that he drew more from the reformist wing of the civil rights movement that was led by Martin Luther King, Jr. In his important book *Black Awareness*, Jones points out that African Americans have several interpretations of black theology. According to Jones, black theology is an indispensable part of the 'black revolution', in which black America is involved. In a context in which theology is the domain of white people, black theology becomes a protest against the traditional way theology is done. Jones states: 'Black theology differs from traditional theology by the simple reason that it may not be as concerned to describe such traditional themes as the eternal nature of God's existence as it is to explore the impermanent, paradoxical and problematic nature of human existence' (*Black Awareness* [Nashville, TN, 1971], p.13). Hence an important task of black

theology is the reclaiming of black America from humiliation.

The black experience becomes an important source in the articulation of black theology. Black theologians claim that any theology in America that ignores the black experience runs the risk of becoming irrelevant to black people. The importance of the black experience as a source for the doing of theology is highlighted in a statement made by the National Committee of Black Churchmen at the Interdenominational Theological Center in Atlanta, Georgia, on 13 June 1969:

> Black theology is a theology of black liberation. It seeks to plumb the black condition in the light of God's revelation in Jesus Christ, so that the black community can see that the gospel is commensurate with the achievement of black humanity. Black theology is a theology of 'blackness'. (*Black Theology*, I, p. 102)

In a more recent book, *Christian Ethics for Black Theology*, Jones points out that the social location of the theologian is of first importance in helping the black person to give a different answer from the white person who is confronted with the question 'what ought I to do?'. According to Jones: 'The answer to this question depends on who is asking the question, and the answer may be made in the light of what the person has become. If he is black the answer may be one thing: if he is white, it might be quite another' ([Nashville, 1974], p.16). Jones concludes that because black theology takes the black experience as the point of departure for theological reflection it is not only a theology of protest against the neglect of the black American experience by white religionists, but it also constitutes a new approach to theology. Black theology becomes a theology of blackness.

J. Deotis Roberts, Sr speaks to some of the themes highlighted by Jones as he articulates for us how the identity of the black community is related to theological reflection. He sharpens the focus:

> The black man in recent years has become color conscious in the sense that he is aware that he is black and that to the white majority, which controls both the wealth and the power in this country, he is not equal. This means that any white man, however poor or illiterate, may assume superiority over any black man whatever his wealth, education, or position. Prejudice is a prejudgement at sight, and the black

man is highly visible. ('Black Consciousness in Theological Perspective', in *Quest for Black Theology* [ed. J. Gardiner and J. Deotis Roberts, Sr; Philadelphia, 1971], p. 64)

According to Roberts, the central theological problem confronting American Christianity is racism. This reality forces black Christians to ask about the relationship between black consciousness and theology.

> The black man, who lives in the dark ghetto, in a rented shack and who works under a white boss, whose environment is regulated from city hall, whose landlord is white or Jewish and lives in the suburbs, lives an other-directed, powerless life. What does the Christian understanding of God say to this man whose life is controlled by a white landlord, a white boss, and white politicians? (*Quest*, p. 72)

The immediate task of black people in America, explains Roberts, is black solidarity and black dignity. 'When we know our identity, have gained our self-respect, and are fully confident as a people, we will be in a position to be reconciled to others as equals and not as subordinates. If we can take our black consciousness up into our Christian faith, we will find it not only unmanly but unchristian to be reconciled on less than an equal basis' (*Quest*, p.79; for a more adequate treatment of black consciousness and reconciliation in Roberts's thought, see his *Liberation and Reconciliation*). All three theologians speak of the creation of a new social order that has its basis in the coming reign of God. Hope for these theologians is more than the anticipation of liberation. It is both the motive force and the shape of human liberation. The vision of the eschatological reign of God makes Christians dissatisfied with reality as they know it and provides the courage for them to work for a new social order. To be in the realm of God means to live with two warrants at once. On the one hand, it means accepting God's grace and being willing to give up everything for it. This is what repentance means. On the other hand, to be in the realm of God means to work for the creation of a new world. This is necessary because the Christ we serve is the 'Christ who transforms culture'.

This unwillingness to put asunder what God has joined together – the eschatological and the concrete historical – is what has uniquely equipped black Christians in their march toward freedom and human liberation. It is the encounter of black Christians with the crucified and risen Saviour that provided the inspirational source and the sustaining power for the community of the oppressed as they sought change in the social, economic and political spheres of society. The presence of the crucified and risen Saviour in the community of the oppressed empowers this community to say 'yes' to all that affirms its right to liberation and to say 'no' to all that encroaches on and frustrates its being. Liberation, then, becomes shouting 'no' to exploitation and victimization of all sorts and acknowledging that these evils do not have their foundation in God's will.

The temptation confronting the church is for it to retreat to preaching, praying and business as usual as it avoids the demands of justice in the world of racism, sexism, materialism and classism. Black theology insists that authentic liberation demands a questioning of the structures of injustice that deny all of God's children the possibility and the opportunity to be fully human. This transformation for which black theology pleads must also express itself within the church in a transformation of values. Black theologians point out that there is a danger that the church is aping the dominant culture, making necessary the urgent need for prophetic self-criticism within the church. It is precisely at this point that black theology asserts that in the life, death and resurrection of Jesus of Nazareth there is an unprecedented disclosure of who we are as a people and who we are called to become. It is from the perspective of Jesus Christ that the community defines itself.

Black theology asserts two Christological moments as critical for its self-understanding. The first is the history of Jesus in which he identified with the wretched of the earth, in the end dying between two thieves on a hill far away. Jesus' act of taking human oppression upon himself was not a historical accident but a choice that witnesses to his identification with victims today. The second Christological moment that black theology asserts is that through cross and resurrection, Christ offers victims the possibility of liberation from their present situation. To encounter the risen and exalted Christ is to become impatient with all forms of injustice. Because Christ takes our condition upon himself, we know that we are not what the world says we are. The resurrection of Christ binds him to our humiliated condition and his presence in our community opens up for us liberation vistas of the humanity to which God has called us.

NOEL LEO ERSKINE

FURTHER READING: James Cone, *Black Theology and Black Power* (New York, 1969); *God of the Oppressed* (New York, 1975); *Martin & Malcolm & America: A Dream or a Nightmare?* (Maryknoll, NY, 1991); James Cone and Gayraud S. Wilmore (eds.), *Black Theology: A Documentary History*, I: 1966–1979; II: 1980–1992 (Maryknoll, NY, 1979, 1993); Kelly Brown Douglas, *The Black Christ* (Maryknoll, NY, 1993); Noel Leo Erskine, *King Among the Theologians* (Cleveland, OH, 1994); Cain Hope Felder (ed.), *Stony the Road We Trod* (Minneapolis, 1991); Major Jones, *The Color of God* (Macon, GA, 1987); C. Eric Lincoln and Lawrence H. Mamiya, *The Black Church in African American Studies* (Durham, NC, 1990); Peter Paris, *The Spirituality of African Peoples* (Minneapolis, 1995); J. Deotis Roberts, *Liberation and Reconciliation* (Maryknoll, NY, rev. edn, 1993).

Blumhardt, Johann Christoph (1805–80) and Christoph Friedrich (1842–1919)

Father and son who pastored and led the German evangelical community at Möttlingen and later at Bad Boll. They became renowned for the depth and breadth of their pastoral work, which included a ministry of healing for mental and bodily illness and an extraordinary revival, as well as initiatives in global missions and politics. Due to the relative isolation of their ministry and since the cumulative impact of their work coincided with the First World War, they have remained relatively unknown in the English-speaking world, their writings being largely untranslated. Nevertheless, their conversations with the many visitors to Bad Boll, as well as their collected writings, influenced a scattered but important group of pastors and theologians including *Barth, Thurneysen, *Brunner, *Bonhoeffer, Ellul and *Moltmann. The four volumes of Christoph's collected writings in German have, as their titles, themes corresponding to the four main periods of their ministry. These usefully summarize their thought and reveal how the son's work was grounded in and developed that of the father.

1. Jesus is Victor! Karl Barth adopted this phrase from the elder Blumhardt's dramatic report regarding a certain Gottliebin Dittus, a woman who had been tormented, dominated and persecuted by what Blumhardt could only

regard as a demonic power. At the climax of a seemingly hopeless two years of ministering, Blumhardt dared to ask and to pray, 'Is there then no other power in the world than that of the devil?' In this moment of crisis, Blumhardt took hold of her hands and said, 'fold your hands and pray: Lord Jesus, help me. We have watched long enough what the devil does. Now we want to see what the Lord Jesus can do.' The words 'Jesus is victor!' were spoken as the 'final cry of a routed angel of Satan, and therefore from within the darkest darkness of the world' (Barth, *CD*, IV.3, p. 170). Shortly thereafter, the woman returned to herself. Other remarkable signs followed and a general revival arose. Thus did Blumhardt part from his Pietist companions who had counselled patient resignation in the face of evil. 'Is it a tolerable theological notion that 2,000 years ago the glory of God was proclaimed over the darkness by signs and wonders, while today patient resignation in the power of darkness is to be the last word?' (Barth, *Protestant Theology*, p. 649).

2. Die and Jesus Will Live! Though he established a reputation as a faith healer, Blumhardt held that one should neither be surprised if irruptions from the coming kingdom break in, nor should one build the altar there. 'To be cleansed is more important than to be healed! To have a heart for God's cause, and not to be chained to the world, but to be able to move for the kingdom of God!' (Lejeune, p. 49). The elder Blumhardt again sounded a different note from the Pietism of his day when he chastised a constricting attention on individual life and faith. 'Yes dear Christian, make sure that you die saved! But the Lord Jesus wants more. He wants not only my redemption and yours, but the redemption of all the world. He wants to finish off the evil that dominates in the world and make the whole world free that occupies itself in sheer godlessness.' Thus Blumhardt explored a new (or newly discovered) way of hope. Whereas Pietism focused on the soul, the interior, the human conscience, Blumhardt hungered for the Holy Spirit to be poured out on all flesh, including the healing of body, soul and even community. 'To this degree, Blumhardt's thought is Eastern-Christian and not Western' (Barth, *Protestant Theology*, p. 650).

3. You are God's! 'You men are of God! Whether you are still godless or already devout, in judgment or in mercy, in salvation or in damnation, you belong to God! You man, listen: you are of God, no hell has any claim on you.' In his next period, Blumhardt was led fully into the world, seeking the kingdom of God not in any religious church form. 'The kingdom of God comes onto the streets, where the poorest live, the outcasts, the miserable' (Lejeune, p. 54). Blumhardt came to interpret the working for social justice as a great prophetic sign of God's kingdom. The striving for a new social order was, for him, grounded in his faith that God's kingdom, promised by Christ, was coming to transform the entire created order, including social relationships. Because he now publicly sided with Democratic Socialism, Blumhardt was asked to renounce his title and rank as pastor of the church of Württemberg. He allowed himself to accept a candidacy for the legislative assembly, serving a term of six years (1900–06). Though later he withdrew from such political activity, he continued to view the movement for social justice as both God's judgement and promise. Not content simply chasing ambulances to tend the wounds of the next casualty, Blumhardt insisted that the church's witness address the larger social roots of particular evil situations.

4. God's Kingdom Comes!

'There is a credible tradition that at Bad Boll a coach was kept ready, year in, year out, with all its equipment, ready to begin the journey to the Holy Land to meet the returning Christ, if need be' (Barth, *Protestant Theology*, p. 647). Though the early Christian hope of a new coming of the Lord had been placed under a bushel, Blumhardt again placed the light of this hope upon a lamp stand. His hope was a longing for a real kingdom and government of God which historically begins, continues and is perfected on earth until God is all in all. Blumhardt saw the present world as temporary, not something to accept in resignation, but full of barriers that obstruct God's help and which we should push aside. In the meantime, believers are summoned to wait with an eager longing which does not express passive inactivity but an expectancy that the decisive help comes finally from Christ. Because this waiting is not just for a future coming, though, Blumhardt preferred to say that the Saviour is on the way. 'It is right to say with the apostles, "He is at hand, He will come soon!" He will not only come at some moment which lies in a distant future; our whole life is filled with the coming of the Lord Jesus. Daily we rejoice at His coming' (Lejeune, p. 225).

ROGER NEWELL

FURTHER READING: *Texts:* Karl Barth, *Action in Waiting* (Rifton, NY, 1969), on Christoph Blumhardt, including his 'Joy in the Lord'; R. Lejeune, *Christoph Blumhardt and his Message* (Rifton, NY, 1963), biography and sermons; Christoph Blumhardt, *Evening Prayers for Every Day of the Year* (Rifton, NY, 1975); Johann Christoph Blumhardt and Christoph Friedrich Blumhardt, *Now Is Eternity* (Rifton, NY, 1976); *Thoughts About Children* (Rifton, NY, 1985); *Thy Kingdom Come: A Blumhardt Reader* (ed. Vernard Eller; Grand Rapids, 1980). *Studies in English with significant mention of the Blumhardts:* Eduard Thurneysen, *A Theology of Pastoral Care* (Richmond, VA, 1962); Karl Barth, *Church Dogmatics*, IV.3, 'The Doctrine of Reconciliation' (Edinburgh, 1976); *Protestant Theology in the Nineteenth Century* (Valley Forge, PA, 1976); Eberhard Busch, *Karl Barth: His Life from Letters and Autobiographical Texts* (London, 1976); *Revolutionary Theology in the Making: Barth-Thurneysen Correspondence, 1914–1925* (ed. James Smart; Richmond, VA, 1964); Theodor Bovet, *That They May Have Life: A Handbook on Pastoral Care for Christian Ministers and Laymen* (London, 1964).

Boethius (d. 525/6)

Anicius Manlius Severinus Boethius, born in Rome c. 475–80, was an office holder in the Italian administration of Theodoric the Great. He was also a thinker who deeply influenced theology throughout the Middle Ages. Following the collapse of the western empire in 476, the great families which traditionally supplied the imperial administration began to work for the new masters. Thus Boethius is in all things a Roman of late antiquity (he belonged to the *gens Anicii* and was reared by a member of the *gens Symmachi*). But he was also aware of the new conditions of post-Roman Europe. Today remembered mainly as a writer, in his own day he was also famous as a politician and man of practical genius. These abilities brought him to Theodoric's attention and allowed him to rise rapidly so that he was consul by 510. He appears to have been a just politician: he prevented a famine in Campania, and when a certain Albinus was charged with treason, Boethius defended him. This defence led to his own imprisonment at Pavia and eventually to his execution in 525/6. From the time of Procopius (mid-sixth century), Boethius was presented as a martyr for orthodoxy against the *Arian Theodoric; and as 'Severinus' he is considered a saint by the Roman Catholic Church.

Brought up a Christian, Boethius began to write on philosophical matters at an early age (Cassiodorus [*Variae* I, 45] knew of the fame of these writings in 507) and until his death worked to preserve what was best in classical education and learning. He also made a useful contribution to the clarification of basic problems in theology in Latin. His contribution to theology should be considered under four headings: education; logic; the theological tractates; and the *Consolatio Philosophiae*.

Education. Boethius wrote introductions to the four 'secondary' disciplines – he coined the term *quadrivium* ('four ways') – of geometry, arithmetic, astronomy and music. These disciplines had already been integrated into a Christian curriculum by *Augustine (*De doctrina christiana* II), and the textbooks were widely used. But rather than being manuals for practical education, the works written within the Neoplatonic tradition of viewing number and harmony as a key to the cosmos were used within the Augustinian scheme of viewing the work of the creation as being the numbered work of God. From this perspective they were often the works which first introduced theology to students (see Cassiodorus, *Institutiones* II, 1).

Logic. Alongside his political work, Boethius appears to have devoted a great deal of time to reading and writing. Realizing that a knowledge of Greek was becoming very rare in the west, he set himself the twin tasks of preserving and translating the works of *Plato and *Aristotle, and then showing how they could be reconciled. He succeeded only in translating and commenting on the logical works of Aristotle – seen as the key to the edifice – along with some other basic works on logic. While in the centuries immediately following his death this work appears to have had little impact, in the tenth century it provoked major development in exegesis/theology and was important in the development of scholastic method.

Theological tractates. Boethius made his most direct contribution to theology with five tractates which clarified the treatment of Trinitarian and Christological questions. The underlying aim seems to have been to remove as much confusion as possible by creating a technical vocabulary and laying bare some verbal confusions. These short works, which are deeply Augustinian in inspiration, established the basic meaning for the Latin tradition until recent times of 'nature', 'person', 'substance', 'eternity', and many other words. The first two tractates deal with Trinitarian questions, the third with how we can predicate the 'substance' of God (this tract was known in the Middle Ages as *De hebdomadibus*) and introduced subsequent writers to many Neoplatonic theological notions. The fourth tractate is a catechetical piece, and the fifth (*Contra Eutychen et Nestorium*) is devoted to Christology. The latter effectively makes a bridge between the followers of *Chalcedon and the *Monophysites by clearing away much of the linguistic chaos that set them in opposition. These works were at the core of formal theological education in the central and late Middle Ages, and through commentaries (e.g., *Aquinas) they were the vehicle for important developments.

In the eighteenth century many saw Boethius as the 'last of the classical philosophers': this required presenting him as a pagan and doubting his authorship of these works. Doubts about authorship subsequently disappeared for four of the tractates, but persisted regarding the fourth tractate. However, recent scholars accept it as genuine (see Chadwick, 1981, pp. 175–80).

The Consolatio Philosophiae. Boethius's most famous work is the *Consolatio*, which was written in prison. A work of literary beauty and technical perfection, it is the solace offered him by the personification of wisdom, Lady Philosophy. When he is faced with hardships and disappointments, she reminds him of the providence and order that imbue the universe. Since the work lacks any reference to Christ or any explicit reference to Christian revelation, the faith of its author has often been questioned. To some since the eighteenth century, it was proof that when faced with death its author gave up the pretence of Christianity in favour of the robust paganism of his ancestors. For many Christians its lack of explicit reference to Christianity was evidence of the shallowness of his Christian faith and they invoked the disjunction of Neoplatonist/Christian. However, the work was not written with the immediate prospect of death, and both its view of the creation as that which proceeds from the divine freedom (III, v. 9), as well as its notion of God as providential, are Christian. The medieval view that it is a consciously *philosophical* reflection still has much to recommend it; while a less pre-defined notion of what 'Christian' means in the period yields interesting results: for example, the image of 'Wisdom' in Wisdom 8 who is a counsellor in adversity and a solace in grief is closer to Lady Philosophy than most of the classical models proposed for her. There is still much work to be done on this text.

THOMAS O'LOUGHLIN

FURTHER READING: *Catalogue: CPL* nn. 878–95, and cf. n. 950. *Studies:* H.R. Patch, 'The Beginnings of the Legend of Boethius', *Speculum* 22 (1947), pp. 443–45; K. Dürr, *The Propositional Logic of Boethius* (Amsterdam, 1951); P. Courcelle, *La Consolation de Philosophie dans la Tradition Littéraire* (Paris, 1967); M. Gibson (ed.), *Boethius: His Life, Thought and Influence* (Oxford, 1981); H. Chadwick, *Boethius: The Consolations of Music, Logic, Theology, and Philosophy* (Oxford, 1981); J. Magee, *Boethius on Signification and Mind* (Leiden, 1989); N.H. Kaylor, *The Medieval Consolation of Philosophy: An Annotated Bibliography* (London, 1992).

Bonaventura, Giovanni di Fidanza (1217–74)

The 'Seraphic Doctor' was born in 1217 in Bagnoregio in central Italy at a peak moment in the early development of the *Franciscan Order. Although it is unlikely that Bonaventura ever met St Francis of Assisi, the significance of Bonaventura's theology cannot be separated from the life of St Francis. As a boy he was cured of an illness through the intercession of Francis. In 1234 he went to Paris to study in the faculty of arts. In 1243 he entered the Franciscan Order, taking the name of Bonaventura. He studied under *Alexander of Hales and John of La Rochelle. In 1253 he became a master of theology, and in 1257 doctor of theology. In the same year, he was elected minister general of the order, after John of Parma, suspected of being under the influence of *Joachim of Fiore, was ordered by Pope Alexander IV to resign. As a trained theologian, Bonaventura saw no conflict between Franciscan simplicity and the intellectual life. He thus defended the right of mendicants to teach at the University of Paris, and he opposed the Franciscan Spirituals. He is considered the second founder of the order. In

1273, he was appointed cardinal bishop of Albino, and he died a year later on 15 July 1274 in the midst of the Second Council of Lyons. He was canonized in 1482 and declared a Doctor of the Church in 1588. Among his works are various biblical commentaries, *Commentary on the Sentences, The Tree of Life, The Breviloquium, On the Reduction of the Arts to Theology, The Soul's Journey into God* and *The Life of St Francis.*

Bonaventura is a thirteenth-century scholastic, a master and doctor of theology, part of a great movement of the reintegration of Catholic theology. His Christocentric theology unites *Augustine, *Dionysius the Areopagite, *Bernard of Clairvaux and *Anselm in the spirit of St Francis. Augustine is his master as filtered through *Peter Lombard. In contrast to his contemporary, *Thomas Aquinas, Bonaventura resisted the direct influence of *Aristotle while accepting the ontological argument of Anselm. His creative syntheses are a theology and spirituality at prayer reaching mystical 'excess'.

For Bonaventura, 'Since every science and particularly the science contained in the Holy Scriptures, is concerned with the Trinity before all else, every science must necessarily present some trace of this same Trinity.' Since the good is self-diffusive, the triune God has expressed God's own fecund being in time, thus overflowing into creation and the incarnation, and into nature and grace. Bonaventura teaches that the creation of the world is a creation in time. He opposes Aristotle's view of the possibility of an eternally existent world. Creation itself, being too limited, is not a sufficient receptacle for God's absolute fecundity. The triune self-diffusion is the basis for the Father's generation of the Son and the procession of the Spirit. The Trinity itself is an exemplar for creation *ad extra*. God acts *ad extra* as God is, that is, as triune: 'God would never have been able to bring forth a creature on account of his will, if he had not brought forth the Son on account of his nature.' In the Son are the *rationes aeternae* of all that is created; thus the Son is the eternal exemplar. Because the Son is the exemplary link between the created world and the divine, contemplation of any created object can move directly back to the divine exemplar in the Son. Bonaventura's use of analogy was boler than Augustine's. He argues from the Trinity in the mind to the Trinity in God. The classical Neoplatonic themes of emanation, exemplarity and return structure Bonaventura's theology. The created world moves out from the Father's communicative goodness according to the exemplar of the Son, and it returns to God in the love of the Spirit.

In Christ, humans experience God's true plan for the world. He is the 'hidden centre', the midpoint of all things. The universe is a translucent and sensate revelation of the incarnate Son in that centre; therefore nothing makes sense apart from the triune presence in creation and in the incarnation. In likeness to God, the universe makes more sense: 'the likeness which is the truth itself in its expressive power ... better expresses a thing than the thing expresses itself, for the thing receives the power of expression from it [i.e., from the likeness]'. God condescends in a divine humility to raise up creation in the incarnation of the Son. A raised up creation meets the humility of God in the humanity of Jesus. Bonaventura emphasizes that the cross of Jesus is the supreme act of divine humility. The love of Jesus, in solidarity with humans and with God, suffered on the cross as an exemplar of the divine vulnerablity and condescension. The cross totally reveals God's love; it discloses the totality of the triune movement toward sinful humans. The humility and the poverty of Jesus is a making room for a nuptual self-emptying of the follower of Jesus like St Francis in his embrace of poverty. Poverty reveals the splendid heart of God: 'He was glorious in what caused him to be despised.' Because of this glory found in the poverty of the cross, Bonaventura does not seriously entertain that there could be another order of the world than the one that actually is: 'in the actions of Christ it is always what is most appropriate that happens'. In Christ as he actually is, is God's plan found. In conformity with this actual plan found in the cross of Christ, the human soul is transformed by faith, hope and love into an image of its exemplar. Therefore all theology is truly mystical. The knowledge of the intellect must be transcended by the affective wisdom of love. For Bonaventura, this affective wisdom is the true message of St Francis. His theology is, in the words of Jaroslav Pelikan, 'the most remarkable statement ... of ... "the identification of personal religious experience as an epistemological principle in theology" '.

The influence of Bonaventura has been extensive in the twentieth century. The combination of theology and spirituality, the intimate embrace of nature and grace, the Franciscan experience of Christ, the balance of biblical symbolism and metaphysical speculation, the cosmological Christocentrism and the theology in touch with religious experience have been utilized by theologians as disparate as Romano Guardini, *Karl Rahner, *Joseph Ratzinger and *Hans Urs von Balthasar.

DANIEL P. SHERIDAN

FURTHER READING: H.U. von Balthasar, 'Bonaventure', in *The Glory of the Lord: A Theological Aesthetics*, II. *Studies in Theological Style: Clerical Styles* (San Francisco, 1984); J. Guy Bougerol, *Introduction to the Works of Bonaventure* (Paterson, NJ, 1963); E. Cousins (trans.), *Bonaventure (The Soul's Journey into God; The Tree of Life; The Life of St. Francis)* (New York, 1978); E. Gilson, *The Philosophy of St. Bonaventure* (Paterson, NJ, 1965); Z. Hayes, OFM, *The Hidden Center: Spirituality and Speculative Theology in St Bonaventure* (New York, 1981).

Bonhoeffer, Dietrich (1906–45)

Few theologians of the twentieth century have had such an ongoing impact upon the ecumenical church as Dietrich Bonhoeffer, the German *Lutheran pastor and martyr. An adolescent decision to become a theologian led him to study – first at Tübingen (1923), where he was particularly influenced by the New Testament scholar *Adolf Schlatter, whose biblical theology left a lasting impression. He continued his studies at the University of Berlin (1924–27) under several of the most prominent theologians of the time, including *Adolf Harnack, the doyen of church history and liberal Protestantism, and Karl Holl, a leading figure in the Luther-renaissance. At the young age of twenty-one Bonhoeffer completed his doctoral dissertation *Sanctorum Communio*, supervised by Reinhold Seeberg. Although he never formally studied with *Karl Barth, Bonhoeffer's theological development was deeply influenced by the Swiss Reformed theologian.

Following his studies, Bonhoeffer served his curacy in Barcelona, Spain (1928), studied at Union Theological Seminary in New York (1929–30), was ordained and ministered in Berlin, completed his habilitation, *Act and Being* (1931), and lectured at the University of Berlin (1932–33). Some of his lectures were subsequently published, notably those on *Creation and Fall* and *Christology*. Shortly after Adolf Hitler's appointment as chancellor of the Third Reich in 1933, Bonhoeffer, who was involved in early attempts by some theologians to oppose Nazism, went to England where he served two German congregations in London (1933–35). The escalating church struggle in Germany led to his return home and his appointment as the director of an illegal Confessing Church seminary at Finkenwalde. During these years he played a leading role awakening the ecumenical movement to the church crisis in Germany. Many of his most seminal thoughts found expression in his essays and addresses of this period, notably with regard to the peace issue, the 'Jewish question', and the nature and witness of the ecumenical movement. On the basis of his lectures on the Sermon on the Mount and his experience of community at Finkenwalde he wrote *The Cost of Discipleship* (1937) and *Life Together* (1939).

After a short aborted return visit to the United States in 1939, Bonhoeffer returned to Germany and became a member of the resistance movement centred in the *Abwher* (military intelligence). Reluctantly permitted to travel by the Gestapo to Switzerland and Sweden, Bonhoeffer used these opportunities to assist some Jews to escape and to pass on information about the resistance to the Allies. He also began writing the essays that were posthumously published as the *Ethics*. These reflect the moral dilemmas of those who, like himself, were engaged in the conspiracy. Arrested and imprisoned in April 1943, Bonhoeffer began to reflect on the future of Christianity and the church in a secular world. These reflections were expressed in letters smuggled to his friend Eberhard Bethge. They provide evidence of Bonhoeffer's wide-ranging reading in prison and, in particular, of Wilhelm Dilthey's influence on him. After the publication of Bonhoeffer's *Letters and Papers from Prison*, these fragmentary insights had considerable impact upon theological discussions in the 1960s. Bonhoeffer was murdered by the Gestapo at Flossenburg concentration camp in February 1945 at the age of thirty-nine.

While Bonhoeffer's reflections in prison indicated that he was in the process of breaking new ground in his theology, there is a remarkable continuity in his thought which can be discerned from its early expression in *Sanctorum Communio* through to his *Ethics* and prison letters. The clue to this continuity is the Christological concentration of his theology centred on the question: 'Who is Jesus Christ, for us, today?' This question initially found its answer in the church, understood as 'Christ existing as a community of persons', then, following Luther, in the *Christology* lectures, in the 'humiliated Christ' (*theologia crucis*), and finally in Jesus as the 'man for others'. Bonhoeffer's consistent attempt to relate God's self-disclosure in Christ (following Barth) to the reality of the world (responding to the challenge of nineteenth-century *liberal Protestantism), enabled him to pioneer a way beyond both revelational positivism and Idealism in the interests of a Christian witness concretely related to responsible living the world. This found its most powerful expression in his 'ethics of free responsibility', a central theme in his *Ethics*.

Although there is remarkable coherence in his theological development, the circumstances of his time prevented Bonhoeffer from pursuing an academic career and developing a formal systematic theology. This explains in part the open-ended character of his theology and the reason why his thought has been received and interpreted in varied ways in different contexts around the world. Yet the recent publication of the sixteen-volume critical edition of the *Dietrich Bonhoeffer Werke*, presently being translated into English, is indicative of the extent of his theological legacy and the interest which it continues to attract. While much of this is academic in character, a great deal more has to do with the way in which Bonhoeffer's life and theology, his spirituality and political involvement, combine to challenge and inspire those engaged in Christian witness in secular societies and the struggle for social justice.

JOHN W. DE GRUCHY

FURTHER READING: *Texts: No Rusty Swords: Letters, Lectures and Notes from the Collected Works of Dietrich Bonhoeffer,* I *1928–1935* (ed. and intro. by Edwin H. Robertson; trans. Edwin H. Robertson and John Bowden; London, 1965); *The Cost of Discipleship* (trans. R.H. Fuller; rev. Irmgard Booth; New York, 2nd rev. edn, 1959); *Sanctorum Communio: A Theological Study of the Sociology of the Church* (ed. Joachim von Soosten; ET ed. Clifford J. Green; trans. Reinhard Krauss and Nancy Lukens; Minneapolis, 1998); *Ethics* (London, 1955); *Christology* (London, 1966); *Life Together* (London, 1954); *Letters and Papers from Prison* (London, 1971). *Studies:* John W. de Gruchy, *Bonhoeffer and South Africa: Theology in Dialogue* (Grand Rapids, 1984); *Dietrich Bonhoeffer: Witness to Jesus Christ* (London, 1988); Eberhard Bethge, *Bonhoeffer, Exile and Martyr* (ed. and with an essay by John W. de Gruchy; trans. from the German; London, 1975);

A.J. Klassen (ed.), *A Bonhoeffer Legacy: Essays in Understanding* (Grand Rapids, 1980); Eberhard Bethge, Renate Bethge and Christian Gremmels (eds.), *Dietrich Bonhoeffer: A Life in Pictures* (sup. Ulrich Kabitz; trans. John Bowden; London / Philadelphia, 1986); Charles Marsh, *Reclaiming Dietrich Bonhoeffer: The Promise of his Theology* (New York, 1994).

Boston, Thomas (1676–1732)

Thomas Boston was a Church of Scotland minister who served in the Scottish borders, first in the parish of Simprin (1699–1707) and then in the parish of Ettrick (1707–32). He was a noted and able pastor and preacher, a significant theological scholar, a distinguished Hebraist and a somewhat unwilling participant in ecclesiastical controversy.

Boston's domestic circumstances involved much suffering. His wife, Katherine Brown, suffered ill health for most of her life and six of their ten children died before their parents. Boston himself was subject to ill health and in his *Memoirs* we often see him wrestling with despondency. Boston's oldest son Thomas followed him into the ministry but left the Church of Scotland to become a founder member of the Relief Church, which later joined with the Secession Church to form the United Presbyterian Church.

Boston was a diligent presbyter. He served for a time as clerk of the Synod of Merse and Teviotdale and attended the General Assembly of the Kirk when called upon to do so. Although personally reluctant to engage in dispute, his sense of duty sometimes led him to speak out when others remained silent, not least at the General Assembly of 1728 when he alone protested against the decision not to depose Professor John Simson for heresy. This steely determination was also evident in Boston's consistent refusal to take the Abjuration Oath (by which ministers and others were required to renounce the claims to the throne of the Stuart dynasty), even publishing a pamphlet against it.

As a theologian, Boston's most significant contribution was in helping to clarify the federal theology of the Westminster Confession of Faith in opposition to a legalist strain in Scottish theology. This legalist strain was represented by those who claimed to be federal theologians but who, *inter alia*, believed that the doctrine of limited atonement was incompatible with the free offer of the gospel. Principal James Hadow of St Andrews who, in pulpit and in print, attacked those of Boston's persuasion, believing them to have introduced serious error into the church, led this group.

The controversy which developed between these two parties was called the 'Marrow Controversy' because Boston and his associates had been considerably influenced by a book called *The Marrow of Modern Divinity*. This book, reputed to have been written by Edward Fisher in 1645, was a compilation of extracts from the works of Reformed scholars including *Calvin, *Beza, Sibbes and Rutherford. Principal Hadow took strong exception to the book, believing it to be antinomian and contrary to the teaching of the Confession. He seems to have been unaware that it was on the list of 'approved' books prepared by Joseph Caryl at the request of the Westminster Assembly of Divines.

In 1720 the General Assembly took Hadow's side against Boston and his associates (sometimes called the 'Marrowmen') and *The Marrow of Modern Divinity* was condemned. Despite an appeals procedure, this judgement was sustained. In 1733, after Boston's death, most of the Marrowmen left the Church of Scotland in what is known as the First Secession.

The controversy was not restricted to the matter of the gospel offer. One of the related issues concerned assurance of salvation. *The Marrow* implied that this was of the essence of saving faith, whereas the Confession taught that it often followed saving faith and that there were true believers who would wait a long time before coming to full assurance. This was another of the areas in which Hadow concentrated his attack on the Marrowmen. Boston himself steered a middle course, believing that there was a certain element of assurance required in order that a person might trust in Christ for salvation, while at the same time recognizing that there might be a fuller sense of assurance which followed saving faith.

Another area of controversy was the doctrine of repentance. Hadow believed that repentance comes before saving faith as a condition (albeit he affirmed that it was an evangelical grace produced by the Spirit in the life of the believer). Boston, following the Confession, taught that repentance followed saving faith as a result rather than preceding it as a cause.

In these ways, Boston clarified and faithfully expounded the theology of the Confession and was, with the Marrowmen, wrongfully rebuked by the General Assembly. His rejection of a neonomian or legalist strain in Calvinistic theology and his affirmation of the grace of God in the free offer of the gospel were necessary and important correctives in Scottish theology.

Unfortunately, this contribution of Boston has often been misunderstood. Some scholars persist in the view that Boston was actually protesting against federal theology itself, rather than against a neonomian deviation from federal theology. A cursory reading of Boston's writing, particularly his treatises on the covenant of works and the covenant of grace, clarifies that this is not the case. Boston was not protesting against federal theology, he himself being one of its finest exponents, but rather against a legalistic perversion of federal theology. Boston remains a striking example of a federal theologian who properly understood federal theology as a theology of grace.

Boston himself would probably prefer to be remembered as a faithful pastor to his flock in Ettrick and as writer of the *Fourfold State* which, in its day, was one of the most popular books among devout Christians in Scotland.

ANDREW T.B. McGOWAN

FURTHER READING: *Texts: The Complete Works of the Late Reverend Thomas Boston in 12 vols.* (ed. Samuel MacMillan; London, 1853); *Memoirs* (ed. G.H. Morrison; Edinburgh, 1899). *Studies:* Andrew Thomson, *Thomas Boston of Ettrick* (1895); D.J. Bruggink, 'The Theology of Thomas Boston' (PhD thesis; University of Edinburgh, 1956); A.T.B. McGowan, *The Federal Theology of Thomas Boston* (Carlisle, 1997); Philip Ryken, *Thomas Boston as Preacher of the Fourfold State* (Carlisle, 1995); D. Beaton, 'The "Marrow of Modern Divinity" and the Marrow Controversy', *Records of the Scottish Church History Society* 1 (1926), pp. 112–34; D.M.G. Stalker, 'Boston of Ettrick as Old Testament Scholar', *Records of the Scottish Church History Society* 9 (1947), pp. 61–8.

Bruce, Alexander Balmain (1831–99)

Free Church of Scotland theologian, born at Aberargie, Perthshire, and educated in Edinburgh at the university and at New College. Following assistantships at Ancrum and Lockwinnock he ministered at Cardross (1859–68) and Broughty Ferry (1868–75). From 1875 until his death he was incumbent of the Chair of Apologetics and New Testament Exegesis at the Free Church College, Glasgow. He convened committees which produced the *Free Church Hymn Book* (1882) and *The Church Hymnary* (1898).

At a time when theological dogmatisms of the 'right' and the 'left' – often associated with ecclesiastical strife – were not uncommon, Bruce, whose own faith had been hard won, sought no easy intellectual solutions and declared, 'It does not suit my temper to speak oracularly.' His judiciousness and integrity, coupled with his willingness to remain agnostic at certain points – for example, on the millennium; his sturdy defence of William Robertson Smith; and his unsystematic method, were misconstrued by some as indicative of doctrinal laxity. This, together with Bruce's openness to modern biblical criticism, lay behind the charges brought against him and Marcus Dods at the Free Church Assembly of 1890. Here Bruce was required to defend the views expressed in his *The Kingdom of God: Or Christ's Teaching According to the Synoptical Gospels* (1889). The assembly majority was satisfied that he was not in breach of the Westminster Confession.

Bruce was his own man. He declined the dogmatism of his pupil, *Denney, eschewed the *post-Hegelian idealism of John and Edward Caird, and maintained the general historical credibility of the Gospels against radical critics. Above all, taking his cue from Thomas Carlyle, Bruce set his face against what he called 'Pharisaism' – the supposition that biblicist, theological or ecclesiastical orthodoxies will save the church. 'The temple which endures for ever is founded on Christ ... and built up of "lively stones."' Ecclesiastical strife particularly distressed him, and from this, he said, 'I fled to the teaching of Jesus'.

Bruce's great concern was that the burden of beliefs be reduced, the creed simplified, so that Jesus may be seen as he is and then shown to others. He was persuaded that the New Testament is a sufficiently reliable guide in these matters. The way to the kingdom of God is by the way of repentance, not of outward observance. Faith is not opposed to reason; rather, it is 'a function of the whole mind exercised on religion'. Indeed, if the church preaches without teaching, it fails.

In contemplating Christ himself, Bruce was constrained to elevate the theme of the Saviour's humiliation – an emphasis of kenotic theology for which he was grateful. Along this route, he thought, the ethical heart of Christianity is brought into view. However, he disapproved of the subordinationism to which some kenoticists were led. In his view the union in Christ of the eternal Son of God with the perfect Son of Man is the supreme miracle.

Following Hebrews, Bruce says of Christ that 'while as a Priest He is our representative, as a sacrifice He is our substitute'. Finding insights of value in the prophetic view of the atonement, the moral influence theory, in redemption by sample, and in the motif of Christ as victim (though dissenting from *McLeod Campbell's 'vicarious penitence'), Bruce nevertheless insisted on the objectivity of Christ's saving work.

Apologetics, for Bruce, is not so much a matter of demolishing 'the dogmatic infidel' as of seeking to expel 'anti-Christian thought in the believing man's own heart'. This entails according due place to a person's moral sense, religious insights and faith. To neglect any of these is 'unscientific'. Apologetics also requires that recourse be had to the biblical texts – but to them rather as witnesses (a term of ominous portent to some) than as authorities. Furthermore, apologetics presupposes openness to the intellectual environment – in Bruce's day one imbued with evolutionary thought, to which theme (rather than to specific theories of evolution) Bruce adjusted his thinking. In all, the final authority remains Christ himself.

Not the greatest technical scholar, the most penetrating philosopher, the most learned historian of doctrine, or the most comprehensive systematizer, Bruce knew Jesus and knew people, and he sought to introduce the one to the other. To a group of humble folk in a mission hall he said, 'for myself I have an entire love for the Lord Jesus Christ, and with all my heart I hope that you may come to be able to say the same'.

ALAN P.F. SELL

FURTHER READING: Texts: The Training of the Twelve (1871); The Humiliation of Christ (1876), Cunningham Lectures; The Galilean Gospel (1882); The Parabolic Teaching of Christ (1882); F.C. Baur and his Theory of the Origin of Christianity and of the New Testament (1885); The Chief End of Revelation (1886); The Miraculous Elements in the Gospels (1886); The Kingdom of God: Or Christ's Teaching according to the Synoptical Gospels (1889); Apologetics, or, Christianity Defensively Stated (1892); St. Paul's Conception of Christianity (1896); The Providential Order of the World (1897), and The Moral Order of the World (1899), Gifford Lectures; The Epistle to the Hebrews: The First Apology for Christianity (1899). Studies: DNB, Supp. I, Who Was Who, 1897–1916; W.M. Clow, 'Alexander Balmain Bruce', Expos T XI (1899–1900), pp. 8–11; W. Knight, Some Nineteenth-Century Scotsmen (Edinburgh, 1903); W.M. MacGregor, Persons and Ideals (Edinburgh, 1939); Alan P.F. Sell, Defending and Declaring the Faith: Some Scottish Examples, 1860–1920 (Exeter, 1987).

Brunner, Emil (1889–1966)

Swiss Reformed *dialectical theologian. Brunner served as pastor of the Reformed Church in Obstalden from 1916 to 1924, then as professor of systematic and practical theology at the University of Zurich from 1924 to 1953. Upon his retirement, he was visiting professor at the International Christian University in Tokyo from 1953 to 1955. Brunner became known in the 1920s through his involvement with the 'Dialectical Theology' movement led by *Karl Barth (1886–1968).

Brunner's theological programme is best understood as an attempt to address an increasingly secularized world – which found Christianity to be irrelevant in a modern age – with the power and directness of the biblical and *Reformation message. In addition to *Luther and *Calvin, five key influences can be identified in the development of Brunner's thinking. First, the Swiss 'Religious Socialism' of Hermann Kutter (1863–1931) and *Leonhard Ragaz (1868–1945) impacted Brunner's thinking both in its politico-social interpretation of the Christian message and in its strong Christological focus.

Second, Brunner was indebted to *Immanuel Kant (1724–1804), particularly Kant's 'soberness' in recognizing the limits of unaided human knowledge and his description of the universal awareness of a 'categorical imperative'. In his writings, Brunner consistently championed Kantianism as the philosophical system best suited for Christian thinking (cf. Revelation and Reason [ET London, 1946]).

Two other key influences on Brunner's thought were *Søren Kierkegaard (1813–55) and Ferdinand Ebner (1882–1931). Brunner took on board Kierkegaard's emphasis on the subjectivity of Christian faith and his developmental schema according to which one progresses from 'aesthetic to ethical to religious' spheres of concern as a person. Brunner appropriated Ebner's argument for the essentially relational nature of human being (which Ebner termed an 'I-Thou' relationship). Ebner's philosophy gave Brunner language with which to develop an anthropology based on humanity's responsiveness and responsibility (*Verantworlichkeit*; cf. *Man in Revolt* [ET London, 1939]).

A fifth important influence on Brunner was Karl Barth. Brunner championed Barth's commentary on *The Epistle to the Romans* (2nd edn, 1919; ET London, 1933) as a powerful return to a theology oriented on the word of God. Alongside but independently of Barth, Brunner also called into question nineteenth-century liberal Protestantism (cf. *Die Mystik und das Wort* [Tübingen, 1924]) and developed a 'theology of the Word' – Christian thinking centred on the Bible and thought out in a consistently Christ-centred manner (cf. *The Mediator* [ET London, 1934]). Nevertheless, a serious disagreement with Barth developed over Brunner's exploration of how the gospel 'makes contact' with non-believers. In 1934 (cf. 'Nature and Grace', in *Natural Theology* [ET London, 1946]), Brunner wrote that fallen humanity retains part of the created 'image of God', which he defined as humanity's ability to be addressed by the gospel (cf. *The Divine Imperative* [ET London, 1947]). Thus, preaching and theology must be shaped in order to 'make contact' with this created potential. Barth thoroughly rejected Brunner's position, insisting that the possibility of revelation is created by God alone through the faithful proclamation of Jesus Christ as witnessed to in Scripture (cf. 'No! Answer to Brunner', in *Natural Theology*). Barth's scathing reply brought the Barth-Brunner theological alliance to an end.

To appreciate Brunner's theology, one must read him not as an academic theologian but as a philosopher-evangelist who seeks to present the gospel in a manner persuasive to the modern person. All of Brunner's writings reveal his commitment to evangelism: he described his work as 'Missionary Theology'; he supported the Oxford Movement due to its effectiveness in reaching the 'cultural elite'; and he saw his two years in Japan as the culmination of his 'missionary' career. Even Brunner's doctrinal books were written in dialogue with the questions and objections of modern non-believers, because he saw his task as reformulating and re-presenting the Reformation message in language that would connect with modern thinking.

As part of his 'missionary task', Brunner coined the phrase 'eristics' to describe his style of theology. Derived from the Greek word 'to debate' (*erizein*), Brunner focused his theological work on the philosophical debates of the age, attempting to expose the weak points in secular thinking while heralding how the gospel addresses human need more effectively. Almost all of Brunner's characteristic concepts – law, point-of-contact, 'I-Thou', etc. – were employed to appeal to modern sceptics.

Brunner's mature theology appeared in 1938 with the publication of *Truth as Encounter* (ET London, 1964), in which he shifted his focus away from 'eristics' towards an explication of a 'Reformed and existential' Christian faith. From this book on, 'overcoming the subject-object opposition in Western thought' became the theme of Brunner's theological programme (see his three-volume *Christian Doctrine* [ET London, 1949, 1952, 1962]).

Brunner was especially influential in the English-speaking world, due to his own facility in English, his early lecture tours in the USA (1928) and Britain (1931), and his year as visiting professor at Princeton University (1938–39). By the time the English translation of the second volume of Karl Barth's *Church Dogmatics* appeared (in 1956, eighteen years after its German publication), fourteen of Brunner's books were already available in English.

Brunner always stood in the shadow of Karl Barth; thus, there are only five major works on Brunner in German: H. Volk, *Emil Brunners Lehre von der ursprünglichen Gotten-bildlichkeit des Menschen* (Emsdetten, 1939); L. Volken, *Der Glaube bei Emil Brunner* (Freiburg, 1947); R. Roessler, *Person und Glaube* (Munich, 1965); H. Leipold, *Missionarische Theologie* (Göttingen, 1974); S. Scheld, *Die Christologie Emil Brunners* (Wiesbaden, 1981). There are two major works in English: P.K. Jewett, *Emil Brunner's Concept of Revelation* (London, 1954); J.W. Hart, *Karl Barth vs. Emil Brunner* (New York, 2001). Brunner's theological influence waned at his death – there are very few dissertations written on Brunner after the 1960s.

JOHN W. HART

FURTHER READING: Charles W. Kegley (ed.), *The Theology of Emil Brunner* (New York, 1962); J. Edward Humphrey, *Emil Brunner* (Waco, TX, 1976); David Cairns, 'The Theology of Emil Brunner', *Scot J Th* 1 (1948), pp. 294–308; George S. Hendry, 'Appraisal of Brunner's Theology', *Th Today* 19 (1963), pp. 523–31; Joan E. O'Donovan, 'Man in the Image of God: The Disagreement between Barth and Brunner Reconsidered', *Scot J Th* 39 (1986), pp. 433–59; Trevor A. Hart, *Regarding Karl Barth: Essays Toward a Reading of his Theology* (Carlisle, 1999), pp. 139–72.

Buber, Martin (1878–1965)

Jewish philosopher, born in Vienna. He was active in the Zionist movement, and was editor of *Die Welt*, the Zionist journal. He taught philosophy at the University of Frankfurt, Germany, until, in the face of Nazi anti-Semitism, he was dismissed in 1933. During this time, Buber was the major force behind a Jewish intellectual resurgence in central Europe. In 1938, he returned to the newly founded Hebrew University in Jerusalem.

Buber is often described as an *existentialist philosopher because of his emphasis on the concrete experience of the individual and his protest against systems and abstractions; moreover, his contribution to theology owes more to his existentialism than to his Judaism. Buber's most distinctive contribution to both philosophy and theology is to be found in his most famous work, *I and Thou* (originally published in German in 1922). Here, Buber introduces a distinction between I-It and I-Thou relations in an attempt to describe philosophically the two-fold attitude of human beings towards reality. The I-It attitude involves dealing with objects and persons as things – to be manipulated, utilized and possessed for their instrumental use. This attitude is characterized by a distancing from reality, where the individual does not recognize or appreciate the richness of human existence. The I-It realm utilizes the categories of conceptual knowledge – objectivity, separation, detachment – to manipulate reality. I-It, therefore, is an accurate description of the academic disciplines of philosophy, theology and the natural and social sciences. One of Buber's main points of social criticism is that the modern world is increasingly dominated by the I-It attitude – from the impersonal nature of human relations, to the obsession with scientific progress as a solution to all problems, to the increased institutionalization and bureaucratization of society.

In contrast to the I-It realm, there is the I-Thou realm, which involves a different kind of relation, a relation which can only be spoken with one's whole being. This is a relation which involves a *dialogue* with the other, in which one is a *participant* and not merely a *spectator*. The I-Thou relation goes beyond the realm of conceptual knowledge, and must be experienced in the concrete situation of the person to be fully acknowledged and appreciated. The I-Thou relation is possible in three areas: life with nature, life with other people and – its highest expression – life with God. This experience not only goes beyond the mechanistic world of cause and effect, but it also reveals the inferiority of this dimension of human existence. Buber's main claim for I-Thou relations is that they involve risk and sacrifice, that they are the basis of true freedom and that they lead to the fulfilment of the human person. As he puts it, 'Becoming I, I say Thou' (*I and Thou*, p. 62). He uses the word 'ego' to describe the self when it is not in relation; this is 'the severed I', the source of much alienation in the modern world. The opposite of being self-centred (egotistical) is to be in dialogue with others (personhood). Different levels of I-Thou relation exist between human beings, from the basic level of respect to the deepest level of love.

For Buber, the I-Thou relation is an excellent way to understand our relationship with God; it captures that openness which is an essential part of the relationship, as well as its inexpressibility. Being an actual experience, it also brings home the proper place, and general inadequacy, of academic theology for dealing with the reality of God. God's reality, for Buber, cannot be inferred from a group of propositions – for God is the Eternal Thou. Buber believes that the reality of God can be glimpsed in all I-Thou relationships; it is a reality which gives them their ultimate meaning, and which can either be acknowledged or suppressed by the individual. The relationship with the Eternal Thou gives people an assurance and certainty, a fullness of being, which the I-It world cannot supply.

Buber's 'religious existentialism' was of great influence in later twentieth-century theology. The distinction between the I-It realm and the I-Thou realm, the critique of modern culture and his eschewing of an academic approach to religion and philosophy gave theologians, ministers and students of theology fresh ways to think about human relationships, society and the nature of God and religion. Buber was partly responsible for the emphasis in modern theology on the non-propositional and the non-theoretical nature of religion. Buber is in the same line of thinkers in philosophy as *Ludwig Wittgenstein (1889–1951) and D.Z. Phillips (and before them *Søren Kierkegaard [1813–55]), and in theology as *Karl Barth (1886–1968) and *Paul Tillich (1886–1965), all of whom stressed the experiential nature of religious belief over its propositional content. However, of the thinkers mentioned above, Paul Tillich was probably the only one on whom Buber had a direct influence.

Buber also produced more explicitly theological works, including a translation of the Hebrew Bible (with Franz Rosenzweig). He was also instrumental in popularizing the Jewish movement of Hasidism in his rewriting of the stories of that tradition. Buber wrote several books of biblical commentary in which Israel's dialogical relationship with God motivates his interpretations of the texts. Much of this work is controversial, and has attracted criticism as well as praise. It is probably fair to say that Buber pursued his own unique, but subjective, and often idiosyncratic, path in his approach to biblical theology.

More generally, Buber, like many existentialists, has been criticized for writing in a vague, unsystematic way, and for failing to provide a sufficiently objective description of the I-Thou relationship. But Buber's whole point is that the I-Thou relationship cannot be fully captured in conceptual descriptions, but must be experienced to be fully recognized and appreciated. But it must not be overlooked that the aim of his work was to try to provide a (necessarily inadequate) *conceptual* analysis of the I-Thou realm, a task at which he probably did not succeed as much as his critics might have wished.

BRENDAN SWEETMAN

FURTHER READING: Texts: *I and Thou* (trans. Walter Kaufmann; New York, 1970); *Between Man and Man* (New York, 1965); *The Eclipse of God* (New York, 1953); *The Prophetic Faith* (New York, 1949); *Two Types of Faith* (London, 1951); *Tales of the Hasidim* (2 vols.; New York, 1961). Studies: M. Friedman, *Martin Buber: The Life of Dialogue* (Chicago, 1955); P. Schilpp and M. Friedman (eds.), *The Philosophy of Martin Buber* (La Salle, IL, 1967).

Bucer (Butzer), Martin (1491–1551)

Protestant Reformer of a mediating temper, who led the reform of Strasburg (1523–48). A native of Sélestat in Alsace, he was grounded in Humanism in its grammar school before entering its Dominican House (1506/7). The stamp of his immersion in *Thomas Aquinas's thought would long remain evident in his theology (e.g. in his view of faith as persuasion), but he also encountered *Erasmus's works, including his Greek New Testament. After transferring to the Dominican convent in Heidelberg (1516/17) he attended *Luther's disputation with fellow *Augustinians in April 1518. He took great delight in Luther's commentary on Galatians. By April 1521 he had left the Dominicans and gained papal release from his monastic vows. In mid–1522 he married Elisabeth Silbereisen, a former nun. Excommunication followed as he preached around Alsace. After reaching Strasburg as a refugee in May 1523, he rapidly won authorization to expound John's Gospel in Latin. The next year he became a parish pastor and was soon the *de facto* leader of the city's Reformation. He remained in this position until the imposition of the Augsburg Interim (1548) against his opposition forced him into exile. He went to England at *Cranmer's invitation and spent his last years, not his happiest but not uninfluential, as Regius professor of divinity at Cambridge. There he died overnight on 28 February/1 March 1551.

No eponymous tradition or school emerged to channel Bucer's legacy to evangelical theology. His contribution was diffused rather than sharply focused, and his thought often displayed a flexible responsiveness which even colleagues sometimes judged too accommodating. Yet, through reform movements elsewhere than Strasburg, Bucer's impact was considerable. The Genevan shaping of Reformed Protestantism owed much to *Calvin's close exposure to Strasburg's new church order during his exile there in 1538–41. It was indeed as a draughtsman of Reformed church life that Bucer was peculiarly productive.

The writing of 'church orders' (*Kirchenordnungen*) was a special gift Bucer had, which he exercised for Ulm, Hesse and other centres in Germany, as well in the revision of the *Anglican Ordinal* (1550) and Book of Common Prayer (1552). For Edward VI, Bucer produced *The Kingdom of Christ* (1550), the most comprehensive and detailed blueprint for the Christian Reformation of the whole community drawn up anywhere in sixteenth-century Protestantism. It reflected not only Bucer's commitment to a purified Christendom but also his conviction of the necessity of the firm ordering of the renewed church. Through Calvin more than through Bucer directly, this became a distinguishing feature of the Reformed tradition. From Bucer's Strasburg, Calvin derived his insistence on the four orders of apostolic ministry – pastor, doctor (teacher, lecturer), deacon, elder – and his tenacious pursuit of church discipline independent of political authority. Unlike Calvin, Bucer made discipline a mark of the church alongside word and sacrament, but never secured the autonomy achieved in Geneva. Bucer's emphasis on discipline was in part a response to the critique of reforming Radicals, in part the fruit of struggles in Strasburg to rein in the disruptiveness of the rainbow variety of Radicals attracted to its tolerant ethos.

The critical synods of 1533–34 defined the Strasburg church's doctrine but left its discipline compromised by the city council's final control. Frustrated at the difficulty of promoting spiritual renewal throughout a church coterminous with the city, in the mid-1540s Bucer fostered small discipleship groups of the individually committed. Voluntary submission to mutual discipline often focused on confirmation – for Bucer was a major architect of a new evangelical confirmation service. His experiment with these 'christliche Gemeinschaften' reflected the magisterial Reformers' problems in nurturing a revival of biblical godliness within the confining structures of the old Christendom. Bucer was not alone in entertaining early doubts about infant baptism, but it was required of all in Strasburg. Perhaps the finest pastoral treatise of the Reformation was Bucer's *Von der Waren Seelsorge* (*The True Care of Souls*, 1538), which is largely taken up with pastoral discipline.

Bucer was a leading player in the intra-Protestant 'Supper-strife'. His first considered position supported the symbolism of *Zwingli and *Oecolampadius, but Luther's *Great Confession* (1528) persuaded him that the dispute was more verbal than substantial. For the next decade he worked tirelessly for Protestant concord. After the failure of the Marburg Colloquy (1529), Bucer and his Strasburg colleague Wolfgang Capito drew up the mediating Tetrapolitan Confession (1530) as an alternative

to the Lutherans' Augsburg Confession. In the Wittenberg Concord of 1536 Bucer and *Melanchthon agreed a form of words which leaned in a Lutheran direction (and so failed to satisfy the Swiss). Bucer found himself accused of pursuing a consensus by mere verbal dexterity. Yet his mature position is expounded with responsible sensitivity. By Christ's appointment and gift in the observance of the Supper (not outside it) a 'sacramental union' means that, by and with the bread and wine, Christ's body and blood are 'truly and substantially' presented and received. A local presence is denied, and Christ's human body is in some sense in heaven. On the knotty issue of what the unworthy eat, Bucer distinguishes between the utterly ungodly, who receive nothing of Christ, and the unspiritual believer, who receives Christ but to no benefit. Above all, Bucer emphasizes that the purpose of the Supper is life-giving communion in the whole Christ. A residual elusiveness in exposition seems to characterize all the Reformers, not least Calvin, who were not satisfied with the simplicities of Zwingli or of Luther.

Bucer's ecumenical impulse extended also to conciliation with reforming Catholics. Here too he appealed to the consensus of the undivided early church as a basis for present-day agreement. With Melanchthon he led the Protestant side in colloquies with German Catholic spokesmen during 1539–41. At Regensburg in 1541, agreement was reached on justification, built around the Augustinian and Erasmian concept of justifying faith as 'faith effectual through love' (Gal. 5:6) rather than bare faith. Justification itself rests only on Christ's imputed righteousness, but the latter is inseparable from the imparting of righteousness, the healing of the will by the gift of the Spirit and the infusion of love. This seems to have been largely Bucer's handiwork, in line with his regular advocacy of a twofold justification, again along Augustinian lines, for God rewards good works in believers which are in reality his own gift.

Bucer's versatility in bridging divisions typifies a theologian with a vigorous ethical commitment. On doctrines such as predestination he was uncompromising, perhaps clearer on limited atonement than most of his contemporaries, yet readier than Luther and Calvin to talk of free will in the unregenerate. He advocated an uncannily modern liberalism towards divorce, making the breakdown of the marital relationship sufficient cause and leaning heavily on Genesis 2:18, 'It is not good for man to be alone'. His full theological legacy will become clearer only as more of his works receive modern editions, especially his massively learned biblical commentaries. Yet it is already evident that he holds out suggestive promise for the era of post-Christendom in the west.

DAVID F. WRIGHT

FURTHER READING: A complete edition of Bucer's works is in progress, in three series: German (Deutsche Schriffen, Gutersloh, 1960ff.); Latin (Opera Latina, Paris, 1954–55; Leiden, 1982ff.); letters (Correspondence, Leiden, 1979ff.). Little is yet available in English: 'The Kingdom of Christ', in W. Pauck (ed.), *Melanchthon and Bucer* (London, 1969); selections in D.F. Wright (ed.), *Common Places of Martin Bucer* (Appleford, 1972). Biographies by H. Eells, *Martin Bucer* (New Haven, CT, 1931); German by M. Greschat, *Martin Bucer: ein Reformator und seine Zeit* (Munich, 1990). *Studies:* W.P. Stephens, *The Holy Spirit in the Theology of Martin Bucer* (Cambridge, 1970); D.F. Wright (ed.), *Martin Bucer: Reforming Church and Community* (Cambridge, 1994); G. Hammann, *Entre le Secte et la Cité: Le projet d'Église du Réformateur Martin Bucer* (Geneva, 1984); H.J. Selderhuis, *Marriage and Divorce in the Thought of Martin Bucer* (Kirksville, MO, 1999); A.N. Burnett, *The Yoke of Christ: Martin Bucer and Christian Discipline* (Kirksville, MO, 1994).

Bulgakov, Sergius (1871–1944)

After the 1905 revolution in Russia, Bulgakov became disillusioned with *Marxism and began to rediscover his Orthodox roots. His father was a priest and there had been priests in his family for several generations. In 1909 he was involved with *Nicholas Berdyaev (1874–1948) and others in the publication of the symposium *Vekhi* ('landmarks'). He was removed from his post as professor of political economy at the University of Moscow in 1918 and was exiled from Russia in 1923. After a period in Prague he settled in Paris where he helped to establish what was to become the St Sergius Orthodox Seminary. He became involved with the ecumenical movement and he was one of the founders of the Fellowship of St Alban and St Sergius in England in 1927. Although he wrote on various aspects of Orthodox theology, even writing one of the best introductions to Orthodoxy of its time, *The Orthodox Church* (1935), Bulgakov is mainly remembered for his contribution to sophiology.

It was from Vladimir Solovyov (1854–1900) that Bulgakov developed his interest in Sophia (Divine Wisdom) as a mediating principle between God and humanity. Solovyov had formulated a sophianic theory as a result of his researches into *Gnostic and occult literature as well as into Byzantine and Orthodox Christianity. The Great Church in Constantinople was dedicated to Divine Wisdom (Hagia Sophia) and many other churches throughout the Orthodox world, including Russia, used the same dedication. Early Christian writers had interpreted the wisdom texts of the Bible to refer to the divine Logos, and Christ was given the title of Divine Wisdom on some Byzantine icons. In Russia there were icons which included a female personification of Sophia, and the association of the Mother of God (*Bogoroditsa*) with Divine Wisdom was confirmed by the feminine gender of the name Sophia. Several Russian religious philosophers took up Solovyov's thoughts on Sophia at the beginning of the twentieth century, among them Pavel Florensky (1882–1937) and Bulgakov.

For Bulgakov, Sophia was an all-embracing but unexplored concept that allowed Orthodox Christianity to engage with the thought of the modern world. In his book *The Wisdom of God* (1937) he promotes sophiology as a way out of the dilemma created by secularism on the one hand and traditional dogmatism on the other. He suggests that Wisdom is not just an attribute of God, but that it is part of the divine essence (*ousia*). The Wisdom that exists in the world is the same Wisdom that exists in God: it is both transcendent and immanent. Wisdom has an ontological identity with God which is at once part of God and distinct from him. God is the ultimate source of this identity and distinction, this unity and duality. Wisdom acts as a bridge linking the creator to the creature and bringing about the transformation of nature and the deification of humanity. For Bulgakov, Sophia is a living entity whose primary function in the redemptive process is to sanctify the world. Sophiology offers a means of forging new relationships out of old dichotomies and reconciling traditional opposites such as humanity and divinity and masculine and feminine.

In some respects Bulgakov's speculations on Sophia resemble earlier discussions on the nature of the relations between the persons of the Trinity and on the Palamite distinction between essence and energy. To this extent they are further elaborations of Orthodox theology, but in the opinion of some commentators

Bulgakov appears to ascribe to Wisdom functions traditionally ascribed to the Logos and the Holy Spirit. Certainly his exposition of sophiology caused controversy in some Orthodox circles and his teaching was condemned by the holy synod of the Russian Orthodox Church in 1935. His detractors accused him of turning Divine Wisdom into a fourth hypostasis, but Bulgakov himself always maintained that his concept of Sophia remained outside the Trinity. It remains to be seen whether sophiology has a future among the new generation of thinkers in post-communist Russia.

KEN PARRY

FURTHER READING: B. Jakim (trans.), *Sergius Bulgakov: The Holy Grail and the Eucharist* (New York, 1997); *Sergius Bulgakov: Apoctastasis and Transfiguration* (New Haven, 1997); C. Evtuhov, *The Cross and the Sickle: Sergei Bulgakov and the Fate of Russian Religious Philosophy, 1890–1920* (Ithaca, NY, 1996); J. Pain and N. Zernov, *Sergius Bulgakov: A Bulgakov Anthology* (London, 1976).

Bullinger, Heinrich (1504–75)

Heinrich Bullinger, the leader of the reformation in Zurich after the death of *Ulrich Zwingli, was born in 1504 in Bremgarten (Aargau). While attending the University of Cologne from 1519 to 1522, his interest in theology was aroused by the burning of Lutheran books in the aftermath of *Luther's excommunication. Having given himself thereafter to reading the Church Fathers, Luther's three great treatises of 1520 (*On the Babylonian Captivity of the Church*, *The Freedom of the Christian Man*, and *To the German Nobility Concerning the Reformation of the Christian Estate*) and the New Testament, he returned home in April 1522 an adherent of the *Reformation faith.

His reforming career began in earnest in 1523, when he was appointed head teacher at the Cistercian monastery at Kappel. Under his influence, the Mass was abolished there in September 1525 and a reformed rite established in March 1526.

The most significant personal influence at this early stage in his career was undoubtedly that of Zwingli. Bullinger first met Zwingli in 1523 and later witnessed his first disputation against the *Anabaptists in January 1525. At the next two disputations (March and November 1525), Bullinger acted as clerk. Zwingli's defence of infant baptism against Anabaptist criticisms

introduced Bullinger to the notion of covenant as a theological concept – a point of great significance in terms of his later intellectual development.

In May 1529 Bullinger replaced his father as pastor in Bremgarten but, after the defeat of the Zurich forces at the battle of Kappel in October 1531, Bullinger was forced to flee to Zurich where, in December of that year, he succeeded the late Zwingli as antistes (chief pastor) of the church.

For the rest of his life, Bullinger was to be the guiding force behind the reformation in Zurich, where he both built upon and developed the legacy of his predecessor. Thus, for example, the church in Zurich continued to remain peacefully under the ultimate authority of the civil magistracy. This in contrast to Geneva, where Calvin engaged in a long and ultimately indecisive struggle to place the power of excommunication firmly within the hands of church authorities. As in the matter of predestination, there was thus a basic difference between the respective ideologies of the Zurich and Genevan reformations on the issue of church discipline.

Bullinger exerted a considerable international influence during this time. Most significant in this regard was his co-authorship of the First Helvetic Confession (1536) and his subsequent authorship of the Second Helvetic Confession (1566), an influential document which became the doctrinal standard for all the Swiss churches, with the exception of Basle. In addition, after much correspondence and discussion, he signed the Consensus Tigurinus (1549) with Calvin. This document brought substantial unity to the Reformed churches in the matter of the Lord's Supper and, as a result, reinforced the division between Lutheran and Reformed churches on this issue.

In terms of his international theological influence, Bullinger was as important in his lifetime as *John Calvin and *Philip Melanchthon. Indeed, Bullinger's *Decades*, a collection of fifty sermons covering all aspects of theology, was used as a standard theological textbook in Elizabethan England. In addition, his presence in Zurich made it a centre for foreign refugees and students, a fact which had repercussions far beyond the Zurich city boundaries. For example, the crisis over predestination within the Anglican church under Edward VI can be understood as due, in large part, to the separate cities of exile of its two principle protagonists,

Bartholomew Traheron, who had lived in Geneva, and John Hooper, who had stayed in Zurich from 1647–49 and was a personal friend of Bullinger.

The theological position and impact of Bullinger has been a source of considerable scholarly debate, much of which has focused on his understanding of salvation. The unfortunate result of this focus has been that the achievement embodied in the Consensus Tigurinus in marking a significant stage in the development of Reformed Eucharistic thought has been somewhat eclipsed.

Regarding soteriology, it is clear that Bullinger both adopted and expanded ideas that can be found in the work of his mentor, Zwingli – particularly in the importance he ascribed to the notion of covenant. This concept, utilized by Zwingli in his defence of infant baptism, was broadened and given greater theological scope by Bullinger, as is evidenced by his work *The One and Eternal Testament or Covenant* (1534). In addition to using the idea of the covenant to maintain a Reformed understanding of the sacraments, Bullinger also applied it to the issue of salvation-history and thus brought out the covenant's soteriological and hermeneutical implications in a much richer way than had Zwingli. Some scholars have seen this as Bullinger's most significant contribution to the Reformation, arguing that it represents the start of a Reformation tradition which regarded the divine-human covenant as a bilateral arrangement involving mutual responsibility. This view is in contrast to the unilateral approach to the covenant of those such as Calvin who emphasized the absolute unconditioned nature of God's grace. Other scholars have pointed to the existence of unilateral and bilateral elements within the understanding of covenant in both Bullinger and Calvin, as well as in many other Reformation theologians, and they have thus argued that the differences between the two alleged traditions are ultimately matters of emphasis, not substance.

In assessing this debate, it must be remembered that in Bullinger's theology a vigorous *anti-Pelagian doctrine of predestination and of human inability provides the soteriological framework within which the covenant is operative. It is certainly true that Bullinger and Calvin differed on the issue of predestination: Bullinger held to a single predestination of the elect to glory which he combined with an infralapsarian

understanding of the object of predestination. This then allowed him to avoid making God the author of sin and damnation and clearly lay behind his somewhat lukewarm reaction to the prosecution of Jerome Bolsec in Geneva. Nevertheless, this anti-Pelagian structure, which is so clearly fundamental in the Second Helvetic Confession must, as *Karl Barth pointed out, exert a decisive influence upon the status and function of the covenant conditions. This, then, would seem to indicate that a radical separation of Calvin and Bullinger on this issue is not sustainable in the clear-cut fashion which has sometimes been asserted. By raising the theological profile and significance of the covenant understood in bilateral terms, Bullinger undoubtedly contributed to the development of covenant theology. Whether he is the fountainhead of a discrete tradition or merely one source for a tradition which is too diverse to fall into the neat categories so beloved by scholars is a matter of continuing debate.

CARL R. TRUEMAN

FURTHER READING: *Texts:* H. Bullinger, *Werke* (Zurich, 1972–); *Decades* (ed. T. Harding; Cambridge, 1849–52); *Zwingli and Bullinger* (ed. G.W. Bromiley; London, 1953). *Studies:* J. Wayne Baker, *Heinrich Bullinger and the Covenant* (Athens, OH, 1981); Lyle Bierma, 'Federal Theology in the Sixteenth Century: Two Traditions?' *West Th J* 45 (1983), pp. 304–21; Carl Pestalozzi, *Heinrich Bullinger* (Elberfeld, 1858); Paul Rorem, *Calvin and Bullinger on the Lord's Supper* (Bramcote, 1989).

Bultmann, Rudolf (1884–1976)

Bultmann became the dominant theological voice in Germany after World War II, but he was already internationally known as a pioneer of form criticism and the leading New Testament scholar associated with the *'dialectical theology' of *Barth (1886–1968) and Gogarten (1887–1967) in the 1920s. The 'demythologizing' debate which Bultmann initiated in 1941 made him a controversial figure. But in retrospect it is his theological interpretation of the New Testament that has confirmed his position both within the Lutheran tradition and as perhaps the greatest biblical exegete of his time.

Bultmann's academic background in the *'history of religion school' and his reputation as its flag-bearer among the younger generation made his positive (but not uncritical) response to the second edition of Barth's *Romans* (1921) a surprise. Both had been devoted students of *Wilhelm Herrmann (1846–1922) and both profited from reading *Kierkegaard (1813–55). While Barth broke with liberal Protestantism, however, Bultmann rejected only certain aspects of it, such as life-of-Jesus research, while advancing its radical historical and critical work. Bultmann remained close to Herrmann's existential theology, but he was stimulated by 'the latest theological movement' and the post-war situation to expand his close study of *Schleiermacher (1768–1834), *Troeltsch (1865–1923) and *Otto (1869–1937) with a fresh appropriation of his Pauline and Reformation heritage. Like *F.C. Baur (1792–1860) he also understood the importance of philosophy for biblical interpretation, and he deepened his hermeneutical sophistication by studying Dilthey (1833–1911).

In 1923 Heidegger became professor in Marburg and a fruitful conversation partner whose *Being and Time* (1927; ET 1962) would help Bultmann to interpret Paul's anthropology. Heidegger's conviction that the way to speak of God was by speaking of human existence enabled him to interpret Paul's theology as a whole in a way that made sense for a modern reader such as himself. Bultmann called this appropriate engagement with the texts 'existential interpretation' and insisted that it required theological criticism (*Sachkritik*) of forms of expression inadequate to their subject matter. His later lecture on 'The New Testament and Mythology' (1941), with its provocative slogan 'demythologizing' (*Entmythologisierung*) emphasized this critical aspect. Bultmann rejected the false 'objectifying' of the gospel involved in taking mythological language literally or in speaking of the other-worldly in this-worldly terms. His lecture gave pointed expression to his engagement over the previous thirty-odd years with the problem of interpretation. He also showed his determination to communicate the gospel freed from false stumbling blocks such as a pre-scientific cosmology.

Bultmann had qualified in Marburg with monographs on Paul's use of the cynic-stoic diatribe form (1910), supervised by J. Weiss (1863–1914) and W. Heitmüller (1869–1926), and on the Pauline exegesis of *Theodore of Mopsuestia (1912, published 1984) proposed by Jülicher (1857–1938). After teaching posts in Breslau (1916) and Giessen (1920) he returned to Marburg as full professor in 1921 and remained there until his retirement in 1951. His form-critical classic *The History of the Synoptic Tradition* which appeared in 1921 (2nd edn 1931; 10th edn 1995; ET 1963; rev. edn 1968) summed up a generation's research: including Jülicher on the parables; J. Weiss on literary forms; Wrede (1859–1906) and Wellhausen (1844–1918) on the history of traditions; W. Bousset (1865–1920) on early Hellenistic Christianity; K.L. Schmidt (1891–1956) on the framework of the gospel history; and the less analytic *Formgeschichte* of M. Dibelius (1883–1947). The historical scepticism of *The History of the Synoptic Tradition* antedated but also dovetailed with his new theological orientation to the *kerygma* or word proclaimed, in reaction against idealist theologies of history and 'the fanciful portraits of life-of-Jesus theology'. Pressed to write his own book, *Jesus* (the original German title) was published in 1926. In it he gave an ordered account of the sayings of Jesus he thought earliest and most probably original and explained his aim not to 'view' the history but to lead his readers 'to a highly personal *encounter* with history' by providing information of his own encounter with it (*Jesus and the Word* [New York 1934], p. 13).

Bultmann's sketches of Jesus' proclamation in his *Theology of the New Testament*, I (1948; ET 1951) and *Primitive Christianity* (1949; ET 1956) are illuminating, but he saw them as only 'a *presupposition* for the theology of the New Testament rather than a part' of it. For this theology 'consists in the unfolding of those ideas by means of which Christian faith makes sure of its own object, basis, and consequences' (*Theology of the NT*, I, p. 3). It can therefore arise only when there is a *kerygma* proclaiming 'the Crucified and Risen One to be God's eschatological act of salvation' (*Theology of the NT*, I, p. 3). This controversial denial of theological significance to historical constructions of Jesus was rejected by some of his pupils in the so-called 'new quest of the historical Jesus' in the 1950s and 1960s.

In his interpretation of Pauline and Johannine theology in *Theology of the New Testament*, I and the Meyer commentary on *The Gospel of John* (1941; ET 1971) Bultmann fuses his modern theology with that of enough central New Testament witness to constitute a claim to the degree of correspondence with Scripture classically demanded of a Protestant theologian. Among the New Testament writers, only Paul and John are deemed theologians because their concepts alone are oriented to human exis-tence. It is in view of the contrast between the individual before and after his faith-response when addressed by the *kerygma* that Paul unfolds his anthropological and soteriological terms. Bultmann draws on Heidegger's phenomenological analysis of human existence to clarify Paul's theological meaning. This anthropological focus is appropriate but one-sided. The history of salvation, the future of the world, the Christian community and the sacra-ments all receive too little attention. Further, Bultmann's method allows interpreters to rein-terpret elements in the text (such as cosmology) which contradict their own individual under-standings of the gospel. Although the word of God cannot be questioned or investigated, the human words in which it is clothed are the product of previous believing reflection and are sometimes inadequate to the gospel. They can therefore be not only investigated historically but also criticized theologically (*Sachkritik*). This gives interpreters control over Scripture, unless the community (i.e., other readers of Scripture in Protestantism, the magisterium in Catholi-cism) restrains them by rational argument or ecclesiastical discipline.

An argument against Bultmann's proposals would insist on those parts of Scripture that he neglected and also on matters needed in a modern theology but insufficiently developed by Paul and John (and so by Bultmann), such as social ethics. Exegetical challenges to Bultmann's interpretation of *soma* in Paul, or Christian freedom as *Entweltlichung*, that is, inward separation from the world (cf. 1 Cor. 7:29–32), become at the same time challenges to his own theology.

Bultmann is on stronger exegetical ground in his interpretation of the other major (existential) theologian in the New Testament canon. John is Bultmann's crown witness and credited with demythologizing the earlier tradition's apocalyp-tic language. The source and dislocation theories of *The Gospel of John* and the history-of-religions hypothesis of a *Gnostic redeemer myth being Christianized by the evangelist have been aban-doned, and the Gospel's sectarian and Jewish Christian character better appreciated. But Bultmann's Kierkegaardian paraphrase, conve-niently digested in his *Theology of the New Testa-ment*, II (1953; ET 1955), is full of insight and broadly true to the evangelist's own strengths and weaknesses. Yet even here Bultmann's

interpretation 'de-narrativizes' the text and attributes to a later redactor early catholic and apocalyptic elements which the evangelist himself perhaps accepted and which the church continues to value.

For all its defects, the profundity of Bultmann's hermeneutical theology has contin-ued to provide a resource for critical theologies based on Scripture, and it is now finding admir-ers among conservatives and among Roman Catholics who see its ecclesiological potential. Such a text-based theology can also draw fresh support from literary theory, and its use of Heidegger continues to make connections with other discussions in the humanities.

ROBERT C. MORGAN

FURTHER READING: *Primary*: In addition to the works mentioned above, several of Bultmann's essays from *Glauben und Verstehen*, I–IV are trans-lated in *Faith and Understanding*, I (London, 1969); *Existence and Faith* (London, 1961); *Essays Philo-sophical and Theological* (London, 1955). Other essays are in J.M. Robinson (ed.), *The Beginnings of Dialectical Theology* (Memphis, TN, 1968); and S.M. Ogden (ed.), *The New Testament and Mythology and Other Basic Writings* (London, 1985). Also in Eng-lish: *History and Eschatology* (Gifford Lectures; Edin-burgh, 1957); *Jesus Christ and Mythology* (New York, 1958); *The Johannine Epistles* (Philadelphia, 1973); *The Second Letter to the Corinthians* (Minneapolis, 1985); 27 articles in *TDNT*; and his Marburg ser-mons, *This World and Beyond* (New York, 1960). Some of the contributions to the demythologizing controversy are in H.W. Bartsch (ed.), *Kerygma and Myth* (2 vols.; London, 1953, 1962). For his corre-spondence with Barth, see B. Jaspert (ed.), *Karl Barth-Rudolf Bultmann: Briefwechsel 1922–1966* (Grand Rapids, 1981). *Secondary*: M. Evang, *Rudolf Bultmann in seiner Früzeit* (Tübingen, 1988); D. Fergusson *Bultmann* (Collegeville, MD, 1992); R.A. Johnson, *The Origins of Demythologizing* (Leiden, 1974); J.F. Kay, *Christus Praesens: A Reconsideration of Rudolf Bultmann's Christology* (Grand Rapids, 1994); C.W. Kegley (ed.), *The Theology of Rudolf Bultmann* (London, 1966); J. Macquarrie, *An Exis-tentialist Theology* (London, 1970); S. Ogden, *Christ without Myth* (London, 1962); W. Schmithals, *An Introduction to the Theology of Rudolf Bultmann* (London, 1968); A.C. Thiselton, *The Two Horizons* (Exeter, 1980).

Bushnell, Horace (1802–76)

New England Congregationalist pastor-theolo-gian. Born to a family engaged in farming and 'homespun' weaving near Litchfield,

Connecticut, Bushnell was the son of an Episco-palian mother and a Methodist father who had become covenanted Congregationalists. His youth was characterized by intellectual struggles with Christianity, particularly the established *Calvinism of rural Connecticut. Although he eventually joined the Congregational Church in 1821, religious doubts persisted throughout his college years at Yale (BA, 1827). Following two years as a schoolteacher and journalist, Bushnell returned to Yale to study law. In the midst of a campus revival in 1831, he experienced a conversion and was also profoundly shaped by the intuitive spirituality of *Samuel Taylor Coleridge. Circuitously fulfilling his mother's aspiration that her eldest son follow a career in ministry, Bushnell immediately entered Yale Divinity School (BD, 1833).

The Divinity School ethos was largely determined by the New Haven theology of Nathaniel Taylor, which used Scottish common-sense realism to effect a logical compromise between Congregationalism and the rising revivalism. Although sympathetic to Taylor's support of human free will against Calvinistic predestination, Bushnell rejected Taylor's rational, systematic apologetic in favour of a romantic, evocative approach. As Coleridge declared, 'Christianity is not a theory, or a speculation; but a life – not a philosophy of life, but a life and a living process' (*Aids to Reflection*, p. 201).

In 1833, Bushnell was ordained pastor of the North Church in Hartford, Connecticut, the only congregation he served until his retirement from active parish ministry (due to ill health) in 1859. North Church was founded by an aspiring, middle-class group which split from First Church of Hartford, whose pastor, Joel Hawes, was a successful revivalist. When Bushnell arrived at North Church, he was immediately confronted by a dispute between predestinarian Calvinists (most of whom favoured revivalism) and the 'Taylorites', who held a moral capacity view of salvation emphasizing the continuity between nature and grace. Bushnell resolved this dispute by seeking to 'comprehend' the truths on both sides. Humanity was dependent upon God's grace for salvation, but this transformation took place through one's free acceptance of God's supernatural presence *within* nature. Advocating continuity without collapse of the distinction between the natural and supernatural not only won the loyalty of Bushnell's congregation, but

also continued to characterize his synergizing approach to theology. For example, in *Nature and the Supernatural* (1858) he argued that religion and science constitute 'one system of God'.

The loyalty of Bushnell's congregation was tested in the summer of 1850 when, in response to his book *God in Christ* (1849), the associated Congregational churches of Connecticut came close to bringing him to trial for heresy. Bushnell defended his 'progressive orthodoxy' in *Christ in Theology* (1851). In order to avoid proceedings, North Church withdrew from the consociation. After four years of legal manoeuvring and denominational wrangling, Bushnell was left alone to continue his preaching and writing, becoming a major voice of mainline Protestantism in Victorian America.

Bushnell's relatively affluent congregation was uncomfortable with the vigorous revivalism of First Church ('the New Lights') and rather bored with New England Calvinistic theology ('the Old Lights'). What concerned Bushnell's parishioners was the religious education of their children. In response, Bushnell wrote *Christian Nurture* (1847), which proposed an organic, family-centred model of Christian experience in the church: 'the child is to grow up a Christian, and never know himself as being otherwise' (p. 10).

Bushnell was critical of one-off conversionism, which ignored the values of Christian character modelled by godly parents. Under revivalism, 'We thrust our children out of the covenant first, and insist, in spite of it, that they shall grow up in the same spiritual state as if their father and mother were heathens' (p. 220). Instead, a properly nurtured child did not need a dramatic conversion.

Bushnell maintained that as individuals do not exist apart from an organic society, so Christians do not exist apart from Christian community. Baptism becomes the initiation rite in which children are warmly welcomed into the church family. Education is a self-evocative process which leads children to develop their true identity in a relationship of grace. Through his dynamic, holistic view of the Christian life, Bushnell became 'the patron saint' of much of American religious education.

In February 1848, following critical responses to *Christian Nurture*, Bushnell experienced another spiritual turning point, which led to confirmation of his calling and an imaginative burst of writing. Among other contributions, including a practical defence of the Trinity, Bushnell authored his 'Preliminary Dissertation on Language', which proposed a revolutionary, metaphorical theory of language, foreshadowing developments in late twentieth-century theology.

Since verbal communication is social and symbolic, Bushnell argued that in theology the poetic method, which symbolically evokes truth, should take priority over the logical method, which seeks precise definition. Religious language lacks the precision which dogmatic heresy hunters assume it possesses. Bushnell's romantic view of language offered a new way to appeal 'literally' to the Scriptures and creeds. The possibilities of poetry and other forms of religious imagination shaped biblical and theological interpretation.

Bushnell applied his metaphorical understanding of language practically to a Christian interpretation of his tumultuous times. For example, his Yale sermon 'Our Obligations to the Dead' (1865) interpreted the American Civil War as the expiation of the national sin of slavery. The 'father of American religious liberalism' discovered 'vicarious sacrifice' as a powerful way to revitalize understanding of the atonement for modern Protestantism.

CHARLES J. SCALISE

FURTHER READING: *Texts: Christian Nurture* (1847, rev. edn 1861; Grand Rapids, repr. 1979); *God in Christ: Three Discourses, Delivered at New Haven, Cambridge, and Andover with a Preliminary Dissertation on Language* (1849; New York, repr. 1972); *Nature and the Supernatural, as Together Constituting the One System of God* (1858; New York, repr. 1973); *The Vicarious Sacrifice: Grounded in Principles of Universal Obligation* (1866; London, rev. edn 1880). *Studies:* Sydney E. Ahlstrom, *Theology in America: The Major Voices from Puritanism to Neo-Orthodoxy* (Indianapolis, IN, 1967); Mary Bushnell Cheney, *Life and Letters of Horace Bushnell* (1880; New York, repr. 1969); Conrad Cherry (ed.), *Horace Bushnell: Sermons* (New York, 1985); Samuel Taylor Coleridge, *Aids to Reflection* (4th edn 1840; Port Washington, NY, repr. 1971); James O. Duke, *Horace Bushnell: On the Vitality of Biblical Language* (Chico, CA, 1984), for extensive bibliography, see pp. 95–126; David L. Smith (ed.), *Horace Bushnell: Selected Writings on Language, Religion, and American Culture* (Chico, CA, 1984).

Butler, Joseph (1692–1752)

Joseph Butler was born in Wantage, Oxfordshire, on 18 May 1792, the youngest of eight children. His father was a reasonably affluent, retired draper, a keen and devout Presbyterian. Butler was educated first under an Anglican headmaster at Wantage and then at the Dissenting Academy at Tewkesbury under Samuel Jones, 'no ordinary Academy, no ordinary man'. Here he engaged in correspondence with Dr Samuel Clarke, 'Newton's henchman, a rational, if somewhat Arian, theologian'. Butler revealed at a very young age marked metaphysical and philosophical talents as he criticized Clarke's a priori arguments for God's existence. Confirmed into the Anglican church by Oxford's Bishop Talbot, Butler entered Oriel College, Oxford, to read law and divinity. He graduated BA in 1718, BCL in 1721 and DCL in 1733. His subsequent preferment in the Anglican church owed everything to the patronage of Bishop Talbot and his two sons, especially Charles, who was appointed Lord Chancellor in 1733 and Samuel Clarke and Thomas Secker, afterwards Archbishop of Canterbury. Clarke and Secker drew Butler to the notice of Queen Caroline, and her influence led to his elevation to the bench as Bishop of Bristol in 1738 and his translation to the wealthy see of Durham in 1750. Butler died two years later in 1752. J.B. Lightfoot, a giant amongst nineteenth-century New Testament scholars, spoke of Butler in his enthronement sermon as Bishop of Durham as 'the greatest of the Bishops of Durham'.

Three things can confidently be asserted of Butler. Apart from the bare outline, little can with certainty be affirmed about his life. Compared with the great classical philosophers – *Plato, *Aristotle, *Aquinas, *Kant – his philosophical output was small. Nevertheless, his work exerted an enormous influence in Britain and the English-speaking world. In the nineteenth century his *Analogy of Religion* was a standard text in theological colleges and his moral philosophy was discussed in university philosophy departments up to the 1950s. In the last fifty years his reputation has suffered a sharp decline – he is rarely mentioned nowadays and even less read.

Butler concentrated his attention on two main areas of philosophical discussion – moral philosophy and the philosophy of religion. Unlike the great classical philosophers he did not develop a large, all-embracing metaphysical system within which every branch of philosophy can be accommodated.

While preacher at the Rolls Chapel Butler published a selection of his sermons entitled *Fifteen Sermons* (1725), a volume which enjoyed wide circulation and gained an enviable philosophical reputation for its author. In it, together with his short *Dissertation on Virtue*, Butler elaborates the two central themes of his ethics – that virtue consists in following nature and that conscience is supreme. He draws liberally on the philosophical insights of Aristotle, the Stoics, *Locke, the Cambridge Platonists and Shaftesbury. Man inherits a human nature which is a harmonious system: one acts morally if one acts in accordance with it, and immorally if not. All actions are prompted by particular impulses which are themselves morally neutral. These impulses are governed by the 'rational principles' of self-love and benevolence. Over all presides the rational principle of conscience which possesses supreme authority in this hierarchically-ordered human nature. Adopting a teleological approach familiar to his age, Butler argues that the object or end of all human action is happiness, captured more in Aristotle's sense of *eudaemonia* (well-being) than in *J.S. Mill's balance of pleasures over pains. Butler makes the startling claim that in a cool moment we recognize that the dictates of cool self-love point in the same direction as those of conscience. Duty and self-interest coincide. We need more cool self-love, not less. He thus offers a devastatingly effective dismissal of Hobbes's claim that all human actions are motivated by purely selfish impulses.

Butler's ethics make no explicit appeal to theological presuppositions. Following the Cambridge Platonists he favours the autonomy of ethics. The morally right cannot be defined nor can it be identified with what God wills; conscience is not straightforwardly the voice of God.

This position is abandoned in his longer work of Christian apologetic, *The Analogy of Religion to the Constitution and Course of Nature* (1736, together with the associated 'Dissertation on Personal Identity'). In this carefully-argued work Butler's stress on God's moral government of the world does seem to imply that the voice of conscience is the voice of God.

The *Analogy of Religion* arguments are directed against the deists who, with Butler, believed in God but denied Christian claims concerning special and general revelation. Eschewing a priori arguments, he appeals to the evidence of ordinary experience about the course of nature. His main philosophical tool is probability, 'which is the guide of life'. In matters of the greatest consequence – God's existence and immortality – reason is justified in insisting that the evidence for the truth of Christian belief is more probable than its contrary. By analogy with the course of nature in which things constantly change but remain the same, probability justifies the belief that the soul survives bodily death. By analogy with man's moral experience Butler can argue the probability of God's moral government of the world; the injunctions of conscience coincide with what God wills. In the realm of special revelation Butler makes a reasonable case for the historicity of gospel miracles, and thus raises questions tackled later in *Hume's celebrated discussion of miracles.

The contemporary neglect of Butler – symptomatic of a general decline in the influence of the Christian religion in the west – is a sad loss. Butler's writings are classics of lucid, economical, reasonable discussions of some of the fundamental problems of moral philosophy and of Christian theological belief.

T.A. ROBERTS

FURTHER READING: J.H. Barnard (ed.), *The Works of Bishop Butler* (2 vols.; London, 1900); C.D. Broad, 'Butler', in C.D. Broad, *Five Types of Ethical Theory* (London, 1930), ch. 3; 'Butler as a Theologian', in C.D. Broad, *Religion, Philosophy and Psychical Research* (London, 1953), pp. 202–19; Christopher Cunliffe (ed.), *Butler's Moral and Religious Thought* (Oxford, 1992); A.E. Duncan-Jones, *Butler's Moral Philosophy* (Harmondsworth, Middlesex, 1952); S.A. Grave, 'Butler's *Analogy*', *Cam J* 6 (1952), pp. 169–80; Anders Jeffner, *Butler and Hume on Religion* (Stockholm, 1966); John Kleinig, 'Butler in a Cool Hour', *J Hist Phil* 7 (1969), pp. 299–341; T.H. McPherson, 'The Development of Bishop Butler's Ethics', *Philosophy* 23 (1948), pp. 317–31 and 24 (1949), pp. 3–22; E.C. Mossner, *Bishop Butler and the Age of Reason* (New York, 1936); Terence Penelhum, *Butler: The Arguments of the Philosophers* (London, 1985); Ian Ramsey, 'Joseph Butler, 1692–1752: Some Features of his Life and Thought', in *Friends of Dr Williams Library* (Lecture 23; London, 1969); T.A. Roberts, *The Concept of Benevolence* (London, 1973), ch. 1; T.A. Roberts (ed.), *Butler's Fifteen Sermons* (London, 1970); James Rurak, 'Butler's *Analogy*: A Still Interesting Synthesis of Reason and Revelation', *Angl Th R* 62 (1980), pp. 365–81; Alan R. White, 'Conscience and Self-Love in Butler's *Sermons*', *Philosophy* 27 (1952), pp. 329–44.

Cairns, David S. (1862–1946)

David Cairns was born on 8 November 1862 in Stitchel, Roxburghshire, the son of a United Presbyterian Church minister. His father's family were farmers and shepherds, while his mother was herself a daughter of the manse. His uncle was the Revd Dr John Cairns, who later became principal of the United Presbyterian College in Edinburgh. Both David himself, and his two brothers, would be licensed as ministers of the gospel. The gospel, and the responsibility for proclaiming it, were thus a significant part of the milieu in which he was nurtured; yet Cairns's religious development was marked by two particular crises of faith. First, as a schoolboy, he found himself dismayed and even disturbed by the dogmas of the *Calvinism that marked his theological heritage. 'It seemed to me', he wrote in his autobiography, 'to make God unjust, and something in me rose up in inextinguishable protest against it' (*David Cairns: An Autobiography*, p. 85). The crisis was as much a matter of personal piety as of theological doctrine, and Cairns testifies to having been rescued from the cloud of unhappiness and fear which engulfed him by a small book written by a popular Baptist preacher, *The Gospel in Various Aspects* by one Dr Landels. This slim volume took the heart of the message which he had heard so many times before (although, as he suggests, in an unnecessarily complicated and distorted version) and drove it home as a personal truth with life-transforming force. The second crisis came during his years as a student in the University of Edinburgh. Here he studied humanity (Latin), Greek, mathematics, physics, English literature and moral philosophy. During his third year he very suddenly found himself in the midst of a profound mood of doubt concerning all the central tenets of his personal faith. This lasted for several long and dark winter months, and took a serious toll on his health. He eventually emerged from it, however, with his health intact if permanently weakened, and his faith tested and more securely founded than before. It is worth recounting these biographical details because it seems probable that the shape of Cairns's theology was in no small part shaped by them.

After a break of some three years, Cairns returned to complete his education at the University of Edinburgh, and he then proceeded to the United Presbyterian College of which his uncle was principal, to train for ordination. One of his summers during this period was spent in Marburg where he attended the university and, in the classes of *Wilhelm Herrmann, received a very positive impression of *Ritschlian theology. Apart from the impassioned genius of Herrmann's own presentation, Cairns was impressed by its deep roots in and capacity to feed and sustain personal faith in Christ, and also by its determination to commend the gospel to modern men and women in terms consonant with the genuine insights of the modern natural, social and human sciences. No doubt his own personal struggles and development in faith rendered him especially receptive to these emphases. While his account of Herrmann (in his autobiography) is in other respects quite critical, these were characteristics that duly marked Cairns's own theological writing.

After licensing in 1892, and ministries in Edinburgh, Burnmouth, Selkirk and Ayton, Cairns was elected to the chair of dogmatics and apologetics in the United Free Church College at Aberdeen (Christ's College after the Church Union of 1929) where he remained until his retirement in 1937, latterly as principal.

Cairns's first published work appeared shortly before (and was instrumental in bringing about) his move from the parish to the theological college. *Christianity and the Modern World* (1906) consisted in the main of articles first written for the *Contemporary Review* from his minister's desk. In it, Cairns protests against any tendency simply to view modernity as something to be revoked and undone, and as likely to have an inevitably negative impact upon Christian faith. On the contrary, he argues, the developments of the previous century should be viewed as in some sense part of God's providential purpose in ensuring 'the slow coming to life of a new and nobler world' (*Christianity*, p. xv) and some of its most notable products might furnish a modern day *preparatio evangelica*. In this connection he mentions in particular the preoccupation of many in the last decades of the nineteenth century with establishing the 'facts' about the so-called 'Jesus of history'. This, he avers, had resulted in a renewed and widespread respect for and interest in the historical personality of Jesus among many who might otherwise quickly have dismissed him as an irrelevance. Cairns recognizes frankly that such interest does not constitute 'faith' in Christ; but 'it is the temper out of which faith may be born anew' (*Christianity*, p. 18), and the church should not underestimate its significance.

This striking anticipation of what later came to be described as an approach to Christology 'from below' is just one example of the way in which Cairns assumed a basically positive relationship between 'natural' categories and those rooted directly and obviously in the Christian testimony to God's self-revealing economy, and understood the former as providing solid and secure foundations for the church's proclamation with respect to the latter. Science, history and the rest are not sufficient when it comes to an accounting of God's ways with the world, but they provide a firm base with which that which the Christian knows by 'revelation' is consistent and upon which it may build in persuading others of its truth. This essentially optimistic attitude to the commensurability between the substance of Christian faith and the canons of meaning and credibility subscribed to in the wider patterns of western culture is neatly summed up in the title of his book *The Reasonableness of Christianity* (1918). For Cairns, Christianity could be held with confidence to be 'reasonable' precisely because God's hand was to be discerned at work in all the great movements of human thought and discovery, including that explosion of insight and practical advancement associated with the *Enlightenment and its aftermath. The pointed question which he posed in his writings to other theological trends, more critical of and resistant to any common cause being sought between the gospel and culture, and insistent upon revelation being posited over against any 'natural' human insight, is encapsulated in the following words from *The Riddle of the World* (1937): 'Can any true and final revelation be recognised as such that does not corroborate something that is there before? ... If we have no glimmerings within us of the knowledge of God, how can we recognise His Son as the fulness of His glory?' (pp. 365–66).

Cairns stood unashamedly within a form of liberal evangelicalism which prized reason and culture not for its own sake, but as part of that world of which Christ was already Lord, and as an ally to be embraced rather than an enemy to be subdued in the business of sharing the gospel with the world. His approach to theology was from first to last apologetic, though he would have seen this as a form of, rather than an alternative or supplement to, positive theological witness. Eschewal of such an approach he condemned as likely to result in a failure to communicate with modern men and women, consigning oneself in the process to well-deserved obscurantism and irrelevance. Cairns was one of the most severe, most eloquent and most compelling among Scots critics of the early theology of *Karl Barth, who gave such radically different answers to the questions which Cairns posed. While the differences between the two were not huge in terms of theological substance, their methods were set completely at odds, a matter having to do in part with the very different routes by which they had come to theological maturity, and the different contexts in which they practised their art.

If Cairns is little read today it is perhaps because the mediating position which he represented in his own day was subsequently adopted and developed with such brilliance by *John Baillie. But Cairns remains one of the most interesting and significant among modern Scottish theologians, and his writings have stood well the test of time. For sensitive, critical and positive engagements between the essential Christian message and the late western spirit they are hard to better.

TREVOR A. HART

FURTHER READING: *Texts: David Cairns: An Autobiography* (London, 1950); *Christianity and the Modern World* (London, 1906); *The Reasonableness of Christianity* (London, 1918); *The Faith that Rebels* (London, 1928); *The Riddle of the World* (London, 1937).

Cajetan (1469–1534)

Tommaso de Vio, Cajetan (from his birthplace, Gaeta), was a Dominican theologian and cardinal. Cajetan taught at Dominican institutions in northern Italy before being called to Rome, first to administrative positions within his order (he was Master General 1508–17), then to the cardinalate by Leo X in 1517. Amongst his earliest works are commentaries on Aristotle and considerations of economic matters. Around 1500, Cajetan embarked on a complete commentary on the *Summa Theologica* of *Aquinas, which occupied him for over twenty years. The final decade of his life was devoted to the study of Scripture. His *oeuvre* contains occasional pastoral and controversial works (often commissioned by successive popes), including treatises on the theology of *Luther and *Zwingli, the marriage of Henry VIII of England, the papacy and councils, and the doctrine of the Immaculate Conception.

As a young friar, Cajetan both studied and taught within the predominantly *Aristotelian environment of renaissance Padua; he made use of new humanist texts of Aristotle, and he shared the humanists' esteem for the philosophy of the ancients. Pitting himself against the Averroists and the Scotists (though not always uninfluenced by them), Cajetan emphasized the Aristotelianism of Aquinas, at times overlooking other traditions (e.g. Neoplatonism) that influenced Aquinas's thought. In his economic treatises, while firmly condemning the practice of usury, he formulated conclusions that advanced theoretical support for emerging capitalist practices.

Cajetan intended his theological writing, especially his scriptural exegesis, to contribute to the reform of Christian preaching and teaching. Sending the first Dominican missionaries to the New World, his instructions to them regarding the catechesis and sacramental initiation of new Christians are broad-minded and generous. His clear defence of the rights of the natives against the coercive measures of the colonists was an inspiration to Las Casas. Cajetan sent Dominicans to Pisa to preach against the rebel French-inspired council, upholding a pro-papal position against the conciliarists (*De comparatione auctoritatis papae et concilii*, 1511). He urged the cause of reform at the Fifth Lateran Council (1512–17), gazing not only 'backwards' (to the early church, the apostles and martyrs), but principally 'upwards' (to the heavenly church, a peaceful unity of human and divine, under one incarnate Lord). On a papal mission to the imperial diet at Augsburg in 1518, Cajetan was instructed to examine the Augustinian friar, Martin Luther. While insisting (ineffectively) that Luther recant his teaching on indulgences, Cajetan eventually suspended a similar request concerning the disposition to receive the sacrament of penance because, as he recognized, there was neither a clear consensus among the schools, nor a definitive ecclesiastical judgement.

Though far from being fully prepared for the task, Cajetan set out to correct and comment on the Vulgate in the light of the original biblical languages, endeavouring to produce commentaries that would be of assistance to preachers and pastors (1524–34). Although a number of 'counter-reformations' were produced during this period, there is little evidence in the biblical commentaries that these motivated his writing. Cajetan's attacks on the Reformers are infrequent (confined only to Eucharistic doctrine and practice) and oblique. Rather, Cajetan shared the humanists' enthusiasm for a 'return to the sources'. These commentaries are better seen as an acknowledgement of *Jerome and *Erasmus than as a pursuit of the Lutherans.

Employing only the literal sense of the Bible, which according to Aquinas has priority over the other senses, Cajetan sought to give to his commentaries a sobriety and doctrinal clarity that would contrast not only with the exegesis of heretics, ancient and modern, but also with the more fabulous Cabalistic and Neoplatonistic exegesis of some of his contemporaries. Cajetan consistently favours rhetoric and narrative over allegory and typology. He follows Jerome in his preference for the smaller Hebrew canon of the Old Testament and leans heavily on the authority of Jerome when questioning standard positions (e.g., concerning the authorship of Hebrews, the damaged ending of Mark's Gospel and the proper location of John 8:1–11).

Though he was in no formal sense a sceptic, a number of Cajetan's later views place him to the agnostic side of Aquinas, and in some cases closer to *Scotus and the Averroists. Most notably, he changed his mind concerning the philosophical demonstrability of the immortality of the soul. At first upholding this doctrine (1503), he reversed his view over the course of commentaries on Aquinas, Aristotle (the *De anima*) and Scripture (on Mt. 22, Rom. 9 and Ecc. 3). He concluded both that Aristotle did not assert the immortality of the soul (with Averroës, against Aquinas) and that, philosophically speaking, Aristotle was right. Echoing the conclusions of Pomponazzi, Cajetan claimed that there are no compelling rational proofs, only probable arguments, for the immortality of the soul.

Cajetan died a decade before the Council of Trent began; the reception of his works at that council was mixed. Although his views on the canon of Scripture were rejected, and his views on justification were closer to those of the evangelical minority party (the *spirituali*), his treatise on the sacrifice of the mass (an anti-Lutheran treatise occasioned probably by the Augsburg Confession) contributed significantly to the council's teaching on that matter, as did his writings on the sacrament of penance. Cajetan contributed to the replacement of *Peter

Lombard's *Sentences* with the *Summa Theologica* as the standard text of theological instruction. His own commentary on this text was published with Aquinas's text by order of Pius V (in 1570, with some censorship of opinions considered too 'ecumenical' or 'pastoral') and by Leo XIII (in 1888–1906). As a consequence of this official sanction, Cajetan's work has often been judged successful in the measure that it accurately reproduces the thought of Aquinas.

MICHAEL O'CONNOR

FURTHER READING: A. Bodem, *Das Wesen der Kirche nach Kardinal Cajetan* (Trier, 1971); A.F. von Gunten, 'La contribution des Hébreux à l'oeuvre exégétique de Cajétan', in *Histoire de l'exégèse au XVIe siècle* (eds. O. Fatio and P. Fraenkel; Geneva, 1978); B. Hallensleben, *Communicatio: Anthropologie und Gnadenlehre bei Thomas de Vio Cajetan* (Münster, 1985); M. O'Connor, 'Exegesis, doctrine and reform in the biblical commentaries of Cardinal Cajetan' (DPhil thesis; Oxford, 1997); J. Wicks, 'Roman Reactions to Luther: The First Year (1518)', in *Cath Hist Rev* 69 (1983), pp. 521–62; *Cajetan Responds: A Reader in Reformation Controversy* (Washington, DC, 1978).

Calvin, John (1509–64)

Calvin was born and raised at Noyon in northern France. He studied at the Universities of Paris, Orléans and Bourges and became an admirer of *Erasmian humanism. At some stage in the early 1530s he underwent a 'sudden conversion' (described in the preface to his commentary on the Psalms) and aligned himself with the *Reformation. Persecution forced him to flee France and he settled at Basle. While passing through Geneva in 1536 he was conscripted by *Farel to take part in the ministry in that city. Calvin was to spend the rest of his life there, apart from a time of exile from 1538 to 1541, spent mostly at Strasburg.

Calvin has been misleadingly branded the 'dictator of Geneva', whereas even at the peak of his power his authority was moral rather than legal. He fought hard to protect the church from state control, thus seeking to resist the trend of the times. He also struggled to impose an effective system of church discipline, against the wishes of many of the native Genevans. His ultimate triumph over them was achieved in part as a result of the influx of zealously Protestant French refugees. Many of these came because, like *John Knox, they felt Geneva to be 'the most perfect school of Christ that ever was in the earth since the days of the apostles'.

Calvin was the greatest Reformed theologian of the sixteenth century and is today read far more widely than any other Reformed theologian. This fact can be misleading. Calvin was a second-generation Reformer. The first edition of his *Institutio* was published nearly twenty years after the birth of the Reformation, some years after the death of *Zwingli and less than ten years before the death of *Luther. Calvin's influence was profound, but he was by no means the only influential Reformed theologian of the century. To judge other theologians of his or following generations by their fidelity to Calvin's thought is to mistake his significance. However great he may have been, he stood in a tradition that began before him and on which he was but one of a number of important influences. Just as the Lutheran tradition is more than and wider than Luther, so the Reformed tradition has always been more than and wider than Calvin.

Protestant theology was already well developed by the time that Calvin came on the scene. He was influenced by Luther, of whom he spoke with great respect. He became friends with *Melanchthon, who probably exercised a limited influence upon him. He spoke disparagingly of Zwingli (especially regarding the Lord's Supper) but was nonetheless fundamentally a Reformed rather than a Lutheran theologian and entered into the tradition that Zwingli had initiated. During the years of exile at Strasburg Calvin was strongly influenced by *Bucer, especially but not exclusively in the question of the Lord's Supper. In addition to these major figures Calvin was of course influenced by other French and Swiss Reformers, either through contact or through their writings.

Calvin's genius was to imbibe the existing Protestant (especially Reformed) tradition and to construct out of it his own creative synthesis. The durability of his contribution is due both to the skill with which he created the synthesis and to the 'lucid brevity' with which he expressed it. It is because of his success in both areas that he became and remained the most influential Reformed theologian. His influence waned in the aftermath of the *Enlightenment, but revived in the twentieth century thanks both to the rise of 'neo-orthodoxy' and to the revival of evangelical theology. Since *Vatican II, many leading Calvin scholars have been Roman Catholics.

Calvin was influenced not just by his Protestant contemporaries but also by the early church Fathers and by medieval theologians. He cited the former extensively, especially *Augustine, who appears over a thousand times in Calvin's writings. *Chrysostom and *Jerome are also cited extensively in Calvin's commentaries. Of the medievals he particularly liked Gregory the Great and *Bernard of Clairvaux. The Fathers are used primarily, but not exclusively, as authorities called as witnesses either for the defence (of Calvin) or for the prosecution (of his opponents). Since he names them so often it is relatively simple to study their role in his theology, but it is a mistake to confuse citation with influence. The extent to which the Fathers influenced Calvin's thinking is uncertain and disputed. With late medieval writers the situation is worse in that Calvin almost never names them. There has been considerable debate about the alleged influence upon Calvin of the Scottish theologian John Major, who *may* have taught the young Calvin at Paris. It is safer to think in terms of the influence upon Calvin, not of specific individuals, but of broad traditions of late medieval thought such as the *via moderna* and the *schola Augustiniana moderna*.

Calvin's theology is known supremely by his *Institutio*. The first edition was completed at Basle in 1535 and published there the following year. There were just six chapters. Four cover the law, the creed, the Lord's Prayer and the sacraments – the basic elements of a catechism. The remaining two chapters, on the false sacraments and on Christian liberty, are more polemical in tone. In the dedicatory epistle to King Francis I of France Calvin explained how what was originally intended as a simple handbook of doctrine had also become a confession of faith for the persecuted French Protestants. The second edition, which at some 220,000 words was nearly three times as long, was completed in 1538 and published the following year at Strasburg.

During his time at Strasburg Calvin took part in an important series of Catholic-Protestant colloquies from 1540 to 1541. These made their mark upon the next edition of the *Institutio*, which was largely completed at Strasburg though it did not appear until 1543. There were fewer changes in the fourth edition of 1550. The definitive edition, now with a little over 405,000 words, appeared in 1559. With this edition the material was for the first time arranged into four books, corresponding broadly to the four sections of the *Apostles' Creed, although it would be wrong to see the work as an exposition of the creed. Calvin stated that he 'was never satisfied until the work had been arranged in the order now set forth'. Structure was important for Calvin, but must not be overemphasized. For example, much is often made of the fact that in 1559 Calvin moved his discussion of the doctrine of predestination from its earlier association with providence to the end of Book III, on the application of salvation. While the move has some significance, the doctrine itself had become more, not less, rigid as a result of controversies during the 1550s.

In the 1559 edition Calvin identifies himself as one of those who, like Augustine, 'write as they learn and learn as they write'. The development of Calvin's thought can be traced through the five major editions of the work. And yet with Calvin, unlike Augustine, there is a remarkable consistency throughout and no acknowledged changes of view. Careful study has led to the detection of shifts of emphasis in his thought. This shift normally happened by the addition of new material to the *Institutio*, for Calvin rarely altered, and even more rarely removed, what he had already written. For example, Calvin was accused of teaching in the 1539 edition that grace destroys the faculty of the will, creating a new will in the place of the old. In due course he answered this in the 1559 edition, but he did so by adding new material and not by removing or changing old material.

In the popular imagination Calvin is seen as the systematic theologian *par excellence*. There is an element of truth in this in that the *Institutio* is a carefully ordered work and Calvin does expound his thought with considerable clarity. But it would be wrong to imagine that Calvin's theology is worked out systematically from some single controlling principle. Such suggestions have been made from the nineteenth century, with predestination being the first controlling principle to be proposed. It is now widely recognized that the idea of such a controlling principle originated in the nineteenth century and that modern authors have been guilty of reading their own approach back onto Calvin. Calvin aimed not to deduce doctrine from a controlling principle but simply to present in an orderly form the substance of the Christian faith as revealed in Scripture and, supremely, in Christ. Calvin was also not a systematic theologian in the sense of seeking after logical consistency as a primary goal. Where he discerns apparently contradictory themes in Scripture Calvin is happy to leave them in tension rather than to resolve them in a logical fashion.

Another feature of Calvin's approach that is contrary to much systematic theology is his stubborn refusal to speculate beyond what is revealed. He has been criticized for this by some of his modern expositors and compared unfavourably with his mentor Augustine. While the latter was prepared to offer a philosophical answer to the question of what God was doing before the creation of the world, Calvin by contrast quotes with approval the response that God was preparing a hell for the curious. Calvin has in fact often been accused of speculating beyond what is revealed, especially in his rigid doctrine of providence and in the consequent belief that the Fall took place because God willed it. While it may be true that such a belief does go beyond Scripture, there can be little doubt that Calvin genuinely believed that he was here following the plain meaning of Scripture.

From 1539, each major edition of the *Institutio* was translated into French. Publishing a major theological work in French was an innovation, and Calvin's *Institutio* played a formative role in the development of the modern French language. The translation was also significant as it showed Calvin's desire to reach not just the intelligentsia but the laity as well. Calvin never lost his concern to reach his homeland, and he turned Geneva into a training ground for missionaries to France. *Calvinism was more than just a religious and theological movement. It also made a considerable social and political impact. It influenced the development of capitalism, the Protestant work ethic, democracy and modern science.

Calvin is often seen as the man of one book: his *Institutio*. This is very misleading. While he devoted considerable time to producing the five major editions of that work, he spent significantly more time on biblical exegesis. He commented on almost all of the books of the New Testament and covered much of the Old Testament (Hexateuch, Psalms and all of the prophets except for the second half of Ezekiel) in commentaries or (published) lectures. He also preached regularly through books of the Bible, preaching almost two hundred times a year for much of his time in Geneva. Just as the *Institutio* is widely read today, his commentaries have also remained popular and are among the few pre-critical commentaries still of interest to biblical scholars.

Calvin's first biblical commentary, on Romans, appeared in 1540. In the dedicatory epistle he stated that the particular virtue of a commentator is 'lucid brevity'. Others (such as Bucer) had been too verbose and had indulged in lengthy doctrinal digressions. One way that Calvin sought to avoid this verbosity was by means of his *Institutio*. At the beginning of the 1539 edition he stated how the two projects would relate to one another. The commentaries could remain brief, because the substantive theological discussion would be confined to the *Institutio*. Conversely (although he did not state this), he did not need to engage in lengthy exegetical discussions in the *Institutio*. There is a sense in which the scriptural references in the *Institutio* can be seen as references to Calvin's commentaries, as well as to Scripture itself.

Calvin also published many polemical works, primarily against Roman Catholics but also against *Anabaptists and other radicals and against Lutherans and other Protestants. He also published many works for church use, such as confessions of faith, catechisms and liturgies.

At Calvin's death the leadership of the Genevan church passed to *Theodore Beza. It used to be fashionable to assert a sharp contrast between the humanist Calvin and the scholastic Beza and later Reformed orthodoxy, but recent studies have demonstrated a greater continuity between Calvin and his successors.

ANTHONY N.S. LANE

FURTHER READING: Rodolphe Peter and Jean-François Gilmont, *Bibliotheca Calviniana: Les œuvres de Jean Calvin publiées au XVIè siècle* (2 vols.; Geneva, 1991, 1994 [full bibliography of writings]); Wulfert de Greef, *The Writings of John Calvin: An Introductory Guide* (Leicester, 1993 [more popular bibliography of writings]); Peter de Klerk, 'Calvin Bibliography 1972 [and following years]', *Cal Th J* 7 (1972 [and following years – exhaustive annual bibliography]); *Ioannis Calvini Opera Quae Supersunt Omnia* (eds. G. Baum, E. Cunitz, E. Reuss; 59 vols.; Berlin, 1863–1900 [almost complete edition of works]); *Joannis Calvini Opera Selecta* (eds. P. Barth, et al.; 5 vols.; Munich, 1926–36 and further editions [vols. 3–5: critical edition of *Institutio*]); *Ioannis Calvini Opera Omnia denuo recognita et adnotatione critica instructa notisque illustrata*

(Geneva, 1992– [new major critical edition]); *Institutes of the Christian Religion* (ed. J.T. McNeill; trans. F.L. Battles; 2 vols.; London, 1961 [most recent translation, with full notes]); François Wendel, *Calvin: The Origins and Development of his Religious Thought* (London, 1963); T.H.L. Parker, *Calvin's Old Testament Commentaries* (Edinburgh, 1986); *Calvin's New Testament Commentaries* (Edinburgh, 2nd edn, 1993); A. Ganoczy, *The Young Calvin* (Philadelphia, 1987).

Calvinism

Calvinism is the term generally used to refer to the tradition of Protestant theology which looks to the Reformed, as opposed to the Lutheran, confessional tradition for its doctrinal standards. Calvinism is thus pluriform in terms of its theological roots, since *Calvin never occupied the same dominant position for the Reformed tradition as *Luther did for the Lutherans (hence the very term 'Calvinism' is itself misleading). In the nineteenth and twentieth centuries, through the influence of Abraham Kuyper, Calvinism also came to be associated with a so-called theological world-view and therefore came to denote a much wider range of concerns than those represented by the strictly theological interests of Reformed confessionalism.

Roots and early development. The Reformed churches initially distinguished themselves from their Lutheran counterparts through disagreement over the presence of Christ in the Lord's Supper. These disagreements derived from a fundamental difference in Christology. The Reformed rejected the Lutheran notion that, in the incarnation, the communication of properties took place between the two natures. Instead, they argued that the communication took place within the one person and that both natures retained their fundamental integrity. This divergence over Christology, with its related implications for the Lord's Supper, led to the formal break with Lutheranism at the Marburg Colloquy in 1529. In addition to this major disagreement, however, the Reformed were distinguished from the Lutherans in a number of other ways. For example, while in basic agreement on the content of the doctrine, the Reformed placed less emphasis on justification by faith; they applied the Scripture principle in a more radical way to church practice, leading to a simpler church order; and they held to different views on the relationship between church and state.

Although Calvin despised the *Zwinglian view of the Lord's Supper as a corporate sign and preferred to see it, with Luther, as a gracious gift of God, Calvin's Christology placed him firmly within the Reformed tradition. In this, he was one of a number of significant Reformed thinkers of his time, each of whom made their own distinctive contribution in the early development of Reformed theology. Thus, *Peter Martyr Vermigli (1500–62), Wolfgang Musculus (1497–1563) and *Heinrich Bullinger (1504–75), to name but three, must also be given a great deal of the credit for the development of Reformed theology in the mid-sixteenth century. Each brought to bear his own distinctive perspective, helping to foster a broad theological tradition which stressed the sovereignty of God in creation and redemption, the sinfulness of humanity, the need for revelation grasped through faith as the basis of human knowledge of God, and the centrality of Christ as mediator. In developing this tradition these theologians were not, of course, attempting to innovate, but rather to recapture central biblical themes which they regarded as having been largely obscured by the perceived intellectual corruption of the church in the Middle Ages.

Developments in the later sixteenth and the seventeenth centuries. At this time Calvinism underwent significant changes. As it moved from the church into the university, it inevitably adopted the accepted forms of university pedagogy. Thus, Calvinist theologians began to articulate their theology using the methodological and linguistic structures of medieval and Renaissance Scholasticism. The language of *Aristotle re-entered Protestant discourse, and theology itself began to be expressed in the highly structured fashion of late medieval dogmatic systems, with particular attention being paid to the ordering and interrelation of doctrinal topics. The medieval *quaestio* method also became a common way of explicating theological issues. These developments were not in themselves dogmatically significant and each merely reflected the use of accepted contemporary pedagogical conventions as the means of expressing Reformed theology. Such methodological development reached its apex in the massive theological system of *Francis Turretin (1623–87), published as *Institutio Theologicae Elencticae* (1679–85).

In addition, theologians became more self-conscious about the metaphysical framework of Calvinist theology and, as with their methodology, drew heavily upon the established philosophical paradigms provided by contemporary intellectual culture. Thus, the theology of Dutchman Gisbertus Voetius (1589–1676) shows strong Scotist tendencies in terms of its theological voluntarism and his treatment of contingency, while the Puritan *John Owen (1616–83) leans much closer towards *Thomism in terms of his intellectualist understanding of God and his use of the analogy of being. Such frameworks were not adopted uncritically, however: theologians tended only to use them as far as they were useful in defending the faith as they understood it, and they were generally too philosophically eclectic to allow for simplistic generalizations. William Twisse (c. 1575–1646) openly acknowledged his debt to *Duns Scotus' voluntarism, but departed quite decisively from the latter by arguing against the univocity of being and affirming the real distinction between existence and essence.

Doctrinal development during this period was further marked by the rise of a confessional orthodoxy keen to deal with new theological threats from the *Arminians and the *Socinians. A key moment in this development was the Synod of Dordrecht (or Dort), where the Dutch Orthodox asserted five doctrinal points against their Arminian opponents: total depravity; unconditional election; limited atonement (or particular redemption); irresistible grace; and the perseverance of the saints. These issues were reflected in the much wider-ranging Westminster Confession of Faith (1647). They have come down to posterity as the 'five points of Calvinism' and are perhaps the defining hallmark of the movement in the popular ecclesiastical imagination. Whether Calvin held the third point is still hotly (and, historically speaking, often fruitlessly) debated. Indeed, the Canons of Dort were themselves open to interpretation on this point to the extent that both John Owen and *Richard Baxter (1615–91) felt able to claim with some justice that their mutually incompatible views of atonement were faithful to the Canons. Nevertheless, Dort effectively guaranteed that the extent of the atonement would be a point of continuing controversy, as evidenced by the rise of 'hypothetical universalism' under the influence of *Moses Amyraut (1596–1664) and the Academy of Saumur.

Aside from the controversy over limited atonement, what is evident in the doctrinal development of Calvinism during this time is an increased emphasis upon, and elaboration of, the themes which had emerged as central in early Reformed theology. Primary importance was assigned to Christ as mediator – in response both to the Arminian removal of this idea from its connection to election, and to the Socinian reduction of Christ's mediation to the office of prophet and thus of Christ himself to a mere moral teacher. In addition, Calvinism also sought to bring out the full Trinitarian nature of salvation which had been implicit, though undeveloped, in the work of Calvin and earlier Reformed thinkers, by relating the external economy of salvation to the internal relations of the persons of the Trinity. Such elaboration of Christ's mediatorship in the context of a developed Trinitarianism can be found in the work of William Perkins, and even more so in that of John Owen, but they were not untypical of Reformed Orthodoxy of the seventeenth century in these matters.

The eighteenth and nineteenth centuries.
In the seventeenth century, Reformed Orthodoxy had been vigorously opposed to the emerging *Enlightenment philosophies. The most famous example of such resistance is provided by the great Dutch theologian, Gisbertus Voetius, who engaged in a vigorous debate with *René Descartes. It was not surprising, then, that Enlightenment thinking ultimately came to displace orthodox Calvinism rather than be assimilated by it. As a result, Calvinism ceased on the whole to be a significant intellectual force in the eighteenth century, and was subject to little creative theological development.

One exception to this was the American theologian, *Jonathan Edwards (1703–58). Most famous perhaps for his role in the various religious revivals in New England during his pastoral ministry, he was nonetheless of immense theological significance. His importance can be seen both in his attempts to provide theological rationale for the revivals and in his efforts to restate confessional Calvinist theology using philosophical paradigms and language provided by the Enlightenment, most significantly by *John Locke (1632–1704). In this context, Edwards made a profoundly original contribution to the Calvinist tradition by arguing for the importance of the idea of beauty for the

Christian understanding of God, salvation and moral virtue.

Edwards apart, it was not until the nineteenth century that orthodox Calvinism again emerged as a significant intellectual force. In Scotland, it found an articulate advocate in the person of William Cunningham (1805–61), professor at the Free Church College in Edinburgh. In America, the theologians at Princeton Theological Seminary spearheaded an intellectual revival that once again gave Calvinism intellectual credibility and significant ecclesiastical influence. Using Turretin's *Institutio Theologicae Elencticae* as the basic theological textbook, the faculty adhered to the Westminster Confession of Faith as a doctrinal standard. Its most famous professor, Charles Hodge (1797–1878), later wrote a textbook of systematic theology which replaced Turretin on the syllabus and helped to put yet another philosophical paradigm, that of Common Sense Realism, to the service of the Calvinist faith. Again, scholars have made much of this aspect of Princeton theology, but the thought of Hodge and company still owed as much, if not more, to the philosophical Scotism of Turretin, particularly in its understanding of the relationship between archetypal and ectypal theology, as to its choice of contemporary paradigm.

At the end of the nineteenth century, the dominant Calvinistic theologians were undoubtedly B.B. Warfield (1851–1921) of Princeton Theological Seminary and the Dutchman, Abraham Kuyper (1837–1920). The two men held to different epistemologies and thus represented different approaches to defending essentially the same confessional position. Warfield argued for the place of apologetics in the theological task, while Kuyper stressed the role of differing presuppositions and worldviews in shaping human thought. For Kuyper, then, unlike Warfield, there was no common epistemological ground between believer and non-believer upon which the apologetic task could be pursued. This specific difference in epistemology, to a large extent, reflected differences in the broader historical reactions of the Dutch and American Calvinist traditions to Enlightenment thinking. The former was utterly opposed to the rationalism of the Cartesians, while the latter drew positively upon aspects of the Anglo-Scottish traditions of Enlightenment science and philosophy.

In the context of the late nineteenth century, Kuyper's Dutch contemporary, Herman Bavinck (1854–1921), is also worthy of note as producing one of the most creative and thorough restatements of the confessional Calvinist position since the Enlightenment, his *Gereformeerde Dogmatiek*.

The twentieth century. In the twentieth century, a diverse number of theological positions have claimed to stand within the tradition of Calvin and Calvinism. The orthodox confessional position has continued, most notably in the work of the faculty of Westminster Theological Seminary in Philadelphia. Warfield's influence at an academic level has waned somewhat. Yet the Dutch tradition of Kuyper has undergone significant scholarly development, with its insights being adopted and explored in various realms of cultural endeavour, such as philosophy (Herman Dooyeweerd [1894–1977]) and art and aesthetics (Hans Rookmaaker [1922–77] and Calvin Seerveld). The presuppositionalist theology of Cornelius Van Til (1895–1987) also draws critically upon the Kuyperian legacy.

Outside of the confessional trajectories, the rise of so-called neo-orthodoxy under *Karl Barth (1886–1968) and *Emil Brunner (1889–1966) in the 1920s and 1930s also signalled the development of a new theology which claimed to stand in the tradition of Calvin but which sought to distance itself from orthodox Calvinism by reconstructing various key doctrines, most significantly those of revelation, Christology and predestination. Cultural engagement was also pursued by the neo-orthodox tradition, for example by the Frenchman, Jacques Ellul (1912–94). Ellul's works, both theological and sociological, drew on the Reformed tradition to expose in prophetic style the dehumanizing aspects of technology and the theological significance of the rise of visual culture.

Relations between confessional and neo-orthodox Calvinism have not in general been particularly positive, as epitomized in the polemical critiques of orthodox Calvinists such as Van Til. The later work of the Dutch theologian G.C. Berkouwer (1903–96) and, more recently, the writings of Donald G. Bloesch, however, represent attempts to draw constructively on both traditions in order to articulate the central themes of Calvinist theology in the modern world. While suspicious of Barth's apparent universalism, this 'third way' still finds Barth's theological method, particularly his

Christocentrism and his understanding of revelation, to be a means of overcoming the perceived problems for orthodoxy raised by,
among other things, *Kantian epistemology
and biblical criticism.

CARL R. TRUEMAN

FURTHER READING: *Texts:* Herman Bavinck,
Gereformeerde Dogmatiek (Kampen, 4th edn, 1928–
30); Donald Bloesch, *Christian Foundations*
(Downers Grove, IL, 1993–); John Calvin, *Institutes
of the Christian Religion* (trans. and ann. F.L. Battles;
Grand Rapids, 1986 [1536 edn]); Jonathan
Edwards, *Works* (New Haven, 1957–); Jacques Ellul,
The Technological Society (New York, 1964); Abra-
ham Kuyper, *Lectures on Calvinism* (Grand Rapids,
1898); John Owen, *Works* (24 vols.; Edinburgh,
1850–55); Hans Rookmaaker, *Modern Art and the
Death of a Culture* (Leicester, 1970); B.B. Warfield,
Works (10 vols.; New York, 1927–32). *Studies:* G.C.
Berkouwer, *The Triumph of Grace in the Theology of
Karl Barth* (Grand Rapids, 1956); P. Heslam, *Creating
a Christian World View* (Carlisle, 1998); J.T. McNeill,
The History and Character of Calvinism (New York,
1954); R.A. Muller, *Christ and the Decree* (Durham,
NC, 1986); C.R. Trueman, *The Claims of Truth*
(Carlisle, 1998).

Campbell, John McLeod (1800–72)

Minister in the established Church of Scotland
and theologian, Campbell was born at Armaddy
House, near Kilninver, Scotland, on 4 May 1800.
He was the eldest son of the Reverend Donald
and Mary Campbell. His father, who served as
the minister for both Kilninver and Kilmeford
in Argyll, studied at King's College, Aberdeen,
and aligned himself with the 'Moderate' party
in the church. Donald Campbell was a gracious
and gentle man who reared his young family
alone after the death of his wife in 1806. John
McLeod said that his father had filled the name
father 'with so much meaning', giving him an
earthly model for that even 'better Father'. The
admiration and love was mutual between father
and son. Donald said of John McLeod during
his heresy trial that he would 'never be ashamed
to be the father of so holy and blameless a son'.
In some respects, John McLeod's theological
work was a critical elaboration of the filial love
of God to which his father gave witness during
those formative early years and during the periods of crisis when some deserted him.

John McLeod entered Glasgow University
aged eleven, having received an introduction
to academic discipline and classical languages,

especially Latin, from his father. His course in
arts and divinity took nine years, after which he
attended Edinburgh University, receiving a
license to preach from the Presbytery of Lorn
in 1821. Following graduation he continued in
Edinburgh for four additional years, engaged in
what today would be called 'postgraduate studies'. In 1825, the Duke of Argyll presented him
to the parish church of Rhu (or Row), west of
Glasgow on the Gare Loch.

The enduring lineaments of Campbell's theology developed while he served as minister of
Rhu parish, and of few theologians could it be
said more truly that it is necessary to understand his history in order to understand his
theology. Campbell later wrote that his parishioners seemed burdened down by their Christian faith: 'Whatever I preached, they were only
hearing a demand on them.' Campbell wanted
to awaken his people to an 'enjoyment' of the
God who revealed his love towards them in
Christ. He discerned at the root of his congregation's joylessness a lack of assurance that had its
roots in the high *Calvinist doctrine of election,
a doctrine which resulted in the belief that
Christ died only for the elect. While his congregation affirmed that God loved the elect, they
had no confidence that God loved them, in particular and individually. Campbell confronted
this theological quandary in his preaching.
Christ, he affirmed, died for all humanity. The
personal assurance of God's love is of the
essence of faith.

Glaswegians on holiday on the Gare Loch
returned to their home parishes with reports of
Campbell's preaching. These reports startled
and concerned many of Campbell's fellow ministers because, as Campbell soon discovered, his
views were held to be inconsistent with the
Westminster Standards of faith which ministers
in the established Church of Scotland were
vowed to uphold. By 1829 rumours abounded
concerning Campbell's preaching, and in that
year petitions were sent from a group of Rhu
parishioners to the Presbytery of Dumbarton
objecting to Campbell's views. Presbytery
initially declined to act on these petitions, but
in 1830 a formal petition, or 'memorial', was
presented to presbytery by a faction of the Rhu
church, charging Campbell with heresy. The
presbytery initiated a course of events which cli-
maxed in Campbell's trial for heresy before the
Presbytery of Dumbarton – a process which
stretched from the autumn of 1830 until March

1831. Campbell, having been found guilty of heresy, appealed to the Synod of Glasgow and Ayr, before which he appeared in April 1831. The transcripts for this trial make disturbing and dramatic reading, as the 'Evangelical' and 'Moderate' parties joined together in opposition to Campbell. J.M. Graham is quoted as saying, 'The spectacle of the Church of Scotland depriving herself of her greatest theologian is not a pleasant one.' The verdict of the presbytery was upheld both by the synod and, in May of 1831, by the General Assembly, and Campbell was deposed from ministry in the established Church of Scotland on the grounds that his positions were contrary to the Holy Scripture, to the Westminster Confession of Faith and the Act of the General Assembly of 1720 which condemned the teaching of the book, *The Marrow of Modern Divinity*.

In the years following his deposition from ministry, Campbell lived with his father at Kilninver and preached in the western Highlands before settling permanently in Glasgow. He had many friends, including *Thomas Erskine of Linlathen, Norman McLeod, A.J. Scott, *F.D. Maurice and *Edward Irving, with whom he carried on a lively correspondence, despite the fact that he served a small chapel in Glasgow as, in his words, a 'nobody', the doors of the established church remaining closed against him. Throughout these years, 1833–59, Campbell laboured without pay, unwilling to join the schismatic 'catholic apostolic church', which Irving had founded in London, or to resign from active pastoral ministry.

Against the wishes of some in his family Campbell, in 1838, married Mary, daughter of John Campbell of Ardnahua, Kilninver. His private correspondence to his wife, whom he addressed as 'My own own love', reflects the same gentle warmth that one finds in his statements to his father. This was a man for whom divinity was filled with humanity. By 1859, Campbell's health had deteriorated to such an extent that he was compelled to retire from public ministry to his beloved home, Achnashie ('field of peace', in Gaelic), near Rosneath, across the Gare Loch from Rhu. Honours followed his labours: in 1868, Glasgow University conferred on him the honorary degree of Doctor of Divinity; a group of church leaders from across Scotland presented him with a silver vase inscribed 'in token of their affectionate respect for his character, and their high estimation of

his labours as a theologian'. Campbell died on 27 February 1872 and was buried at the old kirk in Rosneath.

While Campbell wrote *Christ, the Bread of Life* (1851, 2nd edn 1869), a brief study of holy communion, and *Thoughts on Revelation* (1862), in response to the *Essays and Reviews* controversy of 1860, his reputation largely rests on the publication in 1856 of *The Nature of the Atonement*, a work described by *P.T. Forsyth as a 'great, fine, holy book'. This book contains what F.W. Dillistone called 'a magnificent testimony to atonement as seen in the New Testament portrait of the Christ'. James Torrance ranks it with *Athanasius's *De Incarnatione* and *Anselm's *Cur Deus Homo* as 'one of the classics of all time on this doctrine'. In this book, Campbell traces out his mature reflections on the atonement which he began as a young minister. In a manner reminiscent of *Luther and the early Church Fathers, Campbell held that God is towards humanity as God is in God's own eternal being. God is essentially love, therefore what God has done in Christ God has done for all people. God's love is not arbitrary, nor is Christ's life and work for the benefit of only an elect minority.

Campbell's understanding of the atonement rang the soteriological changes in a distinctive manner. He stressed what he called the prospective aspect of the atonement, which he believed had been neglected in favour of a purely retrospective aspect. According to Campbell, God's eternal will for humanity is that all persons should share in Christ's Sonship, his relationship of trustful dependence upon God the Father, through the Spirit. Humanity is freed (retrospectively) from sin and its consequences in order to live (prospectively) as children of God. Thus, for Campbell, the filial purposes of God are emphasized over the forensic or the legal purposes. Christ did suffer, however he suffered not to reveal 'the *measure* of what God can *inflict*' but to show humanity 'what God *feels*', 'that which the Son of God in our nature has felt in oneness with the Father, that into the fellowship of which He calls us in calling us to be sons of God'.

Arguably, the most controversial element of Campbell's thought was his doctrine of the vicarious penitence of Christ, the view that Jesus Christ, though he had no 'personal consciousness of sin', assumed humanity in order to rightly confess our sin to God and to pronounce 'a perfect Amen in humanity to the judgment of God on the sin of man'. Rightly understood, Campbell's teaching here provides a brilliant restatement of Christ's high priesthood, as taught in the epistle to the Hebrews, of substitutionary atonement and of the classical theological concept of the *mirifica commutatio* (the 'wonderful exchange') which one finds in *Irenaeus, Athanasius and *John Calvin. Campbell gives expression to Jesus Christ's priestly work of bearing humanity's burden of sin into the presence of God.

Though even the great Forsyth declined to agree with Campbell at this point, in recent years Campbell has inspired a chorus of assent among those, like F.W. Dillistone, James B. Torrance and *T.F. Torrance, who hear in Campbell the high orthodoxy of the ancient church put into the most intimate and personal terms. As Dillistone said of Campbell,

> Speaking in the simplest terms, we may say that Campbell had realized afresh that the most wonderful thing known to us in human life is for one person to take another's burdens on his own heart and carry them into the presence of God. If the burden is a burden of sin, then suffering is bound to be involved for he cannot fail to see the sin in the light of God's standard of holy judgment, while at the same time his whole heart is set toward the establishing of a condition in which his brother can live as a free son in the family of God. (F.W. Dillistone, *The Christian Understanding of Atonement* [London, 1968], p. 287)

MICHAEL JINKINS

FURTHER READING: *Text: The Nature of the Atonement* (intro. James B. Torrance; Edinburgh / Grand Rapids, 1996). *Studies:* James C. Goodloe IV, 'John McLeod Campbell, the Atonement, and the Transformation of the Religious Consciousness' (PhD thesis, University of Chicago, 1987); Michael Jinkins, *A Comparative Study in the Theology of the Atonement in Jonathan Edwards and John McLeod Campbell: Atonement and the Character of God* (San Francisco, 1993); *Love is of Essence: An Introduction to the Theology of John McLeod Campbell* (Edinburgh, 1993); Christian D. Kettler, 'The Vicarious Repentance of Christ in the Theology of John McLeod Campbell and R.C. Moberly', *Scot J Th* 38 (1985), pp. 529–43; James B. Torrance, 'The Contribution of McLeod Campbell to Scottish Theology', *Scot J Th* 26 (1973), pp. 303–11; Thomas F. Torrance, *Scottish Theology: From John Knox to John McLeod Campbell* (Edinburgh, 1996); Gael Turnbull, 'John McLeod Campbell: His Life, Times and Contemporaries' (New College Library, Edinburgh, 1994);

George Tuttle, *So Rich a Soil: John McLeod Campbell on Christian Atonement* (Edinburgh, 1986); Leanne Van Dyk, *The Desire of Divine Love: John McLeod Campbell's Doctrine of the Atonement* (New York, 1995).

Campbell, R.J. (1867–1956)

R.J. Campbell was a British preacher born of Methodist parents and raised by Presbyterian grandparents who, after confirmation in the Church of England, studied history at Oxford. While *Charles Gore's Anglo-Catholicism satisfied Campbell's spirit, it was the appreciation of his eloquence by Free Church congregations, combined with the absence of any requirement for doctrinal subscription, that led to his call to Union Street (Congregational) Church, Brighton, in 1895. Large congregations gathered to hear the earnest preaching of this charismatic personality.

In 1903, Campbell accepted the prominent City Temple pulpit in London, where thousands heard and read his thrice-weekly sermons. His conversion to socialism put him in touch with the widespread popular indifference to Christianity. Convinced that 'the fundamentals of the Christian faith need to be rearticulated in terms of the immanence of God', he proposed a 'new theology' built on knowledge of 'the Infinite Cause … as we read Him in His universe and in our own souls'. In a 1907 newspaper interview Campbell declared, 'We believe man to be the revelation of God … there is thus no real distinction between humanity and deity … We believe that Jesus is and was divine, but so are we. His mission was to make us realise our divinity and our oneness with God.'

The *New Theology Controversy which ensued was marked by overwhelming negative reaction from other Christian leaders. Campbell responded with a best-selling book, *The New Theology*. Here he insisted that sin was essentially selfishness and its effects predominantly social. More problematic was his assertion that 'sin itself is a quest for God – a blundering quest, but a quest for all that'. Later Campbell added, 'The only sense in which Jesus died for sinners was that in which any Son of God or martyr for truth and righteousness had died for the sake of his mission'. Therefore, the church must champion the kingdom of God, but 'the Labour Party is itself a Church … for it represents the getting together of those who want to bring about the Kingdom of God'.

As the controversy progressed Campbell moderated his views, influenced by Gore's book, *The New Theology and the Old Religion* (1907), and attracted by the sacramental tradition. After purchasing the publishing rights for *The New Theology*, Campbell resigned from the City Temple and was re-ordained by the Church of England. In *A Spiritual Pilgrimage* (1916), he vowed, 'I shall never be a party to religious strife again as long as I live if I can possibly avoid it.' While never entirely embracing orthodoxy, Campbell remained out of the limelight. In a reprise of his earlier ministry, he served in London and Brighton, before becoming canon-teacher in the Diocese of Chichester, where he died at the age of eighty-nine.

LESLIE McCURDY

FURTHER READING: B.G. Worrall, 'R.J. Campbell and his New Theology', *Theology* 81 (1978), pp. 342–48; Keith Robbins, 'The Spiritual Pilgrimage of the Rev. R.J. Campbell,' *J Eccl H* 30 (1979), pp. 261–76; Alec Vidler, *Twentieth-Century Defenders of the Faith* (London, 1965).

Canon Law

The law of the church, so called because during the Middle Ages the Western church adopted ancient Roman legal methods while most secular states were still using customary, or common law procedures inherited from their Germanic forebears. In the course of time, the Roman system ousted common law everywhere but in the British Isles, but the name 'canon law' has continued in use as an exclusively ecclesiastical term.

The laws of the Christian church are ultimately derived from Holy Scripture, but in the course of time it was found necessary to make provision for situations which the original gospel message had not envisaged and which might not be permanent or binding in nature. A classic New Testament example of this is the compromise reached in Acts 15 between Jewish and Gentile believers. This established the principle that tender consciences would be respected as long as no fundamental theological principle was at stake, so that the peace and order of the church might be preserved.

Later centuries saw a growing number of decisions of this kind, many of them taken at different councils convened for the express purpose of resolving such difficulties. In some cases, appeal was made to the leading bishops, especially those of the five patriarchal sees (Rome, Constantinople, Alexandria, Antioch and Jerusalem), or to sayings culled from the writings of the Church Fathers. Beginning with the First Council of Nicaea (325), ecumenical canons were passed which were meant to be applied to the discipline of the worldwide church. This caused problems in 692, when a council, convened in the palace of the Trullum at Constantinople, passed a series of canons which favoured Eastern practices (such as the use of leavened bread in the Eucharist). These canons were rejected at Rome, and from that time onwards the East and West diverged significantly in matters of church order.

The Western canonical tradition remained in a state of disorder until about 1140, when a monk by the name of Gratian composed a harmony of discordant canons, the first legal textbook written in Western Europe. This collection, known nowadays as the *Decretum*, formed the basis of what was to become Roman canon law. Then, between 1188 and 1192, Bernard of Pavia (d. 1213) collected a further one thousand or so canons into five books, known as the *Quinque Compilationes Antiquae*. In 1234 Pope Gregory IX published a supplement to Gratian which is known as the *Liber Extra*, and Bernard's collection gradually fell out of use. This was later followed by other collections, the first of which was the *Liber Sextus* issued by Pope Boniface VIII (1294–1303) in 1298. This was soon followed by two collections issued by Pope John XXII (1316–34). The first of these is known as the *Clementines*, named after Pope Clement V (1305–14), because most of the decretals in it were originally issued by him. Later John issued a second collection, now known as his *Extravagantes* (1325–27). A further collection of 69 decretals was added by Jean Chappuis in his edition of the canons in 1500. In 1503 four more were added, and the whole collection has been known since then as the *Extravagantes Communes*. Taken together, all these documents formed the *Corpus Iuris Canonici*, which became and remained the canon law of the Roman Catholic Church until 1917.

In that year, Rome promulgated a new Code of Canon Law (*Codex Iuris Canonici*), which replaced the *Corpus*, but its weaknesses were soon felt, and in 1983 a second code was issued. In both cases, there were corresponding codes for the Eastern churches in union with Rome, which appeared shortly after the Latin codes were issued.

In the later Middle Ages, as *Scholastic philosophy declined, canon law became the chief intellectual basis of Western theology. It was the chief repository of tradition, and it was considered by many to possess an authority equal to that of Holy Scripture. In practice of course, because it was more detailed and up-to-date, this often meant that canon law superseded Scripture in the life of the church. A classic example of this can be found in the imposition of clerical celibacy. Scripture knows nothing of this, but canon law had imposed it and therefore it could not be questioned. A similar situation obtained with respect to communion in one kind, and so on.

When *Luther revolted against Rome, it was against the dominance of this canonical tradition that his ire was directed. He believed that there was a fundamental contradiction between the canon law and the gospel, and in 1520 he burned the *Corpus* publicly. He envisaged a church which would depend on secular law in matters of temporal or outward administration, but which would be exclusively dependent on Scripture for its own internal, spiritual discipline. This solution was applied in the emerging Protestant countries of Europe, though with certain differences of detail between basically Lutheran and basically *Calvinist countries. In the former, the church was virtually a department of state and enjoyed very little autonomy. In the latter, the church retained an independent administration, but one which accepted secular judgements in temporal matters.

The Church of England presented an anomaly in this respect, and this explains much of its subsequent development. Like Luther, Henry VIII tried to get rid of the ancient canon law, but he succeeded only in abolishing the faculties at Oxford and Cambridge which had taught it. He envisaged creating a new canon law for the church, and draft proposals, now known as the *Reformatio legum ecclesiasticarum,* were eventually submitted to Parliament (1553), but they were not accepted and pre-Reformation canon law continued in force. In addition to the Roman canons, this included the collection of English provincial ecclesiastical legislation compiled by William Lyndwood in 1430 and published three years later as his *Provinciale.* It also included two sets of canons issued by the papal

legates Otho (1237) and Othobon (1268), which were normally published alongside Lyndwood.

When the Protestant settlement of 1559 was imposed by Elizabeth I, many in the church hoped that the proposals rejected in 1553 would be adopted, but Elizabeth would not hear of it. The result was a series of canons (1571, 1575–76, 1584–85, 1597) which responded to the needs of the moment but did not produce an overall system. These were eventually collected and systematized to some extent in 1603–04. There were many attempts to revise these canons in later years, but it was not until 1964–69 that a new set replaced them. Even so, however, the Church of England has never adopted a Code of Canons to replace the medieval ones, which still retain their force unless they have been superseded by subsequent legislation.

Another result of the failure of canon law reform was the growth of a movement for a further, more perfect reformation of the church. This was what we now call *Puritanism, and it determined the course of evolution which English Christianity followed in the later sixteenth and early seventeenth centuries. It is seldom appreciated nowadays that Puritanism is best understood as a reaction to canon law, which in turn was used by the church authorities to suppress it. The differences among English Christians were seldom doctrinal; for the most part they concerned matters of church order and discipline which were the province of the canons, which were administered by the ecclesiastical courts. It is no accident that, when Parliament took control of the government in 1641, the canon law and the church courts were abolished.

The fact that both were restored in 1660 and used once more to persecute dissenters merely added to the dislike which the latter felt for the canon law and the church courts. It was not until a limited religious toleration was granted in 1689 that the force of canon law was dissipated, and even then it continued to influence the lives of most Englishmen, because of the control which the ecclesiastical courts exercised over matrimony and the probate of wills. These jurisdictions were abolished in 1857, and since that time, the ecclesiastical courts and canon law have been largely restricted to the internal affairs of the Church of England. Nevertheless, it is still true to say that the canons define the character of Anglicanism in a way which is not true of other Protestant bodies, and that many of the differences between Anglicans and other Protestants are matters of canonical, rather than of purely theological, significance.

GERALD BRAY

FURTHER READING: J.A. Brundage, *Medieval Canon Law* (London, 1995); G.L. Bray (ed.), *The Anglican Canons 1529–1947* (Woodbridge, Suffolk, 1998); E. Freidberg (ed.), *Corpus Iuris Canonici* (2 vols.; Graz, 1879); R.H. Helmholz, *Roman Canon Law in Reformation England* (Cambridge, 1990); S. Kuttner, *History of Ideas and Doctrines of Canon Law in the Middle Ages* (London, 1992); E.G. Moore and T. Briden, *Moore's Introduction to English Canon Law* (London, 1986).

Cappadocian Fathers

'Cappadocians' usually refers to Basil of Caesarea (330–79), Gregory of Nyssa (331/40– c. 395) and Gregory of Nazianzus, or Nazianzen (c. 330–90). Basil and Nyssa were brothers, Basil and Nazianzen the closest of friends, and Nazianzen and Nyssa more than acquaintances. Less often and thus somewhat unfairly, the term has also included Amphilochius of Iconium (340/45– c. 400), a cousin of Nazianzen, and Macrina (d. 379), the sister of Basil and Nyssa. Although Amphilochius's works were important to ecumenical councils, we now have only fragments. Macrina left no writings, but Nyssa insisted upon her importance. The five had interrelated careers and evidently shared projects with each other although their views were occasionally distinct or even contradictory. Macrina did not visit the famous schools; her education was at home and in the church. Amphilochius apparently studied at Antioch. Nyssa's learning was both broad and deep, but we know little about its details. Basil and Nazianzen probably attended school together as children in Cappadocian Caesarea. Later Basil was educated in Constantinople and Nazianzen in Palestinian Caesarea and Alexandria before they met again in the final stages of education at Athens. The four men all taught rhetoric and later served as bishops. Macrina was the abbess of a small convent. Because of the region of their birthplace, they are named the Cappadocians. That region now lies in central Turkey.

Cappadocian theology grew in the midst of a worshipping, serving community which relied on Scripture and tradition while developing its views in response to internal church conflicts and external cultural demands and opportunities. Even when the Cappadocians insisted on how much they detested Hellenism's faults, they did so in Greek, within Hellenistic rhetoric and with deep knowledge of Hellenistic culture and religion.

Each of the five not only had some sense of Cappadocian Christian tradition, particularly that of Gregory of Thaumaturgas, but they were also familiar with Alexandrian and Antiochene views. Basil and Nazianzen probably constructed the *Philocalia*, which is comprised of selections from the works of *Origen. All of the Cappadocians wrestled with Origen's extensive scriptural commentaries as well as his theological views. Nazianzen wrote a funeral oration on *Athanasius and may have studied with Didymus the Blind while he was in Alexandria. Both Nazianzen and Nyssa constructed Christological views that were in dialogue with treatises from Diodore of Tarsus. Basil and Nyssa responded directly to *Eunomius, Nyssa to *Apollinaris. As a bishop in Constantinople Nazianzen preached against the popular Eunomians and wrote theological letters against Apollinarians. The Trinity was the battlefield with Eunomius, Christology with Apollinaris.

What the Cappadocians knew best was Scripture. Like many elite Christians of antiquity, they memorized large sections. Amphilochius provides a list of biblical books that is important for the history of the canon. Nazianzen mentions shared lists of the words 'holy', 'spirit', and 'Holy Spirit' in the Bible. Such studies led to a kind of concordic scriptural commentary which was helpful in building a biblical basis for other doctrines. Each theologian had at least one Bible and such concordic helps as well as the commentaries of others; theological treatises were not always kept but sent on to some other person in an even larger circle of theologians.

The Cappadocians' knowledge of philosophy was penetrating and their selection from it eclectic. In some ways they were contemporary *Platonists, influenced by some of Plotinus's *Enneads* and thus his interpretation of Plato's dialogues. Nyssa, the best philosopher, used medical interpretations found in Galen to explain the way that the 'power' and 'nature' of any being always appear together – and thus make the Father and Son of the same essence. In the *Hexaemeron*, his sermons on the first six chapters of Genesis, Basil employed the best science of his day. He attacked Eunomius for his dependence upon *Aristotle, but he himself relied upon the Stagarite for various aspects of epistemology and logic. Nazianzen had fuller knowledge of the Aristotelian corpus, including the *Rhetoric* and the *Poetics* as part of the logical treatises. He insisted with Aristotle, against Plato, that language is conventional rather than names revealing essences. Nazianzen employed Ephectic Sceptic models for thinking about the begetting of the Son, and he used Stoic terms to describe the unity of the human and the divine in Christ.

The Cappadocians had an appreciation for Hellenistic *paideia*. Basil specified what to avoid when teaching pagan literature to boys. Nazianzen strongly attacked the pagan emperor Julian's claim that Greek learning belonged only to pagan polytheists. He carefully sifted views from various schools and brought them together with his own rejection of Christian anti-intellectualism and his acceptance of pagan views of investigation. He also integrated their understanding of philosophical rhetoric. Nyssa worked so deeply in developing mystical views of divinity that his philosophical and Christian position provides a rather confident acceptance of Greek *paideia*'s great gifts.

Cappadocian Trinitarian thought has attracted considerable attention. It began within a Jewish-Hellenistic debate about the character of deity. Like earlier apologists the Cappadocians both attacked the moral depravity of the Greek pantheon, one invaded by various Iranian and Egyptian figures, and praised any who spoke of the good God beyond the pantheon. Our knowledge of Greek antiquity was thinned by the sack of Byzantium's libraries in 1204 and 1451. Therefore we cannot even identify all the names of those Greek non-Christian theologians which later Byzantine commentators thought so important to the Cappadocians – both in skewering the Hellenistic deities and in honouring God beyond the gods.

In terms of philosophical precision, Cappadocian Trinitarian thought did advance beyond the phrases which comprise the 325 Creed of Nicaea and the work of its champion, Athanasius of Alexandria. Yet what the Cappadocians did was to attempt to salvage and extend Nicene Trinitarian positions after their savaging in the 360s and 370s. The track is difficult to follow because Basil, who first asked some of the most penetrating questions and thus received the earliest helpful answers,

became embarrassed by the later positions of his teachers. We have correspondence between Basil and Apollinaris of Laodicea about the meaning of *homoousios*, 'of the same essence or nature', and about the distinction between *ousia*, 'essence or nature', and *hypostasis*, 'person'. Basil originally questioned *homoousios*; he apparently knew that Paul of Samosata had employed the term to emphasize the oneness of Father and Son such that their distinct characteristics were either lost or made incidental.

Apollinaris was a helpful teacher regarding this set of issues. He convinced Basil that using such an important non-biblical term served to sharpen the argument's point rather than to destroy the stylus. Basil's deep sensitivity to employing biblical words for biblical subjects had raised its own suspicions. Apollinaris urged Basil to focus on two levels of reality in the Trinity – one in which the unity of the divine nature would be proclaimed and protected, and another in which the particular aspects of each person would be professed and secured. Basil learned the lesson well and evidently shared it with the two Gregories. But later, when Apollinaris's Christology made the Laodicean suspect in Nicene circles which also questioned Basil's consecration as bishop and his theology, Basil chose not to claim Apollinaris as his teacher. To reveal how much he had learned from the Laodicean defender of Nicaea would only have worsened the situation. So he fudged the record, admitting that he had had contacts with Apollinaris but insisting that he owed him nothing of great significance in the structure and content of his own work.

That background offers one reason why the important *Ep. 38*, which deals with levels of unity and difference within the Trinity and is found in the corpus of both Basil and Gregory of Nyssa, is now usually attributed to Nyssa alone. Basil defended *homoousios* strongly, but he did not develop it with the philosophical precision that one finds in Nyssa's works. Almost every position which marks Cappadocian thought as significant can be found in a nutshell within Basil's writings. Their astute logical, philosophical development, however, is often lodged in the work of Nyssa. *Ep. 38* is the *locus classicus* of Cappadocian Trinitarian doctrine. It uses biblical illustrations and depends upon existing Christian theology, but it deftly works out the relationship between Father and Son both in terms of unity and distinction. In his *Catechetical Orations* Nyssa insisted that although Judaism mistook the divine nature of the Word and Hellenism floundered in polytheism, Christian Trinitarianism insisted both on the one God of Judaism and the divine diversity of Hellenism.

The final achievement of full Trinitarian thought, however, appeared in the *Theological Orations* of Gregory Nazianzen, affectionately and penetratingly called 'The Theologian'. Basil and Gregory of Nyssa employed *homoousios* when expressing the relationship of Father and Son, but neither explicitly used the word when speaking of the Holy Spirit. Basil, at least, was deeply concerned that Scripture did not refer to the Spirit as God. Nazianzen insisted that in the same way in which the Old Testament did not directly call the Son 'God' as the New Testament did, the growing contemporary revelation of the Spirit now demanded that *homoousios* and the designation 'God' be applied. The scriptural conservatism of Basil was not enough. Without dangerous innovation, the church needed to confess three persons in one nature: God, God and God. Nazianzen was furious when the 381 Council of Constantinople only slightly strengthened the article on the Holy Spirit. The wide scriptural base of both titles for, and actions of, the Holy Spirit demanded the Spirit's inclusion in the fullest expression of Trinity. Yet at the same time that all the Cappadocians moved toward a full Trinitarian doctrine, they confessed that ultimately the relationships of the Father, Son and Holy Spirit proved impossible to describe.

Basil and Nyssa were convinced by Hellenistic non-Christian theology that the impassible could not suffer passion. The passion of the impassible, which is a poetic phrase used within Nicene and non-Nicene communities alike, had a fascination for them, but only Nazianzen pushed farther. He demanded that not only the human Jesus suffered on the cross; the divine Son and the Father also did not shy away from the pain. God suffered. Christians should dare to speak of the crucified God. All the Cappadocians claimed the rich biblical sense of atonement, but Nazianzen rejected payment to the devil; the evil one was not properly owed anything. Nazianzen developed a sense of movement in the Trinity and a doctrine of creation which fits well with modern ecological concerns. Furthermore he insisted, against the Eunomians, that speaking of

God as a male must be a joke because divinity is beyond human gender.

With Basil providing the questions and significant answers, Nyssa deepening the spirituality through philosophical acuity and Nazianzen shaping the full theology through philosophical rhetoric, the Cappadocians created a balanced understanding of the Trinity which satisfied the east for centuries. Only *Augustine's *On the Trinity* went further. And with his bad Greek Augustine just may have picked up his psychological images and his insistence on relationship as the key to an economic Trinity from Nazianzen.

Basil's *Hexaemeron*, comprising beautiful sermons on God and creation, surpassed a treatise by Nyssa on the same topic. According to Basil one must take the actual verses of Scripture with ultimate seriousness, but those passages did not demand a full-scale attack on science. The observations of Aristotle and others need not force one into a kind of anti-intellectualism. Christians should attack Hellenistic deficiency but also recognize its grand proficiency.

In Christology the Cappadocians also offered an advance. Unlike Athanasius, the Cappadocians found a way to consistently emphasize the full humanity of Jesus and its activity in his person. Basil mentions some writings from Diodore of Tarsus, one which he read with pleasure and another which he found diffuse, but he and the two Gregories rejected certain conceptions of two sons within the Christ. They all used the Stoic conceptions of mixing and blending rather poetically – conceptions which suggest that two entities keep their distinctive characteristics and do not become a third reality and yet are truly united. Amphilochius spoke of an unconfused and unlimited unity in the person of Christ. Nazianzen employed the word *perichoreo* to picture the interpenetration of the divine and the human in Jesus Christ – one whole in which the divine predominates.

Basil and Nyssa wrote long treatises against the errors of Eunomius of Cyzicus, who creatively suggested that while the Son was not like the Father in essence or nature, and was a created being, he was not in the same category with human beings. The Son was the first-born in a class by himself. Nazianzen took on popular Eunomians in Constantinople who vulgarized some of Eunomius's subtle distinctions and who worried about the many weaknesses attributed to Jesus in Scripture. Nazianzen replied, as did

Basil and Nyssa directly against Eunomius himself, that the Son in his incarnate condition, or the human Jesus, was the subject of things unworthy of deity. The Son became man for our salvation. That was the mystery.

Against the Christology of Apollinaris and his followers, which found no place for human intellect and will in the person of the Christ, Nyssa and Nazianzen insisted upon Jesus' full human nature complete with feelings, thoughts and actions. Scripture demanded it. Nazianzen was the first to suggest that there is a similarity between three and one in the Godhead and two and one in Jesus Christ.

Yet the single most important model for the Cappadocian conception of Jesus' identity grew out of what they thought he did for human salvation. Accepting a partial Platonic framework, they drew on both Scripture and tradition to insist that the word 'deification' best described salvation. Basil and Nyssa used biblical terms to speak of humans becoming divine because the divine Son became human. Nazianzen the poet cleaned up the strong Hellenistic word *theosis*, 'deification', and used it frequently.

Looking at least back to Athanasius, the Cappadocians insisted that God became human in order that humans might become divine. Threefold baptism insisted on trinity, but also on the human putting on developing divinity. Apollinarians were wrong to suggest that intellect and will were not present in the person of Christ because what was not assumed by the divine Son could not be saved. Only what he took on himself would be healed. Since intellect and will were as much responsible for sin as the flesh, they had to be saved and must therefore have been assumed. All humans had a modicum of free will which rendered them responsible for their actions. Eunomians were wrong to think that the Son was not fully divine, because we could only be healed and become as divine as the fully divine had become fully human. Pneumatomachians, those who opposed the full divinity of the Holy Spirit, were wrong because baptism into the spirit was not baptism into a creature.

Of the many contributions which Nyssa made, perhaps the most scintillating is his description of eternal life as unending progression in knowledge of God, so well described in his *Life of Moses* and *Commentary on the Song of Songs*. He found contemplative and virtuous growth possible on earth, but essential in heaven. According to him,

his sister Macrina offered some remarkable reflections on human passions. She emphasized their good aspects, making them a positive part of this life and of life hereafter. Nyssa avoided Origen's own epistolary rejection of the devil's salvation and followed the Alexandrian's other hints about universal salvation. His own sense was that for love finally to conquer, all eventually must be healed.

As the Cappadocian most gifted with the confidence and political skills to be a bishop, Basil also provided the deepest conception of the church. His epistles presented the colour of international intrigue and internal struggle. Because being a bishop carried cultural status he often wrote to Roman officials asking for special consideration of those who had asked him to plead their cases. But the bulk of his letters were concerned with the struggle to establish Nicene orthodoxy and vital Christian community. Basil had a rather extensive collection of canon law which he shared for handling daily problems. Almost always confident, he placed his foot wrongly at times. Nyssa actually forged letters in an effort to help Basil with one problem – only to make it far worse. Nazianzen never felt settled in congregational life and warned others of mediocre bishops and squabbling councils that threatened one's soul. It was Basil who created a hospice in Caesarea – first for travellers, then the sick. It was large enough to assist those threatened by an extended regional famine. He cajoled and badgered the rich, and perhaps even an emperor who disliked him, so that the complex of buildings could be referred to as a new city.

In the modern period Amphilochius and Macrina are proof that apparently minor figures can offer major suggestions. Basil the Great has been re-appropriated particularly for his work *On the Holy Spirit*, as well as for his attempts to regularize monastic life through a many-faceted rule. His sense of the church as an institution which moves to help the poor and oppressed would confirm and instruct many liberation theologies. His understanding of creation continues to offer helpful hints on how to deal with modern science. Nyssa has enhanced the contemplative sense of the mystical life. He is rare among Christian theologians for having integrated so well an understanding of God with the life of the soul. He strengthens and guides the burgeoning interest in spirituality at the turn of the millennium. Nazianzen deserves his title

'The Theologian'. His poetic power shapes his theology and dares new formulations. His poetry can be mined for faith which gives fullness to reasoning. His command of logic and rhetoric indicates an analogical rejection of Aristotle's law of non-contradiction which so perfectly describes contemporary physics. Study of all five Cappadocians will prove beneficial.

FREDERICK W. NORRIS

FURTHER READING: David Balas, *Metousia Theou: Man's Participation in God's Perfections According to Saint Gregory of Nyssa* (St Ans 58; Rome, 1966); Sigurd Bergmann, *Geist, der Natur Befreit: Die trintarische Kosmologie Gregors von Nazianz im Horozont einer ökologischen Theologie der Befreiung* (Mainz, 1995); Jean Bernardi, *La Prédication des Pères Cappadociens: Le Prédicateur et son Auditoire* (Publications de la Faculté de Lettres et Sciences humaines de l'Université de Montpellier 30; 1968); Jean Bernardi, *Grégoire de Nazianze: Le Théologien et son Temps, 300–390* (Paris, 1995); Jean Daniélou, *Platonisme et Théologie Mystique* (Paris, rev. edn, 1954); Paul J. Fedwick (ed.), *Basil of Caesarea: Christian Humanist, Ascetic* (2 vols.; Toronto, 1981); Karl Holl, *Amphilochius von Ikonium in seinem Verhältnis zu den grossen Kappadociens* (Tübingen, 1904); Anthony Meredith, *The Cappadocians* (Crestwood, NY, 1995); Frederick Norris, *Faith Gives Fullness to Reasoning: A Commentary on Gregory Nazianzen's Theological Orations* (VCSup 13; Leiden, 1991); Brooks Otis, 'Cappadocian Thought as a Coherent System', *DOP* 12 (1958), pp. 95–124; Bernard Pottier, *Dieu et le Christ selon Grégoire de Nysse: Étude Systématique du 'Contre Eunome' avec Traduction Inédite des Extraits d'Eunome* (Namur, 1994); Philip Rousseau, *Basil of Caesarea* (Berkeley, 1994); Rowan Williams, 'Macrina's Deathbed Revisited: Gregory of Nyssa on Mind and Passion', *Christian Faith and Greek Philosophy in Late Antiquity* (Leiden, 1993), pp. 227–46.

Cassian, John (c. 360 – c. 435)

Monk, writer, and master of ascetic spirituality. Cassian was probably born in Scythia Minor (modern Romania) and was educated in both Greek and Latin. He drank deeply from the wells of communal (coenobitic) and solitary (anchoritic) monasticism, the former while living in a monastery in Bethlehem in the 380s and the latter while interacting with Egyptian anchorites in the 390s. (While in Egypt, Cassian was heavily influenced by the *Origenistic spirituality of Evagrius Ponticus.) Sometime after 400, Cassian moved to Marseilles, where he founded two monasteries (one for men and the other for women) and wrote two works on monasticism and one on the incarnation. His fluency in Greek and Latin and his wandering life uniquely equipped him to bring the treasures of fourth-century eastern monasticism to the west, and Cassian was the primary bridge between the spirituality of the desert fathers and the monastic rule of *Benedict (c. 480 – c. 550).

As a theologian, Cassian is best known for his part in the *semi-Pelagian controversy. Like many monks in Gaul and North Africa, Cassian was concerned that the doctrine of grace not be taught in such a way that human initiative was ignored. He was vitally concerned with the human struggle for moral perfection and virtue, so as to enable one to gain purity of heart and unhindered contemplation of God. This human task of pursuing virtue is the theme of his great monastic writings, *On the Institutes of the Monasteries* (before 426) and *Conferences* (426–29). In the infamous Conference 13, Cassian argues that sometimes God gives grace by drawing people to himself and causing them to seek perfection, but at other times he allows people to make the first move toward him and then aids them in striving for virtue. Conference 13 was bitterly contested by Prosper of Aquitaine (c. 390 – c. 463), who believed that Cassian's teaching constituted a denial of the *Augustinian doctrine that the initiative in salvation always lies with God, never with the human will. The basis for Prosper's criticism was apparently his belief that Cassian saw salvation as a gradual process of ascent through moral virtue, a ladder leading to contemplation of God. However, Prosper almost certainly misunderstood Cassian on this point. It is true that Cassian believed people were able to will the good apart from God's grace, and this placed him somewhat at odds with Prosper and Augustine. But Cassian did not believe that a person's good will was the beginning of salvation. Rather, he argues elsewhere in the *Conferences* that salvation begins with God's gift of himself to people through Christ, a gift by which God draws a person into union with himself and makes him an adopted child. According to Cassian, a person's desire for virtue and moral purity is an attempt to deepen the union he already has with God, not an attempt to aspire to a union which is merely future. In the process of moral purification, God sometimes takes the initiative and sometimes waits for human action, but this entire process is based on God's prior gift of grace to a person.

God always initiates salvation by granting union and fellowship with himself. Cassian was branded a 'semi-Pelagian' largely because his opponents mistakenly believed that his teaching about the pursuit of virtue constituted his entire doctrine of grace and salvation. In fact, that teaching was simply the portion of his understanding of grace most relevant to the monastic task; the monk seeks to appreciate as fully as possible the union he has been given with God, to remove all distractions so as to contemplate the God who has saved him. This teaching about the pursuit of perfection was not the foundation of his soteriological thought at all.

Cassian also played a small part in the Nestorian controversy leading up to the Council of Ephesus in 431. At the request of *Leo (then archdeacon of Rome and later to become Pope Leo the Great), Cassian wrote *On the Incarnation of the Lord* (430) in order to refute Nestorius. This work is often criticized for its confused terminology and apparent vacillation between the extremes of what would later be called Nestorianism and *Eutychianism, and Cassian's Christological thought seems to have had little influence on the subsequent development of the church's doctrine of Christ. (His work is never cited in any later discussions of Christology.) In spite of his sloppy terminology, however, Cassian is significant as a theological thinker because his work represents a Christology very similar to that that of *Cyril of Alexandria and to what would later be called Neo-Chalcedonianism. Cassian clearly sees the personal subject in Christ as the Logos himself, not as the man Jesus or as a combination of divine and human entities. God the Logos took humanity into his own person at the incarnation, so as to live as a man for our salvation. Cassian insists repeatedly that the Word himself was born as a man, suffered as a man, died as a man and rose as a man. It is surprising to find such a 'Cyrillian' Christology in the writings of a Latin theologian of the fifth century, and Cassian's work lends support to the contention that Cyrillian Christology was the norm in both east and west during the fifth century.

DONALD FAIRBAIRN

FURTHER READING: *Texts: On the Institutes of the Monasteries* (*De Institutis Coenobiorum*), *Conferences* (*Conlationes*), and *On the Incarnation of the Lord* (*De Incarnatione Domini*) in *PL* 49–50 (Migne's reprint of Gazet's 1616 Latin text); CSEL 13, 17 (critical Latin text by Petschenig; 1888); *NPNF²* 11 (ET by Gibson; 1894); *Conferences* (critical Latin text with French trans. by Pichery; SC 42, 54, 64; 1955–59); *Institutes* (ed. and trans. Guy; SC 109; 1965); *Conferences* (Mod. ET by Ramsey; ACW 57; 1997). *Studies:* E.C.S. Gibson, Prolegomena to 'The Works of John Cassian', *NPNF²* 11 (1894), pp. 183–97; O. Chadwick, *John Cassian* (London, 1950; 2nd edn 1968); P. Munz, 'John Cassian', *J Eccl H* 11 (1960), pp. 1–22; J. Harper, 'John Cassian and Sulpicius Severus', *Ch H* 34 (1965), pp. 371–80; P. Rousseau, *Ascetics, Authority, and the Church in the Age of Jerome and Cassian* (Oxford, 1978); R.A. Markus, *The End of Ancient Christianity* (Cambridge, 1990); C. Stewart, *Cassian the Monk* (New York, 1998).

Catholic Reformation

The terms 'Catholic Reformation', 'Catholic Reform', 'Catholic Renewal' or 'Tridentine Reformation' are to be preferred to the older and less accurate 'Counter Reformation' with its suggestion that the Catholic Church of the sixteenth century merely reacted to the Protestant *Reformations, for this was simply not the case. This said, with the coming of the Protestant Reformations and the formulation and spread of doctrines which struck at the very heart of the Catholic Church, a reassessment of Catholic teaching regarding the disputed issues became increasingly more urgent.

Since the Middle Ages the Catholic Church had known many reform movements (see Constable, Bolton and Lambert): from within in the form of the reforms of Gregory VII (c. 1023–85) and his successors, through the founding of new religious orders, such as the *Franciscans (1209) and Dominicans (1216), but also in the persons of contemplatives and mystics who included *Hildegard of Bingen (1098–1179) and *Joachim of Fiore (c. 1135–1202); and from without in the heresies, most notably the Waldensians, Cathars and *Hussites. Such late medieval calls for the renewal of the church were generally grounded in the ascetic and theological traditions concerned with spiritual and ecclesiastical renewal through moral reform. In contrast, the Protestant Reformers believed that people could not be reformed by religion unless it was the right religion and so their focus was first doctrinal and practical, then moral. The problem, however, for the Catholic Church was that the very institutions which needed reforming, the papacy and the *Curia*, had much to lose and so resisted calls for reform and delayed in convening a council.

At the dawn of the sixteenth century, there were many devout Catholics who recognized the need for the renewal of the church. Such included the fiery Florentine Dominican, Girolamo Savonarola (1452–98), Giles of Viterbo (1469–1532) who called on the Fifth Lateran Council (1512–17) to reform the church's members and restore its discipline, the Spanish Franciscan, Cardinal Francisco Ximénes de Cisneros (c. 1436–1517), and the humanist Dean of St Paul's, London, John Colet (c. 1466–1519). Others set out to reform the church in practical ways, and these included new religious orders such as the Theatines (1524) and Capuchins (1528), and the Genoese and Roman Oratories (1497 and 1517) who focused on personal spirituality and charitable works. That none of these were reformers or reform movements in the same way as the Protestant Reformers does not mean that they should not be seen as evidence of Catholicism seeking to renew itself, even if this was by means of a return to a piety of a previous era rather than innovative doctrinal and/or institutional reform.

The humanist *Desiderius Erasmus (c. 1466–1536) believed that the hope for the future of the church rested with the laity, while Bishop Gian Matteo Giberti (1495–1543) sought to reform the education and morality of the clergy. Pope Adrian VI (1522–23) recognized the need for the reform of the church from the top downwards but died before he could do anything about it, while his successor, Clement VII (1523–34), finally agreed in 1532 to the ecumenical council for which *Luther had called twelve years previously, but he too died in 1534 before convoking it. The committee appointed by Pope Paul III (1534–49) which composed the *Consilium de emendanda ecclesia* ('Advice Concerning the Reform of the Church', 1537), included leading advocates of reform Gaspar Contarini (1483–1542), Jacopo Sadoleto (1477–1547) and Reginald Pole (1500–58). The *Consilium* criticized the mismanagement of the church's property and held that the leadership of the church had been corrupted by the practices of nepotism, simony, pluralism of benefices, absenteeism, clerical immorality and venality, though their solution was an increased discipline and adherence to the church's laws, rather than innovative reform. For this they were criticized in Luther's German translation of the *Consilium* (1538),

which included a sarcastic preface as well as marginal glosses, and, needless to say, the report was not accepted by the papal court, though it did anticipate many of the reforms later made by the Council of Trent. Even by mid-century, the Catholic scholars of the Italian Evangelism (the *spirituali*, c. 1512–1560s), who agreed with much in the theology of the Reformers, nevertheless disagreed with them on the need for the institutional reform of the church. All such moves were too little too late to preserve even the semblance of a united Christendom, though it must be remembered that Martin Luther's (1483–1546) Ninety-five Theses (1517) were posted by a Catholic monk who sought to reform the abuses of the indulgence sellers: he did not set out to divide the church.

In the early 1540s, Catholics and Reformers met first at Hagenau (June 1540), then at Worms (January 1541), and these meetings led to the Regensburg Colloquy in April 1541, led by the Catholic reformers Johannes Gropper (1503–59), Julius Pflug (1499–1564) and *Johann Eck (1486–1543) and the Reformers *Martin Bucer (1491–1551), *Philip Melancthon (1497–1560) and Johannes Pistorius (d. 1583). A considerable amount of theological agreement was reached on humanity's nature before the Fall, the loss of free will in Adam and its restoration in Christ, the volitional nature of sin and the debilitating effects of original sin. But the compromise formula on 'double justification', whereby justification was seen as, on the one hand, inherent in the just and, on the other, the imputed righteousness of Christ, while finding initial support from Contarini and *John Calvin (1509–64), was rejected by the pope and Luther, and proved insufficient for reunion. Double justification was later condemned by the Council of Trent.

Two significant events for the development of the Catholic Reformation took place during the pontificate of Paul III (1534–49): the founding of the Society of Jesus (*Jesuits) in 1540 under the inspiration and direction of *Ignatius Loyola (1491–1556), and the re-establishment of the Inquisition. Ignatius's Spiritual Exercises were in use in the late 1520s, long before they were published in 1548. They were meditations and rules intended to strengthen and discipline the will to conform to and serve God's will. Members of the Society of Jesus embodied Ignatius's beliefs and emphasized their readiness to serve the pope absolutely, and they became prominent in the Catholic Reformation in general and the proceedings of the Council of Trent in particular. With its roots in the thirteenth century when it was used to counter the Cathar movement (see Lambert, pp. 133–42, 176–88), the Inquisition had been revived in Spain in 1478 and then in Rome in 1542, where Paul III reluctantly allowed it to become established under Gian Petro Carafa (the future Pius IV), under whom it became a means of insulating Italy against the inroads of Protestantism, not least after the failure of the Colloquy of Regensburg and the panic which surrounded the 'apostasy' of two leading Catholic reformers to Calvinism, Bernadino Ochino (1487–1564) and *Peter Martyr Vermigli (1500–62) (see Jedin, 1957, I, pp. 446–47).

However, under Pius IV (1555–59) 'reform took on a darker side and more fearful character. Creativity was distrusted as dangerous innovation, theological energies were diverted into the suppression of error rather than the exploration of truth. Catholicism was identified with reaction' (Duffy, p. 169). A list of prohibited books had circulated since 1521, mainly through the theology faculties of Paris and Louvain, but Pius IV transformed it into a complete list of heretical works and published the *Index librorum prohibitorum* ('Index of Prohibited Books') in 1559, it being modified five years later by Trent. Not only were Protestant works proscribed, but also those by Erasmus, and Boccaccio's *Decameron* and the reading of vernacular Bibles was also forbidden.

From 1537 to 1542, attempts to convene a council proved unsuccessful. However, the Council of Trent (reckoned to be the nineteenth ecumenical council) finally opened on 13 December 1545, and met in three distinct assemblies (1545–47, 1551–52 and 1561–63) comprising a total of 25 sessions, all but two being held at Trent. Its location at Trent was a compromise, lying as it did on the border between the Holy Roman Empire and Italy. The emperor hoped it would achieve the reconciliation of Protestants and Catholics and he insisted that Protestant representatives attend. The pope, however, wanted the council to shore up the Catholic Church and make clear that Protestantism was heretical. Papal reluctance was based on a combination of political and theological concerns. The conciliar movement of the fifteenth century had sought to subjugate papal authority to that of a council, and the pope feared the wish of the Emperor

Charles V (1500–58) for such a council, though there was pressure from many Catholic princes who deplored ecclesiastical abuses and believed a council was the only way of correcting them. Further, Luther's call for a council also implied the conciliarist position, with Scripture as the authority to the exclusion of ecclesiastical tradition. In contrast to the more representative earlier councils of Constance (1414–18) and Basle-Ferrara-Florence (1431–45), voting at Trent was confined to individual bishops, and since the majority were Italian this effectively gave the pope firm control on all that was decided. At Trent, doctrinal decisions took the form of decrees (*decreta*) which included positive declarations of the church's teaching and canons (*canones*), while all opposing (Protestant) teachings were anathematized.

While the possibility of the reunion of the Protestant and Catholic churches remained in the first two sittings of the Council (Protestant representatives even attended the sessions in 1552), with the election of Pius IV all hope of conciliation soon disappeared. The Council of Trent evinced the two overriding concerns of the Catholic Church: opposition to Protestantism and self-renewal. To counter the Protestant *sola scriptura* principle, Trent upheld as dual sources of authority both Scripture and tradition, the latter including the rulings of popes and councils, the final interpreter of both being the magisterium, that is, the teaching authority of the Catholic Church under the pope. To this was added the decree that *Jerome's Vulgate (old Latin) edition of the Bible be given normative status for doctrine. On justification it reaffirmed the role of human co-operation with grace for salvation in opposition to the Reformers' *sola gratia*. In stark contrast to the soteriology of the Protestant Reformations, 'The counter-reformation ... announced that Man – even in the face of his almighty Creator – carried, to some extent, his own fate in his hands' (Evennett, 1970, p. 36). The efficacy *ex opere operato* (by the performance of the rite) of the seven sacraments of baptism, confirmation, Eucharist, penance, extreme unction, holy orders and marriage were reasserted over the Protestant two of baptism and Eucharist. Communion in one kind (the taking of only the bread by the laity) was ratified (which also perpetuated the distinction between the sacerdotal priesthood and the laity), as was the understanding of the Mass as the repetition of Christ's sacrifice, the bread and wine becoming the very body and blood of Christ at the prayer of consecration (transubstantiation). Clerical marriage was forbidden, as was clerical concubinage. Purgatory, indulgences, the veneration of relics and sacred images and the worship of the saints were endorsed, though abuses were corrected.

On 26 January 1564, the bull 'Benedictus Deus' was issued. It confirmed the canons and decrees of the Council and declared that the pope had the sole right to interpret them. This was followed in November by the 'Profession of the Tridentine Faith', a statement of Catholic beliefs to be recited publicly by all bishops and beneficed clergy and which is the symbol imposed on all converts to Roman Catholicism. The work of Trent was carried forward by Pius IV's successors, Pius V (1566–72), Gregory XIII (1572–85) and Sixtus V (1585–90). Pius V founded the Congregation of the Index in 1571 (now the Congregation for the Doctrine of the Faith – the index itself was only abolished in 1966) and Sixtus V undertook the reform of the *Curia* in 1588. Liturgical reform, not dealt with at Trent, came later, with the Roman Catechism (1566) and the revised Roman Breviary (1568) and Roman Missal (1570), which codified a uniform liturgy of the Mass for the whole liturgical year to be used in all Catholic churches. In 1593 the revised Vulgate, ordered at Trent in 1545, was completed under Clement VIII (1592–1605).

Positively, Trent made many significant administrative reforms, including episcopal reforms, and included the creation of seminaries for the education of all new clergy, though it did not provide a consistent doctrine of the nature of the church or of the position of the pope. However, though important changes were effected in administration and new programmes of education and reform, Trent was conservative in both doctrine and practice. When Trent opened, Christendom was still, theoretically, united, but by the time it closed, Christianity was divided. Though Trent failed to accomplish all its goals for the reformation of the faith, the renewal of morality and the reunion of the church, it nevertheless clearly reinvigorated the Roman Catholic Church. It was responsible for formulating Catholic doctrine more clearly than ever before. It was followed by renewed theological education and scholarship, moral reform, missionary endeavour and success, and spiritual growth,

but the Catholic reforms were still in essence personal. The church would be renewed by the renewal of its members who were themselves transformed by a renewed hierarchy.

It is from Trent that the Catholic Church can be truly reckoned to have become the Roman Catholic Church, and this formed the basis of what is known as ultramontanism (the centralization of authority and influence in the papacy), which would be a key factor in much subsequent Roman Catholic theology and practice. After 1563 there would not be another ecumenical council until *Vatican I (1869–70), at which papal authority and infallibility was defined, while the Immaculate Conception of Mary (that from birth she was free of original sin) was issued in 1854, the doctrine of the assumption (that on death Mary was assumed bodily into heaven) following in 1950.

ANTHONY R. CROSS

FURTHER READING: B. Bolton, *The Medieval Reformation* (London, 1983); J. Bossy, *Christianity in the West, 1400–1700* (Oxford, 1985); E. Cameron, *The European Reformation* (Oxford, 1991); G. Constable, *The Reformation of the Twelfth Century* (Cambridge, 1996); A.G. Dickens, *The Counter Reformation* (London, 1968); E. Duffy, *Saints and Sinners: A History of the Popes* (New Haven, 1997); H.O. Evennett, *The Spirit of the Counter-Reformation* (Notre Dame, IN, 1970 edn); E.G. Gleason 'Catholic Reformation, Counterreformation and Papal Reform in the Sixteenth Century', in *Handbook of European History 1400–1600: Late Middle Ages, Renaissance, and Reformation*, II: *Visions, Programs, and Outcomes* (ed. T.A. Brady, H.A. Oberman and J.D. Tracy; Grand Rapids, 1995), pp. 317–45; E.G. Gleason (ed.), *Reform and Thought in Sixteenth-Century Italy* (Chico, CA, 1981); E. Iserloh, J. Glazik and H. Jedin (eds.), *Reformation and Counter Reformation* (ed. H. Jedin and J. Dolan; History of the Church 5; New York, 1986); H. Jedin, *A History of the Council of Trent* (2 vols.; London, 1957, 1961); M. Lambert, *Medieval Heresy: Popular Movements from the Gregorian Reform to the Reformation* (Oxford, 2nd edn, 1992); M.R. O'Connell, *The Counter Reformation 1560–1610* (New York, 1974); J.C. Olin, *Catholic Reform: From Cardinal Ximénes to the Council of Trent 1495–1563* (New York, 1990); *The Catholic Reformation: Savonarola to Ignatius Loyola* (New York, 1992); H.J. Schroeder, *Canons and Decrees of the Council of Trent* (St Louis, MO, 1955).

Cave, Sydney (1883–1953)

Congregational theologian, born in London. He elected to train for the ministry at Hackney

College (1902–08) under *P.T. Forsyth, who had succeeded Cave's uncle Alfred as principal in 1900. Following four months of study in Berlin, Cave was ordained and served under the London Missionary Society at Neyyoor, Travancore, until 1918. During a pastorate at Henleaze, Bristol (1918–20) he lectured at Western College and at Manchester University, proceeding thence to the presidency of Cheshunt College, Cambridge (1920–33). From 1933 until his death he was principal of New College, London.

A devoted scholar, Cave excelled as a teacher. His fair, concise expositions of the ideas of others, based upon wide and careful reading, are interspersed with illuminating critical comments. His theological grounding (to which *A.E. Garvie of New College, London, contributed), coupled with his experience in India, enabled him both to expound Christian doctrine and to consider Christianity in relation to other faiths.

Thus, in *Redemption, Hindu and Christian* (1919), for which he received his London DD, Cave first expounds Hindu thought and then relates Christian teaching to it. He argues that the aspirations of Hinduism may be answered only if Christians understand that Christianity proclaims not only redemption from sin, but from the world – not in the sense of denying or fleeing from the world, but of living out the truth that in Christ the world is overcome and eternity is now. In *Christianity and Some Living Religions of the East* (1929) Cave discusses Islam, Hinduism, Buddhism, Chinese religions and Zoroastrianism from this perspective, concluding (in words which some latter-day critics would contest) that, 'The missionary enterprise is not the imposition of an alien civilisation ... It is not for [the missionary] to condemn or criticise ... [but] to present to the East the Christ whom the West imperfectly obeys.' There followed *An Introduction to the Study of Some Living Religions of the East* (1933); and the Haskell Lectures (Oberlin College) of 1939, *Hinduism or Christianity?: A Study in the Distinctiveness of the Christian Message* (1939). Having compared and contrasted doctrinal and ethical teachings, Cave concludes that Hindu thought and devotion present a challenge to Christianity which can be met only by a deeper grasp by Christians of their gospel and a more faithful witness to Christ, who is 'the Word of God to men of every race'.

Between them, Cave's doctrinal works encompass the principal teachings of Christianity: The *Doctrine of the Person of Christ* (1925), *The Doctrine of the Work of Christ* (1937), *The Christian Estimate of Man* (1944) and the compendium, *The Doctrines of the Christian Faith* (1931). Biblical and historical exposition predominates, but Cave's own views are not hidden. He cannot agree either that Christ is simply the greatest of human teachers, or that the historic creeds are final in content and terminology. He observes that the most severe critics of kenotic Christology deny or ignore Christ's pre-existence, thereby escaping the problem the kenotic theory was introduced to alleviate. Salvaging something from each of the main approaches to the atonement, Cave's practical bent requires him to insist that those who have been grasped by God's holy and forgiving love in Christ are required to learn the way of forgiveness themselves. Having pursued Christian anthropology through the centuries, he interprets election not as a product of God's *horribile decretum*, but in terms of God's holy love which desires the salvation of all. Predestination is not a matter of God's arbitrary choice, but the expression of his gracious purpose to provide in Christ all that is necessary for salvation. The church is not constituted by apostolic orders, but by its gospel, proclaimed in preaching and sacraments. The Trinity is not a primary truth of the gospel, but is 'an ultimate intellectual implicate'. By making the doctrine the foundation of his theology *Barth gives it undue prominence. The Christian hope concerns the present as well as the future: 'Already we have a communion with God which is eternal life, and that communion death is powerless to interrupt.'

Cave also published, *The Gospel of St. Paul* (1928); *What Shall We Say of Christ?* (1932), a work of popular apologetics in the series of Westminster Books which he edited jointly with V.F. Storr; and *The Christian Way: A Study of New Testament Ethics in Relation to Present Problems* (1949) – namely, those concerning the orders of creation, marriage, industry and the state. Christian ethics, Cave maintains, derive from the good news of what God has done in Christ. He also contributed the volume on Acts to *The Study Bible* edited by J.F. Stirling (1926–30).

ALAN P.F. SELL

FURTHER READING: *The Congregational Year Book* (London, 1954), pp. 506–7; *Who Was Who* (London, 1951–60); S. Cave, 'Dr. P.T. Forsyth: The Man and his Writings', *Cong Q* 26.2 (1948), pp. 107–19.

Celtic Theology

No systematic study of Christian celtic theology from the primary sources exists; indeed, the title 'celtic', applied to a church, theology, spirituality and people, is problematic. By the dawn of the Christian era, Brythonic tribes inhabited Britain, speaking early forms of Welsh. Goidelic tribes inhabited Ireland and Man, speaking early forms of Irish/Gaelic. They held diverse pagan theologies difficult now to ascertain due to the lack of early literary evidence and the Christian authorship of later accounts. Society was organized in competing tribal kingdoms, with no 'nations' following modern boundaries until the Norman era. By the early sixth century, Britons had settled in Brittany, and Goidelic tribesmen (Scotti) in Dyfed and Gwynedd, Argyll (Dalriada) and the Western Isles, taking control of north and west Scotland by c. 811. Diversity within both these people groups is now recognized, with tribal loyalties eclipsing any modern romantic idea of celtic solidarity. They would not have used the term 'celtic' of themselves.

'Celtic' is the term popularly applied to early Christianity in these regions, established certainly by 314 when British bishops attended Arles. The (Christian) Roman Empire had been an evangelistic instrument, acting as a vehicle for the faith both in Roman administered Britain where it took root amongst Romanized 'celts', and also in areas not under direct Roman rule, that is Ireland and Pictland, where there was sufficient interaction to communicate the gospel and where the faith grew amongst non-Romanized 'celts'. From c. 407, the Empire withdrew, leaving the tribes to administer their own churches. Coincident with Roman withdrawal came pagan Germanic invasions which challenged, and even wiped out, church and celtic cultures in Britain. In the fifth and sixth centuries, Saxons established control of the south-east of Britain; Angles took control of the north-east as far as the Forth, establishing the pagan kingdom of Northumbria by c. 550. Ireland was largely unaffected by this wave, and the church there prospered. However from c. 793, pagan Vikings first raided and then took control in much of Ireland, coastal and insular Scotland, and Man. The establishment of Norman ecclesial structures from the late eleventh century finally closes the 'celtic' era.

According to Prosper of Aquitaine (c. 390–c. 463), Bishop Celestine of Rome (d. 432) sent Palladius to be 'first bishop of the Scotti [i.e. Irish] who believe in Christ' in 431. Patrick (c. 390–c. 461) went from Britain to Ireland to evangelize the remaining pagan northern Irish from 432 (Annals of Ulster). We have two of his writings, *Confessio* and *Epistola ad milites Corotici*. *Bede (d. 734) says the Roman trained bishop Ninian went to the southern Picts in Galloway, possibly in the late fifth century (A. Macquarrie, *The Saints of Scotland* [Edinburgh, 1997]). The Irish aristocrat Columba (521–97) brought the gospel to the northern Picts from 563 (confirmed by Adomnán, ninth abbot of Iona, whose *Of Holy Places* [c. 688], *Law of Innocents* [697], and *Life of St Columba* [c. 697] are extant). After a failed attempt by the Italian cleric Paulinus, Aidán (d. 651) was sent from Iona to evangelize the Northumbrians (from 634). St Illtyd (fl. 500–47) began a period of restoration in Wales before the evangelization of the Saxons by *Augustine (from 597), producing an independent church. St Samson (c. 490–565) went from Llanilltyd to evangelize the Bretons. His extant *Life* was probably written in the early seventh century.

Celtic church unity has been shown to be a product of modern imagination (K. Hughes, 'The Celtic Church: Is This a Valid Concept?', *CMCS* 1 [1981], pp. 1–20; W. Davies, 'The Myth of the Celtic Church', in N. Edwards and A. Lane, *The Early Church in Wales* [Oxford, 1992]). It is more accurate to think of the *paruchiae* (i.e. the areas and/or churches/monastic houses over which the churches/monasteries established by the cult of a saint had, or claimed, jurisdiction) of Patrick of Armagh, Columba of Iona, David of Mynyw (c. 520–89), Samson of Dôl (fl. 521), and so on. In studying celtic Christianity, and celtic theology, moderns hope to get back to a purer form of the early faith than that altered by medieval western/continental developments. It is the pagan Germanic conquests which are commonly supposed to have isolated the 'celtic' churches from their continental neighbours by blocking land communications. Thus a spirituality, ecclesiology and theology influenced by 'celtic' rather than 'catholic' culture is supposed to have developed. In practice, selectivity has identified a 'purer form' in the guise of the searcher. Some claim celtic Christians retained elements of pre-Christian belief, taking an inclusive approach to pagan mysticism. A reading, for example, of Patrick's *Confession*, or Adomnán's *Life of Columba* (a profoundly theological reflection on the work of the Spirit), demonstrates the powerful rejection of such elements. One collection in particular, Alexander Carmichael's *Carmina Gadelica*, has had a strong influence in building a picture of early Irish/Scottish Christianity, though the provenance of many of its pieces is uncertain.

The celtic isolation theory is challenged on a number of fronts. Communication by sea was, for insular peoples, a standard method of transporting goods and ideas. Archaeological evidence shows that throughout the period of 'isolation', Mediterranean trade flourished in western Britain and Ireland. The libraries identified as being consulted by insular 'celtic' authors Patrick, Muirchú and Adomnán show deep familiarity with mainstream patristic writings (*Athanasius, Basil, *Cassian, *Jerome, *Augustine, Gregory the Great, Sulpicius Severus, etc.), and a concern to be considered part of Roman ecclesiastical polity. The period has left numerous annals, codes of canons, penitentials, biblical commentaries, lavishly illustrated manuscripts and hagiographies (Lapidge and Sharpe, 1985), hymns, poetry and 12,000 Old Irish glosses (*Thesaurus Paleohibernicus* [eds. and trans. W. Stokes and J. Strachan; Cambridge, 1901–03]), which are revealing more of the theological catholicity of the various churches represented, even if some practices diverged.

The greatest challenge to this catholicity was *Pelagius (fl. 383–409/10). He was a Briton (therefore 'celtic') who spent his visible life in Rome and Africa. Some see celtic theology as Pelagian, or 'pre-Pelagian'. That is, it retained an anthropology and soteriology that was not skewed by Augustine's reaction to Pelagian heresy (413 onwards; see Nicholson in Mackey, 1995). The *Lives* of Germanus and Prosper record that in 429, perhaps by request of some British clergy, Celestine sent Germanus (c. 496–576) to extirpate Pelagianism in Britain. Gildas (c. 540) laments the harm done in Britain by Pelagian teaching. One effect may have been to have weakened the Christian stand against pagan Germanic invasions. Christianity was largely wiped out in areas where Pelagianism had strongholds. Faustus Britto, Abbot of Lérins from 437, bishop of Riez from 459, was another Briton to hold semi-Pelagian soteriology. (He was a strong opponent of *Arianism. The language of anti-Arian Nicaea comes across clearly in Patrick [Dales, 1999]). Despite elements of semi-Pelagian thought in celtic sources, Clancy,

Márkus and H. Conrad-O'Briain ('Grace and Election in Adomnán's *Vita S. Columbae*', forthcoming) have begun to show theology in these sources is strongly Augustinian, that is, orthodox catholic, despite the strong influence of semi-Pelagian Lérins.

Through 'the age of the saints', or the age of the missionaries who are credited with establishing Christianity in Ireland, Wales and Scotland, various centres of learning were established – for example, Bangor and Armagh in Ireland; Llanbadarn Fawr and Mynyw in Wales; Whithorn and Iona in Scotland. All of these had extensive sixth–eighth century libraries lost to the Vikings. This tradition of Christian scholarship was exported into paganized Europe by missionaries, the most visible of whom is a product of Bangor, Columbanus (c. 543–615). He read the Scriptures in Hebrew and Greek and, most notably, urged Boniface IV to apply the Fifth Oecumenical Council (Constantinople 553) in rejecting *Eutyches's *Monophysitism. We have his letters, rule and sermons, yet to be theologically systematized. The theological and intellectual minds of Patrick and Adomnán are beginning to be recognized (D.R. Howlett, *The Book of Letters of Saint Patrick the Bishop* [Dublin, 1994]; Jennifer O'Reilly, e.g. in Broun and Clancy, 1999). They reveal a sophisticated pneumatology, particularly regarding the work of the Spirit in realizing the eschatological kingdom, and ubiquitous application of scriptural categories, and patristic understanding. Hardinge (*The Celtic Church in Britain* [London, 1972]) sees the primary influence being Scripture. Celtic Christians held a respect for nature, for ascetic holiness in community (i.e. as *Cassian: not individualistic); hell was the destination of the unredeemed in a fallen creation. Salvation is wrought by God's grace through the merits of Christ. However, they did not love animals to the extent of not eating them. In all this, they were little different to mainstream Catholic orthodoxy. As Márkus says, rather than egalitarian, anti-Roman, pro-women and Pelagian, these churches were hierarchical, subordinate to and in close conformity with Rome, markedly chauvinist and strongly Augustinian.

The age of mission gave way to the cult of saints, with its collection of relics, veneration of shrines, iconography and associated theological interest in eschatology and miracle. The latter abound in the proliferation of hagiographical writings which are slowly being made to reveal historical and theological information. Developments in celtic realms followed continental mainstreams closely. From the late eighth century, a reforming, sometimes referred to as 'evangelical', movement grew under the influence of Mael-rúain of Tallaght (d. 792). His reforming rule is extant. The Céli Dé (clients of God), or Culdees, first associated with Dunkeld to which Columba's relics were brought by 849, sought a return to earlier ascetic faith.

*John Scottus Eriugena (c. 810 – c. 877) is another celtic scholar who worked away from his native Ireland, in the palace school of Charles the Bald. He is chiefly known as an interpreter of Greek thought to the west, but he was involved in theological debate over predestination and election, and the Eucharist. He translated *Pseudo-Dionysius and Gregory Nyssa. His work *De Divisione Naturae* (c. 862) makes no distinction between theology and philosophy. His attempt to demonstrate a rational foundation for Christianity may lead him to pantheism, though he distinguishes God from his creation sharply. In Neoplatonist fashion, he claims God is the only true reality. Eriugena's theology was condemned (Paris 1210, Sens 1225), accused of rationalism, pantheism and agnosticism. Sedulius Scotus (fl. 848–58) established a centre of Irish culture in Liège, from where he compiled an unoriginal collection of writings on Matthew and the epistles of Paul. His *De rectoribus Christianis* is Augustinian. Though neither Irishman is usually linked with 'celtic' Christianity as such, their origins in celtic schools, and their notability, make their theology important to the task of describing 'celtic' theologies.

The late twentieth-century phenomenon of interest in celtic Christianity is based around the erroneous concept of the existence of a pan-celtic church in this era. It is often treated as unified even if caution is signalled, and even where the reality of its organization in competing *paruchiae* based around monasteries administered by abbots, rather than dioceses administered by bishops in provinces, is acknowledged. Groups and individuals, often though not always dissatisfied with current orthodoxy, look here for ideas, ways, 'feels' with which they identify. The rich variety of literature, art forms and artefacts gives ample scope to such eclecticism, and the celtic industry has prospered. The eclecticism proceeds with an ill-defined selectivity. The churches of the celts of

Galatia, for instance, are not included. Much of the modern movement is more concerned that something be celtic than Christian. Though much is made of divergent practice over Easter, the tonsure and the appointment of bishops, celtic individualism, harmony with nature and awareness of the supernatural, these are not coherent celtic universals, and they do not amount to significant doctrinal divergence from Latin orthodoxy. A definition of celtic theology must consider the thought and practice of all Christian celts, perhaps in all times, and will not be singular.

JAMES BRUCE

FURTHER READING: Donald E. Meek, 'Surveying the Saints: Reflections on Recent Writings in "Celtic Christianity"', *Scot Bul Ev Th* 15.1 (Spring 1997), pp. 50–60; 'Between Faith and Folklore: Twentieth-century Interpretations and Images of Columba', in *Spes Scotorum* (eds. Dauvit Broun and Thomas Owen Clancy; Edinburgh, 1999); I. Bradley, *Celtic Christianity: Making Myths and Chasing Dreams* (Edinburgh, 1999); James P. Mackey, *An Introduction to Celtic Christianity* (Edinburgh, 1995); Thomas Owen Clancy and Gilbert Márkus, *Iona: The Earliest Poetry of a Celtic Monastery* (Edinburgh, 1995); M. Lapidge and R. Sharpe, *A Bibliography of Celtic-Latin Literature 400–1200* (Dublin, 1985); R. Sharpe, 'Churches and Communities in Early Mediaeval Ireland: Towards a Pastoral Model', in *Pastoral Care before the Parish* (eds. J. Blair and R. Sharpe; Leicester, 1992); Douglas Dales, *Light to the Isles: A Study of Missionary Theology in Celtic and Early Anglo-Saxon Britain* (Cambridge, 1999); Gilbert Márkus, 'The End of Celtic Christianity', *Epworth R* 24.3 (1997), pp. 45–55; Patrick Sims-Williams, 'The Visionary Celt: The Construction of an Ethnic Preconception', *CMCS* 11 (1986), pp. 71–96.

Chalcedon, Council of (451)

In his letter to Flavian in 448, *Theodoret had warned that *Arianism had never really gone away. Some, notably *Eutyches, were trying to mix the two natures in Christ. They implied that Christ was not so much God as to be of immutable essence and that there was a loss of the true humanity in that the human soul or mind was replaced by the Word. Theodoret denied then, and later at the Council, that he subscribed to any notion of there being 'two sons'. *Leo also sent his advice to Flavian in 449. At Ephesus, however, Eutyches was acquitted, Theodoret was excommunicated and Flavian, the most senior theologian of the church and patriarch of Constantinople, was murdered in shady circumstances. Chalcedon would be an attempt to make good the damage.

The Roman see gained much by standing alone in condemning Ephesus as a 'robber-synod' (*latrocinium*). Pope Leo I leant on the western emperor Valentinian to persuade the eastern emperor Theodosius II to convene a new council, preferably in Italy. Theodosius refused, but after falling from his horse he died (28 July 451). Once Theodosius's sister Pulcheria had married his successor, Marcian, the new emperor determined to humble the Alexandrian party. Marcian arranged a council at Chalcedon even while Leo was left in Rome believing that it was premature.

On 8 October 451, five hundred bishops gathered in the Euphemia Church in Chalcedon. Marcian had called a universal council because smaller synods had not resolved anything, and he appointed 19 commissioners to control and speed the agenda. The easterners faced a coalition of Egyptians, Palestinians and Illyrians across the church. The pope was represented by four legates who placed Dioscorus on trial – not only for defending and seeing to the reinstitution of Eutyches at Ephesus in 449 after the latter's condemnation at Constantinople in 448, but also for his murder of Flavian at the order of Theodosius II. Theodoret, free after a season of house arrest, turned up at the opening of the council – only to be insulted as a *Nestorian. Yet Dioscorus was a convenient scapegoat and many hoped that theological matters could easily be settled. It was an inauspicious opening to the attempt to discuss how to speak of the union in Christ. By 22 October (only two weeks later), the formula was ready: those who denied the *theotokos* and those who believed in a mixing in Christ resulting in one nature were condemned. While the Council of Constantinople (381) was raised to the same level of authority as Nicaea in its protection of the status of the Holy Spirit, the council at Chalcedon saw its own relationship to Nicaea as similar to that of Constantinople. Cyril was used to counteract one extreme, Leo's tome to counteract the other. It seems clear that Eutyches did at least believe in 'two natures before, one nature after the union', and most were prepared to abandon this position which suggested that Christ's humanity pre-existed the incarnation. It would seem that the fear of Eutyches was greater in that there was an actual condemnation of him: Nestorius had been dealt with a generation earlier. Dioscorus and five other bishops were removed from office. To make sure, the 19 commissioners had each bishop present sign the Confession of Nicaea, Constantinople, the canonical letters of Gregory, Basil, *Hilary, *Athanasius and *Ambrose and two letters of *Cyril (to represent Ephesus 431), as well as Leo's *Tome*. The bishops refused to sign but agreed to say 'this is the true faith' when they were read out. The amount of harmony between Cyril and Leo seemed remarkable, even if three sections in Leo's *Tome* were doubted by Illyrian and Palestinian bishops as out of step with Cyril's opinion and the commissioners decided not to make Leo's *Tome* the only criterion. Nevertheless, most in fact did decide for 'two natures', if they were less decided about the mode of Christ's unity.

In Christological doctrine, nature (*physis*) and person (or more specifically the Greek '*hypostasis*', individual reality) became for the first time in a Christological context differentiated, even if not all realized this (e.g., Pope Leo). Amongst Antiochenes, Christ's unity was that of one *prosopon* which meant that which can be seen (Luise Abramowski), while for the miaphysites there was only 'one nature' (*mia physis*) in Christ. What would result in the following decades was the Cyrillian compromise of 'the one nature of the Incarnate Word', which translated into one divine *hypostasis* with a human origin. The popularity of the *theotokos* can be explained: calling her 'God-bearer' demanded Mary's own purity and virginity with the consequence that Christ's human origin came to be viewed as sinless, while Jesus' divinity was preserved by the Holy Spirit.

The most enduring section of the decision of the Council reads as follows:

> We confess God and man with a rational soul and a body, consubstantial with the Father according to the deity and consubstantial with us according to humanity, totally like us except for sin, according to the deity engendered by the Father before the ages, in the last days the same was engendered by the Virgin Mary, mother of God according to the humanity, one and the same Christ Son Lord Only-Begotten, recognised as being in two natures without confusion, without mutation, without division, without separation, the difference of natures being in no way suppressed because of the union, the property of each of the natures being

rather safeguarded and running towards the formation of one sole person (*prosopon*) and one sole hypostasis [cf. 'they run together into a single *hypostasis* and *prosopon*', Gregory Nazianzen, *Orat.* 37.2], one sole and same Christ not being broken nor divided in two persons, but being the one and the same Only Begotten Son, God, Word, our Lord Jesus Christ. (Festugière, p. 64)

If Leo's *Tome* provided the basis for the statement, the phrase 'without confusion or division, change or separation' was a significant addition. Theologians have praised this balancing act, since according to it, the creation is neither overcome nor left helpless. 'Basil of Seleucia declared that Christ is "known in two natures", a formula which in effect echoes Cyril's proviso that the dual nature of Christ is discerned only in the abstract by the reflective mind, not in the concrete by the worshipping soul' (H. Chadwick, Intro. to Festugière, p. 11). But 'known in two natures' would be the downfall of Chalcedon (Festugière, p. 14) amongst the significant minority for whom his unity was just too important. The opposition came from those of a non-abstract spirituality: to the monks and the masses of Egypt and Palestine, the Antiochene and Constantinopolitan theology seemed too philosophical. How could he be known in two natures though worshipped as one?

Mark W. Elliott

FURTHER READING: A. Festugière (ed.), *Actes du Concile de Chalcedoine*, sessions III–VI (Geneva, 1983); R.V. Sellers, *The Council of Chalcedon* (London, 1953); Frances Young, *From Nicea to Chalcedon* (London, 1983); A. Grillmeier, *Jesus Christ in Christian Tradition*, I and II.1 (London, 1975, 1987); B. Studer, *Trinity and Incarnation: The Faith of the Early Church* (ET Edinburgh, 1993).

Chemnitz, Martin (1522–86)

Leading German Lutheran theologian in the first generation after *Luther and *Melanchthon, co-drafter of the Lutheran 'Formula of Concord' (FC), and author of the celebrated *Examination of the Council of Trent* (4 vols.). Although his education was delayed due to the premature death of his father, Chemnitz managed to learn Latin by himself. Thanks to benefactors, he finally acquired some formal training in mathematics and theology at the universities of Frankfurt (1543) and Wittenberg (1545/6). From 1547 he

earned his living as a teacher, and then from 1550 to 1552 he was a librarian and the astrologist of Duke Albrecht of Prussia in Königsberg. In 1553 he returned to Wittenberg to pursue his theological studies. He belonged to Melanchthon's inner circle (even living in his house) and was appointed in 1554 to lecture on Melanchthon's *Loci communes*. Later the same year, however, he accepted a call to become the coadjutor of the general superintendent of Braunschweig, his old friend Joachim Mörlin, who held a Gnesio-Lutheran position.

During the decades that followed, Chemnitz came to play a crucial role in defining Lutheran identity between an extreme Gnesio-Lutheranism (Matthias Flacius) and a synergistic Philippism. While remaining loyal to the anti-speculative thrust of Melanchthon's *Loci communes* and appreciating its usefulness, Chemnitz refused to assign any normative status to Melanchthon's work (cf. FC, Preface).

Appointed as Mörlin's successor in 1567, Chemnitz became more directly involved in the complicated political struggles between the regional Lutheran churches. Despite inner theological tensions between the drafters of the 'Formula of Concord', Chemnitz provided the theological leadership for its completion and political reception (1577–80) and for drafting its less successful 'Apology' (1583).

Chemnitz was among the first to notice the pivotal role of the *Jesuits in the Catholic Counter Reformation. His *Principles of Jesuit Theology* (*Theologiae Jesuitarum praecipua capita*, 1562) was widely read, and the Catholic response elicited his *opus magnum*, *Examen Concilii Tridentini* ('Examination of the Council of Trent', 1565–73). In *Repetitio sanae doctrinae de vera praesentia corporis et sanguinis Domini in coena* ('The Lord's Supper', 1561), he mediated between the view of Johann Brenz that Christ's human nature is naturally omnipresent, and the Philippist rejection of this view, that the human body of Christ can be present wherever and whenever God wishes (the doctrine of 'multivolipresence'). In *De duabus naturis in Christo* ('On the Two Natures in Christ', 1570, enlarged 1578), Chemnitz radicalized the Lutheran doctrine of incarnation by reference to Colossians 2:9 – 'The majesty of God has dwelled among us'. Drawing on patristic studies, he defined the Lutheran doctrine of a threefold communication of attributes (*communicatio idiomatum*) between the divine and human natures of Christ, including the self-communication of the majesty (cf. FC, Solida Declaratio, VIII.31ff.). Chemnitz's lectures on Melanchthon's *Loci communes*, posthumously published in 1591, were in use for more than a century.

After his death, Chemnitz was praised as 'the most outstanding theologian of our age' (Polycarp Leyser) and has often been referred to as the 'second Martin'. As a seventeenth-century adage says, 'If Martin [Chemnitz] had not come, Martin [Luther] would hardly have stood'.

NIELS HENRIK GREGERSEN

FURTHER READING: W.A. Jünke (ed.), *Der zweite Martin der Lutherischen Kirche: Festschrift zum 400. Todestag von Martin Chemnitz* (Braunschweig, 1986); J.A. Preuss, *The Second Martin: The Life and Theology of Martin Chemnitz* (St Louis, MO, 1994).

Christian Socialism

The words 'socialist' and 'socialism' were coined in Europe at the beginning of the nineteenth century to refer to that movement which emphasized co-operation as opposed to competition, mutuality as opposed to individualism, and equality as opposed to hierarchy in the ordering of society. Despite the identification of the church with the ruling class and the Marxian critique of religion as opiate, many recognized an elective affinity between Christianity and socialism which ran all the way back to Acts 4. 'Christian socialism' covers a wide range of options from the mildest reformism to militant *Marxism, from a principled refusal to identify the gospel with socialism to the belief (which the young *Barth embraced) that Christianity is the theory of which socialism is the praxis. There is likewise a variety of theological grounding – distinct, but not mutually exclusive.

Socialism and the scriptural narrative.
Although socialism is a child of the Industrial Revolution, the ideals of justice and equality for which it stands have ancient precursors. Socialists have often appealed to the prophetic critique which alleges that riches can only be accrued at the expense of others (e.g. Amos 8:4). This tradition was taken up by Church Fathers like *Ambrose and *Chrysostom, who were cited by the nineteenth-century Christian socialists

and more recently by Latin American liberation theologians.

*Liberation Theology has been particularly associated with the appeal to the Exodus as a paradigm of the need to leave slavery and take 'the long road to freedom'. That this is not a completely new appeal is instanced by its use in the famous Negro spiritual 'Let my people go'.

Another appeal to Scripture by Christian socialists was to the creation narratives. In the 1381 Peasants' Revolt the theme was: 'When Adam delved and Eve span / who was then the gentleman?'. What is being said here, on scriptural grounds, is what was argued on the grounds of natural reason four hundred years later, namely that class divisions are constructed and do not belong to the original condition of humanity. Inequality is part of the Fall and to be obedient to God we need to get away from it. Gerrard Winstanley also used Scripture in this way.

The demands of the kingdom of God.
When Jesus spoke of the kingdom, and taught his disciples to pray for its coming on earth, he set in train an idea which continues to have the profoundest political consequences. One strand of Christian thinking had set the human city and the heavenly city over against each other, but from the sixteenth century on there were those who insisted that the kingdom seeks an earthly realization. Appeal to the kingdom was at the heart of the Social Gospel movement in the United States, the best-known representative of which was *W. Rauschenbusch (1861–1918), whose *Christianity and the Social Crisis* (1907) was a best-seller. For Rauschenbusch the kingdom is 'a collective conception involving the whole social life of man' and demands not just political but also economic democracy. Jesus believed in the organic growth of a new society, cell by cell. He incarnated a new type of human life and communicated that to his disciples. He worked on individuals and through individuals, but 'his real end was not individualistic, but social'. He was interested not in the new soul, but the new society, 'not in man but Man'. Rauschenbusch represented liberal theology with a social conscience. He adopted the reigning theology of *Harnack, but removed its individualism and cultured pietism.

The logic of orthodoxy. The Christian socialism which began in Britain after the collapse of

Chartism in 1848 involved *F.D. Maurice's (1805–72) very idiosyncratic appeal to the kingdom, and the violent moral polemic of Charles Kingsley's (1819–75) social novels. The theological appeal which came to characterize Anglican Christian socialism, however, was far more to the historic creeds. Conrad Noel's (1869–1942) Catholic Crusade, for example, founded in 1918, was Marxist in outlook, vehemently anticapitalist and anti-imperialist, but derived its moral passion from the *Athanasian Creed. The doctrine that in God there is 'none before, and none after, but one perfect equality' was pasted up in Crusade church doorways. *Bishop Gore (1853–1932) and Scott Holland (1847–1918) appealed more to the incarnation, which revealed the significance of bodies and their well-being, but also established an ontological solidarity between all people which called into question every class distinction.

Christian millenarianism. A very different tradition runs through the medieval millenarian groups, to the *Anabaptists, to the seventeenth-century Diggers, to William Blake, and in the twentieth century into Mennonite radicalism in America, with its emphasis on non-violence, and into the social radicalism of someone like Tony Benn in Britain. A new heaven and a new earth is what is in view. The apocalyptic edge of this strand means that half measures will not do: what is called for is radical action now – land reform and redistribution, the realization of equality, an end to war.

Catholic social teaching. From the inclusion of socialism in the 'Syllabus of Errors' in 1864 to *Cardinal Ratzinger's condemnation of liberation theology 120 years later, the Catholic Church has not been happy with any *rapprochement* between the church and socialism. The Christian democratic parties of the European mainland have nevertheless been nurtured by Catholic social teaching, beginning with Leo XIII's 'Rerum Novarum' (1891), with its appeal to natural law and its attempt to maintain a balance between labour and employers, between a right to property and the principle of common use.

Although there are wide areas of overlap between them, these strands do correspond to genuinely different emphases. The remit of Christian socialism, following that of socialism in general, has broadened to take into account not only class, but race, gender and culture. The collapse of 'really existing socialism' in 1989 is less responsible for this broadening than the inner dynamic of socialism itself, which is concerned to establish the possibilities of true human fulfilment for all. In its emphasis on the body, on the kingdom, and on the radical difference and openness of the promised future, Christianity continues to contribute to this project.

TIMOTHY GORRINGE

FURTHER READING: J.C. Cort, *Christian Socialism* (New York, 1988); C. Raven, *Christian Socialism* (London, 1920); W. Rauschenbusch, *Christianity and the Social Crisis* (Louisville, 1991); R. Groves, *Conrad Noel and the Thaxted Movement* (London, 1967); E.R. Norman, *The Victorian Christian Socialists* (Cambridge, 1987); C. Rowland, *Radical Christianity* (Cambridge, 1988); C. Myers, *Who Will Roll Away the Stone?* (New York, 1994).

Chrysostom, John (c. 349–407)

John Chrysostom, the 'Golden Mouth' as he was nicknamed for his oratorical skills, was born in Antioch to a pagan father and a Christian mother and trained in rhetoric by the pagan teacher Libanius. Chrysostom turned his back on a secular career and along with his friend *Theodore, also a former student of Libanius, devoted himself to Christian asceticism. This Theodore was later to become bishop of Mopsuestia and one of the great exegetes of the Antiochene school. They practised Christian asceticism under instruction from Diodore, later bishop of Tarsus, who was another leading exponent of Antiochene hermeneutics. Chrysostom's disciplined life at this time was similar to that of the 'sons and daughters of the covenant', familiar from the life and writings of *Ephrem the Syrian. In due course he left Antioch to live a solitary life in the surrounding mountains, and on returning to the city he wrote in defence of the monastic way of life.

Chrysostom was ordained priest in 386 and for the next 12 years established his reputation as the leading preacher in Antioch. In one of his sermons of this period he mentions the introduction of the feast of Christmas on 25 December which had been instituted in the west at Rome in 330. In 398 he was taken without his prior consent to Constantinople to be made bishop of the metropolis. Chrysostom's reputation as a preacher attained new heights during the six years he was in office, but it was a period beset with difficulties, some of them of his own making, leading to his final deposition and exile in 404. He made the Empress Eudoxia his implacable enemy, and he was no match for the political intriguer Theophilus, patriarch of Alexandria, who accused Chrysostom of *Origenism for harbouring the Tall Brothers whom Theophilus had persecuted in Egypt. This particular episode saw the arrival of *Epiphanius of Salamis in Constantinople as an ally of Theophilus, only it ended in humiliation for the aged heresiologist when his condemnation of Chrysostom was not endorsed by the synod of bishops.

Chrysostom's zeal for religious and institutional reform upset both the monks and clergy as well as the Byzantine aristocracy. He spoke out against the pleasures of the hippodrome and the theatre, and his so-called 'socialist' views on the equitable distribution of wealth made him more enemies. Although concerned primarily with the see of Constantinople, he also took an interest in the church beyond the borders of the empire, notably in Persia and among the Goths of the Danube region. He was finally hounded out of office by his enemies at the court, but when news of his deposition became known the church of Hagia Sophia in Constantinople was gutted by fire, started either by his own supporters or by those opposed to him. A commission was set up to inquire into the affair, but it was never able to determine who had been responsible for the arson. Chrysostom was exiled to the town of Cucusos in Armenia, where he received many of his followers. Never in good health from his early days of asceticism in the mountains around Antioch, Chrysostom died on his way to further banishment in Georgia. His relics were finally returned to Constantinople in 438 and placed in the church of the Holy Apostles.

Many authentic sermons of Chrysostom's have survived, and some of them show his defence of social justice and the dignity of women in marriage. In recent years he has come to the attention of a wider audience through inexpensive translations of his works published by St Vladimir's Seminary Press in New York. This has enabled a new generation of readers to appreciate the depth of his pastoral concern for the lives of ordinary believers and to see for themselves what made him such a popular preacher in his own day. The Eucharistic liturgy of the Orthodox Church carries Chrysostom's name and he is often depicted on the sanctuary gates of the iconostasis, along with Basil the Great, whose liturgy is also celebrated in the Orthodox Church. Together with Basil and Gregory Nazianzen he is remembered on the feast of the Three Hierarchs on 20 January.

KEN PARRY

FURTHER READING: *Texts: On Marriage and Family Life* (trans. C. Roth and D. Anderson; New York, 1986); *On the Priesthood* (trans. G. Neville; New York, 1984); *On Wealth and Poverty* (trans. C. Roth; New York, 1983). *Studies*: D.C. Ford, *Women and Men in the Early Church: The Full Views of St John Chrysostom* (South Canaan, PA, 1996); J.N.D. Kelly, *Golden Mouth: The Story of John Chrysostom – Ascetic, Preacher, Bishop* (London, 1995); F. van de Paverd, *St John Chrysostom, the Homilies on the Statues: An Introduction* (Rome, 1992).

Clement of Alexandria (c. 150 – c. 215)

The first major Christian writer at Alexandria, which was then the largest and most important intellectual centre in the Greek world and the home of Hellenistic Judaism. Although little is known of its origins, Alexandria also had a flourishing Christian congregation which in the century after Clement's death would have been universally recognized as the theological leader of the entire church. Clement was born to a pagan family at Athens, and it was only after his conversion, about which we know nothing, that he finally decided to settle in Alexandria. The main reason for this was his discovery of the teaching of Pantaenus, a Sicilian Christian who had set up a school in the city sometime about 180. Clement became his avid disciple and eventually succeeded him as head of the school, probably about 200. Shortly afterwards an imperial persecution forced him to flee, and he went to Cappadocia, where he died in or shortly before 215.

Clement was well educated in the classical manner of his time, but he also had a thorough knowledge of both the Jewish and the Christian Scriptures. He realized that if Christianity were to survive in the Graeco-Roman world, it would have to develop a philosophy and literature which could challenge the reigning culture. He made it his goal to achieve this, and it is largely to him that we owe the famous doctrine that all secular learning must be used in the service of theology. He was a prolific writer, and three of his most important treatises have survived. The first of these is his *Exhortation to the Greeks* (*Protrepticus*) which is an evangelistic tract aimed at the conversion of intellectual pagans. In it, he points out the basic emptiness of pagan religion and contrasts it with the prophetic tradition of the Bible, which attained its fulfilment in Christ, the Logos (Word) of God. In its argument, this work is very close to those of the other second-century Christian apologists, and its style reflects patterns which were common to both pagans and Christians of the time.

His second great work is the *Tutor* (*Paedagogus*) which is a continuation of the foregoing. The Tutor is the Logos himself, who comes to lead the young Christian along the path of spiritual perfection. In this work, Clement aims to provide the church with an alternative to *Gnosticism, and it is particularly noteworthy that he deals with practical moral issues just as much as with spiritual speculations. His basic source is the Bible, but he endeavours to demonstrate how the views of various pagan philosophers can be integrated into a Christian approach to life. Nevertheless, however magnificent pagan philosophy may be, Clement insists that knowledge of the Logos can only come by faith, and any truth found among the Greeks is due to the fact that (according to Clement) they had borrowed their ideas from Moses and the Old Testament. He develops this theme at great length in his third book, the *Carpets* or *Stromata* (*Stromateis*), so-called because the book is a miscellany of different ideas. Once again, the form was one which was common in the ancient world, though the content was entirely Christian.

Clement also wrote other works, but they are either very short or extant only in fragments. The most important of these is his lost commentary on the Bible, the first of its kind from a Christian source. In it, Clement borrowed extensively from the commentaries of *Philo of Alexandria (d. 50), who had introduced the Hellenistic allegorical method of interpretation into Jewish exegesis. It was through Clement that this method reached *Origen (c. 185–254) and from him spread to the Christian world as a whole.

The heart of Clement's theology is his doctrine of the Logos, who is the creator of the universe, the God revealed in the Old Testament and the reality incarnated in Jesus Christ. With the Father and the Holy Spirit, the Logos forms a divine Trinity. The rational principle which the Logos incarnates is matched by a more mystical approach to the sacraments, particularly baptism, which he regarded as a true spiritual rebirth. In it the believer is sealed with the Holy Spirit and becomes able to understand the hidden mysteries of God's self-revelation.

In other matters, Clement regarded the sin of Adam as a refusal on his part to be educated by God, and he did not believe in the concept of inherited guilt. This view, which owes more to *Plato than to Genesis, was to exert great influence in the Greek world, where it continues to provide an alternative to the *Augustinian doctrine of original sin as this has been understood by the west. Clement himself preferred celibacy to matrimony, but his defence of the latter is one of the most thorough and impressive to be found anywhere in Christian thought. It is clear that he regarded asceticism as a personal spiritual discipline, but not as something to be imposed on others as a condition of Christian service.

In the history of Christian thought, Clement is recognized as a seminal theologian whose ideas were developed over several centuries by the leading thinkers of Alexandria. In general the latter have overshadowed him, though occasionally modern writers have gone back to Clement's work for inspiration, particularly in the attempt to construct a viable philosophical theology for our own time.

GERALD BRAY

FURTHER READING: *Texts: Works* (ed. O. Stählin; 4 vols.; Berlin, 1906–80); J.-P. Migne (*PG*, VIII–IX); *Clément d'Alexandrie* (SC, 2, 23, 30, 38, 70, 108, 158, 278–9; Paris, 1949–81). *Translation*: W. Wilson, *ANF*, II (1887); G.W. Butterworth (LCL; Cambridge, MA, 1953). *Studies*: H.A. Blair, *The Kaleidoscope of Truth: Types and Archetypes in Clement of Alexandria* (Worthing, West Sussex, 1986); S.R.C. Lilla, *Clement of Alexandria: A Study in Christian Platonism and Gnosticism* (Oxford, 1971); A. Méhat, *Études sur les Stromates de Clément d'Alexandrie* (Paris, 1966); E. Proctor, *Christian Controversy in Alexandria: Clement's Polemic against Basilideans and Valentinians* (New York, 1995); A. Van den Hoek, *Clement of Alexandria and his Use of Philo in the Stromateis* (Leiden, 1988).

The Cloud of Unknowing

The *Cloud* is an anonymous book on contemplative prayer, written c. 1390–95, most probably by a Carthusian of Beauvale Priory (Notts.). While the *Cloud* is not primarily controversial, there are marks of the same concern which is found in *Walter Hilton (c. 1343–96) to present traditional spiritual methods and aims in the face of Lollardy, as well as warning against attachment to the 'heat, sweetness and song' associated with Richard Rolle (d. 1349). There is evidence of some interaction with Hilton, but whereas Hilton addresses overall a wide circle of readers, the *Cloud* (and its corpus) are directed particularly to contemplatives.

The book's title is drawn from the writings of *Pseudo-Dionysius the Areopagite (c. 500), where the author affirms that all the teaching of the *Cloud* may be found in (Pseudo-) Dionysius. The core of Pseudo-Dionysius's apophatic *Mystical Theology* is the search for union at a supra-intellectual level with God, who in his transcendence exceeds both all that may be affirmed and all that may be denied of him. This union occurs in the 'luminous darkness' (exemplified by Moses' ascent of Sinai), or the excess of God's light experienced as darkness, as all that can appeal to sense or intellect is left behind. The *Cloud* speaks of leaving created things under a 'cloud of forgetting', in order to penetrate with a 'sharp dart of longing love' the cloud of unknowing that veils God's presence. The author of the *Cloud* knew Pseudo-Dionysius through such Latin mediators as John Sarrazin (1140–67) and Thomas of Vercelli (d. 1246), who in various respects modified Pseudo-Dionysius. Latin theology makes more explicit that the soul's ascent towards union with God is an act of love, a gift of God's grace. Among other Latin writers in the Dionysian tradition, the *Cloud*'s author certainly knew something also of the *De Mystica Theologia* of the Carthusian Hugh of Balma (1289–1304), echoing (*inter alia*) his account of imageless prayer without premeditation, a movement of love and not of intellect.

In fact the *Cloud* is firmly rooted in the monastic tradition of spiritual guidance, and in Latin theology. There are echoes of *Augustine (354–430), Gregory the Great (c. 540–604), *Bernard (1090–1153) and *Richard of St Victor (d. 1173). Augustine's teaching on the *ordo caritatis*, the rightly-ordered love of God and of neighbour, is fundamental. Humility and charity are the two interdependent virtues in which the whole Christian moral life is implied. The author is also in accord with *St Thomas Aquinas (c. 1225–74) at various points: on the name

'Is' as the most appropriate to God (in contrast to Pseudo-Dionysius, who prefers 'Good'); on the capacity of charity to unite us directly to God while we are unable in this life to know him as he is; and on the theology of 'operant grace'. In the latter mode, as distinct from that of 'co-operant grace', where there is deliberate conjunction of the human will with grace, God moves the will directly and without impediment, yet with the will's consent, ensuring the soul's spontaneous conformity to his will. The *Cloud* sees this as concomitant with 'perfect humility', which has regard only to the greatness of God in his love and worthiness, and so is self-forgetful. In contrast, 'imperfect humility' has regard to one's own qualities, especially to one's own sinfulness, and thus is necessary but is still self-regarding. Entry into the 'cloud of unknowing' opens the way to 'perfect humility'.

The *Cloud* thrice refers in passing to 'another man', who may well be Walter Hilton. The third reference is mildly critical, as if the (Augustinian and Gregorian) approach to God by introversion – the search for the 'image of God' within and yet beyond the soul – favoured by Hilton and by many others might seem to 'localize' God. *The Book of Privy Counselling*, intended to elucidate difficult points in the *Cloud*, answers just such criticisms of the *Cloud's* presentation as the profoundly incarnational Hilton might have made. Comparison of *Cloud* and *Privy Counselling* shows no doctrinal difference between the two books. But what is stated in passing in the *Cloud* is, where necessary, restated more clearly and emphatically in *Privy Counselling*. The latter explicitly identifies the rejection of distinct images of God and the entry into the 'cloud of unknowing' with response to Christ's call to deny oneself and take up the cross (Mt. 16:24), a text used by Hilton in *Scale*, 1. *Privy Counselling* also seems to echo Hilton in its use of John 10:9; 10:1; to insist that conformity to the virtues of Christ in his incarnate life is the only true way to contemplation. Again, *Privy Counselling* has a forceful passage on the sanctifying value of spiritual aridity which goes far beyond anything in the *Cloud* but accords with Hilton. The use of John 16:7 in this context (echoing Augustine) stands close to the use made by Hilton of more particularly Bernard's teaching on the transition from the carnal to the spiritual love of God in Christ. *Privy Counselling* also marches with Hilton's *Scale*, 2 on a fluctuation between aridity and awareness of God's presence within contemplation. Conversely, Hilton's *Scale*, 2 seems to draw on the *Cloud* for its teaching on imperfect and perfect humility, and 'operant grace' as ensuring (for the duration of the experience) conformity to God's will.

There is no evidence that the *Cloud* was known outside England until the late sixteenth century, through an English Carthusian copy used by Benet Canfield (1562–1611) and later by Augustine Baker (1575–1641). Parallels have been drawn between *St John of the Cross (1542–91) on the 'dark night' and the *Cloud* (and Hilton), but St John cannot have known the English writers. However, the *Cloud*'s apophatic and affective theology, in conjunction with Harphius (Henry Herp, d. 1477), Blosius (Louis of Blois, 1506–66), Canfield and Constantin Barbanson (1582–1631), became an important constituent in Augustine Baker's teaching.

JOHN P.H. CLARK

FURTHER READING: *Texts (critical editions): The Cloud of Unknowing and The Book of Privy Counselling* (ed. Phyllis Hodgson; London, rev. edn, 1958); *Deonise Hid Diuinite and other Treatises on Contemplative Prayer* (ed. Phyllis Hodgson; London, 1958); *The Cloud of Unknowing and Related Treatises* (ed. Phyllis Hodgson; Salzburg, 1982). *Texts (modernized versions): The Cloud of Unknowing and Other Treatises* (ed. J. McCann; London, 6th rev. edn, 1952), includes Augustine's commentary on the *Cloud*; *The Cloud of Unknowing* (ed. James Walsh; Mahwah, NJ, 1981); *The Cloud of Unknowing and other Works* (ed. C. Wolters; Harmondsworth, 1961). *Studies:* D. Knowles, *The English Mystical Tradition* (London, 1961); W. Johnston, *The Mysticism of 'The Cloud of Unknowing'* (New York, 1967); J.P.H. Clark, *'The Cloud of Unknowing': An Introduction* (3 vols.; Salzburg, 1995–6); R. Tixier, 'Mystique et Pédagogie dans "The Cloud of Unknowing"' (PhD thesis; University of Nancy, 1988).

Cocceius, Johannes (1603–69)

Johannes Cocceius (Johann Cock or Coch) was the son of Timmann Cock, city secretary and judicial adviser to the guild at Bremen, and Elisabeth Bake. He studied philology, theology and philosophy at the *Gymnasium Illustre* in Bremen from 1620, and then oriental languages in Franeker from 1626. He was appointed professor, first in Bremen in 1630 (*Philologia Sacra*), then in Franeker in 1636 (Hebrew, and after 1643 theology), and finally in Leiden from 1650

to 1669. He married Catharina Deichmann on 5 August 1635 in Bremen. Their son, Johannes Henricus Cocceius, published a complete edition of the works of his father, entitled *Opera Omnia Theologica, Exegetica, Didactica, Polemica, Philologica* (Amsterdam, 1673–75). Cocceius's writings include commentaries on virtually every book of the Bible, disputations on all major subjects in theology, a treatise on the covenant, a complete systematic theology and the monumental lexicon of Hebrew words in the Old Testament. In these writings Cocceius attempted a new formulation and justification of the *Reformed tradition by drawing on his considerable exegetical skills. After 1658 he was increasingly confronted with the consequences of his theological system, so that he clashed especially with the Reformed orthodoxy of his day.

Cocceius's systematic work can be characterized as a form of federal theology. By means of the concept *foedus* (covenant) he sought to do justice, also in systematic theology, to the historical nature of the biblical narrative. His systematic work was an extension of the exegetical and philological research that had brought him international fame. His handling of Scripture has been unjustifiably accused of a baroque arbitrariness. He offered a number of fixed hermeneutical rules and clearly delimited methodological comments that cohered with his whole outlook regarding Scripture. In the preface to his commentary on Romans he wrote:

> The words of Scripture mean what they can mean in the context of the scriptural passage, and in mutual coherence, so that it may be clear that what God has spoken in his wisdom is suitable for our instruction, and may therefore not be interpreted contrary to his intention.

All the emphasis is on the context of the text (*tota compages orationis*). Cocceius differs from earlier and later allegorists in emphasizing the literal and historical meaning of Scripture (*sensus literalis et historicus*). He assigns typology to the *sensus literalis*, and he presupposed the unity of the Old and New Testaments. They are like two eyes, not one of which can be done without. It is anachronistic to dub Cocceius's theology 'biblical' in the sense of being undogmatic.

His *Collationes de Foedere et Testamento Dei* (later *Summa Doctrinae*, etc.), which can be regarded as a standard work of his theology, appeared in 1648. It was published in the form of a monograph in which a large chunk of classical theological material was treated from the perspective of the covenant. In this keyword, inherited from the Reformed tradition – Cocceius himself mentions *Heinrich Bullinger (1504–75), Matthias Martini (1572–1630) and Caspar Olevianus (1536–87) – he believed he had found the secret enabling him to present a biblically based dogmatics. In doing so, he distinguished between two fundamental forms of the covenant in salvation history. The covenant of works (*foedus operum*) was made in the Garden of Eden – before the Fall – with Adam as the head of all humanity. This covenant was broken through Adam's disobedience. The covenant of grace (*foedus gratiae*), established after the Fall with humankind, harked back to a covenanting of the Trinity in heaven (*pactum salutis*). However, the establishment of the covenant of grace did not entail an abrupt end to the original, failed covenant in paradise. Cocceius describes the whole biblical history after the Fall as a series of events by which this original covenant of works is cancelled, or abrogated, step by step: (1) by human sin; (2) by God's decision to establish the covenant of grace; (3) by the promise of the new covenant, which fills the whole Old Testament and is fulfilled in the New Testament; (4) by the detachment from, and the dying to, the old humanity as the believer undergoes sanctification; and (5) by the resurrection of the dead, all the evil effects of the breaking of the covenant of works are gradually removed, until the salvation promised in the covenant of grace is finally revealed in full glory and liberty. By means of this abrogation theme Cocceius infused his view of the covenant with a powerful dynamic and with an eschatological perspective. He elaborates on this in his doctrine of the kingdom of God, following his teacher at the gymnasium in Bremen, Ludwig Crocius (1586–1655), in discerning a development in seven periods: (1) the time of the proclamation of the gospel until the death of the apostles; (2) the Jewish wars; (3) the period from Constantine to Ludwig of Bavaria (i.e., the thousand-year kingdom); (4) the period of the papacy and the antichrist; (5) the time of the Reformation; (6) the Thirty Years War (1618–48); and (7) the end-time. Cocceius believed that this development had been described in the seven letters to the churches in Asia Minor (Rev. 2 and 3). This view of salvation history is also found in Cocceius's interpretation of the last six chapters of Deuteronomy, published under the title *Considerationes ad Ultima Mosis* (1650).

During the mid-1650s the tide began to turn for Cocceius. A conflict erupted which would continue for many years after his death, leaving ineradicable traces on church, school and society – and not only in the Netherlands. The first phase in this struggle concerned the conflict over the Sabbath. Although Johannes Hoornbeeck, a pupil of the Utrecht professor Gisbertus Voetius (1589–1676), had already published his book *Des Heeren dagh heyligingen* in 1655, the conflict only erupted subsequent to Cocceius's treatment of the Sabbath in his lectures on Hebrews. His Leiden colleague Abraham Heydanus (1597–1678) initiated a disputation on the matter (*Disputatio de Sabbato et Die Dominica*, 1657) and lent his support to Cocceius's views. The central thesis of these writings was that the Sabbath spoken of in Genesis 2 did not signify a separation between profane and holy days, but rather the start of the sanctification of all time. The Sabbath commandment of a weekly recurring day of rest was not given in paradise; its origin lay in Israel's desert period.

A new phase in the conflict with his orthodox opponents was initiated by events at the academy of Utrecht. In the summer of 1665 Voetius had a number of Dutch and Hungarian students debate an aspect of the doctrine of justification, the forgiveness of sins, and some views of Cocceius were – without his name being mentioned – roundly condemned. Already in his commentaries on Hebrews and Romans, and in the *Summa Doctrinae*, Cocceius thought it possible to make a distinction between forgiveness in the Old and New Testament dispensations. He based this distinction on two New Testament words for forgiveness: *páresis* and *áphesis*, used in Romans 3:25 and Hebrews 10:18 respectively. Before the coming of Christ, during the Old Testament economy, one may speak of *páresis*, *praetermissio* or non-imputation of the guilt of sin. However, following the completion of Christ's atoning sacrifice as a reality brought about in history, *áphesis* – that is, the actual removal of the guilt of sin – is the order of the day. From this, Voetius drew the conclusion that the believers under the Old Testament could not then be justified in the full sense of the word. Cocceius reacted to Voetius's initial disputations by offering an extended exegesis of the words *páresis* and *áphesis* in his *Moreh Nebochim: Utilitas distinctionis duorum vocabulorum páreseoos et ápheseoos* (1665). Here he pointed once again to the importance of the salvation-historical context in the description of the order of salvation as far as both the Old and New Testament believers are concerned.

Elements of Cocceius's covenant theology were elaborated in the works of a later generation of Cocceians. Some of them, like Franciscus Burman (1632–79), Salomon van Til (1643–1713) and Henricus Groenewegen (c. 1640–92), called 'Green Cocceians', tried to incorporate elements of Cartesian philosophy. Others, like Campegius Vitringa Jr (1659–1722) and Johannes d'Outrein (1662–1722), developed a more pietistic model of covenant theology (they were therefore called 'Earnest Cocceians'). Cocceius did not only influence the later significant Voetian theologians Herman Witsius (1636–1708) and Wilhelmus à Brakel (1635–1711), but also pietistic circles in Germany. Friedrich Adolf Lampe (1638–1729), Theodor Undereyck (1635–93), Philipp Jakob Spencr (1635–1705) and Johann Albrecht Bengel (1687–1752) developed Cocceius's exegesis of biblical prophecies and his chiliastic orientation. Although the term *Heilsgeschichte* was coined in the nineteenth century by the German and *Lutheran theologian J.C. von Hofmann (1810–77) and the Erlangen School, Cocceius can be viewed as the founding father of this concept in the Reformed tradition.

WILLEM J. VAN ASSELT

FURTHER READING: W.J. van Asselt, *The Covenant Theology of Johannes Cocceius* (Studies in the History of Christian Thought; ed. H.A. Oberman; Leiden, 1999); *Johannes Coccejus: Portret van een zeventiende-eeuws theoloog op oude en nieuwe wegen* (Kerk-historische monografieën 6; Heerenveen, 1997), an intellectual biography of Cocceius; H. Faulenbach, *Weg und Ziel der Erkenntnis Christi: Eine Untersuchung zur Theologie des Johannes Coccejus* (Neukirchen-Vluyn, 1973); C.S. McCoy, *The Covenant Theology of Johannes Cocceius* (PhD dissertation; Yale, 1957); J. Moltmann, 'Jacob Brocard als Vorläufer der Reich-Gottes-Theologie und der prophetischen Schriftauslegung des Johann Coccejus', *Z Kg* 71 (1960), pp. 110–29; 'Geschichtstheologie und pietistisches Menschenbild bei Johannes Coccejus und Theodor Undereyck', *Ev Th* 19 (1959), pp. 343–61; G. Schrenk, *Gottesreich und Bund im älteren Protestantismus, vornehmlich bei J.C.* (Gütersloh, 1923; Darmstadt, 1967); S. Strehle,

Calvinism, Federalism and Scholasticism: A Study of the Reformed Doctrine of Covenant (Bern, 1988); D.A. Weir, *The Origins of the Federal Theology in Sixteenth-Century Reformation Thought* (Oxford, 1990).

Coleridge, Samuel Taylor (1772–1834)

Coleridge belongs with his contemporaries *Schleiermacher and *Hegel as a major early nineteenth-century theological mind. Often termed the father of British liberal theology by virtue of his engagement with biblical criticism and his influence on later theologians, he has equally reinforced Christian orthodoxy by his critical engagement with *Enlightenment rationalism. His restless and protean mind, probing all sides of many questions, is today arousing increasing interest. His influence comes as much from his scattered notes as from his poetry and longer writings.

Coleridge differs from his contemporaries in that he is less inclined to appeal to feeling – and so he is more wedded to a quest for rationality – than Schleiermacher, and he is less inclined than Hegel to a thoroughgoing rationalism. While the systems of the two are both, in different ways, in danger of collapsing into pantheism, Coleridge's life project was to sharpen the distinction between pantheism and Trinitarian theism. In this light, the whole of his life's work, poetry and prose alike, represents an essentially religious quest. Afflicted for much of his life with drug addiction and an inability to complete many of his projects, he was yet a voracious reader of immense and wide-ranging learning. His quest was shaped by his personal problems – perhaps partly as their result, he had a more radical doctrine of sin than the two Germans – but was also deeply informed by an awareness of the crisis of western thought and institutions consequent upon modernity.

Indeed, he lived through the crisis in his own career. The young Coleridge was the child of enlightened optimism. For a time a *Unitarian preacher – in marked contrast with his later defence of Anglican establishment – he toyed with plans for a utopian community in America. At this stage he was something of a deist, a disciple of the associationist philosopher David Hartley (1705–57), but he came to see the life-denying implications of a philosophy which effectively made ethics, aesthetics and religion merely the conditioned responses of a mechanical mind. The combination of practical and intellectual questions involved in this critique indicates both Coleridge's Englishness and his drive to integration. While he was unable ever to develop the system of thought which he constantly intended, his perennial interest lies in the fact that everywhere he demonstrates the interrelatedness of all important questions and the relevance of theology to them.

The concern to integrate art, morals and theology marks Coleridge's involvement with the *Romantic reaction to Enlightenment rationalism. Responding to the rediscovery of the pantheist philosopher *Spinoza, he sought in a close involvement with Nature the liberating nearness of the divine that deism had so signally lacked. However, finding Romantic divine closeness as deterministic as deist transcendence, he moved steadily nearer to orthodox Trinitarianism, which he finally adopted in his thirties.

An approach to the third and crucial phase of Coleridge's development can be made through three related features of his thought. First, concerned with a rational account of reality, yet aware that traditional rationalism tends to a dualism between thought and experience, he sought in the imagination a link between the two worlds. In general, rationalist philosophers had seen in imagination a merely constructive faculty, the enemy of reason as the source of myths and fantasies. Coleridge, the poet, drawing on literary rather than philosophical sources, called that the 'fancy', and reserved 'imagination' for those deeper acts in which the human person responds creatively yet faithfully to the creating work of God. Imagination thus bridges sense and reason, the subjective and the objective.

Second, in parallel with this he developed a distinction between understanding and reason. Rationalists had made the mistake of confusing *mere* understanding – the faculty which simply aggregates facts – with reason, which penetrates into the deeper structures of reality. Understanding corresponds to fancy as the more superficial function, while reason goes deep. Here Coleridge calls upon the *Platonist tradition, but, in order to avoid a dualistic approach to reality, he seeks to ally reason with imagination. The result is a dynamic Platonism, with a revised notion of the 'ideas', which are understood as open possibilities for the mind's engagement with reality on a broad front.

The third feature is a pervasive concern with freedom. Although he was never able to accept that philosopher's rejection of metaphysical thinking, *Kant's philosophy of the will liberated Coleridge from mechanistic determinism and provided a way into an understanding of a free relation of God and the world. In sum, the crown of a widening of the terms of intellectual construction was Coleridge's doctrine of the Trinity. The triune God wills the existence of the other, but in such a way that the world and the human agent within it remain free to be themselves. The otherness of the world is grounded in the way in which God has otherness within the structure of his being, as Father and Son linked by the Spirit. The Trinity is for Coleridge the 'idea of ideas' – Platonism Christianized – the central notion by which human beings, employing both imagination and reason, may engage with the mysteries of human sin, redemption and freedom as they are taught by historic Christianity.

The chief weakness of Coleridge's Trinity is its abstractness. While he had come to accept the Christian scheme of redemption, centred on history, the historical details of its outworking were never of much interest to him. He rarely thought in incarnational terms and was unable to develop an adequate doctrine of the Holy Spirit. His importance lies, rather, in his prophetic reading of the signs of the enlightened times and in his awareness of the centrality and function of Trinitarian doctrine.

COLIN E. GUNTON

FURTHER READING: Among Coleridge's theologically important books are *Biographia Literaria* (1817); *Aids to Reflection* (1824); and *Confessions of an Enquiring Spirit* (1840). A collected edition of his works, sponsored by the Bollingen Foundation, is in process. Works not yet published may be found in W.G.T. Shedd (ed.), *The Complete Works of Samuel Taylor Coleridge* (7 vols.; New York, 1853). *Studies:* Owen Barfield, *What Coleridge Thought* (Middletown, CT, 1971); Thomas McFarland, *Coleridge and the Pantheist Tradition* (Oxford, 1969); J.R. Barth, *Coleridge and Christian Doctrine* (Cambridge, MA, 1969); Daniel W. Hardy, 'Coleridge on the Trinity', *Angl Th R* 69 (1988).

Cone, James Hal (b. 1938)

James Cone wrote his dissertation at Northwestern University on 'The Doctrine of Man in the Theology of Karl Barth'. Four years later, he published his first book, *Black Theology and Black*

Power, which became a road map for the development of *black theology. A cursory look at the index of *Black Theology and Black Power* reveals that Cone demonstrates great competence in European theology, with incisive and insightful discussions of scholars as diverse as *Emil Brunner, *Rudolf Bultmann, *Dietrich Bonhoeffer, Gunther Bornkamm, *Karl Jaspers, *Søren Kierkegaard and Richard Niebuhr, to name a few. This should not surprise us as Cone mentions that he was steeped in the writings of white philosophers and theologians throughout his college and seminary education. Cone writes:

> Like most college and seminary students of my generation, I faithfully studied philosophy and theology – from the pre-Socratics to modern existentialism and linguistic analysis, from Justin Martyr, Irenaeus, and Origen to Karl Barth, Bultmann and Tillich. I was an expert on Karl Barth and knew well the theological issues that shaped his theology. I wrote papers in seminary on the Barth and Brunner debates, the knowledge of God in contemporary theology, Bultmann's program of demythologization, the Tillichian doctrine of God as being itself, and concluded my formal education with a Ph.D. dissertation on Barth's anthropology. (*God of the Oppressed*, p. 5)

It was highly improbable that Cone would engage in theological analysis of the black experience without reference to these theologians whose writings he had encountered in seminary and graduate school. Further, because he knew the theologians of the white church very well, this gave him ready access to criticism of the church and its theology. Cone indicates that the fundamental problem with American theology is its attempt to affirm and confirm the language of unreality in the church, rather than call the church to its central task of acting out the gospel. Theology, if it is to save its own soul, must be related to life. That is, the chief problems of society must become grist for the theological mill. According to Cone, a rereading of *Barth's *Church Dogmatics* would make this observation clear, because the revolution which Barth led in the theological arena took place in Hitler's Germany and reflected the political, economic and social problems of that society.

Cone traces similarities between the black religious experience and Karl Barth's theology. Cone writes:

When one relates Barth's theology to the black church experience, there are many similarities. Like Barth's theology, Jesus Christ occupies the centre of the gospel message in the black church. In sermon, song, prayer and testimony, Jesus is the one to whom the people turn in times of trouble and distress, because they believe that he can heal their wounded hearts and broken spirits. He is the one who is called the lily of the valley, the bright and morning star. No black preacher would dare to tell the story without reference to Jesus, because he is the gospel story. Without him there is no story to tell and no gospel to celebrate. (*My Soul Looks Back*, pp. 80–81)

The Christocentric focus of Barth's work, coupled with the confessional nature of his theology, is an important resource for Cone in his articulation of black theology. Barth's insistence that the Bible is the primary source for theology and that the church needs to recapture its primary mission of proclaiming the word of God all find ready response in Cone's approach to the theological task. Cone marvels at how closely the emphasis in Barth's theology on Scripture approximates to this reality in the black church. Cone asserts that the theology of the black church is scriptural. The dependence and reverence which the black church has for the Bible goes back to the experience of slavery. The Bible was often the first book to which slaves were introduced. Many slaves risked floggings and even death by learning to read the good book. Further, Cone points out that Barth's emphasis on the word of God as preached resonates with the witness and the experience of the black church. In the black church, the high point in the worship service is the proclamation of the word of God. In black ecclesiology, the proclamation of the word of God is a miracle – a miracle not of human volition but of divine revelation.

As Cone constructs his theology he uses songs, sermons and testimonies from the black church – in conversation with Barth. But what it is important to note is that Cone uses Barth to go beyond Barth. He asserts that it is one thing to regard Jesus Christ as the focal point of the Christian gospel. It is quite another thing to investigate the meaning of his person and work in the light of the black experience. Black theology has to go beyond Karl Barth's approach to theology and do more than assert that Jesus Christ is the essence of the gospel. Black theology must specify the meaning of Christ's existence in relation to the slave ships that appeared on American shores. Unless Christ's existence is analyzed in the light of the oppressed of the land, we are still left wondering what his presence means for the auction block, the underground railroad and contemporary manifestations of black power.

There are points at which we begin to sense a divergence in Cone's thought from that of Barth. With Barth, Cone agrees that Jesus Christ is normative for the gospel message; but unlike Barth he wants Christ's relationship specified in relationship to the wretched of the earth. Unlike Barth who articulates a Christology 'from above', Cone espouses a Christology 'from below'. The key for Cone is that we dare not separate our questions about Jesus from the concreteness of everyday life. For Christians who have experienced the extreme absurdities of life, the Christological issue is not primarily theoretical but practical. To understand the historical Jesus is not only to learn that Jesus is who Jesus was, but even more importantly to begin to understand that this knowledge of Jesus forces the church to see the identification of Jesus with the poor and marginalized. It must be noted, however, that Cone was not uncritical of Barth's perspective. He faults Barth in particular for his overcommitment to the institutionalized church.

Barth could not bear the weight of black theology, and so in more recent writings Cone places his primary emphasis on the work of Malcolm X and Martin Luther King, Jr. Cone illustrates this for us in the final chapter of his book *For My People*. Here he gives an exposition of what it would look like for the church to become involved in social transformation. He begins earlier chapters with quotations from Martin Luther King, Jr and Malcolm X. In these citations, the church is challenged to engage in the restructuring of American society.

Cone is insistent that the black church needs to create a vision of a new social order that deals with the complexities with which black people live. The challenge facing the church is to build on the vision of our past leaders. Malcolm X's vision of nationalism and King's vision of the beloved community must become foundational as the black church faces the twenty-first century. The new vision of freedom must not only build on the dream of our leaders of the past, but it must also move beyond North America to include the third world. This new vision must be able to analyze world poverty and sickness, monopoly capitalism, antidemocratic socialism, racism and sexism – with a determination to eliminate these evils.

NOEL LEO ERSKINE

FURTHER READING: *Texts: Black Theology and Black Power* (New York, 1969); *A Black Theology of Liberation* (New York, 1970); *The Spirituals and the Blues: An Interpretation* (New York, 1972); *God Of The Oppressed* (New York, 1975); *My Soul Looks Back* (Maryknoll, NY, 1986); *For My People* (Maryknoll, NY, 1984); *Speaking the Truth: Ecumenism, Liberation, and Black Theology* (Grand Rapids, 1986); *Martin and Malcolm and America: A Dream or a Nightmare?* (Maryknoll, NY, 1991), an in-depth study of how the thought of Malcolm X and Martin Luther King, Jr, functions in Cone's approach to theology; James Cone and Gayraud S. Wilmore (eds.), *Black Theology: A Documentary History* I, *1966–1979* (Maryknoll, NY, 1979); *Black Theology: A Documentary History* II, *1980–1992* (Maryknoll, NY, 1993).

Congar, Yves M.J. (1904–95)

Theologian, ecclesiologist and ecumenist. Born at Sedan in the French Ardennes on 13 April 1904, Congar studied at the Institut Catholique in Paris and there entered the Dominican Order in 1925. Earning a doctorate in theology at the Dominican Studium of Saulchoir for a dissertation on the unity of the church according to *Thomas Aquinas, he was ordained a priest in 1930 and taught at Le Saulchoir from 1931–39. Drafted into the army in 1939, he was a prisoner of war from 1940–45 before resuming his teaching at Le Saulchoir. Congar was widely considered one of those suspected of the 'false irenicism' criticized in Pius XII's 1950 encyclical, 'Humani generis', and in 1954, after he published an article in support of the worker-priest movement in France, the ecclesiastical authorities forbade him to teach and subjected his writings to censorship. His situation changed dramatically upon the election of John XXIII as pope in 1958; he was appointed a theological expert for *Vatican II and made crucial contributions to the council's two major documents on the church, and to those on revelation, ecumenism and mission. His reputation rehabilitated after the council, Congar was able to concentrate his energies on research and writing even into his eighties. In November 1994, only seven months before his death on 22 June 1995, he received his final vindication when John Paul II named him a cardinal.

An indefatigable researcher and prolific writer, Congar's published works amount to more than 1,700 items in constructive, fundamental and spiritual theology, and in historical and contemporary ecclesiology. He will be primarily remembered as an ecumenical ecclesiologist. Shortly before his priestly ordination he had received what he considered a special vocation from God to work for the renewal of the church and the reunion of Christians. He realized such a goal would require a renewal of Catholic ecclesiology and various reforms within the church. His scholarly task would be, by way of a 'return to the sources', to recover that broader Catholic ecclesial vision from patristic and medieval times – before the schisms of the eleventh and sixteenth centuries produced the hardened and polemical positions so evident in the post-Tridentine era. Congar thus took his place as one of the 'new theologians' dedicated to the historical retrievals of positive theology.

For nearly five decades Congar wrote the bulletin on ecclesiology for the *Revue des Sciences Philosophiques et Théologiques*, and in 1936 he established the ecclesiological series 'Unam Sanctam'. The first volume was his own *Chrétiens Désunis* (Paris, 1937, ET 1939), in which he offered an ecumenically sensitive explanation of the church's great schisms and sought to work out principles for Catholic involvement in ecumenical dialogue. His next major work, *Vraie et Fausse Réforme dans l'Église* (Paris, 1950), attempted to establish appropriate criteria for the church's renewal and reform, which he saw as an ever-present task given that it may always be asked whether the church's ecclesial forms are fostering or hindering the Spirit. His path-breaking book *Jalons pour une Théologie du Laïcat* (Paris, 1953, rev. edn 1964, ET 1957, 1965) criticized the contemporary reduction of ecclesiology to a treatment of the hierarchy and justified the laity's participation in the priestly, royal and prophetic offices of Christ. Although crucial themes from these books would find later reverberations in the documents of Vatican II, in the decade before the council they were often considered dangerous and suspect.

A few years before the opening of the council, Congar published two profound works, *Le Mystère du Temple* (Paris, 1958, ET 1962), and the two-volume *La Tradition et les Traditions* (Paris, 1960, 1963, ET 1966). The former discusses how the Hebrew and Christian Scriptures understand the mystery of God's presence to creatures, with special reference to God's presence in the Jewish temple, Jesus Christ and the Christian community. The latter offers an exhaustive and nuanced historical and systematic treatment of the relationships among Scripture, the church's essential faith, tradition and the many ecclesiastical traditions of a less binding nature. He argues that God's revelation only occurs concretely when Scripture, tradition and church are intimately combined in a living synthesis.

After the council, Congar wrote two weighty tomes on the history of ecclesiology: *L'Écclésiologie du Haut Moyen Age* (Paris, 1968) and *L'Église de Saint Augustin à l'Époque Moderne* (Paris, 1970). In *Je Crois en l'Esprit Sainte* (Paris, 1979–80, ET 1983), a three-volume work emphasizing the vital importance of pneumatology for western theology and ecclesiology, he suggests that the Roman Church could without loss of faith suppress the **filioque* in the Nicene Creed as an ecumenical action of humility and solidarity with the Orthodox Church.

Congar is one of the most influential Catholic theologians of the twentieth century and one of the predominant architects of Vatican II's legacy. His vast historical investigations have continued to enrich contemporary theology – especially his retrievals of the full and capacious Catholic tradition in ecclesiology and fundamental theology. He does not easily fit into the customary categories: while his methodology, sources and hermeneutical presuppositions mark him as a classically trained theologian, the theses he draws from his broad erudition are often progressive and ecumenically fruitful. The antithesis of the ivory tower theorizer, he often synthesizes the results of his positive theology into a constructive historical theology, which propounds fresh ways of looking at contemporary issues. J.-P. Jossua has rightly called Congar a 'prophet of tradition', a theologian who laboured faithfully to transmit the critical power and inclusive range of the church's heritage for the benefit of all Christians.

GREGORY ROCCA, OP

FURTHER READING: *Texts: Diversity and Communion* (Mystic, CT, 1983); *I Believe in the Holy Spirit* (New York, 1983); *Le Concile de Vatican II – son Église: Peuple de Dieu et Corps du Christ* (Paris, 1984). For Congar's bibliography: J.-P. Jossua, *Yves Congar:*

Theology in the Service of God's People (Chicago, 1968), pp. 185–241; A. Nichols, 'An Yves Congar Bibliography 1967–1987', *Angelicum* 66 (1989), pp. 422–66. *Studies:* T. MacDonald, *The Ecclesiology of Yves Congar: Foundational Themes* (Lanham, MD, 1984); A. Nichols, *Yves Congar* (London, 1989).

Cotton, John (1584–1652)

Cotton was born 4 December 1584 in Derby, England, the son of lawyer Roland Cotton. John's education began in Derby, but by the age of thirteen he gained admission to Trinity College, Cambridge, where he was eventually elected a fellow. From Trinity he moved to Emmanuel College where he served as head lecturer, dean and catechist.

While at Emmanuel, Cotton was regarded as a respected scholar and orator. However, despite the praise he received from academic audiences, he underwent a profound struggle of the soul during these years, especially under the influence of two leading *Puritans: William Perkins, the renowned fellow of Christ College and preacher at Great Saint Andrew's Church, and Richard Sibbes, a fellow and preacher at St John's College and lecturer for the Trinity parish, who would go on to be preacher at Gray's Inn and to be Master of Catherine Hall. It was said that when the young Cotton heard the bell toll for Perkins's funeral he 'secretly rejoiced in his deliverance from that powerful ministry, by which his conscience had been so oft beleaguered'. Thus, Cotton was in the midst of a spiritual crisis when, hearing a sermon by Sibbes, he was 'converted'.

Cotton heralded his conversion to the university community with a sermon he preached at St Mary's Church, the academic pulpit of Cambridge. He delivered a plain sermon in the Puritan style, thus rejecting the arts of oratory and rhetoric which had been his trademark. Some in that academic congregation were reportedly disappointed at Cotton's homiletical transformation, but at least one present, John Preston, the brilliant fellow of Queen's College, credited Cotton's preaching with his own conversion.

In 1612 Cotton left Cambridge to assume the pastoral leadership of St Botolph, Lincolnshire, a position he held for twenty years. From St Botolph he exercised considerable influence in the Puritan movement, communicating with Preston, the venerable Puritan leader John Dod, and others, and receiving students from Cambridge who chose to complete their studies for ministry under his tutelage. Over these years Cotton's non-conformity with respect to the Church of England only increased. He laboured under the strict *Calvinist view that only those liturgical rites and vestments prescribed by Scripture were allowable in worship. It was also during these years that he first made the acquaintance of Anne Hutchinson, a parishioner living in nearby Alford who later followed Cotton to New England, and whose views would bring Cotton into a serious doctrinal controversy with the colonial leadership.

Cotton was forced to flee St Botolph after it was reported that magistrates receiving Holy Communion in his church did not kneel at the sacrament. After finding refuge with John Davenport and consulting with Dod, the forty-eight-year-old Puritan decided that he should emigrate to the American colonies. Cotton departed for New England on the same ship that carried Thomas Hooker and Samuel Stone, both of whom were also in the circle of Cambridge Puritans. Cotton apparently wrestled with his decision to leave England for the New World. He came to interpret his emigration as a mission, not unlike St Peter's, in which God's will ultimately reigned over his own. Cotton's understanding of his mission coincided with and contributed to the Puritan interpretation of their migration to the New World (about fifteen thousand English citizens crossed the Atlantic in the decade before 1640) as an 'errand into the wilderness' to establish the 'New Jerusalem', the 'Holy Commonwealth' in which a full reformation of the church could take place. These themes would echo down through the social, political and religious history of the American colonies and the new nation.

Cotton's ministry in Boston was largely unremarkable from 10 October 1633, when he was ordained to the office of teacher of First Church, until October 1636. At that point the report reached his ears that members of his congregation, led by Anne Hutchinson, were spreading dangerous doctrines concerning the Holy Spirit and the character of the new covenant. Hutchinson had followed Cotton to the New World in 1634, believing that he (and her brother-in-law, John Wheelwright, who would immigrate to the Massachusetts colony in 1636) were the only two ministers that preached the true 'covenant of grace'. After her arrival in the colony, Hutchinson gathered around her a group of men and women affiliated with the Boston church. Meeting in her home each week, they studied Cotton's teachings and interpreted them in Hutchinson's antinomian manner. Cotton's fellow ministers, the elders in the Massachusetts Bay Colony, urged him to take action against opinions they saw as heretical and which they came to suspect were somehow resultant from his teachings. Their concern set in motion a course of events that for a time engulfed Cotton's ministry and threatened his future in the colony. The controversy brings the doctrinal views of John Cotton and his fellow ministers into sharp focus.

John Winthrop, governor of the colony, described the erroneous views which were held by the antinomians and were condemned by the assembly of churches as the following: '1. That the person of the Holy Spirit dwells in a justified person. 2. That no sanctification can help to evidence to us our justification.' The second of these issues figured most prominently in the debates between Cotton and his colleagues in ministry, though the two statements were closely related.

The crucial question was this: Does God, in the divine work of justification and sanctification, use created means, including the capacities of human beings, to accomplish his work? If God does work through such natural means to accomplish supernatural ends, then one should be able to establish objective criteria through the use of which persons can discern the presence of sanctifying grace at work in their lives. This was the position of the Puritan elders of the Massachusetts colony, including Thomas Shepard, Peter Bulkeley and Thomas Hooker. It was this position which was called into question by the teachings of Anne Hutchinson and her antinomian followers. And it was this position which Cotton's teachings seemed to call into question as well.

Cotton advanced an understanding of sanctification that emphasized God's direct action on human beings which overrules their natural capacities, a divine action which transforms persons in spite of any activity of their own. In Cotton's view, God alone, through the Holy Spirit, acts to regenerate persons, and those who are to be saved must simply wait for the Holy Spirit to open their eyes to discern that they have been united with Christ and have been justified. From the perspective of the other ministers of the colony, this view abandoned people

to subjective impressions, bereft of any objective means for testing their election. It also, in their view, came dangerously close to confusing the human person and his/her impressions with the divine Spirit.

Hutchinson, Wheelwright and their followers brought more heat than light to the controversy, charging that the ministers of Boston (except Cotton) were legalists 'preaching a covenant of works' rather than a 'covenant of grace', and were unfit to be called ministers of the gospel. Cotton himself though, in a more guarded statement, said that if one appeals to one's sanctification as the ground on which one builds an assurance of justification then one is continuing on 'in a Covenant of works'. Cotton's critique raised two further questions: What is the proper ground of Christian assurance? And, what is the proper place of law in the Christian life? Both questions were contemporaneously being asked in the Old World by English antinomians such as Tobias Crisp (1600–43), John Traske (d. c. 1636) and John Eaton (1575–1642). Their ideas gained popular support, especially following the eruption of the 'Puritan Revolution'. A careful reading of the Westminster documents reveals that concern over English antinomianism was present in the minds of the Westminster divines as they met (1643–48). Puritan divines throughout the period came to stress ortho-praxy (ethical right practice) and ortho-doxy (doctrinal right teaching/belief) as objective criteria for testing one's justification and sanctification.

By the end of the antinomian controversy in the Massachusetts colony in 1638, Cotton came to an agreement with his fellow ministers. Anne Hutchinson suffered banishment from the colony to Rye, New York, where she died in an Indian raid in August 1643. Cotton's stress on the immediate, intuitive awareness of the Spirit of God as the criterion of God's work of grace emerged within a generation as a third test of assurance of election, the test of ortho-affection (right religious experience). This would be described with elegant precision by *Jonathan Edwards in his classic *Treatise Concerning the Religious Affections* (1746).

Cotton's reputation and influence in New England grew after this controversy closed until, in November 1652, he became ill because of exposure to the elements which he suffered crossing the Charles River on his way to preach to the students at Harvard College. When he died on 23 December 1652 he was mourned throughout the colonies. Cotton Mather, in whose name the two great ministerial houses of New England were commemorated, praised Cotton as 'a most *universal scholar*, and *living system* of the liberal arts', a preacher without peer whose chief art lay in the *'concealing of his art'*.

Among Cotton's theological works are *A Briefe Exposition with Practicall Observations upon the Whole Book of Ecclesiastes* (1654), *A Brief Exposition of the Whole Book of Canticles* (1648), *Christ the Fountaine of Life* (1651) and *Some Treasure Fetched Out of Rubbish* (1660), all of which were apparently written during his English ministry, between 1612 and 1632; *A Treatise of the Covenant of Grace* (1659, probably dating from c. 1636). He also wrote *Sixteene Questions of Serious and Necessary Consequences Propounded unto Mr John Cotton … together with his Answers* (1644, composition dates from 1636 and is crucial for understanding his beliefs during the antinomian controversy), *The True Constitution of a Particular Visible Church Proved by Scripture* (1642, composed c. 1634–35) and *An Exposition upon the Thirteenth Chapter of the Revelation* (1655, composed c. 1639–40). Also of interest is the body of writings and responses between Cotton and Roger Williams over the question of toleration.

MICHAEL JINKINS

FURTHER READING: David Hall (ed.), *The Antinomian Controversy, 1636–1638: A Documentary History* (Middletown, CT, 1968); William Haller, *The Rise of Puritanism* (Philadelphia, 2nd edn, 1984); Michael Jinkins, 'John Cotton and the Antinomian Controversy, 1636–1638: A Profile of Experiential Individualism in American Puritanism', *Scot J Th* 42.3 (1990), pp. 321–49; *A Comparative Study in the Theology of Atonement in Jonathan Edwards and John McLeod Campbell: Atonement and the Character of God* (San Francisco, 1993); Cotton Mather, *Magnalia Christi Americana: Or, The Ecclesiastical History of New England*, I (Hartford, CT, 1853); Perry Miller, *The New England Mind: From Colony to Province* (Cambridge, MA, 1953); Irwin H. Polishook, *Roger Williams, John Cotton and Religious Freedom: A Controversy in New and Old England* (Englewood Cliffs, NJ, 1967); William K.B. Stoever, *'A Faire and Easie Way to Heaven': Covenant Theology and Antinomianism in Early Massachusetts* (Middletown, MA, 1978); Judith B. Welles, 'John Cotton, 1584–1652, Churchman and Theologian', (PhD thesis; University of Edinburgh, 1948); Larzer Ziff, *The Career of John Cotton: Puritanism and the American Experience* (Princeton, 1962).

Cranmer, Thomas (1489–1556)

A Cambridge don tested in diplomatic service, Cranmer was selected to solve the pressing 'privy matter' of Henry VIII's 'divorce'. Found suitable for the royal purpose, he was promoted to succeed Warham as Archbishop of Canterbury in 1533. If his service of the Tudor monarch was unquestionable in its loyalty, Cranmer's mind was equally clear about the obedience Scripture demanded as due under God to the 'godly prince' and supreme head of a sovereign church. By the time of Edward VI's accession moreover, Cranmer had become sufficiently versed in *Reformation 'new divinity' of the kind he set out for vernacular worship in *Books of Common Prayer* (1549 and 1552) to gain recognition as the first Protestant Primate of All England. Deprived for high treason and tried for heresy under the Catholic Mary I, Cranmer was burnt at an Oxford stake (1556) to become the principal martyr of the English Reformation.

Before being propelled into the treacherous world of the Tudor court and *haut politique*, Cranmer had followed the customary routines of late-medieval university life at Cambridge. A first biographer later observed that he was there early 'nosseled in the grossest kynd of sophistry'. But such scholastic obscurities – dismissed in the *Narratives* of Morice (or was it Nevinson?) as 'the dark ridels and quidities of Duns and other subtile questionestes' – were soon exposed to the textualism of *Erasmus who, in 1511, accepted Fisher's invitation to teach Greek in the schools. If no evidence exists of Cranmer's presence at these Cambridge classes, his status as examiner (after securing the doctorate in 1526) would have made him familiar with a developing discipline so biblical that philological or textual exegesis roundly repudiated rationalist speculation. Henceforth careful focus on scriptural, patristic and liturgical texts was to mark the work of a scholar archbishop not only bringing Cranmer into line with Renaissance learning, but also making it easier for him to move ahead and embrace the ideology and doctrines of the European Reformation.

Although in a very special sense Henry's archbishop, and a new kind of ecclesiastical civil servant to the Tudor headship which made Thomas Cromwell vicegerent or 'high vicar over the spirituality under the King', Cranmer kept abreast of the latest scholarship. In particular, his copious commonplaces represent an advance on medieval collections, or *florilegia*.

For with help from chaplain-secretaries who compiled these notebooks, the archbishop assembled a range of definitive texts on many key issues of Reformation principle that, on the basis of his own wide reading, would in time revise the practice of the English Church he served more as a chief pastor than as a high priest of the Roman hierarchy. Such citations – 'notions in garrison, whence the owner may draw out an army into the field on competent warning' (as 'worthy Tom Fuller' later chose to express it) – embraced widely different viewpoints, conservative and radical. *De Eucharistia* (British Library MS Royal, 7B, XI) thus set out *Luther's insistence on a sacramental real presence in key tracts of 1527 and 1528 written to refute *Zwingli. Together with his *Preface* (1540) to the *Great Bible*, such evidence reveals a Cranmer altogether open to the new Renaissance textualism that expounded biblical and patristic priorities. And it was that 'godly and excellent learned man' *Oecolampadius who gave Cranmer his appetite for the early Fathers of the Greek and Latin Church. This taste the archbishop acquired when he was still convinced of the doctrine of real presence. Once the 'veil of old darkness' fell from his eyes however, a certain independence of mind enabled Cranmer to make fuller use of the work of a Basle humanist who ranks only second in importance to Erasmus himself. For with the publication of *De genuina verborum* (1525), Oecolampadius offered a figurative understanding of Christ's words of institution many found more acceptable than Zwingli's bald solution. Since Aramaic has no *copula*, the Basle professor held that the *tropus* was not to be found in *est* but rather in *corpus*. So Christ's original meaning was 'This is the figure of my body', an ingenious explanation based by Oecolampadius on *Tertullian's *figura corporis mei* (with reference to that Father's treatise *Against Marcion*, Lib. 1).

In the *Defence* (1550), Cranmer is much indebted to this approach. He certainly brought his 'old authors' into line as an invaluable support, second only to Scripture, of the fundamental exegetical issue when he chose to confront Roman doctrines of sacrifice and transubstantiation in the Mass. Based as it was on what he upheld as patristic consensus, the idea of Christ calling bread and wine his body and blood provided Cranmer with an important solution to the real difficulty he faced when obliged to answer the traditional arguments forwarded by his rival and foe Stephen Gardiner. The archbishop's ready use of realist patristic language in the fierce wrangle that was sixteenth-century debate also offers a key to grasping the liturgical composition he designed to transform the priestly high Mass into a fellowship meal and communion of the people. For by far his most remarkable achievement was the way Cranmer, after years of both solitary study and difficult drafting in committee, revised the worship of the English Church in *Books of Common Prayer* which skilfully injected old forms and rites with new symbolist meaning.

> I say now as I said before, that neither bread, wine, nor water have any capacity of holiness; but holiness is only in the receivers ... And therefore the marvellous alteration to an higher estate, nature and condition, is chiefly and principally in the persons, and in the sacramental signs it is none otherwise but sacramentally and in signification. (*Answer*, 1551, p. 323)

In short, although Cranmer was no original thinker, he nevertheless played an important part in transmitting the changing theology of continental divines in a way that, suitably adapted, proved crucial to the ultimate survival of English Protestantism.

PETER NEWMAN BROOKS

FURTHER READING: *Texts:* Cranmer's works are no longer readily available in print, but for his *Defence* and the *Answer* to Gardiner, cf. *Writings and Disputations of Thomas Cranmer ... relative to the Sacrament of the Lord's Supper* (ed. J.E. Cox; Cambridge, 1844). *Studies:* J. Ketley, *The Two Liturgies, A.D. 1549 and A.D. 1552 ... set forth ... in the Reign of King Edward VI* (Cambridge, 1844); P.N. Brooks, *Cranmer in Context* (Lutterworth, 1989); *Thomas Cranmer's Doctrine of the Eucharist* (London, 2nd edn, 1992); D. MacCulloch, *Thomas Cranmer, A Life* (New Haven, 1996); G. Bromiley, *Thomas Cranmer, Theologian* (New York, 1956).

Cupitt, Don (b. 1934)

Cupitt is most widely known for his two books *Taking Leave of God* (1980) and in the UK also for his work *The Sea of Faith* (1984; 2nd edn, 1994). The latter is a written account of a series of talks on BBC television the same year, which drew relatively large viewing audiences. It also gave rise to a loosely defined network of sympathizers called 'The Sea of Faith Network'. The major theme of this Network is that 'God' is a human construct, not a being 'out there' who addresses and encounters us as other. God is a projection of the human self, as *Kant and *Feuerbach had proposed.

Taking Leave of God and *The Sea of Faith*, however, belong to a middle period of Cupitt's ever-changing thought. Cupitt acknowledges that 'We love mobility. We don't want creeds' (*Radicals and the Future of the Church*, p. 112). Nevertheless it is easiest to understand his thought by distinguishing between three stages of development. Apart from a curacy in an Anglican parish at Salford, near Manchester (1959–62), Cupitt has spent his entire life at Cambridge. He taught at Westcott House theological college (1962–66) and then became dean of Emmanuel College from 1966 to 1991. He lectured in the University of Cambridge on philosophy of religion from 1968 (Lecturer, 1973) to 1996. Cupitt himself briefly traces his own development from 1968, the year of his full university appointment, in the foreword to Cowdell's *Atheist Priest?*

Earlier years: 1968–79. Cupitt recalls his early interest in the debates of the 1960s about 'images' of God, prompted at the popular level in the UK by *J.A.T. Robinson's *Honest to God* (1963). In *Christ and the Hiddenness of God* (1971) Cupitt shares in this quest to reformulate ways of understanding the transcendence of God within the frame of Christology. He is especially mindful of the Kantian critique of reason, natural theology and notions of God as an object of human thought 'out there'. In *Crisis of Moral Authority* (1972) he presses further Kant's theme of human autonomy, as against repressive human traditions. Like Kant, Cupitt places the autonomous human subject at the centre: truth springs from discovery, rather than from revelation. The role of interpretation begins to become more explicit. In an essay entitled 'One Jesus, Many Christs', also written in 1972, Cupitt starts to pave the way for what will become a later theme drawn from *Nietzsche: that we cannot reach behind 'interpretations', indeed we have only interpretations of interpretations. Jesus, he concludes, would not have been troubled 'by being many Christs' to different interpreters (in *Christ, Faith and History*, p. 143).

Cupitt's most searching book, *The Leap of Reason*, appeared in 1976. Here he draws on *Plato's allegory of the cave, in which shadows play on the walls from the outside world and invite speculations and inferences about how they should be interpreted by the cave-dwellers. But Cupitt's cave has no opening. Reason cannot lead to a notion of what is 'outside'; but a 'leap' of reason may initiate an experience akin to 'waking out of sleep' to some larger reality. This book ascribes a proper role to issues of interpretation and rightly examines limits of pure reason, as in Kant and *Kierkegaard. But the book never draws on the rich traditions of hermeneutics such as those found in Gadamer or *Ricoeur, but instead relies on a simplified social constructivism of the kind proposed in T.S. Kuhn's earlier work. Likewise, *The Leap of Reason* bypasses criticisms of constructivist theory and tends to simplify the complex thought of Kierkegaard. Nevertheless, this book addresses fundamental issues and we see a thinker attempting to grapple creatively with major problems. Kierkegaard's theme of indirect communication receives further attention in *Explorations in Theology* (1979), where Cupitt explores irony, parable and humour 'to awaken perception' (p. 69). There are also useful comments on non-cognitive modes of discourse in religion.

The middle years: 1980–85. In *Taking Leave of God* (1980), Cupitt insists that 'dependency' in religion constitutes a regressive, infantile stage. As against *Schleiermacher, he agrees with Feuerbach and with Freud that this dependence reflects immaturity and reduces the stature of humanity. His catchphrases are 'internalizing, de-objectifying and autonomy'. 'Religious meaning … is to be sought within rather than from above us' (p. 3). God is not an 'object', in the sense that 'God is no longer a distinct person over against us' (p. 85). Such a being would threaten our 'autonomy' by imposing commands or demands, and such a being, Cupitt asserts, *we should reject*. Once again, Cupitt is dominated by Kant's agenda. A God 'above', in Kant's view, either lies outside human thought, or is more probably a mere conceptual construct projected by the categories of the human mind. Cupitt's strategy is to reformulate 'spirituality' in a mode more akin to Buddhism. 'Buddhism … has no trace of dependency' and therefore escapes the critiques of Kant and of Freud (p. 2). In *The World to Come* (1982), Cupitt looks for a 'new order' which effectively brings with it 'the end of theism'. '*We* made all the theories' (p. 9).

The title of *The Sea of Faith* (1984) alludes to Matthew Arnold's poem 'Dover Beach' (1867), which depicts the retreat of a Sea of Faith in the face of the forces of mid-nineteenth century scientific 'modernity'. Cupitt formulates for a popular audience his own assessments of the impacts of such figures of 'modernity' as Kant, Kierkegaard, Feuerbach, Freud and *Wittgenstein. These figures supposedly demonstrate the end of 'theism' and the need for a 'non-realist' God, that is the God of his 1980 book. Many more orthodox theologians experienced extreme frustration since they had lectured almost daily on these thinkers but had drawn entirely different conclusions from their work.

However, a growing body of sympathizers eventually formed themselves into 'The Sea of Faith Network' in 1989. The Network's membership application form for 1993–94 alludes to Cupitt's vision 'of religious faith as entirely human' and states that they seek to promote religious faith *as a human creation* (their italics). Numbers in England grew rapidly. Anthony Freeman's *God in Us* (1993) broadly represents the stance of the Network, although its members emphasize its wide diversity. Freeman's view of prayer precisely reflects Kant on 'churchly' prayer: 'I do not actually believe there is anyone "out there" listening to me ... I was talking to myself' (p. 54). One by-product of such writing was the debate about the limits permitted to Anglican clergy holding the bishop's licence. Bishop Eric Kemp of Chichester took some disciplinary action, largely on the ground that Freeman had had some Diocesan responsibility in clergy training. Several other bishops attempt to contain the issue by sustained dialogue.

The later years: 1986–96. The name of Derrida begins to appear in *Only Human* (1985). But since this volume retains Feuerbach's more 'heroic' view of the human self, this book still belongs to the middle period. *Life Lines* (1986) decisively moves into postmodernity. Gone is the privileging of 'autonomy' and the human subject, for in postmodern rhetoric the self becomes decentred. Everything, including the self, is in flux and on the move. Lines are avenues for travel, in contrast to points where we can stop. Selfhood, meaning and truth all constitute products of social situatedness, which is itself ever-changing from context to context. Here is a decisive repudiation of 'foundations' or metaphysics.

Serious problems emerge, however, not only from the inherent difficulties or half-truths of postmodernity, but from Cupitt's desire to retain some of his earlier perspective alongside the new ones. How can 'God' be 'internalized' within a self that has become de-constructed? 'There is no substantial individual self' (*Life Lines*, p. 198). Denys Turner observes in the context of medieval mysticism that 'the very best reason why the God Cupitt takes leave of does not exist is that his "autonomous consciousness" does not exist either' ('The Mystics and the Objectivity of God', in C. Crowder [ed.], *God and Reality*, p. 126). Moreover, if postmodernity permits no privileged viewpoint or centre, how can Cupitt revert to the language of generalizing assertion, declaration and imperative in his later *Radicals and the Future of the Church* (1989)? 'The religious teacher *must* (Cupitt's italics) use language manipulatively, rhetorically, deceitfully' (p. 111); 'Recent literary theory has shown that absolute integrity ... is a myth' (pp. 106–7); 'Liberal ideology ... has collapsed' (p. 167); 'The more realistic your God, the more punitive your morality' (p. 168). 'We are anarchists ... we love mobility' (p. 112); hence meaning and truth, or reality, 'slips away ... shifting, elusive' (*The Time Being*, pp. 15, 38). On what basis, then, is Cupitt's philosophy of religion (for that is what it is) anything more than an emotive expression of approval, disapproval, or preference, dressed up as *argument* when in practice it serves as *rhetoric*?

At best, D.Z. Phillips perceives 'anti-realist faith' as disengaging religious belief from metaphysical systems (in Runzo [ed.], *Is God Real?*, p. 205). Rowan Williams points out that it perceives God 'as a reality constructed in language', and a recognition that in language we 'negotiate' rather than simply 'represent' or 'refer' (foreword to C. Crowder [ed.], *God and Reality*, p. vi). Crowder sees the stages of Cupitt's thought as moving from 'Christian Buddhism ... a severe inner discipline' to 'a celebration of the world, the body, and the passions which represents a different kind of spirituality' (Crowder, *God and Reality*, p. 8). Indeed, in *After All* (1984), *The Last Philosophy* (1995) and *Solar Ethics* (1995), we encounter what Cupitt calls 'energetic Spinozism', even 'poetical theology'. Yet in one recent essay ('Free Christianity', in Crowder [ed.], *God and Reality*, pp. 14–25), Cupitt still attacks 'metaphysical realism', the belief 'that God made us and has himself taught us ...' (p. 18). He rejects the view that 'we live ... in a stable world' (p. 19); and rejects the orthodoxy of those who 'want us to stand still so that we can be shot' (p. 24). That a theologian should be always on the move may in many contexts be a refreshing sign of openness and self-criticism. What is puzzling and paradoxical is that he writes not in a self-critical style, but with a supreme confidence that borders on the very dogmatism that he seeks to escape.

ANTHONY C. THISELTON

FURTHER READING: *Texts:* D. Cupitt, *Christ and the Hiddenness of God* (London, 1971); *A Crisis of Moral Authority* (London, 1972); 'One Jesus, Many Christs', in S.W. Sykes and J. Clayton (eds.), *Christ, Faith and History* (Cambridge, 1972); *The Leap of Reason* (London, 2nd edn, 1985); *Explorations in Theology* (London, 1979); *Taking Leave of God* (London, 1980); *The Sea of Faith* (London, 2nd edn, 1994); *Only Human* (London, 1985); *Life Lines* (London, 1986); *Radicals and the Future of the Church* (London, 1989); *What is a Story?* (London, 1991); *The Time Being* (London, 1992); *After All* (London, 1994); *The Lost Philosophy* (London, 1995); 'Free Christianity', in *God and Reality* (ed. C. Crowder; London, 1997), pp. 14–25. *Studies:* S. Cowdell, *Atheist Priest?* (London, 1988); C. Crowder (ed.), *God and Reality: Essays on Christian Non-Realism* (London, 1997); A. Freeman, *God in Us* (London, 1993); D.A. Hart, *Faith in Doubt* (London, 1993); B. Hebblethwaite, *The Ocean of Truth* (Cambridge, 1988); J. Runzo (ed.), *Is God Real?* (London, 1993); A.C. Thiselton, *Interpreting God and the Postmodern Self* (Edinburgh / Grand Rapids, 1995), pp. 81–120; S.R. White, *Don Cupitt and the Future of Doctrine* (London, 1994).

Cyprian (d. 258)

Thascius Caecilius Cyprianus, bishop of Carthage from 248/9 till he died a martyr in 258, is known chiefly through a biography by an admirer, and through a collection of letters covering the ecclesiastical controversies of his career as bishop. Only recently converted in middle life, he had sufficient rhetorical training to write good Latin and was a man of stature in the community, perhaps a teacher. Nonetheless, his rapid promotion to the episcopate provoked dissent among the clergy.

The persecution under Decius began late in 249, and it caused large-scale apostasy among Christians in Africa as elsewhere. Cyprian tried to maintain control from a secret retreat, while dissident clergy continued to operate in Carthage. As persecution gradually slackened, many who had defected by offering pagan sacrifices sought rehabilitation in the churches. In Carthage some clergy restored the 'lapsed' without the bishop's consent, following the lead of certain 'confessors'. Confessors were those who had suffered trial, torture or imprisonment for the faith, but had survived the ordeal. Custom allowed them special privileges, and sometimes (as at Lyons in 177) lapsed Christians had been restored at their behest. Cyprian argued that such judgement should be reserved for the bishop, and principles settled by bishops in council.

With Decius's death, Cyprian returned to Carthage. His tract *On the Lapsed* argues the folly of readmitting those who had offended God by idolatry and the need for due episcopal process. In councils of African bishops, rules were agreed covering the varying degrees of lapse: flight, pretending to sacrifice and voluntary and involuntary sacrifice were all carefully differentiated. Communion could be restored to a serious penitent near to death. When renewed persecution later impended, a more general amnesty was agreed.

Before this persecution, however, other troubles intervened. Cyprian's chief correspondent at Rome, where the bishop Fabian had been executed, was the presbyter *Novatian, who shared his hard line on the lapsed and was supported by a group of five Roman confessors. In March 251 Cornelius became bishop of Rome, but it was reported that Novatian had also been elected. Cyprian could find little to say on Cornelius's behalf, except that he was elected first, so Novatian could not be bishop. Cornelius's party favoured a more flexible approach to the lapsed, and Cyprian was obliged to defend actions that he found unpalatable. Novatian's tough line, allowing no restoration for baptized persons who had committed such grave offences as idolatry, adultery or murder, attracted support – not only in Rome, but also throughout the Empire. His dissident, puritan church was to persist for some centuries. In Carthage, Cyprian's earlier opponents continued and eventually set up a rival bishopric, even while Cyprian was defending moderate discipline against those who favoured Novatian. The outcome was a classic tract *On the Unity of the Catholic Church*. In it, Cyprian held that there is only one church, and that those who break away, however pure they appear, are agents of the devil in their breach of fundamental charity. He also wrote works on practical subjects, which to him were the essence of the bishop's task, such as the Lord's Prayer, patience and wrath. A devastating plague in 252 prompted Cyprian to write both *To Demetrian*, taking the plague as a sign of the death of the world, as well as *On Mortality*, containing advice to believers troubled by the enormity of the disaster.

Cornelius died in 253. His short-lived successor, Lucius, was followed in 254 by Stephen, who, as bishop of Rome, adopted policies offensive to Cyprian. When the Spanish churches of Merida and Leon deposed and replaced their bishops for offences classed as idolatrous, the deposed bishops appealed to Stephen, who upheld their cases. Their opponents appealed successfully to Cyprian, who criticized Stephen in a council of African bishops. Similarly, the bishop of Arles in Gaul, Marcian, supported the rigorist policy of Novatian, but Stephen was reluctant to allow his deposition by colleagues: Cyprian rebuked Stephen by letter. But the chief dispute, unresolved when Stephen died in 257 and Cyprian in 258, concerned baptism. Faced with Novatian's denial of all baptisms save those of his own churches, Stephen claimed that this was totally new, and that even heretics recognized each other's baptisms. The believer could only be baptized once, and if it was in an unorthodox or schismatic community, they were traditionally admitted to the Catholic Church by imposition of hands for penance. Cyprian claimed on the basis of past practice that only the true, Catholic Church could give valid baptism: even the formally correct sacraments of Novatianists were demonic, not spiritual. Penitent heretics and schismatics must be baptized (or as some might say, rebaptized). Cyprian won the support of Firmillian in Cappadocian Caesarea, an area where *Montanist baptisms had in the past been repudiated by councils on similar grounds. This dispute remained unresolved when the protagonists died. Cyprian's public execution under Valerian in 258 added prestige to the policies he had espoused. The baptismal controversy was to re-emerge as a chief issue in the Donatist schism of the fourth century, when the church generally adopted the Roman position and recognized any baptism received in the name of the Trinity.

Cyprian saw the church as held together historically and geographically by the episcopate: the believer was one with Christ by communion with a lawful bishop. The church could only be one, and outside it there was no salvation. Hence, sacramental acts by Novatianists or lapsed or dissident clergy were meaningless or diabolic; they breached the law of love. Cyprian cites the uniqueness of Peter among the apostles as representing the unity of the church. The text of *On the Unity of the Catholic Church* 4–5 comes in various versions, some seeming to support Roman papal claims. This interpretation, however, is now rejected – for example by Bévénot. Cyprian's policies and councils mark a development in the casuistry of penance and reconciliation, as churches reacted to the disaster of 249–50. His works provide valuable details of sacramental and liturgical developments: early baptism and communion of infants, and the assimilation of the Eucharist to public sacrifice and of the bishopric to the Old Testament priesthood. His episcopalianism, combined with his disputes with Rome, have made Cyprian useful to Anglican apologists.

STUART G. HALL

FURTHER READING: *For texts and bibliography see:* CPL nos. 38–67; CSEL 3.1–3; CCSL 3, 3A, 3B. *Annotated English versions:* Maurice Bévénot, *De Lapsis and De Ecclesiae Catholicae unitate* (OECT; Oxford, 1971); *The Letters of St Cyprian* (trans. G.W. Clarke; ACW 43–4, 46–7; New York, 1984–89); James Stevenson, *A New Eusebius* (new edn rev. by W.H.C. Frend; London, 1987), nos. 192–246. *Studies with bibliographies:* Maurice Bévénot, 'Cyprian von Karthago', *Th Real* 8 (1981), pp. 246–54; Michael M. Sage, *Cyprian* (Patristic Monograph Series 1; Cambridge, MA, 1975); J. Jayakiran Sebastian, '...*Baptisma Unum in Sancta Ecclesia...*': A Theological Appraisal of the Baptismal Controversy in the Work and Writings of Cyprian of Carthage* (Delhi, 1997).

Cyril of Alexandria (378–444)

Cyril was one of the most powerful leaders of Christian Egypt in the early Byzantine period, and one of the ablest and most influential of the Alexandrian school of theologians. Although the churches of Rome and Syria would demand additional nuances to his scheme at Chalcedon in 451, especially in terms of abandoning the concept of a single physis, it was substantially his Christological doctrine which became established (not without considerable controversy both at the time and afterwards) as the bedrock of the ecumenical teaching of early Christianity, after the councils of Ephesus in 431 (and 449), *Chalcedon in 451 and Constantinople II in 553.

Cyril's early education was patronized by his uncle Theophilus, the archbishop of Alexandria (385–412), and his skills in rhetoric are evident in his work. His knowledge of the previous patristic tradition is reflective, but limited to a few favoured authorities: particularly Gregory Nazianzen and *Athanasius. Cyril was one of the first controversialists to cite written authorities from earlier theologians as evidence of the 'mind of the church', the earlier authentic tradition which he claimed to maintain, and after him this became a standard method of Christian argumentation in the classical period.

In 412 Cyril succeeded his uncle as archbishop. His first six years were turbulent. He had to deal with incidents of riot between Christian and Jewish factions, and continuing tensions between Christians and the old religion's intelligentsia. Cyril continued, though less provocatively than his uncle, an active missionary and apologetic campaign among the common folk who remained devotees of the old gods, particularly Isis. Cyril's control over the violent life of an antique city was certainly not even-handed, but the considerable vilification of his name and character that arose after the nineteenth century is exaggerated. The continuing *animus* against him in popularist scholarship is outmoded, but it served its purpose in allowing the scholarly retrieval of the writings of the Antiochene school which he had overshadowed.

In 428, Cyril was brought to the centre of the world stage. In that year the Syrian *Nestorius was appointed archbishop of Constantinople, and he immediately began a campaign to establish Antiochene Christology as a standard of reference. Nestorius's preferred theologians, Diodore of Tarsus (d. c. 390) and *Theodore Mopsuestia (c. 350–428), had long stood in vigorous opposition to aspects of the Alexandrian Christological tradition which they castigated for 'losing the humanity' of Jesus in the face of an overwhelming advent of divine power in the process of incarnation. In turn, the Syrians witnessed a separatist tendency in describing Christology. Whereas some earlier thinkers had favoured a model of union to describe the incarnation, such as *krasis* (the blending of wine and water), as being the conception best suited to evoke the strong symbiosis of human and divine in Jesus, the Syrians preferred to stress the abiding distinctiveness of the double characteristics. They argued that the relation of the two

should be seen as a profound associative relation (*synapheia*), rather than a union (*henosis*). Their unwavering suspicion of union language caused most Syrians, until late in the debate, to regard Cyril as no more than the heretic *Apollinaris (c. 315–392) redivivus. In fact, Cyril was rescuing the Alexandrian scheme from Apollinaris's understatement of the humanity of Christ, and teaching not the absorption or replacement of the human character of Jesus by the deity of the Logos, but rather its transfiguration. Such a transfiguration Cyril posited as the essential mystery of the incarnation, which was itself the dynamic principle of Christian soteriology – the root motive and entire foundation of the divine advent in Jesus. For Cyril, what he thought to be the insinuation of a double subject in the one Christ by Syrian thinkers utterly destroyed this dynamic of the 'deification' of the human race. He saw the process as initiated personally, concretely (*hypostatically*), even 'physically' in the Logos-made-man, and thence distributed collectively in the process of 'deification by grace' offered to the Christian believer. The Eucharistic mystery became his central paradigm for such transformation thought. He unwaveringly insisted on the single subjectivity of the Word of God assuming flesh, and his thought therefore excluded the possibility of human person in the divine Christ, although he affirmed a full human nature. He met his opponents' objections by the argument that the Word not only assumed human flesh (Apollinaris's scheme) but also a genuinely human life, including its limitations and sufferings. He refused, however, to identify the manner of the life-process (divine or human) with the concept of personal subjectivity, which for him was always none other than the divine Word acting directly in Christ. Because of this intensely close involvement of the Word in his own human life, Cyril insisted on the theological validity of phrases such as the 'Suffering of the Impassible One', which used apparent paradoxes to bring home his message that the Word was the sole subject-referent in all Christ's acts. His logical foundation for this form of speaking (*The Communion of Idioms*) was that the appropriation of the limited by the unlimited was, in Christ, concurrently a genuine experience of limitation and an exercise of divine power and freedom. It was the *kenosis* (emptying out) of God which was simultaneously the exaltation of humanity.

The theological controversy between Constantinople and Alexandria came to a head at the Council of Ephesus (431), but even after Cyril had secured Nestorius's condemnation there, the Syrian church continued to be suspicious of his thinking. Only in 433 did a compromise emerge between the churches (Epistle 39 in Cyril's *opera*) which secured, to mutual satisfaction, the principle of duplicity of nature and singleness of Person in the God-Man. The terms of this Christology continued to agitate the church for generations to come (the *Monophysite schism). Much of the twentieth-century European Christology has reopened similar issues, relating to the subjective unity of Christ, and the nature of incarnational 'models' in theology. There has been lively scholarly debate as to the enduring significance of Cyril's contribution, but his importance as one of the leading theologians of the patristic era cannot be denied.

J.A. McGuckin

FURTHER READING: E. Gebremedhin, *Life-Giving Blessing: An Inquiry into the Eucharistic Doctrine of Cyril of Alexandria* (Uppsala, 1977); L. Koen, *The Saving Passion: Incarnational and Soteriological Thought in Cyril of Alexandria's Commentary on the Gospel According to St John* (Uppsala, 1991); J.A. McGuckin, *St Cyril of Alexandria: The Christological Controversy* (Leiden, 1994); J.S. Romanides, 'St Cyril's "One Physis or Hypostasis of God the Logos Incarnate and Chalcedon"', *Gr Or Th Rev* 10 (1964–65), pp. 82–107.

Cyril of Jerusalem (c. 315–86)

Bishop of Jerusalem from 348. Cyril's birthplace is unknown, though it is usually assumed to have been in that city or its environs. He was initially suspected of Arianism, but soon after his consecration he became involved in a protracted dispute with local Arians and was three times expelled from his see as a result. His longest period of exile was from 367 to 378, after which he took part in the first council of Constantinople (381), where his see was recognized as the fifth of the great patriarchates. He is generally supposed to have died on 18 March 386, the date kept as his feast in both the Eastern and the Western churches.

We know Cyril chiefly for his 24 *Catechetical Lectures*, most of which he delivered in the Church of the Holy Sepulchre and which were taken down in shorthand by one of his hearers. The text is therefore a report of his teaching, rather than his own composition, and it is not certain when the lectures were delivered, though 350 is the most widely-accepted date. The *Catechetical Lectures* are of great importance because they form a primer of Christian teaching, designed to instruct new converts and young believers in their faith. They have a systematic character which is lacking in most patristic writings, and are an invaluable source for our understanding of liturgical practice at Jerusalem in the mid-fourth century. Furthermore, as Cyril was not innovating in his teaching but merely explaining what was common practice, we can assume that what he says represents a much wider consensus in the church of his time.

Cyril concentrates on the meaning of the sacraments of baptism (including what we would now call 'confirmation') and the Eucharist, which he places in the context of Holy Week and Easter. It is quite clear from the text that he was not an Arian, and much of his argument was taken up with a refutation of Arian ideas, though it is noticeable that he avoided using the controversial term *homoousios*. This was probably not because he disagreed with it, but because he did not want to erect unnecessary theological barriers against those who needed to hear and be persuaded by the pro-Nicene Christological argument. Furthermore, in his defence of the Trinity, Cyril's main concern was to avoid Sabellianism, and he may have felt that the word *homoousios* might have lent itself to a Sabellian interpretation.

Cyril's description of baptism is a highly developed sacramental approach, which focuses on the principle of regeneration accompanied by the seal of the Holy Spirit. Baptism, for him, is the key to the Christian life because it represents the death of sin, the ransom of the captive and the new birth, which is the inheritance of the saints in light. In his Eucharistic teaching, Cyril puts forward the idea that in the act of consecration there is a spiritual change in the elements of bread and wine which is brought about by a descent of the Holy Spirit onto the elements (the so-called 'epiclesis'). Because of this idea he is frequently regarded as the originator of the doctrine of transubstantiation, a belief which is reinforced by the fact that he regarded the Eucharist as a 'sacrifice'. However, it has to be said that much of Cyril's language is poetic imagery as much as it is theological affirmation, and it is certainly anachronistic to attribute medieval Catholic beliefs to him. It is more accurate to regard him as a forerunner of the mystical theology of the Eastern church which generally avoids such categories of thought, though even there it is all too easy to read him anachronistically.

In modern times Cyril has often been appealed to by those interested in both liturgical renewal and in ecumenism, and it has even been suggested that his approach might form the basis for Christian reunion, particularly on the highly sensitive matter of the sacraments. However, the tendency for all sides to appropriate him to serve their own ends makes it very difficult to reach a common agreement about what his teaching actually was, and how it relates to modern beliefs on the same subjects.

GERALD BRAY

FURTHER READING: *Texts:* W.K. Reischl and J. Rupp (Munich, 1860); J.-P. Migne (PG, XXXIII), pp. 331–1180; A. Piédnagel and P. Paris, *Cyrille de Jérusalem* (SC, 126; Paris, 1966). *English translation:* R.W. Church and E.H. Gifford, *NPNF*², VII (1894), pp. 1–157. *Studies:* G. Dix, *The Shape of the Liturgy* (London, 1945), pp. 187–209; 349–54; R.C. Gregg, 'Cyril of Jerusalem and the Arians', in *Arianism: Historical and Theological Reassessments* (Cambridge, MA, 1985), pp. 85–109; A.A. Stephenson, 'The Lenten Catechetical Syllabus in Fourth-century Jerusalem' (TS, XV; 1954), pp. 103–16; 'St Cyril of Jerusalem and the Alexandrian Heritage' (TS, XV; 1954), pp. 573–93.

Czech Brethren
(*Unitas Fratrum Bohemorum*)

In the autumn of 1447 (or perhaps in the spring of 1448), a group of *Hussites moved from Prague to Kunvald in East Bohemia, to a fairly isolated place surrounded by forests. They were disappointed with the developments within the Hussite (Utraquist) Church which seemed to compromise the radical biblical vision of its origins. Their intention was to test the possibilities of a truly Christian existence in strict obedience of the biblical commandments as interpreted in the Sermon on the Mount. Their leader was Gregor of Prague (d. 1474), who defined as follows their motive and aim: 'We have resolved to live and to govern ourselves in accordance with the Scriptures and with the Lord Jesus Christ and his apostles as our pattern – in patience, modesty, forbearance and love of our enemies, in well-doing and in prayer for all.'

At the beginning, the Brethren were protected by the Hussite Archbishop Jan Rokycana and the Hussite king George of Poděbrady. But that protection was withdrawn when they broke with the established church by election of their own priests. Royal decrees were then issued declaring the Brethren to be heretics. But the persecution failed to break them. In the spirit of the radical Hussite pacifist Petr Chelčický (c. 1380–1450), they saw their Christian discipleship as a striving for a 'greater justice', as a narrow way very different from the prevailing lifestyles in a traditional 'Christian society'. A brother had to refuse to participate in political life with its instruments of repression in law, government and administration. Above all, military service was ruled out for members of the Unity. Nor could a brother be a merchant or innkeeper. The professions favoured were those that met some basic human need: preferably farming and sheep-rearing, as well as elementary craftsmanship.

This way of life was possible in Kunvald and other rural settlements. But the Unity grew and moved into the towns. Quite a few of their fellow citizens were attracted by the credibility of this resolute Christian way of life. Ought the new members to be simply taken away from their customary living conditions or was it possible to obediently follow the law of Christ even in conditions different from rural simplicities?

Behind these urgent practical questions, the fundamental theological problem was emerging. How was the 'greater justice' to be understood? The 'older Brethren', including Gregor of Prague, were inclined to interpret it as the call to an ascetic lifestyle. But here the 'younger Brethren' raised some doubts. As a protest against secularized, tepid Christianity such a lifestyle was quite understandable. But in the light of the gospel, the alternative to 'cheap grace' can hardly be found only in the direction of an intensified asceticism with its temptation toward 'works-righteousness'. Certainly grace is binding and costly but it is liberation and not compulsion; it is joy and peace in the Holy Spirit. That Spirit leads not only 'into the woods'. Its demands should be matched obediently also in the towns and cities.

It was Lukas of Prague (1458–1528), the 'Second Founder' of the Unity, who showed the majority of Brethren the new way in readiness to enter into the more complex conditions of an urban society. This readiness did not mean just conformity to prevailing practices. The Brethren and Sisters were to remain faithful to the basic insights of their beginnings. They kept their discipline of grace and regarded this emphasis as their particular *charisma*. But that discipline was to be practised not in a wilful isolation but rather in solidarity with their contemporaries.

This new openness had ecumenical implications. Czech Brethren were keen to enter into an ecumenical dialogue. They knew that the church of Christ is greater that any given confession. This was the reason why they called themselves consistently the 'unity' but not the 'church'. A particularly intensive and fruitful dialogue developed between Lukas and *Luther about the relation between justification and justice in Christian life. Lukas agreed with Luther: justification by faith alone is the foundation of our salvation. But Lukas and the whole Unity emphasized more strongly than Luther that the works of gratitude and obedience are inseparable from faith. The joy of justification and concern for justice go hand in hand. This emphasis later led the Brethren closer to the Helvetic (Swiss) reformation. Many of the gifted students of the Unity pursued their studies at the reformed universities like Basle or Geneva.

Even in new spiritual and sociological circumstances, the Czech Brethren remained a tiny minority. Nevertheless, with their combination of deep piety and a creative involvement in the intellectual and cultural life of their nation they exercised an astonishingly effective wider influence. Although for most of its history merely tolerated and even persecuted, the Unity educated a considerable number of the leading figures of Czech history in the sixteenth and seventeenth centuries: in particular Jan Blahoslav (1523–71) and, finally and incomparably, *Jan Amos Komenský (1592–1670). A magnificent translation of the Bible, the Kralice Bible, a rich treasury of spiritual hymns, and also intensive and pioneering educational work, all made the Unitas Fratrum a most outstanding and creative contributer to Czech ecclesiastical and cultural history.

The severe Hapsburg counter-reformation after 1620 put an end to the free life of Czech Protestant churches in Bohemia and Moravia. For a generation, the Czech Brethren carried on their work in exile. Their legacy was taken up with new (pietistic) emphases by Count N.L. Zinzendorf in Herrnhut (1722). Moravian churches in many countries as well as evangelical churches in the Czech Republic look to the 'old Unity' as to their 'fathers and mothers in faith'.

JAN MILIČ LOCHMAN

FURTHER READING: J.T. Müller, *Geschichte der Böhmischen Brüder* (3 vols.; Herrnhut, 1922–31); R. Říčan and A. Molnár, *The History of the Unity of Brethren* (trans. C.D. Crews; Bethlehem, PA, 1992).

Dale, Robert William (1829–95)

Dale was born on 1 December 1829 in London and died on 13 March 1895 in Birmingham. The son of a London tradesman, he was educated at elementary schools, and for the Congregational ministry at Spring Hill College, Birmingham (1847–53), where he took a London University MA, securing a gold medal for philosophy in 1853. In 1877 he gave the Lyman Beecher Lectures at Yale and also received a DD from Yale; he was given an LL D by Glasgow in 1883. (He never used the title 'Revd', and he used 'Dr' with some reluctance only after 1883.) Dale became assistant to the Reverend John Angell James of Carr's Lane Congregational Church, Birmingham, in 1852. He became co-pastor in 1854 and then pastor when James died in 1859, remaining there until his own death. Four churches were planted elsewhere in Birmingham during his ministry. He was chairman of the Congregational Union in 1869 and first president of the International Congregational Council when it was formed in London in 1891.

Dale reacted strongly against the subjectivism of much contemporary evangelical theology and spirituality, including the popular book *The Anxious Inquirer*, written by James. In 1855 he preached a series of sermons on Romans, criticizing the cruder aspects of a penal substitutionary understanding of the atonement. Though influenced by the work of Anglicans such as *Coleridge, *Maurice, Jowett and Robertson, he also sought to reaffirm the significance of earlier theologians such as *Athanasius, Gregory Nazianzen and *Anselm. This was reflected in his Congregational Lecture, *The Atonement* (1875, translated into French and German), which became a classic. Dale emphasized the objective character of the redemption wrought by Christ, but he criticized understandings of it framed in essentially legal categories (especially the idea of Christ's death as a ransom for sin paid to God or the devil), which he felt had deformed both Catholic and Protestant theology. The atonement was more an act of God's love than of God's justice; hence it was vital that the one who suffered was the Son of God, 'God manifest in the flesh'; and he affirmed the significance of the fact that Christ suffered for the sins of others. The Christological emphasis in this view was a criticism both of *Unitarianism and evangelical individualism. (At a practical level, however, Dale was not prepared to exclude from church membership anyone who professed Unitarianism but manifested clear faith in Christ.)

Dale was also critical of both the idea of election associated with *Calvinism and of the emphasis of the evangelical revival on personal experience, which he thought had led to a neglect of the significance of the church and of ethics. He regarded the Declaration of Faith of the Congregational Union of 1832 as manifesting a more subjective approach to the sacraments than the Savoy Declaration of 1658; but he supported the reaffirmation of evangelical principles as the basis of the Union in 1878. His belief in the independence of the local church was reflected in his *Manual of Congregational Principles* (1884) and *History of English Congregationalism* (1907). He opposed state support for religion, and he was prominent in the Nonconformist campaign against the Education Act of 1870 because it allowed publicly funded religious education.

Such support for the secular principle in public life may seem surprising in view of Dale's urging that local and national government should embody moral principles in legislation – 'the civic gospel', as it was called. However, it was based on the view that Christians should campaign on such issues as citizens, rather than as members of churches. As a Birmingham citizen Dale was prominent in educational policy, serving on the school board and the governing body of King Edward's School. But he was as critical of Nonconformist involvement in politics as churches, as he was of the Church of England. In 1886 he sided with his friend, Joseph Chamberlain, rather than with the Prime Minister, William Gladstone, when the Liberal party split over Home Rule for Ireland. After that he took little part in the public life of the Congregational Union, which supported Gladstone. But he was not a secularist in any modern sense, since he believed that 'Everyday Business' was 'a Divine Calling' (to quote the title of one of his essays). In his preaching and in the disciplined life of his congregation, he spelled out the ethical implications of Christianity for modern business. The effectiveness of his civic gospel depended on the quality of those responsible for local government.

Dale's career spans the period when English Nonconformity emerged from the back streets to reach its maximum influence in public life. Based in the leading Congregational church in one of Britain's most important provincial towns, Dale epitomized the complexity and ambiguity of Nonconformity's relationship with the new democratic state. He was a premier preacher in an age of famous preachers. His preaching affected the lives of several who framed municipal policy. He supported the move of Spring Hill College from Birmingham to Oxford (as Mansfield College) in order that Congregationalism should have a voice at the heart of the ancient universities after the University Tests Act of 1871 (and also secured a modification in the doctrinal statements required under its trust deed). His son became a Cambridge don and later first vice-chancellor of Liverpool University. He left a later age to wrestle with the question of whether Nonconformity (and indeed Christianity) can ever be totally integrated with national culture.

DAVID M. THOMPSON

FURTHER READING: *Texts: The Life and Letters of John Angell James* (London, 1861); *The Atonement* (London, 1875); *Nine Lectures on Preaching* (New York, 1877); *The Evangelical Revival and other Sermons* (London, 1880); *The Laws of Christ for Common Life* (London, 1884); *Manual of Congregational Principles* (London, 1884); *Essays and Addresses* (London, 1899); *History of English Congregationalism* (ed. A.W.W. Dale; London, 1907). *Studies:* A.W.W. Dale, *The Life of R.W. Dale of Birmingham* (London, 1899); C. Binfield (ed.), *The Cross and the City: Essays in Commemoration of Robert William Dale, 1829–1895* (London, 2000).

Darby, John Nelson (1800–82)

An evangelical Anglican clergyman who seceded to become the most prominent leader of the Brethren (often miscalled 'Plymouth Brethren') and the effective founder of *Dispensationalism and its distinctive form of premillennialism. Caught up in contemporary excitement over unfulfilled prophecy, and disillusioned with current evangelicalism, Darby gave himself to unremitting Bible study and reflection leading to tireless writing and teaching on three continents (he never married). Disagreements with fellow leaders (e.g. B.W. Newton and G. Müller) split the nascent movement (1845–48) into 'Darbyite' or 'Exclusive', and 'Open' Brethren. In 1881, towards the end of his life, the first of numerous divisions took place within his own section of the Brethren. Though Darby's voluminous writings were

obscure, he was well served by popularizers, notably C.H. Mackintosh and C.I. Scofield.

For Darby, the Scriptures were divinely inspired and supremely authoritative. He stressed the believer's union with Christ and constantly reiterated Pauline and Johannine themes. His emphasis on sanctification as a 'state' rather than a process, and the sharp distinction he drew between the believer's old and new natures, came under frequent criticism. Nevertheless, he retained much of his initial *Calvinism.

His dispensational approach made him distinguish the church as the bride of Christ from Israel as God's earthly people. As an organized structure, the church apostatized before the end of the apostolic era (the church is 'in ruins'), and any attempt to restore it to its pristine condition is both doomed to failure and a mark of apostasy. In such a situation, the believers' resource is to claim Christ's abiding promise to be with them when they meet 'in his name', and to obey his unqualified command to break bread in remembrance of him on a regular basis. Darby never ceased to hold in tension the concept of the oneness of all true believers and the need to separate from evil which he once described as 'God's principle of unity'.

Though Darby insisted on open worship around the Lord's Table and stressed the role of the Holy Spirit in indwelling the church, he came to believe that most of the gifts described in 1 Corinthians 12 and 14 were foundational. Of abiding importance were the gifts of evangelist, pastor and teacher (the last two often conjoined in the same person). He exercised each.

His eschatology revolved around the idea of a two-stage second advent. This will commence with the secret rapture of the church to save it from the seven years of tribulation about to be unleashed on the Jewish people. It will conclude with the return of Christ in glory, together with his church, to initiate the millennial kingdom which, like every other dispensation, will end in failure due to the inevitable rebellion of man. The last judgement and the eternal state will follow.

HAROLD H. ROWDON

FURTHER READING: *Texts: The Collected Writings of J.N. Darby* (ed. W. Kelly; 34 vols.; London, 1867); *Letters of J.N.D.* (n.d.). *Studies:* H.H. Rowdon, *The Origins of the Brethren* (London, 1967); M. Weremchuk, *John Nelson*

Darby (Neptune, NJ, 1992); J.P. Callahan, *Primitivist Piety: The Ecclesiology of the Early Plymouth Brethren* (Lanham, MD, 1996).

Deism

A definition of 'Deism' is hard to come by and is perhaps best given by means of a historical description of it and through examining its proponents. Deism arose in the mid-sixteenth century out of a sense of dissatisfaction with traditional Christianity – with its basis on authority and Scripture, and particularly its foundation on divine revelation. By the 1750s the movement was effectively a spent force, though its influence would extend far beyond its own life. Three main ideas can be identified with it. First, true Christianity is consistent with reason, natural religion and morality. Whatever is incompatible with these is to be jettisoned. Second, true religion is primarily moral, individual and social. Third, enlightened reason is sceptical of all claims of supernatural revelation and miracles – later radical deists rejected these altogether.

The reformations of the sixteenth century had failed to answer all the questions and resolve all the problems of the church. If anything, they created newer and more problems. Instead of being reformed, the church was now more divided than ever and acrimonious theological controversies multiplied: controversy surrounded *Puritanism in Britain, while throughout Europe *Arminians and *Calvinists attacked each other. The seventeenth and eighteenth centuries also witnessed many religious wars: Protestants fought each other in the English Civil War in the 1640s, while in continental Europe Protestant fought Catholic in the Thirty Years War (1618–48). The Protestant *Reformation also inaugurated an intellectual crisis in that they questioned the long-accepted sources of authority and knowledge and also the established methods of thinking, as well as strengthening the belief in the individual's right to decide on such matters. Then, around the middle of the seventeenth century, a new cultural mood known as the *Enlightenment swept Europe. Deism's earliest exponents displayed all the traces of thinkers who sought to understand the Christian religion in terms of Enlightenment categories, particularly its emphases on the omnicompetence of human reason, the attraction of natural religion, a growing scepticism towards traditional institutions and traditions. All this took place against the backdrop of developments in science most closely linked with Sir Isaac Newton (1642–1727), which saw the world as governed by inviolable laws. The new science understood the universe to be like a clockwork machine, created by God but not necessarily requiring his continued involvement. This often led those influenced by Deism to accept God's transcendence but deny his immanence.

Deism developed the thinking of earlier schools of thought (see Brown, 1990, pp. 166–203). The first was that of the late sixteenth-century Christian Sceptics (Pyrrhonists), who argued that experience and reason are unreliable, and that the only attitude to religion was either one of scepticism, where nothing could be established with certainty, or fideism, by which ideas could be accepted by faith. Then there were the rationalist philosophies associated with *René Descartes (1596–1650), *Benedict Spinoza (1632–77) and G.W. Leibniz (1646–1716), which sought to answer the sceptics 'by providing an account of reality, which would show the universe to be a rational whole, accessible to rational thought' (Brown, 1990, p. 173). Thomas Hobbes (1588–1679) combined a high view of reason with scepticism in the development of what is frequently interpreted as his secular philosophy, which is often understood to have excluded appeals to experience and supernatural revelation, while the Cambridge Platonists, who gathered around Benjamin Whichcote (1609–83), contended that reason would answer the materialistic atheism of the likes of Hobbes and the religious fanaticism which they derided.

The father of English Deism was Lord Edward Herbert of Cherbury (1583–1648). In his *On Truth* (1624), he outlined what was later called natural religion. He criticized traditional Christianity's appeal to special revelation, its divisions over doctrine and what he viewed as irrationalism, and in their stead he offered five common notions of religion which he believed to be universal, rational and in accord with nature: belief in God as the Supreme Being; that God is to be worshipped; that virtue is the most important part of worship; that peoples' vices and crimes need to be expiated by repentance; and that there is reward and punishment after this life. All religious truth had to be judged according to these five principles and those which fell short of them, such as the Trinity and deity of Christ, were treated with scepticism.

> The importance of *De Veritate* is that it made it possible for subsequent thinkers to profess belief in God, yet to abjure revealed religion and established Christianity; the liberating effects of such a possibility for thinkers immersed in the daring discoveries of the new scientific age should not be underestimated. (Byrne, p. 105)

Another important influence on Deism was the work of *John Locke (1632–1704), who, while clearly influencing the movement, even making it possible, was not himself a deist as he rejected its more radical views (so Hefelbower). In *The Reasonableness of Christianity* (1695) and other writings, Locke sought to show that many Christian beliefs based on divine revelation were consonant with reason, though he remained vague on the Trinity and deity of Christ. In his treatment of Christianity as a matter of intellectual belief he inverted the traditional view that reason served faith (as in *Anselm and *Aquinas): 'whatever God has revealed is true and must be the object of our faith; but what actually counts as having been revealed by God, *that* must be judged by reason' (Byrne, p. 107). So, while Locke's defence of 'reasonable' Christianity was not Deism as such, it opened the way for its development by opening a gap between revealed religion and that which could be derived from reason without special revelation (Byrne, p. 108).

When the Licensing Act lapsed in 1694, freedom of thought was no longer curtailed and an increasing number who had become disillusioned with and critical of traditional Christianity were able to express and publish their opinions, though they could still be prosecuted under the libel and blasphemy laws. In 1696, the Irishman John Toland (1670–1722) published his *Christianity not Mysterious, Showing that there is Nothing in the Gospel Contrary to Reason, nor above it; And that No Christian Doctrine can properly be Call'd a Mystery*, which portrayed Jesus as a preacher of a simple, moralistic and social religion. He regarded Locke as his teacher, but while the latter disowned him, Toland felt he was carrying to their natural conclusion Locke's views on religion. His basic principle was 'whoever reveals anything, that is, whoever tells us something we did not know before, *his words must be intelligible, and the matter possible*. This rule holds good, let *God* or *Man* be the

Revealer' (in Gay, p. 61). He classified as mysteries anything which reason regarded as unintelligible and impossible and, as intrusions of pagan and priestly ideas, did not belong to true religion or authentic Christianity, for they would require the sacrifice of the intellect which violated the image of God in humanity. That he placed reason over revelation also reflected his rejection of the role of the Holy Spirit in revelation. Toland developed these views into a form of pantheism, a term which he first coined. He labelled religions that change over time, including Christianity, positive religions that must be judged according to the natural religion of reason, which is eternal and immutable.

In *Discourse on Free Thinking* (1713), Anthony Collins (1676–1729) argued that freedom of thought alone was sufficient for discovering truth while raising serious doubts on the authority of the Bible. Later, in his *Discourse on the Grounds and Reasons for the Christian Religion* (1724) and *The Scheme of Literal Prophecy Consider'd* (1727), he denied that prophecies like Isaiah 7:14 and Hosea 11:1 were originally prophecies of Christ, but that they were fulfilled in the time of the prophets themselves. They were, therefore, not supernatural predictions of Jesus, and this meant Christianity was based on allegory, not history. Collins' intention to examine miracles, however, did not materialize, but was taken up by Thomas Woolston (1670–1727), whose six *Discourses on the Miracles of our Saviour* (1727–29) asserted that the miracles were not historical events, but allegories similar to those identified by Collins' study of prophecy. What was more, if the healing miracles of Jesus were genuine, then they must have a natural explanation. He explained the resurrection as the result of the disciples having stolen Jesus' body after bribing the guards. What was a miracle was the belief in the resurrection.

Deism's definitive statement was penned by the Oxford scholar Matthew Tindal (1655–1733), whose *Christianity as Old as the Creation; or, the Gospel a Republication of the Religion of Nature* (1730) became known as 'the Bible of Deism', in which he contended that the purpose of the gospel is not to bring about an objective redemption but to demonstrate the universal natural law that is the foundation and content of all true religion, thereby freeing humanity from superstitious religion. He took the work of Locke and Toland to its logical conclusion, that true Christianity is a rational ethical system against a theistic background. He believed that when traditional Christianity and rational religion clashed, it was the unacceptable doctrines of the former which had to be excised, for instance the Fall, original guilt and the atonement. Though he did not automatically dismiss all claims of special revelations and miracles, he made them dependent on natural religion, their role being to confirm in special ways what was already known through reason. While he considered himself a 'Christian deist' he nevertheless sought to demonstrate 'the impossibility of reconciling the petty and arbitrary God of Revelation with the impartial and magnanimous God of Natural Religion' (Mossner, p. 77).

The deists incurred the wrath of many. Toland's work was highly praised by many of the educated elite of Europe (Byrne, p. 109), but it was also roundly condemned by the church and many leading churchmen. Copies of Toland's book were even burned by the Irish Parliament, while Woolston was imprisoned for blasphemy and spent the remainder of his life serving his sentence. Bishop Thomas Sherlock (1678–1761) answered Woolston in his *Tryal of the Witnesses of the Resurrection* (1729), in which he developed some of Locke's work on the feasibility of testimony. Sherlock drew attention to the fact that the human knowledge of nature is limited and that while human experience makes resurrection highly unlikely, logically we are not able to say it is impossible. But the most important reply to Deism was from the Anglican priest *Joseph Butler (1692–1752). His *The Analogy of Religion, Natural and Revealed, to the Constitution and Course of Nature* (1736) did more to discredit Deism than any other book. While he agreed that there were difficulties associated with accepting special revelation, he observed that there were equally difficulties in the deists' view that the universe is a coherent and orderly system. As both positions were based on probabilities, this enabled him to argue that to an infinite intelligence everything is certain, but to humanity, who does not have this infinite intelligence, probability is the guide to life. As with Sherlock, this had implications for miracles. But the end of Deism came with *David Hume's *Natural History of Religion* (1757), which pointed out that the arguments used to prove the reasonableness of natural religion were inductively very weak, and included the observation that savages were not enlightened deists.

Deism was a numerically small and relatively short-lived movement of English thinkers. However, their influence has been far out of proportion to their numbers and continues to be felt in contemporary theology. While Deism was never widely accepted in Britain, it became very influential in France where it was taken up by Voltaire (François-Marie Arouet, 1694–1778), Jean-Jacques Rousseau (1712–78) and the Encyclopedists (see Brown, 1990, pp. 285–99). In Germany, Tindal's work was used by H.S. Reimarus (1694–1768), whose fragments were posthumously published by G.E. Lessing (1729–81). *Immanuel Kant's (1724–1804) *Religion within the Limits of Reason Alone* (1793) presents Deism from the perspective of transcendental Idealism (see Brown, 1990, pp. 301–30). The deists' legacy also includes the origins of biblical criticism (see Reventlow; Morgan and Barton, *passim*), principally in its reluctance to accept the intervention of the divine into history, not least in the rejection of explaining away of the miraculous. Deism also gave rise to the quests for the historical Jesus (Brown, 1985, pp. 29–55; Morgan and Barton, pp. 52–57). The thought of Spinoza, the Jewish pantheist whose philosophy was based on his study of the Old Testament and the rejection of special revelation, was the main source of Einstein's knowledge of Deism and continues to be a major influence in twentieth- and twenty-first-century French theology and philosophy, such as that of Henri Bergson. In their opposition to miracles the deists anticipated the views of David Hume (1711–76) (see Brown, 1984, pp. 47–100) and the secular interpretation of history exemplified by Edward Gibbons' *The Decline and Fall of the Roman Empire* (Brown, 1990, p. 203). The deists also influenced the founding fathers of the American constitution, Benjamin Franklin, Thomas Jefferson and Thomas Paine, and their successors founded the *Unitarian Church in Britain in 1744 and in the United States in 1785, with its seminary at Harvard Divinity School. Deism also led to the development of *liberal Protestant theology in Europe and North America and provided many of its presuppositions.

ANTHONY R. CROSS

FURTHER READING: C. Brown, *Christianity and Western Thought: A History of Philosophers, Ideas and Movements*, I: *From the Ancient World to the Age of the Enlightenment* (Leicester, 1990); *Jesus in European Protestant Thought, 1778–1860* (Durham, 1985); *Miracles and the Critical Mind* (Exeter, 1984); J.M.

Byrne, *Religion and the Enlightenment: From Descartes to Kant* (Louisville, 1996); P. Byrne, *Nature Religion and the Nature of Religion: The Legacy of Deism* (London, 1989); F. Copleston, *A History of Philosophy*, I: *Hobbes to Hume* (London, 1968); G.R. Cragg, *From Puritanism to the Age of Reason: A Study of Changes in Religious Thought within the Church of England 1660 to 1700* (Cambridge, 1950); *Reason and Authority in the Eighteenth Century* (Cambridge, 1964); W.L. Craig, *The Historical Argument for the Resurrection during the Deist Controversy* (Lewiston, 1985); S.H. Daniel, *John Toland: His Methods, Manners, and Mind* (Kingston / Montreal, 1984); P. Gay (ed.), *Deism: An Anthology* (Princeton, 1968); P. Harrison, *'Religion' and the Religions in the English Enlightenment* (Cambridge, 1990); S.G. Hefelbower, *The Relation of John Locke to English Deism* (Chicago, 1918); R. Morgan and J. Barton, *Biblical Interpretation* (Oxford, 1988); E.C. Mossner, *Bishop Butler and the Age of Reason: A Study in the History of Thought* (New York, 1936); H.G. Reventlow, *The Authority of the Bible and the Rise of the Modern World* (London, 1984); R.E. Sullivan, *John Toland and the Deist Controversy: A Study in Adaptations* (Cambridge, MA, 1982); E.G. Waring (ed.), *Deism and Natural Religion* (New York, 1967).

Demant, Vigo Auguste (1893–1983)

Demant became professor of moral and pastoral theology at the University of Oxford in 1949. This appointment reflects the importance of Demant in England; for about thirty years, from 1930–60, he had a significant following, especially amongst Anglo-Catholics. Demant is best known as the 'thinker' of the Christendom Group. This informal grouping, brought together by Maurice Reckitt, was involved in various publications, including a journal. The group had a significant influence on the thought of *William Temple and T.S. Eliot.

Demant's analysis of society is grounded in natural law. Built into creation, he argues, is a pattern for ethical behaviour appropriate to both individuals and society. Each human person is made in the image of God. This means that humanity is able to transcend nature and the physical world; and the essential nature of humanity has at its centre a spiritual link with, and dependence on, God. When a human person is spirit-centred, then the whole of his or her life settles into an appropriate balance; with each element in the life playing an appropriate role. This means that reason, sexuality, economic elements, etc., are not at the centre of a person's being; but rather they each play an appropriate role around the spiritual centre. The Fall then, for Demant, consists in an elevation of some peripheral element of human life into the centre, thereby displacing the position that the spiritual link with God ought to have. Sin is an attempt to break the dependent link with God. The result is a disordered and unnatural life. This attempt to break the link with God is always unsuccessful. Human existence depends on God. Sin creates a disorder which is always dissatisfying. The spiritual link remains intact, pulling the human person back towards the centre. However, human pride will not settle with the spiritual link reinstated but reacts by swinging to a different element in the periphery.

What is true for the individual is also true for the social whole. There is a natural order for society, with the spiritual dimension at the centre. Human disorder is upsetting the natural order for society, by placing something other than the spiritual at the centre. For example, western society has placed economic life at the centre. However, our unnatural society is a frustrated and dissatisfied society; so there are constant tugs back to the natural order. Humanity, through pride, refuses to recognize our dependence upon God, so we cannot rediscover the natural society. The result is that our society swings from one overemphasis to another, for example, the dialectic from individualism to collectivism.

Given this theological description of the nature of humanity and society, the ethical task is simple. We should apply our theology to contemporary events. This is the task of 'Christian Sociology'. Unlike secular sociology, it assumes the truth of the Christian narrative. In *The Religious Prospect* (1939), Demant applies this analysis to the shift from liberalism to totalitarianism which Europe was facing before World War II. European liberalism is made up of two incompatible elements: the *aims*, which affirm an objective morality and limits to state power; and the *assumptions*, which deny any eternal dimension. Totalitarianism, argues Demant, is simply the logical consequence of the assumptions. In *Religion and the Decline of Capitalism* (1952), Demant applies the analysis to the shift from capitalism to socialism. He sees the shift as a dialectical swing in the search for the balanced natural order. Capitalism represents an overemphasis on the individual and the market; socialism represents an overemphasis on the collective. Both are equally inadequate, because both fail to recognize the spiritual needs of humanity.

Demant's practical solutions to the problems facing modernity have been extensively criticized. He supported Guild Socialism and Social Credit. Guild Socialism was made famous by G.D.H. Cole, who expounded the idea in a volume called *The World of Labour* (1913). Guild Socialism involved the creation of national guilds for each main industry, in which managers and workers would have equal status. Major C.H. Douglas was architect of Social Credit. He spotted the paradox of the 'curse of plenty' (why is it, in a world of such wealth, technological advance and manufacturing success, that there is so much deprivation and poverty?). Douglas then argued that the solution was simple: you must increase the purchasing power of the community by a social dividend. Both Guild Socialism and Social Credit were doomed to failure. However, towards the end of his life, Demant implied that he identified with movements that anticipated the Green Party. He believed that the modern west is using up the resources of the earth much more rapidly than they are reproduced. We need to attend to the natural reproductive ecological system. The social costs of so much industrialization need to be confronted; and the ecological limit to economic growth needs to be acknowledged. In some respects, Demant argued, medieval Christendom was a much more balanced society: the spiritual dependence of human society on God was recognized and human life was much less ecologically destructive.

Despite the fact that Demant has been extensively criticized, certain elements of his approach have endured. Demant described himself as a 'historian of cultures'. In this respect he operates on the same canvas as Alasdair MacIntyre. Demant's unpublished Gifford Lectures of 1957–58 share MacIntyre's pessimism about modernity. His insistence that there is a distinctive 'Christian' approach to sociology has been taken up enthusiastically by John Milbank. Unlike many in the Green movement, he is persuaded that Catholic Christianity is the solution to the ecological crisis of the world, not part of the problem.

IAN MARKHAM

FURTHER READING: *Texts: Religion and the Decline of Capitalism* (London, 1952); *Theology of Society* (London, 1947); *Christian Polity* (London, 1936); *The Religious Prospect* (London, 1939); *God, Man and Society* (London, 1933). *Studies:* I.S. Markham, *Plurality and Christian Ethics* (Cambridge, 1994); R.H. Preston, *Religion and the Persistence of Capitalism* (London, 1979); A. Hastings, *A History of English Christianity 1920–1985* (London, 1986); D. Munby, *Christianity and Economic Problems* (London, 1956); E.R. Norman, *Church and Society in England 1770–1970* (Oxford, 1976).

Denney, James (1856–1917)

James Denney was born in Paisley, brought up in Greenock, and attended university in Glasgow (where he gained a double first in classics and philosophy). He studied for the ministry of the Free Church in the Glasgow College of his denomination. Only after his course did he move to a definite evangelical position through the influence of his wife, Mary Brown. He spent seven years in mission work and parish ministry, during which time he preached the sermons which were the basis of his two contributions to *The Expositor's Bible* on *Thessalonians* and *Second Corinthians*. He also gave lectures on systematic theology in Chicago (*Studies in Theology*). After a brief spell as professor of systematic and pastoral theology in the Glasgow College (1897–99) he was transferred to the chair of New Testament in succession to *A.B. Bruce (1831–99) and became principal in 1915. The academic quality of the College is evident from the fact that his colleagues included *James Orr (1844–1913) and George Adam Smith (1856–1942).

It is for his work as a New Testament scholar that Denney is primarily significant. He wrote a commentary on the Greek text of *Romans*, and an important study of *Jesus and the Gospel*. But his most memorable works are *The Death of Christ* (revised edition [1951, 1997] incorporating *The Atonement and the Modern Mind*) and *The Christian Doctrine of Reconciliation* (reprinted 1998).

Denney's work on the historical Jesus demonstrates his knowledge of the critical writings of the day and his ability to enter into debate with them in order to demonstrate that the church's understanding of the Christ of faith is firmly based on the actual character of the Jesus of history. Although biblical criticism has moved on since his time, a good deal of what has been said by subsequent radical critics is not so different from the positions attacked by Denney, and his general position remains eminently defensible.

Denney's understanding of the atonement starts from the fact of human sin, both in individual acts and in inner character, as deliberate rebellion against God and his moral law. Human sin is so great that people cannot save themselves, but not so great that not even God can save them (a possibility to which, in Denney's opinion, the Westminster Confession came perilously near [*Reconciliation*, p. 199]). Since God is a moral being, his reaction against sin is utterly real; it is summed up in the term 'wrath' and is finally expressed in 'an annihilating sentence' (*Reconciliation*, pp. 209f.).

The atonement, therefore, has to deal not with 'man's distrust of God but with God's condemnation of man' (*Studies*, p. 103). In his death the condemnation of human sin came upon Christ. Denney's understanding of the death of Christ was thus penal and substitutionary.

> The Cross is the place at which the sinless One dies the death of the sinful; the place at which God's condemnation is borne by the Innocent, that for those who commit themselves to Him there may be condemnation no more. I cannot read the New Testament in any other sense. I cannot see at the very heart of it anything but this – grace establishing the law, not in a "forensic" sense, but in a spiritual sense; mercy revealed, not over judgment, but through it; justification disclosing not only the goodness but the severity of God; the Cross inscribed, God is love, only because it is inscribed also, the wages of sin is death. (*Studies*, p. 124)

Denney maintained this position throughout his life:

> Can we say anything else than this: That while the agony and the Passion were not penal in the sense of coming upon Jesus through a bad conscience, or making Him the personal object of divine wrath, they were penal in the sense that in that dark hour He had to realise to the full the divine reaction against sin in the race in which He was incorporated, and that without doing so to the uttermost He could not have been the Redeemer of that race from sin, or the Reconciler of sinful men to God? (*Reconciliation*, p. 273)

In 1915 Denney wrote, 'I have often wondered whether we might not say that the Christian doctrine of the Atonement just meant that in Christ God took the responsibility of evil upon Himself and somehow subsumed evil under good' (*Letters to his Family*, p. 187). In fact

Denney went beyond saying that God simply accepted the worst that sinners could do and continued to love them; rather Christ 'owns the reality of sin by submitting humbly and without rebellion to the divine reaction against it' (*Reconciliation*, p. 234). Denney showed some sympathy for the views of *J. McLeod Campbell (1800–72), according to which Christ saves by acknowledging the justice of God's condemnation of sin, but Denney emphasized that Christ actually bore that condemnation.

Denney's work must be evaluated in its context. In his earlier writings he was essentially reacting to the influential position of *A. Ritschl (1822–89), sharing the latter's distrust of speculation and mysticism, but rejecting his abandonment of the biblical understanding of God and his wrath against sin. Denney was also critical of the broad 'liberalism' of his day, which adopted those biblical ideas which were congenial to modern thought and rejected or reinterpreted those which were not. Fundamentally he stood in the orthodox, Reformed tradition, but he was by no means a traditionalist. He firmly believed in the inspiration of Scripture, but he disliked the idea of verbal inerrancy, and commented:

> The Word of God infallibly carries God's power to save men's souls. That is the only kind of infallibility I believe in. Authority is not authorship. God attests what is in this book as His own, but God is not the author of it, in the sense in which a man is the author of the book he writes. To say so is meaningless. (*Letters to his Family*, p. 23)

Consequently, Denney was open to the practice of critical scholarship, although his conclusions were generally conservative.

There are weaknesses in Denney's thought. He tended to overvalue the place of experience as the criterion of theological truth. He was in danger of overstressing the centrality of the atonement to such an extent that he was almost prepared to derive the doctrine of the incarnation from it: 'the doctrine of the atonement … is the proper evangelical foundation for a doctrine of the person of Christ. To put it in the shortest possible form, Christ is the person who can do this work for us' (*Death*, p. 175). This may also have led him to underemphasize the place of union with Christ and the role of the Spirit in Christian experience (on which see his lengthy article in *Dictionary of Christ and the Gospels*, I, pp. 731–44).

Denney was not simply an expounder of a critical orthodoxy. He could write: 'I haven't the faintest interest in any theology which doesn't help us to evangelize' (*Letters to his Family*, pp. xii–xiii). And again: 'If evangelists were our theologians or theologians our evangelists, we should be nearer the ideal' (*Death*, p. viii). It is little wonder that his theology was centred on the cross, and that he remains the finest expositor of its meaning in the New Testament.

I. HOWARD MARSHALL

FURTHER READING: *Texts: The Epistles to the Thessalonians* (Cambridge, 1892); *The Second Epistle to the Corinthians* (London, 1894); 'St Paul's Epistle to the Romans', in *The Expositor's Greek Testament*, II (ed. W. Robertson Nicoll; London, 1900), pp. 555–725; *Studies in Theology* (London, 1894); *The Death of Christ* (London, 1902); *The Atonement and the Modern Mind* (London, 1903); *Jesus and the Gospel* (London, 1908); *The Christian Doctrine of Reconciliation* (London, 1917); *Letters of Principal James Denney to his Family and Friends* (London, 1922). *Studies:* J.R. Taylor, *God Loves Like That: The Theology of James Denney* (Richmond, 1962 [with full bibliography of Denney's writings]); I.H. Marshall, 'James Denney', in *Creative Minds in Contemporary Theology* (ed. P.E. Hughes; Grand Rapids, 1966), pp. 203–38.

Descartes, René (1596–1650)

Descartes is often referred to as the 'Father of Modern Philosophy' because of the revolutionary influence he exerted on the intellectual world. He is most commonly known for his work in metaphysics and epistemology, but his work had profound implications for the physical sciences, ethics, mathematics and religion.

Descartes received his early education at the *Jesuit college of La Flèche. Although convinced that La Flèche was among the best of all European universities, he was disappointed that none of the ideas encountered in his education, save those of mathematics, was beyond dispute. In the absence of an epistemological foundation that provided certainty, Descartes argued that we have no basis for distinguishing between truth and falsity. This is the impetus behind his decision to doubt everything that is open to any degree of question, however improbable, until he arrived at one indubitable truth.

Descartes' *Meditations on First Philosophy* (1641) begins the quest for certainty by reciting common arguments against epistemological confidence such as the fallibility and limitation on sense experience and our inability to distinguish dreams and hallucinations from rational consciousness. Even the certainty of mathematics was put in doubt by his hypothetical malignant genius capable of distorting the contents of human thought processes.

In the midst of this intense and extensive process of systematic doubting, however, Descartes arrived at the conclusion that one thing was beyond doubt: the fact that he was doubting. From this realization comes his famous dictum, *cogito ergo sum* ('I think, therefore I am'). Doubt is a form of thought, and thoughts require a thinker. Therefore, the act of doubting indicates the certainty of our existence. Even if the malignant genius attempts to deceive us in all that we think, we must exist in order to be deceived. Thus, the deductive process, which bypasses all input from the senses, secures the truth of our existence. Because, however, the correspondence of actual objects to sense perception is still, at this point, susceptible to doubt, the 'thinking thing' that constitutes the 'I' includes only the mind.

With the one unassailable truth of his own existence in place, Descartes now had a foundation from which he could determine the veracity of other claims. His third 'Meditation' presents a modified version of *Anselm's ontological argument for God's existence. Descartes notes that we can conceive of a perfect being. As is the case with every idea, this concept must have a source, and the source of any idea must possess sufficient reality to account for the concept itself. Descartes finds it impossible that we could be the source of the idea of a perfect being. Human beings are capable of doubt and, since doubt is a deficiency, it is clear that we are imperfect. Because no imperfect source, or combination of imperfect sources, can account for the concept of a perfect being, only the actual existence of God explains our ability to conceive of a perfect being.

Descartes' certainty of God's existence then provides the foundation for reversing our doubts about the physical realm. A perfect being would not allow us to be deceived in our belief that ideas of objects originate in the external world. By this means, Descartes argues that, in addition to the existence of minds and God, belief in bodies is justified. While the information provided by our senses about the nature of bodies is susceptible to error, we can avoid mistakes by suspending judgement on matters where reason does not offer clarity.

The difference in the manner that the existence of mind and body are grounded in Descartes' *Meditations* raises questions about the relationship between the types of entities. The mind is an incorporeal substance whose essence is thought; the mind is a thinking thing (*res cognitans*). In contrast, all bodies, including the human body, are extended substances (*res extensa*). Bodies are mechanical objects that exist in space. However, Descartes did not believe the relationship of the soul to the body should be viewed as that of 'a pilot in his ship'. Instead, mind and body are intricately intertwined (by God) so that potential dangers to the person might be immediately known to the mind rather than discovered 'as a pilot perceives by sight if anything is broken on his vessel' (*Meditations*).

Although Descartes asserts that there is a close association between the body and mind, his attempt to explain the means of that interaction is less than satisfactory. He argues that the mind's link to the senses occurs in the pineal gland, a small gland embedded in the brain's interior. However, the means by which one might speak of an incorporeal entity (mind) being in a location, and how it interacts with a body that is essentially a mechanism subject to laws governing cause and effect, are unclear.

Descartes' attempt to erect a unified understanding of the universe by employing a subjective consciousness of the self as a point of departure created a great deal of philosophical controversy. Some fellow rationalists, such as *Spinoza, agreed with the basic methodology, but they argued that Descartes did not recognize the monistic implications of his system. Empiricists were forced to respond to his doubts about sense experience as a proper beginning point for epistemology. Although his conclusions tended to be in conformity with Christian doctrine, many religious philosophers were concerned about the mental world of the self as the proper starting point of epistemology.

STEVE WILKENS

FURTHER READING: Texts: *The Philosophical Writings of Descartes* (trans. J. Cottingham, R. Stoothoff and D. Murdoch; 3 vols.; Cambridge, 1991); *Discourse on Method and Mediation on First Philosophy* (trans. Donald A Cress; Indianapolis, IN, 3rd edn, 1993); Anthony Kenney, *Descartes: A Study of His Philosophy* (New York, 1968); Marjorie Grene, *Descartes* (Minneapolis, 1985); John Cottingham (ed.), *The Cambridge Companion to Descartes* (New York, 1992).

Dialectical Theology

Groundbreaking movement in Protestant theology emerging immediately after World War I in Switzerland and Germany, mainly under the influence of *Karl Barth (1886–1968) and Friedrich Gogarten (1887–1967) but in close collaboration with Eduard Thurneysen (1888–1974), *Emil Brunner (1889–1966), *Rudolf Bultmann (1884–1974) and others.

This talented group came out of German liberal theology. Barth and Bultmann were students of *Wilhelm Herrmann, Gogarten of *Ernst Troeltsch, while Thurneysen and Brunner (and also Barth, to some extent) were influenced by religious socialists such as *Leonhard Ragaz and Hermann Kutter. In the early 1920s they launched a generational revolt and accused their teachers of making humanity rather than God the central subject of theology.

Barth, Bultmann, Thurneysen and Gogarten first met at a religious-social conference in Tambach in September 1919. In his lecture 'Der Christ in der Gesellschaft', Barth claimed that God's history is completely discontinuous with human history, since it breaks into the world 'vertically from above' (*senkrecht von oben*). This lecture triggered a departure from any attempt at reconciling Christianity and culture. God's pure transcendence was emphasized; Paul's expression 'Christ in us' means that Christ is 'above us', and is distinguished from religious feelings. Hence, one cannot attain a knowledge of God independently from the human side ('natural theology'), but only through God's self-revelation. In consequence, the socialist hope of bringing the kingdom of God to flourish within history was seen as theologically misguided.

The publication of the second edition of Karl Barth's *Letter to the Romans* (1922) was a breakthrough, and the spread of 'Barthian' theology among pastors and theological students proceeded apace, especially on the European continent. In the early years, however, it was Gogarten who set the movement's highly polemical tone against the theological establishment. The word of God was opposed to the hollow idols of human idealism, be it in the pietist form of Christian experience (Herrmann), or in a historicist notion of religious progressivism

(Troeltsch). Referring to the cultural breakdown of western culture, Gogarten writes: 'We are only happy about this disaster, for one does not like to live among corpses' (*Zwischen den Zeiten*, 1920). However, the appeal to the freshness of 'the moment' and the call to 'the decision of faith' could not fully disguise the fact that the emergence of dialectical theology was itself deeply influenced by socio-cultural disillusionment. During the 1920s, the term 'theology of crisis' (coined by *Paul Tillich) was widely used to place the movement in the context of expressionism and the pessimistic philosophy of Oswald Spengler's *The Decline of the West* (2 vols., 1918–22).

According to Barth, the term 'dialectical theology' was attached to the movement from the outside. The use of term, however, differs markedly within the group. As explained by Barth in 1922, the dialectical method presupposes both the positive way of doctrinal tradition and the negative way of mystical tradition. God is the incomprehensible truth who – in the event of divine self-revelation – comes forth in the dialectic between the positive insight that God has become a human being and the negative insight that human beings cannot grasp God. God's revelation is only apprehensible in the moment of faith (*Das Wort Gottes als Aufgabe der Theologie*, 1922). This noetic concept of dialectics, however, is grounded in the *Realdialektik* of the 'infinite qualitative difference' (*Kierkegaard) between time and eternity (*Der Römerbrief*, 1922, p. xiii). Barth never gave up this insight. Also, in the *Church Dogmatics* (1932ff.), the gulf between God and world can only be overcome by God's self-revelation. More recent research (Beintker; McCormack) therefore questions the thesis of a development 'from dialectics towards analogy' (*Hans Urs von Balthasar; *E. Jüngel). Throughout Barth's work, there are analogies (from God to world) *and* dialectics (from world to God).

According to Bultmann, the dialectic is grounded in the fact that a knowledge of God is never at our disposal (*verfügbar*). A genuine relation to God is only possible in communication (*Gespräch*); however, communication between God and humanity is asymmetric, since it depends on God's self-revelation to the individual believer here and now (*Die Frage der 'dialektischen' Theologie*, 1926). Under the influence of personalistic I-Thou philosophy, Gogarten and Brunner developed similar concepts of dialectics while emphasizing that God's revelation is a paradox compared with ordinary human self-understanding. God appears only in the midst of contrary statements. After the late 1920s, however, Gogarten reserved the term for the inner-worldly dialectics of historical existence.

Between 1923 and 1933 the circle published the journal *Zwischen den Zeiten*, which helped to clarify both the common ground and the internal differences among its members. After 1924, Barth (followed by Thurneysen) began to develop a positive doctrinal theology, while Gogarten and Bultmann further pursued an existentialist position. Brunner's concern for social ethics moved towards reformulating *Luther's theology of the orders. After 1930, the group began to disintegrate. Barth could not accord any independent role to a theological anthropology, much less to a Lutheran doctrine of God's two regiments. When Gogarten joined the movement of the Nazi German Christians, Barth officially denounced his partnership with him and the journal ('Abschied von *Zwischen den Zeiten*', 1933). In his 1934 publication *No!*, Barth also rejected Brunner's project as a relapse into natural theology. By comparison, the disagreements between Barth and Bultmann were settled in an atmosphere of mutual respect, although they were not clarified until the 1950s. The debate whether the gospel, in its reception by faith, implicitly presupposes a 'pre-understanding' (*Vorverständnis*) of human existence (so Bultmann) or carries its own theological logic (so Barth), shaped the international theological climate until around 1970, when the paradigm of word-of-God theology began to collapse. Also, alternative theological proposals (e.g. Paul Tillich's method of correlation, Wolfhart Pannenberg's theology of history, or *Jürgen Moltmann's theology of hope) had to cope with these reigning paradigms of word-of-God theology (sometimes, though imprecisely, referred to as 'neo-orthodoxy').

The term 'dialectical theology' can best be used as a *historical* term designating the first phase (1919–33) of a broader family of distinct word-of-God theologies.

NIELS HENRIK GREGERSEN

FURTHER READING: Michael Beintker, *Die Dialektik in der 'dialektischen Theologie' Karl Barths* (Munich, 1987); Christof Gestrich, *Neuzeitliches Denken und die Spaltung der dialektischen Theologie: Die Frage der natürlichen Theologie* (Tübingen, 1977);

Wilfried Härle, 'Dialektische Theologie', *Th Real* 8, pp. 683–96; Bruce L. McCormack, *Karl Barth's Critically Realistic Dialectical Theology: Its Genesis and Development 1909–1936* (Oxford, 1995); Jürgen Moltmann (ed.), *Anfänge der dialektischen Theologie* (2 vols.; Munich, 1974); James M. Robinson (ed.), *The Beginnings of Dialectic Theology* (Richmond, VA, 1968); *Zeitschrift für Dialektische Theologie* (vol. 1ff.; Kampen, 1985ff.).

Dionysius the Areopagite

According to the account in Acts (17:16–34), among those converted by the apostle Paul's speech before the council of the Areopagus in Athens was a man called Dionysius, a member of the council (hence: Areopagite). According to an early tradition he became the first bishop of Athens (Eusebius, *CH*, 3.4.10). In the second quarter of the sixth century there emerged a body of writings ascribed to this Dionysius. The 'monophysite' Severus of Antioch quoted from them, and a passage from one of Dionysius's letters was cited in support of the *Monophysite position at a council called by Justinian in 536. Gradually this body of writings gained acceptance in the Christian world, and their authenticity was not called into question until the Renaissance. Their near-apostolic authority lent them immense prestige throughout the Middle Ages. Now, however, it is generally accepted that the *Corpus Dionysiacum* was composed in the early sixth century, not least because the writings betray dependence on the advanced Neoplatonism associated with Proclus, heir to the *Platonic tradition in Athens, who died in 485.

The *Corpus Areopagiticum* consists of four treatises and ten letters, although it presents itself as part of a larger collection of works, the rest of which are lost. Few scholars accept that these 'lost works' ever existed, but regard them as part of the elaborate subterfuge that lies behind the presentation of this corpus. The four treatises are the *Celestial Hierarchy*, the *Ecclesiastical Hierarchy*, the *Divine Names* and the *Mystical Theology*. They present a grand vision of the cosmos as a graded manifestation of God (a 'theophany'), drawing all beings back into union with God. This cosmic vision expresses liturgical and cosmological ideas already developed in Greek patristic theology by such as the *Cappadocian Fathers and *John Chrysostom, though they are articulated through the concepts and vocabulary of late Neoplatonism.

Fundamental to this vision is the circular

movement of rest-procession-return: the cosmos is seen as proceeding from God and striving to return through contemplation. Immediately proceeding from God, or the Thearchy, are the spiritual ranks of the angelic beings, and beyond these angelic ranks lies the graded structure of the church, which involves human beings who are both spiritual and material, and who make use of matter, both as symbols and as sacraments, in order to return to the source of all things, God.

In depicting this glittering array, Dionysius shows considerable fondness for triads. God himself, the Thearchy, is triadic. The angelic beings are arranged in three ranks, each consisting of three orders (in descending order): seraphim, cherubim, thrones; dominions, powers, authorities; principalities, archangels, angels. The church itself ('our' hierarchy: the term 'ecclesiastical hierarchy' only occurs in the title) is formed of the clerical orders of hierarch, priest and minister (as he calls the familiar bishop, presbyter and deacon), and the lay order of monks, the 'sacred people', and catechumens together with those also excluded from communion. The first rank of 'our' hierarchy are the sacraments: illumination, the gathering-together and ointment (the first two evidently baptism and the Eucharist, the last the blended and scented oil used in various sacramental rites).

The word 'hierarchy', which is Dionysius's own coinage, does not primarily mean a graded structure of subordination (as nowadays), but rather the loving outreach of God's self-manifestation in creation, by an infinitely gradual radiation of divine light or revelation, which itself serves to draw the whole creation into union with God. It is 'a sacred order, knowledge and activity, which is being assimilated to likeness with God as much as possible' (*Celestial Hierarchy* 3. 1). This process of assimilation to God is accomplished through yet another triad – the threefold operation of purification, illumination and union or perfection (the origin of the 'three ways' of the western mystical tradition). Union with God involves knowledge of God that transcends (though it does not annul) the discursive activity of the intellect.

Such knowledge of God is called 'theology', and Dionysius distinguishes two types of theology (taking the terminology, though not the notion, which was already familiar in Christian theology, from his Neoplatonic contemporaries): the theology of affirmation ('cataphatic') and the theology of negation or denial ('apophatic'). Cataphatic theology is the theology of revelation: by affirming the concepts and symbols used in Scripture and the liturgy, Christians are drawn towards God who is revealed in them (later western theology extended cataphatic theology to natural theology, but Dionysius shows no interest in this). Apophatic theology is a further stage, born of the realization that concepts and symbols are *about* God, but fall short of God himself: by denying the affirmations that have been made of God one draws close to God himself. Such closeness to God involves renunciation of knowledge and its accompanying power, and surrender to God in a darkness of unknowing.

The influence of the powerful vision of the Dionysian corpus has been immense, and was only enhanced (not created) by its presumed near-apostolic provenance. Within a few decades of its composition, John, bishop of Scythopolis, had prepared an edition with accompanying prologue and scholia (the source of all our manuscripts, save one early Syriac version), which firmly assimilated it to the orthodox tradition of Byzantine theology, a process furthered in the next century by *Maximus the Confessor. In the western Middle Ages interest in Dionysius was profound and diverse. Despite Dionysius's own total lack of interest in the political implications of his cosmological vision, a somewhat distorted form of his own notion of hierarchy became fundamental to the political theology of both eastern and western Christendom.

ANDREW LOUTH

FURTHER READING: Critical text of *Corpus Dionysiacum* (ed. B.R. Suchla, et al.; Berlin, 1990–1 [C. Luibheid and P. Rorem; London, 1987]). *Studies:* A. Louth, *Denys the Areopagite* (London, 1989); P. Rorem, *Pseudo-Dionysius: A Commentary on the Texts and an Introduction to their Influence* (Oxford, 1993).

Dispensationalism

Dispensationalism is less a theology *per se* than a method of biblical interpretation designed to disclose the progress of God's governmental dealings with the world during successive periods of time. The 'dispensations' are periods during which God tests humankind in various ways, with failure, judgement and, eventually, the commencement of a new dispensation the unfailing result.

Usually, seven dispensations are distinguished: 1) innocency (Adam in Eden, the dispensation of 'unconfirmed creaturely holiness', so Charles Ryrie); 2) conscience (from Adam to Noah, during which obedience to the dictates of conscience was humankind's primary stewardship responsibility); 3) civil government (from Noah to Abraham, with humankind's responsibility being obedience to human government); 4) patriarchal rule (from Abraham to Moses, when one family was singled out and given the responsibility of believing and serving God); 5) Mosaic law (from Moses to Christ, during which the people were held responsible to obey God's law); 6) grace (from the first to the second advent of Christ, with human beings responsible to accept God's free gift of righteousness); 7) the millennium (when humankind will be responsible to obey the divine king and obey his laws).

Ultradispensationalists, such as E.W. Bullinger (1837–1913), discern one or more additional dispensations between the first advent of Christ and Paul's prison ministry. Bullinger maintained that the present dispensation commenced with the ministry of Paul after Acts 28:28; held that Paul's prison epistles are the only Scriptures addressed *primarily* to the church; and he denied that baptism and the Lord's Supper are for this age.

Of vital importance to Dispensationalism are its insistence that biblical interpretation must be literal (which does not rule out symbols, figures of speech and typology); and a sharp distinction between Israel as God's earthly people and the church as his heavenly people. The Old Testament prophecies will be fulfilled to the letter in the millennial kingdom, just as relevant ones were fulfilled at Christ's first coming. During the dispensational of grace Jews, as well as Gentiles, who believe the gospel are incorporated into the church.

Dispensationalism includes a highly distinctive eschatology differing from historic premillennialism by its insistence on a two-stage second advent, with a pre-tribulation return comprising the secret rapture of the church followed by a period of intense tribulation for the Jews. This will culminate in the return of Christ in glory, accompanied by the church, to set up his millennial kingdom on earth. This will end with the inevitable rebellion of man, followed by the setting up of the eternal state (during which, it appears, the distinction between the church and Israel will remain).

Dispensationalists like Ryrie specifically deny the charge that they teach a different mode of salvation for different dispensations, asserting that salvation is always by grace and that it is God's 'governmental relationship with man' that differs, not the way of salvation.

Dispensationalists who follow *J.N. Darby all the way regard the structured church as it currently exists as apostate. They make no attempt to restore its outward form but meet together simply as believers, making no pretence of trying to reconstitute 'the church in ruins'. Most Dispensationalists, however, follow Darby in his eschatology but not in his ecclesiology.

Dispensationalism is not necessarily incompatible with *Reformed theology. Darby combined Dispensationalism with some of the doctrines of grace; he converted numerous Presbyterians to it; and The Fundamentals reflect a (temporary) coalition between *Calvinists and Dispensationalists in the battle with theological liberalism. Nevertheless, Dispensationalism tends to combine *Arminian elements with some of Darby's distinctive teachings.

Despite the claim that Dispensationalism was foreshadowed in the distinctions drawn by theologians in the early church such as *Irenaeus, *Clement of Alexandria and even *Augustine, and in more recent times by *Jonathan Edwards and Isaac Watts, there can be little doubt that it was Darby who laid the foundations of modern Dispensationalism. Once almost universally held among Brethren, it has lost some of its attraction, particularly among revisionist 'Open' Brethren. During the late-nineteenth and early-twentieth centuries Dispensationalism gained an influential hearing among evangelicals who were under intense pressure from liberal and (in the UK) High Church theology. From the UK and North America it has been taken by missionaries around the world. The Emmaus Bible correspondence courses which teach Dispensationalism have circulated in millions around the world.

Dispensationalism made its greatest impact in North America. Darby spent a total of more than six years there and, while comparatively few Brethren assemblies resulted, he influenced numerous key pastors in cities such as Saint Louis, Chicago, New York and Boston. Among those who became propagators of Dispensationalism were the Presbyterian pastors J.H. Brookes and W.J. Erdman. It was taught at the numerous Bible and prophetic conferences stemming from the Niagara Bible conferences (beginning in 1875). Though Darby's own writings were turgid, they possessed an attraction of their own, and their message was effectively conveyed in popular form in the writings of men like C.H. Mackintosh. W.E. Blackstone's immensely popular book, Jesus is Coming (2nd edn, 1886) with an ultimate circulation of at least 691,000 in 31 languages, spread Dispensationalism's eschatological message (cf. Hal Lindsay's Late Great Planet Earth, 1970). Even more influential were the writings of C.I. Scofield, whose Rightly Dividing the Word of Truth (1885), Scofield Bible Correspondence Course and, especially, the Scofield Reference Bible (1909), followed by revision and many editions, carried Dispensationalism around the world. Dispensationalism was taught in the growing number of Bible schools, including Moody Bible Institute (1889, with roots going back to 1886), the Bible Institute of Los Angeles (1907) and Dallas Theological Seminary (1925).

HAROLD H. ROWDON

FURTHER READING: L.S. Chafer, Dispensationalism (Dallas, rev. edn, 1951); E. Sauer, From Eternity to Eternity (London, 1954); C.N. Kraus, Dispensationalism in America (Richmond, VA, 1958); A.D. Ehlert, Bibliographic History of Dispensationalism (Grand Rapids, 1965); C.C. Ryrie, Dispensationalism Today (Chicago, 1965); E.R. Sandeen, The Roots of Fundamentalism (Chicago, 1970); J.H. Gerstner, Wrongly Dividing the Word of Truth: A Critique of Dispensationalism (Brentwood, TN, 1991).

Docetism

Docetism is the name given to the idea that the humanity of Jesus Christ was an appearance or illusion. The term comes from the Greek dokein, 'to seem' or 'to appear', and its cognates. About 115 Ignatius of Antioch (or someone using his name about 150) denounces the view that Jesus suffered and rose only 'apparently' (Smyrn. 2; 4.2; Trall. 10). This doctrine, he says, makes the sufferings of the martyrs unreal as well. *Irenaeus and *Clement of Alexandria repeatedly criticize those who hold that Christ's birth and body were only 'in appearance', a view which they attribute to such heretics as *Marcion and various *Gnostics. Early in the third century *Hippolytus attacks Marcion and his teacher Cerdon for the view that 'Christ is the son of the Good, and is sent by him for the salvation of souls.... and that he was revealed as a man, though not a man, and as being in a body when not in a body, manifest in appearance only, subject to no nativity or passion, except only in appearance' (*Haer.* 10.19). Later the Manicheans held similar views.

Some heresiologists write of the 'Docetists' as a distinct sect (early examples are Clement of Alexandria, *Stromata* 7.17; Hippolytus, *Refutatio* 8.2). It is unlikely, however, that anyone ever called himself a Docetist.

Docetic views appear in early apocryphal texts. In *Acts of John* 93 Jesus' body sometimes yields to the touch and is insubstantial, and he walks leaving no footmark. Such ideas may originate from New Testament accounts, as when Jesus escapes mysteriously from pursuit (Lk. 4:30; Jn. 8:59), passes through shut doors (Jn. 20:19), needs no food (Jn. 4:31–32) or walks upon water (Mk. 6:48, etc.). Opposition to docetic views is, however, also already visible in the New Testament. The reality of the resurrection body is emphasized (Lk. 24:39; Jn. 20:27), especially by eating (Lk. 24:41–42). The view that Jesus Christ did not come in the flesh is condemned as 'of the antichrist' in 1 John 4:2–3. Some hold that the Gospel of John is partly or even predominantly anti-docetic (e.g. Richter). This view is, however, generally rejected (Brown; Thyen).

Other doctrinal devices are sometimes loosely called 'docetic', because they immunize the divine Saviour from being contaminated by birth or suffering. Cerinthus held that Christ descended on the man Jesus at his baptism, but separated from him before he suffered (Irenaeus, *Heresies* 1.26.1). Some Basilideans taught that Simon of Cyrene was substituted for Jesus on the way to the crucifixion, and died instead of him (Irenaeus, *Heresies* 1.24.4). In *Acts of John* 97 Jesus talks to the apostle John in a cave while his body is crucified. Serapion of Antioch about AD 180 uses the word *doketai* (*docetae*) of those associated with the *Gospel of Peter*, where Christ's divine power forsakes him before the crucifixion (Eusebius, *CH* 6.12.3–6). In the gospel according to Marcion, Christ first appears from heaven fullgrown in the synagogue of Luke 4:16 (Tertullian, *Marcion* 4.7–8).

Docetic thinking may arise from Greek philosophical ideas of God's transcendence. In *Plato and *Aristotle God cannot be affected by outside agencies, so he cannot suffer or feel passion, nor can he change or be contaminated by the world of becoming. So if Christ in any way shares the divine nature, he cannot suffer or die. The apparent sufferings may have value as examples or manifestations of the divine, but are not intrinsically real or effective. Such a salvation may, however, be adequate if souls, not bodies, are saved. This, too, fits with some Greek ideas. In circles influenced by Pythagoras and Plato the quest for knowledge recalls the mind or soul to its true immortality, out of the world of change and uncertainty and into the timeless divine eternity of true knowledge. For this purpose a docetic Christ is sufficient, or even necessary. What is needed is a summons from the real, spiritual world to wake the inner man from the sleep of passion and ignorance to a true spiritual destiny and knowledge of the truth. Critics like Irenaeus and *Tertullian insist that the world and matter are good, as coming from the one God who was both Creator and Saviour. Christ came precisely in order to save the physical world, which was intrinsically good, though corrupted by sin. Human beings are to be saved by restoration in the image of the divine Christ. For such a work he must be both human and divine. His birth, death and resurrection were therefore physical, like those of other human beings. When humankind is fully restored in the resurrection of the body, there will also be a new heaven and a new earth.

In later times the term 'docetic' is extended to criticize thinkers or doctrines which appear to assert Christ's deity at the cost of denying his full historic reality. *Apollinaris in the fourth century, who held that God the Word replaced the human soul or mind in Jesus Christ, was so attacked. Julian of Halicarnassus in the sixth century, who held that Christ's flesh was incorruptible because of its absolute unity with the divine nature residing in it, was called 'aphthartodocetic' (incorruption- docetist). In modern times, *existentialist interpretations of Christ which separate faith in him from dependence on the historical Jesus, of whom nothing certain can be known, are sometimes called docetic. This use carries on the early tradition, since the term was always one of hostile abuse rather than of sympathetic presentation.

STUART G. HALL

FURTHER READING: Raymond E. Brown, *Jesus, God and Man* (Milwaukee, 1967); *The Community of the Beloved Disciple* (New York, 1979); Aloys

Grillmeier, SJ, *Christ in Christian Tradition* (London, 2nd edn, 1975); J.K. Elliott, *The Apocryphal New Testament* (Oxford, 1993); John Macquarrie, 'Jesus Christus VII: Dogmatisch', *Th Real* 167 (1988), pp. 42–64; Georg Richter, *Studien zum Johannesevangelium* (BU 13; Regensburg, 1977); Tertullian, *Adversus Marcionem* (ed. and trans. Ernest Evans; OECT; Oxford, 1972); Hartwig Thyen, 'Johannesbriefe', 'Johannesevangelium', *The Real* 17 (1988), pp. 186–225.

Duns Scotus, John (c. 1266–1308)

John Duns Scotus was born c. 1266, probably in Duns, just north of the border into Scotland. He joined the *Franciscan order and was ordained in 1291 at Northampton. Scotus studied in Oxford probably between 1288 and 1301, and he taught in Paris 1302–03 and 1304–07, where he was regent master from 1305. He taught at the Franciscan *studium* in Cologne from 1307 until his death in 1308, traditionally 8 November. Scotus was the most influential of all the schoolmen during the Middle Ages through until the seventeenth century, and his thought was central to that of his greatest successor, *Ockham. He was beatified in 1993.

Traditionally known as the 'subtle doctor', Scotus's thought is often of extreme complexity and sophistication. More than any other *scholastic, Scotus emphasizes the scientific nature of theology: truths about God are intrinsically ordered in terms of explanatory priority, such that even God's knowledge of these truths, although timeless, is arranged syllogistically. Human theology (*theologia nostra*) is practical, not theoretical, since its aim is to dispose the theologian to love God.

According to Scotus, God's nature and existence can be shown by natural reason, and they are the objects of the science of metaphysics, the *Aristotelian study of being and the other 'transcendental' attributes (unity, truth, goodness, as well as the pure perfections – attributes which it is simply better to have than not to have – and disjunctive attributes such as necessary-or-contingent, cause-or-caused). Since it is empirically evident that it is possible for something to be caused, it follows that it is possible for something to be a cause and, given the demonstrable impossibility of an infinite regress, it is possible for something to be a first cause. But any first cause will be necessarily uncaused, and thus a necessary existent. So the possible existence of such a being entails its necessary existence. A first cause

therefore exists. Arguing similarly for the existence of a maximally excellent being, Scotus follows *Anselm in holding that God has every pure perfection. These perfections in themselves are the same as the corresponding creaturely perfections, differing merely in their infinite degree. The concepts of the pure perfections are thus univocal to God and creatures. This univocity is required in order to allow for a theory of analogy, according to which, for example, the concepts 'infinite being' and 'finite being' are analogous in virtue of the underlying univocal concept 'being'. Since the pure perfections are different from each other, God's simplicity must be compatible with his possession of different perfections. Scotus holds that the divine perfections are 'formally distinct' from each other – inseparable, but really differing in their definitions.

Scotus uses his formal distinction in his accounts of creatures' individuation, and of the Trinity. A creature is an instance of a common nature – such as humanity – that is really shared by all creatures of a given kind and is numerically distinct in each of its instances. An instance of a nature is unshareable and distinct from all others, in virtue of its unshareable 'haecceity' or 'thisness'. The haecceity is formally distinct from the creature's nature – inseparable from the nature, but not included in its definition. The divine persons are formally distinct from the divine essence. This essence is really shared by the persons, though not thereby divided into numerically many instances. Hence there can be three persons but only one God.

God is radically free, such that he can actualize any logically possible state of affairs. Nothing external to him determines his actions. Hence, the nature of creatures places no constraints on the things he can command them to do. God can thus command as he will – with the exception of those actions whose object is God: God cannot command human beings to hate him. Freedom of the will requires the power (though not the opportunity) to bring about the opposite of an action at the same time as the action itself is brought about. This 'synchronic power for opposites' allows a timeless God to act freely, bringing about by ordained power (*potentia ordinata*) one possible state of affairs out of the complete set of logical possibilities ranged over by his absolute power (*potentia absoluta*). As we know by introspection, human beings are similarly free to choose differently from the way they actually choose. Free human choices are not determined by prior causes – not even by the recommendations of the intellect. Human beings, like God, are free self-determining agents. Original sin does not diminish this freedom. Original sin consists merely in God's holding human beings guilty for failing to have Adam's supernatural gift of original justice, a gift that human beings are obliged by God to possess. God freely predestines the elect to salvation, leaving those not elect to merit their own damnation. God accepts the actions of the just as meritorious of eternal life, and he has contingently determined that a necessary precondition for justification is the possession of habitual grace, a created quality inhering in the soul. This grace is merited by Christ's death, which was also accepted by God as making satisfaction for sins.

Since God always acts in the most well ordered way, willing the end before willing any of the means to the end, his decision to become incarnate did not depend on the Fall of Adam. Even if Adam had not sinned, Christ would have become incarnate as the supreme glorification of creation. Scotus was among the first to defend the doctrine of Mary's 'immaculate' conception (that is, conception without original sin). Preserving someone from original sin – paying the debt that they would have incurred had the payment not been made – is the most perfect way for anyone to be saved by Christ's merits.

The sacraments are complex aggregates of words and deeds; hence they cannot be instrumental causes of divine grace. Rather, God causes the sacraments directly, determining merely that some creaturely actions are the occasions for his direct intervention. Christ's bodily presence in the Eucharist is a case of his body's bi-location – hence, according to Scotus, the (false) doctrine of consubstantiation allows for the real presence as well as the (true) doctrine of transubstantiation.

RICHARD CROSS

FURTHER READING: *Texts: Opera Omnia* (ed. C. Bali, et al.; 11 vols. to date; Rome, 1950–); *Opera Omnia* (ed. Luke Wadding; 12 vols.; Lyons, 1639); *Opera Philosophica* (ed. Girard J. Etzkorn, et al.; 3 vols. to date; St Bonaventure, NY, 1997–). *Collections and translations: God and Creatures: The Quodlibetal Questions* (ed. and trans. Felix Alluntis and Allan B. Wolter; Princeton / London, 1975); *Philosophical Writings* (ed. and trans. Allan B. Wolter; Indianapolis, IN / Cambridge, 1987); *Duns Scotus on the Will and Morality* (ed. and trans. Allan B. Wolter; Washington, DC, 1986, 1997). *Studies:* Richard Cross, *Duns Scotus: Great Medieval Thinkers* (New York, 1999); Thomas Williams (ed.), *The Cambridge Companion to Duns Scotus* (Cambridge, 2000); Allan B. Wolter, *The Philosophical Theology of John Duns Scotus* (ed. Marilyn McCord Adams; Ithaca, NY / London, 1990).

Ebionites

The Ebionites were an early Jewish-Christian sect, concentrated especially in Transjordan, Syria and Egypt. The name is a Graecized form of the Hebrew *ha' ebyonim*, 'the poor', a title used by the Qumran community (1QM 11.9.13; 13.13f.; 1QH 5.22; 1QpHab 12.3. 6.10) and by some of the Jerusalem believers in apostolic times (Gal. 2:10). The Ebionites were legalistic ascetics who espoused poverty and practised vegetarianism, equating economic frailty with spiritual blessing (cf. Lk. 6:20). Their roots lay in the opposition to Paul and the Gentile church at Jerusalem. The Ebionites maintained that since Paul was not an eyewitness of Jesus, his authority was illegitimate, and so too was his theology of justification by faith apart from works. The chief apostle was James. *Epiphanius (*Haer.* 30) quotes fragments of a document which modern scholarship has dubbed the 'Gospel of the Ebionites'. It was written in Greek, east of the Jordan, early in the second century. Much of it is modelled upon canonical Matthew, but it also assumes the Synoptics more generally. Ebionite sources may underlie the pseudo-Clementine writings, the *Homilies* and *Recognitions*. For the most part, however, the Ebionites' beliefs have to be inferred indirectly from the writings of the Fathers.

The Ebionites rejected the virgin birth and saw Jesus as the natural son of Mary and Joseph. He was 'the true prophet' (cf. Deut. 18:15–22), a second Moses, a teacher and reformer. He perfectly fulfilled the Law, but as a man, not as the Son of God. He was not a priest; rather, he came to abolish the sacrificial cultus and to restate the true, spiritual meaning of the Mosaic code. The Pauline construal of the death of Jesus as sacrifice was therefore utterly wrong. The name 'Christ' was given to Jesus at his baptism, when God adopted him as his messianic prophet. The Ebionites maintained a strong eschatological hope: the Son of Man, transfigured into supra-angelic form, would return in glory. The twin foci of Ebionite Christology were thus baptism and parousia, not incarnation and atonement. Conversion to Christ meant conversion to the ultimate reality of the Law of God as propounded by Moses. The Ebionites were vigorous opponents of *Marcionite polemic against the relevance of the Hebrew Scriptures for Christians.

The delay of the parousia led to disillusionment in the Ebionite ranks, and by the fourth century they were few in number. Some elements survived until the seventh century, but were then either absorbed into mainstream Judaism or Christianity or swallowed up by the nascent force of Islam. Symmachus, the late second-century translator of the Old Testament into Greek whose version was recorded in the fourth column of *Origen's *Hexapla*, is said by *Eusebius and *Jerome to have been an Ebionite leader, and there are a number of fourth- and fifth-century references to the Ebionites as 'Symmachians'.

IVOR DAVIDSON

FURTHER READING: G. Howard, 'The Gospel of the Ebionites', *ANRW* 25.5 (1988), pp. 4034–53; A.F.J. Klijn, G.J. Reinink, *Patristic Evidence for Jewish-Christian Sects* (NTSup 36; Leiden, 1973); W. Schneemelcher (ed.), *New Testament Apocrypha*, I (Cambridge, rev. edn, 1991); H.J. Schoeps, *Jewish Christianity* (Philadelphia, 1969); 'Ebionite Christianity', *J Th St* NS 4 (1953), pp. 219–24 (also in E. Ferguson [ed.], *Early Christianity and Judaism* [Studies in Early Christianity 6; London, 1993], pp. 125–30).

Eck, Johannes (1486–1543)

Theologian and controversialist, responsible in large part for shaping the early Catholic response to the challenge of Protestantism. Christened Johann Maier in the city of his birth, Egg (Eck) in Swabia, the precocious young Eck entered the University of Heidelberg at age twelve, transferring to Tübingen the next year. There he received, at age fourteen, the Master of Arts degree (1501). At the University of Freiburg im Breisgau he earned the *Baccalaureus biblicus* (1505), the licentiate (1509) and the Doctor of Theology degree (1510). Shortly thereafter he joined the faculty at Ingolstadt, where he served until his death.

In 1514 Eck published his first theological treatise, the *Chrysopassus*, a study of the doctrine of predestination in which he defended the notion that God predestines on the basis of foreseen merit (*praedestinatio post praevisa merita*). God, Eck argued, is the *causa universalis*, but not the *causa totalis*, thus leaving room for a free human response to the means of grace. In a disputation in Bologna in 1515, Eck also entered into the debate regarding usury, defending the proposition that Christians could charge a modest rate of interest on loans.

Shortly after the publication of *Luther's

Ninety-five Theses, Eck became one of the Protestant Reformation's most important opponents. In Leipzig in 1519, he publicly debated first Andreas Bodenstein von Karlstadt and then Luther. It was Eck's achievement to recognize that the issue of indulgences on which Luther had seized led immediately to that of papal authority. Luther, too, had recognized this implication, but he had resisted taking a public position. Eck defended the notion that the papacy held its authority 'by divine right' (*de iure divino*), forcing Luther publicly to acknowledge that he rejected that claim, thus implicating the Wittenberger in the errors of *John Huss. Eck also played a leading role on the papal commission appointed to draft the bull 'Exsurge Domine', in which Luther was threatened with excommunication. When the bull was at last approved in 1520, moreover, Eck was appointed papal nuncio and charged with publishing it in Germany. During this period of intense opposition to Luther, Eck wrote a defence of papal authority, *De primatu Petri* (1520). Later, he energetically defended other controverted Catholic teachings in his *De purgatorio* (1523), *De satisfactio* and *De poenitentiae* (both 1523), and *De sacrificio missae* (1526). In 1525, he also compiled a 'handbook' for use by Catholic controversialists in confronting the Lutherans entitled *Enchiridion locorum communium adversus Lutherum et alios hostes ecclesiae*, which was reprinted more than a hundred times.

Eck played a central role at the Diet of Augsburg in 1530, where he led the team that compiled the Catholic *Confutatio*. In addition, he led the commission that drafted the official rejection of the Tetrapolitan Confession. He also participated in ecumenical councils with the Protestants, including the Regensburg Colloquy of 1541. In later years, Eck continued his tireless efforts on behalf of the Roman Church, publishing, for instance, anti-Protestant sermon cycles and a German translation of the Bible (1537).

MICKEY L. MATTOX

FURTHER READING: *Texts: Enchiridion of Commonplaces against Luther and Other Enemies of the Church* (1525; trans. Ford Lewis Battles; Grand Rapids, 1979); Pierre Fraenkel (ed.), *Enchiridion locorum communium adversus Lutherum et alios hostes ecclesiae, 1525–1543* (Münster, 1979). *Studies:* Erwin Iserloh, *Johannes Eck, 1486–1543: Scholastiker, Humanist, Kontroverstheologe* (Münster, 2nd edn, 1985); Walter Moore, 'Catholic Teacher and Anabaptist Pupil: The Relationship between John Eck and Balthasar Hubmaier', *Arch Ref* 72 (1981), pp. 68–97.

Eckhart (c. 1260 – c. 1327)

Eckhart, theologian and mystic, almost always called 'Meister Eckhart', was born at Hochiem in Thuringia c. 1260. He entered the Dominican community at Erfurt c. 1275, and he studied at Paris and Cologne, possibly making the acquaintance of Albert the Great (c. 1200–80). He read the works of *Thomas Aquinas (1225–74). He completed his studies with the degree of 'master' in 1302. He served his order in Germany as Provincial of the Saxon province and as reformer of the Bohemian houses. In 1311 he returned to Paris as a teacher. After 1313, he lived at Strasburg, and then at Cologne, where he preached widely to religious men and women in both Latin and German. The Archbishop of Cologne accused him of teaching heresy in 1326. He was tried in Cologne, but appealed to the pope and died in Avignon before the final judgement was reached in 1329. John XXII (1249–1334) ruled in the papal bull 'In Agro Dominico' that of 28 of his sentences, 17 were heretical, while 11 were deplored for tone, but not definitively heretical. Even after, or in spite of, the condemnation of his propositions, his influence has been extensive. Among his students was Henry of Suso (c. 1295–1366), and he influenced Johannes Tauler (c. 1300–61) and the Rhineland mystics. He wrote extensively in both Latin and German, including sermons, biblical commentaries, *Parisian Questions, Counsels on Discernment* and *On Detachment*. The conditions of these texts has been confused, but the critical edition has improved the state of Eckhart scholarship.

For Eckhart, in contrast to the careful distinctions of a fellow Dominican scholastic like Thomas Aquinas, both philosophical reason and revelation in Scripture may reach the same truth, both in content and in the mode of apprehension. Influenced by Maimonides (1135–1204), he adopts a speculative approach to the inner meaning of Scripture in a 'mystical' or 'parabolical' sense that is beyond the literal sense. Following both the Christian Platonist and the negative theological traditions, Eckhart teaches that all things flow out from God in two phases, that of the inner emanation of the Trinitarian Persons and that of the creation of all things. Similarly, they flow back to God in two phases, that of the birth of the Word in the soul and that of the penetration of the soul into the divine ground of God. This divine ground is described both paradoxically and apophatically.

Theology does not so much reveal truths about God as, instead, it establishes for finite minds a paradoxical knowledge of the unknown ground that is God beyond God. The ineffability of God demands multiple strategies for speaking of such a God, none of which are definitive in themselves. No predicate can simply be applied to God. Thus existence, unity, truth and goodness are predicated of God, and at the same time God is stated to be beyond existence, unity, truth and goodness. Therefore, when existence is predicated of God, it must be denied to the finite human creature. Although he most frequently uses *esse*, or existence, to speak of God, Eckhart's preferred predicate for God is *intelligere*, the pure act of intelligence which he teaches is beyond existence. Both predication and analogy, for Eckhart, stress the fundamental difference between God and creature. For him, analogy is an opposition rather than a proportion as in Aquinas. Whichever transcendental is used of God, the application is inexorably dialectical. Thus the transcendentals are applied properly only to God, and not to creatures. Hence the creature is nothing in itself, but it exists only radically within God's existence. God is the existence of all things: 'If my life is God's being, then God's existence must be my existence, and God's is-ness is my is-ness, neither less nor more.' This doctrine, condemned in the papal bull, is the source of the frequent, but false, attribution of pantheism to Eckhart. He defended himself by distinguishing between the 'absolute existence' of God and the 'formally inherent existence' of creatures. In accord with this distinction, what he affirms of creatures can be both denied and affirmed of God. Thus if creatures exist, God does not: 'Nothing is formally both cause and effect if the cause is a true cause. Now God is the cause of all existence. It follows that existence is not formally present in God.' On the other hand, if God's existence is considered, the creature's existence disappears within God's. Eckhart's dialectic is an attempt to combine both a transcendent and an immanent determination of God's reality. It has a theological coherence that has escaped commentators in both the fourteenth and twentieth centuries. In the words of

Bernard McGinn, 'the Meister was after ... a way of speaking about God as simultaneously totally immanent to creatures as their real existence and *by that very fact* absolutely transcendent to them as *esse simpliciter* or *esse absolutum*.' Eckhart affirmed the sharpest possible difference between God and creature as well as the sharpest possible identity between them.

Eckhart as a mystic is disinterested in special states of rapture or of sensible experiences. His teaching on mystical experience displays a 'this-worldliness'. He is not an ecstatic. The purpose of his theology and of preaching was to see the ordinary in a new, true way, to let what is disclose itself. Thus the person who is open to being sees that God and man are one at their deepest ground: 'He can as truly find it and live it and possess it within him as God is God and I am a man.'

Although his language is open to misunderstanding, there can be little doubt of the orthodoxy of Eckhart's theological intentions when he is understood as a *Scholastic theologian and a preacher in two different languages. The boldness of his dialectical method, in both his Latin and German writings, explains the difficulty his contemporaries had with many of his dialectical propositions. To add to the difficulty in interpreting Eckhart, the *Romantics in nineteenth-century Germany saw him as a precursor of German spirit. Some later interpreters have understood him as the prototype Christian mystic (*R. Otto [1869–1937]), or even at the extreme as a proto-Nazi (A. Rosenberg [1893–1946]). He is widely cited in generic studies of mysticism where his specific theological context is lost.

DANIEL P. SHERIDAN

FURTHER READING: *Meister Eckhart: The Essential Sermons, Commentaries, Treatises, and Defense* (trans. and intro. E. Colledge, OSA, and B. McGinn; New York, 1981); V. Lossky, *Théologie Négative et Connaissance de Dieu chez Maître Eckhart* (Paris, 1960); B. McGinn (ed.), *Meister Eckhart: Teacher and Preacher* (New York, 1986); R. Otto, *Mysticism East and West: A Comparative Analysis of the Nature of Mysticism* (New York, 1932).

Ecofeminism

In 1974, in an article entitled 'Le Temps de l'Ecoféminisme', translated as 'The Time for Ecofeminism', the French writer Françoise d'Eaubonne called for a mass movement of women 'to remake the planet around an entirely new model', that of 'egalitarian administration of a world being reborn'. She saw this as a necessity, as 'the planet is in danger of dying, and we along with it'. Ecofeminism was, she said, 'the sole possibility for our species to still have a future'.

This perspective on feminism brought together women's consciousness of their historically constructed domination and a burgeoning consciousness of the crucial role played in environmental degradation by the logic of male domination. Western concepts of mastery over women and over Nature were seen as two sides of the same coin. This synthesis between feminism and ecology is intended to offer a transformative dialectic between them, which both overcomes domination of women and Nature and reconnects Nature and culture.

The relationship between biological and cultural difference, and in particular between human nature and culture, is a hotly debated issue in ecofeminist theory. On the one hand, those who reject any essentialist notion of the relation between women and Nature see this identification as a marginalizing of women. On the other hand, those who emphasize the relation see it as a catalyst for a new consciousness. Others working for social justice fear that women's particular issues, such as the feminization of poverty, will lose focus. All are united in their commitment to non-violence and to the abolition of militarism, and in their concern for sustaining life processes.

The move towards integration of ecojustice and social transformation in ecofeminist consciousness includes a reshaping of the concept of God from one modelled on male rationality ruling over women and Nature to one of God immanent in, while not bounded by, the different life communities which make up the earth community. Models of co-operation, compassion and interdependence are used to evoke a sense of the sacredness of all life. This is expressed practically in women's involvement in peace movements, in groups campaigning non-violently against environmental degradation in their local communities, and in co-operatives of various kinds ranging from literacy and reproductive health campaigns to women's banking systems in rural agricultural communities and high-profile input into the biotechnology debate.

There are also ecofeminist spirituality initiatives which foster a sense of the sacredness of women's bodies as a way of reclaiming the goodness of femaleness, of sexuality and of the earth itself from religious traditions which have systematically disparaged them in favour of a metaphysic which privileges the eternal, the immaterial, the objective and the rational over the changing, the material and over personal feelings. Many ecofeminist rituals mark stages in the individual's life concurrent with or complementing those which celebrate liturgical or seasonal cycles. These help to reinforce the individual's sense of participating at many levels in a network of relationships sustaining diverse earth communities, and of committing ourselves to making those relationships just, non-violent and fruitful.

ANNE PRIMAVESI

FURTHER READING: Carol Adams (ed.), *Ecofeminism and the Sacred* (New York, 1993); Irene Diamond and Gloria Orenstein (eds.), *Reweaving the World: The Emergence of Ecofeminism* (San Francisco, 1990); Maria Mies and Vandana Shiva, *Ecofeminism* (London, 1993); Val Plumwood, *Feminism and the Mastery of Nature* (London / New York, 1993); Anne Primavesi, *From Apocalypse to Genesis: Ecology, Feminism and Christianity* (Tunbridge Wells / Minneapolis, 1991); Karen Warren (ed.), *Ecological Feminism* (London / New York, 1994).

Ecumenical Theology

'Ecumenical theology' is theological reflection aimed at nurturing the unity of the Christian church, or at overcoming schism between divided churches. In this broad sense the practice has ancient roots. Thus, *Athanasius's attempt to rally the various anti-Arian parties around the *homoousios* could be seen as an early venture in 'ecumenical' theology. The same might be said of the Augsburg Confession, drafted by *Philip Melanchthon as a possible instrument of reconciliation between reform churches and Rome. Presupposed in all such efforts is the historic Christian conviction concerning the church's unity, grounded in Jesus' prayer for his disciples: 'that they may all be one' (Jn. 17:20).

In the more usual and specific sense of the term, however, 'ecumenical theology' is a distinctly modern phenomenon. It presupposes the ecumenical movement, born of early twentieth-century efforts at overcoming divisions within Protestantism. The scandalous picture of churches competing in the mission fields of Africa and Asia initially led to calls for various forms of practical co-operation. Yet the question of the churches' specifically *doctrinal* disagreements could not long be postponed. To address these, the Faith and Order Commission was formed in 1927 in Lausanne, Switzerland. A part of the World Council of Churches since 1948, Faith and Order serves as a major forum for ecumenical work among Protestant, Orthodox and Roman Catholic Christians. Among its major achievements has been the 1982 statement titled *Baptism, Eucharist, and Ministry*, often referred to by the abbreviation *BEM*, as well as the 1991 text *Confessing One Faith*, an ecumenical commentary on the so-called *Niceno-Constantinopolitan Creed.

Most mainstream ecumenism assumes that a purely inward or spiritual unity among Christians is not enough. To be faithful to the gift of unity they receive as members of Christ's body, believers are called to manifest this gift in common life, witness and service to the world. Terms like 'visible unity' and 'full communion' are often employed to describe this goal. While just what 'full communion' entails is a contested issue, it is widely agreed that it does not mean uniformity. Just as the triune God is a unity who embraces 'otherness', so there is room for a legitimate pluralism among churches in matters like liturgy, governance and theological tradition, so long as their communion in the apostolic faith is not imperilled. Of course, deciding which differences are and are not church-dividing is one of the major issues at stake in any ecumenical discussion.

Ecumenical dialogue has generated its own peculiar methods and styles of theological reflection. Participants in the dialogues, especially the smaller, more intimate bilateral discussions, regularly comment on the importance of simply listening to what their conversation partners have to say. Coming to recognize one's own faith in the often strange idiom of another tradition helps foster the conviction – one might call it an axiom of ecumenical theology – that the church's unity is an already existing reality, even though hidden under human sin. For this reason the experience of friendship seems to play an even greater role in ecumenism than in other forms of theology. Once Christians from different traditions have intensively worked and prayed together, it becomes harder to believe that the differences dividing them are ultimate.

On a more formal level, two strategies have played an especially important role in ecumenical dialogue. The first is the practice of *ressourcement*. Ecumenical theology has benefited from the same 'return to the sources' of Scripture and tradition that nurtured the great theological revivals of the twentieth century (neo-orthodoxy, *théologie nouvelle*, etc.). This has been the case above all with respect to biblical study. The mere awareness that Paul, for example, was not trying to answer questions posed by *Luther or the Council of Trent can set *Reformation debates over justification in a new light. Historical research can also aid in clarifying the background and precise nature of doctrinal disagreements. To stay with the previous example, Lutheran-Roman Catholic dialogue has gone to great lengths to situate the sixteenth-century controversies within the history of medieval debates on grace, faith and justification. While such historical work does not by itself resolve all differences, it is useful in overcoming entrenched stereotypes, and it can often point to the deeper truths each side is seeking to safeguard in its doctrinal formulations.

The second strategy is the quest for a common language or conceptual framework. A disagreement that seems intractable in its traditional form may look quite different after it has been creatively 'redescribed', perhaps in language drawn from Scripture itself. The debate over the historic episcopate furnishes a good example of this approach. Catholics, Orthodox and some Anglicans have argued that bishops in historic succession are essential to the church's identity; Protestants have been reluctant to make this claim, fearing that it tends to restrict the freedom of the gospel. *BEM* and other dialogues have tried to break this impasse by emphasizing the *function* assigned to bishops, namely a ministry of unity and pastoral oversight (*episcopê*). Since even non-episcopal churches can acknowledge the biblical warrant and practical necessity underlying *episcopê*, the concept offers a shared framework for discussing more contentious issues, for example the relation between episcopal and other forms of ordained ministry. As the example illustrates, this more constructive aspect of ecumenism often relies on the insights achieved by *ressourcement*.

One of the pioneering experiments in ecumenical dialogue has been the Groupe des Dombes, an informal colloquy composed mainly of French Catholic and Reformed Christians. First convened by Abbot Paul Couturier in 1937, the group has met regularly since the end of World War II. Because of its unofficial status the Groupe des Dombes has felt an unusual freedom to broach thorny issues, especially those revolving around ecclesiology, sacraments and ordained ministry. Typical of the Dombes approach is its situating of these doctrines in a robust Trinitarian context. By stressing the agency of the Spirit in the Eucharist, for example, the dialogue has tried to combine a 'Catholic' sense of the sacrament's efficacy with a 'Protestant' stress on its utterly gracious character. In this as in other respects, the Groupe des Dombes has proved prophetic of many of the more official dialogues.

Prior to about 1960, the Roman Catholic Church maintained a wary distance from the ecumenical movement. If non-Catholics wished to foster Christian unity, it judged, they could best do so by returning to the one true Church. This situation changed radically with *Vatican II, whose 'Decree on Ecumenism' (1964) marks one of the watersheds of twentieth-century church history. Since then, the Catholic Church has been an active participant in the work of Faith and Order, as well as in numerous bilateral dialogues. Among the most productive of the latter have been the conversations held with Anglicans and Lutherans. Following a 1966 meeting between Archbishop of Canterbury *Michael Ramsey and Pope Paul VI, the Anglican-Roman Catholic International Commission (ARCIC) was set up to address the theological differences dividing the two communions. Between 1971 and 1976 the Commission published far-reaching statements on Eucharistic doctrine, ministry and authority in the church. The statements on the Eucharist and ministry claimed to have achieved 'substantial agreement', that is agreement sufficient for the two churches to initiate actual steps toward unity. Questions of authority and, in particular, of papal infallibility, proved more intractable, though even here some cautiously hopeful progress appeared to have been made. Yet when the ARCIC Final Report was issued in 1982 it met with a critical response from the Vatican, which held the claimed 'substantial agreement' to be defective in relation to central Catholic teachings (e.g. transubstantiation and the church's role in the Eucharistic sacrifice). Sobering as this reaction was, it raised two key questions that need to be addressed in any

ecumenical dialogue. First, precisely how much disagreement is tolerable when churches seek to enter into communion? And second, how far can theological consensus go in reformulating or 'bending' the received language of doctrine in the interests of unity?

Like ARCIC, international dialogue between Roman Catholics and Lutherans has addressed issues concerning the sacraments, ministry and the church's teaching office. Yet understandably the doctrine of justification by faith has been a major priority, given the key role this doctrine has played in shaping Lutheran identity. Here, indeed, the results have been nothing short of astonishing. Building on a series of rich and detailed historical studies, Lutheran and Catholic theologians have argued that the mutual condemnations of the sixteenth century may have been aimed, so to speak, at non-existent targets. Lutherans were never Manichean pessimists, even if the formula *simul iustus et peccator* (at the same time justified and a sinner) must have sounded that way to their opponents. Likewise, Catholics never taught that human beings can save themselves, even if the Reformers' critique of late medieval theology and penitential practice was to a large extent justified. More positively, each church argues that its own *present* doctrine tries to address the most urgent concerns of the other.

The Lutheran stress on salvation 'by faith alone' affirms rather than denies the necessity of good works; Catholics explain that their emphasis on the fruits of grace is intended as a praise of God's power, not as an affirmation of human self-sufficiency. In the words of the North American Lutheran-Catholic dialogue:

> Our entire hope of justification and salvation rests on Christ Jesus and the gospel whereby the good news of God's merciful action in Christ is made known; we do not place our ultimate trust in anything other than God's promise and saving work in Christ. This excludes ultimate reliance on our faith, virtues, or merits, even though we acknowledge God working in these by grace alone (*sola gratia*).

As in the case of ARCIC, Lutheran-Catholic dialogue on justification has not claimed to have resolved all differences. Yet the differences that remain no longer seem such as to warrant the division of the churches. On this one issue, at least, the sheerly doctrinal obstacles to unity appear to have been overcome.

Of course, Protestant churches have to address not only their relationship with Roman Catholicism but also their divisions among themselves. Among the oldest of these is the bitter division between Reformed and Lutheran bodies over teaching on the Lord's Supper. The Leuenberg Agreement of 1973 officially ended this split among European Protestants, bringing the churches into full Eucharistic fellowship with one another. A similar agreement in the 1990s provided for full communion and shared ministries among Lutheran and Reformed churches in the USA.

As mentioned above, among the most visible ecumenical achievements has been the statement on *Baptism, Eucharist, and Ministry* issued by the Faith and Order Commission. Although it makes for fairly dry reading, *BEM* offers a remarkable brief synthesis of much twentieth-century ecumenical thinking. The main text sets out the theological convergence achieved on each issue, while a running commentary identifies historical differences that have been overcome or areas of continued disagreement.

The importance of *ressourcement* for *BEM* is evident in its discussion of ordained ministry. The document sketches the historical development of various forms of ordained ministry, from the apostles in the New Testament period to the second- and third-century pattern of bishops, presbyters and deacons. Given that forms of ministry were in flux in the early church, it becomes difficult to claim that any one church possesses 'the' biblically-mandated pattern of church order. On the other hand, *BEM* poses the question whether the historic threefold ministry does not exercise a 'powerful claim' on those churches that now lack it:

Although there is no single New Testament pattern ... and although other forms of the ordained ministry have been blessed with the gifts of the Holy Spirit, nevertheless the threefold ministry of bishop, presbyter and deacon may serve as an expression of the unity we seek and also as a means for achieving it.

At the same time, *BEM* is extremely careful to situate its discussion of ordained ministry in the wider context of the ministry of the people of God. The Spirit bestows gifts on all members of the church for the building up of Christ's body. The ordained minister is not a bureaucrat exercising impersonal power, but a believer whose special calling is to remind the church of its 'fundamental dependence on Jesus Christ, and thereby provide, within a multiplicity of gifts, a focus of its unity'.

The end of the twentieth century saw a certain sobering of the ecumenical hopes marking the immediate post-Vatican II period. In many cases great theological progress had been made, only to be followed by apathy or resistance on the part of the churches. It has proved harder than imagined to take concrete steps toward *koinōnía*. Some have proposed that a model of local or grass-roots ecumenism needs to supplement the work of the theologians. More radically, it has been suggested that ecumenical theology reflects a hidden triumphalism on the part of the churches, and that mutual repentance and forgiveness need to precede further 'dialogue'. Both proposals have the merit of reminding us that ecumenical theology cannot create the unity of the church. It can only be an intellectual form of prayer for the Holy Spirit, who alone draws believers into the acknowledgement of 'one Lord, one faith, one baptism, one God and Father of all' (Eph. 4:4–6).

JOSEPH L. MANGINA

FURTHER READING: H. George Anderson, T. Austin Murphy and Joseph A. Burgess (eds.), *Justification by Faith: Lutherans and Catholics in Dialogue VII* (Minneapolis, 1985); Faith and Order, *Baptism, Eucharist, and Ministry* (Faith and Order Paper 111; Geneva, 1982); *Confessing the One Faith: An Ecumenical Explication of the Apostolic Faith as it is Confessed in the Nicene-Constantinopolitan Creed* (381) (Faith and Order Paper 153; Geneva, 1991); Robert Jenson, *Unbaptized God: The Basic Flaw in Ecumenical Theology* (Minneapolis, 1992); George Lindbeck, *The Nature of Doctrine: Religion and Theology in a Postliberal Age* (Philadelphia, 1984); Harding Meyer and Lukas Vischer (eds.), *Growth in Agreement: Reports and Agreed Statements of Ecumenical Conversations on a World Level* (New York, 1984); Ephraim Radner, *The End of the Church: A Pneumatology of Christian Division in the West* (Grand Rapids / Cambridge, 1998); Konrad Raiser, *Ecumenism in Transition: A Paradigm Shift in the Ecumenical Movement?* (Geneva, 1991); Ruth Rouse and Stephen C. Neil (eds.), *A History of the Ecumenical Movement 1517–1948*, I (Geneva, 3rd edn, 1986); Harold E. Fey (ed.), *The Ecumenical Advance: A History of the Ecumenical Movement 1948–68* (Geneva, 2nd edn, 1986); Second Vatican Council, 'Decree on Ecumenism', in *Documents of Vatican II* (ed. Austin P. Flannery; Grand Rapids, 1984).

Edwards, Jonathan (1703–58)

In his dissertation *On the Nature of True Virtue*, written in 1755 but published posthumously in 1765, Jonathan Edwards defines God as 'the Being of beings', the one who, 'as infinitely the greatest being ... is allowed to be infinitely the most beautiful and excellent: and all the beauty to be found throughout the whole creation, is but the reflection of the diffused beams of that Being who hath an infinite fullness of brightness and glory' (*Works*, VIII, p. 550). *True Virtue* was intended to be read alongside the dissertation *Concerning the End for Which God Created the World*, a work which concludes with an assertion of the appropriateness of the eternal damnation of sinners. It is this startling combination of philosophical insight and *Reformed theology or, in this particular, of beauty and horror, that renders Edwards such an intriguing and enigmatic thinker.

Edwards was born on 5 October 1703 in East Windsor, Connecticut, the fifth of eleven children to be born to Timothy Edwards and Esther (née Stoddard) – but the only boy. As early as 1716 he was enrolled as a student at (what was to become) Yale. In 1723 he was awarded a Master's degree, and by May of the following year he had been elected tutor. Even in his earliest writings the same enigmatic combination of ideas and influences is explicit. A genuine polymath, the young Edwards displayed a love of the *Puritans, a fascination for scientific theory and analysis, and a concern to formulate a reflective response to the increasingly dominant empiricism of *John Locke (1632–1704).

In the latter respect Edwards's developing epistemology bears a marked similarity to that of *George Berkeley (1685–1753), though the possible influence of Berkeley on Edwards remains a matter of dispute. For Edwards all knowledge is given by God, and that in a more explicitly Trinitarian dynamic than was suggested by Berkeley. The substance of a thing is the precise and unchanging idea of that thing in the mind of God, an idea of the thing communicated to us by his Spirit. All our ideas are communicated to us directly by God and the continuity of those ideas, which constitutes the coherence of our consciousness, derives from the coherence of those ideas in the mind of God. Hereby the division between knowledge and will is superseded since, as the idea of a thing is communicated to us by God, so also is a sense of the beauty of the thing: human will is simply our inclination towards or away from the idea of the thing.

In 1727 Edwards joined his maternal grandfather, Solomon Stoddard, in the church at Northampton, Massachusetts and, after the latter's death in 1729, Edwards remained as sole pastor. Whether his successive written responses to the phenomena of 'revival' betray a growing caution, or whether the distinctions between them merely reflect distinctions of context and purpose, the underlying understanding of the phenomena was set out in a sermon entitled 'A Divine and Supernatural Light' (1733) and is simply an outworking of the theocentric epistemology already noted. The Spirit, who communicates all ideas to our consciousness, communicates to us his own consciousness of God. And, since this implies no mere notional knowledge but a sensibility of the heart or will, this work of the Spirit issues in a change of affections, and a change of affections is phenomenal – it can be discerned, described and evaluated. Edwards's final written response to the phenomena of revival, *A Treatise Concerning the Religious Affections* (1746), comprises a penetrating analysis of religious experience that remains unsurpassed.

Given this expectation for discernible affections in the converted it is hardly surprising that Edwards came to reject his grandfather's less discriminating policy concerning church membership and admission to communion, a rejection that eventually led in 1750 to Edwards's dismissal from the Northampton congregation. His subsequent appointment as pastor to the 'mission' church at Stockbridge, while not resolving his painful relations with certain prominent New England families, nonetheless gave opportunity for some of his most significant literary work. This output ended prematurely with Edwards's abrupt death following an inoculation against smallpox, leaving some writings to be published posthumously and others, principally comprising notes and jottings collected since his days at Yale, in barely publishable form. In 1757 he had been invited to become president of the newly formed Princeton College: he moved in January 1758, received the inoculation in February, and died on 22 March. His wife, Sarah, died on 2 October that same year.

The recent renaissance of interest in Edwards has sometimes been characterized by an implicit disjunction between Edwards the philosopher and Edwards the latter-day Puritan, between the author of the *Scientific and Philosophical Writings* (*Works*, VI) and the preacher of 'Sinners in the Hands of an Angry God' (1741). Edwards's more perceptive commentators, however, identify the theocentricity that distinguishes and unites the entirety of his thought. The key works from his period in Stockbridge, *A Careful and Strict Enquiry into the Modern Prevailing Notions of Freedom of Will* (1754), *The Great Christian Doctrine of Original Sin Defended* (1758) and *A History of the Work of Redemption* (1774) share with the two dissertations mentioned at the beginning of this article not only a God-centred account of creation and humanity that is typically Puritan, but also a God-centred epistemology that is Edwards's response to *Enlightenment rationalism. The distinction between our will to choose and our will to will forms the basis both of a profound account of the human condition and of an understanding of the dynamic of divine grace. That which remains less easy to resolve is the disjunction between themes of beauty and harmony on the one hand and, on the other, the perception that God's glory is equally demonstrated in the justice of hell and the mercy of heaven. For all the Christocentric anticipations of *Barth this disjunction savours of an unnecessary yet central incoherence.

JOHN E. COLWELL

FURTHER READING: *Texts: The Works of Jonathan Edwards* (eds. Perry Miller, John E. Smith; New Haven, 1957– [invaluable for introductory and textual notes]); *The Works of Jonathan Edwards* (rev. Edward Hickman; 2 vols.; Carlisle, PA, 1974). *Studies:* Conrad Cherry, *The Theology of Jonathan Edwards: A Reappraisal* (New York, 1966); Terrence Erdt, *Jonathan Edwards: Art and the Sense of the Heart* (Amherst, MA, 1980); Robert W. Jenson, *America's Theologian: A Recommendation of Jonathan Edwards* (Oxford, 1988); Sang Lee, *The Philosophical Theology of Jonathan Edwards* (Princeton, 1988); Michael J. McClymond, 'God the Measure: Towards an Understanding of Jonathan Edwards' Theocentric Metaphysics', *Scot J Th* 47 (1994), pp. 43–59; Perry Miller, *Jonathan Edwards* (New York, 1949); Ian H. Murray, *Jonathan Edwards: A New Biography* (Edinburgh, 1987); John E. Smith, *Jonathan Edwards: Puritan, Preacher, Philosopher* (London, 1992).

Enlightenment

The European intellectual and social history known as the Enlightenment covers roughly a period from the English Revolution of 1688 to the French Revolution in 1789. It was principally an eighteenth-century movement, and in practice it can be further broken down into three sub-periods. The first of these is represented by such figures as the political thinker Montesqieu and the political and religious satirist Voltaire. This period can be circumscribed to the first half of the eighteenth century. The representative figures of the second period include *Hume, Rousseau and the French materialists d'Alembert, Diderot, and d'Holbach. Building as the first period had done on *Locke and Newton, they were united by a common proclamation of the methods of the natural sciences based on observation, and the consequent rejection of the authority of revelation, sacred writings and creeds – the basic elements of the Christian tradition. Those who stand out in the third period – the so-called 'deep' Enlightenment, some of whose leading figures represented the contribution of the German enlightenment – are such as Lessing, Wieland and *Kant, especially Kant (1724–1804). Kant's legacy was constituted by the separation of substantive reason, hitherto expressed in religion and metaphysics, into the three autonomous spheres of science, morality and art. Each sphere had its own respective criterion: truth, normative rightness and authenticity or beauty.

The movement of the Enlightenment was by no means unanimous in terms of its aims and convictions. It took different forms at different times in different countries – for example, in England, France, Germany and Scotland. There was, however, a continuity of common commitment to the belief that reason and criticism were a more valid means of knowing the truth, a more likely route to human betterment and lasting dignity, than the prescriptions that had been passed down in tradition from the past. This was no less true of some of the leading figures of the first half of the century who had been deists than of the main thinkers of the second half who, by and large, were atheists. When Kant reflected on his century he was cautious in his praise: 'Are we living in an enlightened age? No, but we are living in a age of Enlightenment' (*What is Enlightenment?*, p. 84). Kant set the agenda for a critical and ongoing reappraisal of the concepts of self, will, freedom, truth, rationality, human identity and nature.

The legacy of Enlightenment (*Aufklärung*), the prelude to modernity as Peter Gay calls it (*The

Enlightenment: An Interpretation, II, pp. 3–12), was primarily the inheritance bequeathed by two of its most distinctive animating forces: *autonomy* and *criticism*. *Autonomy* as Kant used it signalled a moral imperative: 'Autonomy of the Will is a property of it by which it is a law to itself independently of any property of objects of volition' (*Foundations of the Metaphysics of Morals*, p. 59). In the sphere of knowledge, the autonomous will of human beings must be conjoined to a similarly autonomous reason.

> Enlightenment is man's release from his self-incurred tutelage ... man's inability to make use of his understanding without direction from another. Self-incurred is this tutelage when its cause lies not in lack of reason but in lack of resolution and courage to use it without direction from another. ... "Have the courage to use your own reason" – that is the moral of Enlightenment. (Kant, *What is Enlightenment?*, p. 85)

The ethos of intellectual freedom inaugurated by the social, economic and cultural movements of the period was essentially a freedom, as Kant's discussion on the autonomy of the will implies, from external constraint. In the context of the Enlightenment, such a freedom was at once: freedom from the constraints of church authority which believed its interests and those of Christianity to be best served by the control and curtailment of enquiry insofar as this was liable to usurp the eternal truths of religion; and freedom from state authority fearful of, and intent on protecting itself against, what it perceived as the dangers inherent in social change.

In the seventeenth century, reason was embodied in the metaphysical or philosophical systems exemplified by such as Leibniz's monadology. In the eighteenth century, reason was no longer quintessentially of the nature of an objectified form, no longer objectified (as in Leibniz's monads) in system or structure; it was rather more akin to a kinetic *process* whose existence, though inferred, was plainly manifest in the change it brought about:

> The whole eighteenth century understands reason in this sense; not as a sound body of knowledge, principles and truths, but as a kind of energy, a *force* [emphasis mine] which is fully comprehensible only in its agency and effects. What reason is, and what it can do, can never be known by its results but only by its function. (Cassirer, *The Philosophy of the Enlightenment*, pp. 6–7)

Since reason is an operative force (it is, Lessing said, not found in the possession of truth but rather in the search for truth), it was inevitable that autonomous reason came to be embodied in *critical reason*. Reason as a force was understood by the Enlightenment as a tool of *criticism* embodied in analytical measurement and dissection. Hence, the Age of Enlightenment, the Age of Philosophy, is also the Age of Criticism. The Age of Philosophy and the Age of Criticism are 'different expressions of the same situation, intended to characterise from diverse angles the fundamental intellectual energy which permeates the era unto which it owes its great trends of thought' (Cassirer, *Philosophy*, p. 275).

Theology and religious belief were not immune to this energy. Though *Descartes' method of doubt is often cited as the intellectual forerunner of the Enlightenment proper, it is now recognized that it is really John Locke (1632–1704) who is the proto-Enlightenment figure as regards the rationality of religious belief. As a Christian, Locke thought he could meet the apologetic challenge. For about a thousand years, western intellectuals had consulted a unified textual tradition – Paul and Virgil, *Aristotle and *Augustine among others – when faced with the question of what to believe on matters of morality and religion. In the wake of the *Reformation, personified among other things in *Luther's challenge to the church, the European cultural and intellectual tradition split into warring fragments. Amid the proliferation of confessional documents in the sixteenth and seventeenth centuries, religious knowledge and belief had to be reunited around another standard. Locke sought to resolve the moral and religious crisis faced by European intellectuals in the wake of the Reformation by making an appeal to reason: Let reason be your guide!

The emergence of critical apologetics during the seventeenth and eighteenth centuries testified to a fundamental shift in the epistemic stance of Christian theology from a 'faith seeking understanding' paradigm to what may be termed a 'faith requiring justification' paradigm. From the time of Christian antiquity to the Enlightenment, the 'faith seeking understanding' paradigm had constituted the fundamental rationale behind the respective epistemologies of Augustine, *Anselm, *Thomas Aquinas and *Calvin, to name some of the foremost names of the pre-Enlightenment theological tradition. With the demise of antiquity in the seventeenth and eighteenth centuries, this 'faith requiring justification' paradigm became the dominant paradigm for Christian theology.

The 'faith requiring justification' challenge to theology was based on the deeply held moral conviction that unless one had good reason for one's theological beliefs, one ought to give them up. This position contrasted with the epistemology of the pre-critical theological tradition. Pre-Enlightenment theologians such as Aquinas and Calvin did not attach foundationalist conditions to Christian articles of faith. Pre-Enlightenment theologians can be understood as viewing the Christian articles of faith – creation, atonement, redemption – as a set of basic beliefs. (A *basic* belief is a belief that is not, *as a matter of fact*, justified by reference to any other belief. It is not founded on any other belief. It is *basic* to one's theological belief-structure.) In other words, prior to the mindset of the Enlightenment, the faith that is believed is affirmed as a set of basic beliefs. With the advent of the Enlightenment, that same faith is subjected to the strictures of criticism.

God. On the issue of the relation between faith and reason, the critical attitude of the Enlightenment is nowhere better exemplified than in what it regarded as the basic infrastructure of theology and religious belief: the classical proofs of the existence of God. Kant was to classify these proofs in *The Critique of Pure Reason* under the categories of, respectively: the physico-theological proof; the cosmological proof; and the ontological proof. Hume's statement of the argument from (or to) design is an example of the first kind. (Such an argument found later expression in William Paley's deduction of the existence of God from mechanistic laws affirmed by such as Newton [*Natural Theology*, 1807]):

> ... The chief or sole argument for a divine existence (which I never question) is derived from the order of nature; where there appears such marks of intelligence and design, that you think it extravagant to assign, for its cause, either chance, or the blind and unguided force of matter. (Hume, *Enquiry Concerning Human Understanding*, §11, pp. 105f.)

The second category of proof is instantiated by Leibniz's *Contingentia Mundi*, and it proceeds from the observation of the contingent existence of the world. To the cosmological question 'Why is there something rather than nothing?', Leibniz applies his own basic principle of sufficient reason. The cosmological question is deemed to require an answer because the existence of the universe is a contingent fact as opposed to a logically necessary truth:

> Now this sufficient reason for the existence of the universe cannot be found in the procession of contingent things ... So the sufficient reason, which needs no further reason, must be outside the procession of contingent things, and is found in a substance which is the cause of that procession and which is a necessary being containing the reason for His existence in Himself ... and this final reason we call "God". (Leibniz, *Philosophical Writings* [ed. G.H.R. Parkinson; trans. M. Morris and G.H.R. Parkinson; London, 1973], §7–8)

The third category of proof is instantiated by the ontological argument as it was assimilated and understood by the classical philosophical tradition and which name was given by Kant. The argument constitutes the supreme example of a rationalist deductive proof in that it attempted to prove the existence of God from the examination of an a priori concept of God alone. This proof was first developed by Anselm and then criticized and somewhat ambivalently rejected by Aquinas. It was revived by Descartes and accepted by *Spinoza. Leibniz also accepted it, with some qualifications. It was Descartes' version that was rejected by both Hume and Kant.

The rationale behind Leibniz's proof, like that of Descartes and Spinoza's respective approaches to the question of the existence of God, is a rationalist one. According to *rationalism, the whole of our knowledge is based on a few self-evident truths from which all the rest can be derived by deductive reasoning. Without this foundation, the whole edifice would collapse before the onslaught of scepticism. Descartes' *cogito* remains the supreme example of this approach – a foundation that could not rationally be doubted. The empiricists, arguably Locke, but most certainly *Berkeley and Hume, saw the foundation of knowledge as consisting of items of sense-experience. According to Locke, knowledge is built up from 'ideas' that are, in some sense, imprinted on the mind when we use our sense organs. Empiricists such as Berkeley and Hume argued that all knowledge and ideas were derived from sense-experience. (Berkeley turned this epistemology into an ontology, arguing for his radical and ultimately sceptical conclusion that 'to be is to be perceived': *esse est percipi*. In a manner characteristic of Descartes' employment of God as a means of proof for the existence of the external world, Berkeley argued that God was the cause of the ideas which we perceive – the idea of the sun for example – and that he maintained their existence even when they were unperceived. Berkeley held the thesis that we perceive ideas of physical objects, not physical objects themselves.) The concluding paragraph of Hume's *Enquiry* summed up an empiricist manifesto that continued to be an influential force in the twentieth century. It called for all enlightened thinkers to unleash the forces of criticism on dogmatism wherever it existed:

> When we run over libraries, persuaded of these principles, what havoc must we make? If we take in our hand any volume; of divinity or school metaphysics, for instance; let us ask, *Does it contain any abstract reasoning concerning quantity or number?* No. *Does it contain any experimental reasoning concerning matter of fact or existence?* No. Commit it then to the flames: for it can contain nothing but sophistry and illusion. (Hume, *Enquiry*, p. 165)

Corresponding to these two kinds of reasoning, abstract and experimental, were two types of truth – relations of ideas and matters of fact or real existence: 'All objects of human reason or enquiry may naturally be divided into two kinds, to whit, *relations of ideas*, and *matters of fact*. Of the first kind are the sciences of Geometry, Algebra, and Arithmetic ...' (Hume, *Enquiry*, p. 25). The second kind is represented by the empirical sciences of physics, chemistry, history, et cetera. This classification of two types of truth, between on the one hand relations of ideas and, on the other, matters of fact – what has become known as 'Hume's fork' – is what Kant speaks of when crediting Hume with waking him from his 'dogmatic slumber'.

Kant's critical philosophy can be understood as a synthesis of rationalism and empiricism. It is this fact which led him to his sceptical conclusions concerning the possibility of rational proof of the existence of God. Hume rejected the validity of the argument from design. Leibniz affirmed his cosmological argument.

Kant argued that the a priori synthetic categories of the mind imposed limits on theoretical reason such that God was an object beyond the reach of possible experience. His critical philosophy added to Hume's truths of matters of fact and existence what for him was the patent existence of a priori synthetic truths (truths the negation of which was not a contradiction). He did not accept the Humean dichotomy of meaningful propositions because he believed that human beings are in possession of propositions which fall into neither of Hume's two classes; they form a third class whose logical nature, function and systematic connection, with each other and with other types of proposition, is the main subject of philosophy. Not all synthetic truths are a posteriori; some are a priori. A priori synthetic truths are truths that, while known a priori (before experience), were yet synthetic and accordingly informative about the world. By means of these truths Kant attempted to re-secure philosophy's own special identity by recasting it as a *transcendental* science specifying the conditions of the possibility of all experience. Such conditions constituted both a framework and a boundary within which all possible truths of theoretical (as opposed to practical) reason were apprehended. But since God as an object of theoretical reason lay outside or beyond this framework, and was in fact a 'noumenal' as opposed to a 'phenomenal' reality, theoretical reason was invalidated as a means of proving the existence of God. All such proofs were doomed a priori, though Kant saw in practical or moral reason the means of proving God as the precept of a moral postulate, the object of a moral faith.

This is why Kant said of his critical philosophy that it made room for faith: 'I have found it necessary to deny knowledge, in order to make room for faith' (*The Critique of Pure Reason*, 2nd edn, p. 29). Theologians responded to the potential in Kant's position on faith in God in various ways.

One way was to question the validity of the first critique's restriction of theoretical knowledge or cognition, for example (as in the idealistic philosophy) by following out Kant's principle of speculative reason and overcoming the phenomenal-noumenal split. The fundamental rationale behind *Hegel's criticism of Kant's critical philosophy was that it imposed overly narrow limits on reason. While *Marx and *Feuerbach endorsed Kant's maxim *Sapere*

Aude!, they did not endorse Kant's claim that faith was immune from the criticism of theoretical reason. Instead, they preferred to build their critique of religion on Hegel's philosophy of the development of absolute rational objective spirit through history by a process of thesis, antithesis and synthesis.

The central and defining problem of the generation to which Hegel (1770–1831) belonged was the reunification of the two opposing impulses of the time: on the one hand, the ideal of radical freedom as expressed in Kant, and, on the other, the desire for self-expression as a mode of feeling, for reintegration or reconciliation as advocated by *Romanticism. As the immediate intellectual context to their thought, Hegel provided both Marx (1818–83) and Feuerbach (1804–72) with the conceptual apparatus for constructing their critiques of religion and opposition to the veracity of theological thought. Marx understood religion in terms of Hegel's concept of alienation (antithesis). Feuerbach understood the concept of God as an objectification (*Vergegenständlichung*) or projection of the essential qualities of human nature.

Another, more minor, stream in the nineteenth century was the denial of reason's right to establish the point of departure for theology. The Danish Christian philosopher *Søren Kierkegaard (1813–55) rejected reason as the basis of theology on the grounds that the very nature of divine revelation implied that belief in it was neither natural nor reasonable. The only possible means of affirmation was one of existential commitment or what Kierkegaard called 'a leap of faith'.

Yet another stream, which was to be taken up by the *Ritschlian school, was adopted in the light of the perceived failure of the Hegelian synthesis in the second half of the nineteenth century. The model of critical thinking which reasserted itself in the intellectual mainstream during this period was that of the methodology of the natural sciences. The practical and tractable aims and methods of natural science were inextricably linked with progress in the material realm. As a matter of methodological principle, materialism and positivism became respectively the dominant, if not the exclusive, ontology and epistemology. Darwin's *The Origin of Species*, published in 1859, was pioneering in the former respect. In time, it brought about the practical acceptance of materialism as the only feasible

means of ascertaining the truth in the biological sciences. A positivist ethos manifested itself in most intellectual activity of that period – the sciences, philosophy and even theology. In German science, there was the science of Helmholtz, Hertz and Kirchnoff at Berlin. The homogeneous tradition of Austrian philosophy, which had begun with Brentano's *Psychology from an Empirical Standpoint* in 1874, followed the maxim, *Vera philosophiae methodus nulla alia nisi scientiae naturalis est* (the true method of philosophy is none other than that of natural science) as its guiding philosophical principle (Brentano, *Psychology*, p. 93).

Mach, Brentano's successor at Vienna, continued the empirical tradition originating in Hume and defended an anti-metaphysical, therefore apparently presuppositionless, positivism. In general, positivist thinking sought to protect the propositions of natural science from the encroachment of the unverifiable statements of metaphysics and theology. The theology of the German world of the second half of the nineteenth century was consistent with the ethos at large during this period. It betrayed – in the words of *Paul Tillich – 'an attitude of self-sufficient finitude'. It was heavily charged with Kant's conception of the highest good, the animating force behind Kant's notions of duty and moral law. Ritschl's theology was a species of anti-metaphysical moralism content to remain within the finite boundaries circumscribed by the transcendental analytic. It was in this sense that the Ritschlian school accepted in full the Kantian critique of theoretical reason and adopted the moral realm as the basis of thinking theologically. In doing so it conformed to the pressure of the positivism prevailing in the second half of the nineteenth century, a methodological position logically reconcilable with Kant's.

Finally, by far the most widely followed route was to enlarge the category of direct experience by turning to *Gefühl* (*Schleiermacher), *Abhang* (De Wette), or by finding in a fuller 'reason' the possibility of knowing the spiritual (*Coleridge). The most important of these thinkers is Schleiermacher. Schleiermacher had already spelled out the Enlightenment manifesto for a positive affirmation of theology in his *Speeches for the Cultured Despisers of Religion* delivered in 1799. In *The Christian Faith* Schleiermacher agreed with Kant that God cannot appear in a concept (*Begriff*) or judgement (*Urteil*), that this sort of objectification was epistemologically inaccurate. But he rejected Kant's deduction that faith in God and immortality was, if rational, necessarily moral. Instead of treating God in abstract moral terms, Schleiermacher located religion in the realm of feeling or immediate self-consciousness converging on a consciousness of 'ourselves as utterly dependent [*schlechthin abhängig*] or which is to say the same thing, as being in relation to God' (Schleiermacher, *The Christian Faith*, p. 12). To the extent that he opposed the translation of religion and theology into the intellectualistic or moralistic categories favoured by the Enlightenment and contraposed to them the Romantic categories of feeling and intuition, Schleiermacher may be said to have attempted to reassert the *sui generis* identity of religion. Claude Welch comments:

> It is frequently said that the great achievement of Schleiermacher, his creative breakthrough was his fresh interpretation of religion in its own integrity, according it fundamental institution and its locus in feeling or in the immediacy of human existence, whereby the traditionalist-orthodox debate was wholly undercut and a new possibility for understanding religion was opened. This is correct. (*Protestant Thought*, I, p. 68)

Each of these ways indicated a 'turn to the subject', a turn which had its motive-force in Kant's analysis in the *Critique of Pure Reason*. Twentieth-century theological existentialism such as that of the theology of *Bultmann continued to plough this particular field, drawing on Heidegger in a manner that had points of contact with Schleiermacher's essentially idealist self-understanding and Kierkegaardian paradox. In contrast, the theology of *Barth has attempted to restate a new species of theological realism loyal to biblical revelation.

Christology. Historically, the identity of the Christ of faith with the historical Christ testified in the New Testament and prophesied in the Old Testament was taken as foundational in Christian theology. But with the advent of the Enlightenment, a necessary condition of affirmation of the rational status of the divinity of Christ was belief in the miracles attested in the Gospels, and in particular, in what is taken to be the greatest miracle of all – the resurrection of Jesus Christ. Beginning with Locke, the attestation of miracle became central to reflection on

the critical foundations of Christian belief, informing *Bishop Butler's *Analogy of Religion* published in 1736 and Hume's *Enquiry* published in 1748. Hume wrote in the concluding paragraph of the tenth section of the *Enquiry*:

> ... upon the whole, we may conclude that the *Christian Religion* not only was first attended with miracles, but even to this day cannot be believed by any reasonable person without one. Mere reason is insufficient to convince us of its veracity: and whoever is moved by *Faith* to assent to it, is conscious of a continued miracle in his own person, which subverts all the principles of understanding, and gives him a determination to believe what is most contrary to custom and experience.

Hume's general argument is in complete harmony with the ironic tone and content of this passage. The probability of human delusion or fantasy or credulity is far greater than the probability of miracle, given the laws of nature as established by experience. Rational judgement based on experience led one to the conclusion that human testimony was inadequate to establish the occurrence of a miracle. Hume's sceptical principles provided the rationale behind the rationalist assault on miracle.

The Enlightenment in Germany, preceding its culmination in Kant, developed two distinctive approaches to the question of revelation and reason – the latter of which resembled Hume's approach. Christian Wolff (1679–1754), like Locke, held (1) that revelation may be above reason but not contrary to reason, and (2) that reason establishes the criteria by which revelation may be judged. This position was criticized from two directions: neology and rationalism. The contention of neology was twofold: (1) that revelation is real but its content is not different from that of natural religion in general, and (2) that reason may reject those individual doctrines of Christian revelation which are not identical with reason. The identification of reason and revelation is affirmed, but at the expense of emptying revelation of its distinctive content. The significance of neology was that it cancelled traditionally important teachings of the church from the complex of truths of revelation without undermining the idea of revelation itself.

On the other side, Wolff's position was attacked by rationalism. Rationalism agreed with Wolff that reason establishes the criteria to judge revelation. But it argued that reason's criteria judge revelation to be false, leaving reason to exist alone. Revelation is seen to be at odds with reason and therefore must be rejected. This was the position of Herman Samuel Reimarus in the *Wölfenbuttel Fragments* published by Lessing in 1774–78. Reimarus was a rationalist in matters of Christian revelation and argued that Jesus' resurrection from the dead cannot be sustained because it involved contradiction in both the evidence and the logic of the argument. The perceived failure of the argument from miracle compelled theology to base the doctrine of the divinity of Christ on grounds other than miracles. One route taken was to employ the Hegelian understanding of self-revelation in history as an alternative means of understanding revelation. This is essentially the position adopted and adapted by Barth in the *Church Dogmatics*.

The Bible. One fundamental element in the pre-critical interpretation of the biblical stories was the presumption of the *identity* of the world rendered by the biblical narratives with the world of extra-biblical thought, experience and reality. For the pre-critical exegete the two designated worlds were one and the same such that the latter world was to be interpreted in terms of the 'one real world detailed and made accessible in the biblical story – not the reverse' (Hans Frei, *The Eclipse of Biblical Narrative*, pp. 4–5). In the seventeenth and eighteenth centuries, with the advent of historical criticism, this original unity – a once seamless garment – began to come apart: there now arose a logical distinction, and in consequence, a 'reflective distance between the stories and the reality they depict' (Frei, *Biblical Narrative*, pp. 6–7).

Increasingly, what had hitherto simply not been reflected upon – the possibility that this world might *not* be the same world which God had created, might *not* be the very same world in which Jesus Christ had been crucified dead and buried and had risen again on the third day, might *not* be the very same world in which Jesus Christ would come again in glory to judge the living and the dead – that some or all of these things might *not* be true – became a matter for critical reflection. Investigation into the factual truth (or falsity) of the biblical stories became a matter of moral necessity. Nevertheless, Locke, for example, had no doubt of the historicity of the narrated events precisely because he thought there was good reason for believing in the revelation attested in the New Testament.

The subjection of the Bible to critical-historical hermeneutics had negative consequences for theological doctrine. Though not without precedent in textual criticism such as that to be found already in *Erasmus, it reinforced earlier arguments that such doctrines as the two natures of Christ and the Trinity were not to be found in the New Testament. In addition, it was concluded that there was little if no biblical support for the concept of atoning satisfaction, the doctrine of the imputation of the righteousness of Christ, or the Augustinian doctrine of original sin. The Augustinian denial of the human capacity for perfectibility was rejected on other grounds – namely that it was in direct contradiction to the Enlightenment belief in progress in matters natural and personal.

However, the real import of critical-historical hermeneutics emerged in the perception that the Bible had been itself a product of history, and in particular of a historical context which was qualitatively different from the emerging modern one. Pre-critical interpreters such as Calvin presumed that *in itself* the literal sense of the Bible, and the biblical narrative in particular, was sufficient for the rational affirmation of the historical truth-claims it made. With the advent of criticism this assumption was put under severe pressure. The authority of biblical revelation was no longer immune to criticism. The Bible was to be treated by the historian as he or she would treat any other historical writing from the past. This meant, among other things, that the main task of hermeneutics was to understand the texts in terms of the historical context and consciousness of their authors and the mind-set and intentions of the persons whose actions were narrated in them. A reading of the Bible confined to the plain literal sense of the text became increasingly superseded by a historical-contextual reading: what counted for the interpreter was the literal *historical* sense of the biblical text as inferred from historical context.

As a result of this historical-critical method of interpretation, the Enlightenment view of the Old and New Testaments differed significantly from that of its pre-critical predecessors. The typological method of reading the Old Testament was excluded, which meant the rejection of the belief that these texts contained prophecies of Jesus Christ. The Old Testament was to be understood in its essentially pre-Christian historical identity as Hebrew Scripture. Theological dogma, especially Christological doctrine, was increasingly perceived as a later Hellenistic development with no indigenous historical basis in first-century Palestinian consciousness. Biblicism and dogmatism were excluded as theological points of departure on the grounds that a truly critical theology must develop appropriate critical methods of biblical interpretation sensitive to historical context.

The rationalist tradition in Christology took the Bible as someone like Calvin would have understood it and submitted it to a rationalist analysis of the kind found in Hume. It was not until *David Friedrich Strauss's *The Life of Jesus Critically Examined*, published in 1835, that critical-historical hermeneutics opened a new chapter in the history of biblical interpretation. The distinction between faith and reason was reapplied to the Bible in the form of the distinction between faith and history. Drawing on a mythical mode of interpretation, Strauss developed hermeneutical criteria which distinguished between historical factuality and 'ancient' or archaic mythological thinking as regards the Gospel narratives. Such criteria were used to demarcate the real Jesus of history from a Christ-figure who had been the product of a first-century Palestinian mythological consciousness. The basic rationale behind Strauss's hermeneutical criteria later resurfaced in Bultmann's attempts to demythologize the New Testament. Strauss was not primarily interested in a historical reconstruction of what had actually taken place behind the Gospels, but his work constituted a point of departure for those who were. This was a question that was later taken up by *Albert Schweitzer, culminating in the results of the first quest for the historical Jesus. Whatever the inadequacies of these results, there is no doubt that critical-historical hermeneutics remains the mainstream methodology in biblical studies.

In assessing the consequences of the Enlightenment legacy for theology one must be careful not to underestimate its achievements and its undoubted revolutionary impact on the relationship between human beings and the natural and social world, their understanding of their place within the universe. To think that one can ignore and indeed devalue the contribution that the physical, biological and medical sciences have made to an understanding of the physical and human world is philosophically naïve. To criticize the main canons of the Enlightenment for being the inevitable progenitor of a Eurocentric, andro-centric mindset, world war, the ills of global capitalism, or worse, is to employ a historicist framework that goes beyond the evidence. Any alternative framework of understanding, such as postmodernism, has at the very least still to prove itself as fruitful a mode of understanding as its 'predecessor'. However, notwithstanding the Kantian critique, twentieth-century science, notably Einstein's theories of general and special relativity, and quantum mechanics, have been understood by some to provide resources for a revitalized natural theology. The meta-mathematical discoveries of Gödel on the limitations of human thought, in an area where it had appeared to be at its most powerful and successful, have contributed to a renewed appreciation of the mystery and complexity of all real systems that can be mirrored by relatively simple mathematical ones. In the field of the human sciences, the Enlightenment has been less successful. To some extent this may be due to misconceived methodology, but it is also due to the enduring mystery and complexity of the human being. Reformed epistemology has forged a new understanding of the relation between faith and reason which promises much in the way of a reaffirmation of the rationality of belief in the defining articles of the Christian faith and faith in God. Post-critical analyses such as those offered by Karl Barth and Brevard Childs may offer a way out of the current impasse in both historical truth-claiming Christology and biblical interpretation by reasserting the enduring truths of the pre-critical approach to both – but without devaluing the contribution made by the Enlightenment.

NEIL B. MACDONALD

FURTHER READING: Ernst Cassirer, *The Philosophy of the Enlightenment* (Princeton, 1951); Peter Gay, *The Enlightenment: An Interpretation* (2 vols.; New York, 1969); Hans W. Frei, *The Eclipse of Biblical Narrative: A Study of Eighteenth- and Nineteenth-Century Hermeneutics* (New Haven, 1974); Claude Welch, *Protestant Thought in the Nineteenth Century* (2 vols.; New Haven, 1972, 1985); Jürgen Habermas, 'Modernity – An Incomplete Project', in *Postmodern Culture* (ed. H. Foster; London, 1985); David Hume, *Enquiry Concerning Human Understanding and Concerning the Principles of Morals* (ed. P.H. Nidditch;

Oxford, 1975); Immanuel Kant, *The Critique of Pure Reason* (trans. N. Kemp Smith; London, 2nd edn, 1933); *Foundations of the Metaphysics of Morals* (trans. and intro. L.W. Beck; New York, 1959); *What is Enlightenment?* (trans. and intro. L.W. Beck; New York, 1959); Richard Schacht, *Classical Modern Philosophers: Descartes to Kant* (London, 1984); Herbert Schädelbach, *Philosophy in Germany 1831–1933* (trans. Eric Matthews; Cambridge, 1984); F.D.E. Schleiermacher, *The Christian Faith* (ed. H.R. Mackintosh and J.S. Stewart; Edinburgh, 1928); Nicholas Wolterstorff, 'The Migration of the Theistic Arguments: From Natural Theology to Evidentialist Apologetics', in *Rationality, Religious Belief, and Moral Commitment* (ed. R. Audi and W.J. Wainwright; Ithaca, NY, 1986), pp. 38–81; *John Locke and the Ethics of Belief* (Cambridge, 1996).

Environmental Theology

Context defines environmental theology. It presupposes that our reflection on the meaning of God's self-revelation in our lives, and our response to that revelation, is interactive with the evolving composite structure of our environments. It takes its scientific perspectives on this structure from theories such as James Lovelock's Gaia theory, which focus on integrating concepts of the Earth as a tightly-coupled system where its constituent organisms co-evolve with their environment. Organism and environment relate to each other reciprocally, and through these emergent processes they effect the evolution of an environment, where in turn selective forces affect the evolution of each species, including the human.

Environmental theology is itself a product of co-evolutionary processes. As a subsystem of knowledge, it has co-evolved under selective pressures from other subsystems within western culture, in particular those of science and technology. These have themselves, through trans-disciplinary research and multimedia access to its findings, transformed the contemporary environment of knowledge. This transformed environment itself selects new ways of understanding environments, one of which is environmental theology. It includes subsystems of values, beliefs and self-perception that mark a particular stage in human self-understanding of our reciprocal relations with our environments and with God. It marks a new awareness of our place in evolutionary history and of our contingent relationships with different environments throughout that history.

Our fundamental environmental relationship is with the earth's biosphere: the sphere where life exists through an ordered transformation of the sun's energies. It evolved around four billion years ago, but we have been consciously involved in its co-evolutionary processes for only about three million years. This asymmetry means that we must reconsider any claims made about the nature and span of God's self-revelation. In a co-evolutionary schematic, there are no exogenous causes that determine endogenous effects within the system. Nothing is exogenous. God's self-revelation has either been a part of the processes from their inception, or not at all. There were reciprocal relations between God, non-human organisms and their environment from the start. The evolving nature of these relationships ultimately defies definition, but its continuity in some form is essential to any definition of divine revelation. Thomas Berry sees this order of magnitude in the relational field as a challenge to create a new sense of what it is to be human: to transcend our species isolation and enter into the larger community of living species. This change in self-perception gives us a functional role within earth processes and a deep awareness of sacred presence within each reality of the universe.

Contextualizing our thinking about God within time, place and relational, co-evolutionary processes calls for a methodology based on accepting a plurality of systems of reference for our knowledge of and language about God. Scientific, socio-economic, socio-political and cultural analyses, as well as traditional religious sources, become bases for reflection on the relationships between the whole and the part, the cosmos and the individual. One pertinent example of this is Michael Welker's theology of God's Spirit systematized in terms of emergent processes.

Environmental theology also has a practical frame of reference, which places the prophetic traditions of Judaism and Christianity in continuity with contemporary United Nations programmes on environment and development. It takes as its chief interlocutors the poor, women, children, indigenous peoples and, as representative of the stranger in the land, alienated, refugee and migrant groups. This choice of interlocutors has important consequences not only for the interpretation of environmental and socio-economic data and policy. It also affects our perception of God. Who does God stand with at this moment, defined in the Preamble to Agenda 21 of the United Nations as one where 'we are confronted with a perpetuation of disparities between and within nations, a worsening of poverty, hunger, ill-health and illiteracy, and the continuing deterioration of the ecosystems on which we depend for our well-being'?

The stress on active human involvement in creating or destroying environments gives us a concept of person-in-environment which factors in our own moral and religious evolution into the emergent properties of evolving ecosystems. Among these are our desire for power, our thirst for knowledge, our passion for justice, our need for community, our capacity for awe, our consumerist greed, our ability to sacrifice, our freedom to change or not, our technological advances and our potentialities for compassion and for love. Through these manifold and complex interactions we contribute, for good or ill, to our personal environment, to our family environment, to cultural, religious and political environments and to a planetary environment. There is reciprocity and a constitutive bonding within the great community of existence which includes the human community, the life community, the earth community and ultimately, the universe community.

Our reciprocal relations with all these communities are so tightly coupled with them that every interaction contributes to their well being or to their violation. The theologian Marjorie Suchocki describes their violation as sin. It has a dual aspect: the transpersonal, or structural aspect, which does not result from any single person's action or influence, and the personal, which results from an individual's decision and action. The methodological shift in environmental theology is evident here. Instead of considering sin only as a personal offence against God, the victims of transpersonal sin (for example, those affected adversely by transnational economic structures and national environmental policies) are given visibility. The refugee mother and child, the clear-cut forest, economic slavery which deprives women and men of the fruits of their labour, manifest what sin is in the system. The inclusion of all human suffering and of the suffering of non-human life communities expands the definition of sin to embrace all earth communities and their environments as areas of concern and responsibility.

Interaction between reflection and action means that the practice of justice, as well as ideas about justice, becomes the hallmark of an environmental theology. Religious texts are read and reflected on from the perspective of diverse victims of violence. New texts are generated, such as those edited by Boff, Hallman and Race, which assess consumerist culture against the background of the demands it makes and the sufferings it inflicts on communities who find their life-resources continuously and irreversibly depleted.

The God who comes to light in our complex interactions within the earth communities is, for Christians, the liberating Spirit of God: a Spirit testified to through ethical relationships which support, respect and defend the specificity and diversity of other existing beings and their environments. The power of this Spirit recognizes, enlivens and maintains the community of Christ in new ways which resist restricting that Spirit to visible churches, which can themselves be systematically corrupted through concern for their own preservation at the expense of others' well being. Rather, the Spirit becomes more or less clearly recognizable in diverse secular and religious environments. This makes an environmental theology intrinsically ecumenical and committed to positive reciprocal relationships with other faith communities.

Awareness of structural and personal violence and its effects requires appropriate, nonviolent responses to it. At the structural level, however, there is a problem in that no single or obvious individual can be held directly responsible. This can then give rise to further violence, rooted in a sense of helplessness in the face of complex systems. A grasp of co-evolutionary processes can help redress the sense of isolation and powerlessness. Even though our relations with our environments encompass different timescales, ultimately we affect and are affected by all the different life communities with which we are bonded in ways beyond our mere physical, personal presence. Therefore a nonviolent lifestyle contributes to the overall reduction of violence. This self-understanding makes a nonviolent environmental ethic integral to an environmental theology.

This commitment to nonviolence is reinforced by insights from feminist environmental philosophy and feminist theology. They make consistent connections between the destruction of the natural world and the oppression of women: between militarism, environmental degradation and the feminization of poverty.

Women, as members of and carers for poor communities, suffer disproportionately from the environmental effects of industrial and military systems. But, as Shiva and Mies demonstrate, given the existing socio-political structures in those communities women are often the least able to do anything about either the systems or their effects. Many women's movements have, however, adopted appropriate nonviolent direct action for bringing about demilitarization, social and environmental justice, believing that the integrity of all life communities is indivisible.

Environmental theology characteristically engages in a fundamental questioning of God-concepts which, through a conjunction of sacred and political power, may function as a legitimation of violence against any life community. It therefore rejects any concepts of transcendence which make the immanent world profane. The dynamic process of the earth's history is itself the place of God's self-revelation: the primary environment for our encounter with transcendence, however defined. Non-conceptual, non-verbal ways of knowing play their part here. For no theological statement can encompass the mysterious reality we call God, with which all life and death is tightly coupled in ways which overflow thought and word.

ANNE PRIMAVESI

FURTHER READING: Thomas Berry, *The Dream of the Earth* (San Francisco, 1988); Leonardo Boff and Virgil Elizondo (eds.), *Ecology and Poverty* (London / New York, 1995); K. Gnanakan, *God's World: A Theology of the Environment* (London, 1999); Roger Gottlieb (ed.), *This Sacred Earth: Religion, Nature, Environment* (London / New York, 1996); David Hallman (ed.), *Ecotheology: Voices from South and North* (Geneva / New York, 1994); James Lovelock, *The Ages of Gaia: A Biography of Our Living Earth* (Oxford, rev. edn, 1995); Maria Mies and Vandana Shiva, *Ecofeminism* (London / New Jersey, 1993); Anne Primavesi, 'The Recovery of Wisdom: Gaia Theory and Environmental Policy', in *Spirit of the Environment: Religion, Value and Environmental Concern* (ed. David E. Cooper and Joy A. Palmer; London / New York, 1997); *Sacred Gaia: Holistic Theology and Earth System Science* (London, 2000); Alan Race and Roger Williamson, *True to this Earth: Global Challenges and Transforming Faith* (Oxford, 1995); Marjorie Suchocki, *The Fall to Violence: Original Sin in Relational Theology* (New York, 1994); Michael Welker, *God the Spirit* (trans. J. Hoffmeyer; Minneapolis, 1992).

Ephrem (c. 306–73)

Ephrem, theologian and exegete, was born c. 306 in Nisibis, modern Nusaybin in southeast Turkey – an important commercial centre on the Roman side of the frontier with Persia. Although numerous lives of the saint exist, some dating from the fifth century, few of the biographical details they contain are trustworthy. From his own remarks, however, it seems certain that Ephrem was a deacon and a member of a proto-monastic group known as the 'Children of the Covenant', in Syriac (a dialect of Aramaic spoken by Ephrem and the majority of the provincial population of Syria and Mesopotamia) the *bnay qyama*. He lived in an age of theological ferment when religious sects flourished. So his small community of Nicene-Orthodox Christians had to face the challenge both of well-established rivals such as the *Marcionites, Manicheans and Bardaisanites, as well as of powerful newcomers, in particular the *Arians and the pagans (briefly resurgent under the Emperor Julian). After Julian's death in battle with the Persians in 363 Nisibis was ceded to Persia and so Ephrem moved to nearby Edessa, modern Urfa, Turkey, where he died in 373. Known to Middle Eastern Christians as the 'Harp of the Spirit', Ephrem's influence was also felt much further afield through the translation of his writings, along with numerous others falsely attributed to him, into a great variety of ancient languages. This was recognized in 1920 by Pope Benedict XV who proclaimed Ephrem a Doctor of the Church.

Although Ephrem produced some prose works, for example his polemical writings against the heretical groups mentioned above, and several biblical commentaries, the best known of which are those on Genesis and the *Diatessaron* (Tatian's Gospel harmony), he was primarily a poet. The great majority of his surviving poems, more than four hundred in number, are stanzaic hymns, known in Syriac as *madrashe*, which are still sung today, to different music, by the various ancient churches of Syrian origin. (Ephrem's hymns also had a profound formative influence on Greek liturgical poetry, especially the *kontakion*, and on its greatest exponent, Romanos the Melodist.) Ephrem's innovation was to use the hymns in the battle against heresy, in particular Arianism. For the words and tunes were highly memorable and so encouraged the dissemination of orthodox teachings. Indeed Ephrem is reliably said to have formed and trained choirs of women to sing them, thus not only giving women an active role in a church liturgy which was otherwise the preserve of men, but also providing them, and so their families, with some theological education. (This positive attitude towards women is also to be found in the passages of his commentaries dealing with female biblical figures.)

But Ephrem's preference for using poetry as the vehicle for theology was not primarily pragmatic. For Ephrem it was self-evident that God's being so far surpassed human comprehension that it could not conceivably be circumscribed by the philosophical formulae and definitions so beloved of the Greek-speaking theologians. Nor could religious truth, by nature dynamic and multi-layered, be fully expressed in prose with its many limitations. Only poetry, with its multivalent images and its ability to communicate differently to each reader on each reading, was capable of hinting at these realities. It was also the perfect complement to Ephrem's 'symbolic theology'.

A basic presupposition for Ephrem is that there is a vast ontological chasm lying between God the creator and his creation which precludes humans from gaining any knowledge of God by their own efforts. God's initial invitation to bridge this chasm, through the offer of immortality and perfect knowledge made to humanity in paradise, was rejected by them in an act of free will. Humanity would have remained eternally alienated had not God been compelled by his love for them to attempt to draw them willingly back to him, and so back into paradise. This he did through self-revelation in his double incarnation and his use of symbols.

The two incarnations are the incarnation of God into humanity as Christ, the fullest form of divine self-revelation although even this leaves much, such as the eternal generation of the Son, still hidden, and his earlier incarnation into human language. This latter act is often expressed in terms of God 'putting on human names' (there are interesting parallels here with the writings of Gregory of Nyssa and Pseudo-Dionysius), which may be subdivided into 'perfect names' and 'transient names'. 'Perfect names' are those which are eternally applicable such as Creator, Father, Son and King. 'Transient names' are metaphors such as rock, shield and Ancient of Days which reveal some aspect of

the divine, or his purpose, but which are not reflections of his true being and are not essential for faith. It is a permanent source of wonder to Ephrem that God allows himself to be described, so inadequately, by human speech. Ephrem reserves his strongest anger for those, in particular the Arians, who, due to their lack of wonder and faith, abuse these metaphors to attack the eternally divine nature of God the Word.

God placed his 'symbols' (raze) or 'types' (tupse), which reveal some aspect of the divine, or point forward to the coming of Christ and the kingdom, in the two witnesses of creation – nature and the Bible. Since God is the creator of both witnesses these symbols are not the mere products of human fancy or devoid of real meaning. They actually contain within them an aspect of the divine reality (shrara), and so Ephrem effectively has a sacramental understanding of creation (which is in every strand interconnected). If different people (or the same person at different moments) approach these symbols in faith with purity of heart or view them, in Ephrem's own words, with 'a luminous eye', they will find in them an almost limitless variety of meanings. But even so only part of the infinitely complex divine reality will be revealed. Such reflection and meditation will lead humans back to God.

Because of his use of symbolic theology, anticipating such recent thinkers as *Paul Ricoeur, and his perceived rejection of 'European' philosophy, there has been a recent resurgence of interest in Ephrem which shows no sign of abating – not only in the west but also in Asia and Africa.

DAVID G.K. TAYLOR

FURTHER READING: *English translations*: S.P. Brock, *Hymns on Paradise* (Crestwood, NY, 1990); C. McCarthy, *Saint Ephrem's Commentary on Tatian's Diatessaron* (Oxford, 1993); K.E. McVey, *Ephrem the Syrian: Hymns* (CWS; New York, 1989). *Studies*: S.P. Brock, *The Luminous Eye: The Spiritual World Vision of St. Ephrem* (Cistercian Studies 124; Kalamazoo, MI, 1992); A. De Halleux, 'Mar Éphrem Théologien', *Parole de l'Orient* 4 (1973), pp. 35–54; R. Murray, *Symbols of Church and Kingdom: A Study in Early Syriac Tradition* (London, 1975); 'The Theory of Symbolism in St Ephrem's Theology', *Parole de l'Orient* 6 (1975), pp. 1–20; T. Bou Mansour, *La pensée symbolique de saint Éphrem le Syrien* (BUSE 16; Kaslik, Lebanon, 1988). *Detailed bibliographies*: S.P. Brock, *Syriac Studies: A Classified Bibliography (1960–1990)* (Kaslik, Lebanon, 1996); C. Moss,

Catalogue of Syriac Printed Books and Related Literature in the British Museum (London, 1962).

Epiphanius of Salamis (c. 310–403)

Born between 310 and 320, Epiphanius was educated by monks in Palestine and Egypt. By the age of twenty he had founded a monastery at Eleutheropolis near Gaza. As abbot he propagated *Nicene orthodoxy in the controversies of the day. In 367 he became bishop of Salamis (now Famagusta) in Cyprus, and there promoted monasticism. In 374 he published *Ancoratus*, and during the next three years he wrote the great *Panarion*. Active in ecclesiastical controversies, especially in Laodicea and Antioch, he tried to reconcile *Apollinarians and Eustathians. His own support in Antioch for the Eustathian congregation under Paulinus, and for the Roman position against Meletius, was unswerving. He may have attended the Council of Constantinople in 381, and certainly travelled to Rome afterwards with *Jerome, negotiating on Paulinus's behalf. Epiphanius converted the wealthy Roman Paula, Jerome's patroness, to the ascetic life. Between 392 and 395 he produced biblical works and the anti-Origenist *Letter to John*. After Theophilus of Alexandria condemned *Origenism in 400, Origenist monks sought refuge abroad. At Constantinople some were received by the archbishop *John (Chrysostom), whose sympathy for them led to the campaign which would finally unseat him. Epiphanius, by now over eighty years old, went to Constantinople in 402 or 403 to pursue the heresy, but left in obscure circumstances, and died on the way back to Cyprus in 403.

Epiphanius's *Ancoratus* deals with fundamental doctrines. He argues strongly against the 'Pneumatomachi' that the Holy Spirit is both divine and personal, and that there is a consubstantial Trinity. He also criticizes Origen's interpretation of Genesis. *Panarion* ('medicine-chest') is meant to provide cures for heresy, 'an historical encyclopedia of heresy and its refutation' (Williams, p. xvi). In this work, Epiphanius describes eighty sects and heresies, beginning with pre-Christian philosophies and Jewish sects – but at least sixty have some Christian content. He classifies them and systematically relates them to each other, often with no historical justification. Each is verbally abused and refuted, chiefly from texts of Scripture. The design is completed with an account of the church's truth, also known separately as *On the Faith*. Where we can check from earlier patristic writings or from such collections as the Nag Hammadi Library, Epiphanius uses his many sources honestly, but he shows poor historical judgement and hasty work. *Panarion* is nevertheless a useful mine of texts and information about groups, some of which are known (like the *Montanists) and others which are otherwise unknown (like the gnostic Ptolemaeus). *On Measures and Weights* and *The Twelve Jewels* concern biblical details; other exegetical works survive only in fragments.

Epiphanius was very influential in his time, and his works remained popular because of his passionate orthodoxy and curious information, until his unclassical style and dogmatic approach brought him into disfavour with post-Renaissance scholars. We are fortunate now to have Holl's critical text of *Panarion*, and Williams' English version, which open up a useful resource.

STUART G. HALL

FURTHER READING: *Text: PG* 41–43; K. Holl, *Die griechischen christlichen Schriftsteller der ersten drei Jahrhunderte* 25, 31, 37 (rev. edn by J. Dummer; Berlin, 2nd edn, 1985). *English introduction and translation: The Panarion of Epiphanius of Salamis* (trans. Frank Williams; NHS, 35; 2 vols.; Leiden, 1987, 1994); Calogero Riggi, *Epistrophe: Tensione verso la Divina Armonia* (BSR, 70; Rome, 1983), pp. 569–891; 'Epiphanius of Salamis', in *Encyclopedia of the Early Church*, I (Cambridge, 1992), pp. 281–2; Frances Young, *From Nicaea to Chalcedon* (London, 1983), pp. 133–42.

Erasmus, Desiderius (1466–1536)

Erasmus was the greatest of the Renaissance Christian humanists in his work as classical and patristic scholar, satirist and theologian. He was born illegitimate (his father was almost certainly in orders), and thus he was given to others, especially the Brethren of the Common Life, for his care and formation. The regulated life of the monastery gave him a structure, and the monastic library allowed him free rein to pursue extensive reading of both Christian and classical literature. He entered the Augustinian monastery at Steyn and was ordained in 1492. But because his wide-ranging mind sought broader horizons, he became secretary to the bishop of Cambrai and received dispensation to leave the monastery, which he never saw again. Erasmus soon convinced the bishop to allow him to begin studies in theology at the University of Paris about 1495. Erasmus found the study of scholastic theology and philosophy as it was then taught in Paris quite stultifying to his broader sensibilities. Through tutoring British students in Latin he received an invitation to visit England in 1499 and there began to cultivate friendships with noted humanists like Thomas More, John Colet and Bishop John Fisher of Rochester.

Through these humanist contacts Erasmus came to realize that the methods of textual application being developed for classical texts might also be used with works in the Christian tradition. The battle cry of the humanists of '*Ad Fontes!*' (back to the original sources), was used by Erasmus in exploring scriptural sources as well. Returning to the original Greek language in which it was written, Erasmus produced in 1516 (the same year as More's *Utopia*) an edition of the Greek text of the New Testament with commentary and the first new Latin translation of the work since the Vulgate. The audacity of this enterprise stunned the theological world; this text initiated a new spirit and became the basis of many vernacular versions produced during the *Reformation.

Erasmus, however, was much more than a linguist and a translator. As early as 1503 his *Enchiridion Militis Christiani* ('Handbook of the Christian Soldier') was a plea for a more simple biblical spirituality for all people and a view of life as a contest between virtue and vice while subtly undervaluing the prevalent external liturgical forms (the sacraments, etc.). His far-reaching satire on contemporary Renaissance society, both ecclesiastical and lay, *Encomium Moriae* ('Praise of Folly'), was written at the home of Thomas More and is a pun on his name. In part because of this work and others like *Julius Exclusus* (a biting satire in which Pope Julius II is excluded from heaven), Erasmus was considered the most learned man in Europe and was thought by Reformation Protestants to be a likely ally for their cause after *Luther's 95 theses in 1517. But Erasmus was always more interested in reform within the Catholic Church, not in the formation of new religions in place of it.

The Reformers had mistaken the goal of these satires; Erasmus wished to rekindle a purer biblical piety that would reunify all of Christendom. He was fed up with external forms and extreme allegorizing of Scripture, not with the church itself. His publication of the *Colloquies* in 1519, for example, extended his ability to present these themes of satire for reform to wider audiences through dramatic dialogues. His *Adagia* (a collection of classical proverbs with close explanations for students as a ready handbook) had already shown him the way to popular and financial success.

The great translation of the *Novum Instrumentum* (the Latin title of his translation of the New Testament) had been dedicated to Pope Leo X; Erasmus had clearly hoped that the church authorities would support him in his quest to make scholarship the handmaiden of new scriptural studies. But the Reformation soon dashed his hopes for unity and scholarly peace. After the papal condemnation of Luther (and his replies), it became clear that a real revolution had erupted in Christendom, and Erasmus was eagerly courted by both sides in the controversy. His attempt to apply again the literary format of the dialogue in a work dealing with the implications of divisiveness within the church (*Inquisitio de Fide*) no longer worked in the extreme polemicism of the new Reformation debates. The stated wish of Erasmus for 'a courteous disputation' from Luther had been replaced by vituperative diatribe. Even his friend, Thomas More in England, began a series of polemical works against Protestants.

The peaceful way sought by Erasmus was impossible, and in 1524 Erasmus published his treatise on the freedom of the will, making his differences with Protestantism altogether too clear. Luther answered with bitter disavowals and Erasmus replied with two versions of his *Hyperaspistes*, which reiterated his original ideas. Theological communion through careful scholarship and dialogue was at an end. Erasmus moved to Basle in an attempt to avoid more controversy, but it was everywhere in reform-minded Europe. He was attacked by the *Lutherans; the emperor was suspicious of him; and the pope wanted him to come to Rome to head a polemic counterblast. Yet Erasmus admonished the pope to use reason and scholarship, not force and threats, against the acrimonious Reformers. His words went unheeded, of course. There was no way to communicate 'to those who will not hear'.

Erasmus's importance in these areas is great, although his influence perhaps may be felt culturally more than theologically. His plan for a simple biblical piety as a means of reinvigorating a stagnant formalist church was doomed by the sudden onset of the Reformation and the theological contention that it produced. Throughout his life Erasmus demonstrated the aims of Christian Humanism with its dedication to scholarship, its love of texts and its unified view of a world made one by intense study and devout faith. His own deep inclination towards moderation in all things was out of place in a world suddenly at theological war. The search for truth, not the destruction of one's intellectual enemies, was always his highest goal. His biographer Johan Huizinga insightfully calls him a man 'who was too understanding and too moderate to be heroic'. In an irenic rather than a polemic time he might have been the key influence to restructure theological attitudes in a new framework. Now he is seen as an enlightened scholar and educator who by example provides us with possibilities for courteous resolution of intellectual disputes in peace rather than the more common contentious combat that inevitably leads to chaos.

CHARLES M. KOVICH

FURTHER READING: *Texts: The Praise of Folly* (ed. and trans. Clarence H. Miller; New Haven, 1979); *Erasmus and Cambridge* (The Cambridge Letters of Erasmus; trans. D.F.S. Thomson; Toronto, 1963). *Studies:* Marjorie O'Rourke Boyle, *Erasmus on Language and Method in Theology* (Toronto, 1977); A.G. Dickens, *The English Reformation* (New York, 1964); T.A. Dorey (ed.), *Erasmus* (Albuquerque, NM, 1970); Johan Huizinga, *Erasmus and the Age of the Reformation* (New York, 1957); Walter Jacob Kaiser, *Praisers of Folly: Erasmus, Rabelais, Shakespeare* (Cambridge, MA, 1963); Margaret Mann Phillips, *Erasmus and the Northern Renaissance* (London, 1949); Erika Rummel, *Erasmus' Annotations on the New Testament: From Philologist to Theologian* (Toronto, 1986); *Erasmus as a Translator of the Classics* (Toronto, 1985).

Eriugena, John Scottus (c. 810 – c. 877)

We know little about Eriugena's life: c. 810 is conjectured as his date of birth, and 877, or slightly later, fits the known facts for his death. We know he was born in Ireland: Scottus was commonly applied to Irish scholars in the period; and *Eriugena* 'of Irish birth' ('Erigena' is incorrect) he coined for himself (note Virgil's *Graiugena*). His name means 'John the Irishman of Irish birth'. We know he was one of a group of Irish scholars in the Reims area in the ninth century. He first comes to notice in 851, while teaching in the palace-school of Charles the Bald, when Archbishop Hincmar of Reims asked him to refute Gottschalk's position of 'double predestination'. Until his death Eriugena was linked to centres of learning in the area: Reims itself, Soissons, Laon and Charles's palace at Compiègne.

Eriugena was a typical teacher of his time, concerned with the basics of understanding given through the arts: he reveals his familiarity with the standard skills in the way he employed logic in his writings, and in how as a teacher he commented on Martianus Capella's *De nuptiis Mercurii et Philologiae*. Moreover, as a teacher of theology, scriptural exegesis is central to his quest for sure bases in argument: he wrote a commentary on the gospel of John; much of his *magnum opus*, the *Periphyseon*, is exegetical (particularly the *hexaëmeron*); and further evidence of his involvement with Scripture continues to come to light (see below). As a theologian involved in argument, his questions are those of the tradition formed in the aftermath of *Augustine (creation, the manner of God's involvement with the world, grace and human freedom are all recurring themes). However, Eriugena stands apart from his contemporaries in: (1) the originality with which he handled these Latin questions, and (2) his range of authorities. First, most Carolingian theologians saw their task as that of codifying and making accessible the body of material that had come down to them. This was done through excerpting, summarizing and writing commentaries with ever more snippets from the Fathers. Eriugena, for all his citations and shared academic values, began with a systematic framework for the whole of reality – based on his logical *organon* – and then he re-located his sources within that framework.

Thus, while he was not the first Latin to use a rationally established systematic (see the anonymous seventh- or eighth-century work *De ordine creaturarum*), he was the first to integrate questions about creation, revelation and salvation in a single structure. Second, Eriugena was almost unique in that he had access to Greek sources and was prepared to integrate them into his own writing. He translated the Pseudo-Denis, Gregory of Nyssa and Maximus the Confessor into Latin. By using concepts from these writers, principally regarding the negative nature of the creature's approach to God, and of creation as a 'going-out-from and return-to God', in combination with the Latin themes (creation as a history of divine activity), he produced the most original Latin work between Augustine and *Aquinas. However, there has been a tendency to regard Eriugena solely in terms of his originality ('the peak in the plane'), and this has led to distorted views of his work. A more balanced picture requires more research into his Carolingian surroundings.

The *Periphyseon*, in five books, employs the form of the pupil interrogating his teacher about the whole of reality. This format is for Eriugena a synecdoche of the human quest for knowledge and salvation: like the disciples around the word. The quest is for an understanding of the relationships between all that is and is not, and within the realm of being, between the Creator and the creation. Thus Eriugena sees what can be spoken of (*natura*) divided into four: (1) uncreated and creating (God) and (2), its contradictory, uncreated and uncreating (nothing); (3) created and creating (the primordial causes) and (4), its contradictory, created and uncreating (the material universe). Divisions two and three proceed from God and have as their destiny – fulfilled in the Word incarnate – the return to God. Eriugena refers to this process as *deificatio* (rendering the Greek *theosis*). This approach has led some modern readers to present him as a pantheist *ante nomen*; however, this accusation fails to note either the distance he sees between God and the creation, or how he focuses on the tradition of creatio *ex nihilo* – expressed in his use of patristic commentaries on Genesis.

Because its strangeness distanced it from its own academic milieu, Eriugena's work had little impact: appreciation would suppose a systematic framework such as appeared only in the twelfth century. Then it had a form different from Eriugena's, and consequently his work became open to suspicions of heresy: it was neither like recent developments nor like older works then being bypassed. The recovery of Eriugena's thought really only began with M. Cappuyns (1933), and is still in its infancy.

THOMAS O'LOUGHLIN

FURTHER READING: *Catalogue:* M. Lapidge and R. Sharpe, *A Bibliography of Celtic-Latin Literature 400–1200* (Dublin, 1985), nn. 695–713. *Bibliography:* M. Brennan, *A Guide to Eriugenian Studies: A Survey of Publications 1930–1987* (Fribourg, 1989), updated in *Iohannes Scottus Eriugena: The Bible and Hermeneutics [ISEBH]* (ed. G. van Riel, C. Steel and J. McEvoy; Leuven, 1996), pp. 367–400. *Overview:* J.J. O'Meara, *Eriugena* (Oxford, 1988). *Carolingian context:* J.J. Contreni, 'Carolingian Biblical Culture', *ISEBH*, pp. 1–23. *Theological context:* T. O'Loughlin, 'Biblical Contradictions in the *Periphyseon* and the Development of Eriugena's Method', *ISEBH*, pp. 103–26. *Insular context:* T. O'Loughlin, 'Unexplored Irish Influences on Eriugena,' *Recher Th Anc Med* 59 (1992), pp. 23–40; T. O'Loughlin, 'The Mysticism of Number in the Medieval Period before Eriugena', in *The Perennial Tradition of Neoplatonism* (ed. J.J. Cleary; Leuven, 1997), pp. 397–416. *Most recent addition to the corpus of edited works:* J.J. Contreni and P.Ó. Néill, *Glossae divinae historiae: The Biblical Glosses of John Scottus Eriugena* (Florence, 1997).

Erskine, Thomas (1788–1870)

Thomas Erskine, laird of Linlathen, advocate and theologian, was born in Edinburgh on 13 October 1788, the fifth child of David Erskine and Ann Graham. His family was of diverse religious sympathies. On his father's side he was descended from John Erskine of Carnock (1661?–1743), one of those instrumental in bringing William and Mary from The Hague in the revolution of 1688, but a staunch covenanter and an enemy of the union. Thomas's uncle was Dr John Erskine (1721?–1803), minister of Greyfriars in Edinburgh, and a prominent evangelical within the General Assembly. On his mother's side, meanwhile, the influences were rather different. His grandmother (in whose home much of Erskine's childhood was spent) was a Jacobite who held an Episcopalian service in Airth Castle every Sunday and would not permit prayers for King George to be said! The tensions inherent in such an upbringing may help to account for Erskine's later eclecticism and tolerance in matters religious and theological, as well as for some of the things he chose to resist and overturn in his own writings.

Erskine enjoyed a long life and formed some significant friendships (for example with Thomas Chalmers, *John McLeod Campbell, *F.D. Maurice, Thomas Carlyle and Alexandre Vinet), some of which were particularly influential in the shaping of his own theology. His written output, though, was mostly produced during the period 1820–40. This consisted in a string of volumes, some of which ran to several editions and were published in French and German. Some of the volumes were slender in size, but all were profound in their penetration of vital issues and, contemporary testimony indicates, made a mark on their readers.

The first volume to appear was *Remarks on the Internal Evidence for the Truth of Revealed Religion* (1820), in which Erskine sought to hold together the spiritual and ethical core of faith expressed in personal piety with the framework of an orthodox creedal belief. His was a generation in which an experiential religion was being cut loose from doctrinal moorings by some, while others clung fervently to the 'truths' of the faith once delivered while being apparently devoid of the very spirit which granted them meaning and life. The first edition of *Schleiermacher's The Christian Faith* would be published just a year later and, while the two adopt quite different approaches, there is an identifiable shared concern with preventing this false polarization which could only prove fatal for faith and theology alike. Erskine's next venture, *An Essay on Faith* (1822), was also directed towards the big methodological questions at stake in early nineteenth-century theology. In particular it constituted a response to what has come to be known as the theological 'turn to the subject', and insisted that Christian theology must finally be concerned with the distinctive object of faith (God, Christ, the gospel, etc.) rather than offering an analysis of the conditions for and nature and structure of the act of faith itself.

Accordingly, in his next few books Erskine turned his attention more directly to an exploration and unfolding of the gospel's content. In doing so, the immediate forces which shaped his interpretation in various ways were his own background in the *Calvinistic Scottish Presbyterian tradition, his nurture within a more broadly based liturgical tradition within the Scottish Episcopal Church, and his immersion in the Christian Scriptures. The wider influence of his classical education can also be discerned behind much of what he wrote, and his reading of a portion of the New Testament in Greek each day was undoubtedly supplemented by other sources in the same language.

On the Unconditional Freeness of the Gospel (1828) is an unashamed defence of the view that the salvation which God offers to humankind is unconditionally free, and is rooted in a universal forgiving and atoning love for sinners. Such

views were controversial in Scotland, having been at the heart of the so-called 'Marrow Controversy' of 1720. The view which prevailed held such opinions to be at odds with the theology of the Westminster Confession of Faith (1647), the Church of Scotland's chief subordinate standard in matters of doctrine. Erskine remained unperturbed by ecclesiastical strictures, and he appealed confidently to the church's own Scriptures in support of what he supposed to be the truth of the matter. His boldness was the occasion for some personal discomfort (he was asked to part company with the independent congregation to which he belonged for owning 'heterodox' ideas), but being a layman he suffered little by comparison with his contemporaries and theological soulmates John McLeod Campbell and *Edward Irving who were both deposed from their charges for the views which they espoused from their pulpits.

Erskine's relationship with Campbell was of particular significance for his own theological reflection. Campbell was the minister of Row (Rhu) near Helensburgh, though Erskine encountered his preaching for the first time in Edinburgh, not long after *Unconditional Freeness* was published. His reaction was spontaneous and immediate. 'I have heard today from that pulpit what I believe to be the true gospel.' So it was that Erskine chose to spend the next several summers on the west coast of Scotland, sitting under Campbell's preaching and forming a close friendship with him. During Campbell's trial in 1831 Erskine was among his closest supporters.

Erskine's own theology did not stand still in this period, spurred on, perhaps, by his dialogue with Campbell. His next two books, *The Brazen Serpent* (1831) and *The Doctrine of Election* (1837) built on theological foundations which he had already laid, and concentrated on a close reading of the biblical text. Now, though, Erskine stepped deliberately outside the boundaries of an orthodoxy rather broader than that entertained by Scottish Federal Calvinism. Most obvious was his honest espousal of a universalistic eschatology. He remained utterly orthodox in his adherence to the symbols of Trinity and incarnation, and he offered as sensitive and meaningful an account of the doctrine of atonement as any; but he combined all this with a deep and clearly articulated conviction that a God who went all the way to the cross and embraced the 'bruising' of sin for our sakes would never finally abandon any to the fate which otherwise awaited them, but would continue to wait, to love and to persuade until his self-sacrificing love finally won their response of faith and obedience, whether in this life or beyond it.

For the next several decades the flow from Erskine's pen stopped, and he wrote little other than letters to his many friends and associates, a correspondence which in itself makes fascinating reading and is rich in theological and spiritual content. He seems, though, to have lost confidence in print as an effective medium for theological persuasion, and he spent his time instead developing a more Socratic strategy, inviting selected friends and contacts to visit his estate at Linlathen, and spending long hours listening, talking and disputing with them in the hope that his own vision of God's character and dealings with humankind would rub off and duly be passed on through them to others. In his final years, with his eyesight already having failed, he turned again to writing in order to capture and clarify some of his mature perspectives. The result was the posthumously published *The Spiritual Order and Other Papers* (1871).

Erskine presents a fascinating theological figure, and one whose stature and influence within the stream of British theology in the nineteenth century is too rarely appreciated. Measured by the canons of the classical creeds he appears refreshingly orthodox; measured by the more precise canons of his own day in Scotland, less so. But Erskine was unconcerned about such matters, and even his clear incarnational and Trinitarian adherence is more a product of first-hand engagement with the biblical text than concern for traditions. He presents dynamic and narrative accounts of the Father, his Son Jesus and his Spirit sent into the world in power, and perhaps betrays tacitly that impatience with or nervousness concerning metaphysical statement which characterized many in his century. He is, in this sense, above all a 'biblical' theologian, one whose reflection is shaped by close engagement with the stories and theologies of the Old and New Testaments. By all contemporary accounts, he was, throughout his life, also a man of such a sort who might convince a person of the reality of the gospel which he proclaimed by the sheer aura of its reality which surrounded him, and by the conformity of his own personality to its essential shape.

TREVOR A. HART

FURTHER READING: *Texts: Remarks on the Internal Evidence for the Truth of Revealed Religion* (Edinburgh, 1820); *An Essay in Faith* (Edinburgh, 1822); *The Unconditional Freeness of the Gospel* (Edinburgh, 2nd edn, 1870); *The Brazen Serpent or Life Coming Through Death* (Edinburgh, 1831); *The Doctrine of Election and its Connection with the General Tenor of Christianity* (Edinburgh, 2nd edn, 1878); *The Spiritual Order and Other Papers* (Edinburgh, 1871); *Letters of Thomas Erskine of Linlathen* (ed. William Hanna; Edinburgh, 3rd edn, 1878). *Studies:* Henry F. Henderson, *Erskine of Linlathen, Selections and Biography* (Edinburgh, 1899); Trevor A. Hart, *The Teaching Father: An Introduction to the Theology of Thomas Erskine of Linlathen* (Edinburgh, 1993).

Eucherius of Lyons (d. c. 449)

Of Eucherius's life we know little. Born into the aristocracy of late Roman Gaul, he, along with his wife Galla and their children, withdrew to live in the island monastery of Lérins sometime in the early fifth century. There he became a confrère of *Vincent of Lérins and Salvian of Marseilles, and was in contact with *John Cassian and Paulinus of Nola. Later, in the mid-430s, he was elected bishop of Lyons, presided over the Synod of Orange in 441, and died towards the end of the decade.

While Eucherius wrote little, his works must be seen as belonging to the circle of Lérins: short works which were to have a profound effect on the way theology was practised for several centuries. While *Augustine, *Ambrose and *Jerome supplied the matter, these works supplied the form. And, in the case of Augustine, while they developed his work, they mitigated its extremes. Eucherius is a good example of this: he built on the younger Augustine's notion of the mind's ascent through creation, yet he drew back from the older Augustine's denial of a real place for human effort.

Eucherius's most significant contribution was two introductions to exegesis. The *Formula Spiritalis Intellegentiae* presents a theory of three senses in Scripture that was derived from Evagrius of Pontus through Cassian, along with a method of reading the text as a code to a series of spiritual realities. Thus when one meets any person or thing in Scripture, it speaks both of itself and as a sign to what is beyond it. The other work is the *Instructiones*, which is a series of guides to specific exegetical problems. Together these works were the most used manuals (at once a semiotics and a decoding device) of the early Middle Ages and were commended as such by Cassiodorus.

Eucherius's three other extant works are the *Passio Acaunensium Martyrum*, which introduced the legend of the Theban Legion to the west, and two works on the spiritual life – the *De Laude Eremi* and *De Contemptu Mundi*. The latter works, despite their titles, present an image of Christian leisure by which one lifts one's eyes from the form of the creation in its beauty and order to its transcendent source. These writings influenced the seventeenth-century Welsh poet Henry Vaughan and the twentieth-century spiritual writer Thomas Merton.

THOMAS O'LOUGHLIN

FURTHER READING: *Catalogue: CPL* nn. 488–496; and 633 (Ep. 14). *Studies:* T. O'Loughlin, 'The Symbol Gives Life: Eucherius of Lyons' Formula for Exegesis', in *Scriptural Interpretation in the Fathers: Letter and Spirit* (eds. T. Finan and V. Twomey; Dublin, 1995), pp. 221–52; J.F. Kelly, 'Eucherius of Lyons: Harbinger of the Middle Ages', SP 22 (1989), pp. 138–42; C. Mandolfo, 'Le Regole di Ticonio e le "Quaestiones et responsiones" di Eucherio di Lione', *Annali di Storia dell'Esegesi* 8 (1991), pp. 535–46; C. Curti, ' "Spiritalis intellegentia": nota sulla dottrina esegetica di Eucherio di Lione', in *Kerygma und Logos* (ed. A.M. Ritter; Gottingen, 1979), pp. 108–22.

Eunomius (c. 335–394)

Eunomius was born in Cappadocia around 335. He was schooled by Aetius, the first Anomean, whose idea of causality was more Neoplatonist than *Aristotelian (so Barnes). Eunomius delivered his *Apology* at the Council of Constantinople in 360 to maintain a position less extreme than Aetius (the Father and Son's 'likeness according to the Scriptures', not their 'unlikeness'), but also distinct from those *homoiousians*, notably Basil of Caesarea, who thought John 5:19 was evidence for 'likeness'. His efforts there were rewarded when he was appointed to the see of Cyzicus (so Basil), albeit for a short time due to his unpopularity there. Eunomius was exiled to Naxos in 370, but by 380, after Gratian's amnesty for heretics, he was back in Constantinople, eloquently presenting his case. However, Theodosius the co-emperor was not impressed, due to persuasion by his Nicene-Orthodox wife Flacilla. In 383, the patriarch

Nectarius demanded written depositions from groups of doubtful orthodoxy. In his last work, the *Expositio Fidei*, Eunomius defiantly maintains his position. He spent the rest of his life a wanderer in charge of a dwindling sect (he was still alive in 392, according to *Jerome). The *Liber Apologeticus* and the *Expositio Fidei* survive only because they were often bound together in the manuscripts of Basil and Gregory of Nyssa's respective refutations. His counterattack to Gregory, the *Apologia Apologiae* (c. 380) is preserved in Gregory's citations.

In the *Apology*, Eunomius insisted that the 'Son is similar to the Father in accordance with the Scriptures'. He would not say 'similar in essence' (*homoiousios*), which the Council of Ancyra (358) had chosen, far less 'of same essence' (*homoousios*) as *Athanasius and his followers had said. The fourth councils of Sirmium, Nike and Ariminium had shared similar misgivings about any 'similarity of essence' which seemed too easily to lead to an identity of essence between Father and Son, and hence the collapse of any proper distinction between them. For two to share the essence of the unbegotten One would mean division/separation, and this would be unworthy of God since God is altogether free from composition. Furthermore, such division would prompt thought about God as occupying space, which is also inappropriate.

One can analyze essences either (1) as revealed by their names ('the Creator, by means of relationship, activity and analogy, has apportioned names suitable to each thing'; thus the one God who gives names is himself unborn – *agennetos*), or (2) by examining effects in order to discern the essence which caused them: the Son is the product of the Father as the first-born of creation. The Son was a perfect minister of God, his lower status enabling interaction with the lower creation. He received glory from the Father, without participating in the Father's glory. He *became* a man; he did not assume humanity (Eunomius accused Basil of a dualism in Christology). If the three persons of the Trinity have distinct operations, then they must have distinct essences. To think of *any* of God's actions, including his begetting of the Son, as being without beginning would suggest that God was always creating the universe. The divine 'activity produces a work that is like the activity in nature and not like the original essence' (Barnes, p. 218). Eunomius was interested in the natural order of things in which the Trinity took its place as the highest. To worship God one needed a clear concept of him – this resulted in baptism with single, not threefold, immersion: only one of the three energies could be involved. As against the *Cappadocian idea of God's very being as self-communication, which is nevertheless remote from us, Eunomius believed in something more simple and present. It was, in fact, Eunomius who first made the distinction, usually attributed to the Cappadocians, between God's essence and energies.

MARK W. ELLIOTT

FURTHER READING: Michael R. Barnes, 'The Background and Use of Eunomius' Causal Language', in *Arianism after Arius: Essays on the Development of the Fourth Century Trinitarian Conflicts* (ed. Michael R. Barnes and Daniel H. Williams; Edinburgh, 1993), pp. 217–36; R.P.C. Hanson, *The Search for the Christian Doctrine of God: The Arian Controversy 318–381* (Edinburgh, 1988).

Eusebius of Caesarea (c. 263 – c. 340)

Born at Caesarea Philippi, where *Origen had founded his famous school a generation before, Eusebius received a first-class Christian education under the presbyter Pamphilus, who was martyred in 310. Eusebius escaped the same fate by fleeing the city, but in 313 he was elected its bishop and was soon deeply embroiled in the *Arian controversy. His view was that the problem could be solved by compromise on both sides. Eusebius did not believe that Arius was a heretic, but he did think that Arius ought to submit to his bishop, Alexander of Alexandria, who had condemned his doctrine. For this view he was excommunicated at the synod of Antioch in 325, though he managed to pursue his middle course (as he saw it) at Nicaea a few months later. To Eusebius, the *homoousios* formula adopted at Nicaea was Sabellian, because it appeared to merge the Son's identity into that of the Father. In the end he signed the *Nicene confession of faith, but this was more out of a sense of duty than of conviction. It was not long before he was persecuting bishops who were true Nicenes, and in 335 he took part in a synod at Tyre which excommunicated *Athanasius. He was able to get away with such behaviour because of his friendship with the Emperor Constantine, to whom he acted as a theological

adviser. In 326 and again in 336 he preached on the anniversary of his accession, and when Constantine died in 337 Eusebius delivered an important eulogy.

Eusebius was an outstanding scholar, and in this respect his only peer in the ancient church was Origen. He was extremely learned and widely read, but oddly for his time, he lacked a sense of literary style. He was a mediocre theologian, and it is as a church historian that he is usually remembered today. Nevertheless, an impressive corpus of his works survives, and we are able to see many sides of his personality and genius in his writings.

Eusebius's historical works consist of the *Chronicle*, which survives in an Armenian translation. The second part is also extant in Latin. The *Chronicle* is a brief account of the history of the world, beginning with Abraham and seeking to harmonize biblical with Graeco-Roman chronology. This history originally ended in 325, but Jerome later extended it to 378. Much more important is the *Ecclesiastical History*, which is a miscellany of Christian testimonies drawn from earlier sources and which tells the story of the church's triumphant progress down to 324. As many of the original texts are now lost, Eusebius's account remains of fundamental importance in seeking to reconstruct the history of the early church, in spite of its many shortcomings. The *Ecclesiastical History* makes no attempt to be comprehensive in its treatment, and it gives the persecutions a disproportionate amount of space. But it rapidly became a classic, and it has remained such ever since the fourth century.

In addition to these works, Eusebius wrote a history of the martyrs of Palestine and at least three panegyrics on the Emperor Constantine, which present the latter's ecclesiastical policies in the best possible light. He also wrote an introduction to the Christian faith for new converts (*Praeparatio Evangelica*), and followed this up with a sequel (*Demonstratio Evangelica*). A major concern of the second of these was to demonstrate why Christians accepted the Old Testament but rejected the Law of Moses which was contained in it. In the field of biblical studies, Eusebius was the first person to write a *Gospel Harmony*, which became a model for such efforts in later centuries. He also wrote a book on the exegetical difficulties contained in the Gospels and commentaries on the Psalms and on Isaiah. The first of these is now lost, but the second was rediscovered in 1934 and reveals that he was largely dependent on Origen. Another work of interest is his *Onomasticon*, which is a gazetteer of Palestine. It was highly valued in the ancient world and even today it remains our major literary source for the topography of the Holy Land in biblical times. Eusebius also wrote on doctrinal questions, particularly against Marcellus of Ancyra, who was an important advocate of the *homoousios* position in Christology. Oddly enough, in spite of their defence of Arianism, the two works in question, *Against Marcellus* and *Ecclesiastical Theology*, are both still extant. Beyond that, there are only a few minor tracts, sermons and letters which have survived. One of these is a study of the date of Easter, a major issue of controversy in the early church. Eusebius goes over the ground carefully, explaining how the Christian festival was both related to, and distinct from, the Jewish Passover.

In the theological politics of the fourth century, Eusebius stood out as a 'moderate' who was neither fully Arian nor fully Nicene in the Athanasian sense. His name is usually associated with the attempt to solve the Arian controversy by interpreting *homoousios* ('consubstantial') as *homoiousios* ('of similar substance'), although he does not appear to have advocated this himself and it did not become a major subject of debate until some years after his death.

Eusebius has always been recognized as one of the greatest historians of the church, and it is this which has kept his name and reputation alive in spite of his sympathy for Arianism. Today his picture of the early church has been filled out by extensive archaeological investigations. These have revealed a wealth of material not previously available and have made it possible to offer some sort of corrective to his account. But nothing has replaced his unique repository of key sources, and it is certain that his works will retain their importance for as long as the study of church history endures.

GERALD BRAY

FURTHER READING: *Text:* There is a critical edition of his works in 8 vols. by I.A. Heikel, T. Mommsen, et al., (GCS 7, 9, 11, 14, 20, 23, 43, 47; Leipzig, 1902–83); Migne, *PG* XIX–XXIV; G. Bardy, *Histoire Ecclaesiastique* (SC 31, 41, 55, 73; Paris, 1952–58); E. Des Places, et al., *Préparation Évangélique* (SC 206, 215, 228, 262, 266, 292, 307, 369; Paris, 1974–). The main English translation is by A.C.C. McGiffert and E.C. Richardson, *NPNF²*, I (1890).

Studies: H.A. Drake, *In Praise of Constantine* (Berkeley, 1976); E.H. Gifford, *The Preparation of the Gospel* (2 vols.; Oxford, 1903; repr. Grand Rapids, 1981); H.W. Attridge and G. Hatta (eds.), *Eusebius, Christianity and Judaism* (Detroit, 1992); T.D. Barnes, *Constantine and Eusebius* (Cambridge, MA, 1981); W.H.C. Frend, *The Rise of Christianity* (London, 1984); R.M. Grant, *Eusebius as Church Historian* (Oxford, 1980); C. Luibhead, *Eusebius of Caesarea and the Arian Crisis* (Dublin, 1981); R.L.P. Milburn, *Early Christian Interpretations of History* (London, 1954); A.A. Mosshammer, *The* Chronicle *of Eusebius and Greek Chronographical Tradition* (Lewisburg, PA, 1979); G.C. Stead, 'Eusebius and the Council of Nicaea', *J Th St* NS 24 (1973), pp. 85–100; J. Stevenson, *Studies in Eusebius* (Cambridge, 1929).

Eutyches (c. 378–454)

Eutyches is generally saddled with the accusation of a caricatured heresy he is supposed to have produced. The heresy is that of dissolving the human nature of Christ in the incarnation, the product of an over-intense mixture union, in which the divine overwhelms the human. In the textbooks, Eutyches is often portrayed as a maverick, holding a hardly-serious view. He did, however, hold a serious and interesting position which was an important link in the chain leading to *Chalcedon.

The brief facts of the case are as follows: Eutyches was archimandrite (abbot) of a monastery outside Constantinople. He was in favour with the emperor (Theodosius II), although he had already been under suspicion of *Apollinarian tendencies. At a local synod in November 448 he was accused by Eusebius of Dorylaeum of confusing the natures in Christ. Here Eutyches was asked if he accepted: (1) two natures *after* the incarnation, and (2) that Christ is of one being (*homoousios*) with us in the flesh. He replied that he had never used the phrase of Christ being *homoousios* with us, but agreed to do so, if this was insisted. He also eventually admitted that Christ was from two natures *before* the union, but only *one* nature *after* the union. For this he claimed the support of *Athanasius and *Cyril of Alexandria, while denying that he dissolved the human nature into the divine. The synod deposed and excommunicated Eutyches because his acceptance of their test was so ambiguous.

Eutyches then held his ground (with Theodosius's support), and wrote for help to

*Leo the Great. Leo waited until he had read the minutes of the trial and then wrote briefly to Flavian (bishop of Constantinople), condemning Eutyches, and promising a full letter later.

Against the advice of Leo and Flavian, Theodosius called a council at Ephesus (in 449, the second Council of Ephesus or the 'robber synod'). Leo quickly sent his 'longer' letter (*Letter 28 to Flavian*, the '*Tome*'). Dioscorus of Alexandria was president at the council and dominated the proceedings with Egyptian monks and bishops who yelled intimidating slogans: 'Burn Eusebius; as he has divided, let him be divided!' The *Tome* of Leo was not even read. Eutyches's confession (two natures before the union; after the union one nature) was accepted and he was reinstated, while Flavian and Eusebius were condemned. Flavian, apparently, died only days later. History then took a most unexpected turn. Theodosius died in 450 and was succeeded by Pulcheria and Marcion. The Council of Chalcedon was called in 451, and there Leo's *Tome* was taken seriously.

What were the issues and theology at the trial of Eutyches? Eutyches's Christological formula was clearly *monophysite (one* nature). After the birth of Christ, Eutyches worshipped *one* nature, which was that of God made flesh and made human person. He denied that Christ is *from* two natures, or indeed that he is *from* two natures *united hypostatically.*

Why was Eutyches so opposed to acknowledging two natures? He denied that this was to be found in Scripture or the tradition. He claimed that he held to Nicaea and Ephesus and Cyril of Alexandria. He asserted (importantly) that he was unwilling 'to seek to explain God' (*physiologein ton theon*). Yet, while refusing to say that Christ had two natures, or that he was from two natures, Eutyches explicitly asserted that Christ was born of the Virgin and that he was perfect God and perfectly human. He denied vigorously that he thought Christ took his flesh from heaven (which Apollinaris was [falsely] accused of thinking). However, Eutyches maintained, although born of Mary, Christ did not have flesh *homoousios* (of the same being/ nature) as ours.

How does one make sense of this most peculiar ragbag of views? Eutyches tried to confine himself to stating his belief in simple, general terms. His critics were not satisfied and pressed him to give his opinion on more elaborated formulas. Eutyches allowed from *two* natures, but

qualified it by saying this was only *before* the union. *After* the union, he only admitted *one* nature.

The questioning moved on to the issue of Christ being *homoousios* with us. Eutyches allowed an incarnation which was made from the flesh of the virgin (i.e., not flesh from heaven), and of a virgin consubstantial to us, and a perfect inhomination. Flavian tried to force him to accept the formula (which he thought was equivalent) that Christ was *homoousios* with us. Eutyches agreed to accept this, but only on the authority of the synod. And he explained his reluctance to use the formula: a body *homoousios[ion]* to us. He said:

> Until today, I haven't said this since I confess it to be the body of God (Do you understand?). I have not called the body of God *"body of a man"*, but I have called the body *human*, and said the Lord was enfleshed from the Virgin. But, if it is necessary to say "from (*ek*) the Virgin and consubstantial with us", I allow this too, Sir, but [I call him] the Only-Begotten Son of God, Lord of heaven and earth, ruling and reigning with the Father, with whom he is enthroned and praised. For I do not say *"homoousios"* in such a way as to deny that he is Son of God ... (Schwartz, p. 25, no. 522)

When pressed to confess two natures, and to anathematize those who denied the two natures, he refused. He held to the (one nature) doctrine of Julius and Felix of Rome (actually Apollinarian forgeries), of Athanasius, of Gregory of Nazianzus and Gregory of Nyssa. He was unwilling 'to seek to explain God'. But he anathematized Apollinaris, Mani, Valentinus, *Nestorius and those who claimed the flesh of Christ was taken from heaven.

Let us now try to assess these views. Eutyches was obsessively insistent on the phrase 'One nature (*physis*) of God the Word incarnate'. Why? Draguet suggests it is because he understands the word 'nature' as the equivalent of '*prosopon*' (really understood as 'person'). It is clear from his submissions at the trial that Eutyches was not a *Docetist, nor an Apollinarian. That is, he did not deny the reality of the flesh of Christ; he did not attribute to him an incomplete human nature; he did not think the divine and human natures mixed into a new 'third entity'. But what is one to make of (1) his denial that Christ is from two natures *after* the union, and (2) his reluctance to say Christ was 'of the same being (*homoousios*) as we are'?

Cyril of Alexandria himself (and his greatest follower, Severus of Antioch, in the sixth century) accepted the phrase 'from two natures after the union', because it showed that their insistence on 'one nature' did not alter or do away with the elements which were united. If Eutyches was opposed to such a Cyrillian phrase, it could only be because he was so hypersensitive to Nestorianism. After his insistence that Christ was *perfect God* and *perfect human* we cannot accuse him of Apollinarianism because he denied 'from two natures after the union'. What about his reluctance to say 'of the same being as we are'? He explained his anxiety to the synod. He feared that saying 'a body of the same being as we' implied that Christ was not the Son of God; and that it would be interpreted as 'body of *a man*', when really it is the body of God. Draguet suggests that, again, the underlying motive is not Apollinarianism but exaggerated anti-Nestorianism. If the body of Christ was the body 'of *a man*' (of an *individual person*), there would be two natures, a God and a man. That is, to Eutyches, 'a body of the same being as we' seemed equivalent to 'a body of *a man*'. Instead, he suggested 'a *human* body'. By this, he hoped not only to avoid Nestorian division of the natures, but also to preserve the integrity of the human nature.

We do not know why Eutyches held these views. They led him to 'simple' statements of faith (simpler than those of Cyril of Alexandria and Severus of Antioch): The body of God, not the body of a man; yet a human body; the same person is perfect God and perfectly human, he is born of the virgin; his incarnation was real, not apparent. This is not an Apollinarian or Docetist position (whatever the textbooks say).

More generally, some important points emerge about Eutyches. (1) He seems to have taken *physis* (nature) in the sense of *prosopon*. This would have speeded up the terminological separation of *hypostasis* (the rounded-off *physis*) from *physis*, and helped it to acquire the meaning of 'person'. This was beginning in Cyril, and was taken further in Leo and at Chalcedon. So Eutyches was a part of the building material which led to the change. (2) His idea that the human nature in Christ was a *human* body (including a mind), rather than a *man's* body may have accelerated the idea that the human

nature was complete and real, but not personal. This understanding pointed to the way it was taken in the sixth century: Christ's body was *anhypostatos* (real, but non-personal in itself) and became *enhypostatos* (personalized) in the union. That is, the union both brought the human nature into being and personalized it: it was not a pre-existing independent human being.

IAIN R. TORRANCE

FURTHER READING: J.F. Bethune-Baker, *The Early History of Christian Doctrine* (London, 1903); R. Draguet, 'La Christologie d'Eutychès d'après les Actes du Synode de Flavien (448)', *Byzantion* 6 (1931), pp. 441–57; W.H.C. Frend, *The Rise of the Monophysite Movement* (Cambridge, 1972); J.N.D. Kelly, *Early Christian Doctrines* (London, 1958); Eduard Schwartz, 'Der Prozess des Eutyches', *Sitz B Ak Wiss* (Ph-hist Kl 5; 1929), pp. 1–93; R.V. Sellers, *The Council of Chalcedon* (London, 1953).

Evangelical Theology

The term 'evangelical' has been used of *Reformed and *Lutheran churches since the Reformation, because they base their teaching pre-eminently on the 'Gospel'. In Germany and Switzerland, 'Evangelical' (*evangelisch*) has been used of Lutheran churches in contradistinction to *Calvinist bodies (in North America the tendency runs the other way), but in 1945 all Protestant churches in Germany were designated part of the Evangelical Church in Germany. In 'Anglo-Saxon' countries, evangelicals distinguish themselves from Catholic, 'liberal', neo-orthodox and radical Christians, and regard themselves as part of a broad, pan-denominational movement stemming from the eighteenth-century evangelical revivals. In some parts of the world, Protestants generally are designated 'evangelical', as in Latin America where Pentecostalism now contends numerically with Roman Catholicism. Pentecostal or charismatic Christianity is the largest and fastest growing form of religion in the world. It has roots in the Holiness movements of the nineteenth century, which themselves derive from the revivals. Its theology is broadly evangelical, whilst the current 'charismaticizing' of mainstream evangelicalism manifests an increased emphasis on the Holy Spirit.

There is not room to give doctrinal histories of evangelicalism within its multifarious denominational, confessional and geographical groupings. Instead, evangelicalism will be considered as a conceptual unity with identifiable theological characteristics that can be traced historically. Evangelical theology reflects the *sola scriptura* principle of the Reformers, the rational orthodoxy of *Protestant Scholasticism and the experiential emphases of the revivals. Its main characteristics include: emphasizing the authority of Scripture over against reason, tradition and ecclesial authority; prioritizing the experience of becoming a Christian and knowing Jesus as one's personal saviour, not over against right belief – the importance of which is taken very seriously – but over against the sacraments and ecclesial structures; stressing conversion, evangelism and missionary work, and the particularism of Christ's saving work; and focusing on sanctification through holy living along with a corresponding rejection of Christ's presence in the sacraments. Prominent internal disputes have arisen over the nature of biblical authority, the relation between divine grace and human free will, and eschatology.

Theological method. Evangelical theology has developed differently in Britain and North America than in Europe. *John Locke's and Thomas Reid's *Enlightenment philosophies influenced British and American evangelicals, shaping a dominant strand of Reformed thought in which faith was viewed as rational assent to propositions. This has resulted in biblical foundationalism – the conviction that we need a reliable Bible upon which to ground faith – and scholarship directed to the defence of Scripture. European evangelicals, by contrast, view faith as a primary given and a necessary guide to reason. The Dutch Reformed theologians Abraham Kuyper (1837–1920) and Herman Bavinck (1854–1921) challenged American evangelical apologetics by arguing that Scripture's authority could not be proved intellectually, but must be experienced by the testimony of the Holy Spirit as one stands in new life in Christ. From this perspective, Anglo-American evangelical theology appears to make reason rather than (scriptural) revelation its first principle.

British and North American evangelicals have wielded the greatest theological influence on evangelical movements worldwide. They usually start their theology with the doctrine of Scripture; this serving as a prolegomenon in the way that fundamental theology does in

Catholic thought. More primitivist evangelicals seek truth solely from Scripture, and not from the development of theological understanding within Christian tradition. Scripture is regarded as self-evidencing. Protestant scholastic theologians had said that one proves God from God, and the divine origin of Scripture from Scripture itself. They developed the doctrine of plenary (full) verbal inspiration from 2 Timothy 3:16 and 2 Peter 1:20–21. That the Bible is the word of God was taken to mean that its very words are God's own words, and that it must be accurate because God cannot err. The conviction arose, and became a hallmark of 'fundamentalism', that the Bible is a reliable foundation for faith only if it is inerrant (without error). The doctrine of inerrancy was classically formulated by A.A. Hodge and B.B. Warfield of Princeton Theological Seminary in 1881. It emerged alongside new methods of biblical criticism, and it became more rigid when attempts arose to demonstrate by 'better' criticism and 'true' science that the Bible is indeed fully accurate. Some inerrantists expect full scientific accuracy from Scripture, others only freedom from error on religious and moral matters.

Evangelicals tend to do theology by summarizing biblical teaching – in contradistinction to scholastic reasoning from first principles and from modern attempts to begin theology from human experience. Evangelicals often refer to the Bible as the textbook of theology. Some describe their method as 'inductive': collecting biblical texts, like scientists collect data, and gathering them into themes to infer God's revelation on those matters. This can reduce to proof-texting (citing biblical verses out of context to argue a point). Others, notably Black evangelicals, practice a sort of *Narrative Theology – taking Scripture as a whole, and relating its themes and stories to historical developments and to individual lives.

Evangelicals affirm most creedal statements as a matter of orthodoxy, but they have not developed theological thinking on all creedal matters. Notably, there is no distinctive evangelical contribution to the doctrines of the Trinity or of Christ. There are several likely reasons for this. Evangelicalism does not have a strong confessional orientation, due both to its anti-traditionalism and to its theological method of summarizing Scripture, which does not readily yield a confessional system. Evangelical theology is more apologetic or polemic than systematic, defending doctrines as they come under threat. It tends to reflect on those elements of the Christian confession that can best be given rational expression or which directly serve mission, rather than to contemplate divine mysteries. The purpose of revelation is thought to be to make things clear, rather than to draw us in to the mystery of God. Contemplative prayer and spiritual journeying are downplayed in evangelical spirituality, compared to devotional Bible study, intercessory prayer and obedience to the moral teaching of the Bible.

Other theological concerns. For apologetic and evangelistic reasons, evangelicals identify common ground between believers and non-believers. Calvinists explain this ground in terms of common grace: a general grace left to humanity despite the Fall, by which we are able to reason. Evangelicals disagree over the capacity of unaided reason to recognize revelation, but Lutherans posit a greater antipathy between faith and reason. Evangelicals speak of 'general revelation' rather than 'natural theology'. Both concepts preserve a human capacity to know God apart from biblical revelation, but natural theology credits natural reason whereas evangelicals stress the need to hear the redemptive word.

The emphasis on the spoken and written word (more than on the Word incarnate) is apparent in the prominence given to preaching and, architecturally, to the pulpit. In worship, rational involvement and personal application are contrasted with repetitive ritual and enacted ceremonial: hearing is emphasized over sight and smell as employed in Catholic and Orthodox traditions.

The sacraments may not feature in an evangelical account of Christian faith. Baptism and Holy Communion are sometimes called 'ordinances' – a means of pledging oneself and testifying to the community (hence the tendency to favour adult baptism) – rather than 'sacraments', or a means of grace by which Christ pledges his presence. Ordained ministers are not readily called 'priests'. They are differentiated from the laity functionally and often by their greater spirituality, but not ontologically. Evangelicals emphasize the priesthood of all believers, and in sacramental churches sometimes promote lay-presidency at the Eucharist or Lord's Supper. The problem of whether women are able to represent Christ at the altar is not an evangelical concern; whether they have the authority to preach (and to take policy decisions with men serving under them) is. Evangelical ecclesiology ranges from seeing the church as the gathering of regenerate believers to regarding her as an institution created by God through word and sacrament, such that she is God's action and transcends local congregations. With the latter ecclesiology, a justification of infant baptism can be attained.

Anti-sacramentalism relates to evangelical understandings of sanctification: one is made holy through holy living and not by any grace conferred through sacraments. Hence evangelicals emphasize right living, which in *Wesleyan circles takes precedence over right doctrine and has involved abstaining from alcohol, dancing and gambling. Wesleyan Methodists developed a doctrine of 'entire sanctification', or 'perfection', as a 'second blessing' bestowed on a believer instantaneously. This doctrine came via the revivals into the Holiness movement, and it alienated Calvinists because it seemed to undermine the need for ongoing growth in grace. Pentecostal and charismatic movements have a related doctrine of 'baptism in the Holy Spirit', which can seem to imply that Christians who do not manifest charismatic gifts have not received the Holy Spirit.

In the *Romantic era, which celebrated individual autonomy, Calvinists were offended by the Holiness notion that perfection could be attained as a matter of the will. Similar tensions had arisen before concerning the roles of free will and divine grace in our salvation. The Dutch Reformed theologian, *James Arminius (1560–1609), had taught that divine sovereignty was compatible with human free will and that the elect were saved on the basis of God's foreknowledge of a human person's perseverance in faith. This was a repudiation of both supralapsarian (antelapsarian) and sublapsarian (infralapsarian) Calvinist doctrines of predestination: that God predestined people to salvation and damnation either before or after the Fall (the latter doctrine dominating since the Synod of Dort, 1618). That John Wesley held an Arminian position in contrast to George Whitefield's Calvinism created the main theological division of the revivals. The idea that salvation is appropriated through personal decision is evident in evangelism when individuals are invited to receive the gospel, for example, by responding to an altar call. It is also present in strict Calvinist rationalism in the idea that faith is rational assent, which the Holy Spirit subsequently actualizes into saving faith.

Penal substitution is the predominant doctrine of atonement amongst evangelicals (from both seventeenth-century Reformed orthodoxy and the Augsburg Confession): that Christ took on himself the punishment for sin that is rightfully ours. God is often perceived primarily in terms of justice, and the gospel interpreted in light of satisfying the law: God meets his own demands because his wrath cannot be minimized nor his holiness compromised. The classical 'Christus Victor' model is also espoused, especially in Pentecostal/charismatic circles where Christ's victory over the powers of darkness is claimed for present-day spiritual victories. Evangelicals are particularist about Christ's saving work: salvation is through Christ alone. This need not be incompatible with universal salvation. A growing universalism, or at least annihilationism (that unbelievers are extinguished at death rather than condemned to eternal hell), characterizes current 'open' evangelical thought.

Eschatologically, evangelicals disagree over millennialism. Millennialists believe in a long period (literally one thousand years) of peace and righteousness associated with Christ's second coming. Amillennialists interpret biblical references to this period figuratively. Postmillennialists believe Christ will return after the church has established the millennium. Postmillennial optimism prevailed throughout the eighteenth-century revivals, and was advocated by America's leading pre-Revolutionary theologian, *Jonathan Edwards (1703–58). Premillennialists believe that human society will decline until Christ returns to establish his reign. They look for the 'signs of the times'. Historicist premillennialists believe that some of the prophetic Scriptures, especially in the books of Daniel and Revelation, have already been fulfilled. Futurist premillennialists expect their fulfilment only in the 'last days', during which the antichrist will reign (the 'tribulation') before being defeated at the battle of Armageddon. The futurists divide into pre-, mid-, and post-tribulationists, disagreeing over when the righteous will be 'raptured up' to meet Christ in the sky. Premillennial speculation flourished amongst the Puritans and again after the French and American Revolutions.

The *Dispensationalist premillennialism of *John Nelson Darby (1800–82), which is futurist and pretribulationist, has dominated American evangelicalism since the 1870s. It interprets Scripture within a framework of seven ages or dispensations, codified in C.I. Scofield's *Reference Bible* (1909). Premillennialists have typically been politically quietist, concentrating on individual piety, but they have become politicized with the rise of the New Christian Right.

Recent developments. Current sacramental and 'post-conservative' trends amongst evangelicals are partly due to charismatic influences which emphasize the presence of God, de-emphasize rational appropriation, and soften anti-ecumenical tendencies. Evangelical theology is being revitalized with insights from *neo-Barthian, postliberal and Narrative Theology, critical realism, non-foundationalism and challenges to the hegemony of historical study in interpreting Scripture. Mainstream theologians, notably *Wolfhart Pannenberg, now influence evangelical scholars, and evangelical concerns – especially the centrality of Scripture and distinctiveness of the Christian gospel – have entered mainstream theology.

HARRIET A. HARRIS

FURTHER READING: *Introductory:* Louis Berkhof, *Systematic Theology* (Grand Rapids, 1941); Donald W. Dayton and Robert K. Johnston, *The Variety of American Evangelicalism* (Knoxville, TN, 1991); Walter A. Elwell (ed.), *Handbook of Evangelical Theologians* (Grand Rapids, 1993); Stanley J. Grenz, *Revisioning Evangelical Theology: A Fresh Agenda for the 21st Century* (Downers Grove, IL, 1993); Wayne Grudem, *Systematic Theology: An Introduction to Biblical Doctrine* (Leicester, 1994); J.I. Packer, *Fundamentalism and the Word of God,* (London, 1958). *Advanced:* Donald G. Bloesch, *Essentials of Evangelical Theology* (2 vols.; San Francisco, 1978–79); Harriet A. Harris, *Fundamentalism and Evangelicals* (Oxford, 1998); A.A. Hodge and B.B. Warfield, *The Presbyterian Review 2* (1881); Walter J. Hollenweger, *The Pentecostals* (Peabody, MA, 3rd edn, 1988).

Ewing, Alfred Cyril (1899–1973)

British philosopher educated at University College, Oxford, who held university appointments at University College, Swansea (1927–31), Cambridge (1931–54) and Oxford (1954–66). He was also visiting professor at several American universities, including Princeton and

Northwestern (1949), the University of Southern California (1961), University of Colorado (1963) and University of Delaware (1971).

Ewing was a thoroughly convinced theist who commended philosophy as a great aid to theology. His importance to historical theology consists especially in his defence of the enterprise of metaphysics, and in his development of a 'religious metaphysics', or a metaphysics congenial to traditional theistic ideas. His book *Value and Reality* (London, 1973) is the most important source for his execution of both projects.

Ewing's general defence of metaphysics targeted two doctrines of the *Logical Positivism that dominated the intellectual landscape of his time. First was the verifiability criterion of the meaningfulness of genuine statements: a statement is meaningful if, and only if, it is either analytic or empirically verifiable. Ewing demonstrated that this criterion of meaningfulness, so obviously inimical to religious belief, is meaningless on its own terms. Second was the claim that all a priori propositions and inferences are analytic. Ewing argued that there are important synthetic a priori truths that can be known by a special faculty of intuition, including certain ethical truths and the existence of God.

Having defended the enterprise of metaphysics, Ewing turned his attention to the metaphysics of theism, with noteworthy contributions in three areas. First, although he did not accept any particular revealed religion, he was a devoted advocate of natural theology, understood as 'a study of the arguments for God' (*VR*, p. 22). He remarked that 'the chief evidence for God seems to lie in an experience which so far from being a special prerogative of philosophers seems not to be possessed by many of them at all' (*VR*, p. 20). While he acknowledged that metaphysical arguments do not strictly prove the existence of God, he maintained that the best arguments follow the pattern of inference to best explanation and tend to confirm the hypothesis of God's existence. The arguments he favoured were versions of the cosmological, design and moral arguments, arranged in cumulative fashion.

Second, Ewing's conviction that religion requires a doctrine of survival of bodily death prompted him to defend the metaphysical doctrine of mind-body dualism – the claim that there is 'a substance-self which retains its identity through time' (*VR*, p. 85). He held that

mind-body dualism is a necessary but not a sufficient condition for human immortality. He allowed that survival is in principle verifiable by empirical evidence, but he judged that such evidence was presently inconclusive. He did not consider the evidence for the resurrection of Jesus Christ to be much support for the doctrine of immortality.

Third, Ewing sought to elucidate the close connection between ethics and religion. In his view, the relation between the two could not be sustained if either naturalism or subjectivism in ethics is accepted. He devoted considerable energy, therefore, to setting forth objections to each of these alternatives. Nevertheless, he maintained that knowledge of ethical truths did not depend upon first accepting theological propositions since it is possible, by an act of intuition, simply to *see* the truth of the most basic moral propositions. Indeed, Ewing's influence as a philosopher was principally in the field of philosophical ethics, where he achieved the distinction of becoming the last great stalwart of intuitionism.

R. DOUGLAS GEIVETT

FURTHER READING: *Texts: The Morality of Punishment* (London, 1929); *Idealism: A Critical Survey* (London, 1934); *The Definition of Good* (New York, 1947); *The Individual, the State and World Government* (New York, 1947); *The Fundamental Questions of Philosophy* (New York, 1951); *Ethics* (London, 1953); *Second Thoughts in Moral Philosophy* (London, 1959); *Non-Linguistic Philosophy* (London, 1968), includes reprints of some of his most important papers. *Study:* G.R. Grice, 'Alfred Cyril Ewing', *Proceedings of the British Academy* 59 (1973), pp. 499–513, an obituary that includes a valuable exposition and assessment of Ewing's philosophical work.

Existentialism

Existentialism is a type of philosophy which is difficult to define, because it does not have any agreed doctrinal content. It is rather a way of doing philosophy and can lead to very different conclusions. It may, for instance, be either theistic or atheistic.

Existentialism is a philosophy closely tied to living. In the words of the Spaniard Unamuno (1864–1936), the existentialist philosophizes 'not with the reason only, but with the will, with the feelings, with the flesh and with the bones, with the whole soul and the body'. The point is made in less exaggerated terms by

*Kierkegaard (1813–55) who talked of the 'existing thinker'. This thought reverses the Cartesian doctrine 'I think, therefore I am'. We do not think in a vacuum but as beings already involved in the struggles of existence. So existentialism challenges the mindset of modernity, in which philosophers have been regarded as detached spectators, offering an objective, value-free description of the world and of human life.

When existentialists use the word 'existence', they understand it in a restricted sense as human existence. In ordinary speech, we say that stars exist, trees exist, sheep exist, men and women exist. The existentialist, however, does not use the word 'exist' of inanimate objects or even of animals. When existentialists speak exclusively of the human being as existing, they are trying to draw attention to something distinctively human. 'Existence' is being understood in what is supposedly its original etymological sense of 'standing out'. The existent is not just another item in the environment, like stars, trees and the like. These things have a 'nature' that is simply given to them. They have their being simply by lying around, so to speak. The human being exists actively by standing out or emerging through decisions and acts that make this existent the person he or she becomes. The human being has to gain the authentic humanity that is unique to him or her. In a famous, if exaggerated, definition by Jean-Paul Sartre (1905–80), the existent begins as nothing and only afterwards becomes something and forms a nature through its chosen policies and actions.

Already we can see that existentialism is opposed to any philosophies which attempt to present some grand, all-inclusive metaphysical view of the universe. As Kierkegaard pointed out in opposition to *Hegel (1770–1831), such a metaphysic is impossible for an *existing* thinker. It would be possible only for a thinker who could stand outside the universe and see it in its totality, and presumably only God could do that. Furthermore, every existing thinker is living in time and is constantly between one state of affairs and another. The universe itself is in process. So any complete account could come only at the end of history and is impossible while history is in progress.

Is existentialism then a positivism, or at most (as Sartre claimed) a humanism? One could only come to this conclusion if one ignored the existentialists' claim that philosophy is not a product of pure thought but draws on the whole multifaceted experience of being-in-the-world, of willing, feeling, acting, experiencing resistance, suffering and even death. Perhaps one should not speak of an existentialist metaphysic, but certainly some existentialists do go beyond an analysis of human existence and say something about the wider framework within which such an existence is set. In particular, some have spoken of God, while others have been quite atheistic. How is it possible for an existentialist to be either a theist or an atheist, without lapsing into the kind of metaphysics which existentialism has so severely castigated?

Existentialists have little use for the traditional 'proofs' or arguments for the existence of God. Already in the seventeenth century *Blaise Pascal (1623–62) criticized the 'proofs' and suggested that they are more likely to sow doubts than to produce conviction. He made a sharp distinction between the 'God of Abraham, Isaac and Jacob' (God as known in religious experience) and the 'God of the philosophers' (God as conceptualized in abstract speculation). Kierkegaard took a similar line, holding that the truth of God can be grasped only by faith, in an inward passionate appropriation. At the opposite extreme from Kierkegaard, though equally existentialist, was *Nietzsche (1844–1900). His convinced atheism rested not on an intellectual disproof of God's existence, but on his passionate belief that God is incompatible with human freedom and must be displaced by a new breed of human beings (the superman, or *Übermensch*). Heidegger (1889–1976) suggests that a God whose existence needs to be proved is hardly worthy of the name of God.

Are these existentialists who support either theism or atheism simply following their emotions, and if so, have they any title to be considered philosophers? Here many difficult questions arise. What is an emotion? What counts as knowledge? What is truth? Let us try briefly to say how an existentialist might answer these questions, and let us take Kierkegaard as our exemplar.

The most widely read of Kierkegaard's books is *The Concept of Anxiety*. The word 'anxiety' here translates the Danish *aengst*, German *Angst*, words for which there is no exact English equivalent. Sometimes the English word 'dread' is used, though perhaps a word we have borrowed from the French, 'malaise', would be the best available translation, for this word denotes a vague feeling of uneasiness, different from fear but less acute than anxiety in the common sense of the word. *Angst* has no definite object that arouses it. It is the awareness of the fragility of one's existence, as a finite being-in-the-world. Heidegger takes up the idea from Kierkegaard, and treats it as an ontological mood. It is not just a passing emotion but a significant disclosure or revelation of human existence as a finite centre of freedom thrown into a world in which the exercise of that freedom is constantly problematical. Anxiety is the inescapable accompaniment of a finite freedom.

With this word 'freedom' we come to another fundamental term in existentialist philosophy. Indeed, freedom is perhaps the most central and distinctive characteristic of the existent. But freedom, like anxiety, is hardly definable. It tends to be left out in supposedly 'scientific' or objective accounts of the human being. Freedom is not an observable object. In an important sense, freedom is nothing – it is the empty space available for our projects. Freedom is essential to human existence. If there were no freedom, existence in the sense understood by existentialist philosophers would never have emerged. Because freedom is essential to existence, it is sometimes taken to be a value. Sartre seems to think of freedom as the supreme value in human life. But this is a mistake. Freedom is not so much a value as the condition that there may be any values. Freedom makes possible the pursuit of values, but also permits the realization of disvalues. It was André Gide who wrote: 'to gain one's freedom is as nothing; what to do with it is the problem'. Human experience gives ample confirmation of this.

We are now beginning to see possible answers to two of the questions asked above – what is emotion and what counts as knowledge? In the view of the existentialists, emotion is not just some transient *frisson*, but more like a disclosure or revelation, throwing light on one's situation as a being-in-the-world, where one's freedom is constantly threatened by the sheer facticity of one's situation, and where, even when freedom is gained, we may not know how to use it. The answer to the question about what counts as knowledge is that knowledge is not confined to that which is objectively knowable, for there is also a knowledge which arises directly from our participation in existence. *Angst* and freedom

are both important realities which we cannot doubt but which can be known only through our exercise of them or our participation in them.

These points also suggest an answer to the third question, 'What is truth?' There are several kinds of truth besides the common-sense idea of truth as correspondence between proposition and fact. The truth that we learn through the 'lighting up' of our being-in-the-world through anxiety and freedom is like the truth of revelation. It is, as Heidegger claimed, the truth which the Greeks called *alētheia*, a word which literally means 'unconcealedness'. It was unfortunate that Kierkegaard associated truth with subjectivity. He did not mean that truth is simply what an individual says that it is – that would be the abolition of truth. He meant that the most important truths of life cannot be reached by observation but only through inward appropriation. In his own words, 'an objective uncertainty held fast in an appropriation-process of the most passionate inwardness is the truth, the highest truth attainable for an existing individual'.

What about God? Are there experiences of God which the existentialist takes to be self-authenticating? Perhaps there are, though this is a point at which we might ask whether the existentialist has been too quick in dismissing arguments which might support the intuition gained in his experience. *Jaspers (1883–1969), for instance, speaks of 'limit-situations', in which a person at the end of his or her resources and confronted with finitude, strikes against what Jaspers calls 'Transcendence'. Rather similarly, Heidegger describes a deep mood of anxiety in which the things of the world fall away in a kind of mystical experience to reveal 'Being', the mystery that is beyond and prior to all the things of the world. The experiences described obviously have to be taken with the utmost seriousness, but can they be accepted as 'truth' without some supporting argument?

The stress which some of the existentialists lay on anxiety, finitude and death has led to the criticism that there is something morbid and pessimistic in their philosophy. Of course, they may be simply realistic. We should also remember that the idea of freedom has led some of them to stress the idea of transcendence in human existence. If human nature is not given ready-made but has to be formed, then there is the possibility of genuine hope, as opposed to the shallow optimism of the *Enlightenment and the nineteenth century. Transcendence in this sense is the capacity to go beyond every situation toward horizons which open on new possibilities. The theistic and Christian philosopher *Gabriel Marcel (1889–1973) is one existentialist who has given prominence to the notion of transcendence.

Another common criticism of existentialism is that most of its leading exponents have seen human existence in an individualistic way. This was true of Kierkegaard who esteemed the individual above the community, perhaps in reaction against Hegel. It was true also of Sartre, who thought of interpersonal relations as essentially frustrating. On the other hand, Heidegger believed that the existent is not only being-in-the-world but essentially being-with-others, while Marcel understood transcendence as not only transcendence toward the future but as transcendence of self toward the other.

A problem with many of the existentialists is their lack of clear moral teaching. They are suspicious of moral laws, which ignore the individual's uniqueness and impose a common pattern upon all. A good example is Kierkegaard's defence of Abraham's setting aside of morality in order to sacrifice his son, Isaac. He did this in obedience to a supposedly higher law, the command of God. But after all, it was Abraham who decided this was the will of God, and Kierkegaard did not scruple to apply the same casuistry to his own case when he broke off his betrothal to Regine. It is difficult to see that existentialism could provide anything more than a so-called 'situation' ethic, and this has been frequently shown to be quite inadequate.

In spite of its ambiguities, existentialism has had more influence among the theologians of the twentieth century than any other philosophy. Such major figures as *Karl Barth (in his early phase), *Rudolf Bultmann and *Paul Tillich, among Protestants, have been deeply influenced by the movement, and likewise *Karl Rahner, the leading Roman Catholic theologian of the period. Some of existentialism's influences are still visible in the so-called 'postmodernist' theologians, and no doubt some abiding truths of existentialism will continue in the future.

JOHN MACQUARRIE

FURTHER READING: Ronald Grimsley, *Existentialist Thought* (Cardiff, 1955); John Macquarrie, *Existentialism* (London, 1973). *Major texts in English translation:* M. Heidegger, *Being and Time* (London, 1962); Karl Jaspers, *Philosophical Faith and Revelation* (New York, 1967); S. Kierkegaard, *The Concept of Anxiety* (Princeton, 1957); *Philosophical Fragments* (Princeton, 1936); Gabriel Marcel, *The Mystery of Being* (Chicago, 1960); J.-P. Sartre, *Being and Nothingness* (New York, 1956).

Fairbairn, Andrew Martin (1838–1912)

Fairbairn was born in Inverkeithing, Fife, the son of parents who belonged to the United Secession Church. He soon left the church of his parents to join the Evangelical Union, which was founded in 1843 by James Morison (1816–93), following his expulsion from the Secession Church for preaching universal atonement. After a very sketchy early education, Fairbairn entered the Union's academy in 1857, which enabled him to attend some classes at Edinburgh University. He then held two pastorates in Scotland, at Bathgate and Aberdeen, before entering the world of English Congregationalism in 1877 as principal of Airedale College, Bradford. Nine years later he moved to Oxford as founding principal of Mansfield College, where he remained until his retirement in 1909. He was chairman of the Congregational Union of England and Wales in 1883.

Fairbairn was one of the two greatest Congregational theologians of the nineteenth century – the other being his friend R.W. Dale. Fairbairn's theological pilgrimage took him from the narrow outlook of the Secession Church, through the Evangelical Union to a liberal theological system constructed through historical enquiry. The greatest change in his thinking came during a year's study in Berlin in the early 1860s. There he studied primarily under Isaak Dorner (1809–84), F.A. Tholuck (1799–1877) and E.W. Hengstenberg (1802–69). 'Theology changed from a system doubted to a system believed', he later wrote. The theological position he had reached by the time he left his first pastorate in 1872 changed little in the succeeding years, but he thought it through more fully and coherently.

Fairbairn was influenced by *Hegelianism, but broke away from it in the significance *Hegel gave to history. Fairbairn's magisterial *The Place of Christ in Modern Theology* (London, 1893), which ran to twelve editions during his lifetime, was an attempt to provide the groundwork for a system of theology through the historical records of the life of Jesus. Influenced by, though never wholly committed to, the biblical criticism he first encountered in Germany, Fairbairn believed it to be possible for the first time since the earliest years of the church to recover knowledge of the historical Jesus prior to the New Testament interpretations of his life and work. It would thus be possible to enter into

Jesus' own consciousness, 'to conceive God as He conceived him', and so to enter into an understanding of the relation of the Son to the Father. 'The interpretation of God in the terms of the consciousness of Christ may thus be described as the distinctive and differentiating doctrine of the Christian religion' (*Place of Christ*, p. 388). Hence Fairbairn's emphasis on the fatherhood of God, through which he believed the eternal sovereignty should be primarily interpreted. Thus, Fairbairn argued, sin cost the eternal Father suffering, and the sufferings and death of Christ could be construed 'as if they were sacraments, or symbols and seals, of the invisible passion and sacrifice of the Godhead' (*Place of Christ*, p. 485). He provided a comprehensive account of contemporary work on the historical Jesus, but neglected the eschatological dimension which was to be emphasized by *Schweitzer thirteen years later, and which took on greater significance during the cataclysmic events of the First World War.

For Fairbairn, Christianity had not only to be historically investigated, but also 'philosophically construed'; this he attempted to do in *The Philosophy of the Christian Religion* (London, 1902), which ran through five editions in the next six years. Christianity was to claim no special consideration from historian or philosopher. 'For he who advances such a claim practically surrenders either the truth and equity of his religion, or the integrity of the reason which was God's own gift to man' (*Philosophy*, p. x). Fairbairn first developed his interest in the idea of God as expressed in the great religions of the world through the encouragement of F. Max Müller (1823–1900) during his Aberdeen pastorate, and in his experience as Haskell Lecturer in India in the winter of 1898–99. He then used this interest to attempt first an explanation of religion through Nature and man, setting Christianity within the framework of the general development of religion, and then, secondly, a philosophical justification of the principle of the consciousness of Christ as the foundation of Christianity.

Fairbairn always insisted that theology should engage with the thought of the age, and he eagerly entered into controversy. He was vehemently opposed to what he perceived to be a rising tide of sacerdotalism (though he was at the same time fascinated by it), and he gave expression to his views in a series of articles in the *Contemporary Review*, later published as *Catholicism, Roman and Anglican* (London, 1899). Some of these views had led him into sharp controversy with J.H. Newman, whom he accused of philosophical scepticism.

The necessity for the agreement of faith and reason was one of the great principles underlying Fairbairn's thought: 'For in every controversy concerning what is or what is not truth, reason and not authority is the supreme arbiter; the authority that decides against reason commits itself to a conflict which is certain to issue in its defeat' (*Philosophy*, p. 18).

In many respects Fairbairn's theology soon appeared outmoded because it related so closely to contemporary controversy. But he did a great service to his denomination and to the church as a whole in emphasizing the crucial importance of the study of theology – not only for the education of ministers within his own tradition, but also for the intellectual life of a university (see especially 'Theology in the Modern University' in *Mansfield College, Oxford: Its Origin and Opening*, London, 1890).

ELAINE KAYE

FURTHER READING: W.B. Selbie, *The Life of Andrew Martin Fairbairn* (London, 1914); R.S. Franks, 'The Theology of A.M. Fairbairn', *Transactions of the Congregational Historical Society* 13 (1937–39), pp. 140–50; A.P.F. Sell, 'An Englishman, an Irishman and a Scotsman', *Scot J Th* 38 (1985), pp. 41–83; P. Hinchliff, 'Knowing God in History: Scottish Critics and Principal Fairbairn', ch. 8 in *God and History* (Oxford, 1992); Elaine Kaye, *Mansfield College: Its Origin, History and Significance* (Oxford, 1996).

Farel, Guillaume (1489–1565)

Guillaume Farel was the famed Reformer of Geneva and Neuchâtel who was born near the city of Gap in the province of Dauphine, France. He studied under the famed humanist Jacques Lefèvre d'Étaples at the University of Paris, where he converted to the Protestant cause. He then began to preach under the sponsorship of the bishop of Meaux, who was sympathetic to the early Protestants. But, in December 1523, he left for Basle because the reform was not moving as quickly as he would have liked. Basle was a haven for humanists such as *Erasmus and many of the early Reformers like *Oecolampadius. When Farel publicly expressed his belief that Erasmus was more a humanist than a true Reformer, Erasmus responded by influencing the city's

leaders to ask him to leave. Farel went on to preach at Montbeliard, Metz and Strasburg. He became an itinerant evangelist throughout the Swiss cantons and was instrumental in Neuchâtel's move in favour of the Reformation in 1530. Farel was an exceptional preacher, arousing the wrath of the Roman Catholic officials wherever he went and practically forcing his listeners to make a choice either in favour of or against the message of reform.

Farel, however, is most famous for his influence on the Reformation in Geneva. He visited Geneva as an itinerant in 1532 under the sponsorship of Protestant leaders of Bern who desired to expand Protestant territory. After an initial exile, he returned to Geneva in 1535 and was instrumental in persuading the city council to vote in favour of the Reformation on 21 May 1536. Farel realized, however, that he was a better evangelist than an organizer of a church, and when he heard that *Calvin was visiting the city he persuaded him, by threatening God's wrath if Calvin refused, to join in the work in July 1536 of reforming the city.

Farel assisted Calvin in drafting the *Ecclesiastical Ordinances* and the *Confession of Faith* in 1537, which served as the basis for the organization of the church and proper doctrine. In February 1538, the election of the four syndics went against Farel and Calvin, in part a reaction against the strictness of their form of ecclesiastical discipline. The council then ordered the Reformers to follow the practices of Berne regarding the administration of the Eucharist and, when the Reformers celebrated the Lord's Supper in a contrary manner, they were expelled from Geneva. Farel subsequently moved in 1541 to minister primarily in Neuchâtel, where he continued in the cause of the reform and also preached in the Swiss cantons and Protestant Germany.

Farel did not produce any major systematic theology treatises. His gifts were in preaching, although none of his sermons have survived, and in recruiting others whom he felt were more gifted as theologians and pastors. However, he composed the first French evangelical tract entitled *Paternoster et le Credo en François* (1524); *Sommaire et brièfve Déclaration* (1529), the first major statement of Reformed doctrine in French; and the first French Reformed liturgy, *La Manière et fasson* (1528).

His theology was strongly *Zwinglian, and he held to the memorial view of the Lord's Supper whereby the bread and the wine symbolize the body and blood of Christ. Later, under the influence of Calvin, he modified this position to include the concept that the communicant received fellowship with and spiritual nourishment from Christ's spiritual body and blood.

Farel believed in both visible and invisible baptism. Visible baptism is performed publicly with water, but it does not necessarily change one's moral character. To accomplish such improvement one needs invisible baptism, or the baptism of fire and water. Farel generally agreed with the concept of infant baptism but was not as completely opposed to adult baptism as Calvin and the other magisterial reformers were.

He strongly preached the Reformed principles of justification by faith and the priesthood of all believers. Good works come as a result of our faith in Christ, not as a cause of our justification. Good works performed in the power of the Holy Spirit are a means by which we express our gratitude to the Lord. Farel believed that, as a result of the Fall, we are truly depraved and in need of God's grace.

Contrary to his colleague Calvin, Farel did not present a developed doctrine of predestination. He did state that God called the elect before the foundation of the world. He also referred to the reprobate as 'children of wrath ordained to death'. Nothing can prevent them from their path toward destruction while God protects and cares for the elect to prepare them for their eternal destination.

Ecclesiastical discipline was an important aspect of Farel's theology, and he argued that the goal of discipline is to lead the sinner back to the correct path of Christian piety. This should be done in a spirit of love – privately at first, and then by the entire local church. If the sinner fails to mend his or her ways, Farel recommended excommunication whereby the individual would be denied access to the Lord's Table. Farel did not advocate total shunning (as the *Anabaptists practised), in order to leave the door open for the person to return to full communion within the body of Christ.

In his theology of last things Farel was amillennial, as were his Reformed colleagues. At death, the soul enters a period of rest in preparation for the resurrection of the body to take place at the second coming of Christ. Then the Lord will separate the sheep from the goats and usher in the eternal state.

MARTIN I. KLAUBER

FURTHER READING: *Texts: Le Paternoster et le Credo en François* (ed. Francis Higman; Geneva, 1982); *Sommaire et brièfve Déclaration* (ed. Arthur L. Hofer; Neuchâtel, 1980). *Studies:* Don P. Shidler, *Elijah of the Alps* (Smithville, MO, 1972); Henri Heyer, *Guillaume Farel: An Introduction to His Theology* (trans. Blair Reynolds; Lewiston, NY, 1990).

Farmer, Herbert Henry (1892–1981)

Born in Highbury, London in 1911, Farmer entered Peterhouse, Cambridge University, during a particularly stimulating period. Not only were Bertrand Russell (1872–1970) and G.E. Moore (1873–1958) lecturing at Cambridge, but also teaching there was the Hegelian J.M.E. McTaggart (1866–1925), the philosopher and psychologist James Ward (1843–1925) and the Kantian philosopher W.R. Sorely (1855–1935). While challenging the philosophical presuppositions of Russell, Moore and McTaggart, Farmer was clearly influenced by the philosophies of Ward and Sorely, both of whom argued that nature, history and moral experience demand a theistic interpretation.

Shaped by these influences, in 1914 Farmer entered Westminster College, Cambridge, the theological college of the Presbyterian Church of England. Here he met his most significant influence, the professor of systematic theology, *John Oman (1860–1939). Farmer's 'radical personalism' (a theology based on the premise that humans are persons in relation with each other and with God), although his own, is indebted to Oman, whom he acknowledged to be his mentor. This debt is clearly seen in his most important work, *The World and God: A Study of Prayer, Providence and Miracle*, which, dedicated to Oman, rigorously interprets all religious experience in terms of personal encounter. Indeed, while attention is often drawn to the impact on Farmer's thought of *Martin Buber's (1878–1965) book *I and Thou* (Edinburgh, 1937), in actual fact the latter's influence was limited and has been overstated. For although Farmer often used Buber's terminology, he used it to articulate a theology arising out of Oman's thought, not Buber's.

After some time as a farm labourer and gardener (which, as a pacifist, he did instead of military service), in 1919 Farmer began life as a minister, firstly at Stafford and then, in 1922, at New Barnet, London. He remained here until

1931 when he joined the staff of Hartford Theological Seminary, Connecticut as Riley Professor of Christian Doctrine and Ethics. In 1935 he returned to England to succeed Oman at Westminster College. In the following years Farmer held various university lectureships and, in 1949, succeeded C.H. Dodd (1884–1973) as Norris-Hulse Professor of Divinity at Cambridge, a post he held until his retirement in 1960.

Writing during the period when *Karl Barth's (1886–1968) influence was at its height, Farmer was the most significant British theologian to develop a theology belonging to a line of thought that can be traced back through *W. Herrmann (1846–1922) and *A.B. Ritschl (1822–89) to *F.D.E. Schleiermacher (1768–1834). Indeed, unlike much theological discourse of the period, Farmer rarely mentions Barth in his writings. Moreover, not only did Farmer's thought seem out of step with the theological world, but because the Cambridge to which he returned as professor had been intellectually shaped by the philosophizing of Russell, Moore, *Ludwig Wittgenstein (1889–1951), C.D. Broad (1887–1971) and Arthur Wisdom (1904–93), Farmer's thought seemed strange and outdated. However, this judgement is superficial, for although drawing from the well of nineteenth-century liberalism, Farmer didn't simply swallow what was drawn but creatively transformed it and applied it to contemporary problems in accessible and challenging ways. Having said that, it is surprising that he never discusses Wittgenstein and one wonders what interesting fruit such a dialogue would have produced.

Developing the nineteenth-century emphasis on 'natural religion' (which claimed that all persons have an awareness of God), running like a thread through Farmer's work is the conviction that God is constantly revealing himself to human souls. While influenced by Schleiermacher's understanding of divine revelation in terms of religious experience, Farmer builds on it, arguing that because God is personal there must be an objective self-disclosure before anything can be known about him. Moreover, there are two primary elements in a person's experience of God: 'absolute demand' and 'final succour'. We become aware of God as personal by becoming aware of, and responding to, an absolute, sacred and unconditional 'will' calling for obedience literally at

any cost. Inseparable from this awareness of absolute demand is an awareness of ultimate succour. God is not simply the holy creator and sustainer of the moral universe, demanding our obedience, but he is also absolute love seeking our highest good, forgiving us and supporting us when we fail. His demands are the demands of love – holy love. Focusing on Christ's work on the cross, and drawing on such as Ritschl and *John McLeod Campbell (1800–72), Farmer's final book, *The Word of Reconciliation* (1966), carefully unpacks the implications of this thesis for a theology of the atonement.

Early in his theological career Farmer made it clear that one of his principal theological aims was to describe, critically interpret and defend the reasonableness of theistic belief. In opposition to the critiques of theism and the naturalistic interpretations of the world popular at the time, in *Towards Belief in God* he examines religious experience and argues that there are three elements in theistic conviction: (1) the coercive; (2) the pragmatic; and (3) the reflective. As with any belief, if it:

> (1) shines in its own light with a certain inherent compellingness, (2) "works" in the sense both of satisfying our nature and of helping in the practical task of managing our world, (3) reveals on examination both internal consistencies and external harmony with other experience and knowledge, then we have in regard to it as full an assurance of truth as it is possible for a human mind to have and as it ought ever to ask.

With different questions in mind, a similar apologetic task is carried out in Farmer's first series of 1950–51 Gifford Lectures, *Revelation and Religion*, in which he turns to Christianity's relation to other faiths. While this interest is apparent in his early works, it was increased by Oman's *The Natural and the Supernatural* (Cambridge, 1931) and particularly by his attendance at the International Missionary Council Meeting at Tambaram, Madras in 1938. Although disagreeing with the Barthian approach of Hendrik Kraemer (1888–1966) which dominated the meeting, the impact of Tambaram on his thought is evident in a sermon delivered to the Baptist Missionary Society shortly after his return from India. In this sermon Farmer forcefully declared Christianity's discontinuity with other faiths. Twelve years later in his Gifford Lectures, combining this insistence on

Christianity's uniqueness and finality with a 'personalist' understanding of an essence of religion underlying the historical religions, he argues that Christianity is a religion along with other religions and yet distinct from them in that, by virtue of God's revelation in Christ, it is the *normative* form of religion. Hence, working from the perspective of normative religion, his Gifford Lectures survey the religions of the world, discern where and to what degree the essence of religion is present in them, and construct a scale of religious types. *Reconciliation and Religion*, his creative and persuasive second series of lectures (which were never completed for publication), seeks to further establish the distinctiveness and unique adequacy of Christianity as a reconciling faith.

One of the best known and respected preachers of his generation, Farmer published two volumes of well-received sermons, *Things Not Seen* (London, 1927) and *The Healing Cross* (London, 1938), as well as a widely-read classic on the preacher's task, *The Servant of the Word* (1941). Indeed, to some extent, all Farmer's works betray the fact that first and foremost he was a preacher with the needs of ordinary Christians in mind. Convinced of its truth and importance, he laboured to cogently defend and clearly present the Christian faith to a questioning generation.

Although departing from Farmer's thought to varying degrees, among those who studied under him and show his influence at certain points in their development are *J.A.T. Robinson (1919–83), I.T. Ramsey (1915–72), *John Hick (b. 1922), *Lesslie Newbigin (1909–98), and H. Richard Niebuhr (1894–1962).

CHRISTOPHER PARTRIDGE

FURTHER READING: *Texts: The World and God* (London, 1935); *The Servant of the Word* (London, 1941); *Towards Belief in God* (London, 1943); *Revelation and Religion* (London, 1954); 'The Bible: Its Significance and Authority', in G.A. Buttrick, et al. (eds.), *The Interpreter's Bible*, I (New York, 1952), pp. 3–31; *Reconciliation and Religion: Some Aspects of the Uniqueness of Christianity as a Reconciling Faith* (Lampeter, 1998). *Studies:* P. Donovan, 'Phenomenology as Apologetics', *Scot J Th* 27 (1974), pp. 402–7; B. Haymes, 'The Supernatural is Personal', *Bapt Q* 26 (1979), pp. 2–13; F.G. Healey, 'Introduction', in Healey (ed.), *Prospect for Theology: Essays in Honour of H.H. Farmer* (Welwyn, 1966), pp. 7–33; T.A. Langford, 'The Theological Methodology of John Oman and H.H. Farmer', *Rel St* 1 (1966), pp. 229–40; C.H. Partridge, *H.H. Farmer's Theological Interpretation of Religions* (Lampeter, 1998).

Farrer, Austin Marsden (1904–68)

Austin Farrer, son of a Baptist minister, converted to the Church of England while studying in Oxford (Balliol College, 1923–28). Later on, he continued his studies in Bonn (1931, with *Karl Barth) and Zurich (1932, with *Emil Brunner), and in 1945 he took the degree of Doctor of Divinity. In Oxford he worked as chaplain (St Edmund Hall, 1931–35; Trinity College, 1935–60) and as warden of Keble College (1960–68). In 1937 he was married to Katharine Newton. They were contemporaries and close friends of C.S. Lewis and his wife Joy. Farrer published mature works on New Testament exegesis and analytical philosophy and some highly acclaimed collections of sermons, but he is primarily remembered as one of the most brilliant Anglican philosophical theologians of the twentieth century. Apart from numerous articles, Farrer's *oeuvre* comprises approximately twenty books.

As a New Testament scholar, Farrer was considered to be idiosyncratic; his 'wild expositions of Scripture' are one of the reasons why he was never elected to a professorship. His impact on New Testament scholarship was limited, but not negligible; his arguments against Q in his 1955 essay 'On Dispensing with Q' (in D.E. Nineham [ed.], *Studies in the Gospels* [Oxford, 1957], pp. 55–88) generated a lively debate. According to Farrer, Luke used Matthew as well as Mark, and there is no need to postulate a now-lost source for Matthew and Luke besides Mark. Farrer's monographs on the New Testament include works on the Gospels of Matthew and Mark and the book of Revelation.

The Freedom of the Will (the Gifford Lectures for 1957, published in 1958) is Farrer's main work in general philosophy; even here, his motivation to write the book was theological (pp. 1–2, 309–15). He aims at 'completeness and at a synthesis of topics' (p. vii), rather than at making an original contribution to the contemporary debate. Nevertheless, he does defend a position of his own, arguing for an incompatibilist and antideterminist account of human freedom. Theologically, he argues that it is through our free will that we know the divine will (p. 315). The second edition (1963) contains a useful 'Summary of the Argument'.

Farrer's work in philosophical theology is erudite and creative, but it is often difficult to read. Characteristic of his approach is an acute awareness of the role of metaphors and images in religious language and thought. His first mono-graph was *Finite and Infinite* (1943), in which he presented a metaphysics inspired mainly by *Aquinas. In 1948 Farrer gave the Bampton Lectures on revelation, published as *The Glass of Vision*. In these lectures he argued that inspired 'images are the stuff of revelation' (p. 51) and that they must be interpreted according to their own principles. In spelling out these principles, Farrer presented a theological hermeneutics; for him, this was an essential part of philosophical theology. In *Love Almighty and Ills Unlimited: An Essay on Providence and Evil* (1961), Farrer emphasizes that God limits himself by choosing to create finite agents; he commits himself to respect the natural order. However, though God's hand is hidden, the natural world is open to his influence, and he brings good out of evil. Thus, Farrer combines a free will defence with an emphasis on divine agency and providence. In *Faith and Speculation: An Essay in Philosophical Theology* (1967), Farrer starts from the principle 'we can think about no reality, about which we can do nothing but think'. He then characterizes our relationship with God as 'one of mutually engaged activities', and at length discusses divine activity (or agency). He proposes a double agency view of divine agency according to which God acts through the operations of creatures. Here, he also engages in a thoroughgoing criticism of Hartshornian process theology (arguing against divine embodiment and against the idea that God has a need of his creatures). While Farrer's brilliance was widely recognized, his position was so far removed from the main currents of both the philosophy and the theology of his day that his philosophical work remained somewhat neglected. Only toward the end of his life did he meet with enthusiastic recognition in the USA, where (as in the UK) there have been conferences on both his theological and philosophical work.

MARCEL SAROT

FURTHER READING: V. Brümmer, 'Farrer, Wiles and the Causal Joint', *Mod Th* 8 (1992), pp. 1–14; Charles Conti, *Metaphysical Personalism: An Analysis of Austin Farrer's Metaphysics of Theism* (Oxford, 1995), contains a bibliography of Farrer's published writings, 1933–93, and several previously unpublished letters by Farrer – Conti overemphasizes the influence of process metaphysics on Farrer's thought; P. Curtis, *A Hawk among Sparrows: A Biography of Austin Farrer* (London, 1985); J.C. Eaton, *The Logic of Theism: An Analysis of the Thought of*

Austin Farrer (Lanham, MD, 1980); J.C. Eaton and Ann Loades (eds.), *For God and Clarity: New Essays in Honor of Austin Farrer* (Allison Park, PA, 1983), contains a bibliography of works by and about Farrer; B. Hebblethwaite and E. Henderson (eds.), *Divine Action: Studies Inspired by the Philosophical Theology of Austin Farrer* (Edinburgh, 1990), contains indexes to Farrer's main works; A. Loades and Michael McLain (eds.), *Hermeneutics, the Bible and Literary Criticism* (London, 1992), pt. 2; Kenneth Surin (ed.), 'The Interpretation of Scripture with Particular Reference to the Work of Austin Farrer', *Mod Th* 1.3 (April 1985), special issue on Austin Farrer.

Feminist Theology

Women have been contributing to theological thinking and writing throughout Christian history, but feminist theology as a distinct movement may be said to have begun in the nineteenth century as women began to struggle: for access to education, and then to theological education; for voting rights; for the abolition of slavery; against the double standard of sexual morality for women and men; and for economic justice. An American Presbyterian woman, Elizabeth Cady Stanton, in her eighties drew together a team of collaborators to write a commentary on the parts of the Bible which refer to women. The results were published as the best-selling *The Woman's Bible* in 1895 and 1898, and it is still in print. From her famous speech at the meeting of women at Seneca Falls on 19 July 1848, and the Declaration of Principles adopted at that meeting, there is a direct line of descent through to the achievements of twentieth-century biblical criticism – represented in the work of Elisabeth Schüssler Fiorenza and Phyllis Trible, and by the range of perspectives in the recent one-volume *The Women's Bible Commentary* (London, 1992), edited by Carol A. Newsom and Sharon H. Ringe, whose very title recalls Stanton's initiative. Feminist biblical theology remains preoccupied with the limitations and resources of canonical texts. Both intrinsically and in their use, biblical texts may inculcate in women a conviction of their subordination and inferiority to men, conveyed to them not least by their alleged incapacity to 'image' God or Christ, insofar as any human person may. Canonical texts are at least in part implicated in androcentrism, but feminist theologians look also to those texts for resources to transform the present in hope for the future. The second phase of feminist theology resulted from response to the work of *Vatican II, but before turning to feminist theology in this latter part of the twentieth century some further preliminary remarks about feminist theology as a movement may be helpful.

Since there is no one thing meant by 'feminism', any more that there is by 'Christian' or 'theology', so feminist theology, whether biblically based or not, is inevitably diverse. A feminist need not be female by sex, but merely someone who seeks change for the better in terms of justice for women. Above all this requires attention to women's perspectives, dislodging assumptions which suppose males and their experience to represent the normal, even neutral and 'objective' perspective on things, with females and their experience as a variation on or from that norm. Feminist theology is also particularly sensitive to differences of perspective which result from complexities of race, class and colonial expropriation. This sensitivity is reflected in different forms of what for convenience may still be referred to as 'feminist theology' overall, such as African-American 'womanist' theology and *mujerista* theology, to mention only two possibilities. Many of the women who work in feminist theology are inevitably 'lay people', simply by virtue of their sexual difference from men, and this affects how their voices may be heard in their ecclesiastical communities, and the weight which may be given to what they say. It is both recent and still comparatively rare for women to be permitted to teach theology, let alone preach (see 1 Tim. 2:12), given the depths of suspicion of what women might say if allowed to open their mouths.

Reaction to the work of the Second Vatican Council was inevitable, coincidental with campaigns for 'equal rights' by those devalued on account of their sex or race, and, most recently, their sexual orientation. The council documents give little explicit attention to women, despite the formidable presence of some members of women's religious orders, excluded from the council's formal deliberations but not from the ferment of discussion associated with the preparation and drafting of its documents. One of the closing messages of the council is addressed 'To Women' and repays attention as a succinct model of gender relationships as seen by the 'Fathers' of the council. (Such relations arise from biological, social, economic and cultural conditions which vary over time, with issues of power between persons embodied in the practices of their societies.) In response to the council, Mary Daly published *The Church and the Second Sex* (New York, 1968), an apologia for her church in the face of such criticisms of the Christian tradition as may be discerned in Simone de Beauvoir's *La Deuxième Sexe* (1949). Mary Daly was to part company with Christianity as she wrote *Beyond God the Father* (London, 1973). These works helped to focus attention on the key theological issues: the interaction of gender with how human beings relate and are related to God.

Certainly essential has been work which examines authorities such as *Augustine and *Aquinas on the topic of the nature and role of women. It is arguable that they stand in the tradition of those whose ideals of reason have incorporated an exclusion of the female/ feminine, and that femininity in turn has been partly constituted through such processes of exclusion. So in both of these aforementioned theologians, affirmation of the spiritual equality of women with men was associated with their natural subordination to men (see K.-E. Børresen, *Subordination and Equivalence: The Nature and Role of Women in Augustine and Thomas Aquinas* [Washington, DC, 1981]). Inevitably then, theology (from *theos*, 'god-male') would seem to be a male-defined project, and a feminist theology a contradiction in terms, since God could not be associated with the female/feminine.

Competent theologians, however, know that God transcends both sex and gender, and they may well retain the convention of writing 'He' and 'Him' for God precisely as a reminder that God is not anthropomorphically masculine, just as 'She' and 'Her' would or could make the point that God could not be anthropomorphically feminine either. In any case, grammatical gender tells us little about some subjects of our attention – 'majesty', for instance, is 'feminine' in French. We might also argue that the mystery of God positively requires a variety of names, each of which acts as a corrective against the tendency of any particular one to become reified and literal. The fundamental principle which feminist theologians are advancing is that the female/feminine can of and by itself image God in as full and in as limited a way as

God is imaged by the male/masculine, and this is because God is *given* to us in gender-fluid ways (see E.A. Johnson, *She Who Is: The Mystery of God in Feminist Theological Discourse* [New York, 1993]). Recovering the richness of the tradition and becoming creatively responsible for it and the reintegration of liturgy, pastoral practice, ethics and spirituality with theology, too frequently narrowly construed as 'doctrine', may well be one of the gifts feminist theology may bring to the Christian tradition.

Some of the resources are already identified. Phyllis Trible's *God and the Rhetoric of Sexuality* (Philadelphia, 1978) not only relates Genesis 2 – 3 to the Song of Songs, but it also traces the journey of a single metaphor (womb/compassion) in relation to the God in whose image male and female are made. Of great importance is her attention to the text of Isaiah (see 'Women and Isaiah', in J.F.A. Sawyer, *The Fifth Gospel: Isaiah in the History of Christianity* [Cambridge, 1996]), with divine 'womb love' going beyond that of a human mother whose love may fail. The reality-depicting metaphor of God as mother can be direct and explicit as in Isaiah 42:14. Elisabeth Schüssler Fiorenza's *In Memory of Her: A Feminist Theological Reconstruction of Christian Origins* (London, 1983) is a major landmark in feminist interpretation. It is clearly her hope that by paying attention to the movement initiated by Jesus of Nazareth and the women and men associated with him, we can find resources for change to mutual acknowledgement of the full dignity and worth of all human persons. A very important section of *In Memory of Her* is headed 'The Sophia-God of Jesus and the discipleship of women', expressing the gracious goodness of the divine by selective use of 'wisdom' theology, which arguably uses elements of 'goddess' language to speak of God, and made possible Jesus' invitation to women to become his disciples. It must be acknowledged, however, that other interpreters are less confident about the value of this biblical material. Both Judith E. McKinlay in her *Gendering the Host* (Sheffield, 1996) and Celia M. Deutsch in *Lady Wisdom, Jesus and the Sages* (Valley Forge, PA, 1996) see in the texts the final stage of a long process of the masculinization of wisdom. Be that as it may, in *Miriam's Child, Sophia's Prophet* (London, 1994) Elisabeth Schüssler Fiorenza's attention turns to theology and the cross, and to the part played by women in actively shaping early Christian giving of meaning to Jesus' execution, and to

the importance of the future-orientation empty-tomb proclamation of Jesus as the vindicated resurrected one, 'ahead of us'. Feminist theologians position themselves, as it were, within such 'open space' and on such an open 'road to Galilee' as to experience and proclaim divine and life-enhancing power. The task ahead is one of struggle for a world free of injustice.

Although Elisabeth Schüssler Fiorenza has the visible and vocally authoritative presence of women in the church firmly in focus, Rosemary Radford Ruether has been particularly associated with the 'Women-Church' movement, which claims the church for women, and which has fostered feminist attention to liturgy and spirituality, as in her *Women-church: Theology and Praxis of Feminist Liturgical Communities* (San Francisco, 1998). She has also turned her attention to the interrelationship of doctrines of creation, redemption and sacramentality, as in *Gaia and God: An Ecofeminist Theology of Earth Healing* (London, 1992), concerns which she shares to some extent with Sallie McFague in the latter's *The Body of God: An Ecological Theology* (Minneapolis, 1993). Quite apart from other valuable essays (such as one on 'Sin'), there is a valuable discussion of such feminist eschatology by Peter Phan entitled 'Woman and the Last Things' in a collection of essays edited by Ann O'Hara Graff, *In the Embrace of God: Feminist Approaches to Theological Anthropology* (Maryknoll, NY, 1995). Theological anthropology seeks understanding of ourselves 'in the context of our inevitable and primal relationship to God' and learns from the new discipline of feminist psychology as well as from the Christian tradition as hitherto conceived. The scope of feminist theology as it is likely to develop into the areas of theology known as ecclesiology, sacramental and moral theology is indicated by the collection edited by Catherine Mowry LaCugna, *Freeing Theology: The Essentials of Theology in Feminist Perspective* (San Francisco, 1993). Important single-authored volumes are those by Elaine Graham, *Making the Difference: Gender, Personhood and Theology* (London, 1995), together with *Transforming Practice: Pastoral Theology in an Age of Uncertainty* (London, 1996) and Susan F. Parsons, *Feminism and Christian Ethics* (Cambridge, 1996).

ANN LOADES

FURTHER READING: *Introductory:* Ann Loades (ed.), *Feminist Theology: A Reader* (London, 1990);

Letty M. Russell and J. Shannon Clarkson (eds.), *Dictionary of Feminist Theologies* (London, 1996); Lisa Isherwood and Dorothea McEwan (eds.), *An A to Z of Feminist Theology* (Sheffield, 1996). *For further study:* Elisabeth Schüssler Fiorenza (ed.), *Searching the Scriptures*, I: *A Feminist Introduction*; II: *A Feminist Commentary* (London, 1994, 1995); Athalya Brenner and Carole Fontaine (eds.), *A Feminist Companion to Reading the Bible: Approaches, Methods and Strategies* (Sheffield, 1997), see also the Sheffield series *Feminist Companion to the Bible*, published since 1993; Mary Grey, *Feminism, Redemption and Christian Tradition* (London, 1989); Beverly Wildung Harrison, *Making the Connections: Essays in Feminist Social Ethics* (Boston, 1985); Ursula King (ed.), *Feminist Theology from a Third World Perspective: A Reader* (London, 1994); Marjorie Proctor-Smith, *In her Own Rite: Constructing Feminist Liturgical Tradition* (Nashville, TN, 1990); Janet Martin Soskice, *After Eve: Women, Theology and the Christian Tradition* (London, 1990).

Feuerbach, Ludwig (1804–72)

The word that best characterizes the role of Ludwig Feuerbach in the history of theology is 'antitheologian'. For a thinker who despised theology and rejected all religious belief, he has exercised a surprisingly great influence on modern religious thought – one that has earned him a place in both religious studies and the history of Christian thought.

Feuerbach began his career in 1823 as a student of theology in Heidelberg, where Karl Daub introduced him to the philosophy of *Hegel. He transferred to Berlin the following year in order to study with the master himself. Under the influence of Hegel's thought, Feuerbach decided to abandon theology and henceforth considered himself a philosopher and the enemy of faith in all its guises. In 1828 he became a philosophy instructor at the University of Erlangen, but his academic career collapsed almost as soon as it began as a result of the controversy ensuing from the publication of his *Thoughts on Death and Immortality*. He spent the rest of his career as a private scholar, writing books and extending his influence through public lecturing. Feuerbach is often acknowledged primarily for his influence on Karl Marx, but he is an important figure – especially for religious thought – quite apart from his role in the origins of *Marxism.

Despite his original enthusiasm for Hegel's philosophy, Feuerbach began quite early to move away from Hegel, becoming in the end one of his severest critics. Feuerbach's quarrel with Hegel has to do fundamentally with the relationship between thought and nature. Whereas Hegel begins with pure thought and then unfolds it dialectically into a systematic idealism, Feuerbach wants to begin with nature and derive all 'spiritual' attributes from an originally material basis. Like Marx after him, Feuerbach learns to think dialectically from Hegel but then inverts his priorities so as to turn the system against him. Feuerbach's passionate zeal to restore 'spiritual' man to his proper place in nature is epitomized in his best known (and frequently misunderstood) aphorism, 'Man is what he eats' – a pun in the original German: '*Der Mensch ist was er isst*'. This watchword is not the expression of a crude materialism as so often thought (much less a principle of good nutrition!), but rather a way of insisting – against Hegelians, theologians, and other spiritualizers – on the dignity of man's natural existence, not only of the head but also the stomach.

By far the best known of Feuerbach's works is *The Essence of Christianity*, first published in 1841. It contains one of the most powerful critiques ever devised, not only of Christianity but also of all religion. Like his critique of Hegel, Feuerbach's theory of religion is founded on a reversal: in this case of the subject and predicates of religious utterances. Feuerbach is convinced that religious man unwittingly alienates himself from his own most valued human qualities ('predicates') by attributing them to an illusory divine subject. For example, a religious sentiment such as 'God is love' takes the attribute 'love' to be a predicate of the subject 'God'. What is really happening here, however, according to Feuerbach, is that the real human quality is being treated as something alien, the predicate of an illusory divine subject, over against whom religious man makes himself into a passive object. The familiar term for this transaction, 'projection', was actually the contribution of the book's translator, the English novelist George Eliot, who rendered Feuerbach's technical philosophical term *Vergegenständlichung* (literally, 'objectification') with 'projection'. The full critical force of this term would later be felt when Sigmund Freud, consciously borrowing from Feuerbach, employed it in his own psychoanalytic reduction of religion. (Eliot is also the translator of another infamous work of religious critique, *David Friedrich Strauss's 1835 bombshell *The Life of*

Jesus Critically Examined.) Unlike Freud, however, Feuerbach insists that projection is a thoroughly communal affair: it is not the human individual but rather the religious community collectively that alienates its own essential qualities by attributing them to the gods. Feuerbach's zeal is consequently based on human solidarity, for his mission is to restore to human beings those real qualities that religion has taken from them.

If the critical force of Feuerbach's thought makes clear in what way he is an antitheologian, it is equally important to understand him as an antitheologian. He particularly likes to portray himself as the friend of the common religious believer, since he, unlike other philosophers, takes the sensuous and material substance of popular religion seriously rather than assuming that religion is 'really' about thoughts and ideas. In *The Essence of Christianity* he can even reject the label atheist, since he affirms the predicates of religion (e.g., love, wisdom, justice) by treating them as realities. He claims that the theologians are the true atheists, since it is they who demean the predicates by exalting their illusory heavenly subject. But Feuerbach is theological in a more significant way. Unlike the classic atheist (e.g., *Hume or the *philosophes* of the French Enlightenment), Feuerbach affirms the (indirect) truth of religious utterances.

The believer is not wrong in affirming that, for example, God is love, but rather is unaware of the real meaning of that affirmation. Religion is therefore not falsehood but illusion – a most significant difference. It was this 'theological' side of Feuerbach that attracted the admiration of so unlikely an ally as *Karl Barth, who saw him as the one who correctly drew the consequences of the theological liberalism of *Schleiermacher and his heirs. Despite the ultimate triviality of Feuerbach's critique of faith, Barth believes, he was more insightful than the theologians of his day, and he was also right in his affirmation of sensuous human reality. He simply listened to what the theologians were saying and extrapolated their method more consistently than they themselves did. In this way Feuerbach represents the bad conscience of modern theology.

Van Harvey has recently reminded us that Feuerbach did not stop with *The Essence of Christianity* but went on to develop a later, and different, theory of religion, presented most fully in the *Lectures on the Essence of Religion* (1851).

Whereas the theory of religion in the early Feuerbach was a dialectical inversion of Hegel's idealism, the later Feuerbach took religion to be based on erroneous interpretations of the forces of nature. Harvey is convinced that the later theory is superior, but it is more plausible to see it as a reversion to the cruder anti-religious thought of the *philosophes* and other detractors of faith.

What is especially noteworthy in Feuerbach, both early and late, is his insistence that imagination is the engine of religion. As a child of his times, he also made the assumption that religion was therefore false. In this way he shows himself to be the true father of the hermeneutics of suspicion, whose masters (according to *Paul Ricoeur) were Marx, *Nietzsche and Freud – all of whom learned from Ludwig Feuerbach to mistrust the religious imagination. Theologians and scholars of religion in the twenty-first century can be grateful to Feuerbach for his insights into the importance of religious imagination while questioning his automatic assumption that truth can never be mediated by means of the imagination.

GARRETT GREEN

FURTHER READING: *Texts: Gesammelte Werke* (19 vols.; Berlin, 1981–93); *The Essence of Christianity* (1841, ET New York, 1957), Karl Barth's 'Introductory Essay' in the ET is especially noteworthy; *The Essence of Faith According to Luther* (1844, ET New York, 1967); *The Essence of Religion* (1845, ET New York, 1873); *Lectures on the Essence of Religion* (1851, ET New York, 1967); *Thoughts on Death and Immortality* (1830, ET Berkeley, 1980). *Studies:* Hans W. Frei, 'Feuerbach and Theology', *J A A R* 35 (1967), pp. 250–56; John Glasse, 'Barth on Feuerbach', *Harv Th R* 57 (1964), pp. 69–96; Garrett Green, *Theology, Hermeneutics, and Imagination: The Crisis of Interpretation at the End of Modernity* (Cambridge, 2000), ch. 4 is on Feuerbach; Van A. Harvey, *Feuerbach and the Interpretation of Religion* (Cambridge / New York, 1995); Eugene Kamenka, *The Philosophy of Ludwig Feuerbach* (London, 1970); James C. Livingston, *Modern Christian Thought: The Enlightenment and the Nineteenth Century* (Upper Saddle River, NJ, 2nd edn, 1997), Feuerbach is discussed on pp. 221–29.

Filioque Controversy

The name commonly given to the theological controversy over the so-called double procession of the Holy Spirit. The word is taken from the Latin version of the *Nicene Creed, into which it was inserted in the course of the sixth century, probably in Spain. The Greek version of the Creed, as approved at Chalcedon in 451, said that the Holy Spirit proceeds from the Father, an assertion based on John 15:26. But Spanish theologians were confronted with a challenge from their *Arian counterparts, who were claiming that if the Spirit proceeds from the Father (from whom he derives his divinity) but not from the Son, then not only is the Father greater than the Son, but the Son cannot be truly or fully God. To counteract this, the word *filioque* ('and from the Son') was added to the Latin version of the Creed, so that it would read: 'who proceeds from the Father and the Son'. It was this version of the Creed which was proclaimed at the Third Council of Toledo in 589, when the Visigothic king of Spain finally abjured Arianism.

Theologically speaking, the Spaniards believed that they were on firm ground. The doctrine of the double procession had already been clearly taught by *Augustine (354–430), and they had no reason to suppose that it was not universally accepted by all orthodox Christians. Augustine expounded his belief that the Holy Spirit proceeded from the Son as well as from the Father on the basis of such biblical passages as Galatians 4:6. In his Trinity of love, it was essential that the love of the Father for the Son be reciprocated by the Son's love for the Father. In Augustine's scheme of things, this binding love inside the Trinity is the Holy Spirit.

The first person to notice any difficulty with the *filioque* was *Maximus the Confessor (580–662), a Greek theologian who learned of it during his exile in Rome. Maximus did not make too much of it; as far as he was concerned, it was the poverty of the Latin language and its relative inability to express subtle theological concepts which had led the Western church to the *filioque* doctrine. Somewhat later, *John of Damascus (675– c. 749) mentioned in passing that the church did not confess the double procession of the Holy Spirit on the ground that the Father was the unique source of the Godhead, but it is clear from the context that he had no idea that this statement would cause any controversy.

At the Synod of Aachen in 809, Charlemagne's bishops adopted the Spanish version of the Nicene Creed and tried to get the pope to follow suit. The bishops were so ignorant of history that some of them could claim that the Greek church had dropped the *filioque* from the original version of the Creed, and had thus become heretical! Rome refused to add the clause, however, and the pope even went so far as to erect two tablets in St Peter's on which the Creed was inscribed in both Greek and Latin – without the *filioque*. Meanwhile, trouble had erupted in Jerusalem, where some Greek monks had noticed that their Frankish brethren were saying the Creed with this addition. The Greeks resented the recent arrival of the Franks in the holy city, and they were looking for any excuse for a fight. Rioting broke out between the rival groups of monks, but the quarrel was soon pacified and no more was heard of the issue.

The *filioque* surfaced again later in the ninth century, when *Patriarch Photius (c. 810 – c. 893) found it expedient to accuse the Western church of heresy. Most scholars agree that he was politically motivated, but he did develop a clear and consistent theology which excluded the double procession of the Holy Spirit, largely on the same grounds as those already mentioned by John of Damascus. In particular, Photius believed that the Nicene Creed had deliberately not included the *filioque*; what the Fathers of the church had wanted to say was that the Holy Spirit proceeds from the Father *alone*. The Eastern churches could not add this clarification to the Creed itself, of course, but they have believed this ever since Photius's time.

Photius managed to convince the Eastern churches, including the non-Chalcedonian ones, of the rightness of his position on this issue, but he made little headway in the West. The political circumstances which had precipitated his original accusations were soon overcome, and the Western and Eastern churches remained formally united. In the centuries that followed, the *filioque* clause spread throughout the Latin West, and about 1014 it was finally added to the Creed in the Roman liturgy. Still the churches remained united, and even when the pope and the Patriarch of Constantinople excommunicated each other in 1054, the *filioque* played only a minor role in the conflict. But as the crusades brought West and East into contact again, the theological difference represented by the *filioque* was bound to come into prominence once more.

It was during his stay at Bari (then a largely Greek-speaking city) in 1098 that *Anselm of Canterbury felt moved to develop a detailed Western argument for the double procession, based on a thorough analysis of Scripture.

Anselm accepted that John 15:26 made no mention of the Son, but he insisted that this verse must be read in its context, and that, taken as a whole, John 13 – 17 made it quite clear that the Holy Spirit proceeded from the Son as much as he did from the Father. Anselm's treatise was clearly polemical in intent, but its tone is moderate and lacks the bitterness of later times.

Sometime about 1135 another Anselm (of Havelberg) visited Constantinople and engaged in debate with a certain bishop Nicetas. We do not really know what transpired because only Anselm's account has survived, and this naturally attributes theological victory to him. Nevertheless, it is clear that by this time a real controversy over the *filioque* was brewing and that growing contact between the Eastern and Western churches would only encourage it even further. That the two churches were no longer united became painfully clear after 1204, when the crusaders sacked Constantinople and established a Latin empire in the city. The empire was overthrown in 1261, but the issue of church union could no longer be dodged. At the Second Council of Lyons (1274), the Byzantine Emperor Michael VIII (1259–82) signed an agreement for the reunion of the churches in which he accepted the *filioque* as a legitimate part of the Nicene Creed.

The result of this agreement was a deep split in the Byzantine church between the 'Latinizers' and the traditionally Orthodox. The Latinizers were a small group of Greek intellectuals who were familiar with the renaissance of learning in the West, and who began to translate Latin theology, including Augustine and *Thomas Aquinas, into Greek. The Latinizers remained a small, elite minority in the Byzantine world, and as the Turks encroached on Constantinople many of them fled to the West, where they were influential in reviving Greek learning.

Opposition to the Latinizers was not slow to develop. Aware that the main weakness of the Greek position was that it did not clarify the relationship of the Son to the Holy Spirit, Gregory of Cyprus, patriarch of Constantinople from 1283 to 1289, asserted that the Holy Spirit proceeds from the Father and rests on the Son. He likened this idea to the descent of the dove at Jesus' baptism. According to him, the Holy Spirit is the illumination of the Son, the radiance which the disciples perceived on the Mount of Transfiguration. This notion was subsequently incorporated into the spiritual technique known as hesychasm, which under the influence of *Gregory Palamas (1296–1359) became the dominant form of Greek Orthodox spirituality.

Once this idea of the Holy Spirit as illumination was elaborated, the Eastern churches had both a doctrine and a spirituality which could be set against those of the Latin West. At the same time, many Greeks began to regard the *filioque* as the root cause of the growth of the papal monarchy in the Western church, to which they were naturally opposed. The logic behind this association was that if the pope was the vicar of Christ and the church was the kingdom of the Spirit, the pope would have the right to rule the church if the Spirit proceeded from the Son and was logically dependent on him. This line of argument was rejected by the West of course, but it can still be heard from time to time among Orthodox theologians.

In 1439 there was another attempt to reunite the churches at the Council of Florence, where it was agreed that the *filioque* clause could be interpreted to mean that the Holy Spirit proceeds from the Father through the Son by a single act, or spiration as it was called. This was intended to be a compromise formula which would safeguard the presence of the *filioque* clause in the Latin version of the Creed without denying the validity of the Greek position. The Greek delegates signed the agreement on the understanding that they would not have to introduce the *filioque* into their version of the Creed. The Union of Florence, as it is called, became and has remained the basis for the union of the Eastern churches with Rome. It had little effect at the time, but in later centuries there appeared a number of so-called 'Uniate' churches (Catholic churches using the Greek or another Oriental rite), which have adopted this formula as their own.

At the time, the Florentine decision had the predictable effect of splitting the Greek church once again, and after Constantinople fell to the Turks in 1453, the decision was officially repudiated there. The controversy has endured to modern times, when it has figured quite prominently in ecumenical discussions. Many Western churches have been prepared to drop the *filioque* from the Nicene Creed on the ground that it did not belong to the original text, but they have been less clear about the theological issues involved.

There is a great fear among some that if it is

allowed that the Spirit proceeds from the Father but not from the Son, then it will be possible to gain access to the Father in the Spirit without going through the Son at all. This is not the Eastern Orthodox position of course, but the absence of any form of hesychasm in the West makes it difficult for Westerners to appreciate the Eastern point of view, and impossible for them to absorb it into their own spirituality. At the present time, it seems probable that the West will consent to dropping the *filioque* from the Creed for what are essentially diplomatic reasons, but that this will not really help to bring the two divergent traditions together again because the underlying theological context will not have been properly addressed.

GERALD BRAY

FURTHER READING: K. Barth, *Church Dogmatics*, I, 1, pp. 546–57; G.L. Bray, *Tyndale Bul* 34 (1983), pp. 91–144; R. Haugh, *Photius and the Carolingians* (Belmont, MA, 1975); G.S. Hendry, *The Holy Spirit in Christian Theology* (London, 1957); A. Heron, in *One God in Trinity* (ed. P. Toon; London, 1980), pp. 62–77; V. Lossky, *In the Image and Likeness of God* (London, 1975); J. Moltmann, *The Trinity and the Kingdom of God* (London, 1981); A. Papadakis, *Crisis in Byzantium* (New York, 1983); L. Vischer (ed.), *Spirit of God, Spirit of Christ* (Geneva, 1981); K. Ware and C. Davey (eds.), *Anglican-Orthodox Dialogue: The Moscow Agreed Statement* (London, 1977).

Forsyth, P.T. (1848–1921)

British theologian. Peter Taylor Forsyth was born and educated in Aberdeen, spent a semester in Göttingen under *Albrecht Ritschl, then returned to London to study theology and prepare for the Congregational ministry. Following twenty-five years of preaching and pastoral work in England, he taught systematic theology and preaching as principal of Hackney College in London. Thus, Forsyth's life divides neatly into thirds: student, pastor, teacher. There are, however, three more significant moments in his life. In the mid-1880s, Forsyth was converted from theological liberalism in the Ritschlian mould to classical Christianity; in his own words, 'from a lover of love to an object of grace'. In 1896, he confirmed his prominent place in Congregationalism with the preaching and publication of 'The Holy Father', a forceful assertion of God's holiness and a prophetic challenge to the view of God's Fatherhood that featured 'a love slack and over-sweet'. And in 1907 he received widespread recognition both for his Lyman Beecher lectures on preaching at Yale, published as *Positive Preaching and the Modern Mind*, as well as for his leadership in the very public conflict with *R.J. Campbell's so-called *New Theology.

Historian David Bebbington has called Forsyth evangelicalism's greatest modern theologian of the cross. Most notably in *The Work of Christ* (1910), Forsyth presents an atonement doctrine that encompasses such themes as victory, regeneration and reconciliation, while accenting the Old Testament-inspired ideas of sacrifice and satisfaction. The death of Christ was 'the offering of a holy self to a holy God from sin's side', involving 'the idea not only of substitution but of judgment'. The holiness of God is in the forefront of this soteriology. Specifically, there is a dynamic relationship between the Son's sinless obedience and the Father's holy satisfaction – holiness answering holiness. This sacrifice by one with whom the Father was always well pleased elicits the faith and ongoing obedience of believers and establishes a new moral order. God's grace in Christ's cross creates its own response, and in the same work confers a continuing righteousness. And at the same time as the cross justifies sinful humanity, it reveals and justifies God: 'God's account of Himself ... is in Christ and His Cross, or it is nowhere'.

Forsyth applies the theme of sacrifice, so central to atonement doctrine, to the incarnation as well. In *The Person and Place of Jesus Christ* (1909), he makes a provocative contribution to Christology. Faced with the theological polarity between an immutable God for whom incarnation is an uncomfortable innovation, and a changeable deity whose divine attributes are lost by being shrunk to human dimensions, Forsyth proposed a middle way, a nuanced kenotic Christology with at least three attractive aspects. First, he posited the psychological retraction of attributes nevertheless retained.

> We face in Christ a Godhead self-reduced but real, whose infinite power took effect in self-humiliation, whose strength was perfected in weakness, who consented not to know with an ignorance divinely wise, and who emptied himself in virtue of his divine fulness.

Secondly, Forsyth added a complementary *plerosis*, making dogmatic room for Christ's growth in grace, personality and achievement until he was filled with the fullness of God. Thirdly, he convincingly elaborated the vital connection of incarnation with atonement. *Hans Urs von Balthasar, in *Mysterium Paschale*, cites this 'outstanding Congregationalist theologian' as saying that:

> Christ's sacrifice began before he came into the world, and his Cross was that of a lamb slain before the world's foundation ... His obedience as man was but the detail of the supreme obedience which made him man.

The objectivity and priority of grace pervade Forsythian theology. When Forsyth looks at salvation from the perspective of the believer he puts a high value on evangelical experience, but he hedges it with an insistence that the claims of revelation must be met with a receptive rather than a creative attitude. Furthermore, 'We do not stand on the fact of our experience but on the fact *which* we experience.' In the area of spirituality, Eugene Peterson regards Forsyth as an 'utterly trustworthy and immensely energizing' theologian precisely because his theology of grace can turn us away from our pious self-centredness and 'can help us re-establish the primacy of God in our prayers'. Concerning nature and grace, Forsyth considers conscience as both an indwelling word of God and the locus of rebellion against God. Consequently, there is no natural way to know the saving God; a radical act of grace must bridge the divine-human chasm.

Further study on Forsyth will profit from a deeper understanding of his place on the theological spectrum. Who influenced his writing? Paul pre-eminently, but unfortunately not the Fathers; *Bernard of Clairvaux ('my favourite saint'); *Luther and especially, but not uncritically, *Calvin; Thomas Goodwin and *Richard Baxter; *Joseph Butler ('Morality is the nature of things'); *Kant and the neo-Kantians; *Hegel, interpreted by Biedermann and challenged by *Kierkegaard (in German translation – one-third of Forsyth's library was in German); Ritschl, moderated by Julius Kaftan, and replaced by *Martin Kähler; *F.D. Maurice and Baldwin Brown conquered by *R.W. Dale. While such connections illumine, however, they fall far short of explaining the distinctive contribution of a brilliant and original thinker who has attracted considerable attention and respect. Read by *Barth and commended by *Brunner, Forsyth's writings are a current resource for such

theologians as Donald Bloesch and Colin Gunton, among others. Forsyth's books continue to be reprinted, recommended and, more significantly, seriously critiqued, suggesting that his influence will continue for some time.

LESLIE MCCURDY

FURTHER READING: Trevor Hart (ed.), *Justice the True and Only Mercy: Essays on the Life and Theology of Peter Taylor Forsyth* (Edinburgh, 1995), which contains a full bibliography; A.M. Hunter, *P.T. Forsyth: Per Crucem ad Lucem* (London, 1974); William Bradley, *P.T. Forsyth: The Man and His Work* (London, 1952); J.K. Mozley, 'The Theology of Dr. Forsyth', *Expositor* (1923), pp. 81–98, 161–80 (reprinted in J.K. Mozley, *The Heart of the Gospel* [London, 1925], pp. 66–109).

Fox, Matthew (b. 1940)

Born Timothy Fox on 21 December 1940 in Wisconsin, USA, he became Matthew on joining the Dominicans. Ordained in 1967, he received a doctorate from the Institut Catholique de Paris in 1970.

Fox established the Institute in Creation Centered Spirituality (later called the Institute in Culture and Creation Spirituality, or ICCS), first at Mundelein College, Chicago in 1977, transferring to Holy Names College (Oakland, California) in 1983. The appointment of Starhawk (a witch) to his faculty attracted unfavourable publicity, and his orthodoxy was subsequently questioned. A 1984 investigation by the Dominican Order cleared him, but the Vatican became increasingly uneasy and he was first silenced for a year (1989), then expelled in 1993. In 1994 he became an Episcopalian priest, and in 1996 ICCS became the University of Creation Spirituality, still in Oakland but not at Holy Names College.

Fox is a prolific and popular writer. His key texts are *Original Blessing* (1983), *The Coming of the Cosmic Christ* (1989) and *Confessions* (1996), together with editions of some medieval mystics and articles in his own magazine, *Creation Spirituality*. Fox's concern is the need for new postmodern theological paradigms following the collapse of the *Enlightenment consensus. He draws heavily on his experience in Paris in the late 1960s and the insights of his mentor, Marie-Dominique Chenu. Fox also evokes his own personal suffering (he had polio when he was twelve and was later seriously injured in a car crash) as highlighting the need to celebrate and affirm human weakness rather than denying or correcting it.

Fox argues that western culture suffers from the triumph of the fall-redemption model of theology, epitomized by *Augustine, over against an original biblical creation-centred spirituality. Whereas the creation-centred model assumes the goodness of creation and of human nature, as rooted in God, fall-redemption regards people and Nature as alienated from God. Creation-centred spirituality promotes a holistic vision, in which Nature (human and cosmic) is a channel of salvation, but fall-redemption fosters an unhealthy dualism leading to alienation between humans and Nature, and between the physical and the spiritual/rational in people. Historically, the negative self-image this alienation inculcated was projected onto the world at large and became the root cause of today's ecological, social and personal dysfunction. Insofar as there is an 'original sin', it is dualism.

By contrast, creation-centred spirituality begins with 'original blessing'. Here nature is good, and wholeness derives from rediscovering the interconnectedness between all things, leading to an affirmation of diversity – in people and nature – which celebrates plurality, not destructive dualisms. Furthermore, Fox believes this is the authentic Christian position, taught by Jesus, and because the historic Jesus is also the cosmic Christ, this wisdom can be found everywhere.

This creation-centred tradition survived in attenuated form through medieval mystics, especially *Hildegard of Bingen, Mechthild of Magdeburg, Francis of Assisi, *Meister Eckhart and *Julian of Norwich. But since mysticism is the heart of all true religion, the same spirituality is to be found in other traditions, especially those which were victimized by the imperialistic dualism of fall-redemption thinking. Combining all these forces – together with the work of mystical scientists like Brian Swimme, Fritjof Capra, Rupert Sheldrake and Wendell Berry – into a 'deep ecumenism' will destroy dualism in all its forms (science/religion, women/men, east/west, spirituality/social justice, etc.). This will then create a new paradigm focused on panentheism ('everything is in God, and God is in everything') – theism being a product of fall-redemption dualism.

Fox has been subjected to searching criticisms, as follows:

(1) Fox rewrites history to suit himself and ignores inconvenient facts. Augustine was far more sophisticated than he allows, and *Aquinas (one of Fox's heroes) certainly espoused dualism. Fox's editions of medieval mystics are widely regarded as unreliable: he omits huge sections of Hildegard and mistranslates Eckhart. He does the same with Bible texts, imposing meanings on them with no supporting argumentation. Moreover, while the mystics certainly emphasized the creation-centred tradition, they all did so within a fall-redemption framework, which itself suggests the two paradigms are not necessarily mutually exclusive.

(2) Fox is naïve about sin, identifying it with patriarchy/dualism and thinking about it as a relatively recent phenomenon in cosmic history. He argues that 'being natural' through participation in traditions ostensibly untouched by dualism will automatically lead to perfection (hence his preference for rituals like shamanic drumming, sweat lodges, vision quests, etc.). But the historical reality is that in most societies where the 'natural' has prevailed over the rational, innocent victims suffered precisely the kinds of violation that Fox professes to hate. Fox's version of creation-centred spirituality has little to say to those who are marginalized, despite his attempt to claim liberation theology as part of the same movement. There is a contradiction here with his own stated intention to be a prophetic witness promoting social justice.

(3) Some see Fox as a *Gnostic, or a *New Ager. He certainly aims to create an eclectic spirituality drawn from different sources. He also speaks of people becoming divine as they discover their inner creativity, and he makes a distinction between the 'cosmic Christ' (a universal Christ-spirit found everywhere) and the 'historical Jesus' (concern for whom he identifies with the failed Enlightenment agenda, and who in any case was just one 'cosmic Christ' among many).

(4) Fox has no self-critical awareness. He complains that western Christianity is anthropocentric (as opposed to ecological or cosmological), but his own focus is almost entirely anthropocentric, concerned with personal fulfilment, happiness, ecstasy and the idea that people create their own experiences of the world. He hates dualism – yet in *Original Blessing* he provides his own dualistic analysis of the entire Christian tradition, according to the categories of creation-centred versus fall-redemption paradigms, even awarding star ratings to key figures depending on how they fare.

Fox's questions are better than his answers, but that should not divert attention away from the crucial importance of the issues he has raised, especially relating to the need to recover a biblical theology of blessing, mysticism, creativity and art, and the urgency of articulating a credible Christian environmental perspective.

JOHN W. DRANE

FURTHER READING: *Texts: Confessions* (San Francisco, 1996); *Original Blessing* (Santa Fe, NM, 1983); *The Coming of the Cosmic Christ* (San Francisco, 1988). *Studies:* Margaret Brearley, 'Matthew Fox: Creation Spirituality for the Aquarian Age', *CJR* 22 (1989), pp. 37–49; Richard J. Bauckham, 'The New Age Theology of Matthew Fox: A Christian Theological Response', *Anvil* 13.2 (1996), pp. 115–26; Barbara Newman, 'Romancing the Past: A Critical Look at Matthew Fox and the Medieval "Creation Mystics" ', *Touchstone* 5 (1992), pp. 5–10; Colin Noble, 'Matthew Fox's Cosmic Christ – A Critical Response', *Crux* 27.1 (1991), pp. 21–9; Lawrence Osborn, 'A Fox Hunter's Guide to Creation Spirituality', in *Different Gospels* (ed. Andrew Walker; London, 1993), pp. 155–72; Ted Peters, *The Cosmic Self* (San Francisco, 1991), pp. 120–31; Rosemary Radford Ruether, 'Matthew Fox and Creation Spirituality: Strengths and Weaknesses', *Catholic World* (Jul/Aug 1990), pp. 168–72.

Franciscans

Franciscan is the name given to those male and female religious Orders that trace their origins to St Francis of Assisi, born Giovanni Bernardone (1181/2–1226), and to St Clare (Clare of Assisi, 1194–1253). The Order today has male and female members throughout the world who are Roman Catholic and Protestant. Roman Catholic Franciscans see themselves as a large tree whose branches are made up of the Friars Minor (OFM), the Friars Minor Capuchin (OFM Cap), the Friars Minor Conventual (OFM Conv), the Poor Clares, and the Third Order. Anglican Franciscans have a Society of St Francis (SSF), which is divided into Brothers, Sisters of the Community of St Francis, Poor Clares, Third Order Brothers and Sisters, and Associates. The SSF was founded in 1937 in Dorset, England, by amalgamating the Brotherhood of Saint Francis of Assisi with the Brotherhood of the Love of Christ. In 1967 there was further unification with the Order of Saint Francis – a similar community in the Episcopal Church in the United States of America, which had been founded in 1919. Other denominations include the Order

of Ecumenical Franciscans and the Danish group Assisi-Kredsen. The Conventuals remain guardians of the tombs of Saints Francis and Antony of Padua today.

The Roman Catholic Franciscans are further divided into three Orders. The First Order is male and was founded c. 1209; in the early days the brethren were called friars minor or lesser brethren, and grey friars in Britain. Today, the First Order comprises the Friars Minor, the Capuchins and the Conventuals. The Second Order is female and known as either Poor Clares, after their foundress Clare of Assisi, or Poor Ladies of Assisi. The Third Order, originally known as Tertiaries or Order of Penance, is a secular branch made up of members both male and female, married and single. The Third Order is now made up of two sections: the Secular Franciscan Order and the Third Order Regular. These are further subdivided into numerous offshoots. Although the Tertiaries trace their origins back to Francis himself, the Order received its first official Rule from Pope Nicholas IV (1288–92) in 1289. Anglican Franciscans are also divided into three Orders (First, Second and Third): First Order Brothers and Sisters, Poor Clares and Third Order of the Society of St Francis (TSSF).

Origins of the Franciscan Order. Francis of Assisi was the son of a wealthy cloth merchant. He started life as a pleasure-seeking youth who ought to have followed his father's trade. After a brief spell as a prisoner when the town was in conflict with neighbouring Perugia, and then an illness, Francis began to experience 'visitations', and he turned to meditation and prayer. He showed a keen interest in the poor, which went beyond the common practise of alms giving, in that he associated himself with them. This led to symbolic acts such as selling bales of cloth from his father's shop to purchase building materials to repair crumbling churches (in response to a call he had heard from a speaking painted crucifix), and then the renunciation of his father's goods in 1206. By 1209 three other men had joined him, and Francis drew up a simple Rule, based on the Gospels, which focused on ideals of charity and renunciation of possessions. During the same year Pope Innocent III (1198–1215) gave verbal approval to Francis's new Order. The Order expanded rapidly, although members lived lives of deprivation and itinerant preaching modelled on the lives of Jesus Christ and the apostles. Francis and his followers were active first in Umbria and Tuscany, but their influence soon spread to much of western Christendom. Francis himself was a strong advocate of missions, and he set off to Syria in 1219 where he attempted to convert the Sultan of Egypt, al-Kamil. Upon his return, Francis renounced the leadership of his now large band and turned to contemplation. In 1224 he experienced a vision which left him with the imprint of the wounds of Christ (the stigmata) on his own body. This sign was not revealed until after his death on 3 October 1226, but it was hailed as the greatest miracle. Pope Gregory IX (1227–41) canonized Francis less than two years later, on 16 July 1228.

Even before his death, there had been conflict between those who wished to follow a strict adherence to the Rule and pursue an itinerant life of mendicancy (initially called Spirituals, later Observants), and the others who were willing to accept modifications, including life in convents (Conventuals). The thirteenth and fourteenth centuries saw an increase in tension that came in part to focus on the nature of Christ's poverty. After the burning of three friars in 1316, Pope John XXII (1316–34) declared in 1322 the belief in the absolute poverty of Christ to be heretical. The issue of property and poverty remained central to attempts at reform, which gained momentum during the fifteenth century. Amidst those reformers were the followers of Bernardino da Siena (d. 1444), the Poor Hermits of Angelo Clareno (d. 1337), the Amedeans (named after their Portuguese leader Amedeus of Sylva, d. 1482), the Collettines (who followed the reforms of Colette of Corbie, d. 1447) and the independent Discalced (shoeless) in Spain. With increasing tension between the two factions and unsuccessful attempts at reform, Pope Leo X (1513–21) united all the Observants in 1517 and separated them from the Conventuals, who nonetheless remained subject to them in that the election of their leader, the Master General, needed approval from the Minister General who had jurisdiction over the entire Order. Thus, this union was also a division. The two Orders evolved separately until 1897, but this did not put an end to conflict.

Observants. The desire for stricter observance within the Observants led to the creation of new communities, such as the Capuchins and Recollects, and the rivalry between nationalities exacerbated problems. The French Revolution decimated Observant convents in France. Various revivals of religious life were quashed by the Napoleonic suppression and the German *Kulturkampf* towards the end of the nineteenth century. Spain maintained its communities, but they were effectively separated from the rest of the Order. Projects of unification or total separation were put forward, but unification won in the end. On the feast of St Francis on 4 October 1897, Pope Leo XIII (1878–1903) suppressed all divisions within the Observants and combined the Observants, the Reformed, the Recollects and the Alcantarines (Spanish Discalced) to form one Order of Friars Minor. The Conventuals and the Capuchins retained their independence.

Conventuals. The Conventuals lost many of their convents to the Observants in the union of 1517, and Protestantism took its toll thereafter. The Council of Trent, however, settled the question of poverty for the Conventuals in 1563 by decreeing possession in common. Their position became consolidated in France when reformed houses became conventual, though this was short-lived. As it was for the Observants, the Revolution was fatal for the Conventuals – particularly as it stripped them of their property assets.

Clares. Francis received the young Clare in 1212, although she had already shown her independent will and compassion by caring for the poor and underprivileged in Assisi. Francis initially placed her in the protection of a Benedictine nunnery, but not long thereafter a community of women settled at San Damiano, led first by Clare and then by her sister Agnes (d. 1253). Even Ortolana, their mother, joined the community. The Second Order was initially under the care of the Friars Minor, at least in the spiritual sense, until 1263 when they were placed under a cardinal-protector. The biggest dilemma of Clare and her followers was their desire to live in total poverty with no possessions except their houses, as Francis had envisaged. But their cardinal-protector wanted properties to be accepted with ownership subject to the pope. Pope Urban IV (1261–64) approved a Rule in 1263 which favoured the second solution. However, Clare's own Rule, approved shortly before her death in 1253, was directed to the Sisters of San Damiano alone. It differed greatly in that the sisters were to possess no property, either as individuals or as a community. For nearly a century, few of the communities followed St Clare's Rule, preferring to accept property. But reforms occurred in the fifteenth century, particularly through the efforts of St Colette of Corbie. In 1517 the Clares returned to the Observants, who were made responsible for their spiritual direction. The seventeenth century was a period of significant expansion, during which communities followed the Urbanist rule. This was not to last, however, and the eighteenth century saw the Order decline and reach near extinction during the French Revolution and Napoleonic suppression. Communities fled and emigrated to places such as England and North America during this period. Today, although all Clares follow the same Rule and share the same basic Constitutions, each monastery is totally autonomous, led by its own abbess. Poverty, contemplation and claustration remain integral to their way of life.

The Third Order includes those who live together in convents and have professed vows (Third Order Regular), and those who live in the world (Secular Franciscan Order). Their work finds them active in the promotion of peace, justice and issues such as ecology.

Franciscan School. Although Francis of Assisi was ambivalent about education, preferring his brothers to be virtuous rather than learned, he respected theologians and wished to see them venerated. The Franciscan Order has produced a considerable number of scholastic, theological and mystical writers. During the Middle Ages some of their scholars, such as *Duns Scotus (d. 1308) and *William of Ockham (d. 1347 or 49), were *Aristotelian, and great efforts were made to undermine the theories of the Dominican *Thomas Aquinas. Indeed, Scotus became the favoured author of the Franciscan School. The *Augustinian tradition was also crucial, in particular the relationship between the soul and God. Franciscan writers such as *Bonaventura (d. 1274) believed that their founder's zeal to imitate Jesus in poverty and humility was rewarded with the stigmata. Thus, their piety is Christocentric – for them, Christ becomes both one of their brothers and an object of contemplation; his passion is particularly the focus of meditation. Other Franciscans were more scientific in their approach – for example, Roger

Bacon, who held that observations were central to the attainment of truth.

Preaching, conversion and mission were central activities, which found them combating heresy (Antony of Padua, d. 1231) and later Protestantism. Their missionary zeal took them to Africa, Russia, Scandinavia and China during the Middle Ages. The Order also accompanied the Portuguese and Spanish expeditions in the Americas and established communities there. To this day, they have remained committed to missions and have made a political contribution to *Liberation Theology with members such as Leonardo Boff (b. 1938). At the popular level, the Franciscans helped spread the devotion to the Christmas crib (prompted by Francis's own re-enactment of the nativity in the woods at Greccio in 1224), the holy name of Jesus (through Bernardino da Siena), the stations of the cross (through Leonard of Port-Maurice, d. 1751), the holy sacrament (by the Capuchins), the sacred heart and the holy blood. The Immaculate Conception was defended by the Order before it became doctrine and other Marian devotions were promoted.

LOUISE BOURDUA

FURTHER READING: L. Iriarte, *Storia del Francescanesimo* (Naples, 1982), with full bibliography; J.R.H. Moorman, *A History of the Franciscan Order from its Origins to the Year 1517* (Oxford, 1968); J. Schlageter, 'Franziskaner', *Th Real* 11 (1983), pp. 389–97; E. d'Alençon, 'Frères Mineurs', *DTC* 6 (Paris, 1947), col. 810–63; J. Eymard d'Angers, 'Frères Mineurs', *DTC, Tables Générales* (Paris, 1951), col. 1696–1736.

Franks, Robert Sleightholme (1872–1964)

Congregational theologian, son of the Revd W.J. Franks, was born at Redcar, graduated BA (London), read mathematics at Cambridge, theology at Oxford (D Litt), and was an Hon. LL D of Bristol. He was tutor at Mansfield College (1897–1900), minister at Prenton Road, Birkenhead (1900–04), and then lecturer at Woodbrook until 1910, when he began his distinguished career as principal of the Western College, Bristol, where he remained until retirement to Winscombe in 1939. Of a retiring and absent-minded disposition, Franks was greatly loved and trusted by his students and known to the wider theological public through his writings.

In the wake of *The New Testament Doctrine of Man, Sin, and Salvation* (1908), and of Bible notes on *The Life of Paul* (1909) and *The Writings of Paul* (1910), Franks published his major *History of the Doctrine of the Work of Christ* (1918). He here investigates Greek theology, *Medieval Scholasticism, Protestant orthodoxy and modern Protestant theology, with special reference to the most systematic writers who, in their very diversity, pose the crucial question of theological method.

In his Dale Lectures for 1933 on *The Atonement* (1934) Franks defends the *Abelardian theory and is so far in accord with *Hastings Rashdall (see *The Idea of the Atonement*, 1919). Unlike Rashdall, however, he cannot accept that God suffers. Again, where Hicks, in *The Fullness of Sacrifice*, invokes a Eucharistic interpretation of the offering up of Christ's life, Franks places in the centre the moral category of love rather than the biological category of life. Some critics found his position unduly subjectivist and held, against him, that if God is love it must be possible for him to suffer.

In *The Doctrine of the Trinity* (1953) Franks discusses the historical development of the doctrine from New Testament times to *Leonard Hodgson, concluding that 'the Christology of Schleiermacher must be combined with the Trinitarianism of Aquinas as reinterpreted by Barth'. Believing that Christology must be reconstructed through a firmly monotheist doctrine of the Trinity, and while maintaining the immanent distinction of the Persons, Franks set his face against the social analogy, which interprets the Godhead 'as though it were a company of human individuals'.

Throughout, Franks's starting-point is religious experience metaphysically justified – a conjunction which, though exemplified by his mentors *Alexander of Hales, *Schleiermacher and C.H. Weisse – he knew to be currently unfashionable. *Ritschl had shown him how to admit biblical criticism without foregoing the evangelical faith, but on reading *Troeltsch he became dissatisfied with Ritschl's divorce of religion from metaphysics. Karl Heim – especially his recourse to the medieval schoolmen – gave Franks the clue to the resolution of this problem (see *The Metaphysical Justification of Religion* [1929]). Shortly before his death Franks completed an unpublished work, *Enigma*, concerning the relations between religion and science.

It is undeniable – and ominous – that since Franks's death no one within his ecclesiastical tradition or its united successor has brought such massive scholarship to bear upon the Christian doctrines with which he dealt. At his death he was described as 'Congregationalism's most learned theologian in this century'. Nearly half a century on, the judgement may stand.

ALAN P.F. SELL

FURTHER READING: *The Congregational Year Book* (London, 1964–5), pp. 439–40; *Who Was Who* (London, 1961–70); Thomas Hywel Hughes, *The Atonement: Modern Theories of the Doctrine* (London, 1949).

Frei, Hans W. (1922–88)

Considering how little he published during his lifetime, the influence of Hans Frei on Christian theology at the end of the twentieth century is remarkable. His academic career was spent almost entirely at Yale University. At Yale he was the teacher and colleague of numerous scholars of religious studies and theology whose indirect communication of his ideas has been nearly as significant as Frei's own published works.

Born into a secularized Jewish family in Breslau, in the eastern German state of Silesia, Frei was baptized in the Lutheran church. As a teenager he studied at a Quaker school in England before the family sought refuge from the rising tide of National Socialism by emigrating to the United States in 1938. He came to theology via a most unusual path. This path included a degree in textile engineering at North Carolina State University in 1942, a chance encounter with H. Richard Niebuhr that led eventually to a divinity degree from Yale in 1945, a brief stint as a Baptist minister in a small New Hampshire town, and eventual ordination in the Episcopal Church. He taught at both Wabash College (Crawfordsville, Indiana, 1950–53) and the Episcopal Seminary of the Southwest (Austin, Texas, 1953–56) before finally earning his PhD under Niebuhr's direction at Yale in 1956.

By far the greatest theological influence on Frei came not from his Yale teachers directly but from the writings of *Karl Barth, whose monumental *Church Dogmatics* began appearing in a series of volumes and part-volumes before Frei began his theological studies and continued to be published during his years as a student and young theologian. One could argue that Frei's importance lies more in his effective mediation of Barth to the English-speaking world than in his own theological ideas. The two, however, are closely intertwined. Barth's reception in Britain and America had been tainted from the start by the curious caricature of the 'neo-orthodox' Barth, who seemed (in the imagination of Anglo-Saxon detractors) to combine the obscurity and long-windedness of Germanic scholarship with a suspiciously reactionary theological program. The caricature was encouraged by an emergent chorus of 'Barthians', a group from whom Barth took pains to distance himself. Frei was able to combine a deep and sympathetic reading of Barth – always in the original German – with his own questions and concerns. Frei did so in a conceptual and written style very different from Barth's own. Frei's exposure to the New Critics, especially his Yale colleague William K. Wimsatt, and to the Anglo-American philosophical tradition encouraged him to approach issues of theological hermeneutics in ways quite foreign to the philosophical world in which Barth lived and wrote. As a result, Frei has attracted followers who would never have come to Barth on their own, and his influence has been a major factor in correcting the distortions of the 'neo-orthodox' reading of Barth. Frei liked to remark that Barth's theology fitted much better with Anglo-American philosophy in the wake of *Wittgenstein and Austin than with the philosophical traditions of continental Europe. Frei summarizes his interpretation of Barth in two short articles: his brief memorial tribute 'Karl Barth: Theologian' (*Theology and Narrative*, pp. 167–76) and his review of Eberhard Busch's biography of Barth (*Types of Christian Theology*, pp. 147–63).

More important than Frei's occasional comments about Barth, however, are his own historical and constructive writings, which exemplify in a most original manner how Barth's theology can inform the historical and constructive work of other theologians. The book for which Frei is most widely known, *The Eclipse of Biblical Narrative*, is also his greatest achievement as a historical theologian. Using evidence drawn from literary criticism, philosophy and theology, he shows how the western Christian reading of the Bible underwent a fateful change in the eighteenth and nineteenth centuries. This new approach to interpretation created a watershed in modern biblical hermeneutics, dividing the pre-critical reading of the Bible from the principles and assumptions that had governed its interpretation in the past two centuries. A broad consensus of Christians from the early church to the Reformation and beyond took for granted that the literal sense of the biblical stories could be expanded by figural or typological interpretation to include the whole of historical reality. Pre-critical Christians consequently lived in a world shaped and interpreted by Scripture. But since the beginning of the eighteenth century, biblical-historical criticism has assumed that the hermeneutical task is to interpret the meaning of the texts from the perspective of modern secular sensibilities. Frei explicates his thesis – that the narrative meaning of Scripture has been 'eclipsed' by these modern hermeneutical developments – by ranging widely through literary, historical and theological movements in Germany and England. The book also seems to many readers to suggest a theological agenda, a constructive response to the hermeneutical conundrums into which modern thought has stumbled; but the *Eclipse* offers no explicit theological construction.

If one turns to *The Identity of Jesus Christ*, however, which Frei published within a year of the *Eclipse*, the outlines of his own theology begin to emerge. Originally written for a church adult education curriculum, the book employs an eclectic blend of philosophical analysis, literary criticism and dogmatic theology to outline a unique approach to Christology. This approach, significantly, depends centrally on biblical narrative – especially the New Testament stories about Jesus. By contrasting these narratives with various 'Christ figures' in modern literature, Frei develops a Christological position that emphasizes the unique particularity of Jesus, in whose resurrection 'fictional description … merges with factual claim'. The identity of Jesus Christ turns out to imply his presence: 'To know *who* he is in connection with what took place is to know *that* he is.' Though Frei does not make the claim explicitly, this book suggests the sort of theology that is required if biblical narrative is to emerge from its modern eclipse.

More evidence of Frei's theology has come to light since his unexpected death in 1988. Two posthumous works have been compiled by George Hunsinger and William C. Placher from manuscripts and notes that Frei left behind. *Types of Christian Theology* makes available a major portion of his projected work in Christology, including the Shaffer Lectures that he delivered in 1983 at Yale and his 1987 Cadbury Lectures at the University of Birmingham. Here

Frei proposes a typology of Christian theologians on the basis of their relation to two conceptions of theology: as an academic discipline of the modern university and as an activity internal to the life of Christian communities. Like so much of his previous work, his classification of modern and contemporary theology into five main types combines insightful historical analysis with constructive forays into dogmatic theology. Frei's work as a historian of eighteenth- and nineteenth-century theology is always motivated by a passion for theological questions that continue to challenge the church in the late twentieth century, especially the relationship of the Bible to Christian faith, practice and theology.

The other posthumous collection, *Theology and Narrative*, is a more diverse work, consisting of ten essays and lectures (some previously published and some from works published posthumously) representing different periods of Frei's career. If there is a common theme, it is the one suggested by the editors' title – narrative. Though Frei is often cited as an advocate, or even the originator, of 'narrative theology', he was troubled by the label and tried to distance himself from it towards the end of his life. Nevertheless, the importance of the concept of narrative in his theology is undeniable. This collection includes one of his most significant and difficult essays, 'The *"Literal Reading"* of Biblical Narrative in the Christian Tradition: Does It Stretch or Will It Break?'. In this essay he tries to resuscitate the venerable notion of the 'literal reading' of Scripture, even in the face of contemporary phenomenological and deconstructivist hermeneutics. This essay suggests a greater attention than in Frei's earlier works to the communal (and specifically ecclesial) contexts in which the Bible is read, a theme also sounded in *Types of Christian Theology*. *Theology and Narrative* also includes Frei's stated desire for 'a kind of generous orthodoxy' that would combine elements of liberal and evangelical theology.

No attempt to place the work of Hans Frei in context can be complete without a consideration of the label most often connected with his name. Is he, along with his Yale colleague George Lindbeck, a founder of the 'Yale School' of theology? Though Frei was as reluctant to claim this label as that of 'narrative theology', it has become unavoidable. There is an undoubted family resemblance among a number of theologians who taught and studied at Yale during Frei's tenure there, such as those represented in the 1987 volume devoted to Frei's theology, *Scriptural Authority and Narrative Interpretation*. If there is indeed a Yale School, it is due in no small measure to the powerful combination of theological acumen and humane teaching embodied in the career of Hans Frei. His contribution to historical theology remains significant because it is never merely historical but always deeply and uniquely theological at the same time.

GARRETT GREEN

FURTHER READING: *Texts: The Eclipse of Biblical Narrative: A Study in Eighteenth- and Nineteenth-Century Hermeneutics* (New Haven, 1974), appendix contains a bibliography of books by and about Frei; *The Identity of Jesus Christ: The Hermeneutical Bases of Dogmatic Theology* (Philadelphia, 1975); 'Niebuhr's Theological Background' and 'The Theology of H. Richard Niebuhr', in *Faith and Ethics: The Theology of H. Richard Niebuhr* (ed. Paul Ramsey; New York, 1957); *Theology and Narrative: Selected Essays* (New York, 1993); *Types of Christian Theology* (New Haven, 1992). *Studies:* David E. Demson, *Hans Frei and Karl Barth: Different Ways of Reading Scripture* (Grand Rapids, 1997); David F. Ford, 'On Being Theologically Hospitable to Jesus Christ: Hans Frei's Achievement', *J Th St*, NS 46 (1992), pp. 532–46; Garrett Green (ed.), *Scriptural Authority and Narrative Interpretation* (Philadelphia, 1987); Issue on 'Hans Frei and the Future of Theology', *Mod Th* 8 (1992); Nicholas Wolterstorff, 'Evidence, Belief, and the Gospels', *Faith Phil* 6 (1989), pp. 429–59.

Garvie, A.E. (1861–1945)

Alfred Ernest Garvie was born in Poland of Scottish parents on 29 August 1861. Sent to Scotland for the purpose of education, he received his schooling at George Watson's College, Edinburgh before proceeding to the universities of Edinburgh, Glasgow and Mansfield College, Oxford. After coming down from Oxford he served as pastor of two Congregational churches – Macduff (1893–95) and Montrose (1895–1903) – before entering New College, London, first as lecturer and then as principal. Here he remained for 30 years.

The author of 40 books and a regular contributor to learned journals, leading encyclopedias and commentaries, Garvie published his mature, constructive thoughts on basic Christian philosophy as *The Christian Doctrine of the Godhead* (1945), described by *R.S. Franks (1871–1964) as a 'greatly daring' book. Garvie died in London on 7 March 1945.

Garvie's theological contribution may conveniently be summarized under various doctrinal headings:

Revelation. Logically prior to the question 'What do we know about religious truth?' is the question 'How do we know?' What is our final authority in these matters?

In respect of special revelation, Garvie placed Scripture high on the list of trustworthy sources of religious knowing, but it is Scripture with its historical inaccuracies erased by scientific criticism and its moral teachings corrected by Jesus the Christ. Can the historic Jesus be recovered sufficiently for this to be done? Garvie held that we can do so by a historico-literary study, supplemented by observing the effects of Jesus' teaching upon our lives and supported by the testimony of the Holy Spirit.

In respect of general revelation, Garvie held that God approaches all his children. No race is so low in the cultural scale as to be excluded from God's call. Anticipating C.E. Storrs (*Many Creeds: One Cross*, 1945), Garvie observed that other religions, though in many respects so different from Christianity, nevertheless exhibit similarities not explicable by reference to human contact.

Nature of God. As a result of the gift of free will to humans, predestination and absolute prescience must be denied of God. As a corollary,

God's power over humans must be seen as self-limited.

With *Martin Buber (*I and Thou*, ET 1937), Garvie insisted that as the creator of that from which personality evolved, God must be seen as at-least-personal.

Garvie's treatment of God's omnipresence is pan-en-theistic rather than pantheistic. God indwells matter and waits for it to evolve to mind. Writing shortly after Rutherford's team split the atom, Garvie pointed out that the contrast between mind and matter must be regarded as tenuous.

Jesus Christ. Jesus is the perfect human personality, perfectly receptive of and responsive to the perfect communication of God.

Garvie held the incarnation to have been progressive. Jesus was sinless, but not impeccable, and it was through many struggles of soul that he perfected his receptivity and response and, in his glorified manhood, became the Christ. Thus, Jesus the Christ could not have been pre-existent, and his birth was probably a normal one. He was infallible in his revelation of God, but this infallibility need not have extended to other fields.

The Trinity. Garvie rejected the orthodox Trinitarian formula, holding that words like 'substance' and 'person' have physical connotations and introduce the concept of a Tritheism. He suggested that the Holy Spirit should be envisaged as God's influence.

Is faith a gift of the Spirit? No, faith must be seen according to Garvie as an individual's response to the Holy Spirit's illumination.

Humankind. The creation stories in Genesis are mythological, but enshrine the truths that human beings were made by God, have a likeness to God, can enter into a fellowship with him, and have personal liberty and responsibility.

With Lloyd Morgan (*Emergent Evolution*, 1929), Garvie claimed that humankind evolved from lower forms of life. God created, indwelt and gave nisus to matter, that is, gave to matter the power to strive toward a higher level of existence. Humans are born amoral: they become good or bad according to their individual response to the Spirit's prompting.

From what are we redeemed? Not from total death, but from less and less advanced personality, until we return to the lower levels from which we evolved.

The work of Christ. What did the crucifixion achieve? Garvie rejected any interpretation involving a sacrifice brought to appease an angry God. Indeed, the atonement is manward, not Godward.

The purpose of the cross was to impress humans and to express God: impressing humans by an appeal to their moral conscience and religious consciousness as they saw the wholly good suffer; and expressing God's loving concern for all his children. Thus, the cross is revelatory.

The cross is not the sole medium of redemption. The truth Jesus taught, the holiness he lived, the grace he showed – all were redemptive.

The church. The church is a human society which allows itself to be suffused by the light and life of Christ. It is not to be singly identified with any one Christian denomination, but overflows the boundaries of denominations. Thus, we should speak of the church within the churches. The church is found wherever there is acceptance of Jesus as revealer of God, and an effort is made toward a recognizable imitation of his character.

Garvie felt that the sacraments could be viewed as practically useful, in that they appeal to imagination and emotion, rather than singly to intellect. However, he did not concede that a personal relationship with God can be mediated more effectively through material channels than by the gospel, in which Christ is presented to reason, conscience and heart.

Garvie emphasized the importance of the visible church being a unified society, and he became a leading international figure in the earliest and continuing conversations between the Christian churches of the world, as they sought to attain that unity.

DOUGLAS YOUNG

FURTHER READING: J.W. Bowman, *The Intention of Jesus* (London, 1945); A.E. Garvie, *Memories and Meanings of My Life* (London, 1938); H.R. MacIntosh, *The Doctrine and Person of Christ* (Edinburgh, 1912); W.R. Matthews, *God in Christian Thought and Experience* (London, 1930); G.F. Nuttall, *The Holy Spirit and Ourselves* (Oxford, 1947).

Gilson, Étienne (1884–1978)

Son of a Parisian shopkeeper and his Burgundian wife, Étienne Gilson was born at a moment when French culture was especially committed to the pursuit of the contemporary. In the last quarter of the nineteenth century, the social scientist Émile Durkheim and the philosopher Henri Bergson stood out as prominent secular critics of a nonetheless omnipresent secular positivism. This positivism shaped the intellectual world of Paris, even as the architects of the Third Republic, after its birth by executive coup in 1877, earnestly worked to make this up to now enduring effort at democracy take definitive root. Gilson's early studies at the Sorbonne unfolded, then, in an atmosphere largely constituted by the spirits of mathematical empiricism, evolutionary philosophy and secular republicanism. The early nineteenth-century romantic movement embodied in the Catholic providentialism of Joseph Marie de Maistre (1753–1821), the erratic idealism of Félicité Robert de Lamennais (1782–1854) and the Christian liberalism of Henri-Dominique Lacordaire (1802–61) exercised no influence on Gilson's early training. He read instead the classics of modern French philosophy, with special focus on its uncontested progenitor *René Descartes. He successfully defended his doctoral theses with *mention très honorable*, earning recognition from the philosopher Léon Brunschwicg, who pronounced Gilson's work, *La Doctrine de la Liberté chez Descartes et la Théologie* (Paris, 1913), a 'notable progress in the study of Descartes' metaphysics'. It was hence amidst positivistic and rational cultural soil that the seed of Gilson's profound appreciation for Christian philosophy and theology took root and flowered. For Gilson, 'an historian who strayed into the past and looked at the flow of events from the wrong end' (*The Philosopher and Theology* [trans. Cécile Gilson; New York, 1962], p. 5), the pursuit of further progress led him to discover the value of past achievements – especially those of the Middle Ages.

It is generally agreed that, in his more than sixty-year post-doctoral career as a historian of thought, Gilson not only made significant contributions to both the history of medieval and early modern philosophy, but he also achieved eminence in the practice of philosophy. His, however, was not a dual-track career. Rather, to the extent that he interrogated history, seeking its intelligibility, Gilson pursued what he liked to call a 'composite vocation'. The results of his wide-ranging inquiry, which concentrated on the great figures of medieval and modern thought, were rich – in printed form, his bibliography runs to 91 pages – and innovative, especially for the impact that his research had on theology. The origins of Gilson's distinctive approach to both history and philosophy can be traced to a 1914 article for the *Revue de Métaphysique et de Morale* (22 [1914], pp. 456–99) on Cartesian innatism and Christian theology, where the young French scholar turned his attention to *Thomas Aquinas's realist theory of knowledge.

Although the period of modern *Thomism had begun with Leo XIII's 1879 encyclical 'Aeterni Patris', the historical centre of original thirteenth-century Thomism proved inhospitable toward this effort at a modern revival of Catholic intellectual life. Gilson, though deeply rooted in the Parisian milieu, became fascinated with Aquinas, in whom he early on discovered 'metaphysical substance' (*The Philosopher and Theology*, p. 88). After military service in World War I, when even as a prisoner of war he read philosophy, Gilson continued his instruction in the French universities: Lille, Strasbourg and then, in 1921, at the Sorbonne. By the time he arrived at the University of Paris, Gilson was ready to publish the second edition of *Le Thomisme* (Paris, 1922), an initial effort to state the essentials of Aquinas's thought that would enjoy six revised editions. For the rest of his long career, Gilson can best be described as one who read Thomas Aquinas. His commitment, as his biographer notes, 'would never be anything other than [to] the text that Thomas left behind, and his objective would simply be to understand the meaning of that text' (Shook, *Étienne Gilson*, p. 124). Gilson's 'living Thomism', as he himself designated it, catalyzed a half century of concentrated research in medieval philosophy and theology, and still continues to inspire the students that he trained, especially at the Pontifical Institute of Mediaeval Studies, which he founded in 1929 as a research centre located in Toronto.

In the period between the two wars, Gilson divided his instructional time between France and America, where he mostly lectured at Harvard University. As his accomplishments won him international recognition, Gilson was asked to undertake special cultural missions for the French government and was also invited to accept prestigious lecture series in Europe and America. The 1931–32 Gifford Lectures, published as *The Spirit of Medieval Philosophy*, provided the occasion to set forth his notion of Christian philosophy, which he defined as: 'every philosophy which, although keeping the two orders (of reason and faith) formally distinct, nevertheless considers the Christian revelation as an indispensable auxiliary to reason' (trans. A.H.C. Downes; New York, 1961, p. 37). Though the thesis remains a controversial one, it illustrates the distinctive character of Gilson's intellectual project, which requires the interplay of three disciplines: history, philosophy and theology. A former student, Kenneth Schmitz, puts it this way: 'For Gilson, "Clio and Athena were called to serve One greater still"' (*What Has Clio to Do with Athena?*, p. 5). The thesis concerning how a philosophy can be strictly rational, even though it is achieved through the indispensable aid of Christian revelation, reflected Gilson's profound reverence for Christian truth, for which he credited his own good catechetical instruction. Although Gilson considered the medieval assumption that 'truth is universal in its own right' a true philosophical conclusion, and not a theological belief, he was under no illusion that many philosophers who read his 1937 Harvard Tercentenary Lecture, 'Medieval Universalism and its Present Value', would agree with him.

Gilson earned an honorary membership in the *résistance* for his conduct during World War II and was elected to the Académie Française in 1946. He surely ranks among the major architects of twentieth-century French Catholic intellectual life that so much influenced the early stages of *Vatican II (1961–65). Between 1956 and 1975, Gilson exchanged a correspondence with *Henri de Lubac that discloses their shared aversion for the standard Thomism of the day, with its reliance on an alleged *philosophia aristotelico-thomistica*. Moreover, Gilson distanced himself from his own earlier positions regarding *obedientialis potentia* and the relation between nature and grace. For example, in *The Spirit of Medieval Philosophy* he had written earlier of obediential potency that 'it expresses one of the profounder aspects of the Christian natural order', and 'no medieval philosopher could reject what it stands for without abandoning the Christian concept of the world' (p. 377). These are views that pass unmentioned, perhaps even abandoned, in the wake of his later approval for de Lubac's approach to this subject. Yet he did not come to share de Lubac's regard for Teilhard de Chardin's theological writings, while his doctrinal embrace of St Thomas's metaphysics of existence (*esse*) continued unabated.

Indeed, Gilson's work throughout exhibits what one may properly identify as Thomist existentialism. He never lost, however, the intellectual modesty proper to a Christian philosopher: 'God is QUI EST [He Who Is]; in God that which in other beings is their essence, is God's act of existing, the EST. Now, in the proposition *Deus est*, we know that what the proposition says is true, but we don't know what the verb *est* means' (letter of 8 July 1956 to Henri de Lubac). Gilson died on 19 September 1978, fortified by the sacraments of the Roman Catholic Church. In his encyclical letter 'Fides et Ratio' (no. 74), Pope John Paul II commended Gilson's work.

ROMANUS CESSARIO, OP

FURTHER READING: Eric L. Mascall, *He who Is: A Study in Traditional Theism* (London, 1966); Armand A. Maurer, 'The Legacy of Étienne Gilson', in *One Hundred Years of Thomism* (ed. Victor B. Brezik, CSB; Houston, TX, 1981); Margaret McGrath, *Étienne Gilson: A Bibliography/Une Bibliographie* (Toronto, 1982); Laurence K. Shook, *Étienne Gilson* (Toronto, 1984); Kenneth L. Schmitz, *What Has Clio to Do with Athena?: Étienne Gilson: Historian and Philosopher* (The Étienne Gilson Series 10; Toronto, 1987); *Letters of Étienne Gilson to Henri de Lubac: Annotated by Father de Lubac* (trans. M.E. Hamilton; San Francisco, 1988).

Gnosticism

In church history, or the history of doctrine, Gnosticism is a religious movement of the early Christian centuries, denounced as a heresy by such Fathers as *Irenaeus, *Hippolytus, *Tertullian and *Epiphanius. They saw it as the result of a fusion of Christianity with Greek philosophy. Gnosticism was, in *Harnack's phrase, 'the acute Hellenization of Christianity'. But although this was the standard opinion for centuries it is doubtful if this 'traditional' view is any longer wholly tenable.

For the history of religions, the Gnosticism censured by the early Fathers is only one aspect of a much more widely-diffused phenomenon, liable to erupt at any time in the most unexpected places, even to modern times (e.g. the *'New Age' movement). The 'classic' gnostic

systems certainly belong to the second century, but there are affinities with gnostic thought in Manicheism and Mandeism later, to say nothing of other movements. It is not always possible to establish a direct historical continuity between one branch of the gnostic tendency and another. It is the use of certain ideas, terms and concepts in particular ways which makes it possible to group the various systems together from a phenomenological point of view.

It is therefore necessary to understand at the outset that this term 'Gnosticism' and its cognates may be employed in at least two rather different senses: in a narrower sense relating to the 'heresy' denounced by the Fathers and in a broader sense referring to the wider 'gnostic' phenomenon. For full understanding it is necessary to keep the whole phenomenon under review, but in the interest of clarity it is advisable to restrict attention in the first instance to the 'classic' gnostic systems. Manicheism and other systems should be given the labels which are theirs by right.

The name Gnosticism derives from the Greek word *gnōsis*, meaning 'knowledge'; but not every knowledge is a gnostic knowledge. Most religions profess to impart knowledge in some form, and there are numerous references to knowledge of God both in the Hebrew Bible and in the New Testament. The Dead Sea Scrolls also make frequent reference to knowledge, but it is now generally recognized that this is not a 'gnostic' knowledge. Irenaeus calls his work a refutation of 'the *gnōsis* falsely so-called' (cf. 1 Tim. 6:20), which implies that there is a true and authentic *gnōsis*. *Clement of Alexandria can speak quite happily of 'the true gnostic', meaning a Christian who has penetrated more deeply into the faith than the ordinary simple believer. None of these is the *gnōsis* of the gnostics, and therefore not every occurrence of this term is evidence for the presence of Gnosticism.

The significance of the 'gnostic' *gnōsis* is neatly summed up in the statement 'it is not only the washing (i.e. baptism) that is liberating, but the knowledge of who we were, what we have become, where we were, into what we have been cast, whither we are hastening, from what we are delivered, what is birth and what rebirth' (Clem. Alex., *Exc. ex Theod. 78. 2*). This statement requires some explanation in terms of gnostic theory (see below), but the point for the moment is first that Gnosticism was a religion of liberation, and second that for the gnostics it was this *gnōsis* that was the fundamental element in their religion, the true saving power, the longed-for means of deliverance.

The gnostic systems are sometimes dismissed as bizarre and grotesque, as if they were not worthy of serious consideration; but that is a superficial view. Fundamentally, Gnosticism is an attempt to account for the human predicament, to explain and resolve the problems which attach to human existence in this world: the meaning and purpose of life, the origins and the cause of evil, and so on. Gnosticism presents an alternative solution to rival the traditional Christian doctrine which, in Milton's words, begins with 'man's first disobedience' and traces the whole problem to 'the fruit of that forbidden tree whose mortal taste brought death into the world and all our woe'. Moreover, Gnosticism is a solution which removes the responsibility from the shoulders of humanity. For the gnostic, the origins of evil go back a stage further, to a pre-mundane fall. The creator or demiurge is not the supreme God but a lesser deity, variously portrayed but not always hostile to humankind, who mistakenly thinks himself supreme.

A regular feature in all gnostic systems is their disparagement of this world and all that belongs to it. Human beings essentially belong not to this world but to a higher realm ('who we were'). They are so many sparks of divine fire which have become imprisoned in matter. The body is a tomb from which they long to be released ('what we have become', 'into what we have been cast'). The deliverance for which they yearn is not from sin and death, but from imprisonment in the body and in this world, at the mercy of the hostile powers who govern the seven heavens (the demiurge and his 'archons'). Nor is deliverance brought by a redeemer or saviour. It is, rather, effected by the saving *gnōsis* which supplies the knowledge of the truth about our nature, our consubstantiality with the divine, and the pass-words that enable the soul to answer the guardians at the heavenly gates on its journey home ('whither we are hastening'). One characteristic feature of all gnostic systems is therefore a myth to explain how it all came about, and to provide the elements of the saving *gnōsis*.

The 'classic' gnostic systems, as already noted, belong to the second century, but that does not mean that the movement only began then. The writings of such authors as *Philo of Alexandria,

for example, show certain affinities with later gnostic systems, although it is generally agreed that Philo himself was not a gnostic (cf. *Studia Philonica Annual* 5 [1993], pp. 84–92 and references there). It is clear that there were various trends and tendencies of a 'gnostic' or 'gnosticizing' kind even in the first century. On the other hand, attempts have been made to trace the origins of the movement back into pre-Christian times, with the more or less explicit suggestion (a) of 'gnostic' influence upon the New Testament, particularly on Paul and John, or (b) that at the very least the New Testament writers were already reacting against 'gnostic' opponents. This may indeed be true for some of the later writings in the New Testament, but it must be said that to identify motifs in the developed gnostic systems which also appear in the New Testament, describe them as 'gnostic' and then claim them as evidence for 'gnostic' influence, may be to read first-century documents with second-century spectacles.

How far are such motifs in themselves essentially gnostic, and how far do they only *become* gnostic within the context of a gnostic system? It is too easily forgotten that the gnostics not only freely borrowed from other systems, they also frequently adapted their borrowings to suit their own purposes. The similarities found in Orphism or in the writings of *Plato are probably to be explained as due to later gnostic borrowing, which aroused the indignation of such as Plotinus, and not as evidence for the existence of 'Gnosticism' at so early a stage. The fact remains that we have no gnostic document which in its present form can be dated back before the New Testament.

For a long time the only information available about Gnosticism came from the writings of the early Fathers. This information was inevitably suspect as the work of opponents of the movement, bent on countering what they saw as a dangerous heresy and none too scrupulous as to the methods they employed. The original gnostic documents then extant in Coptic (*Pistis Sophia* in the Askew codex in the British Museum, the two *Books of Jeu* and an untitled treatise in the Bruce codex in Oxford) are from a period when gnostic ideas had long run to seed. The contents of the Coptic gnostic codex 8502 in Berlin were known in 1896, but through various circumstances this codex was not published until 1955. Meanwhile an extensive library of Coptic texts (not all gnostic) was discovered near Nag Hammadi in Egypt in 1945. A complete edition of this library has now been produced, containing the texts with an English translation (French and German editions are in preparation). These texts enable us to compare and check the patristic reports, and also to trace the growth and development of gnostic themes within the context of the gnostic documents (cf. the study of the *Apocryphon of John* and related documents by A.H.B. Logan, *Gnostic Truth and Christian Heresy* [Edinburgh, 1996]).

For example, where the Fathers often accuse the gnostics of obscene and licentious practices, the evidence of the texts suggests asceticism rather than libertarianism; but the gnostics would not be the first or the only victims of a vindictive polemic. The slanders brought by pagans against Christians, or by Christians against Jews, show only too clearly how hostility can breed falsehood, or generalize a single incident into an allegedly common practice.

One long-standing problem in earlier research was to determine whether the documents of the *Corpus Hermeticum* should be considered gnostic. The discovery of some Hermetic texts in the Nag Hammadi library shows that at least some readers in the ancient world thought that they belonged in the gnostic sphere; at any rate they had an appeal for those interested in gnostic literature. Gnosticism in the past has often been regarded as a religion of gloom, a counsel of despair. But one of the contributions made by the Nag Hammadi discovery is to give a glimpse of what Gnosticism meant *to a gnostic*. It was a religion of hope, described in terms of waking from a nightmare, or from a drunken stupor, into the dawn of a new day.

A later branch of the gnostic movement, Manicheism, was launched by its founder Mani in the middle of the third century, and at one stage attained to the status of a world religion, reaching as far as China. Fragments of Manichean texts have been found in the Turfan oasis in Chinese Turkestan as well as in Coptic in Egypt. For a time Manicheism numbered *Augustine of Hippo among its adherents, although he later wrote against the Manicheans. In the seventeenth century Manicheism was to attract the interest of Bayle and the *philosophes*.

Later movements such as that of the Bogomils in the Balkans and the Cathari in southern France show gnostic features, although it is not clear that there is any direct relationship. The occurrence of 'gnostic' motifs and concepts does not necessarily mean a historical connection, or that the later movement is influenced by the earlier. It is different with more modern authors like Blake and Thomas Mann, who have consciously utilized gnostic elements derived from their reading of older sources (for gnostic influence in later literature, cf. the plenary addresses in Layton (ed.), *The Rediscovery of Gnosticism*, I [Leiden, 1980], and Richard Smith's 'Afterword', 'The Modern Relevance of Gnosticism', in J.M. Robinson (ed.), *The Nag Hammadi Library in English* [3rd edn, 1988], pp. 532–49; G. Quispel [in Layton, pp. 17–31] deals with the significance of Gnosticism for the psychologist C.G. Jung). One might also mention the gnostic element in Theosophy and Anthroposophy; the reader acquainted with the gnostic texts who turns to some modern 'splinter groups' will find much that is familiar.

R. McL. WILSON

FURTHER READING: Complete facsimile edition of the *Nag Hammadi Library* (Leiden, 1972–84); and editions of the several codices in the NHS series with text, translation and notes. *For detailed bibliography see:* D.M. Scholer, *Nag Hammadi Bibliography 1948–1969* (Leiden, 1971; vol. 2 [1970–94], 1996). *See also:* J.M. Robinson (ed.), *Nag Hammadi Library in English* (San Francisco, 3rd edn, 1988). *Recent full studies:* K. Rudolph, *Gnosis* (Edinburgh, 1983); G. Filoramo, *A History of Gnosticism* (Oxford, 1990).

Gore, Charles (1853–1932)

At the height of his powers Gore was generally regarded as the most powerful Anglican theologian of his day. He exerted a profound influence on *William Temple and *Michael Ramsey, later leaders of the Church of England and the Anglican Communion. But, as a Victorian, Gore's reputation has suffered undeserved eclipse in modern Anglicanism. Gore came from an aristocratic Irish family, though he lived all his life in England. He enjoyed an unselfconscious sense of social and intellectual superiority and command. At Harrow, Gore was influenced by B.F. Westcott to see scholarship as a vocation and to follow a rule of life. A distinguished academic career at Oxford led to his being appointed vice-principal of Cuddesdon Theological College at the age of twenty-six and then the first principal of Pusey House, a research and teaching foundation in memory of the patriarch of Tractarianism. After an unhappy spell as a vicar of a country parish, Gore became a canon of Westminster Abbey until appointed as Bishop of Worcester in 1901.

Gore took the lead in several spheres of Christian thought and action. He pioneered the acceptance of both Darwinian science and German biblical criticism in High Church Anglicanism. He developed a radical, immanentist Christology that stressed the real humanity (but not at the expense of the full divinity) of Jesus Christ. He was a leader in theologically informed social concern and action. He founded and personally partly endowed a new diocese of the Church of England (Birmingham). He was the inspiration behind the founding of a new religious order (The Community of the Resurrection) that could respond to the social and intellectual challenge of modernity with flexibility.

Gore was the successor of the Tractarians and the heir apparent of *Pusey and his lieutenant, Liddon. As bishop of several sees in succession (Worcester, Birmingham and Oxford) and a senior voice in the episcopate, he was the acknowledged leader of the burgeoning Anglo-Catholic party within the Church of England. As a young man Gore dismayed the old guard of the Oxford Movement with what they regarded as his radical theological innovations, and as an old man Gore was regarded as *passé* by progressive Anglo-Catholics. With considerable precocity, Gore developed a distinctive theological position at an early stage and defended it against conservatives and liberals for the rest of his life. His theological consistency has often been challenged, but it can be vindicated. It was at once his strength and weakness that he refused to change with the times. He did not see the need to explain all the workings that led him to his conclusions, but he propounded them with an oracular authority that carried diminishing influence.

Gore first caught the public eye in print as editor of *Lux Mundi* (1889), which emerged from the annual reading holidays of the 'Holy Party', a group of Anglo-Catholics, mainly Oxford clerical dons. This symposium was a brave attempt to establish a creative relationship between creedal orthodoxy (Trinitarian, incarnational, sacramental, biblical and patristic in its theological commitments) and new movements of thought. The group embraced an idealist, immanental, developmental paradigm of God's relation to the world in order to embrace the natural, historical aspects of human origins (Darwin and Genesis), of holy Scripture (not infallible, containing myth and legend, especially in the Old Testament) and of the incarnate Christ (not omniscient, could be mistaken about matters of historical fact).

This immediately posed for Gore (in his seminal contribution on the Holy Spirit and biblical inspiration) the problem of reconciling his acceptance of limitations in the human knowledge of Jesus Christ with the traditional orthodox doctrine of his omniscience as the incarnation of God. A kenotic Christology that postulated a self-emptying of divine metaphysical attributes, such as omniscience, on the part of the pre-existent Logos, provided Gore with the escape route from this impasse. It led him, however, into direct conflict with authoritative tradition, derived from the early councils of the church. Gore rather uncomfortably operated a distinction in practice between the authority of the creeds and that of the councils that produced them. He was scarred by the outrage with which his attempt to reinterpret orthodoxy was met by conservative Anglo-Catholics.

He pursued these Christological explorations further in his Bampton Lectures for 1891, *The Incarnation of the Son of God*. It was not speculative philosophical theology but above all faithfulness to 'the figure of the Gospels', freshly revealed by moderate biblical criticism, that compelled Gore's kenotic Christology. It is notable that his critical methods did not lead Gore to question either the virginal conception or the physical resurrection of Jesus. He defended these beliefs vigorously and harassed clergy under his jurisdiction who militantly denied (rather than humbly questioned) them. He held that the creeds had final authority (supported by Scripture) and provided the parameters for theological exploration by clergy. Thus Gore was unsympathetic to the more liberal direction, evinced by *Essays Catholic and Critical* (1926), that Anglo-Catholic theology began to take in his later years.

Gore also defended a conservative position on liturgy, insisting that the Book of Common Prayer 1662 be used, and that reservation of the sacrament be confined to communicating the sick. *The Body of Christ* (1901) is an impressive statement of Gore's Eucharistic theology, affirming a real presence and a Eucharistic sacrifice but rejecting Roman Catholic ideas of transubstantiation and propitiatory sacrifice. He opposed intercommunion with non-episcopal Protestants and was an inflexible advocate of 'the historic episcopate' as of the *esse* of the true church. Free Churches were spheres of grace only through 'uncovenanted mercies'. His account of the emergence of the monarchical episcopate in the early church in *The Church and the Ministry* (1886) still has to be reckoned with today.

Like many in the Anglican High Church tradition, including the founders of the Oxford Movement, Gore was violently anti-papal. His demolition of *Roman Catholic Claims* (1884 – after *Vatican I) as imperialistic, totalitarian and obscurantist, stands alongside *Orders and Unity* (1909) as representing the parameters of Gore's ecumenical theology. *The Basis of Anglican Fellowship* (1914) is the definitive statement of Gore's position on several fronts: the nature of Anglicanism, the authority of the creeds, liturgy and the conditions of Eucharistic hospitality.

Gore's prolific outlook culminated, after his resignation from the See of Oxford in 1919, in the trilogy *The Reconstruction of Belief* (1921–26). The work follows a Trinitarian pattern (*Belief in God, Belief in Christ, The Holy Spirit and the Church*). It was followed by a fourth volume (*Can We Then Believe?*) in which Gore responded to his critics and clarified his arguments. Though he went on to give the prestigious Gifford Lectures on natural theology (*The Philosophy of the Good Life*, 1930), in which he expounded sympathetically non-biblical religious traditions, the four volumes of apologetics remain his *magnum opus*.

Gore argues on mainly historical and ethical grounds (characteristically underlining the significance of the phenomenon of the eighth-century prophets of the Old Testament) for what we might call a modulated orthodoxy. Gore had long typified this position as 'Liberal Catholicism'. 'Liberal' stands for freedom of conscience and unhampered enquiry, using all the tools of secular scholarship, and it carries no contemporary connotations of scepticism or relativism. 'Catholicism' refers to the ideal of the early undivided church: a universal, structured visible society led by those who had authority handed down from the apostles to teach, administer salvation-bestowing sacraments, and exercise disciplined pastoral oversight. Gore was acutely aware of the deficiencies of Anglicanism, chastising it for lukewarmness and compromise, but he nevertheless believed it to be the closest available approximation to Liberal Catholicism.

Gore practised a method of theological synthesis in which he brought together whatever convinced him of its truth from any tradition. From the early church and the patristic texts that he had mastered in the original languages he learned the importance of the visible, ordered community and its sacramental life. From the *Reformation he accepted the paramount authority of Scripture, the priestly calling of all the baptized and the doctrine of justification by grace through faith. From the Renaissance and the *Enlightenment he received the imperative of unrestricted critical evaluation of all sources, sacred and secular. The *Hegelian school gave him his philosophical framework (a personal, not an absolute idealism) for his theological immanentism. But his firm grounding in the Scriptures, which provided 'the sole final testing ground of dogmatic requirement', ensured that the immanental model was always balanced by the transcendental. Gore did not merge God and the world, deity and humanity, as some *Anglican Modernists appeared to do. For him, the ultimate metaphysical distinction was that between Creator and creation. Gore was the hammer of Modernists, whether in the form of the facile *New Theology of *R.J. Campbell, or in the shape of the Modern Churchman's Union.

PAUL AVIS

FURTHER READING: P. Avis, *Gore: Construction and Conflict* (Worthing, 1988); J. Carpenter, *Gore: A Study in Liberal Catholic Thought* (London, 1960); G.L. Prestige, *The Life of Charles Gore* (London, 1935); A.M. Ramsey, *From Gore to Temple* (London, 1960).

Grosseteste, Robert (c. 1170–1253)

Born into a humble family in Suffolk, England, Grosseteste went on to complete a liberal arts education, probably at an English cathedral school. He was part of the household of the Bishop of Hereford from c. 1192 to 1198, and he later acted as a judge-delegate in that diocese, c. 1213–16. At one time it was thought that he went to Paris to study theology in 1209; however, recent scholarship has demonstrated the distinct lack of evidence for this claim. Grosseteste reappears in the historical record in 1225, when Bishop Hugh of Lincoln awarded him a benefice with cure at Abbotsley. In 1229, he became archdeacon of Leicester and a canon of Lincoln cathedral. Three years later, taking a serious illness as God's punishment for holding multiple benefices, he resigned all save his position as canon. Grosseteste was also a master of theology at Oxford, but there is no consensus as to when his tenure began. The only datable evidence comes from the *Franciscans at the university, for in 1229/30 he was appointed their first lector in theology. Grosseteste taught theology until 1235, the year he was elected bishop of Lincoln. He ruled the diocese for eighteen years until his death on 9 October 1253.

Accounts of Grosseteste's theological outlook have undergone some revision in the last forty years or so. He was initially perceived as an independent thinker out of step with his contemporaries, but it has since been shown that Grosseteste employed contemporaneous methods and themes. As a university master, he engaged in the traditional practices of scholastic theology. He lectured on sacred Scripture, led disputations on various theological and philosophical problems, and preached both before university and lay congregations. At the same time, some of his writings do reflect a desire to pursue theological problems in a unique manner. Two fundamental features of his theological argument are his commitment to a careful reading of the Fathers – beyond the standard cut and paste sources of the various glosses and florilegia – and a strong belief in the role of imagination in discourse. The latter may have been the result of his conviction that the physical world could be represented mathematically, a concept he drew from his reading of Euclid and *Aristotle in his early years. Abstraction (either in terms of division or definition) was thus a natural act of the human intellect and it thrived in the world of images and symbols.

This continual reference to symbols can lead readers of Grosseteste to conclude that he was solely interested in the spiritual exposition of Scripture and showed no interest in literal exegesis. However, like his contemporaries Grosseteste saw, in part, the validity of allegory as grounded in a literal exposition of the sacred text. He is one of the few theologians of the early thirteenth century to delineate rules for both literal and spiritual exegesis. Like so much of his theology, Grosseteste's theory and practice of exegesis took their inspiration from *Augustine, but they were augmented as well by his reading of other Fathers and pagan philosophers.

What actually distanced Grosseteste from other scholastic theologians was his knowledge of Greek. It is unclear what led him to learn this language, but it provided him with access to sources unknown to western medieval theology. His Greek reading began at Oxford with commentators on Genesis and the Psalms (drawn mainly, but not exclusively, from the Cappadocian circle) and culminated in a series of translation projects in the middle years of his episcopate. His translations included the complete works of *Pseudo-Dionysius, the major writings of *John of Damascus, the *Testament of the Twelve Patriarchs* and the first complete Latin rendering of Aristotle's *Nicomachean Ethics*. Grosseteste considered this last text an excellent resource for pastoral theology. Grosseteste may also have learned to read Hebrew while he was bishop, and he may have sponsored the production of a four-column Psalter, which included all the Latin versions as well as an interlinear Hebrew-Latin text.

Generally, Grosseteste's theology revolved around his Christology, but his enquiries were not limited to the economy of salvation. He stated that the subject of theological discourse was the *Christus totus* (the whole Christ), a term he discovered during his lectures on the Psalms. This subject embraced the incarnation in relation to the Trinity, the natural world, the angelic world and humanity. While the person of Christ was essential to salvation history and also the key to Old Testament exegesis, it was also the point of departure for any theological analysis of the created world, including the objects of the intellect. Grosseteste was instrumental in reviving the thirteenth-century reading of *Anselm, and in doing so he strengthened Anselm's doctrine of the necessity of the incarnation. So central was the God-man to Grosseteste that he claimed Christ to be the means by which humanity gained access to all created and uncreated truth. Hence, Grosseteste's Christology is also the context for his teachings on the divine illumination of the intellect and the exemplarist nature of creation, both of which bear the marks of the philosophies of Augustine and Anselm.

Necessity spilled into Grosseteste's ecclesiology, since its nature was connected to the incarnation. The church, as it had metaphysical attributes, was more than simply a social and political reality. Pseudo-Dionysius provided an ideal set of concepts for him to further his ecclesiology, since in the Dionysian universe the church reflected the structure of the angelic hierarchy. As with the celestial hierarchy, the ecclesiastical hierarchy was perfected when each fulfilled his function and did not rise above his station nor abrogate his role. This perspective explains in part why Grosseteste placed such importance on his own episcopal duties, and why he so vociferously castigated the papal court in 1250 concerning abuses in the pastoral care of the universal church. Grosseteste built upon the scholastic view that authority vouch-safed ministry, and the Dionysian framework only added urgency to this perception.

Grosseteste is perhaps best known for his unwavering commitment to pastoral theology. During his lifetime he addressed the sacrament of confession in no less than five separate works. He drew from the traditional sources, but he was also conversant in the psychological theory of medieval Islamic philosophical sources. The human nature of Christ, in confluence with the divine, was his model for the Christian life. Pastors were to use preaching and penance to lead Christians towards that perfection. His most famous work, the *Templum Dei* ('The Temple of God'), survives in over ninety manuscripts from the thirteenth to the fifteenth centuries – a testament to its enduring popularity. The work contains the standard theology of confession, but it is also adorned with useful tables and diagrams which summarized some of the more complex theological discussions on penance.

JAMES GINTHER

FURTHER READING: Much of Grosseteste's work still remains unedited, but in the last thirty years some of his major philosophical and theological works have received critical attention. His Oxford writings have been published in the British Academy's *Auctores Britannici Medii Aevi* series: *Hexaëmeron* (1982), with a recent translation by C.F.J. Martin (1996); *De cessatione legalium* (1986); *De decem mandatis* (1987). A new sub-series in the CCCM dedicated to new editions has recently begun, with Grosseteste's *Expositio super epistolam s. Pauli ad Galatas, Glossarum in s. Pauli epistolas* and *Tabula* (Turnhout, 1995). The editorial team of J.W. Goering and F.A.C Mantello have edited many of Grosseteste's smaller pastoral works, published in various scholarly journals, as well as the *Templum Dei* (Toronto, 1984). Critical editions of Grosseteste's commentary on the Psalms, the *Dicta*, and his translation of and commentary on the Pseudo-Dionysian corpus are all underway. Some of his sermons have also been edited by J. McEvoy and S. Gieben. Grosseteste's *Epistolae* were printed in the Rolls Series 25 (1861). A comprehensive survey of Grosseteste's writings was completed by S.H. Thomson, *The Writings of Robert Grosseteste* (Cambridge, 1940).

For his philosophical and scientific works, see the editions of L. Baur, *Die Philosophischen Werke des Robert Grosseteste, Bischofs von Lincoln* (Münster, 1912), although some are in need of editorial revision. R.C. Dales edited Grosseteste's *Commentarius in VIII libros physicarum Aristotelis* (Boulder, CO, 1963), and P. Rossi rendered an edition of his *Commentarius in libros analyticorum posterium Aristotelis* (Florence, 1980).

The most recent biography is R.W. Southern, *Robert Grosseteste: The Growth of an English Mind in Medieval Europe* (Oxford, 1986), but F. Stevenson, *Robert Grosseteste Bishop of Lincoln* (London, 1899) is still of some use. The collection of essays in *Robert Grosseteste, Scholar and Bishop* (ed. D. Callus; Oxford, 1955) remains essential reading. See also the recent studies in *Robert Grosseteste: New Perspectives in his Thought and Scholarship* (ed. J. McEvoy; Turnhout, 1995). Also relevant is J. McEvoy, *The Philosophy of Robert Grosseteste* (Oxford, 1982) and S. Marrone, *William of Auvergne and Robert Grosseteste* (Princeton, 1983).

Grotius, Hugo (1583–1645)

Born in 1583, Hugo Grotius was even in his youth proclaimed the 'miracle of Holland'. As a latter-day humanist he made a broad contribution to the political and literary life of his times. Having held the office of Advocate-Fiscal of Holland (1607–13), it was in his role as Pensionary of Rotterdam from 1613 that he increasingly identified himself with the defenders of *Jacob Arminius in the growing struggle against a *Calvinist theology which was married to a centralizing political programme led by Prince Maurits of Nassau. The political role Grotius played led to his arrest and imprisonment in the Louvestein castle in 1618. Aided by his wife, he escaped in 1621 and fled to France where he was awarded a pension by Louis XIII. After a failed attempt to resettle in Holland in 1631, he spent his later years in Paris as the ambassador for Queen Christina of Sweden. He died as the result of a shipwreck during the night of 28–29 August 1645.

Today Grotius is known to but a few, and principally as the founding father of a secularized doctrine of natural law and the inventor of the 'Governmental Theory' of the atonement. This remains the case despite the recent republication of a number of major critical editions of works by Grotius with extensive commentary and English translations (see below). Both elements of his current reputation are misleading. He did indeed make a significant contribution to both the philosophy of law and the just war theory with his monumental *De iure belli ac pacis* (1625), but he sits uncomfortably with the progenitors of modernity. The infamous *etiamsi daremus* statement from the prolegomena to the work allows the continued existence of the natural law without the existence of God – but it is a hypothetical thought experiment, quickly rejected. For Grotius, the existence of the universe without God was of course an impossibility, and even within his thought experiment he envisaged the survival of only a weakened form of the natural law. Following the *etiamsi daremus* he explains that nature itself requires the worship of the one God, thus showing that he envisages only a partial continuance of the natural law. In an earlier work defending an Erastian position, *De imperio summarum* (not published until 1647), Grotius goes so far as to argue that worship of the Trinity follows from the principles of natural law (iii.3).

In *De satisfactione Christi* – his answer to the radical view of the atonement proposed by Faustus Socinus (1539–1604) – Grotius does indeed stress the governmental justification of the penal doctrine, which he considers (with good reason) to be the Catholic doctrine of the atonement. He argues that in the doctrine of the atonement God should be considered as Ruler, rather than as Judge (c.2). His point, however, is a limited one: he merely intends to show that the one who transfers punishment from the guilty to the innocent must be a ruler, since a judge is bound by the law. Indeed, in a letter to Gerardus Vossius of 14 June 1618, he states that he does think of God as a judge, even in the doctrine of the atonement – but not the sort of judge who is under the law. When, in speaking of God as Ruler, Grotius draws attention to the governmental aspect of the atonement, he says no more than the apostle Paul, who speaks of God demonstrating his justice in the cross (Rom. 3:25–26) and making by it a public spectacle of the rulers and authorities (Col. 2:13–15).

Furthermore, despite the common reading of *De satisfactione*, Grotius does not convert the substitutionary death of Christ into a penal example rather than the exact equivalent of the punishment deserved by sinners. He uses the language of example merely to emphasize the Pauline theme of public demonstration, not to replace a retributive account of punishment: the two ideas of public example and retribution are not mutually exclusive. When he denies that the performance by Jesus was the same as the punishment deserved by sinners (c.6), he explains the difference purely in terms of the fact that Jesus was not the one intended for punishment but was the one who endured it. In other words, he defines the difference solely by reference to the person punished, not to the measure of the punishment itself. Hence, when Grotius elucidates the nature of the justice manifested in the atonement, he adduces passages from the New Testament which make plain reference to the wrath of God against sinners on the last day (c.1). Grotius does not invent a new doctrine of the atonement which disagrees with that of the Protestant Reformers, but he rather makes an important contribution to the development of the penal doctrine which they had emphasized.

Grotius wrote works on a wide range of other theological subjects which are now less well known. His apologetic work *De veritate Christianae religionis* (1627) proved to be immensely popular; since 1645 there have been over one hundred and forty editions in various languages. He also engaged in detailed exegetical work in his *Annotationes* on the Old and New Testaments (1641–50), which are sometimes cited as an early example of historical-critical scholarship. They do contain some novel opinions derived from a historical-contextual approach unusual for the time, and on occasion the comments even tend in a *Socinian direction against the earlier and more reliable exegesis contained in *De satisfactione*. Again, however, it is wrong to use these writings to locate Grotius at the start of the critical age. His theology as a whole, including his exegesis, properly identifies him as a late-Reformation author following the irenical humanistic approach to theological questions and to the text of Scripture witnessed, for example, in the work of *Philip Melanchthon, rather than as an early proponent of the critical secularism of the *Enlightenment.

GARRY WILLIAMS

FURTHER READING: *Texts: De imperio summarum potestatum circa sacra*, in *Opera Omnia Theologica* (3 vols.; Amsterdam, 1679), 3:201–291; *De veritate Christianae religionis*, in *Opera Omnia Theologica* (3 vols.; Amsterdam, 1679), 3:1–96; *An English Translation of the Six Books of Hugo Grotius on the Truth of Christianity* (trans. S. Madan; London,

1814); *De jure belli ac pacis* (ed. J.B. Scott; *The Classics of International Law* 3.1, photographic reproduction of the 1646 edn; Washington, DC, 1913); Vol. II (trans. F.W. Kelsey, et al.; Oxford / London, 1925); *Meletius sive de iis quae inter Christianos conveniunt epistola* (ed. and trans. G.H.M. Posthumus Meyjes; Leiden, 1988); *Defensio fidei catholicae de satisfactione Christi adversus Faustum Socinum Senensem, Opera theologica* I (ed. E. Rabbie; trans. H. Mulder; Assen / Maastricht, 1990); *Ordinum Hollandiae ac Westfrisiae pietas* (ed. and trans. E. Rabbie; Leiden, 1995). *Studies:* W.S.M. Knight, *The Life and Works of Hugo Grotius* (The Grotius Society Publications 4; London, 1925); L.F.M. Besselink, 'The Impious Hypothesis Revisited', *Grotiana* NS 9 (1988), pp. 3–63; 'Bibliography', *Grotiana* NS 14–15 (1993–94), pp. 63–114; H.J.M. Nellen and E. Rabbie (eds.), *Hugo Grotius: Theologian* (Leiden, 1994).

Gustafson, James (b. 1925)

From his birth in 1925, nurture in a pious family and awakening to modernist approaches to life at Northwestern University to his wider intellectual and theological explorations at the University of Chicago Divinity School (especially under James Luther Adams) and at Yale University (especially under H. Richard Niebuhr), Gustafson was an intellectual leader. He sought to relate theology to the historical, social and natural sciences on the basis of a deep conviction, widely held in the United Church of Christ, into which he was ordained, that theology at its best is not irrational or privileged. Instead, it is a form of public discourse that has as its object the issue of God. Thus theology is also concerned with the questions of the norms for life, the ultimate ends of existence and the awareness that something is more meaningful than our anthropocentric constructions, needs, desires and wants. Gustafson became the chief heir in his generation of the tradition of the great German scholar *Ernst Troeltsch (1865–1923), who shaped his teachers, *Paul Tillich, and many others.

What has attracted many to his work and provided a key point of contention for those doubtful about it, is precisely the attempt to develop a view of God, a 'theocentric perspective', that is rooted in an analysis of the way things 'really and ultimately are'. These are common themes in his teaching at Yale Divinity School, as a visiting professor at Harvard, after his return to Chicago as a university professor, and

subsequently in a rather unique position at Emory University, where he teaches a seminar only for selected professors from many fields.

This theme of developing a theocentric perspective appears also in books and articles stretching from his *Treasure in Earthen Vessels* (1961) and *Christ and the Moral Life: The Church as Human Community* (1968) to his most systematic statement, *Ethics from a Theocentric Perspective* (2 vols.; 1981, 1984), and his most recent *Intersections: Science, Theology, and Ethics* (1996). He has consistently begun his inquiries into the human, affective, social and natural sources of meaning and proceeded to seek the ways in which these reveal and maintain a relationship to God – the non-subjective, objective source and norm of all being, thinking, living and doing.

Gustafson consistently argues that a theological view is necessary for a deep interpretation of the structures and dynamics of time and experience, even if it is only through the relativities of time and experience that we come to the more generic views of the way things 'really and ultimately are'. Further, he holds that a profound hermeneutics of life will unveil a moral realism – a view that ethical matters can be assessed as right or wrong, and not viewed either as a divine command known only to the eyes of faith or merely a construction of our existential experience. Thus Gustafson has taken an alternative position in theology and ethics to both the *Barthian dogmatic and confessional approaches that have dominated much of European and American evangelical thought over much of the last century, and to the tendency of much *Schleiermacherian romantic and 'radical' views of theology that tend to become entirely historicist, subjectivist and situational. Neither has developed a sustained and compelling way of dealing with the more universal dimensions of logic, warrant and integrity that are required for all scientific and moral reflection.

Gustafson remains deeply committed to that form of the liberal theological agenda that is willing to revise, challenge or jettison those biblical views or traditional doctrines that cannot be coherently conceived as converging with what can be known from the best of the humanities and the sciences. Yet he insists that theological issues are at the root of every deep inquiry. His back and forth movements from divinity school to university signal less a path of career advances than they signal the way his mind works as he seeks to fulfil his vocation.

Gustafson presses his students and readers to acknowledge that simply to be in a religious tradition gives one no special knowledge that can override what also can be known in other ways. This is not to say that faith has no noetic content. Rather, every discipline requires faith in and the honest pursuit of the faith that things have, or reflect, or suggest, some ultimate meaning. The exploration of just these matters leads to theology. At the same time, theology may not claim special privilege even if what it points toward is required for and by all.

Few theologians or ethicists in this generation have been as careful about laying out and taking seriously the arguments of others. This appears equally in his treatment of biblical scholars, business executives, university scientists and theologians with whom he does not fully agree. Gustafson's expositions of such Protestant authors as *Walter Rauschenbusch, Reinhold Niebuhr and *Paul Ramsey and those of Catholic thinkers such as Charles Curran, Bernard Haring and *Karl Rahner are judiciously fair (see, e.g., his *Protestant and Roman Catholic Ethics* [1978]). Still, his work in this area has been especially criticized because he does not argue strongly from a position that focuses on Christ, and because the God of which he speaks seems quite dispassionate and even impersonal (see the seven articles, 'Focus on the Ethics of J. Gustafson', *J Rel Ethics* 13.1). These are charges to which he replies with sharp intensity (*J Rel Ethics* 13.2).

However, it is true that Gustafson's emphasis sets aside those accents in traditional theology in which God is viewed as an agent with intellect, moral intentions and will who exercises this wisdom, purpose and care essentially for persons or even humanity at large. God, in his near Stoic view (which has continuities with some Scandinavian Lutheran and Puritan Reformed views), is not androcentric, even if much theology is. Instead, God's reality is the source and norm for the divine governance of all things. Humans ought not to be utterly preoccupied with their own well being, or even salvation; but ought to accept realities that are larger than humankind can reach.

It is from this perspective that Gustafson treats a range of practical issues from moral education, the character of technology, marriage and the family, the church as a community of moral discourse, ecological questions, medical ethics and the nature of modern business, as can be found in *Theology and Christian Ethics* (1974), the second volume of his systematics, a host of essays, and the recent Festschrift written by his close students and friends, *Christian Ethics: Problems and Prospects* (1996). Other theologians and ethicists may have been more widely known in the last decade of the twentieth century, but the work of few others is likely to endure longer into the next.

MAX L. STACKHOUSE

FURTHER READING: *Texts: Treasure in Earthen Vessels: The Church as a Human Community* (New York, 1961); *Christ and the Moral Life* (New York, 1968); *Ethics from a Theocentric Perspective* (2 vols.; Chicago, 1981, 1984); *Intersections: Science, Theology, and Ethics* (Cleveland, OH, 1996); *Protestant and Roman Catholic Ethics: Prospects for Rapprochement* (Chicago, 1978); *Theology and Christian Ethics* (Philadelphia, 1974). *Studies:* L.S. Cahill and J.F. Childress (eds.), *Christian Ethics: Problems and Prospects* (Cleveland, OH, 1996); 'Focus on the Ethics of J. Gustafson', *J Rel Ethics* 13.1 (1985), pp. 1–112 (and Gustafson's reply in *J Rel Ethics* 13.2 [1985], pp. 185–209).

Gutiérrez, Gustavo (b. 1928)

The Peruvian priest Gustavo Gutiérrez Merino was born 8 June 1928 in Lima. After his education and training for the priesthood at universities in Latin America (Lima and Santiago) and Europe (Louvain, Lyons and Rome) he returned to Peru in 1960 to teach at the Catholic University in Lima and act as adviser to the National Union of Catholic Students. His contributions in the late 1960s to the emerging radical Catholic social theology known as Latin American *Liberation Theology were decisive in setting its agenda and winning official support from the Latin American bishops. Since then he has continued to be one of its most influential and respected proponents.

In 1968 the Latin American bishops had signalled a new direction for the church at their Second General Meeting (CELAM II) in Medellín, Colombia. Gutiérrez had served as a theological adviser at the meeting and his contributions encouraged their decisive commitment to the Latin American poor. Just before the meeting, Gutiérrez had started to promote the term 'liberation' in clerical circles to do justice to the complexity of salvation at the political, historical and theological level. Other progressive thinkers in Latin America influenced his use of the term during the 1960s, especially in the social sciences and educational theory. New ways of thinking in other academic disciplines had created an 'atmosphere of liberation' amongst intellectuals across the continent. In left-wing circles 'liberation' had come to be understood as implying an overturning (revolution) of existing procedures and a rejection of dependency.

In 1971 Gutiérrez systematized his work of the 1960s in a book-length study, *A Theology of Liberation* (ET 1973), that was the first and remains one of the most influential statements of Liberation Theology. This work set out a theological justification for making 'liberation' the key term for interpreting Christian faith in Latin America, argued for a pastoral and ethical identification with the Latin American poor and sketched a new methodology that made theology a reflection on praxis. The work reveals a wide range of intellectual influences (including nouvelle théologie, psychology, European philosophy and biblical scholarship) but was controversial due to its adoption of *Marxist analysis and advocacy in some passages of a socialist alternative to capitalism.

Since the early 1970s Gutiérrez's work has developed in a number of ways, but it has always remained consistent with the basic principle identified in *A Theology of Liberation* that 'history is one', and the temporal and spiritual realms are intimately connected. In the 1970s Gutiérrez was greatly influenced by the base community movement in Latin America and started to root his work more directly in the experiences of the communities and the everyday lives of the poor. Although he travels and has taught at international universities, he has continued to serve as a local parish priest in the working-class district of Rimac, Lima.

Much of Gutiérrez's writing originally takes the form of articles, often for the Peruvian pastoral journal *Páginas* or similar publications. Lengthier and more academic articles – such as those published for *Concilium* (for which he served on the international editorial review) are then usually subsequently published in books. *The Power of the Poor in History* (1979, ET 1983) examined the Latin American Church's 'option for the poor' from what he called 'the underside of history'. During the 1980s he and other Liberation theologians faced a period of intense pressure from Rome. Partly in response to this

pressure, his writing moved away from its early 1970s engagement with Marxist analysis and gave greater attention to spirituality and biblical reflection. *We Drink from Our Own Wells* (1983, ET 1984), *On Job* (1985, ET 1987) and *The God of Life* (1982, ET 1991) retain the ethical commitment to the poor that had characterized his work from the outset but show a noticeably different tone from that of *A Theology of Liberation*. These later works engage more directly with the Bible and the experiences of the church and the oppressed in Latin America. During the 1980s Gutiérrez made efforts to extend his analysis of oppression beyond class and colonialism to touch on race, culture and gender. His own *mestizo* (mixed-race) background made him more sensitive to the suffering of the Amerindian indigenous population at home, and his active participation in the Ecumenical Association of Third World Theologians in the 1970s and 1980s extended his awareness of oppression elsewhere.

His collection of writings *The Truth Shall Make You Free* (1986, ET 1990) presented his response to criticisms of his work – especially the Vatican's concern over the uncritical use of Marxist analysis by Liberation theologians. The book – which includes a long piece from his oral exam at the University of Lyons where he was awarded a doctorate on the basis of his publications – provides the most nuanced and careful statement on his willingness to use Marxist analysis. Here he rejects aspects of Marxist philosophy such as atheism and historical determinism. Publication of a revised edition of *A Theology of Liberation* in 1988 also allowed Gutiérrez to clarify his position in the face of previous criticism. Despite continuing suspicion and hostility from the Vatican and some Peruvian bishops, Gutiérrez escaped the official censure suffered by his Liberationist colleagues like Leonardo Boff and Ivone Gebara in Brazil.

The 1990s proved a difficult decade for Liberation Theology for a number of reasons, but for Gutiérrez this decade provided the opportunity to publish a lengthy historical work on Bartolomé de las Casas, *Las Casas: In Search of the Poor of Jesus Christ* (1992, ET 1993). The sixteenth-century Dominican friar known as the 'defender of the Indians' had long served as an inspiration for Gutiérrez, and he had been working on this book for many years. The book is noteworthy as a piece of historical scholarship as well as theological insight. Gutiérrez explores the work of Las Casas and relates it to the challenges faced by the Latin American Church in the twentieth century.

Gutiérrez's overall contribution to post-Conciliar Catholic theology has been immense. In its focus and methodology, Liberation Theology was the first distinctive alternative to the traditional dominance of Europe and North America in Christian theological thought. Gutiérrez has been a leading proponent and interpreter of the movement and has formulated many of its most memorable and incisive ideas in the process. In presenting a theology that stresses social justice and concern for the poor he has inspired many in Latin America and elsewhere to a new understanding of the ethical and political dimensions of Christian faith.

DAVID TOMBS

FURTHER READING: *Texts:* Major works by Gutiérrez: *The Power of the Poor in History* (trans. R.R Barr; Maryknoll, NY / London, 1983), Sp. orig. *La Fuerza Historica de las Pobres* (Lima, 1979); *We Drink from Our Own Wells: The Spiritual Journey of a People* (trans. M.J. O'Connell; Maryknoll, NY / London, 1984), Sp. orig. *Beber en su Proprio Pozo: En el Itinerario Espiritual de un Pueblo* (Lima, 1983); *On Job: God-Talk and the Suffering of the Innocent* (trans. M.J. O'Connell; Maryknoll, NY / London, 1987), Sp. orig. *Hablar del Dios desde el Sufrimiento del Inocente* (Lima, 2nd edn, 1986); *The Truth Shall Make You Free: Confrontations* (trans. M.J. O'Connell; Maryknoll, NY, 1990), rev. from Sp. orig. *La Verdad las Hará Libres: Confrontationes* (Lima, 1986); *The God of Life* (trans. M.J. O'Connell; Maryknoll, NY / London, 1991), Sp. orig. *El Dios de la Vida* (Lima, rev. edn, 1989); *Las Casas: In Search of the Poor of Jesus Christ* (trans. R.R. Barr; Maryknoll, NY, 1993), Sp. orig. *En Busca de los Pobres de Jesucristo* (Lima, 1992); *Sharing the Word through the Liturgical Year* (Maryknoll, NY / London, 1997), Sp. orig. *Compartir la Palabra: A lo Largo del Año Litúrgico* (Lima, 1995); Gustavo Gutiérrez and Richard Shaull, *Liberation and Change* (ed. Ronald H. Stone; Schaff Lectures; Atlanta, 1977). *Studies:* Curt Cadorette, *From the Heart of the People: The Theology of Gustavo Gutiérrez* (Oak Park, IL, 1988); Robert McAfee Brown, *Gustavo Gutiérrez: An Introduction to Liberation Theology* (Maryknoll, NY, 1990).

Harnack, Adolf (1851–1930)

Adolf Harnack (von Harnack from 1914) was the most important representative of theological historicism in Germany. He was the outstanding church historian of his day and one of the most influential academic administrators in the Wilhelmine empire.

Harnack was born a son of the Lutheran theologian Theodosius Harnack (1816–89) on 7 May 1851 in the Baltic city of Dorpat (now Tartu). As early as his student days Harnack had begun to move away from the Christian orthodoxy propounded both by his father and most of his academic teachers. He argued that clarity about the truth of Christian faith would only be gained through a consistently historical approach – an approach that reflected the influence of *Albrecht Ritschl (1822–89), with whose theology Harnack aligned himself closely. Harnack especially took up Ritschl's demand that theology have a secure, historically-grounded, philological foundation. In his own research into texts and history, Harnack made consistent use of the methods of critical analysis which contemporary academic historians were developing. As a result of this, Harnack drew conclusions with respect to some dogmatic questions (e.g. the resurrection, the significance of the historical Jesus) which were vehemently rejected by the *Lutheran Church.

Harnack's academic output was prodigious. After a short time as an external lecturer, he became assistant professor at Leipzig in 1876 and then, in 1879, full professor in church history at Gieflen. He was then appointed to chairs in Marburg (1886) and finally to the Friedrich-Wilhelm University in Berlin (1888), where he taught until becoming professor emeritus in 1921. In Berlin, he covered not only many periods in church history, but he also lectured on modern theology, symbolism and the New Testament. In addition to his university work, Harnack was also director of the Royal Library in Berlin from 1905 to 1921 and, from 1910 to his death, president of the Kaiser Wilhelm Society (later the Max Planck Society), built up by Harnack to become the most important organization for the development of the sciences in Germany.

Much of Harnack's academic endeavour was undertaken under the auspices of the Prussian Academy of Sciences, of which he became a member in 1890. Harnack led the commission undertaking the editing of the works of the Greek Fathers, and he was entrusted with the task of writing the official history of the Academy on the occasion of its two hundredth anniversary (which appeared in 3 volumes in 1900). Harnack was also active in social and political affairs. From 1903 to 1912 he was president of the Evangelical Social Congress. In this capacity, Harnack was engaged in a programme of reform directed towards improved social conditions. He was critical of the ever-increasing economic power of large-scale industry. After 1918 Harnack spoke out in favour of the introduction of parliamentary democracy. His political stance enabled him at times to exert a substantial influence upon the Prussian ministry of education. He was trusted by the ministry of culture as well as by Kaiser Wilhelm II (1859–1941). He died in Heidelberg on 10 June 1930, during a trip undertaken in his role as president of the Kaiser Wilhelm Society. As is evidenced by a posthumously published collection of sermons (*Vom inwendigen Leben* [1931]), Harnack possessed a deep, personal piety. One of Harnack's sons belonged to the resistance movement against Hitler and was executed in 1945.

Harnack first became a public figure in the 1890s as a result of his stance in the dispute about the use of the *Apostles' Creed in the liturgy of the church. Harnack spoke against the rejection of the creed, but he argued in favour of extending people's knowledge about its history. His lectures on the 'essence of Christianity', delivered in the winter semester of 1899–1900 in Berlin and quickly appearing in book form (ET *What is Christianity?*), had an immediate and sensational impact. It was Harnack's intention to expound the Christian faith in a comprehensible way, and with due regard for modern living. The 'Gospel of Jesus', understood to be the original, pure doctrinal heart of Christian faith, was the focal point of his exposition. In a very short time, the book went through twenty editions. An English translation appeared in the same year as the German original. It remains a classic document of the theology of *Liberal Protestantism in Germany. In his *Lehrbuch der Dogmengeschichte* (3 vols., 1886–90; ET *History of Dogma* [7 vols.; 1896–99]), his main academic work, Harnack describes the origin and development of Christian doctrine. In his account, early Christian theology and dogma are seen as the result of a process in which, as a result of the activity of *Gnostic theologians, the gospel became subject to Hellenization to a radical degree.

Harnack linked to his historicist understanding of history the notion, drawn from Idealism, of the ethical progress of humankind, as brought about by Spirit. Following *Schleiermacher, he links religion indissolubly with the pious consciousness of being a child of God. However, he saw the community of the church as the context within which this individual religious sensibility emerges and develops. All through his life Harnack had considerably more respect and sympathy for churches and denominations than his opponents give him credit for. A second basic motif in Harnack's understanding of religion is the relationship between religion and culture. In Harnack's view, religion in modern culture is constantly confronted by secular interpretations of reality. A central task of Protestant theology is therefore to highlight the way in which western culture has been influenced by Christianity on many levels. Faith is not, however, to be derived from culture. He frequently adopts a critical stance towards culture. Misguided movements in culture, such as materialism and atheism, are identifiable, Harnack claims, precisely because of their opposition to faith. In this regard, the criticism launched by *Karl Barth (1886–1968), who in a famous controversy in 1923 accused Harnack of giving up the gospel in favour of culture, misses the mark. Harnack's goal in his theological critique of culture is the activation of the ethical potential of Christian faith. His concern is to render the concept of God ethically effective. In doing this, he seeks to make clear the indispensability of religion for the structuring of life in a humane way. Through this directly practical interest in particular, Harnack reveals the extent to which he represents the theological self-understanding of Liberal Protestantism at the dawn of the twentieth century.

MATTHIAS WOLFES

FURTHER READING: *Texts: Geschichte der altchristlichen Literatur* (3 vols.; Leipzig, 1893, 1897, 1904); *Wesen des Christentums* (Leipzig, 1900; ET *What is Christianity?* [1900 and many later edns]); *Adolf von Harnack als Zeitgenosse: Reden und Schriften aus den Jahren des Kaiserreiches und der Weimarer Republik* (ed. and intro. by Kurt Nowak; bibliographical appendix by Hanns-Christoph Picker; Berlin / New York, 1996). *Studies:* Friedrich Smend, *Adolf von Harnack* (Leipzig, 1927; repr. with additions 1990); Agnes von Zahn-Harnack, *Adolf von Harnack* (Berlin, 1936); Martin Rumscheidt (ed.), *Adolf von Harnack: Liberal Theology at its Height* (London, 1989).

Hegel, Georg Wilhelm Friedrich (1770–1831)

German Idealist philosopher. After a classical education at the Stuttgart Gymnasium, he entered the *Stift* at the University of Tübingen in 1788 as a Lutheran seminarian. Disillusioned by the prevailing scholastic *Lutheranism, he turned to more radical movements in philosophy and culture: *Kantian philosophy, the ideals of the French Revolution and German *Romanticism. Hegel completed his theological studies but was never ordained, choosing instead to work as a tutor. Nevertheless, a number of his early writings are explicitly theological in character, arguing that the Christian gospel is at heart concerned with moral beauty. In 1801 he became *Privatdozent* at the University of Jena, rising eventually to succeed the great Idealist J.G. Fichte (1762–1814) as professor of philosophy in Berlin in 1818. Hegel occupied this post until his death.

Hegel's mature philosophy is a bewilderingly complex synthesis of themes from the whole of western philosophy from the ancient Greeks through to the Idealist movement. In his first major philosophical work, *The Phenomenology of Spirit* (1807), Hegel attempted to set in logical relation the general historical forms taken by human self-consciousness. In this work, and in his later writings, Hegel presented his own thought as the culmination of the history of philosophy, in the sense that he understood himself in relation to this history and as inseparable from it. Although frequently accused of developing a wholly abstract, purely theoretical approach to philosophical truth, Hegel in fact assumes that philosophy can be developed only in relation to historical reality. He therefore assumes the truth of previous philosophical systems, and so attempts to build upon previous intellectual developments. Already in the *Phenomenology*, and again later in his *Encyclopaedia of the Philosophical Sciences* (3rd edn, 1830), he presents the cultural institutions of art, religion and philosophy in ascending sequence as the means by which truth in the form of human self-conscious life is transmitted and known.

Hegel's contribution to the history of Christian theology is considerable. In his doctrine of God, first of all, Hegel emphasizes the divine subjectivity, distinguishing between the idea of God as substance and God as subject. This theme, which is first stated in the *Phenomenology*, can also be found in Hegel's later *Lectures on* *the Philosophy of Religion* (1840, posthumously). Subjectivity alone allows for movement and development within the divine life. The more classical conception of divine substance is not abandoned, but it is regarded as lifeless, and therefore as in itself inadequate. It would be fair to speak of divine subjectivity as Hegel's essential concern in all his constructive thinking concerning God. The concept of God as subject rather than substance subsequently became a central theme in nineteenth-century liberal Protestantism, and even appears prominently in the theology of *K. Barth (1886–1968).

Hegel's philosophy can be understood as a Trinitarian elaboration on the central idea of God as subject. Although both the structure and detail of Hegelian Trinitarianism is disputed, it is clear that Hegel wishes to define his philosophy as a Trinitarian enterprise, and even as a Trinitarian *theological* enterprise, over against the prevailing anti-Trinitarianism of *Enlightenment theology. Hegel's distinctive contribution to the doctrine of the Trinity lies in his conception of the 'passing over' of the Absolute (God) into the finite as a function of the logic of divine freedom. The capacity of the Absolute to be what it is both in itself and in its self-alienation is the root of the Hegelian conception of *Geist*, or Spirit. As Spirit, God is the unity-in-difference of his eternal transcendent being and his self-alienation in the finite. Expressing this in Christological terms, we may say that for Hegel, Jesus can only be fully understood as the incarnate, crucified and risen one who has been exalted to the right hand of the Father, and thus who has been exalted as the Lord of the church.

Hegel had many theological disciples, and his direct and indirect influence on the history of philosophy and theology has been enormous. During the nineteenth century, a variety of important streams of Protestant theology traced themselves back to Hegel's writings. Much of kenotic theory, for example, allied itself with Hegel's philosophy. It is, however, important to note that Hegel was decidedly opposed to the theology of *F. Schleiermacher (1768–1834), whom he knew personally as a colleague in Berlin, and whose thought subsequently prevailed in nineteenth-century Protestantism. Schleiermacher's religion of feeling owes much to the Romantic movement to which Hegel too belonged in his youth, but Hegel's mature position corresponds much more closely to the view stated by *Justin Martyr: those who in any time or place live by reason are Christians. For Hegel, God is supremely rational, while the logic of the divine *Geist* is also the organizing principle of literally the whole of reality – including the reality of human self-consciousness.

In the *Lectures on the Philosophy of Religion*, Hegel argues that his philosophical system attempts, in relation to Christianity, to do in the context of modern philosophy what the ancient Church Fathers attempted to do in their adaptations of *Platonic thought to the Christian gospel. This claim is to be understood in the context of the distinctive Hegelian doctrine of religion as *Vorstellung*, or imaginative, pictorial thinking – as opposed to philosophical thinking. The latter is understood to raise images to more adequate, conceptual form. Hegel's thesis is that this is what the ancient church did in its development of the doctrine of the Trinity. The apparent downgrading of religious imagery which this seems to imply, however, helps to explain why Hegel's own claim of adherence to the content of the Christian revelation is seldom taken by Hegel's theological critics at face value. In fact, Hegel's claim provides what is perhaps the clearest indication of the relation in which he himself stood to the Christian religion, and the sense in which he asks us to understand his philosophy.

GARY D. BADCOCK

FURTHER READING: *Texts: Encyclopedia of the Philosophical Sciences in Outline, and Other Philosophical Writings* (ed. Ernst Behler; New York, 1990); *Gesammelte Werke, Auftrag der Deutschen Forschungsgemeinschaft* (Hamburg, 1969–); *On Christianity: Early Theological Writings* (New York, ET 1948); *Lectures on the Philosophy of Religion* (ed. Peter Hodgson; 3 vols.; Berkeley, ET 1984–85). *Studies:* Karl Barth, 'Hegel', in *Protestant Theology in the Nineteenth Century* (London, ET 1972); Emil Fackenheim, *The Religious Dimension in Hegel's Thought* (Bloomington, IN, 1967); Hans Küng, *The Incarnation of God* (Edinburgh, ET 1987).

Hegelianism

During the decades immediately following Hegel's death in 1831, his disciples divided into two main camps. Crucially, the dispute between them largely concerned religion. In Hegel's philosophy, religion is the truth in the limited form of imagery, or *Vorstellung*. Through philosophy, however, this truth can be expressed in a form more adequate to its content. Some of Hegel's disciples (the so-called 'old' or 'right-wing' Hegelians) understood this to mean that Hegel's philosophy, while ultimately transcending the imagery of religion, allowed religion basically to stand within its sphere as a valid expression of truth, and even as a necessary form of truth's self-expression. The Hegelian philosophy, on such a reading, amounts to a speculative bulwark against the collapse of religious belief in the modern era. Hegel's more radical disciples (the 'young' or 'left-wing' Hegelians), on the other hand, saw fit to lay greater emphasis on the theme of the sublimation of religion in philosophy. On such a reading, Hegel's philosophy is to be understood as an implicit atheism and thus as the end of religion.

In retrospect, we may say that it was the young Hegelians who gained the upper hand. This group included such seminal figures as *Ludwig Feuerbach (1804–72), Friedrich Engels (1820–95), *Karl Marx (1818–83) and *David Friedrich Strauss (1808–74), along with the lesser-known Bruno Bauer (1809–92). Bauer himself, as possibly the most committed Hegelian among the group, believed that he had completed Hegel's imperfect atheism. According to Bauer, the real sublimation of religion lies not in the philosophical idea, as in Hegel's own writings, but in the development of the concrete reality of individual self-consciousness as the locus of truth. All else is abstraction. Strauss, by contrast, left room in his system for human culture, but like Bauer, was sceptical towards religion as religion. Feuerbach, Engels and Marx took a different route, Feuerbach arguing the case for an understanding of the Christian religion as the truth of humanity, while for Engels and Marx, Hegelian theoretical consciousness must be transformed to a practical end, and religion thereby abolished.

The old Hegelians included the Danish theologian against whom *Søren Kierkegaard (1813–55) railed, Bishop H.L. Martensen (1808–84), who taught a distinctive but broadly Hegelian integration of speculative philosophy and *Lutheran Christianity. It is notable, however, that much twentieth-century theology has been preoccupied with either the Kierkegaardian theological reaction against the perceived excesses of Hegelianism or with the anti-theology of the young Hegelians. The work of the more moderate old Hegelians has too often been overlooked. Their number included, however, advocates of kenotic Christology: I.A.

Dorner (1809–84) and *G. Thomasius (1802–73) both forged links between Christology and the philosophy of Hegel. Another of the old Hegelians, *Ferdinand Christian Baur (1792–1860), took a different path as professor of historical theology at Tübingen (1826–60), founding the Tübingen school of biblical criticism. Its best-known contribution to Christian theology is the thesis that primitive Christianity was characterized by a struggle between 'Petrine' Jewish-Christian and 'Pauline' Gentile-Christian thought, the tension between the two being finally resolved in the development of Catholicism. Though now somewhat antiquated, this reading of ecclesiastical history has been very influential, and owes much to Hegel's conception of history as a movement of opposing forces that resolve themselves in a more comprehensive synthesis.

In Britain, Hegelianism took a different, and less divisive, path. Although George Eliot had translated Feuerbach's *Essence of Christianity* into English as early as 1846, the young Hegelians had relatively little impact on nineteenth-century British theology, or indeed on theology in the English language generally. From about 1870 down to as late as 1950, however, a distinctive Hegelian school can be identified within the British universities, including such figures as Edward Caird (1835–1908), his brother John Caird (1820–98), T.H. Green (1836–82), A.S. Pringle-Pattison (1856–1931), the young A.E. Taylor (1869–1945) and Clement C.J. Webb (1865–1954). It was a philosophy allied with religious faith, which attempted to employ Hegel as a means to escape the clutches of the reigning scientific materialism and to envision the universe as a spiritual whole, governed supremely by moral value. To this extent, British Hegelianism is akin to 'old' Hegelianism on the European continent. Its most prominent representatives were identifiably Christian. The Scottish theologian *H.R. Mackintosh (1870–1936), who had been a student of Pringle-Pattison, provides especially in his early theology an excellent example of the constructive direction in which a theological engagement with such philosophy can lead. The Hegelian tradition continued in Scotland, however, well beyond Mackintosh's day. John Macquarrie's teacher C.A. Campbell (1897–1974) was still working within this tradition of British Hegelianism as professor of logic and rhetoric in the University of Glasgow well into the 1950s.

On the whole, however, Hegelianism steadily lost ground following World War I.

In recent years, Hegel's thought has been partially resurrected, firstly within the 'death of God' movement of the 1960s (a new version of 'young' Hegelianism), but also within a certain tradition of constructive Christological and Trinitarian thought. Originating in Germany largely within Barthian circles but also, significantly, in Roman Catholic thought, Hegelianism has been used for approximately the past three decades by a variety of theologians in order to develop an understanding of God as relating himself to the world by 'passing over' into the finite. New resources for the development of a genuinely Christian doctrine of God are thus held to lie dormant within the Hegelian tradition. Among the theologians advocating such an approach in contemporary theology are the Lutherans *Wolfhart Pannenberg and *Eberhard Jüngel, the Catholics *Walter Kasper and *Hans Küng, and the Reformed theologian *Jürgen Moltmann. No contemporary theologian, however, has attempted a re-appropriation of the total vision of Hegelianism.

GARY D. BADCOCK

FURTHER READING: William J. Brazill, *The Young Hegelians* (New Haven, 1970); C.A. Campbell, *On Selfhood and Godhood* (London, 1957); Hans Küng, *The Incarnation of God* (Edinburgh, 1987); John Macquarrie, *Jesus Christ in Modern Thought* (London, 1990); Peter Robbins, *The British Hegelians, 1875–1925* (New York, 1982); Alan P.F. Sell, *Philosophical Idealism and Christian Belief* (Cardiff, 1995); Lawrence S. Stepelevich (ed.), *The Young Hegelians: An Anthology* (Cambridge, 1983); Claude Welch (ed.), *God and Incarnation in Mid-Nineteenth Century Theology* (New York, 1965).

Heppe, Heinrich (1820–79)

One of the leading systematic theologians and church historians of his generation, Heinrich Heppe was born in Kassel in Hesse, the son of an oboist in the court orchestra. He was educated at Marburg and, after completing his doctorate, was appointed pastor at St Martin's Church there in 1845. In the same year he began lecturing on church history at the university, publishing the first of several studies of the Hesse church in 1847: *Geschichte der hessischen Genralsynoden von 1568–1582*. A thorough examination of the Kassel archives convinced him that the origins of the church were not narrowly determined by *Luther, but were 'German-reformed', a position he identified chiefly with *Melanchthon. In 1849 Heppe was appointed *Privatdozent* at Marburg, becoming an 'extraordinary professor' in 1850.

Heppe's defence of the reformed roots of the Hesse church led him into a bitter conflict with the prominent Lutheran confessionalist August Vilmar (1800–68). Vilmar, director of the Gymnasium at Marburg, was also given government responsibility for the administration of the Hesse church in the political reaction after the revolution of 1848. The dispute between them was sparked off by Heppe's 1849 book, *Die Einführung der Verbesserungspunkte in Hessen von 1604–1610 und die Entstehung der hessischen Kirchenordnung von 1657*, and they continued to fight over the minutiae of *Reformation history, especially the role of Philip, Landgraf of Hesse (1504–67). After Vilmar's dismissal from the government and appointment as professor at Marburg in 1855, the dispute became more personalized. The issues, however, lay far deeper than the interpretation of the Reformation: the real battle was between liberalism and the attempt of reactionary forces led by Vilmar to gain control of the church. Vilmar sought to refashion the church on hierarchical lines, maintaining a supernatural understanding of the office of the church and its sacraments which resembled that of his contemporary *Edward Pusey (1800–82), in England. Indeed Vilmar was so opposed to any form of lay representation in church and state that he remarked: 'When I hear the word "synod", it is as if the devil is flying past me'. Vilmar's call for a 'pastors' Church', and the concomitant separation of church and state which rested on his theology of supernatural 'facts', was aimed at providing an alternative source of absolute authority independent of the state. In opposition to such confessionalism and reaction, Heppe identified with the cause of religious freedom against what he saw as an 'unevangelical hierarchy'. Heppe regarded the common 'evangelical' inheritance as of far more importance than mere confessionalism. Indeed, he could not trace the term 'Lutheran' used in distinction from 'Reformed' earlier than 1648 (*Ursprung und Geschichte der Bezeichnungen 'reformirte' und 'lutherische' Kirche*, 1859).

Heppe's support for liberal causes meant that, despite continued applications and recommendations, he was not called to an ordinary professorship until 1864. During this long period of considerable financial hardship as extraordinary professor Heppe was given an immense lecturing load, which became the basis for a number of important works, especially the four-volume *Geschichte des deutschen Protestantismus in den Jahren 1555–1581* (1852–59) and his biography of *Theodore Beza (1861). Heppe continued to add to his vast literary output during his years as ordinary professor, producing major studies of the Reformation, education and mysticism. Alongside his theological and historical work, Heppe was also involved in church reform and helped establish a diaconal house at Treysa. By the time of his death he was the leading member of the Marburg faculty, preparing the ground for what developed into Marburg liberalism under his successor, *Wilhelm Herrmann (1846–1922).

Although the bulk of Heppe's work was in Reformation history, he is remembered today chiefly for his three-volume *Die Dogmatik der evangelisch-reformierten Kirche* (1861; ET *Dogmatics of the Reformed Church*, London, 1950), based on lectures. This work, which consists of a large number of quotations drawn from a wide range of Reformed theologians from the sixteenth to early seventeenth centuries, interspersed with brief comments and dictated sections, was described by *Karl Barth in the foreword to the new edition of 1935 as 'out of date, dusty, unattractive, almost like a table of logarithms, dreary to read, stiff and eccentric on almost every page I opened' (*Dogmatics*, p. v). Despite this judgement, however, Heppe's influence on Barth's theological development was profound. On reading Heppe in 1924, Barth claims he was drawn 'visibly into the wider circle of the church' and led to an appreciation of the biblical roots of the Reformation, more 'meaningful than that stamped by Schleiermacher and Ritschl' (*Dogmatics*, p. v). Whatever its significance for Barth, however, Heppe understood his *Dogmatics* differently: instead of seeing it as a compendium of old Reformed orthodoxy, he regarded it as a conciliatory rather than as a confessional work. Heppe wrote in his tribute to Vilmar in 1868: 'We must not speak of Lutheran and reformed … As far as I see it, I must confess that I do not see myself as a representative of reformed dogmatics … With my Dogmatics, which I lecture on every winter, I am not standing on the ground of reformed systematics, but rather on Schleiermacher's theology … I regard

the differences of the confessions as of no importance' (Bizer, pp. 123f.). Not surprisingly, given its polemical background, Heppe's *Dogmatics* focuses on Melanchthon at the expense of *Calvin, and he does not even rank *Zwingli as an important source of Reformed dogmatics.

Perhaps ironically, given his influence on Barth's change of theological direction as represented in the *Göttingen Dogmatics* (cf. McCormack, pp. 327–74), Heppe fought against a revitalized confessionalism in modern theology, thereby preparing the ground for his liberal successors at Marburg. Similarly, his approach to church history, which he regarded as a branch of cultural history, as well as his return to the sources, were distinctively modern. Unlike Vilmar, Heppe placed a high value on human freedom but exercised his freedom in dialogue with the inheritance of the Reformation. Given the rhetorical and polemical character of much of his writing and his importance as a church historian, it is perhaps unfortunate that he should be judged solely on the basis of his rather dry *Dogmatics*.

MARK D. CHAPMAN

FURTHER READING: *Allgemeine deutsche Biographie*, XVI (Leipzig, 1875–1912), pp. 785–89; *Neue deutsche Biographie*, VIII (Berlin, 1953); *Rel G G*, III (Tübingen, 1957–65), pp. 226–27; E. Bizer in *Lebensbilder aus Kurhessen und Waldeck, 1830–1930*, VI (ed. I. Schnack; Marburg, 1958), pp. 112–26; H. Hermelink, *Das Christentum in der Menschheitsgeschichte*, II (Stuttgart, 1953); Bruce L. McCormack, *Karl Barth's Critical Realistic Dialectical Theology: Its Genesis and Development 1909–1936* (Oxford, 1995).

Herrmann, Wilhelm (1846–1922)

One of the leading representatives of liberal theology of his age, Wilhelm Herrmann was *Privatdozent* in Halle from 1875 and became professor of systematic theology in Marburg in 1879, where he remained until his retirement in 1917. He shared with his teacher *Albrecht Ritschl (1822–89) a vigorous distaste for all forms of metaphysics in theology, which he regarded as a way of circumventing revelation. However, whereas for Ritschl the value-judgement was a precursor to all knowledge, it was transformed in Herrmann to something inward, related to the isolation of the knowledge acquired in Christianity from the rest of knowledge.

Herrmann's theology can be understood as a response to *Kant's epistemological threat to Protestantism. Since in the Kantian view knowledge of the world could not be acquired immediately through the senses but was the work of the subject shaping sense-data in accordance with a priori laws of reason, Kant appeared to threaten the status of the directly revealed or freely given knowledge of faith. Knowledge of God thus had to be of a different kind from that of the natural world: unless we could think of God as 'wholly other', we would have to 'give up the idea of God's distinctiveness from the world and with it religion itself' (*Schriften zur Grundlegung der Theologie*, *SGT* hereafter [Munich, 1966–7] II, p. 27). Greatly influenced by his neo-Kantian Marburg colleague, Hermann Cohen, Herrmann held that Kantian epistemology should restrict itself to its own domain, that of the natural sciences. Religious epistemology, however, was of a quite different kind: there was simply 'no way from the world of science to the world of faith' (*SGT*, I, p. 115).

Herrmann thus sought a certainty which could never be achieved by science. Whereas science was directed towards a provable (*nachweisbar*) reality, religion was directly experienced (*erlebbar*) in the individual. Thus, by attempting to delineate the spheres of faith and science, Herrmann introduced a system of parallel realities which reflects an underlying ontological dualism. On the one hand, there was that mode of being expressed by scientific reality which could never reveal anything of true life while, on the other hand, there was the reality of faith, of 'life', which made manifest a higher realm of absolute or 'authentic' being. This religious experience was self-authenticating: 'it was impossible to give any other answer to the question of how an object can be presumed to be real which cannot be proved to others than by saying "through religion"' (*SGT*, II, p. 232). Religion concerned a higher world experienced in the activity of living, as the ' "whence" which we must accept' (*SGT*, I, p. 107).

For much of his career at Marburg, Herrmann was concerned with ethics, which he conceived as a 'different mode of life which separates itself off from the natural' (*Ethik* [Tübingen, 5th edn, 1913], p. 37). Religion provides the power to escape the conditions of a nature which inevitably conceals the ethical life. Joy is experienced when all the energies of the natural world are cast aside, as the previous life is overcome in faith in God. This power to escape nature emanates from the lips of Jesus who speaks to human beings in the inner experience 'in which we are truly alive' and in which we are given ethical power (*SGT*, I, p. 279). The 'impression (*Eindruck*)' of the personality of Jesus creates a 'certainty that a loving will is the omnipotent ground of all being and that we are called through him to an eternal goodness, to a blessed life in ethical freedom' (*SGT*, I, p. 122).

Herrmann's approach to history is similarly shaped by his epistemology: historical research, because it is forever trapped in the natural world, can reveal nothing of true religion. Criticizing the historical method of the *History of Religions School, he claimed that just as the 'authentic "historical" (*geschichtlich*) fact' of Jesus is not to be found in his ethical teaching or in his understanding of the kingdom of God but in the personal 'impression' which creates a 'life-history' in the individual, so 'real' or authentic experience is that direct self-authenticating experience of being in communion with God. All personal doubts are thus overcome in the appropriation of a revelation which is gained neither from the Bible nor from the church but solely from a direct 'experience' (*Erlebnis*) of Christ (*SGT*, I, p. 254). Knowledge of Jesus as saviour is not a work of human reason, but it is freely 'given' in a faith which has to be 'grasped in the same independent fashion by learned or unlearned, by each for himself' (*The Communion of the Christian with God* [London, 1904], p. 76).

Although Herrmann was subjected to much criticism from both his fellow Ritschlians, including Max Reischle (1858–1905) and Julius Kaftan (1848–1926), and from *Ernst Troeltsch (1865–1923) for his absolute distinction between faith and knowledge, he exerted great influence as a teacher. His students included *Karl Barth and *Rudolf Bultmann, both of whom retain much of his thought in their theologies. In the face of the massive scientific and technological edifice of modern society, Herrmann's system provides an elegant attempt to circumvent Kantian epistemology, without denying its truth for the scientific sphere. Yet Herrmann's solution also presents serious problems: in his thought there seems to be no place left for religion other than in its own sphere. Theology thus becomes a theology *intra muros*, centred in on itself, unable to fulfil its public role.

MARK D. CHAPMAN

FURTHER READING: Michael Beintker, *Die Gottesfrage in der Theologie Wilhelm Herrmanns* (Berlin, 1976); Mark D. Chapman, ' "Theology within the Walls": Wilhelm Herrmann's Religious Reality', *N Z Sys Th* 34 (1992), pp. 69–84; Peter Fischer-Appelt, *Metaphysik im Horizont der Theologie Wilhelm Herrmanns* (Munich, 1965); Simon Fisher, *Revelatory Positivism?* (Oxford, 1988); W. Grieve, *Der Grund des Glaubens* (Göttingen, 1976); Ole Jensen, *Theologie zwischen Illusion und Restriktion* (Munich, 1975); Hermann Timm, *Theorie und Praxis in der Theologie Albrecht Ritschls und Wilhelm Herrmanns* (Gütersloh, 1967); Ernst Troeltsch, 'Grundprobleme der Ethik', in *Gesammelte Schriften*, II (Tübingen, 1913), pp. 552–672; Falk Wagner, 'Theologischer Neukantianismus: Wilhelm Herrmann', in *Profile des neuzeitlichen Protestantismus 2:2* (ed. F.W. Graf; Gütersloh, 1993), pp. 251–78; Joachim Weinhardt, *Wilhelm Herrmanns Stellung in der Ritschlschen Schule* (Tübingen, 1996).

Hick, John Harwood (b. 1922)

Born in Scarborough, Yorkshire, Hick read law at University College, Hull, during which time he 'underwent a spiritual conversion ... [becoming] a Christian of a strongly evangelical and indeed fundamentalist kind'. In 1940 he joined the Presbyterian Church of England and enrolled at Edinburgh University to study philosophy. During his time at Edinburgh he was influenced by the idealist thought of the Kantian scholar Norman Kemp Smith. Following graduation he began research at Oriel College, Oxford under the supervision of H.H. Price (1899–1984). After completing his doctoral work, which was to become his first book, *Faith and Knowledge*, he trained for the ministry at Westminster College, Cambridge. There he was deeply influenced by his professor of systematic theology, *H.H. Farmer (1892–1981), as well as by the work of Farmer's predecessor, *John Oman (1860–1939). Hick can thus be situated at the end of a line of liberal thought which can be traced back to *Schleiermacher (1768–1834). After some time in the ministry (1953–56), Hick taught successively at Cornell University, Princeton Theological Seminary, Cambridge University, Birmingham University and Claremont Graduate School in California, where he remained until his retirement in 1993.

Primarily a philosopher of religion rather than a theologian, Hick's early work was written against the philosophical background of *Logical Positivism, which insisted that religious assertions must be empirically testable. This is particularly evident in *Faith and Knowledge*, his first contribution to the philosophy of religious knowledge – the development of which has remained central to his work. Betraying the influence of *Immanuel Kant (1724–1804) and, to a lesser extent, Schleiermacher as mediated through Farmer's and particularly Oman's thought, *Faith and Knowledge* seeks to develop the notion of faith as 'the interpretative element within religious experience, arising from an act of cognitive choice'. Faith is not assent to the truth of particular doctrinal propositions, it is rather a matter of personal experience. This thesis was developed in a 1968 lecture entitled 'Religious Faith as Experiencing-As'. Making use of *Ludwig Wittgenstein's (1889–1951) discussion of 'seeing-as' which draws attention to ambiguous puzzle pictures (such as Köhler's goblet-faces which can be viewed as either a goblet or two faces), Hick suggests that the world is similarly ambiguous and, according to one's presuppositions, it can be experienced in different ways. Hence the reason for the differing atheistic and theistic interpretations, the latter being derived from an experience of the world as providentially ordered.

Showing traces of Farmer's influence, Hick further argues that the ambiguity of the universe was *intended* by God in order to safeguard human freedom. Created at an 'epistemic distance' from God, humans are preserved from a coerced response to God by the lack of compelling evidence.

In his important book *Evil and the God of Love* Hick seeks to apply this thesis to the problem of evil. Drawing on the thought of *Irenaeus (and again showing traces of Farmer's influence), over against the classical *Augustinian argument that evil originated not in God but in humanity at the Fall, Hick sought to justify the existence of evil by its contribution to spiritual development or 'soul-making'. Created sin-prone, humans are nevertheless able, in an evil world, to progress towards moral and spiritual maturity; 'moral and spiritual growth comes through response to challenges'.

Linked to these arguments, and in response to the Logical Positivist demand for verification, is Hick's account of *eschatological verification*. Concerning the existence of God, the argument is that, although believers may properly claim to know God in this life, the claim involves an assertion which is factually true or false, because it is subject to verification or falsification within future human experience which continues beyond bodily death. The existence of God will be verified in the afterlife.

While Hick's works had been written from an obviously Christian perspective, a shift began to take place in his thought as a result of his move to the multi-cultural milieu of Birmingham (1967). The results of this shift were published in *God and the Universe of Faiths*. Greatly influenced by the writings of Wilfred Cantwell Smith (b. 1916), Hick argued that Christian theology needs a 'Copernican revolution'; it needs to move from a Christ-centred to a God-centred understanding of the universe of faiths. The traditional view of the church is 'ruled out by the Christian understanding of God. For does not the divine love for all mankind ... exclude the idea that salvation occurs only in one strand of human history, which is limited in time to the last nineteen centuries and in space virtually to the western hemisphere?'.

Furthermore, the idea that there is a single transcendent reality, about which many different belief systems demonstrate some awareness, led to Hick's interest in the possibility of a 'global theology', to which he sought to contribute in his comparative study *Death and Eternal Life*. This study surveys and assimilates insights from the major world religions, humanism, contemporary philosophy and parapsychology in order to provide 'a global theology of death'. However, Hick's understanding of a single transcendent reality which informed this work was criticized for being rather ambiguous. Sometimes he used terms which suggested a personal (if not Christian) deity, and at other times he indicated an impersonal concept of the divine. In the early 1980s he addressed this problem by replacing the word 'God' with 'the Real' and argued that the latter lies beyond personal and impersonal understandings. As part of his ongoing development of an epistemology of religious faith, this thesis is worked out in terms of Kant's distinction between things as they really are in themselves before the human mind has interpreted them (the *noumenal*) and things as they appear to us after they have been conditioned and ordered by our minds (the *phenomenal*). Applying this distinction to religious belief, Hick argues that the Real is a noumenal reality which is interpreted by the human mind – a mind which has, in turn, been conditioned and

moulded by a particular culture and stream of experience. Hence, from the perspective of religious pluralism, the world religions represent diverse, culturally-conditioned responses to the Real. This thesis is most comprehensively and cogently worked out in his 1986 Gifford Lectures, *An Interpretation of Religion*.

Finally, perhaps the most controversial work his name has been associated with was the 1977 symposium which he edited, *The Myth of God Incarnate* (London, 1977). Whereas in 1958 Hick had criticized the Christology of *Donald Baillie (1887–1954) for 'failing to express the full orthodox faith', in the 1970s, primarily as a result of his exposure to non-Christian faiths, Hick developed a Christology rather less orthodox than that of Baillie. Along with some biblical and philosophical objections to the doctrine of the incarnation, he argued that its pernicious implication is that 'God can be adequately known and responded to only through Jesus; and the whole religion of mankind, beyond the stream of Judaic-Christian faith is thus by implication excluded as lying outside the sphere of salvation'. Focusing specifically on religious plurality, the same line of thought was followed in a more recent volume co-edited with Paul F. Knitter, *The Myth of Christian Uniqueness* (London, 1987).

Not only is Hick one of Britain's most important radical religious thinkers, but it is difficult to underestimate the significance of his thought concerning the issues raised by religious plurality. As a result of the clarity of his writing and the cogency of his arguments, he, perhaps more than any other contemporary thinker, has forced Christianity to reflect upon its attitudes to non-Christian world-views. Whether from the perspective of missiology, systematic theology or the philosophy of religion, and whether one broadly agrees or disagrees with him, theologians seeking to provide a theological account of Christianity's relationship to other religions have to reckon with Hick.

CHRISTOPHER PARTRIDGE

FURTHER READING: P. Badham, *A John Hick Reader* (London, 1990); G. d'Costa, *John Hick's Theology of Religions* (Lanham, MD, 1987); D. Edwards, 'John Hick and the Uniqueness of Jesus: Is Jesus of Nazareth the World's Only Saviour?', in D.L. Edwards, *Tradition and Truth: A Critical Examination of England's Radical Theologians* (London, 1989), pp. 212–53 (a response from John Hick appears on pp. 306–10); C. Gillis, *A Question of Final Belief* (London,

1989); J. Hick, *Faith and Knowledge* (New York, 1957); *Evil and the God of Love* (London, 1966); *God and the Universe of Faiths* (London, 1973); *Death and Eternal Life* (London, 1976); *An Interpretation of Religion* (London, 1989); 'Straightening the Record: Some Responses to Critics', *Mod Th* 6:2 (1990); R. Mathis, *Against John Hick: An Examination of His Philosophy of Religion* (Lanham, MD, 1985); C. Sinkinson, *J. Hick: An Introduction to His Theology* (Leicester, 1995).

Hilary of Poitiers (312–367/8)

Born in 312 at Poitiers, he became bishop of his home town in 353 and was unfortunate to be exiled by the anti-Athanasian Constantius II in 355 after backing the Nicene Eusebius of Vercelli. Phrygia, the place of exile, was a theological education for him, not least in the history of the disputes (which he recorded) and the subtleties of Trinitarian theology. Hilary became the first Latin-speaker to be familiar with *Origen's commentaries, although he owed more to *Tertullian and Cicero and Seneca (so J. Doignon, *Hilaire de Poitiers avant l'Exil* [Paris, 1971]). *Harnack claimed he was an abler theologian than *Athanasius, Simonetti that he was the first Latin theologian to steer between *Arianism and Sabellianism. Hilary did have the advantage of writing all his major works in his late maturity while the empire espoused Arianism from 357–60. He saw it as his task to play down the differences between the *homoiousion* and *homoousion* positions in order to unite against Arianism proper. The Nicene *homoousion*, he insists, should not be interpreted as meaning there was a prior substance which Father and Son took shares in.

Books 1–3 of Hilary's *On the Trinity*, with their reminiscences of Athanasius, suggest that he felt himself to be a follower of the Alexandrian. The Father and Son cannot be of different natures since God could not co-exist with something other than himself which was also eternal (*De Trinitate* [henceforward *DT*] 2.13). They are *unus* though not *unum*. 'Being' can be predicated only of that which does not come to an end (*DT* 3.17). God's nature cannot be known but may be adored in his infinite power. It is less the ontological equality of Father and Son which is stressed (as in Athanasius) than the (wider issue) of the infinity and unknowability of God. The Arians could be accused of trying to speak of God in a human way. The Father is the origin of the Son by his will (*DT* 2.11; *De synodiis* 37;

58–59), eternally willing to generate the Son. Like the *Cappadocian Fathers (but unlike Athanasius, who disliked the idea that the origin of the relationship between Father and Son had anything to do with will or causation), Hilary is a Latin exponent of the Father's priority if not his superiority. 'According to Hilary, the Son is caused by the Father's will, power and wisdom, while for Athanasius the Son is the Father's will, power and wisdom' (Meijering, p. 135). The Father is greater than the Son in generation not in genus (*Tractatus on Psalms* 138:17). 'The Father is therefore, greater than the Son: for manifestly he is greater, Who makes another to be all that He himself is, Who imparts to his Son by the mystery of the birth the image of his own unbegotten nature' (*DT* 9.54).

Hilary was one of the first in the west or the east, since the anti-Marcionites (e.g. Tertullian), fully to grasp the importance of Christ's humanity. Christ was united to all, but we do not all unite ourselves to Christ. It is not so much a universal humanity which the Word assumes in the incarnation as the universal principle of human life; his humanity has a sanctifying effect by its association with ours (see *DT* 2.24; 10.61; 10.74; 11.16). The incarnation changed the history of humankind, assuming a humanity drawn from the faithful remnant which grows in extent and influence, so as to lead the whole of humanity towards salvation at the end. Similarly, at an individual level, salvation begins with the soul (with the body stigmatized) and ends with the glorified body once the soul has learned to bear its weight. The 'form of God' is equated with the nature of God, in order to elevate humanity to divine form. Thus, for example, on Psalm 53:5 ('For by the power of the judgement human weakness is rescued to bear God's name and nature'), although this applies properly to Christ alone rather than to humanity as such. 'It is one thing that He was God before He was man, another, that He was man and God, and another, that after being man and God he was perfect man and perfect God' (*DT* 9.6). Hilary insists in several places upon distinguishing between the two natures of Christ and clarifying which gospel verses pertain to which. The suffering of the Son of God, for example, belongs to his human nature alone. Hilary denies that there was a kenotic loss of the *forma Dei* when Christ descended, since the divine nature cannot be destroyed or lost.

The implications of this include a tendency towards the denial of a true atonement in the sense of the Son of God becoming fully involved in human sin and redeeming it from within (an emphasis crystallized in the later anti-Apollinarian soteriological claim of some eastern theologians that 'what is not assumed remains unhealed'). Rather, there is, from as early as the *Commentary on Matthew* onwards, a focus on the dynamic life of Jesus culminating in the victory of his resurrection. *De Trinitate* (10.24) reveals a Christ who wept, but not for himself. The concept of *persona*, which unites the natures in Christ, is at best imprecise and his nature is spoken of as divine – as the source of life (*Tr. Ps.* 138:3). Salvation is appropriated through receiving the power of the Word in baptism.

Other important themes are developed in Hilary's commentaries on Psalms and Matthew and in the *On the Mysteries*. The key mystery is that of the Church which had been called through Christ and the Spirit. He did not so much practice allegorical as typological interpretation. There is a tension between the degree of fulfilment brought by incarnation and Pentecost in the church and the remaining completion of that form at the end of time (see *Tr. Ps.* 124:4). Hilary understands the unity of the church as a unity of love reflecting God's unity, which goes deeper than the collegiate unity of bishops (*Cyprian), an understanding which reflects the influence of Origen (so, Figura). The church is sinful, still on the way to a holiness in which she will become fully Christ-like as he makes his perfect humanity available to her. Yet in an important sense the church is already glorified, the wedding has happened. Hilary declares (*Tr. Ps.* 125:6) that Christ *is* the church, holding her in himself through the sacrament of his body. The church as Christ is the form of the future, of paradise for all people who choose to identify themselves with him. The last judgement will be preceded by the appearance of the cross in the sky as well as by the presence of Elijah and Elisha. At the resurrection (similar to Christ's, except he raised himself), souls and bodies will be reunited and, with the restoration of the image of God, paradise regained. Good will be rewarded, though the role of grace in this is not totally explained. Origen lies behind Hilary's idea of believers experiencing a purifying fire, but there is no hint of the former's universalism. The subordination of Christ to the Father in not knowing the hour and in handing over the kingdom is explained on the grounds of what is necessary for our salvation. Hilary's is a western, non-chiliastic eschatology. The original aspect is the idea of the *medii* (who have neither belief nor unbelief): they alone will be judged on merits, and then dispatched to either heaven or hell. There is no third 'place' as such (unlike the hints in *Ambrose). There is, however, a place of *refrigerium* (coolness: Lk. 16:24; Ps. 65:12), but only for the martyrs.

MARK W. ELLIOTT

FURTHER READING: E.P. Meijering, *Hilary of Poitiers on the Trinity: De Trinitate 1, 1–19, 2, 3* (Leiden, 1982); Paul C. Burns, *The Christology in Hilary of Poitiers' Commentary on Matthew* (Rome, 1981); Luis F. Ladaria, *La Cristologia de Hilario de Poitiers* (Rome, 1989); Hans C. Brennecke, *Hilarius von Poitiers und die Bischofsopposition gegen Konstantius II: Untersuchungen zur dritten Phase des Arianischen Streites (337–361)* (Berlin, 1984); M. Durst, *Die Eschatologie des Hilarius von Poitiers: ein Beitrag zur Dogmengeschichte des vierten Jahrhunderts* (Bonn, 1987); M. Figura, *Das Kirchenverstandnis des Hilarius von Poitiers* (Freiburg, 1984).

Hildegard of Bingen (1098–1179)

Hildegard was born as the tenth child of a noble family in the year 1098 at Bermersheim, near Alzey in Rheinhessen. At eight years of age, she was given to the nearby monastery of Disibodenberg, where she was put in the care of the anchoress Jutta of Spanheim. At fifteen she took the habit of a *Benedictine nun and, on the death of Jutta in 1136, she was elected leader of the small community of women attached to Disibodenberg. Hildegard tells us that from an early age she had had visionary experiences and, in 1146, she wrote to *Bernard of Clairvaux, seeking confirmation of her vocation. Passages from *Scivias*, her first visionary work, were read out to Pope Eugenius III at the Trier Synod of 1147–8. He was suitably impressed and urged her 'in the name of Christ and St Peter to publish all that she had learned from the Holy Spirit'. It was perhaps the growth in Hildegard's popularity which contributed to her decision in 1150 to move with her sisters to a new foundation at Rupertsberg, overcoming the resistance of the monks. As a result of her visions Hildegard took on an increasingly public role, undertaking preaching tours in the Rhineland area no less than four times. She also maintained a vigorous correspondence with numerous dignitaries, including the Emperor Frederick I, also known as Barbarossa, Henry II of England and four popes. With the growth of her community she established a second foundation at Eibingen, near Rüdesheim, in 1165. She died peacefully on 17 September 1179. Her cult was sanctioned by Pope John XXII in 1324.

The many works Hildegard produced during her long lifetime can be divided into visionary works (*Scivias, Liber vitae meritorum, De operatione Dei*), scientific works (*Physica, Causae et curae*), letters and songs, as well as a number of miscellaneous texts, including commentaries on selections from the Gospels, the Rule of St Benedict, the *Athanasian Creed and an outline of an invented language. Most of the details of her life are known from the *Vita sanctae Hildegardis*, which was produced some time during the last quarter of the twelfth century. The manuscripts of *Scivias* and *De operatione Dei* were richly illuminated, although the former was lost during the Second World War and now survives only in a modern copy. Hildegard was not herself responsible for these fine illustrations, although the *Scivias* manuscript was probably produced in the Rupertsberg scriptorium during her own lifetime. A body of music written by Hildegard, which is among the earliest of western musical manuscripts, has gained her a special place in the history of Western music. Hildegard's musical compositions show the same originality and organic expressivity as the texts of her songs and hymns, and she is widely regarded as one of the great composers of the Middle Ages.

We find in Hildegard's theological work many of the characteristics of twelfth-century theology. In the first place, her status as visionary is to be distinguished from that of the women mystics of the fourteenth century and later, whose visions had a unitive character. Hildegard understood her own visionary experiences to be essentially didactic, and she successfully combined the honour accorded to high-born abbesses in twelfth-century society with a vocation to a teaching function within the church and a prophetic critique of its mores. She makes subtle use of her femininity in this regard by pointing to her own 'weakness' as a woman in order to underline the divinity of her message which is all the more necessary in this 'effeminate age'. The graphic character of her visions also looks back to the tradition of spiritual personification, with its roots in exegesis (cf. *St Trudperter Hoheslied*) and para-liturgical performance.

Hildegard understands the Christian revelation to be a cosmological event, and her imagery frequently serves to draw together the diverse themes of creation and redemption, heaven and earth, into a unified whole. The appearance of the image of a beautiful young woman to signify the creative wisdom of God and the Holy Spirit as well as Eve, the church and Hildegard's own virgins is an example of this, as is her use of the image of the Word as creative and divine life-force, which 'resonates' through the creation, and which sounds out also in the song of the church's praise. We see the same bridging of the gulf between the human and the divine in the image of 'greenness' or *viriditas*, which is most particular to Hildegard and for which there are no obvious biblical models. On the one hand this represents the action of the Holy Spirit, grace and virtue, while on the other it is physical vigour, fertility and vibrancy of life. Despite the generally visual and narrative character of her visions, therefore, they yield a sophisticated and coherent theology which lays great stress on the immanence of God and on the role of *sacra doctrina* in the unfolding cosmic drama of Christ and his church.

In her rationalistic optimism, her persistent interest in questions of cosmology and her openness to the use of art in the service of theological truths, Hildegard has much in common with the school of Chartres, especially the work of Bernard and Thierry of Chartres. Hildegard may also have been influenced by some of the same *Platonic texts which were read at Chartres, most notably Plato's own *Timaeus* and works by *Scotus Eriugena. The question of Hildegard's sources is difficult to resolve, and without doubt the Scriptures were the chief textual influence upon her, above all the literature of the Wisdom tradition, which would have formed the basis of the daily devotions in the monastery.

OLIVER DAVIES

FURTHER READING: Fiona Bowie and Oliver Davies, *Hildegard of Bingen: An Anthology* (London / New York, 1990); Sabina Flanagan, *Hildegard of Bingen: A Visionary Life* (London, 2nd edn, 1998); Werner Lauter, *Hildegard von Bingen: Eine internationale wissenschaftliche Bibliographie* (Selbstverlag der Gesellschaft fur mittelrheinische

Kirchengeschichte; Mainz, 1998); Barbara Newman, *Sister of Wisdom, St Hildegard's Theology of the Feminine* (Berkeley / London, 1987); *Voice of the Living Light: Hildegard of Bingen and her World* (Berkeley / London, 1998).

Hilton, Walter (c. 1343–96)

Walter Hilton was a spiritual theologian. Incepted in canon law at Cambridge, Hilton was one of a circle of northern clerks retained by Thomas Arundel (Bishop of Ely 1374–88) in his administration. Hilton spent some time as a hermit and joined the Augustinian priory of Thurgarton (Notts.) about 1386. After Arundel's translation to York in 1388, Hilton and others were instrumental in Arundel's policy of imposing rule and structure on a piety influenced by 'enthusiastic' elements in the spirituality of Richard Rolle (d. 1349), where such 'enthusiasm' seemed to open the way to convergence with Lollardy and perhaps with the movement of the 'Free Spirit' existing in mainland Europe. Richard Rolle's 'enthusiasm' was orthodox, though, open to criticism; Lollardy and the 'Free Spirit' movement were fundamentally unorthodox. Several of Hilton's Latin letters and some minor English works are extant. Hilton is credited with a tract in defence of the veneration of images, and with an English version of the popular *Stimulus Amoris*.

Hilton's major works are the two books of the *Scale of Perfection*, completed circa 1390 and 1395, which draw together and develop afresh points made in his 'occasional' writings, within a wider synthesis. The shorter *Mixed Life* is designed to march with *Scale*, 1.

Scale, 1 was intended for those vowed to the contemplative life, as distinct from actives living in the world. 'True contemplation' is knowledge and love of God in the spirit, as distinct from anything that touches the senses or imagination, including the 'heat, sweetness and song' associated with Rolle. Firm faith, humility and intention to God (charity) are needed. Contemplation represents the renewal of the *imago Dei* in humankind, the recovery of that conformity to God which Adam lost in the Fall. The withdrawal of sensible devotion is seen as a call to search for God in a more 'spiritual' manner, by introversion, with the breaking down of that 'image of sin' which occludes the *imago Dei*; indeed, God is seeking us before ever we seek him. The twin virtues of humility and charity

are the most effective means of destroying the seven capital sins of which pride is the chief. Contemplation is to be sought, but remains over the horizon in *Scale*, 1, except as an occasional and fleeting gift.

Mixed Life was written for a devout temporal lord with responsibilities for others. It sets out a careful framework of devotional disciplines, but urges that for the recipient the *ordo caritatis* – the proper service of God and man – precludes him from aspiring to that properly spiritual contemplation to which religious are called. Hilton's contribution here is in applying to secular men those principles of the 'mixed life' of action and contemplation which Gregory the Great (d. 604) had prescribed for ecclesiastical pastors.

Scale, 2, has a different perception of the nature and function of contemplation. The carefully-structured scheme of progress in *Scale*, 1 is replaced with the simpler model of 'reforming in faith' leading to 'reforming' (contemplation). Hilton went on to identify contemplation – a many-sided experience, for which no single designation is adequate – more especially with the awareness of the life of grace – 'a lively feeling of grace'.

More forcefully than in *Scale*, 1, and with a clear eye to the Lollards, Hilton repudiates in *Scale*, 2 the pride of those who, because they have begun to feel some sensible devotion and keep the letter of the law, upbraid others, create division, and despise ecclesiastical disciplines. No one can come to contemplation except through becoming conformed to Christ, in passing through the 'luminous darkness', the passage from the false day of self-love to the love of God. In this process it is again not only those mortifications actively embraced by the soul, but the trials laid on the soul by God, including the sense of dereliction in which one is supernaturally sustained by faith, which are essential on the road to union with God.

This new understanding of contemplation as an awareness of the life of grace seems to build partly on the distinction found in the *Cloud of Unknowing* between 'imperfect humility', based on the sense of our own weakness and so in a sense self-regarding, and 'perfect humility', which looks beyond ourselves to God in his immensity and love. Hilton makes the same distinction. 'Perfect humility' opens the way to docility to the leading of the Holy Spirit, and to the free working of grace in what *St Thomas Aquinas (d. 1274) calls its 'operant' mode, where God directly governs the will without conscious labour or reflection by us. From *Scale, 2, 34* onwards, Hilton's exposition is profoundly Trinitarian; the Holy Spirit, uncreated love, gives himself to us, so that our adoption in Christ may be realized (Rom. 8:14). The interaction of perfect humility with perfect love breaks down the capital sins and makes for conformity to God's will. Reforming in feeling becomes a growing habit of conformity to God, with a fluctuating but progressively constant awareness of grace. Each phase of darkness issues in a deeper sense of union, *unitas spiritus*, yet one which can never be final and unbroken in this life. It is because contemplation, or reforming in feeling, confers such a progressive conformity to God that it is declared in *Scale, 2* to be no optional extra for a few, but it is to be sought by all Christians.

Hilton is explicitly grounded in the tradition of *Augustine (354–430), Gregory the Great (c. 540–604) and *Bernard (1090–1153). His teaching on 'reforming in feeling', where 'feeling' is equated with 'understanding', echoes the tradition of Augustine and *Anselm (c. 1033–1109) on understanding as the corollary of recovery of purity of heart. Hilton's deeply incarnational emphasis draws on Bernard's teaching on the transition from 'carnal' to 'spiritual' love of God in Christ. His teaching on 'fluctuation' within contemplation also echoes Bernard. Other important Cistercian sources are William of St Thierry (c. 1085–1148) and Gilbert of Holland (d. c. 1172). Despite reciprocal influence with the *Cloud of Unknowing*, Hilton bypasses the characteristic apophaticism of *Pseudo-Dionysius.

The *Scale* and *Mixed Life* were printed in 1494. Hilton was a constituent in the teaching of Augustine Baker (1575–1641). Despite convergences between Hilton – and the *Cloud* – with the teaching of *St John of the Cross (1542–91) on the 'dark night', there is no reason to suppose direct influence.

JOHN P.H. CLARK

FURTHER READING: *Critical editions: Scale, Book 1* (ed. A.J. Bliss and completed by M.G. Sargent; London, forthcoming); *Scale, Book 2* (ed. S.S. Hussey); *Mixed Life* (ed. S.J. Ogilvie-Thomson; Salzburg, 1986). *Modernized editions: Scale* (ed. J.P.H. Clark and R. Dorward; New York, 1991); *Ladder of Perfection* (trans. L. Sherley-Price; London, 1988); *Walter Hilton's Latin Writings* (ed. J.P.H. Clark and C. Taylor; 2 vols.; Salzburg, 1987). *Articles*: S.S. Hussey, 'Walter Hilton: Traditionalist?', in *The Medieval Mystical Tradition in England: Dartington 1980* (ed. M. Glasscoe; Exeter, 1980), pp. 1–16; A.J. Minnis, 'Affection and Imagination in *The Cloud of Unknowing* and Walter Hilton's *Scale of Perfection*', *Traditio* 39 (1983), pp. 323–66; J.P.H. Clark, articles in *Down R* 95 (1977), pp. 95–109; 96 (1978), pp. 61–78, 281–98; 97 (1979), pp. 69–80, 204–20, 259–74; 100 (1982), pp. 235–62; 101 (1983), pp. 15–29; 102 (1984), pp. 79–118; 103 (1985), pp. 1–25; 'Augustine, Anselm and Walter Hilton', in *The Medieval Mystical Tradition in England: Dartington 1982* (ed. M. Glasscoe; Exeter, 1982), pp. 102–26; 'The Trinitarian Theology of Walter Hilton's *Scale of Perfection, Book Two*', in *Langland, the Mystics and the Mediaeval English Mystical Tradition: Essays in Honour of S.S. Hussey* (ed. H. Phillips; Woodbridge, 1990), pp. 125–40.

Hippolytus (c. 170 – c. 236)

Although a significant figure in the ante-Nicene church, Hippolytus remains somewhat elusive. The only approximate date that is known about Hippolytus is his martyrdom c. 236, remembered traditionally on 13 August. Speculation places his birth some time close to the mid-second century, perhaps c. 170. What is known is that he was a presbyter and teacher of the gospel in Rome (so *Eusebius), and that he was consequently exiled to the Sardinian mines along with the Roman bishop Pontianus under the intolerant reign of Emperor Maximinus Thrax (235–38). Prior to Hippolytus's exile, he was a central figure in a schism regarding the relationship between the Son and the Father, with traditional scholarship maintaining that he established himself as antipope against Roman bishops Callistus, Urban (222–30) and Pontius (230–35). Inscriptional evidence by Pope Damasus I (c. 304–84) suggests that Hippolytus was not considered to be out of communion with the larger church at the point of his death.

No information concerning Hippolytus's childhood and early development is extant. Much more is known about his theological viewpoints and contributions, and of his relations with other key early church figures. Hippolytus was a Greek whose thinking was influenced chiefly by *Irenaeus (early mid-second century), who was in turn influenced chiefly by Polycarp (c. 70 – 155/160). As a bishop and presbyter Hippolytus wrote many works that provide insights into the ecclesial order and theological developments of the church from the late second to early third centuries. Hippolytus's identification as a schismatic comes from a combination of historical notes and scholarly observations, beginning with Damasus I who made a loose connection between Hippolytus and *Novatian because of the close proximity of their tombs. Hippolytus's literary works reveal a mastery of Greek, a knowledge of a variety of cultures, philosophies and religions, and an ability to synthesize the brief history of Christianity with an interest towards apologetics.

From Pirro Ligorio's discovery of a headless seated statue in 1551 between the via Tiburtina and the via Nomentana to the nineteenth- and twentieth-century excavations of Hippolytus's cult centre located in the same region, modern scholars have learned much about Hippolytus's work and theological contributions to the early church. The significance of the statue to Hippolytan studies lies in the inscriptions (early third century) of Hippolytus's works and two paschal calendars from 222–333 – one for Easter and a second for Passover. The obvious question for debate more recently is whether or not the statue represents Hippolytus the man or Hippolytus's school of thought, and whether the works listed are his alone or products of his school (so Brent). Exclusive of the debate, the works themselves are significant regardless of their sole or multiple authorship, since Hippolytus is, in either instance, a key influence behind them either as author or as founder of a school of thought.

Several of Hippolytus's works reveal him as a theologian preoccupied with the onset of various heresies. Hippolytus was concerned about the preservation of Scriptural authority, and he argued rigorously for a logos doctrine that distinguished between the Son and the Father in a way that makes him appear to be a ditheist. His most significant work is the *Philosophumena* (also known as *kata pason aireseon elegchos*), discovered in 1842. The first four books, the second and third of which are missing, concern Greek, Egyptian, Chaldean and Babylonian astrologies, philosophies and religious doctrines. Books five through nine provide modern scholars with the fullest account of Christian heresies dating from the composition of the Fourth Gospel to the death of Callistus I. Subsequently, the work is of some degree of importance for Johannine scholars who are concerned about the dating of the Gospel. The tenth book

provides a detailed summary of the previous nine. The heresies which Hippolytus castigates are those of the Ophites, Simonists, Basilidians, Docetae and the Noetians. *Syntagma*, a shorter refutation of heresies, was composed by Hippolytus earlier in his life. Still another anti-heretical work by Hippolytus is *Small Labyrinth*. Other monographs against certain heresies include his treaties against *Marcion, the Modalists, the *Montanists, Caius and the more obscure Alogi.

Hippolytus's inflexible position against the Modalists strained his relationship with the bishops of Rome Zephyrinus (198–217) and Callistus I (217–22). His accusations against Callistus were particularly vilifying – that he was a participant in the Modalist heresy of Sabellius, and that he was overly gracious in the case of penitential heretics. Traditional scholarship maintains that Hippolytus was so thoroughly disenchanted and frustrated with Callistus's treatment of the Modalists that he established himself as antipope. This case is, perhaps, overstated since recent insights into early church development do not allow for a monarchical episcopate at this time – preferring a system of house-schools led by various bishops, coexisting in an egalitarian manner.

Certain other of Hippolytus's works reveal him to be a man concerned with the right interpretation of Scripture. Of his many writings on the Old and New Testaments, some of which exist in fragmentary form, only his commentaries on the Song of Songs and on Daniel survive *in toto*. *Apostolic Traditions* bears a degree of Hippolytan influence also – reflecting his, and his school's, concern for a rigorous church order. Works that have at times been ascribed to Hippolytus but which are now challenged or forthrightly rejected are the *Constitutions of Hippolytus* (parallel with the eighth book of the *Apostolic Constitutions*), the *Canones Hippolyti* and *Egyptian Church Ordinance*.

The most recent significant contribution to Hippolytan scholarship is Allen Brent's *Hippolytus and the Roman Church in the Third Century*. This is a commendable, albeit highly technical and painstaking, study that evaluates Hippolytus's works and the evidence provided by his statue in light of more recent scholarship on the ante-Nicene church. Brent challenges the notion that Hippolytus established himself as antipope or that he could even be qualified as a schismatic, suggesting (following P. Lampe,

1989) that the church had developed a monarchical episcopate only in Novatian's time (c. 210–80). However, Brent makes an intriguing and somewhat convincing argument from a historical-critical method of reading statements by Eusebius, Damasus and Hippolytus's school in *Apostolic Traditions* that the presbyter and bishop were already distinct offices in the church of Hippolytus's day.

THOMAS J. BOONE, III

FURTHER READING: A. Brent, *Hippolytus and the Roman Church in the Third Century* (Leiden, 1995); J.M. Hanssens, SJ, *La Liturgie d'Hippolyte* (Rome, 1965); J.P. Kirsch, *The Catholic Encyclopedia* (New York, 1910); P. Lampe, WUNT 2.18 (1989).

History of Religions School

The History of Religions School (*die religionsgeschichtliche Schule*, more correctly translated as the History of Religion School) was, according to Hermann Gunkel (1862–1932), one of its leading representatives, 'a closely connected circle' of primarily New Testament scholars 'who found themselves in Göttingen at the professorial chair of Ritschl' in the late 1880s. Looking back late in his career, the School's 'systematic theologian' *Ernst Troeltsch (1865–1923) referred to it affectionately as the 'little Göttingen Faculty' (CW 34 [1920], cols. 281–83). The most important figure in the formation of a group identity was their *primus inter pares*, the polymathic 'genius' Albert Eichhorn (1856–1926). Also among the circle of young academics were the New Testament scholars William Wrede (1859–1906), Wilhelm Bousset (1865–1920) and *Ritschl's son-in-law Johannes Weiss (1863–1914), the Old Testament critic Alfred Rahlfs (1865–1935) and the student of comparative religion, Heinrich Hackmann (1864–1935). Others who were later associated with the School were Wilhelm Heitmüller (1869–1926), Hugo Gressmann (1877–1927), Paul Wernle (1872–1939), Heinrich Weinel (1874–1936) and Richard Reitzenstein (1861–1931).

This disparate group was united not so much by any explicit common programme (although many of them were later to collaborate on the influential series of popular works, the *Religionsgeschichtliche Volksbücher* and the first edition of the encyclopedia, *Die Religion in Geschichte und Gegenwart*), but rather they were concerned to investigate what Troeltsch called (in a letter to Bousset of 1895) 'the multifaceted religious

movements which surround Christianity in a purely historical manner'.

This approach meant that there was soon a general dissatisfaction with Ritschl's theology, particularly his dogmatic isolation of Christianity from the flux of development and his insufficiently rigorous approach to history. This split can be seen in the theses defended by members of the School as part of the doctoral examination at Göttingen, almost all of which were hostile to their erstwhile teacher (cf. F.W. Graf, *Troeltsch-Studien* I, pp. 235–90). Instead, the young scholars were soon attracted to those who were more thoroughgoing in their approach to history. From beyond the theological faculty they found great stimulation in Ritschl's Göttingen opponent Paul de Lagarde (1827–91), professor of oriental languages, who believed that a 'knowledge of Jesus and the Gospel can be obtained in no other way than that by which historical knowledge in general is acquired' (*Deutsche-Schriften* [Göttingen, 5th edn, 1920], p. 47). Another profound influence was the Göttingen Old Testament professor Bernhard Duhm (1847–1928), who regarded religion as something distinct from dogmatic formulations and marked chiefly by enthusiasm and inspiration. He thereby sought to reduce the 'constriction of religion by theology' (*Büber Ziel und Methode der theologischen Wissenschaft* [Basle, 1889], p. 7).

Under Duhm's influence, the members of the History of Religion School stressed the importance of the 'spirit-filled person', rather than the scholastic theologian, in the development of religion: 'We recognise God's revelation in the great persons of religion who experience the holy mystery in their depths and speak in tongues of fire' (Gunkel, *Israel und Babylonien* [Göttingen, 1903], p. 36). This emphasis on spirit, particularly the effects of the spirit on the individual and in the cultic community, forms one of the leading themes of the School and can be dated from Gunkel's dissertation on the effects of the Holy Spirit in Paul (*Die Wirkungen des heiligen Geistes* [Göttingen, 1888]). Thus, unlike Ritschl and many of the Ritschlians, who were often deeply hostile to anything that seemed to resemble pietism, the History of Religion School was not primarily concerned with the analysis of theological and dogmatic statements, but with the explanation of what Wrede called 'appearances and moods'. History of religion was thus not the 'history of dogma, but the history of piety ... the enormous variety and the fullness of religious ideas and appearances which dominate human thought and the human heart and have determined human wills' (*Vorträge und Studien* [Tübingen, 1907], pp. 65–6). In his great work *Kyrios Christos*, Wilhelm Bousset similarly took as his starting point the 'activity of the cultus and the community's worship of God', claiming that 'the beginnings of Christianity, in which we might include Paul, John and Gnosticism have nothing, I repeat absolutely nothing, to do with the distinctive philosophical literature of the educated classes' (*Kyrios Christos* [Göttingen, 5th edn, 1965], p. 271).

Consequently, rather than concentrating on literary studies of the various books of the Bible, the primary object of investigation of the History of Religion School was the religion expressed by these books. In an important essay, Gunkel wrote:

> From the outset we did not understand history of religion as the history of religions but as the history of religion ... We were convinced that the ultimate purpose of our work on the Bible was to look in the hearts of the people of religion, to experience their thoughts inwardly and adequately to describe them. We did not chiefly want to occupy ourselves with the books of the Bible and their criticism, but rather we sought to read the living religion from these books. (*Reden und Aufsätze* [Göttingen, 1913], p. v)

Not surprisingly, St Paul proved a favourite subject of study, Gunkel viewing him as a 'man of the spirit of a particularly high grade', for whom 'the whole life of the Christian' was 'a work of the spirit – revealing an overwhelming, supernatural divine power' (*Die Wirkungen*, pp. 58, 96). The essence of Pauline religion, Gunkel held, was not to be found in hard and fast doctrines, but in the religious experience of the individual: this meant the study of the historical origins of Christianity served to reveal a spiritual essence which would endure despite all historical criticism.

In the same way as the members of the History of Religion School viewed religion as something primarily of the spirit, so the history of religion became the history of the spirit as it manifested itself in what Bousset called the 'great web of history'. The extent to which the picture of history in the History of Religion School was coloured by the post-Hegelian view

of necessary progress varied between the members of the School. Bousset, for instance, considered that the history of religion was 'a great work of God, a ceaseless upwards attraction, a continual discourse of God with humans and of humans with God' (*Das Wesen der Religions* [Halle, 1906], p. 17). In contrast, few went as far as Troeltsch, who gradually came to consider it impossible 'to construct a theory of Christianity as the absolute religion on the basis of a historical way of thinking or by the use of historical means' (*Am J Th* 17 [1913], pp. 1f.).

Most of the members of the History of Religion School emphasized the immediate grasp of the truth of a religion, which served to free it from the vagaries and relativities of history. The essence of religion was thus primarily to be found, according to Bousset, in 'the life-impulse ... which in actual fact emanated from the person of Jesus and touches and embraces us in his community'. This alone allowed the Christian to gain 'a firm and lasting hold in the whole of the Gospel' (*Die Mission und die religionsgeschichtliche Schule* [Göttingen, 1907], p. 19). In the experience of redemption, the individual was 'liberated' from history 'and released from the natural, sensually determined self, which draws to itself the goal of its life and its strivings. Redeemed means being grasped by God' (*Unser Gottesglaube* [Tübingen, 1908], p. 48). Epistemologically, this emphasis tended to lead the members of the School into semi-mystical philosophies. In particular Bousset, together with *Rudolf Otto (1869–1937), sought to popularize the work of the post-Kantian J.F. Fries (1773–1843), who had earlier been influential on the Old Testament critic W.M.L. De Wette (1780–1849).

In such works as Gunkel's *Schöpfung und Chaos* (Göttingen, 1895) and Bousset's *Kyrios Christos*, the researches of the members of the School made a lasting impact on biblical studies, pioneering new approaches in the study of ancient religion and investigating the broader context for biblical writings. However, the weakest aspect of the method adopted by the School, and particularly of its theory of religion, was the tendency to separate religion from ethics, and even, perhaps ironically, from history itself. As a reaction to the dehumanizing effects of Wilhelmine capitalism, the escape into the individual was unsurprising. Yet, as Troeltsch came to recognize, such 'mystical' religion was ethically 'impotent' (*The

Social Teaching [London, 1931], p. 985). As its systematic theologian, Troeltsch sought to reincorporate such a spiritual understanding of religion into the concrete historical world. But in doing so he distanced himself from the other members of the School.

MARK D. CHAPMAN

FURTHER READING: Mark D. Chapman, 'Religion, Ethics and the History of Religion School', *Scot J Th* 46 (1993), pp. 43–78; F.W. Graf, 'Der "Systematiker" der "kleinen Göttinger Fakultüt" ', in *Troeltsch-Studien*, I (ed. F.W. Graf and Horst Renz; Gütersloh, 1982), pp. 235–90; G.W. Ittel, 'Die Hauptgedanken der "religionsgeschichtlichen Schule" ', *Z Rel Gg* 10 (1958), pp. 20–55; W. Klatt, *Hermann Gunkel* (Göttingen, 1969); Martin Rade, 'Religionsgeschichte', *Rel G G*, IV (Tübingen, 1st edn, 1909), pp. 2183 ff. W.G. Kümmel, *The New Testament: The History of the Investigation of its Problems* (London, 1972), pp. 245–324; Gerd Lüdemann, *Die religionsgeschichtliche Schule in Göttingen* (Göttingen, 1987); John K. Riches, *A Century of New Testament Study* (Cambridge, 1993), pp. 14–49; Dieter Sänger, 'Phänomenologie oder Geschichte: Methodische Anmerkungen zur religionsgeschichtlichen Schule', *Z Rel Gg* 32 (1980), pp. 13–27; Anthonie Verheule, *Wilhelm Bousset* (Amsterdam, 1973).

Hodgson, Leonard (1889–1969)

Hodgson is a mainstream theologian of the modern Church of England, fairly typical in his combination of historical, biblical and philosophical methods and his ability to operate on both sides of the boundary between revealed and natural theology. Theology and philosophy, Hodgson insists, are intersecting circles and the area of overlap is not a no man's land but the proper territory of both. From studies and teaching at Oxford, Hodgson became professor of Christian apologetics at the General Theological Seminary, New York in 1925. In 1938 he was appointed canon professor of moral and pastoral theology at Oxford and in 1950 Regius professor of divinity in the same university. His teaching career culminated in his Gifford Lectures *For Faith and Freedom* (1956–57).

The biblical emphasis is seen in his early work *And Was Made Man*, which was intended as a preface to the study of the Gospels. The developed faith of the early church underlies the Gospels and their Christology. The fourth Gospel is needed in order to interpret the synoptics. There is a role for Christian metaphysics

in the construction of belief. Jesus' human knowledge was limited and his authority emerges from genuine human struggle. He knew himself to be the Messiah, but he had no consciousness of his own divinity. Miracles are not valid proofs of his deity. Hodgson affirms the incarnation but is open about the virginal conception. Christians worship Christ as God.

Hodgson's doctrinal intention is evident particularly in *The Doctrine of the Trinity* (1943) and *The Doctrine of the Atonement* (1951). The Trinity is not explicitly revealed in Scripture but is inferred in Christian reflection under the impact of divine revelation (revelation is primarily in historical events, interpreted with the assistance of divine illumination). Trinitarian theology is worked out within the matrix of Christian fellowship and is a practical, not a speculative, doctrine. Hodgson defends a version of the moral influence model of the atonement: God reveals the extent of his love in the life and death of Christ in order to win our hearts to penitence and faith.

An apologetic concern, to commend the Christian faith in the modern world, underlies all Hodgson's work. *Christian Faith and Practice* (1950) originated in lectures to which all members of the university were invited. Hodgson's consistent method is to build bridges between revelation and reason, theology and philosophy, general significant experience and encounter with God.

> All theology which has any truth in it is to that extent both natural and revealed. Christian theology should be thought of as a specific form of natural theology, differentiated by its seeing in certain events particular acts of God of unique and supreme significance for our understanding of everything. (*For Faith and Freedom*, II, p. 3)

The original form of revelation is inaccessible to us and therefore our theology has an inevitable apophatic aspect, but we can see beyond the historical witnesses and ask, 'What must the truth have been and be if they put it like that?' (*For Faith and Freedom*, II, p. 182).

PAUL AVIS

FURTHER READING: *Texts: And Was Made Man: An Introduction to the Study of the Gospels* (London / New York, 1928); *For Faith and Freedom* (Oxford, 1956–57); *The Doctrine of the Trinity* (London, 1943); *The Doctrine of the Atonement* (London, 1951); *Christian Faith and Practice* (Oxford, 1950).

Hollenweger, Walter J. (b. 1927)

The Pentecostal movement, ecumenism and intercultural theology are the areas with which this Swiss theologian and evangelist has engaged experientially and reflectively. The Bible and contemporary realities provide the reference points for his thinking and enable him to seek to discern the activity of the Holy Spirit, the *ruach Yahweh*, outside as well as within the churches. Hollenweger acknowledges twentieth-century Christianity's amazingly culturally diverse liturgical, doctrinal, missiological, socio-economic and political contexts and dimensions while also recognizing critical scholarship's insights into the nature of the first-century church. The church at Corinth provides a case study of pneumatological, ecumenical and intercultural processes and debates.

A Pentecostal who served as a pastor with the Swiss *Pfingstmission* until 1958 and is now a minister of the Reformed Church, Hollenweger studied theology at the universities of Zurich and Basle (1955–61), and from 1961–64 was research assistant for church history and social ethics (Zurich). He was awarded a DTh in 1966 for his ten-volume *Handbuch der Pfingstbewegung,* published (in an abridged form) in German, Spanish and English. This overview of the worldwide Pentecostal movement became a standard reference. From 1965–71 Hollenweger was executive secretary of the Department on Studies in Evangelism as well as secretary for evangelism in the Division of World Mission and Evangelism of the World Council of Churches, Geneva. He then took the chair of mission at the University of Birmingham and The Selly Oak Colleges in Birmingham, England, from which he retired in 1989.

The continued growth of Pentecostalism since the 1960s has confirmed the importance of the movement as an area of international study. The identification of (at least) three streams – classical Pentecostalism, the charismatic movement within the traditional Protestant and Roman Catholic churches, and the indigenous, non-white independent churches of Africa and Latin America – reveals the complexity of issues and contexts noted by Hollenweger to be significant and offering both promises and problems for mission and theological reflection. Major themes which occur are the importance of oral liturgy and narrative theology, and the contribution of so-called 'non-rational' religious elements such as dreams, visions and healing through prayer. Issues raised include the revision of mission policy in recognition that western culture and theology is not the norm to which all others should conform and that theological, spiritual and cultural insights emerge from groups many do not even recognize as churches. Pentecostals have to ask why non-white indigenous Christians who have the hallmarks of Pentecostalism do not conform to the cultural patterns and ideologies of North American and European Pentecostalism; and the non-white indigenous churches must ask what they are going to do with the western heritage of critical analysis and doctrines. These issues are intimately related to hermeneutics, and Hollenweger draws attention to the need to examine principles of selectivity in biblical usage, arguing for 'a theologically responsible syncretism' in a paper entitled 'Priorities in Pentecostal Research' (in Jongeneel (ed.), 1991, p. 15).

Recognition of the ecumenical nature of Pentecostalism was an important insight Hollenweger carried to his appointment with the World Council of Churches. The World Council of Churches, he noted, while sharing characteristics of ecumenism, church renewal and doctrinal inconsistency, fell short of its intention to be a world movement in its under-representation of 'Third World' Christians, in its operation within a western conceptual framework which precluded easy communication with oral traditions (despite the latter being nearer the form of the Gospels), and in its being eschewed by most Pentecostalists and evangelicals.

Hollenweger can be viewed as an intermediary. He acts as a theological interpreter in his experimentation with narrative exegesis where he draws on the insights and experience of both western and non-western traditional modes for both inter- and intra-cultural communication. This 'bi-lingual' facility is demonstrated in his two contributions to the Bossey Consultation on the Significance of the Charismatic Renewal for the Churches, March 1980 (ed. Bittlinger). Practical application in the form of 'non-colonial' evangelism in a European context is demonstrated in the dramas with music, song and dance which Hollenweger continues to write and facilitate (1996). These incorporate the insights of critical scholarship with the interpretation of the script/text by Christians and non-Christians working together, using affective and physical, as well as cognitive, senses. Participants, through their life experiences, bring contemporary issues to the process of producing a 'body-of-Christ' theology. Hollenweger's approach is in line with the thinking in *The Church for Others*, the controversial 1968 report of the World Council of Churches study (under his secretaryship, following the work initiated by H.J. Margull) on the missionary structure of congregations inspired by *Bonhoeffer's 'church for others' and the idea of 'the world setting the agenda'. Following New Testament examples, Hollenweger asserts that evangelism should be dialogic and situational.

Intercultural theology, according to Hollenweger, is an academic discipline which operates in a given culture without making it absolute and is open to the insights of other cultures, thus mirroring the reality of the universal church. That he practises what he has formulated intellectually on the basis of wide research (and shares through prolific writing) is evidenced in the work of his postgraduate students from a variety of countries and denominational traditions, many of whose work is published in *Studies in the Intercultural History of Christianity* (Frankfurt), of which he is a series editor. The scope of his interests – ranging from *Marxism to the Kimbanguist Church, from prayer to business practice, from *Zwingli to Bonhoeffer – are brought together in his three volumes of intercultural theology (German only): 'Experiences of Life's Realities', 'Engagement with Myths' and 'Spirit and Matter'.

Werner Ustorf sees in Hollenweger's theological approach

> the attempt to unreservedly encounter what is realized as "reality", and to resolutely understand the gospel in relation to this reality, notwithstanding that this may go beyond the framework and constructional patterns of our world-view, our ecclesiological or denominational convictions and our theological fixations. (Festschrift, p. 28).

Hollenweger's contribution to theological history has yet to be appraised; it will be interesting to see how western theological academia, in its present internally-fragmented and socially-marginalized condition, responds.

LYNNE PRICE

FURTHER READING: Walter J. Hollenweger, *The Pentecostals* (Peabody, MA, 3rd edn, 1988 [sequel forthcoming]); *Conflict in Corinth and Memoirs of An Old Man* (Munich, 1978; ET New York, 1982); 3 vols. of intercultural theology: *Erfahrungen der Leibhaftigkeit* (Munich, 2nd edn, 1990); *Umgang mit Mythen* (Munich, 1992); *Geist und Materie* (Munich, 1988) (1-vol. abridged French version: *L'Expérience de l'Esprit: Jalons pour une théologie interculturelle* [trans. C. Mazellier and S. Toscer; Geneva, 1991]); 'Healing through Prayer', *Th* 82.747 (1989), pp. 166–74; 'Theology and the Future of the Church', in Peter Byrne and Leslie Houlden (eds.), *Companion Encyclopedia of Theology* (London, 1995), pp. 1017–35; Arnold Bittlinger (ed.), *The Church is Charismatic* (Geneva, 1981); Jan A.B. Jongeneel (ed.), *Experiences of the Spirit: Conference on Pentecostal and Charismatic Research in Europe at Utrecht University 1989* (Frankfurt, 1991); Jan A. B. Jongeneel, et al. (eds.), *Pentecost, Mission and Ecumenism: Essays on Intercultural Theology* (Festschrift Walter Hollenweger; Frankfurt, 1992 [containing full bibliography up to 1990]).

Hromádka, Josef Lukl (1889–1969)

Hromádka was born in Hodslavice, northern Moravia into the family of a Lutheran peasant. He studied theology in Vienna, Basle, Heidelberg and Aberdeen. In Basle, he was influenced by biblical scholars including Paul Wernle and Bernhard Duhm. In Aberdeen, it was *David S. Cairns who inspired him by his missionary zeal and deep concern for concrete church life. Of decisive significance, however, for the young theologian was his encounter with *Ernst Troeltsch in Heidelberg. Hromádka's wider point of departure was continental cultural Protestantism.

The experience of World War I and the collapse of liberal culture in post-war Europe led Hromádka to question the idealistic presuppositions of liberal theology. Particularly, the lack of understanding for the tragic dimension of human sin made its anthropology less convincing. Biblical faith, with its critical evaluation of human potential and its vision of salvation grounded not in human religious ideas but in the sovereign transcendent Lord, seemed to open more realistic and liberating options for coping with the crisis. At the same time, facing the social upheavals in post-war Europe, Hromádka began to doubt if the capitalist system could solve the grave issues of social justice. In this respect, the Russian October Revolution of 1917 emerged for him as a basically hopeful event.

Theologically, Hromádka struggled for a more biblical orientation within his (now united)

Evangelical Church of *Czech Brethren, rediscovering what he called the 'classical line of Christian thought': *Athanasius, *Augustine, *Anselm, the *Reformers (particularly the thinkers of the Czech Reformation from *Huss to *Comenius); and among his contemporaries *Karl Barth, *Emil Brunner and the religious socialists like *Leonhard Ragaz.

Philosophically, Hromádka was a critical yet faithful disciple of T.G. Masaryk in close cooperation with his philosophical friend Emanuel Rádl. Socially, he moved to the left wing of the political scene. He did not hesitate to join the struggle against the emerging danger of German Nazism. After the German occupation of his country in 1939, he had to leave Prague. He found refuge in the United States and became an influential theological teacher at Princeton Theological Seminary.

After World War II, Hromádka returned to Czechoslovakia. As the dean of the Comenius Faculty he became a leader in attempts to find a positive theological way for the church in the new Socialist, later Communist, society. At the same time, he was active in the ecumenical movement. As one of the 'founding fathers' of the World Council of Churches and as a vice-president of the World Alliance of Reformed Churches he was highly respected but also rather controversial because of his defence of radical social changes in Eastern Europe, and later in China and other countries.

There are several theological motives behind Hromádka's ecumenical and political engagement. First is his belief in God's sovereignty over all historical situations and social systems. For him, the encounter with Communist society was the test case of this belief. With its atheistic totalitarian ideology and practice, this system changed the cultural climate for the churches. Hromádka spoke of the 'end of the Constantinian era' and he was aware of the painful implications of such an event. However, exactly in this situation, Christians should bear witness to the challenge and promise of the gospel: the church of Christ is never totally dependent on cultural or social conditions. She lives by the grace of God and not by the 'grace' of secular powers.

Another accent of the gospel is highlighted by Hromádka. The gospel is good news. It is fundamentally a positive message, an offer and an invitation valid also in adverse situations. The primary task of the church is to proclaim the good news even to those who reject it. The title of the book with which Hromádka encouraged and influenced the Christian-Marxist dialogue indicates his direction: *Gospel for Atheists* (1965). With this vision, he struggled also within the ecumenical movement. No anticommunist crusades but the patient and uncompromising witness to the power of God in the cross of Christ as the hope for all: this is the mission and the legitimate strategy of the church of Christ.

The eschatological perspective of the biblical message as understood particularly in the Czech Reformation is another essential motive in Hromádka's theology and practice. The vision of the coming city of God, of the 'new heaven and new earth' motivates the church as a *communio viatorum* (pilgrim community) to work towards the renewal of human hearts and social conditions. His call 'to take history seriously' is one of his *ceterum autem* (frequent remarks). This obliges Christians to try to recognize the signs of the times.

Hromádka took the risk to combine his theological vision with his social and political analyses. He was, practically all his life, a convinced Socialist. The Munich Agreement of 1938, with its betrayal of Czechoslovak democracy by western European powers, led him to the conclusion that western civilization was incapable of dealing with the burning demands of global social justice. He was attracted by the options of the emerging Socialist experiment. He was aware of the totalitarian tendencies in the 'realized (Communist) Socialism'. But he hoped for the possibility of its renewal. The developments in his country before 1968 seemed to confirm his expectations. These hopes were destroyed by the Soviet invasion and occupation. Hromádka addressed a passionate protest against that invasion. He died shortly after – literally with a broken heart.

At this point, a certain ambiguity in the prophetic theology of Hromádka becomes tragically apparent, namely his combination (and occasional mixture) of fundamental theological insight with a particular pattern of historical interpretation under the strong influence of *Marxism. Karl Barth, his close friend and co-pilgrim, asked critical questions in this respect. After the collapse of Communist regimes in Eastern Europe, many in his own church raised emphatically critical objections. Hromádka's political vision is indeed one-sided and controversial. But his theological motives remain valid: the emphasis on the liberating sovereignty of the gospel as well as his appeal to ecumenical theology to face, never to flee, the challenges of history.

JAN MILIČ LOCHMAN

FURTHER READING: *Texts: Doom and Resurrection* (Richmond, VA, 1944); *Gospel for Atheists* (Geneva, 1965); *Thoughts of a Czech Pastor* (London, 1970); *Looking History in the Face* (Madras, 1982).

Hügel, Baron Friedrich von (1852–1925)

Von Hügel was born of mixed parentage. His father, Carl Alexander Anselm, was an Austrian Roman Catholic and his mother, Elizabeth (née Farquharson), a Scottish Presbyterian, who, however, converted to Catholicism, and had the greater influence on von Hügel's piety. Carl von Hügel, baron of the Holy Roman Empire and Austrian minister to Tuscany and Belgium, provided Friedrich with his title and cosmopolitan outlook. Friedrich was born in Florence and grew up there and in Brussels before moving, on his father's retirement, to Torquay, England, in 1867. Though he continued to live chiefly in England for the rest of his life, he often travelled abroad and regularly spent winters in Rome. In 1873 von Hügel married Mary Catherine Herbert, who, like her husband, had both an aristocratic pedigree (being the daughter of Lord Herbert of Lea and sister of the Earl of Pembroke) and a sickly disposition. In 1870 von Hügel suffered an attack of typhus that permanently impaired his hearing. He and 'Molly' had three daughters.

Von Hügel had no formal education, but he was taught first by an Anglican governess; then by a Lutheran pastor, under the direction of a Catholic historian, Alfred von Reumont; and finally by an English schoolmaster, William Pengelly, who fostered his interest in geology. As an adolescent, von Hügel received spiritual guidance from a Dutch Dominican, Raymond Hocking, and in later life from a French priest, Henri Huvelin. Von Hügel was a gentleman-scholar, whose wide interests in science and philosophy, and increasingly in religious history and theology, were not pursued for the sake of a career, but purely for love of the subjects. It was both the breadth and combination of his interests – the conjunction of science and theology, curiosity and devotion – that led von Hügel to explore those areas where religion and modernity were in contact, and apparent conflict.

Von Hügel was first interested in the problems that historical criticism posed for the historicity and inspiration of Scripture. He learnt Hebrew so as to more closely follow arguments regarding the Mosaic authorship of the Pentateuch. In the wake of Pope Leo XIII's encyclical 'Providentissimus Deus' (1893), he developed a doctrine of biblical inspiration (presented in three articles in the *Dublin Review*, 1894–95) that allowed for the Bible to be a wholly human work, complete with errors, yet also a medium of divine revelation. Von Hügel's interest in these and other matters brought him into contact with most of the leading liberal Catholics of his day, on both sides of the English Channel. Some of them, such as Wilfred Ward, were moderate in their liberalism, looking for a church that would be open to, but not uncritical of, modern scholarship. Others, such as George Tyrrell and Alfred Loisy, wished to reform Catholic teaching in the light of current critical trends, advocating a less historical and more symbolist reading of the Bible, including the New Testament.

Von Hügel's own historical studies and philosophical reflections led him to the more extreme end of the liberal spectrum. In 1908, Tyrrell could write of von Hügel:

> Wonderful man! Nothing is true; but the sum total of nothings is sublime! Christ was not merely ignorant but a téte brulé [sic]; Mary was not merely not a virgin, but an unbeliever and a rather unnatural mother; the Eucharist was a Pauline invention – yet he makes his daily visit to the Blessed Sacrament and for all I know tells his beads devoutly.

Tyrrell may have exaggerated von Hügel's scepticism, and in so far as Tyrrell fairly represents von Hügel's views at the time, they were for private consumption only. Von Hügel's public pronouncements were much more circumspect, being elaborately, often excruciatingly, qualified.

Von Hügel was certainly a 'modernist', but a cautious one, who chiefly worked behind the scenes, fostering and maintaining conversations and correspondence between many of the other modernists, often urging them to write and publish what he was too diplomatic or timid to do himself. Indeed, some thought that von Hügel was the engine of the movement, at least in Britain, and that if it had not been for his influence, Tyrrell would not have developed and published his historical scepticism and immanentist theology to the extent that in 1906 he was expelled from the *Jesuits and eventually excommunicated. It is in this aspect, as an *éminence grise*, that von Hügel appears as the Count Paul d'Étranges in Mrs Wilfred Ward's *roman a clef* of the modernist movement, *Out of Due Time* (1906).

Despite von Hügel's role in the modernist movement, his thought developed in a different direction from that of his modernist colleagues. During the course of his friendship with Tyrrell he became increasingly interested in metaphysical issues, and with the question of transcendence. In *The Mystical Element of Religion* (1908), that had been ten years in preparation, and in his later writings – *Eternal Life* (1912), and the first and second series of *Essays and Addresses on the Philosophy of Religion* (1921, 1926) and *The Reality of God* (1931) – von Hügel articulated an account of human life that recognized both its concrete givenness and the difficulty of describing its diversity. What is known is always encountered within a greater unknown, for 'life, after all, is a stretching out of faith and love to God into the dark'; and Christianity – for von Hügel – is the formation of persons who can so stretch.

For von Hügel, the three elements of religion – its historical instantiation, its speculative enquiry and its spiritual waiting upon the dark – are all necessary for the one end of learning to love God, not beyond but in the concrete complexities of human existence. There is no such thing as a specific mystical experience, but all experience is potentially mystical; all of life is open to the possibility of apprehending, however dimly, that from which all life comes. Von Hügel was a 'panentheist', for whom God is neither located beyond the world, nor identified with the world, but encountered *in* the world.

GERARD LOUGHLIN

FURTHER READING: Texts: *The Mystical Element of Religion as Studied in St Catherine of Genoa and Her Friends* (2 vols.; London [1908], 2nd edn 1923); *Eternal Life: A Study of Its Implications and Applications* (Edinburgh, 1912); *Essays and Addresses on the Philosophy of Religion: First Series* (London, 1921); *Essays and Addresses on the Philosophy of Religion: Second Series* (London, 1926); *Letters from Baron von Hügel to a Niece* (ed. Gwendolen Greene; London, 1928). Studies: Michael de la Bedoyere, *The Life of Baron von Hügel* (London, 1951); Lawrence F. Barmann, *Baron Friedrich von Hügel and the Modernist Crisis in England* (Cambridge, 1972); James J. Kelly, *Baron Friedrich von Hügel's Philosophy of Religion* (Louvain, 1983); Patrick Sherry, 'Von Hügel: Philosophy and Spirituality', *Rel St* 17 (1981), pp. 1–18; Joseph P. Whelan, *The Spirituality of Friedrich von Hügel* (London, 1971).

Hugh of St Victor (c. 1096–1141)

Theologian, biblical commentator, monk and canon of the abbey of St Victor in Paris. About Hugh's early life, little is known. One account indicates that he came from Flanders, another, Saxony. In any case, he entered the community of *Augustinian canons at St Victor (which had been founded in 1110 by William of Champeaux) around 1114, and he served as director of its school from 1120 until his death on 11 February 1141.

Hugh's academic work was clearly set in the context of his role in the preparation of young novices for the contemplative life within the abbey (e.g., *De institutione novitiorum*). His writings range widely across the fields of learning, including geometry (*Practica geometriae*), grammar (*De grammatica*) and philosophy (*Epitome Dindimi ad philosophiam*). Most prominent in this category is Hugh's *Didascalion de studio legendi*, a work that introduces the study of the arts and of theology. In six books, this text sets forth the study of the arts in systematic fashion. The first three books treat worldly learning, including philosophy, logic and the liberal arts and sciences. The last three books take up the science of biblical study, the *sacra pagina*. Biblical study itself is intended to foster the contemplative life; the progression is from the careful reading and analysis of Scripture in its literal sense (*lectio*), to reflection on the biblical text itself (*meditatio*) and, finally, to the contemplation of the divine mysteries (*contemplatio*). The literal sense of the text is foundational to Hugh's hermeneutical approach to the Christian Bible, and he is critical of those who would move too hastily to interpret it allegorically. All mystical exegesis, he argues, is built upon the literal sense and presumes it.

Not surprisingly, then, Hugh was also a significant and original commentator on the biblical text. His biblical exposition includes a commentary on the Octateuch, the *Notulae in Pentateuchum, in librum Iudicium et in libros*

Regnum (modern title: *Adnotationes Elucidatoriae*); on the Psalms, *In quosdam Psalmos*; on Ecclesiastes, *Homiliae in Ecclesiasten*; and on Jeremiah, *In Threnos Jeremiae*. Hugh occupied a central place in Beryl Smalley's classic study of medieval biblical interpretation. She argued that his work on Scripture amounted to a revival of biblical studies. According to Smalley, Hugh's 'great service to exegesis was to lay more stress on the literal interpretation *relatively* to the spiritual, and to develop the sources for it' (Smalley, p. 102).

Hugh's systematic exposition of Christian teaching, *De sacramentis christianae fidei* (*On the Sacraments of the Christian Faith*), is considered the first great *summa* of theology produced in the medieval period. In the two volumes of this work, Hugh's mystical vision not only of Scripture but also of the entire creation becomes apparent. Having constructed a foundation out of the raw materials of the study of the literal meaning of Scripture and the scientific investigation of history and the whole created order, it becomes the theologian's task at last to move on to the divine mysteries which these things figure.

Indeed, the *De Sacramentis* proceeds along historical rather than strictly theological lines – evidence that Hugh had constructed a distinctively Victorine version of the Christian philosophy of history articulated in its classic form by St Augustine. The sacred history recorded in the Scriptures stands at the centre of world history, which implies the Christianization both of history and of the Old Testament. The ages of human history, according to Hugh, may be categorized according to the manner of God's restoration of the fallen creation: the first, the age of the natural law; the second, the age of the Mosaic law; and the last, the age of grace (Bk. 1, Pt. 8, ch. 11). The first book of the *De sacramentis* includes everything from creation to incarnation; the second book discusses last things and the Christian doctrine of the sacraments.

Hugh's writings are simultaneously deeply traditional and strikingly innovative, demonstrating that even in the Middle Ages faithfulness and creativity were not considered mutually exclusive. His learning and influence were so prodigious that his contemporaries sometimes referred to him as the 'second Augustine'. That influence was magnified, moreover, by the incorporation of many of his ideas into the *Libri Sententiarum* (*Books of Sentences*) of *Peter Lombard, and by the biblical work of two of his students, *Richard and Andrew of St Victor.

MICKEY L. MATTOX

FURTHER READING: *Texts: Opera Omnia, PL,* 175–177 (also contains some works doubtfully ascribed to Hugh); 'On the Sacraments of the Christian Faith', partial ET in *A Scholastic Miscellany: Anselm to Ockham* (ed. and trans. Eugene R. Fairweather; LCC; Philadelphia, 1956), pp. 300–18; *Hugh of St Victor on the Sacraments of the Christian Faith* (trans. R.J. Defarrari; Washington, DC, 1939); *The Didascalion of Hugh of St Victor: A Medieval Guide to the Arts* (trans. Jerome Taylor; Records of Civilization: Sources and Studies 64; New York, 1966); *Soliloquy on the Earnest Money of the Soul* (Medieval Philosophical Texts in Translation 9; Milwaukee, WI, 1956). *Studies:* R. Baron, *Études sur Hugues de Saint-Victor* (Paris, 1963); M.-D. Chenu, *Nature, Man, and Society in the Twelfth Century: Essays on New Theological Perspectives in the Latin West* (Chicago, 1968); H.J. Pollitt, 'Some Considerations on the Structure and Sources of Hugh of St Victor's Notes on the Octateuch', *Recherches* 33 (1966), pp.5–38; B. Smalley, *The Study of the Bible in the Middle Ages* (Oxford, 2nd edn, 1951); G.A. Zinn, '*Historia fundamentum est*: The Role of History in the Contemplative Life according to Hugh of St Victor', in *Contemporary Reflections on the Medieval Christian Tradition: Essays in Honor of Ray C. Petry* (ed. G.H. Shriver; Durham, NC, 1974).

Hume, David (1711–76)

Scottish philosopher. Hume was born in Edinburgh, and he enrolled at its university in 1723, aged twelve. He did not take a degree, but there he became enamoured of the 'new philosophy' that, in the wake of Sir Isaac Newton, was promoting an inductive, 'experimental method of reasoning'. Failing to find interest in the study of the law, and failing to become a merchant in Bristol, Hume set himself to write a moral philosophy whose method would be strictly empirical. This would become his first and greatest work, *A Treatise of Human Nature*. It was chiefly written between 1735 and 1737 at La Flèche in Anjou, where Hume was able to use the library of the local Jesuit College, which had educated *René Descartes and had subsequently become a centre for Cartesian *'rationalism'. Hume's *Treatise* offered a sceptical critique of such philosophy, and its belief in the power of reason to secure certain knowledge of God, self and world.

The first two volumes of the *Treatise* – on the 'understanding' and the 'passions' respectively –

were published in January 1739, with the third – on 'morals' – appearing in November 1740. All three were published anonymously, and Hume publicly admitted authorship only posthumously, in his autobiography *My Own Life* (1776) and in the advertisement for *Essays and Treatises* (1777). In his autobiography, Hume declared that the *Treatise* 'fell *dead-born from the press*; without reaching such distinction, as even to excite a murmur among the zealots'. But in fact the 'zealots' had murmured and the *Treatise* attracted hostile comment, both abroad and in Britain. It was because it met with such little understanding that Hume came to believe it had been written too hastily, published too early, and he spent the rest of his life attempting to say better what he had said at the first. Thus in 1748 he published *An Enquiry Concerning Human Understanding*, which in 1751 was followed by *An Enquiry Concerning the Principles of Morals*. The projected fourth and fifth volumes of the *Treatise* – on 'politics' and 'criticism' – though never written as such, were supplied in Hume's *History of England* (1754–62) and in various essays on aesthetic subjects.

Though acclaimed in his own lifetime – James Boswell in 1762 called him the greatest writer in Britain – Hume's work gained general approbation only in the twentieth century. Hume's 'experimental' method was congenial to the positivistic turn in twentieth-century philosophy, which again saw the natural sciences as providing a model for a precise and proven philosophy. With Hume, the positivists of the 1930s (such as A.J. Ayer) would commit to the flames any book that did not contain 'abstract reasoning concerning quantity or number' or 'experimental reasoning concerning matter of fact and existence'. For such books 'can contain nothing but sophistry and illusion', and chief among them are those of 'divinity or school metaphysics' (*An Enquiry Concerning Human Understanding*, sect. XII, pt. III). Furthermore, Hume's concern with the human person as first and foremost a passionate being, in whose interests reason is made to serve, became of increasing interest to a philosophy of human knowing – 'epistemology' – that in the 1950s was itself becoming an 'anthropology of knowledge' (Stuart Hampshire).

In his own day and since, Hume has been read as offering a withering critique of religion and the morality founded upon it, and all the more withering because of his inimitable style

and mordant wit, especially in the posthumously published *Dialogues Concerning Natural Religion* (1779). These were modelled on Cicero's *De Natura Deorum* (*Concerning the Nature of the Gods*) and, in the persons of Cleanthes, Philo and Demea, considered various arguments for the existence of a deity. The principal argument discussed is that from design, which infers the existence of a supreme authoring intelligence from the supposedly self-evident order of the world. This argument would become popular with the publication of William Paley's *Evidences of Christianity* (1794) and *Natural Theology* (1802), but Hume's Philo had already supplied a devastating critique, from which the argument has never really recovered.

However, Hume did not properly engage with Christian theology, but only with 'natural religion', 'theism' or 'deism' (terms he used interchangeably), and it was only because 'theism' had become confused with orthodox Christian faith, by both 'zealot' and 'freethinker', that Hume's coruscating arguments against the one could be supposed to touch the other. It need not be thought that Hume, like *Kant, wished to dispose of 'natural religion' in order to make room for 'faith', but in the *Enquiry Concerning Human Understanding* he did acknowledge that 'faith and revelation' are the 'best and most solid foundation' of 'divinity and theology' (sect. XII, pt. III). As Hume knew, this seems like no foundation at all when it is thought necessary to secure 'faith and revelation' by a preceding 'reason'. But in the twentieth century, after the waning of positivist influence on theology and the growth of a neo-orthodoxy every bit as scornful of 'natural religion' as was Hume, it was possible for Christian theology not only to endorse Hume's critique of 'theism', but also to approve his more general undermining of 'reason' as providing certain knowledge. For Hume, all knowledge rests upon imaginative belief and contains an element of indeterminacy.

However, Hume's satirical *Natural History of Religion* (1757), written at about the same time as the *Dialogues* (early 1750s), is perhaps of more importance for the history of theology, since it announces a more purely secular approach to religion, issuing in nineteenth-century 'anthropology of religion' and twentieth-century 'religious studies'. The *History* claims to show how religion – which waxes and wanes between polytheism and theism – arises from humankind's attempt to control natural events, supposing them to be caused by invisible agents otherwise like itself. It also considers the intolerance to which religion gives rise, and while asserting the self-evident truth of Christian theism, also claims that the best begets the worst, so that the systematic violence of the Inquisition is more terrible than the occasional human sacrifices of the pagans. Hume prefigures nearly all subsequent critiques of religion, including those of *Nietzsche and Freud.

GERARD LOUGHLIN

FURTHER READING: *Texts: A Treatise of Human Nature* (ed. with intro. by Ernest C. Mossner; Harmondsworth, Middlesex, 1985); *Enquiries Concerning Human Understanding and Concerning the Principles of Morals* (ed. and intro. by L.A. Selby-Bigge and P.H. Nidditch; Oxford, 3rd edn, 1975); *Principle Writings on Religion including Dialogues Concerning Natural Religion and the Natural History of Religion* (ed. with intro. and notes by J.C.A. Gaskin; Oxford / New York, 1993); *Selected Essays* (ed. with intro. and notes by Stephen Copley and Andrew Edgar; Oxford / New York, 1996). *Studies:* E.C. Mossner, *The Life of David Hume* (London, 1954); David Fate Norton (ed.), *Cambridge Companion to David Hume* (Cambridge, 1994); N. Kemp Smith, *The Philosophy of David Hume* (London, 1941); J.C.A. Gaskin, *Hume's Philosophy of Religion* (London, 1978); Gilles Deleuze, *Empiricism and Subjectivity: An Essay on Hume's Theory of Human Nature* (trans. Constantin V. Boundas; New York [1953], 1991).

Huss, John (c. 1370–1415)

John Huss was born at Husinec in southern Bohemia. He studied philosophy and theology at the University of Prague with an impressive academic career. His theology was shaped under the influence of the Czech reform movement as represented by Jan Milič of Kroměříž (1325–74) and Matthias of Janov (1355–93). Of particular importance for Huss was the thought of John Wyclif, whose writings were circulating in Prague thanks to the Czech students studying at Oxford. Wyclif's writings aroused a great controversy. Huss agreed with the English Reformer that the historically developed church could not be identified with the true church of Christ. The true church is the *ecclesia invisibilis*, understood as the *coetus electorum*. God alone decides who belongs to this true church. The debate over Wyclif's reforms brought Huss to the very centre of academic life and university policy (in

1409 he was made the rector of the University of Prague).

Huss was even more influential in his role as preacher at the Bethlehem chapel. In his Czech sermons, he contrasted the actual lifestyle of the power-hungry 'Constantinian Church' with the biblical vision of the apostolic community of disciples following Jesus, the 'poor king of the poor'. Huss's resolute opposition to the indulgence preaching sponsored by the Pope proved the critical turning point in his struggle. In 1412 the *Curia* placed the city of Prague under the ban because of Huss. He left for southern Bohemia but refused to discontinue his reformatory work and justified his refusal in a solemn appeal to Jesus Christ. Huss engaged in a wide-ranging tour of open-air preaching and met with surprisingly strong support among his people. He also continued his writing and finished a series of important works in Czech and Latin, among them his great work *De Ecclesia*.

In 1414 Huss decided to defend his cause before the Council of Constance. He made thorough preparations and drafted a series of papers to enable him to counter the charges against him. He did not get a fair hearing, however. Against all the promises made to him, he was arrested and imprisoned. The Council was not really interested in any dialogue with Huss but determined to secure from him an unqualified retraction. Huss was prepared to be corrected by the council, but only if it convinced him by arguments drawn from Holy Scripture. Even when physically weakened, Huss refused to recant. As a 'heretic' he was burned at the stake on 6 July 1415.

The hope of the anti-reform forces that the Hussite movement would be extinguished by the martyrdom of Huss was not fulfilled. On the contrary, practically the whole kingdom of Bohemia rose up in his defence. The Hussites defended their reformation against the series of crusades launched against them. In 1432 the Council of Basle had to acknowledge the right of Hussite *utraquism* (the Lord's Supper was celebrated 'under both kinds', not only with bread but also with the chalice, the symbol of Hussitism).

The teaching and preaching of John Huss has one central concern: the sovereignty of truth. One of Huss's best-known statements is the following exhortation from his Czech *Exposition of the Faith*: 'Therefore, faithful Christian, seek the truth, listen to the truth, learn the truth, love the truth, tell the truth, learn the truth, defend the truth even to death.' This concentration on the motive of truth has manifold implications. In his philosophy, Huss was the (medieval) realist: ideas (universals) are ontologically essential and not merely 'names' or conventional means of communication. Concepts, convictions and creedal formulations are not matters for theoretical games but have their life-shaping consequences. This attitude has theological, and particularly Christological, roots, and applies already to the very concept of truth as such. This concept is closer to the Hebraic *emeth* (the truth as fidelity in the covenant of, and with, God) than to the Greek philosophical *aletheia*, or cognitive insight into the structure of being. Scripture bears the unique witness to this truth and Jesus Christ is its unique incarnation. Hence the reformation appeal of Huss against the church authorities is addressed quite concretely to Jesus Christ as the only true head of the church.

This has ecclesiological and even social implications. The question of the church has to be approached as a question of truth. The church has no independent significance in itself but depends fundamentally on its relation to the truth, to Christ in the Holy Spirit. If it forgets this constitutive relation and claims ultimate authority for itself, it goes astray and is in critical need of renewal and reform. This renewal has not only a theoretical, but also an inseparable practical social dimension. Christ, the heavenly head of the church, is at the same time the Jesus of history – the messenger of the 'good news' for all, but particularly for those who 'labour and are heavy laden'. Consequently, as teacher and especially as preacher, Huss interpreted the gospel as an option in favour of the poor and applied the biblical 'no' and 'yes' not only to the spiritual, but also to the social, condition of his hearers. Huss's successors, particularly the Taborites, developed these emphases into a revolutionary programme with elements of 'apostolic communism'.

In the spirit of the whole Czech reform movement, Huss's theology has a strong eschatological element. Not only his concept of truth, but also his personal reformation struggle, are upheld by confidence in the fidelity and promise of God. This faith strengthened him in his painful decision 'to defend the truth even to death'. The later motto of the Hussite movement (which in turn became the motto of the Czech state), was 'the truth of the Lord prevails'. It is an affirmation of eschatologically inspired and oriented faith in the true spirit of Huss.

JAN MILIČ LOCHMAN

FURTHER READING: *Texts: Tractatus de ecclesia* (ed. S.H. Thomson; Boulder, CO, 1956); *The Letters of Jan Hus* (trans. and ed. M. Spinka; Manchester, 1972). *Studies:* M. Spinka, *John Hus: A Biography* (Princeton, 1968); P. de Voogt, *L'hérésie de Jean Hus* (Louvain, 1960).

Iconoclast Controversy

Although iconoclasm as an imperial policy in Byzantium did not begin until the eighth century, the debate about images had already begun in the seventh century. We can see this from the surviving *Adversus Judaeos* literature of the period, in which the veneration of images is discussed. For example, in his *Apology Against the Jews* Leontius of Neapolis has a Jew accuse a Christian of breaking the second commandment. In response, the Christian points out that God sanctioned image making when he instructed Moses to make the cherubim to put over the ark. The Christian agrees that it is wrong to make an image of the invisible Godhead, but because of the incarnation it is not wrong to make an image of Christ.

The first period of iconoclasm (726–87).

Sometime during the 720s the patriarch of Constantinople, Germanos, engaged in correspondence with three hierarchs of the Byzantine Church in Asia Minor concerning the veneration of images. The contents of the patriarch's letters show that at least one of the hierarchs had gone as far as removing icons from his church. It was the Byzantine emperor Leo III in 726 who took steps to implement an official policy of iconoclasm by removing Christ's image from the Chalke Gate of the imperial palace. In 730 the emperor issued an edict ordering the destruction of images, and as a result the patriarch Germanos was forced to resign. He was replaced by a new patriarch, Anastasius, who signed the iconoclast decree and thus implicated the ecclesiastical hierarchy in the imperial policy of iconoclasm.

The most important defender of images during the first period of iconoclasm was *John of Damascus (c. 665–749). He may have been asked to undertake the defence of images by the patriarch Germanos. In his *Three Orations on the Holy Images* he makes explicit reference to the imperial edict of Leo III and to the exile of Germanos. John's work is the first systematic attempt to develop a theology of Christian image-making, and it remains the definitive statement on the veneration of images in the orthodox tradition.

It was under Leo III's son, Constantine V, that the policy of iconoclasm became more oppressive. There was considerable persecution of icono phile monks, as Constantine found the monks the most stubborn defenders of icons.

The emperor himself composed several short works concerned with iconoclast theology, two of which are preserved in the writings of the ninth-century iconophile patriarch of Constantinople, Nikephoros. In 754 Constantine assembled a synod in Constantinople in order to secure conciliar endorsement for his iconoclast policy. The Council of Hiereia was attended by 338 bishops – an indication of the extent of Constantine's influence on the hierarchy of the church. Only the *Horos*, or definition of faith, of the council of 754 has survived, owing to the fact that it was refuted and incorporated into the proceedings of the Seventh Oecumenical Council of 787. The council of 754 publicly anathematized three iconophiles, including John of Damascus.

When Constantine died in 775 he was succeeded by his son, Leo IV. Leo's wife Irene became an ardent iconophile, and it was probably due to her influence that iconophile prisoners were released and persecution of the monks ceased. Although the policy of iconoclasm remained official, with an iconoclast patriarch remaining on the throne, Leo IV did not pursue it with anything like the same vigour as his father. When the emperor died in 780 his son Constantine VI was still a minor, and so his mother Irene acted as regent.

With the help of a new patriarch, Tarasios, an iconophile like Irene, she summoned an ecumenical council to overturn the policy of iconoclasm. By this means the Byzantine Church could put its house in order, as well as improve relations with the papacy, which had condemned iconoclasm from the beginning. The Seventh Oecumenical Council met in the church of Hagia Sophia at Nicaea in 787. It was attended by 350 bishops, and theologically the most important part of its proceedings is the sixth session which contains the council's refutation of the *Horos* of 754.

Constantine VI ruled as sole emperor from 790 until 797, when he was removed on orders from Irene. The empress herself ruled till 802, when she was in turn overthrown by the emperor Nikephoros I. Nikephoros I seems to have had some sympathy with iconoclasm, but he does not appear to have tried to revive the policy. It was during his reign that the patriarch Nikephoros was appointed, in 806. The emperor Nikephoros I was succeeded by his son-in-law Michael I in 811. The interval between the first and second periods of iconoclasm was an uneasy truce between the two parties. The Seventh Oecumenical Council of 787 succeeded in purging iconoclasm from amongst the ranks of the clergy and the monastic hierarchy, but it does not appear to have had much effect on other adherents of iconoclasm within Byzantine society.

The second period of iconoclasm (813–43). When the emperor Leo V came to the throne in 813 he restored the policy of iconoclasm and ushered in its second phase. He was motivated by the belief that the Byzantine empire had fared better under the iconoclasts of the eighth century. He was supported in this by John the Grammarian, an abbot of a monastery in Constantinople who had once been an icon painter. The emperor engaged in debate with the patriarch Nikephoros in the hope of reaching an accommodation, but Nikephoros refused to compromise over the issue of icons. Part of the compromise involved the patriarch agreeing to the taking down of icons where they were low enough to be kissed and venerated. Eventually the patriarch was deposed and sent into exile, where he wrote several works in defence of images.

With Nikephoros in exile, the mantle of iconophile resistance fell on the shoulders of Theodore the Studite, abbot of the famous Studios monastery in Constantinople. Leo V called a synod in 815 which based its definition of faith largely on that of the earlier iconoclastic council of 754. It repudiated the Seventh Oecumenical Council of 787 and recognized instead the council of 754 as the Seventh Oecumenical Council. The definition of faith of the council of 815 is preserved in the writings of the patriarch Nikephoros. Theodore the Studite was exiled as a result of his opposition to the new iconoclasm, and an iconoclast abbot was appointed to his monastery. Further persecution of iconophile monks and bishops took place, but Theodore continued the iconophile resistance from his place of exile.

The emperor Michael II came to the throne in 821, and tried to place himself above the controversy by recalling the iconophiles from exile. This allowed the return of Theodore the Studite to the capital, but not the restoration of Nikephoros to the patriarchal throne. The emperor suggested that Nikephoros might return if he agreed to remain neutral on the question of images. Theodore the Studite was banished into exile again for refusing to participate in a synod of both parties to discuss the question of images. Michael II appointed an iconoclast to the vacant patriarchal throne, and made John the Grammarian tutor to his son Theophilus.

On the succession of Michael II's son Theophilus in 829, a fresh wave of persecutions began. Theophilus was a cultured and educated emperor who enjoyed the support of John the Grammarian. The emperor made his former tutor patriarch of Constantinople in 834. In 830 Theophilus married Theodora, who turned out to be a fervent iconophile and who was responsible for the restoration of icons in 843. Several iconoclastic edicts issued during Theophilus's reign led to the punishment of iconophile monks. The faces of the two brothers Theodore and Theophanes were tattooed with iambic verses, and the hands of the icon painter Lazarus were branded. This persecution may have been prompted by the emperor's discovery of iconophile sympathies among the women in his household.

When Theophilus died in 842, his widow Theodora became regent for their son Michael III. On the death of Theophilus, the main opponent to the restoration of icons was the patriarch John the Grammarian. Theodora convoked a synod in 843 to restore the veneration of icons with the help of a new iconophile patriarch Methodius. The synod anathematized the iconoclasts and affirmed the teaching of the Fathers of the Seventh Oecumenical Council of 787. It was in 843 that the 'Feast of the Triumph of Orthodoxy' was established on the first Sunday in Lent, a feast which is still celebrated in the Orthodox Church.

Various suggestions have been made concerning the motivations for iconoclasm amongst Byzantine emperors in the eighth and ninth centuries, none of which are fully satisfactory. The loss of so much territory to the Arabs in the seventh century may well have led the iconoclast emperors to see in the aniconic culture of Islam a means of reasserting Byzantine imperial power. The presence of this rival religion provided, if not the initial impetus, then at least an abiding stimulus for the debate about images in Byzantium.

KEN PARRY

FURTHER READING: K. Parry, *Depicting the Word: Byzantine Iconophile Thought of the Eighth and Ninth*

Centuries (Leiden, 1996); A. Giakalis, *Images of the Divine: The Theology of Icons at the Seventh Ecumenical Council* (Leiden, 1994); S.H. Griffith, 'Images, Islam and Christian Icons: A Moment in the Christian/Muslim Encounter in Early Islamic Times', in *La Syrie de Byzance à l'Islam VIIe-VIIIe Siècles* (ed. O. Canivet and J.-P. Rey-Coquais; Paris, 1992); L. Ouspensky, *Theology of the Icon* (2 vols.; New York, 1992); J. Pelikan, *Imago Dei: The Byzantine Apologia for Icons* (New Haven, 1990); D.J. Sahas, *Icon and Logos: Sources in Eighth-Century Iconoclasm* (Toronto, 1986); S. Gero, *Byzantine Iconoclasm During the Reign of Constantine V with Particular Attention to the Oriental Sources* (CSCO 384; Louvain, 1977); *Byzantine Iconoclasm During the Reign of Leo III with Particular Attention to the Oriental Sources* (CSCO 346; Louvain, 1973).

Ignatius of Loyola (c. 1491–1556)

The exact date of Ignatius of Loyola's birth is somewhat uncertain due to the fact that the baptismal records of the church in which he was baptized, the church of San Sebastián in the town of Azpeitia in the Basque province of Guipúzcoa in Spain, were later destroyed by fire. But it would seem that Ignatius was born in 1491 rather than 1495, as Ignatius himself seems to have believed. Ignatius was baptized Iñigo López de Loyola. It was not until later in life that he took the name of Ignatius, perhaps because it was better known or because of his own devotion to St Ignatius of Antioch.

Iñigo had seven brothers and five sisters and was the child of Beltrán Ibañez de Oñaz and Marina Sánchez de Licona. His father was the Lord of Loyola, the name of the family's manor house and its surrounding properties. The surname Loyola alternated in his family with another surname, Oñaz, because the manor houses and lands of two Guipuzcoan families had been joined by marriage in 1261. The Licona family was from the Biscayan town of Ondárroa. According to Iñigo's mother's marriage contract, her father was a member of the king's council. Thus Iñigo came from old and distinguished stock. His family was in contact with the royalty of Spain and possessed a sizeable income from numerous farms, homesteads, the patronage of the church in Azpeitia, blacksmith shops and a mill.

Iñigo's mother died while he was still a child, and his father died when he was sixteen. But a year or two before his death, Ignatius's father received an invitation from the chief treasurer of the Kingdom of Castile, Juan Velázquez de Cuéllar, who was related through his wife to Iñigo's mother's family, the Liconas, to send one of his sons to be raised at his home in Arévalo. Iñigo was sent and spent the next decade as a page in the court of the treasurer of the king, learning the manners of a courtier and being prepared for a career as a gentleman in the king's service.

With the death of King Ferdinand in 1516 Velázquez de Cuéllar lost favour and Iñigo was forced to seek his future elsewhere. Family connections and his years of service at Arévalo helped him find employment under the Don Antonio Manrique de Lara, the duke of Nájera, then the viceroy of Navarre. It was in the service of de Lara that Iñigo was to experience the event that changed his life. The French had invaded the kingdom of Navarre and the city of Pamplona was under siege. The military situation was hopeless, given the superior French forces, but Iñigo refused to abandon the city's fortress and held out against the French until a cannon ball shattered his right leg and wounded the left.

The French allowed him to be carried back to Loyola, where he spent almost a year convalescing. The first setting of the right leg was redone at Loyola, but after this resetting one bone protruded over the other and would have made it impossible for Iñigo to wear the high, close-fitting boots fashionable at that time. Iñigo had the protruding piece sawed off and the leg stretched. In his autobiography dictated two years before his death to a fellow *Jesuit, Iñigo related that during this procedure he said nothing and gave no sign of pain other than clenching his fists.

During his convalescence at Loyola there was nothing to read except a *Life of Christ* and the *Lives of the Saints*. Forced to read them, Iñigo became interested in the great deeds of asceticism practised by the saints and began to ask himself why he could not do likewise. He also daydreamed of a lady-love, someone of too high a station to be his wife. Then he began to notice that his dreams of romance were pleasant while he was experiencing them but did not leave him comfortable after their departure. His thoughts about the deeds of the saints, on the other hand, provided him comfort both while he was having them and afterwards. This was his first lesson in what he would later identify as the discernment of spirits. During these months of convalescence he also had a vision of Mary and Jesus which made it possible for him to turn away from his past sins of the flesh and never again surrender to temptations of this nature.

When he was well again, his resolve was to go to Jerusalem and live there as the saints had lived. On his way to take ship at Barcelona he stopped at the famous shrine of the Black Madonna at the *Benedictine monastery of Montserrat, where he made an all-night vigil, hung up his sword and exchanged his nobleman's clothes for those of a beggar. Then, in an attempt to avoid meeting friends, he took a back road for Barcelona. That detour led him to the small town of Manresa, where he stayed for almost a year. There he prayed seven hours a day, wrote down his reflections and experienced both visions and periods of doubt and dryness which were so severe that he went without food for a week and was tempted to despair and suicide. But afterwards his sense of God's presence returned and he experienced an intellectual vision of many truths of the faith, which he would later say was never surpassed. He left Manresa a changed man.

The visit to Jerusalem was short. The *Franciscans refused to let him stay there. Iñigo went back to Europe and decided to study in order to be able to help others. His first academic attempts were at learning Latin in Barcelona and lasted two years. Then he was ready for university studies at Alcalá. But there he experienced difficulties with church authorities because he had not yet studied theology and yet he spoke to people of God and even distinguished between serious and venial sin. Forbidden to make such distinctions, he left Alcalá and went to the university at Salamanca where he experienced the same difficulties with church authorities. He therefore decided to go to the University of Paris.

He arrived in Paris in 1528. By giving fellow students his *Spiritual Exercises*, the fruit of his year in Manresa, he gathered around himself six others who together with him dedicated their lives to poverty, chastity and future missionary work in Jerusalem.

Ignatius, now a Master of Arts, left Paris in 1535. His plan was to visit his homeland and then to meet his companions in Venice where they hoped to find passage to the Holy Land. His companions, now numbering nine, joined him there in 1537.

When it was clear that their dream of going to the Holy Land was not realizable, they placed themselves at the disposal of the pope for service to the church. The question now was whether they would simply be dispersed in papal service or whether they wished to create a structure which would insure their unity despite this dispersal. They decided for the latter, which meant creating a leadership that would serve this unity. Since they were already vowed to lives of poverty and celibacy, this third component, leadership, would mean adding a vow of obedience and would give them the traditional threefold ingredient of religious life in the church. They therefore decided to petition the papacy to recognize them as a new religious order. At the request of the others Ignatius drew up a sketch of this new order (the 'Formula of the Institute'), which was submitted to Rome in 1539 and approved in 1540. The name they chose for themselves was the companions of Jesus, a name which they had used to identify themselves once they arrived in Italy and which was confirmed by a vision which Ignatius had on his way to Rome in 1537. In 1541, Ignatius's companions elected him as their leader or general.

Ignatius spent the remainder of his life in Rome, writing the *Constitutions*, the rules governing life in this new Society (Company) of Jesus, and directing it by means of letters sent to his fellow *Jesuits now scattered throughout the world. By the time of his death in 1556, the order had grown to a thousand men serving as teachers, preachers and missionaries throughout the world.

GERALD F. FINNEGAN, SJ

FURTHER READING: James Brodick, SJ, *The Origins of the Jesuits* (Chicago, 1986); Cándido de Dalmases, SJ, *Ignatius of Loyola, Founder of the Jesuits* (trans. Jerome Aixalá, SJ; St Louis, MO, 1985); *Ignatius of Loyola: The Spiritual Exercises and Selected Works* (ed. George E. Ganss, SJ; New York, 1991); George E. Ganss, SJ, *The Spiritual Exercises of Saint Ignatius: A Translation and Commentary* (Chicago, 1992); Joseph N. Tylenda, SJ, *A Pilgrim's Journey: The Autobiography of Saint Ignatius* (Collegeville, MN, 1991).

Illingworth, John Richardson (1848–1915)

Illingworth was born and grew up in London, and he was educated at St Paul's School where he was awarded a scholarship to Corpus Christi

College, Oxford, in 1867. After taking a first in 'Greats' he was elected a fellow of Jesus College in 1872 and, in the same year, as tutor at the recently founded Keble College; after which he was ordained. His preaching and lecturing were said by students to be outstanding. But his health broke down and in 1883, having married a nurse, Agnes Louisa, he moved to the Jesus College living at Longworth outside Oxford, where he remained until his death in 1915. During those years, the Lux Mundi group of Anglican theologians gathered annually at his rectory.

Illingworth was a man of considerable humility – turning down preferment because it did not interest him, nor suit his health, and refusing the offer to deliver the Gifford Lectures. He continued, however, to produce books – publishing nine in total as well as several articles, essays and sermons. Important among these latter are three sermons in *Sermons Preached in the Temporary Chapel of Keble College, Oxford* (1878); an essay entitled 'The Incarnation of the Word', in *The Expositor* III (1886), pp. 161–75; another essay with the title 'The Church and Human Thought in the Present Day', *Pan-Anglican Papers* 2 (1907); and two important essays entitled 'The Problem of Pain: Its bearing on Faith in God' and 'The Incarnation in Relation to Development', in *Lux Mundi* (1889). His own books are chronologically: *Sermons Preached in a College Chapel* (1882); *University and Cathedral Sermons* (1893); *Personality, Human and Divine: Being the Bampton Lectures for the Year 1894* (1894); *Divine Immanence: An Essay on the Spiritual Significance of Matter* (1898); *Reason and Revelation: An Essay in Christian Apology* (1902); *Christian Character: Being Some Lectures on the Elements of Christian Ethics* (1904); *The Doctrine of the Trinity Apologetically Considered* (1907); *Divine Transcendence: And Its Reflection in Religious Authority* (1911); and *The Gospel Miracles* (1915). In addition, his wife edited a biography entitled *The Life and Work of John Richardson Illingworth* (1917).

Perhaps in part due to the unavailability of his books, Illingworth has been the subject of often ill-informed pejorative repetitions by scholars – especially that of Idealism. Illingworth is susceptible to this charge particularly because of an immanentist streak in his early writings. But due recognition must be given to the way in which his theology changed decisively later in life. He moved away from immanentism (as evidenced in *Lux Mundi*) to a thoroughly Trinitarian position (so *The Doctrine of the Trinity*) and to a view of the essential ontological otherness of God (so *Divine Transcendence*). Like *S.T. Coleridge before him, whom he greatly admired, Illingworth asserted that the only effective counter to pantheism was the doctrine of the Trinity. Similarly, he became increasingly pessimistic about the nature of humankind, and his later letters and writings show a marked prevalence to speak of the all-pervasiveness of sin.

Another important feature of Illingworth's theology concerns his apophatic tendencies. Illingworth has sometimes been criticized for skating lightly over complex doctrinal issues (for instance, the nature of the immanent Trinity). However, while there is truth in this assertion, it needs to be balanced by Illingworth's deliberate refusal to speculate about the nature of God's inner being. He devoted two complete chapters of *The Doctrine of the Trinity* to a consideration of apophaticism in the Church Fathers and the nature of mystery in God. In this way, Illingworth asserts that the Fathers moved away from a neoplatonic 'exaggeration of His transcendence – His aloofness from the world' to an apophaticism based on their encounter with the transcendent otherness of God. And, as such, they moved closer towards the 'reverential abstinence from the use of God's name, which characterised later Judaism'.

In both *Personality, Human and Divine* and *The Doctrine of the Trinity*, Illingworth is concerned to trace this development of Trinitarian theology from the New Testament through the Fathers; but elsewhere he is equally as emphatic that regarding the doctrines of the Trinity and the incarnation: 'We are no nearer to an understanding of either doctrine than were the Fathers; the most speculative of whom are continually anxious to profess their own incapacity' (*Divine Transcendence*, pp. 130–1). Nevertheless, whilst we should duly note Illingworth's apophaticism, there is no doubt that this occasionally appears as a front for avoiding serious doctrinal complexities. The words of Illingworth's wife are apposite: that he was a writer who 'set himself all along, as it were, more to study of the forest, than of the trees which grow therein' (*The Life*, p. vi).

Even so, it is perhaps his view of the social, yet transcendent, God which so marks Illingworth as a man ahead of his time. Not only did he stress that the absolute nature of God entails his freedom to be unrelated to anything outside himself, but he also urged that God is therefore *in se* perfect personality: three Persons, one God – from whom perfect personality is derived. At the same time, it is precisely because, at root, the doctrine of the Trinity was revealed by a Person that his Trinitarian theology remains ontologically, and not simply functionally, 'social'. While, therefore, he does use Trinitarian analogies (such as subject-object and their relation, and Father-Mother-Child) these are neither more nor less than analogies. It is by the revealed nature of the doctrine that Illingworth ultimately sets greatest store: the 'fact' that Christians have sufficient justification for believing that the existence of the Trinity was taught by Christ himself. The key to understanding Illingworth's theology is that sociality and transcendence must not be divorced from the person of Jesus Christ – a focus which provides parameters beyond which we must of necessity be apophatic.

RICHARD HOSKINS

FURTHER READING: *Texts: Sermons Preached in the Temporary Chapel of Keble College, Oxford 1870–1876* (ed. E.S. Talbot; London, 1878); 'The Incarnation of the Word', in *The Expositor* III (1886), pp. 161–75; 'The Church and Human Thought in the Present Day', *Pan-Anglican Papers* 2 (1907); 'The Problem of Pain: Its Bearing on Faith in God' and 'The Incarnation in Relation to Development', in *Lux Mundi* (ed. Charles Gore; London, 1889); *Sermons Preached in a College Chapel* (London, 1882); *University and Cathedral Sermons* (London, 1893); *Personality, Human and Divine: Being the Bampton Lectures for the Year 1894* (London, 1894); *Divine Immanence: An Essay on the Spiritual Significance of Matter* (London / New York, 1898); *Reason and Revelation: An Essay in Christian Apology* (London, 1902); *Christian Character: Being Some Lectures on the Elements of Christian Ethics* (London, 1904); *The Doctrine of the Trinity Apologetically Considered* (London, 1907); *Divine Transcendence: And Its Reflection in Religious Authority* (London, 1911); *The Gospel Miracles* (London, 1915); *The Life and Work of John Richardson Illingworth* (London, 1917).

Irenaeus of Lyons (c. 130 – c. 200)

St Irenaeus, whose name derives from the Greek word for peace, and who proved himself a peacemaker among his fellow bishops in the Paschal Controversies, is widely regarded as the first theologian of ecumenical stature. As a youth he heard Polycarp preach, which suggests that he may have been native to the region of Smyrna, though it is thought that he received some of his education in Rome. Later he served alongside Pothinus, whom Polycarp had sent as a missionary to Celtic Gaul. After Pothinus's death in the persecution of 177, Irenaeus succeeded him as bishop of Lyons. Tradition commemorates him as a martyr (feast 28 June) on slim evidence, supposing him to have died in the disturbances of 202.

As an extension of his pastoral duties Irenaeus undertook the writing of several theological works. Two of these are extant, though not for the most part in their original Greek: *A Refutation and Subversion of Knowledge Falsely So-called*, commonly known as *Against Heresies*; and a much shorter work, rediscovered in 1904, entitled *Demonstration of the Apostolic Preaching*. Though the former is a scholarly polemical work and the latter more catechetical, both attempt to explore the church's threefold witness to Father, Son and Spirit, in the Scriptures and in the primitive baptismal confession, as an antidote to the major heresies of the second century.

Irenaeus stands out as the church's great champion against *Gnosticism in particular, which together with *Montanism and other esoteric movements was gaining momentum. Older scholarship, mindful of Irenaeus's appeal to a definite 'rule of faith' and to episcopal succession as safeguards against sectarian tendencies, has also presented him as a transitional figure in the shift from the relative informality of the primitive church to so-called early Catholicism. Following F. Loofs, some have supposed Irenaeus's writing to be little more than a patchwork of ideas collected from Scripture, the *apologists, and even from his opponents, proffered under an artificial unity. Neither of these latter claims carries much weight today, however. The first does little justice to the anti-hierarchical character of the churches of Lyons and Vienna, or to Irenaeus's own ecclesiological framework. The second overlooks, in its fascination with source criticism, the operation of a powerful mind spurred by social and theological crises.

Irenaeus arguably offers the first attempt at a dogmatic theology, inasmuch as he works his way out from the creedal and doxological centre of the Christian faith to a refutation of heresy *qua* heresy, exposing not only the heretics' inconsistencies but also the common character of their respective enterprises. This work required reflection not only on the subtleties of docetic doctrine (Marcionite, Valentinian, Basilidean, etc.), but also on the underlying philosophical tradition of Hellenism. Here Irenaeus was forced to go back behind the likes of *Justin and *Theophilus to the leading apostolic theologians, in search of the unique logic of the gospel. The results of his labours were presented with patience and wit; they remain a reliable guide to the heterodoxy, as to the orthodoxy, of his time. More significantly, they contain a number of insights of which the full impact has yet to be felt, for they were quickly overshadowed by the quite different construct of the early Alexandrians, *Clement and *Origen, whose popularity owed much to their willingness to incorporate far more of the Greek tradition.

Irenaeus's theological achievements may be grouped for convenience under three headings, though they admit of no separate treatment. Many others might be mentioned were space to permit.

God and creation. Though carefully emphasizing divine unity against the fragmented deity of Gnosticism, the God-talk of Irenaeus is irreducibly Trinitarian (even if the term itself is anachronistic). Moreover, it is Trinitarian in a fashion that is neither subordinationist, like that of the apologists and Alexandrians, nor merely economic. That is because the bishop was working towards a dynamic concept of divine transcendence that left God free to engage with the world as its creator and redeemer, through the exercise (in Theophilus's metaphor) of his 'two hands', the Son and the Spirit. Irenaeus's Trinitarianism should be connected with his articulation of the doctrine of creation out of nothing, which had hitherto not achieved clear definition; with his firm insistence on the goodness of the entire universe as the divine handiwork; and with his affirmation of temporal process as a positive feature of the divine-human relationship.

Christ and reconciliation. The incarnational language of the later creeds also begins to appear in Irenaeus, who was at great pains to repudiate any distancing of Christ from God, on the one hand, and from humankind on the other. The Gnostics sought to divide Christ from Jesus, but

the Scriptures proclaimed 'one and the same Jesus Christ': the mediator who is 'true God' and 'true man', the guarantee of God's intimacy with the world. Perceptively, Irenaeus recognized that a docetic view of the resurrection is just as much a threat to that guarantee as a docetic view of the incarnation. Either leads to a concept of reconciliation pernicious to human beings – and to a mythologizing of the cross as a symbolic rather than a historical atonement – by detaching the mediator himself from a genuinely temporal and material form of existence. Irenaeus understood reconciliation as a sanctification of human beings from the inside out, in a personal recapitulation of every phase of our individual and corporate history, judgement and death included.

Unlike some of the later Fathers, however, Irenaeus regarded Christ not only as the reconciler but also as the very ground of our existence. The incarnate one, in other words, was the cornerstone of the first creation as well as the new creation. His belated appearance in history was due to his willingness to show solidarity with us even in our fallenness, so that our reformation as well as our consummation might be effected in him. Irenaeus's trademark doctrine of recapitulation requires attention to this double headship, to his doctrine of the Fall, and to a rather complex interpretation of history into which a purely linear or evolutionary view (such as that associated with him by *J. Hick) will not fit.

The Spirit and humanity. Steering away even from the Hellenized logos Christology of the apologists, Irenaeus further distinguishes himself by refusing to locate the image of God exclusively in the intellect. To be in the image is rather to be a recipient, body and soul, of the Holy Spirit. His famous Christological maxim, that Christ became what we are that we might become what he is, has often been misunderstood in terms of a more abstract notion of the divinization of human nature. But Irenaeus interpreted the work of Christ to be one of accustoming the Spirit to dwell with humanity, of introducing the Spirit even into the 'desert' places of human intransigence and corruption, so that what the devil had distorted, and death claimed, might after all become heir to an inexhaustible process of divine beneficence. It is this pneumatological dimension that supports both his Eucharistic realism and his long-suppressed eschatology, the earthiness of which brought it into disrepute in an age when dualism was far from vanquished. Indeed, it is only today that a new appreciation for his holistic perspective has been emerging.

DOUGLAS B. FARROW

FURTHER READING: A good short introduction can be found in H.U. von Balthasar, *The Glory of the Lord*, II (Edinburgh, 1982), pp. 31–94; a helpful introductory monograph is D. Minns, *Irenaeus* (Washington, DC, 1994); other English monographs include F.R.M. Hitchcock, *Irenaeus of Lugdunum* (Cambridge, 1914); R.M. Grant, *Irenaeus of Lyons* (London, 1997), which contains some fresh translation; J. Lawson, *The Biblical Theology of Saint Irenaeus* (London, 1948); G. Wingren, *Man and the Incarnation* (Philadelphia, 1959), a penetrating work. Readers of Spanish will want to pursue the works of A. Orbe; these and other significant foreign language works are listed in Minns. *See also:* G. Aulén, *Christus Victor* (New York, 1961), ch. 2; W. Bousset, *Kyrios Christos* (ET Nashville, TN, 1970), ch. 10; E. Brunner, *The Mediator* (London, 1934), pp. 249–64; Mary Ann Donovan, *One Right Reading? A Guide to Irenaeus* (Collegeville, MN, 1997); D. Farrow, 'St Irenaeus of Lyons: The Church and the World', *Pro Ecclesia* 4.3 (1995), pp. 333–55, and *Ascension and Ecclesia* (Edinburgh / Grand Rapids, 1999), ch. 3; T. Hart and D. Thimell (eds.), *Christ in our Place* (Exeter, 1989), ch. 9; G. May, *Creatio ex Nihilo* (Edinburgh, 1994), pp. 164–78.

Irving, Edward (1792–1834)

Born in Annan, south-west Scotland, educated at the University of Edinburgh in divinity and then a school teacher at Haddington and Kirkcaldy. Whilst at Kirkcaldy Irving struck up a close friendship with Thomas Carlyle that was to continue, in different ways, through to Irving's death.

In 1819, Irving entered the Church of Scotland as an assistant minister to Dr Chalmers in St John's parish, Glasgow. However, it was to be in London that Irving would carve out his career and reputation. In 1822 he took up his call to the Caledonian Chapel in Hatton Garden, London. Irving took to mid-nineteenth-century London quickly and soon became renowned as a reputable speaker drawing large crowds to his churches. The climate suited his classically trained yet romantically inclined temperament and mind. It also suited his desire for discovering new ground, for it was a time of great upheaval – both culturally and professionally.

Culturally, London was a collection point for much that was beginning to take shape in British and European thinking. At home Irving was a contemporary of Carlyle and *Coleridge – he discoursed and enjoyed friendship with both of them. On the continent his contemporaries were *Schleiermacher, *Hegel and Goethe, all of whom vehemently opposed the kind of theology Irving was to develop and preach. Whilst the central doctrines of the incarnation and the Trinity were being undermined and discarded for more contemporary interpretations, Irving's theology, at first, appears anachronistic. However, if he is read as an apologist for all that was being swept aside in the modernist rush to Enlightenment, he begins to take on a more relevant hue.

Professionally, Irving struggled with the same issues which were ultimately to topple both him and *John McLeod Campbell; namely, the legacy bequeathed to Scottish Presbyterianism by federal theology. Both men sought to address the insecurities which federal theology imposed on the believer who, according to this theological scheme, could never know final assurance of salvation. McLeod Campbell sought an answer in the universal scope of Christ's death, whereas Irving sought the point of contact in a particular account of the human nature of Christ. Both solutions resulted in formal charges of heresy and eventual deposition from the ministry of the Church of Scotland.

Irving's career may be understood, externally, against these two backdrops. Internally, his theology can be considered under three clear chapters which are closely interconnected: the theological development; the Christological innovation; and the tongues controversy.

Irving has been renowned and subsequently caricatured for the latter two. He cannot be fully understood, however, without some appreciation of the theological outlook which developed once he took root in Hatton Garden. For it was with this congregation that he began to defend his doctrine of God against the increasingly *Unitarian interpretation of God which late eighteenth- and early nineteenth-century *Deism spawned (see *The Collected Writings of Edward Irving*, vol. 4). It would be true to say that at this point Irving simply unpacks a doctrine of God inherited from the Puritan *Owen and Irving's mentor Hooker. What is significant is the degree to which it engaged with contemporary doctrines of God and sought to establish the centrality of Christ as both the Saviour and eternal Son as well as to refute more heterodox responses, and to do so in a manner that engaged with the issues rather than simply mouthing old formulae. In this, Irving's contemporaneity is to be seen.

Innovation begins, however, when Irving begins to defend his doctrine of Christ against vitriolic attacks from those who opposed any notion that Jesus Christ assumed in incarnation a humanity that was itself in need of restoration. After all, for Irving, that which is not assumed is not healed, and it is a *fallen* humanity that is in need of restoration. It is here, too, that Irving begins to develop his doctrine of the Spirit, clearly in line with Owen; namely, the belief that all Jesus Christ achieved in his humanity he achieved by the enabling power of the Holy Spirit and not by virtue of his own divine nature. In as much as the believer receives the same Spirit through whom Christ overcame fallen humanity, so the believer can be reassured that holiness is not an unobtainable ideal (see *The Orthodox and Catholic Doctrine of Our Lord's Human Nature* [1830], *Christ's Holiness in the Flesh* [1831]).

It was in 1828, however, that the storm erupted with outbreaks of glossolalia on the west coast of Scotland and subsequently, in 1831, in Irving's own London congregation. This charismatic manifestation ultimately led to Irving being ousted from his church, along with over six hundred followers – an event to which, in part, the origins of the Catholic Apostolic Church may be attributed, although this breakaway group was more directly influenced by a small group of millennialists who met under Henry Drummond of Albury, Surrey than by Irving.

In 1833 Irving was summoned to Annan in order to give an account of his 'heretical' teaching concerning the sinfulness of Jesus Christ's human nature. This, obviously, had been fuelled by the remarkable events taking place in his church. It was on the grounds of his Christology, however, that Irving was subsequently deposed by the presbytery of Annan from the ministry of the Church of Scotland.

Left without a parish or ministry, Irving quickly deteriorated in health after the battering received from both public and ecclesial fronts. Convinced of a calling to preach the gospel, Irving ventured to travel north during which he became seriously ill and died. It is ironic, then, that Irving was to be buried in 1834, aged forty-two, in the cathedral of the church that had condemned him and indirectly contributed to his early death.

GRAHAM MCFARLANE

FURTHER READING: *Texts: Christ's Holiness in the Flesh, the Form, Fountain Head, and Assurance to us of Holiness in the Flesh: In Three Parts* (Edinburgh, 1831); *The Collected Writings of Edward Irving in Five Volumes* (ed. G. Carlyle; London, 1864); *The Day of Pentecost or the Baptism with the Holy Ghost* (Edinburgh, 1830); *The Doctrine Held by the Church of Scotland Concerning the Human Nature of Our Lord, As Stated in Her Standards* (Edinburgh, n.d.); *The Orthodox and Catholic Doctrine of Our Lord's Human Nature, Tried by the Westminster Confession of Faith: Set in Four Parts* (London, 1830); *The Prophetical Works of Edward Irving in Two Volumes* (ed. G. Carlyle; London, 1865). *Texts:* G.W.P. McFarlane, *Christ and the Spirit: The Doctrine of the Incarnation according to Edward Irving* (Carlisle, 1996); M.O.W. Oliphant, *Edward Irving* (London, 5th edn, n.d.); C.G. Strachan, *The Pentecostal Theology of Edward Irving* (London, 1973).

Jansenism

Jansenism was an ecclesial movement within Roman Catholicism in seventeenth- and eighteenth-century Europe, especially France. The movement's name derives from the Flemish theologian Cornelius Jansen (1585–1638), whose systematic treatment of *Augustine's anti-Pelagian theology of grace was identified as the informing core of Jansenism's concerns (see his *Augustinus* [1640]). Jansen's work, however, is properly linked to the sixteenth-century Hispano-Flemish controversy over grace and free will (cf. the debate of the *Congregatio de Auxiliis* [1588–1607]), while Jansenism as a movement was a primarily French phenomenon located in the post-Reformation context of church reform within the Catholicism that emerged after the Religious Wars. Despite its theologically 'systematic' cast on the issue of grace, the energy of the movement was centred on pastoral ecclesiology, lay spiritual discipline, Bible reading and catechism.

The originator of French Jansenism was Jean Duvergier de Hauranne, known as the abbé de Saint-Cyran (1581–1643). Saint-Cyran, who had known Jansen as a student, was at the centre of a movement to renew the Catholic Church in France as a missionary force in the face of perceived corruption from within and of Protestantism from without. Saint-Cyran's outlook conformed to the rigourist standards of many Catholic reformers elsewhere (e.g. Charles Borromeo), which he interpreted in terms of the 'pure love' of Augustine's 'irresistible' grace. His influence as a confessor and director for the nuns of Port-Royal, a reformed Cistercian order with houses outside and within Paris, had wider impact in the church, though most of his writings were published posthumously.

Among Saint-Cyran's protégés was the young theologian Antoine Arnauld (1612–94), who had relatives at Port-Royal. Following his mentor's imprisonment and death, Arnauld engaged in a defence of Saint-Cyran through polemical treatises on penitential practice, patristic exegesis and Augustinian theology. Controversial exchanges with the *Jesuits soon involved *Blaise Pascal (1623–62) – whose sister was a also nun at Port-Royal – and other prominent writers like Pierre Nicole (1625–95). Various propositions associated with Jansen's extreme anti-Pelagian theology of grace were condemned by the Vatican (1653), although Arnauld and his followers continued to write on a wide range of topics. Meanwhile, the grounds of the convent of Port-Royal outside Paris became a magnet for lay ascetics like Isaac Louis le Maistre de Sacy (1613–84) and Jean Hamon (1618–87), whose works of Bible translation, exegesis, spiritual direction and education fuelled a broadening movement of scriptural renewal and personal asceticism within the French church.

Official hostility against the movement resurfaced in the late seventeenth century, leading to the destruction of Port-Royal, and the promulgation of the papal bull 'Unigenitus' (1713), condemning many texts taken from the Jansenist Pasquier Quesnel's (1634–1719) devotional manual on the New Testament known as the *Réflexions Morales* (1698; 1st edn 1672). The imposition of the bull on the French clergy caused a profound institutional rift, with many Jansenists refusing to sign and calling for a general council to resolve the matter (this group was known as *Appellants*). The Appellant phase of the movement, which took place in an increasingly persecutory environment, saw Jansenism spread with new vigour to the lowlands and express itself in energetic engagement with ascetic discipline, hagiology, scriptural exegesis and, eventually, prophecy. Appellant bishops continued to press for catechetical and vocational reform in an era of growing religious indifference.

The spectacular occurrence of alleged miracles beginning in the late 1720s at the tomb of a Jansenist ascetic, François de Paris (who died in 1727), in Saint-Médard (Paris) led finally to a split in the movement itself, especially as the Saint-Médardists began to exhibit and promote other more sensationalist religious phenomena, like convulsions and symbolic trances. Late eighteenth-century Jansenism was less a movement than a bunching of disparate religious trajectories with a common source. Some Jansenist political concerns (e.g. Gallican claims for the episcopacy) played into the developing stream of revolutionary events, as far away even as Italy (cf. the Synod of Pistoia in 1786), but the movement as a whole was subsumed and disappeared in the national conflagration that enveloped France.

The theology of grace at the centre of Jansenist identity was less uniform than its enemies alleged. In the reflections of different Jansenist thinkers, it derived, alternatively, from neo-Platonic (Jansen and Gabriel Gerberon [1628–1711]), *Thomistic (Quesnel) and varied patristic influences, and it was distinct from Protestant attitudes towards grace in at least two ways. First, Jansenist deployment of exclusivist Augustinian anti-Pelagianism – the victorious 'love' of, for example, Augustine's *De gratia et libero arbitrio* – was for the purpose of ecclesial purification rather than personal justification. Second, the material outworking of that grace remained tied, traditionally, to the structures of the Catholic Church. Taken together, these readings of 'efficacious grace' as an inescapable historical demand upon individuals to suffer with discipline their spiritual fate within the sovereign bounds of the institution, led to an extreme and peculiar providentialism about most matters. (A major summary of Jansenist views on grace can be found in Quesnel's *La Tradition de 'Église romaine sur la prédestination des Saints et sur la Grace efficace* [1687–90].)

Jansenism, in this regard, was closer to the devotional outlook of the 'French School' of spiritual writing, linked to *Bérulle and the Oratory, wherein divine 'grace' refers, more globally, to the intentional process by which individuals are conformed to the experiential 'conditions' of Jesus' life, reiterated in the church and its members. (Influential Jansenists like Quesnel and Jacques-Joseph Duguet [1649–1733] were members of the Oratory.) By turns illuminist, disciplined, passive and protesting, the Jansenist appropriation of this outlook was notable for its rigour and lay dissemination, and less for its essential novelty within the era's culture of ecclesial renewal. The hostility Jansenism aroused grew out of its more public opposition to the surrounding environment of religious decline.

The movement's rigouristic pastoral concerns produced notorious controversies over penitential discipline and separation from communion (cf. Arnauld's *De la Fréquente Communion* [1643]) and confessional practice (cf. Pascal's *Lettres provinciales* [1656–57]). But there were also anti-Protestant apologies of vast proportions (cf. Arnauld and Nicole's defence of the Eucharist, *La Perpétuité de la Foi Catholique Touchant l'Eucharistie* [1669–74]), designed to dispel doubts and indifference about central Catholic practices. Most of these treatises were fuelled by a common concern with outlining the providential orchestration of Christian experience over time that formed the basis of Jansenism's unique ecclesial theology of history. Combining the archetypal Christ-devotions of

the French School with a thoroughgoing Augustinian scripturalism, Jansenists located the church figurally in time, interpreting its life according to the forms of biblical history – both Israel's and Jesus'. Commitments to pastoral reform were couched in terms of a scriptural history of the church's pneumatic decline and conformity to Christ, and were buttressed by a single-minded sifting of documented historical exemplars.

The shape of this informing figural scripturalism was only touched upon in Jansen's exegesis. Arnauld elaborated its principles, and a blossoming of exegetical reflections followed – see Pascal's *Pensées*, the Bible translations of de Sacy and others and patristic-styled commentaries and, later, Quesnel's New Testament devotions, Duguet's many commentaries, and the elaborate figural exegesis of Jean-Baptiste le Sesne de Ménilles d'Étemare (1682–1770). Even the phenomenon of eighteenth-century Appellant symbolic miracles, in the context of the Jansenist struggle to wed protest with ecclesial unity, can be read in terms of this scripturalist understanding of figural history.

Jansenism's many contributions to modern theological practice are also linked to this underlying historical outlook. In addition to vernacular Bible-translation and reading, Jansenists were pioneers in liturgical renewal based on patristic sources, scripturally-based catechesis (after Claude Fleury's [1640–1723] model), the disciplines of critical church history (cf. Louis Sébastien le Nain Tillemont [1637–98]) and positive theology, including text criticism (cf. critical editions of *Leo the Great, *Anselm, et al.) and, especially after the rise of Jansenist miracles, evidentiary documentation of religious experience (cf. Carré de Montgeron's remarkable *La Vérité des Miracles* [1737], and the clandestine Appellant journal *Nouvelles Ecclésiastiques* [1723–1803]).

As with many reactionary movements, Jansenism reflected characteristics of the culture to which it was opposed – in this case, the historicist and rationalist cast of developing modernism (cf. Arnauld and Nicole's still popular *Logique* [1662]). Jansenist supernaturalism, already apparent in Pascal, also shared many of the rigid features of modern religious 'enthusiasm'. Still, the wedding of a scripturalist institutionalism to this mix was novel and produced a distinctive hermeneutics and ecclesiology that must be judged a creative modern adaptation of traditional Catholicism. Many of its practical outworkings are now an accepted part of contemporary Roman devotion, even while their Augustinian theological roots remain deeply antithetical to modern commitments.

Jansenism's controverted relation with the Vatican has resulted in most Catholic scholars treating it with hostility, until recently. New interest in the religious sociology and history of the *ancien régime* has provoked and revived more respectful study of the movement. In addition, current engagement with philosophical issues of early modernity has stirred interest in limited aspects of, for example, Arnauld's work. There remains little grappling with Jansenism's purely theological concerns, however, and vast areas of theological and devotional material in Quesnel, Duguet, d'Étemare and others are still unexamined. This situation is furthered by the primary literature's inaccessibility and untranslated condition.

EPHRAIM RADNER

FURTHER READING: *Standard narrative:* C.A. Sainte-Beuve, *Port-Royal* (1840–59); theological discussions in L. Kolakowski, *God Owes us Nothing* (Chicago, 1995); and H. de Lubac, *Augustinianism and Modern Theology* (London, 1969); documentary history in J. Orcibal's multi-volume *Les Origines du Jansenisme* (Paris, 1947 ff.); and the many articles of L. Ceyssens; historical overviews in L. Cognet, *Le Jansenisme* (Paris, 1968) and J.-P. Chantin, *Le Jansenisme* (Paris, 1996); R. Ravenaux, *La Vie Quotidienne des Jansenistes* (Paris, 1973); C.-L. Maire, *De la Cause de Dieu à la Cause de la Nation: Le Jansenisme au XVIIIè Siècle* (Paris, 1998); A. Sedgwick, *The Travails of Conscience: The Arnauld Family and the Ancien Régime* (Cambridge, MA / London, 1998).

Jaspers, Karl (Theodor) (1883–1969)

German psychopathologist and philosopher, foundational figure in existential philosophy who considered true understanding to begin with a knowledge of human existence. Jaspers developed a philosophical theology of the Encompassing (*das Umgreifende*), seeing the pursuit of philosophy as being a means and source of human transformation.

Born in Oldenberg, Germany, on 23 February 1883, Jaspers began studying law at the University of Heidelberg in 1901 while also attending classes in philosophy. Feeling unsatisfied, however, with the study of law, and being unfulfilled by the classes in philosophy as they did not explore the experience of being or a way of self-improvement in life, Jaspers turned the following year to the study of medicine. His studies in medicine led on to his research in psychopathology, which in turn led on to his career in philosophy. In 1913, Jaspers began as lecturer in psychology at Heidelberg, and in the following year, with the outbreak of World War I, he began seeing the importance of philosophy to human welfare. In 1916, Jaspers became assistant professor of psychology. He held various positions in the following years and was appointed to the chair of philosophy in 1922. With the rise of Nazism, Jaspers fell into a conflict with the Nazi authorities which came to a head in 1937 when he was declared an enemy of the state since his wife, Gertrude Mayer, whom he had married in 1910, was Jewish. The conflict resulted in the banning of all of his publications and his dismissal from his post at Heidelberg. Though reinstated to his post in 1945, Jaspers felt that the university must be restructured so as to remove all those who had been sympathetic to the Nazi cause, and that the German people must realize a collective guilt for what took place. Disappointingly for Jaspers, his calls for reform of university and society were mostly disregarded and overlooked. In 1948, Jaspers, though receiving much criticism, accepted a professorship of philosophy at the University of Basle, in Switzerland – a post that he held until his death on 26 February 1969.

Throughout his thought, Jaspers established a philosophical theology that centres itself upon the idea that human existence (*Existenz*) finds its true meaning only in relation to transcendence. Humanity is part of the world, part of 'being-there' or *Dasein*, where we are confronted outwardly (objectively) and inwardly (subjectively) by objects, which form the content of our consciousness. But humanity longs and strives for that which is true being, or *Sein*, which is the Encompassing (*das Umgreifende*), the Comprehensive, God, the pervading reality in which all things exist, which is neither subject nor object, but is one reality encompassing both the objective and subjective in a dichotomy. The philosophical study of this Encompassing, or *periechontology* (an ontology of the Encompassing), is that upon which true philosophy builds and through which I am able to reach a knowledge of true Being.

The Encompassing, because it is the dichotomy between the subjective and objective, is beyond all systematizations of doctrine, formula or full definition. As with the image of the Encompassing, the concept of God is unthinkable (*das Undenkbare*), we can know its reality but we cannot understand its essence. However, though it cannot be cognitively captured, we experience the Encompassing, Transcendence, God, through ciphers (*Chiffren*), symbols in myths, art, history and nature, in which the Encompassing is made manifest, but which never capture its reality. To take the great metaphysical theories of fire, matter, mind, etc. as objects is, for Jaspers, completely wrong. We must understand these not as objects, but as 'hieroglyphics of being' devised by philosophers out of their own lives and striving for the Encompassing. Like the Being it seeks to encounter, philosophy itself cannot be placed in objective systems of doctrine, or made an endeavour of objective scientific claims. Though philosophy is linked to science and uses all scientific knowledge as a basis upon which it builds, philosophy is the contemplation of that which is true Being, whereas scientific knowledge is always particularized, embracing only a specific subject. Science affords no aim to life, no answer to the essential problems of humanity, and when scientific knowledge replaces philosophy, or when philosophy is seen to be simply a science, man is reduced to perplexity by confusing knowledge which can be objectively proven with convictions by which he lives.

Because it is through philosophy that I am able to know this Being, this Encompassing, philosophizing is, for Jaspers, part of the essential nature of humanity – providing human existence with meaning. Though never rejecting the idea of faith or the religious nature of philosophy, Jaspers held that one must pursue a philosophic faith (*philosophische Glaube*) in which life is constantly open to that Transcendence which is manifested in the world, and, by practising a philosophical way of life in light of this, secure freedom and fulfilment in one's existence. Such a life, for Jaspers, springs from the forlornness or anxiety that one senses when staring without love as into a void, consumed by the busyness of the natural world, and it is through philosophy that we find ourselves

again. But though the philosophical life is a religious way of existence, it does not centre in the holy 'thing', or sacred place, or fixed form of doctrine. Rather, it demands solitude and a contemplation based on self-reflection, a reflection of authentic being, and a pondering of what should be done at present. Such a life, for Jaspers, is not static (a state) but a constant progression toward being.

The development of Jaspers's thought in the aftermath of World War II, and in the 1950s through the 1960s, saw the development of a world philosophy which emphasized the study of philosophy as a means by which humankind could realize its potential and form a basis for mutual communication. For Jaspers, ethically speaking, though God manifests himself only indirectly, he does so through our love for one another. Through philosophy and the philosophical life, communication (and love between individuals and within humanity as a whole) fosters peace in the world. For Jaspers, true philosophy, which strives to understand human existence and the Encompassing, thus holds the key to a meaningful and fulfilled existence.

DERON S. NEWMAN

FURTHER READING: *Texts: The Perennial Scope of Philosophy* (trans. Ralph Manhim; New York, 1949); *Way To Wisdom* (London, 1951); *Reason and Existence* (London, 1956); *The Great Philosophers* (4 vols.; New York, 1962, 1966, 1993, 1995); *Philosophical Faith and Revelation* (trans. E.B. Ashton; London, 1967); *Philosophy* (trans. E.B Ashton; Chicago, 1969). *Studies:* Paul Arthur Schilpp (ed.), *The Philosophy of Karl Jaspers* (New York, 1957); Oswald O. Schrag, *Existence, Existenz, and Transcendence: An Introduction to the Philosophy of Karl Jaspers* (Pittsburgh, 1971); Walter Kaufmann, *Existentialism from Dostoevsky to Sartre* (New York, 1956), pp. 158–232.

Jerome (c. 347–420)

Jerome was born in Stridon in Dalmatia, the son of prosperous Christian parents. He was educated at Rome, where he was baptized. While spending some time in Trier and Aquileia in his early twenties he developed an interest in the monastic life and decided to move to Syria, where he lived for a time as a hermit at Chalcis, east of Antioch. This training in asceticism made a major impact upon him, but in the end he found his life in the desert an excessive strain and he returned to Antioch, where he was ordained as a priest. He was in Constantinople in the important years of 380–81, and in 382 he went back to Rome and became *de facto* assistant to the aging Pope Damasus. The latter commissioned him to undertake a revision of the existing Latin versions of the Bible and produce one standard edition, a task which was to occupy him for more than twenty years. Jerome stayed in Rome for three years, and during this time he formed close friendships with a number of aristocratic Christian women, to whom he became a spiritual tutor and counsellor. He made himself unpopular with the Roman clergy, however, both for his criticisms of their mores and not least because his own relations with one widow in particular, Paula, aroused suspicions. Following the advent of Siricius he was investigated, condemned and effectively banished from Rome. After a period of travel in the Near East, accompanied by his entourage of devoted women, he settled in Bethlehem in 386 and established a monastic community, financed initially with Paula's wealth. Devoting himself to scholarly activities, he presided over a fairly liberal ascetic regime until his death in 420.

A bibliophile from an early age, Jerome stands out as one of the greatest biblical scholars in the history of the church. His most remarkable achievement was his new translation of the Scriptures. The Latin Bible of the fourth century had, he tells us, almost as many textual forms as there were manuscripts: the new edition for which Damasus had a vision was obviously much needed. Jerome was particularly well equipped to tackle such a task, being competent in Hebrew, Greek and Latin. His first project was a revision of the four Gospels, which was presented to Damasus shortly before the latter's death in 384. This was followed by new versions of the Psalter and parts of the Old Testament, based upon the Septuagint. By 390, however, Jerome became convinced of the need to go back to the 'Hebrew verity' rather than relying on the Greek, and he embarked on a completely new rendering of the Hebrew canon. The work was pursued intermittently and was not completed until 405. But this version, which formed the core of what became known as the Vulgate Bible, represented a huge advance on previous Old Testament scholarship. Not until the Reformation was Jerome's determination to follow the Hebrew taken up again with comparable zeal.

The quality of his erudition can also be gauged from his commentaries and works of textual, historical and philological reference. Jerome wrote on both major and minor prophets, on the Psalms, Ecclesiastes, Matthew's gospel, several Pauline epistles and Revelation. He produced translations of Greek dictionaries of Hebrew etymologies and topographical references, and a textual study of selected passages of Genesis. Exegetically, his tastes were eclectic: the literal sense of Scripture was for him the primary *desideratum*, but he could also accommodate spiritual interpretation. For much of his career, this openness to spiritual hermeneutics was inspired by *Origen, a number of whose homilies he translated into Latin.

After the Origenist controversy of the early 390s, however, Jerome began to repudiate Origen's doctrinal views in no uncertain terms; and here we see the other side to his temperament. He could engage in the bitterest of polemic and deliver the most cutting denunciations of those with whom he disagreed. His contributions to theological debate were, accordingly, seldom acute: in his latter-day opposition to *Pelagianism, for example, he shows a greater ability to vilify Pelagius's supporters than to grasp the doctrinal points they were seeking to make. At the same time, his polemical works and extensive collection of epistles (some of them short treatises in themselves) contain some of the most brilliant satire to be found in late antiquity. In his broadside against the anti-ascetic monk Jovinian, for example, and in his letters describing the corruption of the Roman clergy, Jerome deploys all the skills of vivid caricature and biting wit to express his loathing of his opponents.

Jerome's writings reveal a personality capable of both extreme rancour and intense warmth, and a mind both brilliant and yet obtuse to some of the inevitable complexities of ecclesiastical politics. He could never be less than controversial: throughout his considerable network of acquaintances, he was loved and hated in roughly equal measure. Many of his idiosyncratic taboos and criticisms of his fellow-churchmen turn out, not surprisingly, to be a mirror image of his own character. The Jerome who so zealously promoted female asceticism and monastic virtue was the Jerome who spent his first period in the desert wrestling with carnal desires and who formed a decidedly delicate relationship with his upper-class devotees. The Jerome who had a dream that he was excluded from heaven for being a Ciceronian rather than a Christian and who consequently vowed not to read pagan authors, was the Jerome who was steeped in classical literature and who later came to an accommodation whereby the best of secular learning could be sanctified to the Christian's benefit. The Jerome who anonymously mocked *Ambrose for plagiarizing Greek texts was the Jerome who exploited other authorities himself without a trace of acknowledgement. Jerome remains a truly complex character. As a scholar, literary artist and practitioner of holy wit, he was a giant. As a pioneer of an ascetic lifestyle which also involved serious intellectual activity, he played a crucial role in Latin Christianity. As an exemplar of every pious virtue, he may require more guarded assessment.

IVOR DAVIDSON

FURTHER READING: Overview of texts in A. di Berardino (ed.), *Patrology*, IV (Westminster, MD, 1994), pp. 212–46. *Biographical and contextual studies*: F. Cavallera, *Saint Jérome: Sa vie et son oeuvre* (2 vols.; Paris, 1922); J.N.D. Kelly, *Jerome: His Life, Writings and Controversies* (London, 1975); S. Rebenich, *Hieronymus und sein Kreis* (Stuttgart, 1992); P. Rousseau, *Ascetics, Authority, and the Church in the Age of Jerome and Cassian* (Oxford, 1978). *Studies of Jerome's scholarship and literary art*: D. Brown, *Vir Trilinguis: A Study in the Biblical Exegesis of Saint Jerome* (Kampen, 1992); Y.-M. Duval (ed.), *Jérôme entre l'Occident et l'Orient* (Paris, 1988); A. Kamesar, *Jerome, Greek Scholarship, and the Hebrew Bible* (Oxford, 1993); D.S. Wiesen, *St Jerome as a Satirist* (Ithaca, NY, 1964).

Jesuits

The history of the Jesuits begins in the life of their founder, *Ignatius of Loyola, and his experience of God which he communicated to others by means of his Spiritual Exercises, a month-long retreat which invites those making it to distinguish themselves in the service of Jesus, even to the point of imitating him in bearing humiliations and sufferings, provided that this is for the greater glory of God.

The men who founded the Society of Jesus with Ignatius were his fellow students at the University of Paris who made the Spiritual Exercises under his guidance: Peter Favre, Francis Xavier, Diego Laínez, Alfonso Salmerón, Nicolás Bobadilla and Simon Rodrigues. On 15 August 1534, these seven men went to the small chapel dedicated to St Dennis on the slope of Montmartre in Paris and vowed to lead lives of poverty and celibacy and to go to Jerusalem. Three years later, their studies completed, they went to Venice in order to join Ignatius, who had preceded them there, and to find passage to the Holy Land. By then three more men, Claude Jay, Paschase Broët and Jean Codure, who had made the Exercises under Favre's guidance, had joined the group. In June of that year those not yet priests – Favre, Jay and Broët were already priests – were ordained to the priesthood. Salmerón was the only exception, because at twenty-two he was too young to be ordained.

After two years of waiting it became clear to them that they would not be able to go to the Holy Land because of the war being waged between Christians and Muslims. They therefore fell back on the alternative plan they had already agreed upon: they would place themselves at the pope's disposal. Their offer accepted, they soon found themselves being sent to different places. The question then arose as to whether they would simply disperse or preserve their union despite this dispersal. They chose the second course. This meant that in addition to the vows of poverty and chastity that they had already taken, they would now add a third vow of obedience to a religious superior whose purpose would be to maintain their unity. Thus they had backed into the form of life recognized by the Catholic Church as religious life. They therefore agreed to ask the church to approve of them as a new religious family. Ignatius wrote up a brief document called 'The Formula of the Institute' and submitted it to the Roman authorities. The Pope Paul III approved it in September 1540. In the spring of 1541, all nine members of this new religious community elected Ignatius as their religious superior. His was the only dissenting vote. Ten years later this founding document, emended and expanded on the basis of experience, was again approved – this time by Pope Julius III.

From his election as superior general in 1541 until his death in 1556, Ignatius worked on a more complete articulation of the character of this new religious community. This work, in substance already completed by 1552, consists of two documents, *The General Examen* and *The Constitutions of the Society of Jesus*, and their respective commentaries or explanations, also called *Declarations*.

This new religious order departed from some of the practices of traditional religious life.

Jesuits would not sing or pray the Divine Office in common, nor would they take a vow of stability, as members of monastic orders did. On the contrary, they existed to be mobile, to go wherever they were sent by the pope and their religious superior. Their governing structure, in contrast to that of the older religious orders, would be highly centralized. All major decisions were assigned ordinarily to the order's religious superior, also called the superior general or simply the general, and to a General Congregation representing the entire order which would assemble to decide extraordinarily important issues – for example, to elect a new general or to change the Constitutions themselves.

By the end of the Society's first decade of existence Jesuit missionaries were to be found in India, Japan, Brazil and Africa. What distinguished them was their openness to native cultures. Xavier began this way of proceeding in Japan in 1549. In the next generation Matteo Ricci (1552–1610), followed by Adam Schall, took it to its perfection in China, learning the language of China's educated class, publishing both scientific and religious works in it, and thereby gaining esteem and acceptance for Christian faith. In India, Roberto de Nobili worked for 49 years (1605–54) in the city of Mardurai, dressing and eating as a Hindu monk and learning Sanskrit in order to read the Veda. By the time he left there, he had made four thousand converts.

In South America, Jesuit missionaries distinguished themselves by their attempts to protect the native population from the slave traders. For this purpose they founded the Paraguay reductions, towns built in the jungles beyond the reach of the slave traders where the native peoples, formerly nomadic, were taught farming methods, metallurgy, music and architecture. Europeans visiting these reductions found that the musical instruments and choral works produced in them rivalled those of Europe. The Jesuits laboured in this work for over one hundred and fifty years (1610–1767). By 1767, there were 57 reductions with a population of 113,716 people.

Despite the emphasis on mobility in their founding documents, Jesuits found themselves after 1548 involved in a kind of work which militated against it – namely, the running of schools. They became the first religious order to make schools their apostolate. Ignatius embraced this work because he realized that long-term involvement with people in the same place could produce very good results. He also saw that schools would produce Jesuit vocations and serve as a base from which Jesuits could practise their other ministries. At his death in 1556 there were already 33 Jesuit schools in Europe alone. By 1773, when the Jesuits were suppressed, they were operating some eight hundred schools throughout the world.

The missionary methods of Jesuits, their dominance in education, their teachings in moral theology and their involvement in business and royal politics created powerful enemies for them – especially among those who embraced the *Enlightenment's ideal of the freeing of the mind and the state from the dominance of religion. Thus Jesuits were exiled from Portugal and its possessions in 1759, from France in 1764, and from Spain in 1767. Then in 1773, under pressure from these three powers, Pope Clement XIV published his letter, 'Dominus ac Redemptor' (Lord and Redeemer), which suppressed the Society of Jesus throughout the world.

Empress Catherine of Russia, eager to retain the services of Jesuits as teachers, refused to allow the letter to be promulgated in her domains. Attempts by the Jesuits' superior in Russia to clarify their situation through an appeal to the papal nuncio in nearby Poland, and later to Rome itself, brought conflicting answers. But with the passing of the years Rome's approval became clearer. Finally, in 1814 Pope Pius VII, freed from Napoleon's imprisonment, restored the Jesuits throughout the world by publishing the bull 'Sollicitudo Omnium Ecclesiarum' (The Solicitude of all the Churches).

The restored Society took up its traditional works and once again grew very large, reaching its greatest numbers in the 1960s when there were some thirty-six thousand Jesuits. But to some, the Jesuits of the nineteenth century and the first half of the twentieth century appeared to be a more cautious group of men who looked back with fondness to the days of the union of throne and altar and regarded their contemporary world with fear, if not disdain. Others, however, would explain their caution as appropriate and to be expected of them at this time, given their papal character. For the papacy of this period regarded the world as the enemy of Christian faith. Jesuits therefore shared this stance.

The educational and missionary work of the restored Society produced great results. By the middle of the twentieth century, Jesuits working in the USA had created a system of Jesuit schools that included 28 colleges or universities and 52 high schools. Jesuit missionaries working in India made themselves superfluous by the 1960s because of the number of native vocations. Of the 21,673 Jesuits living in the year 2000, the two largest groups are those in the United States (3,652) and those in India (3,606).

In the last half of the twentieth century Jesuits made major contributions to the life of the church. The French Jesuit Pierre Teilhard de Chardin (1881–1955) attempted to articulate a vision of Christian faith within an evolutionary context. The Canadian Jesuit *Bernard Lonergan (1904–84) and the German Jesuit *Karl Rahner (1904–84) are recognized as philosophers and theologians of the first order. The American Jesuit John Courtney Murray (1903–67) was influential in bringing the bishops of *Vatican II to accept the separation of church and state. The desire shared by these Jesuits was to bring the Catholic Church into dialogue with the modern world. Thus their work prepared the way for the official acceptance of such a dialogue by the church at the Second Vatican Council.

Vatican II, the 1971 Synod of Bishops, and the Latin American Conference of Catholic Bishops at Medellín, Colombia in 1968, and at Puebla, Mexico in 1979, had all expressed a new understanding of Catholic faith which linked it to justice in the political and economic sense. The man elected as General of the Jesuits in 1965, the Basque Pedro Arrupe (1907–91), took this message to heart and preached it to his fellow Jesuits. The response was mixed. While some supported it, others felt that this stress on social justice was reducing the Jesuit vocation to a this-worldly work and leaving out the transcendental character of Christian faith. Outside the Society there was also hesitation. Addressing the 32nd General Congregation of Jesuits in 1974, Pope Paul VI warned them not to lose sight of their priestly character. When Arrupe suffered a stroke in 1981 the new pope, John Paul II, appointed his own representative to assume the responsibilities of an interim general, thereby bypassing the man already designated for this post by Arrupe himself. Arrupe and the Jesuits throughout the world accepted this papal action in a spirit of obedience. In 1983 the government of the Society was allowed to return to its normal mode of operation and a

33rd General Congregation elected a new general, Peter-Hans Kolvenbach.

The joining of faith and justice continued to be a major preoccupation of Jesuit life in the 1980s, especially in El Salvador in Central America, where six Jesuits were murdered by government forces for their attempts to make a concern for justice in society an essential part of their apostolic work, especially their work at the University of Central America. It remains to be seen how this understanding of the gospel will play itself out in the lives of the Jesuits of the twenty-first century.

GERALD F. FINNEGAN, SJ

FURTHER READING: J.C.H. Aveling, *The Jesuits* (New York, 1982); William V. Bangert, SJ, *History of the Society of Jesus* (St Louis, MO, 1972); James Brodrick, SJ, *The Origins of the Jesuits*; *The Progress of the Jesuits* (Chicago, 1986); Geoffrey Cubitt, *The Jesuit Myth* (Oxford, 1993); Cándido de Dalmases, SJ, *Ignatius of Loyola, Founder of the Jesuits* (trans. Jerome Aixalá, SJ; St Louis, MO, 1985); Joseph de Guibert, SJ, *The Jesuits: Their Spiritual Doctrine and Practice* (trans. William J. Young, SJ; Chicago, 1964); *Ignatius of Loyola: The Spiritual Exercises and Selected Works* (ed. George E. Ganss, SJ; New York, 1991); Jean Lacouture, *Jesuits: A Multibiography* (trans. Jeremy Leggatt; Washington, DC, 1995); Peter McDonough, *Men Astutely Trained* (New York, 1992); David Mitchell, *The Jesuits* (New York, 1981); John O'Malley, SJ, *The First Jesuits* (Cambridge, MA / London, 1993); Jon Sobrino, SJ, *Companions of Jesus* (Maryknoll, NY, 1990); George E. Ganss, SJ, *The Spiritual Exercises of Saint Ignatius: A Translation and Commentary* (St Louis, MO, 1992); Joseph N. Tylenda, SJ, *A Pilgrim's Journey: The Autobiography of Saint Ignatius* (Collegeville, MN, 1991).

Joachim of Fiore (c. 1135–1202)

Joachim of Fiore, born at Celico, spent most of his life in Calabria. He entered the *Benedictine Order at Corazzo c. 1171 and soon became prior and then abbot. He was instrumental in the long process of the order's affiliation to the Cistercian Order, but, desirous to be freed from the encumbrances of administration, he retired first to Petra Lata and finally, with disciples who joined him, to the remote Sila plateau to follow a more contemplative life. With papal encouragement, he established his own order of the Florensians at San Giovanni in Fiore which was finally recognized by Celestine III in a bull of 1196.

Joachim's own life of meditation centred on the interpretation of the Scriptures. He went on pilgrimage to the Holy Land c. 1167. Early legends point to the first of three visionary experiences, reputedly on Mount Tabor; the other two are clearly documented in his writings (*Expos.*, f. 39ʳ⁻ᵛ; *Psalt.*, f. 227ʳ⁻ᵛ). From these experiences he drew his conviction that, through patient study, the *Spiritualis Intellectus* would break through the barriers of the letter to reveal the full inner meanings of the symbols and patterns of Scripture.

Joachim believed that through the Spirit he had been given the key to history, and it is for this theology of history that he is best known. This theology springs from his meditations on the inner *relationes* of the three Persons which he expounds in five and seven *modi* (*Psalt.*, ff. 261ᵛ–262ʳ). This mysterious inner life of fellowship is manifested in the happenings of history, for the time-process is the active work of the Trinity. So he reaches his exposition of the three *status* which encompass the whole of history: that of the Father (law), from the beginning to the incarnation, of the Son (grace), to about two generations after Joachim, of the Spirit (liberty and illumination) to the end of time. These *status* are often misinterpreted as three successive stages, each Person in turn being revealed as one stage with its cut-off point – hence the accusations of Tritheism levelled at Joachim. His vision is much more profound. He reiterates that all three Persons operate throughout history, that the three remain one. The unity is inherent in the interpersonal activity and must not be expressed as a separate essence – as he believed *Peter Lombard had done (e.g. *Psalt.*, ff. 277ʳ, 229ʳ). In the Fourth Lateran Council (1216), however, Lombard's view prevailed and Joachim's was condemned, although his reputation was safeguarded.

The fundamental forms of Trinitarian activity are those of *missio* and *processio*: the Father sends the Son; Father and Son send the Spirit; the Son proceeds from the Father; the Spirit from both Father and Son. His emphasis on the double procession of the Spirit established Joachim's Latinity, as against the view which stresses Greek influence on his doctrine. Translated into terms of history this means that the second *status* has its inception in the first *status*, while the third *status* of the Spirit has a double inception, taking its origin from the *status* of both Father and Son. Joachim finds these overlapping beginnings, first, in the time of the Old Testament King Uzziah (for the Son) and the time of Elijah, Elisha

and the sons of the prophets (for the Spirit); secondly, in the time of St Benedict for the third *status* of the Spirit. There is a further ambiguity which blurs the lines between the second and third *status:* in *Expos.*, 12ʳ, Joachim writes as if the life and passion of the Son will be in some sense re-enacted in the third *status*. This foreshadows the conviction of some spiritual *Franciscans that St Francis embodied a 'middle event' of Christ between his coming in the flesh and his coming in judgement.

Yet clearly the message of the three *status* was one of positive progression within the time-process towards a climactic end to history. This constituted a break – probably unintended – with the *Augustinian view that history had already reached its consummation in the incarnation, a view which dominated the Middle Ages. Joachim's doctrine constituted a catalyst for variously expressed hopes of preceding centuries groping towards an expectation that, before the end, history would culminate in a positive apotheosis. Joachim did, indeed, trace through history a double series of seven tribulations to be endured by the faithful ending with the last and worst antichrist. But, still within time, after victory over antichrist (symbolized by the passage across the Jordan) the pilgrim church would enter the promised land of the Spirit, a time of further illumination which would be the sabbath of history, symbolized in the seventh day of creation. But it should be noted that Joachim always distinguished this from the eighth day of full perfection in eternity. Joachim also used the symbol of Satan bound (Rev. 20:2) as a figure of the Sabbath, but he should not be classed as a millennialist since this period – which might be shorter or longer – represents the culmination of history itself rather than a single supernatural intervention in time. This positive vision of history exercised a powerful influence over many imaginations down to the sixteenth century, with strange echoes still evident in the nineteenth century. These forms of Joachimism ranged from the revolutionary claims that the eternal evangel of the Spirit would supersede the New Testament as that had superseded the Old Testament, to the milder visions of achievement in a golden age, before the end of time.

Although there are some ambiguous passages in his works, especially in his latest, unfinished, *Super Quatuor Evangelia*, Joachim himself avoided the logical extremes to which his doctrine could be carried. He did this partly through his complex number symbolisms – in particular, his interweaving patterns of 'twos and threes'. There are only two dispensations in time, embodied in synagogue and church, Old Testament and New. Just as the church of St Peter, superseding the synagogue, will endure until the end of time, so also the New Testament, superseding the Old. Although the pattern of three *status* runs parallel in time, institutionally there is no third church or testament: the *Ecclesia Spiritualis* will be the reformed Latin Church and the third testament will be the spiritual interpretation of Old and New.

Number symbolism lends itself to *figurae*. Joachim was an artist who expressed the complexities of his thought in visual images: intertwined circles, demonstrating the three-in-one of the Trinity, trees of history, setting out the patterns of twos and threes, *figurae* using the letter-shapes of the alpha and omega to reveal the *missio* and *processio* and others. These *figurae* were finally assembled in the unique *Liber Figurarum*.

MARJORIE REEVES

FURTHER READING: *Texts: Liber de Concordie Novi ac Veteris Testamenti* (Frankfurt, 1964); *Liber de Concordia* (ed. E.R. Daniel; Philadelphia, 1983); *Expositio in Apocalypism* (Frankfurt, 1964), bound with *Psalterium decem Chordarum. Studies:* H. Grundmann, *Studien über Joachim von Floris* (Leipzig, 1927); B. McGinn, *The Calabrian Abbot: Joachim of Fiore in the History of Western Thought* (New York, 1985); M. Reeves, *The Influence of Prophecy in the Later Middle Ages: A Study in Joachimism* (Notre Dame, rev. edn, 1993); M. Reeves and B. Hirsch-Reich, *The Figurae of Joachim of Fiore* (Oxford, 1972); M. Reeves, *Joachim of Fiore and the Prophetic Future* (London, 1976).

John of the Cross (1542–91)

Juan de Yepes was born in 1542 at Fontiveros, Spain, three years before the inaugural session of the Council of Trent. He grew up in extremely penurious circumstances. At twenty-one, John entered the Carmelite Order. Upon his profession in 1564 he received permission to follow the older, unmitigated observance of the Order.

From 1564 to 1568 John studied philosophy and theology at the University of Salamanca, residing and also studying at the Carmelite College of St Andrew. His studies exposed him to a number of philosophical, theological and literary influences, including: *Scholasticism,

and its Carmelite representatives Baconthorp (c. 1290–1348) and Michael of Bologna (c. 1320–1400); the 'scripturist' movement then *au courant* in opposition to *Thomist doctrine; Pseudo-Dionysius and Gregory the Great, the subjects of a lost written exercise attributed to John; *Augustine and the Pseudo Augustine of the apocryphal *Soliloquia*; and the Italianizing poets Boscan and Garcilaso, to name those most commonly recognized. To these influences should be added the Bible, the Breviary, and the Rule and other early texts of the Carmelite Order.

In 1567 John made the acquaintance of *Teresa of Avila. The following year they inaugurated the Reform of the Carmelite Order. John held various posts within the Reform until his imprisonment in 1577 by Carmelites opposed to it. He composed his greatest poetry during his imprisonment. After his escape nine months later, he again occupied various posts within the Reform and wrote poetry and prose works.

John of the Cross died on 13 December 1591 in Ubeda, Spain, while subjected to denunciation by a faction within the new Discalced Carmelite Order. He was canonized in 1726 and declared a Doctor of the Church in 1926.

The essential elements of John's ascetical-mystical vision of union with God were developed during his early years of privation, observance of the unmitigated Rule and study. They were amplified from 1568 to 1577 as he matured in his expertise as a novice master, confessor and spiritual director. His poems and their prose commentaries were written and refined from 1578 to 1591, yet they express a vision of contemplation that is essentially unchanging. Although often articulated within a scholastic conceptual framework, and bearing signs of other intellectual and cultural influences, his doctrine of the 'ascent' leading to union with God also demonstrates a singular and unbending reliance upon his own experience as a contemplative, whence comes its remarkable unity. One might characterize the form of his doctrine as proceeding from an 'unutterable' experience of God that is then expressed poetically as a first instance of conceptual mediation, before finding its further conceptualization in the commentaries.

John's vision of union with God is a cornerstone of Christian ascetical-mystical theology. His major works, *The Ascent of Mount Carmel, The Dark Night, The Spiritual Canticle* and *The

Living Flame of Love constitute an integrated doctrine and itinerary of the contemplative 'ascent'. The ascent is from the active and passive 'nights' of the purifications of sense and spirit to the approach, through love, to the 'dawn' of union with God, and finally to the 'day' of total transformation in God through spiritual marriage.

John's doctrine is a further elaboration of two major sources of ascetical mystical theology: the *Dionysian *via negativa* that lies at the heart of mystical prayer and an asceticism born of an Augustinian understanding of the consequences of original sin. Continuing the apophatic mystical tradition dominated heretofore by Pseudo Dionysius, John counsels a practice of prayer that requires the relinquishment of discursive and image-based modes of meditation in favour of a silent and imageless contemplation of the wholly transcendent God. Such contemplation occurs and deepens in conformity to the purification, illumination and transformation, through the working of the Holy Spirit, of the individual flawed by original sin. Spiritual marriage is characterized by the transformation of the intellect into perfect faith, the memory into perfect hope and the will into perfect love. The spiritual freedom attendant upon such union with God then enables the individual's disinterested and compassionate engagement with the world. Although John's vision has been thought to describe the contemplative state of life and is certainly influenced by its expression in sixteenth-century Spain, his own example of ministry attests to the apostolic engagement that spiritual freedom renders possible, since the individual's 'affections' or desires have been transformed by the sole love of God. John states that all the baptized are called to contemplation.

It is important to emphasize the Christological character of John's doctrine. The imitation of Christ lies at the heart of his ascetical vision of active purification. What is more, Christ's revelatory role in relation to the Father constitutes the very foundation of Christian faith because Christ alone makes possible the intellect's adherence to revealed truth. One knows God in and through Christ, yet such knowledge cannot exhaust the mystery of the transcendent God. Rather Christ, the Logos, leads one into the mystery of God.

The 'exceptional' quality of John's doctrine has often been noted. It is thought by many that his itinerary of the 'ascent' to transforming union with God is reserved for those who pursue the contemplative life with a high degree of perseverance and detachment from the world. His vision has, at times, been criticized as finding its origins in too pessimistic an understanding of the human condition in its 'natural' state – that is, prior to the transforming effects of active and passive purification of sense and spirit. His doctrine has also been thought to exhibit a concern with individual spiritual growth that is disproportionate in relation to the just claims of communal experience. In light of this latter concern, his understanding of the 'ascent' is then regarded as lacking a sufficient sense of history.

Because the influence of John of the Cross has not been historically widespread, his impact upon contemporary spiritual theology is perhaps best seen in the individuals who have made his doctrine an integral part of their own spiritual journey and who have then 'translated' it for accessibility to a wider audience. Edith Stein and Thomas Merton are two such examples.

MARIE L. BAIRD

FURTHER READING: Jesus-Marie de Bruno, *Saint John of the Cross* (ed. Benedict Zimmerman; New York, 1932); Jesus Sacramentado de Crisogono, *The Life of Saint John of the Cross* (trans. Kathleen Pond; London, 1958); E.W.T. Dicken, *The Crucible of Love: A Study of the Mysticism of St. Teresa of Avila and St. John of the Cross* (New York, 1963); Saint-Joseph de Lucien-Marie, 'S. Jean de la Croix', vol. 8 of *Dictionnaire de Spiritualité: Ascetique et Mystique Doctrine et Histoire* (ed. M. Viller, et al.; Paris, 1976); Marilyn May Mallory, *Christian Mysticism: Transcending Techniques: A Theological Reflection on the Empirical Testing of the Teaching of St. John of the Cross* (Assen, 1977); Thomas Merton, 'St. John of the Cross', in *Saints for Now* (ed. Clare Boothe Luce; New York, 1952), pp. 250–60; Georges Morel, *Le Sens de l'Existence selon S. Jean de la Croix* (3 vols.; Paris, 1960–61); Steven Payne, *John of the Cross and the Cognitive Value of Mysticism: An Analysis of Sanjuanist Teaching and its Philosophical Implications for Contemporary Discussions of Mystical Experience* (Dordrecht, 1990); Edith Stein, *The Science of the Cross: A Study of St. John of the Cross* (trans. Hilda Graef; Chicago, 1960); Hans Urs von Balthasar, 'St. John of the Cross', in vol. 3 of *The Glory of the Lord: A Theological Aesthetics* (ed. John Riches; trans. Andrew Louth, et al.; San Francisco, 1986), pp. 105–71.

John of Damascus (c. 665–749)

The outstanding Greek theologian of the eighth century and one of the most influential in both east and west. His grandfather Mansur negotiated the surrender of Damascus to the Arabs in 635. His half-brother Cosmas was bishop of Maiuma in Gaza and is known as the hymnographer Cosmas of Jerusalem. As a Syrian Melkite, John served in the administration of the Umayyad Caliph Abd al-Malik at Damascus before entering the monastery of Mar Sabas in Judea. He initially came to prominence during the first period of Byzantine iconoclasm (726–87) when he defended the veneration of icons against the iconoclast policy of Emperor Leo III. Although John was living under the anti-image culture of Islam, he was well placed to defend the icon cult because he was outside Byzantine imperial jurisdiction. His *Three Orations on the Holy Images* is still the definitive statement on the theology of Christian images and the extensive florilegium attached to this work provides valuable information concerning his patristic sources. In Syria his work was continued by his fellow Sabaite Theodore Abū Qurrah (c. 740–820), who defended icon veneration in Arabic against both Muslim and Jewish attacks. In Byzantium, John's iconophile credentials were upheld by the bishops of the Seventh Oecumenical Council in 787, and he influenced such iconophiles of the second period of Byzantine iconoclasm (815–45) as Theodore the Studite (759–826) and the patriarch Nikephoros (758–828).

John's next most important work is his three-volume *Fount of Knowledge* (*Pege gnoseos*). Book one, the *Dialectica*, deals with philosophical definitions, mainly of the *Aristotelian school, and is by far the most comprehensive collection of such definitions from the period. Book two is a compendium of heresies based largely on the earlier work of *Epiphanius of Salamis and other writers. Book three, *On the Orthodox Faith*, is of great theological importance because it attempts to systematize the Greek patristic tradition, especially on Christological matters. *Maximus the Confessor is an important influence in this respect. This third volume also deals with physics and medicine and shows that science and secular knowledge were integral to John's Christian world-view.

The *Sitz im Leben* of his *On the Orthodox Faith* has not been given the attention it deserves. The situation in Syria-Palestine in the first half of the eighth century was not easy for the Greek Church. There was no Greek patriarch of Jerusalem for the second half of the seventh century, while a similar situation persisted at Antioch for the first half of the eighth century. The steady consolidation of Islam brought increasing divisions between the Christian communities. As independent churches, the Syrian Orthodox (Jacobite) and Maronite communities fared better than their Byzantine counterparts with their links with the *ancien régime*. John's *On the Orthodox Faith* must be seen, therefore, in the context of inter-church rivalry on the one hand, and survival under Islam on the other. It was most likely written to inform the Melkite communities of where they stood on questions of doctrine, cut off as they were from their Byzantine roots at Constantinople. Given also that at the time of writing iconoclasm reigned in Byzantium, John may have composed his *On the Orthodox Faith* to remind the patriarchate of Constantinople of its true heritage.

Parts of *On the Orthodox Faith* were translated into Arabic in the early tenth century and into Slavonic by John, exarch of Bulgaria, in the late ninth century. A Latin translation was begun by Burgundio of Pisa in 1148, and a further translation, along with the *Dialectica*, by *Robert Grosseteste, bishop of Lincoln, in 1235. Because *Thomas Aquinas (1224–74) cites extensively from this work, western scholars have spoken of John as a pioneer of *Scholasticism, as well as the last of the Greek Fathers. From an Eastern Christian perspective, however, this is rather misleading. John was the last of the Fathers in Syria-Palestine to write in Greek, but there were other Byzantine Fathers after John, notably *Photius (c. 820 – c. 891) and *Gregory Palamas (1296–1359). In the one hundred chapters of his *On the Orthodox Faith* John demonstrates familiarity with, and mastery of, the technical vocabulary of patristic theology. It is apparent that, in spite of his knowledge of Aristotelian philosophy, his terminology remains largely that of the Fathers and the church councils. By the fourteenth century both Byzantine and Latin theologians were quoting from his *On the Orthodox Faith*, but for different purposes. The one quoted it in support of the hesychast tradition of Byzantium, the other in support of the scholastic method of the schoolmen.

John also wrote homilies and hymns and is credited with composing the *Octoechos* of the Greek Church. The earliest refutation of Islam in

Greek, *The Heresy of the Ishmaelites*, is attributed to him, and he is thought by some to have influenced the development of Muslim *kalām*. A concise treatise on ascetic doctrine, *On the Virtues and the Vices*, is included under John's name in the *Philokalia* of Nikodimos of the Holy Mountain (1749–1809). The *Sacra Parallela*, an extensive florilegium, is ascribed to him, and in Byzantium and the western medieval world John's name was also associated with the story of *Barlaam and Iosaphat*, which is based in part on the life of the Buddha.

KEN PARRY

FURTHER READING: P.B. Kotter (ed.), *Die Schriften des Johannes von Damaskos* (5 vols.; Berlin, 1969–88); D. Anderson (trans.), *St John of Damascus: On the Divine Images* (New York, 1980); K. Weitzmann, *The Miniatures of the Sacra Parallela: Parisinus Graecus 923* (Princeton, 1979); D.J. Sahas, *John of Damascus on Islam: The 'Heresy of the Ishmaelites'* (Leiden, 1972); F.H. Chase (trans.), *Saint John of Damascus: Writings* (Washington, DC, 1958); J. Nasrallah, *Saint Jean de Damas: Son Époque, sa Vie, son Oeuvre* (Paris, 1950).

Julian of Norwich
(c. 1342–1416 or later)

Julian of Norwich was a spiritual theologian. In May 1373 Julian received 16 revelations of Christ. She was subsequently described as an anchoress; Margery Kempe of Kings Lynn was among those whom she counselled. Her epithet may well be taken from the church in Norwich to which she was attached. Julian referred to herself as unlettered, but she could probably read Latin, and presumably she controlled the form in which the revelations were set down. Excellent theological advisers would have been available either through the Benedictine Cathedral Priory or through the four learned mendicant orders resident in Norwich.

Julian rarely quoted Scripture verbatim, but she was imbued with *lectio divina* and the Liturgy. There are two versions of the revelations. The Short Text ('S') was presumably written fairly soon after the event. The Long Text ('L') was not finished before 1393, and Julian may have worked on it into her old age. 'S' begins with the incarnation but is centred on the passion of Christ, passing on to his resurrection and the indwelling of Christ in the soul. Mary has an important subordinate place in association with Christ's incarnation, cross and glorification.

Julian also wrestles with the problem of sin in the context of God's omnipotent love; and she considers prayer as our sharing, through grace, in God's good deeds.

'L' includes practically all that is in 'S', with expansions in the sections dealing with the problem of evil and with prayer. More especially, the traditional (Augustinian) appropriation of power, wisdom (*sapientia*) and love or goodness to the Persons of the Trinity is adapted. Julian introduces a variant appropriation of truth, wisdom and love (chs. 44, 54), while again it is to Christ as wisdom that motherhood (with mercy) is appropriated (chs. 48, 54, 58, etc.), and lordship (with grace) is appropriated to the Holy Spirit (chs. 48, 58).

The application of female imagery to God has roots in Scripture and some of the Fathers, but Julian is distinctive in appropriating motherhood specifically to Christ as the second Person within a carefully articulated Trinitarian theology. Doubtless there is an element of personal perception here, and there are occasional adumbrations in 'S'. But the appropriation of wisdom to the second Person is most probably the point of departure. Scripture speaks of wisdom, in female terms, as God's agent in creating and conserving the world. Julian seems to echo something of this.

Julian saw the orders of nature and redemption as cohering in Christ, our mother in nature ('kind') by our creation and our mother in grace through assuming our humanity. She feels her way in portraying the work of the three Persons in willing, working and confirming; in nature, mercy and grace (ch. 59).

Already in 'S' Julian has asked how, in the face of the real effects of sin, she is to understand the Lord's assurance that 'all shall be well'. Echoing the language of the Easter *Exultet*, 'O happy fault, O truly necessary sin of Adam ...', she has gone on to see herself as representative of all falling and rising Christians in whom the 'goodly will' is maintained by God, and she has found this a ground of hope. She eschewed any dogmatic universalism, but in 'L' (ch. 36) she looked forward to the 'great deed', incomprehensible to men, which will vindicate God's almighty love.

In 'L' she speaks of two judgements: God's judgement, regarding our 'substance', which is inseparably united to him, and human judgement, regarding the 'sensuality' which is changeable and a source of pain, often hindering us from perceiving the love of God which is always active in us (ch. 45). In Christ the 'substance' and 'sensuality' are united. This concept is summed up in the vision of the lord and the servant, introduced into 'L' (ch. 51). The lord (God the Father) sends his servant (who is both Adam [or everyman] and Christ), to do his will. In his eagerness the servant falls and is badly hurt, unable to raise himself. But the lord, looking on his good will, regards him with pity rather than with blame, and raises him to higher dignity than he had before the fall. The 'fall' represents both Adam's fall and Christ's descent into Mary's womb; in God's sight, in contrast to our perception, Adam's fall (and ours) is subsumed within Christ's saving work.

Julian's biblical overtones include echoes of John and especially of Paul. No doubt her links with affective devotion in, say, the *Franciscan tradition, might be explored. But it is repeatedly *Augustine (354–430) who provides a point of departure – often interpreted or applied in a way that stands within the parameters of orthodoxy but offers something new. In 'L' she brings out even more explicitly the common operation of the Trinity in the passion of Christ, and the mutual indwelling (circumincession) of the three Persons. Her teaching on prayer as a participation in God's activity is deeply rooted in the Augustinian theology of grace. And the exposition of the vision of the lord and the servant is a reworking of elements found in Augustine, especially in *De Trinitate* 2.5.9 on the temporal disclosure of the Word who was with God in the beginning – a passage familiar to medieval theologians especially through the *Sentences* of *Peter Lombard (c. 1100–60), a standard work in the schools. We should love to know more about the Norwich theologians of Julian's day.

Julian's teaching will have appeared difficult and problematic to some in her own time. The *Revelations* were preserved by exiled English religious following the dissolution and printed in France in 1670. It is in the present century that she has come into her own, as a theologian who is faithful to the received tradition and at the same time finds sometimes surprising resources for exploration and development in it. Much has been written about her, especially from feminist viewpoints; the doctrine of the divine motherhood in Christ has to be evaluated in the context of Julian's profoundly orthodox approach to the mystery of the Trinity and of grace.

JOHN P.H. CLARK

FURTHER READING: *Texts: A Book of Showings to the Anchoress Julian of Norwich* (ed. E. Colledge and J. Walsh; 2 vols.; Toronto, 1978); *Julian of Norwich: A Revelation of Love* (ed. Marion Glasscoe; Exeter, rev. edn, 1993 [Long Text]); H. Kempster, 'Julian of Norwich: The Westminster Text of A Revelation of Love', *Mystics Q* 23 (1997), pp. 177–246. *Modernized version:* Elizabeth Spearing, *Julian of Norwich: Revelations of Divine Love* (Harmondsworth, 1998). *Studies:* P. Molinari, *Julian of Norwich: The Teaching of a Fourteenth-Century English Mystic* (London, 1958); B. Pelphrey, *Love Was His Meaning: The Theology and Mysticism of Julian of Norwich* (Salzburg, 1982); R. Maisonneuve, *L'Univers Visionnaire de Julian of Norwich* (Paris, 1987); Joan M. Nuth, *Wisdom's Daughter: The Theology of Julian of Norwich* (New York, 1991); Ritamary Bradley, *Julian's Way: A Practical Commentary on Julian of Norwich* (London, 1992); Margaret Ann Palliser, *Christ, our Mother of Mercy: Divine Mercy and Compassion in the Theology of the 'Shewings' of Julian of Norwich* (Berlin, 1992); Denise N. Baker, *Julian of Norwich's 'Showings': From Vision to Book* (Princeton, 1994); J.P.H. Clark, 'Time and Eternity in Julian of Norwich', *Down R* 109 (1991), pp. 259–76; 'Julian of Norwich and the Blessed Virgin Mary', in *Mary is for Everyone: Essays on Mary and Ecumenism* (ed. W. McLoughlin and Jill Pinnock; Leominster, 1997), pp. 236–50.

Julian of Toledo (642–90)

Julian has been called 'the last of the Spanish fathers'. He belonged to the Janus-faced culture of Visigothic Spain just before the arrival of the Saracens. It was a culture which perpetuated a classical past in language and learning. At the same time, it anticipated many of the characteristic habits of medieval thought and produced some of its widely used textbooks. Julian not only grew up in that culture, but consciously sought to protect and enhance it. He is a fitting end to the century that began with Isidore, whom he equalled in erudition and surpassed in originality. Julian became Archbishop of Toledo in 680 and presided over four synods (Twelfth to Fifteenth Councils of Toledo). In these councils he sought to establish the primacy of Toledo within a more unified Spanish church, and he came into conflict with the See of Rome over its privileges. Independently of Rome he approved the acts of Constantinople III (680) and for this received a rebuke from Pope Benedict II. Later he had to defend one of his own writings (the *Apologeticum*) against a Roman accusation of Christological unorthodoxy.

Julian's writings range from a 'history' of contemporary Spain to a Latin grammar, and from theological textbooks to contributions to the Mozarab liturgy. Like other Spanish writers of his time he shows an intense desire to collect materials, edit them with *breuitas* and reproduce their contents in an easily accessible form. Julian's biographer listed 17 books by him, but at present we can only identify six with certainty; and of these six only three had any wide currency during the Middle Ages. Of these three, the *De comprobatione aetatis sextae* was the least used. A polemical anti-Jewish work, its purpose was to prove to its Christian audience (though it claims to be written for Jews), using the arithmetic of millennia based on Daniel 9:24–6, that the Messiah has come. It is indicative of the increasing anti-Semitism of Visigothic Spain. Julian's most copied work was the *Prognosticon futuri saeculi*: a patristic florilegium on dying and eschatology. It funnelled many stern and fear-inspiring patristic warnings into later preaching. Although not the most copied, Julian's *Antikeimenon* was the book with the greatest impact. It gathers 221 cases from the Fathers of solutions to scriptural contradictions and simplifies them – giving preference to logic-based solutions. This work lies behind much Carolingian exegesis, was a forerunner of *Abelard's *Sic et non*, and can be seen as a foundation of *disputatio* in later scholastic method.

THOMAS O'LOUGHLIN

FURTHER READING: *Catalogue*: CPL 1258–1266, and see 1252, 1555 and 1997 (note misprints: n. 1260 should read: *CC, t.c.*, *p. 143–212*; and n. 1261 *PL xcvi*, *595–704* [i.e., to date no new edition of the *Antikeimenon*]). *Studies*: J.N. Hillgarth, 'Introduction' to CCSL 115 (1976), pp. viii–lxxiv; T. O'Loughlin, 'Julian of Toledo's *Antikeimenon* and the Development of Latin Exegesis', *Proceedings of the Irish Biblical Association* 16 (1993), pp. 80–98.

Jüngel, Eberhard (b. 1934)

Professor of systematic theology and philosophy of religion at the University of Tübingen, and a leading German Protestant thinker. Raised in the Stalinist German Democratic Republic, Jüngel studied with some of the leading figures of German theology in the 1950s, and taught in East Berlin and Zurich before moving to Tübingen. He has written extensively in many areas: New Testament, dogmatics, the theologies of *Luther and *Barth, classical and modern philosophy. He is a renowned preacher and commentator on church and public life.

Jüngel's work is deeply influenced by both *Bultmann's Christian existentialism and the Christocentric dogmatics of Barth. His first specialization was New Testament, where he learned much from Bultmann's pupil, Ernst Fuchs. In his doctoral dissertation *Paulus und Jesus*, Jüngel developed an account of Jesus' proclamation of the kingdom of God as an eschatological, interruptive word, found above all in the parables. This parabolic word is no mere illustration or symbol, but the real presence of the kingdom in language (the debt to the later Heidegger is explicit). This 'speech event' breaks apart and remakes human life; and the word evokes faith as the shape of human life remade by grace. This sharp focus on Jesus' parables, coupled with a strong emphasis on the cross as the *telos* of Jesus' mission, continues to shape Jüngel's Christology. Jüngel sought to combine this eschatological Christology and theory of language with aspects of Barth's theology of revelation and the Trinity. In Barth, Jüngel found (and continues to find) an example of 'theological theology', that is, a dogmatics which is free from anxiety about foundations and undertakes the task of expansive description of Christian verities under the guidance of biblical revelation. In particular, Barth's rooting of all doctrine in a Trinitarian Christology set the frame for much of Jüngel's constructive dogmatic work. A fine early study of Barth, *The Doctrine of the Trinity*, formed the first of a series of remarkably penetrating interpretations of Barth. Here Jüngel argued that Barth's identification of God-for-himself and God-for-us not only helps hold together classical Christian emphasis on divine aseity and the anthropological concerns of Christian existentialism, but also articulates how, in identification with the crucified Jesus, God can suffer and die without collapsing into contingency. This latter theme (the 'death of God') has furnished the theme of some powerful writing, often in conversation with *Hegel or leading atheistic thinkers.

In the later 1960s, Jüngel's work followed a number of different directions. Partly under the influence of an intense study of Luther's doctrine of Christian righteousness, Jüngel began to write on the metaphysical, anthropological and ethical aspects of the doctrine of justification by faith. One of his chief emphases became the priority of divine agency, before which the human person, defined by faith, is primarily a passive hearer of the word and only secondarily a moral agent. This developed into a critique of the stress on self-realization through activity which Jüngel believes to dominate modern technological culture, and which he traces back to *Aristotelian anthropology. The critique involves him in deploying an ontology in which actuality (realized through activity) is subservient to possibility (which is generated by God's presence and activity as word).

Alongside this, Jüngel wrote much on life after death and its relation to the message of the cross and resurrection (most of all in his book *Death*). He sketched out some initial lines of a natural theology. He continued to work on Barth's thought, most of all in response to the final section of the *Church Dogmatics*, where Barth rejected the sacramental status of water baptism. Jüngel published important interpretative essays on this material which not only clarified the ethical aspects of Barth's purpose, but also shaped Jüngel's own theology of the sacraments, a topic on which he also worked in conversation with *Karl Rahner. His work on theological and philosophical aspects of language took on increasing sophistication, especially in studies of metaphor, anthropomorphism and analogy in which some of the eschatological emphases of his earlier material were refined. In addition, the steady stream of interpretative studies continued, treating not only Luther and Barth but *Spinoza, Hegel, *Nietzsche, Heidegger and others.

In 1977 Jüngel published his *magnum opus* to date, *God as the Mystery of the World*. It is a wide-ranging book, which operates on a number of different levels – part history of the fate of Christian theology within a foundational framework supplied by philosophical theism, part theory of language and revelation, part Trinitarian dogmatics, part anthropology. One of the chief tasks of the book is to trace the fate of thought and speech about God since *Descartes, who represents the attempt to base certainty of God on the self-certainty of the self-conscious knower. In reply, Jüngel recommends a realist theological epistemology, in which thinking follows the speech event of revelation in which God comes to the world. This speech event is transformative; and Christian language thereby takes the form of an 'analogy of advent', in which the renewing power of God is indicated. At the dogmatic level, Jüngel here extends and refines themes he first articulated in the 1960s, notably the suffering and death of God as a Trinitarian act of divine freedom and love. This cross-centred doctrine of God is then used as a lever against what Jüngel construes as the failures of metaphysical theism. Though the book does not always develop its axioms to the fullest extent, it remains an extraordinarily perceptive account of modern theological history as well as an important dogmatic proposal.

Since the publication of this book, Jüngel has concentrated on consolidating the positions developed there and elsewhere. He has continued to interpret the work of others (now including *Schleiermacher and *Kierkegaard). He has expounded the ramifications of the doctrine of justification, and particularly its political consequences, with great vigour. He has often done so in polemical divergence from political theologies, which Jüngel believes to privilege the human moral act over divine agency. He has turned with renewed interest to questions of ecclesiology and sacramental theology, and he has written with considerable effect on the centrality of prayer in the theology of worship and Christian ethics. By now, he is established as one of the handful of leading German Protestant thinkers, and his work has been widely translated and discussed in continental Europe. His work has, however, made relatively little impression on English language theology.

Jüngel's best work is often done in close commentary on major theological and philosophical texts, and his thought is a model of serious engagement with some of the great writings of the philosophical and theological traditions of the west. Of all those who have been deeply influenced by Barth, he has given great attention to questions of metaphysics and ontology, without thereby falling into apologetics. Jüngel has done much to demonstrate that the alliance of theology and idealist metaphysics has introduced some basic distortions into Christian doctrine. His ontology of possibility and becoming, and its application to theological anthropology, is of very great significance as an example of the attempt to spell out the metaphysical dimensions of Christian faith, without subsuming Christianity within an external scheme. He is a suggestive and evocative thinker, less concerned to analyze his own basic convictions, and more prescriptive in tone. The compensation in his work is that he is without equal as one who has sought to foster a genuine conversation between the theology of revelation and the history of modern philosophical culture.

JOHN WEBSTER

FURTHER READING: *Texts: Paulus und Jesus* (Tübingen, 1962); *Unterwegs zur Sache* (Munich, 1972); *Death, the Riddle and the Mystery* (Philadelphia, 1975); *The Doctrine of the Trinity* (Edinburgh, 1975); *Entsprechungen* (Munich, 1980); *Barth-Studien* (Philadelphia, 1982); *God as the Mystery of the World* (Edinburgh, 1983); *Karl Barth – A Theological Legacy* (Philadelphia, 1986); *Theological Essays* (2 vols.; Edinburgh, 1989, 1995); *Wertlose Wahrheit* (Munich, 1990). *Studies:* E. Paulus, *Liebe – das Geheimnis der Welt* (Wurzburg, 1990); R. Spjuth, *Creation, Contingency and Divine Presence* (Lund, 1995); J. Webster, *Eberhard Jüngel* (Cambridge, 1991); J. Webster (ed.), *The Possibilities of Theology* (Festschrift E. Jüngel; Edinburgh, 1994).

Justin Martyr (d. c. 165)

Justin was executed, together with some of his pupils, in Rome about 165. We know of his life only by a martyrology and some autobiographical passages in his own writings. He was an uncircumcised Palestinian from Samaria who, after conventional education, sought a true philosophy. He says he studied successively with Stoic, Peripatetic and Pythagorean teachers and was then won to *Platonism, with its sense of invisible reality. An encounter with an old man finally convinced him – through an exposition of the Old Testament prophets – that Christianity was true. The account is somewhat idealized and his knowledge of philosophy superficial. The historian *Eusebius says that Justin's *Dialogue* with Trypho records a historic debate in Ephesus, implying that he lived there for a time. Justin certainly ended up running a Christian school in Rome, where he made enemies. His death may have resulted from the professional jealousy of another philosopher.

Justin wrote controversial works against *Marcion and the *Gnostics, which are lost. We possess two *Apologies* (i.e., reasoned defences of the Christian faith). The first is addressed to the Emperor Antoninus Pius and his sons, and it is thus dated between 137 and 161. The second is addressed to the Romans, apparently near his death. His longest work, the *Dialogue with Trypho the Jew*, is aimed to refute Jewish objections to Christianity. The authenticity of a further work, *On the Resurrection*, which deals with specific objections to the doctrine of the resurrection of the flesh, is doubtful.

The chief purpose of the first *Apology* is to refute the charge that Christians are atheists. From the viewpoint of the Roman imperial cult, Christians repudiated the gods on whom the social fabric relied. Justin argues that slanders against Christian conduct are themselves the work of these evil demons, the false gods. Christians hold to one God, the morally perfect Father and maker of all, who needs no sacrificial cult. The truth about him came through Jesus Christ his Son, who with the angelic host is worshipped 'in the second place', together with 'the prophetic Spirit in the third rank'. Such rudimentary Trinitarianism belongs to the baptismal confession, but like other apologists Justin speaks more often of God and his word (Logos) than of Father, Son and Spirit. This is because it is a point of engagement with contemporary philosophical vocabulary which he is seeking to exploit.

Some contemporary Platonism was theistic. It retained belief in an absolute transcendent unchanging God, but it postulated a secondary 'divine mind' which mediated existence to the world. Albinos taught this in Asia Minor in the middle second century, when Justin may have been there. So Justin himself asserts that God is totally beyond description, unchanging, not in any place, as well as totally good. The God of the Bible, who acts and reacts towards the world, who appears and intervenes (who is 'immanent') is a distinct being – his Word or Son. So the angel who appears to Moses in the bush is not the Father, but Jesus Christ his Son. The title 'Word' or Logos is particularly convenient. In Scripture it is the means by which God achieves things and makes himself known. In philosophy it stood for the rational principle – not only of articulate speech, but also of all thought and of the rational order of the universe. This ambiguity is already exploited in the first verses of John's Gospel, and the notion that the universe is created in or by the Logos of God can be understood philosophically. Justin held that past philosophers had known this truth (which they had plagiarized from Moses) and Socrates was tried and executed at the behest of the same demons (false gods) that were now inspiring anti-Christian persecutions.

Useful as it was to account for the relation between the active God of Scripture and the transcendent God of Platonism, and for

Christian veneration of Jesus as divine, this distinction between God and his Logos met with opposition from thoughtful Jews. The *Dialogue with Trypho the Jew* is an attempt to meet such objections. Whether or not the dialogue ever actually happened, Justin's literary version of it gives us valuable insights into the Jewish polemic and exegesis of his day and, among other things, into the difficulties caused by differing versions of the text of Scripture. Justin himself relies on the Greek version of the Old Testament (LXX) which he inherited as authoritative. From it he tries to prove that, correctly read, the Scriptures point clearly to the new dispensation in Jesus and the church: the expected Messiah must suffer, and Jesus fulfils what was prophesied. In particular, we find the argument that in creation God put forth his Word (Logos). God was always rational, and he had his Logos within him. When God says, 'Let there be light' (Gen. 1:4), this Word goes forth and becomes 'another beside himself with whom he may hold converse'. That conversation begins when God says, 'Let us make Man in our image ...' (Gen. 1:26). Here Justin clearly implies that when God first spoke, the Logos immanent within him was expressed as Word. Justin's Trinity (or at this point Binity) is therefore functional or 'economic' rather than eternal, a view that would soon be repudiated by *Origen and *Athanasius. A further point where Justin fails by later orthodox standards is with regard to the matter of creation. He suggests that the chaotic void of Genesis 1:2 was the same as Plato's notion of formless matter, on which form is imposed when God utters his Word (Gen. 1:4). (The presence of a similar thought in the treatise *On Resurrection* is one of the strongest arguments for its authenticity.)

The *Second Apology* was inspired by a particular trial and execution and is a protest against punishing Christians merely for their name, and not for their actual conduct. It includes one important idea borrowed from philosophy. Stoics called the generative principle of the universe, or of an individual thing, its *logos spermatikos* ('seminal thought/word'). Justin says this 'seminal Word' makes known to wise men, ancient and modern, the truth that is fully known only in Jesus Christ. (In Barnard's version, *logos spermatikos* is translated 'logos, the Sower'.)

Justin differs from other early apologists in two important ways. (1) He writes freely about Jesus Christ, whose conception in a virgin he portrays as a miracle like those in which pagans also believe. (2) He gives explicit descriptions of Christian worship, specifically baptism and the Sunday Eucharist, which are of enormous value to liturgical scholars. He does this chiefly to give the lie to accusations of cannibalism and other monstrous secret practices, and to show that the sacraments too have pagan parallels.

STUART G. HALL

FURTHER READING: *Texts: Corpus apologetarum christianorum saeculi secundi* I–III (ed. J.C.T. Otto; Jena, 3rd edn, 1876–79 / Wiesbaden, 1969–71); *Die ältesten Apologeten* (ed. Edgar J. Goodspeed; Göttingen, 1914, 1984 / New York, 1950); *The Acts of the Christian Martyrs* (ed. and trans. Herbert Musurillo; OECT; Oxford, 1972). *English versions:* Leslie William Barnard, *St Justin Martyr: The First and Second Apologies* (ACW 56; New York / Mahwah, NJ, 1997); A. Lukyn Williams, *Justin Martyr: The Dialogue with Trypho* (London, 1930). *Studies with bibliography:* Leslie William Barnard, *Justin Martyr: His Life and Thought* (Cambridge, 1967); Erwin Ramsdell Goodenough, *The Theology of Justin Martyr* (Jena, 1923 / Amsterdam, 1968); Eric Francis Osborn, *Justin Martyr* (BHT 47; Tübingen, 1973); Oskar Skarsaune, 'Justin der Märtyrer', *Th Real* 17 (1988), pp. 471–78.

Kähler, Martin (1835–1912)

Martin Kähler was a key figure in German Protestant theology at the turn of the twentieth century. Often classed as a 'Bible theologian', he offered a major challenge to the dominant liberalism of his day, and he sought consciously to rework *Reformation emphases in theology for the modern era. Born in 1835, Kähler switched to theology after beginning to study law at the University of Königsberg. He studied further at Heidelberg, Tübingen and Halle, being heavily influenced in Heidelberg by the lectures of Richard Rothe (1813–85), especially on ethics and the life of Jesus, and at Halle by Julius Müller (1801–78) and August Tholuck (1799–1877), whose 'mediating theology' encouraged Kähler himself to turn to the contemporary reformulation of traditional doctrinal themes. After three years as a tutor in Bonn (1864–67), Kähler became professor of systematic theology and New Testament exegesis in Halle, where he remained till his death in 1912.

Three main emphases are apparent in Kähler's thought. Kähler stressed, first, the priority of preaching about Christ over historical enquiry into the figure of Jesus. In his highly influential slim volume *The So-called Historical Jesus and the Historic Biblical Christ* (Leipzig, 1892, ET 1964), Kähler questioned the assumed theological importance of the many 'lives' of Jesus being written in the nineteenth century. He argued for the greater significance of an interpretation of Jesus as the Christ – as prepared for throughout the Old Testament and as found in the New Testament. The interpreter of the New Testament should be concerned with *kerygma* (the biblical, 'preached Christ'), not the results of historical research.

Second, Kähler reasserted the importance of the Bible in theology in a manner different from many of his conservative contemporaries. Though respectful both of the personal piety and of the love of the Bible shown by his Tübingen teacher Johann Tobias Beck (1804–78), Beck's dodging of some of the issues of biblical criticism proved unsatisfactory for Kähler. In *Zur Bibelfrage* ('On the Question of the Bible', 1907, untranslated), Kähler offered a series of studies locating the Bible's continuing significance for theology less in its being a record of revelation, than in its being source-material for proclamation. Half a century before Gerhard Ebeling (b. 1912), Kähler recognized the necessity for theologians to see church history as the history of the Bible's impact. In this sense, the Bible is the 'church's book', and the church's theology must always remain biblical. Furthermore, the kerygmatic quality of the whole of the New Testament led Kähler to stress both the Bible's function as a book of mission as well as the Christian responsibility to engage in proclamation to the world.

Third, Kähler placed the doctrine of justification at the centre of Christian thought and practice. In *Die Wissenschaft der christlichen Lehre* ('The Science of Christian Doctrine', 1883, untranslated), described by contemporary American Lutheran theologian Carl Braaten as 'perhaps the greatest one volume work of dogmatics to appear between Schleiermacher and Barth', Kähler attempts an exposition of Christian faith in three main steps, beginning with 'apologetics' and ending with 'ethics'. With this procedure he wishes to show that the central core of his exposition – the doctrinal treatment of the doctrine of justification – will prove inadequate if not related to the practicalities of Christianity when viewed as a religion ('apologetics'), and to the consequences for a believer shaped by Christian doctrine ('ethics'). This major work, then, is not, strictly speaking, a comprehensive dogmatics. It is, however, a bold and original effort to render the Reformation's central doctrinal theme comprehensible in a fresh way at the turn of the twentieth century. A major conversation partner, if rarely explicitly, throughout this work – as on many other occasions – was *Albrecht Ritschl, with whose understanding of justification and reconciliation, and of the relationship between them, Kähler interacted critically. For Kähler, both in *Die Wissenschaft der christlichen Lehre* and in *Zur Lehre von der Versöhnung* ('On the Doctrine of Reconciliation', Leipzig, 1898, untranslated), reconciliation was much more of an objective occurrence – being an act of God in Christ – than Ritschl's understanding seemed to allow. The reconciliation between God and humanity had already been brought about in and through the death of Jesus Christ. In Kähler's view, Ritschl's insistence on the awareness and outworking of reconciliation in the believer as the starting point for theological exploration, even if certainly not the ground of the theological conviction, weakened the inevitable objectivity of the doctrine.

There is more to be said about the Kähler-Ritschl debate. It does, however, highlight the way in which Kähler was part of, and anticipated, neo-orthodox critique of Ritschl, his school, and the many diverse liberal theologians of the late-nineteenth/early-twentieth century. In discussion about the objectivity of the being and action of God in relation to the justification and reconciliation of the Christian believer, nothing less than the potential over-assertion of arrogant humanity was at stake.

Kähler's critics have labelled him a biblicist or, pejoratively, as a 'Pietist'. He was comfortable with the latter label, claiming to keep both the Reformation and Pietism together in his thought and practice. He can be called a 'biblicist' only to the extent that he took the Bible seriously. If his practical concerns are evident in his bibliography (many of the 165 items collected together by Ernst Kähler are occasional pieces for concrete, church settings), and in the fact that he dedicated his one-volume dogmatics to his local pastor, this is indicative only of what he viewed his theological endeavour to be for: the service of both church and world. He created no school, and he is difficult to locate satisfactorily within the currents of his day. But even if his 1892 Jesus book will prove his main, lasting legacy, it will be valuable indeed – not least for its direct impact on the likes of *Barth, *Bultmann and *Tillich.

CLIVE MARSH

FURTHER READING: *Texts: Die Wissenschaft der christlichen Lehre* (Neukirchen-Vluyn, 1966; repr. of 3rd edn [1905]), with an introduction by Martin Fischer; *Aufsätze zur Bibelfrage* (Munich, 1967), comprising three long essays from the six originally published as *Zur Bibelfrage* (1907). *Studies:* Carl Braaten: 'Revelation, History and Faith in Martin Kähler', in Martin Kähler, *The So-called Historical Jesus and the Historic Biblical Christ* (Philadelphia, 1964), pp. 1–38; Anna Kähler (ed.), *Theologie und Christ: Erinnerungen und Bekenntnisse von Martin Kähler* (Berlin, 1926); Ernst Kähler, 'Verzeichnis der Schriften Martin Kählers', in Martin Kähler *Geschichte der protestantischen Dogmatik im 19. Jahrhundert* (Munich, 1962), pp. 290–307; Hans-Georg Link, *Geschichte Jesu und Bild Christi: Die Entwicklung der Christologie Martin Kählers* (Neukirchen-Vluyn, 1975); J. Wirsching, *Gott in der Geschichte: Studien zur theologiegeschichtlichen Stellung und systematischen Grundlegung der Theologie Martin Kählers* (Munich, 1963).

Kant, Immanuel (1724–1804)

One of the greatest of all philosophers, Kant has had a tremendous influence on the history of theology (see *Kantianism). His voice was the most important one in German philosophy during the *Enlightenment, representing a watershed in western thought. Born in Königsberg, East Prussia to a pious but humble Lutheran family, Kant was educated, lived and died in the same area (called Kaliningrad when part of the USSR). He graduated from the University of Königsberg, where later he held the chair in logic and metaphysics (1770–96). His early interest in natural philosophy and science turned to questions of epistemology. Learned in the tradition of rationalism on the Continent, Kant tells us that he was awakened from his 'dogmatic slumbers' by the empiricism of *Hume ('Prolegomena', *Werke*, IV, p. 260). Kant's system of critical philosophy represents a brilliant synthesis of continental rationalism and British empiricism.

His mature, critical system of philosophy begins with the first of three great critiques: the *Critique of Pure Reason*, published in 1781 (cited as 'A'; 'B' is the 2nd edn, 1787). In this work, Kant seeks the foundations and limits of human reason – especially speculative and scientific reason. Kant distinguished between analytic propositions (which Leibniz called truths of reason) and synthetic propositions (truths of fact). He also believed that some truths can be known 'independent of all experience' (B, p. 2), which he called a priori knowledge. A posteriori knowledge, on the other hand, comes through experience.

Kant was interested in the following question: scientific knowledge of the world is certain knowledge, but how is this possible? Where does the certainty come from? Kant argued for a combination of empirical and rational sources. Scientific knowledge is synthetic a priori truth. What looks like pure experience is not: all perception is guided by the mind.

The use of a priori concepts is the condition of the possibility of experience, or, in Kant's terms, they are 'transcendental'. Two of these transcendentals are space and time, which Kant argued are given by the understanding to structure the world of appearance (phenomena). They are not part of the world as it is (things-in-themselves, or the *noumena*). In grounding scientific knowledge in a priori rational principles, Kant drove a wedge between the world of appearance and the world as it really is. Humans can know nothing about the *noumena* except for their bare reality. This is the transcendental limit of speculative and scientific reasoning.

With one slice of his transcendental scythe, Kant undercut traditional metaphysics and natural theology. He was interested in, but rejected, all traditional arguments for the existence of God in the first critique (B, pp. 618–58). In his second critique, the *Critique of Practical Reason* (1788), Kant brings back in as assumptions for practical reason what he rejected for pure reason: God, immortality and human freedom. These are postulates of morality which we cannot prove (by pure reason) but must assume in order to live an ethically pure life, and fulfil our moral duty (practical reason). Kant is famous for his rational, ethical system, which bases morality on rational principles of duty rather than on the consequences of our actions. God, the immortality of the soul and the freedom of the will are necessary postulates for a practical reason which decides what we ought (rationally) to do. With respect to God, reason demands a providence that matches goodness with reward, and evil with punishment. Since such moral matching is not found on earth, there must be a God and a life after death, which supplies them ('Practical Reason', *Werke*, V, pp. 122–32). Thus Kant's God cannot be known through pure or theoretical reason, but is known as a necessary postulate or presupposition for morality. In a famous phrase, Kant claimed 'I had to do away with knowledge in order to make room for faith' (B, p. xxx).

In the third critique, the *Critique of Judgement* (1790), Kant treats beauty and final causes (teleology). Under the theme of teleology, he returns to the notion of God whose nature is beyond the grasp of human knowledge (pure reason), but who is needed as an assumption for both reason and ethics. For Kant, reason requires the notion of a perfect Being who is 'an Author and Governor of the world, who is also a moral Lawgiver' ('Judgement', *Werke*, V, p. 455). Kant develops in this later work a transcendental type of teleological argument for God's existence, as an assumption reason demands beneath the *noumena* ('Judgement', *Werke*, V, pp. 461–66).

Kant's philosophy of religion is in keeping with his ethical focus. In *Religion within the Limits of Reason Alone* (1793), Kant puts forth his rationalist theory of religion, which is individualistic and moralistic. For the most part, Kant rejects the corporate, historical, traditional and liturgical aspects of religion. For him, the religious life is the moral life of individual obedience to duty. True religion consists in this: 'that in all our duties we regard God as the universal legislator who is to be reverenced' ('Religion', *Werke*, VI, p. 103). Anything else we might do to please God, is 'mere religious delusion and spurious worship' ('Religion', *Werke*, VI, p. 107). As for Kant's theology, in his lectures on the subject he did advance a rational and critical concept of God as a Perfect Being. Through a kind of *via negativa* which he called 'transcendental theology', some of the traditional metaphysical attributes for God were developed (*Lectures on Philosophical Theology* [1783?]). The argument is transcendental, that is, based upon the need of both pure and practical reason for a perfect, personal ground of being. Kant rejects any appeal to revelation, since that must be tested by the individual's own reason in order to be admitted.

Kant helped turn philosophy away from traditional metaphysics toward a rational, critical reflection upon the grounds of knowledge and morality. He developed a critical system of philosophy in which the individual, rational, free agent was supreme. His philosophy represents the rejection of tradition, community and canon in favour of autonomous reason and the free individual. He presented, and still presents, a profound challenge to traditional Christian theology.

ALAN G. PADGETT

FURTHER READING: The standard German collected works, the Akademie edition (*Werke*) is the *Gesammelte Schriften* (ed. German [formerly Royal Prussian] Academy of Sciences; 29 vols.; Berlin, 1900–). Page references to this edition are standard in commentaries and translations, including *The Cambridge Edition of the Works of Immanuel Kant* (ed. P. Guyer and A. Wood; 14 vols.; Cambridge, 1992–). *Selected works about Kant:* Ernst Cassirer, *Kant's Life and Thought* (New Haven, 1981); P. Guyer (ed.), *The Cambridge Companion to Kant* (Cambridge, 1992); H.J. de Vleeschauwer, *The Development of Kantian Thought* (New York, 1962); R.C.S. Walker, *Kant* (London, 1978); C.C.J. Webb, *Kant's Philosophy of Religion* (Oxford, 1926); Allan Wood, *Kant's Moral Religion* (Ithaca, NY, 1970); *Kant's Rational Theology* (Ithaca, NY, 1978).

Kantianism

Kantianism refers to the thought of *Immanuel Kant, and its impact upon the later history of philosophy and theology. It is difficult to overestimate the importance of Kant for the history of western philosophy and theology, especially in German. Kant turned both theology and philosophy inwards. He made consciousness and the possibility of thought and experience the starting points for sophisticated philosophy. He helped to turn religion and theology away from abstract metaphysical reflection towards practical reasoning and ethics. For Kant it was morality, and not doctrinal speculation, that was the essential aspect of religion. His work marks off the beginning of a new age in the history of Christian thought, and it has left a lasting impression upon academic theology.

Kant's writings became required reading in German academic circles, and yet the interpretation and significance of his thought were received in very different ways. While there was no uniform school of Kantianism, his works caused a great sea change in theology. A thorough history of the impact and importance of his ideas would require many volumes. There are at least five areas in which Kant's thought influenced theology and religious reflection after him. These areas or themes provide a kind of portrait of Kant's influence, without specifying a system. First, many philosophers and theologians accepted Kant's rejection of traditional metaphysics and natural theology as a *fait accompli*. Both *Albrecht Ritschl and *Karl Barth exemplify this trend in their rejection of metaphysics in theology, despite the fact that these two theologians are so different in other ways. Second, Kant's focus on morality as the essential part of religion also found numerous followers. In his own time, J.G. Fichte is one follower who accepted Kantian moralism. In the late nineteenth century, the Ritschlian tradition offers another example. Indeed, Ritschl is remembered as one who deliberately sought to return to Kant's insights after the work of *Schleiermacher and *Hegel earlier in the century had, in different ways, sought to move beyond Kant.

Third, Kant opened up the possibility of knowing about God through experience and aesthetics in his third *Critique*. This possibility was developed through the *Romantic movement, which found brilliant expression in two classics of the period: Schleiermacher's *On Religion* (1799), and *Coleridge's *Aids to Reflection* (1825). Both of these works are impressive monuments to Kant's impact in religious thought.

Fourth, Kant's thought had the effect of pushing religious epistemology to the forefront of Christian theological consideration. Kant was not alone here, as the entire *Enlightenment focused attention on rational foundations, but his was a major voice. Schleiermacher again provides a good illustration of this focus on epistemology. In his *Dialectics* (a published set of philosophical lectures) and in the first part of his famous *The Christian Faith*, Schleiermacher takes the work of Kant as basic for his own, making issues of method and epistemology central to both theology and philosophy (as he understood them). A similar emphasis on the epistemology of religion can likewise be found in *Ernst Troeltsch's failed quest for a 'religious a priori'. Even Barth, by beginning his *Church Dogmatics* with the doctrine of the word of God, and in his wider reformulation of a doctrine of revelation, was identifiably replying to this emphasis upon religious epistemology, its possibilities and conditions – so dominant was it in the German tradition of theology and philosophy of religion in which he had been educated.

Fifth, also in terms of method, Kant developed a transcendental approach, which some theologians have followed. A transcendental approach seeks a critical examination of what makes knowledge, consciousness or experience possible in the first place. The French Jesuit *Joseph Maréchal is one example of this trend, and one of the first Catholics to follow Kantian methods in fundamental theology. Maréchal in turn influenced *Karl Rahner, who likewise followed a transcendental method. In both the content and methods of theology, then, Kant has had tremendous influence upon the nineteenth and twentieth centuries – perhaps more than any other philosopher of his age. In many ways we are only now, at the start of the twenty-first century, beginning to move beyond Kant towards a genuinely postmodern theology.

ALAN G. PADGETT

FURTHER READING: Adina Davidovich, *Religion as a Province of Meaning: The Kantian Foundations of Modern Theology* (Minneapolis, 1993); Johann Gottlieb Fichte, *Attempt at a Critique of All Revelation* (trans. G. Green; Cambridge, 1978); Simon Fisher, *Revelatory Positivism? Barth's Earliest Theology and the Marburg School* (Oxford, 1988); Joseph Maréchal, *A Maréchal Reader* (ed. J. Donceel; New York, 1970); Albrecht Ritschl, *Three Essays* (trans. P. Hefner; Philadelphia, 1972); Helmut Thielicke, *Modern Faith and Thought* (trans. G.W. Bromiley; Grand Rapids, 1990); Ernst Troeltsch, *Religion in History* (trans. J.L. Adams and W.E. Bense; Minneapolis, 1991); Steve Wilkens and Alan Padgett, *Christianity and Western Thought*, II: *The Nineteenth Century* (Downers Grove, IL, 1999); Claude Welch,

Protestant Thought in the Nineteenth Century (2 vols.; New Haven, 1972, 1985).

Kasper, Walter (b. 1933)

German Roman Catholic theologian. For many years professor of dogmatic theology on the Catholic faculty of the University of Tübingen, Kasper is widely regarded as one of the most important of contemporary German theologians. In 1989, he was consecrated Bishop of Rottenburg-Stuttgart.

A variety of themes characterize Kasper's theology. In contrast to much Protestant theology in the twentieth century, he is a staunch defender of the Catholic tradition of natural theology. Kasper distinguishes, however, between a purely philosophical, rationalistic natural theology, and an approach informed by Christian faith. The latter, he believes, is the route taken by the Church Fathers and by the great theologians of the medieval era, and it is therefore the only approach consistent with the classical sources of Catholic thought. It is nature understood as creation, for example, which attests the cogency of Christian claims in versions of the cosmological argument. Thus the arguments for the existence of God make final sense only within the context of faith.

Ordained a priest in 1957, Kasper's theology is very much in keeping with the renewal in Catholic theology associated with *Vatican II (1962–65). He draws on two main sources in developing his own approach: first, the theology of the Tübingen Catholic school, which resists the imposition of rigid theological definition and which instead emphasizes the organic development of doctrine; secondly, German Idealism, and in particular the philosophies of F.W. Schelling (1775–1854) and *G.W.F. Hegel (1770–1831). Kasper maintains that Idealist philosophy can enable us to conceive of God as love in his innermost essence. In particular, the Hegelian 'passing over' of God into the finite is used to explain the logic of the creation of the world and of the incarnation of the Word.

Kasper is best known for his work in Christology. In keeping with his approach to natural theology generally, he distances himself here from a purely historical-critical approach to Scripture and to the mystery of Jesus Christ as attested in Scripture, insisting on an interpretation informed by faith. In his Christology, Kasper argues that the Sonship of Jesus can be understood in two senses: from the standpoint of the assumption of flesh by the Word, and from the standpoint of the unction of the Spirit which makes him the 'Christ'. The latter is Kasper's primary point of departure. His views are developed in relation to a presupposed theological anthropology. As a human being, Jesus shares the historical and developmental character of human nature generally. His Sonship, therefore, is established dynamically and cross-temporally rather than statically; it presupposes a life-story, acts of concrete obedience and the theological virtues of faith, hope and love. Jesus can only be Son of God in his actual human existence in time in this sense, however, by virtue of the anointing of the Spirit.

At this point, Kasper is deeply indebted to the 'transcendental christology' of *Karl Rahner (1904–84). It is Rahner's theology which enables Kasper to relate his Spirit Christology to the doctrine of the hypostatic union. As in Rahner, human nature is understood in terms of its potentiality for obedience to and love for God. The very condition of the possibility of the event of the incarnation is precisely such human nature. According to Kasper, however, the hypostatic union which is effected when the Word assumes human nature into a personal union with itself is, and can only be, brought about across time, since human nature is temporal in its essence. The hypostatic union takes place, therefore, through a human life. The medium of this union, according to Kasper, is the anointing of the Spirit, which enables Jesus as a man to be constantly open to the divine 'self-communication'. Although sometimes understood in a *Nestorian sense, Kasper's Christology appears orthodox when seen in the light of Rahner's theology.

GARY D. BADCOCK

FURTHER READING: Walter Kasper, *Jesus the Christ* (ET London, 1976); *The God of Jesus Christ* (ET New York, 1984); *Theology and Church* (ET New York, 1989); Eberhard Schockenhoff, et al. (eds.), *Dogma und Glaube* (Mainz, 1993).

Keble, John (1792–1866)

Anglican parish priest, poet and leader of the *Oxford Movement. John Keble was born in Fairford, Gloucestershire, where his father, an old High Churchman also named John Keble, was parish priest. At the age of fourteen he went up to Corpus Christi College, Oxford, where he gained high honours and was elected to a Fellowship at Oriel College. Ordained in 1815, he assisted his father, at Eastleach and Coln St Aldwyn, country parishes near Fairford. In Oxford he pioneered a pastoral role for the college tutor, having a profound influence on some of his pupils – notably *John Henry Newman (1801–90), Isaac Williams (1802–65) and Hurrell Froude (1803–36) – all of whom were to play significant roles in the Oxford Movement. Newman recognized in his *Apologia pro vita sua* (1864) that Keble had underlined for him both the importance of a sacramental understanding of creation and *Bishop Butler's maxim 'probability the guide of life' in relation to religious truth. In 1827 Keble published *The Christian Year*, a volume of poetry based on the services and calendar of the Book of Common Prayer. The poems often draw on biblical texts taken from the lessons set for the day, and they exhibit a sacramental understanding of the world that was characteristic of both the *Romantic movement and the Catholic revival in the Church of England. They were appreciated by Wordsworth and the book became a staple of Victorian devotion and supplied some texts which became popularly sung as hymns.

In 1833 Keble was invited to preach the Assize Sermon at Oxford and he determined to make this an occasion of protest against what he saw as a government attack on the church and secular interference with apostolic ministry, particularly in proposals to reduce the number of bishoprics in the Church of Ireland. The sermon, entitled 'National Apostasy', was preached on 14 July and was reckoned by John Henry Newman as the beginning of the Oxford Movement and Catholic revival in the Church of England. Its impact was telling, not so much because of the content of the sermon, but because of Keble's standing as a priest of exemplary piety and pastoral diligence. Keble contributed to the *Tracts for the Times* (nos. 4, 13, 40, 52, 54, 57, 50 and 89), mostly concerned with defending and promoting the doctrine of apostolic succession in relation to the ministry of the church. Tract 89, *On the Mysticism Attributed to the Early Fathers of the Church* (1841), was the most significant. In this tract Keble explored and defended the allegorical interpretation of Scripture (particularly as found in the Alexandrian Fathers) and set out a doctrine of religious 'reserve'. As with much of Keble's writing, there is a concern to hold together theology and

spirituality, and to acknowledge the place of the *via negativa*, the silence of the apophatic tradition alongside the affirmation of symbol and sacrament. In his *Sermons Academical and Occasional* (1847) he defended the importance of implicit faith.

In 1836, the year Keble became vicar of Hursley near Winchester where he remained until his death in 1866, he published a major edition of the works of Richard Hooker (c. 1554–1600). In his substantial preface Keble writes of Hooker's grounding of church ceremonies in a sacramental understanding of creation which is at one with the mystical interpretation of Scripture found in the Fathers. In the same year, in a sermon on primitive tradition, Keble warned against the 'Nominalism' of his day – 'the habit of resolving the high mysteries of the faith into mere circumstances of language, methods of speaking adapted to our weak understandings, but with no real counterpart in the nature of things'. Two years later, in 1838, he became one of the editors of the *Library of the Fathers*, and he himself contributed the translation of the works of *Irenaeus, though this was not published until after his death.

Keble's *Lectures on Poetry* (*Pralectiones Academicae*) (1832–41) were among his most original contributions – delivered (in Latin) as professor of poetry at Oxford and dedicated to Wordsworth. Largely a study of classical poetry, they enabled Keble to develop a theory of poetry as disciplined catharsis, and to set out a relationship between poetic symbolism, inspiration and sacramental theology. In his tract *On Eucharistical Adoration* (1857) Keble defended a doctrine of the Real Presence, and he argued for the legitimacy of adoration of the sacrament, writing that 'wherever Christ is there He is to be adored'. After Keble's death, a complete set of his sermons was published in 1879.

John Keble consciously eschewed originality in both theology and preaching, but he played a significant part in reawakening an awareness of the Fathers, the importance and character of tradition and sacramental devotion. Newman said of him that it was his great contribution to 'make the Church of England poetical'. It is perhaps in his exploration of the nature of poetry and his awareness of the sacramental and poetical character of religious language that his greatest theological contribution lies. Keble College in Oxford was founded in his memory and preserves his library and many of his papers.

GEOFFREY ROWELL

FURTHER READING: *Text: Keble's Lectures on Poetry, 1832–1841* (trans. E.K. Francis; Oxford, 1912). *Studies:* G. Battiscombe, *John Keble: A Study in Limitations* (London, 1963); Brian Martin, *John Keble: Priest, Professor and Poet* (London, 1976); W.J.M. Beek, *John Keble's Literary and Religious Contribution to the Oxford Movement* (Nijmegen, 1959); Charles R. Henery (ed.), *A Speaking Life: John Keble and the Anglican Tradition of Ministry and Art* (Leominster, 1995); G. Rowell, *The Vision Glorious: Themes and Personalities in the Catholic Revival in Anglicanism* (Oxford, 1983); A. Härdelin, *The Tractarian Understanding of the Eucharist* (Uppsala, 1965).

Kierkegaard, Søren (1813–55)

Kierkegaard's life was unremarkable and, apart from a brief sojourn in Berlin in 1841–42, was spent wholly in Copenhagen. The immediate cause of his 'authorship' (the conventional term adopted by Kierkegaard scholars to refer to his writings) was his breaking of his engagement to Regine Olsen. At one level, his authorship can be read as an attempt to come to terms with this traumatic experience. At a deeper level, however, Kierkegaard's authorship is a profound analysis of the human condition and the nature of the human being's relation to God.

Kierkegaard is a notoriously difficult thinker to interpret owing to the deliberately unsystematic nature of his writings and his employment of 'indirect communication'. It was his conviction that existential and religious truths cannot be taught 'directly' in the way that a teacher can teach a pupil mathematics or woodwork. Existential and religious truths, he argues, are only properly understood when the individual 'becomes' them by actualizing them in his or her own existence. This principle of indirect communication colours Kierkegaard's authorship in two ways. Firstly, he deliberately avoids presenting his readers with 'results', that is, with neatly worked out answers to existential questions. Instead he offers them a series of 'existence possibilities', leaving it up to each reader to choose which one he or she believes is most appropriate. Secondly, in order that his own personality should not interfere with his readers' existential decisions, Kierkegaard concealed his own identity by publishing his works pseudonymously. Despite the principle of indirect communication,

however, Kierkegaard does not present existential possibilities neutrally, as if the human being's mode of existence were merely a matter of personal preference. He is concerned, rather, to educate the reader to make the correct choices. It is this concern that underlies Kierkegaard's theory of the stages of existence, according to which the individual passes through 'aesthetic' and 'ethical' modes of existence before arriving at the highest sphere of existence, namely Christianity.

The pseudonymous works are not Kierkegaard's only works, however, for it was his custom to publish alongside them 'edifying' or 'upbuilding' discourses. These consist of meditations on biblical texts and are more overtly religious than the pseudonymous works. The relation between these two types of authorship – the pseudonymous and the non-pseudonymous – is a perennial problem in Kierkegaard scholarship. It seems likely, however, that the discourses are meditations on religious themes hinted at in the pseudonymous works.

The work which first brought Kierkegaard to the attention of the general public was *Either/Or* (1843), a two-volume work dealing with the aesthetic and ethical spheres of existence. The aesthetic individual, described in volume one, understands the purpose and meaning of life to consist in the fulfilment of one's talents and the satisfaction of one's urges. In the second volume of *Either/Or*, Judge William, a magistrate representing the ethical sphere of existence, attempts in two lengthy letters to convince the aesthete of volume one that the enjoyment and fulfilment for which the latter is striving can be achieved only when aesthetic values are grounded in the ethical. For example, the aesthetic ideal of romantic love, the judge argues, is only fulfilled when it is given an ethical grounding in the form of marriage. The book ends, however, by giving the reader the first indication that the ethical sphere is itself flawed and is ultimately an invalid mode of existence for the human being. This is hinted at in the concluding piece in *Either/Or*, the 'Ultimatum', a sermon written purportedly by a country parson on the theme that, 'In relation to God we are always in the wrong'. This is a first indication that the judge's assumption that the human being's relationship to God can be fully expressed in ethical categories is mistaken.

The themes of *Either/Or* are taken up and developed in *Repetition* (1843), *Fear and Trembling*

(1843) and *Stages on Life's Way* (1845), in which the religious sphere becomes distinguished ever more clearly from the ethical sphere. Of particular interest is Kierkegaard's introduction in *Fear and Trembling* of the concept of the 'teleological suspension of the ethical'; that is, the idea that God may require the believer to override or suspend ethical norms. The classic example of this is God's command to Abraham to sacrifice his son Isaac. Although this has been interpreted by some commentators as evidence of his 'moral nihilism', Kierkegaard is not claiming that ethics is irrelevant or that God is immoral, but merely that the God-relationship can never be confined within the ethical structures created by human beings.

A work of particular importance in the subsequent development of existential philosophy is *The Concept of Anxiety* (1844). Anxiety is the simultaneous fear of, and attraction to, freedom and the choices and decisions with which freedom confronts the human being. In Kierkegaard's words, anxiety is 'a sympathetic antipathy and an antipathetic sympathy', in which we are both drawn to and repelled by our possibility. Yet at the same time anxiety is an educator of the human being, making individuals aware of the inadequacy of their mode of existence and the necessity of faith, the only antidote to anxiety.

In *Philosophical Fragments* (1844) and its sequel *Concluding Unscientific Postscript* (1846), Kierkegaard attempts to make clear Christianity's distinctiveness from 'Socratic religiousness' or 'religiousness A', that is, non-Christian forms of religiousness. Religiousness A is based on the principle that there is a fundamental affinity between existence and the eternal, or God. The eternal is seen as undergirding existence, as being the foundation upon which existence rests. With regard to truth, this affinity between the eternal and existence means that the human being is understood to be in innate but initially unconscious possession of the eternal truth. The existential task is to 'recollect' this truth and structure one's life in such a way that one's existence comes to express ever more fully the eternal truth and the relationship with God that undergirds it. The role of the teacher in religiousness A is that of the 'Socratic midwife' who enables the pupil to 'give birth' to the truth that he or she innately possesses.

But what, Kierkegaard asks, if the human being is *not* in innate possession of the truth?

This, he argues, is the claim of Christianity and is what distinguishes Christianity from non-Christian forms of religiousness. Christianity, or 'religiousness B', claims that in Christ the eternal has entered time, God has become human. Eternity and time, God and the human, are, however, mutually exclusive opposites. The fact that these mutually exclusive opposites are nevertheless conjoined in Christ means that he is the 'absolute paradox'. Furthermore, the eternal's presence in time posits a breach between existence and eternity, the consequence of which is that there is *no* affinity between eternity and existence and the underlying continuity between the human being and eternal truth is dissolved. In such a situation a Socratic midwife is useless, for there is now no innate truth for the midwife to bring to birth. Another sort of teacher is required – one who is able to provide the individual with the truth which he or she lacks. Such a teacher is the God-man, Jesus Christ, who in his own person graciously bestows upon human beings the truth necessary for their salvation. The human response to this gift is faith, which for Kierkegaard is the highest form of human existence and the means by which the gulf between the human being and God is bridged.

It is in the course of deliberating in the *Concluding Unscientific Postscript* on the nature of the human being's relationship to Christianity that Kierkegaard introduces his controversial claim that 'subjectivity is the truth'. Kierkegaard is certainly not claiming, as some commentators have held, that truth is a matter of personal preference. Rather, he asserts that in the case of existential and religious truths it is not enough that the individual should give merely notional assent to the truth; the individual must live out this truth in his or her everyday existence.

Kierkegaard intended to conclude his authorship with the *Concluding Unscientific Postscript* and then enter the priesthood. However, his concern at contemporary political events and his increasing disquiet with the state church led him to abandon this plan. The gospel would be better served, he concluded, not by entering the church, which was little more than a branch of the civil service full of self-serving clergymen, but by making clear through his writings how far Danish society had fallen short of the Christian ideal. From this point onwards, Kierkegaard's authorship became more overtly Christian and he made less frequent use of pseudonyms. Among the most significant of the non-pseudonymous works of this period are *Purity of Heart is to Will One Thing* (1847) and *Works of Love* (1847). Kierkegaard's last two pseudonymous works are intended to be radical demonstrations of the Christian ideal. *Sickness unto Death* (1849) is an explication of the concept of despair, a state of spiritlessness which Kierkegaard believed to be endemic in contemporary Denmark. *Practice in Christianity* (1850) is a reworking of themes treated in *Philosophical Fragments*, but with far greater emphasis on the necessity of the Christian's suffering in the world.

Kierkegaard's impact on his own century was minimal. In the twentieth century, however, he was rediscovered and came to exert an important influence on both philosophy and theology. He has been described as the father of *Existentialism and is a forerunner of *dialectical theology. More recently, some have seen in Kierkegaard a precursor of *postmodernism.

DAVID R. LAW

FURTHER READING: *Texts: Either/Or* (ed. and trans. Howard V. Hong and Edna H. Hong; 2 vols.; Princeton, 1987); *The Concept of Anxiety* (ed. and trans. Reidar Thomte; Princeton, 1980); *Fear and Trembling and Repetition* (ed. and trans. H.V. Hong and E.H. Hong; Princeton, 1983); *Philosophical Fragments and Johannes Climacus* (ed. and trans. H.V. Hong and E.H. Hong; Princeton, 1985); *Stages on Life's Way* (ed. and trans. H.V. Hong and E.H. Hong; Princeton, 1988); *Concluding Unscientific Postscript to Philosophical Fragments* (ed. and trans. H.V. Hong and E.H. Hong; 2 vols.; Princeton, 1992); *Christian Discourses* (trans. Walter Lowrie; London, 1939); *Edifying Discourses* (ed. and trans. H.V. Hong and E.H. Hong; Princeton, 1990); *Søren Kierkegaard's Journals and Papers* (ed. and trans. H.V. Hong and E.H. Hong; 7 vols.; Bloomington, IN, 1967–78); *The Sickness unto Death* (ed. and trans. H.V. Hong and E.H. Hong; Princeton, 1985); *Practice in Christianity* (ed. and trans. H.V. Hong and E.H. Hong; Princeton, 1991). *Studies*: Patrick Gardiner, *Kierkegaard* (Oxford, 1988); Alistair Hannay, *Kierkegaard* (London, 1982); David R. Law, *Kierkegaard as Negative Theologian* (Oxford, 1993); George Pattison, *Kierkegaard and the Crisis of Faith* (London, 1997); Robert L. Perkins, *International Kierkegaard Commentary* (Macon, GA, 1994); Murray A. Rae, *Kierkegaard's Vision of the Incarnation* (Oxford, 1997); Mark C. Taylor, *Kierkegaard's Pseudonymous Authorship: A Study of Time and the Self* (Princeton, 1975); Julia Watkin, *Kierkegaard* (London, 1997).

Kirk, Kenneth (1886–1954)

Kenneth Kirk was the leading Anglican moral theologian of his day. His most important books were written during the 1920s and 1930s when he was teaching in Oxford, at Keble College, Trinity College (where he was fellow and chaplain) and Christ Church (where he was Regius professor of moral and pastoral theology). In 1937 he became Bishop of Oxford, remaining the Church of England's leading spokesman on moral theology and heading the Anglo-Catholic wing in the House of Bishops.

His first major book, *Some Principles of Moral Theology and their Application* (1920), illustrates Kirk's conviction that Anglicanism is well placed to achieve the right balance between authority and freedom. Concerned primarily with the minimum standards to which conduct must conform if it is to be called Christian, Kirk drew on the long Catholic tradition of priestly counselling to set out both the guiding principles of Christian formation and their practical application under present-day conditions. He stressed at once the church's educative role and the individual's right to search out and act upon the most probable opinion. He also underlined the practical importance of the distinction between mortal and venial sin.

Kirk's second major book, *Ignorance, Faith and Conformity: Studies in Moral Theology* (1925) drew attention to the notion of invincible ignorance. Without denying the importance of the church's customary teaching, Kirk's non-legalistic approach allowed a greater tolerance of conscientious dissent within the Christian family than is found in Roman Catholicism.

His third major book, *Conscience and its Problems: An Introduction to Casuistry* (1927), deals with the guidance of conscience where differing views prevail, or where specific precepts are found to be in conflict. What is needed is a wise casuistry, drawing on the church's long experience, yet sensitive to the fact that circumstances alter cases. The book contains a balanced assessment of the ethics of compromise.

Kirk's masterpiece, *The Vision of God: The Christian Doctrine of the Summum Bonum* (1931), grew out of his 1928 Bampton Lectures. It traces in detail the Christian tradition's understanding of the ultimate goal of human life in the disinterested love of neighbour and of God. Growth towards such love and enjoyment of God may – but not necessarily – entail self-sacrifice in this life. But the promised life of heaven is not love's motive; it is love's reward, simply in the sense of being the inevitable consequence of disinterested love.

Kirk's work has shaped all subsequent Anglican moral theology. It has been suggested that he anticipated the later school of situation ethics. But his was far from being an antinomian position. The wealth of custom and the long tradition of casuistry handed down in the church, within the framework of its overarching hope of the vision of God in heaven, enabled Kirk to steer this quintessentially Anglican path between authority and freedom. On some issues, however, such as the indissolubility of marriage, he remained inflexible, just as he did, outside the sphere of moral theology, over the alleged invalidity of non-episcopal orders.

BRIAN HEBBLETHWAITE

FURTHER READING: In addition to Kirk's four main books, mentioned above, see also E.W. Kemp, *The Life and Letters of Kenneth Escott Kirk* (London, 1959); V.A. Demant, 'Kenneth Kirk as Moral Theologian', *Ch Q R* (1957), pp. 423–34; R.H. Preston, 'Re-Review: Kenneth Kirk's *The Vision of God*', *Mod Ch* NS XXV.2 (1982), pp. 36–9.

Knox, John (1513–72)

Protestant Reformer, preacher, theologian and historian, Knox is the best known, most admired and most hated man of his generation in Scotland. Little is known of his early life until he came under the influence of the Zwinglian Reformer, George Wishart, to whom he acted the part of bodyguard. While Knox acknowledged the authenticity of Wishart and the *Lutheran Reformer, Patrick Hamilton, Knox regarded Geneva as 'the most perfect school of Christ that ever was upon the earth since the time of the apostles'. While he is usually remembered as a Scottish Reformer, it is worth noting that much of his life was spent outside Scotland – in France, England, Germany and Switzerland.

Knox was born at Giffordgate on the outskirts of Haddington in East Lothian. He received a good education, probably at St Andrews University during the time that John Major was teaching there. Despite Major's trenchant criticisms of the existing ecclesiastical order, Knox was ordained priest before 1540 and practised as a papal notary in the archdiocese of St Andrews. He makes no reference to his conversion, but on his deathbed he asked his secretary to read the

seventeenth chapter of John's Gospel for it was there, he said, 'I cast my first anchor'.

When he met George Wishart, Knox was employed as tutor to the sons of two Lowland lairds, both of whom were committed to the pro-English Protestant party in Scotland. After the capture of St Andrews castle following the execution of Wishart and the assassination of Cardinal David Beaton, Knox was ordered to bring his pupils to the castle. During his stay there he received a call to become a preacher of the gospel, and somewhat reluctantly he agreed. The recapture of the castle by the Regent, assisted by the French, meant for Knox a period of nineteen months as a galley slave in France. He was, however, able to write a summary of a work on justification by his friend Henry Balnaves during this time. This was smuggled back to Scotland, and Knox later commented that this summary contained 'the sum of his doctrine and confession of his faith'.

Knox was released from the galleys in March 1549, probably due to the intervention of the English government of Edward VI, which was pushing forward the Protestant *Reformation there and saw Knox as a useful agent. He was sent to Berwick, which was then in the diocese of Durham where the bishop was not sympathetic to reform. Because the Prayer Book of 1549 was unknown in the north of England, Knox was able to devise his own much simpler order of service, giving much more prominence to the sermon. A fragmentary manuscript gives an outline of the practice of the Lord's Supper at Berwick. Communicants received the bread and wine seated at tables. From this period come the first of Knox's many attacks on the Mass, a term still used in the 1549 Prayer Book. The Prayer Book of 1552 dropped the use of the word 'Mass', but Knox was unhappy about the rubric that directed that the elements should be received kneeling. At his insistence, a comment was added which stated that no adoration of the elements was thereby implied. This has become known as the 'Black Rubric' because it was printed at the last minute in black, not red.

Knox was deeply disturbed and hurt when the accession of Mary Tudor to the throne of England forced him to flee to the Continent. He had come to love England and was appalled at the return to papistry merely because a woman desired it. From his exile he wrote to the faithful in England, urging them not to participate in the idolatry of the Mass. In *A Faithful*

Admonition to the Professors of God's Truth in England, written from Emden in 1554, he makes an attack on rule by a woman: 'But the saying is too true, that the usurped government of an affectionate [i.e., emotional] woman is a rage without reason'. A description of Emperor Charles V as 'no less enemy unto Christ than ever was Nero' in the same pamphlet led to his expulsion from Frankfurt. Knox also sought the guidance of various Reformers like *Calvin, Viret and *Bullinger on the problem of obedience to a magistrate who enforced idolatry and condemned true religion. Their answers did not satisfy him, and he developed his own doctrine of resistance which had its most famous expression in *The First Blast of the Trumpet against the Monstrous Regiment of Women*, which unfortunately appeared just as Mary's sister Elizabeth succeeded to the English throne. This prevented Knox from ever returning to England.

Knox had made a brief return visit to Scotland in 1555 during which he urged those favouring reform to cease attending Mass. He celebrated the Lord's Supper for them in various baronial halls. He was recalled to Scotland from Geneva in 1559 as the Reform movement was reaching a crisis. His vehement preaching gave fresh courage to the waverers, but it also provoked some riots and damage to church interiors. The crisis was resolved by the sudden death of the Regent, the Queen Mother, Mary of Guise in June 1560.

It is doubtful whether Knox thought of himself as a theologian. He was primarily a preacher, but in fulfilment of that vocation he became a theologian. Surprisingly few of his sermons survive but they are supplemented by many other writings, letters both to individuals and to congregations, polemical pamphlets and his massive *History of the Reformation in Scotland* which in many ways is an *apologia* for his own ministry and summarizes some of his sermons. His only theological treatise, *An answer to a great number of blasphemous cavillations written by an Anabaptist and adversarie to God's eternal Predestination* was written in Geneva in 1558 but not published until 1560. As its ponderous title indicates, it is an attack on what Knox regards as erroneous views rather than a systematic account of his own views.

Knox was not a clone of Calvin, much as he admired him and his achievement at Geneva. In several respects he goes beyond Calvin, notably in relation to the doctrine of resistance to idolatrous rulers and the place of the sacrament of the Lord's Supper. The circumstances of his exile first from Scotland and then from England made him take a more radical stance than Calvin in resisting rulers inimical to the gospel. His celebrations of the Lord's Supper in Scotland in 1555, well before the Reformation was accomplished, show that he regarded the sacrament as constitutive of the church and not just the worship of an established congregation.

Knox contributed to the *Confession of Faith* adopted by the Estates of Parliament in 1560 and also to the largely ignored *Book of Discipline* of 1561. Both would appear to be compromise documents, which do not fully represent Knox's views. The latter is based in part on the *Consultatio* prepared for the archdiocese of Cologne in 1546. The *Book of Common Order* authorized by the General Assembly in 1562 was based on the service book for English-speaking exiles used by Knox at Frankfurt and Geneva.

HENRY R. SEFTON

FURTHER READING: *Texts: John Knox's History of the Reformation in Scotland* (ed. William Croft Dickinson; Edinburgh, 1949); *The Works of John Knox* (ed. David Laing; Edinburgh, 1895). *Studies:* Lord Eustace Percy, *John Knox* (London, 1937, rev. edn 1964); Jasper Ridley, *John Knox* (Oxford, 1968); W. Stanford Reid, *Trumpeter of God: A Biography of John Knox* (New York, 1974); Henry R. Sefton, *John Knox: An Account of the Development of his Spirituality* (Edinburgh, 1993); Roger A. Mason (ed.), *John Knox and the British Reformations* (Aldershot, 1998).

Kohlbrügge, Hermann Friedrich (1803–75)

Kohlbrügge was born in 1803 in Amsterdam, where, after the completion of his theological studies, he worked as an assistant pastor in a Lutheran congregation. His protests against the rationalistic preaching of one of the Lutheran pastors led to his suspension. Having obtained his doctorate in Utrecht, he sought to be admitted to the Reformed (*Hervormde*) congregation there, but his request was refused on formal grounds. After the death of his young wife, he came into contact with Wuppertal Pietism during a journey along the Rhine. G.D. Krummacher (1774–1837) invited him to preach, and during his preparation for a sermon on Romans 7:14 he discovered the comma between the words 'of the flesh' and 'sold'. This discovery brought about the great turning point in his life: A Christian is not sold under sin insofar as he is of the flesh, but he is rather wholly of the flesh. His sermon was generally well received, but it also evoked some resistance from, among others, his Revivalist (*Reveil*) friend, Isaac de Costa (1798–1860), who accused him of antinomianism. In 1845 Kohlbrügge settled with his family – he had remarried by then – in Elberfeld, where he was ordained in 1848 in the (breakaway) *Niederländisch Reformierte Gemeinde*, where he served until his death in 1875.

Kohlbrügge pitted himself against three different fronts. First, he opposed rationalism, with its plea for autonomy and historical criticism of the Bible. Kohlbrügge insisted on unconditional submission to the inspired word of God. Secondly, he fought against subjectivism, as he encountered it in certain circles where people still sought sustenance in the writings of eighteenth-century Pietism. He shared their emphasis on the applicative work of the Holy Spirit, but he was critical of their introversive attitude. He found solid ground only in the 'objective' Christological salvation, toward which the subject is outwardly oriented. Thirdly, Kohlbrügge pitted himself against legalistic activism, which he discerned, for instance, in de Costa, and in certain missionary circles in the Wuppertal. Kohlbrügge pleaded for a passivity of faith in which one expects everything from God alone. His strength was his spiritual depth, rather than the breadth of social criticism.

The sources from which Kohlbrügge drew can be depicted as three concentric circles. The Church Fathers and the Reformers form the widest circle. The middle circle represents a healthy Pietism in which reformational ideas are not reduced to subjectivism, but in which there is a certain stress on the applicative dimension of soteriology. The innermost circle (and the most significant for historical theology) is that of *Luther's theology of the cross, with its strong emphasis on justification, the paradoxical nature of revelation and the way the latter gives rise to a faith assailed by temptation.

Kohlbrügge did not write a systematic theology. His doctrine can be gleaned from a number of treatises, and especially from his (strongly pastoral) preaching. The following elements are typical of his theology: Humans were created in God's image and glory. Through sin they stepped out of that image and became flesh.

Only through God's sovereignty can they be saved. That sovereignty is synonymous with God's merciful love. This insight implies a Christocentric, asymmetrical doctrine of election, somewhat reminiscent of *Bullinger's. God reveals himself in the concealment of the incarnation and the cross. The fact that Christ became flesh means that he identified with human misery. As the one most profoundly assailed by temptation, he could fulfil God's righteousness only through faith. The most important gift of the glorified Christ is the Spirit who creates faith – by which one condemns oneself and justifies God, but also by which one receives Christ's righteousness and holiness. Thus sanctification is no quid pro quo, but purely a gift. It consists of a practice of discipleship, envisaged in very concrete terms. Kohlbrügge attaches great importance to the Law. It must be done. The believer (the *simul sanctus et peccator*) can do it by abiding in Christ, in whom every commandment is a promise. Temptation, in which one constantly observes the contrast of what is believed, keeps the Christian permanently in a state of beggary. The theology of the cross and Pietism form the two pillars of Kohlbrügge's spirituality. On the one hand, there is a contrast between faith and the experience of the present; on the other, faith contracts its own unique experience of the Spirit as the pledge of glory.

Kohlbrügge's sermons, whether translated or not, were already quite warmly received during his lifetime. Various factors contributed to this. First, there was a circle of like-minded people in Holland, where, to this day, a foundation called 'Friends of Dr H.F. Kohlbrügge' publishes its own bulletin ('Ecclesia', formerly '*Kerkblaadje*'). Secondly, a number of young theologians did apprenticeships under Kohlbrügge, and they took what they had learned to congregations in Germany and Switzerland in particular. Thirdly, the work of Kohlbrügge's productive son-in-law Edward Böhl (1836–1903), professor of dogmatics in Vienna from 1864–99, deepened contacts with Bohemia and Moravia. Fourthly, *Karl Barth responded positively to Kohlbrügge. Fifthly, Kohlbrügge had a profound impact on some influential Dutch theologians, especially O. Noordmans (1871–1956) and K.H. Miskotte (1894–1976). To this day, Kohlbrügge is appreciated in the church in both dialectical ('faith-critical') and pietist ('experiential') circles.

ARIE DE REUVER

FURTHER READING: *Texts (selected): Specimen philologico-theologicum inaugurale, exhibens commentarium in Psalmum XLV* (Amsterdam, 1829); *Gastpredigt über Römer 7:14* (Elberfeld, 1833); *Das siebente Kapitel des Briefes Pauli an die Römer in Ausführlicher Umschreibung* (Elberfeld, 1833); *Betrachtung über das erste Capitel des Evangeliums nach Matthäus* (Elberfeld, 1844); *Wozu das Alte Testament?* (Elberfeld, 1846); *Zwanzig Predigten im Jahre 1846 gehalten* (Halle, 1857); *Passionspredigten in den Jahren 1874, 1848, 1849 gehalten* (Elberfeld, 1870); *Festpredigten* (Elberfeld, 1878); *Die Lehre des Heils in Fragen und Antworten* (Elberfeld, 1903); *Briefe von Dr. Theol. H.F. Kohlbrügge an Johannes Wichelhaus* (Elberfeld, 1911), the latter four are useful for an initial probe into his work. *Selected English translations: The Seventh Chapter of the Epistle of Paul the Apostle to the Romans* (London, 1854); *Sermons on the First Epistle of Peter* (London, 1855); *Sermons on the book of Jonah the Prophet* (London, 1885), see also J.H.F. Kohlbrügge, *Lijst van werken en geschriften van en over H.F. Kohlbrügge* (Amsterdam, 1887). Most of the original manuscripts are kept in the 'Kohlbrügge Archive', University Library, Utrecht. *Studies:* J. van Lonkhuyzen, *Hermann Friedrich Kohlbrügge en zijn prediking in de lijst van zijn tijd* (Wageningen, 1905), useful bibliography; O. Noordmans, *Geestelijke perspectieven* (Amsterdam, 1938), pp. 15–37; H. Klugkist Hesse, *Hermann Friedrich Kohlbrügge* (Wuppertal-Barmen, 1935), biography; Theodor Stiasny, *Die Theologie Kohlbrügges* (Düsseldorf, 1935), brief survey; W. Kreck, *Die Lehre der Heiligung bei H.F. Kohlbrügge* (Munich, 1936); K. Barth, *Protestant Theology in the Nineteenth Century, its Background and History* (London, 1972); A. de Reuver, *Bedelen bij de Bron: Kohlbrügges geloofsopvatting vergeleken met Reformatie en Nadere Reformatie* (Zoetermeer, 1992); A.H. Bogaards, 'Die christologie van Hermann Friedrich Kohlbrügge' (diss.; Potchefstroom, 1997).

Komenský, Jan Amos (Comenius, 1592–1670)

Comenius was born into a family of *Czech Brethren in southern Moravia. The Brethren took charge of his education after he was orphaned in early childhood. He was sent to *Calvinistic-oriented colleges in Herborn and Heidelberg and served later as a pastor in a parish of the *Unitas Fratrum* in Fulnek. In 1620, a radical and tragic change took place in Bohemia and Moravia when the Protestant Estates lost in the war against the Catholic Hapsburgs. A pitiless counter-reformation was pursued in which the Protestant priests had to leave the country. After that, Comenius had to live as an exile, first in the city of Lissa in Poland where he served the Czech Brethren as school director. It was here that he wrote a series of educational works which soon brought him an international reputation. One call followed the other. He worked as an educational reformer in many countries including Hungary, England, Sweden and Holland.

In all this work, an even more ambitious programme was beckoning Comenius. He envisaged a universal reformation and renewal having as its aim a root and branch improvement not only of the schools but of all the main realms of church, culture and society. He entitled his life-long project *De rerum humanarum emendatione consultatio catholica*. The large part of his monumental work (in seven volumes) remained unpublished in his lifetime. The bulk of manuscripts came to light in 1935. Innumerable other works by Comenius – pedagogical, theological and visionary – appeared and made their author one of the most appreciated Europeans of his time. He died in Amsterdam and is buried in Naarden. Although Comenius's work is classic in the theory and practice of education, he himself considered it as his essential vocation to work as a theologian.

Comenius's thinking rests on a fundamental assumption that the human world, God's world, is to be viewed and claimed in its fundamental unity. In view of its true origin and its true goal the world is a whole – indeed a basically positive, harmonious whole. This fundamental confidence is grounded in the belief in the God of Christian faith, in the triune God. Comenius was an enthusiastic Trinitarian thinker. As the Father, Son and the Holy Spirit, '*Deus non est solitarius*' (God is not alone). He is, in his essence, '*summe communicativus*' (the ultimate communicator). As we are created in his image, we are called not to live as solitary, but as truly communicative, beings. This indicates the true direction for our human, and even for our scientific, orientation: no human person and no human science should be 'self-contained'. They should never forget that all human perspectives are only fragmentary and, therefore, respect the whole and seek communication with other persons and other sciences.

Comenius was well aware that the present state of humankind contradicts this vision. The biblical story of Adam and Eve, as well as his personal experience, allow for no illusion. Humanity broke out from the inclusive wholeness and harmony of the creation and unilaterally cancelled the communication with the creator and other beings within the creation. Our world is a veritable 'labyrinth' (the title of the famous Czech novel by Comenius).

Nevertheless, Comenius was not immobilized by the sight and experience of a world out of joint; quite the contrary, they mobilized his determination and his energy for reform. For he saw not only the first but also the second Adam, Christ, at work in our human world. In his *Didactica magna* he urges his readers: 'It is scandalous and disgraceful and a plain sign of ingratitude that we are for ever bemoaning the corruption but say never a word about the restoration (*restitutio*); that we readily acknowledge the power of the old Adam in us but never give the power of the new Adam, Christ, a try …'

Comenius developed his Christology in the spirit of the Czech Reformation. He was a theologian of strong personal piety. Yet Jesus Christ is not only the saviour of the soul. He is the Lord of the church and the world. In the traditional language of the threefold office of Christ, Comenius emphasized (with a critical side glance at his *Lutheran friends): it is not enough to ensure that Christ not only has the pulpit as teacher and the altar as priest, but the throne is also to be erected for him as king.

There is a strong eschatological element in this emphasis on the kingship of Christ. Comenius saw Christ as the *Christus renovator*. Faith in the coming Christ is the ultimate ground for his reformatory pathos, his world-transforming hope. In this connection, the controversial question of his millenarianism (*chiliasm*) has to be raised. Already in his lifetime he was accused by Dutch reformed theologian Samuel Maresius as '*Fanaticus, Visionarius et Enthusiasta*'. Comenius defended his position and was not shy to accept the charge of chiliasm. '*Audeo pronunciare verum chiliasmum verum christianismum, antichiliasmum vero esse antichristianismum.*' ('I dare to pronounce that true millenarianism is true Christianity, and to be anti-millenarianism is truly to be anti-Christianity.') The qualification *verum* (true) must not be overlooked. Comenius does not stand for any type of millenarianism. But true chilianism, the hope in the eschatological kingdom of God, is integral to Christianity – and this indeed not marginally but centrally.

In his preface to *Lux e tenebris*, Comenius explains what he means by this qualification.

The true way of Christians leads between 'Scylla and Charybdis', between and through two constant temptations. The rock 'Scylla' is the crude and fanatic type of millenarianism. But there is also, on the other hand, the whirlpool 'Charybdis': a spiritualizing piety oriented on heaven alone which, in fear of materialistic reading of the images, falls victim to an idealistic spiritualization of the Christian hope. By such attitudes, the church betrays the world, shrinks God's eschatological promises, and dismisses Christ into a private corner or into a dead past. This was the danger Comenius saw in the orthodoxy of his day and in the major part of established Christianity. In contrast to this, he openly accepted the legitimate concern of chiliasm, emphasizing however that the hope which sustains Christians already concerns and illuminates earthly history and sets it in motion in the direction of the kingdom of God.

Comenius's diverse activities can be understood in this light. The programme of a complete renewal of the church, culture and society was developed in a down-to-earth way in the eschatological perspective of the coming of *Christus renovator*. It is from here that the impetus ultimately comes for his educational, pansophist and irenic plans.

JAN MILIČ LOCHMAN

FURTHER READING: *Texts: Opera omnia* (Prague, 1957); *The Labyrinth of the World and the Paradise of the Heart* (trans. H. Louthan and A. Sterk; New York, 1998). *Studies*: M. Spinka, *John Amos Comenius* (Chicago, 1967); M. Blekastad, *Comenius* (Oslo, 1969); J.M. Lochman, *Comenius* (Hamburg, 1982).

Küng, Hans (b. 1928)

Hans Küng may be the most prolific theologian of the late twentieth century, both in terms of the number of books he has written or edited and in the range of topics he has considered. Küng has sought to make Christianity understandable to modern people, to build bridges to other religions, and to recast the Roman Catholic Church in a more democratic form. In each of these areas, he has shown himself ready to give up what others consider essential aspects of Christianity and Catholicism, and this has aroused strong opposition.

Born in Switzerland in 1928, Küng studied at the Gregorian University in Rome and the Sorbonne in Paris. In Rome he was trained in the Neo-Scholasticism of pre-Vatican II Catholicism, and in Paris he was introduced to the modern biblical-critical methods that were beginning to influence Roman Catholicism. In Paris Küng wrote *Justification* (1964), his celebrated study of *Barth's view of justification which concluded that Trent and the *Reformers held compatible views on the doctrine. After two years as a parish priest, he went to Münster to teach and to write his study of *Hegel's value for developing future Christologies. In 1960, Küng joined the Catholic Tübingen faculty. During *Vatican II, Küng was a theological adviser to the German bishops, the youngest theologian at the council to have such a role. He was among the progressives at the council and has continued to advocate a liberal agenda, developing further what he considers to be the achievements of the council.

At Tübingen, Küng was influenced greatly by Käsemann's biblical criticism and applied it to Catholic teaching about the church. He also concluded that early Christian doctrine had been distorted by Hellenistic philosophy. Küng came to see human experience as a crucial element in theology and, because human experience is historical and limited, concluded that doctrine must be understood in relation to its context. This historical turn, which occurred just before the first session of Vatican II, caused Küng to question those theological teachings he considered underivable from Scripture. Following the council, Küng wrote several books challenging papal infallibility and the hierarchical structure of the Catholic Church as unbiblical. He offered a modern statement of Christian belief and practice in *On Being a Christian* (1976), which also contained an equivocal Christology. Küng then examined Christianity's relationship to the modern world in *Does God Exist?* (1980), *Art and the Question of Meaning* (1981), *Eternal Life?* (1984), *Freud and the Problem of God* (1990), *Theology for the Third Millennium* (1988) and *Global Responsibility* (1993). Küng has applied Thomas Kuhn's concept of paradigm shift to theology in *Paradigm Change in Theology* (1989), examined Hegel's contribution to Christology in *The Incarnation of God* (1987), and joined the dialogue among world religions with *Christianity and the World Religions* (1986), *Christianity and Chinese Religions* (1989), *Judaism* (1992) and *Christianity* (1995). In 1993, he edited the papers of the World Parliament of Religion. Although Küng's thinking can be

described in four phases, each phase has concerned him throughout his career.

Küng's attack on the structure of the Catholic Church led Pope John Paul II to withdraw his *missio canonica* and force his removal from the Catholic Tübingen faculty in 1979. Küng remains at Tübingen as director of the Institute for Ecumenical Research. His equivocal Christology has been only slightly less controversial than his ecclesiology. For Küng, Jesus is at the centre of Christian thought, but it is the man Jesus of Nazareth, not the God-man of the creeds. Believing that only a Christology 'from below' can speak to modern culture, Küng is uncomfortable with traditional Christological titles and language, which he calls Hellenistic distortions. He considers the Bible to be the norm for all Christian theology, but this Bible is the product of modern critical study. Küng approaches theology functionally, so what is most important is not theory but faith in Christ and following Christ. Küng's theology gives priority to function over being and practice over belief.

Küng's theological method has come to be characterized by the concept of paradigm shifts. This provides for discontinuity and plurality in theology, enabling Küng to present Christianity to modern culture on its terms. Christianity interprets Christian history in terms of five paradigm shifts, arguing classical creedal language comes from an outdated paradigm and must be reformulated for the modern world. This relativizes doctrinal language by making it both time- and culture-bound. The most important result of this paradigm concept lies in Küng's belief that each world religion provides its own valid offer of salvation. Each religion has only a partial grasp of truth, so none can claim superiority over the others.

Küng differs from most Catholic theologians not in disagreements about specific doctrines, but in a different concept of doctrine that denies many later doctrines are legitimate developments from Scripture. His attitude toward tradition and doctrinal development stands in sharp contrast to that of the Catholic Tübingen tradition. Nonetheless, Küng sees himself as the heir of the early Catholic Tübingen School, sharing with it a concern for history and the need to communicate the gospel in the language and concepts of contemporary culture.

Küng's theology continues to develop in a pluralistic direction. The conflict with Rome, however, has increasingly marginalized him within the Catholic Church. The success of his work results from his clear writing style and apologetic concern, not its consistency with Catholic tradition.

DOUGLAS MCCREADY

FURTHER READING: Comprehensive and balanced evaluations of Küng's theology can be found in Catherine Mowry LaCugna, *The Theological Methodology of Hans Küng* (Chico, CA, 1982); John Kiwiet, *Hans Küng* (Waco, TX, 1985); and Werner Jeanrond in *The Modern Theologians* (ed. David Ford; Cambridge, MA, 2nd edn, 1997). Sympathetic studies come from Leonard Swidler, *Küng in Conflict* (Garden City, NY, 1981); Hermann Häring and Karl-Josef Kuschel, *Hans Küng: His Work and His Way* (London, 1979); and *Hans Küng: New Horizons for Faith and Thought* (New York, 1993); and Robert Nowell, *A Passion for Truth: Hans Küng and His Theology* (New York, 1981). Leo Scheffczyk offers a conservative German Catholic critique in *On Being a Christian: The Hans Küng Debate* (Blackrock, Ireland, 1982); and Robert Butterworth, *Hey J* 18 (1977) questions Küng's approach to tradition.

Lactantius (c. 250 – c. 324)

Lucius Caecilius Firmianus Lactantius was born in North Africa. There he studied with Arnobius, the author of a lengthy attack on paganism called *Against the Nations* written after his conversion c. 295. Lactantius became a teacher of rhetoric, and as such, he was intimately acquainted with the courts of two emperors. Therein rests his importance. Emperor Diocletian brought him to Bithynia to teach in the newly established school at Nicomedia, a city that Diocletian elevated to the eastern imperial capital. That position ended with the outbreak of persecution in 303, but as *Jerome said (*De viris illustribus*, 80), in extreme old age, apparently c. 314–17, Lactantius became the tutor of Constantine's ill-fated son, Crispus (the son was executed by his father in 326). As a young man, Constantine may have known Lactantius from the time of his own education at Diocletian's Nicomedian court. But it was Lactantius's subsequent reputation that must have encouraged Constantine's attention. After leaving the chair of rhetoric in 303, Lactantius wrote the *Divine Institutes*, a lengthy defence of Christianity as the only sure source of Roman security and prosperity, which he completed by 309, probably in North Africa. After persecution ended in the eastern empire in 313, he wrote *On the Deaths of the Persecutors*, a pointed defence of the preference Constantine showed for Christianity ever since he succeeded his father in 306. Lactantius completed it between 313 and 315, probably after resuming the chair in rhetoric at Nicomedia. Lactantius referred often to contemporary events in his writings. It is difficult to imagine that he would fail to mention Constantine's final victory over Licinius, Emperor (Constantine's last pagan imperial rival) in 324. The only allusions to events around 324 are invocations to Constantine in the *Divine Institutes* (1.1.13ff., 7.26.11ff.) that Lactantius appears to have revised around that time. Therefore, scholars suspect that Lactantius died shortly before Constantine's final victory or soon after the victory, but before he could more substantially revise the *Institutes* to reflect recent events. Hence he witnessed the triumph of Christianity in imperial government but, lacking conclusive evidence, the question of whether he influenced those events by swaying Constantine or whether he himself was swayed by the emperor remains a matter for endless debate.

The *Divine Institutes* is an eloquent witness to the passions of a learned Christian at a time when Christianity had suddenly attracted growing numbers of learned people. It displays an unswerving conviction that between Rome's mythical Golden Age and the coming millennium, the worship of the Christian God is the only guarantee of justice and the only guarantee that Roman civilization shall endure. The threat to Rome's survival was the not insignificant matter of her traditional gods, whose cults Diocletian's reforms aimed to revive for the benefit of the empire and who were to Lactantius, in the manner of Christian apologists, the divine disguises of so many *daemones*. This main argument was embellished with refutations of pagan philosophy and a thorough attempt to reconcile Christian teaching with Roman cultural and philosophical ideals; it drew from Arnobius and presaged *Augustine's *On the City of God*. Lactantius became justifiably famous and beloved by Latin Christian writers ever since, especially in the *Reformation, when humanists were drawn to this 'Christian Cicero' and when another writer of *Institutes*, *John Calvin, must have been irresistibly drawn to Lactantius's claim that his argument was all about providence (*Divine Institutes*, 1.2.6).

In spite of orthodox approval, the reader finds within the *Divine Institutes* a fascinating variety of what were to become, through the course of the fourth century, unorthodox ideas – if they were not so already. There is, in this pre-Nicene work, the expected ambiguity about the Son of God's divine nature. The Son was, to Lactantius, generated before the creation of other angelic sons and is alone worthy of the divine name. But he was above all a teacher who came to the world to teach virtue and justice and who gave this office to disciples who established churches to do the same – promoting the very things that would preserve Roman society. In the *Divine Institutes*, the Son's moral excellence earned him the divine name and the rule of the future kingdom. Beyond such *Origenistic and Sabellian-sounding ideas, which later in the century would have quickly raised an outcry, scholars have uncovered a number of *Gnostic and dualistic tendencies. Lactantius's syncretism displays well the intellectual curiosity of the new learned Christians just before the coming of the Christian empire, still unsullied by debates over *Athanasius and the *Nicene doctrine of the Son's consubstantiality with the

Father. Also reflecting the sensibilities of the newly converted learned pagan is the comfortable juxtaposition of Sibylline oracles and the *Hermetica* with Scripture in Lactantius's major work.

On the Death of the Persecutors (written between 313 and 315) is much studied by historians for what it says about Diocletian's reforms and the rise of Constantine, but it was written with a tendentious theological purpose. It proves the simple point that emperors who support Christianity win, and everyone else loses, by reason of the same providence explained in the *Divine Institutes*: the supporters are on God's side. The argument is presented as an ideology for Constantine and Licinius, Emperor, who defeated their respective co-regents in 312 and 313, paving the way for Constantine's final consolidation of power in 324. In addition, between 313 and 324 Lactantius wrote an *Epitome* of the *Divine Institutes* that expanded his denunciation of paganism and removed a condemnation of Christian military service. In the same period, he wrote *On the Anger of God* against Stoic and Epicurean views. An earlier work, *De opificio Dei* (c. 303), shows that the human body reflects divine artifice.

CHRISTOPHER OCKER

FURTHER READING: *Texts: Institutions Divines* (SC 204, 205, 326, 337, 377; 1973–); *De mortibus persecutorum* (ed. and trans. J.L. Creed; Oxford, 1984). *Studies:* T.D. Barnes, 'Lactantius and Constantine', *J Rom St* 63 (1973), pp. 29–46; P.S. Davies, 'The Origin and Purpose of the Persecution of 303', *J Th St* 40 (1989), pp. 66–94; E.D. Digeser, 'Lactantius and Constantine's Letter to Arles: Dating the *Divine Institutes*', *J E Chr St* 2 (1994), pp. 33–52; E. Heck, *Die dualistischen Zustäze und die Kaiseranreden bei Lactantius* (Heidelberg, 1972); V. Loi, *Lattanzio nella storia del linguaggio e del pensiero teologico pre-niceno* (Zurich, 1970); C. Ocker, '"Unius arbitrio mundum regi necesse est": Lactantius' Concern for the Preservation of Roman Society', *Vig Chr* 40 (1986), pp. 348–64; M. Perrin, *L'Homme Antique et Chrétien: L'Anthropologie de Lactance, 250–325* (Paris, 1981); A. Wlosok, *Laktanz und die philosophische Gnosis* (Heidelberg, 1960).

Leo the Great (d. 461)

Leo, whose date of birth is unclear, is best known for his leadership as bishop of Rome (440–61) over the worldwide church at the time of the Christological crisis of the mid-fifth century. Diplomacy was an essential quality in

Leo's efforts to promote the Roman see as *primus inter pares* (see his epistle to Marcian, 449). He had represented imperial Ravenna on a tour of Gaul shortly before his election to the see of Rome in 440. It was St Peter's *authority* which made Leo, his successor from 440–61, the primate of all the bishops (a theme from Leo's earliest sermons onwards). As Mark looked to Peter, so should Alexandria to Rome. Alexandria may have accepted Leo's patronage (so Camelot), but it is much less apparent that the other patriarchates did. Leo argued that unresolved problems in the provinces should not go directly to him but should find their resolution through the regular synods of a fortnight's duration. Yet the synod should concur with the pope's view, since the same Spirit inspired each. For Leo, *Nicaea (325) proclaimed timeless and irrevocable principles, not least because its canons assured Rome's priority, but also because it reflected the *Apostles' Creed (which Leo took to be genuinely by the apostles). After 451 *Chalcedon too became fundamental, and its authority ever enduring.

According to Leo, the pope was entrusted with preaching the gospel as handed down, inspired by the Spirit, and teaching the council of bishops, whose job in turn was to pronounce who the heretics were (so Sieben). The pope was not *to define* the faith – which was the technical term used for conciliar and imperial decisions – but rather *to preach* it. The faith, the *regula fidei*, is clear enough (*Ep.* 38). Thus Leo's own teaching has a material rather than a formal authority, and the question the conciliar bishops had to ask was: was it sufficiently lucid? Horn thinks it more likely that Leo saw the church's reception of the pope's voice as proof he had indeed spoken the gospel, while the bishops, for their part, were so divided among themselves that they needed the reconciling decisiveness of the pope. That is why they accepted his Petrine principle. This would mean that the emperor was less able to manipulate any council: Rome would be both the church's conscience and its convener. Leo's own theology was a convenient mix of the Cyrillian and the Antiochene theologies so that the Council of Chalcedon did not see him only as Peter's interpreter, but even as a second Peter who agreed with at least *Cyril's two canonical letters as read at Chalcedon. The collection of bishops was merely the means of communicating the truth around the churches. In order to keep the spiritual and secular apart,

Leo argued that the apostolic seat should *not* follow the imperial throne to 'New Rome' – whatever Canon 28 of Chalcedon had decided, as he wrote to Emperor Marcian in 452. The Nicene 'priority of Rome' was in no way anachronistic, and in 453 (21 March) Leo pronounced Canon 28 invalid.

At the point of convocation by Theodosius II of the synod of Ephesus to deal with the problem of *Eutyches, in his letter to Pulcheria (the emperor's sister) in 449 and in the letter to Flavian (the famous *Tome*), Leo set out his own and the church's teaching. Although in epistolary form, this was really a collection of passages from his sermons made by a secretary. It was reissued, supplemented by a collection of supporting authorities and sent to the Council with the papal legates in 451.

Leo's *Tome* teaches that each 'nature' in the incarnation retains its own property, and the two natures come together in a single *persona* (cf. *Augustine, *Enchir.* 11.36 and *Tract. in Jn.* 78.3). Because Christ is one Person, Scripture speaks of the Son of man 'descending from heaven', and the Son of God's being crucified: 'the unity of the person in each nature'. Eutyches had relied on his own human wisdom and had ignored the fact that the Son, who is co-eternal with the Father, had in fact been born in time for the purpose of taking a true body, a soul endowed with human reason, and the same nature as his mother. The virgin birth removed nothing human from him. The key phrase was: 'the property of each nature remaining and coming together in one person' (with a debt to *Tertullian in the phraseology). 'Nature' meant for Leo that which was real or substantial, not shadowy. The form of God did not suppress the form of the slave, and vice versa. The Word and the flesh operate what is proper to them; there is a person/operation distinction. Due to the unity of the Person one can, however, affirm with the creed that the Son of God was crucified and buried.

Leo's was a soteriological teaching which lacked the precision demanded by many in the East, and which tended to be more interested in what happened to the human nature than to the divine. He owed a large debt to Augustine's use of *persona*. The *Tome* stressed that God came in person to drive out the devil from human nature and when the devil, deceived by the form of a human (though not by God as such), tried to hold Christ, he could not. This is a

mystery, a sacrament, but also an example for our moral-spiritual lives. For Leo, as perhaps for Augustine, one does not meet God in Christ but rather the way to God as the 'in two natures' teaching stresses. 'But not even he knew how to make clear that Christ's unity is based on the fact that only the second person of the Trinity is incarnate (*Serm.* 64.2)' (Studer, p. 479). There Leo claimed that, since the Son made human nature and in that sense, of the three in God, was closest to it, it was fitting that he should restore it. But the personal unity is the result rather than the cause of the incarnation. One gets the feeling that the Person of the Son in heaven is not quite the same as the Person of Christ. The Magi 'honoured the kingly person with gold, the human person with myrrh and the divine person with incense' (*Tr.* 33.2; Grillmeier, p. 160).

There was a second *Tome* (458), the content of which reveals that behind Leo's severer criticism of Eutyches than of Nestorius lay a genuine terror of the spread of Manicheism, manifested in the Egyptian Timothy Aelurus' denial of two natures in Christ. What is new in the second *Tome* in contrast to the first *Tome* is Leo's emphasis on the death of Christ as a sacrifice.

                                                          MARK W. ELLIOTT

FURTHER READING: Basil Studer, 'Leo the Great', in *Encyclopedia of Early Christianity* (Cambridge, 1992); A. Grillmeier, *Christ in Christian Tradition* (Oxford, 2nd rev. edn, 1987), pp. 93–194; H. Arens, *Die Christologische Sprache Leos des Grossen* (Freiburg, 1982); H. Sieben, *Konziliengeschichte: Die Konzilsidee der Alten Kirche* (Paderborn, 1979); Stephen O. Horn, *Petrou Kathedra: der Bischof von Rom und die Synoden von Ephesus (449) und Chalcedon* (Paderborn, 1982).

Leontius of Byzantium (c. 500–43)

Very little is known of the life of Leontius, except that he was a Palestinian monk who lived in Constantinople in the 530s and early 540s. He is not to be confused with his namesake and contemporary, Leontius of Jerusalem (c. 485 – c. 543). Six of his works have survived intact: five were written explicitly to defend the formula of *Chalcedon, that Christ is one concrete individual (*hypostasis*) in two natures (*physeis*); the sixth is an anthology of *Apollinarian ideas, with notes explaining how erroneous they are. Leontius is a sophisticated, demanding writer, who uses *Aristotelian categories with dialectical aplomb. Modern scholarship has been divided, however, over how to classify his contribution to the Christological tradition.

To Leontius, the Christian faith hinges upon a right understanding of the 'unconfused union' of divine and human in Jesus Christ. The Chalcedonian position is a *via media* between the opposing extremes of *'Nestorianism', which divides the unity of Christ, and *Monophysitism, which reduces Christ to a single nature. The one Christ does not have two *hypostaseis*; nor does the convergence of divine and human produce a new, synthetic entity, as the Severan Monophysites maintained. Both ideas are based on the misconception that *hypostasis* and *physis* are interchangeable terms. Leontius adopts the *Platonist and *Cappadocian distinction that *physis* describes a generic set of characteristics, differentiating one entity from another, while *hypostasis* is the particular instance of these features in an actual case. Every human being represents a union of soul and body, without confusion: each dimension functions according to its own laws; yet both come together in a given individual. The incarnation is a similar union. Christ is unique, not in the structure of relations that forges his two natures into one person, but in the fact that no other individual unites humanity with the divine Word.

The term which Leontius (followed by other eastern writers) uses to describe the concrete existence of the human Jesus is *enhypostatos*. This has traditionally been taken to mean 'hypostatic *within*' the Word (Loofs). Thus Leontius assumes, with *Cyril of Alexandria, that Christ's human nature is strictly *anhypostatos* – it lacks personal subsistence of its own – but affirms that it *is* personally centred because it is actually in union with the Word (Lynch). For *Barth, *enhypostatos* expresses the structure of grace: the human nature of Christ derives its origin only from the divine; the human Jesus is not of himself, he is *in* the divine (*CD* 1.2, 163f.; 3.2, 70; 4.2, 49f., 91f.). Attempts have been made to argue that Leontius brilliantly anticipated modern psychologies of personhood in which it is consciousness that is said to give substantial existence to an intellectual nature (Relton; Otto).

More recently, a very different interpretation has been advanced. According to one ancient source, Leontius had associated with *Origenist monks in Palestine, and it has been suggested that his whole Christology is Origenist (Evans). Both the divine and the human natures of Christ are enhypostatized in the particular *hypostasis* of Jesus, but that *hypostasis* is not the *hypostasis* of the Word.

The traditional construal is weakened by a basic misunderstanding. *Enhypostatos* does not mean 'hypostatic *within*' the Word, but simply 'having a concrete existence' (Daley). Great caution is thus required when we are tempted to read back modern psychological categories into Leontius's ontology. But an Origenist construction is no less problematic: only by ingenious reasoning can it be established that Leontius is proposing a hypostatic *tertium quid*. In fact, Leontius's achievement lies precisely in his determination to ground Christology in faith's apprehension of the concrete actuality of the man Jesus Christ, and its ability to see *in him* the existential relatedness of God and the human. The language may be difficult and abstract, but Leontius's argument turns out to be historically focused. It is in the contingent life of the real Jesus that we see the two realities comprised in a single personal unit, unconfused yet integrated in reality. Leontius offers a defence of Chalcedonian Christology that is both soteriologically constitutive and ethically evocative.

IVOR DAVIDSON

FURTHER READING: *Texts:* In *PG* 86; new edn by B.E. Daley in CCSG. *Studies*: B.E. Daley, 'The Origenism of Leontius of Byzantium', *J Th St* 27 (1976), pp. 333–69; ' "A Richer Union": Leontius of Byzantium and the Relationship of Human and Divine in Christ', SP 24 (1991), pp. 239–65; D.B. Evans, *Leontius of Byzantium: An Origenist Christology* (Washington, DC, 1970); A. Grillmeier, *Christ in Christian Tradition* 2.2 (London, 1995), pp. 181–229; F. Loofs, *Leontius von Byzanz und die gleichnamigen Schriftsteller der griechischen Kirche* (TU, 3.1–2; Leipzig, 1887); J.J. Lynch, 'Leontius of Byzantium: A Cyrillian Christology', *Th St* 36 (1975), pp. 455–71; J. Meyendorff, *Christ in Eastern Christian Thought* (Washington, DC, 1969); S. Otto, *Person und Subsistenz* (Munich, 1968); H. Relton, *A Study in Christology* (London, 1917); M. Richard, *Opera minora* II (Louvain, 1977); F. LeRon Shults, 'A Dubious Christological Formula: From Leontius of Byzantium to Karl Barth', *Th St* 57 (1996), pp. 431–46.

Liberal Protestantism

The term 'liberal Protestantism' admits of no simple definitions. Further, it has been used to describe both those Protestants whose relationship to Christian orthodoxy has been one of radical criticism, as well as those who, while considering themselves wholly orthodox, have sought to reconcile Christianity with modern thought. However, although the word 'liberal' is similarly vague, most liberals of whatever shade have accepted, at least to some degree, the guiding principles of *Enlightenment thought, particularly its criticism of the supernaturally-justified authority of Scripture or dogma. Theological liberalism has thus to be understood as one aspect of a more general reaction to the authority structures of the university, church and state which survived largely intact after the *Reformation. As a particular approach to authority, liberalism regarded no institution, however hallowed, as beyond the scope of criticism. Those liberals who also regarded themselves as Protestants (which is a similarly slippery term) felt a consonance between the Reformers' criticism of the claims of the medieval church and their own post-Enlightenment criticism of dogmatic and supernatural authority. In addition, the Reformation reliance on faith alone allowed all people the liberty to criticize tradition in the light of a higher truth.

Since the course of the Enlightenment proceeded very differently in different countries, however, liberal Protestantism developed strong national characteristics. Although the following survey is necessarily selective (and fails to address important movements in France and Scotland), the three examples from England, Germany and America illustrate continuities and divergences within liberal Protestantism.

England. In England, partly because of the tolerance and degree of parliamentary representation expressed in the constitution, liberalism presented less of a political threat than elsewhere in Europe. Liberalism could be seen as a reflection of the general ideology of progress which accompanied technological advances and had come to dominate the English establishment by the end of the nineteenth century. As part of a wider world-view theological liberalism came to be associated, through educational reformers and theologians like Thomas Arnold (1795–1842), Benjamin Jowett (1817–93) and Frederick Temple (1821–1902), with the

Enlightenment ideal of growth into human maturity. Indeed, there was no right, Temple wrote in the notorious collection *Essays and Reviews* of 1860, 'in all exercise of the intellectual powers ... to stop short of any limit but that which nature, that is, the decree of the Creator, has imposed on us ... If we have made mistakes ... the enlightenment of the understanding is the best means to show us our folly' (pp. 57f.). Christian truth constituted thus no special knowledge apprehended through God's direct communication. It was, rather, known in the same way as any other knowledge and open to the same means of verification.

When applying this understanding to theology, English liberals, unlike many of their continental counterparts, followed the eighteenth-century lead and tended to focus on the reconciliation between the claims of the natural sciences and those of religion. Liberalism thus often amounted to apologetics for the rationality of Christian belief as, for instance, in Temple's Bampton Lectures *The Relations between Religion and Science* of 1884, which sought to harmonize religion and modern scientific method. This search for synthesis has been one of the leading characteristics of English liberalism, exemplified in the twentieth century by the Modern Churchmen's Union under Henry Major (1872–1961). Outside the established church, a more radical breach with tradition was represented by the Congregationalist *R.J. Campbell (1867–1956), whose *New Theology* (1909) offered 'a religion of science', which was in reality little more than a shallow monism. An emphasis on the unity of thought also led liberals, including *Hastings Rashdall (1858–1924) and B.H. Streeter (1874–1937), to downplay the supernatural element in religion – which resulted in widespread controversy within the churches.

Germany. The position of liberal Protestantism in Germany in the nineteenth century was quite different from that in England. In so far as the church functioned as the spiritual arm of a conservative and anti-democratic regime, theological liberalism was perceived as part of a broader social and political movement. This movement was associated with efforts towards the democratization and rationalization of institutions, including the churches. The Enlightenment in Germany was thus far more explicitly political than in England or Scotland. *Immanuel Kant's

(1724–1804) critical philosophy, for instance, is a critique of the claims of reason outside its own sphere. But it is also a critique of all forms of authority based on dogmatic and supernatural revelation. For Kant, enlightenment meant the gradual emancipation from the tutelage of the past towards the glorious liberty of the rational kingdom. Although he made space for God as the necessary postulate for ethically meaningful activity, the shock waves of Kant's attack on authority reverberated throughout the nineteenth century. Other problems were raised by Gotthold Ephraim Lessing (1729–81), whose claim that history could contain no absolutes, but merely probabilities, threatened the survival of a religion founded on a historical revelation.

Throughout the nineteenth century, theologians in Germany addressed these problems. Most importantly, *F.D.E. Schleiermacher (1768–1834) sought, without contravening the principles of the Enlightenment, to identify a distinctive sphere for religion and to ensure that Christianity might retain its rootedness in history. At the same time, he engaged actively in ecclesiastical and university politics, seeing theology as something affecting the whole of culture rather than as simply confined to its own sphere. Although the dominant strands of German theology later in the nineteenth century were anti-Enlightenment and associated with political and ecclesiastical conservatism, a number of theologians continued in Schleiermacher's path. Most influential was *Albrecht Ritschl (1822–89), professor of theology at Göttingen from 1864, who, in his *magnum opus* entitled *Justification and Reconciliation* (1870–74), tried to show how God and the world were to be combined in an all-embracing system, thereby displaying the liberal quest for a unified vision of truth. At the same time he accepted the basic tenets of Kant's theory of knowledge, refusing to accept the possibility of any scientific demonstration of the truths of Christianity. Instead, faith was dependent upon a value-judgement whereby the believer was able to exercise dominion over the natural world.

Ritschl exerted a great deal of influence from the 1880s, with many of his followers refining his ideas but also criticizing his historical work. *Wilhelm Herrmann (1846–1922), for instance, maintained a similar sharp distinction between faith and knowledge. Unlike Ritschl, Herrmann moved towards a position of extreme dualism in which faith seemed to exert no influence over the world. *Adolf von Harnack (1851–1930),

perhaps the most important of the liberal Protestants, similarly sought a certainty of faith in the historical essence of Jesus' gospel, the 'infinite value of the human soul' (*What is Christianity?*, 1904, p. 51). While attracting a vast readership both in Germany and beyond, such an approach was historically implausible and little more than a vague pietism.

Other theologians retained Ritschl's unified vision of religion and ethics but took modernity far more seriously. *Ernst Troeltsch (1865–1923), for instance, suggested that modernity placed such constraints on traditional Christianity that Christianity itself would have to change to remain a potent force. This apparent compromise of Christianity with modernity led critics to label such theology 'culture Protestantism'. This is, however, misleading: most liberal theologians displayed a critical engagement with modernity rather than any religious legitimation of the prevailing culture. Indeed, despite its frequent compromises, German liberal Protestantism, with its integrated vision of church and society united in accord with enlightened principles, functioned as one of the most important channels of opposition in an authoritarian society.

America. The fate of liberal Protestantism was different still in the United States. Liberalism posed far less of a threat to the established order than it would otherwise have done after the official political ideology had embraced the principles of the Enlightenment. However, the rigid separation of church and state had led to a 'private Protestantism' (Martin E. Marty, *Religious Empire: The Protestant Experience in America* [New York, 1970], pp. 177–87), relegating religion to the sphere of individual piety. Towards the end of the nineteenth century there was an increasing dissatisfaction with this approach. Theologians began to relate Christianity to modernity in several seminaries, most importantly in Andover, Massachusetts, which saw the rise of the so-called 'progressive Orthodoxy' (1885). Despite frequent controversy, a moderate liberalism which sought to embrace human reason and a scientific study of history spread throughout the country after the 1880s. The influential Union Theological Seminary in New York, for instance, came under the control of liberals such as A.C. McGiffert (1861–1933) and William Adams Brown (1865–1943). The latter's *Christian Theology in Outline* (1906), greatly influenced by Ritschl, represents a synthesis of liberal theology, emphasizing religious experience and the quest for an essential Christianity purged of dogmatic accretion.

Most important in the success of liberalism, however, was the new Divinity School at Chicago (1895) which was established on the principle of a close interaction between sociology, ethics and theology, where theory and practice were related in the attempt to ameliorate social problems. Instead of merely reproducing the traditional theological seminary, the Divinity School was guided by the study of sociology as the discipline best suited for equipping ministers for their tasks. Under the influence of Shailer Mathews (1865–1941), dean of the school from 1908–33, theology came to rely no longer on its own peculiar method but had to some extent to adopt the method of the social scientists. Reacting against his pietist upbringing, he looked for a new method which took society seriously. Mathews claimed to derive the ethical ideal of social individuality from the teachings of a Christ viewed as the proto-sociologist: it was Jesus himself who legitimized the fraternal goals of an ameliorative sociology. Later, the Chicago socio-historical school under Shirley Jackson Case (1872–1947) sought to carry out sociological investigations into biblical texts, viewing them chiefly as products of their environment.

Professor *Walter Rauschenbusch (1861–1918) at Rochester Theological Seminary moved in a similar direction, influenced by Ritschl and Harnack. He formulated an explicitly social gospel which focused on the kingdom of God 'as a great synthesis in which the regeneration of the spirit, the enlightenment of the intellect, the development of the body, the reform of the political life, the sanctification of industrial life and all that concerns the redemption of humanity shall be embraced' (*Selected Writings* [New York, 1984], p. 76). Like other liberals, Rauschenbusch, who was prepared to engage in the detailed study of economics and sociology, sought after the unity of thought and action in a synthesis aimed at social and political regeneration.

Conclusion. What these three examples from around the world reveal is that, although there were significant differences, there were nevertheless unifying threads in liberal Protestantism. In general, liberals sought to include theology within the broader sphere of scientific and critical knowledge, but they sought to do so with the wider aim of re-shaping society in accordance with a rational end. Liberal Protestantism was thus the public theology *par excellence*.

While never ceasing to exert an important influence in the mainline denominations, liberal Protestantism has nevertheless been in decline since its heyday at the beginning of the twentieth century. World War I, with its shattering of optimism, was of decisive importance in this decline. In Germany, theology gradually began to distance itself from the public debate and to retreat into its own sphere. The concept of a pluralist public realm vanished as Protestant theologians, including many liberals, either gave up the search of a mutually shared public truth altogether or fell victim to totalitarianism. In England, where the effects of the war were less catastrophic, liberalism was infected by theological insularity. Particularly within the Church of England, liberal Protestantism tended (with notable exceptions) towards a theological amateurism often unaware of developments elsewhere, epitomized by the anti-ritualist mathematician-bishop, E.W. Barnes (1874–1953). Liberal Protestantism's influence was frequently eclipsed by a more catholic-minded theology chiefly concerned with specific issues in ecclesiology. In the United States, liberal Protestantism similarly declined during the 1920s and 1930s, particularly after the Depression. Partly under the influence of the continental *dialectical theologians, many erstwhile liberals reinvigorated orthodox teaching on sin, thereby questioning the optimism of the social gospel and its idealization of the liberal American ideology. Most important among these was Reinhold Niebuhr (1892–1971). Others, however, sought refuge in a conservatism which refused even to engage with modern culture. With the demise of liberal Protestantism, academic theology has become ever more distant from the secular university and from public life. Whether this distance will render theology increasingly irrelevant in public discourse is a matter of some importance for the future of the discipline.

MARK D. CHAPMAN

FURTHER READING: C.H. Arnold, *Near the Edge of Battle* (Chicago, 1966); K. Cauthen, *The Impact of American Religious Liberalism* (Lanham, MD, 1962); K.W. Clements, *Lovers of Discord* (London, 1988); W.R. Hutchinson (ed.), *American Protestant Thought*

In Latin America in recent years Liberation Theology has addressed the question of the practice of popular religion, and in particular the Pentecostal and charismatic groups. Although the progressive elements of the historic churches have opted for the poor, the poor apparently have opted for these new churches. Some from within the Liberation Theology movement have criticized unrealistic talk about the vision of a new society. They are now asking whether socialism was ever a historical option for Latin America in the early 1970s. Many of the poor, particularly women, are asking how faith can sustain them in the daily struggle for survival and in their resistance to discrimination in all its forms. In other parts of the world, the question of alliances with people of other faiths in the struggle to overcome violence is an important question. In yet others, truth and reconciliation in the return to democracy after brutal dictatorships is the main issue. Some theologians, after the end of the Communist system, are turning to the apocalyptic writings of the Judeo-Christian tradition to find ways of interpreting theologically the total, closed 'empire' of global capitalism and western culture.

Conclusion. Liberation Theology marks the beginning of an epoch in which the church of the south has asserted its independence from the predominant theologies of the North Atlantic. It has demonstrated the latter's cultural and social biases and, therefore, limitations, and has called into question its pretensions to be a universal theology. It has explored systematically the relationship between theoretical thinking and concrete action, between social analysis and theological reflection and between the faith of the church based on the Bible and its structures and practices. It makes the claim that what the church does is a surer indication of what it believes than what it says. It has restored a prophetic-critical dimension to theology, quite different from either the sceptical tradition of post-Enlightenment theology or the 'fideism' of post-liberal theology in Europe and North America.

Liberation Theology could be criticized for a too selective approach to the Bible. In particular, it has been noted how little the theology of Paul and the epistles features in comparison with the Gospels and prophetic books. There has been a tendency to minimize the personal element of faith in Jesus Christ and to maximize the social

and political dimensions of Christ's death. Thus, evil in the world is seen more in terms of the injustices of a collective system and the idolatries of power structures than of the intrinsic sinful nature of human beings in rebellion against the God who created, sustains and loves them. Without a return to the complete gospel of the New Testament, neither Liberation Theology nor any other theology will account for the failure of projects for social change, the uninhibited spread of an alienating economic system or the turning to new religions and spiritualities, nor will it be able to supply the tools to sustain people's trust in God for the future.

J. Andrew Kirk

FURTHER READING: Gustavo Gutiérrez, *A Theology of Liberation: History, Politics and Salvation* (London, 1974); Curt Cadorette, Marie Giblin, Marilyn Legge and Mary Snyder (eds.), *Liberation Theology: An Introductory Reader* (Maryknoll, NY, 1992); Juan Luis Segundo, *Signs of the Times* (Maryknoll, NY, 1993); Jon Sobrino and Ignacio Ellacuria (eds.), *Systematic Theology: Perspectives from Liberation Theology* (London, 1996); James Massey, *Down Trodden: The Struggle of India's Dalits for Identity, Solidarity and Liberation* (Geneva, 1997); Chris Rowland and John Vincent (eds.), *Liberation Theology UK* (Sheffield, 1995).

Lidgett, John Scott (1854–1953)

Born on 10 August 1854 into middle-class London Wesleyanism – his grandfather, John Scott, was principal of Westminster College – he was a BA and MA of University College, London in logic and philosophy by the age of twenty-one. Accepted for the Wesleyan Methodist ministry, he was tutored by William Burt Pope (1822–1903), the leading Methodist systematic theologian, instrumental in altering the Wesleyan Catechism from 'What is God – an infinite and eternal Spirit' to 'Who is God – our Father'. Pope insisted that 'Christ is not the Substitute of God in atonement but his Representative; and not otherwise our Substitute than as our Representative also' (*The Person of Christ*, 1875, p. 51). Here was Lidgett's theological agenda.

After 15 years in Methodist circuits, urged on by W.F. Moulton, Lidgett pioneered the Bermondsey Settlement, on the pattern of Toynbee Hall, where he remained from 1891–1946.

Scott Lidgett, who has been called the greatest Methodist since *John Wesley, claimed that his many interests in education, mission alongside the poor, ecumenism and politics, stemmed from his theology.

His systematic theology emerges in five books – *The Spiritual Principle of the Atonement* (1897), thought at first dangerous by some Wesleyans; *The Fatherhood of God* (1902); *The Christian Religion, its Meaning and Proof* (1907) and later two theological commentaries on Ephesians and Hebrews, *God in Christ Jesus* (1915) and *Sonship and Salvation* (1921). Lidgett sees God's sovereignty expressed in his fatherhood – Victorian fatherhood. His Wesleyan stress on the doctrine of universal love merges with *F.D. Maurice's assertion of Christ as the head of humanity. His doctrine of the atonement moves on from that of W.B. Pope and *R.W. Dale (1829–95). Christ's absolute filial obedience to the Father is the key. This is not a 'moral influence' theory but it avoids the harshness of some transactional theories. It must be admitted that, though linking with the thinking of *Charles Gore and *A.M. Fairbairn, his style is ponderous, with relentless detail compared with *P.T. Forsyth or *R.C. Moberly. His vision of salvation builds on John Wesley's doctrine of Christian perfection, seeing the whole of life as redeemable – the world of politics as well as the world of the church.

The Christian Religion takes the argument into a more apologetic style, reflecting the challenge of immanentalist theories (the *New Theology* of *R.J. Campbell was contemporary), of evolution and the great religions. The climax of the argument is, again, fatherhood. 'All that God is or can be to men throughout the whole of their life-history, as Creator, Sustainer, Redeemer, Sovereign, Judge – all that He can manifest to them as gracious and merciful, righteous or wrathful, springs out of and fulfils the meaning of the all–comprehending relationship of fatherhood' (p. 509). The two biblical expositions are notable, if rather stolid. Ephesians was always central to Lidgett's theology. Phrases like the 'Divine Commonwealth' anticipate C.H. Dodd, the exposition of 'sonship' in the book on Hebrews reflects a Methodist stress on 'adoption' which is typical of Lidgett. *God, Christ and the Church* (1928) and *God and the World* (1943) contain shorter articles illustrating more briefly the basic themes of the major works.

Theology and life, reflection and action were one for the immensely active Scott Lidgett. He was editor of the *Methodist Times* from 1907–18 and joint editor and frequent writer in the *Contemporary Review*. A liberal of Gladstonian persuasion, modified by T.H. Green's assertion that the state should 'remove hindrances to freedom', he served on the London County Council, being leader of the Progressives from 1918–28. He was involved at every level of education, culminating in the vice-chancellorship of London University from 1930–32. His support of Free Church unity led to him being president (1906) and moderator (1923–25) of the National and Federal Councils of the Free Churches. Election as president of the Wesleyan Methodist Conference in 1908 led to him playing a crucial theological role, with Professor A.S. Peake, in the union of the three major branches of Methodism which finally took place in 1932 and over which he presided in that year. The important doctrinal clauses of the Deed of Union bear Lidgett's stamp, asserting Methodism's catholicity. The Companionship of Honour followed the reception of an Oxford DD at that time.

Lidgett was a leading supporter of the Lambeth Appeal for reunion of 1920. 'Where there are no differences our watchword must be *union*; where they are comparatively slight *federation*; where they are more serious yet not destructive of the fundamental agreements of Christianity *co-operation* ...' (*Apostolic Ministry*, 1908, pp. 115–16). Catholicity was more than a mere catchword. *God, Christ and the Church* contains five major articles on this theme. Lidgett's two autobiographies, *Reminiscences* (1928) and *My Guided Life* (1936), contain astringent comment on theological and educational issues, as does his significant, if brief, *Victorian Transformation of Theology* (1934) which eulogizes Maurice as the most significant theologian of the previous century – showing, again, the importance of the change from sovereignty to fatherhood and the crucial role of the incarnation. His Beckly lecture *The Idea of God and Social Ideals* (1938) saw Lidgett at his more radical and most Methodist. 'That the relationship of God to mankind has come to be conceived of as that of universal Fatherhood is more directly due to the pervasive influence of Methodism than any other cause' (p. 83).

Later in life a series of short devotional works set out his view of the person and work of Christ. He died on 16 June 1953, aged ninety-eight, at Epsom.

Boyd Hilton, in his *The Age of Atonement* (Oxford, 1988), is right to stress the shift in Victorian theology from atonement to incarnation. In Methodism the two were held in tension by W.B. Pope, Lidgett and W.F. Lofthouse (1871–1965), whose *Ethics and Atonement* (1906) and *Altar, Cross and Community* (1921) develop Lidgett's position in a more radical direction with a stress on the effect of atonement in the community.

Scott Lidgett was still active after the Second World War, not fully retiring until 1948, but his theology was essentially late Victorian. It was evangelical *Arminianism tinged with the insights of Maurice and late-Victorian liberalism. His influence on 60 years of Methodist history was immense, even if his theology was not read much outside Methodist circles.

JOHN MUNSEY TURNER

FURTHER READING: R.E. Davies (ed.), *Scott Lidgett: A Symposium* (London, 1957), esp. E.G. Rupp, ch. 3; R.E. Davies, 'John Scott Lidgett: Architect and Man of the Match', *Meth Rec* 6608 (1984), p. 11; R.E. Davies, A.R. George and E.G. Rupp (eds.), *History of the Methodist Church in Great Britain*, III (London, 1983), esp. W. Strawson, ch. 4, 'Methodist Theology 1850–1950'; Maldwyn Edwards, *Methodism and England* (London, 1943), pp. 90–5; Graham Slater, 'William Burt Pope 1822–1903', *Epworth R* 15.2 (1988), pp. 59–66; William Strawson, 'W.F. Lofthouse 1871–1965', *Epworth R* 13.3 (1986), pp. 21–7.

Limborch, Philippus Van (1633–1712)

Born in Amsterdam and the son of a lawyer, Limborch was the great nephew of the famed Remonstrant theologian Simon Episcopius. He studied law at Leiden and Utrecht and then studied theology in Amsterdam under Vossius and Barlaeus. He pastored in Gouda and Amsterdam before becoming a professor of theology at the Remonstrant Seminary in Amsterdam in 1668. He held this position for 45 years, becoming the most prominent *Arminian theologian of his generation.

Limborch's major theological work was his *Theologia Christiana*, later translated into *A Compleat System*, or *Body of Divinity*. He also composed a biography of Episcopius and a brief history of the Synod of Dort. His correspondence with Isaac Orobio, a Jew from Spain who fled the Inquisition to settle in Amsterdam, was published as *De veritate religionis christianae, amica collatio cum erudito Judaeo*.

As a Remonstrant, Limborch opposed many aspects of *Reformed theology that he considered to be pernicious, especially the doctrines of predestination and reprobation. He also held to an 'evidential' approach to apologetics, rejecting *Calvin's interior witness of the Spirit. Fulfilled prophecy and biblical miracles served as primary evidences of the truth of the faith. He also argued for the historical accuracy of the New Testament based on the eyewitness testimony of the apostles.

Natural theology played a prominent role in Limborch's theological system, but he maintained the authority, infallibility and perspicuity of Scripture. All that we need to know for salvation, he argued, is clearly revealed in Scripture. He cautioned against what he considered to be the excessive creedalism of the Reformed movement, which he feared could lead to the authority of creeds and catechisms being asserted over that of the Bible. He also believed that the Reformed insistence on minor points of doctrine such as predestination served to divide rather than unify the body of Christ.

Limborch asserted that God first gave to man a law of nature that closely corresponds to the higher moral law of the New Testament. Man's intellect was not affected by the Fall, but man's will and disposition to be obedient to God was impaired. Limborch's elevation of the intellect contributes to his positive view of natural theology – so man, by use of reason, can discern much about God without the need to resort to biblical revelation. As a Remonstrant, Limborch was careful to protect the freedom of the will as well as divine sovereignty. He argued in favour of God's middle knowledge (*scientia media*) that came before God's free act of his divine will. According to this middle knowledge, God has perfect foreknowledge of future contingent events.

Limborch held strongly to the concept of religious toleration and expressed much affinity for the English Latitudinarian movement as well as the philosophy of *John Locke. He preferred a practical system of theology, which pointed the believer towards a moral life and ultimately towards union with God in the next life.

MARTIN I. KLAUBER

FURTHER READING: *Texts: Theologia Christiana ad praxim pietatis ac promotionem pacis christianae unicè directa* (Amsterdam, 1686), ET: *A Compleat System, or Body of Divinity* (trans. William Jones; 2 vols.; London, 1702, 1713); *De veritate religionis christianae, amica collatio cum erudito Judaeo* (Gouda, 1687).

Locke, John (1632–1704)

According to Gilbert Ryle, 'It is not much of an exaggeration to say that one cannot pick up a sermon, a novel, a pamphlet or a treatise and be in any doubt, after reading a few lines, whether it was published before or after the publication of Locke's *Essay on Human Understanding*, which was in 1690. The intellectual atmosphere since Locke has had quite a different smell from what it had before Locke'('John Locke', in *Critica* 1.2 [1967], p. 3). Locke is commonly credited with having laid the foundations of the empiricist tradition in philosophy. Empiricists have held that knowledge comes to us through sense perception, though that does not necessarily mean – and did not in the case of Locke mean – that it is confined to what the senses perceive. Locke worked this out principally in the *Essay* to which Ryle refers. However, the work's attempt to see what our understanding could and could not handle originated in discussion of the principles of morality and revealed religion and Locke's closing brief treatment of faith and reason is of importance not just for his philosophy of religion, but for his overall enterprise. In these chapters, Locke distinguished between propositions derived from reason and propositions derived from revelation. The latter are apprehended by faith. But even where reason can not deduce the propositions that faith receives from revelation, it must nevertheless test the claim that such propositions are indeed revealed and refuse to accept anything which (1) contradicts what it knows, (2) is unintelligible or (3) shows no evidence that it has truly come from God. Locke sought to avoid the extremes of rejecting anything which was deemed 'above reason' and of denying that reason had any role to play in religious knowing. Roughly speaking, this amounted to the rejection of the *deist and the 'enthusiastic' positions.

How successful Locke was in this enterprise is a matter of debate. Several recent or contemporary theologians, including *Thomas Torrance, Colin Gunton and *Lesslie Newbigin, hold that Locke played a fatal role in the development of western thought by making faith subordinate to reason, thus reversing the sounder *Augustinian notion that faith is the basis of understanding, and inaugurating a typical *Enlightenment and post-Enlightenment tendency to confine faith to the sphere of opinion, while reason is paraded as a source of knowledge. This judgement is at least questionable. In *The Reasonableness of Christianity*, written in 1695 and followed by lengthy *Vindications*, Locke sought to show that belief that Jesus is the Messiah is sufficient for salvation, if accompanied by repentance. Such a proposition is received on faith, and faith is justified because Jesus gave miraculous evidence of his divine credentials. The different components that made up his moral teaching might in principle have been discovered independently, but only with exceeding difficulty and, taken in its entirety, his moral teaching never was. However, Locke does not always emphasize the weakness of natural light in this way, and his writings in social and political philosophy must be consulted to get the wider picture. These include influential treatises on social contract and government that limited the absolute authority of the monarch, and epistles on toleration. These writings must naturally be understood in their historical context. The Civil War of the seventeenth century was followed by the Stuart Restoration in 1660, but the advent of William of Orange in 1688 secured a Protestant succession to the throne of England which had been joined with that of Scotland in 1603. During this period, questions of political and religious settlement and political and religious authority were inextricably linked. Locke sought to offer a philosophical framework for religious belief and a generally philosophical, religious and moral framework for political society. Again, how successful he was is a matter of debate.

Locke worked as political secretary as well as occasional medical adviser to the first Earl of Shaftesbury and in this capacity served in exile in the Netherlands as well as in his native England. He can be viewed either as generally conservative or radical in his religious convictions, or as a mixture of both. In any assessment, one must remember the way in which contemporaries would have understood his words in a context where the expression of religious opinion had to be more guarded than it does in contemporary democracies. Locke's influence extended to the political, religious and philosophical thought of both what became the United States and the continent of Europe. His grounding of knowledge and opinion in sense perception encouraged many to go much further than Locke had done and arrive either at sceptical conclusions about the knowability of anything beyond the bounds of the senses, or at a materialist philosophy which regarded thought as a function of matter. Scepticism could lead to practical atheism; materialism was a (possibly *the*) major tributary of theoretical atheism in the modern world, mediated particularly through the radical wing of the French Enlightenment.

Today, Locke's religious thought in particular appears to many largely outmoded, allegedly operating with a pre-critical view of Scripture and a mistaken concept of universal and natural reason. But his influence remains, and his attempts to combine more traditional religious views with a world-view owing much to the general advance of the sciences may yet turn out to be interesting in the future.

STEPHEN WILLIAMS

FURTHER READING: Clarendon Press (Oxford) has reproduced many of Locke's works under the general editorship of Peter Nidditch, who himself edited the *Essay on Human Understanding* (1975). V. Chappell (ed.), *Cambridge Companion to John Locke* (Cambridge, 1994). Very general introductions are furnished by J. Yolton, *Locke: An Introduction* (Oxford, 1985) and J. Dunn, *Locke* (Oxford, 1984). On his religious thought, see W.M. Spellman, *John Locke and the Problem of Depravity* (Oxford, 1988) and Alan P.F. Sell, *John Locke and the Eighteenth-Century Divines* (Cardiff, 1997). For biography see Maurice Cranston, *John Locke: A Biography* (Oxford, 1985).

Logical Positivism

Logical Positivism is the name given to a movement in analytic philosophy which began in Europe in the early part of the twentieth century. Also known as 'logical empiricism', this movement is associated with the work of the so-called 'Vienna Circle', headed by Moritz Schlick (1882–1936). Members of the Circle, and like-minded philosophers such as A.J. Ayer, spread the doctrines of Logical Positivism throughout the world. Members of the Circle also eventually left Vienna for England and America because of World War II (the most influential being R. Carnap [1891–1970]). With its similarity to the 'logical atomism' of Bertrand Russell, and some elements of the early thought of *Ludwig

Wittgenstein, Logical Positivism of various sorts dominated English-speaking philosophy for much of this century.

The tenets of Logical Positivism can be gained from the manifesto of the Vienna Circle, 'The Scientific World Outlook' (1929, in Neurath, 1973): (1) Scientism. Science is the best, or only, form of rational knowledge. (2) Logical analysis. The new formal logic, developed by G. Frege, B. Russell and A.N. Whitehead, is a pure instrument to analyze the often confusing and ambiguous sentences of natural language. (3) The verification principle. The meaning of a proposition is its means of verification. In other words, a sentence expresses a meaningful idea (statement, proposition) if, and only if: (a) it is true or false by logical factors alone (a tautology, an analytic statement); or, (b) it can be verified by sensory experience. (4) The unity of science. Since observable things are the only basis for rational knowledge (apart from mathematics and logic), natural and social science must progress toward a pure, scientific language which will describe all true facts about the world. It was the avowed purpose of this movement to sweep all metaphysical claims from the field of rational knowledge. These last two points (3 and 4) were not held by Russell or Wittgenstein, but they are characteristic of the Vienna Circle. An English version of the teachings of the Vienna Circle was published by A.J. Ayer as *Language, Truth and Logic* (1936) – a very popular and influential work.

The Vienna Circle began with a *neo-Kantian philosophy and a strong sense that only a scientific philosophy can bring reform and regulation to the current crisis in Europe. The implications of the verification criterion for meaning were vast and sweeping. The so-called truths of ethics, metaphysics and theology alike were, on this principle, neither true nor false, but simply meaningless. Since moral, metaphysical and religious statements are not verifiable through sense experience, and they are not true by logic alone, they cannot be meaningful. While not all analytic philosophers from 1930–60 (the heyday of Logical Positivism) would accept every tenet of the Vienna Circle's sweeping program, the general issue of how religious language could possibly be meaningful (much less true!) was pressed hard by analytic philosophers. While not all analytic philosophers would accept the verification principle (which was subject to serious criticism), they were quite empiricist in their thinking. How could theologians and believing philosophers respond to this claim? A.N. Flew, among others, pressed this problem in a very influential book of readings exploring the meaning of the new logical empiricism for theology. 'What would have to occur or to have occurred to constitute for you a disproof of the love of, or the existence of, God?' (Flew followed a 'falsification' version of the verification principle, i.e., an empirical sentence is meaningful if, and only if, it can be falsified by experience).

As a generalization we can say that analytic philosophy of religion began as a response to the challenge of Logical Positivism. Some theologians simply ignored the problem, seeing it as a technical difficulty of no lasting importance, or simply irrelevant to theology. This was, in fact, not the case. The Logical Positivists raised an important issue: how shall we understand religious language? The issue of the empirical foundations of religious language, especially the meaningfulness of that language as well as its truth or falsity, and the various uses that religious symbols, rules, statements and prayers are put to, is an important problem which theology should not ignore. A second possibility was to accept the verification criterion, or something like it, yet still reinterpret religion so as to make it meaningful. This usually led to some kind of behavioural interpretation of religion which reduced it to ethics. *J. Hick, however, argued that religious language is 'verified' in the next life, a view few accepted. A third position was to insist that the methods of Logical Positivism were fine for factual knowledge, but to insist also that belief in God is not a simple matter of empirical fact. Faith involves seeing the world in a certain way, they would argue, and living life in the light of that viewpoint. Ian T. Ramsey was an early exponent of this latter move. Such a response was made much more plausible with the growth of Wittgenstein's later philosophy of language. Because he was very critical of his own early work (and that of Logical Positivists), and because he grounded meaning in use, 'language-games' and 'forms of life', it was possible to see religious beliefs, language and practices as part of a meaningful 'language-game' like other human pursuits. D.Z. Phillips makes a good example of this Wittgensteinian move (in Mitchell, 1971). A further response was to loosen the strictness of the verification principle to allow some room for both metaphysics and theology, while accepting the general empiricist challenge to provide evidence for theism. This response came from philosophers influenced by traditional Christian philosophy, such as F.C. Copleston, *E.L. Mascall and *Austin Farrer, and from process theologians like C. Hartshorne. They insisted that religious language was meaningful, responding to an empiricist philosophy of language. They also developed more clear and precise arguments for the existence of God. R. Swinburne later provided an ample expression of this position. Fourth, and finally, the eventual demise of Logical Positivism in mid-century opened the door to completely new epistemologies within analytic circles. No dominant school since the Positivists has arisen. This situation allowed Christian philosophers such as Alvin Plantinga to propose epistemologies much more friendly to religious belief. While Logical Positivism as a movement is over, its concerns and questions are with us still.

ALAN G. PADGETT

FURTHER READING: A.J. Ayer, *Language, Truth and Logic* (London, 1936); A.J. Ayer (ed.), *Logical Positivism* (Glencoe, IL, 1959); F.C. Copleston, *Contemporary Philosophy* (London, 1956); A. Flew and A. MacIntyre (eds.), *New Essays in Philosophical Theology* (London, 1955); J. Joergensen, *The Development of Logical Empiricism* (Chicago, 1951); Victor Kraft, *The Vienna Circle* (New York, 1953); Basil Mitchell (ed.), *Philosophy of Religion* (London, 1971); Otto Neurath, *Empiricism and Sociology* (Dordrecht, 1973); Hans Reichenbach, *The Rise of Scientific Philosophy* (Berkeley, 1951); Bertrand Russell, *Mysticism and Logic* (New York, 1918).

Lombard, Peter (c. 1095/1100–1160)

Peter Lombard is a significant figure in the history of the development of theology, yet he is poorly known and misunderstood. In spite of his very popular and enduring work, the *Sentences*, and his remarkable rise through the ecclesial hierarchy, no contemporary or disciple ever wrote about him. Moreover, aside from his exegetical and theological works, there is scant material to draw on which could help to illumine our understanding, as a discrepancy of five years in his date of birth shows. In fact, beyond identifying the region of Navara, the place of Lombard's birth remains a mystery. This enigmatic personality, in combination with the perceived lack of originality in his works, has caused many scholars to dismiss Lombard's contribution to theology as a relatively unimportant part of *Scholasticism.

The problem with this assessment of Lombard is that it fails to account adequately for his contemporaries' and colleagues' high esteem of his life and works. *Bernard of Clairvaux, for instance, bears witness in his letters to Lombard's promise as a scholar and a theologian. It was for this reason that Bernard sent Lombard to Paris: so that an already keen intellect could be given the best theological training. Lombard did not disappoint; within ten years of arriving at Rheims he was described as one of the celebrated theologians of the church. No small accolade for anyone, but this is brought into sharper relief when one considers that this was in comparison to some of the brightest minds in Europe. Before examining Lombard's theology in more detail it is also worth mentioning his appointment as canon at Notre Dame. This is a significant development in Lombard's life because it was exceedingly unusual at this time for anyone to become a canon at Notre Dame unless they were members of, or closely linked to, the Capetian line. Lombard did not fall into either category. The only other probable reason for his appointment was that he stood out as a promising theologian with an impressive intellect. If, then, we take these appraisals of Lombard's ability seriously, perhaps a closer examination of his literary legacy is not entirely unfitting.

When looking at the order of Lombard's writings the first thing we notice is that he wrote exegetical works before he wrote theological treatises. This is an instructive fact, for so often Lombard is associated solely with his much later work, the *Sentences*, without any reference to or consideration of the groundwork that was laid in his biblical commentaries (glosses). Indeed, even at the end of his life, we discover that Lombard's library consisted mainly of commentaries on books of the Bible. What is remarkable about these commentaries is that, at least with respect to their form, they look very much like modern commentaries. Lombard was in the habit of quoting the sentence or section of the relevant book before commenting on it. This was not the usual procedure for twelfth-century commentators. Many commentators of this period summarized, in one way or another, the text under examination and expected the reader to be able either to remember the appropriate passage or have the Bible (or other reference material) at hand. Lombard's practice, therefore, marked a shift in pedagogy. Lombard had begun to include enough material that the reader would have most of what he needed contained in one work. Sound pedagogical procedures were not, however, the only way in which Lombard's early works affected his later theology. The most important aspect of Lombard's commentaries is that they show us that he did not lecture or write on doctrines *per se* until he had given due attention to exegesis.

And yet, we would be remiss if we did not note that even in his exegetical works Lombard wrestled with other authors. Furthermore, we cannot neglect the fact that as much as Lombard's early exegetical work influenced and informed his later theology (e.g. his *Sentences* and *Homilies*), he did alter his views over time. Any number of examples could be used to demonstrate this, but Lombard's theory of the atonement will have to suffice.

In Lombard's commentary on Romans he states that while God could have saved humanity in some other way, the way God chose to act was most fitting (a position he reiterates in other commentaries). What strikes the reader first about this position is that Lombard cites *Augustine and *Ambrose in support, but he does not mention *Anselm. Anselm was, after all, the most recent and forceful proponent of this imputation interpretation of the atonement. In addition, it is interesting that Lombard should choose to describe God's activity in the way Anselm did by referring to fittingness. Nevertheless, Lombard clearly allied himself with a more objective view of the atonement. In his *Sentences*, however, Lombard adopts an Abelardian stance and argues that in so far as one mimics and appropriates the ethical purity exemplified in Christ's life, redemption is made possible. Like *Peter Abelard, Peter Lombard understood love as the true motivation for right action and the power that can turn sinners away from their sins. In Lombard's conception Christ's death is not necessary in the light of his life, but it is still instructive as it demonstrates the extent of the love that Christ's sacrifice demands of us. Consequently, Lombard aligned himself later with a more subjective view of the atonement.

While Lombard's opinion on this and other matters changed over time (in the case of the atonement, change would have been difficult to resist since Abelard's ideas were well circulated and defended during this period), what remained constant was his continual integration and evaluation of accepted authorities with scriptural passages. In other words, although the conclusions Lombard reached on any given doctrine were open to change, his theological method was preserved. Lombard's chief concern was that the process of discerning doctrines should begin with scriptural exegesis elucidated by authoritative commentators, and that it should be finally established by a judicious application of reason and thoughtfulness. Thus, even in his *Sentences*, Lombard makes numerous references back to earlier works of exegesis. The modern scholar should, therefore, take care to distinguish between earlier and later works and the developments in them, but he or she should not divide Lombard's works in such a way that their interrelation is ignored.

To be sure, the conclusions Lombard reached on matters of doctrine were rarely momentous, but his command of the scholarship of his day and his ability to integrate it with careful exegesis to produce texts which met pedagogic exigencies for hundreds of years should surely qualify him as a theologian worthy of attention.

DAVID S. HOGG

FURTHER READING: *Text: Sententiae in IV Libris Distinctae* (ed. Ignatius C. Brady; 2 vols.; Grottaferrata, 3rd rev. edn, 1971–81); Marcia Colish, *Peter Lombard* (New York, 1994); J. de Ghellinck, 'Pierre Lombard', in *DTC* 12, cols. 1941–2019; G.R. Evans, *Old Arts and New Theology* (Oxford, 1980); M.-D. Chenu, *La Théologie au Douzième Siècle* (Paris, 1957).

Lonergan, Bernard (1904–84)

Bernard Lonergan was born in Buckingham, Quebec on 17 December 1904. He entered the *Society of Jesus on 29 July 1922, and he was ordained priest on 23 July 1936. He taught at the Society's English Canadian theologate, at Rome's Gregorian University, and, from 1964 until his death on 26 November 1984, at various North American institutions.

Although Lonergan exercised no direct influence on *Vatican II, his studies of *Aquinas and the philosophical bases of modern science had immense influence on Catholic theology. Methodology remained his lifelong interest, but his treatises on the Trinity and the incarnate Word

are masterpieces of dogmatic speculation. Lonergan's doctoral thesis, *Grace and Freedom* (New York, 1981), tackled the problem of grace's causality. He pictured creation as a network of natures and causal series set in motion by God. Men's wills are moved by their intellects which are bound to phantasms presenting the circumstances and ideas of culture, thereby forming an objective *Geist*. Except for sin, a 'non-act', man's acts would be determined. But sin disrupted the universe's unity and *Geist*. Since adequate reflection before all free acts is impossible and the matter-spirit tension renders failures probable, only special actual graces can prevent human sin – even if man is theoretically free in every act. When Christ entered this fallen world he established a new causal series, the church, and an absolute *Geist*, as the norm of thought and action. Correspondence between these external 'premotions' and grace's internal premotions assures God's purpose.

Within that objective schema Lonergan analyzed human knowing. *Verbum* (Notre Dame, 1967) studies Aquinas's doctrine of the interior word, the act of understanding which provides the analogy for the Word's eternal procession from the Father. Understanding resides in a double insight into the phantasm previous to conceptualization. Understanding answers the question *what* the phantasm is, and in judgement it weighs objective evidence to answer *whether* it is. Judgement involves critical self-awareness and possesses the truth through which reality is both known and known to be known. Its self-transcendence moves the intellect to God as uncreated light in which it participates. Knowing thus involves movement among God, knower and known external reality. Through its reflective synthesis, which unifies self, concept, sensibility and existential reference, judgement avoids an infinite regress in the quest for truth.

Insight (New York, 1957) confronts the epistemological problems of modern physics. Is reality grasped by the senses or by theoretical reconstructions? Are quantum mechanics' statistical probabilities or classical physics' universal, invariant laws ultimate? Distinctions are necessary: between common sense knowledge and science, as between description (things known in relation to us) and explanation (things known in themselves). A preconceptual insight releases the invariant function from experience to establish a primitive circle of terms (concepts) and relations: 'the terms fix the relations, the relations fix the terms, and the insight fixes both'. Thus scientific truth refers primarily to theoretical constructions known in judgement. 'Inverse insight' recognizes when empirical evidence contains no special intelligibility. Their condition of possibility is the 'empirical residue', or the empirical data without immanent intelligibility but which is linked to a higher intelligibility. Research studies this 'non-systematic manifold' to derive statistical laws that yield to classical laws. The latter provide parameters within which new statistical laws are recognized. Thus arise 'schemes of emergent probabilities' that provide ever higher viewpoints, from which a reconciliation of physical theories may be attained. Besides theories are 'things', that is unities, identities, wholes grasped initially in data as individual. A 'thing' is not independent of the knower but is real as verified by experience, insight and judgement. Judgement reveals an underlying pure, detached, disinterested desire to know which goes beyond all revisable theories to grasp a virtually unconditioned (which 'involves three elements, namely: (1) a conditioned, (2) a link between the conditioned and its conditions, and (3) the fulfillment of the conditions' [*Insight*, p. 280]). Judgements are revisable, but, as relevant questions dry up, they become invulnerable and approach the limit of certitude. Hence true judgements are possible and allow the knower to affirm himself.

Since the real is what is affirmed, *Insight* develops an epistemological metaphysics. Being, anticipatively grasped in judgement, extends beyond the actually known and is what is to be known by the totality of true judgements, that is, by the complete set of answers to the complete set of questions. The unrestricted desire to know all reveals the structure of proportionate being and drives beyond all central and conjugate forms (cognitional equivalents of substantial and accidental forms) to Subsistent Understanding, who comprehends all – even contingency. Alongside this natural drive for the beatific vision, Lonergan retains the validity of concepts and postulates a propositional supernatural revelation tied to the church (Cosmopolis) to respond to the problem of evil.

God, known as Subsistent Understanding, undergirds Trinitarian and Christological doctrine. The first divine procession is conceived analogously to the judgement with which the human mind is identical and distinct in self-consciousness. The Spirit is proceeding love, identically the divine act of love. Thus the divine nature's operations ground personal distinction. 'Person', defined as 'distinct subsistent in an intellectual nature' is applied to Trinitarian subsistent relation and Christology. The person of the Word is a complete being in two incomplete beings, the divine *esse* and human nature. The human nature, with its subordinate *esse*, depends on the divine *esse* just as an ultimate disposition depends on a form's acceptance. The Word knows himself as God's natural Son through the human nature's operation (beatific vision). Knowing himself as God directly and through his human nature, he is one conscious person in two consciousnesses.

After 1964 Lonergan gradually abandoned 'faculty psychology', or analyzing human action in terms of intellect and will, in favour of 'intentionality analysis', or concentrating on the unified subject of knowing and loving. *Method in Theology* (New York, 1972) adapts *Insight*'s four levels of intentionality: empirical (gathering data), intellectual (seeking intelligibility), rational (true judgements) and responsible (action and value). Along them the spirit spontaneously advances in self-transcendence to intellectual, moral and religious conversions. Religious conversion, understood as unreservedly falling in love, culminates the hierarchy of intentionalities. Faith occurs in response to God's love and finds expression in various religious traditions. In Judaeo-Christian tradition the exterior word corresponds to the interior word of God; both attain their peak in the incarnation. Lonergan reverses the priority of knowing over loving (once determinant for the order of Trinitarian processions) and places 'faith' before propositional 'beliefs'. Doing theology involves eight functional specialties. Four 'field specialties' correspond to the four levels of intentionality: research, interpretation, history and dialectics. They lead to conversion. Thereafter theology develops four 'subject specialties' which reflect the same intentionality levels in reverse order: foundations, doctrines, systematics and communications. No mechanical task, theology depends on the theologian's authentic conversion.

Though his earlier works manifest greater speculative genius, Lonergan's later works dealing with hermeneutical questions draw more attention. The distinctions between experience and conceptual expressions as those between faith and beliefs place Lonergan in the same intellectual quagmire as Heidegger, Gadamer and *Ricoeur: how can the finite knower attain an absolute standpoint guaranteeing knowledge? Though Lonergan always resisted *Modernism, accepted ecclesial dogmas and upheld conceptual knowledge, his final writings reveal the tensions between concept and judgement, essential and existential orders, and nature and grace, which he balanced more successfully in his earlier writings.

JOHN M. McDERMOTT, SJ

FURTHER READING: *Texts: De Constitutione Christi Ontologica et Psychologica* (Rome, 2nd edn, 1958); *De Deo Trino* (2 vols.; London, 3rd edn, 1964); *De Verbo Incarnato* (Rome, 3rd edn, 1964); *Collection* (New York, 1967); *Method in Theology* (New York, 1972); *A Second Collection* (London, 1974); F. Crowe and R. Doran are editing a critical edn of Lonergan's *Collected Works. Studies:* P. McShane (ed.), *Foundations of Theology* (Notre Dame, 1972); J. McDermott, SJ, 'Tensions in Lonergan's Theory of Conversion', *Gr* 74 (1995), pp. 101–40; 'The Sacramental Vision of Lonergan's *Grace and Freedom*', *Sap* 50 (1995), pp. 115–48; J. Stebbins, *The Divine Initiative: Grace, World-order, and Human Freedom in the Early Writings of Bernard Lonergan* (Toronto, 1995); the magazine *Method* is devoted to publishing articles on Lonergan.

Lossky, Vladimir (1903–58)

Lossky, an exiled Russian intellectual, departed his homeland in 1922 and arrived in Paris in 1924, regarding it as his task to introduce the Russian philosophical/theological tradition to the west. He did so by pointing to all that was distinctive in the Eastern Orthodox tradition compared with its western counterpart. In interpreting orthodoxy to the west, Lossky both represented it and was critical of it, and he always stressed the underlying shared Christian tradition. He had an ambivalent relationship to *St Augustine, who developed the western tradition through his doctrine of the sinfulness of humanity and its consequence of inherited original sin. He found in *Meister Eckhart a mystic of the west who was yet close to the eastern tradition. Lossky published his final study on Eckhart in 1960 under the title *Théologie Négative et Connaissance de Dieu chez Maître Eckhardt*.

Lossky's own masterpiece of introduction to eastern thinking was, however, *Essai sur la Théologie Mystique de l'Église d'Orient* (Paris, 1944; ET *The Mystical Theology of the Eastern Church* [1957]). In two more works on the eastern tradition he extended and deepened his own esteem of his proper theological identity: *Vision de Dieu* (Paris, 1962) and *A l'Image et Ressemblance de Dieu* (Paris, 1967; ET *In the Image and Likeness of God* [1974]).

Lossky indicated in these three books his own Eastern Orthodox preferences. In *The Mystical Theology of the Eastern Church* he underlined that the whole salvatory function of Christ is deification/divinization. The 'Economy of the Son' is the centre of his entire presentation. On the one hand he stresses that Christ assumed our nature, and that this implied his voluntary submission to 'all the consequences of sin' and taking upon himself the responsibility for our error. This ended in the cross. But, on the other hand, Lossky sees the incorruptibility of our nature as having been revealed in the resurrection. Yet he underlines that this happens in the form of mystical union only, and this mystical union is, to him, communication through the 'uncreated energies' of the Holy Spirit – the doctrine first developed by *St Gregory Palamas. Lossky traced the presuppositions of Palamas already in the *Cappadocian Fathers, and found them clearly expressed in *St Maximus the Confessor. At this point Lossky met opposition from a number of western theologians. In *The Vision of God* Lossky pointed out that this vision among Christian mystics is Trinitarian. This fact implies that God is manifold, and yet unitary. The three aspects of divinity are 'personal', hypostatic, and this implies that the secret of 'Three-In-One' is basically a mystery of 'persons'. For the three persons are one and manifold at the same time.

In his book *In the Image and Likeness of God* Lossky explores the delicate problem of the 'theological notion of the human person'. Here he stresses, on the one hand, that the 'human person' coincides with the 'human individual'. On the other hand, however, we have to give a new sense to the term 'human person', for, according to the dogmatic statement of the Council of Chalcedon, the human person receives its individuality from its 'nature', so that these two coincide. That is, the individual transcends his particularity in being both an individual and essentially the same. In this context Lossky develops his understanding of Palamism as the logical outcome of patristic thinking on the deification of man.

Although sympathetic to many aspects of western spirituality Lossky always underlines basic differences between the Christian east and west. He goes so far as to say that 'the cult of the humanity of Christ' is foreign to the former, and that the way of imitation is never practised in the spiritual life of the east. Finally, of course, the proceeding of the Spirit within the Trinitarian unity is from the Father alone.

LARS THUNBERG

FURTHER READING: Texts: *Théologie Négative et Connaissance de Dieu chez Maître Eckhardt* (Paris, 1960); *The Mystical Theology of the Eastern Church* (London, 1957); *The Vision of God* (London, 1963); *In the Image and Likeness of God* (New York, 1974). *Studies:* Olivier Clément, *Orient-Occident. Deux Passeurs: Vladimir Lossky et Paul Eudokimov* (Geneva, 1985).

Lubac, Henri de (1896–1991)

French Roman Catholic theologian, born in Cambrai on 20 February 1896, died in Paris on 4 September 1991. After entering the Society of Jesus in 1913, he was mobilized in World War I and severely wounded in 1917. He then resumed his studies in England (1919–26), completed his theological training in Lyons, and was ordained to the priesthood in 1927. From 1929 to 1960, with some interruptions, he taught fundamental theology at the Catholic faculty of Lyons. His thinking on faith and reason was profoundly influenced by Maurice Blondel, Joseph Maréchal and *Pierre Rousselot. Appointed to a new chair for history of religions at Lyons in 1930, de Lubac developed a special interest in Buddhism and its relationship to Christianity.

De Lubac's first book, *Catholicism* (1938), celebrated the power of Catholic Christianity to transcend all human divisions and sought to substantiate this claim from many patristic texts. To promote familiarity with the Fathers, he and Jean Daniélou founded a collection of texts and translations in 1941, *Sources Chrétiennes*. In 1940 he was a co-founder of *Cahiers Clandestins du Témoignage Chrétienne*, underground publications that denounced the anti-Christian ideology of National Socialism.

De Lubac also collaborated in founding the collection *Théologie* for which he wrote two volumes: *Corpus mysticum* (1944), a study of the medieval theology of church and Eucharist, and his most famous work, *Surnaturel* (1946). In the latter he contended that human beings are created with an innate desire for a supernatural vision of God, which can only be received as a gift from God. His criticism of the appeal to 'pure nature' and 'natural beatitude' in *Cajetan, *Suárez and the Neo-Scholastics aroused accusations that he was advocating a 'new theology'. In fact, he was returning to the position of *Augustine, to which *Thomas Aquinas himself subscribed. After the encyclical 'Humani generis' (1950), the Superior General of the *Jesuits removed him and several other Jesuits from their teaching positions, but de Lubac continued to write on non-Christian religions, especially Amida Buddhism, which he viewed with respect but found deficient in comparison with Christianity.

In 1956 de Lubac was permitted to return to Lyons, where he began research for his major study *Exégèse Médiévale* (1959–64), a four-volume work in which he demonstrated the fruitfulness of the 'spiritual' interpretation of Scripture. Some exegetes accused him of neglecting the literal or historical sense of Scripture, but he maintained that the 'spiritual' sense, while going beyond the literal, does not negate the latter.

In 1960 Pope John XXIII appointed de Lubac a consultant for the preparations for *Vatican II. He then served as an expert at the council (1962–65), which in its teaching sustained many of his own positions, especially on Christology, revelation, non-Christian religions and missionary activity. At the council he developed a friendship with the future Pope John Paul II, who was to name him a cardinal in 1983.

In the early 1960s, at the request of the Superior General of the Jesuits, de Lubac composed several works to defend the substantial orthodoxy of his friend Pierre Teilhard de Chardin, who had died in 1955. These works helped to stave off a condemnation, which at the time seemed likely.

Fascinated by the problem of atheism, de Lubac wrote not only on Buddhism but also on modern European secular humanism. The atheistic humanists were correct, he believed, in rejecting certain naïve concepts of God, who far surpasses all human comprehension. Christian mysticism guards against idolatry and protects the divine transcendence by asserting the inadequacy of all human concepts of God. Mysticism, however, becomes inauthentic when it strives to dispense with God.

Having resigned from the editorial board of *Concilium* in 1965, in 1975 de Lubac took part in the foundation of a new international journal, *Communio*. In these years he opposed the tendency of some Catholics to be critical of Catholic tradition in the light of contemporary secularity. For de Lubac there could be no doubt about the uniqueness of Jesus Christ as universal redeemer and the necessity of the church as his instrument for the redemption of all. His ardent love of the church shines forth in many of his writings: *The Splendor of the Church* (1953), *The Church: Paradox and Mystery* (1967), and *The Motherhood of the Church* (1971).

In his study on *Particular Churches in the Universal Church* (1971), de Lubac cautioned against the excessive influence of national episcopal conferences, which some regarded as having doctrinal authority over diocesan bishops. In a 1980 essay 'The "Sacrament of the World?"' he sharply criticized *Edward Schillebeeckx for treating the world itself as 'implicit Christianity' and for maintaining that anyone struggling for a better world must be considered implicitly a Christian. For de Lubac, the mystery of salvation revealed in Christ comes to meet the individual through the mediation of the church, which is charged with bringing the light of Christ into a world that does not know him. But de Lubac continued to esteem all that was good and beautiful in the human person created in the image of God. He frequently quoted from *Irenaeus: 'The glory of God is the living human person, and the life of the human person is the vision of God' (*Heresies* 4.20.7).

In his autobiographical work *At the Service of the Church* (1991), de Lubac modestly summarized his achievement: 'Without claiming to open up new avenues to thought, I have sought rather, without any antiquarianism, to make known some of the great human areas of Catholic tradition. I wanted to make it loved, to show its ever-present fruitfulness' (p. 143). His works continue to ignite love for Christ and the church in the hearts of many readers.

AVERY DULLES, SJ

FURTHER READING: *Text: Oeuvres Complètes* (projected 50 vols.; Paris, 1998–). *Studies:* Hans Urs von Balthasar, *The Theology of Henri de Lubac* (San Francisco, 1991); Jean Pierre Wagner, *La Théologie Fondamentale selon Henri de Lubac* (Paris, 1997); Susan K. Wood, *Spiritual Exegesis and the Church in the Theology of Henri de Lubac* (Grand Rapids, 1998).

Luther, Martin (1483–1546)

The diverse symbolic roles which Martin Luther has played in subsequent religious and cultural history have ensured continuing controversy over the development, structure, content and significance of his theological teaching. Modern Protestant and Catholic interpretations have, for different purposes, tended to stress the novelty of his theology over against the previous doctrinal, spiritual and theological traditions of the church. While this vein of interpretation has by no means been exhausted, contemporary research is also bringing into focus the rich and subtle ways in which Luther's thought is embedded in wider traditions of Christian thought and practice.

Approach to theology. Luther's early thought (c. 1514–18) is marked by his struggle for a new form of theological discourse, centred in a close reading of Scripture and oriented towards the preaching and pastoral life of the church. Luther thus brought the concerns of medieval monastic theology (e.g. *Bernard of Clairvaux) and vernacular theology (e.g. Tauler and the *Theologia Germanica*) into the university context. Like Bernard, Luther criticized scholastic tendencies to treat the conceptual elaboration of Christian belief as an end in itself; the aim of theology is rather to bring the apostolic word to bear transformatively on human life, to rebuke and console the conscience, as well to reform and build up the church. Theology so conceived is the attempt to identify and learn to practise the *modus loquendi apostolicus*, the 'apostolic mode of discourse', the distinctive logic and grammar of gospel proclamation.

These concerns brought Luther into conversation with humanism, whose hermeneutical organon he substantially appropriated. Yet despite his scorching attacks on the scholastic 'sophists', in some ways he remained more closely bound to the scholastic tradition than many of his contemporaries. While he collaborated with *Philip Melanchthon in the humanist reorganization of studies at Wittenberg, he never ceased to make creative use of the sophisticated analytical techniques acquired in his *Ockhamist schooling, putting the logical tools of *Scholasticism in service to the rhetorical and pastoral goals of the monastic and vernacular traditions. This continuing bond with Scholasticism bore fruit in his efforts to revitalize the custom of public theological disputation at the

University of Wittenberg in the 1530s and 1540s.

Early development. Along with these concerns, Luther's early thought is characterized by a protracted engagement with the *Augustinian theology of grace, in the course of which he became alienated from the Ockhamist theology in which he had been formed. As Luther understood it, this teaching betrayed the Augustinian tradition at two crucial points. Though technically non-Pelagian, it made of grace only a qualification of good works which we can achieve by our own strength. Thus Ockhamist theology underestimated both the corruption of fallen humanity and the disruptively transforming effect of divine grace. Grace, Luther came to believe, is no mere qualification of the religious and moral achievement possible for human beings dominated by sin and the devil; it means the death of the 'old Adam' and the painful birth of a new humanity.

These were the concerns that Luther took into the struggle over indulgences, which exploded unexpectedly in the wake of his famous theses of 31 October 1517. Luther regarded indulgences chiefly as a cheap substitute for the pain of authentic transformation, and he saw deep connections between their popularity and the nominalist soteriology he had rejected in his academic work.

However, in the course of the conflict, Luther was forced to attend seriously to sacramental theology, perhaps for the first time, and to consider the role of the sacraments in the working of grace. While Luther's development remains a focus of debate, many scholars believe that his thought achieved its mature configuration only *after* the indulgence controversy was underway, as the outcome of this new consideration of the sacraments. Key to the new dimension in his thought, on this view, is the doctrine of the *outward word of the gospel*, and the associated account of faith as confident trust in God's promise.

Justification by faith alone. At the centre of Luther's mature thought is the doctrine of justification *sola fide*, 'by faith alone', which Luther describes as the 'chief article', the criterion of authentic Christian teaching and practice. Yet 'justification by faith alone' turns out to summarize a teaching of considerable complexity, not so much a single doctrine as a way of

understanding the coherence of Christian doctrine as a whole. Luther's theology of justification juxtaposes two bodies of teaching in particular: teaching about Jesus Christ and teaching about the *verbum externum*, the 'external' or 'bodily' word, Luther's code-phrases for the public ecclesial practices of preaching and sacrament. It is the specific interrelation of these themes that constitutes the distinctiveness of Luther's doctrine of justification.

Luther teaches that we are saved by an *alien justitia*, often translated 'alien righteousness' but literally meaning 'the righteousness of another person'. Luther insists very strongly that Christ himself, in the unity of his divine-human person, is the righteousness by which human beings are saved. This is connected with his central understanding of Christ as the one who is utterly *pro nobis*, 'for us'. The Son of God has assumed mortal flesh and become the ally of sinners, not for his own sake, but for ours. His whole incarnate existence is thus sheer gift, sheer benefit to the needy. On the cross, Christ endured and overcame in his own person all that threatens sinful humankind – sin, death, God's wrath and curse – and triumphed over them in the resurrection. 'And so all who adhere to that flesh are blessed and freed from the curse' (*WA* 40/1:451).

Luther therefore defines the faith by which we are saved as *fides apprehensiva Christi*, 'a faith which takes hold of Christ'. Salvation involves an intimate union of the believer with Christ, not only a mental connection but a joining in 'one body and flesh … so that his flesh is in us and our flesh is in him' (*WA* 33:232). This union brings both free forgiveness and acceptance by God: 'Faith justifies because it grasps and possesses this treasure, the present Christ … Therefore the Christ who is grasped by faith and dwells in the heart is the Christian righteousness on account of which God reckons us righteous and gives us eternal life' (*WA* 40/1:229). Those who take hold of Christ by faith are received with him into the Father's favour, their sins forgiven for Christ's sake. At the same time, Christ's presence does not leave believers unchanged; he lives and acts in them by the Spirit and grants them new life.

This all takes place by means of the 'external word', the preached and sacramentally enacted *gospel* of Christ. For Luther, the gospel is defined primarily by its Christological content; it is 'a chronicle, history, or tale about Christ, who he is, what he has done, said, and suffered … a discourse about Christ, that he is God's Son and became a human being for us, suffered and rose again, and has been appointed a lord over all things'(*WA* 10/I/1:9). But just because Christ is the one who is unreservedly 'for us', *pro nobis*, the telling of this tale is at the same time the conferral of a blessing, the presentation of a gift. Or as Luther likes to put it: this story constitutes a *promise* on God's part which cannot be received by any answering achievement on our part but only acknowledged in thankful trust and confidence.

The preaching of the gospel and its enactment in the sacraments are the instruments of the Spirit by which he 'brings us to the Lord Christ to receive the treasure' (Large Catechism, Third Article of the Creed). Luther's insistence on the work of the Spirit is the background for his denial of the 'free choice of the will' (*liberum arbitrium*), most uncompromisingly stated in *The Bondage of the Will* (1525). The freedom to respond to God in faith is not an abstract property of the individual, like the power to lift heavy objects; it is a freedom granted by the Spirit's concrete intervention in a human life through the bodily word of the gospel.

Hearing and trusting this word of Christ, moreover, the believer encounters Christ himself and is joined to him. Without this concrete presence, Luther believed that the redemptive work of Christ in the flesh would lose its graciousness. We would be trapped in a new legalism, with the salvation won by Christ as the elusive prize that we must seek anxiously to appropriate by good works and devotion. To forestall this, the Spirit brings us the treasure of salvation, which is inseparable from Christ himself, and 'lays it in our laps' (Large Catechism, Third Article of the Creed) through the word and the sacraments. In this way faith is freed to be pure receptive acknowledgement of God's mercy in the particularity of its bestowal.

Conflicts and controversy. The doctrine of justification thus construed is for Luther not so much a 'systematic principle' from which other teachings are derived as a constant critical reference point with which all other teaching and practice in the church must be co-ordinated. In his efforts to carry out the testing and sifting this implies, Luther entered into a series of conflicts in which various aspects of his thought underwent further development.

Luther initially came into conflict with the Roman See against his own expectations and intentions. Nevertheless, as the conflict escalated Luther accused the Roman Church not only of teaching a false doctrine of justification, but also of making false ecclesiological claims. Luther believed that the papacy claimed absolute authority to prescribe the doctrine and practice of the whole church, in such a way that whatever wastaught by the Roman See had authoritative force simply *because* it was taught by the Roman See. By contrast, Luther came to hold that formal authority in the church – authority inhering in a person, office or institution by virtue of its position within the Christian community – could only acquire legitimacy from its substantive faithfulness to the apostolic gospel, which all church authority is appointed to serve.

At the same time, Luther also rejected any absolute division of the church into rulers and ruled. Christ established the church not by endowing a special clerical group with power to form and govern a community in his name, but by entrusting the message of salvation to his apostles. The whole church has received the gospel, and with it the anointing of the Holy Spirit, from the apostolic company; the distinction between pastors and people, which Luther by no means wanted to erase, must be placed within the context of this common reception of salvation. This is Luther's doctrine of the *universal priesthood* of the faithful; its theme is not so much the rights of the individual as rather the shared reality of salvation in Christ, which is the foundation of the church. Authority in the church must be exercised in such a way as to acknowledge this shared relationship of all members of the body to Christ their head. Authentic church governance therefore seeks the 'Amen' of the Spirit-anointed people of God by its intelligible appeal to Holy Scripture as the authoritative word entrusted to the whole church.

By the mid-1520s, Luther was engaged in a whole series of new controversies on very different fronts. Most vehement was the conflict with a range of opponents, most prominently the Zurich Reformer *Ulrich Zwingli, who denied the bodily presence of Christ in the Eucharist, and who more broadly called into question the relation of faith to 'external things', such as preached words and sacramental signs. Luther believed that the gospel was just as much at stake in this conflict as in the conflict with Rome; without the concrete bestowal of Christ's presence in public, bodily acts, faith is once again condemned to anxious insecurity. Or, as he wrote of Andreas Bodenstein von Karlstadt, an erstwhile faculty colleague who denied the Eucharistic presence: 'he mocks us and brings us no further than to show us the holy thing in a glass or container. We can see it and smell it until we are full, indeed we may dream of it, but he does not give it to us, he doesn't open it up, he doesn't allow it to be our own' (*WA* 18:203).

Luther was also alarmed in these years by the emergence of anti-Trinitarian groups, and he devoted much attention from the close of the 1520s until the end of his life to working out the interrelations of the theology of justification and the ecumenical Trinitarian and Christological doctrines. This concern can be seen especially in his extended expositions of Johannine texts from those years, but it is also visibly present in the great *Commentary on Galatians* of 1535.

Mention should be made also of Luther's involvement with the Saxon Church Visitation of 1528, an official inspection of the parishes of Electoral Saxony. The ignorance and disorder brought to light thereby brought home to Luther in a powerful way that legalistic works-righteousness was not the only enemy with which an evangelical theology had to contend. This experience was an important motivation for the writing of the two Catechisms of 1529, undoubtedly the writings by which Luther has exercised the widest influence in subsequent history. It is remarkable that the Small Catechism, intended to be taught to the lay faithful, never speaks explicitly about justification by faith; the point of the doctrine is communicated indirectly in an exposition of the Ten Commandments, the Apostles' Creed, the Lord's Prayer and the sacraments.

Moreover, the emphasis on repentance and the Decalogue to which the Church Visitation brought Luther and the other Wittenberg theologians provoked a bitter controversy years later (in 1539) with Johannes Agricola of Eisleben, originally a close adherent of Luther's. Agricola taught that divine law had no place in the proclamation of the church. God in Christ meets sinners with no demand but only with the sheer mercy embodied in the crucified. Luther argued in response that the good news of God's mercy in Christ was only intelligible in the context of the condemnation of sinners under the law.

Therefore the law must be proclaimed precisely for the sake of the gospel. Furthermore, Christ by his death on the cross has not only merited forgiveness of sins for us; he has also gained for us the gift of the Spirit so that we might begin to obey the law. Thus the gospel of Christ makes it possible for us to love the commandments of God, despite our sin; Christ's office, Luther says, is not to abolish the law but to 'render the law pleasing and undefiled' (*WA* 39/1:372–3).

A legacy of tensions. Luther's greatest influence has undoubtedly been exercised through the Catechisms, in the nurture of faith and the formation of life far beyond the academic sphere. For theology, however, Luther's legacy has been controversial from the first; both by its own internal complexity, and through its involvement with epochal historical shifts, it has often seemed a legacy chiefly of acute tensions, a few of which should be noted.

The doctrine of justification notoriously gives rise to critiques of church teaching and church practice: do they promote trust in Christ alone or do they deflect trust from Christ to human achievement or indeed to the church's own institutions and officers? Yet this critique does not lead Luther, as it has some Protestants, to disengage salvation from church, so that 'faith alone' becomes synonymous with 'private experience alone'. For Luther, salvation remains tied to public ecclesial practice, to preaching and sacramental rites. The result is a tension between *critique and affirmation of the visible ecclesial community* that is by no means easy to negotiate.

A related tension is that between *continuity and discontinuity in Christian history*. Luther's critical posture towards the existing western church took extreme and apocalyptic shape in his belief that the papacy as an institution was the antichrist prophesied in Scripture. Yet, for Luther, salvation itself depended on the continuous integrity of core ecclesial practice, on the ongoing presence of the true gospel and the sacraments in the church through time. Therefore Luther found himself arguing that the Roman Church was both the dominion of antichrist and the vehicle through which the gospel had been brought into his own day. He thus came into conflict with both the traditionalism of his Roman opponents and the radicalism of those for whom the Roman provenance of a practice was already reason to reject it.

On another front, Luther's thought generates tension concerning the relationship between *faith and renewal of life*. We never have confidence in God on the basis of any achievements or qualifications of our own; Christ alone remains our righteousness. Our good works in themselves are never more than Isaiah's 'filthy rags' (Is. 64:6). Yet the faith that grasps Christ as its righteousness can never leave the believer unchanged; believers are joined to Christ by faith and Christ is neither weak nor idle. The believer is therefore both 'a sinner and righteous at the same time' (*simul peccator et iustus*), which means both 'still defiled inwardly but accepted by God for Christ's sake', and 'truly transformed but no less utterly dependent on the undeserved mercy of God in Christ'.

Finally, there is the tension in Luther's thought between *law and gospel*. The gospel is the word which presents Christ as God's gift of righteousness. Law, by contrast, makes known the will of God without providing for its accomplishment. If heard accurately, it is a death sentence on sinful humanity; if distorted, it motivates the doomed quest for self-justification. Yet, as we have seen, Luther does not draw the conclusion that the church should proclaim gospel and renounce law. Both modes of discourse are necessary in a complex interplay that responds equally to the inner dynamics of Scripture and the diverse modes of human confusion and misery. The resulting tension between critique and affirmation of the discourse of law has been another of Luther's enduring legacies.

DAVID S. YEAGO

FURTHER READING: Carl E. Braaten and Robert W. Jenson (ed.), *Union with Christ: The New Finnish Interpretation of Luther* (Grand Rapids, 1998), the most challenging recent departure in Luther-interpretation; Martin Brecht, *Martin Luther* (3 vols.; Philadelphia, 1985–), standard and extensive biography; Bernhard Lohse, *Martin Luther's Theology: Its Historical and Systematic Development* (Minneapolis, 1999), will now be the standard overview; Heiko A. Oberman, *Luther: Man Between God and the Devil* (New Haven, 1989), lively study emphasizing Luther's apocalypticism; Otto Hermann Pesch, *Hinführung zu Luther* (Mainz, 1983), ecumenically-oriented study by an important Roman Catholic interpreter; Hermann Sasse, *This Is My Body: Luther's Contention for the Real Presence in the Sacrament of the Altar* (Minneapolis, 1959), still the best study in English of this controversy – important corrective to interpretations of Luther which focus too exclusively on the controversy with Rome; Jared Wicks, *Luther's Reform: Studies on Conversion and the Church* (Mainz, 1992), lucid essays by one of the most important Roman Catholic interpreters of Luther.

Lutheran Confessions and Catechisms

Origin. The Lutheran confessional tradition originated with a work which has never achieved official 'confessional' standing in the Lutheran churches – *Martin Luther's Confession Concerning Christ's Supper of 1528. In the third part of that work, following his extensive polemic against *Zwingli, Luther presented an overview of his teaching, in order to hinder the use of his name in support of error after his death: 'I want in this work to confess my faith, point by point, before God and the whole world. I mean to abide in this faith until death, and in it to depart from this world (may God help me so to do) and come before the judgement seat of my Lord Jesus Christ' (*WA* 26:499).

Luther's personal confession was not only a crucial source for other confessional writings, especially the Augsburg Confession, but it also shaped in an abiding way the Lutheran understanding of what is at stake in confessions of faith. A confessional statement is not only an instrument of church order or an expression of negotiated consensus; it is always also an eschatological declaration, a public account of that by which a community pledges to live and die and stand before divine judgement. In the background are the words of Jesus in Matthew 10:32: 'Everyone therefore who acknowledges me before others, I also will acknowledge before my Father in heaven; but whoever denies me before others, I also will deny before my Father in heaven' (NRSV). This eschatological dimension of 'confessions' should not be forgotten even as other factors in the development of Lutheran confessionalism are taken seriously. Two such factors are of particular importance.

In the first place, in sixteenth-century Europe questions of religious faith were inevitably *public* questions, which engaged civil society as a whole. It was thus necessary for those who accepted the Wittenberg Reformation to give a public account of their doctrine before the larger Christian community, within which church and state were not easily disentangled.

This is the background especially of the Augsburg Confession (1530), its *Apology* (1531), the Schmalkaldic Articles (1537) and the *Treatise on the Power and Primacy of the Pope* (1537). A second factor was the internal need of the Lutheran churches themselves. The Saxon Church Visitation of 1528 disclosed a level of ignorance and disarray in the congregations which Luther and his colleagues found shocking. Luther's Small Catechism (1529) and Large Catechism (1529) were written in part to address this situation. Another form of internal need arose from intra-Lutheran controversy, especially after Luther's death, when the unity of the German Lutheran churches was nearly shattered by contending parties claiming to represent the true legacy of the Reformer. This was the background to the 'Formula of Concord' (1577), as well as to the gathering of the whole body of Lutheran confessional writings in the *Book of Concord* (1580).

The following summary follows the order in which the Confessions appear in the *Book of Concord*, which deviates from chronological sequence in its placement of the Catechisms.

The three chief symbols or creeds of the Christian faith.

The *Book of Concord* begins not with sixteenth-century writings but with three texts from the ancient church: the *Apostles' Creed, the *Nicene Creed and the so-called *Athanasian Creed. This was not an afterthought of the compilers but corresponds to the content of the sixteenth-century confessions themselves, which persistently refer to and ground themselves on the creedal inheritance represented by these documents. The Augsburg Confession begins by affirming the 'decree of the Council of Nicaea' as 'true and to be believed without any doubting' (Art. 1). The Schmalkaldic Articles likewise begin with the 'high articles of the divine Majesty' (Pt. 1), the Trinitarian and Christological dogmas of the ancient church. At the centre of the Catechisms is the exposition of the Apostles' Creed. The 'Formula of Concord' pledges itself to the creedal orthodoxy of the ancient catholic church and describes the Lutheran Reformation as continuing the struggle of the Fathers on behalf of pure doctrine. This consistent and unambiguous affirmation of continuity in faith with the ancient church is of considerable importance for the interpretation of the confessional writings as a whole.

The Augsburg Confession.

On 21 January 1530, the Emperor Charles V summoned a diet to address the widening religious division in the empire, 'so that we might all live in one fellowship, church, and unity' ('Preface', citing the imperial summons). The imperial estates met in Augsburg starting in May of that year. The Augsburg Confession (or *Confessio Augustana*, sometimes referred to simply as the '*Augustana*') was produced there on behalf of the evangelical estates amidst a complex process of negotiation, going through multiple drafts and redrafts in a comparatively short period of time. *Philip Melanchthon acted as chief theological adviser to the evangelical princes and city governments, and he was the chief author of the confession. Luther, who was outlawed in the empire, could not attend but stayed restlessly at Castle Coburg, where he was consulted by letter. The confession was written in both German and Latin; while it was the German text which was publicly read to the emperor, both versions have been regarded as authoritative in the subsequent Lutheran tradition.

The initial assumption of the Wittenbergers was that the diet would chiefly discuss disputed points of church practice, since the imperial summons seemed to assume that all parties shared a common faith. Upon arriving at Augsburg, however, they discovered a much chillier atmosphere than anticipated. The emperor was in any case inclined to defend established belief and practice, and Luther's old enemy, *Johann Eck, had presented him with a list of 404 heretical statements drawn both from the Wittenberg theologians and their opponents on the left. The catholic faith of the evangelical estates and churches was therefore under attack. It was in this context that the confession took its eventual form.

As finally presented to the emperor on 25 June 1530, the Augsburg Confession falls into two main parts. The first part (Art. 1–21) deals with matters of faith. In Articles 1–3, the evangelicals declare their agreement with both the Trinitarian and Christological teaching of the ancient church, and the western *Augustinian consensus on original sin. Articles 4–20 set forth the evangelical theology of salvation, treating the themes of justification, church, sacraments and newness of life, as well as a handful of miscellaneous issues. The second part (Art. 22–28) takes up a series of disputed points of church practice: the distribution of the cup to the laity in the Lord's Supper, clerical marriage, the Mass, private confession, rules regarding fasting and other ceremonies, monastic vows and church government.

The overall strategy of the Augsburg Confession is to argue (1) that the faith of the evangelicals is grounded in Scripture and not contrary to the teaching of the universal church; and (2) that in view of such agreement in faith, differences in practice do not give the old-believing bishops and estates legitimate grounds to break church fellowship, for example by the bishops refusing to ordain evangelicals to the priesthood. In its historical context, therefore, the *Augustana* was anything but a denominational declaration of independence; it was an ecumenical appeal written not to justify, but if possible to prevent, the division of the church.

Signed by seven princes and the representatives of two free cities, the Augsburg Confession nonetheless speaks on behalf of 'the churches among us' and thus claims ecclesial significance. Given its solemn and highly public character, as well as its own intrinsic merits, it quickly became an authoritative identity marker for the churches of the Wittenberg Reformation; eventually it was recognized in law as the confessional basis for the Lutheran estates within the empire. Thus, contrary to its original ecumenical intention, the *Augustana* came to function as the charter of a special denominational tradition within a divided church.

Philip Melanchthon, it should be noted, continued throughout his life to regard the confession as an instrument of Christian unity. However, he put this concern into practice by periodically rewriting the text to address new ecumenical junctures, not only with Roman Catholics but also with the Reformed. This was greeted with suspicion and anger by many other Lutherans, who regarded the text as the public property of the Lutheran churches, no longer under its author's control. Thus subsequent Lutheran tradition often refers pointedly to the 'Unaltered Augsburg Confession' (*Confessio Augustana Invariata*) of 1530 as the authoritative text.

The Apology of the Augsburg Confession.

On 3 August 1530, the Roman party at Augsburg presented the emperor with a point-by-point rebuttal of the Augsburg Confession, known as the *Roman Confutation* (*Confutatio Pontificia*). The emperor demanded that the evangelicals admit on the spot that their views had been refuted, and he refused to allow them to have a copy of the *Confutation* until they did so. Instead, Melanchthon was assigned the task of writing a response on the basis of notes taken during the reading; though a draft was prepared by 22 September, the emperor refused to receive it. After his return to Wittenberg, Melanchthon continued to revise and enlarge his response, finally acquiring the text of the *Confutation* in October. The completed *Apology of the Augsburg Confession* was published at the end of April or the beginning of May of 1531. Originally appearing as a private work of Melanchthon, it acquired corporate standing when it was adopted as a statement of faith by the Schmalkaldic League in 1537.

In character, the *Apology* is unmistakably a theological treatise. It deals extensively with the points at which the *Roman Confutation* rejected the doctrine of the Augsburg Confession, especially the doctrine of justification. The original Augsburg strategy is continued: Melanchthon argues that the teaching of the *Augustana* is founded on Scripture and consistent with the consensus of the Fathers, differing only from the distortion of the faith by late-medieval scholastic theologians, especially the *nominalists.

The *Apology* is in certain respects unique among the Lutheran confessional texts. On the one hand, its presence in the confessional tradition prevents the much starker formulations of the Augsburg Confession from being received in too bare and schematic a fashion, for Melanchthon's defence roots the confessional formulations deeply in the history of doctrine and thus provides them with a richness of resonance that would otherwise be lacking. On the other hand, how is its authority as public doctrine to be understood, if it is not to bind the whole subsequent theological tradition to Melanchthon's particular development of Reformation themes? The 'Formula of Concord' (*Solid Declaration, Rule and Norm*) suggests that it be read as an interpretive guide to the Augsburg Confession, which thus retains its central place. On the basis of the *Apology*, readings of the *Augustana* that caricature or distort its doctrine can be ruled out, and the precise scope of its positive teaching can be clarified.

The Schmalkaldic Articles.

In June 1536, Pope Paul III called a council to meet in Mantua the following year. Though the council did not actually convene until 1545 in Trent, the papal summons presented the Lutherans with a challenge. The elector of Saxony responded by asking Luther to draw up a statement distinguishing those issues on which the faith itself was at stake from those on which concessions might be made. Luther complied despite severe illness and produced what later became known as the Schmalkaldic Articles, which were reviewed, amended and signed by a small group of theologians in December of 1536.

The subsequent history of the Articles is a complex lesson in the dynamics of the reception of doctrine in the church. The elector took the Articles with him to Schmalkalden in February of 1537 in the hope that they might be adopted as an official statement of the Schmalkaldic League, a defensive alliance of the evangelical estates. Yet despite these hopes, and despite the name eventually attached to them, the Schmalkaldic Articles were *not* adopted by the Schmalkaldic League at Schmalkalden. Philip Melanchthon, who had signed the Articles in December, was instrumental in persuading the representatives of the League that they would be counterproductive if officially adopted (Luther was present at Schmalkalden, but he was bedridden the entire time). At the same time, the Articles were signed by a large number of the theologians and clergy who were present. Luther published the Articles in 1538, and over subsequent decades they came to be widely acknowledged as an authentic witness to Lutheran teaching and were received as such into the *Book of Concord*.

In the background is the character of the Articles themselves, and the circumstances of their composition. Luther was suffering with excruciating attacks of kidney stones and gallstones while he wrote them, and he believed quite soberly that he was dying. Thus the Articles are an intensely personal document, written in Luther's least accommodating style – clear, pointed and almost flamboyantly polemical. The division of the evangelicals from the 'Papists' is declared to be eternal and irreparable, and the pope is solemnly declared to be the antichrist prophesied in Scripture. Their character as 'Luther's theological testament' added immensely to the authority of the Articles in the churches, while at the same time rendering them less plausible for the purposes of the League. The tension between the ecumenical hopefulness of the Augsburg Confession and the apocalyptic defiance of the Schmalkaldic Articles is perhaps impossible to resolve. At the same time, the Articles contain some of Luther's most lucid theological writing, including the strongest articulation within the confessional writings of the characteristic Lutheran doctrine of the essential role of the 'outward' or 'bodily' word (Pt. III, Art. 8).

The Treatise on the Power and Primacy of the Pope. This brief essay was written by Melanchthon at the request of the authorities assembled at Schmalkalden; unlike Luther's Articles, it was adopted officially by the League, along with the Augsburg Confession and the *Apology*. The *Treatise* was commissioned as a supplement to the Augsburg Confession, which had deliberately avoided any discussion of the papacy; by 1537 it had become clear that the issue was inescapable. The *Treatise* attacks the claims of both pope and bishops to govern the church by divine right; its arguments must be carefully situated against the background of late-medieval papal and episcopal theories, and it should not be assumed to respond directly to subsequent accounts of papal and episcopal authority. In the course of its primarily negative arguments, the *Treatise* sets forth many important principles of the early Lutheran understanding of church, ministry and authority.

The Small and Large Catechisms. Luther's Catechisms were written in response to the internal needs of the evangelical churches. As early as 1525, Luther had delegated the writing of a handbook of religious instruction to his friends Justus Jonas and Johannes Agricola, but this did not take place, and in the context of the Saxon Church Visitation of 1528 Luther himself undertook the task. Drawing on three series of sermons preached in 1528, Luther started writing the Large Catechism in the autumn of that year and began the Small Catechism in December. The Large Catechism was published in April 1529 as the German Catechism; it received its present title after 1541. The completed Small Catechism was published as an illustrated pamphlet in May 1529.

The Catechisms are, in essence, commentaries on five basic Christian texts: the Ten Commandments, the Apostles' Creed, the Lord's Prayer and the biblical passages in which baptism and the Lord's Supper are instituted. Both Catechisms in their final form deal also with private confession and absolution; the Small Catechism incorporates a brief liturgical order for this rite. The Small Catechism also adds instructions for family prayer, and a 'Table of Duties' (*Haustafel*), made up of Scripture passages which specify the obligations of the various members of the household. In addition, many editions of the Small Catechism have included Luther's 'Baptism Booklet' (*Taufbuchlein*) and 'Marriage Booklet' (*Traubuchlein*), liturgical orders with theological prefaces. Some editions have also included the 'German Litany'.

The two Catechisms are independent, if closely associated, works. The Small Catechism is not merely an abridgement of the Large Catechism, nor is the latter an expansion of the former. The Small Catechism, written in question-and-answer form with lucid simplicity and a complete absence of polemic, was intended for laypeople – and especially for children. Its resonant phrasing lends itself to memorization. The Large Catechism is a manual for those with the responsibility for teaching, especially pastors and schoolmasters. More discursive, and therefore more polemical than the Small Catechism, it nonetheless displays a comparable clarity and vigour, as well as a disciplined focus on the basic structure and inner coherence of the faith.

Despite their independence in detail, the two Catechisms display a common theological structure. The Ten Commandments and the First Article of the Apostles' Creed are bound together as instruction about the will of the Creator, who calls human creatures to live before him in fear, love and trust. The Second and Third Articles of the Creed describe God's rescue of human beings when we had fallen under the tyranny of the devil: the Son of God has acquired our salvation by shedding his holy and innocent blood on the cross, and the Holy Spirit distributes this salvation through the word and the sacraments in the Christian church. The exposition of the Lord's Prayer then depicts the embattled holiness of the little flock, which is sanctified by the Spirit in daily conflict with the world, the flesh and the devil. The presentation of the sacraments describes the concrete means by which we are protected from the devil's spite and brought to Christ in order to live under his gracious rule. Thus the five main parts of the Catechism form a sort of triptych, with the Decalogue and the First Article of the Creed as one side panel, the Third Article, the Lord's Prayer and the sacraments, as the other, and in

the centre the exposition of the Second Article, focused in both Catechisms on the confession of Jesus Christ as 'Lord'.

The Catechisms were immediately popular, and they had been through many printings and been included in several church orders and collections of confessional documents before they were received into the *Book of Concord*. Their significance in the Lutheran tradition is indicated by the description given them in the 'Formula': they are 'the layperson's Bible, in which everything is contained which is treated more extensively in Holy Scripture, and which is necessary for a Christian to know in order to be saved' (*Epitome, Rule and Norm*). The Small Catechism in particular has been not only a textbook but also a prayer book for generations of Lutherans; it has perhaps shaped *Lutheranism as a form of lived and practised Christianity as much or more than the Augsburg Confession.

The 'Formula of Concord'. Martin Luther died in 1546, and in 1547 the evangelical estates suffered crushing military defeat at the hands of the emperor. German Lutheranism entered the 1550s demoralized and dispirited, and under strong pressure to seek religious and political alliances in either the Reformed or the Roman direction.

During the 1550s, moreover, theological tension mounted between rival theological factions. On the one side were the so-called 'Gnesio-Lutherans', (the 'authentic' Lutherans) who took their stand on what they believed to be Luther's teaching, while at the same time often pressing his thought to extreme conclusions. Thus Matthias Flacius Illyricus, the brilliantly obdurate theologian who was the most distinguished representative of this tendency, taught that after the Fall sin has become the very essence of the human creature; while Nicholas von Amsdorf, an old comrade-in-arms of Luther's, taught that good works were actually detrimental to salvation. Both theologians were making serious points, but at the price of a rupture with the western theological tradition which other Lutherans were not willing to countenance. On the other side were the so-called 'Philippists', named after their teacher, Philip Melanchthon, who were ready to make concessions to Rome on both the doctrine of grace and issues of church practice, and to Geneva on the theology of the Eucharist. A whole array of secondary controversies arose at the same time to complicate the situation. By 1557 it had become clear that the Lutherans were seriously divided, and attempts by evangelical princes to negotiate a truce in 1558 and 1561 were ineffective.

The 'Formula of Concord' was the outcome of a process of consensus-formation led by a diverse team of younger theologians – especially Jakob Andreae and *Martin Chemnitz – who were convinced that the authentic Lutheran ground lay somewhere between the two conflicting parties. Like the Gnesio-Lutherans, they were committed to a robust reception of Luther's teaching on justification and the sacraments; but they shared with the Philippists a commitment to articulating Lutheran themes in substantial continuity with the western theological tradition. With financial support from a group of evangelical princes, these theologians orchestrated a large-scale doctrinal colloquy that lasted from 1568 to 1577. Draft texts were produced by individuals or small committees of theologians and circulated to universities, conferences of clergy and distinguished colleagues, and then new drafts were prepared on the basis of comments received. The final text in the process was achieved at Bergen Abbey in 1577, and it largely achieved its goal of halting the disintegration of German Lutheranism by marking out a common ground capable of wide acceptance. Between 1577 and 1580 it was signed by three electors, 20 dukes and princes, 24 counts, four barons, 35 imperial cities and 8,188 theologians, pastors and teachers.

The 'Formula of Concord' in its final form consists of two parts, the so-called Epitome and the Solid Declaration. The Epitome is a relatively concise summary of the Solid Declaration, which is itself the final text of 1577, the so-called 'Bergen Book'. The 'Formula' contains an opening account of the criteria of pure doctrine and the confessional basis of Lutheranism, followed by twelve articles which address the divisive issues of the previous three decades: (1) original sin, (2) grace and free will, (3) the righteousness of faith, (4) good works and salvation, (5) the distinction of law and gospel, (6) the function of the law for believers, (7) the Lord's Supper, (8) the person of Christ, (9) his descent into hell, (10) church practices not commanded by divine law (known as *adiaphora* or 'things indifferent') and (11) divine election. The twelfth article repudiates a disparate bundle of miscellaneous errors ascribed to *Anabaptists,

Schwenkfelders and anti-Trinitarians. A *Catalog of Testimonies* was also added to the 'Formula', which was essentially an anthology of patristic citations supporting the Christological teaching of Article 8.

The 'Formula' was decisively important for the definition of Lutheranism as a particular confessional theology in the post-Reformation divided church. Combining a strong emphasis on *sola scriptura* with a lively appreciation for church doctrine, an austerely Augustinian theology of sin and grace with rejection of *Calvinist double-predestinarianism, a forensic account of justification with an articulate concern for sanctification and renewal of life, and a high doctrine of Christ's bodily real presence in the Eucharist with rejection of transubstantiation and the sacrifice of the Mass, the 'Formula' marked out the distinctive ground Lutherans would occupy for centuries to come – and at the same time it set up tensions that would motivate, energize and sometimes frustrate the subsequent Lutheran theological tradition.

***The* Book of Concord.** A last stage in the formation of the Lutheran Confessions was the assembly and publication of the *Book of Concord* itself by the same team of theologians who had produced the 'Formula'. The establishment of a normative canon of confessional texts is itself necessarily a confessional act – a point not wasted on the theologians, who saw to it that the *Book of Concord* was published on 25 June 1580, fifty years to the day after the presentation of the Augsburg Confession to Charles V. The collection was introduced by a preface discussing at some length the preceding history and describing the nature of the doctrinal 'concord' achieved; this preface was written in the name of the princes and city governments who accepted the *Book of Concord* as a body of public doctrine in their territories, and it is they who are its signatories.

Reception and interpretation. The 'Formula of Concord' was addressed primarily to the woes of the Lutheran churches in Germany, and it was never received as a normative confession of faith in the churches of Norway, Denmark and Iceland. Indeed, in 1580, the sovereign of all three realms, Frederick II, fearing the introduction of the German controversies into his dominions, declared it a capital offence to import, sell or possess a copy of the 'Formula'!

Even in Germany, moreover, acceptance of the 'Formula' by the Lutheran territories was not universal, though it was sufficient to redefine the Lutheran theological centre.

Still today, the Lutheran churches of the world receive the Lutheran confessional tradition in different ways. Particular Lutheran church bodies accept different documents as normative and ascribe different weights to the documents they receive. Three patterns of reception are most common. Some churches receive the entire *Book of Concord* as a unified body of doctrine without internal differentiation among its parts. Other churches receive the *Book of Concord* in a differentiated way, giving special weight to the Augsburg Confession and the Small Catechism. Finally, still other Lutheran bodies accept only the Augsburg Confession and the Small Catechism as normative.

These differences in reception are complicated by differences in the way the Confessions are interpreted. In the post-Reformation period, the confessions of faith received by a particular church came to have the force of public law, prescribing the boundaries within which church life and theological teaching were constrained to proceed. Since these legal arrangements came to an end all over Europe in the nineteenth century, and since they were never operative to begin with in non-European Lutheran churches, issues of confessional hermeneutics have been continually under discussion among Lutherans.

Some Lutherans have regarded the *Book of Concord* as a body of essentially timeless theological teaching, all of which is normative in the same way. Other Lutherans have insisted on reading the Confessions historically: they record normative decisions made in specific historical circumstances in the face of specific challenges. It is these *decisions* which are confessionally normative on this view, and not necessarily the conceptualities in which they are articulated, or the terms in which the alternatives are described.

In another direction, many Lutherans have viewed the Confessions primarily as exegesis of Holy Scripture. For some, the Confessions faithfully gather and present the revealed truths taught in Scripture, so that agreement with Scripture and agreement with the Confessions turn out simply to coincide with one another. For others, the relation between Scripture and Confession is more complex. The Confessions

provide a perspective on Scripture, a way into its essential dynamic, yet at the same time it is possible that the fullness of Scripture exceeds the scope of the confessional formulations and may indeed correct them.

Still other Lutherans have interpreted the Confessions with primary reference to Christian experience. For some Lutherans coming out of the nineteenth-century revivals, a full account of the inner experience of the converted individual required the whole panoply of confessional doctrine. Other Lutherans have thought more in terms of corporate experience: the Confessions represent the theological underpinnings of the Christian communal life form in its purity. This perspective helps recapture the intertwining of faith and common life that is especially visible in different ways in the Augsburg Confession and the Catechisms, but without the reference to Scripture it risks devolving into a view of the Confessions as the charter of denominational or even ethnic folkways.

Finally, Lutherans differ in the way they relate the Confessions to the ecumenical situation of the divided church. One hermeneutic of the Confessions reads them as constitutive of a distinctive and self-contained form of Christianity; the very function of the Confessions is to found the separate reality of 'Lutheranism' as a mode of corporate life and individual believing irreducible to any other. A different hermeneutic takes its lead from the priority of ancient creeds within the *Book of Concord* and the ecumenical intentionality of the Augsburg Confession. On this account, the Confessions propose to the whole church a way of receiving the faith and life of the ancient catholic church in fidelity to the gospel. Thus for this hermeneutic the ecumenical hope of the Augsburg Confession remains valid, while the other regards the sixteenth-century disappointment of that hope as having permanent normative significance for the way in which the Confessions must now be read.

DAVID S. YEAGO

FURTHER READING: Charles P. Arand, *Testing the Boundaries: Windows to Lutheran Identity* (St Louis, MO, 1995); *Die Bekenntnisschriften der evangelisch-lutherischen Kirche: Herausgegeben im Gedenkjahr der Augsburgischen Konfession 1930* (Göttingen, 12th edn, 1999), the standard edition of the primary texts; George W. Forell and James F. McCue (eds.), *Confessing One Faith: A Joint Commentary on the*

Augsburg Confession by Lutheran and Catholic Theologians (Minneapolis, 1982), an ecumenical milestone; Günther Gassmann and Scott Hendrix, *Fortress Introduction to the Lutheran Confessions* (Minneapolis, 1999); Eric W. Gritsch and Robert W. Jenson, *Lutheranism: The Theological Movement and Its Confessional Writings* (Philadelphia, 1976); Robert Kolb and Timothy J. Wengert (eds.), *The Book of Concord: The Confessions of the Evangelical Lutheran Church* (Minneapolis, 2000); Wilhelm Maurer, *Historical Commentary on the Augsburg Confession* (Philadelphia, 1986), detailed study of the development of the text which also pays significant attention to theological issues; Albrecht Peters, *Kommentar zu Luthers Katechismen* (5 vols.; Göttingen, 1990–), theologically rich study; Edmund Schlink, *Theology of the Lutheran Confessions* (Philadelphia, 1961); Gunther Wenz, *Theologie der Bekenntnisschriften der evangelisch-lutherischen Kirche: Eine historische und systematische Einführung in das Konkordienbuch* (2 vols.; Berlin / New York, 1996–), magisterial study.

Lutheranism

The genesis of Lutheranism. The term 'Lutheranism' refers both to the normative beliefs of those post-Reformation confessional churches that trace their origin to the Wittenberg movement whose central figure was *Martin Luther, as well as to the theological tradition which has attempted to explicate those beliefs and their implications. As the name indicates, Lutheranism has at all times been much engaged with the theological legacy of Martin Luther, but he was by no means the exclusive founder of the Lutheran tradition. Almost equally influential was his friend and colleague *Philip Melanchthon, who provided the first orderly presentation of the Wittenberg theology in the successive revisions of his *Loci Theologici* ('Topics in Theology').

Lutheranism further received a more or less classical formulation in the work of the second-generation Lutheran theologians who produced the 'Formula of Concord' of 1577, especially *Martin Chemnitz (1522–86), a Melanchthon student whose own *Loci Theologici* (published posthumously in 1591) takes the form of a commentary on his teacher's work. Chemnitz defined normative Lutheranism over against Rome in his *Examen Concilii Tridentini* ('Examination of the Council of Trent') (1565–73) and over against the Reformed in his *De duabus naturis in Christo* ('On the Two Natures in Christ') (1578) and his

Fundamenta Sanae Doctrinae de Vera et Substantiali Praesentia Domini in Coena ('Basic Principles of Sound Doctrine concerning the True and Substantial Presence of the Lord in the Supper') (1570). The work of these theologians coincided with the statutory consolidation and regulation of church teaching and practice in the various German principalities as the Holy Roman Empire made its first, ultimately unsuccessful, attempt to come to terms with unresolvable religious division.

Chemnitz's titles indicate some of the contours of Lutheranism as it emerged from the *Reformation era as a distinctive confessional theology. Over against Tridentine Catholicism, early Lutheranism shared many commitments with Reformed Protestants, especially with regard to justification, the sacrifice of the Mass, ecclesiology and the authority of Scripture. On other issues, however, particularly the sacraments, Lutherans seemed closer to Rome, or at least to the broader Catholic tradition, than to other Protestants.

Contours of historic Lutheran conviction. Following the Augsburg Confession (1530), Lutherans affirmed that a sinner is justified before God freely, for Christ's sake, by faith alone. Thus reception into God's favour is not the goal of the Christian life, which must be sought anxiously through the performance of meritorious works, albeit with the assistance of grace, as the Council of Trent was rightly or wrongly believed to teach. Reception into God's favour on the basis of gratuitous and undeserved mercy is rather the starting point and abiding foundation of the Christian life. The word and the sacraments of the gospel offer this mercy to all without any qualifying conditions, in such a way that it can be received only by confident trust, which believes what God promises.

These shared commitments of the mainline Reformation received a distinctive shape in Lutheranism, however, from Lutheran convictions concerning preaching and sacrament. The word and the sacrament do not merely speak *about* God's mercy and invite the sinner to receive it; rather God acts in and through the actions of the proclaiming and celebrating church to awaken faith and bestow his mercy. God's own saving word and act impinge on us concretely in the witness and celebration of the Christian assembly, and faith is invited to rest with assurance in the promises, declarations and signs thus articulated.

It is this identification of the saving word and action of God with the word and sacraments proclaimed and celebrated in the church that chiefly distinguished Lutheranism from other forms of non-Roman Christianity after the Reformation. Lutheran preoccupation with the *distinction of law and gospel* arises directly from this identification; the law-gospel theme brings into focus the *hermeneutics* of an ecclesial discourse which faithfully embodies God's own liberating and gift-bestowing word of mercy.

The distinctiveness of Lutheranism at this point became most visible, however, in the doctrine of the Lord's Supper. Like other Protestants, Lutherans repudiated what Rome was believed to teach about the sacrifice of the Mass, that the sacrament is a rite of propitiation by which the church seeks to win God's favour. But at the same time, though Lutheranism rejected transubstantiation, it held to a strong doctrine of the *bodily real presence* of Christ 'in, with, and under' the elements of bread and wine in the sacrament.

Christ's presence in the Supper was said to be 'bodily' in at least three senses: First, it is the whole Christ, in his bodily humanity as well as his deity, who comes in the Supper to the whole human being, to the body as well as to the soul. Second, this encounter takes place through the bodily acts of eating and drinking the bread and wine of the Supper in obedience to Christ's command. In the context of the Supper, the faith that receives Christ's promise cannot be separated from these bodily acts of eating and drinking, but rather includes them and indeed takes form in them. Third, if by eating and drinking the bread and wine the communicant encounters Christ in his bodily humanity, then there must be posited a distinctive relationship between Christ and these bodily elements. Lutherans called this relationship a 'sacramental union'; in an incomprehensible way, Christ binds the bread and wine of the Supper to his own glorified humanity in such a way that whoever encounters them, encounters him.

Non-Lutherans have often described this as a doctrine of 'consubstantiation' or 'impanation', but nearly all Lutheran theologians have rejected both terms, as implying either a conjunction of two masses in physical space, or the physical coalescence of two substances into one. The presence of Christ was held by Lutherans to be 'real' and 'bodily' but non-spatial; the sacramental union was no sort of physical connection between objects in space but a relation *sui generis*, analogous only to two other incomprehensible unions – the union of the two natures in Christ and the union of Christ with the believer in faith. The point of the doctrine is not to describe theoretically the mode of the union but to insist with all possible force that the officiating minister may offer the bread and wine to the communicant and say with simple truth, 'Here is the body of Christ, given for you; here is the blood of Christ, shed for you'. Those who take what the minister holds out therefore encounter Jesus Christ in his concrete bodily-personal reality, and they must either welcome him by faith or turn from him in denial. This is the doctrine of the *manducatio impiorum*, which teaches that even unbelievers who share in the sacramental eating and drinking come thereby into contact with Christ.

In connection with this Eucharistic teaching, Lutherans strongly affirmed the concrete inseparability of the two natures in the one person of Christ. They argued that the flesh of Christ shares in both the freedom and the life-giving power of his deity. A deep affinity with the Christology of *Cyril of Alexandria was recognized already by Chemnitz. This Christological teaching was given classic shape in the 'Formula of Concord' in a distinctive Lutheran doctrine of the 'communication of attributes' in the person of Christ. There is no action or presence of Christ's divinity 'apart from' (*extra*) his humanity, as the *Calvinists were understood to teach (the so-called *extra Calvinisticum*); all actions and attributes of Christ are actions and attributes of the one person who is divine and human at the same time. Therefore the humanity of Christ shares in the divine actions and attributes: it is *Jesus*, not an unfleshed Logos, who sits at God's right hand and is therefore present everywhere and rules over all things.

In the doctrine of the church, Lutherans like other Protestants denied that the church was bound by divine law either to the Pope or the existing episcopate, and affirmed the validity of ordinations performed outside the historic succession of bishops. Unlike some other Protestants, however, Lutherans did not reject the traditional polity of the western church in favour of some other mode of organization believed to be prescribed in Scripture. Lutherans denied that Scripture prescribed *any* detailed church order, beyond the centrality of the assembly around the word and the sacrament and the institution of the gospel ministry to preside in that assembly. Organizational structures beyond this were obviously needed to serve the mission of the gospel and the unity in faith and communion of love among the churches, but they were nonetheless matters of human law and custom.

Thus Lutherans were more open than some other Protestants to *functionally* episcopal church order; the *Apology of the Augsburg Confession* in fact commends the traditional episcopal polity, saying that 'it was on a good and useful plan that the order of the church was set up by the fathers in the way the ancient canons describe' (*Apology*, art. XIV). This same attitude was carried over into other areas, especially liturgics: what was 'scriptural' was not exclusively that which could be *derived* from Scripture, but rather that which served the gospel to which the Scriptures bear witness. Therefore Lutherans tended to receive and reform the traditional practices of the western church rather than replace them with new and supposedly more 'biblical' forms.

Lutherans argued vigorously for the material sufficiency of Holy Scripture and its supremacy as the norm of all teaching and practice in the church. Furthermore, the capacity to understand and interpret Scripture has been given to all the faithful through the baptismal gift of the Spirit, and is not the monopoly of the clergy. Therefore the *magisterium* or teaching office of the church's ministers, which Lutherans did not deny, must establish the legitimacy of its teaching through continuous and credible public appeal to the Scriptures.

While sharing these convictions with other Protestants, however, Lutherans were more confident than some in the ability of the church, led by the Spirit, to formulate scriptural teaching in a permanently valid and binding way. While all church teaching must be tested by Scripture, the consonance of *some* church teaching with Scripture was a known and settled thing. This was the case with the Nicene and Chalcedonian doctrines of the ancient church, Lutherans believed, and likewise with the teaching of the Augsburg Confession and Luther's Catechisms. Thus Lutherans did not urge a purely inductive exegesis but taught that Scripture was to be interpreted 'in accordance with the rule of faith' embodied in creed and catechism. 'Public doctrine', formulated church teaching, has therefore played a stronger and more significant role in Lutheranism than in some other forms of Protestantism, and it has not so frequently been placed in an adversarial relation to *sola scriptura* ('Scripture alone').

Tensions and controversies within Lutheranism. Lutheranism is not only a historic configuration of belief and practice but also a tradition of exposition and interpretation, and such traditions are in large measure traditions of tension and controversy. Three especially volatile points of intra-Lutheran conflict should therefore be mentioned.

Firstly, there was the debate over 'Pietism' and 'Orthodoxy'. The stereotype that divides all seventeenth-century Lutherans into warm-hearted Pietists and cold-hearted Orthodox scholastics has been exploded by historical research; in reality, there was in seventeenth-century Lutheranism a broad concern for spiritual renewal and the practice of piety in which different Lutheran figures and movements participated in complex ways. The Orthodox were on the whole more pious and the Pietists more orthodox than their subsequent reputations would indicate.

Nonetheless, there can be discerned in this period a certain polarization, which continues today in a form only distantly related to the historical realities of Pietism and Orthodoxy. Some Lutherans have always insisted that true faith must be a *serious* and *transforming* inner engagement with God, even at the expense of faith's confident trust in the outward word of promise. Other Lutherans, in reaction, have tended to present justification in ever more exclusively forensic terms, as the free and unconditional acquittal of the guilty for Christ's sake, even at the expense of any intelligible connection between justification and newness of life. The strength of the second perspective in academic Lutheranism may be seen in a certain minimalism common in Lutheran theological ethics, as well as in what might be called an 'antinomian drift' which has difficulty seeing how any normative formation of life is compatible with the gospel. A coherent and widely accepted integration of free forgiveness and renewal of life has eluded Lutheran theology through most of the past century.

A second polarization of Lutheranism, that between the inner and the outer, has taken form as Lutherans have encountered cultural modernity and its definition of religion as a mode of private inwardness within a demystified outward or public world free of supernatural presence and fully describable by secular reason and its scientific instruments and methods. One tendency in modern Lutheranism has taken certain classic Lutheran dualities – works and faith, law and gospel, etc. – as already anticipating modern ways of sorting out the private and the public, the religious and the secular. The outer world of modern secularity is described as the realm of law and works, while salvation engages the inner person in the subjectivity of faith. A very different Lutheran tendency has taken its start from the Lutheran doctrine of the external word, and especially from the traditional Lutheran theology of Christ's bodily presence in the Lord's Supper, and has thus found itself in a far more critical and uncomfortable relationship to cultural modernity.

The chief point of controversy between these two construals of Lutheranism has been the doctrine of the *church*, over which Lutherans have been in more or less continuous conflict for the past two centuries. For the first tendency, the church as an outward social phenomenon is a strictly secular reality, constructed by groups of believers on strictly utilitarian grounds. For the second tendency, the visible church is itself an eschatological phenomenon, the public body of Christ, gathered and configured around Christ's public presence and action in the word and the sacraments. This divergence leads to conflict across a broad range of questions concerning the outward order of life and worship: are there forms of common life with an appropriateness intrinsic to the eschatological nature of the church, or are all forms essentially arbitrary, contingent on aesthetic taste and missionary tactics?

The third area of tension has been that between identity and ecumenicity. Lutherans have reacted with both caution and enthusiasm to the twentieth-century ecumenical movement, and world Lutheranism remains deeply divided over the compatibility of authentic Lutheran identity with ecumenicity. Three main viewpoints are in evidence.

Conservative Lutherans, including most Lutheran churches outside the Lutheran World Federation, identify the existing ecumenical movement with doctrinal indifference and compromise. Lutheran identity for them involves subscription to a body of teaching whose substance cannot easily be separated from its precise linguistic formulation in the Lutheran Confessions and the classic Lutheran teachers of the sixteenth and seventeenth centuries. They do not recognize authentic agreement in faith short of wholesale acceptance by other Christians of that body of teaching in its classical linguistic form. Many of these bodies also deny the existence of 'open questions' in theology; thus church fellowship is possible only where there is agreement on *all* points of theological conviction.

Within the ecumenically involved churches of the Lutheran World Federation, there is a strong body of opinion that calls the ecumenical enterprise into question on other grounds. These Lutherans do not read the Confessions as a body of irreformable doctrinal propositions, but rather as the secondary theological expression of Martin Luther's epochal 'Reformation discovery', an insight into the basis and structure of Christianity as a whole. Founded on this singular existential and theological breakthrough, Lutheranism is *systematically* incompatible with other forms of Christianity, especially Catholicism. Therefore ecumenical *rapprochement* with other Christians based on discussion of particular doctrinal issues only conceals the radical morphological incompatibility, the 'basic difference' (*Grunddifferenz*), which underlies historic points of confessional conflict. In the process, the integrity of the Lutheran form of Christianity is inevitably corrupted.

By contrast, ecumenically engaged Lutherans typically hold that Lutheranism shares in the common doctrinal and ecclesial *Gestalt* of catholic Christianity. The Lutheran Reformation on this view was a cleansing and clarifying, but not a repudiation of the historic form of catholic Christianity. These Lutherans therefore believe that what is essential to Lutheran identity can be sustained, and even strengthened, within the context of *rapprochement* with other Christians. Church fellowship is sought by way of 'differentiated consensus', an agreement in faith which does not pretend to eliminate all points of difference or even disagreement between Christian traditions, but which seeks to achieve mutual recognizability of gospel proclamation and core ecclesial practice despite continuing diversity. The accompanying vision of Christian unity is thus often described as 'reconciled diversity'.

This third perspective has been the basis for the ecumenical activity of the Lutheran World Federation and many of its member churches. It celebrated its greatest triumph to date with the signing of the *Joint Declaration on Justification* on 31 October 1999 by representatives of the Federation and the Vatican, affirming that Lutherans and Roman Catholics no longer have church-dividing differences over the doctrine of justification. Nevertheless, the intense controversy over the *Joint Declaration* that continues in the Lutheran world reveals how little consensus there is within the Lutheran community on the relation between confessional identity and ecumenical involvement.

All parties to each of these conflicts make appeal to Luther and to aspects of the early Lutheran consensus. Indeed, Lutheran debates over theological identity and ecclesiastical policy frequently take the form of arguments about the interpretation of Luther and the Confessions. There is room to question, however, whether these deep and persistent tensions within the Lutheran family can truly be resolved in this way. It may be that new configurations of belief and practice are taking form within the Lutheran world, each of which derives in some way from the Lutheran Reformation while being at the same time divided with increasing sharpness from the others.

DAVID S. YEAGO

FURTHER READING: Karen L. Bloomquist and John R. Stumme (eds.), *The Promise of Lutheran Ethics* (Minneapolis, 1998); Martin Chemnitz, *Examination of the Council of Trent* (4 vols.; St Louis, MO, 1971–); *The Lord's Supper* (St Louis, MO, 1979), crucial studies by a defining figure in post-Reformation Lutheranism; Eric W. Gritsch, *Fortress Introduction to Lutheranism* (Minneapolis, 1994), recent introductory study; Heinrich Holze (ed.), *The Church as Communion: Lutheran Contributions to Ecclesiology* (Geneva, 1997); Lutheran-Roman Catholic Joint Commission, *Church and Justification: Understanding the Church in the Light of the Doctrine of Justification* (Geneva, 1994); Charles P. Krauth, *The Conservative Reformation and its Theology: As Represented in the Augsburg Confession, and in the History and Literature of the Evangelical Lutheran Church* (Philadelphia, 1871), classic statement from the nineteenth-century revival of confessional identity; Philip Melanchthon, *Melanchthon on Christian Doctrine: Loci communes, 1555* (trans. and ed. Clyde L. Manschreck; New York, 1965), enormously influential in the formation of the Lutheran theological tradition; Hermann Sasse, *Here We Stand: Nature and Character of the Lutheran Faith* (New York, 1938), emphasizes the centrality of the incarnation in historic Lutheranism; Heinrich Schmid, *The Doctrinal Theology of the Evangelical Lutheran Church, Verified from the Original Sources* (Philadelphia, 3rd edn, 1875), still the best window onto the Lutheran dogmaticians of the seventeenth century; Theodore G. Tappert (ed.), *Lutheran Confessional Theology in America, 1840–1880* (New York, 1972), documents the struggle to define Lutheranism in nineteenth-century North America; Vilmos Vajta (ed.), *The Lutheran Church, Past and Present* (Minneapolis, 1977), essays on Lutheran faith and life in global perspective.

Mackintosh, Hugh Ross (1870–1936)

Professor of systematic theology/Christian dogmatics, New College, Edinburgh, 1904–36. Mackintosh was ordained as a minister of the Free Church of Scotland (United Free – 1900, Church of Scotland – 1929) in 1897, having previously studied at the University of Edinburgh and New College, Edinburgh. During his studies he was particularly influenced by the philosopher Andrew Seth Pringle-Pattison (1856–1931), whose Personal Idealism undergirds much of Mackintosh's theology. The New College professors A.B. Davidson (1831–1902) and John Laidlaw (1832–1906) were also influential upon his developing thought, and the latter is the most likely source of Mackintosh's interest in the theology of *Albrecht Ritschl (1822–89). In common with many Scottish theological students, Mackintosh spent semesters studying in Germany under *Martin Kähler (1835–1912) at Halle and *Wilhelm Herrmann (1846–1922) at Marburg. As a result, he established a firm understanding of developments within German theology, and this remains a feature of his subsequent thought. An indication of the general orientation of his early thought is to be found in the title of his Edinburgh University DPhil dissertation on 'The Ritschlian Doctrine of Theoretical and Religious Knowledge' (1897). Thereafter, Mackintosh was a joint editor of the English translation of Ritschl's *The Christian Doctrine of Justification and Reconciliation*, III (Edinburgh, 1900), and later joint editor of the English translation of *Friedrich Schleiermacher's (1768–1834) *The Christian Faith* (Edinburgh, 1928). Thus, Mackintosh may be regarded as exemplifying the influence of German thought on Scottish theology in general, and of Ritschlian thought in particular. However, Mackintosh's engagement with the latter was in no way uncritical, and it is a characteristic of his theology that it resists classification and offers instead a distinctive synthesis of biblical and modern thought leavened by historical theology.

Nowhere is this more evident than in his earliest significant work, *The Doctrine of the Person of Jesus Christ* (Edinburgh, 1912). Here Mackintosh offers a thorough exposition of the Christology of the New Testament, followed by a similar exposition of Christological formulations from the second to the nineteenth centuries. In the light of this he offers a constructive statement of his own position in which he seeks to lay equal emphasis on the human personality of the historical Jesus and on the incarnation of the Son of God. Mackintosh subjects the formula of the Council of *Chalcedon (451) to particular criticism and contends that our faith in Christ is not to be linked to any particular Christological formulation. However, although not stated as such, it is the legacy of Chalcedon that underlies Mackintosh's most significant contribution to Christology – that is, his rehabilitation of kenotic Christology. Thus, his attempt to formulate an understanding of the self-limitation of God in Christ implicitly wrestles with the difficulties inherent in Chalcedon. Mackintosh recognizes the weaknesses of earlier kenotic Christologies and suggests that the attributes of deity, rather than being laid aside, are in fact 'transposed', such that they:

> …may come to function in new ways, to assume new forms of activity, readjusted to the new condition of the Subject. It is possible to conceive the Son, who has entered at love's behest on the region of growth and progress, as now possessing *all* the qualities of Godhead in the form of concentrated potency rather than of full actuality. *Person of Jesus Christ* (p. 477)

In *God Was in Christ* (London, 1948), *D.M. Baillie (1887–1954) strongly critiqued Mackintosh's position. Nevertheless, Mackintosh's treatment highlights the crucial interrelationship between Christology and soteriology in a manner which is sensitive to the points at which these doctrines mutually inform one another.

Thereafter, Mackintosh's most notable contributions focused on the question of eschatology in *Immortality and the Future* (London, 1915) and then, in the 1920s, on the nature of Christian experience in works such as *The Christian Experience of Forgiveness* (London, 1927) and *The Christian Apprehension of God* (London, 1929). In both of these works, the influence of Ritschl and Herrmann and others remains marked.

Mackintosh's final book, the posthumous *Types of Modern Theology* (London, 1937) traces the development of modern theology via Schleiermacher, *Hegel, Ritschl, *Troeltsch, *Kierkegaard and *Barth. In particular, Mackintosh seeks to assess the contribution of Barth, and in so doing he has been typically interpreted as rejecting the stream of theology influenced by Ritschl, in favour of that influenced by

Barth. Thus, J.W. Leitch in *A Theology of Transition: H.R. Mackintosh as an Approach to Barth* (London, 1952) contends that Mackintosh 'would seem to represent the remarkable – and indeed unique – spectacle of one who, starting as at least in some sense a Ritschlian, finally completely changed his direction and found himself in close proximity to Barth' (pp. 33–34). This line of interpretation is endorsed by *T.F. Torrance and R.R. Redman. However, this interpretation cannot be sustained. In fact, Mackintosh judges that the aim, if not the performance, of Ritschl and Barth is basically identical. Further, while offering a rigorous critique of Ritschl, he specifically exempts Herrmann from the criticisms he makes of Ritschl's own position, and suggests that Herrmann's conception of the nature of God's revelation in Christ is one which is consonant with the New Testament. Therefore, Mackintosh may be regarded as offering, to the end of his life, a continuing openness to Ritschlian thought which was not understood as preventing the approbation of the theology of Barth. The synthesis which his mature theology represents is one which is profoundly spiritual and pastorally sensitive, and which offers access to a theological legacy which is worthy of being revisited.

JOHN L. MCPAKE

FURTHER READING: *Texts: The Person of Jesus Christ* (London, 1912); *The Originality of the Christian Message* (London, 1920); *The Divine Initiative* (London, 1921); *Some Aspects of Christian Belief* (London, 1923); *Sermons* (Edinburgh, 1938), with a memoir by A.B. Macaulay; 'Leaders of Theological Thought: Karl Barth', *Expos T* 39 (1928), pp. 536–40. *Studies:* R.R. Redman, *Reformulating Reformed Theology: Jesus Christ in the Theology of Hugh Ross Mackintosh* (Lanham, MD, 1997); T.F. Torrance, 'Hugh Ross Mackintosh: Theologian of the Cross', *Scot Bul Ev Th* 5 (1987), pp. 160–73.

Macmurray, John (1891–1976)

Distinguished Scottish philosopher who argued, against the prevailing trends in his discipline, for an understanding of the self as essentially embodied, social, religious and active. This relational account of the person has continued to influence the social and theological sciences after Macmurray's death.

Macmurray was educated at schools in Aberdeen before proceeding to Glasgow University and Bailliol College, Oxford. His studies in philosophy were interrupted by the outbreak of war in 1914. He was awarded the Military Cross after the Somme, but his experience of war left him critical of establishment politics and the institutional church. Despite being deeply religious and untroubled by doubts about the existence of God, he remained without any organized religious community, until in his retirement he and his wife became Quakers. The pacifism of the Society of Friends and its lack of doctrinal definition attracted him.

After holding teaching posts in Manchester, Johannesburg and Oxford, Macmurray was appointed in 1928 to the Grote Chair of the Philosophy of Mind and Logic at London University. In 1944 he returned to Scotland to the chair of moral philosophy in Edinburgh. He was regarded as an inspirational lecturer and teacher. Several key publications arose out of a series of popular radio broadcasts in the 1930s. His Gifford Lectures delivered in Glasgow in 1953/4 constituted his most significant work. The two published volumes comprise *The Self as Agent* and *Persons in Relation*.

Macmurray's philosophy is grounded upon a conviction regarding the unity of theory and practice. Every theory serves some form of action and it is in practice that all theories must be tested. The truth of judgement cannot be divorced from the rightness of action. His epistemology is strongly realist. The mode of knowledge is shaped by the nature of the object of enquiry. This holistic approach enables Macmurray to tilt at a range of characteristic dualisms in western thought: body and mind; spirit and matter; reason and emotion; God and the world. There are three types of reality which exist in hierarchical relation. These are the material, the organic and the personal. At the material level, the behaviour of entities is marked by consistency and predictability. At the organic level, behaviour is marked by growth, change and the evolution of life. At the personal level, beings can act freely and rationally according to their nature. The goal of personal life is friendship or communion. Human identity is thus fulfilled by living in, through and with others. From this perspective, further features of Macmurray's philosophy can be discerned.

His sympathy to *Marxism, particularly in his writings for the Christian Left in the 1930s, derives from the view that material and organic processes must be used for the sake of personal freedom. A just socio-economic order and a classless society are necessary conditions of genuine human community. Nonetheless, Macmurray's early affinity with Marxism did not extend to its radical criticism of religion. While hostile to other-worldly forms of Christianity, he insisted that religion can enhance personal life. Religion exercises a vital social function in uniting persons across national and racial boundaries. It enables us to overcome our fear of death and of one another. Fear, not hatred, is the antithesis of love. In this respect, ritual and fellowship are primary in religion; belief and doctrine are secondary. Macmurray was here strongly influenced by Hebraic thought forms over against Roman and Greek traditions. In the Old Testament, religion is not a compartment of life. It shapes all of personal, social and national life. The significance of Jesus resides in his transforming Judaism from a national to a universal religion. His central vision is of the kingdom of God on earth. Yet whether eschatology and the transcendence of God can be so easily downplayed in the religion of Jesus is arguable and may indicate some problems in Macmurray's account.

In his Gifford Lectures, Macmurray presents his philosophical vision with greater precision. The egocentric and disembodied self of Cartesian thought is roundly attacked. Macmurray substitutes the 'I do' for the 'I think'. The self is more adequately described in terms of agency than thought. The agent is rooted in a material and social world in which identity is determined relationally. In his analysis of the mother-child relationship, Macmurray argues that the child's identity is shaped by the intentions of its mother. Skills are acquired through linguistic communication rather than by mere instinct. All experience is thus shared experience, and all existence irreducibly social. The child's well being is dependent both upon the mother's continual love and her willingness to enable her child to become a free agent. A family is maintained by bonds of mutual affection and friendship between all possible pairs of its members. In this respect, a family is a model for every society. The task of politics is to apply this model under the conditions of economic and social life.

Macmurray's influence continues to grow, as is evident by the recent reissue of his major publications. His philosophical work can now be seen as one of several twentieth-century protests against the distorting effects of Cartesianism. The relational and holistic description of the self Macmurray presents has attracted the attention of social scientists. His vision of human society has appealed to recent communitarian trends in political thought. In theology, his account of the person has resonated with recent Trinitarianism and anthropology, with comparisons being drawn *inter alia* with *Richard of St Victor's Trinitarian doctrine. His distinction between the organic and personal forms of being has been viewed as a useful corrective to some recent trends in *environmental and *feminist theology, which tend to depersonalize the God-world relation.

DAVID FERGUSSON

FURTHER READING: *Texts: Freedom in the Modern World* (London, 1932); *Reason and Emotion* (London, 1935); *The Self as Agent* (London, 1957); *Persons in Relation* (London, 1961); *Search for Reality in Religion* (London, 1965); *The Personal World: John Macmurray on Self and Society* (ed. Philip Cornford; Edinburgh, 1996). *Studies:* A.R.C. Duncan, *The Nature of Persons* (New York, 1990); David Fergusson, *John Macmurray: The Idea of the Personal* (Edinburgh, 1992).

Marcel, Gabriel (1889–1973)

French, existentialist philosopher, born in Paris. He converted to Catholicism in 1929. Marcel never held a formal third-level position as a philosopher, but he worked as a lecturer, reviewer, playwright and drama and music critic.

Marcel belongs to the line of thinkers, which includes *Søren Kierkegaard (1813–55) and *Martin Buber (1878–1965) in philosophy, and *Karl Barth (1886–1968) and *Paul Tillich (1886–1965) in theology, who emphasize the non-theoretical nature of religious belief and moral experience. Marcel's phenomenological analysis of the human person is based on his critique of the 'spirit of abstraction' at work in modern culture, a critique which leads to his famous distinction between problem and mystery. Marcel argues that the realm of conceptual knowledge (or primary reflection) typically deals with *problems* of various kinds. Problems require conceptual generalizations, abstractions and an appeal to what is universal and verifiable in human experience. However, the realm of the problematic cannot give an adequate account of what Marcel calls the *being-in-a-situation* of the human person, the person's *fundamental involvement* in the world at the level of personal experience. This involvement takes place, according to Marcel, in the realm of *mystery*, a realm where the distinction between subject and object breaks down. Many of our most valued and profound experiences occur at this level. These experiences are all mysterious because they intimately involve the questioner in such a way that the meaning of the experience cannot be fully conveyed by means of an abstract conceptual analysis. This realm of mystery includes the 'concrete approaches' of love, hope, fidelity and faith. These experiences are being lost in the modern world – a loss that is ushering in new forms of alienation (a theme of many of his plays). From the philosophical point of view, such experiences can be recovered by means of *secondary reflection* – a general term which refers to both the act of critical reflection on primary reflection, and the realization or existential assurance of the realm of mystery, beyond primary reflection.

At the level of mystery, Marcel believes, human life is endowed with value by virtue of its very existence. It is possible to refuse to recognize this value, but this is still a refusal – and not a result arrived at by means of an analysis of the evidence. To refuse to recognize the value of being for Marcel means that one withdraws from the intersubjective nature of human relations, and the behaviour appropriate to these relations, and focuses instead on one's self as the centre of meaning and value. To adopt this attitude is to become 'unavailable' (*indisponible*) for the other, whereas what we urgently need is a kind of 'spiritual availability' (*disponibilité*) towards our fellow human beings.

Marcel holds that the experience of value also leads to the experience of the *transcendent*. For human existence is already endowed with value, which no individual created, but which we recognize, and which will exist after we are gone. This glimpse of the transcendent can lead to the affirmation of God. While Marcel believes that one cannot prove the existence of God in the philosophical sense, he argues that the transcendent aspect of human relationships, and the notion of availability, only make ultimate sense if God exists. Marcel's conclusion is that the commitment underlying the various promises which are at the heart of authentic human relationships only makes sense if it is understood as grounded in an absolute, transcendent reality.

By means of his 'theistic existentialism', Marcel wishes to challenge the scientism of the twentieth century and the increased bureaucratization and institutionalization of the modern era, and in so doing to preserve the dignity and integrity of the human person – all ideas which became prominent in twentieth-century theology.

BRENDAN SWEETMAN

FURTHER READING: *Texts: The Mystery of Being* (2 vols.; London, 1950); *Being and Having* (London, 1951); *The Philosophy of Existence* (London, 1956); *Creative Fidelity* (New York, 1964); *Homo Viator* (Paris, 1952). *Studies:* Kenneth Gallagher, *The Philosophy of Gabriel Marcel* (New York, 1975); Clyde Pax, *An Existential Approach to God* (The Hague, 1972); P.A. Schilpp and L. Hahn (eds.), *The Philosophy of Gabriel Marcel* (La Salle, IL, 1984).

Marcion (d. c. 154)

Marcion was a second-century heretic who was known for his work as a reformer, biblical critic, canon-maker and theologian. He was born at Sinope, a seaport city in the province of Pontus (modern-day northern Turkey). The son of a bishop and a very prosperous shipowner, Marcion travelled to Rome where he taught from 137 to 144. While there he came under the influence of Cerdo, a *Gnostic teacher who gave Marcion the conceptual framework for developing his theology. After elucidating his beliefs to the church leaders in Rome he was excommunicated in 144 and soon afterwards founded his own church. Like most of the later Protestant Reformers, Marcion did not wish to start a new church or claim doctrinal innovation, but he maintained that he was testifying to the original message of Jesus which the church of his day had distorted.

So successful and rapid was the spread of his ideas that by c. 150 his contemporary, *Justin Martyr, tells us that a vast number of his churches could be found scattered throughout the entire Roman Empire and posed a serious threat to the doctrinal purity of the faith. This assertion is supported by the numerous extant writings of geographically separated patristic writers who specifically opposed Marcion. Marcion died as a heretic c. 154, with the peak of his influence lasting until c. 200. By the end of the third century, most of the Marcionite communities were absorbed in Manicheism. Though little is known about them, a small number of Marcionite communities continued in the west until c. 300 and especially flourished in the east until as late as 692, when the Council of Trullo provided guidelines for the church's reception of Marcionites into the orthodox faith.

The growing influence of Gnosticism clearly linked Marcion to the intellectual trends of his day. The extent of Gnostic influence on Marcion has been debated. The traditional view, represented by *Irenaeus of Lyons, sees Marcion as a Gnostic: 'Marcion of Pontus succeeded Cerdo and developed his doctrine' (*Heresies* 1.27.2). Contemporary scholarship agrees that there are many similarities, but underscores important differences as well. For example, Marcion fails to develop the Gnostic belief in a series of ages that emanated from the One divine spirit (though hints of this idea are reflected in portions of his thought). Marcion believes that humans are the product of the Creator's work and therefore without the innate divine spark from the One divine spirit, and he rejects allegorical methods of exegesis that make myth the foundation for doctrine. Thus, the growing scholarly consensus is that Marcion was not a fully developed Gnostic but was strongly influenced by Gnosticism and therefore may be considered a broadly atypical Gnostic of his day.

The principal points of Marcion's theology which contributed to his role in shaping the development of Christian thought can be seen in his world-view and in his understanding of the boundaries of the biblical canon. The reconstruction of his theology, however, comes not from his own writings, which are no longer extant, but from the anti-Marcionite polemics of various Church Fathers, especially *Tertullian. Moreover, Marcion's influence can be seen in the history of Paul's impact on the development of theology outside the New Testament period. For it was Marcion who first challenged the church to determine what was the message of the 'true' Paul, since Marcion relied heavily on the Pauline corpus in the development of his own heterodox conclusions.

Following particular Gnostic emphases of his day, and at points modifying them, it was Marcion's faulty Christology which proved to be the fatal virus infecting his overall system of belief. Marcion held to a *docetic Christology which denied both the human origin of Christ's existence and that his body was material (since matter was an unworthy dwelling for divinity). The Saviour was pure spirit, and the body in which he appeared on earth was only a ghost-like substance that could, nevertheless, assume the appearance of real flesh – as in the case of angelic appearances. Marcion's positive account of the relation between the human and divine in Christ, however, cannot be reconstructed due to the lack of available evidence.

Marcion's cosmology, anthropology and soteriology are logical corollaries of his Christology. In his cosmology, the God of the Old Testament was the evil Demiurge God of Gnosticism who created matter, and who was thus the author of evil. As such, this God is himself evil, imperfect and self-contradictory. The anthropological consequences which flow from this are that humans became the fleshly material product of an evil God and now stand in need of being freed from the ignorance of their human predicament. Hence, Marcion's version of the Christian gospel was structured around a series of antitheses between the Old and New Testaments. The God of the Old Testament was not the same God as that of the New Testament; the Old Testament deity was a God of wrath, the New Testament deity a God of love; the Old Testament brought bondage, the New Testament announced freedom through Christ; the Old Testament Law stood at odds with the New Testament gospel; the predicted Messiah of the Old Testament could not be the same Messiah of the New Testament. Soteriologically, therefore, Christ could not be the offspring of the Old Testament God, but of the One pure spirit who manifested himself in the redemptive acts and person of Jesus. This God revealed his identity by sending his Son to redeem humans from the evil God of the Old Testament and his creation, with Christ's crucifixion playing a major role in human redemption. Evil for Marcion was more the physical reality of suffering, and not the moral reality of sin. The difficulties of the human predicament and environment concerned him more than the theological meaning of sin as revealed in Romans 3 and elsewhere. Emphasizing the metaphor of 'purchase', it is clear that Marcion's interpretation of the shed blood of Christ was not so much for the purpose of forgiving sinners as it was to cancel the evil Creator's claims upon his creatures and their bondage to creation itself. Such a view arose from his dualistic presuppositions about the two deities and the antithesis between matter and spirit. Thus an inadequate conception of sin, which allowed for little or no punishment, made the need for forgiveness almost obsolete.

From these assumptions it was only natural that Marcion's canon of Scripture excluded the entire Old Testament due to the latter's unworthy character. Even his New Testament excluded the Gospels of Matthew, Mark and John and all the non-Pauline writings including the pastoral epistles and Hebrews (considered non-Pauline) – all due to their doctrinal corruption by Jewish laws and precepts. Even this abbreviated canon underwent the knife of Marcion's further editorial cuts, as described in his treatise titled *Antithèse* (more or less an 'Introduction to the New Testament' that reappears in the refutations of the Church Fathers). Utilizing a literal method of biblical exegesis, as opposed to allegory, all verses which upheld the Mosaic Law were cut out or textually modified to create harmony with Marcion's theological presuppositions. This left Marcion's canon with only an edited version of the Gospel of Luke (a companion of Paul and thus a purer Paulinist) and ten Pauline epistles. While some scholars have asserted that Marcion was the first person to compile a canonical collection of New Testament Scriptures, this seems unlikely given the church's ability to reject it based on a previously existing, loosely organized collection of New Testament writings, and the witness of the New Testament itself concerning an earlier collection of Paul's epistles that were considered by Christians to be on a par with sacred Scripture (2 Pet. 3:16).

Contemporary scholarship on Marcion is indebted to *Adolf von Harnack, who collected a wealth of material and argued for a more sympathetic appreciation of Marcion's Paulinism and reforming spirit. Harnack's arguments are impressive and forceful in style, but his views tend to be misleading because they are not based on a close reading of the primary sources. He overestimates the importance of Marcion in the formation of the canon, and he often fashions him more into an image of the Protestant *Luther than he actually was. R. Joseph Hoffmann, however, has recently attempted to alter the direction of post-Harnack research by correcting Harnack's oversimplification of Marcion's image of Paul and Marcion's role in the history of the development of the New Testament canon. Nevertheless, Harnack's work continues to set the pace for the field.

BRADLEY NASSIF

FURTHER READING: Adolf von Harnack, *Marcion: The Gospel of the Alien God* (trans. J.E. Steely and L.D. Bierma; Durham, NC, 1989); R. Joseph Hoffmann, *Marcion: On the Restitution of Christianity* (Chico, CA, 1984); David W. Bercot (ed.), *A Dictionary of Early Christian Beliefs: A Reference Guide to More Than 700 Topics Discussed by the Early Church Fathers* (Peabody, MA, 1997); Arland Hultgren and S.A. Haggmark (eds.), *The Earliest Christian Heretics: Readings from their Opponents* (Minneapolis, 1996); Arland Hultgren, *The Rise of Normative Christianity* (Minneapolis, 1997); E.C. Blackman, *Marcion and His Influence* (London, 1948); Hans von Campenhausen, *The Formation of the Christian Bible* (London, 1972); D. Balas, 'Marcion Revisited: A "Post Harnack Perspective"', in W.E. March (ed.), *Texts and Testament: Critical Essays on the Bible and Early Church Fathers* (San Antonio, TX, 1980), pp. 95–108; Robert M. Grant, 'Marcion and the Critical Method', in P. Richardson and J.C. Hurd (eds.), *From Jesus to Paul: Studies in Honour of Francis Wright Beare* (Waterloo, Ontario, 1984), pp. 207–15; R.S. Wilson, *Marcion: A Study of a Second-Century Heretic* (London, 1932); John Knox, *Marcion and the New Testament* (Chicago, 1942).

Maréchal, Joseph (1878–1944)

Maréchal was a native of Charleroi, Belgium. He entered the *Jesuit order in 1895 and gradually completed his required spiritual and intellectual formation despite his recurrent episodes of ill health from adolescence onwards. After further philosophical training, he studied the natural sciences at the University of Louvain and earned a doctorate in natural science, summa cum laude, in 1905. Upon completion of his theological studies, he was ordained in 1908.

Maréchal's most prolific period of writing spans the years from 1915 to 1935. His primary works were a two-volume study of religious psychology and Christian and comparative mysticism, *Études sur la Psychologie des Mystiques*, and his five-volume *magnum opus*, *Le Point de Départ de la Métaphysique*. In volume one of the latter masterful work, *De l'Antiquité à la fin du Moyen Âge: La Critique Ancienne de la Connaissance*, Maréchal traces the rise and fall of the realist epistemological tradition at the heart of the Aristotelian-Thomistic synthesis. In volume two, *Le Conflit du Rationalisme et de l'Empirisme dans la Philosophie Moderne avant Kant*, Maréchal attempts to demonstrate how the sundering of

*Thomistic realism under the attacks of late medieval *Nominalism laid the groundwork for the continual conflicts between rationalists and empiricists in pre-Kantian modern philosophy. Maréchal's balanced and largely favourable treatment of *Kant in volume three, *La Critique du Kant*, led to his being held suspect in certain ecclesiastical quarters. As a result, Maréchal dedicated himself directly to the publication of volume five of *Le Point de Départ*, *Le Thomisme devant la Philosophie Critique*, in which he tries to defend the orthodoxy of his then daring attempt to correlate Thomistic realism and Kantian transcendentalism in a positive fashion. Volume four, *Le Système Idéaliste chez Kant et les Postkantiens*, Maréchal's critique of German Idealism, was published posthumously based on manuscripts he had left.

Maréchal always considered himself a dedicated Thomist and never genuinely called into question the epistemological realism that was the centrepiece of *Aquinas's philosophical method. However, he realized that Thomism had to enter into a critical dialogue with modern philosophical movements if it was to be more than a Catholic curiosity and have any real impact on modern intellectual life. In this sense, Maréchal differed markedly from the neo-Thomist programme that had been highly influential in Catholic circles since the mid-nineteenth century. Neo-Thomists such as Joseph Kleutgen argued that all modern systems of philosophy were inherently flawed by the subjectivist turn in philosophy since *Descartes and, thus, dialogue with them would be fruitless and vain.

Central to Maréchal's Transcendental Thomism is the contention that the epistemology originally developed by *Aristotle and refined by Thomas Aquinas, which portrays our senses and intellectual faculties operating in a coordinated and complementary fashion, cannot be abandoned if we are to develop a coherent theory of knowledge. Furthermore, Aquinas's doctrine that our concepts or ideas are not the direct object of knowledge (*id quod intelligitur*) but the means by which we come to know reality directly (*id quo intelligitur*) must serve as a bulwark against both idealism and scepticism in philosophy. The goal of his extensive analysis of the history of western philosophy is to demonstrate that when thinkers strayed from these epistemological principles as the point of departure for their philosophizing, what resulted

were caricatures of cognition. According to Maréchal, Kant's great achievement was to recapture the necessity of presenting a harmonious account of sensation and intellection, thus pointing a way beyond the impasse between rationalists and empiricists that had bedevilled philosophical thought from Descartes to *Hume. But Kant was prevented from retrieving a full-bodied realism by his overly static view of the role of human understanding in its search for knowledge. Maréchal tried to show that when the dynamic nature of our intellectual striving is fully realized, then Kant's own critical idealism, as well as nineteenth-century absolute idealism and twentieth-century agnosticism, can be overcome. In the fifth volume of *Le Point de Départ*, Maréchal daringly argues that, even beginning with a subjective starting point (our own content of consciousness), a rigorously pursued transcendental method will reveal the necessity of objective affirmation or epistemological realism.

What Kant failed fully to appreciate in his *Critique of Pure Reason* was the way in which our primordial intellectual orientation toward the absolute or God undergirds all our attempts to come to know finite things. In Maréchal's view, every attempt at knowing finite realities must be seen as a partial step in the overarching quest of human intelligence for intellectual union with God. As Maréchal puts it, 'Every particular volition is inspired by the natural volition of the last end. Hence no activity of our intellect, no intellectual assimilation is possible but in virtue of the deep yearning whose saturating end would be the intuition of the absolute real' (*Mélanges Joseph Maréchal*, I, p. 89). Hence, for Maréchal, this intellectual striving toward God is a necessary pre-condition of the knowing process itself. He believed that a fully orchestrated transcendental analysis reveals the indirect but still actually existing and necessary reference to God as the ultimate animating dynamism of all cognitive operations. As a result, 'our quest for an adequate metaphysical vision of reality is necessarily ongoing, unfinished, and self-correcting for it has as it goal nothing less than the grasp of God. It is, in its deepest and most fundamental sense, a quest for the absolute' (*Quest for the Absolute*, p. 143).

Maréchal's Transcendental Thomism had a formative influence on the emergence of the so-called New Theology within Catholic circles. It likewise inspired the work of *Karl Rahner and

*Bernard Lonergan, arguably the most influential Catholic thinkers of the second half of the twentieth century. Most importantly, Maréchal showed that intellectual isolation within a Catholic citadel mentality was not in keeping with the spirit of the Angelic Doctor, Thomas Aquinas. Like the great medieval master, those who worked in the Thomist tradition should open themselves to critical and open conversation with the intellectual currents of their time.

ANTHONY M. MATTEO

FURTHER READING: *Texts: Le Point de Départ de la Métaphysique* (5 vols.; Paris, 1964); *Mélanges Joseph Maréchal* (2 vols.; Paris, 1950); *Studies in the Psychology of the Mystics* (Albany, NY, 1964). *Studies:* Joseph Donceel (ed.), *A Maréchal Reader* (New York, 1970); *The Searching Mind* (Notre Dame, IN, 1979); Anthony M. Matteo, *Quest for the Absolute: The Philosophical Vision of Joseph Maréchal* (Dekalb, IL, 1992); Gerald A. McCool, *Catholic Theology in the Nineteenth Century* (New York, 1977).

Maritain, Jacques (1882–1973)

French Catholic philosopher, born in Paris; Maritain was brought up as a *liberal Protestant. In his early life, he fell under the influence of scientism and secularism. Maritain married Raïssa Oumançoff in 1904, and they converted to the Catholic faith in 1906. In 1914, he became chair of modern philosophy at the Institut Catholique de Paris. Maritain spent the war years 1939–45 exiled in the United States. In 1945 he returned to Paris and was appointed French Ambassador to the Vatican. In his later years, he returned to the United States, where he lectured widely and held various teaching posts.

Maritain is one of the foremost modern scholars and interpreters of the thought of *St Thomas Aquinas, and his insights and influence contributed much to a *Thomistic revival in this century. Maritain supports the classical view of philosophical realism that there is nothing in the intellect that is not in things; he holds that being is real, and can be known because of the essential conformity of the intellect to being. One initially comes to know being as such through intuition, a term that Maritain inherited from Henri Bergson (1859–1941), a philosopher under whom he studied in his early career. Unlike Bergsonian intuition, however, which was non-conceptual, for Maritain the intuition of being reveals that being is *transcendental*, that is, that being is real and is all there is. It also

reveals to the intellect an insight into the *analogical* nature of being – that, although all existents have being in common, they differ by means of their individual essences.

In *The Degrees of Knowledge*, Maritain's major work in epistemology, he refers to a type of knowledge that is non-conceptual, called 'connatural knowledge'. This is knowledge that occurs when the individual subject becomes 'co-natured' with the object of knowledge. In such knowledge the intellect does not operate alone or primarily by means of concepts, but it operates also with the affective inclinations and the dispositions of the will, and is guided and directed by them. Maritain believes that this notion of connaturality has particular relevance in philosophy and theology. In *Approaches to God*, after presenting in contemporary language Aquinas's five ways of demonstrating the existence of God, Maritain proposes a new 'sixth way', which is initially guided by connaturality. He argues that when a person is engaged in an act of purely intellectual thought, he has an intuition that the thinking intellect is outside time (for the spiritual operation of thought is superior to time). It is impossible for the self in the act of thinking to conceive a time when it did not exist; this leads to the insight that the immaterial intellect always existed, not necessarily in its own being, but in a super-personal existence, a Being of transcendent personality (God). This argument, which begins as a preconceptual intuition, can then be elaborated philosophically. A similar type of experience is possible in art and poetry. The artist, whatever his ideological position, in so far as he is in touch with beauty itself, goes *beyond* art and comes in touch with God, who is the source of beauty. The artist may not acknowledge God, but he or she is nevertheless touching the transcendent in human experience.

Maritain was very concerned with the philosophical justification of, and the application of, the Christian world-view in modern, pluralist societies, and it is in the area of social and political philosophy that he had most influence. Here he addresses some of the most significant matters for twentieth-century Christians. Maritain argues that people of different belief systems, as long as they are committed to the basic principles of democracy and the common good, can agree on basic human rights and values – such as equality and justice, the rights of the family, rights of association and the function of authority. Maritain's ideas were influential in promoting a consensus view on human rights in the United Nations.

The dream of all-encompassing secular and rationalist philosophies collapsed in twentieth-century catastrophes, Maritain pointed out. He went on to argue that the proper philosophical justification for the rights in the United Nations charter must ultimately belong to natural law, for natural law is the imprint of God's eternal law on human beings, and, just as important, it is discoverable through reason. Nevertheless, a theocracy is out of the question in the secular, democratic, pluralist state; so what is required today is 'a secular faith', where the state imposes and promotes practical truths that most democratically-minded people agree on, but it makes no commitment to any particular theory of justification of these truths. Although freedom of religion must be guaranteed and the separation of church and state must be maintained, Maritain held that, from the perspective of the Christian philosopher, the body politic is nevertheless inspired by Christianity (and other world-views in so far as they agree with Christian social philosophy). In addition, Christian virtues are both the inspiration for a modern democratic society and will be strengthened in such a society.

Maritain was often criticized on these latter points, especially for his claim that natural rights were derived from the Christian gospel, and for adopting a too apocalyptic tone in his critique of modern society. However, he believed that his view was a reasonable position for a committed Christian to hold, and a pluralism that does not advocate a similar approach to the general question of theoretical justification (even if one's justification is not based on Christianity) must inevitably end up in scepticism about truth and moral relativism about values.

Maritain's thinking championed modern ideas long before they became fashionable within the church: ecumenism, natural rights and liberal democracy, the critique of capitalism, the condemnation of anti-Semitism. These issues were all the subjects of major pronouncements by *Vatican II (1962–65), on which Maritain's thought had a significant influence, and the conclusions of which he welcomed. In recognition of Maritain's work, the 'Letter to Intellectuals' was presented to him by Pope Paul VI at the close of the Council, a fitting tribute to

Maritain's influence on the twentieth-century church. But before his death Maritain strongly criticized (in *The Peasant of the Garonne*) what he regarded as the later abuses and distortions by modern theologians of the Council's recommendations.

BRENDAN SWEETMAN

FURTHER READING: *Texts: The Degrees of Knowledge* (1932; Notre Dame, IN, 1995); *A Preface to Metaphysics* (1934; New York, 1939); *Integral Humanism* (1936; London, 1941); *The Rights of Man and Natural Law* (1942; San Francisco, 1986); *Christianity and Democracy* (1943; London, 1945); *Man and the State* (Chicago, 1951); *Approaches to God* (1953; London, 1955); *Creative Intuition in Art and Poetry* (1953; London, 1954); *The Peasant of the Garonne* (1966; London, 1968); *The Collected Works of Jacques Maritain* (ed. Ralph McInerny; 20 vols.; Notre Dame, IN, 1995–). *Studies:* James V. Schall, SJ, *Jacques Maritain: The Philosopher in Society* (Lanham, MD, 1998); Brendan Sweetman (ed.), *The Failure of Modernism: The Cartesian Legacy and Contemporary Pluralism* (Washington, DC, 1999).

Marxism

The term 'Marxism' as a description of a world-view owes more to the leaders of the Second International (1889–1914) than to Karl Marx himself. The Russian revolutionary thinker Plekhanov (1856–1918) developed the idea of 'dialectical materialism', which understood the work of Marx as a fully materialist version of *Hegel's system. Both Plekhanov and Kautsky (1854–1938) were much influenced by the reigning evolutionary 'biologism' and scientific positivism of the end of the nineteenth century. Marx himself (1818–83) was concerned first and foremost with developing a critique of political economy (*Capital*, 1867; *Theories of Surplus Value*, 1861–63) and with historical materialism – the insistence that ideas and concepts can only be understood in relation to their social and economic situation (*German Ideology*, 1846). Not only is he not interested in propounding a metaphysic, but he is highly ironical about those who are more concerned with ideas than with real social change. His scepticism made him ill-disposed to the construction of all-embracing ideologies.

Marx became an atheist shortly after leaving school, and he was never seriously interested in religion. His famous description of it as 'the opium of the people' and his view that 'the critique of religion is the origin of all critique'

(*Critique of Hegel's Philosophy of Right*, 1843) belong together. *Feuerbach accounted for religion, to Marx's satisfaction, as a form of projection. For 'God', read 'what human beings aspire to become'. Marx went beyond this abstract point and understood religion as the expression of a distorted society. He could appeal to many contemporary Christian writings, and especially to A. Ure's *Philosophy of Manufactures* (1835), to show how religion could be cynically used to dispel critical or revolutionary thinking. Marx believed that as society changed and became more just, religion would die away (*On the Jewish Question*, 1843).

Engels (1820–95) was more interested in religion and contributed a brilliant analysis of the German Peasants' War in terms of class analysis (1850). In *Anti-Dühring* (1877) he went further in analyzing religion as the projection of an alienated society and paved the way for the materialist metaphysic of Plekhanov. For the Second International, 'Marxism' or 'scientific socialism' was now an all-embracing worldview. On the other hand, Kautsky portrayed Jesus as a proletarian Messiah who wished to found a kingdom on earth. Jesus' revolutionary ideals had been eroded by the growth of hierarchy but were now taken over by socialism, which was the true heir of the gospel (*Foundations of Christianity*, 1908). The early Bolsheviks, while theoretically recognizing freedom of religion, in fact actively discouraged it. Under Stalin (1879–1953), who was seminary educated, many Russian churches were closed and there was some persecution, though it was not as severe as that directed at the 'kulaks', or dissident members of the Communist party.

Soviet hostility to Christianity dominated the perception of Marxism for almost half a century following the revolution. Occasional Christian supporters like Hewlett Johnson, the 'Red Dean' of Canterbury, or active communists like Alan Ecclestone (1904–92), were regarded as eccentrics or blacklisted. Theologians like Reinhold Niebuhr (1892–1971), who were socialist in the 1930s, became vigorous opponents of communism during the cold war (1947–89). Within the Soviet bloc, however, theologians like the Czech Protestant *J. Hromadka (1889–1969) sought to respond more positively, with the strong support of *Karl Barth, while the East German Church understood itself as a 'loyal opposition'. This work prepared the way for the Christian-

Marxist dialogue of the 1960s, made possible by the 'Prague Spring' of 1967 on the one side and *Vatican II on the other. The dialogue appealed above all to Marx's early Paris manuscripts in which he explored the impact of capitalism in terms of alienation – a term which had already been used in existentialist theology as a synonym for sin. Czech Marxists like V. Gardavsky and M. Machovec, for their part, found religious figures like Jacob or Jesus examples of liberated subjectivity, and they rejected the thin rationalism of earlier Marxist critiques of religion (Gardavsky, *God is Not Yet Dead*, 1973). Machovec argued that Christianity had resources to understand and critique society which Marxism lacked (*A Marxist Looks at Jesus*, 1976). This dialogue was largely extinguished by the Russian invasion of Czechoslovakia in 1968. *J. Moltmann's dialogue with the heterodox Marxist E. Bloch, whose *Principle of Hope* had appeared in the 1950s, was more fruitful and influenced European political theology (*Theology of Hope*, 1965).

The year 1968 also saw the emergence of liberation theology on a continent where the cold war struggle had quite a different significance – Latin America. Liberation theologians had to try to understand why 'development' and 'aid' led only to greater poverty and debt. They found help in the Marxist analysis of economy and society, above all in the account of private property (by J. Miranda) and of the fetishization of commodities (by F. Hinkelammert). Miranda claimed that the Marxist concern to free people from oppression found its authentic precursor in the liberating God of the Scriptures, while encyclicals such as Paul VI's 'Populorum progressio' (1967) effectively summarized Marxist teaching (*Marx and the Bible*, 1971). After the accession of John Paul II, whose background was in Stalinist Poland, the Vatican launched a counter-attack with the highly critical 'Instruction Concerning Liberation Theology' (1984). This document claimed that Marxism was incompatible with Christian faith and that liberation theology confused the biblical 'poor' with the Marxist proletariat. These views were somewhat modified two years later in the 'Instruction on Christian Freedom and Liberation'.

After the collapse of 'really existing socialism' in 1989, some of the heat has gone out of the official church opposition to Marxism. Many theologians, not only in Latin America but also in the United States, continue to acknowledge a debt to Marx – primarily in terms of his economic analysis. In this they are more faithful to his original intentions than some of his followers. The need to use Marxian analysis is likely to continue while capitalism remains the dominant mode of the organization of economy and society.

TIMOTHY GORRINGE

FURTHER READING: F. Hinkelammert, *The Ideological Weapons of Death* (New York, 1986); N. Lash, *A Matter of Hope* (London, 1981); A. MacIntyre, *Marxism and Christianity* (London, 1968); D. McLellan, *Karl Marx* (London, 1973); Marxism and Religion (London, 1987); J. Miranda, *Marx and the Bible* (New York, 1974); D. Turner, *Marxism and Christianity* (Oxford, 1983).

Mascall, Eric Lionel (1905–93)

Anglo-Catholic theologian and philosopher. He conducted parish work from the time of his ordination in the Church of England (1932) until his academic career, first at Christ Church, Oxford (1945–62), and then as professor of historical theology at King's College, London (1962–73). His distinguished lectures included the Bampton Lectures at Oxford (1956; published as *Christian Theology and Natural Science*), the Boyle Lectures (1965–66; published as *The Christian Universe*) and the Gifford Lectures (1970–71; published as *The Openness of Being: Natural Theology Today*).

Mascall's contribution to theology lies especially in three areas: natural theology, dogmatic theology and the special project of relating Christian theology to the natural sciences.

His lifelong work in natural theology was inaugurated with the publication in 1943 of *He Who Is: A Study in Traditional Theism* and carried further in the 1949 sequel *Existence and Analogy*. His main project was to demonstrate the rational grounds for asserting the existence of God, and to solve special problems that arise in connection with his distinctive approach to such demonstration. He followed what he called 'the existential approach to God' as manifest in the metaphysics of *Thomas Aquinas. That God's existence is necessary follows from the need to explain the existence of finite beings. But the sort of existence and causal power that God must have in order to account for finite existence is radically different from what is found in the world of finite creatures. Hence, the demonstration of God's existence raises the problem of how to think and speak intelligibly about such a transcendent and wholly other being. To solve this problem Mascall set forth a detailed analysis of the scholastic doctrine of analogy. In his little book *Words and Images* (London, 1957) Mascall sought to show the relevance of this doctrine for answering the *Logical Positivists, who construed all theological language as meaningless.

In dogmatic theology, Mascall's aim was to promote the unity of the historic Christian church and at the same time protect it from heterodoxy. The former aspect of his work is especially well illustrated by his book *The Recovery of Unity* (1958) and numerous essays, including contributions to volumes edited by other churchmen. The latter aspect is confirmed by his extensive polemical work in defence of traditional Christian orthodoxy. This work is characterized by detailed and incisive assessments of the theological literature produced by his contemporaries. For example, the book *Theology and the Gospel of Christ: An Essay in Reorientation* (London, 1977) is a defence of the deity of Jesus Christ against the onslaughts of liberal New Testament scholarship.

Mascall was convinced of the need for collaboration between scientists and theologians. His erudition and versatility as a theologian are amply attested by the wide-ranging treatment of scientific topics from a theological perspective in the book *Christian Theology and Natural Science* (1956). This book explores the bearing of scientific theory and discovery on such subjects as the problem of evil, the virgin birth of Jesus, the doctrines of the incarnation and the atonement, and the nature of the human soul and the possibility of human freedom. Even with the tremendous advances of science since the middle of the twentieth century, these discussions continue to be relevant in ways that reward study.

R. DOUGLAS GEIVETT

FURTHER READING: *Texts: Christ, the Christian and the Church: A Study of the Incarnation and Its Consequences* (London, 1946); *Corpus Christi* (London, 1953, rev. 1965); *Via Media: An Essay in Theological Synthesis* (London, 1956); *The Importance of Being Human: Some Aspects of the Christian Doctrine of Man* (New York, 1958); *Grace and Glory* (London, 1961); *The Secularisation of Christianity: An Analysis and a Critique* (London, 1965); *The Christian Universe* (London, 1966); *Theology and the Future* (London, 1968); *Nature and Supernature* (London, 1976).

Maurice, Frederick Denison (1805–72)

The son of a *Unitarian minister, Maurice was exposed to religious controversy as a child. Refusing to take his Cambridge degree because he would have to subscribe to the Thirty-nine Articles, he paradoxically transferred after an interval to Oxford and defended subscription on matriculation as the salutary condition of study within a community committed to specific beliefs, rather than as an arbitrary imposition at the end of it (*Subscription No Bondage*, 1835). Maurice was liberated into Trinitarian orthodoxy by the power of fervent (actually revivalist) Scottish *Calvinism through the influence of *Edward Irving. As chaplain of Guy's Hospital, Maurice wrote his seminal work of theological synthesis *The Kingdom of Christ* (1838) – 'hints' to a Quaker (who by definition rejected the institutional form of the church) on 'the Principles, Constitution and Ordinances of the Catholic Church'. The catholicity of the church is grounded in its historical existence as a concrete society, united in the sacraments and other means of grace, including the ministry.

Appointed professor of English literature and history at King's College, London, in 1840, Maurice became chaplain of Lincolns Inn and professor of theology at King's in 1846. Increasingly exercised about social questions, Maurice was involved with Kingsley and others in the *Christian Socialist Movement (which was not socialist) and founded the Working Men's College in 1854. Deprived of his London chair because of an outcry against his rejection of everlasting punishment in his *Theological Essays* (1853), his manifesto against Victorian religiosity, Maurice's career came full circle when he was appointed Knightsbridge Professor of Moral Philosophy at Cambridge (1866).

Maurice baffled thoughtful contemporaries, such as *J.S. Mill, who could not see what he was driving at, and he remains a misfit on the theological scene. His insights are found at the axiomatic level of theological method, rather than in specific theological positions (though he does not lack these). Maurice saw himself digging deep for theological principles, for the ground of all divinity. He has been championed as a theologian of synthesis and reconciliation by *A.M. Ramsey and Alec Vidler.

Maurice has been placed (e.g. by Sanders) among the Broad Church theologians, but though he had the reputation of a radical (on hell and on Christian 'socialism'), he was no true liberal. His affinity with *Newman, within a 'common tradition' centred on a Burkean sense of the corporate nature of Christian existence and the power of sacramental actions and hallowed religious language to sustain that tradition, has been brought out by Coulson. There have been few stronger defenders of tradition – as a living matrix, not as a catalogue of binding precedents – than Maurice. But Maurice was an implacable opponent of Newman (whose theory of the development of doctrine he particularly attacked) and of other Tractarians whom he accused of opposing the spirit of the age with the spirit of a past (i.e. medieval) age rather than with the Holy Spirit. He is best seen perhaps as a disciple of *Coleridge, whom he revered, and as an exponent of Coleridge's method of polarity, of holding truths in tension. To that extent, Maurice is connected to the Broad Church through the primary source of its inspiration.

Together with Coleridge and Julius Hare, Maurice provided a more historically objective understanding of the *Reformation than that promoted by the Tractarians. Though Maurice romanticized the Reformation and championed *Luther, he preserved sufficient critical detachment to expose what he saw as the degeneration of a living movement into scholastic aridity in the seventeenth century. *The Kingdom of Christ* and the major work *Moral and Metaphysical Philosophy* (1872) reveal Maurice's method in theology and philosophy. Maurice followed Coleridge in maintaining that thinkers were usually right in what they positively affirmed, but that they were often wrong in what they denied. At the heart of every distinct tradition there was a living insight or principle that, reflecting a real experience of God, had brought spiritual renewal, but had become corrupted into an insular and intolerant system of speculation. The Coleridgean method of polarity aimed to bring to light these positive principles, to liberate them from their stifling systems and to hold them together through imaginative power and historical empathy. Thus Protestantism stood for the principle of the supreme claim of the individual conscience before God; Catholicism for the corporate nature of the church. Neither could be compromised; both must be affirmed to the full.

God must be at the centre of theological reflection. Maurice professed his intention 'to ground all theology upon the name of God the

Father, the Son and the Holy Ghost; not to begin from ourselves and our sins; not to measure the straight line by the crooked one'. This was the approach of the Bible itself. 'There everything proceeds from God; he is revealing himself; he is acting, speaking, ruling.' The next step 'is to ground all human morality upon the relation in which man stands to God' (*The Doctrine of Sacrifice* [1879], p. xli). Maurice saw Luther as an exemplar of this theological objectivity grounded in revelation and claimed that it was the great merit of the Thirty-nine Articles. His conviction of the reality and informative content of revelation led Maurice to challenge (in *What is Revelation?*, 1859) Mansell's apophatic (negative) theology which contained too much agnosticism for his liking.

Maurice strikes us as above all a paradoxical figure: a searcher after clarity, whom people could not understand; a defender of the institutional church who was dismissed from his post; a man consumed by a passion for unity who engaged in ceaseless polemic against some of the most formidable adversaries and entrenched shibboleths of his age.

PAUL AVIS

FURTHER READING: *Text: The Life of Frederick Denison Maurice: Chiefly Told in His Own Letters* (2 vols.; London, 1885). *Studies*: P. Avis, *Anglicanism and the Christian Church* (Edinburgh, 1989), ch. 16, on Maurice and the Reformation; O. Brose, *Frederick Denison Maurice: Rebellious Conformist* (Athens, OH, 1971); T. Christensen, *The Divine Order: A Study in F.D. Maurice's Theology* (Leiden, 1973); J. Coulson, *Newman and the Common Tradition* (Oxford, 1970); F.M. McLain, *Maurice: Man and Moralist* (London, 1972); A.M. Ramsey, *F.D. Maurice and the Conflicts of Modern Theology* (Cambridge, 1951); C.R. Sanders, *Coleridge and the Broad Church Movement* (Durham, NC, 1942); A. Vidler, *F.D. Maurice and Company* (London, 1966).

Maximus the Confessor (c. 580–662)

Byzantine theologian, saint and martyr. The personal life of Maximus reflects the political and ecclesiastical situation of his time. He was born into a family of high reputation in the imperial capital and was well educated. At that time there was a relatively high degree of harmony in the empire, and the emperor of his early manhood, Heraclius, made him into a kind of personal secretary of state. Yet after some time he left the court to become a monk,

first in Asia Minor, and later – because of the circumstances after the invasion of Persia – in North Africa (Carthage). There he became a disciple of Sophronius, patriarch of Jerusalem.

In many ways Maximus's theology covers the whole range of classical topics. However, he was no systematic theologian. His chosen subjects were mostly inspired by questions or difficulties put to him, especially within the circles of monastic life. Besides more practical instructions – such as his *Capita de Charitate, Liber Asceticus*, his *Commentary on the Lord's Prayer* and his meditation over the divine liturgy, called *Mystagogia* – his two main works are his explications of Bible texts. These works are *Quæstiones ad Thalassium* (addressed to a fellow monk and his surroundings) and *Ambigua* (addressed to the abbot Thomas), which includes his comments to difficult passages, particularly in Gregory Nazianzen. In addition to these, his best-known work is his polemical dispute with Pyrrhus (once patriarch of Constantinople): *Disputatio cum Pyrrho* (where Maximus developed his doctrine on the two wills of Christ).

Pyrrhus agreed with him at first, but he changed his mind again. Rome, however, supported Maximus's doctrine. The pope Martin was later tried before the imperial court in 654, and he was sent into exile where he died. In 656 the patriarch Peter attempted a reconciliation with Maximus, but in vain. In 662 he was brought to Constantinople to be heard by a monothelite council which condemned him. The right hands and tongues of Maximus and his friends were cut off. Maximus was sent to the south-east shore of the Black Sea where he died in the same year. His cause, however, was soon victorious, at the Sixth Oecumenical Council of Constantinople in 680–81, where the doctrine of two wills in Christ was promulgated.

It would, however, be misleading to regard Maximus's theological vision as primarily polemical. He based his doctrine on the statements on the hypostatic unity of the two natures in Christ, made by the Council of Chalcedon in 451. From this position it became more and more clear to him that Christ must have two wills and energies as well. In the opposite monothelite position he saw a reminiscence of *Monophysitism. He confessed Christ's full humanity, and one of his main points was his insistence that God always wants to incarnate himself. He stated three forms of divine embodiment: in the principles (or *logoi*) of creation, in the words (or *logoi*) of Scripture and in the incarnate Logos/Christ the Man. Consequently, he also rejected the *'Origenist' position of a double creation (although he had a high veneration for Evagrius Ponticus as an ascetic, whose doctrine of the hierarchy of eight capital vices he accepted). Also in his relation to *Pseudo-Dionysius the Areopagite, influenced by Neoplatonism, he was selective. He saw the created universe as a dialogical counterpart to God, and man as both a reflective microcosm and a mediator in Christ to serve human deification and creational transfiguration.

In his understanding of humanity's mediating function Maximus was influenced by Nemesius of Emesa. The whole world is successively humanized through humanity in Christ. Yet human sinfulness is a very serious affair, and an area where Maximus's thinking seems to come very close to *St Augustine, though without a doctrine of predestination. Did he learn about Augustine in North Africa? We do not know. Deification and the mutuality between God and humankind are basic points in his doctrine of salvation. He expresses himself in the formula that 'God and man are exemplars one of another'. This is fully seen in Christ. The doctrine of the duality of natures implies a circumincession between them (in Greek *perichoresis*) which is not only passive on the human side.

Yet the fullness of the divine likeness in humanity, built upon our being created in the image of God, is not yet developed in Adam's original state. Maximus came very close to *St Irenaeus at this point. He underlines that Adam fell in sin at the very moment when he came into being. What lies before him is a process of deification through the ascetic development of virtues and the communion with the Logos in his *logoi* (an active contemplation in the species of creation, in the words of Scripture and in the sacramental fellowship with the incarnate through baptism and the Eucharist).

Maximus understands the *logoi* not only as ideas in the Platonic sense but as divine intentions, so that what he calls 'the *logos* of nature' may become 'the true *tropos* of existence' (the equivalent of human likeness unto God). Participation in the *logoi* as divine intentions implies an activation of the dynamic forces inherent in both God and creation. At this point it may be

that Maximus is a forerunner of the vision of uncreated divine energies, found much later in *St Gregory Palamas.

LARS THUNBERG

FURTHER READING: The corpus of Maximus's writings is not yet edited in critical form, yet new translations have appeared in recent years. The most important new English translations are George C. Berthold (ed.), *Maximus Confessor: Selected Writings* (London, 1985) and Andrew Louth, *Maximus the Confessor* (London / New York, 1996). Both books are extensively commented. *Recent studies*: Aidan Nichols, OP, *Byzantine Gospel: Maximus the Confessor in Modern Scholarship* (Edinburgh, 1993); Lars Thunberg, *Microcosm and Mediator: The Theological Anthropology of Maximus the Confessor* (Chicago, 2nd rev. edn, 1995); Jean-Claude Larchet, *La Divinisation de l'Homme selon Saint Maxime le Confesseur* (Paris, 1996); *Maxime le Confesseur, Médiateur entre l'Orient et l'Occident* (Paris, 1998).

Mediating Theology

This term is applied to an approach to Christian doctrine which largely flourished in German Protestantism in the earlier part of the mid-nineteenth century. Its beginning may be assigned to the founding of the Heidelberg journal *Theologische Studien und Kritiken* in 1828, to which many of its leading exponents contributed. Its programme was defined by K. Ullmann (1796–1865), one of the founding editors, as follows:

> Mediation is the scientifically tracing back of relative oppositions to their original unity, through which an inner reconciliation and higher standpoint is gained by which they are transcended, the intellectual position arising out of this mediation being the true, healthy mean.

In their writings, a variety of mediations seem to have been covered by this formula: between academic knowledge and the historic Christian faith, between *rationalism and supernaturalism as well as between the positions of *Hegel and *Schleiermacher. A further possible mediation would be between theology and the life of the contemporary church, for it is noticeable that many of the practitioners of mediating theology were highly committed to the development of the life of the ecclesiastical bodies to which they belonged. The principal German exponents of this school were I.A. Dorner, Julius

Müller and Richard Rothe. Among theologians from other lands who shared this approach were Alexander Schweizer (1808–88), professor at Zurich, and H.L. Martensen (1808–84) of Denmark, who is possibly remembered best for being the butt of many of *Kierkegaard's attacks on the religious establishment in his later years.

I.A. Dorner (1809–84), the most influential of the mediating theologians, held a number of important posts in Germany, culminating in his appointment in 1862 to the most prestigious chair of the time at Berlin. His most significant writings were *The History of the Development of the Doctrine of the Person of Christ* (1846–56, ET 1861–63) and *The System of the Christian Doctrine of Faith* (1879–81, ET 1885–88). Throughout his writings, Dorner had a deep positive appreciation of what he felt was being offered by the Idealism of his day, namely, that it helped to overcome the tension inherent in *Reformation thought between faith as its subjective principle and Scripture as its objective standard. Starting from the Schleiermacherian position that faith needed no validation beyond itself, he was nevertheless concerned to show that this approach must not end in the phenomenology of the religious consciousness, but it must rather be the doorway to objective knowledge. Pious consciousness could not be validated by an extraordinary history as narrated in the Scriptures, or on the grounds that it was a symbolic adumbration of the truth which reason eventually would verify. Rather, such consciousness pointed directly to the human awareness of the need for moral redemption, and therefore the God required as a counterpart to this self-awareness was one whose nature was holy love.

On this basis, Christian affirmations about God were to be thoroughly reinterpreted, particularly the divine simplicity and immutability, which must not determine abstractly how the moral characteristics of God are to be understood. God is to be thought of as primarily an ethical personality, in a Trinitarian fashion, but not as having an inner hypostatic life. Rather, in God there are the two poles of the ethically necessary and the ethically free, held together by the life of the Spirit – a very different understanding of the divine interiority than that generally put forward by classical expositions of the Trinity. In order to realize this ethically free aspect of his being, the world is required for God's proper self-expression – a world which will include free creatures with whom moral interaction can take place.

The culmination of such interaction is the coming of Jesus, in which the ethically free pole in the Godhead expresses itself in a receptive human life. As with all God's external activity, the giving and the receiving are progressive. Thus we have not only a developing incarnation, but we also bypass recurrent problems about the nature of the hypostatic union, as according to Dorner's account what we now have is the divine ethically free principle becoming a human personality in Jesus. This understanding lies at the heart of his resistance to the kenotic theory associated with the contemporary *Lutheran Confessional theologian, *G. Thomasius (1802–75), who argued that in order that the Logos might be made flesh, certain eternal powers of the Godhead needed to be retracted or temporarily laid aside. For Dorner, the incarnation meant divine fulfilment rather than temporary withdrawal into potentiality.

The system of doctrine so developed illustrates well the eclectic use of German Idealism typical of the mediating theologians. Beginning with the basis of Christian self-consciousness taken from Schleiermacher, Dorner proceeds to interpret the human condition according to the *Kantian analysis, and then he proceeds to view the divine being fulfilling itself in the production of the world-process after the manner of Hegel. What is remarkable, however, is that the argument is marked at every turn by reference to the Christian tradition, which Dorner certainly knew well, and whose inner truth he believed he was bringing to the fore.

Julius Müller (1801–78) was professor at Halle, and his reputation rests upon one work, the massive *Christian Doctrine of Sin* (1839/44, ET 1852 and 1866). This writing, whatever one makes of Müller's conclusions, is both learned and thorough, whilst his discussions of the various approaches in this field are still valuable for their searching examination of the various issues. Like Dorner, Müller started from Schleiermacher's position that the Christian consciousness is the ultimate theological datum to which even Scripture has a secondary role in providing exemplification. However, Müller finds embedded in this consciousness a deep sense of alienation from God, to which neither the systems of Schleiermacher nor Hegel are able to do justice, for both tend implicitly to deny human freedom. Schleiermacher denies this by explaining sin as being due to the priority of sensuous influences over the gradually awakening God-consciousness, whilst Hegel's solution is rejected as insinuating that evil in a fashion is necessary for the development of the divine in personal form. Müller's own understanding of God is that of the ultimate person, arguing from this that human beings only attain personality because God as a personal will stands over against them. As Schleiermacher denies any distinction between possibility and actuality in God's external activity, thus undermining any notion of the divine freedom, so Hegel achieves the same result by assimilating God to the cosmic process. Thus, Müller would argue, if God is not essentially free it is impossible either to attribute a genuine freedom to human beings or to justify the sense of the gravity of sin implicit in the Christian consciousness.

The next crucial step in his argument is to clarify what is meant by human freedom. Here he distinguishes between two kinds of freedom: real freedom, which is the conformity between the individual and his proper nature, and formal freedom, or the choice between good and evil. Real freedom, however, is only gained through the right use of formal freedom, and the problem is that, for all human beings, that real freedom is already impaired by sin, in the Kantian sense that evil maxims are present as motivating our actions. An *Augustinian solution which views original sin as some kind of hereditary disease does not provide any solution, as that situation can only have arisen through the individual's misuse of his formal freedom. What, then, can account for this universal condition? Müller's somewhat startling answer, reminiscent of *Origen, is that we should presuppose that every individual soul misused its formal freedom in a pre-temporal existence, and hence has undermined its historical real freedom. Not only does the Kantian analysis provide for Müller his basic understanding of human freedom, but he reverts to a procedure akin to the transcendental method to account for the invariable sinfulness of the human condition. So Müller, who perhaps more than any other mediating theologian was aware of the deficiencies of Idealism, has still in the end to rely on one of its techniques to deliver his argument from a fundamental impasse.

Richard Rothe (1799–1867) spent most of his academic life as professor at Heidelberg, and his main work, unfortunately lacking an English translation, is the *Theologische Ethik* (1845–48). Similar to Dorner and Müller, Rothe's starting point was the pious consciousness as delineated by Schleiermacher, but then his argument took a strikingly Hegelian turn. Just as Hegel argued that overall truth could only be gained through the logical analysis of the act of knowledge, so Rothe argued that the relationship between God and the cosmos, which are essentially correlative to each other as the Absolute, might be deduced from what is implicit in the pious consciousness. What Rothe offers is a system of speculation grounded in faith. Somewhat like Dorner, he interprets the world as a process of self-development on the part of God, who will gain fulfilment in having a realm of spirits vis-à-vis himself. The physical world is to be seen as the way in which God through materiality, and even through sin as sensuousness, makes it possible to give these spirits a genuine independence as his partners. It is extremely interesting that in an age taken up with the notion of evolution, Rothe has already put in place an idealistic interpretation of such a process – though when the Darwinian storm broke few, it seems, took notice of it.

There are also supernaturalistic overtones in Rothe's scheme, as God is thought of as providing stimuli, together with inspiration, to lead the developing spirits to turn to himself. It is along these lines that Rothe also interprets the role of Christ and the miracles that are found in the biblical history. One particularly interesting facet of his thought is that he only envisaged a temporary role for the church in the development of humanity, as he regarded that society as having only an authoritarian, educative role, which could be dispensed with when people generally were able to appropriate the truth for themselves. Eventually, then, the state, considered as a moral community rather than as a political organism, would take over the church's function – a state of affairs that Rothe does not seem to have envisaged as being too far distant in the future.

The mediating theologians were immensely learned, sophisticated in the handling of doctrinal method, and generally highly involved in the life of the church. Yet their influence, at least in Germany, was extremely short-lived – largely because it seems they did not offer an immediate and as clear-cut an answer to the encroaching problem of scientific naturalism as did

*Ritschl, with his eschewal of the task of ontological reconstruction. Towards the end of the nineteenth century it appears that the mediating theologians had some significant influence on theology in Britain, particularly that of the Scottish churches and the English Free Churches. However, their suggestive structures of doctrine have on occasion proved to be sources of stimulus and insight to those who are not afraid to wrestle with theological complexity.

STANLEY H. RUSSELL

FURTHER READING: R. Holte, *Die Vermittlungstheologie: Ihre theologischen Grundbegriffe kritisch untersucht* (Uppsala, 1965); E. Hirsch, *Geschichte der neuern evangelischen Theologie*, V (Gutersloh, 3rd edn, 1964), ch. 52; K. Barth, *Protestant Theology in the Nineteenth Century* (ET London, 1972), chs. 21–23; C. Welch, *Protestant Thought in the Nineteenth Century*, I (New Haven / London, 1972), ch. 12; S.H. Russell, 'I.A. Dorner: A Centenary Appreciation', *Expos T* 96 (Dec. 1984), pp. 77–81; 'Two Nineteenth-century Theologies of Sin – Julius Müller and Kierkegaard', *Scot J Th* 40.2 (1987), pp. 231–48.

Melanchthon, Philip (1497–1560)

Born in Bretten, Germany, son of Georg Schwartzerdt, an armourer in the employ of Elector Philip of the Palatinate, and Barbara Reuter, daughter of an important merchant family in Bretten. After his father's death in 1508, Philip attended the Latin school of Georg Simler in Pforzheim. There the famous German humanist and jurist, Johannes Reuchlin, Philip's relative by marriage, bestowed on him the Hellenized form of his family name –'*melan*' (black) '*chthon*' (earth) – in recognition of his precocity in Greek. After receiving university degrees at Heidelberg (1511) and Tübingen (1514), Melanchthon became (upon the nomination of Reuchlin) the first professor of Greek at the fledgling University of Wittenberg in August 1518. There he remained practically without interruption until his death in 1560.

He quickly fell under the influence of *Martin Luther's theology and received under Luther's direction his first (and only) theological degree, the bachelor of Bible, in 1519. He lectured in both the arts and theology faculties throughout his career. Besides contributions in theology and biblical exegesis, he also authored a variety of important confessional documents for the emerging evangelical (Lutheran) churches, including the Augsburg

Confession and its *Apology* (1530/31), the Saxon Confession (1551) and the Mecklenburg Examination of Ordinands (1552). After Luther's death in 1546, he became embroiled in a series of intra-Lutheran theological battles, beginning with the adiaphoristic dispute over the Augsburg Interim in 1548 and including major disputes over free will and original sin, justification by faith and the Lord's Supper. Melanchthon influenced not only a generation of Lutheran theologians, including such major authors of the 'Formula of Concord' (1580) as *Martin Chemnitz, Nicolaus Selneccer and David Chytraeus, but also other *Reformation theologians, such as Johann Brenz, *Martin Bucer and *John Calvin.

Philip Melanchthon's theology represented a unique blend of humanist method and style with the basic theological principles of the Reformation. Already before the Reformation, he had begun to develop a method of interpreting texts, based upon certain suggestions of the German humanist Rudolf Agricola, that used both rhetoric and dialectics. Melanchthon defined a fourth genre of speech (beyond the classical deliberative, demonstrative and judicial), called the didactic (*genus didaskalion*). In place of purely rhetorical rules of invention, this genre, constructed for the classroom, employed the basic questions of *Aristotelian logic (such as, what a thing is, its genus, species, parts, opposites, causes and effects). From this genre arose Melanchthon's peculiar use of commonplaces (*loci communes*), which he understood – in contrast to *Erasmus, who used commonplaces as topics in which to sort classical texts – as the basic (intrinsic) categories of a particular subject.

Under Luther's influence, Melanchthon came to organize Reformation theology using these Renaissance humanist principles. He was the first to analyze the Pauline epistles under the strict rules of classical letter writing. Thus, he argued for a rhetorical and theological consistency often ignored or disputed by earlier patristic, medieval and even fellow humanist exegetes, including Erasmus. From what Melanchthon determined were the basic topics of Paul's letter to the Romans (including sin, grace, faith, Law and gospel), he developed an alternative to *Peter Lombard's *Sentences* and in 1521 published the first Protestant handbook of theology, the *Loci communes theologici*. Twice he thoroughly rewrote the text (1535, 1543), and once he even translated it into German (1553) himself.

Like Luther, one of Melanchthon's basic theological categories was the distinction between Law and gospel, not simply understood as definitions (command and promise), but also in terms of their effects (God's terrifying and comforting word). Upon this distinction rested his interpretation of justification by faith as a movement from contrition (understood as terror for sin worked by the Law) to faith (comfort in forgiveness declared to the sinner on account of Christ). When some radical reformers in Wittenberg, such as Andreas Bodenstein von Karlstadt, insisted on the use of Mosaic Law in civil affairs and denigrated the role of the humanities for Christians, both Luther and Melanchthon developed in 1521–22 a distinction between two kinds of righteousness. Civil righteousness had its place within this world and human relations and was based upon principles of (natural) law embodied in the Ten Commandments – what Melanchthon later called the first use of the Law. Evangelical, or divine, righteousness came from God's word of forgiveness (the 'second use' of the Law and the gospel). This distinction allowed Melanchthon to teach in both the arts faculty (where he lectured on Aristotle, Cicero, history and Greek and Latin literature and language) and the theology faculty (where he produced important commentaries on Romans, Colossians and Proverbs as well as the *Loci communes*). Against certain antinomian challenges by Johannes Agricola and others, Melanchthon insisted that the Law also functioned in Christian lives, and in 1534 he defined a third use of the Law as a guide for the Christian life.

Melanchthon's theological method stressed clarity in theological expression. As a result, in the *Loci communes*, in biblical interpretation and in confessional statements, Melanchthon strove to develop clear statements of faith both to ward off false teaching and to provide a basis for agreement among Protestants. Thus, in the 1530s Melanchthon rejected a certain (*Augustinian) understanding of justification, championed even by the Lutheran reformer Johannes Brenz, which held that God declared sinful human beings righteous on the basis of the anticipated work of the Holy Spirit to make them righteous through their actions. Melanchthon argued more and more consistently that God justified sinners forensically, based upon the sure declaration of forgiveness on account of Christ alone, without taking into account any intrinsically righteous deeds that may result. In the early 1550s this resulted in a debate with the former Nuremberg preacher and later professor at the University of Königsberg, *Andreas Osiander, over the nature of Christ's righteousness in justification. Furthermore, Melanchthon attempted to avoid the charge (by certain Roman Catholic polemicists) that the Reformers had developed a Manichean understanding of sin by stressing human responsibility. This resulted in disputes with the strict Lutheran theologian, Matthias Flacius, who charged Melanchthon and his students with synergism. On the question of the Lord's Supper, Melanchthon altered his early unambiguous support for Luther's position of Christ's real presence over against *Ulrich Zwingli. With Martin Bucer, he authored the Wittenberg Concord in 1536, which brought about an agreement between certain south German cities and Wittenberg that Christ was present 'with the bread and wine' in the Lord's Supper. This compromise language was reflected in Melanchthon's rewriting of the Augsburg Confession in the early 1540s, the so-called 'Variata'. Only after Luther's death did Melanchthon's understanding of Christ's 'actual presence' in the celebration of the Lord's Supper come under attack by Lutherans who perceived him as capitulating to the Swiss.

TIMOTHY J. WENGERT

FURTHER READING: *Texts: Opera quae supersunt omnia* (ed. Karl Bretschneider and Heinrich Bindseil; Corpus Reformatorum 1–28; 28 vols.; Halis Saxonum, 1834–60); *Melanchthons Briefwechsel* (ed. Heinz Scheible; 10+ vols.; Stuttgart, 1977–). *Studies:* Günter Frank, *Die theologische Philosophie Philipp Melanchthons (1497–1560)* (Leipzig, 1995); Wilhelm Hammer, *Die Melanchthonforschung im Wandel der Jahrhunderte* (4 vols.; Gütersloh, 1967–96); Sachiko Kusukawa, *The Transformation of Natural Philosophy: The Case of Philip Melanchthon* (Cambridge, 1995); Clyde Manschreck, *Melanchthon: The Quiet Reformer* (New York, 1958); Wilhelm Maurer, *Der junge Melanchthon* (2 vols.; Göttingen, 1967–69); Heinz Scheible, *Melanchthon: Eine Biographie* (Munich, 1997); Timothy J. Wengert, *Human Freedom, Christian Righteousness: Philip Melanchthon's Exegetical Dispute with Erasmus of Rotterdam* (New York / Oxford, 1998); *Law and Gospel: Philip Melanchthon's Debate with John Agricola of Eisleben over* Poenitentia (Carlisle, 1997).

Meyendorff, John (1926–92)

Born to Russian immigrant parents in France, Meyendorff studied at the Sorbonne and joined the staff of the St Sergius Seminary in Paris. He moved to the United States where he taught at Harvard and Columbia as well as at St Vladimir's Seminary in New York. He was appointed dean of St Vladimir's in 1984. He first came to prominence with his study of *Gregory Palamas, published in French as *Introduction à l'Étude de Grégoire Palamas* in 1959. This was subsequently published in English as *A Study of Gregory Palamas* (1964) and led to a revival of interest in the writings of Palamas and the hesychast controversy in fourteenth-century Byzantium. Meyendorff's more popular and richly illustrated book on the subject, *St Gregory Palamas and Orthodox Spirituality*, first published in French in 1959 and translated into English in 1974, set Palamite theology and hesychast prayer in the wider context of Orthodox art and thought.

Meyendorff's book *Byzantine Theology: Historical Trends and Doctrinal Themes* (1974) established him as a leading authority on Byzantine and Orthodox thought in the western world. This book remains the only readily accessible study of the subject in English, and it has become something of a classic. In it Meyendorff locates the main concerns of Byzantine theologians in the context of their time and, in doing so, he sheds new light on several important issues. Above all, he shows that there was a legitimate Christian tradition of theologizing which was distinct from the Latin west and which is worthy of study in its own right. Although confined to a historical period ending in 1453, the theological legacy of Byzantine Christianity has continued to influence Eastern Europe and Russia through to the present day. If there was one thing that united Meyendorff's critics, whether they were Protestants or Roman Catholics, it was their reluctance to accept the idea of a separate non-western theological tradition. Meyendorff's book did much to remind scholars that Christianity was, and still is, a multifaceted phenomenon.

In other books, such as *Christ in Eastern Christian Thought* (1975) and *Imperial Unity and Christian Divisions* (1989), Meyendorff explored further his interest in Greek patristics and the period of the separation of the churches in the East. These works furthered his reputation as a first-class scholar of the early Christian period in the East. His interest in Byzantino-Russian relations was developed in his study *Byzantium and the Rise of Russia* (1981) and in the collection of articles *Rome, Constantinople, Moscow: Historical and Theological Studies* (1996), published posthumously. Both these books reflect the breadth of Meyendorff's knowledge and insight into Orthodox Christianity and the factors that helped shape the history and culture of Eastern Europe and Russia.

Like other Orthodox theologians living in the west, such as Georges Florovsky (1893–1979) and *Vladimir Lossky (1903–58), Meyendorff became an authoritative interpreter of Orthodoxy for many Christians living under Communism. He was actively engaged in ecumenical dialogue between the Eastern Orthodox and the Oriental Orthodox churches, as well as with the Roman Catholic and Protestant communities. Unfortunately, in the post-Soviet period extreme conservative elements in the Russian Orthodox Church have publicly destroyed Meyendorff's books because of his perceived concession to ecumenism and western requirements. Despite this, his writings continue to exercise considerable influence in many Orthodox countries, and there seems no doubt that he will be judged one of the most important writers on Byzantine and Orthodox theology in the English-speaking world in the twentieth century.

KEN PARRY

FURTHER READING: *Texts: Byzantine Theology: Historical Trends and Doctrinal Themes* (New York, 1974); *Christ in Eastern Christian Thought* (New York, 1975); *Imperial Unity and Christian Divisions: The Church 450–680 AD* (New York, 1989); *Byzantium and the Rise of Russia* (New York, 1981); *Rome, Constantinople, Moscow: Historical and Theological Studies* (New York, 1996).

Mill, John Stuart (1806–73)

John Stuart Mill is best known to most as a leading advocate of utilitarian ethics, women's rights and democratic political thought. His education was supervised by his father, and he began with training in Greek at the age of three. The elder Mill also tutored his son in Latin, philosophy, political theory, economics and history. The younger Mill was employed for 35 years by the East India Company, and his job provided ample opportunity to engage in writing. Mill's political ideas and promotion of women's suffrage were strongly influenced by

Harriet Taylor, whom he married in 1851. He served three years in Parliament, where he was a fervent proponent of women's rights.

Mill's empiricism represents an attempt to find a middle road between a priori approaches to epistemology and the sceptical empiricism of philosophers such as *Hume. His inductive approach relies on the uniformity of Nature and its process. This uniformity does not require the complex metaphysical justifications attempted by earlier empiricists. Instead, experience is the source of all ideas. Since these ideas have a consistency from which we can make generalizations about specific processes, these consistencies serve to ground belief in Nature's uniformity.

Mill employs this empirically derived concept of uniformity to matters beyond the physical sciences. Human activity is subject to the same types of restrictions (which we express in terms of law) as may be found in the non-human realm, thus inductive logic applies equally to the social domain. However, given the complexity of human activities and our imperfect knowledge of the relevant laws, the social sciences will always be inexact in their predictions. In spite of this, the science of human behaviour is sufficient to make probable forecasts concerning future actions.

While Mill describes human activity as lawful and therefore accessible to a scientific approach, he does not embrace causal determinism. Instead, he argues that the causes behind human behaviour are partially subject to our control. Our actions are not compelled by unbending necessity, but they are instead part of invariable sequences. Many have found this attempted avoidance of determinism less than satisfying, but some degree of human freedom is a necessary assumption of his social, political and ethical thought.

The centrality of freedom is nowhere more evident than in his *On Liberty*, where Mill argues that individuals should be afforded complete liberty to do or say as they wish provided that their actions or utterances cause harm to no one else. In short, the role of government is to protect us from others. Society should not prohibit individual members from engaging in activities that harm only themselves, although it is proper to seek to persuade them to avoid such activities. This emphasis on debate and persuasion, Mill believes, is a safeguard against human fallibility. In the past, governments have taken actions against individuals (e.g. Socrates and Jesus) whose ideas have later proved valuable to society. Thus Mill believes coercive measures threaten to hinder moral development, and he takes the more optimistic perspective that moral progress is best facilitated by free exchange of ideas.

A second advantage of individual liberty is its role in promoting democracy. Mill believes a symbiotic relationship exists between ethics, individual freedom and democracy. We are moral beings only when we act for the benefit of the whole of humanity, and such actions carry moral weight only when free of compulsion. This freedom from coercion is possible only within a democratic political system in which all people are given the right to self-determination. While Mill is a fervent supporter of democracy, he is concerned that pure democracies are always in jeopardy of descending into a 'tyranny of the majority'. Thus he argues for a representative form of democratic government.

Mill is perhaps best known for his advocacy of utilitarian ethics. Given his inductive method as a starting point, he does not seek to ground ethics on a metaphysical basis. Instead, the test of right and wrong is utility, or usefulness. As Mill defines it,

> The creed which accepts as the foundation of morals Utility, or the Greatest-happiness Principle, holds that actions are right in proportion as they tend to promote happiness, wrong as they tend to produce the reverse of happiness. By happiness is intended pleasure and the absence of pain, by unhappiness, pain and the privation of pleasure. (*Utilitarianism*)

Mill finds it unnecessary to justify happiness, of the consequence that ethics uses happiness as its guide. The fact that all naturally seek happiness is sufficient reason for its place in ethics. However, he hastens to add that utilitarianism does not find individual happiness in tension with social happiness. An individual's happiness is, instead, dependent on the greatest happiness for the greatest number. Temporary sacrifices that benefit the whole ultimately result in a personal increase in happiness.

Mill, though probably the best-known utilitarian philosopher, is not the originator of this theory. His contribution to this ethical model is his qualitative approach. His most famous predecessor (and close friend of Mill's father), Jeremy Bentham, took a quantitative approach to happiness. Mill, on the other hand, argues that the quality of happiness should be our primary concern. This, of course, raises the question of how we determine which forms of happiness are of higher quality. Mill's answer, as we might expect, is based on experience. 'Of two pleasures, if there be one to which all or almost all who have experience of both give a decided preference, irrespective of any feeling of moral obligation to prefer it, that is the more desirable pleasure' (*Utilitarianism*). Mill is confident that those who have experience with various type of happiness will find those which appeal primarily to the intellect to be the more desirable.

Mill was not so much an innovator as a popularizer. He is a significant figure because he was at the vanguard of movements – such as women's rights, liberal democratic political thought and a utilitarian approach to ethics – which anticipated the spirit of social trends predominating in the late-nineteenth and early-twentieth centuries.

STEVE WILKENS

FURTHER READING: *Texts: Collected Works* (ed. John M. Robson, et al.; 33 vols.; Toronto, 1963–91); *Three Essays on Religion* (New York, 1969); *Autobiography of John Stuart Mill* (New York, 1944); *Utilitarianism* (ed. George Sher; Indianapolis, IN, 1979); *On Liberty* (ed. Elizabeth Rapaport; Indianapolis, IN, 1978). *Studies:* William Thomas, *Mill* (Oxford, 1985); Alan Ryan, *J.S. Mill* (London, 1974).

Moberly, Robert Campbell (1845–1903)

R.C. Moberly was the third son of George Moberly, headmaster of Winchester College and later bishop of Salisbury. His upbringing brought him close to the priest and poet *John Keble, whom he revered. He was educated at Winchester and New College, Oxford, and he was ordained in the Church of England (deacon 1869, priest 1870). In the early years of his ministry, he undertook a variety of tasks – tutoring in classics as a senior student (i.e. junior fellow) of Christ Church, Oxford, acting as domestic chaplain to his father, and assuming the principalships successively of St Stephen's House, Oxford and the Diocesan Theological College at Salisbury. In 1880 he married Alice Sidney Hamilton and was appointed vicar of Great Budworth in Cheshire. As a parish priest he was both pastorally effective and intellectually active, gaining the approval of the Bishop of Chester (Stubbs, later bishop of Oxford). In 1892 he was appointed Regius professor of pastoral theology at Oxford and canon of Christ Church, in which post he exercised considerable influence in the church at large until his untimely death in 1903.

Moberly belonged to the second generation of Tractarians who faced the challenge of carrying forward, in changed circumstances, the inheritance of the pioneers. A man of scholarly gifts and irenic temperament, he possessed the ability to argue discriminatingly from large principles to the details of practice, and to engage sympathetically yet firmly with the beliefs of his opponents. He first came to public attention in 1884 by his determined campaign against the legalization of marriage to a deceased wife's sister, a *cause célèbre* of the time. In 1886 he published a pamphlet entitled 'Is the Independence of Church Courts Really Impossible?', in which he maintained that independent ecclesiastical jurisdiction did not conflict with the principle of establishment. A more philosophical inclination appeared in his contribution to the famous volume *Lux Mundi*, an essay on 'The Incarnation as the Basis of Dogma' which defended both the general validity of dogma in its dependence on the authority of truth, and the particular dogma of Christ as 'very God and very man' as the lynchpin of Christian belief and practice. The essay, though subtle, now seems inconsequential, but it identified Moberly with those Anglo-Catholics who felt compelled (to quote *Charles Gore's preface) 'to put the Catholic faith into its right relation to modern intellectual and moral problems'.

The rise of the Tractarians had brought to prominence the doctrine of 'apostolic succession' through episcopal ordination as the key both to the authority of the church independent of the state and to the validity of Anglican Orders. By the 1890s, research into the history of the early church had cast doubt on the assumption that the threefold ministry of bishop, priest and deacon had existed from apostolic times, and in 1896 clerical insecurity was intensified by the issue of the papal bull 'Apostolicae Curae'. This document declared Anglican Orders 'absolutely null and utterly void' on account of the absence of intention to ordain a sacrificing priesthood, and it seems to have impelled Moberly to publish six lectures on the ordinal, together with an extended chapter on 'What is Priesthood in the Church of Christ?' and an appendix rebutting Roman Catholic objections to Anglican Orders.

The resulting book, *Ministerial Priesthood* (1897), has become a classic. Moberly criticizes the theological assumptions implicit in the historical analysis of Edwin Hatch and J.B. Lightfoot, and he argues that the ordained ministry is a representative organ, exercising on behalf of the whole body the functions and powers which belong to the whole. He distinguishes between the universal priesthood of the laity and the ministerial priesthood of those who act not vicariously but so as to enable the laity to fulfil their priestly vocation. He claims, on the evidence of New Testament and subapostolic times, that the ordained ministry exists by divine commission and its authority is transmitted from Christ through the episcopate. Finally, Moberly traces priesthood to its origin in the sacrifice of Christ as the expression of the divine love under the conditions of sin. The church is to be priestly, both outwardly in Eucharistic worship and inwardly in the spirit of sacrifice, while the ordained priesthood is the specialized personification of that vocation, uniting the priestly and pastoral roles in a typical Anglican synthesis. It may be thought that Moberly (characteristically) claims too much for his church and tradition, but the book is judicious in style and conciliatory in tone.

Moberly's Christological interest found full expression in his greatest work, *Atonement and Personality* (1901), which offers an alternative to Protestant doctrines of penal substitution and integrates the atonement closely with other Christian doctrines. He argues that the purpose of punishment is not primarily to inflict pain upon wrongdoers but to promote penitence, but that for sinful creatures penitence, like forgiveness, can come only from the creative act of God which is consummated in holiness. The atoning work of Christ is to be understood on the analogy of one human being bearing with another in love. In his life and death, Christ offers to God not only perfect obedience which provides the basis for the renewal of human personality but also perfect penitence which cancels the guilt of the past through sympathetic identification with both God and sinful humanity. The link between objective and subjective atonement comes only through the indwelling of 'the Spirit of the Incarnate', leading to the fulfilment of true selfhood in holiness. The

environment of this transformation is the sacramental and ethical life of the church. Moberly's theory of 'vicarious penitence' recalls *John McLeod Campbell's concept of the 'vicarious confession of sin' by Christ, not least in the dubiousness of its logical coherence. The argument also relies on contestable philosophical assumptions about human personality current in nineteenth-century Idealism, but its original and morally sensitive approach continues to appeal even when the conclusions are not accepted.

Moberly repeatedly defended the dominant position of the Church of England in the educational system. He also published *Sorrow, Sin and Beauty* (1889), *Reason and Religion* (1896) and *Christ Our Life* (1902). A posthumous collection, *Problems and Principles* (1904), also appeared.

CHRISTOPHER M. JONES

FURTHER READING: W. Sanday, 'Robert Campbell Moberly', *J Th St* 4 (1903); A.T. Hanson, 'Introduction' to reprint of *Ministerial Priesthood* (London, 2nd edn, 1967); E.R. Moberly, *Suffering, Innocent and Guilty* (London, 1978).

Modernism, Anglican

Anglican Modernism was part of a continuum, beginning in the liberalism of the nineteenth century (but Bethune-Baker sees its roots in the *deists, *The Way of Modernism*, p. 2) and evolving into the radicalism of the late twentieth century. It was never a unified 'school', but a method or, more accurately, an attitude. The term covers various attempts to present the gospel in contemporary terms, taking account of discoveries in biblical criticism, church history and the sciences. It has been exhaustively examined by A.M.G. Stephenson in the Hulsean Lectures of 1979–80.

The liberalism of the second half of the nineteenth century was identified with the Broad Church, which saw itself as a third party, neither evangelical nor tractarian. Liberal theology was slow to gain recognition and only in 1889, with the publication of *Lux Mundi*, did the results of biblical criticism begin to be received. In 1884 F. Temple declared the theory of evolution not contrary to revelation and denied any threat to the Christian religion in placing miracles within the natural order. In 1898 *Rashdall's *Doctrine and Development*, Percy Gardner's *Exploratio Evangelica*, W.R. Inge's *Mysticism*, and James M. Wilson's *The Gospel of the Atonement* were all published. These works, and the abundance of books and articles which poured out in the early decades of the twentieth century, exemplified in one way and another Streeter's dictum that 'The world … cannot accept a religion if its theology is out of harmony with science, philosophy and scholarship' (*Foundations*, Intro.).

More positively, Rashdall wrote in 1904:

> In modern language, I think we might say that we adhere to the three great essentials of the Christian religion – belief in a personal God, in a personal immortality and (while not limiting the idea of revelation to the Old and New Testaments) in a unique and paramount revelation of God in the historic Christ. (*Christus in Ecclesia*, p. 335)

For Rashdall, adherence to these three essentials – but not necessarily all teaching derived from them – was required of all ministers of the Church of England.

Christology was at the centre of the controversy. The modernists were seen to narrow, if not deny, the gulf between divinity and humanity, and to advance a 'degree Christology'. W.H. Fremantle in 1911 maintained that God is at work in all nature and all men, and that it is within this total divine presence that Christ was morally supreme. Fremantle also denied the miraculous character of Christ's birth. In the ensuing furore Fremantle was defended by Dean (of Westminster) Armitage Robinson, who warned against confusing belief in the incarnation with belief in a 'mode' of the incarnation.

For *W. Temple, Christ reveals 'the actual life of God' and 'the ideal life for man'. Temple concludes, '[W]e are all drawn in … till all men come to constitute "One Perfect Man", the measure of the stature of the completion of the Christ' ('The Divinity of Christ', *Foundations*, p. 263). In the same volume, W.H. Moberley ('The Atonement') insisted on the 'inclusive' view of Christ's saving work, taking points from both the liberal exemplary and pedagogical explanation and the conservative legalistic transactional teaching, while rejecting both in their entirety. Moberley argues that Christ's temptations were real, and his death 'the most conspicuous martyrdom in history' (p. 312). The crucifixion and resurrection are both historical facts and 'facts in heaven', illustrations of eternal principles.

On the other hand, H.D.A. Major, while agreeing that Christ's birth was not miraculous, held a modified Logos Christology, teaching that the moral and rational principle of the universe dwelt in Jesus Christ. He was aware of God's fatherhood, and, Major argued, the correlative of divine fatherhood was divine sonship. 'Jesus regarded himself as the anointed Son and God and Vicegerent of the Kingdom of God, thus possessing a relationship to God shared by no one else.' 'What seems clear', Major continued, 'is that the Incarnation process is not the mechanical addition of a Divine Personality to a human personality, but the development of human consciousness until within the sphere of human limitations it may be said to coincide with the Divine consciousness' (Major, *A Modernist View of the Incarnation*, p. 22, quoted in Stephenson, p. 91).

The like-minded organized themselves. In 1870 the Church Reform Association was founded and was the precursor to the Churchman's Union, begun in 1898. The association's voice, *The Broad Churchman*, began publication in 1873. The custom of yearly conferences was begun; they were intended 'to unite the body of Churchmen who consider that dogma is susceptible of re-interpretation and re-statement, in accordance with the clearer perception of truth attained by discovery and research' (Stephenson, p. 57). The 1899 meeting pledged:

> To give all the support in their power to those who are honestly and loyally endeavouring to vindicate the truths of Christianity by the light of scholarship and research, while paying due regard to continuity, to work for such changes in the formularies and practices of the Church of England as from time to time are made necessary by the needs and knowledge of the day.

The Churchman's Union was seen by some to be too radical, by others to be too moderate, but it continued to attract members. The appeal lay in a desire 'to clear away the accumulation of the dust of ages which lies about the foundation of the Christian creed, and to see wherein the foundation really consists' (Percy Gardner, *Exploratio Evangelica*). Gardner also held that '[doctrinal] truth is after all not to be taken too literally… . At best man can but adumbrate in words any divine idea, he cannot enclose it in words' (address to the Churchman's Union, 1899; Stephenson, pp. 66–67).

Major started the *Modern Churchman* in 1911, and he was an active defender of other modernist writings such as J.M. Thompson's *Miracles in the New Testament*, and B.H. Streeter (ed.), *Foundations: A Statement of Christian Belief in Terms of Modern Thought*. The rejection of the miraculous was common modernist ground, but Major pointed out that the overthrow of the miraculous did not mean the overthrow of the supernatural (Stephenson, p. 91).

Christology was the focus of the Girton conference in 1921, and here the *liberal Protestant theology which had to this time characterized Anglican Modernism came into conflict with the findings of Foakes-Jackson and Kirsopp Lake, expressed in the first volume of their *Beginnings of Christianity*. Lake accused the Church Union members of having 'lost the historical Christ, and ... regained Him by converting Him into a social reformer, a moral legislator, a revealer of a new conception of God'. The Christ preached by the primitive church was rather 'a Risen Saviour who was expected to come quickly to judge the quick and the dead' (Stephenson, pp. 114–15).

There was also great and bitter resistance to a paper by Rashdall. Not only did he deny the virgin birth and other miracles, but he insisted that Jesus did not claim divinity for himself, nor was he omniscient. Rashdall's, too, was a degree Christology. God is revealed to a greater or lesser degree in all persons.

> [There was a] gradual, continuous, and on the whole progressive revelation of God ... [until the belief] that in one Man the self-revelation of God has been signal, supreme, unique... . The character and teaching of Christ contains the fullest disclosure both of the character of God ... and [God's] will for man... .[T]hat is ... the true meaning for us of the doctrine of Christ's divinity. (Stephenson, p. 118)

There were other reactions against the liberal theology of Modernism. A. Richardson, in *The Redemption of Modernism* (1935), on the one hand welcomed liberalism which he described as 'the acceptance and assimilation of the scientific attitude towards historical theology' (p. 15). He assessed it as 'the greatest revolution in Christian thinking since its beginnings in the first century of our era' (p. 16). On the other hand, he saw the liberal spirit betrayed by the post-war Modernists. 'Modernism', he wrote, 'is essentially a method rather than a system' (p. 19); it includes intellectual sincerity, intellectual adventure, and it is not the property of one party. 'Modernists will have to dissociate the

spirit of their inquiry from the particular conclusions to which that inquiry has led ... [that is,] the conclusions and outlook of pre-war Modernism' (pp. 20–21). He advocated a new liberalism which would follow 'the road of the more classical Christianity' (p. 52).

Gore also was very critical of 'the men of Girton'. He accused them of denying Christ's divinity, but Rashdall denied this charge. This and other exchanges evoked much publicity, and the continuing controversy was the reason for the appointment in 1922 of the Commission on Doctrine. Its report, which came only in 1938, was seen as a vindication by the modernists.

JOANNE MCWILLIAM

FURTHER READING: J.F. Bethune-Baker, *The Way of Modernism* (Cambridge, 1927); Percy Gardner, *Exploratio Evangelica* (London, 1907); A.L. Lilley, *Modernism: A Record and Review* (London, 1908); Alan Richardson, *The Redemption of Modernism* (London, 1935); Charles R. Sanders, *Coleridge and the Broad Church Movement* (Durham, NC, 1942); Alan M.G. Stephenson, *The Rise and Decline of English Modernism* (The Hulsean Lectures 1979–80; London, 1984), with an extensive bibliography; B.H. Streeter (ed.), *Foundations: A Statement of Christian Belief in Terms of Modern Thought* (London, 1913), by 7 Oxford men.

Modernism, Roman Catholic

The term 'Roman Catholic Modernism' is somewhat ambiguous since it can refer to both a reform movement and a theological system. This movement and system together constituted a crisis for Roman Catholic theology and church discipline in the first decade of the twentieth century. The *movement* consisted of a small, loosely-connected group of Catholic scholars, working chiefly in France and England between 1885 and 1910. Their general aims were: 1) to bring theology into dialogue with modern scientific thinking in its various forms and, 2) to establish human experience as a fundamental element of theological reflection. Some of their work anticipated the developments of *Vatican II. Modernism as a *system* was abstracted by the Roman authorities from the more extreme elements of the modernists' work and was condemned in 1907. In subsequent decades the same authorities waged a determined campaign to root out any trace of what it called this 'compendium of all heresies'.

At the movement's centre was *Baron Friedrich von Hügel (1852–1925), whose organizational ability and epistolary zeal brought many of the modernists into contact with one another. They were far too diverse to constitute a school, but in various ways they all attempted to reform the authoritarian, centralized and juridical church of their day by challenging the prevailing *neo-scholastic method of theology. That method was static, abstract and intellectualist, construing Christian revelation as a set of propositions. It organized these into a system and demonstrated its truth by deductive reasoning and by establishing it upon a philosophical foundation. This approach was called integralism, since the system stood or fell as a whole.

The modernist movement received its initial impulse with the work of Maurice Blondel (1861–1949) in the area of philosophical apologetics. Within Neo-Scholasticism, philosophy's role was to prepare for belief by demonstrating that the possibility of a supernatural revelation is reasonable. The doctrinal facts of Christianity are proven to be revelation by Jesus' miracles and the resurrection, for these are the signs which manifest his supernatural mission and authority. That authority has been given to the church, which now hands on the revelation. Against this, Blondel noted that miracles are convincing signs only for those who already believe. Moreover, the doctrines which the signs supposedly make credible have no intrinsic connection with the believer. They are to be accepted simply on the evidence of miracles and thus imposed authoritatively from the 'outside', irrespective of whether they are credible in themselves or whether they respond to human experience. In place of this extrinsicist apologetics, Blondel's *Action* (1893) developed the method of immanence, which begins *within* human experience. We apprehend God not in reason alone but in 'action', understood in the broadest sense as our whole being, including willing and feeling. Blondel's phenomenology of human action showed that implicit within our willing of anything finite there is always a desire (or 'exigence') for the infinite. Belief in a revealed religion is therefore reasonable, because the dynamism of our concrete activity, reflecting a vital force inherent within human nature itself, demands a supernatural response.

An outspoken Oratorian priest, Lucien Laberthonnière (1860–1932), anticipated many later developments in promoting Blondel's approach. He offered a theological justification for the method of immanence in *Le Problème Réligieux* (1897), where he argued against the strict separation of the natural and supernatural spheres by contemporaneous Neo-Scholasticism. No part of our lives is simply natural; pure nature does not exist. Our destiny is supernatural and gratuitous since grace *already* joins the two spheres *prior* to any conscious act of faith. With his notion of 'moral dogmatism', Laberthonnière contended that mere intellectual assent to truth claims is insufficient. The truth of a doctrine can be grasped only by living it, by realizing it in our experience – hence every doctrine is a 'moral work'.

Perhaps the best-known modernist was the exegete Alfred Loisy (1857–1940). His most famous book, *The Gospel and the Church* (1902), was written in response to the liberal Protestant *Adolf von Harnack's What Is Christianity? (1900), which had argued that, when stripped of the 'husk' of doctrines, the 'kernel' of the gospel is simply Jesus' message of the fatherhood of God and love of neighbour. Loisy argued that a more historically accurate and less reductivist metaphor is that of the mustard seed. The seed of Christianity is the kingdom of heaven, planted by Jesus. Loisy's oft-quoted statement that 'Jesus preached the Kingdom and behold, it is the Church that has come' is meant positively, for the seed grows to fullness only as the church develops its organization and doctrines in response to its historical-cultural environment. The church is necessary for the gospel in order that the latter can penetrate 'with its spirit the whole existence of man'.

During his modernist period Loisy viewed doctrine in increasingly functional terms. Some of his work, especially the articles written under the *nom de plume* of A. Firmin, seems to reflect a belief that Christian truth claims are historically relative and merely symbolic. Another modernist and Bergsonian philosopher, Edouard Le Roy (1870–1954), proposed a theory of doctrine in a 1905 article (*Qu'est-ce qu'un dogme?*). He said that doctrines state nothing positive; their function is to rule out errors and to give guidelines for action.

Blondel was unhappy with Loisy's insistence upon a complete methodological separation of historical research from belief. In his *History and Dogma* (1904) Blondel rejected both the historicist view (Loisy's, without naming him) that history is the normative way of gaining access to Christ's authentic message, and the extrinsicist notion of tradition as simply handing on revealed facts. Instead, Blondel saw tradition as a 'living synthesis' of the gospel and believers' historical experience that extends from Jesus and his disciples to the present. The very survival of the tradition demonstrates the truth of the church's teachings, since they have been tested and verified by the lived experience of generations of Christians.

The English modernist George Tyrrell (1861–1909) focused upon the crisis in the spiritual lives of modern Catholics who, he believed, found institutional Catholicism irrelevant. Catholicism makes no attempt to dialogue with modern science and philosophy, nor does it revise traditional doctrinal expressions to make them more compatible with modern culture. Like Loisy, Tyrrell was strongly influenced by *liberal Protestantism, yet also like Loisy, he sought to distance himself from it. He distinguished between revelatory religious experience and its doctrinal expression. To confuse the two, as did the integralists with their notion of revelation as a fixed deposit of propositions, results in what he called 'theologism'. Rather, the function of doctrines is to evoke the religious experience out of which they originally arose. Hence doctrines are to be tested by experience, a test that is not simply pragmatic, but spiritual.

In July 1907, 65 propositions abstracted for the most part from Loisy's works were condemned by the decree 'Lamentabili'. Though often referred to at the time as a new 'Syllabus of Errors', the document was seen as fairly moderate. Blondel for one was happy in that it made no mention of his method of immanence. This changed, however, with Pius X's encyclical 'Pascendi Dominici Gregis' in September of the same year, the tone of which was harsh and vindictive. 'Pascendi' understood Modernism to be a complete system confronting integralism. It condemned the following assertions, which it regarded as Modernism's chief systematic principles: 1) religion is simply the product of human needs and aspirations, without any external revelation; 2) the meaning and truth of doctrine is historically relative and mutable; 3) Scripture and tradition are subject to scientific analysis independent of dogma.

The condemnation of Modernism was institutionalized by the proclamation 'Sacrorum Antistitum' of September 1910. This proclamation required bishops to root out any modernists in their dioceses, and it made all clerics and their teachers take a detailed anti-modernist oath. The resulting atmosphere of suspicion essentially ruled out any attempt to find alternatives to Neo-Scholasticism until the 1940s. Most recent commentators regard the condemned system as not truly reflecting the work of the modernists themselves, or as reflecting only their more extreme or careless statements. This is especially the case with Blondel and von Hügel, both of whom subsequently had respectable careers as Catholic scholars. It has also been suggested that, legitimate theological concerns aside, the excessive reaction of the authorities was due to their view that Modernism was all of a piece with contemporaneous social and political challenges to traditional authority, especially in France. There Modernism had a short-lived social-activist component in Marc Saugnier's pro-democratic group *Le Sillon* (founded in 1894), which was suppressed at the instigation of the reactionary political movement *Action Française*.

NICHOLAS M. HEALY

FURTHER READING: *Texts:* Maurice Blondel, *The Letter on Apologetics and History and Dogma* (ed. and trans. A. Dru and I. Trethowan; Grand Rapids, 1994); Alfred Loisy, *The Gospel and the Church* (trans. Christopher Home; London, 1908); J. Neuner, SJ and J. Dupuis, SJ (eds.), *The Christian Faith in the Doctrinal Documents of the Catholic Church* (London, rev. edn, 1983); G. Tyrrell, *Christianity at the Crossroads* (London, 1963). *Studies:* Gabriel Daly, OSB, *Transcendence and Immanence: A Study in Catholic Modernism and Integralism* (Oxford, 1980); Roger D. Haight, SJ, 'The Unfolding of Modernism in France: Blondel, Laberthonnière and Le Roy', *Th St* 35.4 (1974), pp. 632–66; Lester R. Kurtz, *The Politics of Heresy: The Modernist Crisis in Roman Catholicism* (Berkeley, 1986); M.R. O'Connell, *Critics on Trial: An Introduction to the Catholic Modernist Crisis* (Washington, DC, 1994); David G. Schultenover, SJ, *A View from Rome on the Eve of the Modernist Crisis* (New York, 1993).

Möhler, Johann Adam (1796–1838)

Johann Adam Möhler was the most prominent figure of the early Catholic Tübingen School. Writing in the early 1800s, Möhler established the school's reputation and anticipated developments in Catholic theology over the next 130 years, particularly in the areas of ecclesiology, doctrinal development and liturgy. Recognized only a century after his death as a valuable resource for responding to the problems confronting Catholicism in the modern world, Möhler was a major influence on the developments of *Vatican II.

Möhler was born in 1796 in a small town in southwestern Germany. At nineteen, he entered the seminary that would soon become the Catholic theological faculty of the University of Tübingen. Ordained in 1819, he spent a year as a parish priest before returning to Tübingen to teach church history, patristics and canon law. Between 1823 and 1835, he became embroiled in controversy, first with the German Catholic hierarchy and then with *F.C. Baur and the Protestant Tübingen faculty. Möhler then taught briefly at the University of Munich before his death in 1838.

Möhler's theology developed through three phases. The first phase understood the church juridically as a subcategory of society – a fairly traditional view. In the second phase he focused on the church as an organism whose guiding principle is the Holy Spirit, and he played down the visible aspects of the church. Möhler finally came to see the church in Christological terms – where the Spirit is the Spirit of Christ and the church is the continuation of the incarnation of the Son of God.

The latter two phases are evident in his two best-known books, *Die Einheit in der Kirche* (1825) and *Symbolik* (1832). The *Einheit* reflects Möhler's early *Romanticism with its organic, Spirit-centred concept of the church and its doctrine. This organic understanding of the church would lead him to conclude that doctrine is an unfolding of the initial scriptural deposit, so all doctrine can be understood as a true product of apostolic teaching. This development results from the Spirit's activity in the community, that is the church. The essence of Christianity is the indwelling of the divine Spirit, not doctrines and creeds. This concept of the church left little room for the visible church. Möhler at this point saw the church in organic rather than structural or hierarchical terms. The *Einheit* provoked controversy and placed Möhler at odds with the German Catholic hierarchy, especially the bishop of Cologne. Möhler's later writings would offer a more balanced ecclesiology, but he steadfastly refused to repudiate or modify what he had written in the *Einheit*.

Both his teaching responsibilities and the influence of Romanticism led Möhler to a careful study of the Church Fathers. This study resulted in a major work on *Athanasius (1827) and a long article on *Anselm of Canterbury (1827–28). This study would prove to be the turning point in Möhler's theology – from an emphasis on the Spirit to one on Christ. It can also be seen as a shift from the subjectivity he had learned from *Schleiermacher to an objective understanding of Christianity based in revelation and possibly influenced to some degree by *Hegel. *Athanasius der Grosse* challenged Schleiermacher's adoptionist Christology without denigrating Christ's real humanity. It was in *Athanasius* that Möhler first described the church as the continuation of Christ's incarnation. The article on Anselm began to develop the understanding of human reason Möhler would use in his concept of doctrinal development.

Möhler's most influential work is *Symbolik*, which was already in its fifth edition at the time of his death. Here he compared Roman Catholic and Protestant confessional documents, trying to show that Catholicism is the one true religion and Protestantism is heretical because it was the product of individuals and not the community. Möhler charged Protestantism with misunderstanding human nature as originally created and this, he contended, caused the remainder of its theology to be wrong. Möhler's approach was Christological, emphasized the visible nature of the church, and applied *Chalcedon's 'two natures' Christology to the church. He based the authority of the church's doctrine and its visible existence on Christ, and argued that the oneness of Christ requires the corresponding visible oneness of his church. Möhler's intent was to restore to Catholicism those who had left during the Reformation and to begin this process through dialogue with the Protestant Tübingers. Instead, he became embroiled in a heated debate with F.C. Baur over the role of myth in Baur's interpretation of Christianity. This debate forced Möhler to leave Tübingen for Munich.

Möhler's legacy to Catholic theology includes the idea of the church as the continuing incarnation of Christ, an ecclesiological understanding of doctrinal development as 'living tradition', and an organic relationship between Scripture, tradition and the church. All of these concepts would find their way into the teaching of Vatican II. Möhler drew on such contemporaries as Schelling, Schleiermacher, and Hegel, but always selectively because he considered their worldviews faulty. Conservatives and liberals both have claimed Möhler as one of theirs. For the former he was the post-Enlightenment restorer of Catholic tradition, for the latter he was the forerunner of modern Catholicism. Seen in its entirety, Möhler's career appears most consistent with the first interpretation.

DOUGLAS MCCREADY

FURTHER READING: J.R. Geiselmann has prepared critical editions of both *Die Einheit in der Kirche* (Darmstadt, 1957) and *Symbolik* (Koln, Olten, 1958). He has also written *Lebendiger Glaube aus geheiligter Überlieferung* (Freiburg, 2nd edn, 1966); *Die theologische Anthropologie Johann Adam Möhler* (Freiburg, 1955); and *Die katholische Täbinger Schule* (Freiburg, 1964). Möhler's two major works have been translated as *The Unity of the Church* (trans. P.C. Erb; Washington, DC, 1996) and *Symbolism* (trans. J.B. Robertson; London, 1997). Secondary literature in English is limited. The most important include Michael J. Himes, *Ongoing Incarnation: Johann Adam Möhler and the Beginning of Modern Ecclesiology* (New York, 1997); Donald J. Dietrich and Michael J. Himes (eds.), *The Legacy of the Tübingen School* (New York, 1997); and Herve Savon, *Johann Adam Möhler: The Father of Modern Theology* (trans. C. McGrath; Glen Rock, NJ, 1966). Additional literature in German and English can be found in the bibliography of Douglas McCready, *Jesus Christ for the Modern World: The Christology of the Catholic Tübingen School* (New York, 1991).

Molinism

The term 'Molinism' is best taken to refer to any theory or conglomerate of theories in which the theory of Middle Knowledge plays a key role. The term can also be taken to refer to the theories which were originally proposed by the Spanish *Jesuit, Luis de Molina (1535–1600), who in 1588 published the first edition of his *Liberi Arbitrii cum Gratiae Donis, Divina Praescientia, Providentia, Praedestinatione et Reprobatione Concordia* ('The Compatibility of Free Choice with the Gift of Grace, Divine Fore-knowledge, Providence, Predestination and Reprobation'), or shorthand, *Concordia*. An even more influential, revised edition came in 1595.

The theory of Middle Knowledge is explained along the following lines. In medieval theory about God's knowledge, it was common to distinguish two 'types' of divine knowledge. On the one hand, God knows himself and all other possibilities outside himself. This knowledge is independent of his will and is often called 'natural knowledge'. On the other hand, God knows the complete reality of past, present and future, 'after' he decides with his will which possibilities should be reality. This type of divine knowledge is called 'free knowledge', because it is preceded by an act of divine free will. Especially those states of affairs which depend on a created free will seem to pose a problem for God to know, since he cannot will them in a direct way. If he were to *cause* the 'free' actions of creatures directly, that would make them unfree. For their own free will does not seem to function in their actions. But if God cannot directly *will* states of affairs depending on a created free will, how can he *know* certainly which states of affairs will be the result of a created free will if he cannot *cause* them by his will to be so? In his *Concordia*, Molina answers the question by proposing a third kind of knowledge, in between (hence its name: middle) natural and free knowledge. He introduces it after having defined natural and free knowledge:

> ... the third type is *middle* knowledge, by which, in virtue of the most profound and inscrutable comprehension of each faculty of free choice, He saw in His own essence what each such faculty would do with its innate freedom were it to be placed in this or in that or, indeed, in infinitely many orders of things – even though it would really be able, if it so willed, to do the opposite ... (*Concordia*, IV.52.9)

Thus, God sees in his essence not simply what each free creature *could* do in any circumstance – that is already included in his natural knowledge – but what it *would* do in any circumstance or 'order of things'. By this knowledge *and* knowledge of his own decision to actualize specific circumstances, he perfectly knows the states of affairs resulting from a free creaturely act of will. One of the questions regarding this Middle Knowledge is: what kind of connection are we supposed to hold between circumstances and free act? This must be a non-necessary or contingent relation. For if the relation between circumstances and creaturely act were necessary, then it would as such be an object of God's *natural* knowledge and it would not be helpful at all. Another question is: how can Molina prove or explain *that* God has Middle Knowledge? For it seems counter-intuitive for a person to be able to know, with absolute certainty, what a not-yet-existing person would freely do in not-yet-existing circumstances. But is it counter-intuitive for a *divine* person to know this? Furthermore, Molina holds the contents of Middle Knowledge to be independent of God's will or decision. For Middle Knowledge is *pre*-volitional. God cannot affect it, as he cannot affect natural knowledge either.

Molina also proposed connected theories in the domain of providence, grace and predestination. God's co-operation or concurrence, without which a free creature cannot act at all, should be understood not as an action of God moving the free creature's will, but rather as an action directly on the effect of the free creature's will, that is the free act itself (called 'immediate causation', see Freddoso, pp. 17–19). According to Molina, there is no intrinsic difference between sufficient and efficacious grace (*Concordia*, III.40.11), a point of view which seems to imply that it is up to the creature's choice to make the sufficient means it obtains from God efficacious. The same structure can be discerned in Molina's view of predestination: it is the way in which the means are distributed about which God sees that they will bring a creature eternal life (*Concordia*, VII.1.11.2; Rabeneck, p. 539). This 'seeing' should be understood as Middle Knowledge. One does not predestinate oneself, however, for as Molina explains – once again relying on Middle Knowledge:

> it is not in the power of any predestined person to make himself predestined, for it is not in his power to accomplish that God chose from infinitely many orders the one in which he saw that the predestined person by his own freedom would choose eternal life, instead of another order. (*Concordia*, VII.1.11.31; Rabeneck, p. 557)

The *Concordia*, containing such theories, ignited a controversy. Could the views presented here be called orthodox? Was free will here pushed beyond its proper boundaries? Was the sovereignty of God threatened? Were predestination and grace not at the creature's disposal instead of at God's? Molina found significant allies and opponents. The former were, for example, the Jesuits *Francisco Suárez (1548–1617), *Robert Bellarmine (1542–1621) and the Dutch Protestant theologian *Jacob Arminius (see Dekker, 1996). Suárez and Bellarmine, while accepting Middle Knowledge, developed a slightly modified theory of grace, which came to be known as 'Congruism'. They tried to circumvent the statement that a human being can render grace efficacious or not, by claiming that God seeks 'fitting' or 'congruent' grace for those persons whom he has predestined before. The

Dominicans Domingo Bañez (1528–1604) and Francisco Zumel (1540–1607) vigorously attacked Molina's theories. The controversy was not confined to the Iberian peninsula, the domain of Molina, for in 1597 some leaders in Spain and Portugal invoked the help of the pope, at that moment Clement VIII. He established the so-called *Congregatio De Auxiliis*, a theological commission, '... thus initiating a ten-year period of intense study and public disputation which rendered the *Concordia* one of the most carefully scrutinized books in Western intellectual history' (Freddoso, p. viii). This commission could not reach a decision, and in 1607 Pope Paul V decreed that the parties were forbidden to call each other heretical and that the Holy See would resolve the issue at an opportune time – which has yet to arrive.

In the seventeenth, eighteenth and nineteenth centuries, Molinism remained much debated, not only in the Roman Catholic Church (see Vansteenberghe), but in Protestant circles as well (cf., e.g., Dekker, 2000). Only with the decline of *Scholasticism did the debate come to rest. But not for very long. For in the twentieth century, the concept of Middle Knowledge was reinvented in circles of analytical philosophy of religion. In the 1960s, the more general debate on the (in)compatibility of divine foreknowledge and human freedom – which has never been completely absent, of course, in theological circles – was revitalized. It was Alvin Plantinga who in the context of this more general debate proposed, in 1973 – then unaware of Molinism – a theory very much like that of Molina's theory of Middle Knowledge. The other tenets of Molinism do not receive equal attention nowadays. The contemporary debate focuses on the philosophical tenability of Middle Knowledge. Among the defenders are, next to Plantinga, William L. Craig and Thomas P. Flint. The theory is attacked by, for instance, Robert M. Adams and William Hasker.

EEF DEKKER

FURTHER READING: *Texts:* L. de Molina, *Liberi Arbitrii cum Gratiae Donis, Divina Praescientia, Providentia, Praedestinatione et Reprobatione Concordia* (ed. J. Rabeneck; Madrid, 1953); *On Divine Foreknowledge* (Pt. *IV of the Concordia*) (trans. and intro. and notes by A.J. Freddoso; Ithaca, NY / London, 1988), contains a particularly lucid translation and a very informative introduction); Francisco Suárez, *De Scientia Dei Futurorum Contingentium*, in *Opera Omnia* (ed. C. Berton; vol.

11; Paris, 1856–78). *Studies:* Eef Dekker, 'Was Arminius a Molinist?', *Sixteen Cent J* 27 (1996), pp. 337–52; *Middle Knowledge* (Leuven, 2000); Thomas P. Flint, *Divine Providence: The Molinist Account* (Ithaca, NY / London, 1998); William Hasker, David Basinger and Eef Dekker (eds.), *Middle Knowledge: Theory and Application* (Frankfurt am Main, 2000), contains a large number of reprinted contemporary articles and a bibliography; Sven K. Knebel, 'Leibniz, Middle Knowledge and the Intricacies of World Design', *Studia Leibnitiana* 28 (1996), pp. 199–210; E. Vansteenberghe, 'Molinisme' and 'Molina Louis', in *Dictionnaire de Théologie Catholique* (ed. A. Vacant, E. Mangenot, É. Amann; Paris, 1930–72), vol. 10–2, pp. 2094–2187 and 2090–92; Linda T. Zagzebski, *The Dilemma of Freedom and Foreknowledge* (New York / Oxford, 1991), ch. 5 is on Middle Knowledge.

Moltmann, Jürgen (b. 1926)

German Protestant systematic theologian, born 1926, professor of systematic theology at Tübingen (1967–94).

Moltmann's major works comprise two series. There is the trilogy of early works: *Theology of Hope* (*Theologie der Hoffnung*, 1964), *The Crucified God* (*Der gekreuzigte Gott*, 1972) and *The Church in the Power of the Spirit* (*Kirche in der Kraft des Geistes*, 1975). These approach theology from three complementary perspectives: eschatology, the cross and pneumatology (including ecclesiology). The second series, called 'contributions' to theology, make up a dogmatics. Five volumes have appeared: *The Trinity and the Kingdom of God* (*Trinität und Reich Gottes*, 1980); *God in Creation* (*Gott in der Schöpfung*, 1985); *The Way of Jesus Christ* (*Der Weg Jesu Christi*, 1989); *The Spirit of Life* (*Der Geist des Lebens*, 1991); and *The Coming of God* (*Das Kommen Gottes*, 1995). A final volume on the foundations and methods of Christian theology is planned. In many of his other works he develops further the implications of his theology for praxis in church and society.

Characteristic of Moltmann's theology is the way it is constantly mediating three poles: the biblical sources of Christian faith, traditional Christian doctrine and the contemporary world. In his work, the central doctrines of the tradition are constantly revitalized from fresh insight into their biblical sources and by engagement with the contemporary world, to which they prove to have wide-ranging relevance. An early emphasis on praxis, insisting that theology's role is not merely to interpret but also to change the world, is supplemented in his later work by a stress also on the importance of contemplation and doxology, implying that theology is the kind of participatory knowledge in which the subject is open to the reality of the other. The development of Moltmann's theology has been an essentially continuous one, in which the key themes of his early work maintain their importance in the later work. But it has also been a development characterized by considerable creativity, as the range of his work has expanded and fresh concerns (such as feminism or the ecological crisis) have been taken on board. He has also engaged with and learned from a variety of Christian traditions – not only the Protestant and Roman Catholic traditions of Europe, but also the liberation theology of the Third World, the Orthodox churches, the churches of the *Anabaptist tradition and Pentecostalism. A dialogue with Jewish theology runs through much of his work. He has also engaged with the challenge of atheism – especially in its more theological forms, such as that of the *Marxist philosopher Ernst Bloch, whose philosophy of hope provided a kind of model for Moltmann's early theology of hope. Owing to the sense of theological excitement and contemporary relevance that his work evokes, as well as to his personal contacts with many parts of the worldwide church, he must be the living German Protestant theologian most widely known and read today.

Thematically Moltmann's theology is notable, first, for rehabilitating futurist eschatology as not only credible but essential to contemporary Christian faith; secondly, for addressing the theodicy problem 'after Auschwitz' from the perspective of the suffering of God in the cross of Christ; thirdly, for developing a thoroughly Trinitarian understanding of God; fourthly, for conceiving the relationship of God and the world as reciprocal and as internal to God's own Trinitarian relationships; fifthly, for breaking out of the modern paradigm of reality as human history and giving theological weight to the reciprocal relationship of humanity and the rest of Nature. In broad terms, most of these themes are shared with his German theological contemporaries, notably *Pannenberg and *Jüngel, but in Moltmann's particular development of them they are intimately linked in ways characteristic of his particular theological project.

In his earliest work Moltmann established his theology's *Christological centre*, in the particularity of Jesus' history, and its *eschatological orientation*, in hope for the whole of God's creation, along with the inseparable connection between the two. The two events of Jesus' cross and resurrection are understood dialectically, representing the contradiction between what reality is now, in its subjection to sin, suffering and death, and what God promises to make it in new creation. Because Jesus in his death was identified with the world in its godlessness, godforsakenness and transitoriness, his resurrection is God's promise for a new future, in God's presence in eternity, for all reality. It is this all-embracing eschatological perspective that grounds Moltmann's consistently holistic view of both theology and the church's mission. Christian hope is not for the spiritual rather than the material, or for the individual rather than the social, or for the personal rather than the political, or for humans rather than the rest of creation. Nor is it for another world but for the transformation by God of this present world. Therefore this eschatology does not promote withdrawal from the world, but rather involvement in the world – promoting change in anticipation of the coming kingdom and openness to the future that only God can give his creation.

On the other side of the dialectic, the cross is God's loving solidarity in love with the godless and the godforsaken. By recognizing God's presence, as the incarnate Son of God, in the abandonment of the cross, Moltmann brings the dialectic of cross and resurrection within God's own experience. God's love is such that it embraces and suffers what is most opposed to God in order to overcome the contradiction. Moreover, this suffering is internal to God's own Trinitarian relationships. On the cross Jesus suffers dying in abandonment by his Father, while the Father suffers the death of his Son in grief. As such, the cross is the act of divine solidarity with the godforsaken world, in which the Son willingly surrenders himself in love for the world and the Father willingly surrenders his Son in love for the world. At the point of their most painful separation Father and Son are united in their love for the world, and from this event of suffering love comes the power of the Spirit to overcome all that separates the world from God.

In Moltmann's understanding, the cross does not solve the problem of suffering but meets it with the voluntary fellow suffering of love. The theodicy problem cannot be solved but requires a dialectical openness of theology to the suffering of the world until the promise of the resurrection is fulfilled in the eschatological future, when God will finally take his whole creation beyond evil and suffering and death.

In *The Crucified God* Moltmann's theology became strongly Trinitarian, since he interpreted the cross as a Trinitarian event between the Father and the Son. From this point he developed an understanding of the *Trinitarian history* of God with the world, in which the mutual involvement of God and the world is increasingly stressed. God experiences a history with the world in which he both affects and is affected by the world, and which is also the history of his own Trinitarian relationships as a community of divine Persons who include the world within their love. This Trinitarian doctrine dominates Moltmann's later work, in which the mutual relationships of the three Persons as a perichoretic, social Trinity are the context for understanding the reciprocal relationships of God and the world. The dialectic of cross and resurrection, now developed in a fully Trinitarian way, becomes the decisive moment within this broader Trinitarian history. It retains the eschatological direction of *Theology of Hope* and the crucified God's suffering solidarity with the world, but it also goes further in taking the whole of creation and history within the divine experience. Essential to this Trinitarian narrative of God and reality is the third divine Person, the Holy Spirit. From *The Church in the Power of the Spirit* onwards, Moltmann's thought becomes increasingly pneumatological. He recognizes the Spirit as the immanent presence of God in creation at the same time as he recognizes the Spirit's equal role as one divine Subject in the fully reciprocal relationships of the Trinity.

With Moltmann's understanding of the Trinity as constituted in the loving and changing relationships of three divine Subjects goes a general *principle of relationality* and reciprocity in Moltmann's thinking about God and the world. This principle governs the way he thinks about the relationship of the church to other movements and forces in world history, including the world religions; about the relationship of persons in society and in the church; about the relationship of humanity and other creatures;

and about the relationship between God and creation. In all these areas Moltmann thinks of relationships of mutuality rather than of dominance or even hierarchy. Whereas 'monotheism' (i.e. *Unitarianism) has in Moltmann's view constantly legitimated human domination, both of other humans and of Nature, social Trinitarianism understands God as in himself a fellowship of love, and so finds relationships of free friendship between humans as most adequately reflecting God and constituting his 'kingdom'. In the political sphere, this principle of mutuality grounds democracy; in the ecclesiological sphere it coheres with Moltmann's vision of the church as an open society of friends; while in the ecological sphere it highlights the interdependence of humanity and the rest of Nature.

Moltmann also applies to such relationships the traditional Trinitarian term: perichoretic. It is in their perichoresis, or mutual indwelling in love, that the three divine Persons are both three and one. Similarly, God's relationship to his creation is one of mutual indwelling. Because God is transcendent beyond the world it dwells in him, but because, as the Spirit, he is also immanent within the world, he dwells in it. With this dominant notion of the Spirit in creation, Moltmann is able also to take the non-human creation into his general concept of the Trinitarian history of God. The whole of creation from the beginning is oriented towards the future goal of its glorification through divine indwelling. The Spirit in creation co-suffers with creation in its bondage to decay, keeping it open to God and to its future with God. Humanity's eschatological goal does not lift us out of the material creation but confirms our solidarity and relatedness with it.

RICHARD BAUCKHAM

FURTHER READING: A bibliography of Moltmann's works up to 1987 is in D. Ising, *Bibliographie Jürgen Moltmann* (Munich, 1987), and further bibliography of Moltmann's works in English translation (together with secondary literature) in R. Bauckham, *The Theology of Jürgen Moltmann* (Edinburgh, 1995). Texts: *Theology of Hope* (London, 1967); *Theology and Joy* (London, 1973); *The Crucified God* (London, 1974); *The Church in the Power of the Spirit* (London, 1975); *The Trinity and the Kingdom of God* (London, 1981); *God in Creation* (London, 1985); *The Way of Jesus Christ* (London, 1989); *The Spirit of Life* (London, 1991); *The Coming of God* (London, 1996); *God for a Secular Society* (London, 1999). Studies: R. Bauckham, *Moltmann: Messianic Theology in the Making* (Basingstoke, 1987); R. Bauckham (ed.), *God Will Be All in All: The Eschatology of Jürgen Moltmann* (Edinburgh, 1999); R.B. Bush, *Recent Ideas of Divine Conflict: The Influences of Psychological and Sociological Theories of Conflict upon the Trinitarian Theology of Paul Tillich and Jürgen Moltmann* (Lewiston, NY, 1991); A.J. Conyers, *God, Hope, and History* (Macon, GA, 1988); C. Deane-Drummond, *Ecology in Jürgen Moltmann's Theology* (Lewiston, NY, 1997); M.D. Meeks, *Origins of the Theology of Hope* (Philadelphia, 1974).

Monophysitism

'Monophysitism', which means 'one nature-ism', is the name given to a wide range of one-sided perspectives upon Christology. A number of those who adopted a Monophysite perspective were heretics (Arius, *Apollinaris and possibly *Eutyches, although his position is unclear). But the perspective was not necessarily heretical, and some of the greatest theologians of the early church were Monophysites (*Cyril of Alexandria and Severus of Antioch).

To explore and assess the Monophysite perspective (the belief that in Christ we encounter *one nature* of God the Word incarnate'), it is helpful to distinguish a number of overlapping strands.

A question of *terminology* (the limitation of vocabulary) goes hand in hand with the question of Christological *vision* (theological instinct). Throughout the post-Nicene patristic writers there was a general acceptance that only one who is really God can save, and for 'saving' to take place there must be real engagement with what is really human. This theological *instinct* was most famously summed up in the statement of Gregory Nazianzen: 'That which is not assumed is not healed'. This instinct threw up two different (but equally sincere) strategies: one was to lay enormous stress on a real unity of the divine and the human in Christ. There was a real engagement with humanity. This tended in a Monophysite direction: *one* nature of God the Word incarnate. It is mirrored by modern 'Christologies from above'. The other strategy was to lay enormous stress on preserving the undiminished integrity of both natures in Christ: we encounter *real* God and *real* humanity. This tended in a Dyophysite direction (*two* natures) and is mirrored by modern 'Christologies from below'.

In assessing Monophysitism, a first point to

make is that vision was often out of step with available terminology. That is, some theologians could have a burning understanding that Christ is one being, not a relationship merely of inspiration, but yet not have an adequate way of expressing the oneness. There were a number of false starts, and patristic Christology advanced by marking out and subsequently avoiding certain 'danger areas'. A false start was shown by Apollinaris, who was so desperate to avoid Dyophysitism, which he saw as an avoidance of incarnation, that he depicted the union of the human and divine in biological, organic terms. It was a *living union*, like the union of body and mind in a person. Here his instincts were laudable, but his model and terminology were inadequate (on his understanding, God the Word replaced the human mind, so it followed that the human nature was deficient). A promising start was made by Cyril of Alexandria, when he explained to Succensus that not all things which are *single* (*one* nature) are *simple*. This more complex vision opened the way for stretching the vocabulary of 'oneness', though it took years for more adequate models to emerge.

We should turn next to models of oneness. Apollinaris was genuinely creative in his *living union* or *organic union* model. The mysterious union of a body and life exercised lasting influence on the patristic imagination. Another model was to look at the way fluids mix. But that in itself was no simple matter. Mixture had been discussed by *Aristotle, who distinguished between 'juxtaposition' (as of beans and wheat, dry solids), 'confusion' (or flowing together, as when a cup of wine is absorbed and overwhelmed by the sea), and 'mixture' (when two or more ingredients do not overwhelm each other, but, as it were, balance each other, producing a new 'third entity' which is different from all of them). This was part of the background chemistry of the day. Another model was to look at the way fire apparently interpenetrates iron when it is red-hot. They do not disturb or destroy each other (their own integrity is maintained), there is no confusion, but they are totally inter-involved. Parallels to this model were the permeation of air by a sweet scent, or the action of light in the air (the interpenetration of two apparent solids). This raised questions of how *space* (location) was to be understood. Here, the contemporary physics had a considerable bearing on how union could be achieved and expressed.

These models, or variations on them, practically mesmerized certain early Christian thinkers and dominated the ways in which the incarnation was understood. And part of the difficulty was that these models illustrated union *in static terms*. It followed that the union, to many, came to be seen as something performed upon two static, pre-existing entities. Static understandings of union brought out the worst, most heretical tendencies of Monophysitism. For example, in the sixth century Julian of Halicarnassus was accused (probably mistakenly) of aphthartodocetism (the understanding that the body of Christ was incorruptible prior to the resurrection). He came adrift partly because he extended the fire model too far. The red-hot coal becomes all fire, and similarly, the body of Christ becomes suffused with the divine glory. Because in the background Julian probably had a controlling picture of the union as something *static*, the qualities of God (glory) were transferred to the human body in such a way that they became the body's own qualities. There was a kind of interior divinization, which threatened the reality of the human nature.

The best of the Monophysites (Cyril of Alexandria and Severus of Antioch, though we actually also see this in Apollinaris) resisted seeing the union in static terms, because they did not see the union as being an end in itself. The Word did not become incarnate just for fun, but did so *for our sake*. Hence the union was always to be understood as something which was purposive, probing, healing and creative. The union was *dynamic*, not static; it was not self-contained or only inward looking. The best of the Monophysites maintained this dynamism by using language about *kenosis* (self emptying, self humbling) and the picture of a journey (the eternal Word came down from heaven, and returned there, clothed with our humanity). Here we see the necessary complicating of the pictures and the vocabulary.

However, this developing theology tended to put more and more pressure upon the ability of the one-nature terminology to express it. By the middle of the fifth century (after the *Council of Chalcedon, which was openly Dyophysite), the Monophysite paradigm was beginning to look rather old-fashioned. In actual fact, a change of meanings had gradually been taking place. The old Nicene/Athanasian terminology understood the three words *ousia*, *physis* and *hypostasis* as all meaning much the same thing, and referring to *being*. However, Basil of Caesarea, to help him in discussing the Trinity, had distinguished between *ousia* and *hypostasis* (the Trinity is *one* God but *three* Persons). And this distinction (the new Nicene/Chalcedonian terminology) fed into Christological discussion as well, so that Christ was said at Chalcedon to be one *Person* in two *natures*. The Monophysites of the fifth and sixth centuries reacted bitterly to the dominance of the Dyophysite (two-nature) paradigm at Chalcedon, and they refused to accept the council. They accused it and Pope Leo of being *Nestorian (that is, of separating the two natures of Christ, and so effectively undoing the incarnation), and they broke away to form their own Monophysite churches, which still exist and today are called the Oriental Orthodox Churches (the Copts and the Syriac churches).

Were the Chalcedonians 'Nestorian'? That is still debated, but it can certainly be argued that Chalcedon tended in a dualist direction, as it could be taken as affirming the *independence* of the two natures in Christ, rather than simply their *integrity*. This suggested that the Dyophysite terminology itself needed to evolve. This was done by sixth-century neo-Chalcedonian theologians who developed the idea that something could be *anhypostatos* (real, but without a prior independent personhood) and then *enhypostatos* (brought into having a personal existence). This became a mechanism for expressing the real integrity but not prior independence of Christ's humanity, which was brought both into union and personhood at the same time. And this distinction, interestingly, passed into *Calvinist Scholasticism, and then into the twentieth-century Christology of *Karl Barth and *T.F. Torrance.

The classic, non-heretical Monophysitism of the kind we find in Cyril of Alexandria and Severus of Antioch was capable of dealing with these subtleties (both of them use the word *anhypostatos*). And it could (at a pinch) speak movingly and illuminatingly about the traditional difficult questions: Which suffers, the divine or the human nature? (the theopaschite issue); Did Christ have a genuine, free human will? (the monothelite issue); Was Christ ever ignorant? (the agnoetic issue). But ultimately it came to be seen as having lost elasticity, and as being hampered by an unnecessarily restricted vocabulary.

IAIN R. TORRANCE

FURTHER READING: P.T.R. Gray, *The Defence of Chalcedon in the East (451–553)* (Leiden, 1979); Aloys Grillmeier with Theresia Hainthaler, *Christ in Christian Tradition*, II, pt. 2, 'The Church of Constantinople in the Sixth Century' (London, 1995); W.H.C. Frend, *The Rise of the Monophysite Movement* (Cambridge, 1972); J. Lebon, *Le Monophysisme Sévérien: Étude Historique Littéraire et Théologique sur la Résistance Monophysite au Concile de Chalcédoine jusqu'à la Constitution de l'Église Jacobite* (Louvain, 1909); Iain R. Torrance, *Christology after Chalcedon: Severus of Antioch and Sergius the Grammarian* (Norwich, 1988); W.A. Wigram, *The Separation of the Monophysites* (London, 1923).

Montanism

This movement was named for Montanus (c. 170), a self-proclaimed prophet from Phrygia who believed that his revelations fulfilled the promises of the New Testament and heralded the imminent end of the world. Montanus was a gifted organizer and he attracted a considerable following among the peasants of Asia Minor. His movement was based in the villages of Pepuza and Tymion, which were not far from Laodicea and Colossae, although they have resisted all attempts at locating them precisely. Almost everything we know about Montanus comes from hostile sources and has been contested, though most scholars agree that he was a charismatic figure who proclaimed the coming of eschatological perfection in Christian communities which would resemble the heavenly city of Jerusalem.

In its own day Montanism was called the 'new prophecy', and there is no doubt that it had a charismatic flavour about it which probably reflected a grass-roots reaction to the increasing bureaucratization of the official church. The Montanists were accused of speaking in ecstasy and may have practised glossolalia, but we cannot be certain. It is certain, however, that the vehicle of the Montanist revelations was the 'Paraclete', who is normally equated with the Holy Spirit, following John's Gospel. The content of the prophecies was not really exceptional in the context of its time, being largely concerned with matters of moral discipline and the coming end, both of which were widespread themes in the late second-century church. Nevertheless, the mainline church refused to accept the genuineness of the prophetic claims made by Montanus and his followers and denounced their sayings as false.

The Montanists were apparently unusually rigorous in their demands for a strict regime of fasting, and they also advocated sexual continence within marriage and celibacy after the death of a partner. This may seem extreme to us today, but in its own context it was a normal, even moderate, line to take in such matters and compares well with what came to be the accepted norm in the mainline church.

Montanism spread to Rome and from there to other parts of the Mediterranean world, notably to North Africa, where it attracted the attention of the great *Tertullian who saw in the Montanists spirits akin to his own. Montanism seems to have lingered on until the fifth century, though by then it was far removed from its charismatic origins and in many places cannot have been more than a vestigial remnant of its former self. Its most lasting effect seems to be that it hastened the fixing of the New Testament canon. An official statement that prophecy of the Montanist type had effectively ceased in the Christian church accompanied the fixing of the canon.

It has frequently been postulated that Tertullian's 'conversion', about the year 207, took place within the Montanist sect. It would be better to say, however, that he welcomed it as an authentic manifestation of the kind of Christianity that he was already advocating. In moral terms Tertullian no doubt reflects Montanist rigorism reasonably well, but it is difficult to say how far his writings can be used as evidence of original (or authentic) Montanist beliefs. It is also not clear whether he joined an already existing Montanist group at Carthage or whether he founded one, which was subsequently known as 'Tertullianist' and which survived until it was reintegrated into the Catholic Church in 388.

A special feature of Montanism was the prominence that it gave to women. Two women in particular, Priscilla and Maximilla, played a major role in the original prophecies and may well have been the prime movers of the sect. It is unclear to what extent the influence of women spread beyond Asia Minor, but if Perpetua and Felicitas can be regarded as Montanists, then the North African church also experienced an important female ministry under the Montanist umbrella. It is of course clear that female ministry was procured at the price of sexual continence, and that it would not have been tolerated otherwise. The enemies of Montanism frequently accused them of debauchery because of the prominence of women in the sect, and had such accusations been true there is little doubt that Montanism's claims to a higher form of spirituality would have suffered an irreparable blow. In fact, the Montanists do seem to have lived exemplary moral lives and it appears that the opposition was motivated mainly by the fact that the church establishment felt threatened by their apparent extremism.

Montanism was not a heresy in the doctrinal sense, though it was later condemned as such. As far as we can tell, its adherents remained fully orthodox, even if occasionally their theological formulations were inadequate or archaic in relation to the Christological and Trinitarian controversies that tormented the mainline church. It is possible that some Montanists pictured Christ in a female form. If so, they would have strayed beyond the bounds of theological orthodoxy, but it all depends on how the evidence is interpreted and who is included in the Montanist category.

In later centuries Montanism was generally regarded as an early example of the kind of chiliast sect which sprang up in the later middle ages, and *John Wesley imagined that it was the last remnant of authentic New Testament Christianity. Today, however, such views have been generally discounted and Montanism is treated as a charismatic movement which was rooted in the circumstances of its own time and which died out without leaving any trace beyond the end of the ancient world.

GERALD BRAY

FURTHER READING: W.H.C. Frend, 'Montanism: Research and Problems', in *Archaeology and History in the Study of Early Christianity*, VI (London, 1988); R.E. Heine, *The Montanist Oracles and Testimonia* (Macon, GA, 1989); W. Tabbernee, *Montanist Inscriptions and Testimonia: Epigraphic Sources Illustrating the History of Montanism* (Macon, GA, 1996); C. Trevett, *Montanism* (Cambridge, 1996).

Müntzer, Thomas (c. 1489–1525)

Until recently, Thomas Müntzer was viewed through *Luther's eyes as an unstable 'Schwärmer', or visionary, whose militancy led his gullible followers into the catastrophe of the Peasants' War. *Marxist scholars, on the other hand, viewed him in primarily social and political terms as the prophet of the common people. Today he is generally regarded as a theologian of considerable importance. His humanist concerns for the renewal of the apostolic church, his liturgical creativity, the mystical and apocalyptic dimensions to his thought and his hermeneutical insights continue to attract wide attention. The flood of publications on the five hundredth anniversary of his birth in 1989 emphasized the significance of his anthropology, Christology, pneumatology and ecclesiology. Müntzer may be the outstanding theologian of the Radical Reformation.

Little is known about his early life, and even his date of birth is uncertain. Ulrich Bubenheimer underscores his debt to Humanism and the nexus of relatively prosperous family relationships, including merchants and goldsmiths, from which he emerged. Müntzer described himself as coming from Stolberg in the Harz, and he appears to have studied in the universities of Leipzig and certainly at Frankfurt an der Oder (1512) and Wittenberg (1517–18), becoming a Master of Arts and a Bachelor in Scripture. His career as a young priest and teacher was typical enough on the eve of the *Reformation.

Müntzer read widely in the mystical works of Tauler and Suso, deepened his knowledge of the early church through the new editions of *Augustine, *Cyprian, *Eusebius, *Hippolytus, *Tertullian and others; above all he devoured Scripture. His own published works show a remarkable breadth of biblical interest, from the Law and the Prophets, the historical books, to the writings, Gospels and epistles. He was deeply influenced by Luther, whom he hailed as his patron and father in the faith. However, contacts with Agricola, *Melanchthon, Karlstadt, and the humanist Aesticampianus were equally important. There are many parallels between his thinking and the mystical language and participatory ecclesiology of Karlstadt.

By 1519 he had a reputation as a fiery preacher, and he probably attended the famous Leipzig Disputation, where Luther's 'Hussite views' were challenged. In 1520, the *annus mirabilis* of the Reformation, Müntzer was a preacher in the important city of Zwickau, where he clashed with the *Erasmian moderate, Egranus. This conflict sharpened his awareness of the importance of the Old Testament and of a personal relationship to God. His confrontational manner led to his dismissal in April 1521. He made the short journey eastwards to Prague. Although he was at first welcomed with open arms as an ally of Luther, his independent theological profile soon became evident.

Müntzer had already evinced a pronounced interest in the apocalyptic thought of Daniel, and he saw himself as a new Elijah. He saw the imminent reformation of the church beginning in Prague, where the Hussite traditions remained strong. His 'Prague Manifesto', written in Latin, German and Czech (hinting at its universalist ambitions), yoked a moralizing denunciation of the clergy of the Old Church to a clarion call to study the living Word of God 'from the mouth of God himself'. After his expulsion from Prague, a time of poverty and uncertainty ended with the most significant ministry of his career, in the little Saxon town of Allstedt, from 1523–24.

Here his six published tracts and liturgical writings were published, and most of his extant correspondence written. His German Mass and German Church Service were pioneering, well before Luther's, and they attracted huge audiences from the surrounding countryside. He wrote a lucid defence of vernacular, contextual services. Worship was to be a training ground for the 'lazy elect', led by earnest preachers, and free of 'mumbo-jumbo'. He encouraged a high degree of lay participation. The whole congregation consecrated the bread and wine together with the presiding minister. His little tracts, 'Protestation or Proposition' and 'On Counterfeit Faith', underlined the importance of every Christian coming to a first-hand experience and understanding of faith. A mere parroting of biblical texts was not enough. He did not reject infant baptism, but the inner baptism of the Spirit was the priority. His 'Sermon to the Princes', delivered to the dukes of Saxony on 13 July 1524 and based on Daniel, articulated his theology of history and his vision of a theocratic society. The persecution of sympathizers of the Reformation by the secular authorities led Müntzer to an impatience with Luther's spiritual understanding of Christian liberty. The poor in spirit were being robbed of their birthright, both spiritually and materially. His final two writings, 'A Manifest Exposé of False Faith' and 'A Highly Provoked Vindication and Refutation of the Unspiritual Soft-Living Flesh in Wittenberg', written under the pressure of his last hectic weeks in Allstedt, equated the Wittenberg theologians with the scribes and Pharisees of biblical times, especially 'Dr Liar' (Luther).

His understanding of the immediacy of revelation included a cautious openness to dreams, and he shows an unusual awareness of other religions. Müntzer was drawn into the Peasants' War, which he saw as a covenantal struggle for justice, and indeed was one of its main leaders. After being tortured, he was executed on 27 May 1525.

Müntzer's theological writings were fragmentary and occasional. He was primarily a pastor, spiritual counsellor and advocate of the underdog. He read Scripture as the deposit of a historic revelation which should spur each generation to plumb anew the depths of doubt and despair until Christ is reborn in the abyss of the soul. A mystical theology of the cross, conformity with Christ in his suffering and obedience, pervaded all his work. It was yoked to an apocalyptic expectation of the restoration of the divine 'order of things'. All property and power was to be held in stewardship. Whether he developed a theology of revolution remains controversial, and no clear blueprint for the future was advanced. However, his analysis of cultural and political oppression was acute, and couched in unforgettable language, and his hymns remained popular long after his death.

PETER MATHESON

FURTHER READING: *Text: The Collected Works of Thomas Müntzer* (trans. and ed. Peter Matheson; Edinburgh, 1988). *Studies:* Andrew Bradstock, *Faith in the Revolution: The Political Theologies of Müntzer and Winstanley* (London, 1997); Ulrich Bubenheimer, *Thomas Müntzer Herkunft und Bildung* (Leiden, 1989); Hans-Jürgen Goertz, *Thomas Müntzer Mystiker-Apokalyptiker-Revolutionär* (Munich, 1989), ET *Thomas Müntzer: Apocalyptic, Mystic and Revolutionary* (trans. Jocelyn Jaquiery; Edinburgh, 1993); Tom Scott, *Thomas Müntzer: Theology and Revolution in the German Reformation* (London, 1989); Siegfried Bräuer and Helmar Junghans (eds.), *Der Theologe Thomas Müntzer: Untersuchungen zu seiner Entwicklung und Lehre* (Berlin, 1989); Günther Franz (ed.), *Thomas Müntzer Schriften und Briefe* (Gütersloh, 1968).

Myth of God Controversy

In July 1977 the most heated theological controversy in Britain since the publication of *J.A.T. Robinson's (1919–83) *Honest to God* (London, 1963) was sparked off by the publication of a volume of essays entitled *The Myth of God Incarnate*. The contributors (soon to be referred to as the 'Seven against Christ')

were *Don Cupitt, Michael Goulder, *John Hick (editor), Leslie Houlden, Dennis Nineham, Maurice Wiles and Frances Young. In an attempt to 'make Christian discipleship possible for our children's children', they called for a revision of the traditional doctrine of Christ which, they insisted, was no longer intelligible to persons living in a modern, western, scientific, religiously plural culture. They urged Christians to recognize that 'Jesus was (as he is presented in Acts 2:21) "a man approved by God" for a special role within the divine purpose, and that the later conception of him as God incarnate ... is a mythological or poetic way of expressing his significance for us'. The church had mistakenly substituted the metaphors of the New Testament for a metaphysical understanding of Christ as God. The result of this is the incarnational faith which affirms that Jesus is uniquely and necessarily both fully human and fully God, the second Person of the co-equal Trinity. The aim of *The Myth* is to demonstrate that not only does the doctrine lack internal coherence and credibility in the twentieth century, but also that it is a deviation from what the New Testament tells us about the historical Jesus.

The prominence of most of the mythographers and the publicity surrounding the book's launch incited an immediate response in the form of letters to newspapers, radio and television programmes and a barrage of generally hostile reviews in the religious and secular press. Much of the sense of scandal was undoubtedly caused by the provocative title of the book. Rather than understanding 'myth' technically as the use of imagery to communicate truth, many understood it in the popular sense of fantasy or fabrication. Was the central doctrine of the Christian faith no more than a fairy tale? Moreover, the problem was not helped by the fact that the mythographers' use of 'myth' was inconsistent.

Within six weeks of the book's publication, excited booksellers were displaying *The Myth* alongside a more reasoned critique in the form of a volume of essays entitled *The Truth of God Incarnate*. The contributors to the latter were Christopher Butler, Michael Green (editor), Brian Hebblethwaite, John Macquarrie and Stephen Neill. A little later the same year George Carey produced his own counter-offensive, *God Incarnate*, and the Church of England Evangelical Council called for the Anglican contributors of *The Myth* to resign their orders. Such was the interest caused by the furore that within the first eight months *The Myth* sold thirty thousand copies, twenty-four thousand of which were bought in Britain alone. Finally, a year after its publication, Hick and Goulder arranged a colloquy at Birmingham University (from 10 to 12 July 1978) between the mythographers and a small group of their critics. The papers from this gathering were published in 1979 in *Incarnation and Myth: The Debate Continued*. However, by this time interest in the controversy itself was waning and by the early 1980s it was all but spent.

In the final analysis, the controversy the book provoked was out of all proportion to the intrinsic merit of the essays, some of which were too technical for many of those who bought it, and others, it was frequently pointed out, were rather poor. In fact, although the book served to highlight some central Christological and methodological concerns, there was nothing new about the arguments. In the first place, similar critiques and restatements of the incarnation been recently provided in England by J.A.T. Robinson in *The Human Face of God* (London, 1973), Wiles in *The Remaking of Christian Doctrine* (London, 1974) and Geoffrey Lampe (1912–80) in his 1976 Bampton Lectures, *God as Spirit* (Oxford, 1977). Further, readers of *The Myth* with any knowledge of the rise of modern theology from *Schleiermacher onwards will feel a sense of *déjà vu*. Indeed, it is surprising that the book did provoke such a furore. Readers will also feel rather surprised, as many did at the

time, at the lack of discussion of the work of important theologians who have not only faced the issues raised by the book, but have developed incarnational Christologies in the context of twentieth-century western culture. For example, there is hardly any mention, if any at all, of *Karl Barth (1886–1968), *Hans Urs von Balthasar (1905–87), *Karl Rahner (1904–84), *T.F. Torrance (b. 1913), *Walter Kasper (b. 1933) and *Wolfhart Pannenberg (b. 1928).

It is perhaps an indication of our changing culture and the increasing prevalence of such views in the church that when, ten years later, Hick co-edited with P.F. Knitter a similar symposium, *The Myth of Christian Uniqueness* (London, 1987), the sense of scandal was nowhere near that provoked in 1977.

CHRISTOPHER PARTRIDGE

FURTHER READING: G. Carey, *God Incarnate* (Leicester, 1977); D. Cook, 'Significant Trends in Christology in Western Scholarly Debate', in V. Samuel and C. Sugden (eds.), *Sharing Jesus in the Two Thirds World* (Grand Rapids, 1983), pp. 251–76; K.W. Clements, *Lovers of Discord: Twentieth-Century Theological Controversies in England* (London, 1988); M. Goulder (ed.), *Incarnation and Myth: The Debate Continued* (London, 1979); M. Green (ed.), *The Truth of God Incarnate* (London, 1977); J. Hick (ed.), *The Myth of God Incarnate* (London, 1977); A. Heron, 'Doing Theology Without the Incarnation?', *Scot J Th* 31 (1978), pp. 51–71; G. Newlands, 'On The Myth of God Incarnate', in S. Sykes and D. Holmes (eds.), *New Studies in Theology* (London, 1980), pp. 181–92; A. Harvey (ed.), *God Incarnate: Story and Belief* (London, 1981).

Narrative Theology

Christian Narrative Theology is a hybrid created from investigations into the disciplines of literary theory and theology. A narrative theology attempts to address biblical truth-claims and their ontological status within a pattern of textual coherence. Most 'narrative theologies' do not measure truth-claims within a scientific model of verification and falsification. Rather, they rely upon truth as textual coherence, a type of literary formalism.

In recent years, there has been a drop-off in first-order theological reflection. It has been suggested that Derrida's 1966 lecture, 'Structure, Sign and Play', began a process which effectively ended formalist readings within the human sciences. Likewise, Lyotard's claim of 'incredulity towards meta-narratives' seemed to further this attack on structural coherence. However, Hayden White proposes that:

> ... to raise the question of the nature of narrative is to invite reflection on the very nature of culture and, possibly, even on the nature of humanity itself. So natural is the impulse to narrate, so inevitable is the form of narrative for any report of the way things really happened, that narrativity could appear problematical only in a culture in which it was absent ... or refused. (White, p. 1)

The competing claims of these varied hermeneutical theories has led to a rampant pluralism which the modern theologian finds him or herself needing to address. Due to these new developments within the humanities, first-order theological reflection has been set aside with questions of method coming to the fore.

The French philosopher *Paul Ricoeur maintains that there are gains to be made in pursuing a theology based on narrative. His essay on Narrative Theology states at the outset that although he is concerned with the difficulties of a narrative theology, he would not exert such effort if he did not believe that a narrative grounding of theology was 'sound'. A narrative theology is fundamentally 'better' than a speculative theology (which rids discourse of reference to stories), a moral theology (which is atemporal), or an existential theology (which rids theology of a historical basis and ultimately focuses too much on the individual). Ricoeur believes that the contemporary need for a narrative theology comes from the loss of tradition and authority inherited from the

*Enlightenment quest coupled with technological advances allowing the human will to control and manipulate the environment. This creates a situation of 'an increase of forgetfulness, especially that of the past sufferings of human kind [which leads] to a loss of storytelling' (Ricoeur, 1995, p. 238). For Ricoeur, the conceptual basis of a narrative theology finds its roots in the elements of literary theory.

The Yale theologian *Hans W. Frei has been widely recognized as the seminal figure in the formulation of modern Narrative Theology. In his 1974 work *The Eclipse of Biblical Narrative: A Study in Eighteenth- and Nineteenth-century Hermeneutics*, Frei traces the breakdown of 'realistic' readings of the biblical narratives. He contends that a confusion between the categories of history and what he calls the 'history-likeness' of biblical narratives caused a shift to occur within hermeneutics. Scholars subsequently began a lengthy and, in his mind, misguided investigation into the historical veracity of the biblical narratives.

The disciplines of narratology and theology are not prima facie compatible. The relationship between biblical narratives and the status of narratives in general (narratology) is tenuous because biblical narratives exemplify different traits than most narratives. Eric Auerbach's work on mimesis analyzed the difference between classical Greek literature and the biblical narratives and suggested that the

> ... Bible's claim to truth is ... tyrannical – it excludes all other claims ... Far from seeking, like Homer, merely to make us forget our own reality for a few hours, it seeks to overcome our reality: we are to fit our own life into its world ... (Auerbach, pp. 14–15)

His analysis concludes that there is a difference in the authorial stance towards the material; the biblical writers were not suggesting a way-of-being-in-the-world, rather they claim exclusive exposition of authentic humanity.

Frei notes several factors that preclude the writing of a narrative theology. He discusses the problem of the self-referentiality of the text and a text's failure to imitate the world (the mimetic function of texts). Frei calls this view 'artificial' (Frei, 1993, p. 141) since the biblical texts must refer beyond themselves. The text shapes the world of the reader, for if the text does not refer to reality in any manner, then it would have no grounds for inviting us to enter into *Karl

Barth's 'strange new world'. Theologically, Frei and his colleague George Lindbeck are committed to the view that the text invites the reader to dwell in the world it creates. Frei also advocates Lindbeck's 'cultural-linguistic' approach in regards to the way doctrines are used: 'the function of church doctrines that becomes most prominent ... is their use, not as expressive models or as truth claims, but as communally authoritative rules of discourse, attitude, and action' (Lindbeck, p. 18). Within this model, the formal/structural analysis of the texts which had previously privileged a 'realistic narrative' reading of the biblical narratives gives way to an emphasis on the community's way of reading. Ultimately, the gains of a narrative theology are not based exclusively on narrative but work in conjunction with the other modes of discourse found in all biblical texts.

Narrative investigations into theology have offered promise. The work of Frei and Ricoeur (though not similar) has given us insight into the theoretical problems facing any narrative theology. However, we can see glimpses of the possibilities opened by the marriage of the disciplines of literary theory and theology. It may prove to be the case, however, that post-structuralist readings, such as deconstruction, may forever plague any form of theology heavily dependent upon textuality.

EDWARD L. NANNO

FURTHER READING: Eric Auerbach, *Mimesis: The Representation of Reality in Western Literature* (trans. Willard R. Trask; Princeton, 1953); Karl Barth, 'The Strange New World Within The Bible', in *The Word of God and the Word of Man* (trans. Douglas Horton; London, 1928); Gary Comstock, 'Truth or Meaning: Ricoeur versus Frei on Biblical Narrative', *J Rel* (1986), pp. 116–40; Stanley Hauerwas and L. Gregory Jones (eds.), *Why Narrative? Readings in Narrative Theology* (Grand Rapids, 1989); Hans Frei, *The Identity of Jesus Christ: The Hermeneutical Bases for Dogmatic Theology* (Philadelphia, 1975); '"Narrative" in Christian and Modern Reading', in *Theology and Dialogue: Essays in Conversation with George Lindbeck* (Notre Dame, IN, 1990); *The Eclipse of Biblical Narrative: A Study in Eighteenth- and Nineteenth-century Hermeneutics* (New Haven, 1974); *Theology and Narrative: Selected Essays* (ed. William Placher and George Hunsinger; Oxford, 1993); Paul Ricoeur, *Figuring the Sacred: Religion, Narrative, and Imagination* (trans. David Pellauer; ed. Mark I. Wallace; Minneapolis, 1995); 'The Narrative Form', *Semeia* 13 (1978); *The Rule of Metaphor: Multi-disciplinary Studies of the Creation of Meaning in Language* (Toronto, 1977); *Time and Narrative* (trans. Kathleen McLaughlin and David Pellaeur; 3 vols.; Chicago, 1984, 1985, 1988); George W. Stroup, *The Promise of Narrative Theology* (London, 1984); Ronald Thiemann, *Revelation and Theology: The Gospel as Narrated Promise* (Notre Dame, IN, 1985); Garrett Green (ed.), *Scriptural Authority and Narrative Interpretation* (Philadelphia, 1987); W.J.T. Mitchell (ed.), *On Narrative* (Chicago, 1981); Hayden V. White, 'The Value of Narrativity in the Representation of Reality', in *The Content of the Form: Narrative Discourse and Historical Representation* (Baltimore / London, 1987).

Neopaganism

'Neopaganism' refers to a wide range of attempts to recover or recreate in late-modern western culture the practice and presumed benefits of pre-Christian polytheistic and animistic religions – particularly (but not exclusively) those of Britain and northern Europe. There is much disagreement (both in the movement and outside it) over the question of whether Neopaganism is the surfacing of a long-concealed folk-religion, or a recent invention tailored to the tastes of the late twentieth century. It is necessary, therefore, to understand Neopaganism in terms of (1) its relationship to 'old' paganism, (2) its origins as a contemporary religious expression and (3) the reasons for its recent growth in a postmodern and post-Christian civilization.

Whether one concludes that Neopaganism is a modern invention or a genuine recovery of older pagan traditions, however, the movement is growing both in Great Britain and in North America. Estimates of adherents range (in 1998) as high as a hundred thousand in both countries, with many times that number assumed to be sympathetic. Hundreds of small publications are devoted to Neopaganism. Also in recent years, Neopaganism has a lively existence on the Internet.

The word 'pagan' is derived from the Latin *paganus*, which means simply 'a dweller in the country'. ('Heathen' and 'heath' are similarly related.) The word assumed its mainly negative connotations early in the Christian era, probably by the fourth century when Christianity became the state religion. Because Christianity grew mainly in urban areas, the older polytheistic ways came to be associated with dwellers in the country. So, as Christianity became established and official, the word pagan gradually lost its meaning of 'old fashioned' and 'countrified', and assumed its more common meaning of idolatrous worship.

Neopaganism, on the other hand, sees that association with old ways – particularly with the religious meaning of the rhythms of nature, which are more evident in the country – as a positive thing. Neopaganism is pursued as a reaction to the nature-destroying modern era, and to the Christianity which is supposed to have nurtured and encouraged this destruction. Ironically, therefore, Neopaganism today is mainly an urban movement, drawing on the sophisticated and well-educated for its support.

'Neo-pagan' is a general term, which includes many attempts to recover pre-Christian religious ways. There are some attempts to draw on continuing aboriginal practice – in certain areas of Australia and North America, for example, where vestiges of primal religion remain. (This is a minor theme, however, since in those communities the native religion is an important part of cultural survival, and the curiosity of the dominant culture is not particularly welcome.) Most of those who would call themselves neo-pagans draw on the shadowy legacy of pre-Christian religion, mainly in Britain. The largest and most coherent attempt to recover this pagan legacy is in the practice of Wicca.

The word Wicca has been variously traced to an Indo-European root *wic*, meaning 'to bend or shape', and alternatively to the words 'wit' and 'wise'. In any case, the word 'witch' has ancient and powerful meaning, describing one who is able to exercise control over natural – and perhaps supernatural – forces, sometimes for good (as in 'white witch') and sometimes for evil ('black magic'). The contemporary Wiccan revival can be traced largely to the work of the English Egyptologist and folklorist Margaret Murray, whose 1921 work *The Witch Cult in Western Europe* argues the thesis that the witch trials of the sixteenth and seventeenth centuries were directed at the practice of a genuine religion. Murray's 1933 work *The God of the Witches* develops the idea of the Wiccan religion as being essentially duotheistic, a worship of the great goddess of fertility and the somewhat lesser horned god of the hunt. Though Murray was a genuine scholar, much of her argument has since been discredited by her failure to see that the content of the Wiccan religion as it is reported in the witch trials is a kind of Christian parody provided mainly by the questioning of the accusers.

Nevertheless, the weight of Murray's reputation helped launch in 1954 the much more dubious – and more influential – *Witchcraft Today* by Gerald Gardner, to which she wrote a preface. Gardner, a retired civil servant who had been impressed by observance of occult practices in Malaya, claimed to have been initiated in 1939 into a surviving coven of witches in the vicinity of the New Forest in England. He sets forth considerable detail of practice and liturgy: meditative attunement with Nature, worship of god and goddess, celebration of the eight pagan festivals (Samhain, Imbolc, Beltane and Lammas, together with the solstices and equinoxes), and dance, chant and celebration in a circle. Though the quality and originality of Gardner's influence continues to be debated, he is still considered to be the father of the neo-pagan movement.

Another well-defined branch of contemporary Neopaganism is an attempt to revive the practice of druidry. Of this the largest group is ADF (standing for the Irish *Ar nDrafocht Fein*, 'Our own druidry'), presided over by Isaac Bonewits. ADF is introduced on the Internet home page in words that characterize the eclectic breadth of the neo-pagan movement – as well as its casual attitude towards historicity:

> ADF is … a completely independent tradition of Neopagan Druidism. Like our sisters and brothers in other Neopagan movements, we're polytheistic Nature worshippers, attempting to revive the best aspects of the Paleopagan faiths of our ancestors within a modern scientific, artistic, ecological and wholistic context.

The phrase 'independent tradition of Neopagan Druidism' points up the distinctively postmodern paradox of all neo-pagan movements: though it seeks to draw spiritual strengths from ancient ways, at the same time it acknowledges little or no continuity with or authority from those ways. Thus Margot Adler, acknowledging that there is little historical warrant to the widespread Wiccan myth – of a goddess-worshipping golden age supplanted by aggressive patriarchal monotheism – at the same time warns against those scholars who have '… refuted the literal accuracy of the myth and then wrongly dismissed the modern Craft itself as a fraud' (*Drawing Down the Moon*). Rather, she says, the ability of Neopaganism to distance itself from the myth of its origin 'is a lesson in the flexibility of the revival'. The paradox of an ostensibly ancient movement with little concern for its historicity is perhaps best resolved in the words of Ronald Hutton, who in *The Pagan Religions of the Ancient British Isles* concludes that 'modern paganism might well be a recent creation which draws upon ancient images but employs them in a new way and for modern needs' (p. 340).

Several aspects of late-twentieth-century culture have contributed to the growth of Neopaganism. One, mentioned above, is a reaction against modernity and its tendency to 'desacralization' of the natural world. Since modernity is generally assumed to have roots in Christian monotheism, many neo-pagans hope that a pre-Christian polytheism might lead to a revitalization of the sense of the sacred in Nature. Another common argument is in reaction against Christian exclusivism and in favour of a plurality of spiritual paths. Margot Adler sums up the attitude in two epigraphs to her chapter on 'The Pagan World View'. One, from James Breasted, is 'Monotheism is imperialism in religion.' The other is from the fourth-century Greek Symmachus: 'What does it matter what practical system we adopt in our search for the truth? Not by one avenue only can we arrive at so tremendous a secret.'

Another closely related influence is the movement of 'deep ecology', which argues that environmental problems will be solved not by technological 'fixes', but rather by inward, spiritual change, a change usually defined as being a recognition of the sacred or the divine in the natural. Feminism also has been a major influence on the growth of Neopaganism – particularly in its critique of monotheism and patriarchy, and its positing of a long goddess-worshipping period of peace at the dawn of history. Closely related is the rich tradition linking the earth with the feminine, a connection given added force by the popularization of the 'Gaia' hypothesis. Gaia, the ancient Greek goddess of the earth, was chosen by the British scientist James Lovelock as the name for his widely influential hypothesis of the planet as a self-regulating organism. The 'gaia' idea is an important theme in *'Ecofeminism', and in many aspects of 'goddess spirituality'.

A subtler contributor to the growth of Neopaganism is a growing subjectivism in both ethics and epistemology. Suspicion of all forms of external authority (whether proposed by the scientist or the priest) as a relic of patriarchalism has led to an elevation of the notion that 'I can create my own reality'. From this stem the casual attitude towards whether or not the 'pagan' sources are historical and the appeal of 'shaping' or 'weaving' reality from inside one's own magic circle. (Indeed the popularity of Neopaganism on the 'net' or 'web' of cyberspace is perhaps related to the near-magical feeling of power one can have in front of a computer screen with its linkages to various virtual realities.)

A Christian evaluation of the various neo-pagan movements might well begin with an acknowledgement of Christian complicity in the witch-burning hysteria of the sixteenth and seventeenth centuries. Though it is unlikely that very many of the people who suffered in this movement were 'witches' or 'pagans' by any definition, the era has certainly coloured Christian thinking about Neopaganism today – as it has coloured neo-pagan attitudes toward Christianity.

On the other hand, there is certainly no room in Christian thought for the animism and polytheism which is at the core of Neopaganism. But inasmuch as the movement is a longing for the divine – and a critique of Christian 'desacralization' – it is important to note that the Christian theology being rejected by Neopaganism is far more a kind of deism (portraying a God who is only transcendent). It does not seem to be rejecting the triune God of Scripture (who is both transcendent and immanent). A fully fleshed-out Trinitarian theology would have much to say to contemporary Neopaganism. At the same time, much of the neo-pagan affirmation of the divinity in Nature turns out in fact to be an elevation of the idea that the self is god. The idea is thus prey to all the dangers which result when human persons begin to pretend that they are gods and not creatures.

LOREN WILKINSON

FURTHER READING: Margot Adler, *Drawing Down the Moon: Witches, Druids, Goddess Worshippers and Other Pagans in America Today* (New York, 1986); Irene Diamond and Gloria Feman Orenstein (eds.), *Reweaving the World: The Emergence of Ecofeminism* (San Francisco, 1990); Ronald Hutton, *The Pagan Religions of the British Isles: Their Nature and Legacy* (Oxford, 1991).

Nestorianism

Contemporary use of the term Nestorianism often connotes three related, but distinct, notions. First, it refers to the teaching on the person of Christ propounded by Nestorius, archbishop of Constantinople between 428 and 431 – particularly as that teaching was received by his opponents, and denounced by them as the implied doctrine of two personal subjects within Christ. Secondly, it connotes the actual doctrine of Nestorius which shows him to have been attempting to represent traditional teachings of the Syrian church, notably of its leading fourth-century theologians Diodore of Tarsus, *Theodore Mopsuestia and *Theodoret of Cyr. Thirdly, Nestorianism refers to the Christian church that from the fifth century developed independently of Byzantium and flourished in the Persian Empire, a communion which never concurred with Nestorius's condemnation, and which regards him as one of its 'Great Lights'.

It was Nestorius's great personal misfortune to have ranged against him, in theological dispute, *Cyril of Alexandria. By the time Nestorius succeeded to the throne of Constantinople in 428, Cyril already had sixteen years' experience of high political and religious office. The imbalance between the two on the level of political acumen is obvious, and it cost Nestorius dearly. It is also evident in the manner in which Cyril took great pains to publicize, explain and vindicate his teachings through widely diverse methods and by applying a range of popular and scholarly styles, whereas Nestorius adopted a method which relied excessively on semantic exactness and also favoured a rhetorical style which applied *reductio ad absurdum* to positions of which he did not approve; thereby alienating not only his Alexandrian theological opponents but also large sections of his own monks and laity in Constantinople, many of whom did not have much empathy for the Syrian tradition which Nestorius had brought with him and was determined to apply with a reformer's zeal as a standard of orthodoxy.

In the Constantinople of 428, the Alexandrian tradition of Christology had high status. Even in the time of Gregory Nazianzen's leadership in the capital (379–81), the doctrine of *Athanasius had been set up as paradigmatic. By contrast, even a Syrian theologian as famous as *John Chrysostom had been at Constantinople (398–407) did not advance the particularly 'Syrian' elements of the Christological tradition to the extent which Nestorius chose to do. Nestorius used his close friends to assist him in a preaching campaign that explained the inadvisability of using the title *theotokos* (Mother of God) in so far as this was an example of loose and undisciplined thinking about the incarnation. He was concerned to explicate the form of the Christological union: the manner in which godliness and humanity could be conceived as joined in Christ. Alexandrian thought was believed by many Syrian theologians still to be tainted with *Apollinaris's premises whereby the deity of the Logos so overwhelmed and absorbed the humanness of Jesus that the manhood all but disappeared: a model that ran dangerously close to *Docetism. The Syrians based their thought on an exegesis of Scripture that resisted *Origen's thesis that all biblical texts represented an 'absolute' perspective (the voice of the Logos spoken in history) and accordingly were best interpreted by the allegorical method, Their teachers advanced a historical contextualization of Scripture which, in terms of the Christological problem, gave their thought a realist and 'Pauline' quality that has proved attractive to many modern Christological thinkers too. They spoke of a discrete humanity and discrete godliness in Christ. The way in which they explained the coming together of such diversity was by the preferred terms of 'God's good favour' (*eudokia*). The grace of God effected a dynamic correlation with the life of a man. Nestorius repeated most of Theodore's theology, less originally and brilliantly than his teacher, but with a comparable stress on the foundation of the Christological dynamic being 'grace', and on the practical acknowledgement of the harmony of divine and human being the single worship the church gave to the Christ. The discreteness of the human and divine were maintained, however, because the Syrians continued to affirm that the concept of 'united natures' implied an abiding compositeness, whereas the Alexandrian theologians insisted that the logic of the term 'union' demanded a transformation to oneness, in some form or other. Syrian theology thus preferred the Christological term 'correlation' (*synapheia*, association) to that of 'union' (*henosis*). Nestorius thought he had expressed the manner of the harmony clearly enough by pointing to the single worship the church offered its Lord: 'On account of the one who lies hidden (The Logos), I worship the one who appears (The man Jesus)', or again, 'Let us confess the God in man, let us adore the man who is to be worshipped together with God because of the divine conjunction (*synapheia*) with God the Creator'.

Many of his hearers, both in Constantinople and then further afield in Alexandria and Rome, had never before been presented in such stark terms with the Syrian tradition of Christology. To some ears it sounded like the same honorific ascription of deity which the anti-Arian theologians had exposed as logically incoherent. Others misheard the Syrian habit of speaking of the 'Man Assumed' to be a revival of the Adoptionist heresy of earlier centuries. Cyril applied these apologetic arguments mercilessly, drawing out the implications of such an approach. He argued that the diversity of natures Nestorius was proposing had overstepped its mark into a doctrine of 'Two Sons'. Here he pushed the doctrine to extremes, pressing its implied conclusion, as he saw it, of a double subjectivity in Christ. He argued that if the Syrians were right that there was a Son of God, and a separate Son of Man, such that some acts in the Scripture could be attributed to one, and some to another, then the dynamic of the redemptive sacrifice of Christ (death on the cross) was voided, for it was no longer capable of being seen as a divine act. In many ways this oversimplified the meaning of Diodore and the later Syrian tradition, including Nestorius himself; nevertheless the pressing of the implications of various doctrines to logical extremities was a standard part of ancient rhetorical argument. Cyril has been much criticized for this, but it is exactly the way in which his own teaching was caricatured by many Antiochenes as Apollinarism.

Nestorius's demands for semantic exactness in distinguishing scriptural attributions often led him to regard the traditional pieties of Christian faith (titles such as 'Mother of God', or strong paradoxes such as those favoured by Gregory Nazianzen: 'The selfsame passible and impassible, circumscribed and uncircumscribed' [*Ep.* 101]) as evidence of feeble-mindedness. In the course of arguments with bishops gathering at Ephesus to adjudicate the case between himself and Cyril, Nestorius appears to have lost his temper with one who was asking the simple question: 'Why cannot a Christian simply describe Jesus as God?' To this he replied: 'We must not call the one who became man for us,

God.' He added: 'I refuse to acknowledge as God, an infant of two or three months old.' This lack of discretion and scorn for traditional pieties went a long way in alienating the great majority of bishops at Ephesus (431) who proceeded to his synodical condemnation for heresy.

It might be said that Nestorius's lack of care in propagating Syrian thought caused his downfall. More subtle Syrian theologians active in the same controversy, such as Theodoret of Cyr, Andrew of Samosata or John of Antioch eventually came to terms with Cyril's thought, and Cyril himself was always convinced that the Syrians who accepted the necessity of a single subject in the Christ were not at all the same as Nestorius who had lost the logical right to claim he taught anything other than two distinct Sons, two personal-centres in Christ. The exiled Nestorius continued to maintain that he had been much misrepresented. With the rediscovery for the west, in the early twentieth century, of the *Book of Heracleides of Damascus* (formerly mistranslated as *Bazaar of Heracleides*), a fuller and primary resource was once more available for the study of his authentic teaching. It has, however, proved difficult to establish a common scholarly judgement, for much turns on the question of how much that treatise, composed in his post-Ephesine exile, perhaps twenty years after the events, represents hindsight or the theology he was elaborating at the time. Here Nestorius clearly wishes to demonstrate how the interrelation of divine and human in Jesus may be articulated, and he gives a fuller account of personal (prosopic) unity than any of the hostile excerpts cited against him at Ephesus manage to offer. All told, however, his Christological thought in this book remains confused and unclear. It was to fall more to Theodoret of Cyr, taking on some of the Cyrilline terminology after Ephesus, to represent the Antiochene Christological tradition. It was probably Theodoret who drafted the terms of the 'Formula of Re-Union' (in Cyril's *opera* as *Ep.* 39) and to that extent resolved the crisis initiated by Nestorius.

Nestorianism is sometimes used as a common misnomer for the 'Church of the East', which was centred in antiquity on the archiepiscopal throne of Seleucia-Ctesiphon. The church's theology was rooted firmly in the school of Edessa and so the tradition overshadowed in Byzantium, in the course of the suppression of

Nestorius, continued to hold a dominant place as the church developed outside the imperial boundaries in Persian territory. From this base it extended its influence and missions to Arabia and Egypt, even as far afield as India and China. Its extent in antiquity was very significant, but by the fourteenth century it had been depleted by Mongol oppression. In the sixteenth century certain parts of the church moved for union with Rome, which then declared a Chaldaean Patriarchate. Today the title of Chaldean is often used of those in Roman communion, while the designation of Suraya (Syrian Christians) is preferred by the main body. In Britain the title of 'Assyrian Church', popularized by the nine-teenth-century Anglican missionaries, is some-times applied.

J.A. McGuckin

FURTHER READING: C.E. Braaten, 'Modern Inter-pretations of Nestorius', *Ch H* 32 (1963), pp. 251–57; S. Brock, 'The "Nestorian" Church: A Lamenta-ble Misnomer', in *The Church of the East: Life and Thought* (ed. J.F. Coakley and K. Parry; Bulletin of the John Rylands University Library of Manchester 78.3; 1996), pp. 22–29; R.C. Chesnut, 'The Two Prosopa in Nestorius' Bazaar of Heraclides', *J Th St* NS 29 (1978), pp. 392–408; R.A. Greer, 'The Image of God and the Prosopic Union in Nestorius' *Bazaar of Heraclides'*, in *Lux In Lumine: Essays to Honour W.N. Pittenger* (ed. R.A. Norris; New York, 1966), pp. 46–61; J.A. McGuckin, 'The Christology of Nestorius of Constantinople', *P B Rev* 7.2–3 (1988), pp. 93–129; 'Nestorius and the Political Fac-tions of Fifth-century Byzantium: Factors in his Personal Downfall', in *The Church of the East*, pp. 7–21.

New Age

An eclectic, syncretistic movement that emerged as a discrete entity in the late 1970s and early 1980s. Definition is a major problem. It is easier to describe specific New Age people than to characterize the entire phenomenon. Some who appear to belong in this category also eschew the term itself. The New Age is variously described as a 'metanetwork', or network of networks (Ferguson, 1980), or a 'segmented polycentric integrated network' (SPIN) (York, 1994). *Wittgenstein's 'family resemblances' provide another useful model for understand-ing the movement.

The New Age is scarcely new, but it is the recy-cling of beliefs and practices culled from differ-ent times, places and cultures and applied to the exigencies of western life. Some describe it in terms of eastern philosophies moving west. Others regard it as a revivalist movement within those esoteric metaphysical circles historically associated with Swedenborg, Blavatsky or the Transcendentalists. The New Age also parallels aspects of ancient *Gnosticism and Catharism, with other connections to occult movements, Wicca and paganism. But the New Age is primarily a product of contemporary cultural change, inspired by dissatisfaction with the val-ues of modernity. It is motivated by the belief that for the human race – indeed, for the entire cosmos – to survive, a transformational shift in consciousness is required, which will result in the replacement of traditional western values by a new paradigm rooted in a transcultural global spirituality. The New Age is therefore a manifestation of postmodernism, though para-doxically it is also an expression of the forces of modernity, intermingled with other notions that are clearly pre-modern.

The New Age alleges that western culture has marginalized spiritual values in favour of a mechanistic, rationalist and reductionist out-look. A workable paradigm for the future will need to reverse that trend through a rediscovery of spirituality. Spirituality is not generally defined, though it is assumed that because of the church's role in western culture traditional Christian insights are irrelevant – unless history can be deconstructed so as to reveal a different way of being 'Christian' that was suppressed by those who came to be dominant. Overall, how-ever, there is little concern with theology as such – which explains why the New Age can combine things that might otherwise appear incompatible and logically contradictory.

The major concern in the New Age is with paradigms for practical transformation, and the most popular options fall within one of four dominant categories:

Non-western world-views. A simplistic view of the collapse of the *Enlightenment consensus assumes that since the problem has been created by what is modern and western, the resolution will come through things that are ancient and eastern. Western forms of Taoism and Buddhism are particularly attractive.

First nation beliefs. Historically, western values were spread by the displacement of other cultures: Native American, Aboriginal, Maori and so on. These banished world-views now look to have been more spiritually orientated than that of the west. Reinstating these world-views might not only provide new hope for the future but could also enable the west to expiate some of the guilt of the past.

Creation centred. European culture itself was 'spiritual' long before the arrival of classical 'western' values, reinforced through Greek philosophy and, later, the spread of Christendom. Concern to rediscover an indigenous pre-Christian western spirituality is seen in the popularity of ancient *Celtic spirituality, goddess worship and the rise of *Neopaganism, as well as in the effort to redefine Christianity in these terms.

Person centred. Many New Agers see religion in general – not just Christianity – as the problem. For them, a new paradigm will only emerge from within the human psyche. Psychotherapies of various sorts, especially transpersonal psychology, provide this kind of 'secular' person with access to transformational experiences similar to those found in mystical religious traditions, but without the initially unwelcome baggage of religious dogma.

New Agers themselves adopt different stances toward the evident syncretism found within the movement. Some are cynical about the effects of individuals constructing their own eclectic spiritualities. They prefer to identify one spiritual path that can be followed with integrity and despise those who 'unwittingly become spiritual strip miners damaging other cultures in superficial attempts to uncover their mystical treasures' (Starhawk, 1989, p. 214). Others are more optimistic about combining disparate materials into a new world-view, and on the whole they are the ones who attract the most followers. Spangler and Thompson envisage 'reimagining our world. We are taking hunks of ecology and slices of science, pieces of politics and a sprinkle of economics, a pinch of religion and a dash of philosophy, and we are reimagining these and a host of other ingredients into something new' (Spangler and Irwin, 1991, p. xvi).

Although it is hard to identify core beliefs that would be widely shared in the New Age, some occur more frequently than others. There is a strong rejection of classic Christian dualism, but this does not necessarily lead to monism. Some New Age circles are themselves strongly

dualistic, emphasizing communication with angels, extraterrestrials and lost civilizations such as Atlantis or Lemuria. Nevertheless, this dualism is generally combined with the view that people are metaphysically identical with such other-worldly entities, and therefore a kind of pantheism or panentheism is also widespread. Astrology is another major influence: the 'new age' is the age of Aquarius (the water bearer, identified with the Spirit), which astrologically succeeds the age of Pisces (the fish, identified with all things Christian). The western concept of individualism is another major driving force in the New Age, enabling beliefs taken from elsewhere to be reformulated. Belief in reincarnation is widespread but is generally without a moral foundation, for in the New Age people choose the form of their own present life. This is one of the major flaws in the New Age world-view, leading as it does to the conclusion that there is no such thing as good or evil, but only the free choices of individuals.

JOHN W. DRANE

FURTHER READING: William Bloom, *The New Age: An Anthology of Essential Writings* (London, 1991); John Drane, *What is the New Age Saying to the Church?* (London, 1991); Marilyn Ferguson, *The Aquarian Conspiracy* (Los Angeles, 1980); J.R. Lewis and J.G. Melton (eds.), *Perspectives on the New Age* (Albany, NY, 1992); Shirley Maclaine, *Going Within* (London, 1990); Ted Peters, *The Cosmic Self* (San Francisco, 1991); David Spangler and William Irwin Thomson, *Reimagination of the World* (Santa Fe, NM, 1991); Starhawk, *The Spiral Dance* (San Francisco, 1989); J.L. Simmons, *The Emerging New Age* (Santa Fe, NM, 1990); Michael York, 'The New Age in Britain Today', *Rel T 9.3* (1994), pp. 14–21.

New Theology Controversy

A pre-World War I debate in Britain concerning the immanence of God. Although the term 'New Theology' had previously signified disparate theological ideas, it acquired specific meaning in 1907 to describe the revisionist theology of the most prominent Congregational minister in London, the *Reverend R.J. Campbell. Grounded in the philosophical idealism of *Hegel, inspired by the nature-mysticism of the Romantics and carried along on a liberal wave represented by Sabatier, the *Catholic modernists, and, to a lesser extent, *Harnack, Campbell's thought posited the unitary nature of all reality and the immanence of God in the creation.

The leading voice in opposition to Campbell was *P.T. Forsyth. When Campbell's theology made headlines in 1907, Forsyth's initial comments were offhand and ill-advised, referring to the New Theology as 'amateur' to signal Campbell's lack of theological education, and 'like a bad photograph – under-developed and over-exposed'. Within days, however, a more composed Forsyth replied to Campbell's views. Immanence was valuable, he wrote, because it 'rescued us from a distant deism', but taken to extremes it is not Trinitarian, and not even theist. Moreover, 'it discourages the sense of guilt and the miracle of grace'. What is required, Forsyth argued, was not immanence but incarnation, not an ideal Christ but a historic revelation of God, not an inert 'divine principle' but a reconciling Redeemer. 'For moral life we must have a dualism.' Forsyth advanced discussion on several other fronts: pressing for higher educational standards for ministry within the Congregational Union, examining the immanence/transcendence dialectic in a scholarly forum, and arguing for Christian social responsibility in his 1908 book, *Socialism, the Church and the Poor.*

Other voices continued the debate, particularly in the *British Weekly*, which was edited aggressively by W. Robertson Nicoll. Week after week, church leaders of several denominations weighed in against Campbell's views. Proponents of the New Theology replied in the pages of *The Christian Commonwealth*, which carried Campbell's sermons week by week. In its pages, Forsyth was not only opposed but vilified, and then he was given a mock obituary under the headline 'A Lost Leader'.

As 1907 progressed, apologists of the New Theology made frequent conference addresses, and Campbell published two more books, *Christianity and the Social Order* and *New Theology Sermons*. The Progressive League gathered supporters and proposed international alliances with other liberal Christians. Subsequently, however, disagreements diminished the impact of the movement. James Warschauer broke with Campbell, accusing him of pantheism. And Campbell himself was alarmed by the Christ-myth doctrine of ally K.C. Anderson. In 1912, the City Temple preacher cancelled all outside involvements, enthusiasm for the movement dissipated, and its demise was confirmed by World War I's death blow to optimistic liberalism.

LESLIE MCCURDY

FURTHER READING: Keith Clements, *Lovers of Discord: Twentieth-Century Theological Controversies in England* (London, 1988), ch. 2; C.H. Vine (ed.), *The Old Faith and the New Theology* (London, 1907); Robert McAfee Brown, 'P.T. Forsyth and the Gospel of Grace' (PhD thesis; Columbia University, 1951), Appendix 1.

Newbigin, Lesslie (1909–98)

Lesslie Newbigin was a Protestant missionary and bishop in India from 1936 to 1974, except for the time he spent leading the integration of the International Missionary Council into the World Council of Churches (1961–65). His most fruitful and influential period, theologically speaking, started when he returned to the UK after his retirement.

By then, Newbigin discovered that in the UK, as in western Europe as a whole, Christian faith had almost totally vanished from the public sphere. In a series of books published during the 1980s, Newbigin investigated the cultural backgrounds of this phenomenon and explored a missionary approach to counter it. Pinpointing the post-Enlightenment separation of public, scientifically attested facts on the one hand from private values on the other as the most important presupposition behind the marginalization of religion, Newbigin challenged this fact-value split as an unwarranted cultural bias, just as he had done before with the syncretist presuppositions of Hindu culture in India.

Drawing upon the philosophical work of Michael Polanyi and Alasdair MacIntyre, and endorsing the postmodern insight that human thought is inevitably historically located, Newbigin argued that modern science, far from being governed by reason alone, is like religion largely based upon faith commitments, authorities and traditions. From this point of view he criticized the reigning *Enlightenment rationalism: there is no neutral institution called 'pure reason', producing indubitable knowledge and passing objective judgements on competing moral and religious truth claims. Rather, the search for truth – in science as well as in religion – requires a strong personal commitment, and a willingness to have one's discoveries tested in the public arena. Thus, if the Christian story is true at all, it must be true *for* all, and it must be possible for Christians by indwelling this story to show its unique capacity in making sense of life. Newbigin therefore stimulated Christians to have 'proper confidence' in the gospel and to relativize the modern plausibility structures in its light instead of becoming domesticated in them.

Newbigin made it clear that he was not striving after a restoration of the Constantinian era; indeed, there is no resemblance to fundamentalist absolutism in his theological thinking. What he emphasized, however, is that it is not true to the Christian faith to present it as a form of privatized religion. Rather, as public truth it continues to have a bearing on public issues; and this should reverberate in, for example, educational curricula (which should not assume that real truth lies in detachment from all religious claims). Newbigin's attempt to help the western church understand its pluralist situation and to restore boldness instead of timidity in fulfilling its missionary task echoed throughout western Christianity; in the UK it led to the launching of the *The Gospel and our Culture Programme* by the British Council of Churches.

GIJSBERT VAN DEN BRINK

FURTHER READING: *Texts: Foolishness to the Greeks* (London, 1986); *The Gospel in a Pluralist Society* (London, 1989); *Unfinished Agenda: An Autobiography* (Edinburgh, updated edn, 1993). *Studies*: George R. Hunsberger, *Bearing the Witness of the Spirit: Lesslie Newbigin's Theology of Cultural Plurality* (Grand Rapids, 1998); Gijsbert van den Brink, 'Lesslie Newbigin als postmodern apologeet', *N T T* (1992), pp. 302–19.

Newman, John Henry (1801–90)

The greatest of nineteenth-century British theologians, and the only one to have had a major influence beyond the English-speaking world. He is also an important Victorian literary figure, as the master of one of the most entrancing and musical prose styles of the nineteenth century. His works were published in his own lifetime in over forty volumes, and many more have been published from his private papers since. His correspondence, which is being published in 31 volumes, shows him as one of the great letter-writers of the nineteenth century. Three of his poems remain in common use as hymns, 'Lead, Kindly Light', 'Praise to the Holiest in the Height' and 'Firmly I Believe and Truly'; the last two come from his longest poem, 'The Dream of Gerontius', set to music by Elgar. The annual bibliographies of works about him, compiled by the Sisters of the Work at Littlemore, near Oxford, the publication *Newman Studien* and

the many university Newman Societies bear witness to his continuing relevance to Christian thought.

Newman's adolescent conversion to evangelical *Calvinism in 1816, after the failure of his father's bank, gave him a dogmatic creed to defend. But as an undergraduate at Trinity College, Oxford and then a fellow of Oriel (from 1822) he encountered the High-Church tradition in the Church of England, and he redefined this creed against what he saw as the threat of liberalism, the principles that religion must be provable and that one religion is as good as another. As vicar of the University Church of St Mary the Virgin from 1828, his understated preaching cast an enchantment on the undergraduates in his congregation. His *Parochial Sermons* (6 vols.; 1834–42), on the fundamentals of the Christian life, eventually enjoyed a readership outside as well as inside the Church of England, and they were republished by an Anglican friend after Newman's own conversion to Roman Catholicism.

Newman's first book, *The Arians of the Fourth Century* (1833), sought a cure for modern liberalism in the writings of the early Christian Fathers, and showed a special dedication to the fourth-century Alexandrian champion of orthodoxy, *St Athanasius. Newman's recovery from a near-fatal illness in Sicily in 1833 convinced him that he had a work to do in England, and in September he began, with his High-Church clerical friends *John Keble (1792–1866) and Richard Hurrell Froude (1803–36), what was later called the *Oxford Movement. In 90 *Tracts for the Times* (1833–41), the Movement set out to recall the Church of England to a true Catholic understanding of herself, as occupying a *via media* or middle way between Roman Catholicism and popular Protestantism. The *Tracts* provoked violent controversy with Anglican Protestants and liberals, a division eventually embodied in the three Anglican schools of High, Low and Broad Churchmanship.

Newman's chief contributions to the prolific literature on the Anglo-Catholic *via media* were his *Lectures on the Prophetical Office of the Church* (1837) and his *Lectures on the Doctrine of Justification* (1838). In 1841, however, in *Tract 90*, he raised a storm by arguing that some of the Tudor Thirty-nine Articles, supposedly the bulwark of the Church of England's Protestantism, could be interpreted in an anti-Protestant and 'Catholic' sense – even in some cases in a Roman Catholic one. *Tract 90* was the last of the *Tracts*. Newman retired from Oxford to the hamlet of Littlemore, where he translated the writings of St Athanasius. He had now abandoned the basis of the old High Church static conception position that whatever is true is not new, and whatever is new is not true, by arguing in his *Essay on the Development of Christian Doctrine* (1845) for a principle now accepted by critical scholars, that Christian dogmas like the Trinity were implicit in Scripture and had been 'developed' by church authority through Christian history.

The *Essay* was Newman's apology for his submission to Rome on 9 October 1845. He was ordained a priest in Rome in 1847 and introduced an Italian institute of secular priests, the Oratory, to England in 1848, making his permanent home in Birmingham. His versatility was expressed in two novels, *Loss and Gain* (1848) and *Callista* (1856), the first a satire on Anglicanism, the second about a North African Christian martyr, and in two works rich in satire, the *Lectures on Certain Difficulties Felt by Anglicans* (1850) and the *Lectures on the Present Position of Catholics in England* (1851). He was also rector (1851–58) of a new Catholic University in Dublin, and he delivered the classic lectures on Christian higher education as the reconciliation of Hellenism and humanism with the Catholic faith which were later published in their definitive form as *The Idea of a University* (1873).

Newman felt, moreover, increasingly isolated in the church by the devotion of other Catholics to Pope Pius IX, who was confronted with the loss of the Papal States to a united Italy. In 1859, Newman was briefly the editor of a liberal Catholic journal, *The Rambler*, the creation of the liberal Catholic Richard Simpson and John Acton, and he was reported to Rome for an article 'On consulting the faithful' in which he urged that when the church makes a dogmatic definition, the laity are at least passively consulted. From this point he wrote little until 1864, when the novelist Charles Kingsley attacked him in *Macmillan's Magazine* for having, like the Roman clergy, no respect for truth. Kingsley thus provoked him to write, in a great rush, his *Apologia Pro Vita Sua*, the greatest of English spiritual autobiographies after Bunyan's, embodying Newman's own conviction that faith is personally appropriated and not simply a matter of intellectual conviction or formal proof.

The *Apologia* established Newman in the pantheon of great Victorians as an Englishman of whom any other Englishman might be proud. It also, however, put him in a classic Victorian duo, like Gladstone and Disraeli, with his fellow convert Henry Edward Manning, from 1865 Archbishop of Westminster. Manning thwarted Newman's plan to establish an Oratory at Oxford, and was a strong Ultramontane and a leading figure in securing the definition of papal infallibility at the *First Vatican Council (1869–70). Newman believed in the doctrine but thought it inopportune to define it, as he worried about the intellectual difficulties which it was causing other Catholics. It was, however, Manning who prevented Rome from censuring Newman's moderate defence of infallibility against Gladstone in his *Letter to the Duke of Norfolk* in 1875. Subsequent theological developments have justified Newman's position. His preface to the *The Via Media* (1877), a two-volume collection of his Anglican writings, argued for a classic constitutionalist conception of the church in which the intellectual or prophetical office of the theologian and the worshipping office of the priesthood and people are to be held in creative tension with the regal authority of the pope and *Curia*. Some of these themes were to be echoed at the *Second Vatican Council (1962–65).

In his old age, Newman also completed his *Essay in Aid of a Grammar of Assent* (1870), a systematic exploration of the relations between faith and reason, arguing for the validity of a personalist informal logic, in religion as in other areas of life. He had already tentatively explored this theme in his *University Sermons* (1843), and philosophers like Michael Polanyi have taken it further. One aspect of the *Grammar* anticipates *Wittgenstein and previews the attempts by modern writers to show the rationality – the internal grammars – of subjects other than empirical science and formal logic.

Pope Leo XIII made Newman a Cardinal-Deacon in 1879. He died in 1890 in a blaze of sacred cardinalate purple glory, his sins against the Church of England and Roman authority having been forgiven him. There is a cause for his canonization, and Rome declared him Venerable in 1991. He remains an inspiration to Roman Catholics who believe in the possibility of a critical but orthodox Roman Catholicism, and to Christians who delight in him as the stylistically haunting and intellectually sophisticated defender of a Christianity which bridges the gap between pre- and post-modernity. His legacy to the Church of England of warring church parties remains a doubtful one, although he is still an icon to many High Anglicans. His scholarship on the Greek Fathers and the theology built upon it has attracted favourable comment from the Orthodox. There is a continuing relevance to his exposition of doctrinal development and his insistence that the laity and the theologian should have a place in the ecclesiastical sun. He continues to fascinate historians as a leading figure in the two great spiritual dramas of Victorian Oxford and nineteenth-century Rome. The *Apologia* still makes disciples. He will no doubt achieve a wider cultus if the church raises him to her altars.

SHERIDAN GILLEY

FURTHER READING: *Texts: Parochial Sermons* (6 vols.; New York, 1843); *The Arians of the Fourth Century* (London, 1919); *Tracts for the Times* (London, 1840–42); *Lectures on the Prophetical Office of the Church* (London, 1837); *Lectures on the Doctrine of Justification* (Westminster, MD, 1966); *Essay on the Development of Christian Doctrine* (New York, 1992); *Lectures on Certain Difficulties Felt by Anglicans* (Dublin, 1857); *Lectures on the Present Position of Catholics in England* (Chicago, 1925); *The Idea of a University* (London, 1873); *Apologia Pro Vita Sua* (London, 2nd edn, 1865); *Essay in Aid of a Grammar of Assent* (London, 1870); *University Sermons* (London, 1943). *Studies:* Ian Ker, *John Henry Newman: A Biography* (Oxford, 1988); *Newman and the Fullness of Christianity* (Edinburgh, 1993); Owen Chadwick, *Newman* (Oxford, 1983); Thomas J. Norris, *Newman and His Theological Method* (Leiden, 1977); John R. Griffin, *Newman: A Bibliography of Secondary Studies* (Front Royal, VA, 1980); D. Brown and H. Chadwick (eds.), *Newman: A Man for our Time: Centenary Essays* (London, 1990); Sheridan Gilley, *Newman and his Age* (London, 1990).

Niceno-Constantinopolitan Creed

The so-called Niceno-Constantinopolitan Creed is assumed by many to have been produced in 381 at the Council of Constantinople. However, no contemporary record exists of the council's proceedings, nor is any creed given. The text surfaces only when it is read out at the Council of *Chalcedon in 451. The initial solution to this puzzle was that the creed originated not at the Council of Constantinople but was perhaps a local creed, used at a baptismal or episcopal consecratory ceremony, that came to be attached to the proceedings of the Council of Constantinople. Recent studies, though, have drawn attention to hints of its existence prior to 451 and have concluded that it almost certainly was produced in 381 at the Council of Constantinople.

Another common assumption is that the Niceno-Constantinopolitan Creed is in fact merely the Nicene Creed, which was produced at Nicaea in 325, with additions – particularly relating to the Holy Spirit. There are, however, clear differences between the two. The presence of some minor differences suggests that this is not in fact an expanded version of the Nicene Creed (why make such alterations?). The more substantial differences include the omission of the words (concerning the Son) 'that is, from the substance of the Father', 'God from God', and (referring to the Son's work in creation) 'things in heaven and things on earth'. Also absent are Nicaea's anathemas against anyone who says 'there was a time when he (the Son) did not exist', 'that he came into being from nothing', that he is 'alterable and changeable'. The major addition concerns the Holy Spirit. All this has led scholarship to conclude that the Council of Constantinople was not modifying or expanding the text of the Nicene formulary, but that it was either drafting its own text *ab initio* or, more likely, was adapting some other, essentially similar, baptismal creed. Whatever the differences, however, the underlying thought of the creeds of 325 and 381 is clearly very similar.

Christian theology underwent substantial development in the years 320–81, largely triggered by the *Arian controversy. Up to the beginnings of this controversy, theology had a strong cosmological flavour – occurring as much of it did within the Greek philosophical context. This was particularly marked in the Logos-theology of the *apologists and *Origen and *Athanasius's early work, *Contra Gentes et De Incarnatione*. The fundamental conception of the Logos of God, and of the Trinity, was one which tended to link them with the creation – with little or no emphasis being given to their eternal inner life within the Godhead. In this cosmological setting the Logos was often conceived (as in Greek philosophy) as a mediator, acting between God and the world and mediating the creative power of God.

With Origen, the generation of the Son and the coming into existence of the world were interconnected, on account of his doctrine of the eternal existence of rational souls. On this basis, a real distinction between God and creatures proved difficult to maintain. Problems then arose, never satisfactorily solved by Origen, as to the exact status of the Son/Logos – in particular whether he existed primarily in relation to God or in relation to creation.

The Arians sharpened radically the difference between God and creatures, ruling out any inherent kinship between the two. While there is no record of their espousing the principle (embedded in Middle *Platonism) that that which acts on something is superior to it, they almost certainly adhered to this principle. This assumption, together with the radical distinction between God and creatures, entailed a strong rejection of any hierarchical system of divinity. Consequently, decisions had to be taken as to the status of the Son. The Arians opted for the term 'creature' as a basic description of the Son, believing they were in accord with Scripture. With the vast distance in being between God and creatures, the Son was given a mediatorial role between God and the world – creatures being unable to endure the direct hand of God. This mediatorial role was largely explicated in terms of creation's existence, rather than, as for the Nicenes, the mediation of the Son being propounded in terms of incarnation and salvation.

The battleground between the Arians and the Nicene party might at first sight seem primarily to concern the status of the Son, but it concerned salvation also. Arian soteriology, which is exceedingly hard to pinpoint, appears to centre in the alterable and changeable Son who, by grace, held faithful to God. God, foreseeing this obedience, created him first, 'a creature but not as other creatures'. As he won through, so may others by grace.

The Nicene Creed of 325 was drawn up to counter the Arian challenge. Various key phrases occur. Athanasius wrote some years later that the Arians, when denoting the Son, had no difficulty agreeing to 'God of God, Light of Light, true God of true God, begotten not made'. The particular sticking point for Arius and others lay in the phrase 'of one substance (*homoousion*) with the Father'.

Though only three refused to sign the creed, many were wary of the word *homoousion*, due to (1) its being non-biblical, (2) its possibly conveying the materialistic notion that Father and Son were separable portions of a single

substance, and (3) its embodying Sabellian ideas in which Father and Son were not each distinct realities. Assurances had to be given, in regard to (2) and (3), that neither was being promulgated. In regard to (1), it was argued that the word *homoousion*, though non-biblical, expressed precisely the thought of the Bible, and moreover was the only word that excluded Arianism. To counter any possible misunderstanding, the anathemas, already referred to, were added.

The creed also contains the phrase 'And in the Holy Spirit'. It is noticeable that where theology occurs in a cosmological setting, or where the Son is given a mediating role between God and creation, little tends to be said of the Spirit, with the Spirit's functions being subsumed under the Logos. It was not until the inner life of the Godhead came more under scrutiny that a doctrine of the Spirit could develop, as in Athanasius's *Orationes Contra Arianos*.

The original creed of Nicaea in 325 (for the text see Hall, *Doctrine and Practice in the Early Church*, p.130) is identifiably shaped by the church's engagement with Arianism. Its key affirmations and its anathemas have Arian doctrine clearly in their sights. In the years following Nicaea, Arianism itself waxed and waned, before reaching its ultimate challenge at the hands of the *Cappadocians – Basil of Caesarea, Gregory Nazianzen and Gregory of Nyssa. These three built on the foundation laid by Athanasius, who argued decisively against any subordination within the Godhead. Athanasius's terminology in speaking of the second person of the Trinity changed dramatically from his *Contra Gentes et De Incarnatione* where 'Word' is the overwhelming choice, to more or less equal usage for both 'Word' and 'Son' in his *Orationes Contra Arianos*. 'Word' tended to convey a cosmological sense of God, whereas 'Son' tended to indicate the inner relationship with the Father in the Godhead. By contrast, Athanasius also developed an understanding of 'Son' in relation to the world, where creatures are given to share in the incarnate Son by the Spirit, and the Word is discussed in terms of his inner relationship with God.

To counter Arianism, Athanasius had to think through the inner connections between the Trinity, the incarnation and salvation, distinguishing what God is in himself, and what God is towards his creation. The *homoousion* (the key phrase in the creed produced by the Nicene Council in 325, according to which the Son is 'of one substance with' the Father) provided for him the epistemological ground for salvation, revelation and knowledge of God. Without the *homoousion*, all these were uncertain.

Athanasius rarely, however, employed the word *homoousion* – perhaps out of deference to those still finding the word itself difficult – and he was happy with words such as 'like in substance', as long as what *homoousion* stood for was adhered to. Muddying the whole meaning of *homoousion* was the ambiguity in the terms *ousia* and *hypostasis*. While Nicaea had seemed to equate the two, it was perceived at the Council of Alexandria in 362 that different people could use each word in different senses. This council took steps to name and clarify the confusion, and it suggested *ousia* as the word for the being shared by Father, Son and Spirit, with *hypostasis* as the word for the Three, in distinction from the others.

Arianism, however, still flourished – especially where backed by emperors with strong Arian leanings. Different forms of Arianism arose, some more extreme than others, including Homoeans (the Son is 'like' the Father) and Anomeans (the Son is 'unlike' the Father). A further group, called Macedonians, accepted the *homoousion* in regard to the Son's relationship with the Father, but denied it to the Spirit, on the grounds that nowhere in Scripture is the Spirit called God or worshipped. The Spirit was reduced to the level of an angel. He may be divine, eternal and Lord, but he is not God. His being 'sent' reveals him to be inferior, a special gift not to be identified with the giver.

Athanasius, in his *Epistulae ad Serapion* concerning the Holy Spirit, met the challenge head-on, almost in despair that a battle similar to that fought over the Son's relationship with the Father had now to be fought over the Spirit's relationship to the Godhead. The three Cappadocians followed Athanasius's lead, carefully locating the Spirit within the Godhead. Their arguments appeal variously to the baptismal formula in which Father, Son and Spirit are named together, the long tradition in the church of worshipping the Spirit, the affinity of the Spirit with God, and the work of the Spirit. It is in the Spirit that creatures share in the Son and behold the Father. Basil did not hesitate to say 'Glory be to the Father with the Son with the Holy Spirit', alongside the more traditional 'Glory be to the Father through the Son in the Holy Spirit'.

For the Cappadocians, God is Three in One and One in Three. The Three are together a dynamic, interconnecting and intermingling (*perichoresis*) unity. If there is no communion there is no God. The very way in which God is God is as Three. When the One is thought of, the human mind leaps to the Three, and when the Three is pondered the One springs to mind. God is God in a way that only God can understand. It is hidden from human eyes how the Godhead is, how the Son is begotten and how the Spirit proceeds from the Father. According to Gregory Nazianzen, humans may be given an occasional insight, like a flash of lighting, before the veil is drawn once more. God's infinity and essence cannot be known, but he can be known in his activity, as he accommodates himself to humanity in creation and incarnation.

The Cappadocians still wished to maintain the Father as source, as 'fountain' or 'root' of the Trinity, but without any sense of subordination. The principle that that which acts on something is superior to it, so deeply rooted in theology at the turn of the fourth century, was now finally set aside in anything to do with God's triune being. No difference of rank or status is permissible within the Trinity. There could now develop an understanding of God in his inner relations, as far as God gives himself to be understood.

The Niceno-Constantinopolitan Creed echoes much of the way theology had developed over the preceding 65 years, since the onset of Arianism. Trinitarian theology had been, or was now able to be, released from a primarily cosmological setting which embodied hierarchical notions with the Logos perceived as mediator existing for the sake of God's creative relation to the world. The Nicene *homoousion* was reaffirmed. Nicene judgements relating to the incarnation and salvation are developed in the creed of 381, revealing the increasing perception of salvation stemming from the Trinity, through the incarnate presence of Christ. Constantinople incorporates statements on the Son's kingdom as having 'no end', on the 'one holy, catholic and apostolic church', on the 'one baptism for the forgiveness of sins' and the waiting for 'the resurrection of the dead and the life of the world to come'. The major theological departure relates to the Spirit, 'the Lord, the giver of life, who proceeds from the Father, who with the Father and the Son is worshipped and glorified, who spoke by the prophets'.

In later years the *filioque* and the precise

nature of Christ's humanity and divinity demanded yet more rigorous debate, although the roots of the issues were already present by 381. The journey through Origen to Arius to Athanasius to the Cappadocians, via many others in between, had seen the church grow in understanding, in discernment and in worshipping the whole Trinity.

JAMES B. WALKER

FURTHER READING: S. Hall, *The Doctrine and Practice of the Early Church* (London, 1991); R.P. Hanson, *The Search for the Christian Doctrine of God* (Edinburgh, 1988); T.A. Hart, 'Creeds, Councils and the Development of Doctrine', in *The Early Christian World* (ed. P.F. Esler; London, 2000); J.N.D. Kelly, *Early Christian Creeds* (London, 1972); T.F. Torrance, *The Trinitarian Faith* (Edinburgh, 1988); F.M. Young, *From Nicaea to Chalcedon* (London, 1983); *The Making of the Creeds* (London, 1991).

Nietzsche, Friedrich (1844–1900)

German philosopher. The son of a Lutheran pastor, Nietzsche was born in Saxony and attended university at Bonn and Leipzig. A brilliant scholar, he was appointed in 1869 to the chair of classical philology at Basle. Having contracted syphilis as a youth, however, Nietzsche was ultimately forced to take early retirement from the university in 1879 on grounds of ill health. Until 1889, he lived a reclusive life in France, Italy and Switzerland, devoting his energies to literary-philosophical work. He was insane from 1889 to his death in 1900.

Nietzsche stands in no philosophical tradition. Though in his early years he had read the philosophy of Arthur Schopenhauer (1788–1860), from whom he possibly derived the idea of the centrality of the will, his philosophy in its final form is wholly unique. It is deliberately unsystematic in character, polemical and decisively anti-Christian. Nevertheless, in both style and content it is characterized by a marked sense of what one might describe as the 'prophetic burden'. In *The Will to Power* (1901), a collection of Nietzsche's aphorisms published posthumously, he described himself as the first European to emerge from the nihilism of Christian civilization, on the one hand, and from the cultural nihilism following the collapse of Christianity, on the other. What he proclaims, by contrast, is the philosophy of the future. Christianity is nihilistic, according to Nietzsche, because of its tendency to affirm what is anti-natural – above all, weakness rather than strength.

With the death of God that Nietzsche first proclaimed in the distinctively modern sense in *Thus Spoke Zarathustra* (1883–91), however, modern culture is also afflicted with a nihilistic crisis of meaning. Nietzsche calls for an affirmative stance in relation to the death of God and what it entails in the realm of truth and value. Meaning is consistently understood by Nietzsche as a human creation; indeed, the recognition that meaning is the creation of finite human beings is the root of the death of God, for it entails that God too is a psychological and cultural artefact. In the light of this, Nietzsche claims, there is no longer room either for God as the infinite source of creation, or for the categories of truth and falsity, good and evil – but only for the naturalistic categories of 'better' and 'worse', 'superior' and 'inferior'. In *On the Genealogy of Morals* (1887), Nietzsche develops these theories as the basis of his famous condemnation of the Christian ethic as a 'slave morality'.

Central to Nietzsche's philosophy is the notion of the will to power, and the idea that the will to power is expressed in a myriad of dysfunctional ways. The will to power is a 'subterranean', pre-rational force within the self which nevertheless determines the shape of the characteristic forms of human consciousness. Christian slave morality, for example, which exalts the weak at the expense of the noble, is the authentic expression of the relentless will to power of the weak. Nietzsche's thesis is that an inferior human type has achieved dominance in western civilization, and that the chief mechanism of this dominance is the Christian religion. Nietzsche singles out religious leaders for special criticism: these are the most decadent of all human beings, the 'ascetic priests' whose will to power is turned explicitly and even professionally against natural instinct. According to Nietzsche, in fact, the interior life of the soul is entirely their creation: it is as they have turned against natural life, which is outward, sensuous and empirical, that the spiritual inner-worlds and other-worlds have been created by a kind of psychological *via negativa*. It is notable that it was largely on the basis of his reading of Nietzsche that Sigmund Freud (1856–1939) developed his theory of the subconscious self. Both Nietzsche and Freud understand the human being as fundamentally a sub-rational, instinctual psychological entity.

Nietzsche's negative assessment of Christianity is unambiguous; his estimate of Jesus, however, is more difficult to determine. In *Zarathustra*, Nietzsche speaks of Jesus as 'noble' enough to have 'learned to love the earth' had he only lived long enough: he would, in other words, have recanted his otherworldly teaching given more time. This relatively positive view is developed further in *The Antichrist* (1888), in which Nietzsche grapples with the historical sense of his time, distinguishing between the original Jesus and the Jesus of the church's faith. The latter, the saviour and judge of the world, becomes for Nietzsche a symbol of the utter corruption of human life which the Christian church embodies in the fabric of its values. Jesus himself, however, is presented as a childlike innocent for whom life itself was blessedness. Jesus is thus, in fact, fundamentally a Nietzschean 'yea-sayer' to unredeemed natural existence.

Nietzsche's philosophy was somewhat tainted by association with the German war effort during 1914–18, and then it was much more seriously damaged by its adaptation by the Nazis. Following World War II, however, his philosophy was widely rehabilitated in the context of Existentialism, both on the European continent and in the USA. *Martin Heidegger's important study *Nietzsche* (2 vols.; 1961; ET London, 1981–84) helped to reinforce this association with the existentialist movement. The understanding of Nietzsche as an existentialist, however, is improbable. Above all, the characteristic existentialist theme of freedom is not his concern. Similarly, the American Walter Kaufmann's study, *Nietzsche* (Princeton, 4th edn, 1974), fails to deal adequately with the radical character of Nietzsche's thought. According to Kaufmann, Nietzsche's ideal is the human being who has overcome his animal nature and sublimated his passions. Such a human type would, however, actually differ little from the arch-decadent ascetic priest of the *Genealogy of Morals*. Nietzsche seems to have in view instead a human type who does not *need* to sublimate passion, whose instincts are simply spontaneously noble. Such a human type affirms the earth, the body and the self without shame, and without inward struggle. Crucially, this is also connected in Nietzsche's thought with an emphasis on concrete human history. In the final analysis, it is at this point that the existential interpretation breaks down, for Nietzsche is committed to the ideal of natural existence, and hence to 'monuments in stone' rather than to an inward life. To this extent, the appeal to Nietzsche's philosophy within Nazism was not entirely aberrant.

Nietzsche also replaces the mythological hopes held forth in religion with two related ideals: the so-called 'eternal recurrence of the same', and the doctrine of the *Übermensch*. Neither is affirmed as literal reality or possibility, but they crystallize the Nietzschean vision in the following respects. The doctrine of eternal recurrence is the affirmation of the absoluteness of the this-world of natural life and existence, over against the religious obsession with the other-worlds of heaven and hell. To be able to affirm one's present constitution *as if* it were to recur eternally is, for Nietzsche, the mark of true greatness. Nothing else is desired; nothing else could be. The *Übermensch*, for its part, embodies a vision of a human type who has the strength to affirm the absoluteness of the finite in this sense. Nietzsche's view is that humanity as a whole does not have such strength. Lacking courage to embrace its own finitude, humanity flees from its awesome implications into a false security: the state, morality and religion are the most likely sources of refuge from one's radical aloneness in the universe. It is only an *Übermensch*, a super-human, who could truly accept the fact that there is no God, with all its implications. Nietzsche thus proclaims the death of humanity, as traditionally conceived, even more than he proclaims the death of God. It is perhaps for this reason that in recent years his philosophy has come to be associated with the new philosophical movement, or movements, known as postmodernism.

GARY D. BADCOCK

FURTHER READING: R.J. Hollingdale, *Nietzsche* (London, 1973); Karl Jaspers, *Nietzsche* (Tucson, AZ, ET 1965); Friedrich Nietzsche, *Werke* (ed. Karl Schlechta; 3 vols.; Munich, 1954–56); John T. Wilcox, *Truth and Value in Nietzsche* (Ann Arbor, MI, 1974).

Nominalism

Properly, the theory that universals – (the referents of) abstract nouns such as 'humanity', 'wisdom', 'redness' – are to be identified merely with the nouns themselves. The term is also used to designate the theory that universals are to be identified with concepts (the contents of mental acts, not extramental things) – a theory also known as conceptualism. The two theories can be traced back to *Boethius's commentary on Porphyry's *Isagoge*, where four possible theories on the status of genera and species (for example, animal and man) are identified. One of these is the theory that genera and species are merely words (Nominalism properly speaking); another that they are merely concepts (conceptualism).

The first theory appeared on the theological scene in the 1090s. According to Roscelin, canon of Compiègne, *Anselm of Canterbury held that the three Persons of the Trinity are just one thing – a belief which entails that all three Persons became incarnate. Anselm responded by noting Roscelin's false presupposition that universals such as Godhead are merely spoken words. If such universals are somehow extralinguistic and extramental, then according to Anselm it is clear that the divine nature can be common to three distinct Persons, without this commonness entailing that the three Persons are just one thing – and thus without entailing that the incarnation of one requires the incarnation of the others.

The version of Nominalism attributed to Roscelin is so implausible that no other thinker in the Middle Ages defended it. *Peter Abelard is usually thought to have defended some version of the second theory (conceptualism), and the theory can be found too in later twelfth-century followers of Abelard. Conceptualism does not reappear until *William of Ockham, who defends it against the moderate realism of *Duns Scotus (according to whom extramental common natures are shared and divided among their instantiations) and Walter Burley.

Ockham's theory, contrary to the opinion of scholars prior to the middle of the twentieth century, does not have any intrinsic link with the orthodoxy or otherwise of Ockham's thought. Ockham explicitly denies that the predicability of universal concepts of particular individuals is merely a matter of convention. So Ockham has no problem formulating true universal propositions of the sort required for *Aristotelian science, and hence for metaphysics. After Ockham, many medieval thinkers – though by no means the majority – accepted some version of the denial of extramental universals: most famously, Gabriel Biel. *Luther, some two hundred years after Ockham, professes himself always to have been a nominalist (a 'terminist') in philosophy (*WA* 56, p. 419).

'Nominalism' and 'conceptualism' are neologisms. 'Nominalist' was used in the twelfth century to designate Abelard and his school; they were the *nominales* referred to in twelfth- and early thirteenth-century writings. What distinguished the *nominales* from others was their approach not to metaphysics but to logic – though many of the logical theories more or less result from a denial of extramental universals. The term 'nominalist', along with the associated 'terminist', reappears in the fifteenth century, associated in German universities (though not elsewhere) with the *via moderna*, the teaching of logic in arts faculties expressly along the lines found in Ockham – in contrast to the *viae antiquae* – the *via Thomae* and the *via Scoti*. These *viae* do not indicate that there were distinct schools of theological thought in German universities of the fifteenth century – the division into *viae* did not extend beyond the arts faculties. The logic of the *via moderna* relies, distinctively, on conceptualist foundations. In the eighteenth century, *Bishop Berkeley described *Locke's brand of conceptualism as conforming to 'the opinion of that sort of Schoolmen called Nominals'.

It is quite wrong to identify Nominalism with any sort of school of Ockham – in contrast to the use of *nominales* to refer to the followers of Abelard. Historiographically, accounts of medieval philosophy written with *Thomist bias, and histories of medieval theology written with Protestant bias, have tended to identify a group of followers of Ockham, either fideist or *Pelagian (or both), whose thought is destructive of both philosophy and theology in the 'decadent' period of later *Scholasticism. This analysis is now known to be false. There are no extant writings of putative philosophical followers of Ockham in Oxford – the fourteenth-century Oxford logicians (and theologians) were either realists on the question of universals, or else (like Adam Wodeham) sufficiently independent of Ockham to disqualify themselves. So the realist Wyclif's 'sign doctors', long thought to have been followers of Ockham in Oxford, do not seem to be anything other than straw men. In Paris, the arts faculty statutes passed in 1339 and 1340 (with attendant oaths imposed in 1341) against 'Ockhamist' teaching and the errors of 'Ockhamists' appear to have been directed against a small group of students; in any case the relevant ban appears to have been lifted sometime between 1355 and 1368. The 1341 oath was imposed again in 1474, and rescinded in 1482;

but there is no evidence that there was any sort of school of nominalists or Ockhamists in Paris University in the late fifteenth century. The claim that there was a school of theologians who both accepted Ockham's Nominalism and consciously followed his theological teachings is now known to be false too. For example, theologians as diverse as Gregory of Rimini and John of Mirecourt accepted some version of Nominalism, but they held widely differing views on questions such as the nature of grace and merit. Overall, generalizations about a supposedly 'nominalist' theology are demonstrably false. Neither should it be thought that official reaction to the denial of extramental universals was always negative. The condemnation of Wyclif and the execution of *Huss – both avowed realists – led in the early fifteenth century to a theological reaction against certain forms of realism, at Paris under Gerson (not himself a nominalist) and at Heidelberg. Still, there is no evidence of any real or even perceived direct connection between Realism and the heresies of Wyclif and Huss.

RICHARD CROSS

FURTHER READING: Marilyn McCord Adams, *William Ockham* (2 vols.; Publications in Medieval Studies 26; Notre Dame, IN, 1987); W.J. Courtenay, 'Nominalism and Late Medieval Religion', in *The Pursuit of Holiness in Late Medieval and Renaissance Religion: Papers from the University of Michigan Conference* (ed. Charles Trinkaus and Heiko Oberman; Studies in Medieval and Reformation Thought 10; Leiden, 1974), pp. 26–59; 'Was There an Ockhamist School', in *Philosophy and Learning: Universities in the Middle Ages* (ed. J.F.M. Maarten, J.H. Hoenen, Josef Schneider and Georg Wieland; Education and Society in the Middle Ages and Renaissance 6; Leiden / New York / Cologne, 1995), pp. 263–92; Zenon Kaluza, *Les Querelles Doctrinales à Paris: Nominalistes et Réalistes aux Confins du XIVè et du XVè Siècles* (Quodlibet 2; Bergamo, 1988).

Novatian (c. 250)

Possibly of Phrygian origin, Novatian was apparently baptized after a serious illness and was subsequently ordained a presbyter in the Roman church, though not without considerable opposition from those who felt that his 'conversion' was opportunist and insincere. In spite of this disapproval, however, he was in a position of influence at Rome by 250. It was he who corresponded with *Cyprian of Carthage about the line to adopt with respect to those who apostatized in times of persecution. He

agreed with the 'rigorist' position in North Africa, but he seems to have been overruled by the Roman church, which chose the 'laxist' Cornelius as its bishop in 251. This appointment drove Novatian into an even more extreme position, and he became the leader of a schism at Rome. This schism lasted for several centuries in different parts of the Roman world, but it never amounted to anything more than a form of puritanism. Novatian and his followers were excommunicated, but it is possible that he is the same person as the deacon who was martyred at some point in the third century and whose statue was rediscovered in 1932.

Novatian seems to have been a prolific author, though only four of his works are known to have survived. The most important of these works is a book on the Trinity, which is dependent on his predecessors in the field, including *Tertullian, but which nevertheless exhibits considerable originality. Most of it is taken up with a defence of a type of two-natures Christology which can fairly be described as *Chalcedonian *avant la lettre*. A second work deals with Jewish dietary laws, which Novatian regarded as typological forerunners of Christian moral precepts. Other works, on public amusements and on (female) modesty are reminiscent of Tertullian, whose tracts on those subjects probably inspired Novatian.

Novatian's theology was fully orthodox, and he made a major contribution to subsequent technical terminology in the field. Among the many words which he used for the first time, *praedestinatio* would enjoy a particularly distinguished career, though it cannot be said that Novatian developed the doctrine of predestination to any significant extent.

In Christian tradition Novatian has always had a recognized place among the early Fathers of the Latin church, although little attention has been paid to his teaching as such. Normally he is regarded as a bridge between Tertullian and *Augustine, between whom his stature as an independent thinker tends to be obscured.

GERALD BRAY

FURTHER READING: *Text: PL*, III, pp. 861–970; G.F. Diercks (CCSL 4; Mechelen, 1972). *English translation:* R.E. Wallis, *ANF*, XIII, pp. 293–395 and *ANF*, V, pp. 611–44; R.J. DeSimone (FC 67; 1974). *Studies:* C.B. Daly, 'Novatian and Tertullian', *Ir Th Q* 19 (1952), pp. 33–43; J. Vogt, *Coetus sanctorum: Der Kirchenbegriff des Novatian und die Geschichte seiner Sonderkirche* (Bonn, 1968).

Oecolampadius (1482–1531)

Johannes Huszgen, or Oecolampadius, was a hero of the *Reformation whose reputation is comparatively unsung. His education was eclectic and thorough: Bologna, Heidelberg, Tübingen and a spell as the Elector Palatine Philip's appointed tutor at Mainz before becoming a 'preacher-confessor' (an increasingly popular way of supplying for absentee incumbents) in his home town of Weinsberg. He was almost as good as *Erasmus at Greek (he wrote his 1515 Heidelberg lectures into a grammar – 1518 and many editions) and, encouraged by Reuchlin and the Jewish convert Adrianus, he was no mean Hebraist. He followed W. Capito to Basle to work in the printers Johannes Froben and assisted in the preparation of Erasmus's New Testament: 'a large number of the Hebrew *adnotationes* came from Oecolampadius, perhaps over a hundred, a high proportion in Matthew' (Rupp, p. 9). In 1515–16 he started the nine-volume project of *Jerome's works as assistant to Erasmus and added an index (1520). By 1516, after opposing the practice of 'Easter laughter' in churches, he had matriculated at Basle and begun his doctoral work. Finishing this work in Augsburg, he then took a year out to consider *Luther's radical views. He came out in favour and would defend Luther, parting company with Erasmus. During the early Reformation, Oecolampadius avoided the public arena of disputes. From 1523 onwards he lectured in Basle in German, and he became lieutenant to Zurich's *Zwingli. His editorial work included editions of Theophylactus on the four Gospels, *John of Damascus's *Exposition of the Faith* and *Chrysostom on Acts. He was not averse to introducing the works of the Fathers to a wider public while sometimes amending 'his text so as to emphasise salvation by faith' (Backus, p. 20). On the matter of praying for the dead, he makes it seem that the issue is about good works of the deceased, which of course do not avail for salvation (he asserts that one should only pray on behalf of those who had been faithful in life), while the real controversy was about whether good works (by saints) on behalf of the deceased were valid. His hard work at the Berne disputation led to Basle accepting the Zwinglian faith as the city's faith.

First paying attention to what the Scripture writer said to his own situation, one could then go on to explore *many* mystical senses. God does not speak through angels, as *Dionysius would have it, but directly to hearts: angels are there to illustrate God's glory. In the same way, Oecolampadius insisted against *Eck that God invites us to pray directly to him ('our Father') and for one another on earth – and not to the saints or for the departed, since there was no proof that there was a purgatory between death and resurrection. The word of Christ to the thief on the cross was conclusive against the existence of such a place: if there had been one, such a person would surely have gone there (cf. *De gaudio resurrectionis*). At Marburg in 1529, Luther exclaimed that the Zwinglian camp differed from him on other questions: the Trinity, the two-natures doctrine, original sin, baptism, justification, the Word and purgatory. Oecolampadius replied that there was not such a difference between the two camps. As for the question of idolatry, God dislikes inner mental images as much as physical ones. If the somewhat 'carnal' Old Testament outlawed images, how much more the more spiritual New Testament. He disagreed with Jerome and Lyra that Isaiah 49:7–13 is about Christ (it is about the church), yet Isaiah 42 does speak of Christ's ascension. Emphasis is placed on communal thankfulness and charity. Yet ultimately the word of God is where the church is and not the deposit of tradition: doctrine must not be founded on texts from books like Maccabees. God's name may be derived either from the verb 'to see' or from the verb 'to run around', but for the Hebrews, *elohim* means 'strength'.

In *On the True Sense of the Words of the Lord* (1525), the watchword 'Scripture is full of tropes' appears. The New Testament speaks figuratively on certain occasions: for example Jesus' words to Mary, 'Behold your son'. The Gospel is not suggesting that John the beloved disciple actually changed into her son. Similarly, when it comes to the Lord's Supper, Christ feeds the soul, not with his body, but 'in the promises through Jesus Christ the eternal life of the soul is given', while the bread is eaten only in memory and as a thankful action for his death. *Augustine has shown how Christ is like manna, which was *spiritual* bread. Luke did not write 'this is the cup', but 'this cup'. Those learned in Hebrew know that in place of a substantive word Hebrew is happy to use a pronoun or an adverb. Unbelievers do not truly communicate.

The impious sample the flesh in appearance but they contaminate it always with unbelief and uncleanness. And so the Word holds back from it. On the other hand, the Word dwells in all who receive in wholesome faith such great mysteries of the incarnation ... But as he is truly present in heaven, there we should not take there to be anything said about transubstantiation or consubstantiation (to use the words of our opponents).

Oecolampadius followed *Tertullian in taking 'body' to be *'figura corporis'*. Yet after the Marburg Colloquy with the Lutherans he insisted that the Lord's Supper was no mere memorial but 'a wonderful work of the sanctifying Holy Spirit' (Staehelin, p. 609). Further, it is the mode of Christ's presence, not the fact of it, which is the source of disagreement (contra Nathanael). Grace cannot be poured through the elements like a conduit. Through the Lord's Supper our hearts are raised to God – to Christ the head – so that we become the *mysticum corpus*. Such due reverence means (here his mind seems to have changed somewhat) that unbelievers eat unworthily and sinfully, even though they receive only symbolically.

In a sermon on 12 June 1521, Oecolampadius declared that confession is intended to make one feel lighter, not more burdened – a view he owed to Luther. Apart from faith granting direct access to God in prayer and thereby hope (since God is love), one could confess to the priest but should not neglect 'brotherly confession'. Jesus offers various ways of confessing sins – as long as we realize that the act of confessing itself does not merit forgiveness. Believers are to do God's will, which is their sanctification. Oecolampadius aimed to free the gathered church from civil control, and he was saddened when this battle was lost. Church courts were required for matters of spiritual consequence beyond the magistrate's competence. Oecolampadius translated Gregory Nazianzen's moral works, and in 'On the duty of loving the poor' exercised his conviction that Christ rules through the State, and it should not be so lacking in its duties that voluntary societies had to look after the poor. Poverty was a material matter and should be the responsibility of the civil authority. His ethical focus was due to a careful reading of the Old Testament prophets. Christ is a peace-bringer, but this includes bringing sins to attention and the requirement for repentance to follow. Oecolampadius saw himself as a pastoral theologian (so Hammer) who was not good enough for priesthood.

MARK W. ELLIOTT

FURTHER READING: Robert C. Waltin, 'Oecolampadius', in *Encyclopedia of the Reformation* (ed. Hans Hillerbrand; 4 vols.; Oxford, 1967), III, pp. 169–71; E.G. Rupp, *Patterns of Reformation* (London, 1969); E. Staehelin, *Das theologische Lebenswerk Johannes Oekolampads* (Leipzig, 1939); K. Hammer, 'Der Reformator Oekolampad, 1482–1531', in *Reformiertes Erbe*, I (ed. H. Oberman; Zurich, 1992), pp. 157–70; I. Backus, 'What Prayers for the Dead in the Tridentine Period?', in *Reformiertes Erbe*, I, pp. 14–23.

Oman, John (1860–1939)

John Wood Oman was born in the Orkneys and studied at Edinburgh University, before proceeding to the United Presbyterian Theological Hall for his ministerial training, which included semesters at Erlangen and Heidelberg. Failing to find a charge in Scotland, he entered the ministry of the Presbyterian Church of England and became minister of the church at Alnwick. He remained there until 1907, when he was called to the chair of systematic theology and apologetics at that church's ministerial training centre, Westminster College, Cambridge. In 1922 he became the principal of the college, from which he retired in 1935.

The decisive incentive to his pursuing a theological career came from the Robertson Smith case in the late 1870s, which impelled him on a lifelong exploration as to how religious belief may be honestly appropriated. His theology was dominated by the problems set at the outset of the nineteenth century by *Kant, *Schleiermacher and *Hegel, of whom he had a deep and acute knowledge, but the agenda he constructed from these was very much his own. His knowledge of theologians before the seventeenth century, though extensive, tended to be of a secondary nature.

His first published work, a translation of Schleiermacher's *Speeches*, appeared in 1893. Schleiermacher's basic thesis that religion was an inalienable element in human life, whose validity did not need to be established by any extrinsic reasons, always remained one of the foundations of Oman's own position. However, he believed that Schleiermacher's chief defect was that he did insufficient justice to the individual freedom of moral personality. These themes were taken up in Oman's major work of historical theology, *The Problem of Faith and Freedom in the Last Two Centuries* (1906), a review of theology in that period centring around the problem 'how Faith is to be absolute and Freedom absolute, yet both one' (p. 4). Though he had considerable reservations about the Kantian dualism between the moral individual and the impersonal cosmos, Oman nevertheless found this to be a better foundation than the merging of the individual with the world-whole as found in Schleiermacher. On similar grounds he was critical of Hegel, who made moral freedom subsequent to cultural participation.

Oman's first strictly theological treatise, *Vision and Authority* (1902), encapsulated his lifelong theological concerns, which were still being repeated in his posthumous volume of sermons, *Honest Religion* (1941). The validation of external religious authority lay in its appeal to what is latent in humanity, and therefore revelation must be thought of as being directed to inner liberation. God's Christ 'must be recognized as the complement of the nature God has given us, as the satisfaction of the aspirations He has awakened in us, as the response to the call of conscience and the voices of the heart' (p. 120). He went on to show how the principal Christian doctrines spoke specifically to the human condition: our ignorance is removed by the incarnation, our sin by the atonement, whilst our weakness is dealt with by grace and our sense of evanescence by the gift of eternal life. The role of the church is to be seen in its nurturing the inner spiritual appropriation of individuals, a theme that is followed up in a subsequent work, a theological sketch of church history, *The Church and the Divine Order* (1911). Thus the institution exists for the sake of the fellowship, and though the necessity of some structure is acknowledged, ecclesiastical authority needs to be subservient to the inner liberation of believers.

Without a doubt, Oman's most influential work was *Grace and Personality* (1917). Its starting point was the continuing impasse between *Augustinianism and *Pelagianism with their modern counterparts, *Romanticism and the *Enlightenment. What lay at the heart of the conflict was the presupposition that God provided infallible authority and that he worked by irresistible power. Once God is thought of as infinite force, the problem then becomes that a place has to be found for humans as finite forces, and God is conceived of as the manipulator of pressures and appetites. Rather, God must be thought of as a party in a personal relationship, working patiently and

subtly by persuasion in order to win people to the truth. Oman did not regard this as being a capitulation to Pelagianism, as unless there is a deep sense of the priority of the divine action, morality is bound to become self-obsessed.

Oman's *magnum opus, The Natural and the Supernatural* (1931), is a work in philosophy of religion, rather than in Christian theology proper, but in it he aims to provide an epistemological underpinning for his basic convictions. He argues that human knowing is determined by interest, and that one primary interest has been the Supernatural, sensed as the holy and valued as the sacred, by which human beings have attempted to find meaning in their environment. This is followed by a survey of types of world religions (on lines made familiar by Hegel and *Troeltsch) to show how their respective understandings of the Supernatural influenced their adherents' attitudes to their environment. These culminate in 'prophetic religion', in which the world is accepted as being reconciled to, and in the course of being redeemed by, God. The direct theological content of this work is elusive, and there has been considerable debate as to how God is related to the Supernatural, which appears to be the realm of personal meaning through which God manifests himself.

Besides his major theological treatises, Oman also engaged in New Testament study. He produced two works in which he argued for a reordering of the text of Revelation, but these seem to have had little influence upon scholars in this field. More significant is the work which reflected the pastoral heart of his theology, *Concerning the Ministry* (1936), a writing of theologically-informed practicality which is probably the nearest equivalent in the early twentieth century to *Richard Baxter's *The Reformed Pastor.*

In the 1920s and 1930s Oman had a high reputation as a philosophical theologian, particularly at Cambridge, where his stimulus was acknowledged by F.R. Tennant, C.E. Raven and above all by his pupil, *H.H. Farmer. After his death, Oman's influence rapidly declined for a variety of reasons; in an age which increasingly demanded clarity of expression, his oracular and allusive style, together with an occasional imprecision in the use of terminology, militated against taking the substance of his thought seriously. Furthermore, not only was he antipathetic to the thought of *Karl Barth, but he was also somewhat oblivious to the factors underlying that position – the hermeneutic of suspicion in regard to religious experience associated with *Feuerbach, the denial of morality enunciated by *Nietzsche, together with the questions as to how God could communicate with sinful humanity raised by *Kierkegaard. On the other hand Oman provided, along with others such as *Buber, *John Macmurray and Michael Polanyi, a definite contribution to the strong personalist influence which has pervaded British theology during the middle and latter part of the twentieth century.

STANLEY H. RUSSELL

FURTHER READING: *Main texts: Vision and Authority* (London, 1902; 2nd edn, 1928); *The Problem of Faith and Freedom in the Last Two Centuries* (London, 1906); *Grace and Personality* (Cambridge, 1917); *The Natural and the Supernatural* (Cambridge, 1931). *Major studies*: F.G. Healey, *Religion and Reality – The Theology of John Oman* (Edinburgh, 1965); S. Bevans, *John Oman and His Doctrine of God* (Cambridge, 1992). *Articles:* H.H. Farmer, 'Theologians of Our Time: John Wood Oman (1860–1939)', *Expos T* 74 (Feb. 1963), pp. 132–35; J.S. Morris, 'Oman's Conception of the Personal God in the Natural and the Supernatural', *J Th St* 23 (April 1972), pp. 82–94.

Origen (c. 185 – c. 254)

Origen is one of the great thinkers in Christian theology, passionately committed to God, to Jesus, to faith, to prayer and to the Bible. As a scholar he is unsurpassed in the early church in literary output. As a creative thinker he had immense impact on succeeding generations. As a guide in the spiritual life his contribution is acclaimed. As a churchman he sought martyrdom in his early teens and his Christian commitment is shown in his preaching and ascetic lifestyle.

For all this excellence, however, and for all his vigorous defence of Christianity and his seeking to evangelize the intellectual world, he could never quite free himself from the effects of *Platonism.

Origen lived in a period when Platonism had undergone, at the hands of the Middle Platonists, a considerable revival and was vying with Christian theology for the adherence of the intellectuals of the day. He accepted much of the Platonist structure as sound, though he was also aware of some of its limitations and failures. His concern was not primarily

apologetic, for he was convinced that true answers to the questions about God, the soul and the world lay within the Christian faith.

He gloried in the incarnation. He defended passionately, especially in his *Contra Celsus*, God's accommodating himself in Jesus to humanity. He argued for the reality of miracles and for the truth of many of the stories of Jesus and of Israel. He recognized that it was within history that God had acted, that the gospel was available to the intellectual and to the simple alike and that Jesus had profoundly changed people's lives. He recognized that without the Word become flesh and without the reality of history, the gospel would take no root in the lives of ordinary people.

He pressed for the study of Scripture, for people to move on from spiritual milk to real food. He argued for the spiritual interpretation of passages, including obvious historical ones, in order to discover what God was saying to his church. Scripture, he maintained, had three levels – body, soul and spirit – though effectively he worked with two – body and soul/spirit. The former had to do with history, with miracle, with flesh; the latter with spiritual meaning and with hidden knowledge. The bodily level included anthropomorphic notions of God, but the spiritual involved true thinking of God who is spirit and mind. Christians must always think worthily of God and think of God according to the nature of God.

Added to this, Origen had a profound sense of God as Trinity, albeit understood in a subordinationist way, for this is how he understood Scripture. The Son, he held, is named in Scripture as a 'creature', yet is also clearly God, not 'by participation but in virtue of his own being'. The Son is eternally begotten, and the whole Trinity is vastly different in being from the rest of creation, which is brought into existence by the creative hand of God, mediated through the Word. Origen's doctrine of the Spirit is unclear, as most of the Spirit's functions tend to be subsumed by him under consideration of the Word.

God 'comprehends' the world, thereby instilling into it rationality, limit, space and time, order and purpose. God's constant providence over creation enables him to be present in every part, making room for himself wherever he wishes, without his moving from one part to another. With a created rationality embedded within the world, humans can begin there, rising to a knowledge of the divine. Christians move from faith to knowledge to wisdom. Origen daringly suggested that God himself cannot be infinite, for only the finite can be comprehended and God must 'comprehend' himself.

For all this, however, there is another side to Origen, pulling his thought in a different direction. Certain late Platonist principles were endemic in his thought, such as: (1) in the hierarchy of being, that which produces is superior to what is produced, (2) like is known by like and (3) sensible things belong to an inferior category whereas intelligible things belong to the category of the real.

Origen's notion of the eternal existence of rational souls is affected by these ideas. In his *First Principles* he argued that God's almightiness entails that there must always have been souls over which he is almighty – otherwise God changes. Origen proclaimed the unity of God, almost a monad-like God. Because God produces, albeit eternally, the Word, this Word must be 'a second God', a lesser God, yet within the genus of the being of God. This Word in turn creates – under the providence of God and as an intermediary – a world of eternal souls, free to respond to God or not. Origen cannot conceive of rational souls knowingly rebelling against God, and so he conceives of the Fall instead in terms of apathy and sloth. The Fall involves souls' attachment to, and their being encased within, bodies. Their rise reveals their kinship with God.

Out of God's continuing love, the Word accommodates himself to humanity, so that at that bodily level people might begin to be formed like 'the Word become flesh'. (Strictly, however, for Origen, 'Word become flesh' means that the Word took the one soul that did not fall and this soul, acting as a 'medium' between God and flesh, united with a body – it being the property of souls to unite with bodies.) Beginning with the Word become flesh, people are gradually led by the Word to a knowledge of himself before he took flesh. Origen's intention is that people should arrive at a right conception of God, freed from all bodily association; but, allied to the third principle listed above, it meant a downgrading of the incarnation, creation, history and faith. Origen cannot even hold that the Word became flesh. People may begin with the incarnation, with history, with the plain meaning of Scripture, but they are encouraged to penetrate through them

and leave them aside in order to discover the eternal truths of God. The Platonic dualism between the intelligible world and the sensible world has had a devastating effect.

Origen is tied into a cosmological understanding of God, and so the second Person of the Trinity is thought of primarily in terms of Word rather than Son, as was the case in virtually all apologist thinking in the early church. What it meant for the second Person to be Son in relation to the Father would be fought out later in the *Arian controversy.

JAMES B. WALKER

FURTHER READING: H. Crouzel, *Origène et la Philosophie* (Paris, 1959); *Théologie et l'Image de Dieu chez Origène* (Paris, 1956); *Origen* (Edinburgh, 1989); J. Daniélou, *Origen* (London, 1955); B. Drewery, *Origen and the Doctrine of Grace* (London, 1960); W. Fairweather, *Origen and Greek Patristic Theology* (Edinburgh, 1901); E. de Faye, *Origène, sa Vie, son Oeuvre, sa Pensée* (3 vols.; Paris, 1923–28); R.P.C. Hanson, *Allegory and Event* (London, 1959); *Origen's Doctrine of Tradition* (London, 1954); M. Harl, *Origène et la Fonction Révélatrice du Verbe Incarné* (Paris, 1958); J.W. Twigg, *Origen: The Bible and Philosophy in the Third-Century Church* (Atlanta, 1983).

Orr, James (1844–1913)

Scottish theologian, apologist and polemicist. Born in Glasgow, he identified as a young man with the minority United Presbyterians (UPs) and their egalitarian tradition. He studied at the UP Divinity Hall, Edinburgh (1868–72) and Glasgow University (MA, 1870; BD, 1872; DD, 1885) where, under the tutelage of John Veitch (one of Scotland's last Common-Sense philosophers) and the Neo-Hegelians John and Edward Caird, he acquired a respect for reason's role in theology. After a pastoral ministry of 17 years in the Scottish Borders town of Hawick, he delivered a lecture series which was published as *The Christian View of God and the World* (1893). This work, which proved to be his greatest, launched him on a prolific academic career. In the remaining two decades of his life, while serving first at the UP College in Edinburgh (1891–1900) and then at the United Free Church College in Glasgow (1900–13), he wrote 16 books, edited a magazine and a major reference work, contributed hundreds of articles and reviews, and frequently lectured in North America. The cumulative effect was that his voice seemed omnipresent in his day.

During the 1870s Orr was among those who campaigned for modified subscription to the Westminster Confession. He helped draft the UP Declaratory Statement of 1879, which qualified and effectively relaxed the extent to which a minister was obliged to affirm the content of the church's subordinate standards. The UP approach was accorded the flattery of being imitated by the other main wings of Scottish Presbyterianism, and it served to undermine the rule of *Calvinism in Scotland.

The central thesis of Orr's *The Christian View* is that there is inherent in the Christian faith a uniquely adequate and coherent interpretation of existence. Though Christianity is a religion and not a philosophy, it does offer among its benefits a supremely satisfying world-view. It is the coherence of the Christian world-view, its harmony with reason and moral experience, that makes it compelling. Thus the systematic presentation of evangelical doctrine (which is nothing other than the setting forth of this world-view) is in fact the most comprehensive apologetic for the Christian faith. Accordingly, *The Christian View* does not begin with an apology for Scripture and then proceed to confident deduction therefrom. The Christian system of belief is commended on the basis of its own intrinsic merits and the correspondence assumed to exist between its claims and humanity's capacity to recognize truth intuitively and rationally. In this sense, then, the Christian faith is self-authenticating.

Having retreated from a strict adherence to confessional Calvinism, Orr gave notice in *The Christian View* of what he considered the Christian faith to be; namely, a religion of personal redemption necessarily undergirded by the classic doctrines of evangelical belief. 'I do not believe', he said, 'that in order to preserve [the Christian view] one single truth we have been accustomed to see shining in that constellation will require to be withdrawn' (p. 347). This comment set the tone for Orr's subsequent theological contribution, which may best be described as a call for continued adherence to the central tenets of evangelical orthodoxy. In the course of his career he urged such continuity in the face of challenges from *Ritschlianism, Old Testament criticism, evolutionary theory and the quest for the historical Jesus.

Orr was one of the earliest and principal British critics of *Albrecht Ritschl's thought. In his *The Ritschlian Theology and the Evangelical Faith* (1897)

and elsewhere, Orr insisted that Ritschlianism was opposed to genuine Christianity and was intellectually untenable because of its limitation of the role of reason in Christian thought and experience. In *The Progress of Dogma* (1901), Orr tried to counter Ritschlian *Adolf Harnack's negative verdict on the history of dogma by arguing that it has unfolded according to a recognizable inner logic. By regarding this logical movement as a manifestation of God's hand in history, Orr sought to vindicate the orthodox doctrines which that movement produced.

In *The Problem of the Old Testament* (1906), prompted partly by his Glasgow colleague George Adam Smith's advocacy of the documentary hypothesis, Orr argued for the 'essential Mosaicity' of the Pentateuch, and for a traditional construction of Old Testament history. Orr treated Charles Darwin's theory of humanity's origin as a serious threat to the Christian doctrines of humanity and sin. Initially he appeared comfortable with theistic evolution, but later, in *God's Image in Man* (1905), he stressed the necessity of supernatural interruptions of the evolutionary process to account for the human being as an embodied soul, and still later, in *Sin as a Problem of Today* (1910), he argued that the idea of moral evolution (as articulated by F.R. Tennant and others) undermined the seriousness of sin and humanity's accountability for it. Finally, he held firmly to orthodox Christological formulations in the face of alternative assessments of the historical Jesus. Among his reasons for doing so was his pragmatic conviction that nothing less would be sufficient to sustain the vitality of the church's practical religious life. In such works as *The Virgin Birth of Christ* (1907), he defended theologically as well as biblically the virginal conception of the Mediator.

In the course of all these initiatives, Orr made allowances that later fundamentalists would consider unthinkably concessionary. He welcomed Ritschl's emphasis on kingdom expansion; he made qualified allowance for evolutionary development; he was unconcerned to defend a literal interpretation of the early chapters of the book of Genesis, and he took the view that an insistence on biblical inerrancy was actually 'suicidal' (see his *Revelation and Inspiration* [1910], p. 198).

Nonetheless, a fairly widespread academic resistance to his views, combined with his own deep-seated populist instincts and common-sense convictions, led Orr in later years to direct his appeals primarily towards the Christian public (see, e.g., his *The Bible Under Trial* [1907], *The Faith of a Modern Christian* [1910], and his contributions to *The Fundamentals* [1910–15]). His last great work as general editor of the five-volume *International Standard Bible Encyclopaedia* (1915) – according to its preface, a reference tool 'adapted more directly to the needs of the average pastor and Bible student – constituted a substantial and enduring means of extending conservative orthodoxy's line of defence.

Orr's contribution was decisively shaped by the convictions that evangelical orthodoxy is ultimately self-authenticating, that truth comprises a unity or interconnected whole, and that genuine Christian belief implies a two-storey supernaturalist cosmology. The significance of Orr's theological contribution lies not in its pervasive originality, but in the breadth of his grasp of classic doctrine, the exhaustiveness of the reading upon which his conclusions were based, and the vigour with which he defended and diffused his views. His personal emphasis on supernaturalism, as well as his populist sympathies, were certainly hallmarks of later fundamentalism; in very few cases, however, were the breadth of his scholarship, or the firm but cordially inclusive tenor of his apologetic efforts, matched among his conservative successors. For these and other reasons, J.I. Packer has recently recommended Orr as a mentor for evangelicals now pursuing *rapprochement* with Roman Catholics and Orthodox Christians.

GLEN G. SCORGIE

FURTHER READING: J.I. Packer, 'On from Orr: The Cultural Crisis, Rational Realism, and Incarnational Ontology', *Crux* 32.3 (1996), pp. 12–26; Glen G. Scorgie, *A Call for Continuity: The Theological Contribution of James Orr* (Macon, GA, 1988); 'James Orr', in *Handbook of Evangelical Theologians* (ed. Walter Elwell; Grand Rapids, 1993), pp. 12–25; Alan P.F. Sell, *Defending and Declaring the Faith: Some Scottish Examples, 1860–1920* (Colorado Springs, CO, 1987), ch. 7.

Osiander, Andreas (c. 1496–1552)

German theologian responsible, with Lazarus Spengler, for introducing Protestant reforms in the city of Nuremberg. Born in Gunzenhausen in Franconia, Osiander was educated at the University of Ingolstadt, where he was also influenced by Humanism. He learned Hebrew and Aramaic and became interested in Cabbalistic traditions through the work of Johannes Reuchlin. Later he spoke out publicly against the slanderous charge of ritual murder against the Jews. Ordained priest in 1520, he became a teacher of Hebrew at the cloister of Augustinian Friars in Nuremberg, where he devoted his attention to a revision of the Vulgate Bible, which he published in 1522. That same year he was called to serve as pastor in Nuremberg's Saint Lorenz church. He also became involved in a controversy, sparked in part by his own conversion to the *Reformation, over the reception of both kinds (i.e., bread and wine) in the Lord's Supper. He married in 1525, and thereafter he worked closely with Spengler to introduce doctrinal and liturgical reforms consistent with Reformation teaching, work that ultimately bore fruit in the Brandenburg-Nuremberg Church Order of 1533.

Osiander represented Nuremberg at the Marburg Colloquy in 1529, where he opposed *Zwingli's Eucharistic theology in favour of *Luther's, and again at the Diet of Augsburg in 1530, where he was critical of the irenic posture adopted by *Philip Melanchthon. In 1537 he attended the Schmalkald Colloquy, and he signed both the Schmalkaldic Articles and Melanchthon's treatise 'On the Power and Primacy of the Pope'. While at Schmalkald, however, he also preached a sermon critical of Luther, a move that emphasized his independence but did little to endear him to his colleagues. In 1543, at the invitation of Count Ottheinrich, he drafted a church order for the Palatinate-Neuburg. That same year, he wrote an apparently unsolicited and thereafter unappreciated preface to Nicholas Copernicus's *De Revolutionibus Orbium Caelestium*, thereby associating himself for ever with the rise of modern science.

When the Protestants lost the Schmalkald War in 1547, the city of Nuremberg soon adopted a new order of worship in line with the Leipzig Interim, a move made without Osiander's participation or approval. Osiander moved to Königsberg in East Prussia, where he served as pastor and as professor of theology, a position in which he was required to set forth his theological opinions in systematic fashion. He soon clashed with Joachim Mörlin, who had studied in Wittenberg under Melanchthon and Luther between 1532 and 1540, over some of the intricacies of Melanchthon's doctrine of justification. Osiander had injudiciously attacked this doctrine in the disputation (against the young *Martin Chemnitz) conducted on the occasion of his inauguration as professor. Osiander argued that Melanchthon's notion of forensic justification – that is, that the free pardon of God is imputed to the sinner for Christ's sake alone as a strictly juridical act – was unfaithful to the teaching of Luther. To the contrary, Osiander claimed, the free pardon of God constitutes only the preparation necessary for justification. Justification itself consists not in a mere juridical pardon, but in the indwelling of the divine nature of the Logos, Jesus Christ. Christ in the Christian justifies, he claims, and then becomes the basis of the Christian's renewal in the image of God. Here Osiander had recourse to *Duns Scotus's idea that the Son of God would have become incarnate whether or not humanity had fallen into sin. Since there is nothing accidental in God, Osiander reasoned, there can be no alteration of God's original creative purposes. The incarnation thus becomes for Osiander the fulfilment of the eternal will of God according to which humanity was to be created in the image of Jesus Christ. Adam was made for God, for union, that is, with the divine nature. His creation is to be understood as an anticipation of Christ's incarnation, and justification is nothing but the fulfilment, in spite of the Fall, of the divine intent behind Adam's original creation.

To his opponents, Osiander's doctrine of justification seemed simultaneously to bear the taint of *Nestorianism – on account of his tendency to separate the human and divine natures of Christ – and to result in a peculiar recatholicization of Protestant theology – since Osiander's notion of the indwelling of Christ's divine nature sounds something like the Catholic notion of 'infused grace' (*gratia infusa*). Just when the controversy was reaching a fevered pitch, on 17 October 1552, Osiander suddenly died – leaving the debate for others to decide. For confessional Lutherans, their nearly unanimous rejection of Osiander's ideas was expressed authoritatively, and explicitly, in the 'Formula of Concord'. Justification must be understood as a forensic act if there is to be any assurance of salvation in this life. Likewise, Geneva's *John Calvin vehemently rejected Osiander's ideas, adding to the 1559 edition of his *Institutes of the Christian Religion* a lengthy

and passionate refutation of the 'strange monster' of essential righteousness (*Institutes*, 3.11.5–12). The penetrating criticisms of Calvin and the orthodox Lutherans notwithstanding, Osiander had raised important issues, ones which troubled the Lutheran tradition up to at least the publication of the 'Formula' in 1580, forcing it to articulate its own account of the relationship between saving faith and the renewal of life.

MICKEY L. MATTOX

FURTHER READING: *Text: Osianders Werke, Gesamtausgabe* (ed. Gerhard Müller and Gottfried Seebass; 10 vols.; Gütersloh, 1975–95). *Studies:* Claus Bachmann, *Die Selbstherrlichkeit Gottes: Studien zur Theologie des Nürnberger Reformators Andreas Osiander* (Neukirchener, 1996); E. Hirsch, *Die Theologie des Andreas Osiander und ihre geschichtlichen Voraussetzungen* (Göttingen, 1919); W. Müller, *Andreas Osiander: Leben und ausgewählte Schriften* (Elberfeld, 1870); Gottfried Seebass, *Das reformatorische Werk des Andreas Osiander* (Einzelarbeiten aus der Kirchengeschichte Bayerns 44; Nuremberg, 1967); Martin Stupperich, *Osiander in Preussen, 1549–1552* (Arbeiten zur Kirchengeschichte 44; Berlin / New York, 1973); David C. Steinmetz, *Reformers in the Wings* (Grand Rapids, 2nd edn, 1981), see ch. 8 for a helpful biography and careful explanation of the distinctive points in Osiander's theology.

Otto, Rudolf (1869–1937)

Lutheran theologian and philosopher of religion, born in Peine, Germany and reared in a pietistic Lutheran family. From 1888 to 1898, Otto studied theology at Erlangen and Göttingen. At the latter, he earned the degree of licentiate of theology. Otto became a *Privatdozent* in the University of Göttingen in 1899 and moved to Breslau in 1914, becoming a full professor in 1915. In 1917, Otto assumed the chair of systematic theology at Marburg. He retired in 1929 and resided in Marburg until his death.

An overview of Otto's publications suggests two phases to his career. After a generally disappointing reception of his book *Leben und Wirken Jesu* in 1902 (ET *The Life and Ministry of Jesus*, 1908), Otto grew disenchanted with theological liberalism and focused his attention on the philosophy of religion. Naturalism (Darwinism) and the historical-critical method were his principal rivals. Otto's *Naturalistische und religiöse Weltansicht* of 1904 (ET *Naturalism and Religion*, 1907) offered a response to the former. He believed that support for traditional Christian faith against historical criticism could be found in a modified form of *Kant's philosophy. He was not a Kant exegete, however. Instead, the work of Fries and De Wette influenced him to formulate a new conception of religious belief and experience as an amendment to Kant's philosophy. Otto developed this idea in his *Die Kant-friesische Religions-Philosophie* of 1904 (ET *The Philosophy of Religion*, 1931).

Otto's thought, particularly in this initial phase, was largely indebted to the influence of *Ritschl and *Troeltsch and the writings of *Luther and *Schleiermacher. With Ritschl, Otto accepted the autonomy of religious consciousness. He came to understand ultimate meaning as a derivation of this consciousness and, developing Troeltsch's idea of the religious a priori, sought to provide a religious theory that accounted for both the rational and the non-rational components of religion. Otto learned from Luther the importance of faith and its relatedness to a distinctly religious category of meaning and value. His reading of Schleiermacher reinforced this idea. Scheiermacher's 'Sense of the Eternal' provided Otto with an insightful yet underdeveloped point of departure for his system. Otto's classic *Das Heilige* of 1917 (ET *The Idea of the Holy*, 1923) expanded upon the work of Fries and Schleiermacher and provided perhaps the most credible critique of religious reason and experience in the twentieth century.

Following the success of *Das Heilige*, Otto's writings displayed a keen effort to expound his religious theory from philosophical, religious and theological points of view. His *Religious Essays* of 1931 put into one text the seminal insights of various philosophical addenda to his religious theory. *West-Östliche Mystik* in 1926 (ET *Mysticism East and West*, 1932) and *Die Gnadenreligion Indiens und das Christentum* in 1930 (ET *India's Religion of Grace and Christianity*, 1930), as well as his translations of several sacred texts of the east, brought his system to bear concretely upon the field of comparative religions. *Reich Gottes und Menschensohn* in 1934 (ET *The Kingdom of God and the Son of Man*, 1938) exemplified Otto's mature Christology.

Otto distinguished between four rational 'outlooks' or perspectives – the empirical, the moral, the aesthetic and the religious – and disavowed those philosophical theories that explained religion solely in terms of reason's non-religious perspectives. Appealing to phenomenology, Otto found religious experience to have three distinct features: the *mysteriosum*, the *fascinans*, and the *tremendum*. These words were not meant to capture meaning; instead, reason schematizes them and substitutes the rational equivalents of absoluteness, grace and wrath. The science of religion enriches our understanding of religion by examining these rational/mystical feelings in their religious manifestations worldwide. Otto was not a universalist, however. 'The degree in which both rational and non-rational elements are jointly present, united in healthy and loving harmony, affords a criterion to measure the relative rank of religions – and one, too, that is specifically religious'.

Although Otto is perhaps best known for articulating the non-rational dimension of religious experience, he argued that this could only be done after a critique of the rational dimension had been completed. He delineated the rational dimension under the term 'the category of the holy'. As the chief constituent of the religious experience, the category of the holy enables human beings to grasp the 'over surplus of meaning' unique to religious experience. Otto called this over surplus 'the feeling of the numinous'. Though not universal, the numinous feeling is a potentiality which must be 'awakened' in us. In the 'deep abyss' of reason, humans have a hidden 'predisposition' for holiness. The faculty of divination, when it is operative, maintains a healthy religious outlook by 'genuinely cognizing and recognizing the holy in its appearances' and by contemplating what these experiences ultimately mean.

Otto influenced two of the twentieth century's most influential theologians: *Karl Barth (1886–1968) and *Paul Tillich (1886–1965). After penning his commentary on Romans (1918), Barth wrote in a letter, 'I read Otto's *The Idea of the Holy* with considerable delight. It opens the way for a basic surmounting of Ritschlianism'. Like Otto, Barth recognized the objectivity and reality of the source of revelation. They disagreed, however, on the respective importance of philosophy and theology in explicating it. Otto felt that revelation required rational analysis prior to fully understanding it, while Barth believed that the divine word stands before all systems as the crisis of religion. Tillich also appreciated Otto's accomplishment. In his *Autobiographical Reflections*, Tillich wrote,

'When I first read Rudolf Otto's *The Idea of the Holy*, I understood it immediately in the light of [my] early experiences, and took it into my thinking as a constitutive element'. Tillich's mature writings reveal strong affinities with Otto's and can be read fruitfully as a creative expansion of Otto's thought into the realm of philosophical theology.

There continues to be a dearth in the supply of systematic treatments of Otto's thought. Two notable exceptions are Davidson's *Rudolf Otto's Interpretation of Religion* (1947) and Almond's *Rudolf Otto: An Introduction to His Philosophical Theology* (1984). The former offers a capable summary of the context of his writings, while the latter provides a careful analysis of important highlights in his life and thought.

CHRIS L. FIRESTONE

FURTHER READING: Philip C. Almond, *Rudolf Otto: An Introduction to His Philosophical Theology* (Chapel Hill / London, 1984); D.A. Crosby, *Interpretive Theories of Religion* (Berlin, NY, 1981); Adina Davidovich, *Religion as a Province of Meaning* (Minneapolis, 1993); Robert F. Davidson, *Rudolf Otto's Interpretation of Religion* (Princeton, 1947); Thomas Idinopulus and Edward A. Yohan (eds.), *The Sacred and its Scholars* (New York, 1996); J.M. Moore, *Theories of Religion with Special Reference to James, Otto and Bergson* (New York, 1938); N. Smart, *Philosophers and Religious Truth* (London, 1964).

Owen, John (1616–83)

A leading *Puritan theologian, Owen was of Presbyterian conviction within the established English church but took the position of an Independent (Congregationalist) after being persuaded that the local congregation should be relatively autonomous. Called to preach before the Council of State, Owen caught the attention of the Protector, Oliver Cromwell, and was invited to be his chaplain on military expeditions to Ireland and Scotland. As a friend and adviser to Cromwell he played an active role in the affairs of the Commonwealth and Protectorate. In 1651 Parliament appointed Owen dean of Christ Church, Oxford and in the following year Cromwell made him vice-chancellor of the university, a position he kept until 1657 when he opposed moves to make Cromwell king. At the end of the Protectorate (1660) Owen was ejected from Christ Church and moved on to London where he continued to preach and write. Under the restored monarchy he enjoyed the favour of King Charles II and was able to provide support to a wide number of ejected Puritan ministers and their families.

From his student days Owen, along with other Puritans, was deeply concerned by the attempt of Archbishop Laud (1573–1645) to forcibly impose liturgical uniformity as a way of countering the prevailing *Calvinistic theology in England. Owen's first work, *A Display of Arminianism* (1643), was a defence of the Reformed position. Although it relied rather too heavily on the disputational style in which he was trained, it nevertheless gave early notice of the careful logic and broad perspective of a gifted theologian. His writing had matured considerably by the time he published *The Death of Death in the Death of Christ* (1647), the classic defence of the doctrine of the 'limited atonement'. Although the principle is suggested in the writings of *Augustine and *Calvin, limited atonement was first distinctly formulated in response to the *Arminian Controversy at the Synod of Dort (1618–19), which proposed that the death of Christ was sufficient for all but efficient only for the elect.

Owen's comprehensive treatise on the subject is the richest development of Reformed thought in an area which is perceived by many as the weakest point of the 'Calvinistic' system. His fair treatment of the major arguments of his opponents contributes to its persuasive force. Owen's thesis is derived from his consideration of the purpose of the Father in the atonement and the effectiveness of the Son's self-sacrifice. God's intention, he argued, was not that the atonement might provide merely the possibility of salvation for those who hear the gospel, but rather that it would effectively reconcile sinful men and women to God. To distinguish between those for whom redemption was procured and those to whom it is applied is an error which fails to recognize that the death of Christ purchased not only salvation, but also the means of salvation – that is, faith, holiness and grace. The efficacy of the atonement, if taken seriously, means that all those for whom Christ died will believe and experience eternal salvation. One could say that Owen contended for an 'effective' atonement. It is interesting that in more modern times *Karl Barth's similar emphasis on the divine initiative in reconciliation has also resulted in an 'effective' atonement in which no distinction is drawn between those for whom redemption was purchased and those to whom it is applied. Yet because Barth believed reconciliation was won for all, his theology constantly pushed him towards universalism.

The rise of the *Socinians (Unitarians) in the seventeenth century posed a threat not just to Reformed thought but to the orthodox faith as a whole. The Socinians presented a carefully considered, biblically developed understanding of Jesus which emphasized his subservience to and dependence on God in a way which undermined the idea of a substantial identity of Father and Son. Not since the triumph of *Athanasius's party over Arianism had the church been required to face so thorough an intellectual challenge to the divine status of Christ.

When John Biddle (1615–62) introduced Socinian ideas to England, the Council of State requested John Owen to reply to his writings. Owen's thorough knowledge of the Church Fathers meant that he was well able to articulate the classical doctrine of the incarnation, as he did in his response to the Socinians in *Vindicae Evangelicae* (1655). But in his later studies, *An Exposition of the Epistle to the Hebrews* (1674) and the *Discourse on the Holy Spirit* (1674), it is apparent that Owen was aware of the inadequacy of the orthodox presentation of Christ's person and its vulnerability to Socinian attack. He believed that the New Testament also presented Jesus as a person dependent on the Holy Spirit, open to temptation and trial and living as a man before God in a way that was not substantially different from our own human experience. Could such a view of Jesus be integrated with an orthodox understanding of the incarnation? Owen was able to achieve this by arguing that the human nature, which the Son of God assumed into substantial union with himself, knew and experienced God always through the Holy Spirit. In short, the human nature of the incarnate Christ was in no way different from our own, even in its experience of and dependence on God.

Consequently, Owen's theology was able to affirm that Jesus Christ was both the giver and the receiver of the Spirit. He was the incarnate Son of God, but he was also a man with a nature like our own, a paradigm of the Christian person living in faith before God. Working within the framework of orthodox incarnational theology, Owen was able to present a coherent exposition of the person of Jesus, the man, which seemed to be far more in harmony with the Gospels' account of his life than that generally emerging from the creeds.

The fall of the Puritans from political power at the Restoration and the ejection of their ministers from the pulpits of England contributed to the comparative neglect of Owen's theology in the years that followed. It meant that the questions raised by the Socinians were not adequately answered, which might well be why much of English Nonconformity fell prey to *Unitarian thought in the eighteenth century. There was, therefore, no generally accepted theological framework which held together ideas of Jesus Christ as both the incarnate Son of God and as a man like ourselves inspired by the Spirit. The absence of this framework helps to explain the rise in later centuries of the movement which sought to discover the historical Jesus behind the trappings of external dogma. It also helps to explain its failure, in general, to give an adequate account of why we should worship him. It is of interest that a further two hundred years passed after Owen before there appeared, in the writings of *Edward Irving (1792–1834), another clearly-articulated account of Jesus Christ as the incarnate Son of God who was yet dependent on the Holy Spirit for his life of holiness and his walk of faith.

As to his direct influence today, it is part of the irony of history that John Owen, whose massive theological mind has been compared to that of *Jonathan Edwards, although he possessed a far greater learning than the renowned American, should be almost unread by serious theologians. One reason for this might be that, whereas the Americans are generally proud to affirm their Pilgrim or Puritan heritage, the English have tended to view their own Puritan past as a historical aberration and have largely neglected what is arguably their richest period of spiritual and theological literature.

ALAN SPENCE

FURTHER READING: *Texts: The Works of John Owen*, 16 vols. (ed. William H. Goold; vols. I–XVI of 1850–53 edn; repr. London, 1965–8); *An Exposition of the Epistle to the Hebrews*, 7 vols. (ed. William H. Goold; vols. XVIII–XXIV of 1855 edn; repr. Grand Rapids, 1980). *Studies:* Sinclair B. Ferguson, *John Owen on the Christian Life* (Edinburgh, 1987); James Moffatt, *The Golden Book of John Owen* (London, 1904); Alan Spence, 'Christ's Humanity and Ours: John Owen', in *Persons Divine and Human* (ed. Christoph Schwoebel and Colin E. Gunton; Edinburgh, 1991); Alan Spence, 'John Owen and

Trinitarian Agency', *Scot J Th* 43.2 (1990); Peter Toon, *God's Statesman: The Life and Work of John Owen* (Grand Rapids, 1973).

Oxford Movement

The name 'the Oxford Movement' is characteristically used for that movement of Catholic revival within the Church of England, which began in Oxford with the preaching of the Assize Sermon on 14 July 1833 by *John Keble (1792–1866). Keble, *John Henry Newman (1801–90) and *Edward Bouverie Pusey (1800–82) are usually reckoned as the leaders of the Movement, which is traditionally considered as running from 1833 to 1845, when Newman was received into the Church of Rome. Some would argue, however, that it was the Gorham Judgement of 1851 which is the better *terminus ad quem*, the former dates having been too much coloured by Newman's personal account of his religious opinions in his *Apologia pro vita sua* (1864). It is increasingly recognized that the old High Churchmen of the Hackney Phalanx and earlier had done much to revive the High Church tradition, and the Oxford Movement has to be seen in the context of a much wider diocesan revival. The Movement expressed its thinking in the series of *Tracts for the Times* published between 1833 and 1841, giving rise to the appellation 'Tractarian' for those adhering to the Movement. The concurrent Gothic revival, and the concerns of the Cambridge ecclesiologists under the leadership notably of Benjamin Webb (1819–85) and John Mason Neale (1818–66), contributed to the transformation of worship and Anglican church buildings which reflected the sacramental and theological concerns of the Oxford Movement.

The catalyst of the Oxford Movement was the perceived threat to the identity of the Church of England consequent upon government legislation which modified the 'confessional state', repealing legislation imposing penalties on Nonconformists and Roman Catholics, and opening Parliament and civic office to non-members of the Church of England. Conservative High Churchmen saw this as a threat to Anglican identity, given that the Church of England had no mechanism of government apart from Parliament. Hence the characteristic appeal of the Oxford Movement to the doctrine of apostolic succession, and the emphasis on episcopacy as the divinely appointed pattern of church government and ministerial order. Another contributing factor to the Movement was a reaction to what was seen as a growing liberalism, and the need for ecclesial authority rather than a religion of private judgement. Influenced to a varying extent by the contemporaneous *Romantic movement, with its stress on imagination and its interest in symbol and image, the Oxford Movement emphasized the centrality of sacramental worship, ordered liturgy and the call to holiness. In common with earlier generations of High Churchmen, the Tractarians appealed not only to the Scriptures but to the Fathers, as well as to the writings of seventeenth-century High Churchmen such as Lancelot Andrewes (1555–1626), Joseph Bramhall (1594–1663) and William Laud (1573–1645). They translated a significant body of patristic writing in *The Library of the Fathers* and assembled earlier Anglican texts in *The Library of Anglo-Catholic Theology*.

The *Tracts for the Times*, initially short pungent pamphlets, developed into more substantial essays with Pusey's major tract on baptism, stressing baptismal regeneration, which was to be a cardinal doctrine of the Oxford Movement. Later tracts included one by Isaac Williams (1802–65) on the theme of 'reserve in communicating religious knowledge', defending a doctrine of economy in revelation and with a stress on a theology of mystery. The same theme occurs in the theology of both Keble and Newman. *Tract XC*, the last of the *Tracts for the Times*, was Newman's endeavour to reconcile subscription to the Anglican formularies with the Council of Trent. The Oxford Movement saw a notable revival in preaching, particularly Newman's *Parochial and Plain Sermons* preached for the most part in the University Church at Oxford, and his *University Sermons*, in which Newman developed a discussion of the relation of faith and reason which was ultimately to lead to his much fuller exploration of the issue in *The Grammar of Assent* (1870). Of Tractarians who were to join the Church of Rome following the Gorham Judgement of 1851, Henry Edward Manning (1808–92), later Cardinal Archbishop of Westminster, is now recognized as a more substantial theologian than had previously been thought, and his Anglican *Sermons* show a profound pneumatological ecclesiology (later to be developed in a Roman Catholic context). Robert Isaac Wilberforce (1802–57) was the author of three significant theological works,

The Doctrine of the Incarnation (1848), *The Doctrine of Holy Baptism* (1849) and *The Doctrine of the Holy Eucharist* (1853).

Newman's writings from the Oxford Movement period may be judged the most substantial theological works produced by the Movement. His *Arians of the Fourth Century* (1833) explored in part the development of the doctrine of the Trinity as well as Christological issues, and it paved some of the way for his 1845 *Essay on Development*. A succinct presentation of his theology of development can be found in his university sermon on the subject of 1843. His *Lectures on the Prophetical Office of the Church* (1837) defended the Anglican *via media* between Rome and popular Protestantism and developed ideas of prophetical and episcopal tradition, which set creedal and doctrinal statements within a wider matrix of prayer, liturgy and devotion. The *Lectures on Justification* (1837) were a creative attempt to explore disputed territory between Protestants and Catholics, and they reflect the characteristic Tractarian concern with sacramental realism in opposition to rationalist abstraction or a theology of feelings.

The Tractarians stressed both church and sacraments as means of grace and developed an understanding of the church as an extension of the incarnation. In its present reality the church was seen as existing in three branches – Catholic, Orthodox and Anglican, all of which adhered to the three-fold apostolic ministry and gave an authoritative place to the tradition of the early centuries.

Following the moves to Rome of some of its most distinguished leaders, the influence of the Oxford Movement continued to spread in the Church of England and the growing Anglican Communion, especially in relation to more elaborate and liturgical worship which led later in the nineteenth century to the ritualist controversies. The contributors to *Lux Mundi* (1889), who were all heirs of the Oxford Movement, enabled the sacramental and ecclesiological concerns of the Tractarians to be taken forward into a new generation with an openness to biblical criticism and an acceptance of contemporary evolutionary theory.

GEOFFREY ROWELL

FURTHER READING: Peter B. Nockles, *The Oxford Movement in Context: Anglican High Churchmanship 1760–1857* (Cambridge, 1994); G. Rowell, *The Vision Glorious: Themes and Personalities of the Catholic Revival in Anglicanism* (Oxford, 1983); A. Härdelin, *The Tractarian Understanding of the Eucharist* (Uppsala, 1965); Owen Chadwick, *The Spirit of the Oxford Movement: Tractarian Essays* (Cambridge, 1990); E.R. Fairweather, *The Oxford Movement* (New York, 1964), a selection of texts; D.H. Newsome, *The Parting of Friends: A Study of the Wilberforces and Henry Manning* (London, 1966); L.N. Crumb, *The Oxford Movement and its Leaders: A Bibliography of Secondary and Lesser Primary Sources* (Matuchen, NJ, 1988, suppl. 1993).

Palamas, Gregory (1296–1359)

One of the most prominent theologians and monastic personalities of the Eastern Orthodox Church, St Gregory Palamas lived in the fourteenth century – an exceptionally creative and critical period of theological, liturgical and spiritual development in the Byzantine East. Representative of an entire tradition or 'school', which came to be known as 'hesychasm', Palamas wrote about the transformation of the human person and the created world. He described the experience of God in paradoxical terms of nearness and distance, transcendent mystery and immanent presence. Like his predecessor in tenth-century Constantinople, *Symeon the New Theologian (949–1022), Gregory spoke of God as divine light; unlike Symeon, however, Gregory is condemned by his critics for this teaching. Finally, Gregory formulated more precisely the doctrine of the distinction between the essence and the energies of God. The theology of Palamas might best be summed up in the word '*theosis*' or 'deification' – a term that signifies the sanctification or glorification, but not the absorption or annihilation, of our created personal identity, both spiritual and material.

Born to a Constantinopolitan family of the aristocracy in 1296, Gregory decided to become a monk after receiving a sound secular education and after the death of his father. Together with his two brothers – his mother and two sisters entered the convent of the city – Gregory went to Mt Athos, a monastic peninsula in northern Greece. For over twenty years, he lived most of his life in silence and prayer. It is during this time that Gregory began to write – his first treatise being a symbolic interpretation of the life of the Virgin Mary as an archetype for all devout Christians (c. 1334). When in 1337 the Athonite emphasis on the central importance of the Jesus Prayer (the rhythm and repetition of the words: 'Lord Jesus Christ, Son of God, have mercy on me') and the hesychast (which literally means 'silence' or 'stillness' in Greek) experience of divine light was attacked by *Barlaam of Calabria in southern Italy, Gregory, perhaps rather unwillingly, came out of his seclusion and became the spokesman for the monks. Gregory's most notable work, the *Triads in Defence of the Holy Hesychasts*, was written during this period. Several significant local councils in Constantinople were convened between 1338 and 1351, affirming Gregory's teaching. In 1347, he was elected Archbishop of Thessalonika. Thus, although he began his life in seclusion, Palamas ended it in pastoral responsibility, thereby combining the mystical and the social life. He died in 1359 and was proclaimed a saint only nine years later.

The criticism of Barlaam of Calabria raised questions about the knowledge of God and the kingdom of heaven. It also raised issues concerning the role and the sacredness of the human body and the material creation. Barlaam argued that God is radically unknowable except indirectly. He claimed that any direct experience of or immediate union with God was reserved for the age to come. He believed that the light which the monastics claimed to see in prayer and silence was not the divine light of God, but a physical, created light. He also denounced the physical techniques of the hesychasts as superstitious, dismissing them as 'people who had their souls in their navels'.

Gregory's response was based on Scripture and tradition, but at the same time it was profoundly innovative. Palamas agreed that God was transcendent, above all being and every essence. Yet he insisted on the distinction between God's essence (or inner being, which was totally inaccessible) and God's energies (or free acts, which were accessible and communicable). Therefore, Gregory claimed, humanity is able to have direct knowledge of, and mystical union with, the energies of God in a face-to-face relationship – even in this present age, even in this world. Gregory stressed divine transcendence as well as divine immanence. This theological distinction preserves the uniqueness of each person – divine and human – while affirming the union between God and humanity. Although the eastern part of the Christian empire was not involved in the early dispute between *Augustine and *Pelagius, the Orthodox Church developed its own discussion and doctrine of divine grace in the fourteenth century, with the hesychast controversy, when it finally confirmed that grace was not a thing, but indeed the personal God himself in revelation and relation to the world.

Consequently, Gregory emphasized that the light experienced by the hesychasts on Mt Athos was precisely the energies of God, which were manifested to the disciples of Christ on the Mount of Transfiguration, or to Paul the apostle on his journey to Damascus. This light is immaterial and spiritual, uncreated and divine, infinite and eternal.

Finally, Gregory's teaching has clear anthropological and cosmological implications. The whole human being, soul and body, experiences the divine light. Gregory's doctrine is deeply Scriptural, appealing to the incarnation and referring to the sacrament of the Eucharist. His teaching about salvation is unitary and universal. It is in this context that Palamas defends the hesychasts, including their physical method of prayer, which involved particular technical aids and bodily postures for use by beginners in the early stages of prayer. We are not, Palamas, believed, angels; we are to use and to transform our bodies too. Although the divine light is spiritual, the human body is able to share in this illumination, and indeed even to become all light, being transformed into that which we contemplate, 'transfigured from glory into glory' (2 Cor. 3:18). All of this is anticipated already from this age, Gregory likes to repeat, 'even now', 'so far as this is possible'.

In this way, Palamas emerges as a theologian of personal experience. Through the persisting influence of the *Philokalia* – the vast collection of texts on prayer and the spiritual life, dating from the fourth to the fifteenth century, and edited by St Nikodemus of Mt Athos (1749–1809) and St Macarius of Corinth (1731–1805) – the hesychast teaching and the theology of Gregory Palamas himself has continued to shape the life and thinking of the Orthodox Church to this day, representing perhaps the most central and creative element in contemporary Orthodox spirituality.

JOHN CHRYSSAVGIS

FURTHER READING: *Texts: Triads in Defence of the Holy Hesychasts* (CWS; ed. N. Gendle; New York, 1983); *The Philokalia* (ET by G. Palmer, P. Sherrard and K. Ware; 5 vols.; London / Boston, 1979–). *Studies:* I. Hausherr, *The Name of Jesus* (Cistercian Studies 44; Kalamazoo, MI, 1978), on the Jesus Prayer; G. Mantzaridis, *The Deification of Man: St. Gregory Palamas and the Orthodox Tradition* (New York, 1984); J. Meyendorff, *Triads in Defence of the Holy Hesychasts* (2 vols.; Louvain, 1959), Greek text and French trans.; *A Study of Gregory Palamas* (London, 1964); *St. Gregory Palamas and Orthodox Spirituality* (New York, 1974); K. Ware, 'The Hesychasts', in *The Study of Spirituality* (ed. C. Jones, G. Wainwright and E. Yarnold; London, 1986).

Panikkar, Raimon (b. 1918)

Raimon Panikkar, a contemporary theologian of interreligious encounter, was born in Barcelona in 1918, of an Indian Hindu father and a Spanish Catholic mother. He has lived and studied in Spain, Germany, Italy, India and the United States, taking his PhD in philosophy in 1945, his DSc in chemistry in 1958 and his DD in theology in 1961. He was ordained a priest in 1946. In his early years he was associated with Opus Dei. Panikkar became a citizen of India and retired in Spain. He has authored more than thirty books and more than three hundred major articles. His most important work theologically is *The Unknown Christ of Hinduism* (1964 and 1981), the two editions of which show a theological progression in Panikkar's position from an inclusivist theology of religions to a pluralist theology.

In the first edition of *The Unknown Christ*, Panikkar proposed that Christ is present in Hinduism and in other religions. Christ is the point of encounter between Christianity and Hinduism since Christ is the point of encounter between the human and the divine. The question arises whether the point of encounter between Hindus and what they consider the ultimate reality is also Christ. If it is affirmed that Hindus encounter Christ then it is also true that an encounter of Christianity with Hinduism is also a mutual encounter of each with Christ. 'Christianity and Hinduism meet in a common endeavour, which has the same starting point and the same "ontic" goal' (Panikkar, 1964, p. 6). Christ is the point of encounter, at the start and at the goal. The point of encounter is not a doctrine; it is 'ontic-intentional', or called by different names in Hinduism and Christianity. 'Neither will contest that the "ontic-intentionally" is the same in both religions: the greatest possible oneness with the Absolute' (Panikkar, 1981, p. 36). Christians call this common intended ontic reality Christ. Hindus call this reality by various names – Rama, Siva, Krishna, etc. What Panikkar proposes as 'unknown' is the Christ known by Christians and not known by Hindus, under that name, and not yet known by Christians as being present in the ontic intentionality of Hinduism. The unknown Christ of Hinduism is the Christ hidden from Christians and Hindus, but known by both in their separate traditions: 'In the wake of St. Paul we believe we may speak not only of the unknown God of the Greeks, but also of the *hidden Christ of Hinduism* – hidden and unknown and yet present and at work because he is not far from any one of us'

(Panikkar, 1981, p. 168). Panikkar specifically names this common ontic reality as Christ and not as the Father. Christ, and not simply God or Father, is found at the point of encounter. Since an unknown Christ is found, an unknown Trinity is found. Panikkar explains this by analyzing the second verse of an important Hindu text, the *Brahma Sutras* of Badarayana: 'Whence the origin etcetera of this.' Panikkar interprets this text as 'Brahman is that from which all things come forth, into which they return and by which they are maintained.' If Brahman is cause of the world, could Brahman be transcendent enough to be truly transcendent? 'If without due discrimination we make Brahman responsible for the world, if we, as it were, tie Brahman to the world, then it appears difficult to maintain the transcendence, the absoluteness of Brahman' (Panikkar, 1981, p. 145). The Hindus wrestled with the same problem as *Thomists. Panikkar proposes that 'the relation of God as First Cause of the World is not a *real* one, that the reality of the effect and its variations do not affect the simplicity and independence of the cause, that divine causality is precisely of a unique type that results in a dependence that is only one-sided' (Panikkar, 1981, p. 145). Hindus solve this dilemma by postulating the existence of *Isvara*, 'Lord', through whom all things were made. *Isvara* is equal to God, but originates in God. Panikkar sees an extremely close homology between *Isvara* and Christ. Although there is the unknown Christ the Son in Hinduism, the more profound unknownness of the Father is essential to the Godhead's very being, and this unknownness of the Father is at the root of Hindu religious experience. The experience of the actual Triune God is common between Christianity and Hinduism.

Of course, Christians assert that 'Jesus is the Christ.' In his Christology, Panikkar affirms that, although it is correct to say that 'Jesus is the Christ', one may not so simply say that 'the Christ is Jesus' with the same affirmation of identity. Panikkar separates the Christ of faith, and of interreligious experience, from the Jesus of history: 'To say "Jesus is Lord" may be considered as the epitome of the Christian confession of faith, but this sentence is not reversible without qualifications' (Panikkar, 1972, pp. 51–52). In his later works, he defends this position by means of distinction between belief and faith. He cites *Aquinas: 'The act of faith does not terminate in the enuntiable, but in the reality.' Faith reaches a reality that it intends, but it is unable to adequately enunciate what it reaches in its intention. When it speaks, it declares beliefs which fall far short of what it intends. Thus he concludes:

> The Christian encounter with Hinduism … is essentially neither a doctrinal dialogue nor the mutual comprehension of two cultures. It is a historical encounter of religions in the concrete meeting of Men in society. This encounter can take place, because it is an encounter in the Presence of the one who is already present in the hearts of those who *in good faith* belong to one or the other of the two religions. (Panikkar, 1981, p. 58)

Raimon Panikkar has thus emerged as a leading proponent of a pluralist theology of religions in which, first, he de-emphasizes the relationship of Jesus of Nazareth and the Christ, and second, distinguishes faith from belief. These two moves enable Panikkar to affirm a possible co-validity and co-efficacy to other religious traditions like Hinduism: 'The Christian cannot but believe (as the buddhists have also said with the same words and practically all religions in similar ways) that all that has been said about truth, goodness, and beauty are aspects of the Mystery which each tradition calls by its own name and the christian calls Christ' (Panikkar, 1996, p. 269).

DANIEL P. SHERIDAN

FURTHER READING: *Texts:* 'Faith and Belief: A Multireligious Experience,' in *The Intrareligious Dialogue* (New York, 1978); *Salvation in Christ: Concreteness and Universality. Supername* (Santa Barbara, CA, 1972); *The Trinity and the Religious Experience of Man: Icon-Person-Mystery* (New York, 1973); *The Unknown Christ of Hinduism* (Maryknoll, NY, rev. edn 1981 [1964]). *Studies:* E. Cousins, 'Panikkar's Advaitic Trinitarianism', G.J. Larsen, 'Contra Pluralism', and D. Sheridan, 'Faith in Jesus Christ in the Presence of Hindu Theism', in J. Prabhu (ed.), *The Intercultural Challenge of Raimon Panikkar* (Maryknoll, NY, 1996); K. Mitra, *Catholicism: Vedantic Investigations of Raimundo Panikkar's Attempt at Bridge Building* (Lanham, MD, 1987); R. Williams, 'Trinity and Pluralism', in *Christian Uniqueness Reconsidered: The Myth of a Pluralistic Theology of Religions* (ed. Gavin D'Costa; Maryknoll, NY, 1990); R. Smet, *Le Problème d'une théologie hindoue-chrétienne selon Raymond Panikkar* (Louvain-la-Neuve, 1983).

Pannenberg, Wolfhart (b. 1928)

German Lutheran systematic theologian. After narrowly escaping death as a teenage conscript in the final days of the Third Reich, Pannenberg turned from student interests in *Nietzsche and *Marx to study theology at Heidelberg (where he received his doctorate in 1954). There the watchword was 'history', and he was influenced by von Rad (Old Testament) and von Campenhausen (church history). Already in his dissertation on *Duns Scotus, Pannenberg considered the relationship between God and future contingency. He taught at Wuppertal with *Jürgen Moltmann, with whom he was loosely associated as a 'theologian of hope'. In 1967 he went to the University of Munich, where he has also directed the ecumenical institute (serving, e.g., in Lutheran-Roman Catholic dialogue).

Pannenberg burst on the theological scene in 1961 as a leader of the 'Heidelberg Group' with his essay 'Dogmatic Theses on the Doctrine of Revelation', in *Revelation as History* (1961). Even here one finds the enduring themes of the indirect revelation of God through history and anticipation of the eschatological revelation. *Jesus – God and Man* (1965), offering a classic 'Christology from below', gained notoriety for Pannenberg with its strong claim for the historicity of the resurrection of Jesus. In the following years Pannenberg published major works on individual *loci*. His study of theological and scientific method, *Theology and the Philosophy of Science*, typically stressed a rationality accessible to all (with *Barth as the implied opponent). Consistent with this is his interest in all branches of human knowledge, especially the natural sciences (e.g., *Toward a Theology of Nature* [1993]). His *Anthropology in Theological Perspective* understood human nature as 'basic trust' and openness-to-the-world (and, as such, essentially religious). Because of this view, Pannenberg is often understood as a foundationist (as *Hans Frei). His essays collected in English as *Basic Questions in Theology*, I-II, sought the substance of Scripture 'behind' the text, but then placed its historical content against an eschatological horizon. There also Pannenberg sought to overcome modern subjectivism and to deploy a modern emphasis on freedom by his concept of the 'God of the future', who 'exists only in the way in which the future is powerful over the present' (*Basic Questions*, II, p. 242). Both these ideas and their criticisms awaited the culmination of his career, *Systematic Theology*. Volume I (1988) treats method and the doctrine of God, volume II (1991) anthropology and Christology, and volume III (1993) ecclesiology and eschatology proper.

'Everything else ... remains insecure in theology, before one has made up one's mind on the doctrine of God' ('Autobiographical Sketch', in Braaten and Clayton, 1988). Pannenberg's concept of God's Trinitarian nature became more complex with 'The Subjectivity of God and the Doctrine of the Trinity' and 'Christology and Theology' (found in vol. II of *Basic Questions* [German, 1980]). His main view may be summarized in the following way. The consummation is the 'locus of the decision that the Trinitarian God is always the true God from eternity to eternity' (*Systematic Theology*, I, p. 331). From the future God 'puts himself in play', exposing himself to history in his Son, who through the Spirit raises the creation back in praise to the Father. Thus the future, already God's, occurs historically in Jesus and is 'inclusively' available to the creation in the risen Christ. To describe this doctrine of God, Pannenberg borrows the image of the field from physics in order to conceive of the one God as a web of relations between three distinct centres of action. Thus Pannenberg enriches his more abstract definition of God as the 'One who determines everything'.

Futurity, then, is the key concept for Pannenberg (*Jüngel). Thus theological statements depend on the analogy not of being (*Aquinas) or faith (Barth), but of the future, in accordance with their different relationships to it. (Here one can note that Pannenberg's *Habilitationsschrift* was an analogy although he, following his teacher Schlink, would prefer the term 'doxology' – see 'Analogy and Doxology' in *Basic Questions*, I). Human beings, met by God, are receptive because of their essential openness to that future. So each of Pannenberg's anthropological works fortifies this claim: *Theology and the Philosophy of Science* finds that all disciplines assume a future totality of meaning (building on Dilthey), and *Anthropology in Theological Perspective* concludes that our human essence is open historicity. Likewise, the contestation of the religions hinges on their capacity to take account of historical change and futurity into themselves (see especially 'Toward a Theology of the History of Religions', in

Basic Questions, II). Finally, Pannenberg's *Metaphysics and the Idea of God* seeks to give an ontological account of the future.

From this perspective we can understand the relationship between theology and philosophy. The latter fills a critical role in the field of open contestation for truth (here the debt is to Popper's critical rationalism), and defines God only in abstract terms as the 'infinite'. Christian theology goes further by conceiving of God as the 'concrete universal' (with debt to *Hegel) who not only transcends but also encompasses the finite as love. In his *Systematic Theology* Pannenberg makes Christianity's case by offering a reconstruction of all *loci*, in light of the Trinity, to demonstrate the latter's explanatory power. For example, he shows how the self-transcendence of creaturely life is a trace of the Trinity (*Systematic Theology*, II, 7.I.3). Seen as parts of this reconstruction, all the controversial ideas listed above come to take on a more traditional look.

Pannenberg's *Systematic Theology* is one of the great theological achievements of this century, but certain questions abide. How exactly do Pannenberg's anthropological, rationalist views fit together with his systematic, Trinitarian moments? Does his importation of a concept of eternity undo that of futurity (Jenson)? Is his theology of religions equally friendly to the answer of pluralism (Knitter)? Is his doctrine of the atonement underdeveloped (McGrath)? More generally, does he offer the crowning answer to modernity just when people are ceasing to ask the question (Huetter)?

Finally, a practical note about reading Pannenberg is in order. Due to his view of the history of transmission of tradition (with a debt to Gadamer), Pannenberg gives a voluminous account of every question before offering his own construction. Thus one may count on him for thorough background to most any debate, or one may move directly to the end of the section for Pannenberg's own argument.

GEORGE R. SUMNER, JR

FURTHER READING: *Text: An Introduction to Systematic Theology* (Grand Rapids, 1991). *Studies:* Philip Clayton and Carl Braaten (eds.), *The Theology of Wolfhart Pannenberg* (Minneapolis, 1988), American peers comment on his work; Stanley Grenz, *Reason for Hope* (New York, 1990); Jan Rohls and Gunther Wenz, *Vernunft des Glaubens* (Munich, 1988), essays by a distinguished group of colleagues and students.

Pascal, Blaise (1623–62)

Although Pascal never wrote a systematic account of any issue in theology or philosophy, his reflections on the nature and defence of Christian faith were important features of seventeenth-century European thought and continue to exercise considerable influence in theology and philosophy. Pascal's thinking on faith and reason, particularly as contained in his *Pensées*, continues to spark scholarly interest. To a lesser extent, his reflections on divine grace and morality found in *The Provincial Letters* have also generated contemporary study. Part of Pascal's appeal lies in the fact that he was a masterful literary stylist, whose aphorisms are well known.

Pascal was born in Auvergne, France. Following his mother's death in 1626, he and his two sisters were raised by their father, Étienne, a lawyer. Pascal was educated at home by his father, and he showed precocious talent in science. As a youth, Pascal participated in scholarly discussion on mathematics with some of the leading thinkers of the day, including *René Descartes (1596–1650), with whom he often disagreed on matters of science and philosophy.

As a scientist, Pascal is known (among other things) for his invention of the first functional calculating machine (which he constructed to help his father tabulate taxes for the French government) and for his experiments demonstrating the existence of a vacuum in nature. This was a matter of great controversy, since the consensus was that God would not leave any portion of creation empty: 'nature abhors a vacuum'. This fact, many claimed, could be known a priori. Pascal, however, favoured an experimental method for determining the facts of Nature, and he found nothing impious in his results. These efforts helped establish a more empirical, inductive and inquisitive approach to Nature – a matter of intense debate in seventeenth-century Europe. Descartes, for example, favoured a more deductive and rationalist approach. In his 'Preface to the Treatise on the Vacuum', Pascal wrote, 'Whatever the weight of antiquity, truth should always have the advantage, even when newly discovered, since it is always older than every opinion men have held about it.'

Pascal's specifically religious thought never challenged the legitimacy of his scientific endeavours. Nevertheless, after a mystical experience on 23 November 1654 (recorded in 'The

Memorial'), he devoted most of his efforts to the defence of the Christian faith against unbelievers and those whom he believed would compromise its integrity for the sake of popularity (the *Jesuits). Pascal's theological sensibilities and doctrine were decisively influenced by the *Jansenists, a group of Catholic reformists who championed the teachings of *Augustine as interpreted by Bishop Cornelius Jansen (1583–1638). Jansen's posthumously published three-volume work *Augustinus* (1640) had stirred debate within the Catholic Church concerning the effects of sin and the work of grace in the believer's life. (Five propositions attributed to Jansen were later deemed heretical by the Roman church.) Pascal defended Jansenist thought in a series of 19 individually released 'provincial letters' (1656–57), which evidenced keen wit, rhetorical flair and theological acumen. Pascal argued that the Jesuits denied the sovereignty of God and the sinfulness of humanity; therefore, they adjusted their notions of grace and ethical behaviour unbiblically.

Pascal is best known for his proposed but unfinished *Apology for the Christian Religion*, published as *Pensées*. After his death, a variety of written fragments were found among Pascal's belongings. These were published posthumously in 1670 and in many later editions. These pieces (some very short and others more developed), nevertheless, present a discernible orientation to the defence of the Christian faith. Pascal says,

> Men despise religion. They hate it and are afraid it may be true. The cure of this is first to show that religion is not contrary to reason, but worthy of reverence and respect. Next, make it attractive, make good men wish it were true, and then show that it is. Worthy of reverence because it really understands human nature. Attractive because it promises true good.

Instead of engaging in 'metaphysical proofs for God' (or natural theology), Pascal laboured to uncover the obstacles to faith that lie in the human self, such as the proclivity to diversion and the careless scepticism that dismisses religious questions. Although sometimes interpreted as being a fideist (largely because of his emphasis on 'reasons of the heart'), Pascal did not shun reason in favour of an irrational faith. 'If we submit everything to reason our religion will be left with nothing mysterious or

supernatural. If we offend the principles of reason our religion will be absurd and ridiculous.'

An important part of Pascal's argument is that Christian faith gives the best explanation for the human condition. In a set of arresting observations, Pascal depicts humans as 'deposed kings'. We bear the traces of royalty yet remain 'wretched' because of our mortality and moral failings. Our intellectual abilities catapult us far above the rest of creation, but a mere drop of water may slay us. Merely human philosophy ('proud reason') cannot solve this 'contradiction' of human greatness and misery. However, revelation tells us that we were made in the image of God and now are mired in original sin. This uniquely explains our contradictory condition. Christianity can also provide a unique way of liberation: 'Knowing God without knowing our own wretchedness makes for pride. Knowing our own wretchedness without knowing God makes for despair. Knowing Jesus Christ strikes the balance because he shows us both God and our own wretchedness.' While *Enlightenment thinkers such as Voltaire (1694–1778) dismissed Pascal as a misanthrope because of his reflections on human misery, Pascal recognized human dignity as well, and he had hope for those who come to Christian faith.

A legacy of Pascal's thought is his famous 'wager argument', which claims that in the face of uncertainty concerning God's existence, it is prudentially wiser to believe that God exists than not, given the consequences of unbelief should God exist. This argument is often caricatured and ridiculed, but it contains complexities and subtleties that philosophers continue to explore and apply. Further, Pascal did not rest his entire apologetic on this argument. It was reserved for those sceptics who would not be completely convinced by the rest of his apologetic.

Pascal's fertile mind and passionate faith make him a perennially important figure in the history of theology and philosophy, and his significance continues to be widely examined.

DOUGLAS GROOTHUIS

FURTHER READING: *Texts: Oeuvres Complètes* (Paris, 1963); *Pensées* (ed. A.J. Krailsheimer; New York, 1966); *Provincial Letters* (ed. A.J. Krailsheimer; New York, 1967). *Studies:* F.X.J. Coleman, *Neither Angel Nor Beast* (New York, 1986); Douglas Groothuis, 'Wagering Belief: Examining Two Objections to Pascal's Wager', *Rel St* 30 (1994), pp. 479–86; 'Deposed Royalty: Pascal's Anthropological Argument', *J Ev Th S* 41.2 (June 1998), pp. 297–312; Leszek Kolakowski, *God Owes Us Nothing: A Brief Remark on Pascal's Religion and the Spirit of Jansenism* (Chicago, 1995); Alban Krailsheimer, *Pascal* (New York, 1980); Peter Kreeft, *Christianity for Modern Pagans* (San Francisco, 1993); Marvin R. O'Connell, *Blaise Pascal: Reasons of the Heart* (Grand Rapids, 1997).

Pelagianism

A theological tendency in western Christendom in the early fifth century, Pelagianism was named after its reputed founder, the British-born layman Pelagius. Pelagianism, an outlook which constantly reappears in Christian thinking, emphasized human freedom and the ability and responsibility of the individual to obey the divine commandments through the natural powers of a will created by God and enlightened by the teachings of the gospel. It therefore saw no need for any particular enabling grace, except in the case of adult converts to Christianity, who needed the grace of baptism to wash away their sins and restore them to a state of primal innocence, after which they could, if they so willed, lead a sinless life.

For this reason it was the distinguishing mark of Pelagianism to deny traducianism, or the transmission of the guilt of Adam's sin to his descendants: every child is born in a state of primal innocence. Logically, this view removes any need for infant baptism for the remission of sins. In practice, however, the Pelagians regarded infant baptism as desirable, thinking it made the child a member of the kingdom of heaven. This left them without any clearly-defined answer to the question of the fate of infants who die unbaptized. *Augustine accused Pelagians of inventing an intermediate state between heaven and hell, thereby anticipating the medieval *limbus infantium*, but there is no evidence that they actually held such a doctrine. At heart, Pelagianism was concerned to exhort individuals to live according to their Christian profession, and its theology regarded the adult convert, who would almost inevitably be a sinner, as the typical baptismal candidate.

Owing largely to the polemics of Augustine, Pelagius has come to be regarded as the founder of Pelagianism; but it is not, in fact, easy to determine the degree of his influence. Pelagius's aristocratic disciple, Caelestius, actually initiated the controversy. Augustine's admirer, Marius

Mercator, considered that the real inspirer of Pelagianism was an eastern monk called Rufinus the Syrian. This Rufinus has been frequently, if not uncontroversially, identified with the priest Rufinus of St Jerome's monastery at Bethlehem, who resided at Rome with Jerome's friend Pammachius about 399. He has been further identified, again not uncontroversially, with the priest Rufinus of the province of Palestine, the author – according to the colophon of a manuscript now at St Petersburg – of a treatise *De Fide*, published by Jacques Sirmond in 1650. This work, which contains very forceful denunciations of traducianism, was noticed by the manuscript copyist to be Pelagian in character. Marius Mercator asserted that Rufinus disseminated his heretical teaching during the pontificate of Pope Anastasius (399–402), but discreetly, using Pelagius as his mouthpiece. This may be true.

Pelagius, in his commentary on the epistle to the Romans 5:15, quoted arguments against traducianism, from *De Fide* 40, without directly endorsing them. But Pelagius's real interest was in ascetic theology and in persuading men and women to live a monastic life. His theology was particularly concerned with the problem of the nature and operation of the human will and the need to defend Christian asceticism against any charge of Manicheism, while at the same time asserting that a sinless life was possible for any Christian who sought to live it. Thus he could tell Demetrias, the aristocratic Roman maiden who took the veil in 414, that to say that virtue was impossible was 'blind folly and profane rashness', as if God had imposed commands too heavy for human beings to bear.

Similar ideas were expressed by an unknown Pelagian writer, variously called 'the Sicilian Briton', 'the Sicilian Anonymous', and 'the Pelagian Anonymous' who, in a series of treatises, urged a doctrine of extreme asceticism as the proper way of Christian living. Pelagius was more moderate; but behind his moderation lurked the harshness which characterized Pelagian morality. 'In the day of judgement no mercy will be shown to wicked sinners, but they will be burned in everlasting fires' (quoted by Augustine, *De gestis Pelagii* 3,9; Jerome, *Dialogus adversus Pelagianos* I, 28). Historical Pelagianism had little of the optimism sometimes attributed to it in later ages.

Caelestius seems to have been more affected by the ideas of Rufinus the Syrian than was his master Pelagius. In 409, when the Goths menaced Rome, he and Pelagius fled to North Africa. Pelagius then went on to Palestine, where many Roman exiles had gathered, but Caelestius remained at Carthage and propagated anti-traducian ideas. For this he was accused in 411 of teaching heresy by a Milanese deacon named Paulinus (probably the biographer of *St Ambrose), on six counts: that Adam was created mortal and would have died, whether he sinned or not; that Adam's sin injured only himself and not the human race; that newly-born infants are in the same state as Adam before the Fall; that humanity as a whole did not die through Adam's death and sin, nor rise again through Christ's resurrection; that the Law had the same effect as the gospel in bringing people into the kingdom of heaven; and that even before the coming of Christ there had been sinless human beings.

These charges may possibly have misrepresented Caelestius's teaching, but as a whole they provide a convenient epitome of how Pelagian theology would have seemed in North Africa, where belief in the Fall and original sin was an article of faith. Caelestius argued that such belief was a matter of opinion, not faith. Challenged to provide examples of Catholic Christians who denied traducianism, he cited 'the holy priest Rufinus, who resided at Rome with the holy Pammachius. I heard him say that there is no transmission of sin' (Augustine, *De Gratia Christi* I, 3–4, 3).

As might be expected in Africa, Caelestius was found guilty and left Carthage for Antioch, where his opinions were apparently acceptable and he was ordained presbyter. The first attack upon Pelagian theology had been made in the area where, partly as a consequence of the Donatist controversy, the question of the nature of baptismal regeneration was a major theological issue.

Pelagius had not hitherto been much involved in controversy over his doctrinal teaching. In Jerusalem, however, he was on bad terms with *St Jerome, perhaps reopening a quarrel going back to the controversy over Jovinian in the early fifth century. In 414 Pelagius published his book *On Nature*, in which he spoke of grace in terms of creation, illumination and baptism, seeking to establish the possibility of sinlessness during earthly life and supporting his arguments by quotations from various authors, including Augustine's work, *On Free Choice*. It seems likely that it was this which swung Augustine into direct opposition, and he replied in a treatise, *On Nature and Grace*, which, while not naming Pelagius and admitting his good intentions in rousing sinners to a devout life, flatly opposed his teaching on grace as inadequate.

There was, however, worse to come from Augustine's point of view. In 415 Augustine's admirer, the Spanish priest Orosius, arrived in Jerusalem and accused Pelagius of heresy on the authority of his heroes, Jerome and Augustine. Pelagius declined to regard their teaching as the rule of faith and contrived to clear himself at a diocesan synod held at Jerusalem on 30 July 415 and then at a provincial synod at Diospolis (Lud) at the end of December. This was alarming in itself; but the situation was made worse by the fact that Bishop John of Jerusalem had accused Orosius of teaching that the Fall had so deeply corrupted human nature that man could not avoid sin, even with the grace of God.

It appeared that to a Greek theologian like Bishop John, Orosius's doctrine, avowedly based upon Jerome and Augustine, seemed to resemble that of the Messalian heretics. The latter maintained that evil was so deeply entrenched in human nature that baptism could only remove past sins, while leaving the soul of the baptized person untouched, so that only continuous prayer could expel the indwelling demon. Thus, the theology of the African church expounded by Augustine was equated with the teaching of an oriental heretical sect.

The news of the decisions of the synods of Jerusalem and Diospolis stirred the African bishops to action. Pope Innocent I (402–17) was persuaded to excommunicate both Pelagius and Caelestius on 27 January 417, and when his successor, Zosimus (417–18), attempted to reopen the case, the Africans flatly refused to recognize his power to do so. They brought pressure upon the imperial court at Ravenna, perhaps assisted by judicious bribery, so that on 30 April 418 the Emperor Honorius issued a rescript condemning those who denied the Fall. The next day, 1 May, a pan-African council at Carthage passed a series of nine canons against Pelagianism, expressing the doctrines of original sin and the damnation of unbaptized infants in the harshest terms. Under the pressure of imperial and African condemnation Zosimus gave way and condemned Pelagian theology.

For Pelagius, these condemnations meant ruin. He attempted to placate Augustine by confessing that grace is necessary, not only for every hour or moment, but for every individual action of our lives. Augustine, however, declared that he had never found any adequate admission of the need for enabling grace in Pelagius's writings and declined to accept his confession. Expelled from Palestine, Pelagius departed for Egypt and thereafter vanished from history. An attempt by Caelestius to enlist the support of *Nestorius of Constantinople in 430 only led to his own condemnation by the Council of Ephesus in 431, in language which ascribed to him the leadership of the Pelagian movement. Thereafter he, too, vanished from history.

After the condemnation of Pelagius and Caelestius in 418, a rearguard action in their support was fought by 18 Italian bishops, led by Julian of Eclanum. Julian naturally denied any transmission of original sin and emphasized human freedom – man was, in a famous phrase, 'emancipated from God' (Augustine, *Opus imperfectum* I, 78), and 'to will' was 'a movement of the soul without any exterior pressure' (*Op. imp.* V, 41). Julian delighted in repeatedly quoting Augustine's own definition of sin as 'the will to commit or to maintain what justice forbids and from which we are free to abstain' (Augustine, *De duabus animabus* 15, quoted in *Op. imp.* I, 44;82;104; II, 38;80, etc.), and there is a note of genuine moral indignation in his demand: 'Why attribute a crime to God? You say that God Himself judges in this way, is Himself a persecutor of the newly-born, Himself consigns to eternal fires for an evil will little children whom He knows to be unable to will either good or evil' (*Op. imp.* I, 48). Modern scholarship has paid tribute to Julian's ability, and he certainly angered and exasperated Augustine more than any other opponent.

Augustine's insistence on the divine initiative in bestowing grace brought him, at the end of his life, into conflict with theologians of southern Gaul, led by *John Cassian, to whom his doctrine smacked of fatalism and discouraged effort on the part of believers. While opposed to Augustine on this particular issue, they had no sympathy with Pelagius, and although commonly called semi-Pelagians would be better termed semi-Augustinians. Their outlook helped to moderate extreme Augustinianism in later medieval theology.

GERALD BONNER

FURTHER READING: *Original texts: Pelagius' Commentary on St Paul's Epistle to the Romans* (trans.

Theodore de Bruyn; Oxford, 1993); *The Letters of Pelagius and his Followers* (trans. B.R. Rees; Woodbridge, 1991); *Rufini Presbyteri Liber de Fide* (ed. and trans. M.W. Miller; Washington, DC, 1994). *Modern studies:* Gerald Bonner, *Augustine of Hippo: Life and Controversies* (Norwich, 2nd edn, 1988); *God's Decree and Man's Destiny* (London, 1987); *Church and Faith in the Patristic Tradition* (Aldershot, 1996); Peter Brown, *Augustine of Hippo* (London, 1967); *Religion and Society in the Age of St Augustine* (London, 1972); Robert F. Evans, *Pelagius: Inquiries and Reappraisals* (London, 1968); B.R. Rees, *Pelagius: A Reluctant Heretic* (Woodbridge, 1988); Rebecca H. Weaver, *Divine Grace and Human Agency: A Study of the Semi-Pelagian Controversy* (Macon, GA, 1996).

Philo the Theologian (15 BC – 50 AD)

Philo of Alexandria, the great Jewish exegete and philosopher, was a contemporary of Jesus Christ. He has been called the 'first theologian' (W. Bousset). The title is appropriate for at least two reasons. Philo's thought, as revealed in his copious writings, is relentlessly theocentric. The word for God (*theos*), which is but one of God's names, occurs nearly 2,500 times in Philo's works. Moreover, Philo is the first thinker in the Judaeo-Christian tradition who, clearly under the influence of Greek philosophy, develops and articulates a doctrine of God – albeit not in a systematic fashion. Philo's ideas, which exerted a much stronger influence on the Church Fathers than on the Rabbis, are foundational for the development of Christian theology.

Philo's context. Philo's thought can only be understood against the background of his historical and social environment. He lived all his life in Alexandria as a prominent member of the Jewish community. Although the community maintained strong ties to Jerusalem, Greek became the language spoken there, and in the educated circles to which Philo belonged there was a positive attitude to the achievements of Hellenic culture. Philo received an excellent training in Greek philosophy and showed a strong partiality for *Platonism, which was undergoing a revival at this time (i.e., the beginnings of so-called Middle Platonism). Philo's loyalty to Judaism, however, was unquestioned. Fundamental to the identity of the Jewish community was the Greek translation of the Bible, the Septuagint. Philo was convinced that the Septuagint translation of the books of Moses, the Pentateuch, represents God's word to his prophet no less than the Hebrew original (which he probably could not read). Philo thus undertook as his life's work the task of expounding the writings of Moses. Making extensive use of the allegorical method, but not neglecting the literal meaning, Philo wrote three extensive commentaries on the Pentateuch. The direct pretext for almost all theological statements in Philo are biblical texts. In his expositions he incorporates many ideas from earlier Jewish exegetes in Alexandria, but overlays them with his own mode of thinking, which is predominantly influenced by Platonism (but also includes themes from other Greek philosophical sources). Philo was convinced, however, that these ideas are present in the biblical text, as written by Moses, 'who had climbed to the very heights of philosophy' (*On the Creation of the World*, 8).

The central motifs. Philo's theological ideas can best be understood in terms of a fundamental distinction between God as he is in himself and God as he is in relation to what comes after him – that is, his creation. This point of departure results from combining Greek ontology with the interpretation of important biblical statements. The theology of God as he is in himself is largely negative, emphasizing what cannot be known. The theology of God in relation to his creation is more positive. God has created the universe and exercises care over what he has made. God's relationship to what comes after him, however, is often articulated with reference to hypostasized entities, a method which runs the risk of undermining fundamental Jewish monotheistic assumptions. A further central theme in Philo is God's relation to humankind, a two-way relationship which enabled Philo to develop a powerful new mode of theocentric spirituality.

God in himself. In Exodus 3:14 God reveals himself as *ho ōn*, 'he who is', or 'Being *simpliciter*'. By means of this remarkable Septuagint translation, Platonist ontology can be located in Mosaic Scripture. God is also emphatically One (though the *shema* is never actually cited by Philo). Crucial for Philo is the distinction between God's existence and essence. The former can be discerned with certainty via

creation. The latter is beyond the reach of humankind, as illustrated by Moses's ascent in Exodus 33, when he is unable to contemplate the fullness of God's being. Because names are indicative of a thing's nature, God is also unnameable ('Being' expresses that God is, but does not express his essence). The biblical names 'God' and 'Lord' indicate his relation to creation. They are revealed to the patriarchs out of compassion and as a reward for their virtue.

God as creator. The biblical account in Genesis 1–2 indicates that God is the maker of the universe and all it contains. God wills to create the cosmos because he is good (another Platonic theme). Philo affirms that God is the sole author and principle of created reality, and he has a strongly positive view of the cosmos' beauty and order. It is, however, a matter of controversy whether Philo regards creation as taking place *ex nihilo* (out of nothing). It is perhaps significant that he does not attain clarity on this issue. For Philo, matter has a negative colouring and is regarded as a source of evil, though not of the absolute moral evil which is committed by humankind through the agency of its free will.

The Logos and the divine powers. In describing the act of creation, Philo invokes the concept of God's Logos, which is clearly related to the repeated 'and God said' of Genesis 1 (Logos as 'word'), but is also conceived in philosophical terms (Logos as 'reason'). The Logos is the location of the transcendent divine ideas, which form the model for creation and represent a higher spiritual realm. The Logos is also represented in an immanent role as instrument of the divine creative activity which divides and orders the material realm. Closely related is the doctrine of God's powers, which are linked to the two chief divine names. The name of God (*theos*) represents God's creative power, the name Lord (*kyrios*) God's role as ruler and judge. The Logos and the powers are best interpreted in terms of the distinction between God 'in himself' and God 'in relation'. They are 'the face' of God (or of 'Being') as it is turned to created reality. Philo undeniably shows a tendency to hypostasize the Logos and the powers, as if they were separate from God himself, and in one famous text speaks of the Logos as the 'second God' (*Questions and Answers on Genesis*, 2.56). It is equally clear that Philo does not regard these theological conceptions as controverting the fundamental Jewish conviction that there is but one God.

The Logos and humankind. According to Genesis 1:26–27, humankind was created 'according to the image of God'. Philo interprets this text in Platonic terms. The image of God is his Logos. Humankind resembles its creator not as people with souls and bodies, but because human beings are endowed with intellectual and spiritual powers. These powers enable humankind to turn away from the body and material things and turn to the things of the mind or spirit – an ascent which may culminate in gaining sight of God and knowledge of him, to the extent that this can be attained. Many passages in Philo may be called mystical because they testify to a powerful sense of God's presence. Philo does not, however, speak of mystical union in the Plotinian or even *Augustinian sense. God's transcendence is too overwhelming, as illustrated by the Platonic image of blinding rays of light.

God and Israel. In his commentary on the Law, Philo writes: 'What the disciples of the most reputable [Greek] philosophy gain from its teaching, the Jews gain from their customs and laws, knowledge of the highest and most venerable cause of all things, whereby they reject the error of worshipping gods who have come into being.' Philo is particularist in his loyalty to Judaism and his strict observance of the Law, including the command to eliminate all forms of idolatry. At the same time, he is universalist in his conviction that reason is embedded in creation and in humankind, and that the study of Greek philosophy can lead to a deeper insight into the biblical text when it speaks about God.

Philo and Christianity. Philo's writings antedate the writings of the New Testament by a few decades. No direct influence can be discerned. The closest parallels are found in the gospel of John (especially the doctrine of the Logos), in the epistle to the Hebrews (the heavenly tabernacle) and in the Pauline corpus (*sophia* and *ōsis*, Christ as heavenly Adam). The New Testament is not, however, Hellenized and Platonized to the same profound extent as Philo's thought has been. Shared themes were noted by the Church Fathers, first in the Alexandrian tradition (*Clement, *Origen, *Eusebius) and later in wider circles (Gregory of Nyssa,

*Ambrose, Augustine). Philo was adopted as a Church Father *honoris causa*, and his influence on the development of Christian theology was considerable. Examples of such influence are the doctrine of the Logos in Alexandrian theology and *Arianism, the doctrine of the immutability of God in Origen, and the theme of the infinite quest for knowledge of God in Gregory of Nyssa. The Rabbis, on the other hand, did not approve of the Hellenized nature of Philo's thought and never cite him. Paradoxically, Philo's writings, the major corpus of Hellenistic Judaism, would have been lost if they had not been preserved by the Christian church.

DAVID T. RUNIA

FURTHER READING: H. Braun, *Wie Man über Gott nicht denken soll: dargelegt an Gedankengängen Philos von Alexandrien* (Tübingen, 1971); J. Dillon, *The Middle Platonists: A Study of Platonism 80 BC to AD 220* (London, 1977), esp. pp. 155–68; G. May, *Creatio ex nihilo: The Doctrine of 'Creation out of Nothing' in Early Christian Thought* (Edinburgh, 1994), esp. pp. 9–20; L.A. Montes-Peral, *Akataleptos theos: der unfassbare Gott* (Leiden, 1987); G. Reale and R. Radice, *Filone di Alessandria: La filosofia Mosaica* (Milan, 1987), pp. liv–cxxiv; D.T. Runia, *Philo of Alexandria and the* Timaeus *of Plato* (Philosophia Antiqua 44; Leiden, 2nd edn, 1986), esp. pp. 433–75; 'God and Man in Philo of Alexandria', *J Th St* 39 (1988), pp. 48–75 (reprinted in Runia, *Exegesis and Philosophy: Studies on Philo of Alexandria* [London, 1990]); G. Sellin, 'Gotteserkenntnis und Gotteserfahrung bei Philo von Alexandria', in *Monotheismus und Christologie: zur Gottesfrage im hellenistischen Judentum und im Urchristentum* (ed. H.-J. Klauck; Freiburg, 1992), pp. 17–41; T.H. Tobin, 'Article "Logos"', *ABD* 4 (New York, 1992), pp. 348–56; D. Winston, *Logos and Mystical Theology in Philo of Alexandria* (Cincinnati, 1985); H.A. Wolfson, *Philo: Foundations of Religious Philosophy in Judaism, Christianity and Islam* (2 vols.; Cambridge, MA, 1947, 1968).

Photius (c. 810 – c. 893)

Patriarch of Constantinople 858–67 and again 878–86. He followed a career in the imperial service as a young man and was still a layman when elected patriarch. He was first elected with the support of Emperor Michael III (842–67) to replace Ignatius, who was patriarch 847–58 and 867–77. Ignatius's supporters appealed to Pope Nicholas I (858–67), who refused to accept Photius as legitimate patriarch and sent legates to investigate the matter, but Nicholas subsequently rejected the report of his legates when they found in favour of Photius. In 863 he declared Photius deposed and excommunicated, and in a rebuke to the emperor lectured him on the authority of the Roman see. Spurred on by Byzantine displeasure over Roman missionary activity in Bulgaria, Photius convened a synod in Constantinople in 867, which excommunicated Pope Nicholas and declared him deposed.

In the same year, Emperor Basil I (867–86) murdered Michael III, deposed Photius and reinstated Ignatius. This failed to improve relations with Rome, however, as Ignatius was just as determined as Photius to defend Constantinople's jurisdiction in Bulgaria, and he acted to resolve the conflict between Latin and Greek missions in Bulgaria in favour of the Greeks. Photius was restored on Ignatius's death, and at a council in 879–80 he was reconciled with Rome, but when Leo VI became emperor in 886 Photius lost favour and was deposed once again.

Photius exercised considerable influence in several spheres of Byzantine thought and culture. He was the first to write an apology, *The Mystagogy of the Holy Spirit*, explaining the Greek rejection of the addition of the *filioque* to the Nicene Creed and maintaining that the Holy Spirit proceeds from the Father alone. The addition of the *filioque* became an issue for Photius through its introduction in Bulgaria by Roman missionaries. He is still cited as an authority on this question by Orthodox theologians in ecumenical dialogue with other denominations. His interest in philology and classical literature is evident in his *Lexicon*, while his collection of essays entitled the *Amphilochia* reflects his interest in a variety of theological topics, including biblical criticism. He is probably best known, however, for his *Bibliotheca* – a collection of critical entries on his reading of 279 books. It was compiled at the request of his brother Tarasius and was probably written around 838. It is an invaluable source of information about books and their availability in ninth-century Byzantium. His many letters and homilies are also of considerable historical and theological interest.

KEN PARRY

FURTHER READING: Texts: *The Mystagogy of the Holy Spirit* (trans. J. Farrel; Brookline, MA, 1987); *The Bibliotheca* (trans. N.G. Wilson; London, 1994); *The Homilies of Photios Patriarch of Constantinople* (trans. C. Mango; Cambridge, MA, 1958). Studies: P. Lemerle, *Byzantine Humanism: The First Phase*

(Canberra, 1986); N.G. Wilson, *Scholars of Byzantium* (London, 1983).

Platonism

In much contemporary theology Plato is viewed, along with the *Enlightenment, as one of the two major corrupting influences in the intellectual shaping of Christianity. While the Enlightenment is held to have brought with it an unhealthy rationalism and excessive confidence in the methods and results of biblical criticism, Platonism is blamed for an otherworldliness and dualism that is seen as fundamentally in conflict with Scripture, especially Scripture's stress on a this-worldly eschatological hope. While some major contrasts cannot be denied, the reasons for the popularity of Platonism are explored below – first by examining it as a philosophical system in its own right and then by tracing its influence across the centuries upon historical Christianity.

Platonism as a philosophy. Plato (427–347 BC), as a former pupil of Socrates (d. 399 BC), initially followed his teacher's presumed interests in exploring the nature of the virtues and their possible definition. He did this through a number of dialogues; the *Euthyphro*, for example, considers piety, the *Laches,* courage. Although the need for habitual reinforcement is stressed, the key is found to lie in intellectual knowledge of what constitutes the good, and it is this insight that leads Plato to develop Socrates' thought in a more metaphysical direction. In exploring the nature of justice in his most famous dialogue, the *Republic*, Plato concludes that all items in the world are only intelligible insofar as we understand their teleology – what they are trying to be good at. A knife, for instance, only has intelligible reality insofar as it is good at a knife's characteristic function, cutting; a circle, at achieving its *raison d'être*, the circumference at all its points perfectly equidistant from its centre; and so on. But neither such a circle nor a knife capable of cutting absolutely anything exists in our world. So, Plato concludes, the 'forms' or 'ideas' or things that give intelligibility to our world are in fact to be found in another, non-material world, as also the supreme form upon which all other forms depend, the Form of the Good. It is into this context that Plato's attack on art must be placed (*Republic* X), for, assuming that art seeks to represent the visible world, it becomes an imperfect copy of what is itself an imperfect copy (the world imitating the forms). Although not conceived of as personal, in introducing the Form of the Good Plato uses quasi-mystical, religious language (VI, esp. 508–9). Another dialogue, however, the *Timaeus*, does offer a 'story' of creation, in which a creator-god, the Demiurge, creates by bringing order to disordered, inchoate matter and looking to the forms for inspiration. Life is given to matter through a 'world-soul' and 'soul' is how Plato understands human identity, in particular our ability to know that other world of the forms. Yet another dialogue, the *Phaedo*, offers four arguments for the immortality of the soul. However, it would be a mistake to think that Plato thought physical reality unimportant or that he regarded it as evil. In the *Symposium* he defends physical or erotic love as a vehicle towards more profound types of knowledge, while his attitude to the arts is nuanced not only by his careful attention to literary style but also by the fact that in the *Phaedrus* he concedes to poetic inspiration a divine source. What is true is that he regarded anything material as necessarily a lower order of reality, however closely it might aspire to the world of the forms; various degrees of 'imitation' and 'participation' remain the order of the day, rather than complete perfection. It should also be noted that Plato was very willing to face difficulties in his own position, as in the *Parmenides* where he mentions objections to the theory of forms in the course of discussing the relation between the One and the many – although he offers no resolution.

Plato's most famous successor in developing his views was Plotinus (AD 205–70). His system, known as Neoplatonism, succeeded a period in the centuries immediately preceding and following Christ's birth that was characterized by eclecticism. During this time, figures such as Plutarch, Alcinous, Numenius and Apuleius borrowed freely from other ancient philosophical systems and attempted to give Platonism a more explicitly religious dimension. This transitional period is commonly known as Middle Platonism. One disputed element was whether Plato had ever intended his 'story' of creation literally. Plotinus doubted it, and so he produced a system of emanation whereby the world emerges from the overflowing abundance of the divine, with the three transcendent elements in Plato's thought now codified (in descending order) as the One (or Good), the

Divine Mind or *Nous*, and the World-Soul. In this system, the activity of the World-Soul is seen as inferior to the kind of intellectual thought that the Mind enjoys. But the activity of the Mind is viewed in turn as inferior to the mystical existence beyond division in the One, only made possible where the Mind is no longer forced to distinguish itself from the objects of its thought in order to reflect upon them. To understand such a mystical claim, one might compare situations where a human being becomes so wholly absorbed in contemplation that awareness of self evaporates. It is therefore no surprise that the proper goal of human beings is seen in similar terms. In his famous phrase, 'the flight of the alone to the Alone' (*Enneads* VI, 9), the divisions of the personality and of the world are wholly transcended. Once again, though, it is important not to interpret such sentiments as a rejection of the world, but only as an assertion of its limitations. Indeed, now that the world is seen as having its source directly in the divine, it has also become in a sense divine. Plotinus explicitly attacks *Gnostics who declare the world to be evil (*Enneads* II, 9).

Platonism and Christianity. Some biblical scholars have detected the influence of Platonism in the Gospel of John and in the epistle to the Hebrews. Although any direct influence is perhaps unlikely, to read John's reference to the Logos not only as an allusion to the opening chapter of Genesis but also to the philosophical notion of Logos as a principle of intelligibility or explanation (a notion found in both Platonism and Stoicism) could be seen as giving added power to the passage: Christ is not only God's Word but also our primary clue to understanding ourselves and our world. Such a sense had already been exploited by *Philo (d. AD 40) on behalf of Judaism, and in second-century Christianity it plays a large role in the writings of the *Apologists. The best known among them, *Justin Martyr, even detects an allusion to the cross in Plato's *Timaeus* (*Apology* 60). In the third century, *Clement of Alexandria and *Origen are often identified as 'Christian Platonists'. Origen may even have shared the same teacher with Plotinus, Ammonius Saccas. Some centuries later, Origen's writings were to be condemned as heretical, but it remains incontestable not only that he was the greatest Christian intellect before *Augustine but also that his Platonism was pursued through active engagement with the Scriptures, on which he produced numerous scholarly commentaries.

In trying to comprehend the attractiveness of Platonism to the Church Fathers, a number of key factors can be identified. First, as Origen's own interest indicates, there are in fact quite a number of biblical passages which quite easily lend themselves to a Platonic reading, not only in John and Hebrews but also in Paul (e.g. 2 Cor. 4:16 – 5:5). Secondly, Platonism is useful as a missionary strategy as it expresses faith in categories already familiar within contemporary Gentile culture. Thirdly, unlike the other obvious candidate, Stoicism, which reduced the divine to a wholly immanent, material reality, Platonism insisted upon the transcendence of the divine. Yet it was a transcendence that remained accessible to human beings, because Platonism saw them as sharing the same fundamental identity as non-physical realities – souls. Notions such as creation or the divine image thus admitted of easy expression. Fourthly, both John and Paul had used images of participation in Christ, and that meant that the significance of Christ could be seen in some ways as the perfect 'form' of humanity with our 'reality' or salvation dependent on how far we are able to imitate or participate in that perfect humanity. Fifthly, the Platonic language of participation seemed to offer the possibility of a realist approach to the sacraments that could nonetheless avoid the complete equation of symbol and reality that the later *Aristotelian approach appeared to require. Finally, Neoplatonism had already developed a clear triadic structure for the Godhead, and, if Origen retained its implied subordinationism, Augustine (354–430) succeeded in integrating some of its key elements into *Nicene orthodoxy. The forms had become 'ideas' in the mind of Augustine. Yet Platonism's continuing influence is perhaps most clearly seen in the prayer with which his *De Trinitate* ends, as in effect it expresses the hope that Augustine may be one even as God is One.

Some later writers, though, are much more explicitly Platonic than Augustine, among them Pseudo-Denys (c. 500) or *Dionysius the Areopagite. He was hugely influential on later thought in part because of the mistaken identification of this anonymous author with the Greek who heard Paul preach on the Areopagus Hill in Athens (Acts 17:34). God is beyond all description, but 'deification' or union with him

becomes possible once we take seriously the symbolic, hierarchically ordered nature of the universe. Although the rediscovery of Aristotle's writings meant that the primary influence on *Aquinas (1225–74) was Aristotle, whom Aquinas constantly refers to simply as 'the philosopher', Augustine and Denys are also frequently quoted; so it is not true that Platonism ceases to be influential from this point on. One of Aquinas's five arguments for God's existence, for instance, is thoroughly Platonic, based as it is on degrees of goodness (his 'Fourth Way'). Nonetheless, Aquinas does mark a significant departure. Human knowledge of the divine was now seen as necessarily mediated through the empirical world, and so the body was viewed as indispensable in understanding who and what we are. While this new focus on the empirical world undoubtedly contributed towards the rise of science, there was also a negative impact on theology. Whereas Platonism spoke of participation, Aristotelianism identified a gap that needed to be bridged, and, while Aquinas was confident that this could be done, theologians of the later Middle Ages often assumed that this was only possible by divine fiat. There was thus increasing emphasis on the arbitrary exercise of divine power that continued into the *Reformation with *Luther and *Calvin. The other side of that coin, though, should not be forgotten, in their stress on the graciousness of God in Christ and the unique value given to revelation in bridging the gap.

Yet it is by no means the case that the influence of Platonism ceased with the Reformation. The immortality of the soul was, for instance, enshrined as an article of faith in the Westminster Confession; yet this only really makes sense on Platonic dualist assumptions that we are two entities, body and soul, and not just one, a psychosomatic unity. But it is elsewhere that we must look for a deeper impact, and particularly to the Florentine Academy under Marsilio Ficino (d.1499) and Pico della Mirandola (d. 1494). These two had a profound impact on Renaissance thought (and also art, as in the work of Michelangelo), not least through Ficino translating the entire corpus of Plato and Plotinus into Latin. Hitherto the *Timaeus* had been the most influential work within that corpus, whereas now a more rounded picture became available, including aspects that pulled further away from orthodox Christianity. The latter is particularly evident where Christianity,

Neoplatonism and Jewish Kabbalistic thought were intertwined, as in the writings of Jacob Böhme (1575–1624), which were influential upon Christian thinkers as diverse as *Wesley and *Hegel. More traditional attempts at integration are, however, to be observed – among them the work of the seventeenth-century Cambridge Platonists. Ralph Cudworth (d. 1688), Henry More (d. 1687) and their associates were concerned with what they saw in the writings of *Descartes and Hobbes as the alienation of the natural world from any deep divine involvement. They responded by giving the Holy Spirit some of the characteristics of the Platonic World-Soul, while their reaction to what they viewed as the arbitrary character of Calvin's God was to insist that reason characterized every aspect of his activity.

*Schleiermacher (1768–1834) is often regarded as the founder of modern theology. His interest in hermeneutics was in part generated by his decision to translate the Platonic corpus into German. The impact of Plato is still to be seen in his mature theology, perhaps most notably in his presentation of Christ as the *Urbild* or ideal form for humanity, and in his understanding of God as the unifying force underlying the world's pluriformity (a position that was to lead to accusations of pantheism). In England, the enormous influence of *Joseph Butler (d. 1752) ensured the continuing impact of Aristotle, and this is reflected in the writings of *John Newman (d. 1890), but both *Coleridge (d. 1834) and *F.D. Maurice (d. 1872) indicate the beginnings of an alternative trend in nineteenth-century England. If stress on the Logos and the presence of the universal in the particular are perhaps predictable, more surprising is the prominence given by them to the notion of truth as the reconciliation of opposites – really a development of later Neoplatonism but often attributed to Plato himself in the *Parmenides*. Benjamin Jowett (d. 1893) was largely responsible for making Plato a compulsory part of the Oxford philosophical syllabus (hitherto confined to Aristotle and Butler), and it seems likely that this played its part in giving a more Platonic character to later Anglo-Catholic thought, with its focus on the incarnation and the sacramental character of the world. *Charles Gore (1853–1932), for instance, was responsible for the teaching of Plato while a fellow of Trinity.

Pope Leo XIII's encyclical 'Aeterni Patris' of 1879, in effect making the study of Aquinas compulsory in all seminaries, ensured a demotion of Plato in Roman Catholic circles during the twentieth century, while the dominance of *Barth (d. 1968) in Protestant theology exercised a comparable restraining influence among Protestants. Even so, there were some contrary trends, but with Platonism usually mediated quite indirectly. So, for example, some parallels can be seen in the writings of *Karl Rahner (d. 1984), but these have probably been mediated through, among others, Schleiermacher, just as with *Paul Tillich (d. 1965) they initially came through his enthusiasm for Schelling, a contemporary of Hegel. On his key contrast between essence and existence Tillich is prepared to declare that 'on this point the Platonic and the Christian evaluations of existence coincide' (*Systematic Theology* II, p. 23), while his notion of God as the reconciliation of conflicting 'polarities' (I, pp. 181ff.) has much in common with later Neoplatonism. In late twentieth-century England, though, the most influential voice for a Platonist approach to Christianity was not, strictly speaking, a theologian at all but the philosopher and novelist, Iris Murdoch (d. 1998).

At the dawn of a new millennium, the influence of Plato now seems very weak. In some ways little else could be expected. Defenders of a dualistic understanding of human identity are now few and far between, and, as science brings mind and brain ever closer together, it looks as though we can survive death, if at all, only by bodily resurrection and not through the immortality of the soul. Yet other aspects might still continue to present a challenge. The question, for instance, remains whether Scripture can bear all the weight that Barth puts upon it, or whether a more participatory relation between the world and God is not required, if biblical revelation is not to be seen as an absurd and implausible exception. Even Plato's views on art have acquired a new relevance, since abstract artists such as Kandinsky, Klee and Mondrian argued that art in any case should not proceed by imitation of Nature but through intuiting the world's underlying spiritual reality.

DAVID BROWN

FURTHER READING: M.J.B. Allen, *The Platonism of Marsilio Ficino* (Berkeley, 1984); L.P. Gerson, *God and Greek Philosophy* (London, 1990); L.P. Gerson (ed.), *The Cambridge Companion to Plotinus* (Cambridge, 1996); J.P. Kenney, *Mystical Monotheism: A*

Study in Ancient Platonic Theology (Hanover, NH / London, 1991); R. Kraut (ed.), *The Cambridge Companion to Plato* (Cambridge, 1992); R. Kroll, R. Ashcraft and P. Zagorin (eds.), *Philosophy, Science and Religion in England, 1640–1700* (Cambridge, 1992); A.O. Lovejoy, *The Great Chain of Being* (New York, 1960); A. Louth, *The Origins of the Christian Mystical Tradition: From Plato to Denys* (Oxford, 1981); I. Murdoch, *Metaphysics as a Guide to Morals* (London, 1992); D. Newsome, *Two Classes of Men: Platonism and English Romantic Thought* (London, 1974); J.M. Rist, *Augustine: Ancient Thought Baptized* (Cambridge, 1994); G.C. Stead, *Philosophy in Christian Antiquity* (Cambridge, 1994).

Postliberal Theology

'Postliberalism' is a term used to describe certain interests shared by a cluster of theological research projects of Yale scholars in the 1970s and 1980s. (The original political background of the term was a more radical sense, in the 1970s, of moving beyond liberalism. Brown and Devaney, however, point out in 'Postliberalism', in *Blackwell's Encyclopedia of Modern Christian Thought* [ed. A. McGrath; Oxford, 1993], that, by the 1980s, the term had taken on a more conservative ring.) The term itself is derived from the final chapter of *The Nature of Doctrine* (pp. 113–35) by George Lindbeck, one of the seminal scholars in question. The primary common interest was hermeneutics, though not of the grander philosophical sort represented by Gadamer or *Ricoeur. In spite of the Old Testament scholar Brevard Childs' own explicit doubts about and distancing from the 'Yale School' (see, e.g., his criticism of Lindbeck's 'functionalism' in *Biblical Theology of the Old and New Testaments* [Minneapolis, 1992], p. 22, and his own reference to the 'Yale School' in *The New Testament as Canon: An Introduction* [Philadelphia, 1985], pp. 541–6), Childs, Lindbeck and the theologian *Hans Frei all shared, in their various ways, the conviction that there is a distinctively Christian way to read the Bible, and that this involved retrieving a 'pre-critical' mode of interpretation. The latter assumption implied that modernity had in various ways distorted the reading of Scripture for Christians, but that one could not naïvely suppose that a simple rejection of the historical-critical method sufficed. Rather, each scholar offered, in addition to a critique of modern theology, complex arguments which combined functional-social scientific, descriptive-historical and more

normative, properly theological warrants in support of a 'post-critical' hermeneutic for the church (see Michael Polanyi in his *Personal Knowledge* [Chicago, 1958]). Though each inherited the *Barthian suspicion of making the apologetic task too prominent (lest it render theology captive to culture), ironically the work of these scholars, independent though convergent, has amounted to an extended apologetic argument for the credibility of such a hermeneutic. An interesting case in point is William Placher's introduction to the major sources and issues in postliberalism, *Unapologetic Theology: A Christian Voice in a Pluralistic Conversation* (Louisville, 1989). By placing postliberalism among contemporary thinkers like Rorty, MacIntyre and Geertz, Placher offers a kind of apologetic for postliberalism itself.

Noting postliberalism's theological and philosophical antecedents will be helpful. Both Frei and Lindbeck (we will focus on these authors; for Childs, see *Canonical Theology*) were Yale students of H. Richard Niebuhr, whose influence is evident in their work. The interest in story found in Niebuhr's *The Meaning of Revelation* (New York, 1941) and in careful sociological analysis found, for example, in *The Social Sources of Denominationalism* (New York, 1929), are obvious antecedents. The latter dovetails, secondly, with an interest in the close study ('thick description' in the congenial phrase of the anthropologist Clifford Geertz) of particular religious traditions with the help of the social sciences. Thirdly, one may point to an interest in and the influence of the theology of Karl Barth. His *Anselmian insistence that theology must be 'faith seeking understanding', that one could discover the 'strange new world of the Bible' on the far side of the liberal project, etc., characterized their theological environment. Fourthly, one can readily see the influence of Yale's philosophical theologians in their formative era. William Christian studied the logic of the official doctrines of particular religious communities. The fruit of his career's work may be found in *The Doctrines of Religious Communities* (New Haven, 1987). Paul Holmer reflected on the application to theology of the philosophy of *Ludwig Wittgenstein, who focused on the meaning of words as they are used in communities and used terms like 'rule' and 'grammar' to characterize such uses (see, e.g., *The Grammar of Faith* [New York, 1978]).

Hans Frei argues in *The Eclipse of Biblical*

Narrative that, until the modern period, the 'words and sentences [of the Bible] meant what they said' (p. 1). This priority of the literal sense implied that the story described actual historical occurrences, that it constituted 'a single world of one temporal sequence' when read figurally, and that the faithful reader could and should 'fit himself into that world' (pp. 2, 3). But eighteenth-century interpreters, both radical and conservative, came to find the meaning of the text in its referent behind the text, and so to create a distance between the stories and the reality they describe. What, then, might a hermeneutic appropriate to the Bible's 'history-like' narrative look like? In Frei's *The Identity of Jesus Christ* the passion-narrative, in contrast to literary presentations of the Christ-archetype, renders Jesus' intentional identity even as he moves from power to powerlessness. In the resurrection, for the believer and as related by the Gospels, Jesus' identity implies his presence; Frei finds here a unique analogue to Anselm's ontological argument. Finally, *Types of Christian Theology* draws the implications for systematic theology. The logic of 'coming to believe' is multifarious and different from that of the logic of 'belief'. So, accounts of the Christian which allow external philosophical criteria to dictate the substance of theological claims are problematic.

George Lindbeck, a veteran of ecumenical dialogue between *Lutherans and Catholics, introduces his *The Nature of Doctrine* as a response to an ecumenical conundrum: how can participants of differing confessional backgrounds come to new agreement without abandoning venerable (and conflicting) doctrinal commitments? In reply Lindbeck offers, first, an understanding of religion, and second, a theory of doctrine. On the first count, he begins by laying out a typology of religion: the propositional, which sees claims as true or false regardless of context; the experiential-expressivist, which understands religious claims as ways of speaking of pre-linguistic, universal states of the human subject; and the cultural-linguistic. This last alternative understands the particular language and practices of a community to be conditions for the experiences possible within it. This leads to Lindbeck's regulative theory of doctrine, namely that doctrine serves as second-order rules for the boundaries of appropriately Christian talk, while allowing a wide variety of actual, first-order ways of speaking. At the same time one must also pay attention to the practices and virtues distinctive to the Christian form of life; a crusader who says 'Christ is Lord' with a raised sword disqualifies his own claim. The main criterion of truth in such a view is 'intrasystemic' coherence, though Lindbeck does allow that religions as a whole may be seen, holistically, as massive 'propositions' whose 'correspondence' to the truth will only be known at the eschaton. In the meantime, a religion might prove particularly potent in assimilating the claims of its surrounding environment. This relates to the practice of 'intertexuality', by which one absorbs the world into the scriptural text. Lindbeck has also wondered in what sort of church this kind of reading might take place. Earlier in his career Lindbeck speculated that, in the present liberal, secular environment, the church would have to become more sectarian in a sociological sense while retaining a more catholic vision of theology in order sufficiently to socialize its members into its practices (see 'The Sectarian Future of the Church', in *The God Experience* [ed. J.P. Whelan; New York, 1971], pp. 226–43). More recently, Lindbeck has turned his attention to ecclesiology proper and emphasized the 'Israel-like' identity of the church (see 'The Church', in *Keeping the Faith: Essays Marking the Centenary of 'Lux Mundi'* [Philadelphia, 1988]).

Every brand of theology has some pervasive question. Each of postliberalism's major authors has a concern for the safeguarding of Christian identity in its concrete particularity. For Frei, the gospel narrative renders the unsubstitutable identity of the crucified and risen Christ. Lindbeck shows how doctrines operate as a distinctively Christian grammar, so that the Scriptures can be read according to the 'rule of faith' and the world 'absorbed' in a myriad of contexts. Childs sets that gospel narrative in the wider setting of the canon, within whose diverse, bipartite confines the Christian interpreter must listen. Likewise, Stanley Hauerwas explores those distinctive Christian practices (most prominently peacemaking and hospitality) which become the conditions for understanding within the church. Previously of Notre Dame, and then at Duke University, Hauerwas has written, among main titles, the following: *Community of Character: Toward a Constructive Christian Social Ethic* (Notre Dame, 1981) and *Resident Aliens: Life in the Christian Colony* (with William Willimon; Philadelphia, 1988). He has worked extensively in ethics, but eschews the distinction between it and theology. His indebtedness to Frei may be seen in the prominence of the category of 'story', and to Alasdair MacIntyre in his emphasis on distinctive practices and virtues.

These seminal thinkers set out a program, but it awaits a subsequent generation of theologians who will move beyond prolegomena to produce works on specific *loci*. One can offer examples of younger theologians who have taken up this challenge. Ronald Thiemann's *Revelation and Theology: The Gospel as Narrated Promise* (Notre Dame, 1985) offers a postliberal theology of revelation first by dissociating it from post-Enlightenment foundationalism, the philosophical requirement of a norm of truth independent of the Christian Scripture and tradition. Bruce Marshall in his *Christologies in Conflict* (Oxford, 1987) shows how a theological proposal like *Karl Rahner's, which commences with a general consideration of human openness to transcendence, can never find the particular identity of the individual Jesus of Nazareth necessary. Only commencing with a narrative rendering of Jesus' identity (as Barth does), can do so. Kathryn Tanner in her *God and Creation in Christian Theology* (Oxford, 1988) offers a 'rule' for Christian talk about God's relation to and activity in creation, namely that God is free to act through or directly upon the created order. Joseph DiNoia in his *The Diversity of Religions* (Washington, DC, 1992) explores Lindbeck's suggestion that different traditions pursue distinctly different goals.

What are the standard criticisms of postliberalism, and how might it respond? Postliberalism has been attacked from many sides, though all the critiques fall under the general rubric of 'ghettoism' (James Gustafson, 'The Sectarian Temptation: Reflections on Theology, the Church, and the University', *Cath Th S Pr* 40 [1985], pp.83–94). Liberal theological critics have claimed that postliberalism amounts to fideism, the ostrich-like refusal intellectually to engage the culture around it. By contrast, liberationists would point to an ethical intransigence, an in-built 'preferential option' for the inherited and venerable. An interesting example of this critique may be found from within the 'postliberal' Yale fold in Kathryn Tanner's *Theories of Culture: A New Agenda for Theology* (Minneapolis, 1997). The book is at the same time an example of the risk that postliberalism can trail off into a

more extreme historicism. Criticism also comes from the evangelical side of the aisle. Carl Henry, in an exchange with Frei, worried that an emphasis on narrative was incapable of standing in for a full doctrine of inspiration. (See particularly George Hunsinger's 'Can Evangelicals and Postliberals Learn From One Another? The Carl Henry-Hans Frei Exchange Reconsidered', in *The Nature of Conversion: Evangelicals and Postliberals in Conversation* [eds. Timothy Phillips and Dennis Okholm; Downers Grove, IL, 1996], pp. 135–50. In general, this book gives a good account of the conversation between the two groups.) Alister McGrath has attacked Lindbeck's position for shirking the questions of history and truth (see *The Genesis of Doctrine: A Study in Foundations of Doctrinal Criticism* [Oxford, 1990], though one may note that the alternative McGrath offers sounds quite Lindbeckian), while others have found the approach overly historicist. Evangelicals, though intrigued by postliberalism, also worry that its notion of different religions speaking different 'languages' undercuts the imperative of evangelism.

Postliberalism might reply that it contributes first and foremost a series of insights in the service of retrieving a way of reading the Bible for the church. Here we can note the contribution of David Kelsey, also a Yale theologian, to postliberalism. His analytic study, *Uses of Scripture in Recent Theology* (Philadelphia, 1975), emphasized that to speak of the Bible as Scripture is to speak of a particular function the writings play for the community. The book's section on Barth contains an important discussion of the function of the Gospels in rendering identity. Postliberalism, then, would insist that its 'generous orthodoxy' (Frei's phrase) not be mistaken for an effort at repristination. Furthermore, the grammar of doctrine makes meaningful disagreement possible (see here Alasdair McIntyre, the moral philosopher who has been influential for postliberals, esp. *After Virtue* [Notre Dame, 1981]). On the questions of truth and engagement it encourages apologetics, but of an *ad hoc* sort (to use Frei's phrase). It offers its claims with 'universal intent'. This phrase of Polanyi's is used often by *Lesslie Newbigin, the missiologist and theologian of culture influenced by postliberalism (see particularly his *Foolishness to the Greeks: The Christian Gospel and Western Culture* [Grand Rapids, 1986]). Still, these claims have their primary meaning within the tradition of faith, and thus conversations with other traditions require their translation (with attendant loss of meaning). Postliberalism has to do with second-order perceptions of epistemic conditions, with how Christians are for the truth, while it nonetheless assumes that it is the truth about which it makes claims.

GEORGE R. SUMNER, JR

FURTHER READING: *Major works by and about postliberals:* Hans Frei, *The Eclipse of Biblical Narrative: A Study in Eighteenth- and Nineteenth-Century Hermeneutics* (New Haven, 1974); *The Identity of Jesus Christ: The Hermeneutical Bases of Dogmatic Theology* (Philadelphia, 1975); *Types of Christian Theology* (eds. George Hunsinger and William Placher; New Haven, 1992); Garrett Green (ed.), *Scriptural Authority and Narrative Interpretation* (Festschrift for H. Frei; Philadelphia, 1987); George Lindbeck, *The Nature of Doctrine: Religion and Theology in a Postliberal Age* (Philadelphia, 1984); Bruce Marshall (ed.), *Theology and Dialogue: Essays in Conversation with George Lindbeck* (Festschrift for G. Lindbeck; Notre Dame, 1990).

Postmodernity

Postmodernity denotes a cluster of interrelated themes and attitudes, not a single system of thought. Its definition and scope may vary from context to context, not least because within postmodernism historical and socio-political context is thought radically to condition or determine all meaning. More specifically, much depends on whether we perceive postmodernity as standing in contrast to modernity, or as a stage or phase within modernity. In its most radical form, Gianni Vattimo (b. 1936) elaborates a perspective drawn largely from *Nietzsche (1844–1900) to the effect that what counts as 'truth' or 'knowledge' owes more to power-interests than to rational claims to truth. 'Distinctions between truth and falsehood, essence and appearance, the rational and the irrational must be dissolved', for we supposedly have no ground or foundation on the basis of which such 'differences' can be sustained in a stable way (*Translator's Introduction to Vattimo* [1991], p. xii). Nevertheless postmodernity is understood by many in less nihilistic ways. Some theologians of both radical and evangelical sympathies even regard postmodernity as liberating and constructive. Hence we must consider what lies behind the problem of definition and such diverse evaluations.

Problems of definition and differing relations of 'modernity'. Many regard postmodernity as standing *in contrast* to modernity. The case for this can readily be made. The era of 'modernity' broadly coincides with the elevation of notions of value-free reason, especially from *Descartes (1596–1650) and Newton (1642–1727) to *Kant (1724–1804) and the success of the sciences and technology. A 'timeless' rationality has roots in *Aristotle, in contrast to the more history-conscious notions of truth in biblical traditions. Only perhaps with *Hegel (1770–1831), followed by *Marx, Dilthey, Heidegger, Gadamer (b. 1900), Foucault (1926–84) and Derrida (b. 1930) did the importance of the historical context and social 'situatedness' (cf. Heidegger's *Dasein*, 'being-there') come fully to light as a factor in determining what the human subject might *count* as true or rational. Thus, whereas Descartes and Kant had placed the self at the very centre of the problem of knowledge, for Gadamer, Foucault and Derrida history and society already throw up prior constraints which define the self as *this* or *that* self within a context of culture, race, class and gender. The self, if this is pressed, becomes little more than a social construct, as R. Rorty seems to imply.

J. Habermas (b. 1929) recognizes the validity of the claim that social 'interests' (in the sense of power-interests) decisively shape what is accepted as 'knowledge'. He approves the agenda whereby philosophy offers an emancipating critique which exposes what masquerades as value-free 'objective' knowledge as reflecting the interests of some dominant tradition. But Habermas's view of rationality remains broader than that of Rorty. Postmodernity, he convincingly insists, remains parasitic upon the traditions of modernity which it seeks to deconstruct by irony, parody and iconoclasm. It may be a degenerative phase of an exhausted modernity.

J.-F. Lyotard agrees that a continuity exists between modernity and postmodernity, but he inverts the sequence. In *The Postmodern Condition* (French 1979; ET 1984), he perceives modernity as *derivative from* the postmodern condition. For modernity gives privilege to a rationalistic, scientific, technological method of knowledge by virtue of its becoming *a socially dominant tradition* through its pragmatic success in a mechanistic, industrial society. In our post-industrial age, a return to the postmodern condition exposes the pseudo-objectivism of modernity as illusory. This resonates with the more positive assessment of postmodernity found among various theologians. They, too, apply iconoclastic approaches to the over-privileging of a single 'scientific' tradition as a supposedly comprehensive and universal horizon for all enquiry, even that which concerns God.

Differing evaluations in theology: confusions with 'anti-foundationalism'.

In North America a full-blown debate concerning foundationalism has obscured many issues about postmodernity. Some British scholars would like to see the terms 'foundational' and 'anti-foundational' banned from theological discourse. If theology has no foundation in the broadest common-sense (English) use of the term, religious believers simply say how it is for them. In some evangelical circles this is perceived as at long last offering a level playing field after nearly two hundred years of dominance by 'the historical-critical method' (as if there were only one). In this context an alliance with postmodernity appears to allow theology to speak for itself. In this sense, R.W. Jenson describes *Karl Barth as the first postmodern theologian, who has liberated theology from the eighteenth- and nineteenth-century paradigms of 'modernity', that is, from liberal rationalism which places the human self at the centre of enquiry. Graham Ward (1995) develops this approach to Barth further.

Nevertheless, narrative theology (to which this approach often leads) demands continuities of past, present and future, and an active self (as in *Ricoeur) which cannot be identified with postmodernity in its fullest sense. More radically, appeals to community-narrative in effect place more reliance on rhetoric than on argument in the public domain. To be convincing, the life-style and coherence of a narrative testimony must implicitly appeal to criteria concerning what counts as good, commendable or persuasive. Otherwise it collapses into fideism. But the postmodern condition disdains 'meta-narrative' (Lyotard). It allows no criteria beyond those internal to the social, political and rhetorical context within which they function. The value of this perspective lies primarily in its disengaging theology from *one specific philosophical tradition*, namely rationalism from Descartes to Kant. But to call this 'anti-foundational' is to imply (falsely) that either theology has rationalist foundations or that it has none.

Differing evaluations in theology: context, 'deferral' and rhetoric.

If we press home the philosophical stance of Heraclitus (c. 500 BC), to say anything twice is to say something different, since a new context gives the same formal utterance a new meaning. Both Derrida and Vattimo draw on hermeneutics or semiotics to try to establish that meaning can never be brought to 'closure'. Since the sign-system is never closed, but is repeatedly revalued through new 'interests' (especially those of race, class, gender and power-guilds), meanings are 'deferred', in recognition of each new contextual redefinition of criteria of meaning. Kevin Hart and John Caputo perceive a Derridean 'erasure' of stable or established meanings in theology as an iconoclastic demolition of an idolatrous thematizing of divine presence. They associate it with the negative theology of *Eckhart or *John of the Cross which remains reticent in the face of divine transcendence, otherness or difference. J.D. Crossan, Mark Taylor and Graham Ward explore parallel approaches. Ward observes: 'Postmodern thinking forces open a new space for theological thinking by paying attention to the pre-emptive foreclosures of systems' (in Ford [1997], p. 587). On the other side, however, Rowan Williams doubts whether 'the Derridean construal of the arbitrariness or contingency of communication' is to be identified with the kind of divine 'otherness' which nevertheless freely chooses to give itself to the other in grace (in Berry and Wernick, esp. pp. 78–9).

*Don Cupitt utilizes explicitly postmodern perspectives for theology in his work after 1985, in contrast to his 'middle' and 'early' periods. But this raises a difficulty to which Christopher Norris draws attention in his incisive critique of Richard Rorty. Postmodernists insist on a *pluralistic* understanding of truth. Yet Rorty (and Cupitt) make pronouncements, assertions and declarations. Norris objects to 'this use of a liberal rhetoric to frame an authoritative message' which appeals in the end only to contextual pragmatism (Norris [1985], p. 159). Similarly, R.J. Bernstein asks how Rorty can ridicule the very notion of 'judicious critique' while appearing to privilege his own (1991, p. 6). Does not postmodernity, by relativizing all criteria radically in terms of each context, replace argument by rhetoric? But in the case of Jewish, Christian and Islamic theologies, how can truth about God as Creator and End surrender its trans-contextual universal dimension? In Paul's theology the cross explicitly transcends the social constructivism of gender, class and race: 'You have all put on Christ; there is no such thing as Jew and Greek, slave and free, male and female; you are all one person in Christ Jesus' (Gal. 3:28). Paul does not deny that the perceptions and criteria of Jew and Gentile, social elite and socially vulnerable ('strong' and 'weak') differ (1 Cor. 9:20–22). But this 'difference' of context is itself relativized by the gospel. This becomes the burden, in postmodernism itself, of J. Baudrillard's critique of Foucault. Even Foucault's postmodernity can become virtually a system of thought which invites followers. Thereby it mirrors 'the power it describes … Foucault's discourse is no truer than any other' (*Forget Foucault* [1987], p. 10).

Church, self and society. If no agreed criteria of meaning, rationality and truth are thought to operate across boundaries of gender, race, class, history and religious tradition, society is doomed. For where argument and rational dialogue fail, this generates resentment and anger, since oppression arises from the power-interests of other groups, not as a mere fact of life (Thiselton [1995], pp. 11–17, 121–44; Denzin [1991], pp. vi–xi, 1–18). Postmodernity flourishes best in those cultures where 'rights' and 'freedoms' are already embedded in a constitutional history, especially in the USA. Here it goes unnoticed that postmodernity sells truth to the loudest, smoothest, most pious or least pious talker. The reality appears in societies plagued by anarchy, where one person's 'freedom' means another's oppression, and where the weak are unprotected against a brutal regime. Yet in a recent volume of essays by evangelical theological writers D.R. Striver, among others, writes that 'postmodernism may be more ally than enemy' (in Dockery [1995], p. 250).

Here, however, postmodernity tends to become confused with non-foundationalism, and with a legitimate recognition of some degree of contextual pluralism in hermeneutics. However, Gadamer's consistent attack on manipulative assertion and *Wittgenstein's recognition that language-games interact and overlap place them in a different category from Derrida or Rorty. We cannot call 'postmodern' whatever fails to match the rationalism of Descartes and the *Enlightenment, or Kant's view of the self.

As against Gadamer and Ricoeur, postmodernity disdains the continuity of selfhood and of tradition. There is only the instantaneousness of fast food, the disposable cup and the demands of the consumer. The self as agent, however, is more than a construct of race, gender, class and the moment, to which the self falls victim under the constraints of another's will to power. The gospel embodies issues of accountability, responsibility, memory, hope, and above all a promise that spans the generations and provides continuities within a public and intelligible tradition. The church is more than a conglomerate of local like-minded groups at a single moment in time. It is not an in-group with its own private language and truth-criteria. It offers norms of truth which transcend context, for the protection and liberation of the weak and for the salvation of humankind.

Conclusion. It is impossible either to define or to evaluate postmodernity as a uniform or even single phenomenon. Depending on what themes within postmodernity we select for examination, the stance involved may offer liberation either from a narrow rationalism, from a world-view dominated by science and technology, or from a naïve failure to recognize the importance of context, social power-interests and shifting criteria. Alternatively, it can dissolve fundamental differences between true and false, good and bad, right and wrong, into the mere preferences of specific classes, genders and races. Postmodernity is consumerist.

ANTHONY C. THISELTON

FURTHER READING: J. Baudrillard, *Forget Foucault* (ET New York, 1987); R.J. Bernstein, *The New Constellation: The Ethical-Political Horizons of Modernity/Postmodernity* (Cambridge, 1991); P. Berry and A. Wernick (eds.), *Shadow of Spirit: Postmodernism and Religion* (London / New York, 1992), includes Mark Taylor, Carl Raschke, Don Cupitt and Rowan Williams; Don Cupitt, *The Time Being* (London, 1992); N.K. Denzin, *Images of Postmodern Society* (London, 1991); J. Derrida, *Speech and Phenomena and Other Essays on Husserl's Theory of Signs* (ET Evanston, IL, 1973); D.S. Dockery (ed.), *The Challenge of Postmodernism: An Evangelical Engagement* (Wheaton, IL, 1995), includes Thomas Oden, Carl Henry and Stanley Grenz; H.L. Fairlamb, *Critical Conditions: Postmodernity and the Question of Foundation* (Cambridge, 1994); M. Foucault, *The Order of Things* (ET

New York, 1970); *The History of Sexuality* (3 vols.; ET New York, 1978–86); D. Harvey, *The Condition of Postmodernity* (Oxford, 2nd edn, 1989); D. Lyon, *Postmodernity* (Buckingham, 1994); J.-F. Lyotard, *The Postmodern Condition* (Manchester, Eng. repr., 1992); C. Norris, *The Context of Faculties: Philosophy and Theory after Deconstruction* (New York, 1985); *The Truth about Postmodernism* (Oxford, 1993); J. O'Neill, *The Poverty of Postmodernism* (London, 1994); R. Rorty, *Contingency, Irony and Solidarity* (Cambridge, 1989); *Objectivity, Relativism and Truth* (Cambridge, 1991); A.C. Thiselton, *New Horizons in Hermeneutics* (Carlisle / Grand Rapids, 1992); *Interpreting God and the Postmodern Self* (Edinburgh / Grand Rapids, 1995); G. Vattimo, *The End of Modernity* (Cambridge, 1991); G. Ward, *Barth, Derrida and the Language of Theology* (Cambridge, 1995); 'Postmodern Theology', in *The Modern Theologians* (ed. D.F. Ford; Oxford, 2nd edn, 1997), pp. 585–601.

Process Theology

Philosophy has acted as the handmaiden of theology over the centuries. Process theology as it has developed in the twentieth century has employed some of the categories of the philosophy of process, particularly as expounded by Alfred North Whitehead (1861–1947), the Cambridge philosopher who latterly taught at Harvard University. Process philosophy has an ancient parentage, drawing on the ideas of *Plato (427–347 BC), Faustus Socinus (1539–1604), *G.W.F. Hegel (1770–1831), F.W.J. Schelling (1801–87), J. Lequier (1814–62), Charles Pierce (1839–1914), Josiah Royce (1855–1916), H.L. Bergson (1859–1941) and *N.A. Berdyaev (1874–1948), among others.

Process thought has been characterized as 'panentheistic'. The designation of 'panentheism' (coined originally by K.C.F. Krause) has been revived to distinguish the process position from 'pantheism' on the one hand and 'classical theism' on the other. Against traditional theism, it maintains that God is not in all senses independent of the cosmos. On the contrary, as all finite things are related to him they can in a sense be said to be included in him (hence 'panen-theo', 'everything-in-God'). But God is more than the sum total of all finite things. His relation to the cosmos represents only one aspect of God. Because there is another aspect of God which transcends the cosmos, panentheism is clearly to be distinguished from pantheism.

As expounded by Whitehead, the system begins with the intuition that the cosmos is 'alive'. Things change in our world – everything is on the move. Either this movement is meaningless or there is some point or purpose to it. 'Process' opts for the latter view and seeks to investigate the circumstances which must obtain if this is so. An appropriate metaphysic is constructed, called by Charles Hartshorne (b. 1897) 'neo-classical metaphysics'. This is a metaphysic not of 'being' or 'substance' but one in which 'events' are primary, relativity is not considered inferior to absoluteness, nor possibility to necessity. Ultimate reality is in a state of dynamic process, taking evolution into account as well as the dynamics of both the physical world and human personality.

The basic unit of reality is an individual unit of becoming, or a process of feelings or an 'actual entity' or 'occasion'. It is the interplay between actual entities (and 'societies of entities', e.g., a table or a human being) which forms the 'process' – a vast network of ever-more complex relationships.

The process is not in a final state of chaos because it depends on a unifier, an envisioner of possibilities, an experiencer of all that happens, a synthesizer, a direction giver – a reality which (or who) experiences all and surpasses all and is capable of bringing harmony out of increasing complexity – that is, God. For most process thinkers, without God there could be no process. God can indeed be spoken of as creator. 'He is the lure for feelings, the eternal urge of desire'. This means, of course, that in so far as God ceaselessly relates himself to a changing world, there is a sense in which change must be attributed also to God. Yet God remains immutable in his purpose, his relativity – in Christian terms, in his love.

Another common aspect of process philosophy is the notion of dipolarity. Every actual entity or occasion has two aspects or 'poles' – a physical pole and a mental pole (the capacity to realize one possibility rather than another). This dipolarity implies that every actual entity has a measure of 'freedom' (though this freedom may be so minuscule as to be capable, for practical purposes, of being ignored). The movement of an atom, for example, is neither determined nor random – there is something akin to 'freedom' there. This notion of dipolarity extends from the least to the greatest. It also, therefore, applies to God.

In process thought, God has two poles or natures or aspects, one 'primordial' (Whitehead) or 'abstract' (Hartshorne), the other 'consequent' (Whitehead) or 'concrete' (Hartshorne). In the former aspect God is to be regarded as infinite and eternal, but unconscious and deficient in actuality. In the latter pole or nature, God is to be thought of as finite, temporal, fully actual and conscious. God's primordial nature or abstract aspect is an abstract realm of possibilities and generalized intentionality. In his consequent nature or concrete aspect God is to be thought of in relation to the actual world or cosmos. This concrete nature results from his 'prehension', or taking account of the world and everything that goes on in it. God thus relates himself to the world, and because something is always going on in the world something is always being added to God in this nature.

This dipolar concept of God is to be contrasted with the classical theistic concept of God, described as monopolar. Given certain pairs of contraries – for example, one/many, permanence/change, being/becoming, absolute/relative – classical theism affirms one and denies the other so that the highest form of reality involves purifying one pole at the expense of the other, hence 'monopolar'. The dipolar concept allows both contrary attributes to be applied to God but in his different natures. Thus he is infinite, independent and absolute in his primordial nature but in his consequent nature, because he relates himself to a finite cosmos, he is finite, supremely dependent and relative.

As far as God's knowledge is concerned, he is omniscient, knowing as actual everything that is actual and knowing as possible everything that is possible. But even God cannot know as actual what is unactualized or only possible. This insight has ramifications in theology where the notion of a divine 'plan' is abandoned in favour of an understanding of creaturely freedom with God's 'luring' or 'persuading', but not imposing, the actualization of possibilities, which are directed towards the goal of ever-increasing harmonization and 'complexification'.

Also basic to process thought is the principle of 'creativity'. For Whitehead, this is 'the universal of universals', the principle of novelty. 'The process of creative advance is the application of this ultimate principle of creativity to each novel situation which it originates'. According to Hartshorne, 'becoming or creativity itself is necessary and eternal because there is nothing more general or ultimate above it'. This principle of creativity, therefore, extends beyond

human beings to literally everything – in the non-human as well as in the human world.

The fact that God is said to be related to everything that is does not, however, imply denial of transcendence. Transcendence is to be conceived as an unlimited capacity to adapt, without loss of integrity, to everything. Unity of purpose is not lost. God comprehends and so includes everything in the cosmos, but he transcends it because he integrates, unites it and leads it on. God surpasses the cosmos, but God is unsurpassable – except by himself. He is surpassable by himself because, as a living, active subject he is, as it were, 'on the move'. His divine life is enriched by anything and everything that contributes to his purpose.

Personality (in the modern psychological rather than in the traditional logical sense) is not denied the God of process theology. In that God has will, purpose and maintains his own integrity and identity he can be termed 'the supreme Person, maximizing relativity as well as absoluteness. Indeed, God as personal is not merely an expression of the absolute (Hegel). Rather, the divine person contains the absolute, being absolutely related to everything that is. One could even say that because of his relativity, God is the supreme person.

The respective roles of God and the creature in the process of creation can be summarized as follows. In any given situation God presents to the creature a range of possibilities – extending from that possibility which, if actualized, would lead to maximum harmony to that possibility which, if actualized, would lead to minimum harmony. The range is not infinite. For example, the choice open to people is limited by their own past and a whole variety of external factors. Nevertheless, the choice is not limited to one (that would be determinism). Each person has freedom to choose one possibility rather than another, and in choosing that person brings about a new state of affairs and so participates in the process of creation. This new state of affairs is not unrelated to God. God knows it and, as it were, adapts himself to it, setting before the person another range of possibilities for the next choice to be made. In this way, the process goes on – and on. As already indicated, what applies to human beings applies also to the non-human world. This does not mean that a stone or a table or an eye can choose from a range of possibilities. But it is claimed that the atoms, molecules and nerve-cells, since they respond to stimuli and display signs of spontaneous activity, do indeed participate in the process, so that creativity (though not consciousness) may be attributed to them. This feature of process thought has proved of considerable interest to theologians concerned with ecological issues.

Process theology denies a beginning to creation: the process is eternal. This does not mean that this world did not have a beginning; only that the process of which it forms part did not have a beginning. This view only conflicts with the traditional understanding of creation (i.e., 'creation out of nothing') if this latter is understood to be a pseudo-scientific account of 'how it all began'. If, instead, as most theologians would now prefer, creation is to be understood as speaking to the relationship between God and the creature, there need be no conflict.

Process theology rejects the model of God as divine dictator or emperor wielding power by fiat or imposing it by a system of rewards and punishments. Rather, preference is given to Whitehead's development of Plato's concept of 'persuasion'. The agency of God in the world is not that of coercion but of persuasion – by the possibilities God continually sets before entities in it. Or again, God is 'the poet of the world, with tender patience leading it by his vision of truth, beauty and goodness'.

Philosophers like Whitehead and Hartshorne have been criticized for developing a concept of God and his creative relationship with the world without developing a Christology – even though they have paid tribute to the unique, decisive role and work of Christ and their writings seem imbued with the spirit of Christ. Later process theologians, however, have been concerned with Christology. Accepting a 'process' conceptuality, they acknowledge that Jesus Christ has made a decisive difference to the world. They assert the total, unqualified humanity of Jesus. They are suspicious of traditional two-nature Christologies as undermining the true humanity of Jesus and, in any event, they presuppose a metaphysic at odds with contemporary ways of understanding the world. These theologians reject any notion of God's 'intrusion' into the world in Jesus that is in any way an exception to 'the creative process'. Rather, God's incarnating activity is understood as not being 'confined' to Jesus – God incarnates himself to the extent that his purpose is actualized, his 'initial aim' accepted – but it is 'defined' by him. In Jesus, divine action and human response are so combined that Jesus can be said to be 'the classic instance of divine activity in manhood', literally 'love "enmanned"' (Norman Pittenger). Jesus is God's decisive act because he is the decisive revelation or representation of a certain possibility for human existence on the one hand, and of God's being and action on the other (Schubert Ogden). The vision of reality expressed through Jesus' sayings and action is the supreme expression of God's character, purpose and mode of agency, the self-expression of God (David Griffin). John Cobb, in particular, has offered a distinctive Christology which considers Jesus in terms of his authority, as revelation, as example and as Lord and Saviour, introducing a new structure of existence in which Christians participate. Cobb went on to develop, without abandoning process conceptuality, a full *logos* Christology which attempts to be reconcilable with the pluralism of our age. Christ is present wherever and whenever 'creative transformation' occurs. These Christologies have been criticized for so stressing the humanity of Christ that his divinity is jeopardized. The question of 'sin' and the need for atonement tend to be given cursory treatment. But contemporary process theologians are not insensitive to these criticisms and wish to address them. Process Christology is itself, it may be said, 'in process'.

As regards the 'end' of creation, there is real divergence in process theology from traditional Christian doctrine – whether 'end' is understood as temporal (*finis*) or as final purpose (*telos*). For process thinkers there can be no temporal end: if the creative process ends, God ceases to be God. It is the *telos* that is important. This is 'the attainment of value in the temporal world' (Whitehead), or to achieve 'a creative harmony present in all things from atoms to deity' (Hartshorne). The *telos* is variously expressed as the continuing consummations of all things in the life of God; or as the kingdom of God not as a state of being but as the fulfilment of God's being in relation to every creature, an infinite realm of creative life. Some expound a doctrine of 'objective immortality', whereby, because of his omniscience everything is preserved eternally in the memory and life of God, being transformed there for use in the ongoing process of creation (Hartshorne). More specifically, 'Christ enables those who follow him to live authentic life in love – and to the extent that life is so lived, a constant consummation occurs' (Pittenger).

'Objective immortality' has been found inadequate by others who have tried to take the resurrection of Jesus and its implications as something more than a synonym for the actualization of authentic existence. John Cobb, for instance, does this by developing Whitehead's concept of the kingdom of heaven as an image of hope and setting it alongside other images of hope such as the city of God and 'the resurrection of the dead'. For Whitehead, persons as persons inhabit the kingdom (i.e., in God's 'consequent nature') not simply in their objectivity but in their subjectivity as well. '[I]n God the occasion experiences an enlarged and enlarging world which contains new occasions as they come into being'. In the kingdom, events and persons are open to each other and to God. The message of Jesus makes the kingdom real in anticipation; the structure of Jesus' existence foreshadows what existence in the kingdom is to be.

Criticisms of process theology have been in the main that it is dominated by an alien metaphysic (Whitehead's); that it does not deal adequately with the reality of evil or the need for atonement; and that its Christology and eschatology are too much at variance with traditional Christian doctrine. Process theologians have tried to answer these criticisms in their own way, certainly not to the satisfaction of all. Yet in its concept of God and his relativity; its understanding of creativity and creation; its taking account of the findings of modern science; its insistence on purpose; and its claim that the life of Christ has introduced a new structure of existence, process theology offers an important resource for Christian thought, worship and life.

D.W.D. SHAW

FURTHER READING: A.N. Whitehead, *Process and Reality: An Essay in Cosmology* (New York, 1929; London, 1979); *Religion in the Making* (Cambridge, 1926); *Adventures of Ideas* (New York, 1933; Cambridge, 1947); C. Hartshorne, *The Divine Relativity: A Social Conception of God* (New Haven, 1948); *A Natural Theology for our Time* (La Salle, IL, 1967); N. Pittenger, *The Lure of Divine Love* (Edinburgh, 1979); J.B. Cobb, *A Christian Natural Theology* (London, 1966); *Christ in a Pluralistic Age* (Philadelphia, 1965); *The Structure of Christian Existence* (Philadelphia, 1966); J.B. Cobb and D.R. Griffin, *Process Theology: An Introduction* (Belfast, 1967); D.R. Griffin, *A Process Christology* (Washington, DC, 1980); D. Brown, et al. (eds.), *Process Philosophy and Christian Thought* (Indianapolis, IN, 1971); D.D. Williams, *The Spirit and the Forms of Love* (Washington, DC, 1981).

Przywara, Erich (1889–1972)

Przywara was born in 1889 at Kattowitz, Germany and died in Munich in 1972.

Przywara entered the Society of Jesus at Exaten, Holland, in 1908 and completed the normal philosophical (1910–13) and theological (1917–21) studies at the *Jesuit seminary in Valkenburg, Holland. As part of his Jesuit formation, he also spent three years (1914–17) as prefect of music at the Jesuit college, Stella Matutina, in Feldkirchen.

After his ordination in 1922 until his death, Przywara was part of the Jesuit writers' community for the periodical *Stimmen der Zeit* in Munich. He published numerous articles and books and lectured widely. He became known as a major spokesman for the Catholic viewpoint and its philosophy in relation to Protestantism and many modern intellectual and cultural movements. Przywara's original approaches in Neo-Scholasticism and Jesuit spirituality inspired fellow Jesuits *Karl Rahner and *Hans Urs von Balthasar. His poetry and inspirational works appealed to everyday believers. After the war he was handicapped by illness but nevertheless continued to publish – mainly on spiritual and biblical subjects.

Przywara's interests ranged from philosophers and theologians: especially *Augustine, *Thomas Aquinas, *Kant, *Kierkegaard, *Newman and Max Scheler to literature, poetry and spirituality. In fact, throughout all his work there is an attempt to discern a polar 'balance in tension' that begins in the concrete world of human culture and culminates in a final 'tension' between the world and God as 'ever greater'. As a Jesuit preacher and writer he is a faithful son of *St Ignatius, intent on service of God's majesty. For Przywara this means demonstrating philosophically how God is present in all things and discerning this presence in ongoing writers and trends.

Thus, an early work, *Gottgeheimnis der Welt* (or, 'The Mystery of God in the World', 1923) – originally lectures for Catholic teachers – consists of a philosophical and theological analysis to find God within, yet transcendent 'above', contemporary cultural movements. Throughout his career, in dialogue with Protestant theologians such as *Karl Barth, he defends the Catholic principle, (the 'analogy of being'), against the Reformation's dialectical or 'tragic' thought.

Przywara's major contribution to Catholic philosophy is undoubtedly his work on the analogy of being. Although using Neo-Scholastic language, he refused to be confined by Neo-Scholastic technicalities and effectively demonstrated the broader implications or 'dynamic' of analogy. His outpouring of articles and books effectively demonstrated that the philosophical issues were alive in the 'concreteness' of this world. His other contribution is to the field of spirituality, especially Ignatian spirituality (cf. *Deus Semper Maior: Theologie der Exerzitien* or, 'God Ever Greater: Theology of the Exercises'). Among lengthy elaborations of the anthropological basis and (frequently fanciful) scriptural resonances which he finds in the text of the *Spiritual Exercises*, we find genial insights into their structure and meaning.

JAMES V. ZEITZ

FURTHER READING: *Texts: Schriften* (3 vols.; Einsiedeln, 1962); *Religionsbegruendung: Max Scheler – J.H. Newman* (Freiburg, 1923); *Deus Semper Maior: Theologie der Exerzitien* (2 vols.; Munich, 1964); *Logos* (Düsseldorf, 1964). *Studies:* J. Teran-Dutari, *Christentum und Metaphysik* (Munich, 1973); J. Zeitz, *Spirituality and Analogia Entis according to Erich Przywara* (Washington, DC, 1982); Leo Zimny, *Erich Przywara: Sein Schriftum 1912–1962* (Einsiedeln, 1963).

Puritanism

The pejorative label applied to the spontaneous religious activism which emerged in the reign of Elizabeth I (1558–1603). The title came to be accepted by some participants but was rejected by most. Many of those to whom it was applied viewed themselves as the 'godly' element of society, thus inviting the sarcastic sobriquet from others. In time, however, 'Puritanism' gained acceptance as a formal label for the movement.

Puritans called for greater liturgical and governmental reforms than were allowed by Elizabeth in the Religious Settlement of 1559. Puritans resisted episcopal polity, ceremonial liturgies and priestly wardrobe, holding them to be unbiblical remnants of Roman Catholicism. Instead they called for Presbyterian polity, an emphasis on preaching in church services and the use of ordinary teaching attire by preachers. Theologically, Puritans were aligned with the continental *Reformed tradition. Thus, with the emergence of *Arminianism in the late seventeenth century, Puritans were closely identified with controversies over strict predestinarian theology – so-called *Calvinism. Puritanism

continued to the end of the interregnum (1660) and well beyond, if measured by the persistence of its core values.

Puritanism, then, may be viewed as a moderate and rather general resistance movement, binding participants together in opposition to problems they perceived in the church. The movement is difficult to characterize more explicitly because it remained informal, lacking a confessional centre or a distinct social structure. Indeed, in many applications the term may be overly broad and misleading. Even when the label is accurate in capturing part of the movement, confusing inconsistencies are present. Some Puritans, for instance, were unhappy with fellow Puritans who conformed to the Act of Uniformity (1559), while remaining of one mind in opposing Arminians. The unity of the movement, then, was rather fragile. When the bonding pressures of external opposition ended during the interregnum, serious divisions quickly emerged.

Puritans were identifiable by their private and sometimes public support of, or participation in, religious conferences, pulpit exchanges, challenging sermons, acts of Nonconformity (or marginal conformity) and personal correspondence in support of reforming goals. This was done in the face of varied levels of civil and episcopal opposition. Collectively, the Puritans formed a broad-based but loosely knit network.

Puritans were not only concerned with the more extrinsic values already noted. Beneath such concerns lay more basic impulses. These included a rigorous devotion to the Bible, affective piety, personal exercises of devotion and strains of strict moralism. The underlying theology reflected primitivist values, holding that the New Testament era church offered God's preferred ecclesiology. The regulative principle, which held that activities not expressly approved or demonstrated in the Bible are unacceptable for the contemporary church, was tied to this. Puritans also viewed God's grace in more relational than sacramental terms. Puritans, however, debated whether grace is more immediate, expressed by the motions of the Spirit experienced within; or strictly indirect, working through 'means' such as preaching and praying. Either way, they resisted views of non-Puritans that proper worship is essentially ceremonial, defined by hypostatized agents such as the communion table and chalice. 'Puritanism' thus characterized those in England who sought to broaden the distance between the English church and her Roman Catholic heritage, as they pressed for adoption of values similar to those of the continental Reformed churches.

Tudor-era Puritans. While the movement began during the reign of Elizabeth I, it was to some degree an extension of the reforming impulse in England that included John Wyclif, the Lollards and, in the early sixteenth century, *William Tyndale. These Reformers held the Bible to have primacy in matters of theology and church practice. Early Reformers also called for vernacular translations of Scripture to be made widely available, supported by biblical preaching and moral reforms in church and society.

Reformation theology formally came to England under *Thomas Cranmer as the Archbishop of Canterbury (1533–56) and grew more distinct with the accession of Edward VI (1547). The eclectic content of England's protestant theology included *Lutheran, Swiss and German Reformed sources, but the Calvinist tradition began to predominate, especially in the 1552 Book of Common Prayer. The English church, however, retained strong Erastian values, reflecting its first establishment under Henry VIII.

Accession of the Roman Catholic queen, Mary Tudor (1553), reversed the English Reformation and drove many of its most avid proponents to the Continent. There they were more fully exposed to a church polity that was free of Erastian assumptions, an experience that helped seed subsequent factions among the Puritans in matters of polity. *John Knox, the Scottish Reformer and chaplain to Edward VI, promoted Presbyterian polity as leader of the English congregation in Geneva. Near the end of Mary's life he published a gender-based challenge to the legitimacy of her rule in *The First Blast of the Trumpet against the Monstrous Regiment of Women* (1558). Thus, when Elizabeth became queen in 1558, Knox was an unfortunate representative for Genevan church polity. Not only was his *First Blast of the Trumpet*, against women serving as rulers, echoing through England as Elizabeth took the throne; but Knox, by his Presbyterian convictions, was also opposed to the episcopal polity of both Henry VIII and Edward VI. Elizabeth, on the other hand, saw the Erastian benefit of controlling the church to be a political necessity in the face of Catholic challenges to the legitimacy of her reign.

Elizabeth imposed a settlement of the religious question by defining a *via media* between the conservative forces of old Catholicism and Puritan calls for a full reformation as measured by continental Protestantism. Elizabeth restored the Reformed theology of Edward's era through legislation and required use of the 1559 Book of Common Prayer, taken, with minor changes, from Edward's 1552 version. Queen Elizabeth, however, staunchly resisted calls to discard use of vestments and surplices. Furthermore, she rejected calls by Thomas Cartwright, among others, to allow a Presbyterian polity. With the succession of Elizabeth's archbishops, from the more Puritan Edmund Grindal to Cartwright's long-time opponent John Whitgift, Puritan efforts to promote Presbyterianism were stifled.

For the balance of the Tudor era, Puritans found other means to promote church reform, including the support of ministers who held Puritan values and the gathering of ministers at prophesying conferences meant for mutual encouragement and the improvement of preaching skills. The promotion of more biblical preaching was a chief Puritan strategy, aiming to reform the church from within. Prominent laymen were prepared to assist these activities, as illustrated by the then Chancellor of the Exchequer, Sir Walter Mildmay, who founded Emmanuel College, Cambridge (1584) to train preachers. Emmanuel quickly became a centre for Puritan activism.

Stuart-era Puritans. Puritans were hopeful that the accession of King James I (1603) from Presbyterian Scotland would open the door to their desired reforms. A delegation of Puritans presented the king with the Millenary Petition upon his arrival in London. In it they called for relief from certain ceremonial requirements. James subsequently met with selected bishops and Puritan leaders at the Hampton Court Conference (1604) to allow some debate and to respond to the petition. The initial petition avoided any call for the king to set aside episcopacy, but the issue was raised by John Reynolds at the conference. James's response was blunt: 'No bishop, no king' – the Erastian political benefits appreciated by Elizabeth had been embraced by the new king. While James was open to some reforms at the conference, the Puritans also impressed on him the disruptive potential of their movement. They failed to engage his support.

James, then, maintained a measured response to the Puritans. As Elizabeth before him, he used the Act of Uniformity as a lever. The more radical ministers were removed from their posts, but the moderate Nonconformists and the conforming Puritans were generally left alone. On the other hand, respected Puritans filled many positions of social and political influence. For example, Richard Sibbes served as preacher at Gray's Inn, London, and as master of St Catherine's Hall, Cambridge, and John Preston served as chaplain to Prince Charles, as master of Emmanuel College and as preacher at Lincoln's Inn, London.

There were disruptive religious events during James's reign that redirected some of the Puritan energy for reform. The logically rigorous supralapsarian theology in William Perkins's *Armilla Aurea* (1590; later the *Golden Chaine*) stirred a reaction among some in the Cambridge University faculty. Perkins's view was supported by William Whitaker, Regius professor of divinity. The result was a sharpened division between Calvinist and anti-Calvinist (or Arminian) forces at Cambridge and elsewhere.

Richard Montague emerged as a spokesman in opposition to predestinarian theology. He also successfully labelled the Perkins-Whitaker position as Puritan, which enlarged the circle of those who bore the label. Efforts to prosecute Montague for his beliefs helped polarize the educated classes. This, along with religious debates in Parliament, resulted in political disruption and increased favour for the Arminians in royal circles.

Charles I, upon his accession to the throne (1625), outlawed public debates over predestination – thus virtually silencing the Puritans. Later, in 1629, he chose not to call the Parliament, thus inaugurating his extended Personal Rule. In this period, William Laud was among those who sympathized with the Arminian position and embraced the *via media*. Laud was noticed and promoted by Charles – first to be Bishop of London, then as Archbishop of Canterbury. Laud actively suppressed any expressions of Puritan Nonconformity or religious activism. This rigorous containment policy drove some Puritans to separate from the church and others to exile. Prominent Puritans departed from England, with *William Ames moving to the Netherlands, while *John Cotton and Thomas Hooker chose New England. The Puritans in New England adopted a 'non-separating' independence from episcopal oversight – the precursor to Congregational polity.

The interregnum. The English Civil War was fed by pent-up religious frustration. The Parliament, finally called by the king to finance his war against rebels in Scotland (1640), unleashed legislation supportive of Puritan causes. With the defeat of Royalist forces and Charles's subsequent execution (1649), the major goals of Puritanism were achieved: an overthrow of church episcopacy, a rejection of conservative liturgical regulations and relief from prior restrictions on Puritan preaching. In the release from external Laudian restrictions, however, a variety of disparate religious tendencies were also unleashed – including various forms of separatism and religious excess. Congregationalists debated Presbyterians about polity. The Society of Friends – the Quakers – explored aspects of existential spirituality, and various antinomian parties examined the implications of their doctrines of grace. Fifth Monarchists called for the kingdom of God to be achieved through the direct rule of gathered churches.

Despite such challenges, an enduring product of interregnum Puritanism emerged: the Westminster Assembly (1643–49) became a Puritan forum in the attempt to define a new religious order for England. Selected ministers and laymen, representing major parties within Puritanism, along with delegates from Scotland, debated matters of creed and polity. The resulting confession and catechisms served as guides for the Presbyterian tradition after the monarchy was restored in 1660.

Despite attempts to maintain a limited range of religious freedoms under Oliver Cromwell's Protectorate, divisions among 'the godly professors' were obvious; growing sectarianism was a problem. This came, in part, through the emergence of lay preaching, which often placed the former functions of educated ministers into the hands of the roughly educated. It was also a time of more conspicuous irreligiosity for some under the voluntarism of the period. Thus, the difficulties associated with religious freedom did much to convince the English that the Puritan experiment had ended badly. Soon after Cromwell died in 1658, the nation invited Charles II back from exile to restore Stuart rule. With Charles II came a renewed religious uniformity aligned with the former *via media* rather than with the values of the Puritans.

R.N. FROST

FURTHER READING: T.D. Bozeman, *To Live Ancient Lives: The Primitivist Dimension in Puritanism* (London, 1988); Patrick Collinson, *The Elizabethan Puritan Movement* (Oxford, 1990); Kenneth Fincham (ed.), *The Early Stuart Church, 1603–1642* (Basingstoke, 1993); William Haller, *The Rise of Puritanism* (New York, 1947); Geoffrey F. Nuttall, *The Holy Spirit in Puritan Faith and Experience* (Chicago, 1992); John Spurr, *English Puritanism, 1603–1689* (Basingstoke, 1998); Tom Webster, *Godly Clergy in Early Stuart England* (Cambridge, 1997).

Pusey, Edward Bouverie (1800–82)

Anglican priest, Regius professor of Hebrew at Oxford, and leader of the *Oxford Movement. Edward Pusey was born into a wealthy family and after education at Eton and Christ Church, Oxford, he was elected to a fellowship at Oriel College in 1823. Two years later he went to Germany, where he studied Hebrew, Arabic, Syriac and other Semitic languages as well as making the acquaintance of many of the leading biblical critics and theologians, notably F.A.G. Tholuck (1799–1877), with whom he maintained a close friendship for the rest of his life. Alarmed by what he saw as the rationalist tendency of German theology he published in 1828 *An Historical Enquiry into the Probable Causes of the Rationalist Character lately predominant in the Theology of Germany*. In this work he argued that this was a consequence of spiritual deadness, against the position maintained by Hugh James Rose (1795–1838) that it was a result of laxity in relation to creeds and church ordinances and the absence of episcopacy. He was ordained the same year, and at the young age of twenty-eight he was appointed as Regius professor of Hebrew and canon of Christ Church, a post which he held until his death in 1882, though sadly his early promise as an innovator in Hebrew and biblical scholarship never came to fruition. His later ultra-conservative stance was reflected in his *Lectures on Daniel the Prophet* (1864), and in his defence of the eternity of hell against F.W. Farrar (1831–1903), *What is of Faith as to Everlasting Punishment?* (1880).

He completed the work of his predecessor, Alexander Nicoll, in cataloguing the Arabic manuscripts in the Bodleian Library, but he was soon drawn into support of the nascent Oxford Movement. He changed the character of the *Tracts for the Times* by contributing major essays on fasting and on the theology of baptism, in which he strongly defended the doctrine of baptismal regeneration, and he taught a strict doctrine concerning the remission of post-baptismal sin. Later he came to emphasize the importance of sacramental confession – and was himself much sought after as a confessor – publishing in 1878 an English edition of the Abbé Gaume's *Manual for Confessors* with an extensive introduction. In his exploration of penitence Pusey preached two notable sermons, *The Holy Eucharist, a Comfort to the Penitent* (1843), which was condemned by the vice-chancellor and six doctors of divinity because of its high doctrine of the Real Presence (many of the condemned phrases were in fact quotations from *St Ephrem), and *The Entire Absolution of the Penitent* (1846), in which he strongly affirmed the reality of priestly absolution in the Church of England. In his Eucharistic doctrine he closely followed the teaching of *Cyril of Alexandria.

Following the secession of *John Henry Newman to the Roman Catholic Church in 1845, Pusey became increasingly looked to as the most significant leader of the Catholic revival. He continued to wrestle with issues of ecclesiology, culminating in his *Eirenicon* of 1865 in which he sought to encourage Rome to clarify what doctrinal agreement was required for reunion between the Church of England and the Church of Rome, believing that the obstacles were not so much in official teaching as in popular devotion. In other words, Pusey sought a declaration from Rome as to what was not *de fide* as well as what was *de fide*, going on to argue in the manner of *Tract XC* that the decrees of the Council of Trent and the Thirty-nine Articles were compatible. Newman, famously, described the *Eirenicon* as an olive branch discharged from a catapult, taking Pusey to task for not distinguishing doctrine and devotion, or taking sufficient account of the cultural colour each derived from its local circumstances. A second *Eirenicon* in 1869 examined the doctrine of the Immaculate Conception, and a further essay, *Is Healthful Reunion Impossible?* (1870), grappled with the issues of purgatory, the deuterocanonical books and Roman supremacy.

In common with *John Keble and other Tractarians, Pusey developed a particular interest in typology, and in 1836 he delivered a series of lectures on 'Types and Prophecies of the Old Testament'. Although these remained unpublished, Newman ventured the opinion that it was in the symbolical theology developed in these lectures, with their stress on the power of the imagination, that a proper response to the reductionist theology of *D.F. Strauss (1808–74) could be found.

Pusey's theology and spirituality emphasize the indwelling of the Spirit, transfiguration into the likeness of Christ and salvation understood as deification. Deeply read in the Fathers, Greek, Latin and Syriac, Pusey was also widely familiar with later writers in the Christian mystical tradition. His substantial corpus of sermons is evidence for Yngve Brilioth's claim that Pusey was the *doctor mysticus* of the Oxford Movement, the only one of the Tractarians who might be described as ecstatic. His sermons are replete with quotations from the Fathers and later spiritual writers, such as *St Bernard, Ruysbroeck, St Catherine of Siena, Surin and Avrillon. Prodigiously learned, Pusey believed passionately that theology must serve the pursuit of holiness, and it is as a preacher, spiritual guide and director, and as a fosterer of the revival of the religious life in the Church of England, more than as an academic theologian, that his reputation is founded. Pusey House in Oxford was founded in his memory and houses his library and many of his papers, as well as other substantial collections relating to the Oxford Movement.

GEOFFREY ROWELL

FURTHER READING: Standard *Life of Edward Bouverie Pusey* by H.P. Liddon (4 vols.; London / New York, 2nd edn, 1893–97), including a list of Pusey's writings; P. Butler (ed.), *Pusey Rediscovered* (London, 1983); D.A.R. Forrester, *Young Doctor Pusey: A Study in Development* (London, 1989); H.C.G. Matthew, 'Edward Bouverie Pusey: From Scholar to Tractarian', *J Th St* NS 32 (1981), pp. 101–24; A. Geck, 'The Concept of History in E.B. Pusey's First Enquiry into German Theology and its German background', *J Th St* NS 38 (1987), pp. 387–408; G. Rowell, *The Vision Glorious: Themes and Personalities of the Catholic Revival in Anglicanism* (Oxford, 1983), pp. 71–97.

Quick, Oliver Chase (1885–1944)

Oliver Quick, the son of a clergyman, was educated at Harrow and Corpus Christi College, Oxford, where surprisingly he took a Third in Greats. Ordained in the Church of England in 1911, he later served as vice-principal of the Leeds Clergy School and was resident chaplain to Archbishop Davidson of Canterbury (in 1917 he married Mrs Davidson's secretary, Winifred Pearson). Quick's intellectual qualities flowered as he held a succession of canonries at Newcastle (1920–23), Carlisle (1923–30), St Paul's (1930–34), Durham (1934–39) and Oxford (1939–44) – the latter two as professor of divinity. He was an influential member of the Archbishops' Commission on Christian Doctrine, which sat from 1922 to 1938, and he was a close friend of its chairman, Archbishop *William Temple. His tenure of the Regius chair at Oxford was cut short by illness, which forced him to retire in 1943, and he died shortly afterwards.

Quick's theological work is marked by the attempt to work from first principles, to proceed by analysis of key conceptual distinctions, and to seek a measure of synthesis. He used philosophy to illuminate theological issues in the belief that reason is God-given and Christian truth must cohere with all other truth; he was unsympathetic to what he saw as the irrationality of *'Barthian' theology. He attached high importance to Scripture as the touchstone of Christian belief and to the inheritance of patristic orthodoxy, yet he was ready to break new ground if intellectual integrity demanded. His churchmanship was broadly Catholic, tempered by the breadth of the Anglican tradition, and he was notably independent of ecclesiastical parties and academic fashions.

Most of Quick's characteristic ideas appear in a book published in mid-career, *The Gospel of Divine Action* (1933). First, he makes a primary distinction between signs and instruments, which he believes to be fundamental to the understanding of both human and divine life. Signification or symbolization (which expresses truth) and action (which accomplishes a purpose) are interwoven and mutually conditioning, but to emphasize one or the other has divergent consequences for understanding God and the universe. The first leads typically to a (supposedly) Hellenistic preoccupation with knowing unchanging truth and the latter to a Hebraic recognition of the acts of God in history. The interrelation between symbolism and

instrumentality is carefully expounded in *The Christian Sacraments* (1927), where Protestant theology is regarded as one-sidedly symbolic and Catholic theology as excessively instrumental, and it informs the discussion of God's relation to the world in Quick's other major work, *Doctrines of the Creed* (1938).

Quick then proceeds via the thought of St Paul and St John to discuss Christology. This remained at the centre of his theological concerns from the Paddock Lectures on *Liberalism, Modernism and Tradition* (1922) to his unpublished Oxford lectures of 1941–42. He argues that for St John the incarnation is primarily the unique revelation or expression of God's love, whereas for St Paul the atonement is primarily a supremely effective act, and both emphases are necessary to articulate the uniqueness and the universality of the person of Christ. In *The Christian Sacraments*, Quick had already anticipated later thought in making Christ himself, as incarnate and atoning, the paradigm and source of sacramentality, and his last years were devoted to deeper exploration of the mysteries of incarnation and salvation.

Quick had earlier criticized both the 'humanitarian' Christology of *liberal Protestantism and the evolutionary modernism which bypassed historical criticism. *Doctrines of the Creed* affirms the Christology of *Chalcedon and its rooting in what can be known historically about Jesus (including the resurrection as a fact inseparable from judgement of its truth and value). The regulative truths of Christology are the revelation of God in person and act, the gospel of the redemption of humanity, and the fulfilment of human goodness – which point to the doctrine of Christ as both divine and human. Yet Quick's orthodoxy is not uncritical: in a nuanced discussion which echoes the 1938 Doctrine Report, he suggests that the historical and theological arguments in favour of the virgin birth, while strong, are not decisive. On the humanity of Christ, he defends a form of kenotic theory, that the knowledge proper to the Godhead was present in Jesus within historical and human limitations, and he argues that his moral perfection consisted in his being the instrument of the divine love in salvation. Most radically, the doctrines of creation and incarnation require that God be understood as 'relatively passible' in virtue of his self-willed relation to the world.

During his Oxford years, Quick developed the sacrificial theory of the atonement which he had sketched in *Doctrines of the Creed*. In his 1942–43 lectures, posthumously published as *The Gospel of the New World*, he places salvation in the context of creation and evil and shows his awareness of New Testament scholarship by relating the atoning death of Christ both to his risen life and to God's eschatological purpose. In this impressive synthesis he vindicates his own lifelong conviction that the self-surrender of Christ is the authentic manifestation of divine omnipotence in overcoming evil and renewing humanity in fellowship with God.

Finally, Quick interprets the church and the sacraments as symbols and instruments of the love of God. His approach to Eucharistic sacrifice and presence reflects in philosophical mode his desire to reconcile 'Catholic and Protestant elements in Christianity' (the title of an early book of 1924). But, with the exception of his treatment of the Holy Spirit in relation to freedom and authority, he is not at his best in discussing ecclesiology, where his schematic distinctions tend to wear thin. His hostility to 'Augustinian' notions of sacramental validity and his preferred 'Cyprianic' model of ordination as the transmission of authority lead him to commend episcopacy as an effective sign of unity and apostolicity, while holding that divisions within the church render all ministerial orders relatively defective. This was, in his day, a fairly enlightened but not immediately influential view.

Quick's premature death must be regarded as a grievous loss to Anglican theology, comparable to that of Temple shortly afterwards. Although his thought is inevitably dated, his aliveness to matters of fundamental importance and his wholeness of vision and clarity of expression ensure its continuing power to illuminate and stimulate.

CHRISTOPHER M. JONES

FURTHER READING: *Texts: Liberalism, Modernism and Tradition* (London, 1922); *Catholic and Protestant Elements in Christianity* (London, 1924); *The Christian Sacraments* (London, 1927); *The Gospel of Divine Action* (London, 1933); *Doctrines of the Creed* (London, 1938); *Christianity and Justice* (London, 1940); *The Gospel of the New World* (London, 1944). *Studies:* J.K. Mozley, 'Oliver Quick as a Theologian' (2 parts), *Theology* 48 (1945); P. de N. Lucas, 'Oliver Quick', *Theology* 96 (1993); D.M. MacKinnon, 'Oliver Chase Quick as a Theologian', *Theology* 96 (1993).

Ragaz, Leonhard (1868–1945)

One of the leading Christian socialists of his generation, Ragaz was born in Tamins in German-speaking Switzerland, the son of a farming family. As a boy Ragaz experienced financial hardship, which sparked off an interest in politics and public affairs. Because of the relative ease of winning scholarships he studied theology at Basle. He also spent a period in Jena and Berlin where he developed an admiration for German culture. He was ordained in 1890 to a pastorate at Heizenberg but gave it up in 1893 to teach religion in a school. It was at this stage that he read the works of Thomas Carlyle (1795–1881), Charles Kingsley (1819–75) and Friedrich Naumann (1860–1919) and became increasingly attracted to *Christian socialism. Throughout his life Ragaz regarded Anglo-Saxon thought as of 'decisive significance for my thinking and acting' (*Mein Weg*, I, [Zurich, 1952], p. 261). In 1895 he became pastor at Chur, where his position grew increasingly radical. Under *Albrecht Ritschl's (1822–89) influence Ragaz came to see the kingdom of God as the most central Christian idea. In 1902 he was called to the Basle Münster and again took up issues of social justice. In 1903 he preached a sermon during a bricklayers' strike which suggested that Christ was on the side of the oppressed. In 1906 he founded the socialist journal, *Neue Wege*, to which he contributed nearly a thousand articles. Ragaz associated with Hermann Kutter (1869–1939) of Zurich, who in *Sie müssen!* (1903) regarded the social movement as doing more than the church to realize God's purposes on earth. Similarly, for Ragaz, the social movement was 'a divine work that is accomplished before our very eyes' (*Signs of the Kingdom* [ed. P. Bock; Grand Rapids, 1984], p. 12). In contrast, the church was 'a preacher's church' rather than a community. However, against Kutter's call to wait patiently for God's kingdom, Ragaz urged Christians to involve themselves in the social struggle. This led to a conflict between the two, with Kutter accusing Ragaz of politicizing the gospel.

In 1908 Ragaz became professor of practical theology at Zurich where he again involved himself in labour politics and in the peace movement. During World War I Ragaz came to see violence as the chief product of the 'kingdom of evil' and, deeply critical of the Versailles settlement, he contributed to the effort towards international reconciliation (*Die neue Schweiz*, 1917). Ragaz was an admirer of Woodrow Wilson and his pacifism was never absolute but always related to the complexities of international relations. In 1913 he joined the Social Democratic Party, applying his critique of violence to the theory of socialism: socialism was not the name of a party, but 'the principle of solidarity in economic life as in all other aspects of life' (*Neue Wege*, II [1908], p. 268). Freedom and community were thus crucial: *Marxism found it all too easy to sacrifice the former in the name of the latter (*Sozialismus und Gewalt*, 1919). Ragaz was instrumental in persuading the Swiss socialists not to join the Third International. Later he became increasingly critical of Marxist materialism with its denial of the realm of the spirit (*Von Christus zu Marx – Von Marx zu Christus*, 1929).

The rise of *dialectical theology, and especially *Barth's attack on 'hyphenated Christianity' in 1919, meant that religious socialism began to decline in influence. Ragaz, however, continued his involvement in workers' causes and adopted an ever-more-radical stance. Increasingly it was religion, which he regarded as 'the strongest reactionary power in the world today' (*Signs*, p. 37), that became the object of his attack. 'Jesus,' he remarked in 1917, 'does not have the slightest interest in making people pious' (*Signs*, p. 31). Instead, what was important was the kingdom of God, which stood in judgement of all human religion. In 1921, increasingly disillusioned with the compromises involved in operating within the institutional church which merely 'comforted' the world (*Signs*, p. 65), Ragaz resigned his chair and moved to a working-class suburb of Zurich. Here he founded an educational centre modelled on the English 'settlements'. Although of limited success, the centre gave him the opportunity to spread his message far beyond the academic world. During this time he wrote extensively on the Bible, producing a seven-volume commentary (*Die Bibel: Eine Deutung* [Zurich, 1947–49]). Again he found inspiration in prophecy and in the imperatives of the Sermon on the Mount, which he saw as travestied in dialectical theology. Ragaz was bitterly critical of the rise of Nazism as well as abuses of power during World War II.

Ragaz's thought has been influential on contemporary political theology and shows affinities with *Liberation Theology as well as the work of *Jürgen Moltmann. Although he has been criticized for reducing the kingdom of God to political ideology, his position was more subtle: the kingdom of God was always a transcendent goal which was critical of all political systems. Nevertheless, human beings were given the responsibility to realize the ideals of justice, fraternity and peace, even if no political expression would be absolute. For Ragaz, works were every bit as important as faith. In a commentary on the *Apostles' Creed (1942), he summarized his position: 'The Kingdom comes from God alone, but man can and should do three things: he can and should wait for it; he can and should pray for it; he can and should place himself at its disposal. Otherwise the Kingdom cannot come' (*Signs*, p. 104). Ragaz's thought is perhaps best understood as a set of oppositions between ideal and real, future and present in which both sides are given equal weight. In all this he sought a new world order freed from the rule of materialism and ruled instead by love, hope and justice. For Ragaz, Christianity and socialism belonged together.

MARK D. CHAPMAN

FURTHER READING: *Text: Gedanken* (Bern, 2nd edn, 1951; contains bibliography). *Studies:* M. Mattmüller, *Leonhard Ragaz und der religiöse Sozialismus* (2 vols.; Zurich, 1957–68); A. Lindt, *Leonhardt Ragaz* (Zurich, 1957); J.S. Martin, *Reich Gottes und Revolution* (Hamburg, 1976); U. von den Steinen, *Agitation für das Reich Gotes* (Munich, 1976); K.-O. Benn (ed.), *Leonhard Ragaz* (Darmstadt, 1986); U. Jäger, *Ethik und Eschatologie bei Leonhardt Ragaz* (Zurich, 1971); E. Beuss and M. Mattmüller, *Prophetischer Sozialismus* (Freiburg, 1986).

Rahner, Karl (1904–84)

Karl Rahner has been aptly called 'the quiet mover of the Roman Catholic Church' and the 'Father of the Catholic Church in the twentieth century'. His four thousand written works indicate that he wrote on all significant theological topics, on sensitive ecclesiological questions, and even on devotional practices. A great ecumenist, he entered into dialogue with atheistic, Buddhist, Jewish, Marxist, Muslim, Protestant and scientific thinkers the world over. He may well be *the* theological titan of the twentieth century.

Rahner was born the middle of seven children of a respected *Gymnasium* professor and a 'courageous' mother in Freiburg im Breisgau, Germany. He entered the *Jesuit Order in 1922, where he received training both in Ignatian spirituality

and in predominantly *neo-scholastic philosophy and theology. His first serious publications (1932–34) and the 1939 book, *Aszese und Mystik in der Väterzeit*, bear witness to his intense research in the Christian spiritual-mystical tradition. Of special importance in this regard was the collaboration with his brother Hugo on both patristics and the spirituality of *St Ignatius of Loyola – the latter indelibly stamping Rahner's theology of grace, prayer, discernment of spirits and existential ethics.

On 26 July 1932, Rahner was ordained priest, and in 1934 he returned to his home town of Freiburg to study for the doctorate in philosophy. Because of Heidegger's Nazi leanings, Rahner selected Martin Honecker as his dissertation director, but he attended seminars taught by Heidegger – the only professor he ever called a great master. Honecker eventually rejected the dissertation, a creative interpretation of *Aquinas's epistemology influenced by the transcendental *Thomism of *Joseph Maréchal (1878–1944). The rejected dissertation is the now famous *Spirit in World*, published in 1939, and translated into many languages. Because Rahner had already been reassigned to teach theology in Innsbruck, the failure meant nothing. In route to his new post, he delivered a series of fifteen lectures in Salzburg – eventually published in 1941 as *Hearer of the Word*, his second foundational work.

Only a year after Rahner's arrival in Innsbruck, the Nazis took over the university, and Rahner went to Vienna. There, as a member of the diocesan Pastoral Institute, he spent most of the war years – the final year as a parish priest in the Bavarian village of Mariakirche. In Munich in 1946, he preached his now famous Lenten sermons, later published under the title *The Need and Blessing of Prayer*.

In so many ways, Rahner's theology is supremely pastoral. Perhaps his pastoral work in war-ravaged Europe during and after the Second World War further developed his already spontaneous inclination towards the pastoral care of individuals and the concerns of a church in 'diaspora'. In fact, many of his writings are essays written for particular occasions or in response to questions as they arose, and do not exhibit the overly systematic and encyclopedic approach considered typical of German theologians of his age. Rahner's pastoral side shows itself in yet another significant way: his theology often begins and ends in prayer. In fact, explicit prayers and penetrating reflection on prayer punctuated his entire theological life, as his widely read *Encounters with Silence* and *Prayers for a Lifetime* illustrate. Thus, Rahner stands in a long line of great Christian theologians who were likewise great teachers of prayer.

In 1948 Rahner began to teach in the reconstituted theology faculty at Innsbruck and began his incredibly prolific period of writing, lecturing and publishing. The first three volumes of his monumental 23-volume *Theological Investigations* were published from 1954–56. He also edited the twenty-eighth to the thirty-first editions of Denziger's *Enchiridion Symbolorum*; co-edited the 13-volume *Lexikon für Theologie und Kirche* (1957–65); the six-volume *Sacramentum Mundi* (1967–69); the five-part volume *Handbuch der Pastoraltheologie*; the 30-volume encyclopedia *Christian Faith in Modern Society* (1980–83); the five-volume compendium of dogmatic theology, *Mysterium Salutis* (1965–76); the 101-volume (at his death) *Quaestio Disputatae* (1958–84); and founded the international theological journal, *Concilium*, in 1965. He also contributed many articles and volumes to these works. During his 1961 summer vacation Rahner and Herbert Vorgrimler wrote the immensely popular *Dictionary of Theology*.

Rahner never ceased his pastoral activities during this period. In 1959 he published 24 articles on a variety of pastoral themes, translated in English as *The Christian Commitment*, *Theology for Renewal*, and *The Christian in the Market Place*. His letters to young people in *Is Christian Life Possible Today?* evince his personal style of spiritual direction; both *The Priesthood* and *Spiritual Exercises*, his prowess as a retreat director. *The Great Church Year* shows why Rahner ranks in the tradition of Christian theologians who were also great preachers.

Difficulties with Rome – due mainly to Rahner's views on Eucharistic issues and Mariology – came to a head in 1962. A short-lived special censorship ended in October 1962 when Rahner was appointed one of the official *periti*, or theological experts, of *Vatican II (1962–65), a council whose theological outlook he influenced decisively. During this period, he also became the successor to Romano Guardini in the chair of Christian Weltanschauung at the University of Munich, where he taught from 1964 to 1967. He was then appointed professor of dogmatic theology at the University of Münster, where he taught from 1967 until his retirement in 1971. One of the courses he gave over two semesters both at Munich and Münster was subsequently published under the title, *Foundations of Christian Faith: An Introduction to the Idea of Christianity*. Translated into many languages, this highly acclaimed book may be the closest thing to a systematic, architectonic summary of his theology.

Living at the Jesuit writers' house in Munich from 1971 to 1981 and afterward in Innsbruck, Rahner continued his unrelenting worldwide lecturing, writing and pastoral activity. Seeming retrenchment on Church reform, unfair criticism of the official Church, and the loss of ecumenical zeal concerned him at this time. He and Heinrich Fries authored the ground-breaking book *Unity of the Churches: An Actual Possibility* in 1983. Becoming ill a few days after the celebrations of his eightieth birthday, he died on 30 March 1984.

Grace as God's self-offer to every person stands at the centre of Rahner's theology. The 'supernatural existential' transforms human nature and bestows a 'transcendental' or 'primordial revelation', even prior to any human response. Every person's deepest experience – albeit often implicit, denied or repressed – is of a God whose mystery, light and love have embraced the total person. Thus, 'the immanent Trinity which is the economic Trinity' works in all persons' lives as the mystery to whom they must freely respond with the inmost yes or no of their entire persons. This is salvation or its opposite.

Because the human person is 'spirit-in-world', an individual-social-bodily transcendental being making history, the supernatural existential results in the religions of the world. Rahner viewed them as the social-historical incarnations – with greater or lesser degrees of success – of God's transcendental self-communication. Thus, grace can also be found in non-Christian religions. Even the agnostic or atheist who truly accepts life's deepest mystery is an 'anonymous Christian'. Still, Rahner never denied Christianity's absoluteness, that all grace is the grace of Jesus Christ.

Jesus Christ is the high point of God's historical self-communication and its acceptance by human beings. In Christ, God's self-communication and the human acceptance of God have become one by God's action. Rahner skilfully interlaced an evolutionary Christology 'from below' with a Christology 'from above'. Thus, in

Christ, God's victorious grace has become unsurpassably, irrevocably and eschatologically present. The crucified and risen Christ also grounds Rahner's Christian pessimism and optimism: everything must die, but God's forgiving, healing love has overcome sin and death. Thus, Rahner believed that we can hope that all will be saved.

In line with the Greek Fathers and *Duns Scotus, Rahner defended the thesis that God created in order to communicate self, that even without sin the incarnation would have still occurred. The church is the sacrament of God's victorious self-offer to the world. It is the social-historical visibility of the Christ-event, the community of those gathered together by the 'absolute saviour' in faith, hope and love. Due to the Second Vatican Council, this formerly Eurocentric church became a genuine 'world church'. To Rahner, however, this indefectible, holy church can also be sinful – even at its highest level.

Prodded by the insights of Johann Baptist Metz, Rahner moved *somewhat* in the direction of liberation and political theology by developing his well-known thesis that love of neighbour is love of God and stressing the socio-political ramifications of the gospel for contemporary Christianity. He rejected contemporary 'anthropoegoism', which claims that God exists for us.

Perhaps the secret of Rahner's appeal is his synthesis of two elements: critical respect for the Christian tradition and unusual sensitivity to the questions and problems of contemporary life. Rahner never doubted the Christian tradition's ability to speak to the 'catechism of the human heart'. If revitalized, even the oldest fossils of the Christian faith could become the keys to unlock the various locks in the human person to release contemporary human authenticity.

Impelled by his 'Ignatian mysticism of joy in the world' and by finding God in all things and all things in God, Rahner's theology moved in two directions. He compressed all Christianity into three mysteries – Trinity, incarnation and grace, and from them developed his well-known 'short formulas' of the Christian faith. He also unfolded these mysteries into every dimension of human life, even into a 'theology of everyday things' – a theology of work, of seeing, of laughing, of eating and sleeping and the like. Rahner not only explained critically and precisely what the Christian faith is and gave

reasons to believe it, but he also sought to *unite* people with it. To Rahner, theology is more than faith seeking understanding; it is as well a mystagogy that gives the people of God experiential union with the faith by leading them into their own deepest mystery. Thus, he was more a 'sapiential' than an academic theologian.

HARVEY D. EGAN, SJ

FURTHER READING: *Texts: Theological Investigations* (23 vols.; London, 1961–92); *Foundations of Christian Faith: An Introduction to the Idea of Christianity* (New York, 1997); *Concise Theological Dictionary* (with H. Vorgrimler; London, 2nd edn, 1983). For anthologies, see *The Practice of Faith* (London, 1985) and *The Content of Faith* (New York, 1993). For an overall view, see William V. Dych's *Karl Rahner* (London, 1992); Harvey D. Egan, SJ, *Karl Rahner: The Mystics of Everyday Life* (New York, 1998); R. Kress, *A Rahner Handbook* (Atlanta, 1982); H. Vorgrimler, *Understanding Karl Rahner: An Introduction to His Life and Thought* (London, 1986).

Ramsey, Arthur Michael (1904–88)

Michael Ramsey was born in Cambridge and brought up as a Congregationalist. He was discomfited by the atheism of his brilliant elder brother Frank (who died young) and traumatized by the death of his mother in a motor accident. Ramsey read classics and law at Magdalene College, Cambridge, becoming an active Liberal and president of the Union, and he seemed destined for a legal or political career. From his schooldays, however, he had felt increasingly drawn to Anglo-Catholic worship and belief, and at Cambridge he came to realize that he cared most about religious and spiritual matters. In 1926 he began to study theology under Sir Edwyn Hoskyns, a New Testament scholar who was not only an Anglo-Catholic but also a proponent of the anti-liberal theology of *Karl Barth. Ramsey's attachment to Hoskyns was formative but costly: for many years it debarred him from academic advancement in Cambridge.

Ramsey spent an important year at Cuddesdon Theological College and was ordained in 1928. From 1930–36 he served as sub-warden of Lincoln Theological College, where he made his name with his first book, *The Gospel and the Catholic Church*. In 1940 he was appointed Van Mildert Professor of Divinity at Durham and canon of the cathedral, where he married Joan Hamilton in 1942. He enjoyed scholarly success, and in 1950 he was unexpectedly elected Regius professor of divinity at Cambridge. His academic career was soon disrupted by his return to Durham as bishop in 1952. He was appointed Archbishop of York (1956) and, almost inevitably, Archbishop of Canterbury (1961). He retired in 1974 and was made a life peer as Lord Ramsey of Canterbury. He died at Oxford in 1988.

Ramsey's theological career may be viewed in three phases. First of all, the writing of *The Gospel and the Catholic Church* (1936) was an astonishing achievement for a man of thirty whom many regarded as an out-of-touch eccentric. As the title suggests, the book was an essay in evangelical catholicism, grounding church order in the gospel of Christ's death and resurrection. Ramsey brought together the Tractarian emphasis upon sacraments and priesthood and the biblical theology he had learned from Hoskyns to argue that baptism, Eucharist, apostles, Scriptures and creeds express and safeguard the church's dependence on the redemption once wrought by Christ and shared in the life of his body. Episcopacy and the other features of Catholicism are neither a betrayal of the gospel nor extrinsic to it, but they develop from it organically. This thesis was supported by wide-ranging surveys of the Greek and Latin Fathers, equivocal assessments of the *Reformers, and commendation of the Anglican fusion of Catholic and evangelical insights (with special reference to *F.D. Maurice).

The 'structure of thought' which Ramsey built had broad and deep foundations. In scholarly terms he was primarily a teacher of the New Testament. He accepted the methods of historical criticism but came to moderately conservative conclusions about Jesus and the apostolic faith. His outlook embraced the Eastern Orthodox tradition, which testified to the symbiosis of theology, prayer and worship, but his otherworldliness coexisted with strong doctrines of creation and incarnation. Nor was he a reactionary: his perception of the complexity of the Christian tradition and his knowledge of doctrinal controversies disposed him to insist that theological disagreements must be argued out and not suppressed by authority. He identified with the socialist strand in Maurice and the Tractarians, supporting the cause of the poor and needy and advocating a critical stance towards the powers that be, not least in defending the independence of the church of God.

From 1936 to 1963, Ramsey was engaged in consolidation. At Durham he became an exponent of 'Biblical theology', producing studies of *The Resurrection of Christ* (1945) and *The Glory of God and the Transfiguration of Christ* (1949). The latter, his favourite work, epitomized his understanding of the unity of doctrine and spirituality. In the churches, he became known as a discerning spokesman for Anglo-Catholicism, chairing an Anglican group which reported on catholicity (1947) and participating in the ecumenical movement. He acknowledged a long-standing debt in his lectures on *F.D. Maurice and the Conflicts of Modern Theology* (1951). As a bishop, his scholarly work was curtailed, but he published collections of occasional pieces marked by his characteristic blend of erudition and penetrating simplicity: *Durham Essays and Addresses* (1956) and *Canterbury Essays and Addresses* (1964). While at York, he wrote *From Gore to Temple* (1960), a survey of Anglican theology between 1889 and 1939.

In 1963, the Church of England was rocked by Bishop *John A.T. Robinson's *Honest to God*, which in its critique of traditional notions of divine transcendence, prayer and Christian ethics focused the disquiet of an age of rapid intellectual and cultural change. Ramsey initially reacted strongly against Robinson's restatements, but he came to think that he must respond more constructively. His teaching and writing became more attentive to contemporary questioning and drew on modern theologians in Europe and North America. *Images Old and New* (1963) was a brief, lucid and sensitive reply to *Honest to God*. *Sacred and Secular* (1964) discussed the idea of 'religionless Christianity' which Robinson had taken from *Dietrich Bonhoeffer. *God, Christ and the World* (1969) explored secularity, the 'death of God' and demythologizing, concluding that the proper corrective to inadequate theisms was a more Christocentric theology. *The Christian Priest Today* (1972) was a collection of ordination charges. Ramsey respected the integrity of doubters and searchers, and he sought to recover a sense of the transcendence of God in the midst of secular life and not apart from it. He wrote frequently on Christian unity and social responsibility, reflecting his many-sided practical involvement. In retirement he published three further books: *Holy Spirit* (1977), *Jesus and the Living Past* (1980) and *Be Still and Know* (1982).

It is significant that the collection of sermons and lectures published on Ramsey's retirement was entitled *Canterbury Pilgrim*. In his theology as in all things, he combined an unshakeable devotion to Jesus crucified and risen, and a serene awareness of the joy of heaven, with an openness to the life of the world which kept him on the move, always learning and growing. His teaching conveyed the reality of God and enabled Christians to think and act with confidence in an era of disorientation.

CHRISTOPHER M. JONES

FURTHER READING: *Texts: The Gospel and the Catholic Church* (1936; London, 2nd edn, 1956); *The Resurrection of Christ: A Study of the Event and its Meaning for Christian Life* (1945; London, 2nd edn, 1961); *The Glory of God and the Transfiguration of Christ* (London, 1949); *Durham Essays and Addresses* (London, 1956); *Canterbury Essays and Addresses* (London, 1964); *Sacred and Secular: A Study in the Otherworldly and This-Worldly Aspects of Christianity* (London, 1965); *God, Christ and the World* (London, 1969); *Canterbury Pilgrim* (London, 1975). *Studies*: G.S. Wakefield, 'Michael Ramsey: A Theological Appraisal', *Theology* 91 (1988); Owen Chadwick, *Michael Ramsey: A Life* (Oxford, 1990).

Ramsey, Paul (1913–89)

The scholar who became the elder statesman of the Society of Christian Ethics and professor of Christian ethics at Garrett Evangelical Theological Seminary before joining the Princeton University Department of Religion, began as a Methodist minister's son in Mississippi in 1913. Given to engaged and engaging debate since his youth, Ramsey became the ethicist who, more than any other, elaborated the concept of 'tough love' in our time. Although theologians *Karl Barth, *Dietrich Bonhoeffer and *Paul Tillich all have scholarly bodies organized by admirers and disciples to carry on their work, the only ethicists of this century who have that honour are James Luther Adams and Paul Ramsey.

Many ethicists set out a systematic, coherent approach to the establishment and justification of norms in the discipline of ethics, then move step by step toward judgements on particular issues. Ramsey chose another path. He presumed that much of the ground-breaking work had been done by his forebears, from *Augustine and *Aquinas through *Luther and *Edwards to H. Richard Niebuhr, his mentor, and Reinhold Niebuhr, whose work on public issues he sought to extend.

Like his preferred theologians, Ramsey saw Christian love as the centre of ethics. Indeed, he approved of Richard Niebuhr's characterization of his work as natural law transformed by love. He also came to agree with Reinhold Niebuhr's turn from idealism, pacifism and socialism to realism in political and social matters, and he agreed that justice could only approximate, and never attain, the sacrificial love of Christ. But only rarely did Ramsey provide an overview of why he held these ideas together the way he did, although he attempted it in his first and, many agree, least successful book, *Basic Christian Ethics* (1950). Nevertheless, D. Attwood argues that an enduring part of Ramsey's thought is expressed therein. For only in this book does Ramsey draw significantly on Karl Barth, and it allows him to reach beyond his own tradition and training.

> Barth speaks of the basis or precondition of covenant, and covenant as the meaning and goal of creation … Ramsey borrowed this language to use it in ways that Barth never did … [C]ovenant expresses the thought of transformation and the asymmetry of the relation between natural law and love very well. (*Paul Ramsey's Political Ethic* [1992], p. 22)

Ramsey did not oppose dealing with methodological or fundamental issues; he trained many of his students to do this better than he himself did. Yet he would simply plunge into a debate and try to sort the issues from the inside, as can be seen in *Christian Ethics and the Sit-In* (1961) and *War and the Christian Conscience* (also 1961), as well as in several key volumes of the next decade: *Fabricated Man: The Ethics of Genetic Control* (1970), *The Ethics of Fetal Research* (1975) and *Ethics at the Edges of Life: Medical and Legal Intersections* (1978). Ramsey often jumped in because he thought that the ways in which these issues were being handled were mistaken or ideological. He was a consistent advocate for those least able to offer their own arguments for life with dignity – the minorities seeking integration and inclusion, the victims of war, the subjects of biological experimentation, the infant, the very sick and the elderly.

Ramsey's writing and teaching, then, was an intense and disputatious, if also collegial, dialogue with the issues. He adopted the character of a lawyer in a trial, recognizing that he, the opposition, the jury of readers and the supreme judge were all part of the court of moral opinion. He had, therefore, to treat them all with respect while attempting at each point to show that the opposition's construal of the facts was implausible and that their knowledge of the first principles of moral law was not fully informed.

It was not easy to break conversation with Ramsey. He was relentless as a conversation partner. His *Nine Modern Moralists* (1962) represented a disputatious indebtedness with, arguably, the best ethical minds of the previous century, and the issues he raised are still debated – often less well. His *Deeds and Rules in Christian Ethics* (1965, expanded 1967) represents two decades of debate between Ramsey's more classical and principled approach, several proto-postmodernists and some explicitly anti-principial approaches. He engaged especially Paul Lehmann, who advocated 'contextual' ethics, and Joseph Fletcher, who spoke of 'situationalism'. Both of these stances were, in some ways, early signs of 'liberationist' thinking. The issues of this dispute are vital in both scholarly and popular circles, for they have to do with the practical implications of love.

In three areas, particularly, Ramsey opposed these directions. One was the issue of war. Almost alone among American Protestant ethicists during the post-World War II period, Ramsey rehabilitated the classical use of the 'just war doctrine'. He showed that this doctrine had great pertinence for assessing the US policy in regard to both nuclear weaponry and Vietnam, and that the use of that doctrine allowed both the judicious use of coercive, even lethal, force under certain conditions and the limitations of it in others. Ramsey's books in this area (*The Limits of Nuclear War*, 1963; *Again, the Justice of Deterrence*, 1965; *The Just War: Force and Political Responsibility*, 1968; and *Speak up for Just War or Pacifism*, 1988) became central to national debate and brought Protestant thought closer to Roman Catholic discussions.

A second area in which Ramsey opposed the 'liberationist' tendencies of Lehmann and Fletcher was that of revolutionary liberation movements, as advanced by major leaders of the World Council of Churches. Not only did they support the decolonialization movements around the world, but they also adopted quasi-Marxist modes of social analysis and identified Christianity with this reading of history. Ramsey thought they were dead wrong. (See *Who Speaks for the Church? A Critique of the 1966 Geneva Conference on Church and Society*, 1967.)

Third, Ramsey persistently argued that contextual and situational approaches to love, as they appear in the treatments of sexuality and marriage, distorted the character of sexual love. (See *Deeds and Rules in Christian Ethics*; *Norm and Context in Christian Ethics*, with G. Outka, 1968; and *One Flesh: A Christian View of Sex Within, Outside and Before Marriage*, 1975.) When Lehmann argues that the loving thing to do is that which is 'humanizing and liberating', and when Fletcher claims that it is liberating to do the most loving thing and uses (as Ramsey points out) some dozen mutually contradictory definitions of love, Ramsey rises to his polemical best. 'The question is simply whether there are any general rules or principles of virtues or styles of life that embody love, and if so what these may be' (*Deeds and Rules*, p. 112).

This opposition to 'contextual' or 'liberationist' thinking in several areas cast Ramsey as a conservative in a liberal epoch. But as the reputation of 'liberalism' has undergone change, it is precisely this quality that has attracted post-liberationist liberals and anti-liberationist conservatives to his side. In some ways Ramsey's ideas are more accepted today than when he wrote, although fewer people know his name or work.

MAX L. STACKHOUSE

FURTHER READING: *Texts: Basic Christian Ethics* (London, 1953); *Christian Ethics and the Sit-In* (New York, 1961); *War and the Christian Conscience* (Durham, NC, 1961); *Fabricated Man: The Ethics of Genetic Control* (New Haven, 1970); *The Ethics of Fetal Research* (New Haven, 1975); *Ethics at the Edges of Life: Medical and Legal Intersections* (New Haven, 1978); *Nine Modern Moralists* (Englewood Cliffs, NJ, 1962); *Deeds and Rules in Christian Ethics* (Edinburgh, 1965, expanded 1967); *The Limits of Nuclear War* (New York, 1963); *Again, the Justice of Deterrence* (New York, 1965); *The Just War: Force and Political Responsibility* (New York, 1968); *Speak up for Just War or Pacifism* (University Park, PA, 1988); *Who Speaks for the Church? A Critique of the 1966 Geneva Conference on Church and Society* (Nashville, TN, 1967); *One Flesh: A Christian View of Sex Within, Outside and Before Marriage* (Bramcote, Nottingham, 1975); with G. Outka, *Norm and Context in Christian Ethics* (London, 1968). *Study*: D. Attwood, *Paul Ramsey's Political Ethic* (Lanham, MD, 1992).

Rashdall, Hastings (1858–1924)

Hastings Rashdall was one of the leading liberal Anglican theologians of the early twentieth century. He was also an important historian and moral philosopher. He taught in Oxford at Hertford College and New College, combining this latter post for some years with a residentiary canonry at Hereford Cathedral, before moving in 1917 to become dean of Carlisle. In 1905 he married Constance Makins. There were no children. In Oxford, he was every inch a college man, and the Rashdalls' hospitality was much appreciated in Oxford, Hereford and Carlisle. Rashdall was a leading light in the English Social Union, an Anglican society devoted to the application of Christian values to all aspects of social life. He was also much in demand as a speaker on behalf of the Modern Churchmen's Union and its liberal views. In his later years, before the onset of the illness that proved fatal, Rashdall gained some national notoriety for the paper on 'Christ as the Logos and the Son of God' which he delivered at the Girton Conference of the Modern Churchmen's Union in 1921. In claiming that in Christ 'the world has received its highest revelation of God, a revelation, however, which is still being continued and further developed by the work of God's Spirit in other human minds ...', Rashdall appeared to many to be rejecting the doctrine of the incarnation.

Rashdall's philosophy of Personal Idealism was already evident behind his early historical work on *The Universities of Europe in the Middle Ages* (1895); and it was the deep inter-penetration of mind and spirit characteristic of the great medieval universities that he believed to be essential to all good education. This philosophy is sketched out in his contribution to *Contentio Veritatis: Essays in Constructive Theology,* by six Oxford tutors (1902) – an essay entitled 'The Ultimate Basis of Theism', in which he argues that the world requires a rational mind and will as its ground and that the moral values it contains point inexorably to the personality and goodness of God.

Rashdall's two main works were *The Theory of Good and Evil,* a two-volume treatise on moral philosophy which appeared in 1907, and his Bampton Lectures, *The Idea of Atonement in Christian Theology,* which appeared in 1919. The former, in its first volume, contains a fine exposition of Ideal Utilitarianism, the view that what makes an act good is its tendency to promote the ideal good of justice and benevolence. The treatment here of justice, non-retributive punishment and forgiveness is particularly noteworthy. The second volume deals with the individual and society, arguing that the individual needs the authority of tradition, while social ideals ultimately depend upon the judgement of individual consciences. The most appropriate metaphysical underpinning for this moral philosophy is provided by personal theism. God cannot include other consciousnesses, however. Consequently God is not the Absolute. Rather, the Absolute is God and all other Spirits. Here Rashdall distances himself from the philosophy of Absolute Idealism. In theology, Rashdall's conviction that every individual consciousness is exclusive of every other is the basis of his hostility to mysticism and his categorical rejection of social Trinitarianism. Rashdall's philosophy and theology are brought together in another, shorter, treatise, *Conscience and Christ* (1916), in which the exemplary role of Jesus and his teaching about human brotherhood are stressed.

Rashdall's Bampton Lectures constitute the ablest defence of an 'exemplarist' understanding of the atonement to be found in English theology. A thorough treatment of the history of the doctrine of the atonement culminates in a powerful presentation of the *Abelardian thesis that Christ's life and teaching – not simply his death – reveal, as nowhere else, the morally compelling nature of forgiveness and the love of God. Again, it is Rashdall's conviction of the primacy of individual moral responsibility that leads him to reject on moral grounds any substitutionary view of the atonement.

While the philosophy of Personal Idealism soon fell foul of the dominant philosophical movements of the twentieth century, Rashdall's theological liberalism remains influential in one strand of the contemporary theological spectrum. His work continues to be held in high esteem within the Modern Churchmen's Union (now the Modern Churchpeople's Union), and the non-Trinitarian and non-incarnational tendencies of contemporary *liberal Protestantism, evident in the work of Maurice Wiles, Geoffrey Lampe and the authors of *The Myth of God Incarnate,* have much in common with Rashdall's theological views. But his most lasting influence is due to his two main works. *The Theory of Good and Evil* remains one of the most persuasive accounts of Ideal Utilitarianism, and *The Idea of Atonement in Christian Theology* remains one of the most compelling defences of a 'subjective' view of the atonement.

BRIAN HEBBLETHWAITE

FURTHER READING: *Texts: The Theory of Good and Evil* (2 vols.; Oxford, 1907); *Conscience and Christ* (London, 1916); *The Idea of Atonement in Christian Theology* (London, 1919); *Jesus, Human and Divine* (London, 1922). *Studies:* M. Marsh, *Hastings Rashdall: Bibliography of Published Writings* (Powys, 1993); A. Dyson, 'Hastings Rashdall as Social Theologian', in *Worship and Ethics: Lutherans and Anglicans in Dialogue* (ed. O. Bayer and A. Suggate; Berlin, 1996); P.E. Matheson, *The Life of Hastings Rashdall* (Oxford, 1928); C.C.J. Webb, 'Rashdall as Philosopher and Theologian', in Matheson (above).

Rationalism

The term rationalism denotes all those views that consider reason (Latin *ratio*) the most important human faculty. According to rationalists of any kind, it is predominantly if not exclusively by means of reason that we may attain reliable knowledge and in this way get a firm grasp on reality. Rationalism can take various forms depending on the way in which 'reason' is defined and the faculties with which it is contrasted. In its narrowest sense, 'rationalism' points to the specific philosophical outlook developed by *René Descartes (1596–1650): Human reason is informed by certain innate ideas, which establish the basis of all possible knowledge. In its widest sense, the term refers to the general spirit of optimism connected with the *Enlightenment belief in scientific, moral and social progress. In theology, 'rationalism' stands for approaches that contrast the deliverances of reason with those of divine revelation and/or ecclesiastical authority, using the former as a criterion to judge the latter. Following historical lines, we will explore these three main contexts in which the term occurs in turn.

Epistemological rationalism. That reason is the sole source of reliable knowledge was already a central insight in *Plato's philosophy: The transcendent reality of the forms, of which our sensible world is merely an imperfect image, is not accessible by means of the senses, but only by means of rational thought. Nevertheless, in the history of philosophy the term rationalism is usually reserved for the first philosophical systems of the modern period, especially those of

Descartes, *Baruch de Spinoza (1632–77) and Godfried Wilhelm Leibniz (1646–1716). Here, the basic idea of rationalism was developed into largely consistent and elaborate philosophical systems. Common to these systems is the view that in the end our knowledge stems from certain innate ideas.

A leading motive behind Descartes' philosophical programme was his wish to surmount a by then widespread epistemological scepticism (M. de la Montaigne, P. Bayle, P. Gassendi, et al.). Descartes decided not to accept as true anything that did not present itself to his mind so clearly and distinctly that he had virtually no occasion to doubt it (as was the case with his famous insight *cogito ergo sum* – 'I think, therefore I am'). Ideas of this kind cannot stem from the senses, for the 'adventitious' ideas that stem from sense experience are always confused and doubtful; neither can these ideas be identified with the 'factitious' ideas that are constructed by the imagination. Therefore, our clear and distinct ideas must be innate in the sense that they are implanted in the human mind by God.

Our concept of God is a primary example of such an innate idea known directly by reason. According to Descartes we cannot produce this idea as a mental construct of our own, nor can we derive it from our experience of the external world. For clearly, both we ourselves and the external world are finite, whereas God is infinite. And in some way the idea of the infinite must precede that of the finite. 'For how could I understand that … I was not wholly perfect, unless there were in me some idea of a more perfect being which enabled me to recognize my own defects by comparison?' (Descartes, *Third Meditation*, p. 1641). Thus, the concept of God can only be laid down in our minds by God himself. Similarly, other clear and distinct ideas that occur in our minds, such as the ideas of mind and matter, fundamental mathematical insights and even basic intuitions on the universal laws of physics, are inborn. It is only from such innate ideas that scientific knowledge can be deduced.

To say that these ideas are innate does not imply that babies are born with them as full-fledged concepts in their minds. Rather, we are born with a disposition to form such concepts, a disposition that starts to operate as soon as it is triggered by certain empirical experiences. Thus, innate ideas are forms of thought or ways of conceiving things, which are initially employed unconsciously, but then evoke in us clear and distinct beliefs about the way the world is. Although sense experience and empirical experiments certainly play an additional role in Cartesian rationalism, the way in which we gain knowledge of the world is largely determined by our a priori intuition of these basic ideas and the demonstrations which we can deductively infer from them. And this is true for the other continental rationalists (e.g. Spinoza, Leibniz) as well. Despite the large mutual differences between their systems, all of them sought to extend the deductive structure of mathematics to the other sciences; intuition and demonstration were considered to lead to a much more certain and permanent type of knowledge than sense perception could ever deliver.

At this point, British empiricism as represented by *John Locke (1632–1704), *George Berkeley (1685–1753) and *David Hume (1711–76) forms the historical counterpart of continental rationalism. Although the adequacy of this traditional classification is sometimes questioned (since it tends to overemphasize the differences and obscure the points of agreement between rationalists and empiricists), it certainly continues to make sense. According to the empiricists, there are no such things as innate ideas in the human mind, either implicitly or explicitly. Rather, when coming into existence the mind is a *tabula rasa*, a white paper without any characters (so Locke, *An Essay Concerning Human Understanding*, 1690). All our ideas stem either from experience or from reflection on experience. So there is nothing in our mind which was not in our experience before. And, apart from logical truths, propositions can only be known to be true from sense perception.

The debate between continental rationalism and British empiricism came to a conclusion in the critical philosophy of *Immanuel Kant (1724–1804), who proposed a largely convincing synthesis between elements from both traditions. Kant moulded these elements into a new epistemological paradigm, in which he neither privileged reason over the senses nor the other way round. He instead ascribed distinctive roles to each of these in the process of knowledge formation, and thus he limited the significance of both to these roles.

Rationalism as a world-view.

With Kant, we enter the heyday of the Enlightenment. In relation to this era, sometimes referred to as the 'Age of Reason', the term rationalism receives a novel connotation that deviates in at least two important respects from that discussed above.

First, the concept of reason as employed by Enlightenment thinkers is much wider in scope than the Cartesian concept of reason as a separate source of knowledge apart from sense experience. Rather, the Enlightenment view of reason subsumes all our intellectual capacities under this concept. Kant's famous dictum *sapere aude* – 'have the courage to use your own brain!' – was representative of this conception of reason. When it comes to the process of knowledge formation, Enlightenment thinkers such as Voltaire (1694–1778), impressed as they were by the successes of Newtonian empirical science, were really empiricists rather than continental rationalists.

Second, the alternative instance in contrast with which reason is acclaimed in the Enlightenment is not sense experience or even feeling, but faith and revelation. In our attempts both to gain knowledge of the world and morally to improve the world, we should choose human reason as our sole guide and stop trusting traditional authorities such as the ecclesiastical tradition and the Bible. In this sense, whereas the systems of the seventeenth-century epistemological rationalists attributed a crucial (though sometimes, as in Spinoza, unorthodox) role to God, the rationalism of the Enlightenment is thoroughly opposed to religion in general and traditional Christianity in particular. 'The age of religion has been replaced by the age of science', d'Alembert (1717–83) characteristically wrote in the introduction of the famous *Encyclopédie* (1751–80). Most of the Enlightenment rationalist philosophers were deists; some of them professed a materialistic variety of atheism.

It is because of its wide definition of 'reason', its presenting itself as an alternative to traditional religion, and its concomitant practical character (with much attention to proper human conduct), that Enlightenment rationalism must be conceived as a comprehensive world-view. Indeed, the world itself was viewed as being rationally structured. This metaphysical aspect of Enlightenment rationalism (i.e., the idea that reality as a whole and in its parts is purely rational) originated in continental rationalism and found its apotheosis in the philosophy of *Hegel, who confidently equated the real with the rational. In this connection, we can also see why the Enlightenment emphasis on reason was accompanied by a strong preoccupation with Nature: the rational form of all spheres of human conduct was to be found in reality in its purest form, that is, in Nature. Thus, natural rights were distinguished, a natural education was recommended (Rousseau), as well as natural morality and natural religion. The third key concept which characterizes the rationalist world-view of the Enlightenment (apart from 'reason' and 'Nature') is no doubt 'progress'. The thinkers of the Enlightenment had high expectations of the extent to which the unrestricted use of reason would lead to scientific and moral improvement, to a maximization of human happiness and to the establishment of a harmonious social and political order.

It is for the supposed naïvety of this huge confidence in the power of the human intellect that the use of the term rationalism as a designation of the Enlightenment world-view is often derogatory. In fact, the term rationalism originated as a polemical tag for the view that reason has precedence over religion.

Rationalism in theology. Mentioning the original context in which the term rationalism arose leads us to a discussion of its use in theology. For it was by theologians such as Daniel Hoffmann (1538–1611) that, at the end of the sixteenth century, both certain *Aristotelian philosophers and the early followers of Descartes were called *rationistae*, or *rationalistae*. By means of these terms Hoffmann meant to criticize the view that philosophy forms a separate source of knowledge in matters of faith, next to revelation. Taken in this sense, rationalism in theology is fairly old, and it can be found already in *Aquinas, who also held that there are certain truths about God which may be known by reason alone without any aid of revelation. The rationalist tendency in theology becomes much more prominent, however, when under the influence of the rise of modern philosophy the view that all theological truth-claims have to pass the test of rational vindication finds acceptance.

In Locke, this view leads to the declaration of the *Reasonableness of Christianity* (1695). Other thinkers, however, such as Lord Herbert of Cherbury (1583–1648), distinguished between a core of very general religious convictions which can indeed be vindicated by reason, and a large belt of much less reliable beliefs which were added in a later stage on the basis of special revelation. These other beliefs, usually of a much more specifically Christian nature, were often contested in religious wars, could not stand the test of reason, and should therefore be rejected. By this attempt to purify historical Christianity and reduce it to 'natural religion', Herbert became the father of English *Deism. This Deism was also propagated by John Toland (1670–1722) and Matthew Tindal (1655–1733), the latter of whom also became influential in Germany.

In Germany, the view that any recourse to divine revelation is no longer necessary, since human reason can establish all we need to know in matters of religion, led not only to conflicts between 'rationalists' and 'supranaturalists', but also to the rise of biblical criticism (inspired by H.S. Reimarus, 1694–1768, J.S. Semler, 1725–91, et al.). At the centre of rationalist religion stands a Jesus who is no longer the saviour of fallen humanity, but a simple Galilean teacher showing us how to lead a morally virtuous life. In the course of the nineteenth century, the term rationalism came to be equated with secularism, atheism or agnosticism. Attempting to achieve a more positive reputation, rationalists began to prefer calling themselves humanists.

In the twentieth century, rationalism in theology came to be sharply criticized for its self-complacency by *dialectical theologians such as *Karl Barth (1886–1968). Later on, the very idea of a universal concept of reason by means of which it would be possible to judge over truth and falsity in moral and religious matters, propagated so strongly in the Enlightenment, became the object of profound suspicion and critique in postmodernism.

GIJSBERT VAN DEN BRINK

FURTHER READING: A.W. Benn, *A History of English Rationalism in the Nineteenth Century* (London, 1906); E. Cassirer, *The Philosophy of the Enlightenment* (Boston, 1960); J. Cottingham, *The Rationalists* (Oxford, 1988); R. Descartes, 'Meditations on First Philosophy', in *The Philosophical Writings of Descartes*, II (ed. John Cottingham, Robert Stroothoff and Dugald Murdoch; Cambridge, 1984); A. Kenny, *Rationalism, Empiricism and Idealism* (Oxford, 1986); P. Kondylis, *Die Aufklärung im Rahmen des neuzeitlichen Rationalismus* (Stuttgart, 1981); A. MacIntyre, *Whose Justice? Which Rationality?* (London, 1988); J. McCabe, *A Rationalist Encyclopedia* (London, 1948).

Ratzinger, Joseph (b. 1927)

Cardinal Joseph Ratzinger, since 1982 the prefect of the Sacred Congregation for the Doctrine of the Faith, was born in Marktl am Inn in Bavaria on Holy Saturday, 16 April 1927. His father was a modestly paid police constable. The Ratzinger family was unfriendly to the national socialist ideology, but the sixteen-year-old Joseph was conscripted to serve in the German army during World War II – first in an anti-aircraft unit near Munich and then in building fortifications on the Austrian-Hungarian border. At the end of the war Ratzinger lived in an open-air camp as a prisoner of the Americans for six weeks.

Ratzinger was ordained a priest in 1951. He did his doctoral dissertation on *St Augustine and his habilitation thesis on *St Bonaventure. He held professorships at Bonn, Münster, Tübingen and Regensburg. At *Vatican II he was a young but highly influential *peritus* under Cardinal Joseph Frings. Ratzinger was made archbishop of Munich-Freising and cardinal in 1977.

Ratzinger's works on Augustine and Bonaventure signal his involvement in a theological venture known as *ressourcement*, or the 'return to the sources'. This movement entailed going beyond the theology manuals, which often relied on a rather narrow reading of *Aquinas, to retrieve a wide range of scriptural, patristic and medieval perspectives. Romano Guardini and *Hans Urs von Balthasar particularly influenced Ratzinger in his approach. In his 1960 (ET 1966) study *The Open Circle: The Meaning of Christian Brotherhood*, he drew upon scriptural and patristic sources to explore the significance of Christian community.

Ratzinger embraced the developments of Vatican II, especially the council's historical sensibilities, its stress on an ecclesiology of communion and its focus on a renewal of the liturgy. His 1968 (ET 1970) *Introduction to Christianity* remains a model for bringing a historically conscious faith into dialogue with modern concerns. Ratzinger took part with many other theologians in the founding of the journal *Concilium*, which was intended to help implement the reforms of the council.

Already in his early work, however, there are indications that Ratzinger's interpretation of the council differed from that of his progressive colleagues. Even at the time of its drafting, he was suspicious of the optimism concerning the modern world expressed in *Gaudium et spes*. Whether it was while reading Augustine or while experiencing the bombings of Munich, Ratzinger had adopted a highly critical outlook toward modernity. Moreover, while many of his colleagues were touting local diversity and the importance of inculturation, this man who had grown up in Nazi Germany was expressing concerns about nationalism and the need for a strong church universal.

In 1974, along with *Henri de Lubac, *Hans Urs von Balthasar and Karl Lehman, Ratzinger helped to launch the journal *Communio*, which stood in reaction to the more liberal *Concilium*. Many saw this as an about-face for Ratzinger, but he maintained that it was his progressive colleagues who had changed. They had begun to implement advances in the 'spirit' of Vatican II, or according to the 'trajectory' of Vatican II, rather than in harmony with the council's actual teachings.

Since becoming prefect of the Sacred Congregation for the Doctrine of the Faith in 1982, Ratzinger has had a reputation for being a conservative watchdog. He rightfully maintains that his work as prefect must be distinguished from his work as a private theologian. Also, he notes that his ecclesiastical involvements have prevented him from writing the major theological works that he might otherwise have produced. His several books include the collections of essays *Church, Ecumenism, and Politics* (1987; ET 1988) and *A New Song for the Lord* (1995; ET 1996). Many of his theological opinions are available through two book-length interviews, *The Ratzinger Report* (1985) and *Salt of the Earth* (1996; ET 1997).

Ratzinger's main theological contributions have been in ecclesiology, particularly concerning the nature of the church as a communion; ecumenism; the church-world relationship; and liturgy. Yet his most grounding concern has been Christological. Ratzinger holds that contemporary Christian spirituality is threatened by both a new form of *Arianism that neglects the divinity of Christ as well as by a new form of *Nestorianism that separates the Jesus of history from the Christ of faith. He favours renewed attention to the doctrine of *Chalcedon, read through the lens of later doctrinal developments, as a way of promoting Jesus Christ as the human being who is the revelation of God.

One of the points that Ratzinger makes most frequently is that the church, while tied in many ways to politics, ultimately transcends the realm of the political. Ratzinger stresses that the church is finally the body of Christ, a mystery that in its essence remains beyond the grasp of sociologists and reformers. The church constitutes an invitation to share in the divine life of the Trinity, and as such it is not simply the receiver of revelation but also a dimension of what has been revealed. Ratzinger recognizes that many historical developments have taken place and that many structures have changed. However, he emphasizes that there are essential structures, such as the world-wide episcopacy, the papacy, the sacraments and the male-only priesthood which, despite evolution in form, represent the will of Christ and so must be maintained.

Ratzinger's strong focus on Christ and the church as the channels of God's grace to the world contrasts with *Karl Rahner's stress on the already present nature of God's grace in all of creation. Ratzinger's emphatic linking of the church, despite its failings, with Christ, contrasts with *Hans Küng's stress that the church is basically a human fellowship radically in need of structural reform. Ratzinger insists that, granting historical complexities, the church still guards an established deposit of faith. This view contrasts with Liberation theologian Leonardo Boff's emphasis on truth emerging from praxis and on 'orthopraxy' preceding orthodoxy.

Ratzinger's positions are sometimes labelled 'restorationist'. His harshest critics believe he is trying to restore the church to its pre-Vatican II mentality. He and his supporters maintain that he is simply trying to restore the direction of conciliar reform to its original path.

DENNIS M. DOYLE

FURTHER READING: *Texts: The Open Circle: The Meaning of Christian Brotherhood* (New York, 1966); *Introduction to Christianity* (New York, 1979); *Church, Ecumenism, and Politics* (New York, 1988); *A New Song for the Lord* (New York, 1996); with Vittori Messori, *The Ratzinger Report* (Leominster, 1985); with Peter Seewald, *Salt of the Earth* (San Francisco, 1997). *Study:* Aidan Nichols, *The Theology of Joseph Ratzinger: An Introductory Study* (Edinburgh, 1988).

Rauschenbusch, Walter (1861–1918)

A leading figure, and the most prominent theologian, in the American Social Gospel movement in the early years of the twentieth century. A Baptist minister, he experienced two 'conversions' in his life – one in his teenage years in the context of the German Pietism of his home, the second when he discovered the centrality of the kingdom of God for all Christian life and thought. In a relatively short life (he died of cancer in 1918, aged fifty-seven), affected throughout by a hearing disability, he sought to maintain in creative tension both personal piety and social activism, and to urge the churches of his day to face the challenges brought by social, economic and industrial change.

Rauschenbusch was born on 4 October 1861 into a pious home. His family history included *Lutheran clergy going back many generations. His father had been a Lutheran missionary who became a Baptist. German Pietism therefore mixed with American evangelicalism in Rauschenbusch's religious upbringing. He studied on three occasions in Germany, as a child (1865–69), after high school (1879–83), and then again when on sabbatical as a Baptist minister (1891–92). Most of his life was spent in Rochester (New York), where his father became professor of German at the university. Rauschenbusch himself studied there (1883–86) and went back to teach there, first in the German department (1897) and then as professor of church history (from 1902). Though it was this final phase of his life which saw him at his most productive in terms of writing, it was undoubtedly a pastorate in central New York (1886–97) which left the decisive mark upon Rauschenbusch as both person and thinker. This period shaped all his later writings. It was here that Rauschenbusch's commitment to the Social Gospel was born, through his seeing the need for the church and Christian theology to respond to urban deprivation in all its many forms, not least bad housing, unreliable employment and lack of income.

Rauschenbusch's work, never collected into a single or critical edition, included newspaper articles, pamphlets and popular books and booklets as well as scholarly works. Collections of extracts of his writings appeared in 1950, 1957, 1966 and 1984. As a theologian he is best known for three titles. *Christianity and the Social Crisis* (New York, 1907; re-issued Louisville, 1991) was his first main attempt to spell out the significance of social change for Christianity. Rauschenbusch locates his concerns within the tradition of the Hebrew prophets, the life and teaching of Jesus and the sociology of the early churches before assessing how and why Christianity lost these emphases. The fifth chapter spells out the nature of the present social crisis, and the last two chapters offer proposals for how the churches can become involved in 'the social movement'. *Christianizing the Social Order* (New York, 1912) appears to have more in keeping with a work of social policy or economics than theology, though Rauschenbusch insisted that it was a thoroughly theological work. It is perhaps the most optimistic of his major works, leading to the charge of his being weak on the doctrine of sin, and it reveals him as 'a precursor of modern democratic socialism' (so Dorrien). *A Theology for the Social Gospel* (New York, 1917) can be regarded as the Social Gospel's main systematic theology, though it is not as comprehensive as the ascription suggests. Its major topics are sin, the kingdom of God and salvation, though the doctrines of God, Holy Spirit, baptism, the Eucharist (Lord's Supper), eschatology and atonement also feature. *The Righteousness of the Kingdom* (Nashville, TN, 1968), a manuscript dating originally from 1891–92 which only came to light in the 1960s, may be regarded as a foundation for these three main works.

There are common themes and emphases across all Rauschenbusch's work. The kingdom of God became the theological focus of his ministry and theology, both as a result of his critical reading of the Synoptic Gospels, and because of his need to find a way of making theological sense of his inner-city experience in New York. Reacting to the individualism both of the piety of his youth and the society around him, Rauschenbusch sought to locate and rework theological concepts in a manner which took society and social contexts seriously. If he was prone to 'ethicize' the kingdom of God too much, he nevertheless saw the kingdom as both a theological and ethical challenge to much of what passed for Christian thought and practice in his day. Rauschenbusch adopted and commended a critical approach to the Bible and Christian tradition. Leaning heavily on the German Protestantism he had encountered through reading and study in Germany – above all *Schleiermacher, *Ritschl and *Harnack – Rauschenbusch was not afraid to point out where the church throughout its history had deviated from its true purpose. He took up too

readily the 'Hellenization' theory from Harnack, according to which early Christianity simply went astray when trying to accommodate Hebrew thought to Greek culture. He was resistant to some of the latest developments in New Testament study at the turn of the century (stimulated by Johannes Weiss and *Albert Schweitzer) which read the kingdom of God in eschatological terms, thus challenging his ethical interpretation. Yet despite these limitations, Rauschenbusch's approach was creative in being critical, recognizing fully (as did liberals and modernists) the nature and extent of the challenge facing Christianity in the modern age. Rauschenbusch's adoption of a critical approach remains unusual in being closely allied to a piety that is still identifiably also 'evangelical'. A third emphasis in Rauschenbusch's work was on the social dimension of evil. Following both Schleiermacher and Ritschl, Rauschenbusch resisted a solely individualistic understanding of sin, desiring to draw attention to sin's systemic aspects: the way that people are dragged down within the social structures of which they are a part. In this respect, Rauschenbusch was clearly a forerunner of *theologies of liberation. The attention he gave to the topic, and without denying the importance of individual sin, counters some of the criticism levelled against his thought at this point.

If Rauschenbusch's thought is clearly over-optimistic at times and in need of further development in the light of later political, social and economic thought and experience, he was far from being as naïve as his critics sometimes suggest. Respected by both Reinhold and H. Richard Niebuhr, and influential upon Martin Luther King Jr, Rauschenbusch's legacy still carries weight. The challenge to Christian theology to reconsider its doctrines in the light of contemporary social questions, which he clearly recognized, has arguably even now not adequately been taken up.

CLIVE MARSH

FURTHER READING: Gary Dorrien, 'Walter Rauschenbusch and the Legacy of the Social Gospel', ch. 2 in *Reconstructing the Common Good* (Maryknoll, NY, 1990); Winthrop S. Hudson (ed.), *Walter Rauschenbusch: Selected Writings* (New York, 1984); Robert T. Handy (ed.), *The Social Gospel in America 1870–1920* (New York, 1966), pp. 251–389; 'Walter Rauschenbusch (1861–1918)', in *Makers of Christian Theology in America* (ed. Mark G. Toulouse and James O. Duke; Nashville, TN, 1997), pp. 341–47; Paul M. Minus, *Walter Rauschenbusch: American Reformer* (New York, 1988).

Reformation

The Reformation is the name given to a series of reforms and reorganizations of the Western church at the local, regional and national levels in the sixteenth century. In a wider sense, however, the term can also be applied to the period from the beginning of the fifteenth to the close of the seventeenth century. The phenomenon was essentially a religious and theological one, but it was strongly influenced by – and in turn influenced – wider cultural, social, economic and political developments in the late-medieval/early-modern period.

As one of the most important events in western history, which largely determined the political as well as the religious shape of Western Europe and its colonies, the Reformation has been subject to a variety of interpretations by historians. In the nineteenth century it was regarded as the religious wing of the Renaissance, which together with the Renaissance made the decisive break with the Middle Ages and ushered in modernity. It did so both by contributing to the decline of papal power and the emergence of sovereign nation states, as well as by removing economics from the realm of canon law and so permitting the rise of capitalism and the urban middle class. In Britain, the inheritance of the Reformation helped to provide a national identity (due to the widespread popularity of John Foxe's *Book of Martyrs* in England, for instance). In the United States of America, by contrast, the same inheritance was credited with initiating the era of religious toleration, and at least in certain respects paving the way for the separation of church and state. The twentieth century, with its two world wars, saw a reaction against such progressive, optimistic ('Whig') views of history. From the 1960s, the Reformation was seen as having more in common with the late-medieval traditions from which it emerged than with modernity. Its religious thought was seen as preventing rather than hastening the emergence of the nation state (the late development of Germany as a unified nation was, for instance, attributed to *Luther's own preference for regional monarchies). *Marxist and social historians saw the possibilities for genuine social change in this period not in the predominantly bourgeois Reformation but in the German Peasants' War of 1524/5. Further, it was noted, the toleration of minorities and the improvement of the state of women had to wait until the *Enlightenment and after. At the end of the twentieth century, there are signs that the progressive view of the Reformation is returning. These signs include the 'confessionalization thesis' proposed by continental historians (which again interprets the Reformation as part of the process of state-building) and the 'revisionist' approach to the English Reformation (which again emphasizes the discontinuity of Protestantism with the late-medieval tradition).

The significance of the Reformation as a theological event was also decisive. It was not primarily concerned with the fundamental Christian doctrines of the Trinity and Christology (as the Patristic period had been): with the exception of some *rationalists, there was general agreement on these basic tenets of the faith. Rather, the concern of the Reformation period was with 'applied' theology in the broadest sense, and in this respect it can be seen as developing the theological concerns of the high and late-Middle Ages. The Reformation's significance for historical theology is evident in three main areas, which will be considered below. First, it posed in a particularly acute form the question of theological authority, especially in relation to the relative claims of Scripture and tradition. Secondly, it raised vitally important questions about soteriology which the medieval discussions had failed to resolve. Thirdly, it raised questions for Christian existence, in reconciling the demands of the gospel with the demands of urbanization and the money-economy, and in reconciling one's existence as a member of the universal church with one's existence as a subject or a citizen in a sovereign nation state.

The classification of the various Reformation movements most valuable to the historical theologian is a division into three confessional strands, with each strand capable of further subdivision: (1) the Protestant Reformation (comprising the Lutheran, Reformed and Anglican traditions); (2) the Radical Reformation (a portmanteau term covering a diverse range of *Anabaptists, Spiritualists and Rationalists); and (3) the Catholic Reformation (which includes the Council of Trent's work of church reform and doctrinal clarification as well as developments associated with the reform of some religious orders and the creation of others). In most cases it is possible to detect four main phases of Reformation. The first involved communication of the primary religious insight, by which for example Martin Luther (1483–1546), *Thomas Müntzer (c. 1489–1525) and *Ignatius Loyola (c. 1491–1556) attempted by the dissemination of their message to replicate in others their own conversion experiences. The second phase was characterized by systematization of this insight, often in the form of theological *summae* by second-generation reformers, such as the *Common Places* of *Philip Melanchthon (1497–1560) or the *Institutes* of *John Calvin (1509–1564). The third phase saw conflict between different exponents of the same primary insight (for instance between the Gnesio-Lutherans and the Philippists). The fourth and final phase realized authorization of an agreed formulary or confession (e.g. the Reformed Heidelberg Catechism of 1562 or the Anglican Thirty-nine Articles of 1563), though further conflict arose after the adoption of an agreed formulary, as in the controversies over grace involving Michel Baius (1513–89) and Domingo Báñez (1528–1604) which followed the Council of Trent.

The development of the distinctive themes of Reformation theology begins in the late medieval period (c. 1350–1500). For the intellectual context of the Reformation one must look to the arts and theology schools of the medieval university. Because, in spite of their polemic against *Scholasticism, most of the early Reformers were university-educated. Arts faculties, in which all students would pursue a course of study, tended to teach philosophy according to one of two ways. The *via antiqua*, the 'traditional way', took a realist approach to epistemology, positing a direct relation between particulars and their universals, and therefore between perception and reality. The *via moderna*, the 'new way', regarded universals as mere names (*nomina*) or constructs, having no necessary existence in reality. The modernists, or 'nominalists', who followed the teaching of *William of Ockham (c. 1285–1347), adopted a radically fideist stance towards the acquisition of divine knowledge. They argued that as no universal concept can be deduced from sense-perception, neither can any knowledge of God come to us except by revelation, to be received by faith. Luther was trained in the modernist arts faculty at Erfurt University, and

regarded himself as a good Ockhamist throughout his life. The scholastic critique of Scholasticism adopted by his philosophy tutors Bartholomaeus Arnoldi von Usingen (1465–1532) and Jodocus Trutfetter (c. 1460–1519), who established a hierarchy of authorities with Scripture and the early Church Fathers at the top and the scholastic theologians at the bottom, assisted Luther in developing his 'theology of the cross'. The impact of *Nominalism on his doctrine of salvation was more equivocal. On the one hand, its insistence that God was bound to reward good works only because God had freely covenanted to reward them, and not because they were intrinsically meritorious, held open the theoretical possibility that God might choose to save people without any reference to their own merit. On the other hand, the covenant itself, by which God would give grace to whomsoever did 'what was in them' to love God above all things by their own efforts, was practically *Pelagian, which explains the vehemence of Luther's attacks on the scholastic 'pig-theologians'. The Swiss and south German Reformers were more influenced by the *via antiqua*. *Ulrich Zwingli (1484–1531) came to conclusions similar to Luther's own from realist (specifically *Platonist) first principles. In his popular pamphlet *That One Should Live for Others and Not for Oneself* of 1523, *Martin Bucer (1491–1551) essayed an evangelical ethic on the basis of a *Thomist exposition of the integratedness of all being.

The Reformation also drew on the traditions of spiritual renewal which characterized the late Middle Ages. Luther himself was able to find a way through his religious difficulties due largely to the guidance of the vicar-general of his order, Johann von Staupitz (c. 1468–1524), a renowned spiritual director. At Staupitz's suggestion, Luther immersed himself in the sermons of Johannes Tauler (c. 1300–61), and his first published work in 1516 was a partial edition of the Taulerian tract *A German Theology*. The same tract became a major influence on Anabaptist and Spiritualist radicals such as Andreas Bodenstein von Karlstadt (c. 1480–1541), Hans Denck (c. 1495–1527) and Sebastian Franck (c. 1499–c. 1542). The Catholic Reformation was also inspired by the medieval mystical tradition, and in the retreats and missions of the *Jesuits one finds a clear desire to 'democratize' this mysticism, so that it comes to inform the spirituality of the home and workplace as well as of the cloister.

The cultural context of the Reformation is provided by Renaissance Humanism – so much so that no Reformer of note was unaffected by Humanism. The rebirth of classical literature and values was a pan-European phenomenon. But in the north it took on a more explicitly Christian flavour as *Desiderius Erasmus (c. 1466–1536), among others, applied the same desire to return 'to the sources' (*ad fontes*) that motivated their recovery of the Greek and Latin classics to the sources of Christianity, namely the Bible in its original languages and the early Fathers. Erasmus's 1516 Greek New Testament, edited according to the best available manuscripts and accompanied by a close Latin translation, can be regarded as a *sine qua non* of the Reformation itself. Advances were being made in the realm of hermeneutics as well as textual criticism. The Psalms commentary of Jacques Lefèvre d'Étaples (c. 1455–1536) was to have a decisive influence on Luther – arguably the Reformer least open to the New Learning. Calvin was among the most open, and with its combination of elegant style and measured content, his *Institutes of the Christian Religion* must rank as one of the finest expressions of Christian humanism of the sixteenth century. Finally, we may simply note the fact that Humanism's concern with education left an indelible mark on both the Protestant and Catholic Reformations.

The Reformation's ecclesio-political context is provided by two medieval controversies. Alarmed by the papacy's increasingly absolutist claims over the church and by its pretensions to authority over secular powers, conciliarists on the one hand and the German emperor's apologists on the other set about restricting papal authority. By 1500, both controversies were settled: conciliarism was practically dead (and was certainly buried by the Fifth Lateran Council in 1512–17), while the papacy ceased to make any but routine claims to secular jurisdiction outside its own territories. But the arguments echoed far into the sixteenth century, and *William of Ockham (who provided the theoretical underpinning for both conciliarism and imperialism by insisting that faith was the mark of the true church), opened the way for the principle of devolved authority characteristic of the Protestant churches.

Theological authority. The Nominalist application of Ockham's razor to the sources of revelation, and the humanist call for a return to the literary headwaters of Christianity, combined to elevate Scripture and to destroy the synthesis of theological authorities which characterized the high Middle Ages. 'Scripture alone' became a watchword of the Protestant Reformation, but with significant variations. Luther's conviction that 'the Word of God', that is, Christ and the forgiveness of sins he both effected and proclaimed, was prior to Scripture allowed him to be both literal (e.g. in basing his belief in the Real Presence on Christ's words 'This is my body/blood') and liberal (e.g. in decanonizing Hebrews, James, Jude and Revelation for not fitting the Pauline template). Calvin made God's word practically synonymous with Scripture, and therefore made no qualitative distinctions between its parts: in particular, both Calvin and Bucer gave the Torah a more positive Christian role than Luther did. Protestants routinely inveighed against 'the words/traditions of men'; but that their rejection of tradition was by no means complete was demonstrated by the extreme position taken by the Radicals. Their desire to re-form the church to its pre-Constantinian, and not simply its pre-papal, state led the *Socinians, for example, to reject the doctrines of the Trinity and of the incarnation as the impositions of imperial councils which could not simply be read off the sacred page. (The complete rejection of Scripture came with the Spiritualists, who claimed direct inspiration by the Holy Spirit and therefore had no need of the 'dead letter'.) Luther's and Calvin's belief that Scripture is its own interpreter did not prevent them from preparing guidelines for Bible study: in Luther's case, his famous series of biblical prefaces; in Calvin's, the *Institutes* itself. In recent years it has been argued that such an attitude was not very different from that adopted by the Fathers at Trent. In declaring that Scripture and tradition should be equally revered, they understood by tradition not some independent source of authority but rather that body of teaching which testifies to the prior truth of Scripture. Those Catholics influenced by Nominalism and/or Humanism certainly had such an understanding of the issues; but for the dominant, Thomist party at Trent, belief in the synthesis of authorities, all equally inspired by the Spirit and all equally possessed by the church, persisted.

Soteriology. At the heart of Luther's reformation lay his doctrine of justification by faith alone. Social historians have doubted that such a 'theological' doctrine could ever have attracted mass support of itself. But the personal testimony of the likes of Hans Sachs and Albrecht Dürer, together with the flood of pamphlets which poured forth in German-speaking lands in the early 1520s, indicate that it was precisely this doctrine, and its liberating message, which drove early popular support for the Reformation. Concerned with the damaging effect on public morality the doctrine was believed to entail, second-generation Protestants put equal emphasis on sanctification. Meanwhile Luther's own deputy, Melanchthon, sided with Erasmus in the free-will debate, and at the Regensburg Colloquy (1541) endorsed a scheme of double justification quite at odds with his leader's wishes. Radicals routinely rejected justification by faith alone. Anabaptists rejected it because it drew attention away from spiritual regeneration, Spiritualists (notably Denck) because it opposed the emphasis on minute regulation of behaviour which direct inspiration dictated, and Rationalists both because of its insistence on a divine saviour and because of its low estimate of human abilities. In various modified forms, the doctrine had its supporters among the Fathers at Trent, particularly among *Augustinians who welcomed the emphasis on grace (notably Girolamo Seripando [1492/3–1563]), among *Franciscans who heard in the principle of imputed righteousness an echo of the Scotist doctrine of divine acceptation, and among contemplatives such as Reginald Pole (1500–58). In the balanced formulation of the Tridentine decree on justification a clear attempt was made to accommodate these minority opinions; but ultimately the Thomist view of the Dominican and Jesuit contingent prevailed.

Christian existence. By the later Middle Ages, popular devotional movements along with increasing literacy were blurring traditional definitions of 'lay' and 'clerical'. Jean Gerson (1363–1429) saw the key to reform in restoring in the clergy a sense of their distance from, and superiority to, the laity. His approach inspired that branch of sixteenth-century Catholic clericalist reform which included Josse Clichtove (1472–1543). Luther's approach to reform demanded, on the contrary, a recognition of the laity's right to be heard, a concern which permeates the Ninety-five Theses and which remains an important theme until the Peasants' War.

Nonetheless, Luther continued to envisage, in a cluster of associated doctrines, a Christian way of life in which the traditional distinctions were eclipsed. The doctrine of vocation taught the equality of all Christian callings, whether religious or secular. The priesthood of all believers taught an equality of obligation to preach the gospel and to intercede for, even sacrifice oneself for, one's neighbour. The 'two kingdoms' doctrine taught that God rules both the church and the world, the first by love and the ethics of the Sermon on the Mount, the second by the sword. The two kingdoms doctrine, with its pessimistic *realpolitik*, was developed in the context of a regional monarchy, where the rule of a godly prince might be wished for and occasionally granted, but never guaranteed. The semi-democratic city-state offered a better prospect for the creation of a theocracy, and Calvin eventually succeeded in turning Geneva into a godly city, despite the many conflicts between council and Consistory. The Radicals refused all compromise with secular authority, whether monarchical or oligarchic. Their response to the challenge of living out the Sermon on the Mount in 'the real world' was either flight (e.g. of south German and Austrian pacifist Anabaptists to Moravia, where they created their own communities) or fight (as preferred by the Spiritualist Müntzer and the bloody Anabaptist regime in Münster). The pacifists, though harshly persecuted, survived, and can make a claim to having pioneered the principles of toleration and of the separation of church and state. Within the Catholic Reformation, monasticism (the traditional means of creating a protected space in which to follow the radical gospel ethic) not only survived but developed, in many cases adopting a greater stress on charitable activity outside the cloister. The challenge of the new political system in the empire after the Diet of Augsburg in 1555, whereby each territory was to follow the religious allegiance of its ruler, was met by the Jesuits who saw it as their mission to offer spiritual, and often political, direction to the crowned heads of Europe. Parallel to this, a massive educational campaign insured that the hearts and minds of the people were as securely Catholic as those of their prince.

Overall, the late-medieval/Reformation period can be seen as marking a paradigm shift in which the 'synthetic' approach of the high Middle Ages, expressed in the multiplication of theological authorities, was replaced by a tendency towards antithesis, embodied in Ockham's razor and in the great Protestant *solas* ('grace alone', 'faith alone', 'Scripture alone'). This antithetical tendency was no less clearly expressed in the separatism of the Anabaptists and can also be found, for instance, in the stark choice between the battle-standards required of the Ignatian retreatant. The tendency was itself a result of the sixteenth-century emphasis on simplicity and clarity. Theology, or rather the gospel, was to be expressed simply and clearly because it had to be communicable. As the Renaissance is characterized by its desire for eloquence, so the Reformation is characterized by its desire for communication (the Word of God, the printing press, education and overseas mission). As a consequence, theology in the Reformation period moved out of the lecture hall and into the public domain to an extent rarely paralleled in the history of Christianity.

DAVID V.N. BAGCHI

FURTHER READING: B.J. Kidd (ed.), *Documents Illustrative of the Continental Reformation* (Oxford, 1911); Gerald Bray (ed.), *Documents of the English Reformation* (Cambridge, 1994); Euan Cameron, *The European Reformation* (Oxford, 1991); Hans J. Hillerbrand (ed.), *The Oxford Encyclopaedia of the Reformation* (4 vols.; New York, 1996); Eamon Duffy, *The Stripping of the Altars: Traditional Religion in England, 1400–1580* (New Haven / London, 1992); H.O. Evennett, *The Spirit of the Counter Reformation* (ed. with a postscript by John Bossy; Cambridge, 1968); Carter Lindberg, *The European Reformations* (Oxford, 1996); Alister E. McGrath, *Reformation Thought: An Introduction* (Oxford, 2nd edn, 1993); Bernard M.G. Reardon, *Religious Thought in the Reformation* (London, 2nd edn, 1995); Heinz Schilling, *Religion, Political Culture, and the Emergence of Early Modern Society* (Studies in Medieval and Reformation Thought, 50; Leiden, 1992). See also the bibliographies for the entries on individual Reformers.

Reformed Confessions and Catechisms

The *Reformation of the sixteenth century was, without qualification, the great era of Protestant confessional theology. The writing of the great confessions of the Protestant churches was a primary manifestation of reform-impulse. In virtually the same breath that the Reformers attacked abuses and strived to set aside non-biblical elements of late medieval religion and theology, they also endeavoured to state clearly the essentials of the Christian faith in and for the community of believers. This positive and constructive side of the Reformation is perhaps most evident in the many confessions and catechisms produced by the Reformers and their successors. Among the 'Reformed' churches in particular, the writing of confessions and catechisms was tied to the rise of state or municipal churches – with the result that each independent political jurisdiction that followed the Reformed trajectory of the Reformation tended to write a distinct confession.

It is, accordingly, important that we overcome some of the historical imperialism and reductionism of the last two centuries and view *Calvin in the context of the development of Reformed theology accomplished by several important writers before him and by a series of major thinkers of his own generation. In particular, it is of paramount importance that we do not imagine a relationship between Calvin and *'Calvinism' analogous to that between *Luther and *Lutheranism. Luther was, without doubt, the pre-eminent Reformer of the first generation and the great wellspring of Protestant theology. The Lutheran Church rightly looks back to his theology as the primary source of its distinctive insight into the meaning of the gospel. The Reformed churches, however, have no such progenitor: they look back to the theologies of *Martin Bucer, *Ulrich Zwingli and, certainly, to that of Luther. Calvin appears as a member of an impressive second generation of Reformed writers, including *Heinrich Bullinger, *Peter Martyr Vermigli, Wolfgang Musculus and Pierre Viret, whose work belongs to a movement which has already seen its initial confessional codification. It is the theology of all these thinkers in its variety and its broad consensus, together with the theology of the next generation, that of *Ursinus and Olevianus, the authors of the Heidelberg Catechism, that we call Reformed. We should not allow the currency of the term 'Calvinism' to restrict our view and blind us to the breadth and richness of the tradition. Rather, then, than seek the unity of the Reformed faith in the thought of a single theologian or a single major confessional document, like the Second Helvetic Confession or the Westminster Confession of Faith, we must seek out instead a sense of broad consensus arising out of diversity in expression, of a unified tradition defined not by any single confession or by any attempt at harmonization but by the limits to expression established by a series of confessional boundary-markers.

It is also of considerable importance to recognize that the history of confessions stands somewhat distinct from the history of Reformed doctrine in general. In some cases, confessional statements stand prior to major doctrinal developments and provide a positive basis for elaboration, whereas in other cases confessional documents are responses to doctrinal disputes and problems. Thus, the earliest Reformed confessions and the great national confessions of the mid-sixteenth century provided a framework within which later Reformed theology developed, whereas later confessional documents, like the Canons of Dort or the Helvetic Consensus Formula were responses to perceived problems. In addition, there are some theological developments and controversies – like the *Cocceian theology of the seventeenth century and the debates it caused – the detail of which goes far beyond the confessional paradigms and that, therefore, stand outside of the confessional history.

Theology of the earliest Reformed confessions: c. 1520–55

(1) The confessions of the 'Zwinglian Reformation'. The confessions and articles written either by Ulrich Zwingli or by the German Swiss Reformers of the early Reformation in close association, or with the co-operation of Zwingli, evidence a certain unity and distinctiveness of character. Between 1523 and 1531, a substantial series of confessional documents came forth directly from Zwingli's pen: the Sixty-seven Articles and the *Exposition of the Sixty-Seven Articles* (1523), the *Short Christian Instruction* (1523), the *Fidei ratio* (1530) and the *Christianae fidei brevis et clara expositio* (1531). To these we add the Ten Theses of Berne (1528), over which Zwingli exercised some influence and, in addition, a final editorial function.

Like the later Ten Theses of Berne, the genre of the Sixty-seven Articles is not so much a confession of faith as a series of propositions for debate. Nonetheless, the proclamatory character of the document and the way in which it both declared and, in the aftermath of the debate, defined the Reformed faith in the canton of Zurich gave it confessional status. Zwingli's exposition, moreover, functioned as a systematic elaboration, albeit not of confessional status, that defined clearly the scope and content of the early Reformed faith and provided an initial framework within which the confessions of the Zwinglian Reformation could find their substance and direction. The two documents together, the articles and their exposition, identified and shaped the early Swiss confessional development.

The Sixty-seven Articles begin with a strong statement concerning the priority of Scripture over tradition and over the teaching office of the church: 'All who say that the Gospel is nothing without the approbation of the Church, err and cast reproach upon God.' There follows an immediate appeal to Christ as the centre and meaning of the gospel, as the fulfilment of revelation, and as the one redeemer: 'The sum of the Gospel is that our Lord Jesus Christ, the true Son of God, has made known to us the will of his heavenly Father, and has redeemed us by his innocence from eternal death, and reconciled us to God.'

The next two articles or conclusions state the Christological focus of the Reformed faith positively as doctrine, and then negatively against Roman abuses like the invocation of saints, works-righteousness, indulgences: 'Therefore Christ is the only way to salvation for all who were, who are, and who shall be', and 'Whosoever seeks or shows another door, errs – yea, is a murderer of souls and a robber.' The argument is stated highly polemically and in such a way that a sharp line is drawn between the Reformers' conception of biblical truth and their view of later medieval theology. It is not at all difficult to show that the great medieval doctors, even a late medieval semi-Pelagian like Gabriel Biel, did not consider penance, indulgences and the invocation of saints to be an alternative door to salvation, separate from the door opened by Christ. Nonetheless, in the popular piety, which could not comprehend the niceties of scholastic discussion, the separation had been made.

The Ten Theses of Berne (1528) are more concise and arguably more important as a Swiss Reformed confessional document than the Sixty-seven Articles. A conference between the Reformers of eastern German Swiss cantons – Zwingli, *Oecolampadius, Haller, Bucer and others – and a contingent of Roman theologians headed by *Dr Johann Eck – the Eck of the famous Leipzig Debate with Luther and Carlstadt – held in May of 1526 resulted in the beginnings of Reformation in Berne, the most powerful of the Swiss cantons. Both for the sake of the solidification of gains made in Berne and for the sake of undoing the damage done to Reform in the German Swiss cantons by the Baden disputation between Eck and Oecolampadius (May 1526), Haller and Kolb produced ten theses, to be presented publicly at a meeting arranged in Berne by the local magistracy scheduled to be held on 19 successive days – from 6 to 26 January 1528.

Zwingli's *Fidei ratio* (1530), and the *Christianae fidei brevis et clara expositio* (1531), are both to be counted as full confessions of faith. The former document, prepared by Zwingli for the Diet of Augsburg, stood beside the Augsburg Confession of the Lutherans and the Tetrapolitan Confession of the free cities in order to represent the Swiss Reformed to the emperor and the princes. Formally more like the Tetrapolitan Confession than the Augsburg, Zwingli's *Fidei ratio* surveys the Trinitarian faith of the church before dealing with controverted articles. The latter confession, not as brief as its title might indicate, offers a broader and more detailed view of the Reformed faith as requested by the French ambassador, Maigret, for the perusal of Francis I and his advisers. If the treatise had as its primary intention the favourable presentation of Reformed Protestantism to the Roman Catholic monarch, it fell short of its purpose on several counts and received sharp rebuke from Protestants as well as Catholics.

(2) The early German, Swiss and Dutch Reformed confessions, c. 1530–45.

Early on in the Reformation, a series of Reformed confessions appeared – the most notable being the Tetrapolitan Confession (1530), the Articles of the Synod of Berne (1532), the First Confession of Basle (1534), the First Helvetic Confession (1536), the Lausanne Theses (1536), the Geneva Catechism and Confession (1536), and the series of Calvin's catechisms (1537, 1541, 1545) – that stood outside of the Zwinglian paradigm, having some affinity with but also some contrast to the Lutheran perspective. Very much like the *Apology of the Augsburg Confession* (1530) and the Schmalkaldic Articles (1537), but in some distinction from the purely Zwinglian confessions, the First Helvetic Confession announces that justification by grace alone through faith is 'the primary and principle' article of the church's teaching and adds, in the

German text, that this doctrine ought to be announced 'in all preaching' and 'impressed on the hearts of all people'. Each of these early Reformed confessions, moreover, emphasizes justification and the solely gracious gift of salvation in Christ without following Zwingli in introducing the doctrine of election into their confessions. (Calvin, similarly, left election out of his 1541 catechism.)

It is to these confessions, moreover, even more directly than to the Zwinglian, that we look for what was to become the distinctively Reformed pattern of confessional organization, signalled by the foundational discussion of the priority of the Holy Scriptures. The Oecolampadius-Myconius First Confession of Basle concludes with the qualifying statement,

> ... finally, we submit this our confession to the judgment of the books of holy Scripture (*Sacrae Biblicae Scripturae*): if, moreover, we are instructed by the same Holy Scriptures in a better [confession], we declare our willingness at any time to yield to God and his holy Word with great thanksgiving.

The other two confessions, the Tetrapolitan and the First Helvetic, both set this view of the priority of Scripture first and foremost in the order of topics, as the foundation on which all else must be built. The Tetrapolitan Confession offers, moreover, not merely a *doctrine* of Scripture, but also a statement of the reason for the priority of the scriptural norm in the church: the perpetuation of godly preaching. The first article of the confession is entitled, 'Concerning the subject-matter of sermons'. This biblical emphasis arose, as the confession proceeds to state, directly out of the debates and disputes over religion that characterized the first decade of the Reformation. 'We enjoined our preachers', the confession states, 'to teach from the pulpit nothing else than is either contained in the Holy Scriptures or has sure ground therein.' The fundamental interpretative rule of the Reformation here becomes a confessional principle for the Reformed: authoritative Christian doctrine must either be explicitly stated by Scripture or available by rational argument based on Scripture. The Tetrapolitan Confession thus echoes Luther's statement at Worms that he would recant only if shown wrong by 'Scripture and right reason', and it looks forward to the precise hermeneutical declarations of later confessions in the Reformed tradition, including the Westminster Confession.

Like the Augsburg Confession, the Tetrapolitan Confession was presented at the Diet of Augsburg and met by a strenuous opposition on the part of the Catholic theologians present – and, like the Augsburg Confession, it was 'confuted' at length by Johannes Eck, Johan Faber, Conrad Wimpina and Johannes Cochlaeus. The Augsburg Confession was defended in the *Apologia* by *Melanchthon, and in perfect historical parallel, the Tetrapolitan Confession was defended in an extensive apologetic commentary by Bucer. Bucer's *Apologia* was not received as a confessional document and has not attained the fame of the *Apology of the Augsburg Confession*. It remains, however, a highly significant theological testament and, from the point of view of the history of Reformed confessional theology, a most significant commentary on and elaboration of the Tetrapolitan Confession. Characteristic of Bucer's work, including the Tetrapolitan Confession, is a reluctance to allow any norms for doctrine (including those of a secondary creedal status) other than Scripture. Unlike many of the major Reformed confessions, particularly the great national confessions of the mid-sixteenth century like the Belgic and Gallican Confessions and the Thirty-nine Articles, the Tetrapolitan Confession offers no acknowledgement of the *Apostles' Creed or the great ecumenical creeds of the early church. It does, however, briefly note the standard Trinitarian and Christological terms for the sake of clarity in doctrine.

Eucharistically, these confessions appear neither Zwinglian nor Lutheran, but hold for an intermediary position. The Tetrapolitan Confession can state that Christ gives us 'his true body and true blood to be truly eaten and drunk for the food and drink of souls'. Although the two confessions of Basle clearly take a step beyond Bucer towards the eventual doctrine of Calvin and Vermigli, similar comments might just as easily be made of their teaching. Neither looks towards Zwingli and, even before the Augsburg Confession of 1540 (the 'Variata'), they sought, in some accord with Bucer, a mediating view of the presence of Christ's body and blood in the Lord's Supper. Christ is confessed in the former document to be 'present in His holy Supper for all who truly believe', albeit (as the confession declares in its margin) 'sacramentally, through a faithful recollection, by which the mind of the individual is raised up to heaven'. Although the 'bread and wine remain bread and wine', 'the

true body and blood of Christ are set forth and offered, conjointly with the bread and wine, according to the words of institution'. This language surely provided the basis for dialogue with the Lutherans, since it manifests opposition not to Luther's teaching or to the doctrine of the Augsburg Confession, but rather to the theology of Zwingli's several statements of sacramental theology, particularly to Zwingli's confessional offering at the Diet of Augsburg, the *Fidei ratio*. There is strong evidence that Melanchthon, on the Lutheran side, had early on believed that there was ground for discussion and potential agreement between the Lutheran and Reformed churches over this kind of Eucharistic language. The accuracy of Melanchthon's assessment of the issue was evidenced by the relative success of discussions in 1536 between the Strasburg theologians, Bucer and Capito, and Luther that resulted in the Wittenberg Concord.

(3) *From the earliest English catechisms to the Edwardine Articles.* Although there are consistent reflections of the continental Reformation and its major epochs in the history of the church in Britain in the sixteenth century – such as the significant impact of the early Lutheran Reformation on the work of English Reformers like *Tyndale and Coverdale, or the influence of Bucer, Vermigli and Bullinger (in the cases of the latter two thinkers, particularly during the reign of Edward VI), or the publication of the Thirty-nine Articles in the era of Protestant confessional flowering between 1559 and 1566 – the Reformation in the British Isles far more closely follows the patterns of English politics represented by the reign of Henry VIII (1509–47) and his successors, Edward VI (1547–53), Mary (1553–58) and Elizabeth I (1558–1603). The progress of the English Reformation from its beginnings under Henry VIII to the promulgation of the Forty-two Articles of Religion or, as they are frequently called, the Edwardine Articles, in 1553, the last year of Edward's reign, was from a state-sponsored redefinition of the church in England as the national Church of England under Henry, with little concern for a change in the church's theology, to an increasingly Lutheran and Melanchthonian movement both outside of the churchly hierarchy and eventually within it, to an increasingly Reformed or Calvinistic movement during the brief reign of Edward. The reign of Mary, with its brutal return to Roman Catholicism, marks the end of the first phase of English confessional development.

Henry's own sentiments, together with those of a large, conservative group of bishops and clergy, were manifest in 1539 when he rejected further dialogue with the German Lutherans and issued the theologically Roman Catholic Six Articles. Although he made no attempt to heal the political and ecclesial breach with Rome, Henry clearly moved to identify the theology of the Church of England with Roman Catholicism in direct opposition to the Reformation. The first of the Six Articles defined transubstantiation as the sole correct and necessarily believed doctrine of the presence of Christ in the Lord's Supper. The second article rejected communion in both kinds in favour of the Roman practice of distribution of the host only. The third article re-instituted clerical celibacy and the fourth commended vows of chastity. The fifth and sixth articles re-instituted and argued the necessity of private Masses and auricular confession. Except for a brief suspension in 1540 at the insistence of Thomas Cromwell, the Six Articles effectively set aside the Lutheran and Melanchthonian direction of *Cranmer and Latimer from the time of their publication until the death of Henry VIII in 1547.

The confessional background of the Edwardine Articles is dominated by the Thirteen Articles written by a committee of English theologians and clergy under the supervision of Cranmer. These articles, in turn, reflect Cranmer's dialogue with Lutheran theologians and evidence a strong reliance on the Augsburg Confession. Whereas the attempt to link the two communions with an official pronouncement came to an end in 1539 with the promulgation of the Six Articles, the Lutheran language of the Thirteen Articles carried over at certain points into the Edwardine Articles.

Archbishop Cranmer himself, together with Nicholas Ridley, had moved, by the end of 1548, from a Lutheran view of the bodily presence of Christ in the Lord's Supper to a Reformed view of the 'figurative' and 'spiritual' presence of Christ in the elements. When the revised Book of Common Prayer was published in 1552, the theological change was evident. Where the first Prayer Book of Edward's reign (1549) had instructed that the bread and wine be distributed under the spoken rubrics, 'The body of our Lord Jesus Christ which was given for thee,

preserve thy body and soul unto everlasting life', and 'The blood of our Lord Jesus Christ which was shed for thee, preserve thy body and soul unto everlasting life', the revision offered, 'Take and eat this in remembrance that Christ died for thee, and feed on him in thy heart by faith, with thanksgiving', and 'Drink this in remembrance that Christ's blood was shed for thee, and be thankful'. The theological change evidenced by the successive editions of the Prayer Book was forcefully defined in the Forty-two Articles, where the explicit polemic against transubstantiation also contains a typically Reformed rebuttal of the Lutheran doctrine of ubiquity.

(4) The era of the Zurich Consensus and the Geneva Consensus in Switzerland: c. 1545–55. The *Consensus Tigurinus* or Zurich Consensus of 1549 arose out of theological dialogue between Calvin and Bullinger and marks the beginning of explicit harmony among the French and German Swiss on the doctrine of the Lord's Supper and the beginning, properly so-called, of a Reformed confessional theology concerning the sacraments. Within three years, the two cities and their theological representatives had examined the other great focus of polemics between the Reformed and their various adversaries – the doctrine of predestination – and had produced another 'consensus' document, the Geneva Consensus of 1552. It is no exaggeration to state that these two documents paved the way for the acceptance of Bullinger's confession of faith as the Second Helvetic Confession.

The origins of the Consensus can be traced to the problems encountered by the several groups of Reformers in reaching some accord on the doctrine of the Lord's Supper, beginning with the Wittenberg Concord of 1536. There, Bucer had made a series of concessions to the Lutheran view of corporeal presence, leaving much doubt as to the tenability of a genuine middle ground between the Lutheran and Zwinglian doctrines of the Supper. Calvin was mistrusted on one side by the Zwinglians, who viewed him as too close to Bucer and, therefore, to the Lutherans – and on the other side by the Lutherans, who were not disposed to distinguish between Zwingli's and Calvin's teaching, given that both refused to interpret the words, 'this is my body' in a literal sense. When controversy began between Luther and the Zurich theology in 1545, Calvin and Bullinger saw the need for consensus – since Calvin, after all, had not led Geneva towards a Lutheran doctrine of the Supper, and Bullinger had moved beyond Zwingli's purely memorialistic teaching.

In 1546, Bullinger sent Calvin a copy of his treatise on the sacrament, together with a letter requesting Calvin's opinion of his teaching. Although Calvin's somewhat critical response troubled Bullinger, this exchange in fact set the stage for further discussion during the following two years. In November 1548, Calvin proposed 24 propositions on the Lord's Supper which were then annotated by Bullinger. Calvin offered a response to the annotations in January 1549. After a conference with Bullinger in May, at which *Farel was also present, Calvin drew up a final set of 26 articles, which were subsequently adopted as representative of the Reformed faith by the churches of Zurich, Geneva, St Gall, Schaffhausen, the Grisons, Neufchâtel and Basle. The articles were published in 1551.

Although it can hardly be called the source of difficulties over the Eucharist between Reformed and Lutheran theologians, the *Consensus Tigurinus* did provide the occasion for a renewal of hostility between the Lutherans and the Reformed. Joachim Westphal was a pastor in Hamburg, a Wittenberg-trained student of Luther and Melanchthon who had only recently proved his 'true Lutheranism' by championing the Flacian cause against his former teacher, Melanchthon. In 1552, the year following the publication of the Consensus, Westphal published his *Compilation of Confused and Divergent Opinions concerning the Lord's Supper, taken from the Books of the Sacramentarians*. The *Compilation* took particular joy in posing Geneva against Zurich and in citing the compromises of the Consensus as still further proof of confusion and bad theology. In this work, and in a treatise on the words of institution published in the following year, Westphal accused the Reformed not only of confusion, but of heresy, and he pointed out that they now posed a great danger to the future of Christianity, inasmuch as they were preaching energetically in France, England, the Low Countries and even portions of Germany.

Reformed confessions and the beginnings of Protestant orthodoxy, c. 1555–1620

The time between the middle of the sixteenth century and the beginning of the Thirty Years War was the great era of the formulation and solidification of Reformed confessional theology. It extended from the time of the second-generation Reformers and their fundamental codification of Reformed teaching in such works as Calvin's *Institutes*, Melanchthon's *Loci communes*, Bullinger's *Decades* and *Compendium* and Musculus's *Loci communes*, to the full development of early Reformed orthodoxy in the writings of Polanus, Perkins, *Ames, Gomarus, Walaeus, Maccovius and others during the time of the *Arminian controversy and the Synod of Dort. The role of the confessions in this process of doctrinal development and solidification ought not to be underestimated. The great confessions of the mid-sixteenth century – the Gallican Confession, Belgic Confession, Thirty-nine Articles, Scots Confession and Second Helvetic Confession, together with the Geneva and Heidelberg Catechisms – provided clear summaries of the basic doctrines of the Reformed churches, definitive resolutions of debated articles like the Lord's Supper, justification and predestination, and both a basis for further development and formulation and a set of broad guidelines within which such development could take place. The confessions and catechisms of the mid-century provided, in other words, the churchly right doctrine or 'orthodoxy' in the light of which larger structures of theological system could be developed and taught.

(5) The era of the great national confessions.

(a) The Gallican and Belgic confessions. During the era of intense religious persecution of Protestantism in the first half of the sixteenth century, French Protestants found a safe haven in Geneva. They also found a powerful impetus in the person of John Calvin and a new theological unity in the confession penned by Antoine de la Roche Chandieu and adopted by the first national synod, which met at Paris in May of 1559. Chandieu, also known as Sadeel, had studied in Geneva and his work manifests the influence of Calvin. Indeed, many studies of the Gallican Confession argue the editorial hand of Calvin in the draft that reached the national synod. The confession is doctrinally in harmony with the other Reformed confessions of the period, but it has one very interesting structural feature: it does not move from Scripture to God like the Swiss Reformed confessions but rather from God to revelation to Scripture. This model is followed in the Belgic Confession (1561). In both instances, a more positive role is given to natural revelation, which is recognized as incomplete but nonetheless genuine revelation in creation and providence, than is the case in other Reformed confessions. The Gallican Confession also contains a powerful identification of the church as the place where the word is preached and the sacraments rightly administered: it is the 'company of the faithful' and not the 'assemblies of papacy'.

The theology of the Belgic Confession stands in the direct line of the earlier Reformed confessional works like the First Helvetic and Gallican Confessions. Much like the Gallican, it contains an elaborate doctrine of Holy Scripture (iii–vii) in which the normative doctrinal authority of Scripture as the word of God, the sufficiency of Scripture for salvation and the limits and contents of the canon of Scripture are all stated in detail. The lengthy discussion of the Trinity (viii and ix), together with the chapters specifically dealing with the full and co-equal divinity of the Son and Spirit (x and xi), sets the confession apart from the other Reformed confessions of the century which are not nearly so detailed in their Trinitarianism. It also reflects, perhaps, the growing pressure of anti-Trinitarian radicalism upon the churches of the magisterial Reformation.

The Reformed doctrine of a real spiritual presence in the sacraments, developed and solidified in the early, non-Zwinglian, German and Swiss confessions, received consistent emphasis in the Gallican Confession and the Belgic Confession, both of which reflect the mature views of Calvin. On the one hand, the Gallican and Belgic confessions insist that the bread and wine of the sacrament are unchanged by the pronouncement of the words of institution and that they remain, substantially, bread and wine. The Reformed, moreover, deny both impanation and consubstantiation and thus refuse to allow any corporeal or bodily presence of Christ somehow 'with' or 'under' the bread and wine. Virtually identical language is found in all of the Reformed confessions. Indeed, even in Bullinger's Second Helvetic Confession, where we might expect to find some remnant of the teaching of Zwingli embodied in the confession of his successor, there is a clear statement concerning the real, though spiritual, presence of Christ's body and blood for the

inward nourishment of believers. Bullinger's language goes considerably beyond that of the First Helvetic Confession in stating the manner and mode of presence.

(b) The Thirty-nine Articles. In order to understand the English Reformed theology known to us as *'Puritanism', we need to look first to the accession of Elizabeth I of England in 1558. When Elizabeth came to the throne, England returned to the Protestant fold after a four-year period of vigorously prosecuted Roman Catholicism under her elder sister, Mary. With the revival of Protestantism, exiled clergy who had fled to the Continent for their lives came back to England, bringing with them a distinctly Reformed type of theology from Strasburg, Geneva and Zurich. A Reformed theology had early on competed with a Lutheran or 'Martinian' type of Reformation thought – chiefly in the persons of Bucer and Vermigli who taught at Cambridge and Oxford before the time of Mary – but after 1558 the Lutheran impact diminished and the Reformed influence increased.

Beyond the varied sources of English Protestant thought, the distinctive character of English Protestantism can also be traced to the specific issues it faced during the crucial, formative period of the Elizabethan settlement. In the second year of her reign, Elizabeth's Parliament passed the Act of Supremacy and the Act of Uniformity. The former act reaffirmed the national church in England with the monarch as its supreme head and required all clergy, magistrates and royal retainers to swear an oath of loyalty to the established religion. The Act of Uniformity imposed a regular form of worship as set forth in the Prayer Book. Servants of the crown and clergy who refused the oath were immediately suspect of allegiance to the papacy and were removed from office. The Prayer Book was virtually that of Edward VI with, however, a series of emendations which broadened the theology of the book to create a settlement capable of uniting diverse groups in one church. In that breadth, though, lay the seeds of dissent. The doctrine of the Lord's Supper was vague, and if the Reformed clergy were pleased by the provisions for the removal of images from churches and for catechetical training of youth, many were disturbed by the requirement of clerical vestments and a few were distressed at the prospect of an episcopal hierarchy in the church. In addition, some objected to the establishment of a book of homilies for church use.

The first four years of Elizabeth's reign brought about a slight shift in the religious policy that had produced the broad tolerant lines of the Prayer Book. The young queen had found it to her advantage to support Protestantism on the continent – in particular to offer limited support to the Huguenot cause against the staunchly Roman Catholic Guise family. A parallel pattern emerged, moreover, in English politics: even as the Guises and Rome supported the claims of Mary Stuart to the English throne, so did Elizabeth find her chief support among the English Protestants and, in particular, in her highly Protestant Parliament. In 1563, Parliament enacted, with the consent of the queen, the Thirty-nine Articles as the confessional standard of the English church. Whereas the Prayer Book had been quite acceptable to those of Catholic sympathies, the Articles were specifically written as a broadly Protestant statement – acceptable to most Protestants, but quite exclusive of the Roman Catholic position which was being formulated contemporaneously at the final sessions of the Council of Trent.

(c) The rise of German Reformed theology in the Heidelberg Catechism and the Confession of Frederick III. The era of the great national confessions did not see the production of many confessions among the German Reformed, but one of the documents that appeared during this time has overshadowed virtually all of the other national confessional documents of this or any other era – the Heidelberg Catechism. Together with the catechism, though of a somewhat later date and potentially to be numbered among the early orthodox confessions of the German Reformed churches, is the Confession of Frederick III (1577). Since this latter work was intended as a personal testament from the elector who had commissioned the Heidelberg Catechism, and since by his wishes it was often appended to that document, it is rightly considered here.

The Reformation came relatively late to Heidelberg. Lutheran forms of worship were introduced only in 1546 when the hesitant elector Friedrich II yielded to the pleas of his nephew Duke Otto Heinrich of Pfalz-Neuburg and Philip Melanchthon, as well as to the demands of his people for reform. Friedrich II died in 1556 and was succeeded by Otto Heinrich. The latter was already a staunch Lutheran,

though of a Melanchthonian sympathy. The brief reign of Otto Heinrich (1556–59) saw the adoption of the 1540 'Variata' version of the Augsburg Confession as a standard of faith and the rise of Lutheran controversy in Heidelberg between Gnesio-Lutherans, Crypto-Calvinists and the Reformed.

When Friedrich III succeeded Otto Heinrich in 1559, he was faced with a massive debate between the Gnesio-Lutheran Tilemann Hesshus, general superintendent of the Heidelberg churches, and the Crypto-Calvinist Wilhelm Klebitz. In its positive doctrine, the new catechism written for the palatinate in 1563 combines the concern of the Reformed that the doctrine of a real, spiritual presence of Christ in the Lord's Supper never be understood as an infringement of the Christological principle of the integrity of Christ's human nature in the incarnation and, by extension, of the local presence of his resurrected body in heaven alone, with the fundamental Protestant insistence that the New Testament teaching concerning the once-and-for-all, full sufficiency of Christ's sacrifice be taken with utter seriousness. In the partaking of the Supper in faith, we are truly engrafted into Christ – but we are to worship the risen Lord in heaven and not the elements of the Supper, as if Christ were physically there present and sacrificed again daily. On these grounds, the Mass must be rejected.

Vehement opposition to the Heidelberg Catechism came from the Lutheran princes of the empire who viewed the catechism as Zwinglian or Calvinistic in its teachings, particularly in its sacramental theology. Frederick continued to claim allegiance to the 'Variata' and argued that the confession and his new catechism were not in conflict. His argument was not well received among Lutherans: even the Philippist faculties at Wittenberg and Marburg repudiated the catechism. Among the Gnesio-Lutherans, both Flacius and Hesshus polemicized against the catechism – not as Philippist but as Calvinist. The mediating theologians of Tübingen, Brenz and Andreae, angered by the Eucharistic theology of the catechism, also drew up an attack. This latter group, however, saw room for conciliation and, under the auspices of their patron, Duke Christopher of Wurtemberg, arranged with Frederick to call a colloquy at the cloister of Maulbronn in 1564.

The Maulbronn Colloquy in April 1564,

between the Wurtemberg theologians Brenz, Andreae and *Lucas Osiander and the Heidelberg theologians Ursinus, Olevianus, Boquinus and Dathenus, marks an important stage in the development of the two orthodoxies. Its importance lies in the inability of the two sides to come to any agreement and the subsequent clearer definition of German Reformed theology over against Lutheranism. The Heidelberg theologians had initially hoped to restrict debate to the Lord's Supper, but the colloquy gravitated, almost immediately, to the logically prior issue, the Christological problem of the *communicatio idiomatum* and the doctrine of ubiquity. Ursinus, the most prominent Reformed voice at the colloquy, held firmly against any mingling of the two natures of Christ – against a communication of proper qualities *in abstracto* – viewing such theories as prejudicing the humanity of Christ and so moving towards *Eutychianism. Andreae, who followed Brenz's highly developed doctrine of *communicatio idiomatum in abstracto*, could only perceive Ursinus's teaching as tending to abolish the union of the natures and as moving towards *Nestorianism.

Despite the Elector Friedrich's subsequent appeals to the Augsburg Confession in the altered (1540) version, he and the catechism were viewed as apostate from the Lutheran cause and called to account before the imperial Diet of Augsburg in 1566. With some support from the Elector Augustus of Saxony – then influenced by his Philippistic faculty at Wittenberg towards a Crypto-Calvinist doctrine of the Lord's Supper – Frederick escaped censure and assured the future of Reformed theology in Germany. This was only insofar, of course, as it could be interpreted as a variety of Lutheranism. His successful defence of his reforms and of his catechism led to its sanction by the Diet and to the legal establishment of the Palatine theology as a form of Lutheranism, in allegiance to the Augsburg Confession, within the empire. Only in 1648, with the Peace of Westphalia, did the Reformed faith as such obtain a legal status in the German lands. Until then, German Reformed theology, as offered in the catechism, stood as a form of Lutheranism, guaranteed its confessional legitimacy by adherence to the much-debated 1540 'Variata'.

(6) The confessional diffusion of Reformed faith to Eastern Europe. From the fourth and fifth decades of the sixteenth century onwards, the Reformers of Bohemia, Hungary and Poland were drawn towards the Reformed faith rather than to Lutheranism as they sought to find a position between Roman Catholicism and the radical, anti-Trinitarian movements that had gained strength particularly in Hungary and Poland.

In Poland, the Reformation arrived as early as 1518, when the city of Danzig advocated Lutheran reforms. Other cities followed, particularly along the Baltic coast, as far to the north as Lithuania. The efforts of King Sigismund I in 1526 to press Danzig back into the Roman Catholic fold were unsuccessful. The papal legates who attempted to enforce the decrees of Sigismund were met with strong resistance – as at Torun or Thorn in 1529 when the papal legate was stoned and forced to flee after he had attempted to burn publicly various books by Luther. A shift towards the Reformed faith began as early as 1544 through the work of Stanislaus Lutorminski, and the *Unitarian faith prospered briefly during the reign of Sigismund II, who was converted to an anti-Trinitarian faith.

In 1555, the Synod of Petrikau demanded the abolition of clerical celibacy, the use of the Polish language in the Mass and the use of the cup by the laity. In 1556, the year after the synod, Johannes à Lasco, the Polish-born Reformer of the Netherlands, returned and began his work as the great organizer of the Reformation in Poland. His teachings provided a further impetus to the Reformed faith, but they also led to a clarification of the debate between the various Protestant parties in Poland – notably the Reformed, the Unitarians and the Lutherans. The translation of Scripture into Polish that he superintended was, in part, a response to another translation, completed in 1552, largely through the efforts of *Socinian theologians and exegetes. At the Synod of Sendomir (1570), the Reformed and the Lutherans joined together, albeit briefly, to produce a confessional consensus for the Polish Protestant churches, against both the Roman Catholic and the Unitarian alternatives.

The Reformation began somewhat later in Hungary than it did in Poland, because of the power of the Roman Catholic Church in firm alliance with the crown of Hungary at the beginning of the sixteenth century. A diet held in 1523 promulgated a decree forbidding

Protestantism and ordering the arrest of Protestants and the burning of the unrepentant as heretics. The defeat and death of King Lojos (Louis) II at the hands of the Turks in the battle of Mohacs (1526), left the country leaderless, divided between the Christians and the Turks, and torn by war between pretenders to the throne. In these radically altered political circumstances, Protestantism was able to gain a foothold and flourish.

In 1549, Leonhard Stöckel wrote a lengthy confession of faith that was favourably received by Ferdinand of Austria, who had managed to wrest power from the hands of his political rival, Zapolya, and to take the throne of Hungary. More than a decade later, the *Compendium doctrinae christianae, quam omnes Pastores et Ministri ecclesiarum Dei in tota Ungaria et Transsylvania, quae incorruptum Iesu Christi Evangelium amplexae sunt, docent ac profitentur* was adopted by the Synod of Tarczal in 1562 and ratified by the Synod of Torda in 1563. This document is a nearly verbatim adoption of *Theodore Beza's *Confessio christianae fidei* (1558). It therefore signals the close intellectual ties between the Hungarian church and the Swiss Reformed, and it offers direct evidence of the influence of major theologians of the late Reformation on Reformed confessional development.

(7) The 'Harmony' and the 'Concord': The hope for a churchly standard at the close of the sixteenth century. When the Lutheran Church was emerging from its controversies and approaching concord, a series of synods in the Reformed churches determined that there was a pressing need for confessional unity among the Reformed also. There had been little internecine struggle in comparison to the Lutheran strife, but – also in contrast to the Lutherans – the Reformed had little confessional unity to begin with. There was considerable theological agreement but great confessional diversity. A synod held at Neustadt in 1570, under the auspices of Friedrich III of the Palatinate, resolved to seek Reformed unity through the writing of one confession acceptable to all.

In 1577, the year following Friedrich's death, his son Casimir became the focus, on the Continent, of a Reformed attempt to frame a response to the 'Formula of Concord' and to further confessional unity among the several Reformed nations and states of Europe. With the encouragement of Queen Elizabeth of England, he arranged for a conference to be held at Frankfurt in the autumn of the year. Delegates arrived in September from England, the Netherlands, France, Navarre, Poland, Hungary and the Palatinate. The Swiss and the Bohemians sent no delegates but expressed their approval of the conference and their interest in its outcome. It was decided that a new creed be written as the basis of common consent. A draft was to be prepared by Ursinus and Zanchi, together with a delegate selected by Queen Elizabeth. This draft was to be circulated for comment among the delegates at Frankfurt and sent for advice to Beza in Geneva and Gualter in Zurich. A consensus document would be drawn up in 1578.

These plans did not materialize in the Reformed Palatinate. Ursinus, aged and ill, proved unable to devote any energy to the project. The English delegate remained unchosen – and the task of writing was left to Zanchi. He prepared a lengthy confession but, by the time the document was ready, opinion had shifted and most of the Reformed states involved in the deliberations saw greater wisdom in a Reformed book of confession than in a single confessional document. A 'harmony' of Reformed confessions, based on the Second Helvetic Confession, was prepared in Geneva in 1581. Zanchi continued his work and published it, as a personal testament, in 1586. Zanchi's confession, although never adopted by any Reformed body, exerted considerable influence upon the development of Reformed theology. It was especially well received in England, where it was published both in the original Latin (1586) and in English translation in 1590.

The National Synods of the Reformed Churches of France held at St Foix in 1578 and at Figeac in 1579 did, however, accept the proposal of the Frankfurt synod and resolve to examine any forthcoming document in its own assemblies under the guidance of a committee of review. One of the clergy nominated to this latter committee was Antoine de la Roche Chandieu, who had worked with Calvin and others to prepare the Gallican Confession of 1559.

At approximately the same time, the resolution of Frankfurt was having its impact among the Swiss Reformed. The clergy of Zurich were favourable to the proposal but saw difficulties in the expectation that any single document might be written that would universally supersede the confessions already in force in the many Reformed churches. As a modification of the plan, they suggested that a harmony of confessions be written in which the documents would be conflated into a single outline without textual alteration and each division be augmented by an explanation of the theological consensus represented in the original documents. A similar opinion was held in Geneva where, under the auspices of Theodore Beza, Lambert Daneau, and A. Salvart, a kind of *Loci communes* based on the confessions was constructed in the years 1579 and 1580.

The product of these efforts was published in Geneva in 1581 under the title *Harmonia Confessionum Fidei Orthodoxarum et Reformatarum Ecclesiarum ... Quae omnia, Ecclesiarum Gallicarum et Belgicarum nomine, subjiciuntur libero et prudenti reliquarum omnium judicio* (a 'Harmony of the Confessions of Faith of the Orthodox and Reformed Churches ... Which things are submitted for the free and prudent judgement of all others in the names of the churches of France and Belgium'). The document itself is rather remarkable: not wanting to begin with a pattern that might be criticized – but rather with a pattern already representative of a Reformed consensus – the Genevans selected the Second Helvetic Confession written by Heinrich Bullinger as the pattern for the 'Harmony' and as the leading statement of doctrine in each chapter. In addition, the Augsburg Confession – on the Lord's Supper citing both the original of 1530/31 and the 'Variata' of 1540, with a lengthy explanation – and the confession of the English church written in 1562 by Bishop Jewel and included in his *Apology*, are present in the 'Harmony'. Also included are the Tetrapolitan Confession, the First Helvetic Confession, the Saxon Confession (1551) of Melanchthon, the Würtemberg Confession of Brenz (1552), the confession of Friedrich III of the Palatinate, the Gallican and Belgic Confessions, the Confession of Basle (1534) and the Bohemian or Waldensian Confession (1573). The 'Harmony' is an inclusive rather than an exclusive document – at least as far as the magisterial Reformation is concerned.

The 'Harmony' was well received. A National Synod of France held in 1583 at Vitry approved the volume and ordered it translated and published with a letter of commendation to the French churches. In 1601 the National Synod

(Gergean) reaffirmed the recommendation and urged publication of the French version together with a new set of explanatory notes. An English translation appeared at Cambridge in 1586 and as late as 1720 the Swiss churches approved the volume in a set of testimonials published by Jean Alphonse Turretin at Geneva, referring to the 'Harmony' as a 'moderate and peaceful' attestation to the 'concord' of Protestantism.

(8) British confessionalism from Lambeth to the Irish Articles. The intentional breadth of the Thirty-nine Articles of the English church was not without troublesome results. The language of the chapter on election was vague enough that, both in the late-sixteenth and in the early-eighteenth centuries, the question of a more synergistic reading of the Articles was raised. In 1581, the eminent Puritan and Reformed teacher Laurence Chaderton warned his colleagues and students in Cambridge University about the danger of synergistic views on salvation held by the Huguenot professor of theology, Peter Baro. Controversy did not break forth, however, until 1595, when Baro – in an anticipation of the Arminian controversy which would shortly trouble the Dutch church – argued against the Reformed doctrine of predestination in favour of a conditional decree. William Whitaker, the Regius professor of divinity at Cambridge, vowed 'to stand for God against the Lutherans'. Archbishop Whitgift favoured the position of Whitaker against Baro and, in order to resolve the controversy, called a conference of theologians and churchmen at Lambeth in November of 1595. A set of nine articles, drawn up by Whitaker against Baro, was debated and modified by the conference. The final draft was then published under the formal auspices of Whitgift, archbishop of Canterbury, and Richard Fletcher, bishop of London, with the further endorsement of Matthew Hutton, archbishop of York. These Lambeth Articles are uncompromisingly predestinarian and look directly towards the Irish Articles (1615) and the Canons of Dort (1619).

The Lambeth Articles begin with a succinct declaration that 'God from eternity hath predestinated certain men unto life; certain men hath he reprobated'. Then, against Baro, the articles declare that 'the moving or efficient cause' of predestination is the 'good will and pleasure of God' alone and not a foreknowledge of faith or works. This argument is then clarified by articles dealing with the certainty of the number of the elect and with the damnation of the non-elect for their sins. Next, the perseverance of the saints and the possibility of assurance of salvation are declared and the concept of a resistible grace and the notion of an acceptance of Christ not grounded in election denied. The final article reads, pointedly, 'It is not in the will or power of everyone to be saved.'

The Articles, although of major theological significance, were of little churchly impact: their primary author, William Whitaker, died in the year of the Lambeth conference and was succeeded by John Overall (1560–1619). Overall had spoken out against the predestinarian theology of Perkins as Regius professor and subsequently, as bishop, completely abandoned Whitaker's Reformed stance by protesting against the Lambeth Articles and championing the cause of Baro. Overall would continue to argue against the Reformed doctrine of predestination and would, at the Hampton Court conference (1604), join with other synergistic bishops in blocking the addition of the Lambeth Articles to the doctrinal standards of the English church.

(9) German Reformed confessions of the early orthodox era.

The German Reformed confessions, written between the decade of the great national confessions of France, the Netherlands, Scotland, England and the Swiss federation and the time of the Synod of Dort, represent an important, if neglected, aspect of developing Reformed theology. Because virtually all of these confessions were local writings, having authority only within small cities and principalities of the empire, they are seldom listed among the major Reformed confessions of the age. Nevertheless, they are hardly lacking in the confessional fervour and religious eloquence that has made the great national confessions works of enduring value. Indeed, because of the embattled existence of Reformed theology in the German empire before the Peace of Westphalia, these confessions stand together with the Heidelberg Catechism as monuments that identify and define a significant national contribution to Reformed doctrine and practice, equal in importance to the varieties of Reformed Christianity represented in the more famous documents of the era.

In the early orthodox era we count some seven confessions from the German Reformed: the Confession of Nassau (1578), the *Repetitio Anhaltina* (1579/81), the Bremen Confession (1595/98), the Confession of the Heidelberg Theologians (1607), the Hessian Confession (1607/08), the Confession of Sigismund (1614) and the so-called Brandenburg Confession, or Confession of the Reformed Churches in Germany (1615). It is quite clear, moreover, that the German Reformed theologians of the seventeenth century valued these confessions highly and referred to at least some of them as on a par in authority with the more famous national confessions of the sixteenth century. Thus, Marcus Friedrich Wendelin responded to his Lutheran opponents by declaring his doctrine to be in accord with the French, English, Palatine, Brandenburg, Hessian, Swiss and Belgian confessions, not to mention the teaching of the *Synodus Belgicae* against the Arminians.

(10) Arminian theology and the Synod of Dort.

If the Reformation, in the persons of its two greatest theologians, Luther and Calvin, stands as a fundamentally *Augustinian movement with a primary emphasis on the doctrine of salvation by grace alone and a parallel stress on the inability of the individual to save himself or even to initiate the process of his salvation, then the two greatest internecine conflicts of the two major Reformation churches – Lutheran and Reformed – were concerned with the denial and exclusion of theological alternatives which diverged from the Augustinian pattern and emphasized human co-operation in the approach to salvation. The Lutheran dispute, confessionally resolved in the 'Formula of Concord' (1580), did not result in the formation of a new confessional body. However the Reformed argument over predestination, grace, and free will, as centred on *Jacob Arminius (1560–1609), ultimately produced a systematic alternative to Reformed theology and a separate confessional stance.

When Arminius died in 1609, the battle lines had been formed and the anti-predestinarian party had acquired enough strength and enough able support in the theological community to tear the Dutch church asunder. In the university, Simon Episcopius carried on Arminius's theology – Episcopius was a pupil of Arminius and Gomarus who espoused the cause of one and debated the other. Episcopius (1583–1643) is the great developer and systematizer of

Arminian or, as it came to be called, 'Remonstrant' theology. Whereas Arminius left no system but only a series of disputation outlines (probably the basis of a projected system), Episcopius produced both the *Confession of the Remonstrant Pastors* (1622) and a massive, though incomplete, *Institutions of Theology* (c. 1640). Episcopius was also instrumental in the composition of the so-called *Articles of the Arminians or Remonstrants* issued in 1610 to express the views of his party. The Calvinist or Reformed side immediately produced a *Contra-Remonstrance*. Debate polarized and led to the National Synod of Dort, 1618–19. The Synod of Dort drew delegates from Britain – including the bishops of Chichester and Salisbury and the professor of divinity from Cambridge, Samuel Ward. Theodore Tronchin came from Geneva, a duo of eminent German Reformed theologians (Alting and Scultetus) came from Heidelberg, and a trio of renowned thinkers (Martinius, Isselburg and Crocius) came from Bremen. Basle, Berne and Zurich also sent representatives – as did all the Dutch provinces and universities. The combination of learning with diversity of views within a churchly consensus produced at Dort a document far from extreme and quite representative of the Reformed theology of its day.

The decision reached by the synod after six months of discussion and 154 formal sessions was, at least in a negative sense, a foregone conclusion. The Arminian articles were condemned and the Belgic Confession, against which the Arminians had protested, and the Heidelberg Catechism, which they sought to reinterpret, were affirmed as the standards of the Dutch church, together with the five Canons of Dort, in which the Arminian position was refuted. The standard acrostic has some virtue as a way of remembering the contents and implications of Dort: TULIP (Total inability; Unconditional election; Limited atonement; Irresistible grace; Perseverance of the saints). Like the Canons themselves, these points are never to be used as a system but read only in the context of the other confessional documents as a refutation of the five essential points of the *Remonstrance*. We also note that the acrostic indicates the contents, but not the actual divisions, of the Canons.

The Arminian *Remonstrance* is therefore a necessary starting point for understanding the work of the Synod of Dort. Article one of the *Remonstrance* contains a distillate of the doctrine of predestination found in Arminius's *Declaration of Sentiments*: it defines predestination as the eternal purpose of God in Christ to save those who believe and to damn those who reject the gospel and the grace of God in Christ. Here already the implication is synergistic and the will of God is viewed as contingent upon human choice. Next (article two), the *Remonstrance* speaks of the universality of Christ's death: Christ died for all and the limitation of the efficacy of his death arises out of the choice of some not to believe. The third article argues the necessity of grace if fallen man is to choose the good and come to belief. In the fourth article, this insistence upon prevenient grace is drawn into relation with the synergism of the first two articles. Prevenient and subsequent assisting grace may be resisted and rejected: ultimately the work of salvation, in its efficacy and application, rests on human choice. The fifth and final article of the *Remonstrance* argues continuing gracious support of believers by God but refuses to decide on the issue of perseverance.

It is clear from the outset that the Synod of Dort could not have been expected to receive these points for debate with a hope for compromise and the ultimate incorporation of some Arminian theology either into the Belgic Confession or into a new confessional document. The Arminian or Remonstrant position was inimical to the confessional stance not only of the Dutch delegates but also to that of the British, German and Swiss delegates. No compromise was possible – and in this sense, the Canons are indeed a foregone conclusion. The synod could only result in the condemnation of Arminianism. What was not a foregone conclusion, but was the substance of the six months of discussion and debate, was the manner in which an international Reformed body such as the synod ought to frame the soteriology of Reformed Christendom over against the *Remonstrance*. The tone and the terminology of the Canons are, therefore, of utmost importance to an understanding of early Reformed orthodoxy.

The first section, 'Of Divine Predestination', is a detailed exposition of Reformed doctrine in 18 articles. It covers the first two letters of the famous acrostic, total inability and unconditional election, with emphasis upon the doctrine of election. The first five articles of this section provide a prologue, indeed a theological context, in which the decree must be understood. The doctrine of predestination here springs out of what J.B. Mozley long ago denominated as the original Augustinian as opposed to the more speculative, scholastic ground. All humankind lies locked in sin and unable to redeem itself, cursed by the Fall of Adam and destined for eternal death. But God in Christ has manifested (art. 2) his saving will and his promise of salvation to believers. God has also graciously (art. 3) called sinful humankind to repentance and belief. Only those who fail to respond to the call of God receive his wrath.

Out of this context of human sinfulness and inability and of the divine offer of salvation in Christ arises now (art. 6–11) the doctrine of election itself. It appears not as a speculative condition for the formulation of other doctrine but rather as the link joining together the lost of the world and the grace of God in Christ. Although the Canons include no discussion of the logical ordering of the decree and, thus, make no attempt to argue the points at issue within the Reformed churches between supra- and infralapsarians, they point, in this first Canon, towards an infralapsarian formulation of the doctrine. The decree is formulated in the context of the problem of sin and posited as divine remedy, as the answer to the question of why some have faith and others do not (cf. art. 6).

The seventh and eighth articles need to be singled out – the former as a perspicuous definition of election and the latter as a response to the excessively speculative character of Arminianism. The seventh article reads, in part,

> Election is the unchangeable purpose of God, whereby, before the foundation of the world, he hath, out of mere grace, according to the sovereign good pleasure of his own will, chosen, from the whole human race, which had fallen through their own fault, from their primitive state of rectitude, into sin and destruction, a certain number of persons to redemption in Christ, whom from eternity he appointed the Mediator and head of the elect, and the foundation of salvation.

Again, the position taken is essentially infralapsarian in its direction and anti-speculative in its formulation. The Canon is framed entirely upon the Reformed exegesis of Scripture and bears witness to the moderate nature of the assembly at Dort: we must disagree with the

frequently seen comment that the majority at Dort were supralapsarian. The eighth article, moreover, insists – against Arminian speculation – that there is only one decree which includes the entire plan of salvation in both testaments.

Since God's election rests on an eternal sovereign decree, the elect are no more deserving of salvation than the non-elect or reprobate. Election does not rest on human merit or even on divine foreknowledge of faith (art. 9), but it is itself 'the fountain of every saving good', resting upon the good pleasure of God (art. 10). Election is therefore unalterable: the elect cannot be cast away, nor their number diminished (art. 11). The remainder of the argument guards against abuses and misconceptions of the doctrine of election. Assurance of election is possible through examination of the spiritual fruits of election such as faith in Christ and thirst after righteousness, but lack of such assurance ought not to inculcate despair – rather the individual ought to desire to be turned towards God (art. 12, 13, 16). This doctrine does not make God the author of sin, but only its judge and avenger (art. 15). Finally, the Canon insists that such doctrine, as the depth of divine wisdom, ought not to be questioned but should, rather, be accepted to the glory of God.

The 'second head of doctrine', nine articles on the death of Christ and man's redemption, covers the topic frequently denominated as 'limited atonement'. From the outset we should recognize that the term 'limited atonement' is ill chosen, a misnomer which does not at all denote the issue at the heart of the debate between Arminian and Reformed. The term attempts to describe the limited salvific intention and application of Christ's otherwise all-sufficient payment or 'satisfaction' for sin. The debate is not over the broad, vague category of 'atonement', but over the limitation of the application of the *satisfactio Christi*. The terminological problem is easily seen when we recognize that Arminian and Calvinist alike agreed that Christ bore the weight of all sin, and that they also agreed that not all human beings were beneficiaries of Christ's death. On the first count, both assume 'unlimited atonement' and on the second both insist on limited redemption as opposed to universalism. The question raised in debate between the Reformed and the Arminians has to do, instead, with the nature of the limitation of the efficiency or effectiveness of Christ's death or satisfaction – and whether Christ, in the strictest sense, can be said to have died or worked satisfaction for all people or for the elect only.

Dort rests its formulation on the proclamation of God's mercy and justice and also on the recognition that no human being can make satisfaction for sin. Since God's infinite justice demands punishment for sin, no sinner can escape unless satisfaction is made – but since such a work of satisfaction cannot be performed by a sinner, God in his infinite mercy gave his only Son 'that he might make satisfaction to divine justice on our behalf' (art. 1–2). The Canons then move on to define the satisfaction of Christ (art. 3) in terms of the traditional distinction between the sufficiency of Christ's work for all sin and its efficiency for the elect only. The perfection of Christ in his humanity, the fullness of his divinity, the weight of divine wrath that fell upon Christ and the universality of the call of the gospel all attest to the infinite value of Christ's death. Dort so emphasized the extent of atonement to all sin that a subsequent article (art. 6) concludes that the failure of some to repent and believe implies no insufficiency in Christ's work but only the failing of humanity. All who believe are 'delivered and saved' (art. 7).

We note that, to this point, no limitation has occurred, and that the term 'limited atonement' hardly fits the case: Christ's satisfaction is infinite. In fact, the first seven articles of this second head of doctrine are an exposition of the first half of an age-old formula defining the work of Christ: Christ's satisfaction is sufficient for all sin, but efficient only for the redemption of the elect. The formula derived from *Peter Lombard's *Sentences* and was accepted by virtually all Reformed writers in the sixteenth century, if properly explained. It was the will of God that the 'saving efficacy' of Christ's death 'should extend to all the elect', which is to say to those given by Christ to the Father. In these, grace has made faith possible, sin has been forgiven and purged away (cf. art. 8).

The Canons now move to counter the 'third and fourth heads' of the *Remonstrance* under a single series of seventeen articles on 'the Corruption of Man, his Conversion to God, and the Manner thereof', in short, 'total inability', now argued at greater length than under the first head, and 'irresistible grace' in conversion. Here too, as in the previous sections, the issue of the Canons is to argue upon a scriptural basis and

not to indulge in speculative theology. This is not to say that the framers of the Canons were not *Protestant scholastics but that here, as in the framing of the Westminster Confession in the middle of the next century, scholastic theologians were attentive not only to definition but also to *genre*: a confessional document is not a systematic theology. Articles one through eleven juxtapose the fallenness of humankind with the universal call of the gospel and pose the question, why are all called and only some saved? Is the fault with Christ and the gospel?

The problem cannot be with Christ, whose work was sufficient payment for all sin, nor can it be in the gospel: 'as many as are called by the gospel are unfeignedly called; for God hath most earnestly and truly declared in his word what will be acceptable to him ...' (art. 8). Those who refuse the gospel, therefore, refuse it because of their obstinacy in sin – yet those who accept the word, in the midst of sin, do not act out of merit or greater ability. Obedience to the call of the gospel does not arise out of 'the proper exercise of free-will' (art. 10), but out of the eternal election of God in eternity and the effectual calling of God in time, out of the grace of God which confers faith and repentance upon the elect.

God's work in the elect is accomplished both inwardly and outwardly: the gospel is preached to the church and the Holy Spirit works inwardly, illuminating the mind and quickening the will by an infusion of 'new qualities' (art. 11). This work of the Spirit is the new creation, the regeneration of the creature, to the end that not only are mind and will transformed, but they also become active – actually believing and actually willing to follow the word of God (art. 12). From this it becomes clear (art. 16) that salvation implies no coercion done to the will. Men are not treated as 'stocks and blocks', nor is violence done to human life. Rather, a gracious healing and correction occurs, bringing about a 'true and spiritual restoration and freedom of our will'. We note that the phrase 'stocks and blocks' comes from the synergistic complaint of the Philippists against extreme monergism: here the argument intends to show that monergism does in fact respect the human will. Human beings do in fact experience a choice for belief and repentance (cf. art. 12) – the issue is merely the ground for that choice in the grace of God.

Finally, the fifth head of doctrine, 'of the Perseverance of the Saints', simply affirms the consistency of divine grace. Since salvation, mercifully, depends upon the grace of God and not upon the human will, it cannot be undone. Election cannot be lost. This means, according to Dort, not that Christians will press on towards perfect sanctification in this life, but rather that the dominion of sin, once defeated by God, cannot begin again to claim the elect. Those who have been regenerated will continue to sin, continue to have spiritual weaknesses, and they will continue to be in need of Christ and the means of grace (cf. art. 1–2). The third article sums up beautifully the position of Dort: 'But God is faithful, who having conferred grace, mercifully confirms and powerfully preserves them therein, even to the end.' Perseverance, therefore, refers not to the merit of believers or to an assurance of salvation founded in works, but only to the power of God and to the assuring work of Word and Spirit, which is to say, to the continuing work of grace in believers (cf. art. 9–14). The Canons of Dort mark the full confessional codification of early Reformed orthodoxy, not as an independent systematic statement of doctrine but rather as an interpretive codicil to the Belgic Confession and the Heidelberg Catechism in which the major deviations from the Reformed confessional consensus are outlined and refuted.

The confessions of the seventeenth century, c. 1620–99

The development of Reformed confessions and confessional theology in the seventeenth century was characterized by a consistent pressure towards closer and more detailed definition of doctrine, particularly among the English and the Swiss Reformed. In contrast to the great confessions of the sixteenth century, which were concerned primarily to define the magisterial Protestant position over against Roman Catholic teaching on the one side and *Anabaptist doctrine on the other, the confessions of the seventeenth century manifest a greater interest in the problems between Reformed and Lutheran theology and in the difficulties caused internally among the Reformed by variant forms of doctrine, such as the Arminian and the *Amyraldian. None of the major confessions of the seventeenth century, not even the Westminster Standards, failed to understand the distinction in form and content between churchly confession and dogmatic system, but the increased sharpness of definition, precision

of argument, and detail of topical division is nonetheless apparent in most of the documents.

This last confessional period did not produce a great array of churchly confessions. Indeed, if we look only to those documents granted official status by a synod or assembly, the century between 1580 and 1680 appears less productive than either of the earlier eras of codification – despite their considerably shorter duration. If, however, we take into account the number of catechisms and personal confessions written for use in the Reformed churches – for the purposes of instruction and witness – this period is as rich as any other. This must be recognized both for the sake of identifying the historical pedigree of major confessional documents like the Westminster symbols and for the sake of setting aside the often made but profoundly erroneous generalization that the age of Protestant orthodoxy or Scholasticism, the seventeenth century, was an age untouched by the piety and fervour of the Reformation. The age of orthodoxy was also the era of a great flowering of Protestant congregational singing and hymnody.

(11) The German Reformed confessions.

The German Reformed confessions of the high orthodox era are only two in number, but both are highly significant theological documents: the formula resulting from the Leipzig Colloquy of 1631 and the Declaration of Thorn from 1645. In the background of the Colloquy of Thorn was the great Lutheran syncretistic controversy in which the irenic Helmstedt theologian Georg Calixt was opposed by a majority of the Lutheran teachers and pastors of the era and most pointedly and vociferously by Abraham Calovius of Wittenberg. Calixt, in brief, argued that Christians could find agreement on fundamental articles, as witnessed by the faith of the first five centuries of the church, while at the same time recognizing that disagreement on secondary or logically consequent doctrines ought not to disturb the larger ecumenical unity of the church. The stricter orthodox in Wittenberg counselled against any such 'syncretism' – the adjustment of ideas or setting aside of differences to find a common ground among Christians of different confessional persuasion.

The turning point in debate, after which Calixtus's teaching became the centre of the major controversy in seventeenth-century

Lutheranism, came at the Colloquy of Thorn, called in 1645 by King Wladislas IV of Poland in order to resolve disputes between Roman Catholic, Lutheran and Reformed factions within the Polish domains. It was held on the more or less neutral ground of the free city of Thorn in West Prussia and organized around the presentation by each party of a confessional document for discussion and dialogue. The colloquy ended in discord with the Roman Catholics contesting the Reformed use of the term 'catholic' in the title of the Reformed confession and with such rancour between parties that the Lutheran statement never was read in public. Neither the Reformed nor the Lutheran confessions were included in the published 'acts' of the colloquy.

Calixtus not only approved the proposal for a colloquy to mend the religious wounds of Christendom, but he also hoped to be a prime mover in the reconciliation. He therefore petitioned the several rulers and free cities involved in the colloquy to accept him as their delegate. These acts aroused the fears of Lutheran orthodoxy. Theologians who had not yet attacked Calixtus but who doubted the wisdom of his views moved to prevent his official attendance at the colloquy. Abraham Calovius, then of Danzig, successfully opposed Calixtus's election as delegate from that city and then, when Calixtus was elected from Königsberg, succeeded in pressing the election of Johann Hülsemann as leader of the Lutheran delegates – a post which Calixtus had desired for himself. Calixtus further enraged the strictly orthodox party at the colloquy by meeting amicably with the Reformed and offering suggestions concerning the final form of the Reformed document. When the conference concluded in discord, Calixtus was better loved among the Reformed than the Lutherans. Indeed, the strict orthodox saw him even more clearly as an enemy of right doctrine.

(12) British confessionalism from the Westminster Standards to Salters' Hall.

English Puritanism, considered doctrinally as a manifestation of Reformed orthodoxy, reached its full codification and scholastic elaboration in the era of the Westminster Assembly. Preparation for such a synthesis is evident in the turning of the English towards theological system in the years following the death of William Perkins. In addition to Ames's famous Medulla (technically an import, though spiritually in the line of Perkins), the first half of the seventeenth century saw James Ussher's *Principles* and John Downham's *Summe of Sacred Divinity* (both major systematic efforts), John Ball's catechism and his *Treatise of the Covenant of Grace*, and, from the pen of the Edinburgh theologian John Sharp, a fully developed early orthodox summation, the *Corpus theologiae*.

The identification of a single line of doctrinal development in seventeenth-century English theology is quite impossible, nor can we define as easily in England as on the Continent a series of distinct Reformed schools of thought, like the federal theology, the Salmurian theology or the Swiss Reformed thought embodied in the Helvetic Consensus Formula. But this problem in no way relieves us of the task of discussing English theology as representative of the age of orthodoxy. The English, as much as the Dutch and the Swiss, fall into the mood of orthodoxy, just as their theology was formulated consistently in dialogue with continental developments – the theological perspective which assumes a positive relationship of revelation and reason, religious discourse and discursive logic, and which identifies the theological task as the establishment of right teaching.

There is good reason to view the development of English theology – from Lambeth and the Irish Articles through the thought of Ussher, Downham, Ball, Leigh and their contemporaries, to the Westminster Standards – as a cohesive movement in Reformed theology. The central issues confronting the Reformed in this movement – divine sovereignty and human responsibility and the doctrinal *loci* of Scripture, predestination, covenant and the Person of the Mediator – were drawn together into a confessionally defined orthodoxy. Some irony appears in the fact that the author of the Irish Articles and of one of the two systems which had the most direct impact on Westminster, James Ussher, was a bishop of the English church who refused formal invitation to sit in the Westminster Assembly. He does stand, nevertheless, as a major witness to the continuous development of Reformed scholastic orthodoxy in seventeenth-century England.

John Ball (1585–1640) must be counted with Ussher as one of the theologians most influential in the development of English Reformed theology in the transition from the early orthodox position of Perkins and its immediate result at Lambeth and in the Irish Articles to the full development of Puritan and Presbyterian theology in the Westminster Standards. Ball's first two attempts at system, both issued anonymously, provide statements of the content and structure of theology: *A Short Treatise: Contayning all the Principall Grounds of Christian Religion* (1629) and *A Small Catechism containing the Principles of Religion* (1639). The former is the more systematic work; the latter reduces the system to a series of questions and answers for more popular consumption. Both works were used as points of reference by the Westminster divines.

Ball also wrote two major doctrinal treatises. The first, *A Treatise of Faith, divided into two parts, the first showing the nature, and the second the life, of faith*, appeared in 1630 and represents both a major dogmatic essay and a realization of the tendency, already noted, of English authors to link doctrine and practice. Ball's other major work, the posthumous *A Treatise of the Covenant of Grace* (1645) explains, together with Fisher's *Marrow* (1645), published in the same year, why the English were capable of producing a complete federal system in Reformed theology so much in advance of their continental brethren. Much like Cocceius, but in a far more normative theological statement, Ball attempted to draw out the covenant of grace as the *locus* in and through which the whole body of doctrine might be understood.

The Westminster Confession and the two catechisms stand, thus, at the peak of a great development of English Reformed theology and represent a federalism complete and fully integrated with orthodox system decades prior to the integration of continental federalism with mainline Reformed orthodoxy. Contrary to the arguments set forth in several recent works, it is impossible, from a historical point of view, to interpret Westminster and the federal theology either as a 'modification' or as a 'distortion' of 'Calvinism'. The 'Calvinism' that we have traced to this point was, from its beginnings, a highly diverse phenomenon, forged not by one but by many leaders – a phenomenon more accurately termed 'Reformed' than 'Calvinist'.

The Westminster Confession itself, though not a scholastic system, could not have been written apart from the intellectual background of Protestant Scholasticism. It bears a systematic design, built upon the two *principia* of Scripture and the triune God, lacking only the prior *locus*, or theology, in which the basic definition of the subject was set forth. The absence of this first *locus* is easily explained by the fact that this is a confession and not a system properly so-called. The subjects included as propositions in the first two chapters of the confession compare almost exactly with the subjects of the *loci de scriptura* and *de deo* of the scholastic systems. In short, the Westminster Confession is a product of the age of scholastic orthodoxy – but it is also a product that respects the difference in *genre* between system and confession. Its doctrinal statement contains little that is unique, although two issues need be mentioned. First, the confession contains a doctrine of predestination that has more supralapsarian accents than any of the previous Reformed confessions, although it continues the basic infralapsarian approach of the confessional Reformed tradition.

More importantly, the Confession offers the first major Reformed confessional exposition of the two covenant schema – the covenant of works and the covenant of grace. The Confession thus documents the increased importance of covenantal thinking to the Reformed faith, indicating particularly an architectonic model in which the righteousness of God and of God's law stand over against human sinfulness as a fundamental or original standard. After the Fall, this standard serves to underscore human inability and to identify the requirement of perfect righteousness to be fulfilled by the Mediator. The covenant of grace provides the otherwise unattainable salvation, grounded in the good will of God and the substitutionary work of Christ as mediator, bestowed freely by God on his elect, and revealed in the history of God's people in the Old and New Testaments.

(13) The era of the Helvetic Consensus Formula. The path towards universal acceptance of the Second Helvetic Confession in the cantons and free cities had been long and arduous – a theological pilgrimage of some thirty years. Reception of the Canons of Dort in Switzerland was mixed, and their acceptance as of equal confessional authority as the great Second Helvetic Confession was not possible either theologically or politically. Not a few Swiss pastors and theologians viewed the Canons on Christ's satisfaction as standing in conflict with the position of Bullinger's Confession. There Christ had been called 'the unique and eternal Savior of the human race, and thus of the whole world, in whom by faith are saved all who before the law, under the law, and under the Gospel were saved, and however many will be saved at the end of the world'. Christ, moreover, 'took upon himself and bore the sins of the world, and satisfied divine justice'. The Confession could not be read in an Arminian manner, for it grounded the entire salvation of humankind and faith itself in the sovereign gracious election of God and cancelled out all synergism – but neither did it broach the question of the limitation of the value of Christ's death.

The most important variations in the patterns and definitions of Reformed theology in the seventeenth century, apart from the federalism of the Cocceian school, were those proposed by the faculty of Saumur: John Cameron, Moses Amyraut, Joshua la Place and Louis Cappell. The latter three were the authors of the celebrated *Theses Salmuriensis*, the doctrinal curriculum of the school of Saumur. As a group, they represent the 'left wing' of Reformed orthodoxy.

The question arises as to whether Amyraut was, as he himself claimed, a more accurate follower of Calvin than his opponents – even more pointedly, was he simply doing greater justice to the language of infinite sufficiency of Christ's satisfaction that was ensconced in the Canons of Dort? Of course, it can be argued that neither Calvin nor the delegates at Dort intended so speculative an elaboration of doctrine as that produced by Amyraut. In addition, the hypothetical universalism of Saumur raises an issue that neither Calvin nor Dort wanted raised – that in the infinite sufficiency of Christ's satisfaction there was, hypothetically, an atonement made and completed for their sin, awaiting application but never applied. At least in the eyes of his contemporaries, this notion moved Amyraut towards Arminianism.

La Place, or Placaeus, proposed a modification in Reformed orthodox doctrine of original sin. It seemed unjust to him that the sin and guilt of Adam be imputed immediately to the descendants of Adam prior to any actual sinfulness on the part of individuals. As an alternative to this doctrine, he proposed a 'mediate imputation' of sin, which is to say, an imputation of sin and guilt with the actual sinfulness of the individual mediating between the sin of Adam and the imputation of Adam's sinfulness to the individual. The sin and guilt of Adam, under this definition, are imputed mediately or on the basis of an actual, inherent sinfulness in the progeny of Adam. Response to La Place was at least as bitter as response to Amyraut. The problem in his formulation was not so much its effect on the doctrine of original sin (which was, in fact, minimal), but rather its effect upon the parallel structure of the immediate imputation of righteousness to believers in Christ.

The modifications of system proposed at Saumur were, in the final analysis, not alterations of the doctrines of Reformed orthodoxy in terms of practical effect. Hypothetical universalism, for all the more gentle tone of its language, issued in a theory of the limited efficacy of atonement. Mediate imputation of sin, for all its appearance of clearing God of the charge of being the cause of human sinfulness, did nothing to alter the Reformed teaching on the original sinfulness and total inability of humanity. The Saumur speculation, far from being a rebellion against Scholasticism, was scholastic to its very core – and a manifestation of the profound effect of logic and subtle distinction upon Protestant theology in the seventeenth century.

The work of Louis Cappell, although condemned with the doctrines of Amyraut and La Place in the Helvetic Consensus Formula, represents a tendency in seventeenth-century Protestant thought quite distinct from the scholastic modification of doctrine. Cappel stood at the forefront of the critical method in biblical studies in his day. He was the first Protestant writer to utilize the theory of the late (sixth- and seventh-century) origin of the vowel points in the Hebrew Bible as a basis for the analysis of text. In one sense Cappel was in continuity with the Reformers: neither he nor they harboured excessive fears concerning the relation of a human and therefore uninspired origin of the system of vocalization to the authority of Scripture in matters of faith and practice. In a more crucial sense, however, Cappel departed from the Reformers. His assertion of the priority of ancient versions – the Syriac and the Chaldee – over the Masoretic text amounted to an assertion of the autonomy of the rational exegete. Here, his method meant the abandonment of the analogy of Scripture as the primary interpretive device of the exegete when study of the verse or passage itself yields no definitive result.

Controversy over the teachings of Saumur began as early as 1645 in Geneva over the views of the Saumur-trained Alexander Morus. Debate intensified during the next several decades until, in 1669, the Zurich theologian Johann

Heinrich Heidegger and the antistes (chief pastor) of Basle, Lucas Gernler, proposed a new creedal statement, limited in its content to the refutation of the problematic elements of Salmurian theology. They viewed such a formula as an augmentation, and not a replacement of the older Swiss confessions and as a 'special' rather than a 'general' declaration of orthodoxy, patterned on the Canons of Dort and not on the Second Helvetic Confession. In addition, the proposed formula would be couched in an irenic manner – there was to be only a refutation of error and not an attack on persons, only a declaration of incorrect doctrine and not an anathematization of heresies. Heidegger, with the assistance of Gernler and *Francis Turretin, prepared the final draft of the formula in March 1675. The resulting document argued a definite divine intention in Christ's work of satisfaction over against Amyraut's hypothetical universalism, the immediate imputation of Adam's sin (paralleling the immediate imputation of Christ's righteousness) against La Place, and the Mosaic origin, if not of the vowel pointing system of the Old Testament, then of the sounds represented by the points, against Cappel. The Helvetic Consensus Formula had a brief confessional life: its acceptance by most of the Swiss cantons and cities came between 1675 and 1678 – and it was abandoned in the very next generation, opposed by J.A. Turretin, among others. By 1725 all of the Swiss cities except Berne and Zurich had set it aside. The great confessional period of the Reformed churches was at an end.

RICHARD A. MÜLLER

FURTHER READING: E.J. Bicknell, *A Theological Introduction to the Thirty-Nine Articles of the Church of England* (rev. R.J. Carpenter; London, 3rd edn, 1955); Arthur C. Cochrane (ed.), *Reformed Confessions of the 16th Century* (Philadelphia, 1966); Peter Y. DeJong (ed.), *Crisis in the Reformed Churches: Essays in Commemoration of the Great Synod of Dort, 1618–1619* (Grand Rapids, 1968); Robert J.W. Evans, 'Calvinism in East Central Europe: Hungary and her Neighbours, 1540–1700', in *International Calvinism, 1541–1715* (ed. Menna Prestwich; Oxford, 1985), pp. 166–96; William Robert Godfrey, 'Reformed Thought on the Extent of the Atonement to 1618', in *West Th J* 37.2 (Winter 1975), pp. 133–71; W. Ian P. Hazlett, 'The Scots Confession 1560: Context, Complexion and Critique', *Arch Ref* 78 (1987), pp. 287–320; James M. Kittelson, 'The Confessional Age: The Late Reformation in Germany', in *Reformation Europe: A Guide to Research* (ed. S. Ozment; St Louis, MO, 1982), pp. 361–81; Martin I. Klauber, 'The Helvetic Consensus Formula (1675): An Introduction and Translation', *Trinity J* 11 (Spring 1990), pp. 103–23; 'Jean-Alphonse Turrettini and the Abrogation of the Formula Consensus in Geneva', in *West Th J* 53 (1991), pp. 325–38; Ernst Koch, *Die Theologie der Confessio Helvetica Posterior* (Neukirchen, 1968); John Leith, *Assembly at Westminster: Reformed Theology in the Making* (Richmond, VA, 1973); E.F. Karl Müller, *Die Bekenntnisschriften der reformierten Kirche: In authentischen Texten mit geschichtlicher Einleitung und Register* (Leipzig, 1903); Wilhelm Niesel, *Reformed Symbolics* (trans. David Lewis; Edinburgh, 1962); Bodo Nischan, 'The Second Reformation in Brandenburg: Aims and Goals', in *Sixteen Cent J* 14.2 (1983), pp. 173–87; M. Eugene Osterhaven, *Our Confession of Faith: A Study Manual on the Belgic Confession* (Grand Rapids, 1964); Jan Rohls, *Reformed Confessions: Theology from Zurich to Barmen* (trans. John Hoffmeyer; intro. by Jack Stotts; Louisville, 1998); Philip Schaff, *The Creeds of Christendom: With a History and Critical Notes* (3 vols.; Grand Rapids, 6th edn [1931], repr. 1983); Richard Stauffer, 'Brève Histoire de la Confession de La Rochelle', *Bul Soc H Prot Fran* 117 (1971), pp. 356–66; Bard Thompson, H. Berkhof, et al., *Essays on the Heidelberg Catechism* (Philadelphia, 1963); Peter N. VandenBerge, 'Protestant Symbols: A Survey with Bibliography', *Am Th L Assoc Proc* 18 (1964), pp. 80–97.

Revisionism

This term entered into the English-speaking theological vocabulary in the 1970s. Originally self-descriptive, in *A Blessed Rage for Order* Roman Catholic theologian David Tracy (b. 1939) denotes as revisionist his own approach to theology. He argues that this approach is followed by a number of contemporary theologians, both Protestant and Roman Catholic. Since Tracy's introduction of the term, revisionism has come to have both a technical and popular meaning. In its technical use, revisionism denotes a hermeneutically sophisticated rethinking of: (1) the ecclesial form of Christian teaching in light of contemporary challenges; and (2) modern conceptions of human destiny in light of the Christian witness. As a popular term, revisionism suggests an ideologically motivated rationale for changing the specific language and practice of the Christian tradition. The former use of the term identifies an important and ongoing theological project. Revisionism has been employed popularly as a term of abuse in *Marxist debates throughout the twentieth century.

As a movement in academic theology, revisionism emerged out of two historical developments – one in Roman Catholic theology and the other in Protestant thought. *Vatican II (1962–65) ended the dominance of *Neo-Scholasticism in Roman Catholic theology. As a result, questions that Neo-Scholasticism had suppressed, or answered without engaging modern philosophy and critical theory, emerged as dominant concerns. These included questions about the historicity of Christian revelation, the linguistic and experiential mediation of truth, modern secularization and an increasingly powerful scientific and technological consciousness. Roman Catholic theologians entertained these questions in the 1950s and 1960s. *Karl Rahner (1904–84) introduced a post-Kantian view of the transcendental conditions for subjective appropriation of revelation. *Bernard Lonergan (1904–84) engaged modern scientific method. These two seminal figures operated within an ecclesiastical context still dominated by Neo-Scholastic habits of thought, and they fashioned their theological systems accordingly. In the Roman Catholic context, then, revisionism signals the efforts of Rahner's and Lonergan's students to extend reflection in theology beyond their teachers. This entails opening theological reflection more fully to the seminal insights of modernity, as well as disengaging theological reflection from the immediate influence and interference of ecclesiastical authorities.

Revisionism in Protestant circles did not arise from the dramatic eclipse of a dominant intellectual tradition and events of international scope. Instead, it grew out of circumstances unique to North America and the elite divinity school culture of the war and post-war decades. The optimistic theological liberalism of the earlier half of the twentieth century fell before the critical energy and scriptural content of neo-orthodox theology. In the midst of these intellectual developments, increasingly egalitarian educational principles brought a number of talented young students from pre-critical backgrounds and denominational colleges to elite graduate institutions. For these students, the neo-orthodox combination of relevance and revitalized emphasis on classical doctrine was most cogently represented in the work of *Paul Tillich (1886–1965). It offered them a path toward a critical engagement with contemporary ideas and social movement that was, at the same time, an immersion in the doctrinal tradition of Nicene-Chalcedonian Christianity. To use terms popular during the Second Vatican Council, neo-orthodoxy was approached by the post-war generation of graduate students as an *aggorniamento*, or updating of the tradition. It was also a genuine *ressourcement*, or return to the doctrinal and symbolic fullness of the Christian tradition. As this generation embarked on scholarly work the civil rights movement, the anti-war movement, the rise of the New Left and feminism changed the social landscape. Further, elite educational culture in the United States became more fully secular. As a result, the terms of critical engagement changed and the neo-orthodox program required extensive rethinking. In Protestant circles, then, revisionism denotes a reprise of neo-orthodox return to fundamental doctrinal commitment, now revised in the context of the new moral imperatives and the new intellectual culture of the second half of the twentieth century.

In spite of different contexts for development, the two impulses towards revisionism converge and produce a unified approach to theology. The diminished ecclesial influence over elite graduate study in theology facilitated this convergence. But more importantly, revisionism coalesced around common theological judgements. A significant consensus emerged about the proper form of critical questions for theology and a more diffuse consensus formed regarding techniques for answering such questions, even as no consensus developed regarding particular Trinitarian, Christological and ecclesiological conclusions.

Unlike non-cognitivist approaches to theology, revisionism does not reduce faith to personal meaningfulness. Revisionism insists that Christian faith involves beliefs about God, the world and human destiny that are public and open to critical scrutiny and informed judgement. No distinction between inner and outer, private and public can protect Christianity from challenge and excuse the theologian from the general intellectual responsibility of articulate defence. Further, against distinctions between reason and revelation, nature and grace, the authority of the intellect and the authority of Scripture, revisionism treats the Christian witness as an always divine and human complex that cannot be dissected into these constituent parts. This view leads revisionism to repudiate a sectarian approach to theology. Revisionism insists that one cannot speak theologically without, at the same time, speaking philosophically. One cannot speak to the church without, at the same time, speaking to the world. As a consequence, responsible theological inquiry must formulate its questions in such a way that extra-Christian criteria of truth are as relevant as intra-Christian criteria.

This combination of extra-Christian and intra-Christian criteria provides revisionism with its distinctive method. Theological questions are doubly formed, both with general cultural categories and within the framework of traditional Christian faith and practice. Answers to these questions must reflect this dual aspect: they must be both public and subject to a general intellectual scrutiny. At the same time, answers must be relevant to the formation of faithful discipleship and the governance of ecclesial communities. This method has been called, following Tillich's terminology, 'correlation'. For example, a theological inquiry into Christ's redemptive work takes shape intra-ecclesially according to the primary sources of Scripture and tradition, as well as to the specific needs of contemporary religious communities. At the same time, such traditional concepts as substitution and sacrifice, obedience and kingly rule, suffering and expiation, are critically examined through an engagement with philosophical, anthropological and ethical theories and judgements. The traditional claims about Christ are then correlated, or are brought into mutually critical engagement with, these general theories and judgements. Each side of the correlation then supplies critical perspective upon and correction to the other. The upshot, then, is a theological judgement both ecclesially significant and culturally relevant.

Within the process of correlation, revisionism consistently adopts a hermeneutical or phenomenological view of both correlates. Revisionists accept the post-Kantian consensus that cognitively significant elements of human life are mediated through language and experience. Given this consensus, the proper task of understanding involves distinguishing between the essential elements of cultural phenomena and the particular verbal forms through which they are mediated. According to hermeneutical theory it is impossible for essential content to be fully separated from its mediating forms. However, a sophisticated understanding of the ways in which human beings both express and receive meanings, as well as practised interpretive judgement, allow for an accurate re-articulation of past truth in new ways. Thus, the correlation practised by revisionism does not split the difference between the correlates. Instead, the goal of correlation is a genuinely revised understanding of religious truth, one both more apt to Christian faith and more fruitful for contemporary culture.

Because revisionism is popular as a term of abuse, it is apparent that correlation does not yield theological judgements apt to Christian faith. This pejorative view of revisionism may stem from two sources. First, *postmodernism has exposed and heightened the ideological content of western intellectual culture. As such, the contemporary correlates to classical Christian teaching are unlikely to be the scientific consciousness or secularization of earlier decades. Instead, the correlates have a greater normative charge – for example, a commitment to liberate sexual desire or a theory of the intrinsic violence of western metaphysics. The sheer urgency and demand of these typical postmodern gestures destabilizes the method of correlation, making the desired combination of ecclesially apt and culturally fruitful restatement of theological truths increasingly difficult to attain. In a postmodern atmosphere of hypercritique, restatements of traditional doctrine read like renunciations. Second, a dismissive use of the label 'revisionism' can derive from a rejection of the post-Kantian philosophical tradition that treats the task of understanding as based in an understanding of linguistic and experiential mediation. In such a view revisionism, for all its hermeneutical sophistication, is reduced to a late twentieth-century reprise of early twentieth-century theological liberalism in which the objective content of Christian revelation is sacrificed to the subjective needs of modern believers.

R.R. RENO

FURTHER READING: *Examples:* Edward Farley, *Ecclesial Reflection* (Philadelphia, 1982); Gordon Kaufmann, *An Essay in Theological Method* (Missoula, MT, 1979); David Tracy, *A Blessed Rage for Order* (New York, 1975); *The Analogical Imagination* (New York, 1981). *Evaluations:* James J. Buckley, 'Revisionist and Liberals', in *The Modern Theologians* (ed. David F. Ford; Oxford, 1997); David Nicholls, 'Modifications and Movements', *J Th St* NS 25 (1974), pp. 393–417; Hans W. Frei, *Types of Christian Theology* (New Haven, 1992); William C.

Placher, *Unapologetic Theology* (Louisville, 1989); Ronald F. Thiemann, *Revelation and Theology* (Notre Dame, 1985).

Richard of St Victor (d. 1173)

Mystical theologian and exegete. Little is known of his early life, but his place of birth appears to have been Scotland. He became a 'canon regular' (*Augustinian) at the Abbey of St Victor in Paris sometime after 1142, rising to become prior in 1162. A prolific and highly original writer, Richard's theology was widely disseminated during the twelfth and thirteenth centuries. He influenced a number of important spiritual movements, including the *Franciscan order. His influence certainly extended to England, for Richard intervened on at least two separate occasions on behalf of the Archbishop of Canterbury Thomas Beckett (c. 1118–70) in his jurisdictional disputes with King Henry II.

Richard's central concern is the life of prayer, and specifically contemplation. In his theology he approaches this subject mainly by way of exegesis. He employs a threefold rule of interpretation: the historical or literal sense leads on to the allegorical sense, and thence to the tropological or figurative sense. Richard's exegesis is directly inspired by *Hugh of St Victor (d. 1142), his great Victorine predecessor, whose writings emphasized the foundational status of the historical sense. In his *Liber exceptionum*, Richard presented a summary of Hugh's teaching concerning the anthropological and scientific principles that enable the scholar to establish the literal sense. The allegorical sense in Richard's exegesis is less free than the tropological. Allegory relates to theology, the content of which is in a certain sense objective, whereas the tropological sense has reference to the spiritual life, which is susceptible to more creative development.

The greatest examples of Richard's fusion of exegesis and spiritual theology are the so-called *Benjamin minor* and *Benjamin major* (ET *The Twelve Patriarchs* and *The Mystical Ark*, 1979). The *Benjamin minor* has the preparation of the soul for contemplation as its theme: the children of Leah (justice) and of Rachel (wisdom) are treated as allegorically representative of the virtues needed for the contemplative life. Its sequel, the *Benjamin major*, is a tropological exposition of scriptural texts concerning the ark of the covenant. Here, Richard develops a doctrine of the contemplation of God in six stages, beginning with imagination. There is movement up and down this scale of knowledge – appropriate both to the capacity of the knower at any given time as well as to the mode of knowledge. The ascent to the highest form of rational contemplation corresponds to a journey into the self: the contemplative is understood as a temple of the Holy Spirit, so that the true ark of the covenant is found within the human soul.

At the summit of the contemplative life stands Richard's exposition of the two cherubim that overshadow the ark. These are taken to represent the highest stages of the contemplation of God, attained when one withdraws into one's innermost self. The first cherub stands for what is above reason but yet not beyond reason, the prime example being the simplicity of the divine essence. The second cherub represents what is above reason and what *seems* contrary to reason: the doctrines of the Trinity, incarnation and Eucharist are cited as examples. Though the two are distinct, they finally harmonize in the mystical life – just as the two cherubim jointly turn their faces to behold one mystery. The same imagery and broad conceptuality is later employed by the Franciscan *St Bonaventure (1217–74) in his classic contemplative work, *Itinerarium mentis in Deum* (ET *The Soul's Journey into God*, 1978).

Richard's most important and original work is his *De Trinitate*, in six books preceded by a preface. His theology at this point makes a radical departure from the prevailing Augustinianism of Latin Trinitarian theology. The central idea in Richard's approach is a Johannine one: God is love. From this premise, Richard deduces in Book III of the *De Trinitate* that the God who is love is *necessarily* a community of persons, and indeed a Trinity. Love cannot exist, he maintains, where there is solitary existence; therefore God the Father must have a Son, for otherwise he could and would not be love. Richard also makes the profound psychological observation that the love of two persons is incomplete, or what we might call narcissistic, when it is not open to more than a selfish possession of a single other. Therefore, as Richard argues, the most perfect charity would be unable to subsist in God were God not a Trinity of Persons.

Richard's Trinitarianism is important for a number of reasons. First of all, it presupposes a redefinition of the concept of the person. The standard medieval definition had been provided by *Boethius (c. 480 – c. 524): a 'person' is an individual substance of rational nature. In Richard's theology, by contrast, 'person' is much more a relational concept, defined supremely by the capacity to offer and to receive love. Secondly, Richard rejects the Augustinian 'psychological analogy' of the Trinity – for with his sense of the term 'person', memory, understanding and will can scarcely be seen as analogous to the Trinitarian persons. Thirdly, Richard's Trinity is a community, and his doctrine is a version of the 'social' Trinity. Augustine's doctrine of the Trinity – and even more the 'Augustinian' doctrine codified by *St Anselm (c. 1033–1109), *Peter Lombard (c. 1100–60) and *St Thomas Aquinas (c. 1225–74) – is, by contrast, radically overshadowed by the regulative unity of a single consciousness. Finally, Richard's doctrine has important implications for the human community of the church. The church is an image of God when it exists in love, and the human person can find spiritual fulfilment in the full religious sense only in the context of a loving community.

Richard's approach to the doctrine of the Trinity has come to prominence in recent years in a number of contexts. In ecumenical theology, for example, there has been a recognition that Richard's theology takes a middle way between the theology of the Christian East and the standard Augustinianism of the Latin tradition. His understanding of the person has also been noted in theological discussion in connection with the ideas of human nature and of the human community. Chiefly, however, Richard's doctrine of the Trinity has come to great prominence in the context of the renewal of interest in the doctrine of the Trinity which characterizes much post-*Barthian and post-*Rahnerian Protestant and Catholic theology. His theological importance has been noted repeatedly by the Reformed theologian *Jürgen Moltmann, while his theology is an important source for Catholic theologians such as Heribert Mühlen.

GARY D. BADCOCK

FURTHER READING: Jean Châtillon, 'Richard de Saint-Victor', in *Dictionnaire de Spiritualité*, XIII (Paris, 1932–), cols. 593–654; Richard of St Victor, *La Trinité* (SC 63; 1959); Richard of St Victor, *Opera omnia* (PL, 196), cols. 1–1366; *The Twelve Patriarchs, The Mystical Ark, Book Three of the Trinity* (CWS; London, 1979).

Ricoeur, Paul (b. 1913)

French philosopher and *Reformed Protestant. Ricoeur is best known, along with Hans Georg Gadamer, for his hermeneutical approach to philosophy and for his interpretation theory. He is also known for his contributions to other disciplines such as psychology, history, social theory, literary theory and religious studies. Ricoeur mediates a 'hermeneutics of suspicion' that criticizes surface appearances with a 'hermeneutics of belief' that retrieves the power of creative language (e.g., metaphor and narrative). This offers exegetes and theologians a way of reading the Bible that is theologically and existentially fruitful in a situation marked by the extremes of historical criticism on the one hand and deconstruction on the other.

The project: A philosophy of the will.
Ricoeur stands in the tradition of reflective philosophy which aims at self-understanding through self-reflection. However, unlike *Descartes, who begins in certainty about the subject ('I think therefore I am'), Ricoeur begins with the question of the subject ('*Who* am I?'). He then follows Jean Nabert in claiming that human existence – the effort to exist and the desire to be – cannot be grasped through direct inspection but only *indirectly* through an interpretation of the signs and acts that disclose it. What is required is a hermeneutics of the 'I am'.

The persistent refrain underlying Ricoeur's work is, to rephrase *Calvin: 'There is no knowledge of self without the interpretation of signs'. Indeed, a number of Reformed themes reappear in Ricoeur's works: the finitude and fallibility of humans as agents and thinkers, the priority and the transformative power of Scripture, the importance of all parts (viz., literary genres) of Scripture and eschatology (i.e., the hope for individual and social transformation).

Ricoeur's ultimate aim – his 'poetics of the will' or 'Second Copernican Revolution' – has as its goal a displacement of the autonomous subject. Transcendence takes the place of the *cogito*: there is a presence, a creative word, that precedes one's own power of self-attestation. Freedom is ultimately realized not by works but rather by something more akin to grace: the regeneration of the will occurs through the appropriation by the imagination of a creative word that bestows new possibilities for existence.

Ricoeur's earliest works treat philosophical anthropology – the attempt to answer *Kant's question 'What is man?'. In the context of post-war France, in which Sartre (1905–80) defined man as 'a useless passion' and existentialist angst threatened to demoralize society, Ricoeur's philosophical style was conspicuous by its positive charge. Ricoeur challenges Sartre's and Heidegger's decision to take anxiety as the fundamental 'mood' of human being. He follows his teacher *Gabriel Marcel (1879–1973) in arguing that joy and hope have equal claim to be regarded as the basic clue to the meaning of human being. There are properly philosophical reasons for describing human being's relation to the world in terms of belonging rather than alienation – reasons that approximate the Christian affirmation of creation.

Ricoeur employs Husserl's phenomenological method to explore the volitional dimension of incarnate existence. The result is an ambitious, and unfinished, trilogy on *The Philosophy of the Will* (1950–60). To be human is to exist in the tension between freedom and nature, possibility and actuality – between the infinitude of one's imagination and the finitude of one's corporeal nature.

Ricoeur's focus on the will enables him to deal as a philosopher with questions of guilt, evil and freedom – the staple of theological discourse as well. *Freedom and Nature: The Voluntary and the Involuntary* (1950) analyzes the structural possibilities of human being. *Fallible Man* (1960) argues that the disproportion between freedom and finitude in human being is the condition of fallibility, not of actual fault. Because evil cannot be read off the fundamental structures of human willing, the phenomenon of fallenness can only be studied indirectly, through the symbolism of evil. Accordingly, the description of the structures of willing (*Existentialism) gives way to a study of actual human existence and to an interpretation of the symbols and myths that express the human condition (hermeneutics). Ricoeur thinks the two problems – the meaning of human being and the meaning of language – belong together, since self-understanding is mediated by symbols and stories. The 'poetics of the will' thus requires a lengthy 'detour' into the role of language and literature. 'Existence via semantics' became the new axiom of Ricoeur's hermeneutic philosophy. Through reading we grasp the range of human possibilities; literature is the laboratory of existential possibilities. The hermeneutical 'wager' that concludes *The Symbolism of Evil* (1960) also funds his subsequent

work: 'The symbol gives rise to thought … I believe [in symbol] in order to understand [the self]'.

The 'detours': responding to the masters of suspicion.
Ricoeur's 'long route' to the meaning of human being thus takes a necessary 'detour' through language. Challenges to the very notions of meaning and subjectivity forced him to take yet more detours: the meaningfulness both of the sign and the self have repeatedly come under philosophical threat in the twentieth century. A growing interest in Freud, Saussure and eventually Derrida among intellectuals in Paris during the 1960s displaced Husserl's phenomenology and Heidegger's existentialism.

Freud, *Marx and *Nietzsche are for Ricoeur the 'masters of suspicion' who, in different ways, put language and consciousness into question. In *Freud and Philosophy* (1970) Ricoeur confronts a 'hermeneutics of suspicion' with a 'hermeneutics of belief': do symbols mediate truths about human existence or do they dissemble? Freud is partly right: consciousness can be false, a projection of unconscious drives and desires. 'The subject is never the subject one thinks it is' (*Freud and Philosophy*, p. 392). Henceforth Ricoeur acknowledges that 'consciousness is not a given but a task'. While recognizing its legitimacy as an episode in the critique of the illusions of consciousness, Ricoeur disputes Freud's reductionistic explanations. Symbols do not only express (or repress) one's past, then, but may *impress* and affect one's future. Creative language is not necessarily illusory: thanks to the imagination, man is 'the prophet of his own existence'. The symbolism of hope, then, may indeed speak a distorted language of desire, or it might possibly be a manifestation of the divine.

Further detours by Ricoeur deal with subsequent 'movements of suspicion': structuralism, 'death of God' theology and deconstruction. Structuralism detaches meaning from subjectivity and relocates it in impersonal and autonomous systems of signs defined by their internal relations only. Ricoeur incorporates the dimension of explaining linguistic structures into his interpretation theory, but argues that structuralism excludes some important dimensions from its hermeneutics, in particular, any reference to the real world.

Ricoeur responds indirectly to Nietzsche and

the death of God movement in a number of articles in the 1970s pertaining to atheism and the critique of religion. As he had earlier appropriated Freud and structuralism, so he appropriates Nietzsche's suspicion that God is a projection of the human will to power as a necessary critical moment in his hermeneutics. In criticizing certain cultural representations of God, the masters of suspicion perform the iconoclastic service of cleansing the temple, thus enabling a new kind of hearing: 'to smash the idols is also to let the symbols speak' ('The Critique of Religion', in *The Philosophy of Paul Ricoeur: An Anthology of his Work* [1978], p. 219). Authentic 'postreligious' faith must henceforth take the long detour through atheism. Ricoeur distrusts theology that fails to think through the properly symbolic moment of religious language, a failure shared by Fundamentalists and *Bultmannians alike in their haste to move to the level of concept and existence respectively.

Jacques Derrida's (b. 1930) deconstruction represents perhaps the greatest challenge to hermeneutic philosophy. Faced with the late-twentieth-century despair of language, Ricoeur displays a firm confidence in 'the institution of language'. And whereas Derrida responds to Descartes' absolutizing of the subject by eliminating it, Ricoeur situates himself in between his modern and postmodern compatriots: his hermeneutics of the self is 'at an equal distance from the apology of the *cogito* and from its overthrow' (*Oneself as Another*, p. 4). Ricoeur's is the constructive side of post-structuralism, a believing postmodern alternative to deconstructive scepticism. His interpretation theory responds to twentieth-century challenges to the meaningfulness of language with an approach that combines analytical precision and existential testimony. Ricoeur's work, like his career, represents a fusion of Anglo-Saxon and continental philosophical horizons.

Hermeneutics of the text: Discourse, metaphor, narrative.
Ricoeur's rehabilitation of the imagination for philosophy and his concept of the text are of special significance for Christian theology. Ricoeur's hermeneutic philosophy is ultimately at the service of the creative imagination, best seen in poetic texts, which in turn are the condition for the possibility of hope. Such texts mediate existential possibilities: ways of seeing and ways of being in the world.

Ricoeur distinguishes semiotics (the science of the sign) from semantics (the science of the sentence). Language is discourse: something said to someone about something. Discourse has both sense (an intrinsic structure of verbal meaning) and reference (a relation to the extra-linguistic world). The text, as writing, is autonomous from its author and its original situation. It has 'semantic autonomy': what it signifies is no longer confined to what the author meant. The text contains its own 'world' and projects its own horizon of meaning. Ricoeur calls this event of world-disclosure 'revelation' and suggests that it is interpretation's *raison d'être*. Interpretation is the process by which the reader opens his or her world to an encounter with the world of the text, and thus to the possibility of transformation.

Ricoeur's interpretation theory holds critical distanciation and existential appropriation in creative tension. There must be both a critical engagement with texts (even suspicion) and a personal engagement with the text's subject matter. Ricoeur speaks of a 'hermeneutical arch': a dialectic between 'explanation' (analyzing the text's sense or structure) and 'understanding' (appropriating the text's reference or 'world'). The text is thus the key to Ricoeur's mediation between belonging to a tradition (Gadamer) and taking a critical distance from it (Habermas).

Imagination in language is best seen at work in metaphor. Metaphors do not simply repackage what can be seen and said literally, but enable new ways of seeing the world. They suspend the first-order reference to literal objects in order to liberate a second-order reference to new possibilities. Ricoeur criticizes the standard 'substitution theory' which considers metaphor a replacement for literal meaning. Again, suspicion has its (penultimate) place: the literal sense must die so that the metaphorical meaning can live. Metaphors refer to reality, not by describing but by redescribing it. Metaphors thus offer the reader expanded views of seeing, and being-in, the world.

Among the many kinds of texts that disclose and transform human existence, Ricoeur accords pride of place to narrative, for only narrative articulates human temporality (i.e., the distinctive mode of human being according to Heidegger). Narrative creates meaning by grouping together heterogeneous events, persons and settings into a unified plot. Ricoeur brings fiction and history closer together by stressing the common configuring work of *emplotment* (i.e., that synthesizing work of the imagination that makes a unity out of events) and the common reference to human being-in-time. Emplotment combines the givens of historical existence with the possibilities of a meaningful interpretation of the whole. Stories and histories alike contribute to the project of self-understanding: without narrative, we would not know what it is to be human.

Hermeneutics of the self: Narrative identity. In his 1986 Gifford Lectures, *Oneself as Another*, Ricoeur returns to his original philosophical project. Self-understanding is now a matter of narrative identity; the *cogito* here becomes a thoroughly hermeneutical subject. We only know ourselves in the light of our lived, and narrated, stories. Ricoeur mediates the extremes of the *Enlightenment's autonomous self and *postmodernity's decentred self. Selfhood is a matter of how one relates with and responds to others (and God). Like the text, so the 'other' introduces a critical self-distanciation which enables a deeper self-understanding. How one treats others is the critical test to which every attempt at self-understanding must submit. It is only through 'dying' to self – through dialogue and deeds of love – that one finds oneself. Self-knowledge is never certain nor autonomous. Rather, the self 'attests' its identity as it recognizes and refigures itself as a character in an ongoing narrative with others.

'Post-Hegelian Kantianism'. While Ricoeur keeps theology and philosophy separate (the one arising from historical testimony, the other from universal experience), there are several aspects of his interpretation theory (e.g., the revelatory world-of-the-text, the wager of faith) that approximate Christian themes. He has, moreover, written provocative interpretations of the opening chapters of Genesis, the book of Job, the parables and the Gospel narratives, as well as a number of essays on biblical themes (e.g., revelation, time, testimony) which examine the respective contributions of the diverse canonical genres. In 'Biblical Hermeneutics' (*Semeia* 4 [1975]), Ricoeur describes his position as a 'post-Hegelian Kantianism'. With Kant, Ricoeur carefully respects the limits of reason; with *Hegel, he explores reason's many forms, both figurative and conceptual (e.g., of history, poetry, culture and religion). Against Hegel,

however, Ricoeur refuses to let conceptual language swallow up figurative language. Ricoeur respects the limits of knowledge yet expands the limits of thought to include a reflection on creative language – on language that enables freedom in the light of hope. Interpretation may be the work of concepts, but philosophy begins from the fullness of language and its proper aim is not theoretical knowledge but the practical realization of human freedom. The existence of God cannot be proved by philosophy, yet Ricoeur repeatedly attends to the diverse literary strategies for naming God in Scripture. Both the conceptual rigour of the philosopher and the exegete's attention to the figurative and literary dimensions of the biblical text are necessary for a hermeneutic philosophy of religion. Theology is not a matter of pure reason, but of hermeneutical reason – of reason reflecting on historical testimonies to the divine.

The 'second naïveté'. By 'second naïveté' Ricoeur means that the sacred is encountered, beyond criticism, in Scripture. The first naïveté, characterized by a belief in the literal meaning of religious language, is no longer open to modern men and women. Hermeneutic philosophy suggests a way forward for postcritical theology, a way beyond the Barth-Bultmann methodological impasse. With regard to biblical revelation, one might say, Bultmann eliminates the level of symbol, *Barth the level of criticism. Ricoeur's critical hermeneutics of revelation works a creative mediation, imaginatively overcoming, like metaphor, things that appear on one level to be too distant and irreconcilable. In fact, Ricoeur owes something to both theologians. With Barth, he believes in the priority of the word over the interpreting subject. Interpretation is about opening the world of the reader to the world of the text. Yet, with Bultmann, Ricoeur philosophically prepares the way for this word, establishing the conditions of meaningfulness for creative language in general. Interpretation is about expanding the range of one's existential possibilities. What we are left with is a kind of 'post-Bultmannian Barthianism' in which the world of the text is revelatory, yet the content of that revelation is human possibility. The question arises, however, as to how distinctive and unique a poetic word Ricoeur considers the biblical testimony to the possibility of resurrection, in particular, to be.

Ricoeur's hermeneutic philosophy seeks to

justify the hope that beyond instrumental reason and empirical experience there may be transcendent possibilities, mediated by metaphors and narratives, that can transform the world of the reader. Hope corresponds to reason in its most expansive mood: we cannot know whether our hopes are well-grounded rather than illusory, but there is a kind of existential verification when faith not only seeks but enables greater self-understanding. Ricoeur's is ultimately a believing philosophy: he wagers that if he attends to the diverse forms of biblical discourse – laws, prophecies, wisdom, narratives, hymns – they will invite him to see the world and live in the world in liberating ways which, without these texts, would not otherwise be possible. An early *cri de coeur* sums up the central aim of his hermeneutic philosophy as a whole: 'Beyond the desert of criticism we wish to be called again' (*The Symbolism of Evil*, p. 349).

Only when philosophy is nourished by poetic, or revelatory, texts, can it fulfil its vocation as a means for human self-understanding and for the realization of freedom. For Ricoeur, hermeneutic philosopher and Reformed thinker, the poetic word is never empty, but will accomplish the purpose for which it has been given.

KEVIN J. VANHOOZER

FURTHER READING: *Texts: Interpretation Theory* (Fort Worth, TX, 1976); *The Rule of Metaphor* (Toronto, 1977); *Hermeneutics and the Human Sciences* (Cambridge, 1981); 'On Interpretation', in *Philosophy in France Today* (ed. A. Montefiore; Cambridge, 1983); *Time and Narrative* (3 vols.; Chicago, 1984–88); *Oneself as Another* (Chicago, 1992); *Figuring the Sacred: Religion, Narrative, and Imagination* (Minneapolis, 1995). *Studies:* James Fodor, *Christian Hermeneutics: Paul Ricoeur and the Refiguring of Theology* (Oxford, 1995); John Van den Hengel, *The Home of Meaning: The Hermeneutics of the Subject of Paul Ricoeur* (Washington, DC, 1982); Kevin Vanhoozer, *Biblical Narrative in the Philosophy of Paul Ricoeur: A Study in Hermeneutics and Theology* (Cambridge, 1990); Mark Wallace, *The Second Naiveté: Barth, Ricoeur, and the New Yale Theology* (Macon, GA, 1990).

Ritschl, Albrecht (1822–89)

Albrecht Benjamin Ritschl can be considered the most influential systematic theologian in late nineteenth-century German-speaking Protestantism. He was born in Berlin on 25 March 1822. His father, Georg Carl Benjamin Ritschl

(1783–1858), was pastor of the Marienkirche in Berlin and later became bishop of the Prussian province of Pommern. Albrecht Ritschl studied theology from 1831 in Bonn and Halle. As a student he devoted much time to the study of *Hegel's philosophy, as a result of the influence of *Ferdinand Christian Baur (1792–1860). After graduating, Ritschl allied himself closely with Baur. Ritschl's first work, on the origin of the Gospel of Luke, was published in Tübingen in 1846. Ritschl lectured in New Testament from 1846 to 1852 in Bonn. It was during this period that he developed his own views about Christianity's early history (*Die Entstehung der altkatholischen Kirche* [Bonn, 1850; 2nd edn, 1857]). In this early work, Jesus is portrayed as the bearer of a new religious principle. He is the focal point of the kingdom of God, the concept used by Ritschl to express the new life of the community gathered around Jesus. In terms of church politics, Ritschl stood close to the supporters of the church union between *Lutherans and the *Reformed. He gave his first dogmatics lectures in the winter semester of 1853–54 and became a full professor in 1859, having been assistant professor since 1852. Central to his academic work throughout this period were the study of Reformation history and biblical exegesis.

In 1864, Ritschl moved to one of the most distinguished chairs in theology at that time, at the University of Göttingen, as successor to Isaak August Dorner (1809–84). He lectured in Göttingen until the end of his life, and it was here that his scholarly endeavours reached their peak. He turned down offers of chairs in both Berlin and Strasbourg. Throughout the 1870s and 1880s, his theology proved deeply attractive to younger theologians. He died on 20 March 1889 in Göttingen, as the acknowledged head of a distinct school of thought.

Ritschl's theological impact rests largely on the significant works of his later years. He had laid the foundations during his Bonn years for his three-volume *magnum opus*, *Die christliche Lehre von der Rechtfertigung und Versöhnung* (Bonn, I 1870, 3rd edn, 1889; II 1874, 3rd edn, 1889; III 1874, 4th edn, 1895; ET *The Christian Doctrine of Justification and Reconciliation*, I [Edinburgh, 1872; III 1900, 2nd edn, 1902; II remains untranslated]). Ritschl's approach begins with a thorough review of the history of doctrine (vol. 1) and continues with an exploration of biblical material, intended to serve as a model of the 'biblical theology' for which Ritschl strives (vol. 2). The third volume, designed to relate closely to the second, offers a contemporary exposition of the doctrine of reconciliation. A summary of his entire position can be found in his *Instruction in the Christian Religion* (Bonn, 1875; ET 1901), a text written for use in schools. Only in this short work did Ritschl succeed in giving equal weight to both the doctrinal and ethical aspects of religion. In his major work, the ethical dimension is severely underplayed. In his later years Ritschl turned towards the study of Pietism (*Geschichte des Pietismus* [3 vols.; Bonn, 1880, 1884, 1886]). Both Reformed and Lutheran Pietist traditions are considered by Ritschl to be relapses into Catholicism. The basic tendency of his theological thought, and its orientation towards an understanding of faith governed by the Reformation, led him to a wholesale rejection of attempts to define piety in subjective terms (cf. *Fides implicita* [Bonn, 1890]).

Ritschl saw the goal of his endeavours to be a 'biblical theology', the main content of which was the doctrine of justification. By 'justification' Ritschl means 'the acceptance of sinners into communion with God'. The judgement which justifies the sinner, seen by Ritschl in neo-Kantian terms as a 'synthetic judgement', is based on the work of Christ. Christ is the bringer of revelation and is as such the 'prototype' (*Urbild*) of religious sensibility. His divinity consists in the fact that his ultimate purpose is identical with that of God. Ritschl rejects every reference to legal understandings of the salvific work of Christ. 'Reconciliation' is the term Ritschl uses for actual justification as it takes shape in the life of faith. Such reconciliation can only take place in the context of a religious community. The purpose that God intends is the inauguration of the full ethical community of the kingdom of God. The notion of the covenant plays an important role in this context. In this respect, and in the resulting high regard that Ritschl ascribed to the Old Testament, Ritschl stood apart from most of his Protestant contemporaries.

There is no place in Ritschl's understanding of the task of theology for individual experience of faith. Religion works primarily not in the realm of feeling, but in the realm of the will. For this reason, Ritschl was heavily critical of *Schleiermacher's theory of religion (cf. *Schleiermachers Reden über die Religion und ihre*

Nachwirkungen auf die evangelische Kirche Deutschlands [Bonn, 1874]. However, Ritschl linked a view of the ethical freedom of the individual over Nature with his voluntaristic understanding of religion. In this way he laid the spiritual and religious foundation for a sense of sovereign domination over the world. He thus propounded an individualistic image of the personality, which proved deeply influential in Protestants' understanding of their vocation. At this point, Ritschl's thought reflects the bitter political conflicts in church life in the Bismarck era. Like Schleiermacher, Ritschl understood doctrine to be information about faith, which was organized conceptually and developed from the perspective of the believing community. Theological statements were to be characterized, following Rudolf Hermann Lotze (1817–81), as 'value judgments', and were of necessity dependent upon historical revelation. Ritschl rejected both natural theology and the claim that theology had need of a metaphysical foundation in order to be able to do its work properly. Even so, Ritschl's utterances about the relationship between theology and philosophy are not without their ambiguities (cf. *Theologie und Metaphysik* [Bonn, 1881, ET 1972]; *Rechtfertigung und Versöhnung*, III.29).

MATTHIAS WOLFES

FURTHER READING: Philip Hefner (ed.), *Albrecht Ritschl: Three Essays* (Philadelphia, 1972); Otto Ritschl, *Albrecht Ritschls Leben* (2 vols.; Freiburg im Breisgau, 1892, 1896), with bibliography; Philip Hefner, *Faith and the Vitalities of History* (New York, 1966); David Mueller, *An Introduction to the Theology of Albrecht Ritschl* (Philadelphia, 1969); David W. Lotz, *Ritschl and Luther* (Nashville, 1974); James Richmond, *Ritschl: A Reappraisal* (London, 1978); Stephan Weyer-Menkhoff, *Aufklärung und Offenbarung: Zur Systematik der Theologie Albrecht Ritschls* (Göttingen, 1988); Clive Marsh, *Albrecht Ritschl and the Problem of the Historical Jesus* (San Francisco, 1992); Helga Kuhlmann, *Die theologische Ethik Albrecht Ritschls* (Munich, 1992); Darrell Jodock (ed.), *Ritschl in Retrospect: History, Community, and Science* (Minneapolis, 1995).

Ritschlianism

*Albrecht Ritschl, and the approach to systematic theology that he developed, were already regarded as the focal point of a school within the Göttingen theologian's own lifetime. A great many students associated themselves with Ritschl and his ideas from the 1870s onwards. In a large number of cases, these students had originally come from neo-Lutheran or pietistic backgrounds and later found themselves in conflict with their earlier convictions. Amongst this group were younger theologians who already held teaching offices. *Wilhelm Herrmann (1846–1922), Julius Kaftan (1848–1926), Theodor Haering (1848–1928), *Adolf Harnack (1851–1930), Ferdinand Kattenbusch (1851–1935) and Martin Rade (1857–1940) number amongst the earliest of Ritschl's pupils. Many others attached themselves to Ritschl later, including Wilhelm Bender (1845–1901), Johannes Gottschick (1847–1907), Hans Hinrich Wendt (1853–1928), Otto Kirn (1857–1911), Max Reischle (1858–1905) and Otto Ritschl (1860–1944). All of these contributed to Ritschl's theology gaining widespread recognition in the German-speaking world, through their own theological and historical work. Their particular achievement was to establish, with reference to Ritschl's method and theory of knowledge, a scientifically credible understanding of theology. In this respect, the Ritschlian school was the most effective and influential group of Protestant theologians at the time of Bismarck.

The following motifs from Ritschl's thought became the most significant theological hallmarks shared by members of the school: the radical rejection of all forms of 'natural theology'; the acceptance of the revelation of God in Christ as the sole starting point of dogmatics; the linking of theology with the church. The Christian religion is viewed not as a form of theoretical knowledge, but – following *Kant – as practical ethical activity. Religion and ethics are brought into an indissoluble relationship. The Jesus of history, whose vocation maps out the direction of Christian existence, constitutes the foundation for both. The biblical concept of the kingdom of God is interpreted in moral terms. On this basis it becomes possible to construct a synthesis between the preaching of Jesus and contemporary ethical concerns (cf., e.g. Hans Hinrich Wendt, *System der christlichen Lehre* [Göttingen, 1907]). Christian faith can be verified only in the realm of ethics. Statements of faith are seen as the expression of decisions of the will, and they are thus to be regarded as value judgements or 'ethical judgements of trust'. Absolute value is realized in the historical person of Jesus (Otto Ritschl, *Über Werthurteile* [Freiburg / Leipzig, 1895];

Max Reischle, *Werturteile und Glaubensurteile* [Halle, 1900]).

By the time of the second generation of the Ritschlian school, for whose members the teaching of Kaftan and Harnack was especially important, the conflict with philosophy and the natural sciences came to the fore. Arthur Titius (1864–1936), Johannes Wendland (1871–1947) and Horst Stephan (1873–1954) investigated the relationship of Christian faith with natural-scientific or non-religious interpretations of the world. Key figures here include *Georg Wobbermin (1869–1943), Hermann Mulert (1879–1950), Georg Wehrung (1880–1959) and Heinrich Scholz (1884–1956), who placed the question of theology's scientific character at the centre of their work, in so doing making a direct link with *Schleiermacher.

In spite of agreement about the main theological questions, in no way was there complete uniformity amongst Ritschl's supporters. Differences existed among them both in relation to the foundations of doctrine and with regard to particular theological issues. In addition, and without destroying an essential agreement with Ritschl's basic theological position, his pupils offered criticism of Ritschl at significant points. Harnack, for example, was critical of Ritschl's tendency to move beyond a theological and history of religions interpretation of the gospel of Jesus and to compare Christological statements with the traditional doctrinal formulae of the Lutheran Church. Other pupils also refused to take on the ecclesiastical orientation of his systematic theology, and his Christology in particular. However, the opposite pole was also represented. Ritschl himself had, on occasion, provided the basis for this (e.g. in his opposition to Haering's *Über das Bleibende im Glauben an Christus* [Stuttgart, 1880], in which Haering argues for adjustments in Christology to bring it more in line with traditional doctrine; see also *Zu Ritschls Versöhnungslehre* [Zurich, 1888]). It did not prove possible for Ritschl to secure a consensus amongst his pupils on the points of disagreement. Different factions ended up opposing each other, some more inclined towards historical and doctrinal criticism, others oriented towards a more positivistic approach to dogmatics.

Wilhelm Herrmann in particular developed a distinctive theological vision. Herrmann rejected Ritschl's critique of religious individualism. In this way he was able to lay the foundation for a particular strand within the Ritschlian school which paved the way for the radically anti-historical proposals of *dialectical theology. By adopting the *Reformation understanding of law and grace, Herrmann identified the law with the autonomous moral law. The law's demands can only be fulfilled by human beings when, through encounter with the person of Jesus, they are given the strength to do this. Behind this notion, an opposition to Marburg neo-Kantianism is clear.

Ritschl's own enquiries into the historical basis of his systematic theology provided fresh stimulus for historical research in Protestant theology. Of particular significance was the expansion of the range of church history, inspired by Ritschl, to include sociological aspects and questions about church law. The way was thus opened up for wide-ranging and methodologically reflective research in church history. Some of Ritschl's pupils, who became representatives of the historicist approach to theology, undertook genuinely ground-breaking studies. A new way of looking at the origins of Christianity, in relation to the world of Hellenistic thought, was proposed (Adolf Harnack, *Lehrbuch der Dogmengeschichte* [3 vols.; Freiburg, 1886, 1887, 1890]; ET *History of Dogma* [7 vols.; London, 1896–99]). Fundamental studies of *Luther appeared (Johannes Gottschick, *Luthers Anschauungen vom christlichen Gottesdienst* [Freiburg, 1887]; Ferdinand Kattenbusch, *Luthers Lehre vom unfreien Willen und von der Prädestination* [Göttingen, 1875]). For the first time it became possible, using an appropriate method, to reconstruct the development of doctrine from the very beginning up to the period of Protestant Orthodoxy (Friedrich Loofs, *Leitfaden der Dogmengeschichte* [Halle, 1889]).

Exploration of the different Christian denominations also became a scientific exercise for the first time (Ferdinand Kattenbusch, *Lehrbuch der vergleichenden Confessionskunde* [Freiburg, 1892]). The 'Theologische Literaturzeitung', launched in 1876 by Emil Schürer (1844–1910), became a crucial instrument for the establishing of a scientific approach in theology, and Ritschl himself was a contributor. The key text presenting the historical outlook of the Ritschlian school was the third edition of the *Realencyklopädie für protestantische Theologie und Kirche* (1896–1913), edited by Albert Hauck (1845–1918). Gottschick took on the editorship of the *Zeitschrift für Theologie und Kirche*, the main scholarly journal of the school, which appeared from 1891.

During the 1890s, the historical orientation of the Ritschlians took a radical turn, due to the activity of a group of younger theologians who broadened the scope of research into a comprehensive religio-historical undertaking. Most of the members of this *'History of Religions School' had contact with Ritschl only in an indirect way. Central to the radical turn was the discovery of the eschatological character of the preaching of Jesus (Johannes Weiss, *Die Predigt Jesu vom Reiche Gottes* [Göttingen, 1892]; ET *Jesus' Proclamation of the Kingdom of God* [Philadelphia / London, 1971]). This dealt a major blow to the ethical interpretation of the New Testament concept of the kingdom of God and entailed huge theological consequences. *Ernst Troeltsch (1865–1923), above all, turned his attention to these. In calling explicitly for a metaphysical foundation, his understanding of the philosophy of religion and his programme for a historical theology already represent a change of direction from Ritschl's Christocentric theology of revelation.

It was not only to the scientific basis of theology, but also to the popularizing of modern theological knowledge, that pupils of Ritschl devoted their attention. The latter occurred primarily through the journal *Die Christliche Welt*, founded in 1886 by Rade, along with Wilhelm Bornemann (1858–1946), Paul Drews (1858–1912) and Friedrich Loofs (1858–1928). Its programmatic title clearly indicates the goal of the 'Culture-Protestantism' of the time: the renewal and strengthening of the Christian religion within an increasingly secular environment through the clarification of the religious foundations of modern culture. In this context, theology itself is to be understood and practised as a science of the history of culture. Rade himself followed the same goal in his monumental biography of Luther (*Luthers Leben, Thaten und Meinungen* [3 vols.; Neuensalza, 1884, 1885, 1887]). Other ventures following a similar line of thought included the *Sammlung gemeinverständlicher Vorträge und Schriften aus dem Gebiet der Theologie und der Religionsgeschichte* (from 1896), the *Religionsgeschichtlichen Volksbücher* (from 1904) and the dictionary *Die Religion in Geschichte und Gegenwart* (1908–13).

The immense success of Ritschlian theology in Germany provoked enormous criticism, even in Ritschl's own lifetime. Countless well-known conservative theologians, usually Lutherans, launched attacks against Ritschl and his school. Franz Hermann Reinhold Frank (1827–94) and Johann Tobias Beck (1804–78) should especially be mentioned. Beck developed an understanding of the kingdom of God explicitly to counter Ritschl's. Ritschl's theory of justification received the critique of *Martin Kähler (1835–1912), and his Christocentrism that of Erich Schaeder (1861–1936). Hermann Cremer (1834–1903) vehemently opposed Ritschl's methodological and epistemological presuppositions, and his dependence on Kant in particular. It was in the context of this criticism that the term 'Ritschlianism' was first used.

The impact of Ritschl's theology was not confined to the German-speaking realm. From the 1890s onwards, his theology proved influential first in England and Scotland (John Kenneth Mozley, *Ritschlianism* [London, 1909]; cf. also Alfred Ernest Garvie, *The Ritschlian Theology* [Edinburgh, 1899]). Alongside Mozley (1883–1946) and *Garvie (1861–1945), *Peter Taylor Forsyth (1848–1921) must also be classed as a supporter of Ritschl, however critical of liberalism he later became. In America, links were also made with Ritschl's work from the turn of the century onwards. Henry Churchill King (1858–1934) introduced key elements of Ritschl's thought into American theological discussion in his *Reconstruction in Theology* (New York, 1901). In all these cases, the notion of the moral personality, and the ethical understanding of Christianity that Ritschl represented, were of significance. The unity of Jesus with God is interpreted as a complete union of the will of Jesus with the will of God, and this is contrasted with the classical doctrine of the two natures. The kingdom of God is viewed as an ethical entity that is dependent upon ethical conduct for its realization. The revelation of God, because of its personal nature, can only become a reality in the personal life of the believer. The content of the revelation is the ethical will of God (cf. Henry Churchill King, *Theology and the Social Consciousness* [New York, 1902]).

Alongside King, William Adams Brown (1865–1943), George Burman Foster (1858–1918) and Douglas Clyde Macintosh (1877–1948) also show signs of Ritschl's influence in their theologies. Due to their focus upon the ethical content of the Christian faith, links can also be seen between the American Ritschlians and the representatives of the Social Gospel, Washington Gladden (1836–1918), Richard Theodore Ely (1854–1943) and *Walter Rauschenbusch (1861–1918).

MATTHIAS WOLFES

FURTHER READING: Gustav Ecke, *Die theologische Schule Albrecht Ritschls* (2 vols.; Berlin, 1897, 1904); Johannes Wendland, *Albrecht Ritschl und seine Schüler* (Berlin, 1899); Martin Rade, 'Ritschlianer', in *Rel G G* IV (Tübingen, 1913), pp. 2334–38; Horst Stephan, 'Albrecht Ritschl und die Gegenwart', in *Z Th K* NF 16 (1935), pp. 21–43; Otto Ritschl, 'Albrecht Ritschls Theologie und ihre bisherigen Schicksale', in *Z Th K* NF 16 (1935), pp. 43–61; Joachim Weinhardt, *Wilhelm Herrmanns Stellung in der Ritschlschen Schule* (Tübingen, 1996).

Robinson, John Arthur Thomas (1919–83)

John Robinson was, as he later acknowledged, born into 'the heart of the establishment'; rooted in a comfortable world of cloisters, choirs and libraries. His father, Arthur William (1856–1928), was canon of Canterbury Cathedral, and his paternal uncle, Joseph Armitage (1858–1933), was successively dean of Westminster Abbey and of Wells Cathedral. Robinson was educated at Marlborough College and Cambridge University, where he would work for much of the rest of his life. He was an undergraduate at Jesus College, a postgraduate at Trinity College, and he trained for the priesthood at Wescott House. He was ordained a priest of the Church of England in 1946, the same year in which he married Ruth Grace. Robinson served his curacy (1945–48) at St Matthews, Moorfield, Bristol, where the vicar was Mervyn Stockwood (1913–95). In 1948, Robinson became chaplain of Wells Theological College, but he returned to Cambridge in 1951 as dean of Clare College. When Stockwood became bishop of Southwark in 1959, Robinson was invited to become the suffragan bishop of Woolwich, which he accepted. He remained at Woolwich for the next ten years, before again returning to Cambridge as dean of Trinity College in 1969, though from then until 1980 he also served Southwark as an assistant bishop.

Robinson's hope of the Lady Margaret Chair in Divinity at Cambridge was unrealized, but for nearly forty years – from the publication of his first book in 1950 until his last, posthumously published in 1985 – he was at the forefront of Anglican theology, a distinctive and remarkably consistent voice. Though privileged by family, education and career, and thus perhaps sometimes too accepting of the *status quo*, Robinson nevertheless challenged complacency and promoted reform, in church and society. He could defend the establishment of the church, argue for the early dating of the New Testament and entertain the authenticity of the Turin shroud, while criticizing the nuclear power and weapons industries, arguing for the ordination of women and promoting homosexual rights. In many ways he embodied his own picture of a 'complete Church of England man': a 'both-and' rather than an 'either-or' man, 'Catholic *and* Reformed, priestly *and* prophetic, profound *and* simple, inclusive by temperament rather than exclusive' (*The Roots of a Radical*, p. 21).

Robinson's doctoral dissertation, 'Thou Who Art', was influenced by *Martin Buber's philosophy of *I and Thou* (1923), and its emphasis on personal relations as constitutive of human being. This emphasis would become central in Robinson's own work, though many, on a first or casual meeting, found Robinson himself somewhat impersonal. This was as much due to his shyness as to any lack of interest in other people; though his inveterate name-dropping, in life and in print, betrayed his particular interest in celebrities. Nevertheless, in all he did, Robinson sought to expound his conviction that at the heart of the world is the one who, in Jesus Christ and in his church, addresses us as 'Thou' and draws us into a relationship that constitutes us anew.

All of Robinson's work was rooted in this orthodox teaching, and it is what made him in his own eyes a 'radical' theologian. Yet for many he was a radical in the sense of a reformer, if not a destroyer, of Scripture and tradition. Robinson first acquired this reputation in 1960, by defending Penguin Books' publication of the unexpurgated version of D.H. Lawrence's novel, *Lady Chatterley's Lover*. Robinson defended the book as an attempt to present sex as sacred, which he thought consonant with Christian teaching. This view was unexceptionable, but in a prurient culture it was found newsworthy when advanced by a bishop of the established church. Then, in 1963, Robinson published *Honest to God*, in which he drew on the work of *Rudolf Bultmann, *Dietrich Bonhoeffer and *Paul Tillich, in order to suggest how Christian

faith might be better expressed with metaphors of 'depth' and 'ultimate concern', than with more traditional images of a paternal God 'above'. He also drew on Joseph Fletcher's 'situation ethics' in order to suggest a less legalistic and more pragmatic approach to moral judgements. Robinson criticized forms of 'theism' that objectified God as a thing among things, and he sought to retrieve for the contemporary world an understanding of the divine that was more intimate and relevant to people's lives. But in a theologically illiterate culture, many thought it heretical for a bishop to declare that much religious imagery was mythological, and that 'our image of God must go' (the editor's title for Robinson's front-page article in *The Observer*, 17 March 1963). Archbishop *Michael Ramsey was provoked into denouncing the book on television; though this he later regretted. The book was immensely popular, selling over three hundred and fifty thousand copies by the end of 1963.

Much of Robinson's other work was an attempt to explain in greater detail some of the positions advanced in *Honest to God*. In particular, *The Human Face of God* (1973) attempted the difficult task of presenting an orthodox Christology in non-Chalcedonian terms, using more existential categories. Many of Robinson's other books were concerned with either moral, pastoral and liturgical issues, or with New Testament themes, such as the second coming of Christ or the Pauline notion of the body, Christ's body and the body of the church. In 1977 Robinson gave the Teape Lectures in India, which resulted in *Truth is Two-Eyed* (1979), a brave attempt to think about Christian faith in relation to Hindu beliefs. In the last years of his life, Robinson surprised many by advocating an apparently 'conservative', pre-70 AD dating for the New Testament. But this reaction ignored the fact that in many ways Robinson was first and last a traditionalist, who only appeared radical because he sought new ways to express old beliefs.

Robinson's abiding faith in 'love' as the transcendent ground of human being is nowhere better seen than in the fortitude with which he faced his own impending death, finding God in the cancer that was destroying him, even as the psalmist found God in the depths of hell (Ps. 139:8).

GERARD LOUGHLIN

FURTHER READING: *Texts: In the End God* (London, 1950; 2nd edn, 1968); *The Body: A Study in Pauline Theology* (London, 1952); *Honest to God* (London, 1963); with David L. Edwards, *The Honest to God Debate* (London, 1963); *Christian Freedom in a Permissive Society* (London, 1970); *The Human Face of God* (London, 1973); *Truth is Two-Eyed* (London, 1979); *The Roots of a Radical* (London, 1980); *The Priority of John* (ed. J.F. Coakley; London, 1985). *Study:* Eric James, *A Life of Bishop John A.T. Robinson: Scholar, Pastor, Prophet* (London, 1987).

Romanticism

Up until about the last third of the eighteenth century, the increasingly obvious subjectivity of human perception was commonly seen as a regrettable nuisance. In particular, two centuries of religious conflict in England had shown that theological controversy was not going to be settled by reason, scholarship or debate. If, in what had unwittingly become the world's first pluralistic society, the Bible could still (usually) be ring-fenced as the inspired word of God, certainty was now easier to find in the exploration of Nature, God's 'other book'. Nature, as everyone since Newton knew, concerned not the vagaries of human perception but mathematically quantifiable facts about the material world. It became one of the tasks of philosophy to establish what kinds of knowledge were objective and reliable and what might be undermined by human subjectivity.

*John Locke (1632–1704), the most popular philosopher of the eighteenth century, was concerned with how we know anything at all. 'The understanding, like the eye', he begins, 'whilst it makes us see and perceive all other things, takes no notice of itself; and it requires art and pains to set it at a distance and make it its own object.' There were, he insisted, severe limits on what could be known. Locke's distinction between 'primary' qualities that belonged to things, and 'secondary' qualities that were attributed to them by us, appeared to have been proved by Newton who had, for instance, shown that colour was not a property of objects themselves, but of light and the human eye. Studies of the eye had shown that what we 'see' is conveyed to the brain through the optic nerve by means of an image on the retina. Though humans might think they perceived a concrete and three-dimensional world, that 'reality' was inside the head. This Lockean version of Newton's optics was at once logical and bleak. The world that

people had previously believed they inhabited – full of colour, sound and scent – was now apparently only a fabrication of the brain. The really important world outside was hard, cold, colourless, silent and dead; a world of quantity, a world of mathematically computable motions.

Such was the view of a whole post-Lockean generation of poets and writers: Addison, Akenside, Sterne and Thomson all in their own ways either deplored or celebrated it. Addison's essay on 'The Pleasures of the Imagination' captured the new ambivalence towards the natural world engendered by Locke's epistemology by stressing the ultimate benevolence of the illusions that engulf us. Its tone suggests enforced cheerfulness, as if the only compensation for the loss of a naïve enjoyment of the beauties of Nature is a melancholy pleasure in the sophistication that knows itself undeceived. Since the task of 'poesy' (a much broader literary category than our modern word 'poetry') was not to discover truth, divine or human, but, by imitation, to 'instruct through pleasing', art could, at best, only add 'supernumerary ornaments' to this bleak world picture.

The first challenge to this theoretical position came, unexpectedly, from biblical criticism. Robert Lowth's Oxford lectures on *The Sacred Poetry of the Hebrews* (1753), instead of trying to deduce manifold meanings within the sacred texts, were primarily concerned, almost for the first time, with trying to understand the state of mind of the biblical writers themselves. The result was to transform not merely biblical criticism, but the status of poetry itself.

Lowth's identification of the prophets and poets of the Old Testament meant that the poet could now claim biblical precedent for a new status: not as a decorator or supplier of 'supernumerary ornaments', but as a prophet, seer and mediator of divine truth. Hugh Blair, first professor of rhetoric at Edinburgh University, devoted a whole chapter of his lectures (1783) to summarizing Lowth. They were one of Wordsworth's main sources for his preface to the *Lyrical Ballads*. But not merely did Smart and Cowper, Blake and Wordsworth cast themselves in a biblical *rôle* unimaginable, for instance, to Pope or Gray – the models and canons of literary taste had undergone a corresponding shift. By and large, the principal literary models in 1700 were classical; by 1800 they were more likely to be biblical. Lowth anticipates and sets the agenda for Wordsworth's theory of poetic diction by implicitly rejecting the stilted conventions of Augustan poetic diction and praising instead the 'simple and unadorned' language of Hebrew verse, which gained its 'almost ineffable sublimity' not from artificially elevated diction, but from the depth and universality of its subject matter.

But Lowth's pioneering work had another even less foreseeable consequence. Because Hebrew poetry relied on parallelism rather than the rhymes and rhythms of European verse, it was, Lowth claimed, best translated not into verse, but into prose. As critics such as Blair were quick to point out, this meant that whereas European and even classical poetry was extremely difficult to translate into another language with any real equivalence of tone or feeling, the Bible was peculiarly, and, by implication, providentially, open to translation. This observation had a further unforeseen consequence: that of blurring the traditional distinctions between prose and verse. To speak of prose as 'poetic' could now be much more than a metaphor. Nor was this shift in critical theory dependent on the writer's own religious beliefs. If Blake, Wordsworth and *Coleridge were all Christians of a kind, Shelley had been expelled from Oxford for his atheism. He nevertheless centres his *Defence of Poetry* (1821) on Lowthian principles. 'Poets, according to the circumstances of the age and nation in which they appeared, were called in the earlier epochs of the world, legislators or prophets; a poet essentially comprises and unites both these characters.' 'The distinction between poets and prose writers', he continues, 'is a vulgar error.' 'Plato was essentially a poet' – so were Moses, Job, Jesus, Isaiah, Bacon, Raphael and Michelangelo. In 'defending' poetry he so extends his definition of the word as to embrace the whole of literature – and, indeed, art in general. Following Lowth, the prophetic function of the artist has become more important than any particular linguistic form of poetry. Common to Romanticism right across Europe at this period is a new concept of 'literature' as of inherent value in itself over and above its ostensible subject. The Oxford English Dictionary lists this value-added variant as the third, and most modern, meaning of the word, defining it as 'writing which has a claim to consideration on the ground of beauty of form or emotional effect' – adding the rider that it is 'of very recent emergence in both France and England'.

Lowth's work had had the unintended effect both of transforming the status of secular poetry, and of blurring the distinctions between prose and verse. His stress on the literary power and 'sublimity' of the Bible could only strengthen the growing appreciation of it as an aesthetic work. Though the new secular aesthetic status of the written word has been attributed to many origins, there is no doubt of the part played by the Romantic reading of the Bible. Thus in Germany, what was virtually a new subject, 'aesthetics', had come into being following *Kant's hint (it is little more than that) in the third Critique that the gap between pure and practical reason might be bridgeable by art, and it had become a central plank of Romanticism. But there is a great deal of evidence to suggest that this new value attached to good writing, whether prose or verse, was already gaining ground in both Britain and Germany, before either Lowth or Kant, as an extension of the traditional Protestant approach to reading the Bible. The intense self-searching and self-constructing relationship to the text fostered by the personal Bible study of Protestantism was subsequently transferred first to the study of the 'book' of Nature in seventeenth-century science, then to history and finally, with the rise of the new art form, the 'novel', in the eighteenth century, to the reading of secular fiction as 'literature'. Not least among the many ironies of critical history is the way in which, just at the time when historical criticism of the Bible was making literal interpretation impossible for an educated readership, it was to regain much of its old status in a secularized form, as 'literature'.

In France and Germany, such reappraisals were to take opposite forms at the end of the eighteenth century. Exiled in England from revolutionary and atheistic France, the conservative Catholic aristocrat Chateaubriand (1768–1848) saw in the Bible both divine revelation and the source of a quite new kind of literary consciousness. *The Genius of Christianity* (1802) claims that Christianity is 'a double religion'. Not merely does it have spiritual authority, but it has historically allowed for the creation of a quite new sense of drama and of literary character.

But Chateaubriand was no less conscious of the moral and social dimensions of this new sense of individuality. 'Christianity ... by mingling with the affections of the soul, has increased the resources of drama, whether in the epic or on the stage'. Thus, since pagan antiquity had little interest in an afterlife, classical tragedy ended simply with death. In contrast, in a play like Racine's *Phèdre* the tragic tension is increased by the fact that, as a Christian wife, Phèdre is also jeopardizing her immortal soul. It is, perhaps, not surprising that the Romantics should have increasingly turned away from the classical towards biblical literary models in their search for legitimation.

Thus, Chateaubriand claims, this new sense of individuality and inner space produced by the Bible had transformed poetry. In spite of neoclassical praise for the evocativeness of classical mythology, it had destroyed her real charms. 'Mythology diminished the grandeur of Nature – the ancients had no descriptive poetry, properly so called.' Christianity had demythologized Nature. Not merely do the great religious poems owe their aesthetic sublimity to the Bible, but the entire aesthetic behind Romanticism is the outcome of a Christian and biblical civilization. Such a realization enables us to look back on the past and perceive qualities that could neither have been noticed nor appreciated in earlier or non-Christian societies. 'The growth of descriptive poetry in modern times enables us to see and appreciate the genius of the poets of Job, Ecclesiastes, and the Psalms.' For Chateaubriand, the true aesthetic qualities of the Hebrew Scriptures awaited a modern and specifically Christian appreciation.

Meanwhile, in a Germany both conservative and reactionary, *Friedrich Schleiermacher (1768–1834) was evolving a far more radical view of religion itself. With *On Religion* (1798), he challenged his self-styled 'Romantic' friends, the Schlegel brothers, Fichte and Schelling, in Jena by arguing that religion was as basic to humanity as sense-perception. As professor of theology in Berlin, his theory of hermeneutics – the art of understanding the meaning of texts – began characteristically not from any fixed meaning of a text, nor with conjectures about authorial 'intentions'. It began, rather, with the complex interrelation between reader and text, and, behind that, the totality of the surrounding culture. Just as there is no 'perspectiveless vision', in that all sight was from a particular moment in place and time, so too all texts had to be understood as coming from a particular person at a particular time. In this context there could be no simple key to unlock the Scriptures;

no formula to establish a definitive meaning: 'understanding' is, rather, 'an unending task'.

For Schleiermacher and his successors there was no privileged access to biblical meaning; all interpretations had to be understood within their context. Nor was the present exempt. Just as medieval systems of allegorizing the Scriptures had been part of a universal system, demonstrating (to inspired 'readers') its divine origin, so the discovery of the Hebrew prophets as poets related to contemporary debates about the *rôle* of art in society. Similarly, the historicizing of those who, like Lessing, Schiller or Chateaubriand, saw the Bible in terms of the growth of human consciousness, was part of a much wider Romantic quest to understand the essential difference of the past.

It was against this background that we find Coleridge devoting the last twenty years of his life to literary and biblical criticism. A highly original thinker, there is ample evidence of his acquaintance with contemporary continental sources. *The Statesman's Manual* (1817), for instance, incorporates to a surprising degree not merely the Schlegels' sense of the imaginative and organic unity of the Bible, but even Chateaubriand's broad cultural sweep:

> ... they [the Scriptures] are the living educts of the Imagination ... Hence ... the Sacred Book is worthily intitled the word of God. Hence too, its contents present to us the stream of time continuous as Life and a symbol of Eternity, inasmuch as the Past and the Future are virtually contained in the Present ... In the Scriptures therefore both facts and persons must of necessity have a two-fold significance, a past and a future, a temporary and a perpetual, a particular and a universal application. They must be at once Portraits and Ideals.

Much of Coleridge's later work centred around giving substance to this pregnant summary. Though his ideas were in many cases only to find their fullest expression with such Victorians as *Maurice and *Newman, Coleridge, of all Romantic critics, probably came closest to this ideal of discovering in the Bible (as in Shakespeare) an organic and aesthetic unity that enhanced – and, indeed, was inseparable from – its spiritual content.

A.T. Stephen Prickett

FURTHER READING: *Texts:* S.T. Coleridge, *Aids to Reflection* (London, 1825); *Confessions of an Inquiring Spirit* (London, 1840); Ludwig Feuerbach,

The Essence of Christianity (1841; trans. George Eliot, 1854; New York, 1957); Julius and Augustus Hare, *Guesses at Truth* (1827, 2nd edn 1838, London, 3rd edn 1871); Johann Gottfried Herder, *The Spirit of Hebrew Poetry* (Dessau, 1782–3; trans. James Marsh; Burlington, VT, 1833); Thomas Paine, *The Age of Reason* (New York, 1793); F.C. Schiller, *On the Aesthetic Education of Man* (1795; trans. R. Snell; London, 1954); David Friedrich Strauss, *The Life of Jesus* (1835; trans. George Eliot; London, 1846); C.F.C. de Volney, *The Ruins: Or a Survey of the Revolutions of Empires* (1791; London, 1851). *Studies:* John Coulson, *Newman and the Common Tradition* (Oxford, 1970); Hans Frei, *The Eclipse of Biblical Narrative: A Study in Eighteenth- and Nineteenth-Century Hermeneutics* (New Haven, 1974); Werner G. Jeanrond, 'The Impact of Schleiermacher's Hermeneutics on Contemporary Interpretation Theory', in David Jasper (ed.), *The Interpretation of Belief: Coleridge, Schleiermacher, and Romanticism* (London, 1986); Thomas McFarland, *Coleridge and the Pantheist Tradition* (Oxford, 1969); David Norton, *History of the Bible as Literature* (2 vols.; Cambridge, 1993); Richard E. Palmer, *Hermeneutics: Interpretation Theory in Schleiermacher, Dilthey, Heidegger and Gadamer* (Evanston, IL, 1969); E.S. Shaffer, *'Kubla Khan' and 'The Fall of Jerusalem'* (Cambridge, 1975); Leslie Tannenbaum, *Biblical Tradition in Blake's Early Prophecies* (Princeton, 1982).

Rousselot, Pierre (1878–1915)

Pierre Rousselot was born 29 December 1878, at Nantes in Brittany. He entered the Society of Jesus on 25 October 1895 and was ordained priest in 1908. He died on the battlefield of Éparges on 25 April 1915. In his brief thirty-six years he manifested an immense intellectual energy that changed Catholic theology. First secretary of *Recherches de Science Religieuse* and professor at the Institut Catholique of Paris, Rousselot reacted strongly against *Modernism yet remained open to the attraction of Blondel. Returning beyond *Suárez and *Cajetan to the text of *St Thomas Aquinas, he rediscovered the dynamic, mystical thrust of Thomas's thought and used it to reshape traditional metaphysics, the analysis of the act of faith and Catholic theology.

In his doctoral dissertations at the Sorbonne, *L'Intellectualisme de Saint Thomas* (Paris, 1908) and *Pour l'Histoire du Problème de l'Amour au Moyen-Age* (Münster, 1908) Rousselot laid the foundation for a renewed *Thomism. Instead of understanding intelligence primarily as the passive faculty which receives abstractions from without under the illumination of the agent intellect, he understood intelligence rather as active, as a dynamic desire for the totality of being. Ultimately its final goal, the beatific vision, defined the intellect as *capax Dei*. Consequently, being was known primarily in the judgement, not in a concept. Lest the direct, dynamic orientation of human intelligence to God as its true and good destroy the distinction between intellect and will, natural and supernatural, Rousselot conceived of a double natural order corresponding to man, the paradoxical creature composed of soul and body. The first order was more static, the second dynamic, whose 'mute appeals' were only clearly recognized with explicit revelation as the supernatural order deepened man's natural desire for the beatific vision and guaranteed the possibility of its fulfilment. The static order assured the validity of human concepts lest they be relativized by the intellect's constant transcendence of the finite and by the intelligibility attributed to material singulars. This static order was grasped in the single intellectual-sensible intuition of the primordial Adam, *de facto* Jesus Christ, whose consciousness grounded the stability of the natural order, mediated knowledge of material singulars to God and pure spirits, and limited the temporal-spatial extension of the universe. Once the universe's extension was limited, human abstractions would approach a real limit and not just be referred onward into endlessness. Rousselot always maintained a 'sacramental' vision, preserving the intelligibility of finite realities and concepts without absolutizing them so that they might serve as signs of God in nature and grace.

In 1910 Rousselot modified his synthesis substantially, borrowing insights from *J. Maréchal. He stressed more strongly the intellectual dynamism filled with love of the truth, yet he preserved the concept by seeing it as an essential part of every judgement. This dynamism allowed him to resolve many apparent antinomies in the traditional analysis of the act of faith. How is the external creed or sign linked with the internal grace to produce a single certitude? How can the act of faith be simultaneously most certain and free? An appeal to the intellect's active power of synthesis, that is, judgement, resolves the difficulties. The natural world of facts serves to provide signs, or clues, of a higher significance. So in matters of faith there can be a similarity of representational elements alongside differences of affirmation. One sees and interprets correctly the signs of grace, the other does not understand. The act of faith results from the mutual causality of perception and the perceived. The clue is seen as significant only in view of a greater meaning (the vital whole is greater than the sum of the parts), and the meaning is revealed only through the clue. Thus the natural order serves as a sign of the supernatural reality which envelops, surpasses and perfects it.

To unite certitude and freedom Rousselot made use of his understanding of the spirit's dynamism (from which judgement flows). The dynamic intellect is intrinsically characterized by a basic love to possess itself and God. In the call and response of faith, as in every judgement, will and intellect mutually affect each other. Practical judgement and voluntary election unite in the spirit's dynamism as a supernatural elevation simultaneously expands the soul's fundamental love. There results a growth of love and, concomitantly, of insight. To prevent the soul from being misled by any internal motion or affective tendency whatsoever, Rousselot recognized the need for a revealed external sign. Thus the unity of external sign and interior assent is preserved. The internal assent is attributed to human freedom since a person may reject the grace calling for free homage. Simultaneously, the act of faith is most reasonable because the perceived clue applies the witness of the natural order to the recognized truth. Through this act faith is accepted on the authority of the revealing God since he alone has given the grace of seeing the supernatural significance intended, and the soul recognizes his authority in accepting faith.

In this analysis the material object of faith consisted in propositions guaranteed by God's authority. Yet Rousselot's contributions to the apologetical manual *Christus* (Paris, 1912) followed the lead of his teacher L. de Grandmaison in stressing the centrality of Christ's person as the vital source of his message and morality. This opening to the personal was accentuated by awareness of weaknesses in his own position. Because there is no meaning apart from intentionality, problems emerged about the meaning of a natural sign endowed with supernatural significance, about the intellect-will relation, and about an independent natural order. His own sharpest critic, Rousselot was moving toward a new synthesis based no longer on natures and necessary dynamisms but on freedom and on person as the individual spiritual centre of Thought-Action from which nature and its intellect-will distinction derived. Unfortunately, his premature death terminated the new synthesis to which his private notes witness. The founder of transcendental Thomisin, Rousselot influenced Maréchal, *Rahner, *Lonergan, *de Lubac, *von Balthasar and countless others. Due to censorship, the centrality of Christ in Rousselot's thought was not manifest and often overlooked. Rousselot saw clearly the need to balance concept and judgement, essential and existential order, nature and grace.

JOHN M. MCDERMOTT, SJ

FURTHER READING: *Texts: L'Intellectualisme de Saint Thomas* (Paris, 1908); *Pour l'Histoire du Problème de l'Amour au Moyen-Age* (Münster, 1908); *Quaestiones de Conscientia* (Brussels, 1937); 'Amour spirituel et synthèse aperceptive', *Rev Phil* 16 (1910), pp. 225–40; 'L'Être et l'Esprit', *Rev Phil* 16 (1910), pp. 561–74; 'Les Yeux de la Foi', *Recher Sci Rel* 1 (1910), pp. 241–59, 444–75; 'Métaphysique Thomiste et Critique de la Connaissance', *RNSP* 17 (1910), pp. 476–509; 'Idéalisme et Thomisme', *Arch Phil* 42 (1979), pp. 103–26. *Studies:* E. Kunz, SJ, *Glaube, Gnade, Geschichte: Die Glaubenstheologie des Pierre Rousselot, SJ* (Frankfurt, 1969); J. McDermott, *Love and Understanding* (Rome, 1983).

Schillebeeckx, Edward (b. 1914)

One of the most important Roman Catholic theologians of the period that included *Vatican II, Schillebeeckx was born in Antwerp on 12 November 1914. He entered the Dominican order in 1934 and was ordained priest in 1941. His training began in Louvain, where D. De Petter (1905–71) introduced him to a wider range of philosophical writings than normally permitted to Roman Catholic students, and to an approach to *Aquinas influenced by De Petter's own phenomenology. De Petter's philosophical framework was central for Schillebeeckx, up to the point in the 1960s when he abandoned a single metaphysical system for a more eclectic philosophy. After the end of World War II, he studied for his doctorate ('The Sacramental Economy of Salvation') at Le Saulchoir, Paris. Le Saulchoir was the centre of the movement in Roman Catholic theology known as *ressourcement*, where patristic and medieval sources were used to raise questions about the theological, liturgical and political development of the church in the twentieth century. Here, the main influences were *Yves Congar (1904–95) and M.D. Chenu (1895–1990). Chenu, in his combination of historical study with contemporary social analysis, was a key influence for the whole of Schillebeeckx's career.

Returning to Louvain as a teacher of theology, Schillebeeckx was called, in 1957, to the chair of dogmatics and history of theology at the Catholic University of Nijmegen in the Netherlands and continued in this post until his retirement in 1983. During Vatican II Schillebeeckx served as adviser to the Dutch bishops but was considered too radical to be granted the status of *peritus*, or official theological adviser at the council. His co-editorship of the journal *Concilium* (launched in 1965) kept him at the forefront of the theological exploration of Vatican II's legacy.

Schillebeeckx's earliest published works deal with either philosophical and methodological issues in theology, or with the theology of the sacraments. Many of his early essays are collected in the two volumes of *Revelation and Theology* (London, 1987). His version of *Thomism (less *Kantian than had been common in the neo-Thomism of the late nineteenth century) suggested that Aquinas assigns a role to the divinely-imparted *lumen fidei* that provides human beings with substantial, if incomplete,

concepts of God. In *Christ the Sacrament of Encounter with God* (London, 1963), Schillebeeckx employs the language of relationship and encounter to describe the origin and development of the Christian sacraments. The sacramental is both a general aspect of human experience and the specific manner of God's encounter with us in Jesus Christ. This sacramental encounter with God continues through the whole life of the church and is focused in (though not confined to) the seven sacraments.

Schillebeeckx's main concern in the years up to the end of Vatican II was with the further development of his sacramental theology. He contributed to the *ressourcement* movement by using biblical and historical study to challenge accepted norms and practices. Thus, *The Eucharist* (London, 1968) begins by exploring the radical changes in Eucharistic theology in the thirteenth century, before moving on to suggest that the doctrine of transubstantiation needs to be modified in the direction of transsignification – though without reducing the Eucharistic presence to a mere human construct. In *Marriage: Human Reality and Saving Mystery* (London, 1965), a historical survey suggests that Christian marriage has existed in many forms, depending on the cultural circumstances. There should therefore be no objection to further changes in the present.

Following Vatican II, Schillebeeckx travelled to the USA for the first time. His encounter with other schools of thought led him to abandon his former reliance on Thomistic philosophy as a foundation for theology, and to employ an eclectic approach. In *The Understanding of Faith* (London, 1974) he draws on, amongst others, the hermeneutical tradition of *Heidegger (1888–1976) and Gadamer (b. 1900), the linguistic philosophy of the later *Wittgenstein (1889–1951), and the critical theory of Jürgen Habermas (b. 1929).

In the 1970s Schillebeeckx produced two major works on Christology, published in English as *Jesus: An Experiment in Christology* (London, 1979) and *Christ: The Christian Experience in the Modern World* (London, 1980). In both of these works he combined extremely detailed biblical exegesis with discussion of the relation between revelation and experience and between salvation and the universal conditions of human existence. His Christology, summarized in the description of Jesus as 'parable of God and paradigm for humanity', was investigated by the Sacred Congregation for the Doctrine of the Faith, which suspected that Schillebeeckx was insufficiently loyal to the *Chalcedonian language of the hypostatic union. Unlike *Hans Küng (b. 1928), however, his status as a teacher of Catholic theology was not removed. Schillebeeckx himself made a vigorous defence of his orthodoxy in a book intended to clarify his position, *Interim Report on the Books Jesus and Christ* (London, 1980).

The final phase of Schillebeeckx's career involved work on ministry (*Ministry: A Case for Change* [London, 1981]; *The Church with a Human Face: A New and Expanded Theology of Ministry* [London, 1985]) and ecclesiology (*Church: The Human Story of God* [London, 1991]). Whilst the first book on ministry was polemical in tone and criticized for its lack of historical rigour, the second developed a strong biblical and historical background and applied it to a consideration of the current crisis in the European Roman Catholic Church over the future of the priesthood. His book on ecclesiology sets out Schillebeeckx's vision of the church as the community in which the experience of Jesus Christ is kept alive and renewed, and in which God is revealed precisely in the human experiences of encounter. A democratized church is needed for this vision to continue.

Schillebeeckx's theological career illustrates successive trends in Roman Catholic theology in the second half of the twentieth century. His work has made a significant contribution to those changes, including the work of Vatican II. This contribution may well be more long lasting than his books themselves. By comparison with *Karl Rahner (1904–84), Schillebeeckx does not have philosophical rigour or consistency. His writing, though intended for a wide audience, is less accessible than that of his fellow radical Hans Küng. In spite of these limitations, Schillebeeckx's passion for human experience, his insistence that this is the proper location for the revelation of God, and his concern for the future of the Christian church, make him an engaging partner in theological conversation.

RICHARD CLUTTERBUCK

FURTHER READING: *Text: The Schillebeeckx Reader* (ed. Robert Schreiter; Edinburgh, 1988), includes helpful editorial material by Schreiter. *Studies:* Robert Schreiter, 'Edward Schillebeeckx', in *The Modern Theologians* (ed. David Ford; Oxford, 2nd edn, 1997), pp. 152–61; Robert Schreiter and Mary Catherine Hilkert (eds.), *The Praxis of Christian Experience: An Introduction to the Theology of Edward Schillebeeckx* (San Francisco, 1989); Philip Kennedy, *Schillebeeckx* (London, 1993), the most detailed study available in English.

Schlatter, Adolf (1852–1938)

Born in German-speaking Switzerland, Schlatter influenced generations of pastors and theologians as he lectured for a hundred consecutive semesters in Bern (1881–88), Greifswald (1888–93), Berlin (1893–98), and Tübingen (1898–1930). Primarily a New Testament and rabbinics scholar, he published voluminously (over four hundred items) on a diverse array of topics extending beyond New Testament to dogmatics, ethics, history of philosophy, metaphysics, historical theology and church history. His academic life was intertwined with a robust church commitment involving regular preaching duties as well as speaking for Bible conferences, student missions organizations, women's circles and small group meetings in his Tübingen home.

In autobiographical publications Schlatter stresses the formative influence of his parents' Christian convictions. These helped instil in Schlatter a high regard for the Bible and a sense of the church's importance. Christian love and community were also tangible realities in a home with eight children.

Yet as a student Schlatter wrestled with Christian truth claims. He was confronted in his university training with the scientific scepticism that dominated the Continent in the 1870s. One of his teachers was *Friedrich Nietzsche (1844–1900), and his reading of *Spinoza (1632–77) posed a particular challenge. In the end, however, Schlatter reaffirmed classic Christian belief, albeit with an academic and technical sophistication still being discovered today.

Of all Schlatter's teachers J.T. Beck (1804–78), with his outspoken focus on the Bible, deserves particular mention. But other teachers piqued the thought of the gifted student, too – notably in the areas of philology, philosophy and history. Accordingly, if Schlatter admired Beck's non-Kantian advocacy of the gospel's noumenal claims on the same level as knowledge derived from phenomena, he rejected Beck's ahistoricism. Throughout his life Schlatter upheld history, partial though our access to it is, as integral to human identity and therefore to human knowledge, including theological knowledge. Keenly aware of *Kant's (1724–1804) claim that human knowledge is ultimately determined by the knowing subject, Schlatter trenchantly criticized the post-Kantian idealism associated with *Hegel (1770–1831) and, in more Christian dress, the neo-Kantian construals of Christian theology associated with *Ritschl (1822–89), *Harnack (1851–1930), and *Troeltsch (1865–1923). In a highly original way, Schlatter worked out a critical realist hermeneutic that modelled acknowledgement of the difficulties of valid apprehension (hence critical), yet exuded tenacious conviction that to a considerable degree assured knowledge of reality, including God, was attainable (hence realist). Subjectivity is an inevitable component in the knowing process but need not prevent adequate, object-determined knowledge (*Wahrnehmung*) of what is known.

The Schlatter corpus documents a theological development that grew in breadth, depth, nuance and grounding. There are no radical shifts or new directions. One finds rather an impressive number of research trajectories, each rooted deeply in the original sources (cf., e.g. his investigation of *pistis* [faith] in the New Testament, *Der Glaube im Neuen Testament* [2nd edn, 1896], a study that inspired Kittel's theological dictionary) and cognizant of contemporary thought trends (cf. especially the footnotes of *Das christliche Dogma* [2nd edn, 1923] and Schlatter's history of philosophy, *Die philosophische Arbeit seit Cartesius* [2nd edn, 1910]).

Over thirty books by Schlatter still in print (more than any other theologian of his era) attest to the staying power of his scholarship. His contribution was many-sided. He was far ahead of his times in stressing the importance of Jewish backgrounds for understanding Jesus and the early church, an insight vindicated by discovery of the Dead Sea Scrolls and championed in Schlatter's train today by the likes of Martin Hengel and Markus Bockmühl. His arguments for the validity of theological concerns in critical exegesis, rejected by the liberalism of his own day, retain importance and mark Schlatter as a forerunner to *Barth. Yet unlike Barth (at least the early Barth), Schlatter insisted on a Jesus of history, attested to by Scripture, as of equal importance with the saving Christ of faith. Schlatter sided with *Brunner in the latter's tiff with Barth over natural theology (although he rejected neo-orthodoxy's neo-Kantian doctrine of revelation); he feared that *Bultmann's proposals set the stage for a slide toward atheism. In sum, Schlatter modelled an independence of thought and fidelity of Christian faith that are still suggestive in academy and church today.

For those who understand Christian faith not only in academic but also in pastoral terms, Schlatter's contribution may be gauged by the large number (and continuing heritage) of ministers and students he encouraged. His somewhat fiery free spirit still inspires, as well: Tübingen's first woman theological licentiate, Lydia Schmid, pointed to Schlatter's encouragement in learning and belief. (Other professors at the time fought against the presence of women in the university.) Paul Schneider, the first Christian minister to be martyred by the Nazis (Buchenwald, 1939), experienced his conversion from liberal to historic Christian convictions through interaction with Schlatter's dogmatics, and in *Dietrich Bonhoeffer's (1906–45) last working library the only other author so richly represented and consulted was *Luther. Schlatter's example of rigour in thought, creativity in formulation, courage in expression and artlessness in practical service amply justify the apparent renaissance in Schlatter studies currently underway.

ROBERT W. YARBROUGH

FURTHER READING: Werner Neuer, *Adolf Schlatter* (trans. R.W. Yarbrough; Grand Rapids, 1995), popular-level biography, appendices contain trans. of important Schlatter essays; *Adolf Schlatter: Ein Leben für Theologie und Kirche* (Stuttgart, 1996), definitive biography; 'Schlatter, Adolf (1852–1938)', *Th Real* 30 (Berlin / New York, 1998), pp. 135–43, succinct treatment of all aspects of Schlatter's life and writings with extensive bibliography; Adolf Schlatter, *The History of the Christ: The Foundation of New Testament Theology* (trans. Andreas J. Köstenberger; Grand Rapids, 1997), valuable introductory essay by translator; 'Karl Barth's Epistle to the Romans', in *The Beginnings of Dialectical Theology* (ed. James M. Robinson; trans. Keith R. Crim; Richmond, VA, 1968), pp. 121–25; *The Theology of the Apostles: The Development of New Testament Theology* (trans. Andreas J. Köstenberger; Grand Rapids, 1997), contains useful essays assessing Schlatter's historical placement and importance (pp. 9–22, 417–31); Robert Yarbrough, 'Adolf Schlatter (1852–1938)', in *Historical Handbook of Major Biblical Interpreters* (ed. Donald K. McKim; Leicester / Downers Grove, IL,

1998), pp. 518–23; 'Adolf Schlatter's "The Significance of Method for Theological Work": Translation and Commentary', *S Bapt J Th* 1.2 (Summer
1997), pp. 64–76.

Schleiermacher, Friedrich Daniel Ernst (1768–1834)

Friedrich Schleiermacher, generally reputed to
be the father of modern theology, taught
broadly in the field from 1808 to 1834 at the
University of Berlin, of which he was a co-
founder. Although half his teaching was in
exegetical theology, his fame principally derives
from his epoch-making discourses *On Religion*
(1799, 1806, 1821) and one of the greatest treatises in systematic theology of all times, *Christian Faith* (1821–22, 1830–31). Schleiermacher
was also a full-time pastor for nearly four
decades and founded the modern study of religions. He was a philosopher as well and
regularly lectured in dialectic (conceived as the
art of doing philosophy and combining both
metaphysics and logic), ethics, psychology,
aesthetics, education, politics and history of
philosophy. He was the chief progenitor of
modern hermeneutics (presenting a general theory of interpretation, applicable in the same
way to biblical as to other texts). Schleiermacher
remains the classic translator of *Plato's writings
into German, and he published numerous
addresses on other Greek philosophers and matters such as the theory of translation before the
Berlin Academy of Sciences. Since the 1980s a
new critical edition of his works has been
appearing in Germany, and translations have
been published yearly in several languages,
especially English and Italian.

Born at Breslau, in Silesia, into the home of a
Reformed pastor, Schleiermacher was raised at
a time of social change brought about by
machine production, new agricultural methods,
increasing awareness of distant parts of the
world and spiritualities therein. Educated at the
Moravian pietist school at Niesky (1783–85) and
seminary at Barby (1785–87), his early years
were marked by spiritual discipline, study of
the Greek classics, mathematics, botany and
English. He became dissatisfied with pietist doctrine and lifestyle, doubted the necessity and
morality of Christ's vicarious sacrifice and left
Barby to live under the supervision of his theologian uncle, Samuel Stubenrauch, in Halle.
Here he attended theology and philosophy

lectures at the university before going in 1789 to
Drossen where, in private study, Schleiermacher
continued to become familiar with the publications of literary figures such as Schiller and Goethe. In 1790 he passed his first theological
exams at Berlin and was appointed tutor to the
family of Count Wilhelm Dohna, at Schlobitten
in East Prussia. His essays from this period evidence an extraordinary breadth and intensity.
In *On the Highest Good, On Freedom* and *On What
Gives Value to Life*, he criticized the narrow rationalism and eudaemonism of the *Enlightenment. In particular, he criticized *Kant's
restricted theory of morals which, among other
things, underplayed historicity and individuality. In 1794 Schleiermacher was ordained and
became pastor in Landsberg, where he prepared
notes on *Aristotle, Leibniz and *Spinoza and
began a programme of translation from English
that eventuated in four volumes of sermons by
the great British divines Joseph Fawcett and
Hugh Blair.

In 1796, Schleiermacher moved to Berlin as a
full-time pastor at Charité Hospital. As French
expansion continued and Prussia prevaricated
about forming alliances, Schleiermacher's writings from 1796 to1802 include the beginnings
of significant reflections upon the dangers of
unrestricted monarchy and protection of the
'rights of human beings'. He shared literary and
philosophical interests with his sometime
roommate Friedrich Schlegel, as well as with
Dorothea Veit, Novalis, August Schlegel,
Henrietta Herz (who held one of Berlin's famous
salon's of the time), and other prominent figures. In an atmosphere of emerging German
Romanticism, Schleiermacher contributed to
the short-lived cultural periodical *Athenaeum*
and wrote *On Religion*, in part to encourage
friends who were critical of religion as they
saw it. Among other things, his *Soliloquies*
(1800) and *Confidential Letters on Lucinda* (1800)
expounded the material world as the 'body' of
the Spirit's presence; the relationship between
religion, poetry and philosophy; the unity of
the sensuous and spiritual elements in love;
and self-comprehension as a reflective human
being. He also completed *Principles for a Critique
of All Previous Ethical Theories* in 1803.

In 1804, Schleiermacher was appointed professor of theology and university preacher at
Halle. He left in 1807 after the Napoleonic takeover of the city. In 1808 he began lecturing
in Berlin, thereafter providing key ideas and

leadership toward the establishment of the university in 1810. Between the collapse of the Prussian state in 1806 and the 1813 War of Liberation, Schleiermacher was active in social and political affairs. The openly political character of several of his sermons at that time is remarkable in an era of censorship and poor newspaper reporting. His writings from this period include *Christmas Eve* (1806), a dialogue in which he depicts a gathering of friends and family in celebration conversing about the meaning of Christ's birth; observations on Fichte; a major work on Heraclitus; *On the So-called First Epistle of Paul to Timothy* (1807), in which he questioned its Pauline authorship; and *Luke: A Critical Study.*

In his seminal work *Brief Outline on Theology as a Field of Study* (1811, 1830), Schleiermacher stated that the ruling purpose of theology is practical: to serve all members of the church in their common life and several ministries. He placed 'historical theology' at the centre of Christian theology, flanked by philosophical theology (a means of apologetic, polemical, critical work) and practical theology, of which he also formed the first systematic treatment. He defined historical theology as having a threefold task addressed to clarifying and presenting the understandings of a community of faith. He placed his emphasis on the evangelical (especially *Reformed and *Lutheran) 'mode of faith' in Germany at that time. Historical theology's three interdependent disciplines were: (1) exegetical theology; (2) the history of the church's life, doctrine and ethics since apostolic times; and (3) a combination of dogmatics, Christian ethics and church statistics (which would later comprise the use of contributions from the social sciences).

According to Schleiermacher, there are no absolute divides between Christianity and either culture or science. Christian thinkers are to use the full range of their critical reason and their capacities to investigate and change the real conditions of the world. Aptly dubbed a critical realist, Schleiermacher was appointed president of the Berlin Synod in 1817 and spent much time in the next decade opposing the king and his ecclesial counsellors on issues of church and state. At great jeopardy to himself, he resisted their attempts to impose upon the free functions of congregations and synods in matters of liturgy and church government. He worked to reorganize presbyteries and clergy

into district, provincial and national synods, and he encouraged sharing of the Lord's Supper by Lutheran and Reformed Protestants in services of church union. At the same time, he delivered highly innovative lectures on psychology (1818) which discussed the inseparability of body and mind, the interconnectedness (*Zusammenhang*) of all conscious experience, and the relational and social nature of human consciousness at every stage of life. All his work was rooted in a sense of language, history and institutions as ever-changing, socially contextual features of human life, all comprising both comparatively general and distinctively individual characteristics.

Schleiermacher's grasp of contextual factors in his own time led him to combat every tendency, then quite strong, to reduce anything religious to abstract metaphysics or morals. Religion is a distinct domain critical to the growth of the whole person, though many outlooks and practices that go by the name of religion are counter to it. Thus his greatest work, *Christian Faith*, comprises Christian 'doctrines of faith' that analyze the human capacity for knowledge of God and identify the distinctiveness of Christianity by distinguishing aspects of its witness that have remained constant throughout church history. The first part of *Christian Faith* deals with doctrines expressing this consciousness of God with respect to creation and preservation, divine attributes and the 'original' perfection of the world and humankind. The much longer second part unpacks specifically Christian doctrines that deal with consciousness of sin and grace, and therein expounds the origin and existence of the church. Although Schleiermacher sees religious experience as something that happens in individuals, it is essentially to be conveyed and shared through some communal relationship ('church'), and it is capable of ongoing development in both individuals and communities of faith. In Christian theology, everything is to be related to 'the redemption accomplished through Jesus of Nazareth', and he asserts the need for a modern Christology that elucidates the faith experience of believers. This involves a recasting of traditional doctrine, not least the definition of *Chalcedon, because its confusing terminology does not illuminate Christian consciousness of redemption. He does not hold that Christ existed from eternity or had a share in creation. Rather, he uses the language of creation and new creation to express living communion with God in Christ, through the Holy Spirit.

Schleiermacher is one of those rare figures in the history of theology whose thought, while greatly influential (as his was over the next two centuries), continues to spark new discoveries in a later age. Partly because much of his work was published long after his death, and partly because significant sections of it are only recently appearing – even in German but especially in English – Schleiermacher seems to be coming into his own at the dawn of the twenty-first century as a major influence.

ESTHER REED

FURTHER READING: *Texts: Brief Outline on Theology as a Field of Study* (trans. Terrence N. Tice; Lewiston, NY, 1990); *On Religion: Speeches to its Cultured Despisers* (trans. Richard Crouter; Cambridge, 1988), and all three editions (trans. Terrence N. Tice; Lewiston, NY, 1997); *Dialectic* (trans. Terrence N. Tice; Atlanta, 1996); *Hermeneutics* (trans. Terrence N. Tice; Atlanta, 1997); *The Christian Faith* (trans. and ed. H.R. Mackintosh and J.S. Stewart; Edinburgh, 1989). *Studies:* Karl Barth, *The Theology of Schleiermacher* (Edinburgh, 1982; GE 1978); Martin Redeker, *Schleiermacher: Life and Thought* (trans. John Wallhausser; Philadelphia, 1973); Hans-Joachim Birkner, 'The Critical Edition of Schleiermacher's Works and its Predecessors', in *New Athenaeum/Neues Athenaeum*, I (trans. Ruth Richardson; Lewiston, NY, 1988–).

Scholasticism, Medieval

The term 'Medieval Scholasticism' primarily refers to a method for education and research which was developed in the medieval period. The term refers only secondarily to a period in history in which Scholasticism was widespread. Although it has been customary to divide the period of Medieval Scholasticism into early, high and late Scholasticism, it is more useful to follow L.M. de Rijk's proposal and to talk about the 'early period' (1030–1200), and the 'period of the universities' (1200–1500). In this way, one can avoid regarding *Aquinas (c. 1225–74) or the thirteenth century as the zenith of Scholasticism, and subsequent developments in terms of decline. In the fourteenth century, for example, British logic reached its zenith, a fact which clearly cannot be regarded as decline. In fact, there is a strong scholastic mainstream, running both through the *Reformation towards Reformed Scholasticism and towards Spanish Scholasticism (the latter term

designating, roughly, the activities of philosophers and theologians at the Iberian peninsula in the seventeenth century), rendering the year 1500 (the usual end of the medieval period) rather arbitrary. Emphasizing that Scholasticism is a method also makes it quite clear that there were other forms of intellectual activity in theology and philosophy during the period from 1030 to 1500, for example, mysticism – although people like *Meister Eckhart (c. 1260–1327) were also fully active in the scholastic milieu.

Among the factors which shaped Medieval Scholasticism, the writings of *Boethius (480–526) must be mentioned, for they 'suggested that logical tools and precisely defined philosophical terms could both clarify difficult points of Christian doctrine and provide the means to demonstrate that, given certain fundamental points of doctrine ... heterodox positions involved logical error' (Marenbon [ed.], p. 16).

A second factor shaping Medieval Scholasticism was the 'Carolingian Renaissance' (around 800) in which, after a period of decline, a new interest in the ancient texts and the Church Fathers (especially *Augustine) developed. Under the rule of Charlemagne (d. 814) it was decreed that a school had to be founded at every episcopal church (cathedral). These 'cathedral schools' flourished, especially during the eleventh and twelfth centuries. In the endeavour to establish a school curriculum, books of Roman and early medieval laws and decretals were compiled, as well as various Church Fathers and philosophy books (mostly by Boethius). Marginal comments, called 'glossa', were written for each of these bodies of writings. Like the marginal glosses to the biblical text made up of comments from patristic writers, the glosses were meant to clarify the text, according to grammatical and logical rules. By the middle of the twelfth century, another type of gloss was introduced by the school of Laon, namely contemporary reflections on the text of the Bible. 'This labour of compilation led in itself to more independent work. It showed up the inconsistencies and gaps in the patristic tradition. Scholars could hardly avoid comparing and discussing them, and filling in by their own compositions' (Smalley, p. 38).

For a balanced view on the matrix of Medieval Scholasticism, the role of Christian faith is quite important. Rational activity was embedded in a setting of meditation. In the choirs and cloisters, people practised their readings of the sacred texts, and meditation upon these readings engendered rational argumentation. In this respect, *Anselm of Canterbury (1033–1109) played an important role. This theologian of the Augustinian tradition propounded the approach *credo ut intelligam* ('I believe in order to understand'). Anselm was convinced that faith, by its very nature, tends to seek understanding: *fides quaerens intellectum* ('faith seeking understanding').

Another factor contributing to Scholasticism was the knowledge of *Aristotle's works, although the importance of this factor is commonly overemphasized. Medieval logic had already developed well beyond Aristotelian boundaries before it received a further impetus in the second half of the twelfth century from Aristotle's newly discovered *Prior* and *Posterior Analytics*, *Topics* and *Sophistici Elenchi*. Also Aristotle's non-logical, 'genuinely' philosophical works were hardly regarded as something for which the theologians had been waiting. In the thirteenth century many condemnations of Aristotelian doctrines were issued, of which that of Paris and Oxford by bishops Tempier and Kilwardby in 1277 had the greatest impact.

A fifth, crowning factor for the development of Scholasticism was the rise of the universities. At the end of the twelfth century some types of schools developed into universities, namely Bologna, Paris and Oxford. Shortly thereafter, Cambridge was founded. These universities were distinct from other theological training facilities in that they provided the possibility of obtaining the degree of 'Doctor of Divinity' (*doctor theologiae*). At this time, a theological education normally took more than a decade. Prior to this, an eight-year training in the seven 'liberal arts' (*artes liberales*) was required. The *artes* divided into two groups: the *trivium* and the *quadrivium*. The *trivium* consisted of the subjects *grammatica*, *dialectica* (or *logica*) and *retorica*. They were intended to train students in the composition of an argument. That required mastery of the language (*grammatica*), the drawing of valid conclusions (*dialectica*) and the ability to convey one's viewpoint (*retorica*). The *quadrivium* consisted of the subjects *arithmetica*, *musica*, *geometria* and *astronomia*.

The noun 'scholastic' originally referred to a person attached to a school (*schola*). Such persons were called *scholastici*. It is important to

consider the way in which school and university instruction was organized. It consisted of a number of elements. The first element was the *lectio* ('lecture'). It involved the reading of an authoritative text with the lecturer commenting on it. The *lectio* itself was meant to give a literal interpretation (the *littera*), followed by an exposition of its meaning (the *sensus*), in turn followed by its deeper understanding (the *sententia*). The *lectio* was followed by the *meditatio* ('meditation'; 'reflection'), during which the students were required to appropriate what had been read and explained to them. This led to the last element, the *quaestio*. The students could encounter an intellectual problem, a 'question', in what they had heard. Over the years, the *quaestio* developed into the most important element in the scholastic educational method. Originally, this method had been used especially to come to a decision when two authoritative texts seemed to contradict each other. Later on, the *quaestiones* became a *genre* on their own. They grew more like discussions designed to lead to a firmer understanding of the subject matter. It is here that we find the origin of such books as *Peter Lombard's famous *Sentences*, written about 1155 and basically an Augustinian collection of theological *quaestiones*. These complete discussions of a *quaestio* were called 'disputations', or more precisely, *quaestiones disputatae*. Questions were now followed by a consideration, first, of the arguments against one's own view, then the arguments in favour of one's own view, whereafter a solution was sought. This solution was, of course, supported by arguments. Finally, the initial counter-arguments were answered. In order to train the students, such disputations were continuously held and one person, called the *respondens*, had to defend a particular point against arguments.

It was *Alexander of Hales (c. 1175–1245) who first adopted an approach which was to become extremely popular: he wrote a commentary on Lombard's *Sentences*. In the thirteenth century, every student of theology had to lecture upon the *Sentences* in order to obtain his doctorate, and these lectures, either in students' reports or in authorized commentary versions, are a major source of systematic theology and philosophy in our period.

Up to now, we have been silent about content. In theology, the doctrines found in Lombard's *Sentences* (which form a quite complete systematic theology) are accepted by everyone – although their exact explication may vary. We can, therefore, encounter Albertism, *Thomism, Scotism, Ockhamism and quite a few other 'isms'. Next to its shared doctrinal basis, there are also specific characteristics of this medieval period in terms of a more general nature, which stand in contrast with ancient philosophy. Extrapolating De Rijk (pp. 71–72), we mention three of them: (1) Christian faith can be said to be the main catalyst of Medieval Scholasticism. It is here that we find the occasions for 'thinking hard' about serious matters. (2) There is the independent, and generally underestimated, development of medieval logic, which found its immediate application in theology – exemplified, for example in *Duns Scotus (c. 1266–1308) and Thomas Bradwardine (c. 1295–1349). (3) In the *Franciscan schools, the so-called theory of synchronic contingency was developed, in which the radical dependence of all creaturely beings is formulated. That view changed subsequent metaphysics and epistemology.

What about the doctrines of Aristotle, then? Generally, his non-Christian views, like that of the eternity of the world, were rejected by the theology faculties. When Aristotle was incorporated into a theological system, like that of *Aquinas, we may speak of a 'christian aristotelianism', and ever since Aquinas's age, there has been a debate whether or not such a move is legitimate. We could interpret the medieval discussion between Thomists and Scotists as being concerned with that very question. It has recently been argued that only mainstream Augustinian thought, culminating in an overarching theory of synchronic contingency, can articulate a Christian world-view (Vos, et al.). Scotism, moreover, should be carefully kept apart from *Nominalism. *William Ockham (c. 1285– c. 1349), the father of Nominalism, is in some respects closer to Aristotle than he has generally been considered to be.

It is important to see that to quote an 'authority' (e.g., the Bible, Augustine, Aristotle), in the medieval period was not to claim that the text was to be followed without reasoning, nor was it only an ornament in one's own discourse, but rather, a text was cited which was considered to be intrinsically important because of its truth. Moreover, such a text did not function historically (a notion which was absent in the medieval period), but it was interpreted according to one's own frame of thought. It would be a mistake, therefore, for us to read their authorities historically.

In the fourteenth century, Nominalism, or as it was called, the *via moderna*, became quite influential because its views were taught at the leading university in Paris, the Sorbonne. To what extent the doctrines taught at this university later came to be associated with Scholasticism as such is clear from *Calvin's usage of the word 'scholastic'. In the Latin edition of his *Institutions*, many criticisms are levelled against 'the scholastics'. In the French edition of 1560, that word was translated mostly with '*théologiens Sorbonniques*'. This means that, in the relevant passages, he was attacking those theologians only, rather than all medieval scholastics.

The *via moderna* was criticized not only by the Reformers at a later stage, but also by contemporaries. The human act was seen as a decisive factor in the attainment of salvation. In reaction to this doctrine, an Augustinian revival arose, later called the *schola Augustiniana moderna*. They developed an anti-Pelagian theology, based on the writings of Augustine. Emphasis was put on double predestination, the depravity of humanity and the necessity of grace for every good deed. Thus both the anti-Pelagian Augustine and Nominalism influenced the *schola Augustiniana moderna*. Gregory of Rimini (1300–58) was an important representative of this movement.

Subsequent to the Middle Ages, the word 'scholasticism' came also to be used by many with reference to content. 'Scholastic theology' then refers to the theology taught at the medieval schools, and especially late medieval (in fact Renaissance) semi-pelagian theology. Among Protestants this was sometimes bound up with a negative evaluation.

WILLEM J. VAN ASSELT
EEF DEKKER

FURTHER READING: John Duns Scotus, *Contingency and Freedom: Lectura I 39* (intro., trans. and commentary by A. Vos, et al.; Dordrecht / Boston / London, 1994); A. Kenny, N. Kretzmann and J. Pinborg (eds.), *The Cambridge History of Later Medieval Philosophy: From the Rediscovery of Aristotle to the Disintegration of Scholasticism, 1100–1600* (Cambridge, 1982); U.G. Leinsle, *Einführung in die scholastische Theologie* (Paderborn, 1995); John Marenbon, *Early Medieval Philosophy (480–1150): An Introduction* (London, 2nd edn, 1988); *Later*

Medieval Philosophy (1150–1350): An Introduction (London / New York, rev. edn, 1991); John Marenbon (ed.), *Medieval Philosophy (Routledge History of Philosophy III)* (London / New York, 1998); H.A. Oberman, *The Harvest of Medieval Theology: Gabriel Biel and Late Medieval Nominalism* (Durham, NC, repr., 1983); L.M. de Rijk, *La Philosophie au Moyen Âge* (Leiden, 1985); B. Smalley, *The Study of the Bible in the Middle Ages* (Oxford, 1984); R.W. Southern, *Scholastic Humanism and the Unification of Europe, I: Foundations* (Oxford, 1995).

Scholasticism, Protestant

Research on Protestant Scholasticism in the last few decades has reached the consensus that, in the past, the term 'protestant scholasticism' had been insufficiently defined, and that the definitions that had been given were often charged with value judgements. Recent historical reappraisals of Protestant Scholasticism have concluded that the contrast so often drawn between Scholasticism, *Reformation and Humanism is outdated. When these phenomena are studied in their context, they turn out to be closely related to each other. Modern research interprets Protestant Scholasticism as a methodological approach, rather than a certain type of content. It rejects clear breaks and lines of demarcation, and it emphasizes the continuous development within the history of theology. It is assumed that Protestant Scholasticism was in continuity with the theology of the Reformers as well as with medieval theology. The proposed definition of the term 'scholasticism' as basically a method also guards against the idea that, through the use of the scholastic method, one particular doctrine or concept is necessarily moved to the foreground, thereby assuming the status of a '*Centraldogma*' (so *A. Schweitzer), which may serve as a key to the understanding of the whole system.

In order to give a historical account of Protestant Scholasticism over a period extending from the second half of the sixteenth century to the end of the eighteenth century, a division is unavoidable for the sake of ordering the material. Therefore we can divide the era of Protestant Scholasticism into three periods. Following Richard A. Müller, among others, we shall speak of Protestant Scholasticism during: (1) 'early' orthodoxy (c. 1560–1620); (2) 'high' orthodoxy (c. 1620–1700) and (3) 'late' orthodoxy (c. 1700–90). Such a division, it is true, is of an extrinsic nature. One should therefore not attempt to draw any sharp lines of demarcation between early, high and late orthodoxy.

The term orthodoxy refers to a period in the history of theology. The scholastic method was used during that period. It involves a certain approach applied in theology, which employed, for the sake of both research and instruction, 'a recurring system of concepts, distinctions, analyses of propositions, reasoning techniques, and methods of disputation'. Protestant Scholasticism was facilitated by the increased openness of Protestant theology to the use of reason and philosophy, specifically to the revised *Aristotelianism of the late Renaissance. Moreover, with regard to this reception of Aristotle by the Protestant theologians, one should be careful to distinguish between formal aspects and aspects related to content. Appropriation did occur, but so did antithesis. Even Aristotle's logic was only received from the medieval tradition in a not very Aristotelian form, while his concept of God and his views on the eternity of the world were sharply denounced by Protestant theologians.

As in the Middle Ages, so also during the period following the Reformation, it was the method that gave Scholasticism a recognizable shape and lent it unity and continuity. The quest was to find a way of showing forth, in the light of the Christian tradition, the catholicity of Protestant theology. In their attempt to show that the Protestant tradition was a consistent and defensible interpretation of the catholic tradition, the Protestant thinkers of the post-Reformation era had recourse both to the great medieval systems of *Peter Lombard, *Thomas Aquinas, *Duns Scotus, and others, and to the ongoing philosophical tradition (J. Zabarella, *F. Suárez) that linked them to those systems. Protestant Scholasticism, however, should not be viewed as identical with the medieval systems nor as a reduplication of the theology of the Reformers. Granting developments in logic, rhetoric and metaphysics which took place in the fifteenth and sixteenth centuries, Protestant Scholasticism was 'a form of Protestant theology in its own right' (R.A. Müller). Although a high degree of conformity can be ascertained with regard to method, there were also many clear differences, as far as content was concerned, between *Lutheran and Reformed Scholasticism. The contents of the different confessions that were recognized within the diverging movements determined these differences. Here we shall concentrate on Reformed, rather than Lutheran, Scholasticism.

The practice of theology in Reformed circles during the period of early orthodoxy, from around 1560 to 1620, can best be characterized with the terms confessionalization and codification. Following the Reformation, and due to the collapse of the Roman Catholic organizational structure, the Reformed churches faced the challenge of proliferating and establishing themselves institutionally. A confessional basis had to be established, ecclesial organizations had to be built up, and sound training had to be provided for ministers. During this period, theology tended to take the shape of efforts to develop the confessions into a doctrine, which would determine, both theologically and sociologically, the attitude towards other confessions. The *doctrina* served as a point of departure for further reflection. Reformed theologies published during the first phase of early orthodoxy usually took the form of commentaries on the Apostles' Creed, the Heidelberg Catechism, the *Confessio Belgica* (the Belgic Confession, 1561), or the Gallican Confession (the confession of the French churches, 1559). After the deaths of *John Calvin (1509–64), Wolfgang Musculus (1497–1563) and *Peter Martyr Vermigli (1500–62), the most prominent theologians who belonged to this early orthodox period in Germany were *Zacharias Ursinus (1534–83), Jerome Zanchi (1516–90), Bartholomaeus Keckermann (1571–1609) and Johann Heinrich Alsted (1588–1638). Prominent theologians in Switzerland included *Theodore Beza (1519–1605), Lambert Daneau (1530–95) and Amandus Polanus (1561–1610). In the Dutch Republic were Francis Junius (1545–1602), Francis Gomarus (1563–1641), Johannes Maccovius (1578–1644) and *William Ames (1576–1633). William Perkins (1558–1602) was in England.

In order to gain a clearer picture of the development of Reformed Scholasticism during the first period of its existence, notice must be taken of a number of external factors. The most significant of these was of a negative nature, namely the polemic with Rome. Following the Council of Trent, Cardinal *Robert Bellarmine (1542–1621) in particular subjected the views of the Reformation to continuous and incisive criticism. He combated the Protestants in his monumental work *Disputationes de controversiis christianae fidei adversus huius*

temporis haereticos ('Disputations concerning controversies over the Christian faith against the heretics of our time', 1586), a work that was often reprinted, and which provoked more than two hundred reactions from both Lutheran and Reformed quarters. Bellarmine's offensive was scholastic in nature, so in order to combat him and the other Roman Catholic polemical theologians, use had to be made of the same scholastic apparatus. In the course of this debate an increasingly detailed elaboration of the Protestant theological position came into being. Against this background it is quite understandable that a theological system came into being that was much more comprehensive than that of the first generations. In order to be able to participate in the academic debate, one had to employ philosophical concepts and metaphysical discussions from the Middle Ages, especially in the area of, for example, the doctrine of the divine attributes, and the doctrines of creation and providence.

Another external factor of some importance with regard to the development of Protestant Scholasticism was of an ecclesial and pedagogical nature. After the first and second generation of theologians, who had played such an important role in the establishment of the Protestant church, had passed away, the new generation faced the task of giving expression to the significance of the Reformation in a new ecclesial and academic context. For the Reformed, the establishment of the academy of Geneva in the year 1559 was a major achievement in this regard. Many theologians received a thorough theological education through that academy, so that Reformed theology eventually earned itself a permanent place in the academic world. The Genevan academy also served as a model for other centres of Reformed theology in Europe. Part of the strength of all these academies lay in their association with the church and in their international character. Students often visited more than one academy in Europe. They moved from one academy to the next in order to get to hear the best professors (*peregrinatio academica*). Accordingly, several academies therefore did their utmost to attract the most outstanding professors.

The increasing international diffusion of Reformed theology and the definition of the Reformed viewpoint with regard to the doctrine of predestination at the synod of Dordt (1618–19) may be taken to mark the onset of the period of 'high orthodoxy'. During this period, comprehensive dogmatic works were published in which the results of exegesis, the dogmatic formulation, the polemical element, and the consideration of the practical implications of the doctrine were synthesized into an impressive whole. Thus the Scholasticism of high orthodoxy came to be increasingly characterized by the sophistication of its theological apparatus, the dogmatic material being further expanded. A second formal difference between early and high Scholasticism is the increasing prominence of the polemical element. This involved especially an increase in polemics with the Roman Catholics, the *Socinians, the Remonstrants and the representatives of federal theology like *Johannes Cocceius. The new philosophy of *René Descartes (1596–1650) also evoked some reactions from Reformed quarters during the second half of the seventeenth century. In this period are found such authors as Gisbertus Voetius (1589–1676), *Francis Turretin (1623–87), Peter van Mastricht (1630–1706), Melchior Leydecker (1642–1721), Herman Witsius (1636–1708), Johannes Marckius (1656–1713), Edward Leigh (1602–71) and *John Owen (1616–83).

The onset of the *Enlightenment towards the end of the seventeenth century and the beginning of the eighteenth century serves as a good indicator of the transition from high to late orthodoxy. During the last decade of the seventeenth century, and the period following it in the eighteenth century, Reformed theology was confronted with a number of new developments in science and philosophy. One may speak in this regard of an intellectual change of climate that came onto the scene from the end of the seventeenth century onwards, and which was related to the emergence of the (early) Enlightenment. The period of 'late orthodoxy' had begun. It is usually associated with the period from around 1700 to 1790. This phase was characterized by the mounting pressure that the scholastic method had to withstand from both external and internal factors. The remarkable intellectual strength and spiritual energy so characteristic of Reformed theology at the end of the sixteenth century, and for the greatest part of the seventeenth century, began to dissipate. Nonetheless, even in this altered climate, a more or less traditional Reformed theology continued to be produced by such late orthodox writers as Benedict Pictet (1655–

1724), Bernhardinus de Moor (1710–56), Friedrich Stapfer (1708–55) and Daniel Wyttenbach (1706–99).

Among several causes of this development was, firstly, the shift that occurred in the interests of the theologians of the academies. Philology and attention to history, rather than Scholasticism, came to the fore. Linguistic studies, historical investigation of sources, text-critical studies and the so-called prophetic theology determined the theological climate of that period. Furthermore, natural religion, the ideal of the Enlightenment, worked on the premise that reason, rather than revelation, was the source of truth. Revelation was not wholly excluded, but it was expected to justify itself before reason. Humanity ought to base its knowledge and moral action on reason, without an appeal to any theological or ecclesial authority.

Thus critical ideas about the Bible became increasingly prevalent, thereby forcing Reformed theology in Europe to reflect anew on various biblical issues. The authority of revelation was believed to be in danger – a state of affairs which, it was feared, could lead to various forms of deism, scepticism (rejection of all consent) and even atheism. The biblical-critical works of such diverse figures as Thomas Hobbes (1588–1679), *Benedict Spinoza (1632–1712), Pierre Bayle (1647–1706) and Richard Simon (1638–1712) provoked a torrent of reactions in the period of the early Enlightenment, polemicizing against this criticism of Bible and dogma.

The prominent place given by Enlightenment thought to knowledge of God derived from nature led, among other things, to a very high regard for human reason. Since reason belonged to the domain of so-called 'natural theology', it seemed natural to allocate a relatively independent place to this kind of theology. Thus the possibility had been created for regarding reason as a separate source of knowledge for theology, preceding or accompanying revelation. This in fact spelled a reversal of the tried and tested principle of the medieval and Protestant Scholastics, who had taken revelation as a point of departure and source of knowledge for theology (*fides quaerens intellectum* – faith seeking understanding). Therefore, it is incorrect to view Protestant Scholasticism as having borne the seeds of the Enlightenment in itself and to characterize it as a 'two-sources-theology'.

Furthermore, the origin of Protestant Scholasticism was no 'regression' to medieval thought patterns, but much rather the result of a progressive development related to the impact of the Renaissance. From a historical point of view it is inaccurate to state that the Renaissance, Humanism and the Reformation were by definition anti-scholastic. Here one thinks of the studies of that great Renaissance scholar Paul Oskar Kristeller, who has argued persuasively that Scholasticism continued to develop slowly but surely in the course of the fourteenth century, until this scientific method reached a high point during the sixteenth and seventeenth centuries. In Reformers like Calvin, Peter Martyr Vermigli and Jerome Zanchi, we can already discern those elements that were taken further by the Scholasticism of the seventeenth century.

WILLEM J. VAN ASSELT

FURTHER READING: W.J. van Asselt, et al., *Inleiding in de Gereformeerde Scholastiek* (Zoetermeer, 1998); W.J. van Asselt and E. Dekker (eds.), *Reformation and Scholasticism* (Grand Rapids, 2000); E.P. Meijering, *Reformierte Scholastik und Patristische Theologie: Die Bedeutung des Väterbeweises in der 'Institutio Theologiae Elencticae' F. Turrettins unter Berücksichtigung der Gotteslehre und Christologie* (Nieuwkoop, 1991); P.O. Kristeller, *Renaissance Thought: The Classic, Scholastic and Humanist Strains* (New York, 2nd edn, 1955, 1961); R.A. Müller, *Post-Reformation Reformed Dogmatics*, I: *Prolegomena to Theology*; II: *Holy Scripture: The Cognitive Foundation of Theology* (Grand Rapids, 1987, 1993); 'Calvin and the "Calvinists": Assessing Continuities and Discontinuities Between the Reformation and Orthodoxy' Part I, *Cal Th J* 30 (1995), pp. 345–75; Part II, *Cal Th J* 31 (1996), pp. 125–60; L.M. de Rijk, *Middeleeuwse wijsbegeerte: Traditie en vernieuwing* (Assen, 2nd edn, 1981); C.R. Trueman and R.S. Clark, *Protestant Scholasticism: Essays in Reassessment* (Carlisle, 1999).

Schweitzer, Albert (1875–1965)

Albert Schweitzer was born in Kaysersberg in Alsace on 14 January 1875. His father and maternal grandfather were both *Lutheran pastors from the liberal German tradition, a tradition which was to be central to Schweitzer's theological work. A few years after his birth the family moved to Günsbach in the Münstertal, which was to remain Schweitzer's European home until his death in 1965. After studying at his local school and the *Realgymnasium* in

Mühlhausen, in 1893 he entered the University of Strassburg to study theology and philosophy. It was in the latter subject that he was to write his doctorate on the subject of *Kant's philosophy of religion, which was to be his first substantial publication. On the basis of this piece of work, his research supervisor, Theobald Ziegler, urged him to pursue a career in philosophy. But Schweitzer was convinced that it was in theology, and particularly in New Testament studies, that his future lay. He completed his licentiate in 1900 and his *Habilitationsschrift* in 1901 under the supervision of Heinrich Holtzmann. In 1902 he became a *Privatdozent*, and subsequently the rector of the theological college, the Thomasstift, in Strassburg.

The period from 1902 to 1913 saw the appearance of a number of significant works on New Testament subjects as well as the publication in two editions of his interpretation of Bach's preludes and fugues, the first in French and the second, heavily revised, in German. It was also during this period that Schweitzer made public his decision to give up an academic career in favour of a life of service for others. After some reflection, he decided to become a missionary in colonial Africa (specifically in Lambaréné in the Gabon), but owing to objections to his theological views raised by members of the board of the Paris Missionary Society, to whom he had applied for work, he opted to carry out his duties as a medical doctor. With the permission of the university's authorities, he began his medical studies in 1905. This was to mark the beginning of an exhausting period for Schweitzer, in which he was at one and the same time theological teacher, medical student, rector of a theological college, parish priest and a regular contributor, both in a practical and scholarly way, to the Bach Society of Paris. It is little surprise that at the end of this period he suffered a mental breakdown.

In 1913, now married and having recovered his health, he set out for Gabon. At the outbreak of the First World War he was interned by the French authorities in Africa because he was a German citizen (Alsace was at that time a part of Germany). In 1917 he returned to Europe, first to an internment camp in Bordeaux and subsequently to Alsace. By 1924 he had raised enough money to return to Lambaréné, and from this period until his death in 1965, he was to spend his time in Africa, punctuated by visits to Europe and America to raise funds for his medical centre at Lambaréné. He was also to become one of the most famous figures on the world stage, receiving amongst many honours the Goethe Prize, the Légion d'honneur, and in 1953, the Nobel Peace Prize. The late 1950s were to see the beginnings of a decline in his reputation, in part stimulated by his view that Africans were being handed their autonomy too soon.

Schweitzer's career as a New Testament scholar was to span a relatively short period, from 1901 to 1913 (the fact that *The Mysticism of Paul the Apostle* appeared in 1930 should be accorded little significance – the book had already been conceived and chapters drafted as early as 1913). Running through all of his work is the view that a key to understanding the world out of which the New Testament texts emerged was Jewish eschatology. In contrast to many of the presentations of the life of Jesus prevalent at the time, which often portrayed Jesus as a skilled ethical teacher whose preaching of the kingdom of God was to be understood in strictly moral terms, Schweitzer saw Jesus as a messianic enthusiast who looked for God's redemption in a coming cataclysm. When that cataclysm did not arrive, Jesus determined on bringing about his own execution to force God's hand. In this reconstruction, Jewish eschatological dogma (the term is Schweitzer's) was used as the tool to connect up the disconnected *pericopae* of the Gospels – in particular, Mark and Matthew. This produced a complete picture of Jesus and his aims which contrasted strongly with that portrayed by the liberal lives of which he was so critical, and presented the world with a figure at once enigmatic and strange. Schweitzer's views were partially developed in his early work on the Last Supper (1901), taken further in *The Mystery of the Kingdom of God* (1901), and reached a crescendo in the work translated into English as *The Quest for the Historical Jesus* (1906). In this work, which in 1913 was to appear in a second edition containing some important changes and additions, and which has until very recently never been translated into English, Schweitzer's presentation of Jesus was set against the background of a detailed critique of the historiography of the subject. The quest was portrayed as a heroic movement which proceeded in various stages, each marked by particular polarities of opinion, or, as he put it, 'either-ors'. The last of these was that between an eschatological, or an uneschatological Jesus, and it led inevitably to

the presentation of Schweitzer's own views as the climactic conclusion of nearly 150 years of scholarship.

Schweitzer's work on Paul proceeded along similar lines. He began with a survey of scholarship out of which the fault lines of the debate emerged (*Paul and His Interpreters*, 1911), and this was then followed by his own reconstruction of Paul's thought in perhaps his most accomplished work, *The Mysticism of Paul the Apostle* (1930). Paul emerges as the first great Christian thinker who saw Christians, as a result of Christ's death and resurrection, as living in a new eschatological state which would be brought to completion at Christ's return. Central to this formulation of Paul's theology is no longer the doctrine of justification by faith, but the 'in Christ' formula understood in terms of eschatology. Once one lost sight of the eschatological thrust of Paul's theology, Schweitzer argued, its Hellenization in the hands of subsequent Christians became inevitable.

Schweitzer's work on Jesus and Paul constituted separate parts of what might be termed a total account of Christian origins which was to explain Christianity's developments from Jesus to Paul to the Hellenized faith of the early church (this task was to be taken further by his pupil Martin Werner). Although his attempts to understand Jesus and Paul in an eschatological context were not in themselves original (one thinks especially of the work of Weiss, Baldensperger and Kabisch, all of which had been stimulated by the discovery and publication of Jewish apocalyptic texts), the consistent way in which Schweitzer carried out his task and the almost rhetorical fervour with which he wrote were original. Jesus and Paul are understood in a systematic way as children of the eschatological world in which they moved, a point of considerable importance in Pauline studies where Paul was customarily seen as the Hellenizer of Christianity.

Schweitzer's strange and apparently alienating portrait of Jesus led to some detailed and not entirely consistent hermeneutical reflections. How could 'this stranger to our time', who was so much a product of his own historical context, have any relevance to the modern world at all? In the end, Schweitzer seems to opt for something like a mysticism of the will in which the will of Jesus, ethically conceived, is understood as transcending the context in which it manifested itself. Here, in some sense, there is an attempt to rescue Jesus' ethical teaching, which Schweitzer had famously described as '*Interims-ethik*', for all time, and this in an uncompromising fashion.

Schweitzer's work on Jesus (his two books on Paul, particularly *Mysticism*, were generally more warmly received), received a critical reception in Germany. Reviewers criticized what they took to be his scant regard for source-critical questions, the overconfident and tendentious character of many of his conclusions and the distasteful picture of Jesus which emerged from its pages. A better reception was found in Britain, where initially W. Sanday, then F.C. Burkitt and, amongst others, G. Tyrrell, appeared as enthusiasts for different aspects of Schweitzer's conclusions. In this respect it should be noted that Ernst von Dobschuetz, at that time a professor in the same university as Schweitzer, felt the need to hold a series of lectures in Oxford in 1909, subsequently published in *The Expositor* of 1910, attacking Schweitzer's views. Today, many of Schweitzer's more general conclusions are widely accepted, for example the view that the Jewish context is an appropriate one in which to understand Jesus and Paul and that eschatology is central to an understanding of the world of both characters, although many of the details that are the constituent parts of his own reconstruction have been strongly criticized. Striking reminders of Schweitzer's *Wirkungsgeschichte* in the past few decades are seen in the works of E.P. Sanders and N.T. Wright.

After 1913, Schweitzer moved away from his interest in New Testament studies and began to busy himself with the question of civilization and culture. His two published volumes on the subject came out in 1923 (a third volume, which was never published in his own lifetime, will soon appear). They constitute an attempt to identify the malaise in our present culture and to formulate a solution in terms of ethical regeneration. Out of this emerges Schweitzer's concept of reverence for life which sees ethics as determined by an almost undifferentiated veneration for all forms of life – from human beings to the most insignificant microbes. The same period was also to witness, amongst other things, a number of publications on other religions in which many of the themes of the books on civilization can also be discerned.

Although Schweitzer has often been identified with those who brought about the demise of liberal Christianity, and in many ways he,

along with *Barth and *Bultmann, although from very different perspectives, mark the end of an era in theology, in several respects he remained a liberal to the end of his life. His commitment to the historical enterprise, his concern for the role of reason in the formulation of religious truths and his contempt for theological dogma, his veneration of *Enlightenment values and his essentially ethical understanding of the Christian religion, are but a few of the marks of his liberal heritage. Where he differed from his liberal contemporaries was in his keen appreciation of the 'otherness' of Jesus and the world from which he emerged, an 'otherness' which meant that he could not in any glib way be appropriated for our time. In this respect Schweitzer anticipates many aspects of more recent biblical hermeneutics.

JAMES CARLETON PAGET

FURTHER READING: C.K. Barrett, 'Albert Schweitzer and the New Testament', *Expos T* 87 (1975), pp. 4–10; J. Brabazon, *Albert Schweitzer* (New York, 1975); T.F. Glasson, 'Schweitzer's Influence – Blessing or Bane', *J Th St* NS 28 (1977), pp. 289–302; Eric Grässer, *Albert Schweitzer als Theologe* (Tübingen, 1979); Claus Günzler, *Albert Schweitzer: Einführung in sein Denken* (Munich, 1996); H. Groos, *Albert Schweitzer. Größe und Grenzen. Eine kritische Würdigung des Forschers und Denkers* (Munich, 1974); W.G. Kümmel, *The New Testament: The History of the Investigation of its Problems* (ET London, 1973), pp. 226–44; Robert Morgan, 'From Reimarus to Sanders', in *The Kingdom of God and Human Society* (ed. R.S. Barbour; Edinburgh, 1993), pp. 80–139; W. Picht, *The Life and Thought of Albert Schweitzer* (ET London, 1964); Henning Pleitner, *Das Ende der liberalen Hermeneutik am Beispiel Albert Schweitzers* (Tübingen, 1992); George Seaver, *Albert Schweitzer: The Man and His Mind* (London, 6th edn, 1969); Harald Steffahn, *Schweitzer* (Hamburg, 1998).

Scougal, Henry (1650–78)

Scottish teacher of philosophy and divinity, Scougal is remembered chiefly for his devotional treatise *The Life of God in the Soul of Man*. Scougal was born while his father, Patrick Scougal, was minister of Leuchars in Fife. In 1659 the family moved to Saltoun in East Lothian on Patrick's translation to that parish. During this period Robert Leighton, principal of Edinburgh University and later Bishop of Dunblane and Archbishop of Glasgow, became a close friend and a role model for Henry. When

Patrick was appointed Bishop of Aberdeen in 1664, the family moved to Old Aberdeen and Henry was enrolled as a student at King's College. He graduated with an MA in 1668 and was appointed a regent in the college the following year, though he was only nineteen. He was recommended for licence as a preacher in 1672 and ordained and inducted to the parish of Auchterless in Aberdeenshire in 1673. It was probably while he was at Auchterless that he wrote *The Life of God in the Soul of Man*. In 1674 he was elected by the synod of Aberdeen to the chair of divinity at King's College. This chair had been founded by the synod in 1620 and elections were made on the basis of a written examination until 1927. Tradition has it that this method was adopted to avoid any suspicion of undue bias because the first incumbent was John Forbes, son of the then Bishop of Aberdeen, Patrick Forbes. Sadly, Scougal's tenure of the chair was only four years, for he died of consumption in 1678.

Henry Scougal has enjoyed a lasting reputation amounting almost to sanctity. This is largely due to *The Life of God in the Soul of Man*, which was written as a letter of spiritual counsel to a friend and was passed from hand to hand until it reached Gilbert Burnet, professor of divinity at Glasgow University and later Bishop of Salisbury, who persuaded Scougal to consent to its publication in 1677. This, the only edition issued during his lifetime, did not bear his name and was commended by Burnet in a short preface. It was almost immediately recognized as a devotional classic, and this first edition was reprinted 17 times by 1819. Other editions were sponsored by principal William Wishart of Edinburgh University in 1739 and by Ashbel Green, president of Princeton University, and others in the United States. Two French translations were printed in the Netherlands in 1722 and 1727. German translations were published in Pennsylvania in 1755 and 1756. A Welsh translation was printed at Caerfyrddin in 1779.

In his address to the friend for whom he wrote *The Life of God in the Soul of Man*, Scougal modestly disclaims any originality: 'I know you are provided with better helps of this nature than any I can offer you, nor are you like to meet with anything here which you knew not before.' Despite this, he hopes that 'God's providence perhaps may so direct my thoughts that something or other may prove useful to you'.

Scougal's hopes for his friend have been abundantly fulfilled for many others in the last three hundred years. His book was a favourite with John Newton, and it had a powerful effect on the early Methodists. Susanna Wesley commended it to her sons, *John and Charles. When John was in Savannah, Georgia, he read Scougal's book aloud in public and on one occasion was an effective counter-attraction to the ball held in the town that evening. Charles Wesley introduced the book to George Whitefield, who wrote of it ' I never knew what true religion was till God sent me that excellent treatise by the hands of my never to be forgotten friend.' On either side of the Presbyterian divide in nineteenth-century Scotland, Scougal is commended by Thomas Chalmers and James Cooper. The Bethany Fellowship of Minneapolis, Minnesota published an edition in 1976.

The enduring appeal of this devotional treatise is largely due to its brevity and apparent simplicity. For Scougal, the root of the divine life is faith and its branches are love to God, charity to man, purity and humility. He is well aware of the despondency of those who feel that they are making little progress and he is practical about the aids available to them. In the context of late seventeenth-century Scotland, when both Episcopalians and Presbyterians celebrated the Holy Communion very infrequently, Scougal recommends the 'frequent and conscientious use of that holy Sacrament' and asserts that its neglect 'is one of the chief causes that bedwarfs our religion'.

Scougal's other writings are largely forgotten, but they may be found in various collections of his *Works*. They include *Essays Moral and Divine* and *Nine Discourses on Important Subjects of Religion*. The last of the discourses is a sermon preached before the synod of Aberdeen on *The Importance and Difficulty of the Ministerial Function*. In this sermon, he describes personal counselling as the greatest and most difficult work of the minister. He is also well aware of the difficulty of preaching to people of diverse educational and spiritual attainments. It was the custom then for a reader to conduct the first part of the Sunday service and for the minister to enter the church only to preach the sermon. Scougal refused to do this and insisted on being present throughout worship.

Although *Calvinist in doctrine and preaching, Scougal was interested in religion rather than theology and regarded theological controversies as irrelevant as disputes about Presbyterianism, Episcopacy and Independency.

HENRY R. SEFTON

FURTHER READING: Texts: *De Objecto Cultus Religiosi* (Aberdeen, 1674); *The Life of God in the Soul of Man* (London, 1677); *Reflections and Meditations* (Aberdeen, 1740); *Essays Moral and Divine* (Aberdeen, 1740); *Nine Discourses on Important Subjects of Religion* (Aberdeen, 1759); *Philosophia Moralis Tractatus* (MS 1026, Aberdeen University Library). *Studies:* G.D. Henderson, 'Henry Scougal', in *The Burning Bush* (Edinburgh, 1957), pp. 94–104; Dugald Butler, *Henry Scougal and the Oxford Methodists* (Edinburgh, 1899).

Secularism

Denotes a view of reality which excludes reference to the transcendent or sacred. Secularist world-views thus require the rejection of supernaturalist religious beliefs and involve the claim that all phenomena can be explained ultimately in terms of physical or material causes. Consistent secularism includes the acceptance of the radical aloneness of humankind and the denial of both creation and purpose in relation to the cosmos. Man is summoned to recognize 'his total solitude, his fundamental isolation' (Jacques Monod). However, the response of secular thinkers to this perceived emptiness of the cosmos and its indifference to human hopes and sufferings can take very different forms. The dispelling of the fantastic dreams of religion, the demystifying of the cosmos, is experienced by some as a liberation, releasing human beings to take responsibility for creating the world. By contrast, other secular thinkers and (especially) artists confess to a sense of terror in an empty universe and recognize that the loss of faith in God poses a real threat to human freedom and dignity.

While the modern period witnessed the growth of secularism as a consequence of the *Enlightenment project, the roots of such beliefs are to be found much earlier in human intellectual and cultural history. Studies in the thought of the peoples of the Ancient Near East, of Greece and Rome and the early civilizations of China and India indicate that secularism is 'almost as old as human thought itself and just as widespread' (James Thrower). A substantial body of ethnographic evidence suggests that secular views and attitudes have been far more widespread among primal peoples in so-called tribal societies than has generally been believed.

In respect of the western tradition, classical materialism was outlined in the works of Epicurus (341–270 BC) and Lucretius (94–55 BC). The latter set himself the task of explaining the universe 'without the aid of the gods' and stated as a fundamental principle of secular enquiry that 'Nothing can ever be created by divine power out of nothing'. Four centuries later, Sextus Empiricus developed what amounted to a theory of religion as a human product and an instrument of social control. The gods are said to have been invented by a 'shrewd and clever man' to terrorize ordinary mortals and keep them in their place – a view which clearly anticipates modern secular critiques of religion by thinkers like *Feuerbach, *Marx and Freud.

At the dawn of the modern era classical secularist texts were rediscovered, and they played an important part in the development of the Enlightenment assault on religion. Modern secular thinkers developed sophisticated arguments in their analyses of the social and psychological functions of religion, yet they were conscious of recovering an ancient tradition of unbelief which had been suppressed by the dominance of Christian and Islamic theism. Time and again leading secular theorists, concerned to liberate humankind from what they viewed as the chains of religion, made use of Greek mythology. Thus, the young Karl Marx cited the confession of Prometheus as his own – 'I hate the pack of gods'.

As a self-contained system of belief secularism has attracted relatively few adherents, but it has played a crucial role at the level of the underlying presuppositions of various humanistic projects. For example, Ludwig Feuerbach's *The Essence of Christianity* (1841) was greeted with enthusiasm by young, radical thinkers since, according to Engels, it demonstrated that 'Nothing exists outside nature and man, and the higher beings our religious fantasies have created are only the fantastic reflection of our own essence'. Feuerbach's demolition of the credibility of theology was regarded as a groundbreaking exercise, providing a materialist foundation on which the positive work of Marxist social transformation might be undertaken. Similarly, atheistic *Existentialism took the aloneness of humankind in an empty cosmos as a given. The loss of the Father in heaven meant that, since human nature was not imposed upon from outside by external authority, liberated men and women could assume full responsibility for themselves and so 'come of age'. Perhaps the most widely influential statements concerning the need for a new humanity in a godless world are those of *Friedrich Nietzsche: 'Once you said "God" when you gazed upon distant seas; but now I have taught you to say "superman" '. By the 1960s, views like these had filtered down to the level of popular culture, spread by lyrics like the following from John Lennon:

> Imagine there's no heaven
> It's easy if you try
> No hell below us
> Above us only sky.

However, as we noted earlier, not all secularist thinkers have greeted the loss of religious faith with such equanimity. The *Romantic movement gave expression to feelings of profound *angst* at the prospect of life in a culture which had lost the capacity for awe and wonder. The erosion of meaning and hope, the threats posed by the growth of technology and the terror of death are all reflected in the music of Gustav Mahler, the novels of Franz Kafka and the art of Edvard Munch. In these and many other works of art, modern man appears to be a very nervous Prometheus, increasingly aware of the truth of Albert Camus' memorable statement: 'The sky is empty, the earth delivered into the hands of power without principles'.

Theological responses to secularism vary from a vigorous repudiation of it as apostasy, at one extreme, to the acceptance of the reality of the death of God in modern culture and the quest for what has been called 'a profane form of Christ's presence in the world' at the other. The former, found in various conservative traditions, represents a continuance of the monopolistic claim on truth which characterized Christendom and which, by denying the free expression of alternative views, actually provoked the secularist revolt. The latter, expressed with caution in Arend van Leeuwen's *Christianity in World History* (1964) and, much more controversially, in Thomas Altizer's *The Gospel of Christian Atheism* (1966), runs the risk of conceding normative status to secularism, so abandoning the truth-claims of the Christian revelation. Between these two extremes, however, is a middle way which, founded on the confession of the truth of the gospel, involves genuine dialogue and a frank recognition of the

validity of much of the secular critique of religion. *Lesslie Newbigin's *Honest Religion for Secular Man* (1966) and the works of *Hans Küng and Helmut Thielicke provide excellent examples of this approach. In a world now clearly postmodern, in which the confident assumptions of the Enlightenment are widely questioned, there is an unprecedented opportunity for dialogue between Christians and humanists of various kinds who, in the light of the history of the twentieth century, are compelled to reconsider the view that secularism is a necessary foundation for the building of a new world. It may now be possible to bridge the ideological divide created by the Enlightenment and bring an end to the conflicts over religion which have disfigured western intellectual life for two hundred years.

DAVID SMITH

FURTHER READING: Thomas Alitzer, *The Gospel of Christian Atheism* (Philadelphia, 1966); Rocco Caperale and Antonio Gurnellis (eds.), *The Culture of Unbelief* (Berkeley, 1971); Owen Chadwick, *The Secularization of the European Mind in the Nineteenth Century* (Cambridge / New York, 1975); J.A. Gaskin, *Varieties of Unbelief* (New York, 1989); Phillip Hammond (ed.), *The Sacred in a Secular Age* (Berkeley, 1985); Hans Küng, *Does God Exist? An Answer for Today* (Garden City, NY, 1980); Arend van Leeuwen, *Christianity in World History* (New York, 1964); Ninian Smart, 'Secular Worldviews in Today's World', in *Religion in Today's World* (ed. Frank Whaling; Edinburgh, 1987); Helmut Thielicke, *Modern Faith and Thought* (trans. G.W. Bromiley; Grand Rapids, 1990); James Thrower, *The Alternative Tradition: Religion and the Rejection of Religion in the Ancient World* (The Hague / New York, 1980).

Servetus, Michael (1511–53)

Born Miguel Serveto, Michael Servetus was a theologian and physician from Villanueva, Spain. He was most well known for his confrontation with *John Calvin over his views on the Trinity. His most important works on this topic were *De Trinitatis Erroribus* (1531) and *De Trinitate* (1552), in which he argued that the doctrine of the Trinity was unbiblical and was never taught in the pre-Nicene church. Opposition to his views was so strong that he had to change his name to Michel de Villeneuve to escape the Inquisition. He left his native Spain, settling in Lyons and then Paris, where he studied medicine. He gained expertise in dissection and is said to have discovered the circulation of the blood in the lungs. He lived secretly in Vienna from 1541 to 1553 as the physician of the Archbishop of Vienna. In 1553, Servetus published his refutation of Calvin's *Institutio*, the *Christianismi Restitutio*, in which he argued that the church should return to the purity of the pre-Constantinian age. Servetus was arrested and tried for heresy by the Roman Catholic authorities in Vienna. He was condemned to death, but he escaped and could not resist the temptation to at least visit Geneva and hear Calvin preach. He was recognized, arrested and put on trial for heresy before the Genevan city council. Calvin served as an expert witness for the prosecution. Calvin's opponents, the Libertines, who saw the Servetus trial as an opportunity to discredit Calvin, defended Servetus. He was convicted to death by burning at the stake – the typical method of execution for heresy. Calvin did recommend the sentence of death, but he pled for some measure of mercy by asking that Servetus be beheaded – a more humane form of execution. On 27 October 1553, while the flames were burning around him, Servetus's last words were 'Jesus, thou son of the eternal God have pity on me'. A Trinitarian would have said 'Jesus, the eternal Son of God'. Even at his last breath, Servetus remained steadfast in his denial of the Trinity.

After the execution, Sebastian Castellio, who ran afoul of Calvin for his literal views of the Song of Solomon, penned *Concerning Heretics, whether they are to be persecuted* (1554), in which he argued that one can kill a man but one cannot kill an idea. In fact, to execute the heretic is to advertise his or her ideas. This work advocated religious toleration in an age when execution for anti-Trinitarian views was an accepted practice among Roman Catholics and magisterial Protestants alike. The trial and execution of Servetus became a rallying point for the eighteenth-century *philosophes* such as Voltaire and Diderot in their cry for religious toleration.

Servetus believed that the doctrine of the Trinity served as an unnecessary stumbling block in evangelizing Jews and Muslims. The Bible, he argued, teaches that God reveals himself to human beings through a series of names – such as El Shaddai and Elohim – each designed to express a different message. In the New Testament, the names 'Jesus' and the 'Holy Spirit' are merely terms designed to convey additional teachings about God. Furthermore, all of the

words related to the Trinity, such as *hypostasis*, persons, substance and essence, were not used in the Bible. Biblical references to the Father, Son and Holy Spirit properly refer to various modes or manifestations of God. Furthermore, the ante-Nicene Fathers did not teach the doctrine of the Trinity. For example, although *Tertullian used the term, he did not refer to any real distinction of the Persons of the Trinity.

Servetus believed that Jesus was fully human while being the begotten Son of God. Jesus is the divine Saviour, but was created in time and, therefore, did not exist from all eternity. There was a time when he did not exist. Servetus separated the Word from Jesus, arguing that the Word is eternal but the Son is not. He later modified his view to say that the Word is the Son, but that the Son did not possess any substance until the incarnation. In addition, he argued that God is a single entity containing hundreds of thousands of essences. These essences constitute a portion of us as human beings and we, therefore, are a part of the divine spirit.

In the *De Trinitatis Erroribus*, Servetus argued that the Holy Spirit is not a Person, but the power of God to help believers live the Christian life. There is a level of harmony between the three, and the divine nature of God is shown in what Servetus calls the 'dispositions' of the Father, Son and Holy Spirit. We become Christians by believing in Christ as the Son of God. Later, in the short pamphlet *Dialogorum de Trinitate Libri Duo* (1532), Servetus admitted that the Holy Spirit became a Person by virtue of his dwelling within the hearts of believers.

Servetus also presented some interesting views on the relationship between the Old and New Testaments. He was eager to interpret the Old Testament in its proper historical context, and he thus rejected the excessive use of allegory. He also argued that many Old Testament prophecies were not fulfilled in the New Testament. For example, Isaiah 7:14 does not refer to the virgin birth of Christ because the Hebrew word means 'young woman' rather than 'virgin'. The verse actually refers to the wife of Hezekiah rather than to the Virgin Mary. He also rejected the prophetic character of Isaiah 53, saying that it properly refers to Cyrus rather than to Christ.

Servetus displayed some degree of affinity with the *Anabaptists. He rejected infant baptism, a view based largely on his experience in Spain with the forced baptisms of Jews and

Muslims. He believed that unbaptized children are covered by the blood of Christ and do not need to be baptized until they reach a stage of accountability, around the age of twenty, when they can express their own faith in Christ.

MARTIN I. KLAUBER

FURTHER READING: *Texts: De Trinitatis Erroribus Libri Septem* (1531); *Dialogorum Trinitate* (1532); *De Regno Christi* (1532); *Christianismi Restitutio* (1553). *Studies:* Roland H. Bainton, *Hunted Heretic: The Life and Death of Michael Servetus* (Boston, 1960); Marian Hillar, *The Case of Michael Servetus (1511–1553): The Turning Point in the Struggle for Freedom of Conscience* (Lewiston, NY, 1997).

Socinianism

Socinianism, which up until the late nineteenth century was a common alternative designation for *Unitarianism (especially in circumstances involving *odium theologicum*), is the name given to that form of anti-Trinitarianism which originated with two sixteenth-century Italian humanists, best-known by the Latin form of their surname, Socinus. At first fairly moderate in tone, Socinianism later became increasingly radical and was usually regarded as a particularly insidious heresy. The humanists in question were both members of the Sozzini family of Siena, many of whom had been, for several generations, distinguished jurists. They were, firstly, Lelio Sozini (Laelius Socinus, 1526–62, who, unlike the other members of the family, spelled the Italian form of his name with one 'z'), and secondly, his much better-known nephew, Fausto Sozzini (Faustus Socinus, 1539–1604). It is the latter who is rightly regarded as the originator of Socinianism – partly because of the decisive role which he played in the consolidation of the radical Protestant group known as the Polish Brethren or Minor Reformed Church of Poland. This offshoot of Polish *Calvinism had embraced an anti-Trinitarian theology before it came under his influence, but it was later to become indelibly associated with him, and it deserves to be regarded, therefore, as the original embodiment of Socinianism. But Faustus himself was probably much influenced by his uncle, and Laelius Socinus, therefore, has sometimes been called 'the Patriarch of Socinianism'. He was originally trained as a jurist, but he developed an interest in theology and soon became a moderately radical Protestant. After conferring with leading

*Reformers in several European countries, including England and Poland, he settled in Switzerland, occasionally disputing with *Calvin.

His nephew Faustus was also a native of Siena who had become, despite an inadequate early education, an erudite enthusiast for theology with a leaning towards radical Protestantism. In 1561, he moved to Lyons in France and he was also resident for a while in Geneva, where he became a member of the refugee Italian Protestant congregation. At Lyons, he published a study of John's Gospel, which queried the supreme deity of Christ, and when his uncle died in 1562, he took possession of his books and papers. But in the following year he returned to Italy to serve at the court of Isabella de Medici, outwardly conforming to Catholicism. During this period, he published a brief treatise on the authority of Scripture, his most influential early work, which was at one time greatly esteemed by both Catholics and Protestants. But in 1574 he moved to Basle to further his religious studies and here, in 1578, he wrote a book entitled *De Jesu Christo Servator*. This work remained unpublished until 1594, but it was the source of one of his most distinctive contributions to theology. The fact that he uses the word *servator* (servant) as the title for Christ, rather than the more usual *salvator* (saviour), clearly indicates its tone. It was a bold statement of the *Abelardian or Subjectivist theory of the atonement, affirming that Christ is our Saviour not because his death appeases the wrath of God, but because he has shown us the way of salvation, which we ourselves must follow. This view was to remain always a prominent feature of Socinianism, and Socinus himself says that he had picked it up from Bernardino Ochino, another influential Italian Reformer.

Meanwhile, in Poland, where a measure of religious toleration was permitted under an enactment known as the *Pax Dissidentium*, anti-Trinitarianism and other radical tendencies had begun to emerge in the Reformed Church – partly under the influence of yet another refugee Italian humanist, the controversial theologian Giorgio Biandrata, who had become the Polish court physician. A former member of the Italian congregation in Geneva who had been forced to leave because of his restless questioning of Christian doctrine, Biandrata ultimately became a bitter opponent of Calvin. In 1563 he moved on to Transylvania, where he was to play an important part, with the help of Francis Dávid, in the establishment of the historic Unitarian church of that region. But Biandrata's work in Poland bore fruit, and in 1565 the existence of a radical breakaway group (the Polish Brethren or Minor Reformed Church) was formally acknowledged, and despite some initial harassment, the movement began to flourish. It was much helped by the establishment in 1569 of the city of Raków (or Racovia), founded through the generosity of Jan Sieninski, a tolerant Calvinist nobleman whose wife had become a member of the Minor Church. The new town soon became the Polish Brethren's metropolis, with a very active printing press and an influential international academy to which scholars came from all parts of Europe.

At first what the movement most lacked was strong leadership, but this was ultimately met by the arrival from Transylvania of Faustus Socinus, who by this time was widely acknowledged as a skilful exponent of moderate anti-Trinitarianism. In 1578 Biandrata had invited him to visit Transylvania, where the increasing extremism of Francis Dávid was causing problems. Dávid had begun to argue that the worship of Christ was idolatry and contrary to Scripture. Socinus had never maintained this position and Biandrata hoped that he might be a moderating influence. But the mission was unsuccessful, and in 1580 Socinus settled in Poland, where he associated himself increasingly with the Minor Reformed Church, eventually becoming its revered leader. He organized the church's beliefs into a consistent system, avoiding extremes and excessive radicalism, and he ably defended it in disputes with its opponents – both Catholic and Protestant. Strangely enough, he himself never became one of its members, partly owing to differences with some of the brethren on the question of baptism, nor was he ever resident at Raków.

Faustus Socinus was undoubtedly a man of great personal charm, who, unlike most of his contemporaries, had the ability to argue with calmness and courtesy. This is probably a clue to one of the most persistent characteristics of Socinianism – a firm belief in toleration. Towards the end of his life, Socinus suffered some harassment as a consequence of *Jesuit-inspired persecution. He had for some time been planning a comprehensive statement of his beliefs, but this was incomplete at the time of his death in 1604. However, the preliminary

work which he had undertaken became the basis of the famous *Racovian Catechism*, first published in Polish in 1605. This was an elaborate and lengthy manual of religious apologetic in question-and-answer form rather than a true catechism. But it was the first complete statement of Socinian doctrine. It was compiled by three leading members of the Minor Reformed Church – Valentin Smalcius (Schmalz), Hieronymous Moscorovius (Moskorzowski) and Johannes Völkel. Smalcius and Völkel were both German converts, which underlines the extent to which Socinianism had already become an international movement.

The catechism was later published in Latin and other languages. The first Latin edition of 1609 was dedicated to James I of England, but when he received a copy he repudiated it angrily and it was burnt by order of Parliament in 1614. Though greatly feared and repeatedly attacked, the book remained in circulation for 150 years and was enormously influential. Bible-based throughout, it nevertheless insists that Scripture has to be interpreted on the basis of 'right reason' (*recta ratio*). It presents Christianity as a way of life demanding true knowledge of God and of his will revealed by Christ. (A favourite Socinian text was John 17:3). The catechism also argues that God is emphatically one, and that the Trinity is unscriptural and inherently irrational. Christ is a true man, but also the Son of God, and a fitting object, therefore, of worship and prayer. The Holy Spirit is simply a power of God and not a separate Person within the Godhead. There is much discussion of the moral and civic duties of the Christian, with great emphasis on the necessity of living a Christ-like life, as well as some expressions of disapproval of the bearing of arms, judicial and social violence, the swearing of oaths and the holding of civic office. Christ's sufferings and death are primarily an example, showing us the true way to salvation. Man's will is free, and original sin and predestination are false doctrines. There is only one necessary sacrament – the Lord's Supper, interpreted as a memorial rite – and infant baptism is rejected. There are undoubtedly some very close similarities between some parts of the catechism and the general trend of *Servetus's *Errors of the Trinity*, but Socinus himself firmly denied that Servetus was the progenitor of his teaching.

The Polish Socinians were always called *Arians by their Catholic opponents, a title which they vehemently repudiated on the ground that they did not believe in the pre-existence of Christ. A very curious feature of early Socinian doctrine, certainly endorsed by Socinus himself, was the claim (based on an idiosyncratic exegesis of John 3:13) that at the outset of his ministry, Christ had been temporarily taken up into heaven to receive his divine commission. This was perhaps an attempt to justify Socinian rejection of the pre-existence of Christ.

The early success of the Socinians in Poland was short-lived. During the first half of the seventeenth century they were subjected to increasing persecution – a consequence of the Jesuit-inspired campaign to eradicate Protestantism entirely from Poland. In 1638, the metropolis at Raków was proscribed and suppressed. Its printing press was destroyed and the academy demolished, and by 1660 all 'Arians' had been obliged to convert to Catholicism or go into exile. One group went to Transylvania, where it was ultimately absorbed into the Unitarian church, and others went to East Prussia, where Socinian communities had already been established. The group centred at Andreaswalde continued in existence until 1811.

But quite apart from these specific groups, the influence of Socinianism was soon felt throughout Europe, especially in Holland, and above all in England. Exiled Socinian scholars were very active in Holland, and a number of works were published, including the famous *Bibliotheca Fratrum Polonorum Quos Unitarios Vocant* (Amsterdam, 1668). This was a massive eight-volume book, which was a collected edition (for the first time) of the complete works of Socinus, together with other Socinian writings. Socinian influence in Holland certainly played a part in the emergence in that country of the Remonstrants and the Collegiate movement.

The extent of Socinian influence in England in the seventeenth century can hardly be exaggerated. Socinian literature, including the *Bibliotheca Fratrum Polonorum*, circulated freely and Socinian views were very prevalent in the Church of England, despite a decree from the Convocation of Canterbury proscribing Socinian books. The Latitudinarian movement and some intense Trinitarian controversies were among the consequences of Socinian influence. John Biddle, 'the Father of English Unitarianism', had arrived at anti-Trinitarian views before he encountered Socinianism, but he later became an enthusiast

for the tradition, translating some of its literature into English – including the *Racovian Catechism*, which, like the original Latin edition, was burnt by order of Parliament.

The Dissenters were at first largely unaffected. But in the eighteenth century, some of their congregations, originally orthodox or Arian in belief, moved on to Socinianism, frequently under the influence of the Dissenting academies, where Socinianism had often taken a firm hold. This was to cause some bitter controversy in the early nineteenth century. A source of some confusion is the fact that, by this time, the term Socinianism had come to imply a very radical form of Unitarianism (sometimes known as 'humanitarianism'), which involved a completely human view of Jesus and a 'non-adorationist' attitude towards him. This had never been characteristic of the original Socinianism, which was always 'adorationist'. But thanks to its emphasis on the importance of 'right reason', Socinianism had always shown a tendency to become more and more radical as the years passed. This had already been reflected in the later editions of the *Racovian Catechism*. That of 1668, published in Amsterdam and edited by Andrew Wiszowaty (Socinus's grandson) and Joachim Stegmann, contains a remarkable statement of the necessity of toleration and the inevitability of doctrinal development. Perhaps it is hardly surprising therefore, that Socinianism has often been characterized (and consequently either admired or condemned) as the chief fountainhead of Liberalism and Modernism.

ARTHUR J. LONG

FURTHER READING: E.M. Wilbur, *A History of Unitarianism* (2 vols.; Cambridge, MA, 1947, 1952), esp. vol. 1: *Socinianism and its Antecedents*; Thomas Rees, *The Racovian Catechism – Translated from the Latin with a Sketch of the History of Unitarianism* (London, 1818); O. Fock, *Der Socinianismus* (2 vols.; Kiel, 1847); H.J. McLachlan, *Socinianism in Seventeenth-Century England* (Oxford, 1951); D.B. Parke (ed.), *The Epic of Unitarianism: Original Writings from the History of Liberal Religion* (Boston, 1992).

Söderblom, Nathan (1866–1931)

Historian of religion, Swedish archbishop, ecumenical pioneer and Nobel Peace Prize winner. Söderblom was born the son of the vicar of Trönö in the northern part of the diocese of Uppsala. His father was a pious man marked by evangelical revivalism. Since his son developed in a more open-minded direction, their relationship was sometimes tense. Söderblom accepted critical approaches to the Bible, but he developed an understanding of religion and theology as relationship with a 'living God', and father and son were reconciled.

The academic and, later, the ecclesiastical career of Söderblom was very straight. As a student he developed a close relationship to the international Christian student and missionary movement. Karl Fries (the YMCA leader who later became the general secretary of the World Student Christian Federation, founded in Vadstena in 1895) sent Söderblom in 1890 to an international student conference in Northfield, USA (in D.L. Moody's summerhouse). Here he received lasting impressions which instilled in him a deep concern for the cause of Christian unity. (He wrote in his diary: 'Lord, give me humility and wisdom to serve the great task of the free unity of Thy Church!')

Söderblom passed his primary examination in 1892, and continued his theological studies. He delivered an important speech at the Reformation celebrations in 1893 which drew attention to him. He was married to Anna Forsell (the sister of the famous opera singer John Forsell) in 1894. His intention at this stage was to study the religion of Zarathustra, and thus he learned Persian. His academic career was economically favoured by his call to be residential pastor to the Swedish Embassy in Paris (combined with a ministry to seafarers in Calais).

The Paris years were teaching years for him, both in terms of scholarship and ecumenically. He published the primary results of his research on 'the *Fravashis*', and later his doctoral thesis on 'The future life according to Mazdeism', which was exquisitely recognized at the Sorbonne in 1901. In the same year he was called back to Uppsala as professor of 'Theological Prenotions'. However, in 1912 he was called to Leipzig as guest professor of history of religion. In this last period he travelled back and forth between the two cities. Even after his appointment as archbishop in 1914 he still had to fulfil his teaching duties in Leipzig. He also got acquainted with the *Christian Socialist movement in 1896, both in Erfurt and in London. (It may be added that much later, in his function as the highest leader of the Swedish national church, he upheld very good relations with the Labour movement although he himself was politically fairly conservative.)

In 1914 Söderblom was appointed Archbishop of Sweden – a somewhat surprising decision by the government, and one not much appreciated within conservative circles. Yet his authority became more and more recognized through the years. His extensive correspondence with personalities of both ecclesiastical and cultural status, in the Nordic countries and abroad, made him the centre of some important networks. In 1921 he became a member of the Swedish Academy, and he was awarded the Nobel Peace Prize in 1930.

Söderblom became one of the most prominent pioneers of the modern ecumenical movement (the future World Council of Churches was part of his vision). As the founder of the Life and Work Movement, which had its first meeting in Stockholm in 1925, he drew the decisive lines of future ecumenical strategy in the field of social ethics (yet he also combined this with a concern for faith and order). His Gifford Lectures in 1931 on 'The Living God', published after his death, became his chief legacy. There he confessed: 'God is alive. I can prove it through the history of religion.' Söderblom was buried close to the high altar of the cathedral of Uppsala in July 1931. (Pope John Paul II paid his reverence to the site during his visit to Sweden in 1989.)

Three basic contributions characterize Söderblom. The first is in his function as scholar and professor. He granted the phenomenological aspects of the history of religion an early profile. He made an important distinction between 'mystics of infinity' and 'mystics of personality'. He defined saints as those who demonstrate that God is a living God. He introduced the history of religion as basic to any theological study. His main concept here was that of 'Revelation'.

The second contribution is a practical one, in his diocese and all over the world, to the self-understanding of the church. He dared to talk about 'Roman Catholicism', 'Greek Catholicism' and 'Evangelical Catholicism'. He took part in the renewal of the Swedish Lutheran Church as a universal 'people's church', furthered by the so-called Young Church Movement. He saw the spirituality of the church as based on the interplay between 'Body and Soul', and thus he also furthered the close relationship between the Swedish Church and the Anglican

Church. Finally, he also saw the fellowship of episcopal *Lutheran churches around the Baltic as ecumenically significant (thus anticipating what is now called the Porvoo agreement).

Thirdly, as an ecumenist Söderblom developed a kind of universal *episcopé*. He took part in the foundation of the World Alliance for Promoting International Friendship through the Churches in 1914, and he supported its national committees. Yet he saw that what became the 'Life and Work' movement was necessary. He furthered its continuing work in Geneva and sent his emissary Nils Ehrenström to its headquarters (later developed into those of the World Council of Churches, where Ehrenström was in charge of the department of Church and Society until Evanston in 1954). Söderblom's correspondence with Constantinople was intense, and so were his efforts (albeit unsuccessful) to draw the Vatican into his ecumenical plans. At the end of the Stockholm conference in 1925, celebrated in the cathedral of Uppsala (1600 years after the *Council of Nicaea), he noted that 'John' was there, and 'Paul' was there, but not yet 'Peter'.

LARS THUNBERG

FURTHER READING: Söderblom's own *oeuvre* is very extensive, though mostly in Swedish (except for his scholarly works in French and German). The Gifford Lectures are a qualified summary of his thinking, published posthumously as *The Living God* (Edinburgh, 1932). The most outstanding study about him is Bengt Sundkler, *Nathan Söderblom: His Life and Work* (Lund, 1968).

Spinoza, Baruch (1632–77)

*Rationalist philosopher who influenced *liberal Protestantism in the eighteenth and nineteenth centuries. He was born 24 November 1632 in Amsterdam to Michael del Espinoza and his second wife, Hana Debora. The Espinozas were Jewish refugees who escaped from religious oppression in Portugal and Spain. In the Low Countries, the father made a handsome living as an importer in the tolerant commercial world of the Dutch Republic. Baruch received a rigorous education under Manasseh ben Israel (1604–57), the spiritual leader of Sephardic Jews in Amsterdam. He studied the Hebrew Scriptures, the New Testament, natural science and philosophy. After his father's death in 1654, Baruch took over the family business with his younger brother Gabriel. On the Bourse

in Amsterdam, he made lifelong friendships with Colligiant and Mennonite businessmen who distrusted established religion and defined faith in Christ as ethical service. His acquaintances included Quaker evangelists to the Jews and Johan de Witt (1625–72), Councillor Pensionary of Holland from 1653 to 1672. Spinoza's circle was anti-monarchist, cosmopolitan, capitalist and internationalist. In 1656, Spinoza was expelled from the Jewish community in Amsterdam for heresy because he called into question the understanding of the nature of God, angels and the soul's immortality. He lost control of the import business to hostile family members. He spurned his inheritance, Latinized his name to Benedict and learned the trade of lens grinding (for which he would become internationally famous). Pressure from Jewish leadership drove Spinoza out of Amsterdam in 1660. With the help of Colligiant friends, he found lodgings near Leiden and then in The Hague. In 1663 he published the only essay in his lifetime under his own name, *Descartes' Principles of Philosophy* (*Renati Decartes Principiorum Philosophiae*), which established his reputation as a philosopher.

In 1670 the *Theological-Political Treatise* (*Tractatus theologico-politicus*) appeared anonymously. Spinoza's authorship was quickly recognized. The work was condemned. In 1672 Johan de Witt was murdered by a mob of supporters of William of Orange (1650–1702) who feared the collapse of Dutch independence following a surprise invasion by the French. This shocking event reinforced Spinoza's suspicion of the uneducated multitude of society. In 1673 Spinoza turned down a chair in philosophy at the University of Heidelberg because he could not subscribe to the requirement that the occupant not disturb 'the publicly established religion'. On 21 February 1677, at the age of forty-four, Spinoza died of tuberculosis. Soon after his death, the *Ethics* (*Ethica ordine geometrico demonstrata*) was published along with his *Treatise on the Correction of the Understanding* (*Tractatus de Intellectus Emendatione*). The *Short Treatise concerning God, Man and his Well-Being* was discovered and published in 1852.

The *Theological-Political Treatise* is a landmark work. It is the first essay on biblical criticism to employ recognizably modern methods of analysis and the first theoretical defence of modern liberal democracy. The *Treatise* argues that the driving force of humanity is the fear of the uncertainty of life. This gives rise to 'superstition': the belief that God is the immediate cause of all things and that the priestly class, rituals and canonical documents of a particular religion can discern and foretell divine decrees. All historical religions, including Judaism and Christianity, exemplify superstition. Superstition is dangerous to society because it worsens the inclination towards cruelty and fanaticism found in all nations and tribes. To defeat superstition, religion needs to be under the control of reason. Reason seeks true virtue, that is, the universal moral characteristics of 'love, joy, peace, temperance, and honest dealing with all men'. To separate true virtue from superstition in Judaism and Christianity requires the critical examination of the Bible. This task is to be undertaken by an educated, independent elite that employs reason to interpret Scripture. Such an elite can arise only in a society that honours education, permits freedom of ideas and gives no group, including the priestly class and dogmatic theologians, the power to censure thought. Democracy is the natural political form of a free society because it alone recognizes that there is no standpoint beyond competing claims of individuals and factions striving to exist and exercise power. Democracy allows the political articulation of the true structure of reality that is characterized by the natural heterogeneity of individual attributes.

Rational biblical criticism is grounded in the distinction between truth and meaning. 'Truth' refers to matters of universal significance that reason is able to discover regardless of time and place. 'Meaning' refers to the cultural expressions of particular peoples bound to time and place. This distinction allows the biblical critic to explain epiphanies of the divine, prophecies and miracles, as well as other elements of superstition, as phenomena of meaning. Truth in the Bible appears whenever there are clear and distinct commands to love God and neighbour. Such commands exemplify true virtue. No one less than Christ himself summarizes the truth of the Scriptures as the teaching to love God and neighbour. Spinoza offers this ostensible divine warrant as a theological rationale for his proposal to subject the interpretation of Scripture to the autonomous biblical critic rather than ecclesiastical officials. The rational critic knows that 'the divinity of Scripture must be established solely from the fact that it teaches true virtue'.

In the *Ethics*, Spinoza defends the idea that true virtue is naturally known by rational understanding. True virtue is grounded in God. Spinoza defines God as that 'substance', outside of which there is no limit, and identifies the divine with nature. God (or nature) is the sum total of individual attributes that form one overall system. God is identical with all there is; he represents immanent reality. The highest good is conforming to the purposes of nature, which means the same as obeying the divine. Because of this claim, Spinoza is often tagged in philosophical textbooks as a 'monist', a philosophical insult coined in the eighteenth century by Christian Wolff (1679–1754). This is misleading. The fact is that Spinoza uses the concept of God to legitimate his vision of the multiplicity of truths in reality. It is the pluralistic condition of reality that is defined as divine. The radical distinction between God and humanity, which is the hallmark of biblical religion, is erased in Spinoza's philosophy. Following Spinoza, the assertion that the divine, the natural and the human are intimately bound up together – this assertion being grounded and defended in the practice of some form of rational biblical criticism – became characteristic of liberal theology.

WALTER SUNDBERG

FURTHER READING: *Texts: A Theological-Political Treatise* and *A Political Treatise* (trans. R.H.M. Elwes; New York, 1955); *On the Improvement of the Understanding; The Ethics; Correspondence* (trans. R.H.M. Elwes; New York, 1955). *Context:* Samuel Lewis Feuer, *Spinoza and the Rise of Liberalism* (Boston, 1958); Yirmiyahu Yovel, *Spinoza and Other Heretics* (2 vols.; Princeton, 1989). *Interpretation:* Richard Kennington (ed.), *The Philosophy of Baruch Spinoza* (Washington, DC, 1980); Steven B. Smith, *Liberalism and the Question of Jewish Identity* (New Haven, 1997); Leo Strauss, *Spinoza's Critique of Religion* (New York, 1965).

Staniloae, Dumitru (1903–93)

Romanian Orthodox theologian, widely considered to be one of the greatest Orthodox theologians in this century. Staniloae was born on 16 November 1903 in the village of Vladeni, near Brasov (in the south-west corner of Transylvania) – a traditional isolated Romanian rural community. His whole outlook was marked by the unique fusion of Orthodoxy and Romanian peasant culture characteristic of this area, with its mingling of poetry, cosmic sensitivity, moral values, Christian faith and ritual forms. Encouraged by his mother, Staniloae went to the theological faculty in Cernauti (northern Bucovina). Here he studied from 1922 to 1927 and received a typical 'academic' westernized theological education. During 1927–29 he spent semesters in Athens, Munich, Paris and Belgrade, learning Greek, French, German and Russian in the process. In Paris he acquired photocopies of the works of *St Gregory Palamas from the manuscripts of the Bibliothèque Nationale. In 1928 he completed a doctoral dissertation on 'The Life and Activity of the Greek Patriarch Dositheos of Jerusalem (1641–1707) and his Relation with the Romanian Principalities' (Cernauti, 1929). He was ordained as a married priest in 1932.

In 1929 Staniloae became professor of dogmatics at the Orthodox Theological Seminary in Sibiu, and in connection with his first lectures he translated the Greek handbook of dogmatics by Chrestos Androutsos (Sibiu, 1930). He was not at all satisfied by its academic Scholasticism, though, and as a reaction he began translating from unpublished manuscripts the *Triads* of St Gregory Palamas. This work was published in parts in Romanian in 1932–33 and 1938. Replying to the learned but hostile studies on Palamism by the Roman Catholic scholar Martin Jugie, Staniloae published his first major work, a historical monograph on *The Life and the Teaching of St. Gregory Palamas* (Sibiu, 1938). He thus became a pioneer in the modern Orthodox revival of Palamism during recent decades (anticipating by two decades the far better known monograph of Fr. J. Meyendorff, 1958).

As editor-in-chief between 1934–44 of the church magazine 'Telegraful Roman' in Sibiu, Staniloae wrote about four hundred articles and involved himself in controversial political discussion connected with the so-called 'great debate'. (In the 1930s the Romanian 'intelligentsia' was deeply divided by the conflict between champions of a rapid modernization of Romania through the adoption of the standards of western democratic civilization and the supporters of a national traditionalist, rural Orthodox country ruled by a right-wing, authoritarian regime.) Given his own conservative peasant roots, Staniloae associated naturally with the nationalist Orthodox circle of intellectuals orbiting round the literary review 'Gandirea' ('The Thought' [1926–44]), becoming close friends with its editor-in-chief, Nichifor Crainic

(1889–1972). In a series of articles in 1935–37, Staniloae criticized both the separation between Orthodoxy and nation (advocated by the academic philosopher C. Radulescu-Motru) and their total identification (asserted by the Orthodox philosopher N. Ionescu). The symbiosis between Orthodoxy and nationalism which Staniloae envisaged (see the articles collected in *Ortodoxie si Romanism* [Sibiu, 1939]) was not explicitly connected with right-wing political extremism and authoritarianism. It was, rather, more in the spirit of the Orthodox nationalist movement promoted in the nineteenth century by the celebrated Metropolitan of Sibiu, Andrei Saguna (1808–73).

Much more radical was Staniloae's sharp critique of the pantheistic religious philosophy and cosmology of the famous Romanian poet and philosopher Lucian Blaga (1895–1962). The articles containing this critique were collected in the pamphlet *Pozitia dlui L. Blaga fata de crestinism si Ortodoxie* ('The Stand of Mr L. Blaga towards Christianity and Orthodoxy' [Sibiu, 1942]). In his dispute with Blaga, Staniloae insisted on the irreducible Christological foundation of the genuine Christian faith. Christology was also the focus of the second major work of Staniloae's Sibiu period: *Iisus Hristos sau restaurarea omului* ('Jesus Christ or the Restoration of Man' [Sibiu, 1943]). The major theme of the book is Christ as the only genuine key to the self-understanding of the human person and of human history. The book presents an interesting dialogue and critical confrontation with the 'dialectical theology' of *Barth and *Brunner and the sophiology of *Bulgakov, from the standpoint of patristic Christology (especially *St Maximus the Confessor) interpreted through the modern categories of existential and personalistic philosophy (Heidegger, *Buber, Lavelle and Blondel).

Along with Florovsky (1893–1979) and Popovitch (1894–1979), but independently and following his own path, Staniloae strived to achieve a 'neopatristic synthesis'. He aimed to surpass both theological *rationalism and speculative *Romanticism or psychological pietism, and to create an existential approach to the genuine tradition of the Church Fathers. He dedicated his whole life to this task both by translating and commenting on patristic works and through his own personal creative synthesis. His extraordinary project of patristic translation and commentary deserves particular mention. This includes the 12 massive volumes of the Romanian extended version with commentaries of the *Greek Philokalia (1782) of St. Nicodemos of the Holy Mountain*, I–IV (Sibiu, 1946–48), V–X (Bucharest, 1976–81), XI–XII (Bucharest, 1991). The project also includes several large volumes (approx. 4,000 pages) containing translation with commentary of the most important works of St Maximus (2 vols.; 1983, 1990); *St Athanasius (2 vols.; 1987, 1988), St Gregory of Nyssa (1982), *St Cyril of Alexandria (3 vols.; 1992–93; other 2 not yet published) and *St Dionysius the Areopagite (*Complete Works with the Scholia*; 1996). Far more than simple translations from the Greek, these critical editions include substantial introductions and abundant theological commentaries in the footnotes and constitute works of interest in their own right.

The Soviet occupation of Romania in 1944 and the violent establishment of the Communist regime there seriously affected Staniloae's personal life and activity. In December 1946 he was forced to move to Bucharest as professor of Christian spirituality. But in 1948 his chair and the publication of the *Philokalia* were suppressed by the Communist censorship, which considered them intolerably obscurantist and retrograde. However, in 1947 Staniloae succeeded in publishing a limited edition of his excellent lectures on *Christian Asceticism and Mysticism* – actually an extremely dense systematic analysis of the spiritual life as an 'anthropology of perfection'. The main texts of the authors of *Philokalia* are interpreted here in the light of the modern psychology and existential analysis of Heidegger, Blondel and Binswanger. The general scheme inserts the Evagrian classification of virtues and passions in the ascensional Dionysian movement from purification through illumination towards union with God by means of contemplation, hesychastic prayer and ecstatic love.

From 1948 to 1973 Staniloae was permitted to give lectures on dogmatics, but only for small groups of doctoral students. He was also allowed to publish a significant number of articles and scholarly studies (some very large and heavily documented) in theological reviews with the restricted circulation of the Orthodox Patriarchate in Bucharest. These articles approached virtually all the main topics of church dogmatics, emphasizing the patristic contribution and not avoiding controversial issues.

In the 1950s, Staniloae was also active in a circle of learned laymen and monks of the Antim monastery in Bucharest concerned with hesychasm, the so-called 'Burning Bush' association. In 1958, all members of this group were arrested and sentenced to years of prison and hard labour. Staniloae himself spent his next five years in prison. He was released in 1963 but did not return to his post at the Bucharest Orthodox Theological Institute until 1964. The price for his reacceptance was a couple of articles stating (with dubious argumentation) the ideological and practical 'convergence' of Orthodox communitarian morality and the 'new' collectivistic realities in Socialist Romania. Another series of similarly 'commissioned' articles denounced the Romanian Greek-Catholic (Uniate) Church, suppressed by the Communists in December 1948, as an attempt to 'destroy the unity of the Romanian nation in Transylvania' while celebrating the traditional 'symphonic' unity between Orthodoxy as a servant church and the Romanian people (i. e., the Communist State). These articles were collected in the book *Uniatismul in Transilvania* (Bucharest, 1973).

After paying this 'price', Staniloae was able to continue his work and to publish articles and books using the climate of limited external openness and internal liberalization in Romania after 1965. He was allowed to travel abroad and also to lecture in the west (Greece, Germany, France and England), where he received many honours. He was also included in the Romanian teams active in various ecumenical dialogues (particularly with the EKD [Die Evangelische Kirche Deutschlands], the Oriental Church and the Roman Catholic Church). His essays approached new topics creatively. Responding to the challenges of the modern world and of ecumenism, they developed a dynamic theology of the world as a 'gift of God to man's responsibility' and also a very interesting theory of an 'open catholicity' (*sobornicitate deschisa*) as a means for approaching the Christian churches by going behind the various confessionalisms. He also suggested solutions to ancient controversies attaching to such theological issues as *Monophysite Christology, *filioque and justification.

In 1976 Staniloae succeeded in obtaining permission to publish the remaining volumes of the Romanian *Philokalia* (in 1978 the church was further authorized to publish a 90-volume series containing Romanian versions of the main works of the Church Fathers), as well as his own original major works.

At the centre of Staniloae's creative work lies the elaboration a theological 'trilogy'. This emerged from Staniloae's intention to offer a fresh assessment of Orthodox dogmatics, spirituality and liturgy (1978, 1981, 1987). The volumes of this trilogy represent Staniloae's creative synthesis, the outstanding productions of his Bucharest period. The first part was released as *Teologia Dogmatica Ortodoxa* (3 vols.; 1978; German translation 1985, 1990, 1994; *The Experience of God* [American version of vol. I; 1995]). The work is a neopatristic Orthodox dogmatic theology written as a huge theological and existential commentary on the basic works of the Church Fathers. Staniloae wrote with the specific intention of 'abandoning the scholastic approach to the dogmas as abstract theoretical utterances by exploring their spiritual significance as a response to the deepest needs of the soul in the search of salvation'. The basic patristic theologies of revelation, Trinity, church, sacraments, humanity and eschatology are interpreted here within a general personalist scheme, stressing as the essence of Christianity the eternal dialogue of love between humanity and God as Trinity. This is a dialogue initiated by creation, fully revealed in Christ and permanently activated in the church's pilgrimage to eschatological fulfilment as a communion of deified persons with the Trinity.

The dogmatic theology which emerges, and which embodies the fruits of Staniloae's meditation over more than half a century, retains in its external division the classic academic scheme of the old handbooks. But its neopatristic and existential style and content make it one of the most original theological works of the twentieth century. It is written also in the spirit of a critical dialogue with the major representatives of modern theology: *Lossky, Evdokimov, Schmemann, Yannaras and Karmiris in the east, but also Barth, *Rahner and *H.U. von Balthasar in the west. Its originality lies in the general vision which it opens up, in the vast orchestration of the topics, and in its unique, powerful and inspiring synthesis appealing for a holistic-existential approach.

In 1981 Staniloae finally succeeded in publishing his 1947 lectures on 'Christian Asceticism and Mysticism' under the less provocative title *Spiritualitatea ortodoxa* ('Orthodox Spirituality' [1981]). This appeared as the third volume of a collective handbook of 'Orthodox Moral Theology'. Apart from minor stylistic changes (words such as 'mystic' and 'mysticism' had to be strictly avoided), the work contains a revised and extended version of the 'Introduction' emphasizing more clearly the ecclesial (objective) nature of Christian spirituality, and it could be regarded as lying in the very heart of the 'tryptichon'.

Staniloae eventually completed the 'trilogy' with the large theological commentary on the Orthodox Divine Liturgy and church symbolism in *Spiritualitate si comuniune in Liturghia Ortodoxa* ('Spirituality and Communion in the Orthodox Liturgy' [Craiova, 1986]). The main theme of this work is the ecclesial dimension of the Orthodox experience of God, especially the 'liturgical ascent of the Christian community towards the Kingdom of God as a Kingdom of the Holy Trinity', which alone enables the 'individual ascent to God' of the mystics.

In his last years Staniloae returned to his initial theological starting point, that is the connection between Christology and anthropology. He planned to write a series of biblical meditations on the image of Christ in the Gospels (only one was finished and published [Sibiu, 1992]), in the epistles and in the prophets; a commentary on John's gospel; and other meditations on Christ (some of these are collected in *Jesus Christ, the Light of the World and Man's Deifier* [Bucharest, 1993]). But the most interesting developments of a Trinitarian anthropology, on the theme of humans as a union of contrasting elements and of a relational foundation for human immortality, are those included in his last great work on man, *Chipul nemuritor al lui Dumnezeu* ('The Immortal Image of God' [Craiova, 1987], completed by the large study on 'Man and God' in *Studii de teologie ortodoxa* [Craiova, 1991]).

There is, however, a serious limitation within Staniloae's thought. He was convinced that the kind of communitarian personalism which he himself advocated was actually a distinctive feature of the Romanian people's unique fusion of Latin and Orthodox elements. He also believed that within Christian dogma as a whole the Romanians had a special vocation to express balance, convergence and universality by going beyond Greek speculativism and Slav mysticism, beyond the various limitations which he deemed to characterize the theologies of east and west. Moreover, he believed the Christian Romanian rural communities to be the best concrete realization of communitarian personalism. These convictions are expressed in one of his last printed books, *Reflections on the Spirituality of the Romanian People* (Craiova, 1992). Notwithstanding such uncritical concessions to a certain sort of ethnocentrism, it can be stated without exaggeration that 'Fr. D. Staniloae occupies a position in present-day Orthodoxy comparable to that of K. Barth in Protestantism or K. Rahner in Catholicism' (K. Ware).

IOAN I. ICA, JR

FURTHER READING: A complete bibliography of the works of Staniloae, together with other essays and references, is now available in the international Festschrift *Persoana si Comuniune, Prinos de cinstire pr. prof. acad. D. Staniloae la implinirea a 90 de ani* (ed. Ioan I. Ica, Jr; Sibiu, 1993), pp. 1–71.

Strauss, David Friedrich (1808–74)

David Friedrich Strauss was born in 1808 in Ludwigsburg, Württemberg. He pursued studies towards ordination at Tübingen, where he also lectured in philosophy under the influence of *Hegel. His first and greatest book, *Das Leben Jesu, kritische bearbeit* (1835, ET *The Life of Jesus Critically Examined* [1846]), was also his most important, and a landmark in New Testament criticism. It provoked a storm of controversy at the time of publication. As a result of the controversy, Strauss was dismissed from his post of *Repetent* (occasional lecturer) at Tübingen. In 1839 he was offered the chair in dogmatics and church history at Zurich, but opposition to his appointment resulted in him being pensioned off before he could begin. His second substantial work, *Die Christiche Glaubenslehre*, was a review of Christian dogma (1840–41). *Das Leben Jesu, für das deutsche Volk bearbeit* (1864, ET *A New Life of Jesus* [1865]) attempted to take into account the latest results of biblical criticism, and in particular *F.C. Baur's criticism that Strauss had not taken into consideration the question of Gospel sources. Strauss's final book, *Der alte und der neue Glaube* (1872, ET *The Old Faith and the New* [1874]), combined *Hegelianism and materialistic metaphysics inspired by Darwinism. Strauss died in 1874.

Strauss's focus in *The Life of Jesus Critically Examined* was theological or dogmatic (or rather, anti-dogmatic), rather than historical. Strauss combined the negative assumption that the causal order excluded the possibility of supernatural intervention in history and, by implication, the miraculous phenomena attested in the Gospel story, with the positive criterion that the representation of such phenomena bore the marks of myth. Myth could be recognized by *form* (e.g., poetry) and *content* (e.g., Jewish legend, genealogy and prediction). By this means he sought to distinguish fact from fiction in the Gospel records concerning Jesus and to give a genetic account of the origin of the writing of the non-historical stories. He judged previous attempts to do this to be unsuccessful. Reimarus had argued that the origins lay in dishonesty and deception: the disciples had hidden Jesus' body and afterwards said that Jesus had risen. H.G. Paulus of Heidelberg argued that, rather than lying, the disciples had misunderstood what had actually happened. The disciples had not really seen Jesus walking on water; he had actually been walking on the side of the shore. For Strauss, the non-historical stories had originated from an unconscious myth-making 'folk' consciousness in which the belief that Jesus was the Messiah led to the supernatural events recorded in the Gospels being derived from the Old Testament. This was the common source of: the virgin birth narratives, the supernatural motifs of Jesus' baptism, the miracles, the transfiguration, his resurrection and ascension. Though Strauss attempted to render a (Hegelian) philosophical interpretation of myth as an early stage of the self-development of 'spirit' or 'Idea' in history, and in this sense preserve traditional dogmatic 'Messianic' Christology, the fact that he dispensed with the crucial historical truth-claims of the Gospel narratives undermined the project from the outset.

Strauss's analysis has been criticized on grounds that his employment of the category of myth was far too broad and undiscriminating. In particular, the work of *Karl Barth, Erich Auerbach and *Hans Frei has indicated that many of the miraculous phenomena – including the resurrection appearances – are not represented in legendary or mythical modes of presentation, but are instead, notwithstanding their subject matter, presented in the form of realistic narrative. The question of their status as historical truth-claims has thereby re-emerged in academic theology. Moreover, it is arguable that the rationality of such truth-claims precludes the validity of Strauss's genetic account in much the same way that the rationality of theistic truth-claims precludes the validity of theories of the origins of religion such as those proposed by *Feuerbach, *Nietzsche and Freud.

NEIL B. MACDONALD

FURTHER READING: *Text: The Life of Jesus Critically Examined* (ed. with intro. by Peter C. Hodgson; London, 1973). *Studies:* Hans W. Frei, 'David Friedrich Strauss', in *Nineteenth-Century Religious Thought in the West* (ed. Smart, et al.; Cambridge, 1985); Horton Harris, *David Friedrich Strauss and his Theology* (Cambridge, 1973); Marilyn Chapin Massey, 'The Literature of Young Germany and D.F. Strauss's *Life of Jesus*', *J Rel* 57.3 (July 1979), pp. 298–323; Albert Schweitzer, *The Quest of the Historical Jesus: A Critical Study of Its Progress from Reimarus to Wrede* (Baltimore, MD, 1998); Claude Welch, *Protestant Thought in the Nineteenth Century*, I (New Haven, 1972).

Suárez, Francisco de (1548–1617)

Jesuit philosopher, theologian and jurist, the unofficial master of *Jesuit theology. Suárez's principal works grew out of his teaching and expounding of *Aristotle and *Aquinas in Jesuit colleges in Spain and Rome (*De deo incarnato*, 1590, *Disputationes metaphysicae*, 1597). In other works, Suárez contributed to contemporary theological controversy. He wrote treatises on grace and freedom during the *De auxiliis* controversy (published posthumously). His *De defensione fidei* (1613), written at the request of Pope Paul V, argued against the views on the divine right of kings held by James I of England (this work was welcomed by Philip II of Spain, burned by royal command on the steps of St Paul's, London, and prohibited by the parliament of Paris).

Suárez's scholarship is prodigious and erudite; he noted exhaustively and dispassionately the opinions of the patristic and medieval writers before offering his own judgement. To assist this process, he developed the practice of attaching theological notes, or indices of doctrinal authority, to theological propositions. Though closest to Aquinas, Suárez accepted key elements from Scotism (voluntarism, univocity of being, autonomy of philosophy). He employed precise distinctions, where possible, to try to reconcile Aquinas with *Scotus and the *nominalists.

Suárez contributed significantly to the establishment of metaphysics as a distinct discipline. The *Disputationes metaphysicae* became a classic text in both Catholic and Protestant universities in the seventeenth and eighteenth centuries. 'Suárez classes' were established in several universities, including Valladolid, Salamanca (1720), Alcalá (1734); some scholastic authors began to write 'ad mentem Sáii'. *Spinoza, Leibniz, Wolff, *Berkeley, *Grotius, Schopenhauer and Vico were familiar with and, to some extent, influenced by his thought. Suárez presented metaphysics as an organic whole for the first time on this scale (not as a commentary on Aristotle). Metaphysics was accorded its own position, anterior to (and not within) theology; Suárez avoided or apologized for digressions on theological topics. Although he saw metaphysics as Christian, as an instrument of theology, and although he explicitly favoured opinions most consistent with devotion and doctrine, Suárez's method inevitably contributed to the separation of theology and philosophy, of faith and reason. In this, his contribution to the advent of modernism may be judged as significant as that of *Descartes.

On the much-debated issue of the motive for the incarnation, Suárez sought to reconcile the opinions of Scotus and Aquinas by means of a distinction between the order of intention and the order of execution. In the order of intention, God chose to complete and perfect the work of creation with the incarnation of the Son. It was God's initial intention to communicate himself *ad extra* through his Son, who is the head and the first of creation. By his knowledge of future conditionals (the divine *scientia media*), God planned the incarnation of the Son as the crown and completion of creation, whichever kind of creation came to be.

In the order of execution, God chose to execute the incarnation by way of redemption, by the way of humble suffering and redemptive incarnation rather than the way of triumph and glory; this way, Suárez argued, is most pleasing to divine mercy, justice and wisdom. In a sense, once God had 'decided' that the way of redemption was the best, then he was bound to create a world in which the conditions for that outcome existed: the world of original justice, with divine permission for original sin. Although original sin is the responsibility of Adam and Eve, it is envisaged and permitted by God, and the initiative remains with God.

Suárez claimed to have worked his way back to Aquinas without losing the best of Scotus: the purpose of the incarnation is the manifestation of Christ as head of creation (Scotus), but this was most realizable, and was indeed realized as Scripture teaches (Aquinas), by way of redemption. The latter achieves the former most perfectly, therefore the two distinct moments of predestination are indivisible.

Although taking no formal part, Suárez was active behind the scenes in the *De auxiliis* controversy – in which, broadly speaking, the Jesuits accused the Dominicans, especially Báñez, of *Calvinism and the Dominicans accused the Jesuits, especially *Molina, of *Pelagianism. Suárez's elaboration of Molina's system of congruism, which seeks to understand the Christian life as a partnership between human freedom (independence) and divine grace (dependence on God), became the official Jesuit position after 1617. According to Suárez, God does not cause free human acts (as in the Dominican view). Rather, by his knowledge of future conditionals (*scientia media*), he brings about the salvation of the elect by granting to them particular graces, in accordance with the particular human circumstances in which he foresees those graces will be put to best use (*gratia congrua*). Although insisting, in this scheme, that the will becomes the proximate cause of conversion, Suárez nonetheless maintained a doctrine of predestination antecedent to foreseen merits.

Suárez must also be counted amongst the founders of international law, and his greatest contribution and widest influence may be in the field of jurisprudence (principally *De legibus*, 1612). He was a powerful advocate of the principle of subsidiarity in civil society, insisting that the powers of the state originate in the free consent of the people, and that the source of authority in all societies resides in the community. His doctrine of *ius gentium*, or international natural law, is based on the principle of a universal love, transcending all distinctions of nationality or race and antecedent to all positive political determinations.

MICHAEL O'CONNOR

FURTHER READING: J.-F. Courtine, *Suárez et le système de la métaphysique* (Paris, 1990); J. Gracia, 'Francisco Suárez: The Man in History', *Am Cath Ph Q* 65 (1991), pp. 259–66; B. Hamilton, *Political Thought in Sixteenth-Century Spain: A Study of the Political Ideas of Vitoria, De Soto, Suárez and Molina* (Oxford, 1963); J. Iturrioz, 'Biografia Suareciana', *Pensamiento* 4 (1948), pp. 31–89; L. Mahieu, *François Suárez: Sa Philosophie et les Rapports qu'elle a avec sa Théologie* (Paris, 1921); J. Montag, 'Revelation: The False Legacy of Suárez', in *Radical Orthodoxy* (ed. Milbank, Pickstock and Ward; London, 1999); R. De Scoraille, *François Suárez de la Compagnie de Jésus* (2 vols.; Paris, 1912, 1913).

Symeon the New Theologian (949–1022)

Byzantine monastic reformer, mystical theologian and hymnographer. His political career in Constantinople led to high rank in the imperial service, but at the age of twenty-eight he entered the Studios monastery to become a disciple of the spiritual elder Symeon Eulabes. After a year at the Studios he moved to the monastery of St Mamas, where he was made abbot. According to his biographer Nicetas Stethatos, there was at least one revolt against the discipline Symeon imposed upon his monks during the 25 years he was in charge at St Mamas. Around 1003 he began to clash with the patriarch of Constantinople on several matters, notably the saintly cult he had established for the elder Symeon, and he was obliged to resign as abbot. Forced to leave Constantinople after a trial in 1009, Symeon spent the rest of his life in exile at the monastery of St Macrina, across the Bosporus, which he rebuilt with the aid of funds donated by wealthy followers.

Symeon was very critical of those who claimed that no one now could keep the gospel commandments and be as worthy of grace as the apostles. For him, the worst kind of heresy was not to believe that the Christian life was a living encounter with the risen Christ. He declared repeatedly that all Christians were capable of knowing God directly. Although it was not the custom in Byzantium for theologians to speak openly of their own religious experiences, Symeon's writings contain many references to his. Yet he did not mention them in order to bolster his own standing, as he declared himself unworthy of the grace to write about his experiences, but to encourage others in their quest for spiritual perfection. His honesty did not find favour with those of his contemporaries who considered that he was setting himself up as equal with the apostles.

The issue of spiritual authority was one that concerned Symeon throughout his life. His elder Symeon Eulabes was a controversial figure who attracted criticism for his eccentric behaviour both in and out of the Studios monastery. He appears to have exhibited many of the characteristics of a holy fool, such as consorting with prostitutes in order to convert them and appearing naked without shame. In defence of his spiritual father, Symeon interprets his unusual behaviour in terms of his charismatic gifts and personal authority as a religious teacher. He speaks of his complete dispassion (*apatheia*) and discerning judgement (*diakrisis*) in matters relating to the spiritual life. In the eastern tradition of the spiritual elder, the thoughts (*logismoi*) of the disciple are disclosed and confessed on a daily basis. For Symeon, absolute obedience to an elder is a prerequisite for spiritual development within the monastic life. In turn, he tried to embody that same compassion and concern for his own monks that he himself discerned in Symeon Eulabes.

Symeon speaks of his religious experiences as visions of divine light, and in this he anticipates the writings of *Gregory Palamas in the fourteenth century. The mystical theology of Palamas was very much a synthesis of Symeon and other Byzantine writers on the nature of hesychast spirituality. Although the ultimate state of contemplative prayer is apophatic and imageless, Symeon mentions having visions of the mother of God and Symeon Eulabes. In his *Catechetical Discourses* he frequently calls upon his monks to practise repentance and humility. There is a persistent theme of contrition and mourning throughout Symeon's writings, which draws upon earlier writers such as John Climacus and Isaac of Nineveh. He seems personally to have known the gift of tears, and in his statements on compunction (*penthos*) he claims that Christians should never receive communion without tears.

Symeon's title 'The New Theologian' has been variously interpreted. The accusation of 'newness' or 'innovation' may have been made by those opposed to his radical, although in fact traditional, interpretation of Christian monasticism. He is also known as Symeon the Younger (*neos*) to distinguish him from the elder Symeon Eulabes. 'New' (*neos*) also distinguishes him from the elder Symeon, while 'Theologian' refers to the experiential nature of his teaching; the word '*theologos*' in Byzantium meaning one who knows God not only by discourse but by direct experience. This title also demonstrates his esteem in relation to John the Divine and Gregory Nazianzen, the only other two theologians to whom the title 'Theologian' is traditionally ascribed.

KEN PARRY

FURTHER READING: A. Golitzin, *St Symeon the New Theologian: On the Mystical Life. The Ethical Discourses* (3 vols.; New York, 1995–97); H.J.M. Turner, *St. Symeon the New Theologian and Spiritual Fatherhood* (Leiden, 1990); B. Krivocheine, *St. Symeon the New Theologian: Life, Spirituality, Doctrine* (New York, 1986); P.A. McGuckin, *Symeon the New Theologian: The Practical and Theological Chapters and the Three Theological Discourses* (Kalamazoo, 1982); C.J. DeCatanzaro, *Symeon the New Theologian: The Discourses* (London, 1980).

Temple, William (1881–1944)

William Temple was the younger son of Beatrice (née Lascelles) and Frederick Temple (1821–1902), Archbishop of Canterbury, 1896–1902. Educated at Rugby and Balliol, he was fellow of Queen's College, Oxford, 1904–10. He became bishop of Manchester (1921–29), archbishop of York (1929–42) and Canterbury (1942–44).

He revered both his parents. His father initiated him into the resources of the Anglican tradition, and especially the liberal catholic sense of incarnation, church, worship and sacrament. Rugby and Balliol stimulated both his intellect and social conscience. At Oxford he was immersed in the dominant British *Hegelian tradition, especially by Edward Caird, Master of Balliol, with his stress on personality. Temple developed a Christian philosophy. In *Mens Creatrix* (London, 1917) he declared the philosophic task was to think clearly and comprehensively about the problems of life. He assumed that the universe was rational, and that the human mind could in principle grasp it whole. The world's principle of unity was not purely intellectual, but it embraced imagination and conscience too: the sciences, the arts, morality and religion. These all converged, yet did not meet, in an all-inclusive system of truth. Temple then adopted the Christian hypothesis, centrally the incarnation, to supply the missing unity.

The shock of the First World War did not deter Temple from his search. In *Christus Veritas* (London, 1924) he worked from the world to Christian faith, but he also confessed that he was writing from an avowedly Christian standpoint. Integral here were four social principles: the dignity and freedom of each individual; fellowship; service; and sacrifice. These were deployed at the 1924 ecumenical Conference on Christian Politics, Economics and Citizenship (COPEC), chaired by Temple, to make critiques of society and suggest broad directions for its future.

The idealism of COPEC was called into question first by the miners' strike of 1926 and the unsuccessful attempt of a group led by Temple to intervene, and then by the economic crises of 1929 onwards. Temple's Gifford Lectures, published as *Nature, Man and God* (London, 1934), comprised his most mature work of Christian philosophy. Tracing the emergence of mind and spirit from matter, he argued for a sacramental universe and invoked the notion of purpose to claim theism alone could offer a satisfying explanation of such a universe. The importance of character and the radical nature of human evil were also prominent: human beings needed consistently to direct their purposes to God, but they pursued the wrong ends.

This thinking was sharpened by the spectacle of Nazi power and by Temple's growing contacts with European and North American theologians such as *Emil Brunner and Reinhold Niebuhr, particularly for the conference on Church, Community and State at Oxford in 1937. In the late 1930s Temple wrote that it was no longer possible to aspire to a Christocentric synthesis, for much in this evil world was irrational and unintelligible. Christians were being pressed from a theology of incarnation to one of redemption. The task was not to explain the world but to convert it. This had to be the work of divine grace.

Temple's change of mind was not simple. He did not just repudiate his earlier quest. His social principles were at the heart of an enquiry he initiated in 1934 into long-term unemployment, and they were repeated in *Christianity and Social Order* (Harmondsworth, 1942), which summarized his social theology (though sacrifice is omitted as beyond the capacity of nations). However, he did lay greater stress on the need to face reality: for expertise over technical questions, and for Christians to repudiate utopianism in politics and to pursue justice rather than love, by harnessing self-interest and checking their narrower loyalties with wider ones. Temple's *Readings in St. John's Gospel* (London, 1939–40, but the fruit of many years' meditation) affirmed the materiality and sacramentality of the Christian religion, centred on the light of the incarnate Christ shining in the darkness of the world.

Temple also responded to the Anglo-Catholic Christendom Group, which included *V.A. Demant and T.S. Eliot and was trying to define an authentically Christian social order against totalitarianism and liberalism. He gave the group prominence at the Malvern Conference of 1941, commended study of the catholic tradition of natural law, and in 1943 addressed the Aquinas Society on *Thomism and modern needs. 'What Christians Stand for in the Secular World' (1944, in *Religious Experience* [London, 1958]), which Temple wished to be remembered by, gave hints of a theology of the cross. He spoke not of principles but of basic decisions: for God who has spoken, for neighbour, for man as rooted in nature, for history, for the gospel and the church. Following Demant he agreed the need was not to proclaim ideals and appeal to the will to attain them, but to heal the gulf between people's ideals and their ultimate assumptions. Following Niebuhr he stressed the need to face egoistic use of power and to pursue justice.

Temple's strength lies both in his determination to see the whole of life in Christian perspective, and also in his acknowledgement that the possibility of synthesis had slipped away and a fresh start was needed. He was right to seek positive relationships between theology and philosophy (although he was ambiguous in his views) and indeed every aspect of human experience. He was also right to sketch a reworking of the Thomist tradition for modern times, thus anticipating *Vatican II. His ideas on a sacramental universe have been influential, for example with John Macquarrie; recent interest in the arts and theology confirms Temple's concern, as does current emphasis on the growth of character within the worshipping community of the church.

Temple certainly overplayed his philosophical hand. As Demant and Donald MacKinnon argued, the incarnation was not the crowning glory of evolution but more a profound cutting across the flow of history and so inseparable from the cross. It is significant that subsequent English social theology (e.g. by Ronald Preston) has stiffened the thought of Temple with Niebuhr. In today's vastly more pluralistic world, the challenge of rethinking which Temple recognized remains pressing.

ALAN M. SUGGATE

FURTHER READING: R. Craig, *Social Concern in the Thought of William Temple* (London, 1963); J.F. Fletcher, *William Temple: Twentieth-Century Christian* (New York, 1963); F.K. Hare (ed.), *The Experiment of Life: Science and Religion* (Toronto, 1982), papers at a Temple centenary conference at Trinity College, Toronto, 1981; F.A. Iremonger, *William Temple, Archbishop of Canterbury, His Life and Letters* (London, 1948); J. Kent, *William Temple: Church, State and Society in Britain 1880–1950* (Cambridge, 1992); C.W. Lowry, *William Temple: An Archbishop for All Seasons* (Washington, DC, 1982); J.F. Padgett, *The Christian Philosophy of William Temple* (The Hague, 1974); W.R. Rinne, *The Kingdom of God in the Thought of William Temple* (Abo, 1966); A.M. Suggate, *William Temple and Christian Social Ethics Today* (Edinburgh, 1987); O.C. Thomas, *William Temple's Philosophy of Religion* (London, 1961).

Teresa of Avila (1515–82)

Teresa was born in Avila, Spain on 28 March 1515, the daughter of Alonso de Cepeda and his second wife, Beatriz de Ahumada. During her lifetime, it was thought by some that her family was descended from a 'Hebrew Christian' family, followers of Judaism who were forced to convert to Roman Catholicism, although Teresa said simply that she was the daughter of God. There exists today some evidence that she was, indeed, from a family of *conversos*.

Early in her life, Teresa had imbibed the fervour of Spanish Catholicism, which focused on heroism and willingness to die a martyr. Memories of the Visigoth invasions and Muslim victories turned popular devotion towards salvation by suffering. At the age of seven, with her brother Rodrigo, Teresa attempted to leave Avila to go to Moorish lands where they might die a martyr's death. Only the intervention of an uncle who happened to be passing stopped them from the trip.

An intelligent and gifted child, Teresa could read and, by age twelve, was reading the Bible and many novels of adventure and romance. When Teresa was about fourteen her mother died, leaving ten children. Teresa was disconsolate. She begged the Blessed Virgin to become her mother and took comfort in her sense of the Virgin's care for her. Don Alonso entrusted Teresa to the *Augustinian nuns at Santa Maria de Gracia in 1531 where she studied as one of the *doncellas de piso*, a 'boarding scholar'. At this time, the reform of *Luther had affected many of the convents of Augustinian nuns in Germany but had little influence in Santa Maria. The convent retained strict observance. Although Teresa's intellectual and spiritual life flourished, her health failed and she returned home at age seventeen. While recuperating Teresa read the letters of *St Jerome and decided to enter the convent, a decision which her father opposed. On 2 November 1535, with the help of one of her brothers, Teresa ran away and entered the Carmelite Monastery of the Incarnation at Avila. The following year she received the habit. Shortly after, Teresa's health began to fail. Her condition worsened despite many attempts at a cure, and she fell into a four-day coma. Although she revived, her legs remained paralyzed for three years. In 1537 she returned to the Convent of the Incarnation.

For about eighteen years Teresa lived the regular life of the convent and, gradually, she began to have mystical experiences in prayer. For much of her life Teresa searched for an intelligent confessor to whom she could speak with ease. *Jesuit and Dominican priests were often her confessors. Her life of prayer and mysticism was often criticized by her confessors as coming from the devil. When Peter of Alcantara, in 1560, affirmed her visions and prayer as God's work and counselled her to continue, Teresa experienced relief and new interest in growth in prayer.

Convents in the sixteenth century were large, with as many as 120 members. Reading materials frequently included adventure novels, and many Sisters spent part of every day in the 'speak room' where they would visit with relatives and townspeople. The conversation was often of the 'things of God', but this interaction did interfere with regular community life. In 1560, after a conversation with some other friends, Teresa began to think seriously that a return to the primitive Carmelite Rule was both possible and necessary. Shortly after, she had a vision in which she understood that Christ wanted her to establish just such a foundation and she began to plan for its establishment. At first, Teresa received wide encouragement. Quickly, however, the opinion changed – largely in response to the protests of the townspeople. Ultimately she received permission from Rome to start a new Reformed or 'discalced' foundation. With the help of her sister and brother-in-law, Teresa secured a house and began to ready it as a convent. Although she had been assigned to Toledo, Teresa nevertheless continued her plans. On 24 August 1562 the new convent, San Jose, was established, under the jurisdiction of the local bishop. There followed five peaceful years in her life during which she wrote the *Way of Perfection* and the *Meditations on the Canticle*. Her raptures and visions were frequent and noted by others.

In 1567, the Carmelite General Superior commanded Teresa to establish other convents. Soon convents were established at Medina del Campo (1567), Malagon (1568), Valladolid (1568), Toledo and Pastrana (1569), Salamanca (1570) and Alba de Tormes (1571). While going to Toledo, Teresa met *John of the Cross, then a young priest, who was to be her friend and confidant for the rest of her life.

Hounded by criticism and misunderstanding all her life, in 1575 Teresa was ordered by the general chapter to retire to a convent. During this period Teresa wrote much of her famous *Interior Castle*. This book is generally considered her mature thought on the spiritual life. The interior castle is the soul, in which the Trinity dwells at the centre. The soul is invited to travel or 'journey' through the various rooms in the castle, seeking closer and closer intimacy with God.

There is evidence from her writings that Teresa saw her reform as a part of the larger reform of the Roman Catholic Church begun in the Council of Trent (1545–62). Her writings indicate that the strict poverty of her group was a witness on the part of the Catholic Church that the poverty of the Lord still lived in the Catholic Church.

On 4 October 1582, Teresa died in Alba. Several miracles had been attributed to her in life, and many were attributed to her after her death. It is believed that her body is still intact. Gregory XV canonized Teresa as a saint in the Roman Catholic Church in 1622. In 1617, the Spanish Parliament had declared her the patroness of Spain. Teresa now holds the title of 'Doctor of the Church' in the Roman Catholic Church.

LORETTA DEVOY, OP

FURTHER READING: *Text: The Collected Works of St. Teresa of Avila* (ed. and trans. Kieran Kavanaugh and Otilio Rodriguez; 3 vols.; Washington, DC, 1976–85). *Studies:* Joseph Chorpenning, 'The Literary and Theological Method of *The Interior Castle*', *J Hisp Ph* 3 (1979), pp. 121–33; Stephen Clissold, *St. Teresa of Avila* (New York, 1982); J.M. Cohen, *The Life of Saint Teresa* (London, 1957); Carole Slade, *St. Teresa of Avila: Author of a Heroic Life* (Berkeley, 1995); Catherine Swietlicki, 'The Problematic Iconography of Teresa of Avila's *Interior Castle*', *St Mys* 11 (1988), pp. 37–47; William Thomas Walsh, *Saint Teresa of Avila* (Rockford, IL, 1944).

Tertullian (c. 160 – c. 220)

North African theologian and controversialist who was writing from c. 196 to c. 212. Little or nothing is known for certain about his life. He must have come from a well-to-do family, and he was probably born in Carthage, where he was educated and where he lived his adult life. He was married, but we do not know of any children. Some have thought that he was a presbyter of the local church, and that he was also a lawyer, but neither of these claims can be substantiated from contemporary evidence.

More controversially, the nature of his relationship to the Phrygian sect known to us as *Montanism is unclear. It is usually thought that Tertullian became a Montanist about halfway through his literary career, and there are some who believe that he later left the Montanists to found his own sect, known in later years as the Tertullianists. However, Tertullian's Montanism was rather different from that of Phrygia, and it is misleading to think of him simply as a convert to the sect. There is no evidence that he ever broke with the main church at Carthage, and his writings were preserved virtually intact by future generations – which would be odd if he were a genuine schismatic. His works were not actually condemned until 496. The condemnation had little effect, and he has always been regarded as an important, if somewhat eccentric, Father of the Western church.

Tertullian was probably the first Christian who wrote in Latin, and the number of his surviving works outstrips that of any Christian writer before the fourth century. Equally impressive is their extraordinary range, covering subjects as varied as the nature of the soul, the doctrine of the Trinity, chastity and the Roman circus. Slightly more than thirty of his writings survive, plus one or two others that are attributed to him in the manuscripts but were probably written by someone else. There is a tradition that he also wrote in Greek but, if he did, none of those works has survived, nor has he ever been more than a name in the Greek church. Tertullian is famous for his pithy Latin, which is eminently quotable, and for his controversial style, which he employed to great effect against both pagans and Christian heretics.

Tertullian's theology is characterized by its dependence on Roman legal terminology. Words like *persona* and *sacramentum* (oath) were taken over by him and used in a Christian context for the first time. It is no exaggeration to say that the basic theological vocabulary of western Christendom, with its typically legal cast, was largely created by him. His theological constructions stood up well in the face of the controversies of the fourth and fifth centuries, and a modern reader can study Tertullian's dogmatic works without sensing that they were written at a time when classical orthodoxy had not yet been defined.

Tertullian's extant works may be divided into the following categories:

1. Philosophical. These works include his lengthy and impressive treatise on the soul (*De anima*), in which he defends the Stoic view that the soul is really only a highly refined form of matter. Tertullian is often thought to be an anti-philosophical writer, largely because of his famous statement: 'What has Athens to do with Jerusalem? Or the Academy with the Church?', but this is a misunderstanding. He was deeply, and at times viciously, opposed to *Platonism, which after his time came to dominate Christian thought, but he made considerable use of Stoic principles and even claimed that the pagan philosopher Seneca (d. 65) had been 'frequently one of us' (*saepe noster*).

2. Dogmatic. Tertullian wrote on the incarnation of Christ in a way which clearly foreshadows the decision of the Council of *Chalcedon in 451, though he was less precise than later writers were to be about Christ's two natures. However, his most important doctrinal work was his treatise against the unknown heretic Praxeas (which may have been a nickname for someone else, possibly Noetus of Smyrna). In this treatise, Tertullian elaborates his doctrine of the Trinity against those who believed that 'Son' and 'Spirit' were no more than labels for the One God in his different functions. Mocking those who would thus crucify the Father, as he put it, and expel the Holy Spirit, Tertullian portrayed a Trinity of divine Persons co-existing within the One God. In his mind, God was primarily a 'substance', which he called *holiness*, and the three Persons could be identified as *holy, holy, holy*, according to the prophetic vision of Isaiah (Is. 6:3).

3. Apologetic. Here Tertullian followed the tradition of the second-century Greek *Apologists, though with his own typical slant. He accused the Roman authorities of inconsistency in their treatment of Christians, and he argued that they should be regarded as model citizens who upheld the ancient Roman virtues of loyalty and chastity better than anyone else. It is in these writings that Tertullian developed his theology of martyrdom, which he regarded as the foundation of the church. He encouraged believers to prepare themselves by an ascetic lifestyle, so that when they were thrown to the lions they would be able to demonstrate the courage and self-denial that Christ expected of them.

4. Polemic. In this category are the many writings directed against popular Christian heretics. Tertullian was a major opponent of the *Gnostics, and he ridiculed their fantasies. He clung firmly to the literal sense of the Old Testament, and he spoke out strongly against the use of allegory in biblical interpretation. He was particularly fierce in his denunciation of *Marcion, who rejected the Old Testament altogether, and Tertullian's five books on the subject remain our chief source for that heretic's beliefs.

5. Didactic. This category covers his moral treatises, directed mainly at Christian women. Tertullian was a firm believer in modesty and chastity, even within the marriage bond. He held that matrimony was a God-given ordinance, and that a couple who refrained from sexual intercourse were more highly blessed than ordinary celibates, because although they were exposing themselves to daily temptation, they were resisting it. Tertullian also taught that baptism should be deferred until later life – not for the reasons given by modern Baptists, but because he was afraid that a baptized child would subsequently sin and therefore lose his salvation. As far as Tertullian was concerned, the only way that post-baptismal sin could be forgiven was by martyrdom – the baptism of fire.

6. Miscellaneous. Tertullian wrote a satire on academic dress, which he regarded as frivolous and egotistical. He also advised Christians to stay away from the circus and to avoid taking the military oath to the emperor.

Because of his robust style, Tertullian is often thought to have been an extremist in his views, but this is not altogether fair. For example, he avoided the asceticism which was then becoming increasingly common in the east, and he urged Christians to stand and fight for their cause within the society of their day – not to run away from it and hide, as so many were understandably inclined to do. Above all, he was concerned for holiness and purity in the church, and this imperative guided his approach to everything he wrote. Even today, his works are never boring or beyond the understanding of ordinary readers, and his directness continues to challenge the faith and commitment to Christ of all those who read him.

GERALD BRAY

FURTHER READING: T. Barnes, *Tertullian* (Oxford, 1971); R. Braun, *Deus Christianorum: Recherches sur le Vocabulaire Doctrinal de Tertullien* (Paris, 1962); G.L. Bray, *Holiness and the Will of God* (London, 1979); J. Moingt, *La Théologie Trinitaire de Tertullien* (4 vols.; Paris, 1965–69); D. Rankin, *Tertullian and the Church* (Cambridge, 1994); C. Trevett, *Montanism* (Cambridge, 1996).

Theodore of Mopsuestia (c. 350–428)

Theodore was born into a wealthy Antiochene family c. 350. Along with his friend, *St John Chrysostom, he studied under the pagan rhetor Libanius and later under Christian ascetic Diodore of Tarsus in Antioch. After a brief departure from Diodore's monastery in pursuit of marriage and a career in law, Chrysostom was able to persuade Theodore to return. He continued his studies under Diodore until 378. In 381 he was ordained to the priesthood in Antioch and in 392, he was consecrated bishop of Mopsuestia in Cilicia. His brother Polychronius likewise pursued a career in the church and was consecrated bishop of Apamea in Syria. Theodore died in 428, the same year that *Nestorius was consecrated as the bishop of Constantinople.

Theodore remains one of the most famous representatives of the Antiochene school of exegesis. He has been greatly honoured by the Nestorian church as one of its most revered teachers and is known to them as 'The Interpreter'. It is not surprising, then, that Nestorian writers have provided the most important available lists of Theodore's writings. The most important of such lists may be found in the thirteenth-century *Chronicle of Seert*, as well as in the writings of the fourteenth-century Nestorian Christian, Ebedjesu. Theodore's earliest work was a commentary on the book of Psalms written at the age of twenty. He largely rejected the allegorical interpretations common among those of the Alexandrian school of exegesis. He held that each Psalm should be understood in its historical context and he therefore rejected messianic interpretations of the Psalms.

His commentaries on the Gospels of Matthew and Luke have survived in numerous fragments, while his commentary on the Gospel of John has survived in a Syriac version. Theodore wrote commentaries on the Pauline epistles which have survived in fragmentary form as well.

Among Theodore's most significant non-exegetical treatises are his 16 catechetical homilies, which are concerned with the tenets of faith as found in the *Nicene Creed as well as teachings on the Eucharist, baptism and the Lord's Prayer. His work entitled 'On the Incarnation' was frequently quoted in Christian sources of late antiquity and was written against the teachings of *Arius, *Eunomius and *Apollinarius. Unfortunately, only fragments of this work remain.

During his lifetime, Theodore was considered an important orthodox writer. He was a firm defender of the Council of Constantinople in 381, however, shortly after his death, his writings began to be appealed to by both *Pelagians and Nestorians. Scholars remain divided as to whether Theodore was an originator of Nestorianism.

As a theologian who wrote prior to the *Council of Chalcedon, his Christological terminology was understandably imprecise. His Christology distinguished between Christ's two natures using the formula of 'Word and assumed man'. His problem was explaining *how* the two natures were united in one Person, constituting one Son. He attempted to do so by stating that the union of the two natures occurs *kat' eudokian* (at will) in order to avoid the notion that Christ's freedom from sin was a result of his physical union with God. However, this gave the general impression that he presupposed duality. This was further reinforced by his understanding that this unity was *sunapheia* (conjunction) instead of *henōsis* (union). Finally, pastorally speaking, his insistence that Mary was more properly *anthrōpotokos* (man-bearer), and not *theotokos* (God-bearer), raised the ire of many.

Following the Council of Ephesus in 431, Theodore's orthodoxy began to be seriously questioned. *St Cyril of Alexandria issued strong condemnations of Theodore on the charges of Nestorianism, though Cyril readily admitted that Nestorius was a student of Theodore and not vice versa. He was ultimately anathematized by the Fifth Oecumenical Council in 553.

JAMES V. SMITH

FURTHER READING: *Texts: PG* 66 (Paris, 1846); *Commentary of Theodore of Mopsuestia on the Nicene Creed* (ed. A. Mingana; Woodbrooke Studies 5; Cambridge, 1932); *Commentary of Theodore of Mopsuestia on the Lord's Prayer and on the Sacraments of Baptism and the Eucharist* (ed. A. Mingana; Woodbrooke Studies 6; Cambridge, 1933). *Studies:* Robert Devresse, *Essai sur Theodore de Mopsueste* (Rome, 1948); Rowan A. Greer, *Theodore of Mopsuestia: Exegete and Theologian* (London, 1961); Richard A. Norris, *Manhood and Christ: A Study in the Christology of Theodore of Mopsuestia* (Oxford, 1963); Francis A. Sullivan, *The Christology of Theodore of Mopsuestia* (Rome, 1956); Dimitri Z. Zaharopoulos, *Theodore of Mopsuestia on the Bible* (New York, 1989).

Theodoret (c. 393 – c. 458)

Born in Syrian Antioch c. 393 to a pious family, at twenty-three Theodoret sold his inheritance to join the community monastic life at Nicerte. His previously acquired scholarly skills served the church in promoting the texts of the four Gospels, over Tatian's harmony, among the Syrians. From 423 Theodoret was bishop of Cyrrhus, two days march from Antioch but under the jurisdiction of Hierapolis and on a cultural fault line (Hellenistic-Semitic). Sensitive to the local culture, he appointed educated teachers who were distanced from 'Christendom'. Efforts to win over the still largely pagan small towns and heretics meant that even the Jews were evangelized. He kept monastic status so he could be invited into other dioceses to preach.

In the controversy over the views of *Nestorius, Theodoret held *Cyril to be *Apollinarian (and thus *Arian in the sense that the divinity of Christ was brought low by mixing with the humanity in Cyril's account). He warned against the use in Christology of the anthropological body-soul metaphor beloved of Alexandrians. He declared that Mary was only Christ-bearer (*christotokos*), but the alternative (Cyrillian) title of 'God-bearer' (*theotokos*) was affirmed at Ephesus in 431. Now Theodoret sought to moderate his theology. He was so successful that two of his works survived under his enemy Cyril's name! He was involved in reconciling the parties in the process which led to the Formula of Reunion of 433, although he did not himself sign this since it still required a condemnation of Nestorius (*Ep.* 171). When conflict broke out again in 449, Theodoret was deposed. He only regained his see in 451 at *Chalcedon, in return for agreeing the condemnation of Nestorius's *De sancta et vivifica Trinitate* and *De incarnatione Domini*. He died c. 458.

Theodoret produced four types of works. Firstly, he wrote spiritual histories of monks and ecclesiastical history. Theodoret was keen to show the Mesopotamian origins of Syrian monasticism. The chapters on Simeon Stylites were written last of all in 444. Theodoret should be placed in the tradition of spiritual theologians.

Secondly, he wrote anti-heretical literature and *De Providentia*. His 'Therapeutic for Maladies' was written early, before the expressly theological disputes of 430 onwards. The plan was: (1) faith as making sense, (2) metaphysical/theological treatment of 'God', angels, gods, demons, matter and the cosmos, human nature, providence (with the incarnation as the highpoint), (3) moral teaching including the themes of sacrifices and sacraments, the cult of the martyrs not heroes, laws, true and false oracles and last judgement and (4) true virtue. He considers the Greek poets ('ridiculous'), then philosophers (e.g., Epicurus, whose ideas such as that God turned in on himself and cared for nothing else, remained influential). Theodoret is more sympathetic to *Plato. He agrees that there are human goods (health, beauty, vigour, insightful/watchful wealth), and four divine ones (prudence, moderation and intelligence, justice and courage). It is unthinkable that the Creator-architect would leave lost humanity to neglect, especially when he made the whole rich world for us: this theme is repeated in the *De Providentia*. Providence cannot do everything, or else there would be nothing but the divine. Yet, rather triumphantly, Theodoret asserts that the result of the incarnation is that ignorance and idolatry are in full retreat. Greeks, Romans and Barbarians all recognize the divinity of the crucified and worship the Trinity; martyrs are honoured and ascetic retreats sanctify the furthest flung places. Greek education cannot help people. By 449 he claimed to have converted ten thousand 'heretics', meaning by this that he drew them into the orthodox faith.

Theodoret also wrote commentaries and works on hermeneutics. He was 'Antiochene' in his concern with what we might call the 'narrative logic' (*skopos*) of the whole text and its context – and in the 'moral' or 'dogmatic' meaning which could be discerned in the whole, although he does not follow a three-level interpretation. More than his Antiochene predecessors, Theodoret allowed Old Testament passages (e.g., Ps. 71:1f.; Hab. 3:3,18; Zech. 3:8,9 or Amos 9:11 – *not* Zerubbabel) to be interpreted prophetically of the New Testament, although he is still guarded:

Hosea *is* prophesying Zerubbabel's restoration. He speaks of 'unnamed pretend Christians' (perhaps meaning that the followers of *Theodore of Mopsuestia are Judaizers?) who supposed the Gog and Magog of Ezekiel 38 and 39 to be still to come rather than having a Christian Messianic reference; so too Haggai 2:23. In this there is one eye on *Origen and his employment of the methods of Middle Platonic textual interpretation. In Theodoret's commentary on Romans, Adam and Eve, not ever immortal by nature, are like our teachers who should have known better. Human bodily existence receives the limits of death (the body is the instrument and not the cause of sin), while the immortal soul feels the death of sin. God made the created realm transient in anticipation of human future sin but did not create evil: sin is not possible for God any more than the Father could be the Son and vice versa.

Theodoret also wrote Christological works, and he insisted on the *distinction of natures in Christ*. 'When heat is applied to gold, the gold partakes of the colour and energy of the fire: but it does not lose its own nature; it remains gold while behaving as fire' (*Ep.* 145). In fact, the Word kept his distance behind the humanity. It is significant that the *Eranistes* (his main, late work on Christology cast in dialogue form) has three chapters with the headings: Unchanging; Unconfused; Impassible. One could say that the divine and human persons (*prosopa*) join forces for the sake of the redemption. What mattered most was the creator/creation divide. Unlike the *Cappadocians before him, he does not employ the *ousia-hypostasis* distinction to explain how God can be both one and three. Therefore the idea of the *hypostasis* as that which unites the natures in a fixed ontological way is unfamiliar to him, being more concerned with God's oneness. By 448–50 (*Ep.* 151), he had clearly denied the Nestorian heresy of 'two sons'; yet the characteristics of each nature are distinguished, and in that there is continuity with his early *Anathemas of Cyril* (c. 430). And yet it is as the man that he wins the victory – the man led into the desert and who gives us an example – thus there is a strongly ethical/ascetic tone. It is human obedience, not overwhelming divine power, that makes the difference, and thus 'perfect man' versus the 'Apollinarians' (Alexandrians). Ultimately Theodoret was more interested in soteriology than pure Christology in the sense of how the two relate; the soul-body metaphor should remind us of the difference, the unmixedness. The key term is the 'unmixed union', owing to a creation/creature separation. In a way a *hypostasis* could not unite, but only reinforce, differences as it was meant to do in Trinitarian theology: any union according to nature would mean that two *hypostaseis* would remain while 'pooling' their natures and would imply a Quaternity in God. The grace of the approaching Word gave the body of Christ a higher function, but it did not change its nature: that is what the communication of idioms is about (the analogy if the Eucharist is invoked). His dual origins (heavenly and earthly) are emphasized. Pouring oneself out does not mean mixing, rather it means permeating all of the humanity. Grace means that the divine nature is the active partner, bearing the assumed human nature taken from David's race. So there was a simple conjunction of two natures rather than the strong introduction of a special 'person'; he affirmed one *prosopon* rather than *hypostasis*, but he did not really say what that meant.

Theodoret defended Nestorius with the *Reprehensio XII capitum seu anathematisorum Cyrilli*. This work, and therefore its author, would be condemned by the Fifth Oecumenical Council (Constantinople 553). Hence the work was lost, although some of the text is preserved in Cyril's answer (see *PG* 76, pp. 385–452).

MARK W. ELLIOTT

FURTHER READING: G.W. Ashby, *Theodoret of Cyrrhus as Exegete of the Old Testament* (Grahamstown, 1972); Silke-Petra Bergjan, *Theodoret von Cyrus und der Neunizanismus: Aspekte der altkirchlichen Trinitatslehre* (Berlin, 1994); J.-N. Guinot, *L'Éxégèse de Théodoret de Cyr* (Paris, 1995); F. Young, *From Nicea to Chalcedon* (London, 1983).

Theophilus of Antioch

Late second-century bishop of Antioch and *apologist. *Eusebius (*CH*, 4.24) attributes to Theophilus catechetical books and refutations of the heresies of Hermogenes and *Marcion, but his one extant work is an apology, *Ad Autolycum*. He intends to discredit the myths and philosophical claims of the Greeks and demonstrate the truth of his religion through various 'proofs' from Nature, the consistent, inspired witness of the Hebrew prophets and the antiquity of his tradition.

Theophilus seems to have a special affinity for Jewish modes of thought. His most succinct confession is limited to a single, providential Creator, who has revealed his Law for the moral betterment of humanity (3.9). The righteous, through obedience to that Law, will be rewarded with immortality, while the wicked will be punished (2.27). He defines a Christian as one who is anointed with the oil of God (1.12), but he makes no explicit reference to Jesus Christ either in this definition or elsewhere. Such an omission, however, is not unique among second-century apologists (cf. *Athenagoras, *Legatio*). Theophilus is the first Christian to produce an extant commentary on the so-called *Hexaemeron*, or the first 'six days' of the creation account (2.12–19). Here his reliance on the exegetical methods of Hellenistic Judaism is clear; some have suggested that he also makes use of rabbinical interpretations. His continuity, though, with the theological vision of a variety of New Testament texts is indicated by his many clear allusions to them.

Theophilus's Trinitarian thought reflects in general the fluidity of ante-Nicene doctrine. God is ultimately beyond description, but the names Logos (Word), Sophia (Wisdom) and Spirit may be used to refer to various aspects of God's being, with 'Father' being the most comprehensive title (1.3). He is the first to use *trias* 'Triad' in reference to God: the first three days of creation are types of God, his Logos and his Sophia (2.15). Theophilus makes the Stoic distinction between the Logos *endiathetos*, the immanent Word, and the Logos *prophorikos*, the expressed Word, which is generated by, but not separated from, God (2.22). He affirms that the Logos is God (citing Jn. 1:1), but that the Logos can also be manifested locally as Son when sent by the Father (2.22). Logos and Sophia seem at times to have similar and overlapping roles: both, for example, are identified as agents of creation (1.7). Theophilus is most consistent in identifying the Holy Spirit as the source of prophetic inspiration (e.g., 2.9, 30, 33).

Perhaps Theophilus's most formative contribution is to the doctrine of creation *ex nihilo*. All things were created out of what did not exist (1.4; 2.10, 13), thus matter itself had a definitive point of origin. For Theophilus, the sovereignty and transcendence of God are here at stake. If matter is uncreated, it is immutable and thus equal to God. God demonstrates his omnipotence and superiority to mortal craftsmen by not being limited merely to the formation of available, pre-existent material (2.4). *Irenaeus, writing at roughly the same time, expresses the same thought (*Heresies*, 2.10.4).

HANS SVEBAKKEN

FURTHER READING: *Text:* Robert M. Grant (ed.), *Theophilus of Antioch: Ad Autolycum* (Oxford, 1970). *Studies:* J. Bentivegna, 'A Christianity without Christ by Theophilus of Antioch', SP 13 (1975), pp. 107–30; Jacques Fantino, 'L'Origine de la Doctrine de la Création *Ex Nihilo*', *R S Ph Th* 80 (1996), pp. 421–42; Robert M. Grant, *Greek Apologists of the Second Century* (Philadelphia, 1988); 'The Problem of Theophilus', *Harv Th R* 43 (1950), pp. 179–96; Kathleen E. McVey, 'The Use of Stoic Cosmogony in Theophilus of Antioch's *Hexaemeron*', pp. 32–58 in *Biblical Hermeneutics in Historical Perspective* (ed. Mark S. Burrows and Paul Rorem; Grand Rapids, 1991); William R. Schoedel, 'Theophilus of Antioch: Jewish Christian?' *I C S* 18 (1993), pp. 279–97; Nicole Zeegers, 'Les Trois Cultures de Théophile d'Antioche', *Th H* 105 (1998), pp. 135–76.

Thomasius, Gottfried (1802–75)

Thomasius was one of the most significant German *Lutheran theologians in the middle of the nineteenth century. After university study in Erlangen, Halle and Berlin (where he heard *Schleiermacher and *Hegel), Thomasius ministered to congregations in and around Nuremberg for 17 years – from 1825 until he was called to a chair in theology in Erlangen in 1842. He remained there until his death, combining his teaching duties with more than two decades of work as university preacher.

Like many of his contemporaries, Thomasius was deeply engaged in the debates initiated by post-Hegelian attempts (particularly those of *Strauss and *Baur) to recast classical Christian doctrines in thoroughly modern forms, especially in terms of contingent historical development and consciousness-centred personality. Unlike some of his more radical contemporaries, Thomasius sought to combine a strong defence of classical formulations with elements of modern thought which he saw as conducive not only to the further clarification of the tradition but also to promotion of the genuine inspiration and expression of Christian piety. Thus, the influence of Schleiermacher and a deep appreciation of the 'revival theology', or the academic articulation of the century's evangelical movements, are evident in his work.

Thomasius's chief concern across his major publications, and especially in his *Christi Person und Werk* ('Christ's Person and Work'), was to demonstrate that the classical assertion of the full union of God and humanity in the incarnation (as found in the ancient symbols and developed in such Lutheran dogmas as the *communicatio idiomatum* and Eucharistic ubiquitousness), could be defended successfully against modern attacks only on the basis of a better understanding of the *kenosis* (self-limitation or self-emptying) of the divine Son in his union with humanity in Jesus. For Thomasius, the divinely self-actualized nature of this union was of crucial importance, since only by the Son's voluntarily abdicating such metaphysical properties as omnipresence and omnipotence could the historical incarnation have been possible without either abrogating Jesus' human integrity or not effecting a true union of his natures. But if these properties were 'latent' in Jesus before the crucifixion, his 'humiliated state', they were re-actualized in him with the resurrection, his 'exalted state', in which he is accessible through prayer and the Lord's Supper. Thomasius's attempt to articulate a kenotic Christology, then, was also tied intimately into then-current controversies over sacramental nature and efficacy in Protestantism, and as such it occupied a transitional position between Schleiermacher and Hegel and the 'value-theology' of *Albrecht Ritschl and his followers which arose in the 1870s.

JON K. COOLEY

FURTHER READING: *Thomasius's major publications: Beiträge zur kirchlichen Theologie* (Erlangen, 1845); *Das Bekenntis der evangelisch-lutherischen Kirche in der Konsequenz seines Prinzips* (Nuremberg, 1848); *Christi Person und Werk: Darstellung der evangelisch-lutherischen Dogmatik vom Mittelpunkte der Christologie aus* (Erlangen, 2nd, expanded edn, 1856–63), partially translated in Claude Welch (ed.), *God and Incarnation in Mid-Nineteenth Century German Theology* (New York, 1965), pp. 31–101; *Das Bekenntnis der lutherischen Kirche von der Versöhnung und die Versöhnungslehre D. von Hofmanns* (Erlangen, 1857).

Thomism

The works and teaching of *St Thomas Aquinas (1224/5–74) have given rise to a lively tradition of philosophical and theological inquiry whose practitioners were, by the fourteenth century, being called 'Thomists'. Although Aquinas's literary output included biblical commentaries, commentaries on *Aristotle and other classical works, disputations and treatises on specific topics, liturgical works, sermons and prayers, it was his three theological syntheses in particular that played a prominent role in shaping the intellectual movement that bears his name: the *Scriptum super Libros Sententiae* (a commentary on *Peter Lombard's *Sentences*, then considered the standard theological textbook); the *Summa contra Gentiles* (a summary of the main doctrines of the Christian faith, possibly intended chiefly for apologetic uses); and the famous *Summa Theologiae*. The commentary on the *Sentences* was perhaps most influential in the period immediately following the death of Aquinas, while the two *Summae* came to dominate the Thomistic tradition after the sixteenth century. More recent Thomistic scholarship has enlarged this canon appreciably through renewed study and appropriation of Aquinas's other works, especially the commentaries on Scripture and Aristotle.

From these works, Thomists have been able to derive a relatively coherent body of teaching, as well as a distinctive approach to philosophical and theological issues, which merits the identification of a properly 'Thomistic' school or tradition within the broad intellectual traditions of western Christianity.

In this connection, a factor which must be considered in assessing the perdurance and intellectual vigour of the Thomist tradition is the widespread conviction in the Catholic Church that Aquinas's thought possesses unique resources for the articulation of the Christian faith in its entirety as well as for its integration with non-theological fields of human learning and inquiry. His distinctive contribution in this area earned Aquinas the title 'Common Doctor' and in no small measure accounts for the appeal of his work for countless generations of Thomists. Following the lead of Aquinas, Thomists have striven in their own writings to express the unity of divine truth which arises from the divine simplicity itself and which can be discerned in the order of creation and in the economy of salvation.

But the intrinsic interest and unchallenged excellence of Aquinas's works and teaching do not fully account for the hugely influential role he has come to play both within the Thomistic tradition and beyond it. Certain personal traits – his comprehensive theological knowledge, his

daunting conceptual rigour, his religious consecration and mystical bent, and his acknowledged saintliness – have combined in rendering him an exemplar of the ideal theologian. Thus it is not surprising to find in many of the finest representatives of the Thomist tradition not only a fidelity to the thought of Aquinas, but also a deep attachment to his person. The reverence in which Aquinas is held can be seen, at least in part, to account for the remarkable vitality, as well as the continuity, that distinguish this eight-hundred-year-old intellectual tradition.

Naturally, it would be misleading to exaggerate the continuities within the Thomist tradition to the neglect of the discontinuities. While there is broad agreement among scholars that Thomism represents a relatively coherent endeavour on the part of its exponents to identify, apply and develop principles drawn from the thought of Aquinas, it remains somewhat difficult to construct a single conceptual synthesis in which all Thomists could be said without qualification to concur. A number of interpretative issues converge here. For one thing, the complexity of Aquinas's literary output, not to mention the variety of genres which comprise it and the lines of development which can be discerned in it, make it difficult to field a comprehensive interpretation of his thought that could win the assent of all commentators.

Another source of disagreement among historians of western thought centres on the variety to be found among arguably representative Thomistic authors who, it has been estimated, number more than two thousand individuals between the death of Aquinas and the present day. Questions arise as to whether a particular thinker deserves to be numbered among the Thomists, or whether his thought is sufficiently faithful to the principal theses acknowledged to be indispensable to inquiries pursued in this tradition. Questions of this kind have led some historians to draw a distinction between what might be called straightforward Thomism and eclectic Thomism. On this account, straightforward Thomism designates any author who accords the thought of Aquinas a privileged role in the pursuit of his or her own philosophical and theological inquiries. Eclectic Thomism, on the other hand, includes authors who, while they operate within the broad parameters outlined by Thomistic principles, nonetheless import significant elements from alien and possibly conflicting conceptualities. It is apparent that no hard and fast distinctions are possible here. One might suppose that it is easier to recognize the difference between straightforward and eclectic Thomists than it is to define that difference.

Still, despite the difficulties in interpreting Aquinas's vast literary output and in specifying an entirely agreed-upon doctrinal synthesis among the authors he inspired, historians agree in discerning a remarkable degree of unity within the Thomist tradition overall.

It has been customary to divide the history of Thomism into three broad periods: first, or primitive Thomism (embracing several generations of thinkers, mostly members of the Dominican Order, in the years immediately following the death of Aquinas); second Thomism (marking especially the creative appropriation of Thomism among Spanish and Italian Dominicans and *Jesuits in the sixteenth century); and neo-Thomism (a movement initiated in the mid-nineteenth century and stretching well into the twentieth). But, as might be expected, historians have been unable to agree on where the lines dividing these periods should be drawn, on whether these periods should not themselves be subdivided, and on what factors distinguish one period from another. It seems best, for the purposes of the present survey, to accept the rough outlines of the standard account and to pass over the controversy that surrounds it in respectful silence. Thomists have figured with varying prominence in almost every major period in the history of European thought – and even outside its ambit in places like Byzantium, the Far East and the Americas. They have engaged the thought of Aquinas to address a plethora of philosophical and theological issues, in remarkably diverse intellectual, social, and political settings and geographical regions. One will stay closer to the complexities of the movement by discerning its striking continuities across the temporal and cultural boundaries that defined the divergent contexts in which Thomists lived, worked and wrote.

As far as can be known, Aquinas had few if any immediate disciples among his students. In the aftermath of this death, his fellow Dominican professors were largely taken up with the task of defending his work against the charge that it had introduced innovations which were inimical to the proper articulation of the Christian faith. This charge was levelled mainly by conservative *Augustinian masters, mostly but not exclusively members of the *Franciscan Order, at the University of Paris and elsewhere, who saw in Aquinas's use of Aristotle a departure from standard philosophical positions regarded as crucial to expressing certain truths of the faith. This opposition led to condemnations of certain propositions drawn from Aquinas's writings – in 1270 by Stephen Tempier, Bishop of Paris, and then in 1277 by Robert Kilwardby, Archbishop of Canterbury. Albertus Magnus travelled from Cologne to Paris in 1276–7 in order to defend his former student. Other Dominican professors responded to the charges against Aquinas in works directed against the Franciscan William de la Mare's *Correctorium fratris Thomae* (1279) which, drawing upon Scripture, Augustine and *Bonaventure, 'corrected' 117 passages from Aquinas's writings. The Dominican response – advanced in works with titles such as *Correctorium corruptori fratris Thomae* and *Contra Corruptorem sancti Thomae* – sought to distinguish Aquinas's intellectual legacy from the doctrinally and philosophically problematic Averroistic Aristotelianism with which it was being conflated. Among the early Thomists who dedicated their energies to this task were the English Dominicans Robert Knapwell (d. 1288), William of Hothum (d. 1298), William of Macclesfield (d. 1303) and Thomas Sutton (d. 1315?), as well as continental Thomists like Bernard of Trille (d. 1292), Giles of Lessines (d. 1304?), John Quidort (d. 1306) and Rambert of Primadizzi (d. 1308). The first in a series of Dominican general chapters which defended the teachings of Aquinas was held in Paris in 1286. Subsequent general chapters, particularly after the canonization and vindication of Aquinas in 1323, enjoined the study, promotion and defence of Thomism by Dominican lectors and masters in theology as well as within Dominican educational centres.

Following upon these debates with traditional Augustinian masters, the new challenges posed by followers of the Franciscan *John Duns Scotus (1264–1308) and, after 1320, by those of *William of Ockham (1300–49) caused the philosophical core of Aquinas's intellectual legacy to emerge with a sharper profile. Controversies with Augustinian, Scotist and *Nominalist masters – as the adherents of the chief competing scholastic systems came to be known – impelled the Thomist masters to articulate the distinctive theses they discerned in the natural philosophy, philosophical psychology, moral philosophy and metaphysics of Aquinas. Chief among these were the following: the composition of all physical bodies by matter and form; the individuation of each physical body by determined matter; the real distinction between the essential nature and the activities of entities; the unicity of the substantial form of each individual human being; the social nature of human beings; their right to pursue personal happiness within the frame of the common good; the primacy of virtue in right conduct; moderate realism in epistemology; the possibility of knowing the existence of God on the basis of observation of the natural order; the real distinction between essence and existence; and the analogous character of the concept of being as applied to God, substances and accidental qualities. This philosophical core would continue to the present day to serve as a criterion by which to assess the authenticity of a particular thinker's claim to the Thomist mantle.

One of the greatest representatives of this tradition – a thinker whose unimpeachable Thomist credentials won him the title '*Princeps Thomistarum*' – was John Capreolus (1380–1444). His brilliant *Defensiones Divi Thomae* (*The Books of Arguments in Defense of the Theology of St. Thomas Aquinas*) represented a kind of benchmark in the history of Thomism in being the first comprehensive synthesis of Aquinas's theology. This important work was just one sign of the increasing maturation of Thomism in the fifteenth century – a period which also witnessed, in German universities where Dominican masters were active, the ascendancy of Aquinas's *Summa Theologiae* as the textbook of theology. This development would culminate, in the first decade of the next century, with its introduction as the theology text at the University of Paris by Peter Crockaert. For its part, the work of Capreolus would continue to exert a considerable influence on subsequent generations of Thomists, laying the foundations for the great flourishing of theology and philosophy in the Thomistic vein in the sixteenth century.

One of the most prominent Thomists of the sixteenth century – *Thomas de Vio Cajetan (1469–1534) – had both read Capreolus and lectured on the *Summa Theologiae* at the University of Pavia. Cajetan's massive commentary on the *Summa Theologiae* – which enjoys a unique position in the Thomistic canon by reason of its inclusion in the definitive Leonine edition of Aquinas's works begun in the late nineteenth century – provided a model for later commentaries. Indeed, it may be regarded as a landmark in the accumulating commentatorial tradition that would be perhaps the most significant medium for the transmission of Thomist thought to subsequent centuries. Conspicuous among such commentaries are that of Francisco Silvestri of Ferrara (d. 1528) on the *Summa contra Gentiles*, and those on the *Summa Theologiae* by the Discalced Carmelite theologians at Salamanca (the 'Salmanticensis') in the sixteenth century, by John of St Thomas in the seventeenth century, and by Charles Billuart in the eighteenth century.

Cardinal Cajetan's role as Pope Leo X's official ambassador to *Martin Luther meant that he would be among the first of many sixteenth-century Thomists to address the challenges posed by *Reformation thought. Several of these Thomists played significant roles in the sessions of the Council of Trent (1545–63), among them Bartholomew Spina (d. 1546), Dominic de Soto (d. 1560) and Melchior Cano (d. 1560), whose work *De locis theologicis* was the first to attempt to rank the sources of theology according to their varying doctrinal authority. Thomist theologians were especially influential in the formulation of the council's decrees on justification and grace, on the sacraments and on the Eucharist, as well as in the composition of the catechism based on the conciliar decrees, the Roman Catechism, issued in 1566 by Pope Pius V. During this period, the identification of Thomist theology with Catholic orthodoxy became official when, in 1567, Pius V recognized Thomas Aquinas as one of the four Doctors of the Church.

Throughout this period, the Iberian peninsula supported a high level of theological and philosophical reflection in the Thomistic vein. In addition to several figures already mentioned, this included some Thomists of great distinction: Francis de Vitoria (d. 1546) and Domingo Áñez (d. 1604) at the University of Salamanca, and John of St Thomas (d. 1644) at Alcala. The theologians at Salamanca helped Bartholomew de Las Casas and other Dominican friars in the New World to defend the rights of the natives and to lay the foundations of international law, while John of St Thomas composed influential philosophical and theological courses of study based on Aquinas.

The founder of the Society of Jesus, *St Ignatius of Loyola (1495–1556), studied with the Dominican Thomists in Spain and stipulated that studies in philosophy and theology in the Society should be based on the works of Aquinas. Soon Jesuit professors would join the Dominicans in the work of commentary on Aquinas's writings, although this shared interest in expounding his works did not always guarantee agreement in their interpretation of his thought. In this period, chief among Jesuit commentators on Aquinas were *Francisco Suárez (1548–1617) and *Luis de Molina (1535–1600). Perhaps the most serious disagreement between the Dominicans and the Jesuits concerned the interpretation of Aquinas's teaching on grace and predestination. This disagreement prompted the Holy See to organize an official inquiry, called the 'Congregatio de Auxiliis', which met intermittently from 1599 to 1607 but was inconclusive.

If thirteenth- and fourteenth-century debates can be said to have sharpened the philosophical profile of the Thomistic tradition, then sixteenth-century controversies pressed the distinctive theological theses of Thomism to greater definition. Prominent among these are the following: the reality of the supernatural order revealed by God; the substantial distinction between nature and grace; the necessity of the grace of Christ for salvation; faith and grace as a real participation in the divine life; an intrinsically-ordered harmony between nature and grace and reason and faith; the fully theological character of the virtue of faith; the real efficacy of secondary causes within the universal divine causality, and, thus, the true freedom of rational agents; the primacy of divine omnipotence and mercy in predestination; redemption as the motive for the incarnation; the sacraments as true causes of grace; the capital grace of Christ as the central principle of ecclesiology; and the unmediated character of the beatific vision.

The chief philosophical and theological themes of Thomism converged to assist nineteenth-century theologians in addressing the challenge of modernity. One of the first leaders in the nineteenth-century renewal of Thomistic studies that has come to be called neo-Thomism – the Jesuit Serafino Sordi (1793–1865) – was himself dependent on Thomistic authors active in the eighteenth century. After the restoration of the Society of Jesus in 1814, several Jesuit professors sought to revive the study of Aquinas within the Society. While at first they did not achieve success, they were eventually able to prevail at their Collegio Romano (later the Gregorian University) in Rome where Gioacchino Pecci, the future Pope Leo XIII, was a student. Through the efforts of this circle of Thomists and, later, through the exercise of papal authority, the Cartesian philosophical manuals in use in seminaries began to be supplanted by Thomist textbooks. Perhaps the greatest Thomist during this period was the Jesuit Joseph Kleutgen, who contributed significantly to the formulation of the decree on revelation at *Vatican I and whose five-volume Theologie der Vorzeit (1853–70) argued that modern philosophical systems were less congenial than Thomism to the articulation of the Christian faith. This conclusion was shared by Pope Leo XIII, who in his 1879 encyclical 'Aeterni Patris' commended the study of St Thomas Aquinas as the basis for Catholic higher and secondary education and thus assured the future of the already vigorous revival in Thomistic studies then underway.

The endeavour to reform Catholic education on the basis of Thomistic philosophy and theology continued throughout the first decades of the twentieth century. Joining other potent Catholic efforts to recover the sources of the great tradition (the ressourcement movement), Thomists have contributed to the renewal of medieval studies. Among the greatest Thomists of this century are the philosophers *Jacques Maritain (d. 1973) and *Étienne Gilson (d. 1979). Within the Society of Jesus, two thinkers stand out for their attempt to wed Thomistic thought to the philosophy of *Kant and *Hegel: the philosopher *Bernard J.F. Lonergan (d. 1984) and the theologian *Karl Rahner (d. 1984). Many Thomist theologians, including Rahner, *Yves Congar (d. 1995) and M.D. Chenu (d. 1990), contributed to the work of *Vatican II. In the immediate aftermath of that council, the philosophical strands of Thomism were pursued with perhaps greater enthusiasm than were the theological strands. But the final decades of the twentieth century witnessed a remarkable revival of interest in the theology of Aquinas as such (as distinct from that of the commentatorial tradition) both among Protestant and Catholic theologians. This revival shows no signs of abating and promises to stimulate the continued flourishing and development of Thomism well into the twenty-first century.

J.A. DiNoia, OP

FURTHER READING: Victor B. Brezik (ed.), *One Hundred Years of Thomism* (Houston, TX, 1981); Romanus Cessario, *Le Thomisme et les Thomistes* (Paris, 1998); Leonard A. Kennedy, *A Catalogue of Thomists 1270–1900* (Houston, TX, 1987); Gerald McCool, *The Neo-Thomists* (Milwaukee, WI, 1994); F.J. Roensch, *Early Thomistic Schools* (Dubuque, IA, 1964).

Tillich, Paul (1886–1965)

Paul (Paulus Johannes) Tillich was born 20 August 1886, in Starzeddel, Germany and died in Chicago, USA on 22 October 1965. Son of a Prussian church superintendent, Tillich became a 'theologian of the boundaries' as a result of his experience as a Lutheran army chaplain in World War I. With his second wife, Hannah, who stimulated his interest in expressionist art, he enjoyed the bohemian ethos of post-war Berlin. Challenged by his encounter with working-class conscripts, he became a leader among Christian socialists appropriating *Marxist critiques of political economy.

A student under *Martin Kähler, influenced by *Ernst Troeltsch, Tillich applied the theological doctrine of justification by grace alone through faith to the existential doubts of his generation. Contrasting arbitrary signs with cultural patterns, for example parental nurture revealing divine creativity, he considered all theological language to be symbolic. He insisted that traditional formulations must be reconceived, if secular society is to receive proclamations of saving truth, and he criticized his contemporary, *Karl Barth, for rejecting apologetics. But Tillich's 1925 Marburg lectures on dogmatics showed him to be, like Barth and *Brunner, a *'dialectical' theologian, stressing revelation and opposing nineteenth-century liberal optimism, epitomized by *Harnack.

Tillich was qualified to teach philosophy by two doctoral dissertations on Schelling emphasizing, against *Hegel, a surd depth in God, the 'ground' of being. Only by participating in the infinite life of the divine Spirit can finite humanity address the constant anxiety and threat of potential non-being. The split between our essential communion with and existential estrangement from God and creation, due to our finite freedom, is overcome by 'New Being',

realized in history when the disciples declared Jesus to be the Christ. Jesus' complete, human self-offering enables us to affirm our divine-human destiny in spite of ourselves and the reality of evil.

Tillich was known in Germany primarily as a philosopher of religion, influenced by *Nietzsche and Heidegger and supporting his Jewish colleagues, who founded the Frankfurt school in critical theory. In *The Socialist Decision* (1933) he attacked the idolatry of National Socialism (Nazism). Dismissed from his chair in philosophy, he reluctantly joined Reinhold Niebuhr teaching in New York. There he flourished as a theologian, first gaining acclaim for one of three volumes of sermons for theological students, *The Shaking of the Foundations* (1948).

After Union Theological Seminary and Columbia University (1934–55), Tillich became a university professor (lecturing across faculties) at Harvard University (1955–62), then at the University of Chicago Divinity School until his death. In philosophy he lectured on German Classical Idealism, dismissing the dominant linguistic analysts as positivists and nominalists. He described his own position as one of 'beliefful realism'.

His three-volume *Systematic Theology*, published between 1951 and 1963, shaped a generation of post-World War II theologians in America. Organized by what he called 'the method of correlation', Volume I began with 'Reason and Revelation', addressing current epistemological concerns. Contrasting the depth of reason with controlling, technical reasoning, he looked beyond reason and experience for answers from revelatory encounters with God in history and nature. But 'Being and God' (I-2) gave what he considered the logically prior ontological categories and questions concerning the polarities of individualization and participation, dynamics and form, freedom and destiny. His dialectical key was the divine-demonic power of being affirming love and justice despite the alienating influence of non-being, construed as potential nothingness, not sheer absence.

Volume II, 'Existence and the Christ', along with *The Courage to Be* (1952), which continues to excite new generations of students, represents his most existentialist phase. For Tillich, doctrines of virgin birth and two-nature Christologies have symbolic power, but lose revelatory significance if taken literally. His emphasis on 'the God above the "God" of theism' and his insistence that God is being as such, not an existing entity, led critics unfamiliar with German Idealism to brand him an atheist.

Volume III – comprising 'Life and the Spirit' and 'History and the Kingdom of God' – came late and was less influential. In principle, Tillich believed one could begin at any point and, in fact, the last sections returned to earlier issues from the years in Germany. What Tillich showed with some success was that it is possible to develop a system in theology without deducing one part from the next.

Tillich assumed that a 'global' perspective is possible and that his categories were universally valid. The trajectory of his theology of culture went from art and politics, through depth psychology and existentialism and then finally, during the Harvard and Chicago years, to Christian encounters with other religions. His best work was a critique of modern quasi-religions: nationalism, capitalism (including Russian Communism as a variant form of idolatrous self-assertion) and scientism. Feminists criticized the generalization of self-assertion as sin, but his acknowledgement of the use of female symbols for divine being inspired Mary Daly's *Beyond God the Father* (1973).

If adding to our theological vocabulary is a mark of constructive theology, Tillich must count among the most influential of his generation. Besides translating justification by faith as 'courage to be', he defined religion as ultimate concern, or being concerned unconditionally; he identified 'the Protestant (prophetic) principle' as a key to biblical religion; and he argued for an *Augustinian conception of 'theonomous' culture. Against *Kant's antinomy between autonomy and heteronomy, this posits the dialectic of finite-infinite becoming as the 'depth dimension' of both self and other. Tillich's insistence that we cannot invent living symbols, and his references to 'Catholic substance', attracted Roman Catholic scholars. His *Lutheran sense of the sacramental Word based on a theology of the cross was never matched, however, by a catholic feel for Eucharistic liturgy.

Contrasting moments of divine breakthrough ('*kairos*') with everyday history ('*chronos*'), Tillich affirmed providence but not progress. Of lasting importance is his conception of the demonic in history. The divine affirming of finite becoming in spite of the breaks consequent upon finitude allows moments of fulfilled time when the eternal is seen fragmentarily in the temporal. Demonic distortion is always possible because of creaturely self-assertion. Doubt should foster more profound formulations of belief, not loss of faith.

No Tillichian school exists comparable to the Barthian, but Tillich societies meet in Europe and North and South America. His principal successors include Langdon Gilkey and Tom Driver (USA), Gert Hummel (Germany) and Jean Richard at Laval University, who is producing definitive French translations of the collected works.

PETER SLATER

FURTHER READING: *Texts: Systematic Theology,* I–III (Chicago, 1967); *The Protestant Era* (trans. J.L. Adams; Chicago, 1948). *Studies:* Wilhelm and Marion Pauck, *Paul Tillich: His Life and Thought,* I (New York, 1976); M.K. Taylor, *Paul Tillich: Theologian of the Boundaries* (London, 1987), a comprehensive selection of texts, with intro. and bibliography; A. Thatcher, *The Ontology of Paul Tillich* (London, 1978); R.H. Stone, *Paul Tillich's Radical Social Thought* (Atlanta, 1980); A.C. Irwin, *Eros Towards the World* (Minneapolis, 1991); Pan-Chiu Lai, *Towards a Trinitarian Theology of Religions* (Kampen, 1994).

Torrance, Thomas Forsyth (b. 1913)

Born 30 August 1913, the first-born son of a missionary family, Torrance spent his first thirteen years in the mission community at Chengtu, Szechwan, China. Educated at Edinburgh University and New College, Edinburgh, he was duly ordained to the ministry in the Church of Scotland at Alyth Barony Parish Church in 1940. His doctoral studies under *Karl Barth were interrupted by chaplaincy duties during World War II but were completed in 1946. Following parish ministry in Aberdeen, Torrance became professor of church history at New College in 1950. In 1952 he was appointed to the chair of Christian Dogmatics at New College, which he held until his retirement in 1979. As active in the church as in the academy, Torrance has diligently served the ecumenical movement, especially in relations and discussions with the Anglican and the Orthodox communions. His many honours include appointment as moderator of the General Assembly of the Church of Scotland in 1976 and being awarded the Templeton Prize for Progress in Religion in 1979. He has written well over two hundred books, articles and reviews, co-edited the *Scottish Journal of Theology* for its first 27 years, co-edited a new translation of *Calvin's New Testament commentaries, and co-edited the English translation of Karl Barth's *Church Dogmatics*. His writings range throughout the various fields of theology. He is virtually unique amongst theologians in the depth of his knowledge of the natural sciences.

The central years of Torrance's teaching occurred during the turbulence of the sixties and seventies, when there was a constant concern to reinterpret the gospel in the light of modern assumptions. Torrance came to these tumultuous times deeply influenced by his Scottish theological heritage, coupled with his intense study of Barth's reconstruction of Protestant theology. Barth had exposed the many shared assumptions and unresolved tensions of liberalism and conservatism, Pietism and *Enlightenment, and had sought to reconstruct Christian theology more rigorously on its proper and unique source, namely, Jesus Christ. However, in disengaging theology from its often subtle but constricting marriage to modern culture, Barth gave the appearance to many of leaving a serious disconnection between theology and contemporary culture and science. Torrance, with these concerns in mind, was led beyond Barth to re-examine the underlying structural unity of the created order with the redemptive economy revealed in Christ. During this time, Torrance chose the analogy expressed in the title of his *Theological Science* (Oxford, 1969) to suggest fresh thinking and throw new light on unsolved problems in the Christian claim to know God and the church's attempt to articulate this faith to the contemporary world. Though he continues to write extensively on matters relating to the central doctrines of Christian faith (e.g., *The Trinitarian Faith* [Edinburgh, 1997]), Torrance's passion has been to explore the areas of method raised during these times of questioning and revolt. His writings have included extensive and detailed analyses of the nature of scientific objectivity, the theological and epistemological assumptions of modern science, the nature of rationality, the nature of language, and the history of epistemology and hermeneutics.

Though critical of Barth for failing to bring to light the connections between the rationality of grace and the rationality of natural science, Torrance confirms Barth's decision to reject all natural theology based on a priori, independent conceptual systems. Torrance thus integrates scientific and theological rationality in dialogue with Einstein, Polanyi and Godel as well as with *Athanasius, Calvin and Barth. Such an integration of fields means that boundary conditions between science and theology are co-ordinated within a hierarchical system, where each level is open upward to a higher but not reducible downwards. Hence the independence of both scientific and theological rationality is honoured, but not at the cost of a dogmatic secularism with its dualistic detachment of God from the world. Torrance insists that theological statements should connect appropriately to issues of historical factuality and contemporary scientific cosmology. For instance the incarnation, that is the coming of God in the humanity of Jesus, deepens the critical realist conviction that the physical world is real in its very contingence – even for God. Hence to speak of resurrection without the empirical, historical correlate of a bodily resurrection and ascension may be fantasy, or perhaps mythology, but not theology (*Space, Time and Incarnation*, p. 89). Torrance understands certain foundational theological concepts, including Trinity and *homoousion*, as based not on logical inference but intuitive indwelling of the empirical reality of Jesus Christ. They are to be understood as open structures, used 'postulatively', having a fluid revision the further they penetrate ('Newton, Einstein and Scientific Theology', in *Transformation and Convergence*, p. 274). In this spirit, Torrance offers many conceptual reforms of the ways theology has been crafted under the influence of now outmoded notions of pre-relativity scientific rationality. Torrance discusses the Newtonian mechanistic determinism within which his own *Reformed tradition erroneously formalized the doctrine of election. Torrance also interprets *Bultmann's hermeneutical project as the inappropriate binding of a positive theological interpretation of the New Testament to the now outmoded *Kantian-Newtonian cosmology of a closed continuum of cause and effect.

Torrance's prescriptive style lacks a dialogical quality and this has at times rendered his thought inaccessible to the sceptic. Yet by positively describing theology as a science, Torrance has articulated a clear epistemological approach and outreach for Christian theology in the modern scientific community. However, because it is the nature of science to abstract and to generalize, theology needs other paradigms to explore and articulate for modernity the concrete particularity of the Word made flesh. Torrance's focus on theology as science has meant that his path has, to some degree, fallen prey to his own warning. Namely, to pursue one mode of rationality rigorously to the exclusion of others creates an artificial abstraction 'which nature punishes by limiting our discoveries through it' (*Divine and Contingent Order*, p. 17). A lack of sustained integration of aesthetic rationality and little, if any, discussion of an economic and political translation (praxis) of the gospel account for the intellectualism of which Torrance has been accused. This is no doubt related to his giving priority in theology to interpreting over enjoying (aesthetics) and serving (praxis) (*The Ground and Grammar of Theology*, pp. 156ff.).

ROGER NEWELL

FURTHER READING: *Texts: The Doctrine of Grace in the Apostolic Fathers* (Edinburgh, 1948); *Conflict and Agreement in the Church*, Vol. I: *Order and Disorder*, Vol. II: *The Ministry and Sacraments of the Gospel* (London, 1959, 1960); *Theology in Reconstruction* (Grand Rapids, 1966); *Space, Time and Incarnation* (Oxford, 1969); *Theological Science* (Oxford, 1969); *God and Rationality* (Oxford, 1971); *Theology in Reconciliation: Essays Toward Evangelical and Catholic Unity in East and West* (Grand Rapids, 1976); *The Ground and Grammar of Theology* (Charlottesville, VA, 1980); *Divine and Contingent Order* (Oxford, 1981); *Transformation and Convergence in the Frame of Knowledge* (Belfast, 1984); *The Trinitarian Faith* (Edinburgh, 1988). *Articles about Torrance*: Daniel Hardy, 'Thomas Torrance', in D.F. Ford (ed.), *The Modern Theologians: An Introduction to Christian Theology in the Twentieth Century*, I (Oxford, 1989), pp. 71–91; I. John Hesselink, 'A Pilgrimage in the School of Christ – An Interview with T.F. Torrance', *Ref R* 38.1 (1984), pp. 49–64; Robert J. Palma, 'Thomas F. Torrance's Reformed Theology', *Ref R* 38.1 (1984), pp. 2–46. *Dissertations about Torrance*: Roger Newell, 'Participatory Knowledge: Theology as Art and Science in C.S. Lewis and T.F. Torrance' (PhD thesis, University of Aberdeen, 1983); C. Baxter Kruger, 'Participation in the Self-Knowledge of God: The Nature and Means of our Knowledge of God in the Theology of T.F. Torrance' (PhD thesis, University of Aberdeen, 1989); Robert J. Stamps, 'The Sacrament of the Word Made Flesh: The Eucharistic Theology of Thomas F. Torrance' (PhD thesis, University of Nottingham, 1986);

Wing-Hong Wong, 'An Appraisal of the Interpretation of Einsteinian Physics in T.F. Torrance's Scientific Theology' (PhD thesis, University of Aberdeen, 1992).

Troeltsch, Ernst (1865–1923)

Ernst Troeltsch, one of the leading representatives of liberal theology before the First World War, studied initially at Erlangen, but he became increasingly dissatisfied with his conservative teachers and moved to Göttingen, where he came under the influence of *Albrecht Ritschl (1822–89). Here he formed close friendships with a group of young scholars, which became known as the *History of Religions School. Because of his many contributions to the first edition of the encyclopedia *Die Religion in Geschichte und Gegenwart*, he was later known as the 'systematic theologian' of the School. After a brief spell at Bonn, he was appointed professor of systematic theology at Heidelberg in 1895, where he remained until 1915 when he moved to the philosophy faculty at Berlin.

Although he engaged in many different academic disciplines, and although much of his work was unsystematic, Troeltsch's overriding interest, which permeates nearly all his published work and unpublished lectures, is in the theological, philosophical and ethical response to what he called the 'great fact' of the modern world. The theologian had to understand the phenomenon of modernity as thoroughly as possible by undertaking an investigation of the 'new foundations and presuppositions by which it is essentially differentiated from the ecclesiastical-unified period of European culture'. From the beginnings of his career Troeltsch was thus engaged with the relationships between modernity and the Christian tradition, and during the 1890s he began to look in detail at the implications of the historical method for theology. These researches crystallized into his book on *The Absoluteness of Christianity* (1901, ET London, 1972). Here, as well as in his articles on dogmatics, his theology was expressed in terms of a progressive revelation rather than in the dogmatic rigidity of orthodoxy. Troeltsch, who was greatly influenced by *Kant, also entered into philosophical debate, seeking against *Wilhelm Herrmann, and also *Rudolf Otto and Wilhelm Bousset, to integrate religious and scientific epistemology. Similarly, in his often deeply pessimistic essays on modern culture, he claimed that unless religion could be connected with the rest of reality it would become apologetically irrelevant in the face of the all-pervasive influence of materialism and monism.

In Heidelberg, Troeltsch formed a close friendship with the sociologist Max Weber (1864–1920), becoming increasingly interested in the social forms of Christianity through history. He published his massive study *Die Soziallehren*, in 1912 (ET *The Social Teaching* [London, 1931]), in which he outlined his theories of church, sect and mysticism. He understood this book as preparing the objective 'sociological' basis for the constructive theological task of trying to recreate a unified world-view analogous to the medieval model, but within the constraints of modernity – the most important being the *Enlightenment discovery of autonomy and its criticism of all supernatural authority.

Feeling that he had 'outgrown' the theological faculty, Troeltsch moved to Berlin, concentrating his efforts on trying to understand the First World War, as well as the philosophical analysis of history. Although he was often influenced by prevailing public opinion, he retained a critical distance from the excesses of militarism, and he later devoted his energies to post-war reconstruction. After the armistice he commented extensively on the political situation, becoming an enthusiastic supporter of the Weimar Republic and also assuming practical responsibilities in the Prussian Ministry for Science, Art and Education after 1919.

His great late work *Der Historismus und seine Probleme* (Tübingen, 1922) was in many ways a philosophical refinement of the theological themes that had occupied him early in his career. Again he saw his purpose as reshaping and unifying the present, drawing from the resources of the past. He recognized the cultural relativity involved in any construction, and yet he still believed it was possible to forge a unified world-view from the 'melting pot of historicism'. In his final lectures intended for delivery in Britain in 1923, which his sudden death prevented him from giving, Troeltsch outlined what he called a 'material philosophy of history'. He presented an ethics of compromise, which stems from his recognition that participants in a dialogue have to limit their claims to an absolute standpoint. Troeltsch's final solution rests on a very provisional decision that can always be modified or reversed by proper debate:

> The task of damming and controlling [history] is … essentially incapable of completion and essentially unending; and yet it is always soluble and practicable in each new case. A radical and absolute solution does not exist; there are only working, partial, synthetically uniting positions … In history itself there are only relative victories; and these relative victories themselves vary greatly in power and depth, according to time and circumstance. (*Christian Thought* [London, 1923], pp. 128f.)

Given the proposed audience of his lecture, it is no surprise that Troeltsch makes explicit use of a metaphor of compromise drawn from British politics which he saw resembling his own practical, piecemeal and relative solution.

Since the First World War, Troeltsch has frequently been branded pejoratively as a 'Culture Protestant' despite his frequent criticisms of his own society. Yet he countered such criticism: for Christianity to retain its ethical potency, it simply could not separate itself from the remainder of reality in sectarian purity. Although he believed in the necessity of compromise with the forces of history, regarding all social forms as exercising constraints upon the expression of Christianity, he was nevertheless inspired by a vision of an ideal, which encouraged constant criticism of the present in the hope of something better. Indeed he regarded this critical principle, which prevented the absolutization of any one expression of the Christian ethos, as the Enlightenment's greatest contribution to theology.

MARK D. CHAPMAN

FURTHER READING: *Texts: Religion in History* (Edinburgh, 1991); *Troeltsch-Studien* (Gütersloh, 1984–). *Studies:* Karl-Ernst Apfelbacher, *Frömmigkeit und Wissenschaft* (Munich, 1978); J.P. Clayton (ed.), *Ernst Troeltsch and the Future of Theology* (Cambridge, 1976); Sarah Coakley, *Christ Without Absolutes* (Oxford, 1988); H.-G. Drescher, *Ernst Troeltsch: His Life and Work* (London, 1992); F.W. Graf and H. Ruddies, 'Religiöser Historismus: Ernst Troeltsch', in *Profile des neuzeitlichen Protestantismus* 2:2 (ed. F.W. Graf; Gütersloh, 1993), pp. 295–335; F.W. Graf and H. Ruddies, *Ernst Troeltsch Bibliographie* (Tübingen, 1982); Walter Köhler, *Ernst Troeltsch* (Tübingen, 1941); Robert Morgan and Michael Pye (eds.), *Ernst Troeltsch: Writings on Theology and Religion* (Atlanta, 1977).

Turretin, Francis (1623–87)

Francis Turretin (Franciscus Turrettinus, François Turrettini), Protestant scholastic theologian of the *Reformed tradition, was appointed professor of theology at the University of Geneva in 1653. His systematic work, *Institutio theologiae elencticae* (Geneva, 1679–85), represented that stage of development in Reformed thought from protest to intellectual system. He employed the categories of the scholastics, being influenced by the late medieval theologians, notably *Thomas Aquinas, and the revived *Scholasticism of Francesco Zabarella (1360–1417) and *Francisco de Suárez (1548–1617). Turretin was reluctant to cite sources directly, and he distanced himself from their conclusions on polemical grounds.

The role of reason and philosophy was of major concern. The Reformers' *sola scriptura* principle required reticence in appropriating philosophy, but *rapprochement* with philosophy became necessary as Protestant theology was institutionalized in the universities. A similar dilemma had confronted the thirteenth-century scholastics, and was resolved by Aquinas in terms of order of being: we cannot know God insofar as God is a higher being than we are. The Reformers, and Turretin after them, phrased the problem in terms of human sinfulness and the need to hear the redemptive word. Turretin maintained the priority of revelation over reason, and he accused the medieval scholastics of resting more upon the philosophy of *Aristotle than upon the testimonies of the prophets and apostles. He attacked the *Socinians of his day, whose theology had a strong Cartesian element, for making reason foundational and for using philosophy to interpret Scripture (*Institutio*, I.13.1). He also denounced 'Fanatics and Enthusiasts', '*Anabaptists and Weiglians' who waged war on philosophy (*Institutio*, I.13.1). He professed to take an 'orthodox' middle position, retaining the hierarchy of 'ways of knowing' within the *Augustinian and medieval tradition: 'grace does not destroy nature but perfects it, neither does supernatural revelation abrogate nature, but cleanses it' (*Institutio*, I.13.3). Reason could not be the foundation (*principium*) or norm for how Christian theology determines the objects of its faith, but could adduce certain articles of faith and draw inferences from Scripture or theological arguments. Thus Turretin retained the Reformation teaching on the ministerial, as opposed to the magisterial, role of

reason, and he fashioned theology as the summarizing of biblical teaching.

The two scholastic questions that most shaped Turretin's theology were whether theology is a science, and whether it is speculative or practical. He argued that theology is not a 'science' (*scientia*) – that is, a discipline that rationally establishes truth upon evident principles – because theology 'does not rest on rational evidence, but on testimony alone' (*Institutio*, I.6.5). He employed a prominent Protestant scholastic distinction (generally credited to Franciscus Junius, a pupil of Calvin, in *De theologia vera* [Leiden, 1594] and *Theses theologicae* [c. 1592]) between *theologia archetypa*, known only to God, and *theologia ectypa*, which rests on divine revelation. *Theologia ectypa* is suited to our human condition. It is revealed theology, not natural theology, because it recognizes God (*principium essendi*) and Scripture (*principium cognoscendi*), rather than reason, as its fundamental principles. Its object is not God as he is in himself, but God as he has revealed himself in his word (*Institutio*, I.5.4). Theoretical consideration of God as deity, as performed by most scholastics, is to the destruction of sinners. Instead, we are to consider God as 'our God, that is, covenanted in Christ' (*Institutio*, I.5.4).

Turretin viewed theology as both practical and speculative. A discipline is 'speculative' when the knowledge it yields is an end in itself, and 'practical' when its knowledge is directed to activity beyond the discipline (*Institutio*, I.7.3). If theology were practical, as argued by the Socinians and later Remonstrants, it would aim at obedience and faith in promises but would lack dogmatic knowledge of such matters as the Trinity or the incarnation (*Institutio*, I.7.2). Yet, theology does not rest in knowledge (*cognito*) 'but directs and orders knowledge towards activity' (*Institutio*, I.6.5). Thus Turretin placed greater emphasis on the practical. In this he was partly influenced by an Augustinian understanding of God as the *summum bonum*, the highest good and ultimate object of our enjoyment, and also by the Reformers' emphasis on soteriology.

He championed Calvinist Orthodoxy against the challenges of counter-Reformation theologians, particularly over the nature of the sacred *apographa*. In this he was an ally of the British *Puritan theologian, *John Owen (1616–83). The *apographa* were understood by Reformed (and *Lutheran) dogmaticians to be the faithful copies of the originally inspired *autographa* (autographs), recording for us that word of God in the same words into which the sacred writers committed it under the immediate inspiration of the Holy Spirit (*Institutio*, II, 3–5, 7, 22, 24). Turretin held even the vowel points of the Hebrew manuscripts to be inspired, as did the Lutheran theologian John Quenstedt (1617–88). *Luther and *Calvin had admitted that the pointing in the accepted Hebrew text of their day could be wrong. However, once Roman Catholics (notably, the *Jesuit *Robert Bellarmine, 1542–1621) argued for the reliability of the Vulgate over the Masoretic text, and attributed the pointing to the Masoretes and not to Moses or Ezra, Protestants argued the matter as a doctrinal issue. Reformed theologians, unlike Lutherans, codified their position on the *apographa* in the Westminster Confession (I, 8). Three decades later, Turretin, Lucas Gernler of Basle and Johann Heinrich Heidegger of Zurich, composed the Formula Consensus Helvetica (1675) because of debates over the authority of the Hebrew vowel points at the University of Saumur. The Formula affirms that God committed his word to writing by Moses, the prophets and the apostles, and that he has watched and cherished it with paternal care to prevent its corruption by craft of Satan or fraud of man.

Turretin's *Institutio* was the main teaching text at Princeton Theological Seminary until the 1870s, and the work influenced the development of theological method and the doctrine of biblical inerrancy associated with the dominant Princeton strand of evangelical theology.

HARRIET A. HARRIS

FURTHER READING: *Introductory*: Jack B. Rogers and Donald McKim, *The Interpretation and Authority of the Bible* (San Francisco, 1979); R.T. Kendall, *The Influence of Calvin and Calvinism Upon the American Heritage* (Annual Lecture of the Evangelical Library; London, 1976); Theodore Letis, 'The Protestant Dogmaticians and the Late Princeton School on the Status of the Sacred Apographa', *Scot Bul Ev Th* 8 (1990), pp. 16–42; J.S.K. Reid, *The Authority of Scripture: A Study of the Reformation and Post-Reformation Understanding of the Bible* (London, 1957); Francis Turretin, *Institutes of Elenctic Theology* (trans. G.M. Giger; ed. J.T. Dennison; 3 vols.; Phillipsburg, NJ, 1992–97). *Advanced*: Richard A. Muller, 'Scholasticism Protestant and Catholic: Francis Turretin on the Object and Principles of Theology', *Ch H* 55.2 (1986), pp. 193–205; *Post-Reformation Reformed Dogmatics* (Grand Rapids,

1987); F. Turretin, *Institutio theologiae elencticae* (Trajecti ad Rhenum; Utrecht, 1734 edn includes a 4th vol. containing *De satisfactione Christi disputationes* and *De necessariâ secessione nostrâ ab Ecclesiâ Romanâ disputationes*); Emil Weber, *Die philosophische Scholastik des deutschen Protestantismus im Zeitatler der Orthodoxie* (Leipzig, 1907).

Tyndale, William (c. 1494–1536)

William Tyndale was born in Gloucestershire, England to a large, influential family. Educated both in Oxford and Cambridge, Tyndale is best known for his translation of the Greek Bible into the English vernacular. He lived during the period of the dawning of the printing press, which allowed for various translations of the Bible into French, German, Dutch, Spanish, Czech and Danish. Tyndale introduced this revolution to the English side of the English Channel in 1526. He suffered a martyr's death after being stripped of his Catholic vestments in early August of 1536 (tradition marks his death on the sixth) in the town of Vilvorde as a leader of the English *Reformation movement, being charged with the heresy of not agreeing with the Holy Roman Emperor.

Of Tyndale's childhood not much is known through primary sources. What is more certain occurs from his time in Oxford onwards. While at Oxford, Tyndale seems to have faced a degree of disenchantment regarding the speculative handling of the Scriptures by academicians. Nevertheless, his education in the arts at Oxford provided him with sufficient background in Greek, Latin and modern languages to equip him for his calling as a translator of the Greek Scriptures. His experience at Cambridge passes without much mention. What is known is that he improved his Greek there and perhaps came into contact with the work of *Erasmus, who published a parallel Greek-Latin version of the New Testament which Tyndale later translated. Upon his return to Gloucestershire, Tyndale was preaching, although the date of his ordination is unrecorded. It was at this point that he translated Erasmus's *Enchiridion Militis Christiani* and determined to translate the Scriptures into vernacular English, an unauthorized act. Tyndale moved to London c. 1523. It was in London that he developed a disdain for his ecclesial colleagues, saying of them that 'they bosted them selves and their hye authorite, and beheld the pompe of our prelates ...' ('Penta-teuch'). Tyndale then moved to Germany for the express purpose of translating the Greek New Testament into English. In Germany he encountered a more progressive spirit of refor-mation than was yet present in England. By 1525 he was in Cologne, overseeing the pro-duction of his first version of the New Testament in English, a project which was completed in Worms that same year. Not only did this translation achieve swift and prodi-gious popularity, but scholars reference the beginning of the English Reformation with its publication.

This work commenced a series of literary pieces which Tyndale published from Antwerp, most notably: (1) 'The Parable of the Wicked Mammon' (8 May 1528), which is related to *Martin Luther's sermon, 'Eyn Sermon von dem unrechten Mammon'; (2) 'The Obeydyence of a Chrysten Man' (2 October 1528), which called for ecclesial submission to royal authority; (3) 'The Pentateuch in English' (January 1530); and (4) his revision of *The New Testament in English* (1534), with more extensive notes and intro-ductions. Betrayed by Henry Phillips, a sup-posed friend at the University of Louvain, Tyndale was arrested in May 1535 and removed to Vilvorde, where he was martyred.

Tyndale's role in the English Reformation is undoubtedly the most salient product of his work. However, one must ask what theological interests and motivations piloted his work. Since Tyndale did not expound theology at great length in his writings, there is some debate among scholars regarding the influences upon him, although scholarship has traditionally maintained a *Lutheran connection. Tyndale cannot be understood outside his place in history at a crossroads of varying reactions to the Catho-lic church: showing influences from Wyclif, the Lollard dissenters in England – although one must be careful not to generalize about this group as a unity of thought and creed – and the Lutheran movement. Following in the footsteps of Wyclif and perhaps even the Lollards, Tyndale was resolute in championing the value of Scrip-ture as the authority by which all other authori-ties were to be judged. This was apparently a cornerstone of Lollard thought, and its influence in England undoubtedly affected Tyndale. That the Scriptures were not permitted to be translated into English was offensive to Tyndale, because he maintained that salvation was achieved through an understanding of Scripture *in toto*.

Soteriology pervaded Tyndale's biblical theol-ogy. He maintained that salvation was procured by humanity through God's election, not by humanity's works. The only proper human response to this grace was faith, expressed through obedience to God's law in Scripture. Thus, while they retained an important place in his theology, Tyndale clearly never regarded works as the cause of salvation. Rather, they were the expression of the new life which one experi-ences by means of the faith that comes from justification. 'For the outwarde workes can never please God nor make frende except they springe of faith' ('Mammon'). Likewise, pneumatology occupied a central position, since the Spirit's salvific work was the identifiable product of preaching delivered and responded to among God's elect, a work which manifested itself chiefly in the 'workes' referred to above.

As for the Lutheran influences which scholar-ship has traditionally traced behind Tyndale's thought, these certainly exist. But Tyndale can be distinguished from the wider Lutheran Refor-mation movement with respect to (1) his view of covenant; (2) Gospels as 'promises' rather than as 'proclamations'; (3) his view of the law mandating perpetual ethical obligation for the Christian, as opposed to Luther's forensic account of it; (4) his figurative view of the Eucharist; and (5) his protest against a two-tiered New Testament canon. This area remains a focus for scholarly debate, however, and one must avoid any undue simplification of the issues.

THOMAS J. BOONE, III

FURTHER READING: David Daniell, *William Tyn-dale: A Biography* (New Haven, 1994); Eric Lund, 'Tyndale and Frith on the Eucharist as Sign and Memorial', and Douglas H. Parker, 'Tyndale's Bibli-cal Hermeneutics'; and William S. Stafford, 'Tyn-dale's Voice to the Laity', in John T. Day, Eric Lund and Anne M. O'Donnell (eds.), *Word, Church, and State* (Tyndale Quincentenary Essays; Washington, DC, 1998); James F. Mozley, *William Tyndale* (New York, repr. edn 1971); J.J. Scarisbrick, *The Reforma-tion and the English People* (Oxford, 1984); Donald D. Smeeton, *Lollard Themes in the Reformation Theology of William Tyndale* (Sixteenth Century Essays and Studies 6; Kirksville, MO, 1986); C.H. Williams, *William Tyndale* (London, 1969).

Underhill, Evelyn (1875–1941)

Perhaps the English language's most widely read writer on prayer, contemplation, spirituality, worship and mysticism in the first half of the twentieth century. Her oft-reprinted and multi-edition 'weathered masterpiece', *Mysticism*, may be this century's most significant book on the subject. By recovering forgotten or undeservedly neglected texts, she became the first of many dedicated to disseminating knowledge of the mystical life to a broad public. For Underhill, spiritual-mystical writings attest to a full-blooded, passionate love affair with 'the Eternal'. Therefore, such literature – to be understood properly – must be read and studied with the passion of both faith and love. Underhill's own life was punctuated by spiritual lapses, numerous conversions, paranormal and perhaps even incipient mystical experiences ('the deep mysterious love one wants to keep'). Her 39 books and more than three hundred and fifty articles give indirect testimony to her own spiritual journey from agnosticism, to mystical monism, to her own struggle between 'pure' mysticism and carrying the cross of daily life, and finally, to the joys of a fully incarnational spirituality culminating in both the individual and communal sacrificial worship of God, the 'wholly Other'.

Born the only child of well-to-do parents in Wolverhampton, Underhill was educated first privately and then at Sandgate House near Folkestone before attending King's College, London, of which she eventually became a fellow. In her early years, Underhill was indifferent – if not somewhat hostile – to religion, especially in its institutional manifestations. However, trips to Italy and a visit to a convent of perpetual adoration sparked a religious conversion inclining her to the sacramental-incarnational faith of Roman Catholicism. Her spiritual yearnings also led her to participate for a few years in the occult, hermetic Golden Dawn Society, which she would later claim opened her eyes to a 'Reality' beneath appearances. At age twenty-seven, she published her first of several books of poetry – a genre she considered the crown of mystical literature – and then three novels in the next few years. Quasi-mystical characters living in two worlds and seeing below life's surface are the heroes who experience 'God's first kiss' and eventually see the redemptive value of losing one's seemingly higher vocation to find full human integration in self-sacrificing love of others. As with

Underhill's later works, these novels – especially *The Column of Dust* – illustrate how the mystical quest can go horribly wrong if embarked upon for its own sake. They also evince a long-lasting tension in her own life: Should one pursue the mystical life of ecstatic consciousness or the loving, self-sacrificing folly of the cross in daily life?

At the age of thirty-two Underhill married a childhood friend, Hubert Stuart Moore, a barrister. In 1911 she published *Mysticism*, the book which established her reputation as a spiritual writer. For the next ten years she published a variety of articles, translations and biographical works related to mysticism. Her *Jacopone da Todi Poet and Mystic 1128–1306: A Spiritual Biography* is still one of the best introductions to this fascinating mystic. Worth mentioning, too, is *The Mystic Way* (1913) which reinterprets Jesus as a mystic and the early Christians as a mystical community, a book 'as impressive as it is unconvincing' (Baron Von Hügel). She also collaborated with the eastern mystic Rabindranath Tagore in translating a selection of the mystical poetry of Pseudo-Kabir, the Bengali poet.

During World War I Underhill worked in naval intelligence and actively supported the war effort, undertakings that forced her to contemplate the relationship of the mystical calling to the historical, cultural, political and social environment. Although she said that she owed her entire spiritual life to the distinguished Roman Catholic lay theologian *Baron Friedrich von Hügel, a long-time friend and eventual spiritual director, she became a practising member of the Anglican Church in 1921. In the mid-1920s, Underhill directed retreats and earned a reputation as a spiritual director, a work she prized highly. *Practical Mysticism* (1914), *The Spiritual Life* (1937), *Abba: Meditations Based on the Lord's Prayer* (1940) and the posthumous 1948 book, *Meditations and Prayers*, are good examples of her practical, flexible and sound Christian advice through which she attempted to create an atmosphere in which God could be found in the midst of any life. She also did excellent editorial work for the *Spectator* and, later, *Time and Tide*. She also found time to visit the poor and the sick.

Both the *Mystics of the Church* (1925) and *The Golden Sequence* (1932) – as well as later editions of *Mysticism* – reject her earlier view that mysticism is the 'flight of the alone to the Alone'. She came to see that the God-centred life must fully embody itself in a given historical community.

One likewise sees her emphasis upon the lives of the mystics, their practical love, their 'spiritual fecundity', and her distinction between the mystic and the ecstatic. As much as she esteemed these pioneers of transcendental life, she viewed God as a realist who did not expect all to become mystics.

In *Man and the Supernatural* (1927), Underhill eschewed the progressive anthropocentrism of her day, for she valued only what resulted from one's inner life in God. Christianity, she held, must be God-centred – not simply social action, philanthropy, or the loudspeaker of public opinion. Her finest book may well be her deeply ecumenical *Worship* (1936), a study of the nature and principles of the human response to the Eternal. To Underhill, worship is the church's and the individual's witness to transcendence, a supernatural action which flows from and bestows supernatural life.

Because she felt herself called to respond to the interior problems of individuals, she avoided particular party movements, especially of a religious-political nature. However, in the late 1930s she became an ardent pacifist, as her *Into the Way of Peace* (1940) and *The Church and War* (1941) attest. Intense and unremitting work may have hastened her death from a thrombosis in 1941.

HARVEY D. EGAN, SJ

FURTHER READING: *Texts: The Letters of Evelyn Underhill* (ed. and intro. C. Williams; London, 1943); *Collected Papers of Evelyn Underhill* (ed. Lucy Menzies; New York / London, 1946). *Studies:* Margaret Cropper, *Evelyn Underhill: With a Memoir of Lucy Menzies* (New York / London, 1958); C.J.R. Armstrong, *Evelyn Underhill: An Introduction to her Life's Writings* (London, 1975); Marjorie Vernon in *DNB, 1941–1950* (ed. H.W.C. Davis and J.R.H. Weaver; London, 1965), pp. 897f.; Annice Callahan, *Evelyn Underhill: Spirituality for Daily Living* (Lanham, MD, 1997); Dana Greene, *Evelyn Underhill: Artist of the Infinite Life* (South Bend, IN, 1998).

Unitarianism

Unitarianism is the term usually applied, since the eighteenth century and in some instances at an even earlier date, to the radical form of Christian belief which rejects the doctrine of the Trinity and the unique divinity of Jesus Christ and affirms uncompromisingly the unity of God. Despite some anticipations of this position in the early church, Unitarianism needs to be primarily thought of as a product of the Radical Reformation, reflecting the anti-Trinitarianism which emerged in the sixteenth century among some of the *Anabaptists and Renaissance humanists.

Martin Cellarius, or Borrhäus (1499–1564), sometimes called the first Unitarian, was an *Anabaptist who taught that Christ was a human prophet and not 'very God'. Similar ideas were certainly discussed in the influential humanist circle established in Naples in the 1530s by the Spanish nobleman Juan de Valdés (c. 1500–41), an admirer of *Erasmus.

An independent humanist figure who had come under Anabaptist influence was the erudite Spanish physician and theologian *Michael Servetus (1511–53), author of *The Errors of the Trinity* (1531) and *The Restoration of Christianity* (1553), who was burned at the stake by *Calvin in Geneva.

In the latter part of the sixteenth century, anti-Trinitarian Protestant churches were established in Poland and Transylvania, partly under the influence of refugee Italian humanists. One such was Giorgio Biandrata, or Blandrata (1516–88), a medical man who became court physician in Poland and then in Transylvania. A former member of the refugee Italian Protestant congregation in Geneva, but later a strong opponent of Calvinism in Poland, he played a leading role in the formation of the group known as the Polish Brethren or Minor Reformed Church, established in 1565.

In Transylvania, Biandrata found a kindred spirit in the person of the radical Hungarian reformer Francis David (Dávid Ferencz, born c. 1510). Together they promoted what was later to become the Hungarian Unitarian Church, which, at the Diet of Torda in 1568, secured the patronage of the Transylvanian monarch John Sigismund II. But this early success was short-lived. Francis David, sentenced to life imprisonment on a charge of 'innovation', died in 1579. The church which he founded, however, has survived to the present day, with a few congregations in Hungary and a considerable number in Transylvania (now Romania).

The later development of the Minor Reformed Church in Poland was mainly due to the work of Faustus Socinus (Fausto Sozzini, 1539–1604), perhaps the most important figure in the entire history of Unitarianism. He was another Italian humanist, and he had probably been influenced in a radical direction by his uncle Laelius.

After visiting Transylvania in 1578, where it was hoped he might be able to moderate Francis David's extremism, he settled in Poland. From 1580 he gradually assumed the leadership of the minor Reformed Church, eventually becoming its revered teacher and apologist. The church at first enjoyed considerable success, with a flourishing international university and printing press at its metropolis, the city of Rakow. Here, in 1605, a year after the death of Socinus, the *Racovian Catechism* was published – the first complete statement of Unitarian doctrine, constructed from preliminary work undertaken by Socinus. It was firmly based on Scripture interpreted in the light of *recta ratio*, or 'right reason'. The Church soon came under increasing persecution and by 1660 it had been totally suppressed. But *Socinianism had already spread to other parts of Europe and its influence was particularly strong in Britain.

John Biddle (1615–62), sometimes called the 'Father of English Unitarianism', was perhaps the most notable and articulate of the seventeenth-century British Socinians. His anti-Trinitarian writings (including a tract *Against the Deity of the Holy Spirit* and some translations of Polish works) earned him several periods of imprisonment, and he died in gaol. By the end of the century, despite attempts to suppress it, Socinianism was widespread in the Church of England. Much controversy resulted from *The Naked Gospel* (1690), a tract written by Arthur Bury, rector of Exeter College, Oxford. Thomas Firmin (1632–97), an Anglican layman who wished to see 'Unitarian Societies' within the established church, published a series of *Unitarian Tracts*, which included some of Biddle's writings as well as *A Brief History of the Unitarians* (1687), written by Stephen Nye, a Hertfordshire rector.

Though the Dissenters at this period were for the most part far more orthodox, during the eighteenth century many Presbyterian congregations and a few of the Independents, mainly under the influence of the Dissenting Academies and those ministers who were calling themselves Rational Dissenters, moved steadily in a Unitarian direction. A typical representative of the trend was Joseph Priestley (1733–1804), a Dissenting minister better known as an important figure in the history of science. Most of the General Baptists also became Unitarian, and some doubts about the Trinity persisted in the Church of England. In 1774, Theophilus

Lindsey (1723–1808), an Anglican vicar and friend of Priestley, who had resigned his Yorkshire living, opened in London the first avowedly Unitarian Chapel in Britain. His congregation was eventually absorbed into the growing Unitarian movement, which evolved mainly from the English Presbyterians and the General Baptists, with a few accessions from the Methodists. During the nineteenth century, the movement's ethos was much transformed by the Unitarian theologian and philosopher James Martineau (1805–1900). In the United States, Unitarianism originated mainly among the New England Congregationalists under the leadership of W.E. Channing (1780–1842), and the movement was later much influenced by Emerson and the Transcendentalists.

The term 'Unitarian' undoubtedly originated in Transylvania. It became the official title of the Hungarian-speaking churches from about 1600, and has remained such until the present day. The term was never used by the Polish Socinians, but their spiritual descendants in exile did not object to it, and it eventually became the usual name in Britain and America. The term first appeared in print in Britain in *Controversie Ended* (1673), a tract by the English Socinian Henry Hedworth (1626–1705) directed against the Quakers.

There has always been considerable variety of belief among the Unitarians, but until the late nineteenth century a common thread can be traced in their theology, going right back to the writings of Servetus. Placing supreme emphasis on the unity of God and refusing to recognize either the Son or the Spirit as separate Persons within the Godhead, they rejected the doctrine of the Trinity as unscriptural and irrational – an unwarranted intrusion of false notions derived from Greek philosophy, which had corrupted what they saw as the simple gospel of Jesus. But their Christology was often confused and ambivalent. While insisting that Christ was primarily a man, the early Unitarians also saw him as being in some sense divine – the Son of God, but not God the Son. For this reason, the Polish Brethren were always called *Arians by their opponents. But they repudiated this on the ground that they rejected the idea of the pre-existence of Christ. Some later Unitarians however, particularly in Britain and America, were certainly Arians. But Arianism was one of the beliefs firmly rejected by Thomas Belsham (1750–1829), sometimes described as the last of the Rational Dissenters. Later Unitarians have almost always thought of Jesus as entirely and completely human – 'Perfect Man' but not 'Perfect God'. The main dividing line has always been on the question of 'adoration'. Socinus argued strongly that the offering of prayer and adoration to Christ was necessary and legitimate. The one most firmly opposed to this was Francis David in Transylvania, who had eventually insisted that the worship of the man Jesus was idolatry.

The issue emerged again at a later period, when at least until recent times, 'non-adoration' became the norm within Unitarianism. Following the lead established by the Anglican semi-Arian Samuel Clarke in his *Scripture Doctrine of the Trinity* (1712), Lindsey insisted that worship must be directed towards God the Father only, and Martineau repudiated the liturgical formula 'through Jesus Christ our Lord'. For this reason, the use of 'Socinianism' as an alternative for 'Unitarianism', especially in the late-eighteenth and early-nineteenth centuries, can be confusing, for the original Socinians were certainly 'adorationists'.

But the Unitarians, advocates from their earliest days of toleration and comprehension, have always been prepared to accept a wide variety of different beliefs, and it is hardly surprising that the movement has been characterized as a 'combination of all the heresies' – embracing anti-Trinitarianism, *Pelagianism, *Arminianism, Universalism and the *Abelardian theory of the atonement. The American Universalists, a denomination founded in 1793, eventually became Unitarian, and they were formally united with the Unitarians (now officially known, therefore, as 'Unitarian-Universalists') in 1961. In the last one hundred years, the English-speaking Unitarians especially have become interfaith enthusiasts, and the movement has happily included (though not without some controversy) non-theistic humanists and agnostics.

ARTHUR J. LONG

FURTHER READING: E.M. Wilbur, *Two Treatises of Servetus on the Trinity* (Cambridge, MA, 1932); *A History of Unitarianism* (2 vols.; Cambridge, MA, 1947, 1952); Tomas Rees, *The Racovian Catechism: Translated from the Latin with a Sketch of the History of Unitarianism* (London, 1818); J. Martineau, *The Seat of Authority in Religion* (London, 1890); *Essays, Reviews and Addresses* (4 vols.; London, 1891); A. Gordon, *Essays Biographical and Historical* (London, 1922); D.B. Parke (ed.), *The Epic of Unitarianism: Original Writings from the History of Liberal Religion* (Boston, 1992); C.G. Bolam, J. Goring, H.L. Short and R. Thomas, *The English Presbyterians: From Elizabethan Puritanism to Modern Unitarianism* (London, 1968); B. Smith (ed.), *Truth, Liberty, Religion: Essays Celebrating Two Hundred Years of Manchester College* (Oxford, 1986), esp. R.K. Webb, 'The Unitarian Background'; M. Wiles, *Archetypal Heresy: Arminianism through the Centuries* (Oxford, 1996).

Ursinus, Zacharias (1534–83)

Zacharias Ursinus was born in Breslau (modern Wroclaw), where he may have been taught by Andreas Moiban, the author of a catechism approved by *Philip Melanchthon. From 1550 until 1557 he studied in Wittenberg. Here he developed a lifelong admiration for Philip Melanchthon. In the autumn and winter of 1557–58 he made a study trip, including brief visits to Basle and Geneva and longer periods in Paris and Zurich to perfect his knowledge of Hebrew. Shortly after his return to Wittenberg, he was called to teach in Breslau. Melanchthon wrote the inaugural oration for Ursinus. From the autumn of 1558 until May 1560 he taught Latin and Melanchthon's *Examen Ordinandorum*, described in his inaugural as a catechism for future pastors. Breslau was then involved in debates about the retention of Roman ceremonies that also involved doctrinal questions about the Eucharist. To familiarize himself with the development of sacramental doctrine, Ursinus composed a set of *Theses* that showed his familiarity with the teaching of Geneva and Zurich as well as that of Wittenberg. In several letters from these years he was critical of the *Lutherans who opposed Melanchthon; Ursinus later lumped them together as *Flaciobrentani* (followers of Matthias Flacius Illyricus and Johann Brenz). In the summer of 1560, Ursinus asked the Breslau authorities for a leave with financial support. He first visited Wittenberg – but without Melanchthon, who had died earlier that year, he found the place no longer congenial. He went on to Zurich, where he studied Isaiah in Hebrew with *Peter Martyr Vermigli.

In January 1561 Hubert Languet, Melanchthon's close friend, and Caspar Peucer, Melanchthon's son-in-law, recommended Ursinus for a post in the Palatinate where the elector, Frederick III, undertook to complete the *Reformation begun under his predecessor.

Typical of his attitude towards public action, Ursinus preferred a post in an obscure village, but he was appointed *Loci* professor at Heidelberg University and placed in charge of the *Collegium sapientiae*, the preparatory school for teachers and pastors. These early years are well described by Erdmann K. Sturm, who sees them as preparing Ursinus for his career in Heidelberg as defender of its *Calvinism.

To prepare for his teaching, Ursinus composed the *Catechismus minor* (the least, that a member of the church should know) and the *Catechismus maior* (everything a teacher or pastor should know). When the elector decided on a catechism for the Palatinate Church, one that would define the differences with Rome and with the ubiquitist Lutherans, Ursinus wrote the draft on the basis of his own catechisms. A final version, the Heidelberg Catechism, resulted from committee deliberations. It was recognized as one of the official cathechisms of the *Reformed churches at the Synod of Dordrecht.

During his work in Heidelberg, the influence of Ursinus grew steadily as a result of his role as defender of the Catechism and its doctrines of the sacraments against Flacius and other orthodox Lutherans. Even his polemic with Jakob Andreae over the nature of the Trinity in the *Confessio de uno Deo, persona Christi et coena Domini* (1573) – an exposition of the two natures of Christ – is an attack on the Lutheran doctrine of the *real presence of Christ's body* in the Eucharist. The place of Palatinate theology and that of Ursinus in the confessional developments of the later Reformation was determined by these writings and firmly established in his *Admonitio* ('Warning', 1581) against the Lutheran *Book of Concord*. But perhaps it was the commentary on the Heidelberg Catechism, edited from Ursinus's notes by David Pareus, that was most influential.

Recent scholarship has focused on Ursinus as the source for the Reformed doctrine of the covenant, and Dutch *Arminians in the early seventeenth century made Ursinus, his Heidelberg colleagues and their students responsible for the spread of *Calvin's doctrine of predestination. Although *predestination* is not used in the Catechism, Ursinus expounds Calvin's doctrine in his commentary on Question 54 concerning the nature of the church which consists of the elect. Reformed covenant theology has been said to originate with *Heinrich Bullinger, and little attention is paid to the teaching of Mel-

anchthon who preferred the word *promise* over that of *covenant* as it emphasized the consolation of God's grace. This is also the essential teaching of the Catechism, which calls God's promise the *consolation (of believers) in life and death* that has become reality. Ursinus explains *covenant* in his commentary on Question 18 (on the redeemer). Interesting is his play on the words *eppangelia* and *evangelium*: the first means 'the promise of a redeemer', the second means 'the preaching of the redeemer who is already there'. This consolation runs through Ursinus's letters and it also led him occasionally to soften Calvin's doctrine of predestination. He maintained that the rejection of God's decisions on election makes one like a ship without a rudder, and he also referred to 2 Timothy 2:19. But he counselled a friend, who had read *Beza, to read Melanchthon on Philippians 1:6 and 2:13, where he stresses the consolation of Paul's teaching that God works in us, disposes us towards him and will complete the work he has begun.

After 1577, when the Lutheran son of Frederick III became Elector Palatine, Ursinus moved to Neustadt where the Reformed Johann Casimir, Frederick's younger son, established an academy. In 1570 there was an invitation to Ursinus to teach in Lausanne and there was also the opportunity of going to the University of Bern, but Ursinus left the decisions in the hands of God, of Elector Frederick and Johann Casimir. Both times, he wrote his friends that he was needed in the Palatinate, and he stayed. But it is interesting that he was considered for Bern, whose theology was neither that of Beza's Geneva, nor of Bullinger's Zurich. In a letter of 1582 about the theology of the sacraments Ursinus refers to Beza and the Lutherans and gives the impression that he belongs to neither. In Neustadt he lectured on Isaiah and continued to write in defence of the teachings in the Heidelberg Catechism.

Ursinus had married in 1574 on the advice of friends who felt he needed to be cared for as his infirmities became increasingly painful. The marriage produced one son, about whom little is known. At his death in 1583, Ursinus left a much valued library, and it is reported that a colleague married his widow for the sake of it. Ursinus died shortly before the Lutheran Elector Palatine, whose death opened the way for Johann Casimir to restore the Reformed Palatinate Church of which Ursinus had been a major architect.

DERK VISSER

FURTHER READING: *Texts: Zachariae Ursini Opera Omnia* (ed. Quirinus Reuter; 3 vols.; Heidelberg, 1612); *The Commentary of Dr. Zacharias Ursinus on the Heidelberg Catechism* (ed. and trans. G.W. Williard; Cincinnati, 1851). *Studies:* Fred H. Klooster, 'Ursinus' Primacy in the Composition of the Heidelberg Catechism', in *Controversy and Conciliation: The Reformation in the Palatinate, 1559–1583* (ed. Derk Visser; Allison Park, PA, 1986), pp. 73–100; Charles S. McCoy and J. Wayne Baker, *Fountainhead of Federalism: Heinrich Bullinger and the Covenant Tradition* (Louisville, 1991); Wulf Metz, 'Heidelberger Katechismus', *Th Real* 14 (Berlin, 1985); Erdmann K. Sturm, *Der junge Zacharias Ursin: Sein Weg vom Philippismus zum Calvinismus (1534–1562)* (Neukirchen-Vluyn, 1972); Derk Visser, 'Covenant', in *The Oxford Encyclopedia of the Reformation* (4 vols.; New York, 1996); 'Zacharias Ursinus (1534–1583), Melanchthons Geist im Heidelberger Katechismus', in *Melanchthon in seinen Schülern* (ed. Heinz Scheible; Wolfenbütteler Forshungen 73; 1997), pp. 373–91; *Zacharias Ursinus: Leven en werk van een hervormer tegen wil en dank* (Kampen, 1991).

Vatican Council I

The First Vatican Council – convoked by Pope Pius IX and held in Rome from December 1869 to October 1870 when it was interrupted by the Franco-Prussian war and never re-convened – represents the first significant attempt on the part of the official magisterium of the Catholic Church to address the challenge posed for Christian faith and life by modernity. Nearly 800 (out of approximately 1,000 possible) bishops and other ecclesiastical officials participated in this twentieth ecumenical council. Invitations were issued to the Orthodox and Protestant churches, but these appear to have been *pro forma*, and there were no non-Catholic participants. In a departure from precedent, no representatives of secular governments or rulers were invited to observe.

In comparison with previous ecumenical councils, Vatican I was unique in having a lengthy preparatory phase, which was initiated in 1865, with commissions charged with developing drafts (schemas) of decrees and constitutions to be discussed, revised and promulgated during the forthcoming council sessions. As it happened, the fathers of Vatican I were able to act upon only two of the 51 schemas (dealing with a wide range of issues in doctrine and ecclesiastical discipline) prepared by these commissions. The first of these schemas, after vigorous debate and extensive revision, became the Dogmatic Constitution on the Catholic Faith (*Dei Filius*) and was unanimously approved on 24 April 1870. Only part of the second and more controversial schema on the church was approved on 18 July 1870 as the Dogmatic Constitution *Pastor Aeternus* concerning the doctrine of the supremacy and infallibility of the pope.

Since the *Enlightenment, modern religious philosophy and epistemology had been concerned with examining and challenging the claim, shared in varying degrees by most branches of Christianity, that the truth of this faith is guaranteed by revelation, transmitted in Scripture and tradition, and reliably conveyed in the doctrine, catechesis and teaching of the church. Although many other topics crowded the agenda of Vatican I, it turned out that its principal legacy was to have addressed modernity's complex challenge to the sources of the truth of Christian faith.

It is noteworthy that the constitution *Dei Filius* represents the first extended treatment, at this level of official teaching, of the doctrine of revelation as such. The four chapters and 18 canons of *Dei Filius* take up, in turn: God the creator, revelation, faith, and the relationship of faith and reason. The burden of the constitution is to affirm the existence of God and the possibility of knowing this truth (against atheism), the necessity of revelation and faith for knowing the full truth about God and his purposes (against *rationalism), and the role of faith and reason in apprehending and articulating religious truth (against traditionalism and fideism).

In addition, while interest in the controversy surrounding the declaration of papal infallibility is understandable, the significance of *Pastor Aeternus* cannot be appreciated apart from the critical challenge posed by modernity to the general Christian claim (shared by Catholics and non-Catholics alike) to the possibility of possessing and transmitting certain knowledge about the truth of God and his purposes for the human race. While a number of bishops opposed the promulgation of the dogma of papal infallibility or thought it inopportune, all professed their adherence to it after its affirmation by the council fathers who were present.

J.A. DiNoia

FURTHER READING: Cuthbert Butler, *The Vatican Council, 1869–1870* (Westminster, MD, 1962); Norman P. Tanner, *Decrees of the Ecumenical Councils*, II (Washington, DC, 1990), pp. 800–16.

Vatican Council II

The twenty-first general, or ecumenical, council met in four separate sessions between October 1962 and December 1965. While Pope John XXIII had announced his intention to call a council as early as July 1959 and in June 1960 established 11 preparatory commissions to lay the groundwork for it, the council itself was officially convoked by the pope on Christmas day in 1961. More than 2,600 bishops from all over the world attended Vatican Council II, with nearly eighty non-Catholic observers, and between 200 and more than 400 theological experts (*periti*) in attendance at various sessions during the council. It was thus the largest general council in the history of Christendom, as well as the most genuinely international and ecumenical.

No previous general council enjoyed the benefits of so much meticulous preparation, with a period of world-wide consultation of bishops, curial officials, superiors of religious orders, universities and faculties lasting for nearly one full year. The results of these consultations were compiled and distributed to the preparatory commissions who used them as the basis for the composition of 20 draft texts (schemas) to be considered by the fathers of the council when they convened in the nave of St Peter's basilica on 11 October 1962.

In his opening address that morning, Pope John XXIII urged the assembled bishops to take a positive approach to the agenda of the council, to discount the dark prognostications of 'those prophets of gloom who are always forecasting disaster'. He also urged them to avoid a simple reaffirmation of the church's traditional doctrines accompanied by condemnations of errors contrary to those doctrines, but instead to seek an affirmative and inviting proclamation of the faith, applying 'the medicine of mercy rather than that of severity'. In contrast to most previous general councils, which were summoned to address some doctrinal crisis, the charter of Vatican II was thus seen to be more nearly a pastoral and evangelical one.

The council's charter, thus defined, guided the bishops in their initial review of the schemas they had received from the preparatory commissions. In general, it can be said that the bishops' consideration of these draft texts resulted in their being reduced to 17 in number and thoroughly revised during the course of the council's proceedings.

Its primarily pastoral objectives did not prevent the council from issuing documents of substantial doctrinal content and scope. Prominent among these were the following. The Constitution on the Sacred Liturgy (*Sacrosanctum concilium*) offered a deeply theological reflection on the nature of the worship and sacraments of the church, and on the centrality of the Eucharist in the liturgy. This document also sketched the lines for a reform of the manner in which the liturgy was to be celebrated. The Dogmatic Constitution on the Church (*Lumen gentium*) centred its account of the doctrine of the church on the theology of Trinitarian communion. The Dogmatic Constitution on Divine Revelation (*Dei verbum*) reaffirmed the church's faith in God's revelation and its basis in Scripture and tradition. Among the major documents of the council, the Pastoral Constitution on the Church in the Modern World (*Gaudium et spes*) contained the most complete articulation of the

kind of pastoral engagement with modernity that Pope John XXIII had called for at the opening of the council.

Several documents of the council concerned the theology and reform of various institutions and structures internal to the church's life. The Decree on the Pastoral Office of Bishops in the Church (*Christus dominus*) affirmed the collegiality of the bishops in union with the pope, and mandated the formation of regional episcopal conferences. Eastern Catholic churches, religious life, priestly life and ministry as well as priestly formation, the role of the laity in the church, and the importance of Catholic education and the communications media were in turn addressed by the Decree on the Catholic Eastern Churches (*Orientalium ecclesiarum*), the Decree on the Renewal of Religious Life (*Perfectae caritatis*), the Decree on the Life and Ministry of Priests (*Presbyterorum ordinis*), the Decree on the Training of Priests (*Optatum totius*), the Decree on the Apostolate of the Laity (*Apostolicam actuositatem*), the Declaration on Christian Education (*Gravissimum educationis*), and the Decree on the Means of Social Communication (*Inter mirifica*). Each of these documents contained numerous recommendations, some of which would have a far-reaching impact on the life of the church once they were read, assimilated and implemented in the years following the council.

The council also had a great deal to say about the church's relations with the world at large, with other Christian churches and ecclesial communions, and with the great world religions. In the Decree on Ecumenism (*Unitatis redintegratio*), the council acknowledged the fruitfulness of the ecumenical movement and committed the church to the task of promoting Christian unity. The council cast its glance to a 'wider ecumenism' when, in the Declaration on the Relation of the Church to non-Christian Religions (*Nostra aetate*), it took the unprecedented step of offering positive evaluations of Judaism, Islam, Hinduism, Buddhism and other religions. The council thus welcomed the prospects of officially sponsored inter-religious dialogue, while at the same time it reasserted its commitment to evangelization in the Decree on the Church's Missionary Activity (*Ad gentes divinitus*). Finally, in the Declaration on Religious Liberty (*Dignitatis humanae*), the council insisted on the right of persons to adhere to the dictates of their conscience in matters of religion and to be free from coercion and persecution with regard to their religious beliefs.

Pope John XXIII did not live to see the immense output that would be the legacy of Vatican II. After his death on 3 June 1963, it was left to his successor to continue its work. In his first message to the world on the day after his election, Pope Paul VI announced his intention to do just that and, during the course of the next two years or more, he guided the council through three sessions until its solemn conclusion on 8 December 1965. It was Paul VI who would have the colossal job of initiating and promoting the implementation of the council's decrees.

Even the brief sketch of the titles and contents of the constitutions and decrees of Vatican II provided above will give a hint of the magnitude of the task that confronted Paul VI and the post-conciliar commissions he appointed. So many areas of the church's internal structure and external relations were affected by the conciliar decrees that each document in effect prompted the development of new instructions, apostolic constitutions, declarations, directories and letters indicating how the council was to be implemented. Already by 1975, just three years before the death of Paul VI, a one-volume edition of the conciliar and post-conciliar documents ran to over a thousand pages.

After the brief pontificate of Paul VI's successor, Pope John Paul I, implementation of the council has continued apace during the twenty years that Pope John Paul II has occupied the chair of Peter. Pope John Paul II had himself been among the council fathers, and he has frequently proclaimed the council's immense significance for Catholic renewal. It has been his task to reconcile the sometimes conflicting interpretations of the council's decrees advanced by different groups in the church. These conflicting interpretations can perhaps best be seen in connection with the two trends that led to the council and influenced its ongoing discussion. The first is the agenda of 'return to the sources' (*ressourcement*), which emphasized the recovery and reaffirmation of Catholic identity and the intrinsic attractiveness of the message of the gospel. The second trend, on the other hand, is the agenda to modernize the Catholic Church (*aggiornamento*), which emphasized a dialogical attitude with respect to modernity and a commitment to an activist program in the arena of social justice

and international relations. During and immediately after Vatican II, the modernizing effect of the council received wide notice in the broadcast and print media. It was also quickly felt in several areas: in the rapid transformation of the liturgy, the conspicuous re-structuring of religious life, and in the marked rise in social activism by Catholic priests, religious and laity. The suddenness of some of these transformations delighted some Catholics but unsettled others.

While the agendas of both *ressourcement* and *aggiornamento* are embodied in the council documents and are, in any case, not opposed to each other, the decrees themselves failed to provide an indication of which of these trends should be accorded prominence in the interpretation of the council's actions. In the aftermath of the council, this fact produced a certain tension between groups espousing one or another of these agendas and claiming to be the authentic representatives of the council's legacy. In an attempt to reconcile these competing interpretations of the council with what has been termed a re-centring strategy (*re-accentramento*), the 1985 Synod of Bishops, marking the anniversary of the council, sought to supply a balanced reading of the conciliar documents in which both agendas could find their proper place.

J.A. DiNoia

FURTHER READING: Giuseppe Alberigo and Joseph A. Komonchak, *History of Vatican II*, I (Maryknoll, NY, 1995); Austin Flannery, *Vatican II: The Conciliar and Post-Conciliar Documents* (Wilmington, DE, 1975); Herbert Vorgrimler, *Commentary on the Documents of Vatican II* (5 vols.; New York, 1967–69); Synod of Bishops, 'The Final Report', *Origins* 15 (1985), pp. 444–50.

Vermigli, Peter Martyr (1499–1562)

Pietro Martire Vermigli, born in Florence on 8 September 1499 and named after a medieval saint of Verona, became a leading churchman in Italy and, for the last 20 years of his life, a Reformer in exile. Martyr entered the Lateran Congregation of Augustinian Friars Regular in Fiesole in 1514. He spent eight formative years at the University of Padua (1518–26), living in the monastery of St Giovanni di Verdara, the order's leading academy in terms of both library holdings and salon discussions. Martyr mastered Greek to read *Aristotle, studied

*Augustinian and scholastic writers (especially Gregory of Rimini and *Aquinas), and learned the art of debate. He began an outstanding career in the Augustinian Order. He was a public preacher, vicar at Bologna, where he learned Hebrew (1530–33), abbot of Spoleto (1533–36), abbot of San Pietro ad Aram in Naples (1537–40), visitor of the order and finally prior of San Frediano in Lucca.

Martyr's Neapolitan triennium introduced him to Juan de Valdés, a decisive influence in his search for biblical truth. The Theatines procured a suspension of Martyr because of his sermons on purgatory. But friends at Rome, notably Cardinals Contarini and Pole, had the ban lifted. Besides the *Erasmianism and spiritualism of the Valdesian salon, anonymous works of northern Reformers were being circulated. By the time Martyr went to Lucca he was bent on introducing reforms of doctrine and morals in both monastery and congregation. In this quasi-episcopal position, he established an academy with prestigious teachers, including Girolamo Zanchi and Emanuele Tremelli, what McNair calls 'one of the marvels of the Continental Reformation'.

In July 1542 the Roman Inquisition was resurrected because of the reforming spirit abroad, particularly in Lucca. One of its first acts was to summon Martyr and Bernardino Ochino, the Capuchin leader, for questioning. In August each headed north, meeting in Florence. Martyr stopped in Pisa where he celebrated the Eucharist in the Reformed manner. He settled in Strasburg with *Martin Bucer, spending five years teaching Old Testament (minor prophets, Lamentations, Pentateuch) in St Thomas College. He married Catherine Dammartin, a former nun, who died in Oxford, in 1553. Tension with *Lutherans over the Eucharist was a chief factor in his accepting *Archbishop Cranmer's invitation to England in November 1547.

Martyr was named Regius professor of divinity at Oxford in 1548, lecturing on Romans and 1 Corinthians. He became canon of Christ Church, and his wife was the first woman resident. A signal event was the Disputation of 1549, a four-day public debate on the Eucharist when Cranmer's new Book of Common Prayer was just introduced. The debate was occasioned by Martyr's lectures on 1 Corinthians 10, and precipitated by his predecessor in the chair, Richard Smith. Martyr defended three propositions which denied transubstantiation and

argued for a 'sacramental union' of the elements with Christ's body and blood. While in England he was one of eight responsible for the *Reformatio Legum Ecclesiasticum*, a project cut short by Edward's death and Mary's accession. During Cranmer's imprisonment, he named Martyr as chosen partner in defending the 'whole doctrine and religious order established' under Edward. Martyr was allowed to leave England in 1553.

Returning to Strasburg, Martyr lectured on Judges and Aristotle's *Nicomachean Ethics*, until disputes with the Lutherans, chiefly with John Marbach on sacramental conformity, led him to move to Zurich. Here (1557–62) he lectured on Samuel and Kings. He remarried; no children survived from either marriage. He engaged his colleague Bibliander in public debate on predestination and attended the Colloquy of Poissy (1561) where he joined *Theodore Beza as the chief spokesmen for the Reformed position. He died in *Bullinger's presence on 12 November 1562.

Peter Martyr's writings form a compact corpus of commentary and polemic. An Italian commentary on the *Apostles' Creed was published in 1544. The English lectures were published during his lifetime: the *Disputation* with accompanying *Treatise* in 1549, *1 Corinthians* in 1551, *Romans* in 1558. From the first Strasburg period, *Genesis* appeared in 1569, *Lamentations* not until 1629, and *Propositions from the Pentateuch* in 1583. From the second Strasburg period, *Judges* was published in 1561 and *Nicomachean Ethics* in 1563. The Samuel and Kings commentaries from the Zurich period appeared in 1564 and 1566. Polemical works include *Defensio ... ad Ricc. Smith ... de Coelibatu sac. et Votis monasticis* in 1559; *Defensio* against Stephen Gardiner in 1559 and *Dialogus de utraque in Christo natura* against the ubiquity doctrine of Johann Brenz, was published 1561, with a preface by John Jewel. A collection of prayers from the Psalms was published in 1564. Many of Martyr's scholia from the commentaries were gathered by Robert Masson for the *Loci Communes* of 1576, expanded 1580–83. This publication enjoyed wide circulation during the next century, including 13 Latin editions and Anthony Marten's English translation of 1583.

Martyr's reputation came to rest on his Eucharistic theology, while his method was judged on the basis of the *Loci Communes*. The latter is misleading, since it was a compilation by disciples, although his custom of inserting copious scholia in his commentaries encouraged its creation. In theology he was essentially a biblical commentator, an expert in Hebrew, Greek and Latin. He is a leading example of the recovery of medieval rabbinic commentators (through the Bomberg Bible) for Reformed exegesis. His polemical works were incidental responses to current controversies with Roman and Lutheran opponents. The two doctrines most closely associated with his teaching are predestination and the Eucharist.

The influence of Peter Martyr on both continental and English reform was widespread. He was confidante of queens – Elizabeth of England and Catherine de' Medici – and adviser on Prayer Book and legal reform and on Christological problems confronting the Polish nobility. He wrote the preface for Jewel's *Apology*, 1562. His significance for *Puritan theology and Erastian polity is yet to be measured. A modern revival of interest in Martyr began in the fifties, resulting in a series of English translations of his chief works, *The Peter Martyr Library* (Sixteenth-Century Journal Publishers, Kirksville, MO, 1994–). The fifth volume of the library contains the first biography of Martyr, Josiah Simler's funeral oration.

JOSEPH C. McLELLAND

FURTHER READING: G. Duffy and J.C. McLelland, *Life, Early Letters and Eucharistic Writings of Peter Martyr* (Oxford, 1989); J.P. Donnelly, *Calvinism and Scholasticism in Vermigli's Doctrine of Man and Grace* (Leiden, 1976); J.P. Donnelly and Robert Kingdon, *Bibliography of the Writings of Peter Martyr Vermigli* (Kirksville, MO, 1990). *Biographies:* Philip McNair, *Peter Martyr in Italy* (Oxford, 1970); 'Peter Martyr in England', in *Peter Martyr Vermigli and Italian Reform* (ed. J.C. McLelland; Waterloo, Ont., 1980); M.W. Anderson, *Peter Martyr Vermigli: A Reformer in Exile 1542–62* (Nieuwkoop, 1975); R.M. Kingdon, *The Political Thought of Peter Martyr Vermigli* (Geneva, 1980). *On Eucharistic theology:* J.C. McLelland, *The Visible Words of God* (Edinburgh, 1957); S. Corda, *Veritas Sacramenti* (Zurich, 1975).

Vincent of Lérins (d.c. 450)

Originally a soldier, Vincent was at some point ordained priest and withdrew to the island of Lérins and lived as a hermit near the monastery there founded in 410 by Honoratus, according to Gennadius (*De vir. ill.*, 65). Vincent died during the period of the co-regency of Theodosius and Valentinian – thus some time before July 450, possibly as early as 445 (*Vincentii Lerinensis Commonitorium, Excerpta* [ed. R. Demeulenaere; CCSL 64; Turnhout, 1985]). According to his friend *Eucherius of Lyons, he could hold his own in eloquence but outshone others in wisdom.

The Augustinian Prosper of Aquitaine wrote some *Responses ad capitula objectionum Vincentianarum*; and for some time Vincent was therefore thought to be anti-Augustinian, yet the discovery of his compilation of quotations from *Augustine by Madoz in 1940 confused the issue. The 'Obiectiones Vincentianae' are probably not Vincent's, and in his main work, the *Commonitorium*, he shows his Augustinian colours (sect. 24) and condemns *Pelagius, Caelestius and Julian of Eclanum.

Since the meaning of Scripture cannot always be agreed on, three principles for ruling whether or not a doctrine is orthodox are necessary: universality, antiquity and consent. He believed new doctrine can only be permitted if it is an elucidation of that which was previously obscure. He is clear in his opposition to *Nestorius, the *bête noire* of the 330s and 340s. 'Person' does not mean what it means in the theatre, namely 'role'; the incarnation was not an appearance; the union was at Christ's conception. 1 Timothy 6:20 tells us to avoid novelties and 'guard the deposit', and so councils should play a receptive, not a creative role. Even a doctor like *Origen or *Tertullian could go astray. However, in his reflections on the 'blessed' Council of Ephesus (431) Vincent provides a list of ten authoritative 'fathers': Peter, *Athanasius and Theophilus of Alexandria; the two Gregorys and Basil; Saints Felix and Julius of Rome; and *Cyprian and *Ambrose. The authority of the Roman see is added only as further recognition of the three principles, not as an authority in itself.

Sieben makes the helpful point that Vincent was not so much concerned with differentiating orthodoxy and heresy. He was being *descriptive of how tradition is established rather than prescriptive*, as he looked at the course of church history. His method was inductive, noting that in the past against the *Arians, *antiquitas* had been employed; against Donatists, *universitas*; against Nestorians, *consensio* (or *sententiae patrum*, to be called upon when the church seemed split: this helps us get back to the right message of the

Bible, for heretics sweeten their poisons with Scripture). Perhaps the scheme is best seen as a threefold cord of checks. Admittedly 'antiquity' on its own is weak, but it is less suspect, prima facie, than novelty. This position remained in Catholicism until *Vatican I, despite Döllinger, and in *Newman's thinking. It has been identified with a Protestant frame of mind that allowed the individual to hold the modern church back from receiving new insights and new doctrines.

MARK W. ELLIOTT

FURTHER READING: H.-J. Sieben, *Die Konzilsidee der Alten Kirche* (Paderborn / Munich / Vienna / Zurich, 1979), pp. 148–70.

Weil, Simone (1909–43)

Simone Weil was one of the most remarkable religious thinkers of the twentieth century. Born in 1909 into an assimilated Jewish family, she grew up with a profoundly ambivalent attitude both to Judaism and to the Roman Catholic tradition of Christianity. Her older brother, André, became one of France's most distinguished mathematicians. Apart from such intellectual competition at home, she was influenced by a remarkable teacher, Alain, at her secondary school. There she learned habits of penetrating reflection and criticism which stood her in good stead not only through her years at the École Normale Supérieure (as a contemporary of Simone de Beauvoir), but throughout her short life.

Qualified to teach, in her post at Le Puy from September 1931 she engaged in political action, writing on social and economic problems and committing herself to the causes of the unemployed. Plagued by headaches, she was eventually to leave teaching. She grew up in a Europe living with the consequences of the Versailles Treaty that helped to precipitate Nazism, and she visited Germany in 1932. She was one of the first to perceive the depth of the threat to Europe which Hitler's power represented. A period of time as a factory worker killed her youth, unsurprisingly, but with a period of farm work a little later she systematically made an effort to identify herself with those whose lives were extraordinarily hard. The New Testament category of 'slavery', and the 'imitation of Christ' as in 1 Peter 2:21 began to shape her spiritual identity. Visiting Portugal with her parents, she had the first of a series of encounters with Christianity which mattered most deeply to her. In a Portuguese fishing village she found herself observing a procession of fisherwomen on the day of the local patron saint, singing hymns of 'a heart-rending sadness', and there and then she became convinced that Christianity is pre-eminently the religion of slaves, and that she was among them. A brief period of entanglement, officially as a journalist in the Spanish Civil War, resulted in an accidental burn to the lower part of one of her legs which effectively ended her period of political activism.

It was to be as a writer whose work was to be insistently introduced to the post-World War II world by Albert Camus that her thought was eventually to become so influential. On a visit to Assisi in 1937 she visited the chapel where St Francis used to pray, and there, 'something stronger than I compelled me for the first time to go down on my knees'. In 1938, the year of the German annexation of Austria, she followed the Holy Week services at the great Benedictine Abbey of Solesmes. There she met a young English Roman Catholic who introduced her to George Herbert's poetry, most notably to 'Love bade me welcome', a poem which can be read both as an invitation to the Eucharist and, for some, as an invitation to death. It was during the recitation of this poem, and of the Lord's Prayer in Greek, that Weil was to experience the direct presence of Christ. She remained unbaptized, believing it to be her vocation to be open in the most catholic sense to the truths of other religious traditions. Hitler's invasion of France drove her and her family first to Marseilles, and then in exile to the USA whence Simone Weil returned to the UK, where she died in 1943, identifying herself through Christ with the suffering of those in war-torn Europe.

ANN LOADES

FURTHER READING (all of which contain listings of either primary or secondary material or both): The best biography is that of Thomas Nevin, *Simone Weil: Portrait of a Self-Exiled Jew* (Chapel Hill, NC, 1991). The most recent collection of essays from the international Simone Weil Society is John M. Dunaway and Eric Springstead (eds.), *The Beauty that Saves: Essays on Aesthetics and Language in Simone Weil* (Macon, GA, 1996). On her political thought: David McLellan, *Simone Weil: Utopian Pessimist* (London, 1989). On her philosophical and religious thought: Peter Winch, *Simone Weil: The Just Balance* (Cambridge, 1989); Richard H. Bell (ed.), *Simone Weil's Philosophy of Culture: Readings toward a Divine Humanity* (Cambridge, 1993); *Simone Weil: The Way of Justice as Compassion* (Lanham, MD, 1998).

Wesley, John (1703–91)

John Wesley was the son of Reverend Samuel and Susanna Wesley, former Dissenters turned Anglicans. In 1726 Wesley became fellow of Lincoln College, Oxford. From 1725 he developed an increasingly ascetic concern for inward and outward holiness until his 'evangelical conversion' on 24 May 1738. Thereafter he became a travelling evangelist, creating a chain of highly-organized religious societies which eventually, after his death, became the Methodist family of churches.

At Oxford Wesley was an advanced High

Churchman, influenced by ex-Anglican Non-jurors who used sacramental and disciplinary practices following the early church and particularly the so-called (actually fourth century) 'Apostolic Constitutions'. Under Moravian influence Wesley reacted against what he saw as 'salvation by works' in favour of justification by faith experienced in a sudden conversion or 'new birth'.

In his mature theology, however, salvation was seen as an extended process which he described in terms of repentance, faith and holiness: 'The first ... the porch of religion; the next the door; the third, religion itself'. He stressed the possibility of perfection in this life. This perfection would be an experience of freedom from conscious sin and an uninterrupted relationship of love towards God and humankind (see *Plain Account of Christian Perfection*, 1767). Perfection should be pursued actively by all means of grace but could be given in a moment in response to faith. Assurance of justification and perfection could be evidenced by conduct and 'the Spirit witnessing with our spirit'.

Justification and perfection, Wesley believed, could be lost (and regained), contrary to the *Calvinist doctrine of 'final perseverance'. His *Arminianism, perfectionism and stress on the role of disciplined piety exposed him to Calvinist charges that he was reverting to 'salvation by works'. The balance of his salvation doctrine was certainly weighted more in favour of sanctification than justification. His paradoxical doctrine of a limited perfection allowing for 'infirmities' (e.g. in knowledge) seems to depend on his restricted definition of sin as 'a voluntary transgression of a known law which it is in our power to obey'. To avoid salvation by works he claimed that the 'perfect' are every moment dependent on grace and faith.

Wesley's sacramentalism persisted from his earlier High Church phase. Through the hymns of his brother Charles (1707–88), Wesley's belief in a form of sacrifice and real presence in the Eucharist (though within the contemporary High Church tradition) was expressed in vivid physical language. He also saw the Eucharist, very unusually, as a 'converting' as well as 'confirming' ordinance. Wesley regarded Methodism as an auxiliary to the Church of England and opposed separation. His frequent violations of Anglican order (including conducting his own ordinations), however, supported by his persistent belief that the needs of evangelical mission should determine church order, suggest a strongly pragmatic view of ecclesiology.

The highly eclectic nature of Wesley's theology helps to explain the variety of interpretations offered of his teaching and place in the history of doctrine. His High Church inheritance was not fully replaced by evangelical influences and he appealed to the 'Primitive Church' to justify his later practices. Roman Catholic influences on Wesley included French Quietists like Madame Guyon and Archbishop Fénelon (despite Wesley's criticisms of 'mysticism') and the examples of Catholic holy men as models of perfection. *Puritan divines, purged of Calvinism, also left their mark on Wesley, notably *Richard Baxter. Wesley owed much to the Moravians in doctrine and practice. Some recent scholarship emphasizes the influence of early eastern Fathers on his perfection doctrine. Wesley, however, was very selective in what he borrowed for his purposes from all his sources. Furthermore, his approach to theology and piety was influenced by eighteenth-century attitudes, notably *Locke's empiricism and rejection of innate ideas. In his popular scientific and medical writings Wesley was a thoroughgoing empiricist, reasoning from observation and experience and disclaiming causal explanations. He also wrote of 'a new class of senses opened in your soul' for apprehending religious truth. Within the Anglican tradition of authority for doctrine being derived from Scripture, tradition and reason, Wesley emphasized Scripture above all, but reason was a valued auxiliary and he increasingly stressed experience for determining the meaning of Scripture for shaping practice. He became increasingly hostile to what he regarded as hair-splitting Protestant scholastic arguments on 'merit' and the role of 'works' in salvation. He nevertheless emphasized the infallibility of the Bible and invoked apparently supernatural phenomena as evidence of the reality of the spiritual world and divine intervention.

Wesley's theological achievement and legacy are difficult to estimate. It has been claimed that he produced 'a necessary synthesis of the Protestant ethic of grace with the Catholic ethic of holiness' (G.C. Cell, *The Rediscovery of John Wesley*, 1935). This statement does underline the fact that Wesley was struggling with a long-standing and divisive theological problem and drew on 'Catholic' as well as 'Protestant' sources in an attempt to solve it, unlike other evangelicals. Later Methodism tended to divide his perfectionist legacy, some seeing perfection as a gradual and incomplete process, others as an instant gift. The 'second blessing' or 'baptism of the Holy Spirit' (the latter notion drawing from Wesley's associate John Fletcher [1729–85]) can be seen in nineteenth-century American Baptist and Methodist revivalists and so became an element in twentieth-century Pentecostalism. The Church of the Nazarene is more directly in the Wesleyan tradition. The Oxford Movement's concern for the pursuit of holiness appears to owe nothing to Wesley.

HENRY D. RACK

FURTHER READING: *Texts: Works of John Wesley* (ed. P. Heitzenrater and F. Baker; 26 vols.; Nashville, TN, 1975–); supplemented by *Works* (14 vols.; 1872) and *Letters* (ed. J. Telford; 8 vols.; London, 1931). *Studies:* A.C. Outler (ed.), *John Wesley* (New York, 1964); H.D. Rack, *Reasonable Enthusiast* (London, 1992); R.P. Heitzenrater, *Wesley and the People Called Methodists* (Nashville, TN, 1995); C.W. Williams, *John Wesley's Theology Today* (London, 1946); H. Lindstrom, *Wesley and Sanctification* (London, 1946); J.E. Rattenbury, *The Eucharistic Hymns of John and Charles Wesley* (London, 1948).

Whale, John S. (1896–1997)

The son of a Congregational minister, John Whale trained for the Congregational ministry at Mansfield College, Oxford, and soon returned there to teach church history before moving to Cambridge as president of Cheshunt College (1933–44). The shortage of ministerial students there in the latter years of the war led him to accept the headship of Mill Hill School, marking the end of sustained theological teaching. Of his books, which have continuing influence, the best known, *Christian Doctrine* (1941), was printed many times, penultimately in a popular edition by Fontana and finally by the Cambridge University Press. Based on open lectures given in Cambridge, it remains one of the relatively few general introductions to the subject that can be recommended to students. It was followed by *The Protestant Tradition* (1955), an extended study of the *Reformation, its long-term affects and its modern ecumenical importance. Of broad learning, this book revealed his love for and reservations about his own Dissenting tradition. Whale's best book is probably his study of the atonement, *Victor and Victim* (1960), which is far better balanced and more

perceptive than the earlier and unjustly more famous work alluded to in its title, Gustav Aulén's *Christus Victor*. *Victor and Victim* is a study, full of insight, of the many strands that constitute this topic of theology, illuminatingly calling for assistance on related treatments of the human condition in the arts. Whale's books are written in a vigorous style, revealing a gift for language which enabled him to make judgements and observations tellingly and vividly, in some way reminiscent of *P.T. Forsyth, with whom he shared both an ecclesiastical tradition and a love of the arts – although he cites Forsyth surprisingly rarely.

COLIN E. GUNTON

FURTHER READING: *Texts: Christian Doctrine* (Cambridge, 1941); *Victor and Victim* (Cambridge, 1960); *The Protestant Tradition: An Essay in Interpretation* (Cambridge, 1955).

William of Ockham (c. 1285 – c. 1349)

Born c. 1285, probably at Ockham in Surrey, Ockham joined the *Franciscan order and studied at Oxford, 1309–23. He never incepted (became a regent master) in theology – hence his nickname, the 'venerable inceptor'. He was summoned to Avignon in 1324 under theological suspicion, but his teachings were never condemned. He became embroiled in the debate on Franciscan poverty, and in 1328 he fled with Michael of Cesena to the Holy Roman Emperor, Ludwig of Bavaria, at Munich. Excommunicated by the pope and the Franciscan order, Ockham spent the rest of his life writing on political issues, defending Franciscan poverty and the rights of the emperor against the pope. Ockham died in Munich c. 1349.

Ockham subscribed to the form of *Nominalism known as conceptualism: universals such as 'humanity', 'wisdom' and 'redness' are merely concepts, and they do not have any extramental existence. Earlier in his theological career, Ockham held that such concepts are the mental objects of our mental acts; later, he came to accept that universals can be reduced merely to the mental acts themselves. Such acts are natural signs of the individuals that fall under the general concept. Ockham avoids conventionalism (the denial of any natural relation between thing and concept) by positing that individuals of a kind have real – extramental – relations of similarity to each other that they do not have to individuals of another kind. Ockham argues in favour of his conceptualism by trying to show that the best brand of realism known to him – that of *Duns Scotus – relies on a formal distinction between common natures and the individuals that instantiate them. According to Ockham, the only possible sort of distinction between creatures is real. Hence Scotus's realism on the question of universals must be false. Consequent upon this, Ockham prioritizes intuitive cognition – an intellectual cognition of existent individuals, the basis of all understanding of abstract universals.

Ockham rejected Scotus's attempt to prove the existence of a first efficient cause, since he rejects any attempt to prove the impossibility of an infinite regress of causes. But he accepts a proof for a first conserver of everything. Conservation, unlike causation, entails temporal simultaneity. Hence an infinite series of conservers would entail actually infinitely many things existing at once – a state of affairs that Ockham, following *Aristotle, believed to be impossible. Ockham rejected, however, every argument in favour of the numerical unicity of any such being. That there is one God is a matter for faith. Unlike his predecessors, Ockham believed that tensed propositions can be literally true of God as well as of creatures. This weakening of the notion of divine timelessness leads to a novel theory of God's knowledge of future contingents: contingent future facts can cause the truth of past-tense propositions. Hence God can know, in the past, future contingent states of affairs, since this knowledge is caused by the future facts.

Ockham's Nominalism raises problems for the doctrine of the Trinity. According to Nominalism, there are no really shared universal natures. But orthodoxy, as stated at the Fourth Lateran Council (1215), requires that numerically one and the same nature is really shared by the three divine Persons. So we have to posit a formal distinction between each divine Person and the divine nature in order to allow for the conjunction of the divine nature's real identity with each divine Person with the real distinction of each divine Person from both of the others. The formal distinction flouts some basic rules of thought on the nature of identity. But these rules are inapplicable in the case of the Trinity. The doctrine of the Trinity is coherent, since we learn on faith that some of the rules of thought that we assume are of general

application turn out on inspection to be true only for the realm of creatures.

Ockham's Nominalism also affects his doctrine of the incarnation. According to Nominalism, abstract nouns such as 'humanity' properly refer to individuals. Hence, an individual human being is identical with a human nature, and 'A human being is a humanity' is typically true. But in the case of the incarnation the proposition is false, since the second Person of the Trinity is not identical with his human nature. He possesses his human nature in much the same way as a substance possesses an accident. Ockham's theory here does not generate a contradiction, but it does entail that Ockham's philosophical theories cannot be generalized to cover all theological cases.

Like most of his thirteenth-century predecessors, Ockham made use of the distinction between God's absolute power and his ordained power. The distinction is used to differentiate God's power to do whatever does not involve a contradiction from the power that ranges over what God actually does. This does not mean that God has two powers, or that he could act in a random way not in accordance with laws that he has (or can) set up. Nevertheless – following and developing insights of Scotus's – Ockham loosens the restrictions that divine goodness can set on God's activity. The commonly accepted claim that God has no obligations to creatures entails for Ockham that God can treat creatures as he likes. Whatever God does is just. Consistent with this, Ockham accepted a divine-command meta-ethic with regard to all moral precepts excepting the duty to obey God, which follows automatically from considerations of the divine nature. Theologically, Ockham denies – against *Aquinas – that a created habit of grace or charity is logically necessary or sufficient for salvation. It is logically possible for God to save whomever he pleases, irrespective of their supernatural goodness or grace. Actions are meritorious or sinful merely in virtue of God's acceptance or rejection of the action – his decision to reward or punish that action's agent. Ockham's view is not a form of *Pelagianism, since in the order God has established, grace is necessary and sufficient for salvation. Equally, God predestines people to salvation in the light of their foreseen merits – where both the moral and meritorious features of these actions are the result of God's unrestricted decision to value the actions in a certain way. Pelagianism is avoided by positing that the conditions for moral and meritorious values are wholly set by God. It is wrong to suppose that there is any intrinsic connection between Ockham's philosophical Nominalism and his theological voluntarism. The central insights of Ockham's ethics were derived from the realist Scotus (to whom Ockham's theological debt was vast), and there is no reason for every nominalist to accept them.

RICHARD CROSS

FURTHER READING: *Editions: Opera Politica* (ed. H.S. Offler, et al.; 4 vols.; Manchester, 1974 [2nd edn], 1963, 1956; vol. 4: Auctores Britannici Medii Aevi, 14; Oxford, 1997); *Opera Philosophica* (ed. Iuvenalis Lalor, et al.; 7 vols.; St Bonaventure, NY, 1974–88); *Opera Theologica* (ed. Iuvenalis Lalor, et al.; 10 vols.; St Bonaventure, NY, 1967–86). *Translations: Philosophical Writings* (ed. Philotheus Boehner; 2nd edn, rev. and ed. Stephen F. Brown; Indianapolis, IN, 1989); *Quodlibetal Questions* (trans. Alfred J. Freddoso and Francis E. Kelley; Yale Library of Medieval Philosophy; 2 vols.; New Haven / London, 1991). *Studies:* Marilyn McCord Adams, *William Ockham* (Publications in Medieval Studies 26; 2 vols.; Notre Dame, IN, 1987); A. Stephen McGrade, *The Political Thought of William of Ockham* (Cambridge, 1974).

Wittgenstein, Ludwig (1889–1951)

Born in Vienna, the youngest of eight children of a wealthy industrialist, Wittgenstein was baptized in the Roman Catholic Church. He gave up Christianity in adolescence but remained fascinated with religion. Educated at home and at school in Linz (where Adolf Hitler, his exact contemporary, was two years behind him in class), he took up mechanical engineering, studying in Berlin and Manchester (1908–11). Theoretical questions led him to the philosophy of mathematics; he worked for five terms in Cambridge with Bertrand Russell (1912–13). When war broke out he joined the Austrian army, serving with valour on the Russian and then the Italian fronts. His *Logisch-Philosophische Abhandlung*, completed in August 1918, appeared in 1921, and again in 1922, with C.K. Ogden's English translation, under the more familiar title of *Tractatus Logico-Philosophicus*. Considering his work in philosophy complete, Wittgenstein trained as a teacher and taught in remote village schools in Lower Austria for six years (1920–26). He then spent two years in Vienna, supervising the building of

a mansion for his sister. Discovering in discussion with members of the so-called Vienna Circle that they had founded *Logical Positivism partly on what he regarded as a misunderstanding of the *Tractatus*, he returned to Cambridge in 1929 as a research student. He submitted the *Tractatus*, for which he received his PhD, enabling him to teach philosophy – which he did from 1930 onwards. He succeeded G.E. Moore as professor of philosophy at Cambridge in 1939. During the war (1939–45), he worked as a porter at Guy's Hospital in London and then as a laboratory assistant in the Royal Victoria Infirmary in Newcastle upon Tyne. In 1949 he was found to have inoperable cancer. He continued to write copiously, as he had done since 1929, evidently accepting that his later work would appear posthumously. His *Philosophical Investigations*, with facing English translation by G.E.M. Anscombe, appeared in 1953. Much else has been published since then, including such major texts as *Remarks on the Foundations of Mathematics* (1956, rev. 1978), *The Blue and Brown Books* (1958), *Zettel* (1967) and *On Certainty* (1969), as well as *Lectures and Conversations on Aesthetics, Psychology and Religious Belief* (1966), *Remarks on Frazer's* Golden Bough (1979) and *Culture and Value* (1980), which contain much of more immediate theological interest.

Theologians sometimes cite the final remark of the *Tractatus* – 'Whereof one cannot speak, thereof one must be silent' – either agreeing or being inclined to disagree with the thesis that what may be said at all may be said clearly, and anything else will be nonsense. On the first view, nonsense reveals the limits of sense; vacuous uses of language can exhibit the conditions that govern the possibility of making sense. In effect, this is the logical-positivist reading. On the second view, however, the nonsense somehow manifests ineffable truths about ethics, the meaning of life, etc. In effect, Wittgenstein has a message about a mystical ineffability, that it is for the initiated to cherish privately in wordless silence. In a conversation in Vienna in 1930 he is quoted as saying: 'I can well imagine a religion in which there are no doctrinal propositions, in which there is thus no talking'. When people talk, in religion, 'then this itself is part of a religious act and not a theory' – which is why 'it does not matter at all if the words used are true or false or nonsense' (*Wittgenstein and the Vienna Circle* [1979], p. 117).

On the face of it, however, the *Tractatus* neither limits meaning to the domain of the hard sciences (physics) nor signals deep yet ineffable truths. Rather, it sets out to show that *philosophical* problems arise because of 'a misunderstanding of the logic of our language'. To one who reads the book with understanding it will give pleasure, Wittgenstein says; but it will be understood only by those who have had the thoughts expressed in it – and anyone who understands him will eventually recognize these thoughts as 'nonsensical'. (There is no agreement among philosophers about what Wittgenstein meant here by 'nonsense' – whether ethical statements that do not fit true/false categories are 'nonsense', albeit important nonsense, or whether in fact he really meant that all of his own remarks in the *Tractatus* are 'nonsense'.) The assumption is that philosophers typically suffer from an *illusion* of understanding: the task is not to disagree with what they think, but to show that what they think themselves to be thinking fails to amount to a thought. Once one sees this, one can throw away the ladder; having understood the nonsensical character of the propositions in the *Tractatus* one can see the world rightly.

Wittgenstein's aim, in the *Tractatus* as in the *Investigations*, was 'to teach you to pass from a piece of disguised nonsense to something that is patent nonsense' (*Investigations*, sect. 464). He has no objection to what we say – provided that 'it does not prevent you from seeing the facts' – and then, he adds, 'there is a good deal that you will not say' (sect. 79). His hope was to achieve a clarity which 'simply means that the philosophical problems should *completely* disappear' (sect. 133).

Few philosophers have accepted Wittgenstein's proposal to solve philosophical problems 'by arranging what we have always known' (sect. 109). Philosophers of religion have been charged with propagating 'Wittgensteinian fideism': religion as a 'language-game' intelligible only to insiders, immune to criticism from others. Wittgenstein suggested no such thing (as Hilary Putnam shows). He might have found congenial, on the other hand, attempts by such philosophers as D.Z. Phillips to free religious discourse from distortion by metaphysical theories. In his fragmentary notes on Frazer's *Golden Bough* Wittgenstein seeks to defend the religious practices of primitive peoples against intellectualizing reductionism. At all periods of his life he wrote sympathetically of the Christian religion. In his private journals, which were culled and published in the book *Culture and Value*, for example, he wrote in 1937 about faith, love and Christ's resurrection (p. 33), and in 1950 about proving God's existence (pp. 85–6). George Lindbeck attributes his 'cultural-linguistic' approach to Christian doctrine to his reading of Wittgenstein. On the whole, however, Wittgenstein's later work, repeatedly recalling us to the nature of human understanding against the will to perpetrate philosophical confusions and impose inappropriate scientific theories, has had little impact on theology.

FERGUS KERR

FURTHER READING: *Texts: Tractatus Logico-Philosophicus* (London, 1922); *Philosophical Investigations* (Oxford, 1953); *Remarks on Frazer's* Golden Bough (Retford, 1979); *Culture and Value* (Oxford, 1980). *Studies:* Derek Bolton, *An Approach to Wittgenstein's Philosophy* (London, 1979); George Lindbeck, *The Nature of Doctrine: Religion and Theology in a Postliberal Age* (London, 1984); Fergus Kerr, *Theology after Wittgenstein* (Oxford, 1986); Cyril Barrett, *Wittgenstein on Ethics and Religious Belief* (Oxford, 1991); Hilary Putnam, *Renewing Philosophy* (Cambridge, 1992), chs. 7, 8; D.Z. Phillips, *Wittgenstein and Religion* (Basingstoke, 1993).

Wobbermin, Georg (1869–1943)

Ernst Gustav Georg Wobbermin was one of the most important theologians of German-speaking *liberal Protestantism after 1918. His work took up ideas from psychology of religion in the English-speaking world. Politically, Wobbermin was a supporter of the Third Reich after 1933. Wobbermin was born the son of a secondary school teacher on 27 October 1869 in Stettin (Prussia, Pommern Province). He studied theology and philosophy in Halle and Berlin. *Adolf Harnack (1851–1930) and Julius Kaftan (1848–1926) feature amongst his academic teachers. He received his doctorate in philosophy in 1894, with a dissertation devoted to the topic 'Inner Experience as the Basis of a Moral Proof for the Existence of God' (Berlin, 1894), and a doctorate in theology a year later. After a study year in Greece, Wobbermin completed his qualifying dissertation (his '*Habilitation*') in systematic theology in the faculty of theology in Berlin in 1898. In 1901, his *Theology and Metaphysics* appeared, in which Wobbermin softens *Albrecht Ritschl's (1822–89) stark rejection of metaphysics in theology, by seeking to show that a theology without metaphysical implications is impossible. Wobbermin became assistant professor at the University of Marburg in 1906. A year later, he was appointed to a full professorship in systematic theology at the University of Breslau. In the autumn of 1907, he delivered a series of lectures on the theology of Ritschl at the Yale University Divinity School. The visit gave him opportunity for personal contact with William James (1842–1910). In 1908 he turned down the offer of a chair in systematic theology at the divinity school. Wobbermin published a German version of James's *The Varieties of Religious Experience* (Leipzig, 1907; later editions: Leipzig, 1913, 1920, 1925). Wobbermin's main three-volume work, *Systematic Theology According to the Religio-Psychological Method*, began to appear from 1913 onwards (Leipzig, 1913, 1922, 1925). *Guidelines from Protestant Theology for Overcoming the Present Crisis* (Göttingen) followed in 1929.

In the history of Protestant theology, Wobbermin's name is associated with the 'religio-psychological method' of exploring basic religious convictions, a method that he developed. The 'essence of religion', in Wobbermin's view, can only be grasped with reference to one's own religious experience. Christianity is described by Wobbermin as Trinitarian monotheism, in which faith in God means adopting a particular lifestyle, focused upon the 'God-personality' represented in ideal form in Christ. Christ is the 'signpost and trailblazer of eternal life'; 'God's holy will for love' is contained in him (*Systematic Theology*, III, p. 261, German edn). The task of the religio-psychological method is to demonstrate the presence of these convictions in the religious consciousness. Wobbermin did not, however, envisage by this method the transfer of explanatory categories from the discipline of psychology into theology. In no way did he see himself as a psychologist of religion in the narrow sense, and certainly not as an 'empirical psychologist of religion'. As a theologian, he took up motifs from the psychology of religion and reshaped them both in their content and conceptually, at times giving them a new meaning. Wobbermin's relationship to the research being undertaken in his time in the field of the psychology of religion is therefore somewhat ambivalent. In particular, the material link that Wobbermin himself claimed to make with James's work comprises merely the exploration of the 'logical structure' of the religious

consciousness. Like James, Wobbermin makes the concept of 'experience' central in his work. However, the theory of religion which James developed out of the reconceived structure of the religious consciousness was rejected by Wobbermin.

It was *Friedrich Schleiermacher (1768–1834), rather than James, who was the most important influence on Wobbermin's theological model. Like Schleiermacher, Wobbermin wished to anchor religious experience in the realm of feeling alone. In this way, and with reference to the Trinitarian concept of God, he distinguished between the 'feeling of dependence', constituting the basic religious feeling, 'the feeling of security' and 'the feeling of longing'. The differing intensity of these respective elements of feeling within any individual version of how the three types of feeling interrelate accounts, in Wobbermin's view, for the different understandings of religious subjectivity at different times (*Systematic Theology*, II, pp. 220–22). The central problem of religio-psychological methodology, which *Karl Barth (1886–1968) in particular repeatedly criticized, lies in the fact that, on the one hand, theology considers religious convictions as the object of study while, on the other hand, simultaneously treating personal religious experience as true. The analysis is thus caught in a circle. This 'religio-psychological circle', which cannot be broken, is decisive in Wobbermin's account of the relationship between religion and theology.

Wobbermin belongs amongst the best known of the German Protestant theologians of his time. He was a member of the liberal Protestant group that gathered around Martin Rade (1857–1940) and the journal of 'Culture-Protestantism', *Die Christliche Welt*. Wobbermin was a delegate at countless ecumenical gatherings. Some of his works have appeared in many editions. The second volume of his systematic theology, which dealt with his theory of religion, appeared in English translation (*The Nature of Religion* [trans. Theophil Menzil and Daniel S. Robinson; intro. by Douglas Clyde Macintosh; New York, 1933]). In 1915, Wobbermin became *Ernst Troeltsch's (1865–1923) successor at Heidelberg. In 1922 he moved to Göttingen. He became acting chair in systematic theology at the theology faculty in the University of Berlin in 1935. Politically, Wobbermin had already begun to link up with right-wing and anti-Semitic groups prior to 1914. As an opponent of parliamentary democracy, he rejected the Weimar Republic. He supported the National Socialists from 1932 and became a member of the Nazi party in 1933. He was one of the theology spokespeople for the German Christians, supported the anti-Jewish laws of 1933 in both state and church, and took part later in National Socialist and German Christian initiatives. Wobbermin died on 15 October 1943 in Berlin.

Wobbermin's significance resides in the fact that he took up Schleiermacher's insight and saw theology in terms of a 'doctrine of faith' (*Glaubenslehre*). Along with the entire liberal Protestant tradition, after 1945 in Germany his work exerted no influence for some considerable time. Admittedly, he was in part responsible for such marginalization, not least through his political stance, which he defended on theological grounds.

MATTHIAS WOLFES

FURTHER READING: *Luther, Kant, Schleiermacher in ihrer Bedeutung für den Protestantismus. Forschungen und Abhandlungen. Georg Wobbermin zum 70. Geburtstag (27 Oktober 1939)* (ed. Friedrich Wilhelm Schmidt, Robert Winkler, Wilhelm Meyer; Berlin, 1939); Wolf-Ulrich Klünker, *Psychologische Analyse und theologische Wahrheit: Die religionspsychologische Methode Georg Wobbermins* (Göttingen, 1985); Ralf Geisler, *Kants moralischer Gottesbeweis im protestantischen Positivismus* (Göttingen, 1992); Georg Pfleiderer, *Theologie als Wirklichkeitswissenschaft: Studien zum Religionsbegriff bei Georg Wobbermin, Rudolf Otto, Heinrich Scholz und Max Scheler* (Tübingen, 1992); Matthias Wolfes, *Protestantische Theologie und moderne Welt: Studien zur Geschichte der liberalen Theologie nach 1918* (Berlin / New York, 1999), with bibliography.

Zwingli, Ulrich (1484–1531)

Ulrich Zwingli was born on 1 January 1484 in Wildhaus, located in the Toggenburg Valley. He attended the University of Vienna at age fourteen and then the University of Basle, where the reformed-minded Thomas Wyttenbach was teaching. At Basle, Zwingli received his BA and MA degrees and, at age twenty-two, he was ordained a priest in Glarus, where he spent ten years in the ministry. He then served the parish at Einseideln from 1516 to 1518, when he was called as people's priest at Zurich Minster. Zwingli was a Swiss patriot who opposed the use of Swiss mercenaries to fight in foreign wars. He personally witnessed the ravages of pitched battle at Marignano in 1515, where thousands of his countrymen fell to the French. Ironically, he died on the field of battle, serving as a military chaplain during the battle of Kappel in 1531.

As people's priest in Zurich, Zwingli began to preach exegetically and systematically through the Bible, beginning with the book of Matthew, instead of commenting on the assigned biblical passages. Largely as a result of his method of preaching, the city accepted the Bible as its guide for reform. In the first disputation of 1523, he used Scripture as the norm for religious authority. For Zwingli, only the exegesis of the Bible in the original languages would distinguish truth from what he believed to be the error of the Roman church. One needs faith in Christ to interpret Scripture in a proper manner. One must always interpret Scripture in its proper context, a process that enables the student of the Bible to harmonize apparent inconsistencies. Zwingli's defence of the reform in Zurich came in his *Commentary* on the Sixty-Seven Articles in 1523, in which he affirmed the authority of Scripture and justification by faith. His *True and False Religion* (1525) was his fullest exposition of biblical theology. Zwingli claimed that he developed the doctrines of justification by faith and *sola scriptura* independently from *Luther. Faith was a critical element for Zwingli, and he believed that faith in anything other than Christ amounted to idolatry.

Zwingli was trained as a humanist which, in part, explains his emphasis on the return to original sources in his exegesis of the Bible in its original languages. He also retained an admiration for the classical works of antiquity – even listing Socrates and Cato among the elect.

Zwingli is best known for his controversy with Luther at the Colloquy of Marburg (1529), where Zwingli opposed the physical presence of Christ in the Eucharist. He argued that since Christ died once and for all physically on the cross, we do not eat his body at the Eucharist. He believed according to John 3:6 that whatever is born of the flesh is flesh and whatever is born of the spirit is spirit. As a result, he interpreted the phrase 'this is my body' as 'this signifies or represents my body'. There is real fellowship with Christ in the Lord's Supper, but not a literal eating of body and blood. John 6:63 was the key passage for Zwingli in his 'memorial' view of the Lord's Supper. Christ according to his divine nature is omnipresent, but according to his human nature his body is seated at the right hand of the Father. Christ, therefore, cannot be at the same time physically present in the bread and in the wine. Zwingli accused Luther of confusing the two natures of Christ and even of denigrating the Lord's humanity.

Zwingli's disputes with the Swiss Brethren over the issue of infant baptism led him to emphasize the unity of the covenant between the testaments. A critical passage for Zwingli in this regard was 1 Corinthians 10:11, which states that the Old Testament rites were symbols written for the instruction of the New Testament church. Baptism became, therefore, analogous to circumcision. Although Zwingli admitted that there is no explicit example of infant baptism in the New Testament, he asserted that children were probably included in the baptism of entire households in 1 Corinthians 1 and Acts 16. Furthermore, since there is no obvious prohibition against the baptism of infants in the New Testament, one must look to the Old Testament for guidance. Infant baptism, he believed, served as a source of unity within the church, while *Anabaptism would lead inevitably to division.

In his conception of the church, Zwingli emphasized Christ's headship and opposed the Roman Catholic ecclesiastical structure. The true church should be one, holy, universal and apostolic. The true church is universal or catholic as opposed to the Roman church, which he described as merely a local church. Here Zwingli distinguished between the visible and the invisible church. The visible church contains both wheat and tares, while the invisible church contains only believers. God alone knows the identity of the invisible church. The local church is responsible for the proper administration of the sacraments and for discipline. The purpose of discipline is to bring the sinner to repentance, rather than to ensure the purity of the church.

For Zwingli, the state played a vital role in the process of discipline. In opposition to the Anabaptists, he argued for the unity of church and state in which the believer may legitimately seek to become a godly ruler. The pious magistrate, like a shepherd, is responsible for discipline and the reform of the church. The public official also wields the power of the sword to enforce proper behaviour and is responsible for ordering society according to God's laws. Any magistrate who fails to do so could be rightly removed from office. Such removal should follow orderly procedures rather than rebellion by force.

MARTIN I. KLAUBER

FURTHER READING: *Texts:* The majority of Zwingli's works can be found in *Huldreich Zwinglis Samtliche Werke* (Berlin / Leipzig / Zurich, 1905–). For those not included see the older edition, *Huldreich Zwingli's Werke* (Zurich, 1828–42). Zwingli's major works include the following: *Commentary on the Sixty-Seven Articles* (1523); *The Pastoral Office* (1524); *True and False Religion* (1525); *Baptism, Rebaptism and Infant Baptism* (1525); *The Lord's Supper* (1526); *An Account of the Faith* (1530); *An Exposition of the Faith* (1531). *Studies:* Ulrich Gabler, *Huldrych Zwingli: His Life and Work* (trans. Ruth C.L. Gritsch; Edinburgh, 1999); G.W. Bromiley (ed.), *Zwingli and Bullinger* (Louisville, 1979); W.P. Stephens, *The Theology of Huldrych Zwingli* (Oxford, 1988); *Zwingli: An Introduction to His Thought* (Oxford, 1994).

Index